D0077135

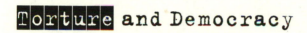

Torture and Democracy

Torture and Democracy

DARIUS REJALI

WITHDRAWN

PRINCETON UNIVERSITY PRESS

PRINCETON AND OXFORD

HV
8593
.R44
2007

Copyright © 2007 by Princeton University Press

Published by Princeton University Press, 41 William Street, Princeton, New Jersey 08540

In the United Kingdom:

Princeton University Press, 3 Market Place, Woodstock, Oxfordshire OX20 1SY

All Rights Reserved

Library of Congress Cataloging-in-Publication Data

Rejali, Darius M.

Torture and democracy / Darius Rejali.

p.   cm.

Includes bibliographical references and index.

ISBN 978-0-691-11422-4 (hardcover : alk. paper)

1. Torture. 2. Torture—Government policy. I. Title.

HV8593.R44 2007

364.6′7—dc22   2007015526

British Library Cataloging-in-Publication Data is available

This book has been composed in Electra

Printed on acid-free paper. ∞

press.princeton.edu

Printed in the United States of America

10 9 8 7 6 5 4 3 2 1

WITHDRAWN

For Gene Rosaschi (1937–2004),
of Yerington, Nevada,
my eighth grade Geography teacher
at Community School, Tehran, Iran

He taught me
that remembering how others live,
knowing the proper names they give
to places, people, and things,
and being observant about how we live
are basic skills for any life well lived.

Contents

Preface

In 2001, I returned to Iran after twenty-four years. This was in itself a risky undertaking. As a feisty publisher said to me, "Dr. Rejali! How nice to meet you! How did you get in? How do you plan to get out?" I had, after all, written a book on modern Iranian torture. On my first day back, still disoriented by travel, I had a further shock. Like all others who have had their lives disrupted, my first instinct was to see the place I used to live. The house no longer existed, of course. The taxi driver chose a route that went right by the gates of the notorious prison at Evin. It had figured prominently in my book, and to see it again and the crowds of anxious relatives milling in front of it, was bracing. Adjacent to it now was a large garden that was rented out for weddings and other festive occasions. I asked about it. "Oh," said the taxi driver, "that is to make it easy for everybody. First you have a wedding and then everybody gets arrested and taken next door!"

Iranians relate to torture as a familiar event of modern life. They know it exists, and they never imagine that it is logically incompatible with telephones, central heating, weddings, elections, and other occasions of modern life. I grew up this way as well. Perhaps this Iranian attitude arose from centuries of violence as successive civilizations burned through the country. The summer I returned, I climbed out to Turab Tapeh, the remains of the great medieval city of Neishabur, with its thirteen libraries and the world's only international university of its time, except Al Azhar in Cairo. In 1221, Mongols executed all 1,747,000 inhabitants and every cat and dog in the city. Historians record about 5 million deaths throughout the region. Neishabur was but one of many places that was devastated; entire cities disappeared. Archaeologists dub a whole section of Khurasan province "the land of lost cities." Neishabur was rebuilt, but not where it once stood. Now, at Turab Tapeh, there were only bits of pottery and mud walls, and not far from it, the solitary grave of its most famous citizen, Omar Khayyam. The genocide still weighs heavily on Iranians eight centuries later. "I never knew what this place was," averred the taxi driver who, braving fields and ditches, had brought me out there. "But I've driven by it a hundred times, and from a distance, I remembered Khayyam's famous poem of the pots who were once men and who cried to those who passed by: 'Who the potter and who the pot?' "

Perhaps as a child, I was more disposed to thinking differently about violence than others. My relation to violence was more intimate. On my Iranian side, royal autocrats in my family had no difficulty ordering torture or genocide when it served their interests. Stories of their deeds are, to say the least, unforgettable. On my American side, we remember General Sherman's march through Georgia. In September 1864, as cannons shelled Atlanta, my ancestor, Harriet Yarbrough, dug a hole in a bank and hid there with her two children. Afterward, she was one of 446 families who stayed behind; she had opposed the war passionately from the outset, but when Union soldiers destroyed the Yarbrough home for firewood, that was the last straw. Undaunted by the situation in which she found herself, she went to find Sherman and unleashed all her fury at him. It did no good, and the site of her home is now part of Olympic Park. She filed for reimbursement from the War Department, and pursued the claim until 1891. She never forgot.

Being an Iranian aristocrat—American Southerner, a Shiite Muslim—Calvinist with a keen sense of history, presents unique intellectual and moral challenges. If you had told me early in childhood that I would write a book on Iranian torture—as I did—I would not have believed you. And I am just as surprised, I think, that this new book is also on torture.

But it seems my family's tales of the dark side of human life have put me in a good position to understand where we find ourselves today. Exactly a hundred years ago, my Iranian great-grandfather fought to defend his autocratic way of life. He did not hesitate to turn cannons on crowds or torture people he considered terrorists and anarchists. His opponents said, there you see, his way of life is a sham, and these people disguise barbaric force behind high-minded talk of honorable values. And who was to say they were wrong? For if honorable men cannot fight fairly and win, who on earth are they, and what do they represent? In the end no one, except a handful of sycophants, mourned the passing of his way of life.

A hundred years later, believers in democracy seem to be ready to make the same mistake as my autocratic ancestor, and I am here to urge them not to. I hope I have written a story that makes us take a second look at ourselves as we enter a new century primed to treat our enemies inhumanely. This book has five aims: (1) to offer a history of the technology of torture around the globe over the past century and use it to engage historical, philosophical, and anthropological claims about modern torture, (2) to raise provocative questions and hypotheses about the historical pattern of torture technology and the factors that shape it, relating the development of this technology to elements not normally considered connected to it, namely, democracy and international monitoring, (3) to change public debate, (4) to offer a riposte to those who defend the use of torture, and (5) to provide a reliable sourcebook for human-rights organizations, policymakers, and politicians, drawing extensively on sources hitherto unavailable in English or so scattered and obscure as to be almost inaccessible.

The title, *Torture and Democracy*, may suggest that I also offer a neat typological chart of regime types and corresponding torture methods, perhaps buttressed by exhaustive statistics. But that would be to read too much into the title. For reasons I will explain in the introduction, our knowledge of modern torture and the events around it is too fragmentary to sustain such firm causal claims; the materials and tools necessary for such a project are simply not available.

This book is far more exploratory. It does focus on a class of torture techniques, those that leave few marks. Popular accounts sometimes characterize these techniques as "brainwashing" or "sensory deprivation," but there are many other techniques less well known and more pedestrian. A complete list of them can be found in appendix A. I call these techniques as a whole "clean tortures," and spend much time puzzling about where they come from and why they have come to be so prevalent. Although the argument is long, the overall structure is simple and modeled on a dialogue:

Are there clean tortures, that is, painful coercive techniques that leave no marks? Yes there are (part 1, introduction). How can you call these techniques torture? What do you mean by torture? (part 1, chapter 1). Do democratic governments torture? What do you mean by democratic? Why do democratic governments torture? Yes some democratic governments do torture, and here are the reasons why (part 1, chapter 2). But don't the techniques democratic governments use come from Nazism and Stalinism? Actually no; if we look at Nazism and Stalinism, we rarely find clean torture techniques (part 2). So where do we find them? Well, electrotorture was first developed in the context of American and French policing and spread outward from there (part 3). But surely that's just one example? Actually, here's the list, and you'll see repeatedly the same pattern: clean techniques begin in British, American, and French contexts and spread outward to other places (part 4). This isn't always the case, but when it's not, we see British, American, and French torturers adapting techniques and innovating on them. Okay, so that's the pattern. Why is the pattern as it is? (part 5, chapter 20). Do these techniques work? (part 5, chapters 21–22). If they don't, why don't we learn? (part 5, chapters 23-24). There are subsidiary dialogues in these divisions, but this is the basic idea.

Torture and Democracy makes a set of factual claims about the global distribution of clean torture techniques, separating myth and mystery from what is genuinely known, identifying puzzles that emerge from these empirical patterns of distribution, and evaluating hypotheses, both plausible and implausible, that purport to explain them. Possibly the most important plausible hypothesis regarding the distribution of clean tortures is this: Public monitoring leads institutions that favor painful coercion to use clean torture to evade detection, and, to the extent that public monitoring of human rights is a core value in modern democracies, it is the case that where we find democracies torturing today, we will also find stealthy torture. I will have more to say about this hypothesis in the introduction and chapter 20.

Because I have privileged the ordinary educated reader in organizing this book, I have not grouped methodological, definitional, and other such matters at the outset, as is often the convention. Rather, I introduce materials and explanations when and where they are needed. Those interested in more technical matters may turn to appendix B and appendix C. Appendix B considers matters of methodology and typology. In particular, I offer my answers to four questions. What is the behavioral measure for grasping the intent of torturers to be stealthy? What is the measure to determine whether states are authoritarian or democratic? And what is the real dependent variable in this study, torture or technologies of physical coercion? What is the difference between torture and punishment? Appendix C is a formal statement of the empirical claims, puzzles, and various explanations of the puzzles.

The effort to centralize so much in one book has its risks. Perhaps, it may be urged, I should have written three books: a historical encyclopedia, a social scientific analysis, and a policy book. Such books would have different audiences, and I am aware that combining the three approaches means that not every page will be equally interesting to all readers. But I hope that the absence of comprehensive, systematic, and historically ambitious books on this subject will allow the work to find its place among more specialized studies. If the worst that can be said is that I spoke too little or too much to this or that discipline, then I am content.

Acknowledgments

Thanks must go first of all to those who helped me take care of myself. Let me thank, then, all the surfers who rode the storm with me at Short Sands (Oregon), Santa Cruz (California), Tauroa Point (New Zealand), and Byron Bay (Australia). Nietzsche once imagined Epicurus staring out onto a brightly lit sea and remarked that only a man who has experienced suffering deeply could imagine a philosophy of pleasure. Perhaps in life there is no light without darkness. Certainly, in writing this book, the beautiful stood out all the more vividly—a harp seal by my board, a sun behind a cloud, the wind bending the great northwestern fir trees by the sea, and above all, a graceful surfer.

Dr. Jeff Parent watched over my fitful sleep, Drs. Michael Booker and James Imatani over my ruptured appendix, and acupuncturist Peggy Rollo over my carpal tunnel. Shamus Roller, Ryan Offutt, Chad Lindner, Cameron Johnson, Marc Visnick, Jay Dickson, Sam Gustin, Josh Phillips, and Marshall Miller played their invaluable part in making sure I didn't forget myself. At many campfires, listeners indulged my accordion, which—perhaps unbeknownst to them—served to heal the sadness as well as express the joy I felt writing this book. Spatial Delivery and the citizens of Black Rock City, Nevada, started this book by enabling me to create, mount, install, and burn the proper sacrifice. The fellas from Burning Boy I and II freed me to burn myself during the middle of it, and the folks from RDO in Aspen helped me celebrate the end of it. You know who you are, and you know what I mean.

My parents David and Sallie, who wish, as I sometimes do, that I worked on more pleasant topics, were always there. Always. Along the way, two Portland writers—Elinor Langer and Martha Gies—who walk occasionally in the shadows as I do took me out to dinner and let me speak my heart. Then there were those who took care of me and fed me when I looked especially haunted in Cambodia, Australia, New Zealand, Alaska, Spain, Norway, Denmark, England, Morocco, Iran, and the United States. How will I ever thank you?

Lois Hobbs guarded the gates to my sabbatical; there was no getting around her, or at least it was a long walk. Lois undertook many important tasks with tight deadlines and impossible odds. Despite cancer and a major car accident, or perhaps because of them, Lois also played the invaluable role of telling me when to stop worrying and move on. Sally Loomis, Jennie McKee, and their staff of determined interlibrary loan assistants gathered obscure documents from small libraries around the world that could not be found at great archives. They were resourceful beyond anything that I imagined. Dena Hutto hunted down government documents, Emma Green designed one cover, and Ben Salzberg and Taylor Smith cast spells on the computer to make things come out beautifully.

Writing is a lonely business; twelve years is a long time. Fortune gave me a string of extraordinarily talented research assistants who kept me company on a dark road: Thomas McElroy (1995–96), Gabriel Lenz (1996–98), Sylvan Bracket (1998), Clay Northouse (2002–3), Chad Lindner (2002–3), Tristan Jean (2002–5), Osman Balkan (2004–5), Adam Bondy (2005), and Peter Miller (2006–7). Another set of fellow travelers kindly read the manuscript, or portions of it, from time to time, including Ian Malcolm, Richard Isomaki, Debbie Tegarden, Tobiah Waldron, Shamus Roller, Lena Eberhart, Karin Purdy, Peter Andreas, Brian Walker, Jamie Mayerfield, Garath Williams, Matt Kocher, Josh Phillips, and the many anonymous readers for Princeton University Press. Ed Peters, John Conroy, Martha Huggins, Phil Zimbardo, Ron Crelinsten, and Michael Geyer—my seniors in this field—unstintingly encouraged me, and this despite surgery, tragedy, and the usual overwhelming nature of academic life.

So many languages went into this book: Portuguese, Spanish, Russian, Romanian, Polish, Korean, Chinese, Japanese, Arabic, Farsi, German, French, Italian, and Norwegian. My own linguistic skills, broad as they are, could never have mastered what was required in such a short time. I am deeply indebted to the many talented translators, especially the Reed College students who gave themselves to this project unstintingly and were wise beyond their years. They include Tristan Jean, Bettina Fairman, Cadi Russell-Sauve, Francisco Toro, Gerardo Lopez Monge, Katherine Fidler, Sallie Rejali, Kasia Bartosynska, Alina Bica Huiu, Sang Woo Kang, Darya Pushkina, Caroline Hurley, Hyong Rhew, Doug Fix, and Randi Leuthold.

Other Reed College students contributed to this book enormously through their curiosity and questions, especially those in my two courses on violence. I am especially indebted to Jenny Benevento, Kathleen Cullinan, Katherine Fidler, Liana Foxvog, Alex Golubitsky, Shankar Mandelkorn, Sam Schaeffer, and Gwyn Troyer from Approaches to Violence, and Scott Beutel, Maria Ochoa, Antonia Keithahn, Will Melton, Peter Miller, Molly Shaver, Josie Jimarez-Howard, and Avy Mallik, from Torture and Democracy.

Library staff, often unacknowledged and underappreciated, aided me in countries around the world. I am especially indebted to Carlos Osorio and Malcolm Byrne (National Security Archives, Washington, DC), Jurgen Matthaus (U.S. National Holocaust Museum Library, Washington, DC), Sven-Erik Braun, Ion Iacos, and Henrik Ronsbo (Documentation Center, the International Rehabilitation Center for Torture Victims, Copenhagen, Denmark), Sopheara Chey (Tuol Sleng Cambodian Genocide Memorial, Phnom Penh, Cambodia), Krista Sajber (Emma Goldman Archives, Berkeley, California), Immanuel Harris (Cook County Clerk), and the very kind staff at the U.S. Library of Congress, the British Public Record Office at Kew, and the Bibliothèque Nationale in Paris. Good xeroxing is an underappreciated art—may many blessings come to Lucas Perkins, Kat Halpenny, Natalie Yager, Dawn Teele, and Caitlin Quinlivan.

Regularly, I required the advice and insight of those far more familiar with regions and countries than I was, including Steve Johnstone (ancient Greece), Joel Revill (France), Ken Brashier and Mark Lewis (ancient China), Peter Zinoman (Vietnam), Shawn Smallman and Martha Huggins (Brazil), John Conroy, Flint Taylor, Geoffrey Klingsporn, Scott Horton, Jackie Dirks, and Ed Segel (U.S. history), João Paulo Coelho (Mozambique), Mark Shaw (South Africa), Simon Thomas (modern China), Lisa Hajjar and George Bisharat (Israel), Craig Etcheson (Cambodia), and Marc Noland, Dae-Sook Suh and Hyon-Sok Ryou (Korea).

Similarly, I was fortunate to receive technical advice on highly specialized disciplines and practices from experts who gave their time generously, including Jeremy Faludi, Hassan Rejali, Andrew Lacy, and Jason Webley (engineering and physics), Tony Williams, Lisa Strauss, John Muench, Lis Danielsen, Kirstine Amris, and Karen Prip (medicine), Sonia Montalbano, Phil Bender, Rob Coleman, Dominik Steiger, and Steve Sady (law), Dan Reisberg, Jeffrey Gray, Phil Zimbardo, Fred Kantor, Thomas Blass, and Rick Bale (psychology), Albyn Jones and Paul Gronke (statistics), Dr. Andrew Charles and Daddy Angel (Gay S&M history), Patrick Bardel (U.S. military equipment), Clifford Shearing, Piet van Reenen, and Brian Rappert (policing), and Gary Sick, John Sifton and Dinah Pokempner (Human Rights Watch).

Assistance of a different sort, moral as well as scholarly, came from my longtime friends Chris Udry, Fred Ross, Paul DeYoung, Mary Catherine King, Christfriede Larson, Joel Pomerantz, Dany Celermajer, Elise Moser, John Calvert, and Stewart, Kenneth, and Peggy Thomas. Likewise, my sister Susan and brother Cameron, as well as my many Iranian cousins, aunts, and uncles, what

I like to call my nuclear extended family, made sure that I knew who I was and where I belonged.

My department chairs, may they live forever, Paul Gronke and Stefan Kapsch, and Dean Peter Steinberger deeply believed in this project and supported it whenever they could with time and finances. A special debt of thanks goes to President Colin Diver and those generous patrons of Reed College who contributed mightily to the forming of the scholarly community I just described. Little would have been achieved without the generous support of the Ducey Fund, the Stillman Drake Fund, and the Levine Fund.

Ian Malcolm at Princeton University Press, it would be safe to say, changed my life. That is a debt not easily repaid.

The Carnegie Corporation of New York greatly facilitated this book, and its successor, *Approaches to Violence* (Princeton University Press, forthcoming), by naming me a Carnegie Scholar in 2003 and extending a generous grant that allowed me to write for two and a half years unimpeded by other concerns.

My Reed colleagues were wonderfully supportive and, despite strong urges to the contrary, thoughtfully left me alone.

Having been drawn inward, I was forced to engage in the painful process of speaking of what I learned. Beth Sorensen at Reed College tirelessly encouraged me during media appearances. Colin Gordon and Daniel Defert invoked for me the thoughts and outspoken spirit of Michel Foucault, thus challenging me to learn the art of speaking fearlessly to power and to do it without a permanent frown on my face or inhuman gravitas. Others gave me important places to stand, debate, and exchange ideas, including Sidney Blumenthal (Salon.com), Finn Stepputat (Danish Institute for International Studies), Henrik Ronsbo (Rehabilitation and Research Centre for Torture Victims, Copenhagen), Martha Huggins (International Sociological Association), Scott Gates, Jon Elster, and Stathis Kalyvas (Peace Research Institute of Oslo), John Sifton, Tom Malinowski, Dinah Pokempner, Ken Roth, and Scott Long (Human Rights Watch), Lili Cole and Joanne Bauer (Carnegie Council on Ethics and International Affairs), and Michael Nutkiewicz, Jose Quiroga, and Ana Deutsch (Program for Torture Victims, Los Angeles).

Four colleagues sadly passed on before this book was finished—Bob Kirschner, Jeffrey Gray, Gene Rosaschi, and Hyon-Sok Ryou. At the same time, my living community grew with the addition of six nephews and nieces (Brandon, Sam, Susie, Ben, Maura, and Hannah) and four who kindly call me uncle (Elliot, Cody, Ilona, and Iris). And I learned a great deal about dependency and vulnerability as well from Kristin's cats and Quillan the Hungarian vizsla.

A book is always a collective project that goes far beyond those whose names can be listed. Inevitably, though some who should be mentioned are forgotten; I hope I will be forgiven.

Throughout this manuscript, I have tried wherever possible to offer the full name of victims. Too often the names of the torturers are well remembered but the victims remain unknown and unnamed. Supplying the name was not always possible, and I hope I will be excused for any errors or omissions.

I write this book at a time when the United States and Iran, the two countries in which I claim a heritage, gear up for even more violence. I wrote and revised this book in both countries—in my study in Portland, Oregon, and in the room in which my great-grandmother and granduncle lived and died in Tehran. And I complete this book now in my balcony study in Spain, overlooking the Mediterranean. Each of these sites has been an awesome perch on which to sit and reflect upon the century that was, the wars, revolutions, and civil conflicts that tore apart societies. If there were gods who sheltered these places, they were exceedingly kind to me.

Three unknown people, Sue Kemsley, Gary Arbuckle, and Fabien Brun, were moved to write me out of the blue with a bright jewel of information. And then there is you the reader: I don't know you either, but I hope you can play a part in making sure the story I tell ends well. For ultimately, this book is not about the past but the future.

Fuengirola, Spain, 2007

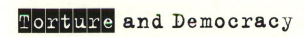

Torture and Democracy

In general, men judge more by sight than by touch. Everyone sees what is happening but not everyone feels its consequences.

—Niccolò Machiavelli[1]

▐ Introduction

On March 3, 1991, police pulled over Rodney King and two other passengers in Los Angeles. Most Americans saw how that incident ended. LAPD officers beat King senseless with metal batons. Many will remember that police fractured King's face and legs. How many remember the number of times police fired electric stun weapons at King during the incident? How many can say how much shock passed through his body as he lay on the ground?

From the start, the King incident was about the sudden remarkable visibility of police violence captured, by happenstance, on amateur video. As the Christopher Commission stated, "Whether there even would have been a Los Angeles Police Department investigation without the video is doubtful, since the efforts of King's brother, Paul, to file a complaint were frustrated, and the report of the involved officers was falsified."[2]

Even a careful viewer of the amateur video would not see the police using electroshock. Sergeant Stacey Koon tased Rodney King thrice, twice prior to when the video started running and once in the course of the video. *To tase* means to use a Tommy A. Swift Electric Rifle (T.A.S.E.R). Tasers fire two darts trailed by long wires. Once the darts catch onto the clothing or body, the operator depresses a button, releasing electric charge from the batteries along the wires to the target. Koon's Taser model possessed two dart cartridges. Koon lodged the first pair of darts on King's back and the second on his upper chest. Each discharge delivered short pulses of 50,000 volts, eight to fifteen pulses per second.[3]

The pain was not trivial. The California Highway Patrol officer said King was "writhing."[4] LAPD officer Timothy Wind stated that King "was shouting incoherently from the *pain* of the taser."[5] Even Koon, who was nine feet away, declared, "He's groaning like a wounded animal, and I can see the vibrations on him."[6] While Officer Laurence Powell beat King on video, Koon depressed the button a third time, draining whatever charge was left in the batteries.[7] This was not a trivial discharge either. LAPD recruits knew that whoever touched a tased victim would also "get zapped. They don't become unconscious . . . they just go down."[8] Officer Ted Briseno claims that he intervened at this point to stop the beating. Koon and Wind believe that "Briseno wasn't trying to stop the violence; he was trying to prevent the TASER charge from hitting Powell and Wind."[9] At any rate, the third tase didn't subdue King, and the beating continued.

If these beatings led to the Los Angeles Riots of 1992, the multiple high-voltage shocks barely impinged on public consciousness. Indeed, what would have happened if King had suffered no fractures, only the mere burn of the Taser? At the trial, the defense produced Dr. Dallas Long to contest whether there even was a burn scar. As Koon puts it, "Rodney King had no burn; a TASER dart doesn't leave one."[10]

A democratic public may be outraged by violence it can see, but how likely is it that we will get outraged about violence like this, that may or may not leave traces, violence that we can hardly be sure took place at all? A victim with scars to show to the media will get sympathy or at least attention, but victims without scars do not have much to authorize their complaints to a skeptical public. A trial can focus on the specific damages of a beating—where did the blows allegedly fall? Were the strikes professional, necessary or neither?—but what precisely can a trial focus on with electric shocks that leave few marks? Some argue we are desensitized to violence we see on the evening news, but about violence we can't see—even when its effects lie before our eyes, shaping very flow of traffic on our streets—we cannot reflect, much less react.

This book explores the disturbing implications of the truth that we are less likely to complain about violence committed by stealth. Indeed, we are less likely even to have the opportunity to complain. I use "we" deliberately, referring to people of modern states, and especially democracies. Dictators generally have no interest in violence that leaves no marks; intimidation can require that they leave bloody traces of their power in every public square. We may think that most clean tortures came to us from Hitler or Stalin, but we would do well to look closer to home.

For wherever citizens gather freely to review public power or name violent injustice, we are also more likely to see covert violence. In democracies, the police, the military, and the secret services are constrained by constitutions and monitored by judges and internal review boards, by a free press, and by human rights organizations. Officers, agents, and soldiers who decide that brutality is required, of their own accord or with quiet encouragement from above, will put a premium on "methods which cause suffering and intimidation without leaving much in the way of embarrassing long-term visible evidence of brutality."[11]

The logic of this dynamic, of the incentives and disincentives created by the tensions between authority and public monitoring, is certainly thought-provoking in itself. This book goes further, arguing that, historically, public monitoring and stealth torture have an unnerving affinity. It is a relationship, moreover, that has been aided by the modern technologies that, put to other uses, make our lives physically comfortable, even pleasurable. I seek to show that where free elections have gone, where monitoring agencies have set up shop, and journalists have taken to the streets and airwaves, they have been followed by electric prods and electroshockers, tortures by water and ice, drugs of sinister variety, sonic devices—and also by methods that are less technical, but no less sophisticated or painful; the modern democratic torturer knows how to beat a suspect senseless without leaving a mark.[12]

But this book does more than describe complex patterns of torture techniques and offer explanations for their distribution. *Torture and Democracy* is also designed as an accessible and reliable sourcebook for citizens. No one these days is particularly surprised that torture has its supporters even in democracies. Since September 11, 2001, American officials have acknowledged using well-known coercive techniques on prisoners, and some influential Americans have justified torture in certain cases.[13] And since Abu Ghraib, the world has become familiar with iconic images of American torture. Most people, though, don't know about the painful but clean tortures that now characterize so much policing around the world. And few would recognize the torture of the Hooded Man of Abu Ghraib or its effects if police used this procedure on someone in their neighborhood.

If global monitoring of torture is to succeed in eliminating these clean tortures, citizens need to understand clearly what these techniques are, where they come from, and what they do. Being able to talk intelligently about these techniques is not simply a cognitive ability that promotes better research on torture, but a necessary civic skill. Citizens who cannot speak competently about cruelty are unable to protect themselves against tyranny and injustice.

Historical Claims

The bulk of this book is devoted to establishing a set of historical claims. These claims describe patterns in the way torture techniques have appeared worldwide over the last few centuries. They are claims of fact, based on the best available evidence, whatever I, or others, make of these claims. The main factual claims of this book are the following.

There exist many painful physical techniques of interrogation or control that leave few marks. I call these *clean* techniques in contrast to *scarring* techniques of torture. Clean techniques are not psychological techniques. A paddle or a fist applied to the body leaves marks if used one way, but not if used another way. Both strikes involve harsh physical blows, and it is deeply misleading, if not deceptive, to call a clean blow a psychological procedure and a scarring blow a physical one.[14]

Clean techniques are physical tortures. The vast majority of clean techniques are not technologically sophisticated. They involve everyday instruments that people commonly have at hand for other purposes (see appendix A).

Most of these techniques appeared first in military punishments, especially among British lists of punishments; in the context of American slavery; in penal institutions; or during policing and military operations in French and British colonies. Virtually all the techniques that appear in conflicts in Afghanistan, Iraq, Algeria, and Northern Ireland, as well as in prisons in France, England, and the United States, are descended from these procedures or subsequent variants.

There is a long, unbroken, though largely forgotten history of torture in democracies at home and abroad, a history in which these techniques were transmitted stretching back some two hundred years. This claim restates the previous paragraph using the conventional designation of France, England, and the United States as the main democracies of modern history, especially prior to World War II.

The alternative claim would be that authoritarian states invented and distributed these clean techniques. However, prior to and during World War II, clean torture techniques rarely appear in other countries notorious for torture, including Russia, Germany, the Austro-Hungarian Empire, and Japan, or their colonies. When they do, they are just as quickly forgotten. However one conventionally designates these states—whether one calls them monarchies, dictatorships, fascist or communist states, totalitarian or authoritarian states—these states are not conventionally or consistently designated as democracies before or after World War II.

By the late twentieth century, the clean techniques that first appeared in the main democracies can be found in countries around the world. In addition, new coercive and clean techniques appeared alongside them in various countries throughout the world. There are, of course, still other techniques of torture that do leave marks, and there are fewer reports of these by the late twentieth century than there were previously.

Moreover, torturers tend increasingly to use clean torture techniques in conjunction with each other. I call this tendency *clustering*. This clustering occurred first in the torture of modern democratic states in the early twentieth century and only rarely in authoritarian torture chambers. By the late twentieth century, the similar clustering begins to appear among authoritarian states, although democratic torturers remain, by far, the most consistent users of clean techniques.

Lastly, clean techniques do not cluster randomly, but appear in predictable combinations. I call these predictable combinations *regimens*, or more commonly *styles* of torture. For example, torturers tend to commonly use electrotorture in combination with various water tortures, a style I call French modern after its first consistent users.

Over the course of a century, then, torture changed worldwide, the kind of sweeping change that is rare with any method of violence. As time has gone by, torturers, on their own or at the direction of others and for whatever reason, seem to have turned more and more toward techniques that leave few marks. This follows from the broad arc of history just described, whether or not one concludes, as I argue, that stealthiness is what makes these clean techniques desirable to torturers. It is possible, of course, that these techniques have some other quality in common besides leaving few marks, and this is why they are used more frequently. I consider this possibility in appendix B, but that is not critical to the factual claim here. The only claim made here is that leaving few marks is *one* quality all these techniques obviously have in common and around which they may be grouped for purposes of analysis, even, if upon further analysis, this is not the only common element.

Lastly, and in short, police and military in the main democratic states were leaders in adapting and innovating clean techniques of torture. French colonial police, for example, developed what became the dominant form of electric torture for forty years, torture by means of a field telephone magneto. They pioneered this clean technique in 1931 in Vietnam, before the Nazis came to power.

This claim is agnostic on how other countries ended up with these techniques and by what route they arrived, if indeed they came from the outside. It does not imply a specific explanation for how torturers around the world came by the techniques they currently use, for example, the CIA did it. All it states is that the techniques that are now commonly used in interrogation rooms and prisons around the world had their roots in the main democratic states.

Puzzles and Cautions

The main historical claims of this book raise some specific, intriguing puzzles. These puzzles include: Why did these techniques first appear in the main democracies and not in other states, democratic or otherwise? Why and how did these techniques migrate from these states to states around the world? And why was there a priority on this class of techniques? Was the reason the evident quality they have in common leaving no marks or some other quality? Regardless, why did this quality become so desirable worldwide in the late twentieth century?

In what follows, I review solutions to these puzzles, some plausible and others unconvincing, and offer my own answers. But before I proceed, two preliminary notes are necessary to explain how I plan to go about doing this in the course of the book.

First, I take my time in offering discrete, disciplined histories of each clean torture, starting with electrotorture, and moving on to techniques involving whips and sticks, water, ice, spices, sleep deprivation, positional and restraint tortures, clean beating, exhaustion exercises, noise, and drugs. Historical "data" comes in certain patterns, and the process of explanation cannot start until one has arrived at a reliable set of claims about the patterns the data forms, identifying what is worthy of explanation. And unfortunately, most explanations of torture, much less torture technology, have relied on misleading and unreliable data—a matter I will document repeatedly in the course of this book.

Getting the patterns right, specifying claims about the shapes of these patterns, is important to any further research, and to see this pattern requires doing the disciplined idiographic studies of techniques. The torture techniques are the protagonists, if you like, of this book, and it is very hard to catch more than glimpses of them as they move from place to place and thus to establish their existence and dispersion. This accounts for this study's 3,400 notes involving approximately two thousand sources in fourteen languages—only a small part of what was actually consulted—covering everything from well-known events, from Vietnam and commercial slavery, to more obscure activities, for example, French prisons in New Guinea and outposts of the Foreign Legion in North Africa or barely known sideshows of World War II where Hungarians tortured Slovak prisoners or Romanians set upon residents of Odessa. Behind each chapter lies a detailed tabulation of techniques, for example, of Gestapo torture by place and year.

All this takes time and care, evaluating alternative factual claims until the pattern is as clear as it can be for the moment. And nothing emphasizes the danger of hastily reaching for theory as the final section of every chapter at the heart of this book (chapters 3–24). These sections, typically entitled "Remembering X and Y," remind the reader of familiar and important factual histories that turned out to be false or misleading in the course of the chapter. Repeatedly, I describe patterns that others have asserted (for example, M.R.D. Foot's assertion that electrotorture was invented by the Nazis), commonly believe (Pavlov was responsible for brainwashing), or are widely trumpeted (torture worked reliably to produce accurate, timely information during the Battle of Algiers) only to show how these historical claims are overstated, misleading, or simply false.

There is, then, a difference between "clean" and "dirty" data, and the problem with most explanations of torture hitherto has been their exclusive reliance on misleading histories. One factor that repeatedly muddies the waters is national memory of torture in various countries. The focus on writing the history of techniques, rather than nations, is deliberate in this respect. I took the unit of analysis as the technique, not the nation, because it serves as an antidote to misleading national memories. Knowing the actual global distribution not only shows how specific national narratives of the history of torture techniques are misleading or simply sometimes conveniently false, but also offers some insight into the way social memory works.

This should not be taken as a rejection of discrete cases studies based on nation-states. The book draws on such studies, and my first book, *Torture and Modernity: State, Society and Self in Iran*, was precisely such a study.[15] But what has long been needed is a large-scale study of the sort I have undertaken, one that puts the local studies in a broad context, draws attention to what kinds of accounts exist elsewhere beyond the horizons of specific area specialists, and brings together in one place what can be known about the history of torture techniques. That is a daunting exercise, and I do not claim it cannot be improved upon.

But what I do claim is that area specialists who focus exclusively on specific nations are at risk of error. I can say this from experience, as my first book, like so many others, accepted certain theses about the origins of torture techniques unthinkingly, theses that proved to be mistaken when I finally learned the specific histories of various techniques. This was a painful realization, not simply from a scholarly point of view, but because it cut against an inherited folklore born out of national trauma that, as a younger man, I absorbed as fact. And as this book shows, in chapter 24 and elsewhere, area specialists are equally vulnerable to this, repeatedly blessing a *folklore* of torture with social scientific legitimacy, simply because they took preconstructed memories as *facts* about patterns of torture.

Second, my approach to explaining the puzzling patterns that emerge from the various histories is going to be more speculative than some might prefer or demand. This is a necessary result of the material that is available for this study. The empirical material I use for the idiographic studies is both too rich and too fragmentary to allow for precise, validated causal claims. By too rich, I mean it comes from so many countries, so many different writers, and in so many styles, guises, and emotional hues (from coldly technical to blatantly cruel, cruelly disingenuous, and literally tortured) that it can be very hard to understand many of the facts in their own contexts, let alone systematically compare them or subdue them under neat hypotheses. By too fragmentary, I mean that I'm often piecing together stories whose most pertinent facts may never come to light, not least because they may have been deliberately obscured or suppressed.

This does not mean that the facts of the history of torture technology are unmanageable or that explanations are impossible, but that one must pay attention to what is achievable. This is why I do not think it wise to try to prove each of my explanations beyond the shadow of a doubt or to explain with fine-grained precision what all the relevant causal mechanisms are behind the spread of torture. What I do offer are provisional claims, plausible in light of what can be known, and I show as well how alternative accounts are, at least as far as can be determined, implausible.

I present these provisional explanations and alternative accounts as empirical patterns emerge from the historical narrative. This is a necessary consequence of the approach I have taken, namely, to provide a plain-language narrative for ordinary educated readers. But here I will sketch broadly some of my main arguments, and in appendix C, I itemize my explanations analytically and list the reasons I reject alternative accounts.

The Priority of Public Monitoring

To reprise briefly, the main historical claims of this study are that there is a long history of torture in the main democracies, that the priority in these cases was on techniques that left few marks, and that democratic police and military were innovators in this area in that techniques they first used appear in many places today around the world. Clean tortures and democracy *seem* to go hand in hand.

But *why* do clean torture and democracy appear to go hand in hand? This is an important puzzle (though by no means the only one suggested by the data). My explanation for this pattern generally is this: *Public monitoring leads institutions that favor painful coercion to use and combine clean torture techniques to evade detection, and, to the extent that public monitoring is not only greater in democracies, but that public monitoring of human rights is a core value in modern democracies, it is the case that where we find democracies torturing today we will also be more likely to find stealthy torture.*

What makes covert coercion valuable is that allegations of torture are simply less credible when there is nothing to show for it. In the absence of visible wounds or photographs of actual torture, who is one to believe? Stealth torture breaks down the ability to communicate. The inexpressibility that matters here is the gap between a victim and his or her community. Stealth torture regimens are unlike other torture procedures because they are calculated to subvert this relationship and thereby avoid crises of legitimacy.

This explanation is logical, but it also fits the available evidence for the most part. Usually, wherever we see these clean techniques in the twentieth century, typically they are in the context of intensive public monitoring—either by churches, the press, politicians, the public, or international organizations. And that is why clean coercive techniques typically show up in democratic states. When we watch interrogators, interrogators get sneaky.

It is not possible to prove beyond a shadow of a doubt that monitoring is the sole source for the emergence of clean torture techniques in democracies. In fact, some histories of torture techniques show that tortures that left few marks had other purposes besides preserving legitimacy in the face of public monitoring of human rights. For example, American slavers developed paddling and bucking because they knew buyers would conclude scarred slaves were a disciplinary problem and not purchase them. Obviously democratic monitoring of human rights had nothing to do with that! What mattered more in this case was the monitoring of potential buyers, which gave slave dealers incentives for using clean techniques. But when police adopted these techniques in the United States, then, yes, based on everything else we know, it is reasonable to believe that their concern was to mislead the public and others, as the Wickersham Report makes amply clear. At any rate, they weren't trying to sell their prisoners to others, so we know *that* was not the reason.

Arguing that public monitoring alters the behavior of state violence workers is not a contentious claim. Most state violence can be committed in ways that draw little or no public attention. Scholars have registered the trend toward stealthiness in how states control street protests, ethnic conflict, and war. They have documented techniques (nonlethal weapons, smart bombs) that states use to sustain legitimacy while dispensing with their opponents quietly.[16] My explanation differs from these only slightly. I maintain that states, especially democratic ones, turned to covert torture earlier than they turned to stealth in other kinds of violence, and torture by stealth spread more widely and involved a greater variety of techniques.

In advancing this monitoring hypothesis, I'm turning away from two alternative ways of framing the puzzle of clean torture and democracy, one that thinks of democracy far more boldly than I do (the regime type hypothesis) and one that is skeptical that there are any real democratic states in the world at all (the ruling elite hypothesis).

Why not say that democracy, not monitoring, explains the pattern of clean torture? This would also seem to fit the pattern of available evidence. After all, public monitoring exists in democracies, not authoritarian states. Democratic states have a free press, human rights groups, and governmental institutions for public accountability, so why not state that democracy causes stealth torture? Let me call this the *regime type* hypothesis.

Certainly several of the main historical claims of this study support this hypothesis, especially those pertaining to the nineteenth and early twentieth centuries. In this case the pattern of torture techniques (clean/scarring) maps onto regime type. But this explanation fails to account for the historical pattern of the late twentieth century, when authoritarian states also adopted techniques that left few marks. Nor does it explain conditions where democratic states do not adopt clean techniques, for example, in some colonial conflicts. Indeed, in many cases, there are extensive intrastate variations in the pattern of torture across geographic areas and over time whether in democratic or authoritarian states. Regime type is a favorite variable among political scientists, but it is too crude a device to explain these variations.

But maybe I have too utopian a view of public monitoring, especially in democracies. Can it really be that torturers care about what church groups and the press think? Those skeptical of this explanation may advance a proposition of their own. They may argue that democratic states are ruled by an elite who, for whatever reason, want to hide their exploitative state in the guise of a democratic government and so order lower-level agents to be stealthy and not make a mess.

There are, indeed, cases where this does appear to be the case. Some elites in the main democracies, particularly political elites, occasionally tacitly or overtly endorse torture, and this often reflects a class distinction. But the main point is this is not really an *alternative* hypothesis. For if the difference between democratic and authoritarian states is that democratic elites want to wear a mask to disguise their tyranny, then one must ask why. And that brings one back to the fact that they believe they are being watched and judged by others in how well they respect human rights, and they believe at least a thin veneer of legitimacy is necessary, one that includes stealth torture.

All that is at stake in the ruling elite hypothesis is this question: *who* is it that insists that torturers should be stealthy, the lower-level agents or the higher-ups or international agents (e.g., the CIA, corporate elites)? This is an empirical question with no universal answer. As the various histories show, the demand for stealth can come from anywhere within institutions, from the head of state and the general to the lowly policeman. When there is evidence for who decided on stealth, I indicate as much, but the evidence is often inconclusive, sometimes pointing to lower-downs and sometimes pointing to higher-ups. This is unfortunately one of those instances where the information is so fragmentary that there is unlikely ever to be adequate evidence to settle the question.

However, the matter is different when it comes to the choice of specific techniques, and here one does get some insight into the world of torturers.

Admittedly, we do find some politicians and institutions issuing lists of torture techniques to interrogators—for example, Secretary of Defense Donald Rumsfeld's orders to military interrogators or CIA manuals—listing a range of techniques that leave no marks. These are rare cases. As chapter 20 indicates, even when politicians authorize torture, there is little evidence of top-down systematic training in specific techniques in the history of modern torture. This is not definitive proof that elites do not have a hand in training because, as I argue, they may prefer backroom apprenticeships that leave no trace.

What is certain, though, is that wherever one finds explicitly approved training in torture techniques, one finds regularly that the interrogators go beyond the approved regulations. As chapters 21 and 23 show, there are several slippery slopes in torture, and one of them is that torturers innovate and introduce new techniques that rapidly become routine. Even if higher-ups *in all cases* really were the people who pushed for stealth and instituted the training, lower agents take things into their own hands fairly rapidly. Torturers appear to be far more independent than is suggested by those who make modern torturers out to be functional appendages of an unholy alliance between big business and big politics. Distinguishing between situations that slip rapidly out of hand and covertly directed operations is always a tricky business, but there are more than enough cases, especially in domestic policing of neighborhoods, to show that torturers do turn to stealth torture on their own.

Variations among States

The historical claims of this study generate a pattern that suggests democracy and stealth torture techniques go hand in hand. The monitoring hypothesis suggests that public monitoring shapes how police and military interrogators behave. It predicts that where public monitoring is present, torturers favor covert coercion, and when it is absent—say in a frontier war or in an authoritarian state—violence, including torture, will be more overt. This proposition is logical and fits the available evidence for the most part.

But there are apparent exceptions to this explanation arising from my main historical claims. These exceptions constitute tests of the monitoring hypothesis. The question here is not whether the monitoring hypothesis is logical or fits the available evidence pertaining to the main democracies, but whether it also works to explain the apparent exceptions better than alternative accounts.

Sometimes, for example, one finds techniques that leave no marks in the absence of public monitoring of human rights, as in the case of American slavery. In these cases, their original adoption was rooted in various religious, educational, moral, medical, or commercial norms not related to the monitoring of human rights. This is especially evident in chapters 12–14. What matters in these cases is not their origin, but why police and militaries adopted and adapted them at particular times and places, and here, it often appears they adopted clean techniques to evade detection or public controversy about rights violations. What appears as an exception in this case is not.

But there is a more important exception of this sort. One important historical claim of this study is that authoritarian states paid little attention to techniques that left few marks in the early twentieth century but many came to adopt these techniques by the end of the twentieth century. Of course, this was not true everywhere. Some states, for example Saddam Hussein's Iraq or Kim Il Sung's North Korea, persisted in using overt, brutal torture. But in many other cases, police and military interrogators seemed to tilt toward torture techniques that leave few marks. Such authoritarian states do not have a free press, autonomous human rights groups, or governmental mechanisms for public accountability such as elections or an independent judiciary. So why would they care whether torture leaves marks or not?

There are two related puzzles here. First, why did authoritarian states in the early twentieth century not use clean techniques, and what explains the few exceptions when they did? And why did authoritarian states in the late twentieth century adopt torture techniques that left few marks? Again, in these cases, I argue that the presence or absence of monitoring made a critical difference.

On my account, it is hardly surprising that authoritarian states did not bother with clean tortures in the early twentieth century. These states were far less accountable domestically and internationally for the violence they performed, and so there was no percentage in using techniques with no marks. What mattered most was whether the torture was painful; whether it left marks or not was a curiosity. In some rare cases, and I document as many as I can find, interrogators consistently used techniques that left few marks. The most famous examples pertain to some prisoners during the various Soviet show trials in the 1930s, but there are others less well known, such as the Nazi treatment of Swedes who aided the Polish Resistance during the war.

When one explores the circumstances around these cases, one finds that for particular reasons, the prisoners in these cases were drawing international attention. Why one case drew international attention while another did not is difficult to say, but when they did, states judged this attention jeopardized their international image or alliances, and it is not too hard to speculate, as historians who document them do, that this is why torturers literally pulled their punches. During the Soviet show trials in the 1930s, for example, defendants had to appear, with no visible signs of torture, to avow their crimes spontaneously before foreign journalists. To this end, Stalin's NKVD favored a procedure involving sleep deprivation, continuous interrogation, and positional tortures dubbed

"The Conveyor," and it is reasonable to conclude that it preferred these techniques because it aimed to be stealthy.

In the early twentieth century, international monitoring of human rights abuses, including torture, was sporadic and selective, as I explain in chapter 1. This situation changed appreciably by the late twentieth century. International human rights monitoring came of age in the 1970s. Certainly, by the 1980s, one can speak of a global human rights regime. In this context, even authoritarian states came to appreciate the value of appearing to conform consistently to such an agenda, especially when foreign aid and legitimacy depended on it. The exceptions to this rule—international pariah states such as Hussein's Iraq or Sung's North Korea—prove the rule. Let me call this the *universal monitoring* (UM) hypothesis.

The UM hypothesis has relatively distinct boundary conditions. It pertains to the pattern of torture only after the formation of a global human rights consensus, enforced by numerous international and national auditors of human rights practices, one that formed roughly in the last three decades of the twentieth century. This kind of consensus is called an international regime, that is, a set of implicit or explicit norms, principles, and decision-making processes that states set up to monitor certain issues in international politics. I make no global claims about the power of monitoring in the period before the formation of this international regime, for example, that the League of Nations or the International Anti-Slavery League constrained the behavior of torturers. Indeed, I hold the opposite view. Before the 1970s, global human rights monitoring was so weak, if it existed at all, that, generally speaking, scarring torture flourished worldwide outside of the main democracies, and it was only in rare cases where states pulled their punches and for highly particular reasons, as I have mentioned.

If the formation of a global, human-rights-monitoring regime drove interrogators to turn to covert coercion, then one would expect a worldwide trend toward clean procedures in its wake. And in fact, the discrete histories of torture techniques repeatedly show a surge in the scope of clean procedures in the 1970s and 1980s. This is most evident in the case of electrotorture (chapters 7 through 9), but it also appears to be the case with many other techniques as well. Moreover, clean techniques tend to cluster around authoritarian states most closely allied with the main democratic states (the United States, the United Kingdom, and France).

This is highly suggestive, but not definitive, and there is another way to explain the timing of these empirical variations. Noam Chomsky and Edward Herman argue, for example, that elites in the United States distributed torture techniques to their authoritarian allies around the world in the 1960s and 1970s. On this account then, the United States distributed clean torture techniques worldwide. Let me call this a *universal distributor* (UD) hypothesis. Chomsky and Herman's UD hypothesis appears to explain why clean techniques spread without referencing human rights monitoring or a global human rights regime as a principal driver.

But that isn't quite true. For this version of the UD hypothesis suggests that a ruling elite (in this case with an international empire) cared about public monitoring too and so trained lower-down agents to use clean techniques. In other words, the difference between the American empire and the Soviet was simply that elites wanted a façade of legitimacy. In that case, monitoring did matter. The only debate here is *to whom* monitoring mattered more—the American elites, the political elites of the client countries, or the lower-downs doing the torturing.

Again, this problem is too shrouded in secrecy to determine with certainty which agent cared more. Consider, for example, the case of an officer in Mobutu's Zaire who stopped his soldiers from beating a prisoner with sticks saying, "It will leave scars and we will get complaints from Amnesty International."[17] It is unlikely this officer had any direct connection to Amnesty. It's possible he knew his immediate superior didn't want a mess, or that he had a circular directly from Mobutu's office on the subject or he was in touch with the local CIA adviser who told him to cool it. The truth is we are unlikely ever to know. All we can say for certain is that *he* cared about international monitoring. It's possible other people around him did too, but who more so than others is anyone's guess.

But there is reason to believe that the United States did not distribute clean techniques to its allies worldwide in the 1970s as a matter of policy. One test is simply this. If the United States really had done so, one would expect a fair degree of continuity in the kinds of clean techniques used. But, as I demonstrate in chapters 8 and 9, such continuity is hard to find, especially outside of Latin America, and even within this zone of American influence, the variations are too great to suggest a single source.

Moreover, even if Chomsky and Herman are right, their hypothesis is a partial one at best. It does not explain the pattern of torture in states like South Africa, which even they concede were not part of the U.S. orbit of influence. Nor does it explain the persistence of clean tortures in the Soviet Union, for example, the notorious Soviet psychoprisons.

Another possibility is that clean tortures were far more widespread before the 1970s than is commonly supposed. Some clean tortures definitely preexisted universal monitoring, but if they were more widespread than is documented here, then the historical pattern I describe is illusory, the effect of better documentation that has become possible with the formation of a global human rights regime after the 1970s. Documentation of torture has certainly improved tremendously since the first global audit in 1973. However, there is little historical evidence that these techniques were widespread before the 1970s, and typically when they appeared, they occurred mainly in democratic states for reasons I have already described.

Lastly, the UM hypothesis may overemphasize international legitimacy at the expense of domestic legitimacy. After all, authoritarian states also need to have some support, however slim, from domestic constituencies. Maybe these states turned to clean tortures to win over those a bit squeamish about overt scarring torture.

But, for better or worse, prison stories do not describe torturers worrying about what other citizens might think as they torture prisoners. Indeed, torturers usually had no trouble finding relatives, neighbors, and friends of prisoners and torturing them in the presence of their captives. Occasional anecdotes suggest that torturers worried more about what international monitors might report rather than a breaking story in the evening paper. The story of the Zairian officer is typical. And logically one would be inclined to say that international monitoring matters more for authoritarian states, whereas for democratic states, domestic monitoring is probably as important. But this cannot be proven with certainty based on the available evidence.

Variations within States

The historical claims in this book generate another set of puzzles more difficult to explain, and these pertain to variations in the pattern of clean and scarring techniques *within* states. British colonial police, for example, showed less concern for cleanliness in torture in Kenya in the 1950s than the Criminal Investigation Division (CID) did in Mandatory Palestine fifteen years earlier. French troops used highly visible tortures on Moroccans in the 1920s, a far cry from the cleaner techniques the French Sûreté used on the Vietnamese in Saigon in 1931. In some cases, the same agents preferred different techniques in different places during the same conflict. French troops in Algeria used far more scarring techniques on the frontiers than they did in the main cities, and a similar contrast appears between tortures that Israeli troops use on the Lebanese frontier and those that appear in the densely populated West Bank.

Some anecdotal evidence suggests that the *quality* of monitoring is what accounts for this difference. As one Israeli soldier observed, on the West Bank, "You need a lawyer next to you all the time," whereas in Southern Lebanon "there aren't hundreds of regulations."[18] Monitoring is more frequent in urban areas, it is logical to assume, and soldiers and police know so. Similarly, the Wickersham Report argues that American police in the 1920s were more likely to change how they behaved if they anticipated institutional monitoring (judges, prison doctors) rather than external monitoring (the press for example) (chapter 3). And British colonial documents indicate that administrators knew that the Anglican Church was monitoring violence in Mandatory Palestine and that the Nazi press was eager to make the most of any overt British violence in its propaganda to Arabs in the Middle East (chapter 14).

Perhaps the most suggestive evidence that the type of monitoring matters comes from the lives of doctors who treat torture victims (chapter 19). Doctors emerged on the front lines of monitoring because they had a specialized set of skills to diagnose the use of some clean techniques. Prison doctors can sink or save a stealth torture operation (as in Northern Ireland in the late 1970s), as can doctors on the outside (whether in a city or a foreign country). As these doctors did their work, torturers abandoned one set of techniques (drugs, for example) for others. Others harassed and tortured health professionals. Maybe all health professionals are radicals, or hunting doctors is better sport than hunting human rights lawyers, but this is unlikely.

What seems more likely is that *someone* inside a torture apparatus is responsive to developments in the kind of monitoring. Usually, prisoners identify their torturers as thus responsive, but this could be an effect of their condition. They only have access to their torturers, not to those who command them. One can list qualities that might affect the potency of monitoring: whether it is frequent or infrequent, comprehensive or scattered, conducted from a distance or proximate, internal or external to the institution, domestic or international, based on local knowledge or conducted by foreigners, and the type of specialization (e.g., medical or lay evaluation). Only more detailed case studies will be able to say which matter more.

National Styles of Stealth Torture

The extent of monitoring may explain *why* torturers turn to or away from clean techniques, but it does not explain *how* they torture. Torturers show distinct preferences for this or that clean technique. Explaining these preferences presents a different set of puzzles.

Take electric torture. Why is it that the French style in electric torture spreads around the world, while other no less painful or clean instruments, notably the Argentine *picana eléctrica*, languish for decades? Why do British colonial police rarely use electricity in interrogation? What explains variation in clean torture techniques between states?

Torturers also show distinct preferences during specific periods. For example, between 1973 and 1984, South African torturers favored forced standing, a well-known positional torture. Forced standing occurred in two-fifths of all cases. Between 1985 and 1989, torturers changed their style. Forced standing faded to a distant one-sixth of all cases, while electric torture and near asphyxiation occurred in nearly half of all cases.[19] Whatever the reason for this variation, it cannot be because forced standing was more scarring than these other techniques.

This book covers dozens, perhaps hundreds, of cases of innovation and adaptation in torture. As these cases pile up, readers will recognize that some common explanations for *how* torture persists cannot adequately explain the shifting patterns of techniques, most notably those that appeal to culture, ideology, and efficiency.

It is not enough to say that torturers favor such and such a technique over time because it stems from the country's cultural legacy. Some techniques, it is true, are closely associated with a country's past, but this does not explain their persistence. Take for example the *falaka*, an old Middle Eastern technique that involves beating the soles of the feet with a rod or cable. While the rod does not break the skin of the victim's soles, it causes excruciating pain along the length of the body and causes the feet to swell enormously. It is not surprising that Turkish police favored it. What then explains the fact that they seemed to abandon the *falaka* rapidly in the early 1990s for techniques involving slabs of ice? Or what explains the fact that, in the 1970s, the *falaka* appeared beyond its customary range, in countries where it had never been used before? Culture and tradition may explain where a technique comes from, but they are too gross to account for intrastate and interstate variations.

The same considerations apply to ideology. Sometimes it appears that variations in ideology map onto the pattern of techniques. For example, in the 1970s, electrotorture reflects the fault line of the Cold War, appearing on the "Free World" side but not often on the Communist side (chapter 9). Communists had their own set of clean techniques (most famously, the notorious Conveyor technique) (chapter 3). In their famous analysis of Communist interrogation practices, Harold Wolff and Lawrence Hinkle argue that the Communists favored the Conveyor technique because Communism strongly opposes overt physical violence.[20]

Perhaps, but there is far greater variation in states that share common ideologies than at first appears. For example, many Eurasian states shared a common ideology ("Communism"), but varied greatly in the techniques they used (chapter 15). Many, such as Romania, abandoned the Conveyor technique for brutal scarring techniques. Others abandoned torture altogether. And the Soviets abandoned the infamous Conveyor technique in the 1940s for warehousing dissidents in psychoprisons in the 1960s (chapter 19).

Similarly, maybe all Latin America and Central American states in the 1970s shared a common "National Security Ideology"(NSI), as is sometimes argued. But this common ideology would have a difficult time accounting for why Argentines favored the *picana eléctrica* or electric cattle prod, the Chileans the *parilla,* or electric grill, and Brazilians the field telephone magneto (chapters 8 and 9).

Some ideologies may require or justify stealthy violence, but they appear useless in explaining the choice of techniques. There are of course variants of Marxism and possibly NSI, but splitting ideologies apart to fit patterns of torture is a notoriously subjective enterprise. Maybe Khruschevism has a deep relationship with the psychoprison just as Stalinism does to the Conveyor technique. But the obstacles to making a persuasive link here are so daunting as to offer a plausible reason to explore alternative explanations.

This brings up the matter of efficiency. Some might hold that police after all are practical people and they favor what gets the job done. It is tempting to think then that considerations of efficiency explain why torture varies over time within a state and between states. Now efficiency is an empty concept in itself; one has to specify a goal before the term takes on meaning. Traveling by bicycle or car may be more or less efficient depending on whether the goal is speed or better air quality.

In torture, the main criterion for efficiency is usually the painfulness of the technique. Consider, for example, sound chambers like the "House of Fun" installed in Dubai Special Branch Headquarters by a British firm. Marketed as "prisoner disorientation equipment," it is a "a high-tech room fitted with a generator for white noise and strobe lights such as might be seen in a disco, but turned up to a volume capable of reducing the victim to submission within half an hour."[21]

We would expect to find such an efficient technique installed widely, if not in squeamish democratic states at least in authoritarian states. Devices like the House of Fun are rather rare; such techniques appear in only a few countries over the past forty years—Portugal, Brazil, the United Kingdom, Israel, and Serbia. On the other hand, electric torture is global. It is the Esperanto, the international language, of torture.[22] Here then are two techniques, both scientific and painful, but one succeeds whereas the other does not. What explains, then, why some efficient techniques succeed or fail? To say that the technique is efficient is clearly not enough.

Torturers, and sometimes those who analyze them, maintain they favor "scientific" methods that are laboratory tested. Very few techniques that dominate the world of torture today come from laboratories. Low-tech tortures, like the *falaka,* are far more common that scientific tortures like the House of Fun.

In case after case, we find availability, habit, and memory shape how torturers choose. Torturers often choose instruments that are available in the station
house or in nearby enterprises (cattle prods from stockyards). In many cases,
torturers favor devices integrally linked to their routine duties, making it difficult to deprive them of it. Would you really deprive us of field telephones,
gas masks, and riot control sticks? In other cases, they favor devices that are
multifunctional, a tub or a hose. There is only one way to use the House of
Fun; human rights activists have an easy time identifying it, and torturers would
have a hard time justifying possessing it. Why bother with something that expensive when plastic bags are readily available for near asphyxiation?

Availability, linkage, and multifunctionality go some way toward explaining
how torturers select their tools. Institutional settings also shape these choices.
Institutions seeking prospective information about the future favor techniques
that generate pain quickly, whereas those seeking coerced confessions about
past events tend to select techniques that may take considerable time. When
there is no urgency, why not resort to days of sleep deprivation and forced
standing until the confession comes (chapters 2 and 3)?

Above all, torturers, like all human beings, remember what was done in
the past. They share stories, recalling terrifying things done in other times and
places. These memories have roots in family histories, schoolboy horror stories,
and boot camp gossip. Often these are traumatic memories of what was done
during a war or nationalist struggle. In the 1990s, Turkish police abandoned the
falaka just as human rights doctors developed techniques that could identify
the *falaka*'s effects up to six months after its use on a prisoner. Police turned to
laying prisoners on slabs of ice, a technique harder to identify, but also one with
a fairly unique history in the Mediterranean region. The British or the Turkish
Cypriots used it on Greek Cypriots in the 1950s, as did the Bulgarians on their
prisoners, and in the 1960s, the Greek junta used it on its dissidents (chapter
13). There are three reports of ice torture from elsewhere in this period (South
Africa in the 1970s; the Philippines and the Soviets in Afghanistan in the 1980s).
But it is hard not to suspect here that one is observing the power of local gossip
as enemies imitate enemies. At any rate, culture, ideology, and scientific efficiency are poorly situated to explain this pattern of diffusion.

In some cases, the memories run deeper. They embrace common mean-
ings, the collective traumas that shaped the narrative of a nation. What is the
worst thing that you remember being done to you? Remember that and do it
to this person. Sometimes, these memories are so terrible that torturers studi-
ously avoid a technique that will associate them with past oppressors. This does
not mean they won't torture; they only torture using things that are similar too,
but not identical with, those of *their* torturers. You see, they seem to be saying,
I'm not one of them. Such memories constitute intersubjective norms among

torturers, institutional norms if you like. For example, during the two Vietnam wars and the Franco-Algerian conflict, French, South Vietnamese, and American troops used electrotorture; indeed, reports of electrotorture came to symbolize these wars (chapters 7 and 8). After the conflicts were over, Vietnamese and Algerian interrogators and guards tortured during the next three decades, but avoided using electrotorture. In both countries, they turned to electrotorture in the 1990s, not using a magneto (the classic technique) but with stun guns and prods (chapters 8 and 9). Perhaps in some cases, a generation must pass before a technique returns, and even then not in its original form.

One striking empirical pattern that emerges from the data is repeated clustering of clean techniques in predictable ways in various countries or regions, what I call "styles of torture." As all the techniques leave few marks, there is no obvious reason why one technique is matched up regularly with another. Some of these conventional bundles have well-known names, such as the Soviet Conveyor technique or the Israeli *shabeh*. Others I have named in order to highlight the predictable clustering and mark its first occurrence. For example, the style of torture American forces used in Iraq and Afghanistan derived from two venerable traditions of torture, French modern and Anglo-Saxon modern. Styles persist not only across time in a country, but also appear in torture in other countries, some of them allies and some of them enemies of the original innovator.

If the choice of technique is entirely arbitrary and random, one would not expect to find national styles of torture. But since they do exist, they need to be explained. My explanation for these persisting styles takes seriously the notion that torture is a craft, not a science (chapter 21). When explaining why regional craftsmen differ in the way they make clothes, one might consider habit and training (this is how we do it here) and availability (we do what we can with what we've got). In the case of national styles, it is plausible to consider historical memory (the old sergeant tells me this is how the Nazis did it), habit and training (this is how we do it here), and availability (torturers do not have a great deal of time for experimentation, particularly in a crisis, and they reach for well-known techniques).

These are reasonable expectations, but they cannot be proven with certainty. And it is frankly impossible to do an ethnographic study of torturers on the job. Nor can one say which of the various factors, availability, habit, or historical memory, matter more. But this explanation is logical, fits with what we know about how some techniques stick together, and is more plausible than variables that point to the state (ideology), modernization (scientific torture), or tradition (culture). These are far clumsier when it comes to explaining why styles develop, persist, and disappear.

If this craft apprenticeship hypothesis is correct, then there is a learning pattern in torture that deserves some reflection. One important historical claim of this study is that torture has changed worldwide, a sweeping change that rarely occurs in methods of violence. But this change is perhaps all the more remarkable in this case for its reliance on hidden networks and subterranean social memory.

War, for example, also changed over the twentieth century, but it did so before our eyes. States may obtain or produce poison gas, atomic weapons, or napalm covertly, but the Somme, Hiroshima, and Vietnam publicly advertised what they should aim for. Modern torture offers no similar universal public reference. Some national styles did briefly draw world attention (most notably the Five Techniques of Northern Ireland and the "brainwashing techniques" in the Korean War (chapters 3, 13, 15, and 18), and some torturers here and there tried to imitate them. But in general, there was no *Janes Torture Weekly*. For most of the century, torturers communicated by ancient methods. Techniques spread through backroom apprenticeships, networks of whispers, and the enabling power of knowing glances and averted eyes. The transformation of torture involved innumerable complex events, many almost lost to modern memory—even to those who have made it their business to monitor torture in the contemporary world. The enormous power of social networks is, in this respect, thought-provoking.

Torture and Democracy

Explaining *how* torture happens is a fairly reliable check on misleading and mistaken stories of *why* torture happens. That a country received Nazi advisers does not mean that its torture techniques came from the Nazis; one has to check, and what one often finds is that analysts moved too hastily from their favorite account of *why* torture happens to an erroneous and misleading account of *how* torture happened. In the various discrete histories, I repeatedly show that it is dangerous to collapse an explanation of *how* torture happens into *why* it happens. Higher-ups may authorize torture and caution police and soldiers to leave few marks, but torturers choose, and explaining these choices means paying attention to the details. Paying attention to the "know-how" throws into question some favorite modern stories about torture (see, for example, "Hell Is in the Details" in chapter 2).

Of course, one should not neglect the question of *why* torture happens, particularly in democratic contexts. This puzzle deserves its own explanation. Why is it that some democratic states torture, while other do not? Can one specify conditions under which torture appears in democratic states?

Let me sharpen this puzzle further. The demand for torture has not waned over the last forty years. At a 1996 conference on abolishing torture in Stockholm, Amnesty International's researchers reported that "torture is as prevalent today as when the United Nations Convention against Torture was adopted in 1984."[23] Three years later, at a similar conference in Chicago, Amnesty's Eric Prokosh suggested that torture is as widespread today as at the time of Amnesty's first Campaign against Torture in 1972. Nigel Rodley, the UN special rapporteur on torture, conceded this might be true, though he asserted that the situation would be far worse if there had not been so many treaties, truth commissions, and newspaper stories.[24]

For those who thought the end of the Cold War, the fall of many dictators and juntas, and the spread of democratization would reduce torture worldwide, this is bitter news. During the Cold War, one could comfort oneself that torture persisted mainly because many states that practiced it, Communist or capitalist, were authoritarian. But evidently regime type does not explain why torture persists or not. The puzzle is no longer, "Does torture persist after the Cold War?" (it obviously does), nor, "Is torture compatible with democracy?" (evidently they can coexist). It is, rather, "How is it that democracy and torture can coexist?"

When I began this book, this puzzle was largely neglected, but today, the danger appears to be to take the answer to this puzzle as self-evident. One might think that the demand for torture in democracies arises mainly during national emergencies. It is easy to imagine that, in war or in the face of terrorism, an imminent threat might lead some to endorse torture and many others to turn a blind eye. This would explain why some democracies turned to torture, for instance the French in Algeria, the British in Northern Ireland, or the Israelis on the West Bank. It would not explain many cases where analysts have documented systematic torture in democracies when an objective or perceived national threat was absent. These cases include such places as Japan, Brazil, the Russian Federation, democratic South Africa, and some American cities, notably Chicago and New York.

There are three ways torture appears in democracies that correspond to these sketches—the national security model, the civic discipline model, and the juridical model. In some cases torture occurs because a national security bureaucracy overwhelms the democratic institutions that were designed to control it. But in other cases, the demand for torture arises out of two other factors: unsound judicial practices and public fear of crime or perceived breakdown in civic order. Police, either on their own or with tacit consent, set about torturing to create safe streets. They hand criminals over to judges with confessions extracted through torture, and they administer curbside justice on marginal populations (transients, aliens, or addicts). In other cases, the demand comes not from local neighborhoods and police but from the judicial system. Some judicial systems value confessions inordinately, and police have strong incentives to secure them by any means.

The models identify important preconditions for torture in democratic states, but these conditions do not obtain in every democracy. These conditions are necessary, but not sufficient for torture to occur. A national security crisis might lead to various massacres but not torture. Police may use psychological tricks, rather than torture, to coerce confessions. The models only indicate that torture has an elective affinity to such conditions, that is, that it is highly probable that torture will appear under these conditions. Pressing beyond this for a fine-grained causal account of the necessary *and* sufficient conditions is currently not possible given the fragmentary knowledge of the empirical cases.

Few empirical cases are as clean as the models. In chapter 2, I review all the known cases of torture and democracy from Athenian democracy to the present, showing the ways they are similar to and differ from the models. The models, in this respect, highlight elements of empirical cases that might be missed otherwise, and more than one model may apply to one empirical case. The empirical cases in turn point to additional elements that sustain torture in democratic contexts. For example, once police seek confessions by any means, they become less skilled at other investigative tasks, and this in turn makes them rely on torture even more. Likewise, hostility between ethnic groups can exacerbate the tendencies set loose in the various models.

Does Torture Work?

The three models of torture in democracies correspond roughly to the three main purposes of government torture: to intimidate, to coerce false confessions, and to gather accurate security information. But do these techniques work?

Certainly, no one can doubt that coercive interrogation techniques can serve to intimidate or generate false confessions in many cases. The heart of the matter is whether an organization can apply these techniques (torture, coercion, "torture lite," call them what you will) scientifically and professionally to generate true and reliable intelligence, intelligence that is qualitatively superior to standard police techniques. That question is at the core of part V.

Despite public denials, the U.S. government's answer to this question appears to be yes in practice. In 2001, reports started describing new American interrogation techniques in the war on terror often dubbed "stress and duress."[25] By 2004, reports confirmed American torture in prisons in Iraq, Afghanistan, Guantánamo, Cuba, and elsewhere.[26] The public debate that has followed the war on terror has assumed the techniques work, and what is left to consider is whether to use them.

There is currently no official report that answers the question, "Does torture work?" No General Accounting Office report weighs how information from "stress and duress" interrogations compares to other intelligence activities (e.g., informers, fingerprinting, and electronic intelligence) in foiling, or failing to foil, terrorist activity. There is no U.S. Army report on what impact these techniques have on the professional behavior and military organization. If the government knows, this knowledge is undoubtedly classified.[27]

What we do know is that these techniques have a history, one that is presented in great detail in part IV. Many of these techniques date back to British, French, and German military punishments in the late nineteenth century, some to American police practice in the 1920s, and some to Soviet practice in the 1930s. We also know something of how these techniques came to be used for interrogation purposes in the late twentieth century.

We also know that, in previous conflicts, militaries have held that torturing for true intelligence can be done professionally, scientifically, and productively. Torture advocates point to the Battle of Algiers in particular, in which French paratroopers dispensed with a terrorist organization in one year with the aid of, among other things, brutal torture (chapter 22).

In the 1990s, many French torturers have written memoirs describing what they did in Algiers. These accounts, not yet translated into English and written by those who did the actual torture, undermine the self-congratulatory accounts that French generals offered after the battle. They explain that there is no "science of torture," nor could there be, given the complex nature of pain; that practicing torture deprofessionalized soldiers; that it fragmented French military institutions; and that the intelligence torture produced during the battle was inferior to work done by informers and other policing activities.

These statements correspond to what we know indirectly about torture from numerous disciplines, from clinical psychology to policing. Hitherto, this material has been too scattered, and I bring all this material together in one book (chapters 21 and 23). This material suggests three points quite strongly. First, torture has not one slippery slope, but three. Torture increasingly takes in more suspects than those approved, leads to harsher methods than are authorized, and leads to greater bureaucratic fragmentation. Moreover, these slopes are slicker and sharper when people are seeking urgent information about the future than when they are securing false confessions about crimes in the past. Lastly, accuracy in torture is exceedingly poor, in some cases less accurate than flipping a coin, and the key successes in gathering information in known cases come from other methods, most notably cultivating public cooperation and informants.

The Battle of Algiers is a textbook illustration of all these points. Indeed, if we go through the entire battle event by event, we find only two instances in which one could say torture generated true, critically timely information, and how one judges what success means in these cases is open to considerable interpretation. Until scholars can give us a more detailed account from the Algerian archives, that is where things stand.

If this is true of the Battle of Algiers, where soldiers used painful water and electrical tortures, it is likely just as true for American "torture lite." The Battle of Algiers—not the movie, but the event—is not the startling justification of torture that it is often taken to be. Nor do other testimonials, offered by torturers in other times and places, bear the weight of historical scrutiny. We live in an age where we substitute movies and storytelling for memory.

It is not then just interrogators whose acts and judgments about torture arise from social memory and the recollection of trauma. We are similar. Memories of collective trauma shape powerfully how we have come to evaluate torture since the World War II. Just as there are myths on the right, there are myths on the left that reinforce a belief that torture works. *The Battle of Algiers*, one might recall, was a left-wing movie; it played to packed audiences in the 1960s that cheered the FLN guerillas.

Memory is not just a great repository of knowledge of times past; it is also a great city in which it is easy to get lost. Many times writing this book I followed well-known memories of torture down broad avenues into blind alleys. As I wrote each chapter, I came to understand that how we remember torture is as much a part of the story I am telling as the actual mapping of the torture techniques themselves. Too often the problems that arose in the mapping arose not from what was done, but from *what was subsequently said* about what was done. Some of us, more than others, are in a position to confront the practice of torture today, but, as I argue in chapter 24, all of us have the responsibility to attend to what we say about torture and to appreciate how important it is to take proper care of our memories.

Who Cares?

The empirical *claims* and theoretical *explanations* in this study raise questions about accepted theses in several disciplines. Let me call these theses disciplinary *interventions*, because they answer to the notorious "Who cares?" question. Not every chapter in this manuscript pertains to these disciplinary interventions. Here, I orient those with specific interests to the relevant chapters, sketching the accepted thesis and indicating ways in which the results of this study challenge them. I'll start with those disciplines that explore the causes of violence (political science, history, sociology) and moving then to disciplines that examine the meaning of violence (philosophy and cultural studies).

International human rights regimes do shape state behavior (chapters 9, 20–24). Simple political realism insists that liberal norms rarely coerce states because in the end, maintaining state power is more important than respecting rights. Short-term advantage trumps political sociability. There are, no doubt, state leaders who believe this. The leaders of Myanmar and North Korea do not care what Amnesty International might say about torture in their countries. In such regimes, torturers value techniques for their painfulness.

Yet today such states are the exception, not the rule, as simple realism would predict. If, as I argue in this book, there has been a global transformation in the means of torture, this is partly because international norms of acceptable behavior are far more robust than is commonly acknowledged.[28] This is a more complex political realism. Most states perceive the advantages of at least appearing to respect human rights. Even repressive states know that bad publicity and human rights monitors can undermine the legitimacy, commerce, and foreign aid on which they depend. These states are caught between their desire to repress "outside the law" and their obligations, juridically codified or externally demanded, to do so without torture.

Stealth torture is one practice that helps states bridge this gap. Political scientists have rarely paid attention to torture in contrast to war, a central preoccupation of international relations.[29] Perhaps they should. Most wars today are civil or secessionist wars, and many involve torture. Watching how torture is conducted in these conflicts may indicate a leadership's susceptibility to international norms. The turn to stealth torture, as well as increases or decreases in its usage, are relevant indicators. This turn indicates that leaders conceive state interests on a broader register and are seeking to integrate themselves, however ungracefully, into the international system.

Moreover, in its broadest sense, this book offers states good reasons to avoid torturing prisoners, quite apart from the prudential considerations of international aid and illegitimacy. Institutionalized torture is the farthest thing from political realism; indeed, it is downright foolish in some cases. The most effective ways of exercising violence and gathering information depend on public cooperation or at least willing informants. Political wisdom suggests that observing human rights habitually in the exercise of violence has benefits far beyond what states can achieve by means of torture. Does this mean that what begins merely in fear leads to routine political sociability over time? Perhaps. The difficulty is that states that torture do not accumulate information on their torture, nor do they analyze its corrosive effect on state power. Indeed, they have strong interests in avoiding such analysis. This is, in part, a perverse effect of the robustness of international norms today: To avoid bad publicity, if not trials before an international criminal court, states keep knowledge of torture classified and hidden from public assessment. Regrettably, many factors still help simple realists fool themselves and others and allow torture to flourish yet another day.

No single nation is the primary, original distributor of modern torture technology (chapters 3–9, 15, and 24). Many people believe that a single nation is the main source of torture training and technology today; this is the universal distributor (UD) hypothesis. For some, this universal distributor was the Soviet Union; for others, Nazi Germany; and for yet others, the United States. Chomsky and Herman's account of U.S. torture described above is just one variant of the UD hypothesis. Unquestionably, the United States and the Soviet Union did shape torture in their zones of greatest influence, Latin America and Eastern Europe respectively, and in Brazil and East Germany in particular. However, beyond these zones, the evidence for the UD hypothesis falls off markedly. Within these zones, states like Argentina, Chile, China, and Romania developed instruments and techniques not used elsewhere in the region.

The UD hypothesis cannot easily explain such regional variations. Since the Nuremberg trials, human rights monitors have held to an important axiom: uniformity of techniques indicates uniformity of intention. When the same practices appear in different places and times within a given country, in the cases of individuals who are unknown to each other, it is hard not to conclude that there is a deliberate state policy to torture. When one finds that other states adopt the same practices, especially states that have established military relationships and receive financial aid, one knows one has identified a distributive network.

However, most versions of the UD hypothesis do not look carefully at the torture techniques themselves. They simply follow the cash and military brass from the principal state to its satellites, substituting this approach for the hard work of studying interstate and intrastate variation in torture techniques. Even Chomsky and Herman, who advance the most sophisticated version of the hypothesis, look only at American military aid and training, not at the specific torture techniques that the aid recipients actually used. While following the cash and the brass can complement a careful mapping of torture techniques, these methods cannot be substitutes for it. Following *only* the cash and the brass generates misleading and often mistaken claims about the origins of torture techniques.

Similar objections can be raised against other UD hypotheses, for example, that the Nazis invented and distributed electric torture or that modern or stealth torture begins with the Stalinist Conveyor technique. In these cases, analysts do not document the incidence, geographic range, and details of a technique or compare it to similar facts about other Nazi or Soviet techniques. Too often, they identify a practice as exemplary when it was in fact limited in range or highly unusual or simply unadaptable to democratic policing. They overstate how much the Nazi and Soviet regimes contributed to the arsenal of clean tortures, passing over the influence of other states that had been using these techniques for years before the Nazis and Soviets even existed. If we could not see how democratic regimes shaped the history of modern torture, this was sometimes because we could not tell the forest from the two tallest trees in it.

Torture is a craft, not a science (chapters 18–21). In the early 1970s, Tim Shallice and John McGuffin warned that laboratory techniques were transforming torture into a science, a claim uncritically repeated by several recent writers.[30] But the last thirty years have not borne out this warning. The tortures at Abu Ghraib do not express an American science of torture and training, for torture worldwide still has all the characteristics of a craft apprenticeship. What torturers do is turn to what is available, what is habitual, what they can get away with, what they have heard from others, what they remember, and what they can learn by imitating others. Most torturers, with the exception of the Greek and the Brazilian, do not report receiving formal training in torture. Even CIA interrogation manuals begin with the proposition that good interrogation technique cannot be taught by manual; manuals are only helpful in reminding one what mistakes should be avoided. These, contrary to popular belief, are a legion. Torturers have to struggle with inadvertent death, decreasing sensitivity of damaged bodies, unconsciousness (which wastes considerable time), failures in timing, and variations in personality that are bewildering. None of this offers much evidence of a science of torture.

Since George Orwell wrote his chilling story of modern torture in *Nineteen Eighty-Four*, we have come to fear that torturers might harness the powers of science. Indeed they have, but not in the way Orwell imagined. Torturers like devices that cause intense pain or save them labor. They appreciate advances that allow them to revive victims for further torture. They have come to appreciate techniques that leave less visible damage. What neither science nor technology has been able to do is offer generalizable and universal rules for breaking victims, and there are good reasons to believe that this will never happen unless the nature of pain itself changes. The belief that torture is becoming ever more scientific is rooted in general preconceptions about technology and progress, not in the empirical study of torture instruments. Torturers may cloak themselves in the mantle of science, but this does not make them so, any more than wearing a white lab coat makes one a scientist.

How well torture technology spreads depends on the strength of the sociotechnical network that carries it forward (chapters 8 and 10). While most torture instruments are local and homemade, a few are technologically sophisticated, including electroshock devices and devices, like the House of Fun, that draw on sensory deprivation studies. Much that pertains to these devices is shrouded in government secrecy; so much has been lost in war, so many stories remain untranslated, that one can understand why we know more about the diffusion of hybrid corn in Iowa than we know about how these techniques spread. The latest books on torture instruments, mainly by English authors, break little new ground in this respect.[31] They illustrate devices with gruesome, glossy pictures and fascinate readers with accounts of how horrible these instruments feel.

What these books do not do well is explain why one sophisticated device fails and another spreads rapidly. They pass over instruments, such as John Lilly's sensory deprivation flotation chamber, that terrified CIA volunteers wonderfully, but found the wrong kind of consumers, not police in authoritarian states, but New Age resorts throughout the West Coast. They do not discuss the many electric devices that never made it, or had incredibly slow starts, or failed to leap the barrier from customary use to police torture.

Social scientists conceptualize innovation and diffusion as a sequence of events in which a technology moves from the world of science to the social and political realm. This sequence begins with identifying a basic need; then doing scientific research to make sure the device works; and then marketing the useful device to society. Then society responds by resisting or adopting it.[32]

The story of electric stun technology, the most successful technology in this book, does not fit this pattern. From the start, the social side of the equation (which theoretically comes last) was integral to the science of stun. John Cover, the inventor of the Taser, organized networks that were simultaneously social and technological. He worked simultaneously on the social side (locating or creating needs; organizing existing or anticipated consumers) and the scientific side (identifying new materials, shaping new connections, conducting different tests); whenever he changed an element on one side, he had to reassemble elements on the other. After assembling several such socio-technical chains, Cover found one that was stable enough to support the Taser. Once the network was stable, other stun devices were developed in the classical form (invention to diffusion) and floated across the network as if the devices were powered by their own inherent utility. There was, however, nothing magical about stun guns.

Whether a device succeeds depends on how strong or weak the network is.[33] In stun technology, we find a chain of agents, human and material, that have to be kept together for the device to work. Multifunctionality and linkage serve to bring more and more allies into a network, stabilizing it against opposition. When the links in the chain are strong, held together by many allies, one can speak of "social resistance" to what looks like inherently useful technology. If the chain is missing a link, if the connection is imperfectly made, if the allies desert or fail, if the technology stands on its own—no matter how sophisticated it is, no matter how many political needs it might satisfy—the technology becomes junk. This, as I will show, is the fate that overtook technology based on sensory deprivation studies.

To know one's pain is to be able to describe it to oneself and others (chapters 2, 11, 17, 19, 20). This book shows repeatedly that communities treat victims that have marks of violence upon their bodies entirely differently from those who have no marks to show. In 1939, Mordehy Petcho, a member of the Jewish guerrilla group Irgun, lay in a cell after being tortured by the British CID. He describes how an old Arab brought food. As he could not eat, the Arab fed him, and when Petcho felt sharp pains, the old man asked to lift the blanket. Then he saw the bruises and "cursed the English as the worst of savages."[34] One can scarcely imagine a stranger scene in which a Palestinian Arab and an Irgun supporter bind themselves in common recognition of each other's humanity. Sixty years later, Palestinians had a hard time appreciating the suffering Israeli positional torture effected on their own relatives, and the Israelis denied torture had happened at all, since it left no marks. It took hard work for people to learn how to read the bodies that were subjected to *shabeh* technique, to question state power and accord respect to its victims.

These events tell us more than the fact that surviving stealth torture is a lonely, miserable experience; they help us understand more clearly that pain is a complex sensation, with cognitive and linguistic components. As Ludwig Wittgenstein observed, we do not have direct access to our pain, if what is meant by this claim is preverbal access to that damn sensation X that fills my mind and drives out the world.[35] Even knowing this sensation, calling it "pain" to oneself, requires some understanding of how to use concepts competently. Such linguistic competence occurs against the background of a common form of life and does not make sense without it.

If pain really did drive one into prelinguistic silence, prisoners would be unintelligible to themselves; phrases like "This hurts!" would make no sense to them, becoming merely babble. Unless they go mad, most prisoners do not lose their ability to recognize and use pain-related language even in their agony. Indeed, torture victims draw sustenance from their pain. Even in their darkest, isolated moments hanging on a hook, their pain roots them powerfully in communities of which they are a part.[36] What they lose in pain is only the ability to express themselves to others. When torturers turn to covert torture, they deliberately induce a breakdown in one's ability to show one's pain to others, stripping their words of the marks that give the speaker credibility. How horrible to be unable to use words in ways that elicit acknowledgment, to be unable to explain, to be uncertain, as in the case of some victims, even about what one has experienced.

This is not, however, how cultural theorist Elaine Scarry describes torture in her important account. For Scarry, torturers reduce victims to a prelinguistic silence. They succeed because of "the inexpressibility of physical pain." "Physical pain does not simply resist language, but actively destroys it, bringing about an immediate reversion to a state anterior to language, to the sounds and cries a human being makes before language is learned." Pain destroys one's world, and, in that silence, torturers impose the myth of the state's legitimacy. The prisoner's pain is "perverted into the fraudulent assertion of power, that the objectified pain is denied as pain and read as power."[37]

Being unable to express pain does indeed have political consequences, but it would be a mistake to confuse the empirical inability to say or think when one is in pain with a philosophical claim that pain is a preverbal sensation, a sensation that has some quality that, in principle, makes it inexpressible. To be sure, pain may drive one into silence, for example during hard work ("Shut up! I'm holding this file cabinet!"). It may drastically shrink one's world, as in torture, forcing one to concentrate on the intense biological effort of getting by. But pain is not an object the torturer makes within me, a sensation to which only I have certain access ("You can't understand *my* pain!").[38]

To know I "have pain" is to invoke linguistic and social conventions that help us make sense of what words mean. The difficulties arise when the conventions we count on to express ourselves breakdown, as they do in stealth torture. The sociologist Veena Das, writing on mass rape in during the partition of India, observes that when we think of pain as Wittgenstein does, we free ourselves "from thinking that statements about pain are in the nature of questions about certainty or doubt over our own pain or that of others. Instead, we begin to think of pain as asking for acknowledgement and recognition; denial of the other's pain is not about the failings of intellect, but the failings of spirit. In the register of the imaginary, the pain of the other not only asks for a home in language, but also seeks a home in the body."[39] Stealth torture denies precisely this home in the body, tangling the victims and their communities in doubts, uncertainties, and illusions.

Scarry is right to draw attention to the importance of expression in torture, but this book distinguishes more carefully between different kinds of inexpressibility that follow from torture. The inexpressibility that matters politically is not the gap between the brain and the tongue, but between victims and their communities, a gap that is cynically calculated, a gap that shelters a state's legitimacy.

Still, eventually communities respond; citizens learn to hear torture victims and read their bodies. Here again Scarry's solution is misleading, at least from a political philosopher's perspective. What enables us to reconstitute our ability to speak with each other about pain is an activity different from capturing pain in works of art, stories, statues, and other objects of worldly making. What it takes is something fundamentally more powerful and fragile, the ability to create a common political space.[40] When the old Arab reached across that prison cell, lifted the blanket, and read Petcho's body, for a brief moment he and Petcho occupied such a space. Such reading has become much harder in modern times, and, consequently, the spaces in which we can appear before each other in our pain have become more scarce. Here, then, is a small offering toward literacy for our times.

I   Torture and Democracy

This won't leave marks; no one will believe you.

—Cambodian policeman to a prisoner, 2000[1]

1   Modern Torture and Its Observers

Today torture exists mainly as a floating word of condemnation. We call many things torture, including rush hour traffic, intrusive in-laws, and office politics. That is not my approach. Torture is the systematic infliction of physical torment on detained individuals by state officials for police purposes, for confession, information, or intimidation. I also consider the activity of some nonstate actors as torture under specific circumstances, as I explain below.

Modern tortures, of which clean tortures are a subset, differ from classical torture in the way they harness pain.[2] Classical torturers marked their victims' bodies as religion or custom required. They often branded or scarred in public, using bodies to advertise state power and deter others from similar behavior. By contrast, modern torturers favor pains that intimidate the prisoner alone. At times, they reach farther than mere behavioral compliance, seeking to apply physical pain in order to touch the mind or warp a sense of self, and thereby shape the self-understandings of prisoners and dispose them to willing, compliant action. Modern torturers may leave scars as they pursue these aims, but these tend to be incidental. When they hide their work from public view using clean techniques, their aims do not change, though the methods do. In either case, religion and custom have little to do with the way they go about inflicting pain. To be sure, some modern tortures have classical roots, and some classical torturers sought to convert minds with fear and pain. There is no mistaking, though, how the emphasis has changed over time.

There are strong temptations to expand or narrow this field of inquiry, but I think they should be resisted. Jurists have always preferred to define torture narrowly, while activists have favored definitions that are quite broad. The latter can be so inclusive as to make the term useless, while the former can be so narrow as to miss important features of modern torture. In this brief chapter, I will discuss each of these definitions in turn, explaining why my definition is clearer and still captures the relevant characteristics of the practice. Then I will explain how we came to monitor torture in the twentieth century. Monitoring torture began with isolated writers. It grew into an international human rights regime, involving numerous organizations that today conduct annual global audits of torture. So this poses an urgent question: how is it that torture flourishes despite extensive global monitoring? For by whatever definition one cares to choose, torture thrives in the twenty-first century. This urgent question leads to several puzzles, which I will try to unravel in the course of this book.

Defining Torture

For the Roman jurist Ulpian, torture was a customary activity judges used "to unearth crimes."[3] "By quaestio [torture], we are to understand the torment and suffering of the body in order to elicit the truth."[4] Indeed, Greeks and Romans did not consider some judicial testimony true unless it was coerced under torture; the torture of slaves, for example, was not merely customary, but compulsory.[5] Over a thousand years later, in 1612, the Italian jurist Sebastian Guazzini likewise defined torture "as the distress of body devised for extracting truth." It was "invented by the Civil Law, as a mode of discovering truth, for the sake of the public welfare, to the end that crimes might not remain unpunished. It is called a species of evidence substituted to supply the lack of witnesses."[6] This was the practice that so outraged Cesare Beccaria, the famous critic of torture, a century later. He understood torture as the jurists did: to compel a criminal before his trial "to confess a crime, to explain the contradictions he runs into, or uncover his accomplices" or "to expose other crimes of which he is guilty, but with which he has not been charged."[7] Beccaria differed from the jurists mainly in that he did not think this activity elicited any truth.

From the start, the activity of torture involved gathering information, not just securing confessions. Witnesses too were tortured to produce evidence in a trial, and "in matters of state, torture was also used to extract information in circumstances not directly related to judicial proceedings."[8] Over time, this element of torture eclipsed the confessional element. In his 1942 directive to the Gestapo, Chief Heinrich Müller emphasized that coerced interrogation could not be used to incriminate the suspect himself. It "may not be applied to induce confessions about a prisoner's own criminal acts. Nor may this means be applied toward persons who have been temporarily delivered by justice for the purpose of further investigation." Torture could only be used if there was preliminary evidence that the "prisoner can give information about important facts, connections or plans hostile to the state or the legal system, but does not want to reveal his knowledge, and the latter cannot be obtained by way of inquiries."[9] Similarly, in 2001, the American civil rights lawyer Alan Dershowitz asked: When is it constitutional to resort to unconventional techniques including torture when someone is in custody? "The constitutional answer to this question may surprise people. Any interrogation technique including the use of truth serum or even torture is not prohibited, all that is prohibited is the introduction into evidence of the fruits of such techniques in a criminal trial against the person on whom the techniques were used. The evidence could be used against that suspect in a noncriminal case—such as a deportation hearing—or against someone else."[10]

All this tells us fairly clearly what the practice of torture is not. The practice differs from war or genocide even though states carry out these violent activities, too. It is not genocide because it does not aim to kill victims; indeed, torture is judged to fail when prisoners die before informing or confessing. Likewise, the practice is not war. In war, soldiers confront each other as free, equal agents on a battlefield, where they act, honorably or not as the case may be. In torture, soldiers or other state officials act upon individuals who are helpless. Soldiers may wound many civilians in war, but it takes a qualitatively different intent to stick a knife into a captive's wound.

The UN *Declaration against Torture* broadens the traditional definitions by including intimidation along with confession and information. It states: "Torture means any act by which severe pain or suffering, whether physical or mental, is intentionally inflicted by or at the instigation of a public official on a person for such purposes as obtaining from him or a third person information or confession, punishing him for an act he has committed, or intimidating him or other persons."[11] On this broader view, state agents can practice torture in closed institutions (camps and jails) on helpless prisoners and even in towns and villages where policing is so intense that life approaches that of a prison.

Modern experience has led us to wonder whether even this more comprehensive view is adequate to capture how states organize torture today. States today parcel out the dirty work of violence, including torture, to nonstate actors. We are all too familiar now with the history of death squads in Latin America (which did not just kill, but tortured, kidnapped, and pursued a variety of other activities) and how state officials colluded quietly with them to induce an atmosphere of terror and intimidation.[12] Since the Bosnian war, we understand how private and public agents work together to produce systematic violence, including genocide, mass rape, and torture.[13] It is important to identify such public and private partnerships, but proving this co-operation is no easy task. One has to show that different groups have members in common, train together, share supplies and information, or use the same characteristic technique. Wherever we can find such evidence, then even though the agent might be a private security guard or an off-duty policeman, I have no difficulty calling this activity torture. This broadens the notion of state involvement in torture farther than legal definitions do, but not unrealistically.

While I am mainly concerned with states in this study, occasionally I also consider torture techniques used by insurgencies and rebel groups, for example, the French or Polish Resistance during World War II. This is because such organizations often act in very statelike ways, providing for public order and dispensing justice, however crudely, in territories under their control. When there is evidence that organizations are providing public goods in this respect, and delegated representatives coerce confessions, extract information, or intimidate prisoners through physical torment, I have no difficulty describing this as torture. However, the more typical guerrilla approach, as near as I can tell, is to resort to executions, rather than torture, as a means of creating terror. This is because guerrillas lack the usual fixed assets that facilitate torture. As a Kenyan guerrilla said about his organization in the 1950s, "We did not have our own jails to hold an informant in, so we would strangle him and then cut his tongue out."[14]

Having expanded the definition of torture somewhat beyond legal definitions, I want to argue that torture is not as elastic a term as much ordinary usage suggests. As a child, I sometimes considered washing the dishes torture. While intuition is sometimes a helpful guide, sentiment must be supplemented with something more durable than a person's moods. Otherwise it would be difficult to say what is not torture. Any human activity is probably torture to someone, and a word that potentially characterizes every human experience is likely to be very slippery indeed.

Since the nineteenth century, some have come to regard any violation of human dignity as torture. Karl Marx, for example, believed that repetitive work on the factory assembly line was "a sort of torture." When little girls iron linen in furnace-hot bleaching rooms for hours, they become nothing but living appendages to machines. Factory work "confiscates every atom of freedom, both in bodily and intellectual activity."[15]

It is not hard to understand why Marx likens social oppression to torture. One can plausibly, though loosely, describe these girls as being there against their will and as suffering for another person's gain. But the pain they experience is not the point of the economic activity. Though managers might cruelly ignore terrible work conditions, such pain is not a prerequisite for factory operation. Marx himself believed that it was possible to organize factories in a way that such suffering would not be a characteristic feature. By contrast, slave economies have always involved deliberate physical torment, and it is difficult to imagine organizing slavery in a way in which such pain would be an incidental feature.[16]

Defining torture as *any* indignity fails to distinguish between cases where the physical pain is incidental and the far graver cases where it is inevitable.[17] Even if one called all these activities torture, one would still explain the causes of each differently. There would be "factory torture," "war torture," "slavery torture" and "genocide torture," not to mention the activity with which this book is concerned ("torture torture"). Whatever this last activity is called, it is still distinct from the others and worth investigating in its own right. Put another way, the loose moral definition of torture simply burdens one with a cumbersome vocabulary when our received vocabulary for violence is more than adequate.

Until recently, legal definitions have concerned physical torment by the state. Some contemporary laws define torture without reference to agents or their purposes. Oregon law, for example, defines torture as the "separate intent to cause intense physical pain." While there is no crime of "torture," torture is an element of many crimes. When private citizens engage in this activity during murder, the prosecutor charges them with aggravated murder. Likewise, aggravated animal abuse in the first degree includes action taken solely to cause pain.[18]

These activities differ from state torture. When citizens detain and assault me, they use only the forces at their disposal. When a state official detains and assaults me for public purposes (to stop crime, to ensure good government), he does so using the authority and instruments with which the public entrusted him. It is not surprising, in this respect, that torture, as it is defined from Ulpian to the United Nations, includes this use or abuse of public trust, something that is absent when a private citizen assaults me. When it comes to the crimes of torture, war, mass rape, or genocide, these are activities for which states and their agents are and should be responsible.

The history of cruelty is undoubtedly related to the activity with which this book is concerned, and I will point out junctures where painful techniques used on animals, slaves, and others pass from private life into the hands of state torturers. Call one private torture and the other public torture, if you wish. But for most instances of violence among private citizens, our received vocabulary on violence already distinguishes between cruelty (any intentional infliction of intense pain) and torture. For the purposes of this book, I will reserve the term *torture* to talk about the state's abuse of public trust.

Monitoring Torture

Today, numerous treaties define legitimate state violence and prohibit torture. Many organizations in turn monitor state compliance with these conventions, including official auditors of the treaties (the United Nations, the Council of Europe), nongovernmental auditors (Amnesty International, Human Rights

Watch), and state bureaucracies (the U.S. State Department's Human Rights Bureau). This monitoring regime watches for violations by all states, whether they are international pariahs or deeply respected governments. This regime is not perfectly even-handed, but it breaks sharply from past practice.

States have always been quick to denounce the torture of their enemies. For example, many states submitted national audits of Nazi violence to the Nuremberg tribunal in 1949, and the American government denounced "Communist brainwashing" in the 1950s.[19] States are less than candid when it comes to their allies or their own troops. During the Cold War, both superpowers overlooked human rights violations on their own side. American policymakers "systematically excluded" human rights issues from their foreign policy decisions, and Soviet decision-makers followed an ideology and statecraft that was "incompatible with respect for individual rights."[20] The French government, when confronted with charges of torture in colonial Algeria, expressed outraged denial, benign indifference, or implicit approval.[21] Likewise, the British Compton and Parker reports, investigating torture in Northern Ireland, blamed rogue policemen and deceitful prisoners.[22] Other states were scarcely better, and mostly worse.

States joined the global monitoring of torture, then, with considerable reluctance. In fact, monitoring began with intrepid journalists, lawyers, and intellectuals, mainly from Europe and the United States, who dared public disapproval. In 1931, Andrée Viollis documented French colonial torture in Vietnam.[23] In 1932, H. Hessell Tiltman surveyed torture in Eastern Europe, boldly including Poland despite Western sympathy for Jozef Pilsudski's government.[24] In 1937, Eugene Lyons, an American Communist journalist, offered one of the earliest accounts of Stalin's torture techniques.[25] In 1938, George Ryley Scott described flogging in western as well as Eastern Europe.[26] Across the Atlantic, George Wickersham and his colleagues at the American Bar Association (ABA) issued a comprehensive account of police brutality in American cities large and small. Their report steadily transformed American police practice over the next three decades and is probably the most important document the ABA has ever produced.[27]

After World War II, independent writers remained the best monitors. In 1949, Alec Mellor's *La Torture* offered the best postwar survey of torture.[28] Mellor noted that torture persisted in France and Latin America and argued that the very modern demand for quick intelligence encouraged police abuse. In 1963, Pierre Vidal-Naquet documented French torture in Algeria.[29] Peter Deeley offered a global survey, as comprehensive as one could find anywhere in print, of torture in the late 1960s.[30] In 1979, A. J. Langguth described the U.S. role in torture in Latin America, while Noam Chomsky and Edward Herman argued that the United States distributed torture techniques worldwide.[31] Most recently, John Conroy has shown how systematic torture entered the Chicago police between 1970 and 1985.[32]

As these writers informed an increasingly alarmed public in Europe and the United States, a grassroots antitorture movement emerged. This movement appeared first in France in the 1950s and then in the United Kingdom in the 1960s. These movements changed the way states handled human rights issues in Europe, and eventually throughout the world.

The French antitorture movement rose in opposition to the war in Algeria. When soldiers arrested French intellectuals in Algiers, groups organized to agitate for their release. These actions soon coalesced into a movement, a movement that broke sharply with the Communist Left. "A whole vigorous independent left wing movement appeared unconnected with the old parties and at times in opposition to them. It even had its own Press since the normal Press was frequently subject to suppression by the government."[33] Editions de Minuit, the movement's flagship press, was originally a clandestine Resistance press under the German occupation established by Jérôme Lindon. Lindon had continued his one-man operation after the war, specializing in avant-garde literature, but he had not forgotten his roots. Never before in modern times had so many prominent Catholic figures and magazines joined an essentially left-wing movement.[34]

Across the Channel, Peter Benenson, a British lawyer, shocked readers by introducing them to torture in democracies: French torture in Algeria and British torture in Kenya. Benenson was no stranger to torture. He had observed trials in Hungary, Spain, and South Africa. He had worked in the Cyprus Emergency. Now the gangrene had spread; faith in democracy was "already flickering in Britain" and might soon "become extinguished."[35]

In 1961, Benenson wrote "The Forgotten Prisoners," appealing for a one-year campaign on behalf of political prisoners. The "Appeal for Amnesty, 1961" grew into Amnesty International. Amnesty organized groups that adopted specific political prisoners, monitored their treatment, and campaigned for their freedom. One can appreciate the speed at which the international antitorture movement grew in the 1960s by comparing Amnesty's first report in 1962 with its twelfth in 1975. In 1962, Amnesty listed 210 prisoners adopted by some 70 Amnesty groups in 7 countries and an annual budget of 7,359 pounds. In 1975, Amnesty had adopted 2,458 prisoners, released 1,403 adopted prisoners in 1974, organized 1,592 groups in 33 countries, and had 70,000 members in 65 countries. Its annual budget was 272,000 pounds and 100,000 pounds in relief funds.[36] Today, Amnesty consists of 1.8 million members, supporters, and subscribers in over 150 countries.[37]

In 1967, a military junta took power in Greece, arresting and torturing opponents. The Greek crisis transformed European politics. The six European Community (EC) members "identified democracy and respect for human rights as prerequisites to membership in the Community"; Greece, Portugal, and Spain would not be accepted into the EC until they met these standards.[38] But Greece was also a member of the Council of Europe. After antitorture activists, including Amnesty International, publicized Greek torture, the Council began an investigation. In 1969, after a bitter dispute, the Greek government voluntarily withdrew from the Council rather than face almost inevitable expulsion.

After the Greek crisis, the European political agenda routinely included human rights compliance. In 1969, the EC transformed détente, explicitly connecting human rights issues to the East-West dialogue in Europe. This new political agenda culminated in the Helsinki Accords (1975) and shaped President Jimmy Carter's human rights policy (1976).[39] By the 1980s, Communist state-controlled media were debating human rights issues. "China's Xinhua news agency increased its usage of the term [human rights] by 1,000 percent in the 1982—94 period, while the Current Digest of the Soviet Press, a selection of key articles, ran 300 percent more stories in 1994 than in 1982." Western media coverage also increased. Reuters's usage of *human rights* increased by 500 percent in this period and the BBC's usage by 600 percent. By the end of the Cold War, "a thin stratum of cultural, economic, and political elites stretching across state borders" was verbally committed to "a shared symbolic world in which the baseline for evaluating social worth is largely set by Western-influenced norms articulated by global auditors."[40] Some called it a "global civil society."[41]

Comprehensive public auditing began in 1973 when Amnesty International issued its *Report on Torture* (1973).[42] This book offered a global survey of torture, a kind of survey that is so common today that many barely think about how unusual it was thirty-five years ago. Before this report, the International Committee of the Red Cross (ICRC) was the only international organization that performed audits of prison conditions and only under limited conditions. Until 1955, these reports were limited to camps for prisoners of war in specific countries. In 1955, the French government and the ICRC arrived at a precedent-making agreement on how to conduct audits of prison conditions in civil wars. The French government allowed the ICRC to investigate conditions of detainees in the Algerian conflict, prisoners whose status under international law was somewhat ambiguous until then. In return, the ICRC agreed to keep its reports confidential. The ICRC conducted several investigations of French prisons in Algeria in the late 1950s as well as British camps for detainees in Kenya in 1957. While the British and French governments quietly shelved ICRC reports, they were important nevertheless in laying the foundations for later public audits in tone and content. Meticulously documented and dispassionately reported, they made it difficult for government officials to deny torture under their watch. The French government discovered the power of this style when a bureaucrat at the Ministry of Justice leaked an ICRC report to the press in 1960; although details of French torture in Algeria were well known by then, the report's tone and content made it impossible to deny.[43]

Amnesty International had long recognized the power of dispassionate documentation of torture, and it harnessed this stylistic voice to powerful effect in its 1973 report.[44] The report's impact was greatly facilitated by the military coup in Chile in 1973, which focused world attention on torture, and Amnesty used the new global attentiveness to broaden its antitorture campaign. Annual global audits now became a standard feature of Amnesty's efforts to move governments and the United Nations to enforce greater compliance with international human rights norms. The Helsinki Accords also generated groups that monitored Soviet compliance. In Eastern Europe, Helsinki Watch Committees formed a nascent opposition that eventually undermined Communist rule. Similar monitoring groups formed in Western Europe and the United States.[45] An American activist, Jeri Laber, launched a broader monitoring campaign. She established groups to monitor U.S. compliance, Americas Watch (1981). Then came Asia Watch (1985), Africa Watch (1988), and Middle East Watch (1989), all of which became Human Rights Watch (1988). Starting with a budget of $200,000 in 1979, Human Rights Watch had, by 2001, a $20 million budget and seven permanent offices worldwide.[46]

Official auditors also appeared. Today, the U.S. State Department's Human Rights Bureau issues country reports, reports that judges worldwide consult in assessing refugees' claims. Under the European Convention on Torture, the Committee for the Prevention of Torture regularly inspects European police, prisons, and psychiatric hospitals. UN special rapporteurs submit to the General Assembly regular reports on human rights conditions in different states.

Today, after the end of the Cold War, we live in an era of unprecedented democratization and global monitoring. Torture has not abated and, by some reports, thrives. What then are we missing?

The general answer is something like this. Global monitoring depends on two strategies: exposing torture to public censure through careful documentation and holding state agents responsible for torture conducted during their watch.

The first strategy has encouraged torturers to invest in less visible, and hence harder to document, techniques. The second strategy has encouraged politicians to find allies for their techniques of enforcement in a public that will not tolerate those who are soft on drugs, illegal immigration, and terrorism. Vidal-Naquet saw this in the Algerian conflict: "Very soon the campaign *against* torture was countered by a campaign *in favour* of torture."[47] By 2000, Amnesty International conceded that "tacit support for torture is a problem particularly when the victim is a member of a despised group—perhaps a homeless teen-ager, a drug addict or a thief."[48]

These responses put new strains on the global monitoring of torture. Monitoring may eventually drive clean torture practices out into the light and eliminate them from police practice. Monitoring may also collapse through political pressures and public indifference. In that case, stealth torture regimens will give way to more visible tortures. What is most likely, though, is that the monitoring system will hobble along and governments will continue to practice clean tortures even as they are scrutinized.

In the following chapters, I explore various dimensions of this likely future. I begin with democratic states, and ask why torture persists despite widespread democratization. I lay out three preconditions that explain why some democracies torture while others do not. I also suggest that democracies today have an affinity for tortures that leave few marks. In parts II, III, and IV, I show that historically, clean torture and democracy go hand in hand. They do so because democracies had to deal with sustained pubic monitoring, domestically and internationally, earlier than authoritarian states. This put a premium on clean torture, and the main democracies were innovators in this area. Authoritarian states did not at first adopt clean torture regimens and followed democracies later when global monitoring of torture intensified in the late twentieth century. In part V, I explore whether states can successfully regulate torture and, if not, whether they can generate successful outcomes by means of it.

The current amazement that the things we are experiencing are "still" possible in the 20th century is *not* philosophical. This amazement is not the beginning of knowledge — unless it is the knowledge that the view of history which gives rise to it is untenable.

—Walter Benjamin[1]

2   Torture and Democracy

As a matter of historical record, torture has characterized democratic as well as authoritarian states. Greek and Roman city-states, Renaissance republics, and modern democratic states have all practiced torture. Of course, I am not claiming that the democratic record is as bad as that of authoritarian states — it is not. Some democratic states have not tortured at all, and some democracies that have tortured have done so intermittently at particular times and places. Still, there is no getting around the fact that some democratic states have legalized torture, treated it as a quasi-legal investigative procedure, or practiced it routinely on the quiet, despite a formal ban. The question then is, how is this possible?

Democracy is a form of government based on amateurism (citizens rule in turn by means of lots or elections in a free choice among competitors) and participation (a significant segment of the society has access to these means). In authoritarian states, by contrast, leaders are self-appointed, or if they were elected, impossible to displace afterward. These leaders typically justify their rule by some claim other than amateurism, most commonly bureaucratic or military expertise, moral and religious authority, or their unique personal qualities such as character or descent. While some authoritarian leaders may allow participation in various national referenda, these electoral processes are highly constrained or the outcomes predetermined.

These fairly simple distinctions are sufficient to pose a puzzle.[2] One would not be surprised if authoritarian states used torture; autocratic leaders have an unfortunate habit of being less than benign when it comes to dealing with those who oppose them. But we tend to assume that democracy and torture could not go together. After all, leaders in democratic states are open to public pressure, and the public does not like to be tortured or to be seen condoning it. Democratic governments are "bargains of leniency."[3] Every group understands that to rule in turn means resisting the temptation to punish, much less torture, one's opponents. Indeed, in *liberal* democracies, constitutions protect citizens from torture. So democracies seem unlikely to torture.

Yet torture can arise nevertheless, either because of or in spite of public opinion. Governments may keep torture covert. Those who would oppose torture might not hear about it for some time, and even then they might be uncertain. Some citizens may even support torture if they believe that it is necessary for public safety, or that it will affect people unlike them, or because it takes place under special conditions (in colonies or war zones). Under these conditions, even liberal democrats may not give much weight to their heritage, preferring instead to be apathetic or even supportive.

Whatever the public may think, it is often the case that powerful processes have already initiated torture long before many people know it is being used in their name. In this chapter, I describe three distinct ways in which this happens in democracies. First torture may arise because security bureaucracies overwhelm those assigned to monitor them. This phenomenon typically begins in colonies or war zones of democratic states, but it may spread backward to the metropole, as I demonstrate in the case of France in the next section. Second, torture may arise because judicial systems place too great an emphasis on confessions. Third, it may arise because neighborhoods want civic order on the streets whatever the cost. Each process generates powerful demands for torture.

The National Security Model

In democracies, legislatures need to make sure laws are applied and elections properly supervised. They establish bureaucracies to perform these tasks. However, bureaucracies are hierarchical, closed institutions of credentialed experts. When the experts decide that legislatures do not have sufficient will or expertise to do the right thing during a political emergency, they may turn to torture. Democrats, as amateurs, are often not in a position to challenge what bureaucrats say is necessary or even what is happening. So bureaucrats can overwhelm democrats.

The most famous instance is the French army in Algeria. In the 1950s, the French police and army were fighting a brutal war with the FLN guerrillas. General Jacques Massu authorized that, under particular conditions, soldiers should use any means necessary to get the information, including torture.[4] Standard military training included the advice, "With these conditions satisfied you have a right to water and electricity." I will describe what these tortures were in a later chapter; for the moment it is sufficient to know that they were "well-known methods of torture which leave little trace."[5]

What is important here is that democratic institutions were unwilling or unable to stop the turn to torture. One after the other, the judicial system, the legislature, the opposition parties, and the press failed. The police and military soon operated outside the law. In effect, they formed a closed state within the state. The military used its privileged position to establish covert torture, delay investigations, shape information, recruit political allies, and mobilize public opinion for the war. The consequences for France were severe. In 1958, the army threatened to intervene in national politics for the first time since Napoleon's coup of eighteenth Brumaire, leading to the collapse of the Fourth Republic. In 1961, the army finally did organize a putsch and failed.[6]

To be specific, above all, the judicial system faltered. Lacking information, prosecutors in Algiers depended on the press to identify the victims. The victims did not always have marks, so how could one bring charges against the police in these cases? And scarred victims feared reprisals; "although the marks of torture were obvious, the Public Prosecutor was unable to persuade the victim to lay a complaint even after he had visited the prisoner personally." In the end, the Prosecutor's Office brought only seventeen cases involving thirty-nine individuals to the Algerian courts. Military prosecutors made far less effort to investigate cases in a timely manner. For example, a military doctor investigated fifteen plaintiffs two or three months after the alleged tortures occurred, time enough for many wounds to heal.[7] Another "examined" a prisoner by asking if he was doing all right, never asking him to remove his clothes to show his bruises.[8]

Then there were the judges.[9] In France, controversial cases went to a M. Jacques Batigne, even though there were one hundred other magistrates available. Batigne was unsympathetic to victims, so much so that one torturer told his victim that he could go complain to "my friend Batigne."[10] Even when judges like Batigne allowed the charge of torture, they excluded the evidence. In one notorious case, the police argued that a plaintiff with clear injuries had mumps. After all, had the examining doctor not said that there was "swelling of the parotid glands and stiffness of the neck, which are the accepted symptoms of this disease"? The judge agreed.[11]

At first, the government disputed press reports and suppressed publications about torture. *La Question*, the prison account of the well-known editor Henri Alleg, became the first book suppressed since the French Revolution. *Gangrene*, a book describing the torture experiences of Algerian detainees in Paris, was seized and the plates smashed. Pierre Vidal-Naquet was forced to publish his masterful account of French torture abroad in English and Italian; it only appeared in French ten years later.[12]

Eventually, the government was compelled to investigate the allegations. It recruited investigators who were sympathetic to the police and military. In France, Judge Batigne was entrusted with the investigation; he returned from vacation saying there was no prima facie case.[13] In Algeria, a separate commission was not much better. The commissioners declined to examine any alleged cases that happened near war operations. They also announced the locations they were likely to visit, which was helpful to the torturers. For example, on June 19, 1957, they announced they would visit the notorious El-Biar interrogation center. "If they had arrived unheralded they would have found Maurice Audin [a young university lecturer and Communist cell member] at the centre, but he, together with Alleg [another cell member] and other prisoners who bore obvious marks of torture, had been transferred for the day to another locality. Two days later Maurice Audin was murdered."[14] The commission chairman appeared more concerned with avoiding embarrassment than restraining the military. When Massu ordered summary executions, the chairman allegedly said to him, "Prepare us all the briefs you like, you can bring us fake witnesses, and I will help all I can, but in God's name withdraw your directive."[15]

The old leftist parties and the press also failed. The internationally minded Communist Party, for example, had its own torture skeletons in the closet, notably Stalin's victims. It did not want to broach the subject of torture. When Henri Alleg, a longtime Communist, brought his book to the Party to publish, it refused. The press at first described "torture victims" in proper inverted commas. Even as the left-wing press became more vociferous, there were notable lapses. The horrible torture of Djamila Bouhired was ignored for three weeks, until a conservative journalist writing in the ultra right-wing *L'Aurore* made it a scandal.[16]

Some military and police commanders broke ranks, resigned and denounced the torture, but there were just as many officers who wrote vociferously in favor of torture and threatened meddlesome amateurs. "You will be made to pay, all you academics. You will pay for lecturing us."[17] Prowar journalists lionized the torturers in popular novels, asking the public: If you knew this terrorist had planted a bomb, would you not torture him too?[18] The secret service recruited an author to write a book of counterpropaganda. The archbishop of Paris was reminded that certain funds might be cut if he was too publicly outspoken.[19]

Max Weber, the noted sociologist, observed that democrats need bureaucrats, but bureaucratic rule, if left unchecked, imperils democracy. For Weber, this was a paradox.[20] For Vidal-Naquet, a bureaucratic faction was in this case a "cancer," a pathology in which a part of democracy turned on itself. It was a slide toward authoritarianism, which stopped just short, because of exhaustion, international opprobrium, General de Gaulle's clever leadership, and tenacious Algerian resistance.[21] Yet, even in the darkest days, an antitorture press still published and activists still agitated. "No country involved in similar horrors," conceded Vidal-Naquet, "has ever permitted publication of such complete documentation on the subject."[22] French democracy survived, though barely.

Military bureaucracies can overwhelm a democracy sufficiently to make it democratic in name only, as in Latin America. In France, bureaucrats carved out a realm in which to practice torture while protected from public scrutiny. There are other examples. In the 1980s, Justice Moshe Landau reported that Israeli General Security Service (GSS) agents had "systematically committed perjury for 16 years, lying about the fact that they used brutal physical and psychological methods to get confessions and information," quoting from "an internal GSS memo, written in 1982, that set out guidelines about what sort of lies should be told."[23]

In the National Security model, as the French case suggests, officers practice torture as part of a proactive strategy to combat an enemy in an emergency. Victims may be locals or foreigners, but they are always chosen because of their suspected political activities. Torturers are interested not in confessions to crimes (for that is already taken for granted), but in information. They torture to secure a complete file on a person's contacts and to recruit their victims as informers (for those who cooperate become dependent and compromised individuals). Other examples of this model include American torture in the Philippines during the Spanish-American War, the British military and police in Kenya, Cyprus, Aden, and Northern Ireland, the Spanish Guardia Civile in Basque country, the Indian army in the Punjab and Kashmir, Turkish forces in the Kurdish regions, and the Russian army in Chechnya.[24] The national security model also helps clarify the conditions in which torture arises among democratic armies operating under the formal jurisdiction of another state, for example, American torture in South Vietnam in the 1960s and 1970s.[25]

The Juridical Model

When modern observers discuss torture in democracies, normally they have in mind the national security model, and thus torture that often takes place far away from the metropole, for example in war zones or colonies.[26] The second way in which torture arises, what I call the juridical model, gets less attention but it is important because it arises at home. I want to explicate that model here, using the example of Italian republics and then turning to some contemporary examples. In this model, torture arises in particular because a judicial system privileges confessions.

In the late Middle Ages, Europe underwent a major legal revolution. The church banned ordeals (duels, trials by water or fire) and replaced them with a new system of proof in which lawyers evaluated evidence and put together a case. In the new inquisitional system, judges and prosecutors prized written documents, and above all confessions. To this end, they revived the Roman practice of torture, a practice that generated additional evidence that could be evaluated with other papers.

Italian city-states, republics, and principalities, adopted the new inquisitorial system in their legal reforms. Republics, though, carefully limited torture to noncitizens and slaves. Citizens had dignity and were thus inviolable, at least normally. Citizens could also fall into ill repute and infamy, *mala fama*, so laws prohibited torture of citizens unless they were of notorious reputation.[27] One jurist advised that judges administering torture should "begin with the culprit who, from the name he bears, is known to belong to a family of criminals, and as examples of such bad names, may be cited the names of Forabosco, Sgaramella, Saltalamachia." He added that family history indicated criminality far more soundly than physiognomy, a pseudoscience that determined, among other things, whether people were criminals from their facial features.[28] Beyond the ancient Roman doctrines of dignity and infamy, there were no doubt practical considerations. Torture must have been especially tempting when evidence was circumstantial and yet everyone "knew" what the family did for a living.

It was not long before Italian podestas, who were responsible for law and order, tortured even citizens of good reputation. Judging by the frantic efforts to limit the podesta's power to torture, the torture of good citizens was a serious problem. According to the statutes of Bologna of 1288, the lord captain had to approve the use of torture before the defendant or one of his family, six consuls, four officials of the commune, and the notary. If the podesta violated this law, he would be excluded from municipal government and required to pay a large fine. If the officials just cited failed to enforce this statute, they suffered the same fate. In Vercelli, a 1241 statute prohibited torture unless the person was a notorious criminal or had an evil reputation. A later addition reemphasized that good citizens should not be tortured and particularly forbade the podesta from circumventing the decree.[29]

Here then is a second model: torture enters democracies through a legal system that highly values the confession of the accused. Here the victims are ordinary criminals. Even when political opponents are arrested, they are presented as criminals. Time does not matter so much in this model; there is no bomb ticking somewhere. Officers take as long as it takes to secure a written confession. And as one might expect, torture is strongly associated with extensive prearrest detention, and not just in the distant past. In the 1920s, American police held suspects in hotel rooms and offices for up to thirty-eight days, in which time they often resorted to torture. In Russia today, police often hold suspects until they confess, using duty rooms and other places where registration is not strict. Likewise, in contemporary Japan, temporary detention has yielded coerced false confessions.[30]

Now false confessions can be achieved by means other than torture. In 1997, for example, police questioned five young men regarding a brutal rape of a jogger in Central Park. The men freely confessed before cameras, falsely, as it turned out when the real rapist admitted the crime five years later. A skilled interrogator can manipulate suspects psychologically to confess to crimes that they never committed.[31] Nevertheless, when prosecutors and judges valorize confessions, police feel the pressure to deliver written confessions by any means, and that can include and has included torture.

Why do modern prosecutors and judges need confessions at all? Medieval European judicial systems, like the Italian ones, had an almost irrational fetish for confessions; confession was the Queen of Proofs. But modern legal systems do not value confessions similarly and, unlike medieval inquisitors, modern prosecutors and judges do not need confessions to convict a suspect. Modern law recognizes circumstantial evidence, and prosecutors can charge suspects along a scale (first-, second-, or third-degree murder, for example) based on the evidence.[32] Nevertheless, prosecutors know that, regardless of circumstantial evidence, a confession by the accused makes their case stronger to juries. Ordinary people value confessions. They regard confessions as believable even when they know or suspect the confessions were coerced. And they give weight to confessions even when the judge tells them the confession is inadmissible, even while claiming to others that the confession did not affect their decisions.[33]

The Italian example suggests one further possibility. Here, the judicial fetish for confessions rested upon a religious ethic, Catholicism, which also valorized penitent confessions. It is possible that wherever there is a long-standing cultural disposition in favor of confessions, judicial systems may also overvalue confessions. Are there democracies with such judicial systems today? Consider the case of Japan.

In Japan, "The vast majority of suspects cooperate voluntarily in their own prosecution." Indeed, Japanese suspects "plead guilty more readily."[34] In a society where sincere repentance matters, a confession generates *ninjo*, warmth and understanding, in officials, "thereby lessening the severity of punishment."[35] The figures are striking. In Japan prior to World War II, 99 percent of all criminal convictions were based on confessions.[36] In 1972, 94 percent of all offenders agreed to a summary judgment, "meaning that a court decided their case on documentary and material evidence without a public hearing."[37] In

1986, 86 percent of all convictions were based on confessions, and 99.99 percent of all cases sent to trial ended in convictions.[38] In 1990, 99.8 percent of cases led to conviction, and 91.5 percent of these cases were based on confessions under arrest.[39] In 1987, the Japanese government offered the following rates for convictions on various charges: 96 percent for homicide, 60 percent for larceny, with an average for all crimes at 64 percent. The average for all crimes in the United States was 21 percent, the United Kingdom 35 percent, and France 40 percent.[40]

No doubt an American prosecutor would find the numbers in Japan enviable, but they mask a darker side. Consider, for example, the case of Masaya Watanabe, who was arrested in December 1977 as a leader of a motorcycle gang. Watanabe was interrogated for six days. During this period, he was struck on the head and hit in the chest with a table. When the interrogators threatened to shame his family, he confessed. He later tried to retract his confession, but was convicted nevertheless. His conviction was overturned in April 1981.[41] The appeals trial revealed that, among other things, the evidence against Watanabe had been gathered under questionable circumstances similar to Watanabe's detention. The police had arrested thirty-six minors and held them in temporary detention. Not only had some of the minors implicated someone named Watanabe, but thirty-one of them also confessed to being one of only three leaders of a motorcycle gang.

Watanabe was held under laws that allow suspects to be detained for up to twenty-three days before the decision to prosecute — "in effect, during the period of investigation."[42] Many detentions centers are not police stations, but rather substitute facilities known as *daiyo kangoku*. In 1988, the government maintained 254 jails at police stations and 1,254 substitute facilities. In the previous decade, it built 36 substitute facilities, but only one police station holding facility, and this despite the fact that the regular police system was only 59 percent full.[43] Nevertheless, Japanese police insist these substitute facilities are essential. If police had to use only formal lockups, investigators would have to travel long distances to ask suspects questions. It would be too expensive to replace these facilities with modern stations. The cost to replace the seventy *daiyo kangoku* in Tokyo alone, given real estate prices, would be astronomical. At any rate, the police urge that officers are well trained and that the high conviction rate "is in part due to cell custody."[44]

David Bayley, a noted sociologist of policing, concedes that this system would alarm Americans, who cannot be held for more than twenty-four hours unless they are charged and who have stronger legal protections while in custody. He argues however, that Japanese police do not resort to lengthy detentions often and that, at any rate, after twenty-three days, they either charge or release suspects. Moreover, Japanese police possess enormous moral authority and "consequently pressure on suspects need not be as intense."[45] Bayley is right that, as a percentage of the Japanese population, the numbers detained for questioning are small, but the absolute numbers are staggering. The government offers the following figures for temporary detention in the mid-1980s: 95,602 (1987), 96,016 (1986), and 100,404 (1985).[46]

Moreover, the number of arrests does not capture repeated detention, *bekken taiho*.[47] Individuals can be arrested and detained repeatedly and if held for the maximum twenty-three day limit, they may be released and rearrested for another period not to exceed twenty-three days. For example, on January 12, 1973, Hideo Hori was arrested, released, and rearrested. Released again, he was rearrested on March 14. He was interrogated daily between eight and sixteen hours a day. The police pulled his hair, yelled at him, and threatened him. He "confessed" on April 4, 1973, but police were apparently unsatisfied with this confession and he was interrogated until May 20. He was granted bail in April 1980, and his trials took place in 1983. He was found not guilty on the charges on May 19, 1983 and December 18, 1983, and the appeals court upheld the acquittal in 1985.[48]

Finally, there is the issue of torture and confession. Torture often appears in conditions where police have extensive power to detain without charging the suspect, and that is a concern in the Japanese case as well. Bayley strongly defends the Japanese police for their professionalism despite their extensive pretrial detention powers. He states:

> Because the psychological compulsion to confess is so strong in Japan, the notion of improper psychological pressure is very subtle. Interrogators may provide a cup of tea to a suspect, but cannot buy him lunch. The implicit obligation formed by the latter act is considered to be too strong. Offering a cigarette is probably all right, say police interrogators, but they would think twice about it. In one case a confession was judged to be involuntary because, among other things, the chief of the police station had visited the suspect in his bath and undertook to wash his back for him. The court thought this created tremendous pressure on the suspect.[49]

Suspects no doubt felt considerably more pressure when police grabbed them by the hair, knocked them on the head, pressed rulers hard into the back of their hands, punched them in the stomach, slapped them on the face (sometimes with a stick or a ruler), banged their head against a table, and shoved them against the walls. All these activities were reported by Futaba Igarashi on behalf of the Japanese Federation of Bar Associations in the 1980s. Igarashi studied one hundred detainees, many of whom—as in the cases cited above— were arrested at the time Bayley was conducting his research in the 1970s. Her findings revealed "a brutal regime guaranteed to break down the resistance of all but the most hardy activists and a system of interrogation that—at least according to its victims—verges on psychological if not physical torture."[50] Several others have since followed Igarashi's study, including Setsuo Miyazawa, Karen Parker and Etienne Jaudel, Human Rights Watch, and Amnesty International.[51]

To understand these abuses, one must appreciate, more broadly, the manner in which Japanese police work. "Japanese detectives work on the assumption that the suspect will confess and that this confession will match the physical evidence." They are assisted in this respect by many legal and cultural forces that prompt such confessions. "Japanese detectives rarely need to apply physical force to a suspect because the legal system of criminal investigations is designed and implemented to give the detained suspect sufficiently strong psychological pressure to admit guilt."[52]

In this legal environment, policing skills decay. Japanese police "do little other than interrogate the suspect." The environment "precluded the development of other investigative skills."[53] As Justice Felix Frankfurter observes, a police that relies "too heavily on interrogation will not pursue or learn other crime detection methods," and he notes "the consequent danger that the police will feel themselves under pressure to secure confessions."[54] In fact, gathering additional physical evidence can cause serious problems for police. When the confession does not match the physical evidence, the detectives panic in the face of imminent public humiliation. "They worry that confessions may be undermined and holes found in prepared evidence. Therefore, judicial scrutiny serves to promote longer, more aggressive investigations and interrogations."[55]

Miyazawa describes these consequences in one case. "Detectives were caught in a vicious cycle of coercive interrogations and false confessions. When one confession did not fit the physical evidence, the detectives simply pressed the suspect to make another confession, which again failed to match the physical evidence. It did not occur to the detectives that their original hypothesis was incorrect." The suspect was eventually indicted for another crime. Had circumstances been otherwise, the police "might have been tempted to use more coercive and manipulative tactics in interrogation in order to *make crime* which fits their hypothesis within the approved time limit." The serious cases— documented by Igarashi and others—"simply magnify the problems inherent in criminal investigation in Japan," but they "are not qualitatively different from more routine cases."[56]

The enabling legal environment, then, plants the seeds of torture. It is true, as Elise Tipton argues, that incidents of torture and brutality in Japan "have been rare (far fewer than in the United States, for example) and highly celebrated as abuses of the system."[57] The comparatively small number is hardly surprising in a system that is designed so that "the suspect will offer apparently voluntary confessions to his captors. It was precisely because of the apparent voluntariness of their confessions that those falsely convicted people . . . had to fight for so many years to secure their freedom."[58] Moreover, as in other democracies, unequal access to justice also makes apparently voluntary confession inevitable. "Most Japanese accused of a crime confess because they are poor, just as poor people do in other countries. They realize that they cannot afford the extremely expensive procedure of defending themselves through numerous courts, possibly all the way to the Supreme Court."[59]

The Japanese case illustrates the main features of the juridical model. A legal environment, reinforced by cultural dispositions, creates an overreliance on confessions: good citizens will confess, and those who do not are clearly bad people. In the few cases where suspects do hold out, police turn to aggressive methods including torture. Extensive prearrest detention creates the opportunity. All this suggests that East Asian democracies, with comparable judicial frameworks and cultural dispositions, are similarly vulnerable to torture—just as the Italian city-states were.

The Civic Discipline Model

There are cases where torture occurs in democracies in the absence of a permissive legal context or a national emergency, objective or perceived. To appreciate these recent cases, it is helpful to begin with ancient Athens. The Athenians, the first democrats, also practiced torture. Their example offers a different model of how torture fits into democratic life, a model that helps capture many examples of torture today.

In ancient Athens, the task of arresting and prosecuting people fell to ordinary citizens. The state would call the jury, but the citizen had to prosecute the case. In this context, torture was a pre-judicial arrangement, a response to charges about one's honor and family. The accused would offer a challenge: "If you don't believe me, torture my slaves."[60] Why torture slaves? Slaves were an important part of the social system of Athens. They assisted in every aspect of life. If something happened, slaves were bound to see or hear it. Indeed, many judicial cases probably arose through slave gossip. Thus, when one citizen offered his own slaves, he was offering up people whom everyone believed would *know* what really happened.

The Athenians considered torture essential when questioning slaves. In practical terms, citizens believed that slaves were more likely to tell the truth under torture. Otherwise, fearing their master's punishment, slaves would lie. Torture was important for a less articulated reason. Because any citizen could offer a torture challenge, every citizen had to act with extreme uprightness even in the privacy of his home. There were, in effect, eyes everywhere. Legalizing the torture of slaves made for good civic discipline. It promoted civic virtue and reduced vice in a decentralized democracy, one without a large bureaucracy or police force.[61]

In ancient republics, torture was tied to citizenship. Torture was inflicted exclusively on noncitizens: slaves, barbarians and foreigners. It is tempting to think this practice followed preestablished categories of "citizen" and "slave," but this is a mistake. For there was a deep anxiety about how one might distinguish "two-footed stock" who looked like citizens from the real thing. The Roman Senate considered, but did not pass, a law "to have slaves dress uniformly in public so that they could immediately be distinguished from free citizens."[62] Torture resolved the anxiety in a different way

> As an instrument of demarcation, it [torture] delineates the boundary between slave and free, between the untouchable bodies of free citizens and the torturable bodies of slaves. The ambiguity of slave status, the difficulty of sustaining an absolute sense of differences, is addressed through this practice of the state, which carves the line between slave and free on the bodies of the unfree.[63]

To the slave belonged brutal tortures whose scars were visible to the naked eye. Citizens could expect, literally, humane punishments, for only Greek and Roman citizens could lead fully human lives.

Such a view is not so far away from our contemporary experience. Only 150 years ago, advertisements like these told any citizen how to read a slave's body in a democratic society. Owners registered their property with recognizable patterns of marks.

> *North Carolina Minerva and Raleigh Advertiser*, August 24, 1809
> RAN-AWAY FROM the subscriber, on the 12th of June, a negro man, named TOM about 26 years old, near six feet high, branded on each check with the letters OG; has one of his ears cropped, and scars on the bottom of his feet.[64]

> *Mississippi Gazette*, July 23, 1836
> Josiah is five feet eight inches high, heavy built, copper colour; his back very much scarred with the whip, and branded on the thigh and hips in three or four places thus: "J.M." The rim of his right ear has been bitten or cut off. He is about 31 years of age.[65]

> *St. Louis Gazette*, November 6, 1845
> A wealthy man here had a boy named Reuben, almost white, whom he caused to be branded in the face with the words; "A slave for life."[66]

The slave and the citizen, not surprisingly, had different civic experiences, and torture (or the lack of it) shaped the bodies and identities of each.

But Americans and Englishmen differed from the Greeks in that they also applied scarring, if not legible, tortures to citizens convicted of crimes, thereby enabling others to read and place them in their proper place, just as they did with slaves. Disgraced citizens were branded with their crimes, Ss for slave stealer, M for malefactor, and B for blasphemer. Commonly, they were branded on the hand so that when they raised their right hand to swear an oath in court, the judge and jury could read their record.[67] Most Americans and Englishmen do not remember that this is why they raise their right hands in court today, but in these societies, as in Ancient Greece, torture was a civic marker.

Here is a third model. Unlike the first two models, here the democratic state is unable or unwilling to provide for public security, perhaps because the territory is too great or its resources too limited. Public security is a partnership of public enforcement and private policing. Torture generates different disciplinary orders, sharpening differences among human beings. Citizens live by a standard of virtue, demanded and expected by their peers. As for quasi citizens and noncitizens, since no virtue can be expected of them, at least they know how to behave.

It is unlikely that modern democratic states will ever be as weak as Athenian democracy. Still, torture in some democracies may resemble the Athenian model more than one might think. Today, torture victims include not simply terrorists and criminals, but street children, vagrants, loiterers, and illegal immigrants. We may not speak of them as slaves, but they fall into a class of quasi citizens that is perceived as vicious. Paul Chevigny, writing about the Brazilian experience, uses expressions that apply elsewhere: "A person may not be a dangerous criminal, but is 'marginal,' a word used constantly by the police, or a 'vagabundo,' hence, is of little account, different from a solid citizen, including a worker."[68]

As in the ancient world, solid citizens are deeply anxious about such people. Who is working legally and who illegally? Who deserves the welfare of the state, and who is a vagrant who abuses it? Who benefits from legal protection, and who deserves no legal protection? How one treats citizens, guest workers, vagrants, immigrants, and the homeless causes great controversy. Torture responds to this anxiety. It does not resolve this anxiety by marking bodies as in ancient Greece. It works on the inside, leaving its traces on habits and dispositions. Different kinds of people know where to go and where not to go, where is venturing too far and where is home. "If you're not waiting for a bus, move out."[69]

This civic discipline model of torture is as much about intimidation as it is about confession. For example, between 1985 and 1986, prosecutors indicted five New York police officers for systematically torturing African-American and Latino youths. The police removed suspected drug dealers from the street by extracting false confessions with stun guns. What is important about such cases is that neighbors and police may look upon such behavior with understanding. "Sometimes, they deserve it," said a neighbor of the suspects. "I think they need some of that lesson when they are 10 and 12 years old, when they're smoking and hanging out, because in 10 years you can't tell them anything."[70] Or as a policeman said, "Stop the auto theft, stop the drug dealing, and we can stabilize these communities. . . . A cop has got to be pretty frustrated when he knows something's going on and he can't seem to do anything about it."[71]

In this case, police set apart those who did and did not belong on the street. Whether one can go here or there without fear of being beaten, whether one can travel in one's car without being pulled over or electrified, these are experiences constitutive of citizenship. Citizenship, after all, is not merely holding a passport, but understanding what treatment is due to one in daily life. This presumably differs from that of noncitizens and constitutes the basis for a common life experience. Our societies offer many finely graded distinctions between citizens, and some citizens soon discover they are not treated equally. These different civic experiences create different expectations and shape future behaviors. Some people expect torture, while others would be shocked to know it was "happening here." These different life experiences amount to, in some cases, insurmountable barriers between groups in democracies. In these cases, torture is not merely following preestablished legal understandings of who is or is not a citizen, falling solely on foreigners. It is conferring identities, shaping a finely graded civic order. It reminds lesser citizens who they are and where they belong.

In such cases, torture is often an "informal arrangement" among policemen in rough neighborhoods.[72] Appreciative residents and businesses aid them by not thinking too hard about why the streets are safe once again. Miyazawa sums up a Japanese police perspective that is no doubt more widely held in the community: "They think that the general public will criticize excessive or illegal actions, but procedural compliance, in and of itself, is not expected."[73] In postauthoritarian countries like Brazil, a sympathetic middle class might denounce obvious torture, but will ignore covert torture and mysterious deaths in custody.[74] The public proceeds in an uncomfortable bad faith, what Bourdieu so aptly calls *méconnaissance*, or misrecognition, so that things move along.[75]

Clean torture, in particular, encourages misrecognition. Clean torture yields an aggrieved voice, but one that complains about something others prefer not to see. Its effects are demobilizing and depoliticizing.

Judges and prosecutors also misrecognize tortured confessions. Such officials have little incentive to create more work for themselves.[76] Often they are constrained by high workloads and poor pay. Sympathetic judges may also think it is useless to investigate, as they have been overruled in the past.[77] Being soft on crime can hurt one's chances for advancement or reappointment.[78] Judges and prosecutors have also been threatened and killed.[79]

The media and politics also play their part. In Russia, "Judges who acquit face often hysterical reactions from the police, media, and the court president."[80] In Japan, police can cleverly manipulate the media, placing considerable pressure on the judicial system.[81] Although doing so was once rare, today American politicians must at every turn speak of being tough on crime.[82] Torture thrives on this insecurity so characteristic of modern democracies.

The privatization of policing also creates pressures for torture.[83] Today, states give national police new legal powers and huge budgets to fight drugs and terrorism.[84] Simultaneously, they cut local police budgets and encourage local police to enter partnerships with private security firms. Private companies now guard malls and industrial parks, and gated residential communities employ security guards or form community vigilance groups. Huge conglomerates now sell security capabilities. "We're not a security guard company. We sell a *concept of security*."[85] In the 1980s, the private security market expanded rapidly in industrialized democracies. The ratio of private police to public police is two to one in Australia and the United States.[86] The largest growth has been in the new democracies. In South Africa today, the ratio is now four to one.[87] In Russia, eight hundred thousand former police and military personnel work in the security business.[88]

These changes seem to generate two effects. On the one hand, police are often understaffed, making torture and other corruption very tempting indeed. On the other, private police don't simply create safe environments; they also engage in violence, including torture. In Russia, security personnel "intimidate honest citizens and business competitors."[89] In San Diego, a security guard who patrolled the Gaslamp Quarter as "Clancy the Cop" used his new stun gun on transients.[90] In South Africa, private security forces attacked a crowd at a train station with electric prods, leading to several deaths. Then there was the security guard who shot dead forty-one alleged burglars over several years in the Eastern Cape. Police did not caution him once, and when charged, magistrates always acquitted him. People Against Gangsterism and Drugs, the most well known of many community vigilance groups, engaged in "terror tactics" including forty-five bomb attacks in 1998.[91]

We do not live in a Robocop universe "in which corporate 'private governments' exist alongside state governments."[92] We do live in a world in which torture is returning to a role it had in ancient Greece, inducing civic discipline and shaping civic order in liberal democracies. It is thus a mistake to argue, as the anthropologist Talal Asad does, that the use of torture by liberal-democratic states "cannot be attributed to . . . governmental techniques for disciplining citizens."[93] This view cannot explain why torture occurs in the huge cities of established democracies (United States, Venezuela, India), among immigrant populations (Austria, Belgium, France, Greece, Hungary, Italy, Switzerland), or in emerging democracies with limited institutional resources (Russia, Eastern European countries, South Africa, Brazil).[94] What drives torture in these cases is neither war nor a permissive legal environment, but informal arrangements among police, residents, and businesses to shape the urban landscape.

Hell Is in the Details

The world we live in is a messy place, and the three models I have just presented do not exist independently of each other. Japan, for example, has problems with terrorism, and its police are sometimes harsh toward immigrants and refugees.[95] Abuses in these cases cannot be explained solely by a permissive legal context. The three models help distinguish three different strands in complicated events, highlighting elements of empirical cases that may be missed otherwise, and more than one model may apply to more than one empirical case.

Moreover, while the models identify important preconditions for torture in democratic states, these conditions do not obtain in every democracy. The conditions are necessary but not sufficient for torture to occur. Some democracies do not resort to torture even when these conditions are present, and that is not surprising. What would be surprising is if torture occurred in democratic states when none of the three preconditions obtained.

The models show that torture has an elective affinity for these three conditions, but pressing beyond this to a fine-grained causal account of the necessary *and* sufficient conditions is currently not possible given the fragmentary knowledge of many empirical cases. But the empirical cases are helpful in pointing to additional factors that may sustain torture once it takes hold. The Japanese case, for example, shows the slippery slope down which police travel once police seek confessions by any means. This tendency means that police become less skilled at other investigative tasks, and makes torture even more likely. Extensive prearrest detention powers, hostility between ethnic groups (such as Japanese hostility toward Koreans), and privatization can also exacerbate tendencies toward torture, tendencies that originally appeared for different reasons. Lastly, politicians and the media can stoke perceptions of a national emergency or a crime wave, creating greater tolerance for reports of torture when they appear.

It may be objected, isn't the purpose of torture the same in all these models: to deter crime and violence? Isn't what matters, from a theoretical point of view, that torture in democracies is simply warfare or deterrence? So why not say this is ultimately the basis for the demand for torture? To do this is to lose one's grip on the phenomenon of torture. One would not be able to explain the particulars of torture as comprehensively or precisely as one could. Each model has consequences for the tortures used, the timing, the rhythm of the interrogations, and why violators behave as they do. Conversely, by attending to these particulars in various historical instances, one can understand more clearly what is driving the choice of particular methods of torture. The details, in other words, matter in assessing the adequacy of explanations of torture. *How* torture happens is an important check on misleading or overly general accounts of *why* torture happens.

Consider timing and rhythm. When officers seek false confessions, they are looking for a performance. They will take as long as it takes until they can secure that performance. The luxury of time allows for more subtle coercive techniques — such as hours of sleep deprivation, continuous interrogation, and forced standing. These methods may grind on for days and weeks until the subject confesses. Timing and rhythm differ when seeking information in war or emergencies. Since World War II, a routine rule of interrogation is that guerrilla organizations change all critical information within twenty-four to forty-eight hours after its members are arrested. This is why officers torture them brutally at first, then ease off. Techniques useful for generating false confessions, sleep deprivation for example, are pointless. Interrogators reach for techniques like electric torture, which are quick. For vagrants and marginals, the brutality is shorter, the helplessness intense, and the techniques involve whatever is at hand. Officers are not interested in information or confession. They only want people to know their place, and then they are let go.

Consider the kind of victim (political enemy, ordinary criminal, or marginal citizen) and the conditions of arrest. These factors affect how much public scrutiny falls on officers, and so the techniques they choose. For example, in the mid-1980s, the Israeli government announced that police had killed two Palestinians during a hijacking. Newspaper photographs, however, showed the two were alive when taken into custody. Suspicion grew that the security officers had killed them, and the scandal led to the Landau Commission that, in turn, confirmed the use of torture.[96] The public and media were less interested in news that Israeli forces tortured Palestinian stone-throwers. There was "a system of regular beatings at a three-story lookout on Prophets Street in Nablus, where people were taken for a 'short treatment.' 'We called it the beatings operation.'"[97] Here few Israelis got into trouble, and the beating of street youth, which was privately endorsed by government and military officials, continued.[98] The security services, on the other hand, had to develop new techniques for interrogating high-profile suspects, techniques that left few marks.

The models point to particular events and practices to look for in torture accounts. Conversely, paying attention to the particulars can save one from faulty assessments of what is driving torture. Consider this messy example, messy because, even though the men here are wearing military uniforms, any analyst who describes what these soldiers did generally as warfare, or deterrence, or even as national security torture, would be misleading us.

In September 1988, Col. Yehuda Meir approached the mukhtar of Hawara, the clan leader of a small Palestinian village, with a list of twelve men wanted by the Israeli General Security Services (GSS). Rather than break down doors, leading to general panic and possible escape, Colonel Meir enlisted the mukhtar's help. None of the men was sought for serious offenses or terrorist activity. The mukhtar assembled the men, including his teenage son; they appear to have assumed that, as in past practice, they would be held for a while, but ultimately released. Colonel Meir and his soldiers of the Nahal brigade took the men three at a time in his bus a short distance down the road to a field. The men were handcuffed and gagged with their own scarves. The soldiers proceeded to beat them with clubs on all the joints, breaking their legs, arms, and ribs. The truck revved its engines so the screaming could not be heard. The soldiers removed the cuffs and gags and left the twelve men unconscious in a muddy field on a winter night.[99]

Some might characterize all this as national security torture. After all, the GSS had listed the names. How odd then that the soldiers did not expect information or confessions. "I didn't expect one of the Arabs to tell me something if we did not hit him. We just hit him. . . . And we didn't expect something to happen and we did not enjoy it." The soldiers knew about the semi-official GSS torture procedures, and they were adamant that they were not interrogating. Indeed, they gagged the prisoners. Nor did the soldiers expect that this beating would deter behavior. "I didn't expect that he would not throw stones the week after. We knew that they would hate us more than ever after this kind of thing."[100]

Nor was this an example of violence in the heat of war. The situation was not out of control. The men at Hawara had not only put up no resistance, they had "arrested themselves," as a soldier put it, reporting when the mukhtar called them.[101] Nor did the soldiers intend to kill the victims; they were supposed to live. Meir and his colleagues had decided in advance that one detainee would not have all his bones broken, so that he would be able to run and inform the villagers: "He ran and fell and ran and fell." The soldiers rejected the view that they were mere automatons carrying out their military duty. "Since the Holocaust, it really sounds bad when someone says, 'I got orders.' I never use this excuse. All my family from my father's side are gone in the Holocaust, and also part of my mother's side. I said in court that I got orders, but that was a fact—it doesn't excuse the things we did."[102]

Explaining what is happening in this example is troubling indeed until we pay attention to what the soldiers say they were doing and the context in which they operated. The soldiers insist that "the purpose was to cause pain, not to break bones."[103] They were instituting order in deeply troubled times: "The Intifada is a name everybody gave it later. [At the time] you didn't know what to call it, you didn't know how to treat it, you didn't know anything about it."[104] They were not the GSS, going after terrorists for information, nor were they the police, seeking confessions. In fact, the soldiers were doing the job of the penal system at a time when the penal system was strained to its utmost limit. "The jails were packed full."[105] The beatings were a brutal but swift way of putting noncitizens in their place. The problem was, as one soldier correctly put it, that the army was given "the job of the judiciary, levying punishment when it did not have the right to punish."[106]

In short, the soldiers described their behavior along the lines of the civic discipline model. The Nahal brigade acted no differently in this respect than police who torture in Rio or security guards in San Diego. Meir himself recognized the similarity. After his trial, he got a job as a private security guard. His notoriety was no handicap in the private security business. He was a man "who knows how to beat Arabs." In two years, he had a company with 150 employees and twenty-five vehicles. He observed, "I think that to go in Los Angeles where the blacks are living is more dangerous than to go into Nablus."[107]

One cannot emphasize enough how important it is to notice what torturers do, how they do it, and what they say about what they are doing. Each contingent particular has theoretical relevance. In the following chapters, I turn to the supply of torture techniques, mapping where different clean tortures come from. As in the study of the demand for torture, the details will matter. Too often, analysts have made assertions about the origins of torture techniques without paying attention to the specific features of the instruments they identify. As these features become evident, these analyses will seem increasingly implausible. In the study of torture, hell is in the details.

II Remembering Stalinism and Nazism

In modern memory, all modern torture comes from either Nazism or Stalinism. In the next three chapters, I review what is known about torture in the Soviet Union under Stalin, Nazi Germany, and the countries under Nazi occupation during World War II. It is important to separate out what was unique to Nazism and Stalinism from what was not. Only then can observers fully appreciate how the main democratic states contributed to modern torture.

These chapters attempt to fill some surprising gaps where modern memory is vague or incomplete, advancing two empirical claims. First, in chapter 3 ("Lights, Heat, and Sweat"), I show that the techniques we now identify as forming the Stalinist "Conveyor" system were common to police forces in the main democracies long before Stalin took power. In part IV, I will complete this claim by offering histories of the component techniques of that system, showing their affinity for democratic contexts. But here, it is sufficient to establish only that these techniques cannot be found in czarist or Leninist Russia, Weimar Germany, or elsewhere in Europe in the early twentieth century. Second, in chapter 4 ("Whips and Water"), I show that "Nazi torture" varied greatly by region, and in chapter 5 ("Bathtubs"), I establish that the techniques we now characteristically identify as "Nazi torture"—most notably electrotorture—occurred mainly in France, usually at the hands of French collaborators, police, and criminals employed by the Gestapo. In part III, I will show that these Frenchmen were not inspired in their choice of techniques by the Gestapo in Germany, but drew instead on inherited traditions of French colonial torture.

These chapters also introduce readers to many painful, simple, physical techniques that leave few marks, distinguishing them from one other and showing how police used them in conjunction. They also advance further the thesis that monitoring drives police to adopt torture techniques that leave few marks. In the American and British cases, observers were well aware that police adopted these techniques because they sought to hide evidence of torture and reduce their culpability. Rank-and-file police officers, on their own or with the consent of the local police chief, used these techniques to intimidate, to interrogate, and to coerce false confessions.

But the practice of stealth was not exclusively a democratic phenomenon. Although Nazi and Stalinist torture was generally scarring, interrogators adopted clean techniques consistently in certain cases where it was obviously advantageous to do so. Likewise, other authoritarian states that borrowed Stalinist techniques also favored scarring techniques, but they also selectively used stealthy regimens. As these chapters document, the best-known cases are those where these states hoped to use prisoners for purposes of international propaganda before cameras or those where they anticipated that external observers would be reviewing treatment of POWs.

He was questioned under blinding lights by the voices of
invisible men.

— *The Report on Lawlessness in Law Enforcement, 1931*[1]

3   Lights, Heat, and Sweat

In 1953, CIA director Allen Dulles hired two noted doctors, Harold Wolff and
Lawrence Hinkle, to study Communist "brainwashing." Dulles had seen films
in which American pilots held prisoner in Korea had recited unbelievable confessions, apparently voluntarily. Had the Communists developed special new
techniques for mind control, techniques that apparently left no marks? Dulles
wanted to know.

The Wolff-Hinkle report is the definitive U.S. government work on "brainwashing."[2] The CIA gave Wolff and Hinkle classified files. It helped them interview former interrogators from the Soviet NKVD and former prisoners from
the Soviet Union and China. The report covers techniques used for the Soviet
show trials, in China, and during the Korean War. Wolff and Hinkle concluded
flatly that there were no special methods: no drugs, hypnotic tricks, secret machines, or new psychological techniques. Rather, the methods used "were
known to police systems all over the world, and many of them are still in use
at the present day."[3]

What the report does not say is what these background practices were. That
is what I describe in this chapter. The common police practice, in Europe and
the United States, was this: Detectives took turns interrogating the suspect for
hours, or even days. They aimed bright lights at the suspect's eyes, aggravating
suspects and preventing them from sleeping. The light and bodies heated the
room. The atmosphere was stifling. In the end, most people confessed.

I shall call this practice *sweating*.[4] European police sometimes supplemented sweating with bruising beatings. In the United States, police beat as
well, but they learned earlier than most other police forces how to use tech-

niques that left fewer visible marks. English police did not beat, but they used powerful psychological pressures and extended interrogations that also yielded false confessions.

Stalinist interrogators adapted from all these traditions. Of course, in most cases arising from Stalin's purges, interrogators rarely held back when questioning, and their use of torture was scarring, if not fatal. Interrogators beat and sweated their suspects until they confessed. But for show trials, victims had to appear in open court before the world press with no bruises. For this far smaller group, interrogators consistently used physical and psychological techniques well known in American and European policing at that time. They coerced confessions using physical techniques that left few marks, and they employed psychological techniques that held prisoners to their confessions in public. They called this combination of techniques "the Conveyor." Stalinist interrogators passed this combination of positional tortures and sweating techniques, what I will call Soviet modern, on to the Chinese and other allied states.

As Wolff and Hinkle say, practicing the Conveyor did not involve any new coercive techniques. The turn to stealth torture had come earlier. It was just that the Stalinist interrogators had learned to use them for new, dramatic purposes, and this is why we remember them. But while today we tend to remember only the Stalinist torturers of the 1930s, patient democratic interrogators had preceded them, quietly assembling many clean techniques.

Sweating and Stealth in America

Washington, DC, 1924: police interrogate a Chinese American, D. C. Wan, in a hotel room for eight days until he confesses. Louisiana, 1925: police hold two men for thirty-eight days, obtaining confessions on the thirty-fourth-day.[5] One could no doubt find earlier examples. To start, it is enough to know that in the years following World War I, sweating became a common police practice in the United States.

In the United States, brutal interrogation was "widespread throughout the country."[6] Torture occurred in back rooms, distant precincts, and secret locations. Interrogators openly slapped, beat, whipped, poked, suspended, or twisted suspects.[7] In 1931, the National Commission on Law Observance and Enforcement of the American Bar Association (ABA) issued a comprehensive account of police brutality in American cities entitled *Report on Lawlessness in Law Enforcement*. The commission, dubbed the Wickersham Commission after its determined chair, George Wickersham, gathered hundreds of affidavits and news reports to reveal an ongoing, persistent pattern of brutality across the United States. It found that police tortured in rural towns (one-third of the cases) and in twenty-nine major cities. It investigated fifteen cities for more detailed case studies, finding that police commonly beat and sweated suspects in ten of them.[8] It emphasized that these were professional departments. Police beat not in the heat of the moment, but as a calculated effort to get confessions.

The Wickersham Commission drew national attention to widespread police abuse, and many books popularized the contents of the commission's report for the public. It was not the first report of police torture, but it was so thorough and complete that the facts were difficult to deny. The report built on public intolerance of police torture over the previous decade. In 1924, George Dougherty, the former deputy commissioner of the NYPD put it plainly: "The bench, jurors, the public are becoming more and more suspicious every day of confessions procured as a result of severe interrogation and examination."[9] Police proved sensitive to this intensified public scrutiny. In some jurisdictions, police abandoned the beating of suspects altogether. In others, police developed clean techniques that enabled them to beat and sweat without raising too much alarm. "Methods are favored which do not leave visible marks, because these attract the attention of the courts and sometimes lead district attorneys not to use the confession."[10]

The Wickersham Commission identified five American cities where police typically combined clean torture techniques to intimidate, coerce false confessions, and gather information without being detected by others. These cities were New York, Cleveland, Chicago, Dallas, and Seattle. And the commission also identified many specific techniques that leave few marks, techniques that, in the course of this book, will commonly indicate a deliberate program of stealth torture when they are used consistently in combination with each other.[11] Some of these techniques were innovations at the time, and some were old but adapted by the police for covert torture (I will describe their full histories in parts 3 and 4); what is important here is that there was an American style of stealth torture by the 1920s, and it consisted of the combination of techniques that follows.

Relay interrogation and sleep deprivation ("sweating"). The most common method was "persistent questioning, continuing hour after hour, sometimes by relays of officers." Depriving suspects of sleep was "the most effective torture and certain to produce any confession desired."[12]

Clean beating. Whips tear and flay the skin; even an untutored eye can see the mark. As an alternative, the Wickersham Commission reported police used heavy objects that did not have edges. There were clubs, rubber hoses, sausage-shaped sandbags made of silk, boxing gloves, all "chosen because, when properly applied, they leave no marks."[13] In Chicago, police even struck suspects on the side of the head with a telephone book. "The Chicago telephone book is a heavy one and a swinging blow with it may stun a man without leaving a mark."[14]

The police struck areas that were unlikely to leave long-term bruises: slaps to the faces and blows over the kidneys, in the abdomen, or in the soft hollows above the hips.[15] They squeezed, twisted, and lifted men by the genitals. They disguised blows as accidents, for example, kicking the shins or pushing the suspect forward unexpectedly.[16]

Light and electricity. Police commonly used "powerful lights turned full on the prisoner's face or switched on and off."[17] In two jurisdictions, police applied electricity directly to the body. In Dallas, it was "a particular device known as the 'electric monkey.' "[18] In Helena, Arkansas, police used "an improvised electric chair" to extract a confession. "Such a method leaves no marks."[19] In Seattle, the police chief forced prisoners into a cell covered with a wall-to-wall electrified carpet.[20]

Positional torture and exhaustion exercises. Positional tortures were those that kept bodies in ordinary positions until they became excruciating. The most common was prolonged forced standing, which can cause limbs to swell painfully.[21] Exhaustion exercises required prisoners to perform common exercises endlessly prior to or during interrogation.[22]

Water and air. Notoriously, police would sometimes tighten a suspect's necktie until he choked and passed out.[23] Some police used sand-blasting guns and ice-cold baths, while others thrust a tube down the prisoner's throat and turned on the tap, painfully distending the internal organs.[24] Southern police favored the "water cure," a "torture well known to the bench and bar of the country." Interrogators tie or hold down a victim on his back. Then they pour water down his nostrils "so as to strangle him, thus causing pain and horror for the purpose of forcing a confession."[25]

Sweatboxes. During the Civil War, the sweatbox was a cell near a very hot stove that produced intense heat. Guards fed the stove rubber shoes, making offensive smells until detainees confessed.[26] By the early twentieth century, sweatboxes were dark, solitary cells like the Denver "black hole." The cells were very cold, hot, or wet.[27]

Drugs and irritants. Some police used drugs (scopolamine or sodium amytal, so-called "truth serum") and alcohol to make suspects talkative.[28] Some police placed victims in enclosed spaces (a room, head in a box) and pumped in tear gas or chloride gas.[29] With addicts, prolonged detention was unnecessary; they would confess if the drugs were withheld.[30]

Positional devices. These devices make it impossible for the prisoner to move. The Wickersham Commission notes the Oregon boot.[31] Other sources describe how police used straitjackets for interrogation in prisons, most notably in the case of Edward Morell.[32]

Americans called all these activities the "third degree." The phrase was originally coined by Major Richard Sylvester of Washington, DC, the president of the International Association of Chiefs of Police. In 1910, Sylvester described police duties as arrest (the first degree), transportation to jail (the second degree) and interrogation (the third degree).[33] Soon, Americans used the phrase *third degree* to refer solely to violence used to obtain confession or information about a crime—in short, torture.[34]

But to the public, torture also meant scarring injuries, and if police were really practicing the third degree in interrogations rooms across the United States, where was the evidence of the wounds and scars on the suspects' bodies? Many American police chiefs denied that police practiced the third degree. In response, the Wickersham Commission not only documented numerous cases of outright scarring tortures, but also showed a sinister change in police practices. It documented how police adopted different techniques in the face of public monitoring. In Buffalo, it observed, where there was no organized protest, police openly beat suspects. In San Francisco, however, the police held back "in outstanding cases of newspaper prominence" and those "who retained lawyers with influence."[35] Lawyers and journalists, though, were not adequate monitors. The Wickersham Commission itemized the tricks police used to appear to conform to the law. They commonly "lost" men in booking even as police interrogated them in a back room.[36] They would strike suspects from behind so that, if charges were brought against the officer, suspects would "be unable to identify him in court."[37] Or another man besides the interrogator would beat the suspect "so that when the arresting officer takes the stand it can not be charged that he used force."[38] And they used torture techniques that left few marks afterward.

The commission emphasized that internal monitoring (doctors, judges, and police chiefs) reduced abuse more effectively than external monitoring (press, public, and lawyers). The Boston police, for example, neither sweated nor beat, and not merely because newspapers were quick to report police brutality. Police could easily sweat suspects in outlying police stations "to which no reporter is assigned." Rather, the commission praised bureaucratic, judicial, and medical officers whose internal monitoring reduced abuse.[39]

The Wickersham Commission transformed American law and, with it, policing in the 1930s. One can see this change in Supreme Court decisions between 1936 and 1944, which sometimes cite the commission's work. In *Brown v. Mississippi* (1936), the Supreme Court struck down confessions secured by whipping and near lynchings of three African-Americans. The Court concluded, "It would be difficult to conceive of methods more revolting to the sense of justice than those taken to procure the confessions of these petitioners."[40]

In *Chambers v. Florida* (1939), the Court overturned confessions based on mob pressure and persistent questioning over five days, including one all-night session. The Court condemned "the protracted questioning and cross questioning of these ignorant young colored tenant farmers by state officers and other white citizens in a fourth floor jail room, where as prisoners they were without friends, advisers or counselors, and under circumstances calculated to break the strongest nerves and stoutest resistance."[41]

In *Ashcraft v. Tennessee* (1944), the Court struck down confessions secured by relay interrogations under bright lights. In 1941, police interrogated Ashcraft for thirty-six hours continuously until he confessed to murdering his wife. The Court finally closed judicial debates about this kind of practice, maintaining that a democratic society would never permit "prosecutors serving in relays to keep a defendant witness under continuous cross-examination for thirty six hours without rest or sleep in an effort to extract a 'voluntary' confession."[42]

When Wolff and Hinkle stated that the techniques used in Communist brainwashing were well-known police techniques, they were describing in part the techniques that characterize American stealth torture. In the 1920s, these techniques were flourishing in the United States as public monitoring of police abuses intensified. By the 1950s, when Wolff and Hinkle wrote their report, the American style of stealth torture had largely disappeared in the United States, but the techniques were well known, as they state, in police systems all over the world. In addition to physical techniques, Wolff and Hinkle pointed out that Communist brainwashing also drew on psychological techniques well known to police worldwide, and again these techniques were well known in the 1920s in the United States and the United Kingdom. These practices also form an important backdrop to Communist practices.

British Psychological Techniques

Unlike the Americans, the English police did not beat during interrogation; this is well established.[43] English judges did note suspicious confessions, however, suggesting that police behavior still was short of exemplary. In 1940, the recorder of Liverpool gave as an example one defendant who had retracted his confession in court. He stated that he had confessed "after repeated promises of release and encouragement by detectives." In his confession, the defendant remembered only those cases known to the police. Not a single sentence described details that "the police did not already know."[44] The recorder refused to admit the statement, saying, "I am not the only one who is amazed at the great increase in the number of confessions tendered by the police in evidence. I have come to the conclusion that these confessions are increasing and, in the interests of justice, ought to be diminished."[45]

In 1929, a royal commission agreed that such confessions "are not only more numerous than formerly, but also longer and more informative, and thus more valuable to the prosecution." It also "found a volume of responsible evidence which it was impossible to ignore, suggesting that a number of the voluntary statements now tendered in Court are not 'voluntary' in the strict sense of the word."[46] They noted "such devices for extracting statements as keeping a suspect in suspense (keeping him waiting for long periods), constant repetition of the same question, bluffing assertions that all the facts are known anyway, that a clean breast will enable them to make things easier at the trial."[47] Some cases, remarked another observer, "revealed a method of questioning which was, at any rate, most unsatisfactory and unfair."[48]

William Sargant, a well-known psychologist and consultant to British intelligence on brainwashing, thought there were special techniques at work. During World War II, Sargant worked in a Maudsley hospital, where police would bring him prisoners from Brixton jail for testing. Many prisoners "had, we found, somehow been persuaded by the police to make full and detailed confessions of crime which would assure them savage sentences in Court, hanging included, and which some of them had subsequently wished to withdraw." Sargant's concerns prompted his research on brainwashing.[49]

There was nothing mysterious here. Peter Deeley, a journalist who documented human rights abuses in the 1960s, listed the techniques from interviews with British officers with long careers in policing.[50] When there was more than one suspect, detectives played the prisoner's dilemma. They separated the suspects and played them against each other, saying or implying that the other partner was about to confess. Faced with the prospect of being convicted more harshly if one remained silent, each tried to confess first. Then there was the "hard and soft" ploy (also called the Mutt and Jeff routine). One officer played the "good cop" and the other "the bad cop." Fearing the bad cop, suspects usually confessed to the friendlier one. Detectives carefully crafted the setting and atmosphere in which they interrogated. They preferred to interrogate alone, so they could use their personality to influence the suspect. They played on the suspect's fears, isolation, anxieties, suggestibility and desire for approval. They strongly preferred suspects not have their lawyer present.

Some of these techniques were also known in the United States. The Wickersham Commission noted, for example, that the police in Newark excelled at the "good cop, bad cop" routine.[51] Nor were these techniques improper or illegal at the time, though eventually the U.S. Supreme Court condemned all of them in the *Miranda* decision (1966), selecting the "hard-soft" routine for particular censure.[52] These were highly problematic techniques because, as we know today, they do not distinguish the innocent from the guilty. Social psychologists know that innocent people will also confess in these circumstances.[53] Philip Zimbardo, a noted social psychologist and a former American Psychological Association president, has shown how New York police generated numerous false confessions using these techniques in the 1950s.[54]

Although the British police mainly used these powerful psychological techniques in interrogations, they were not unfamiliar with American sweating, what they called "extended interrogation."[55] Cases of sweating were uncommon, but they happened. In one case before World War II, a Scotland Yard inspector worked on a suspect for hours. "My boss was tireless, he went on cross examining him all night long, contrary to the rules." In another case, the senior detective set aside the physical evidence and asked the suspect to make a statement: "Before we got to the Old Bailey we had five different statements from him."[56]

The case of Timothy John Evans provoked the greatest scandal.[57] The police maintained that Evans confessed as soon as he arrived at the station. Subsequently, investigators determined that the police interrogated him all night. They recorded three different confessions. In each successive version, Evans added details that more closely resembled the police's circumstantial evidence. For a virtual illiterate, Evans showed a remarkable skill with numbers and words. Evans was hanged in 1949. The true murderer confessed four years later.

When interrogators combine powerful psychological techniques and sweating, they can create remarkable effects. In his book on the Evans case, Ludovic Kennedy persuasively compares Evans's interrogation with Sargant's analysis of brainwashing, and finds that "there is not very much difference."[58] Zimbardo goes further, arguing that such techniques are "more psychologically sophisticated and more effective than the Chinese Communist 'brainwashing' techniques which we have denounced."[59]

Interrogation Elsewhere in Europe

By the 1920s then, American and British police used a distinctive set of physical and psychological techniques in interrogations. But how widespread were they elsewhere at the time? The answer is that they were not very widespread at all. This is not, of course, to say that other countries were better: If there was a general trend in European torture at the time, it was a trend away from sweating and other forms of clean torture toward brutally scarring violence.

In France, police interrogation in the 1920s also sometimes involved torture, but the specific techniques are not as clearly documented as in the American and British approaches. The head of the Criminal Investigations Division of the Sûreté Nationale acknowledged many complained of "physical maltreatment, threats, abuse, [and] the dragging out of an interrogation till the suspect is exhausted." He conceded that these complaints were "not always imaginary."[60] In 1929, for example, inspectors "tortured ferociously" a murder suspect, an Armenian named Almazian.[61] The police named this procedure *passage à tabac*, after the beating necessary for processing tobacco leaves, but loosely meaning "rough handling."[62]

In Germany, "patient interrogations"[63] gave way to *verschärfte Vernehmung*, sharpened interrogations, the Nazi euphemism for torture.[64] Police brutality was rare in Weimar Germany, though not unknown, especially in Bavaria in 1919–21.[65] In the 1920s, the Berlin criminal investigation division recorded two cases: a detective beat a serial murderer (1920) and another sweated two master burglars (1929). These cases were regarded as "a serious breach of police ethics."[66] Nevertheless, some detectives "advocated (and practiced) third degree techniques and summary justice."[67] In 1933, with the rise of the Nazis, one of these detectives took over the department, leading "the fight against crime using methods which I always thought proper, but which could never have been applied, but for . . . the National Resurrection."[68] Soon defendants appeared in courts with "signs of torture," and judges learned to live with such evidence of abuse.[69]

Typically, detectives interrogated the prisoner and then handed him over to the SA or SS until he confessed.[70] But the appearance of prisoners with cuts and bruises in the dock made lawyers at the Ministry of Justice uncomfortable. So on June 1, 1937, the Gestapo and lawyers for the Ministry of Justice established interrogation guidelines. Henceforth, beating was to be regulated: only blows with a club to the buttocks, numbering no more than twenty-five. A physician had to be present after the tenth blow; "a standard club will be designated, to eliminate all irregularities."[71] In 1942, Gestapo chief Heinrich Müller expanded the approved methods. They now included sleep deprivation, starvation, exhaustion exercises, and confinement in dark cells.[72]

The rhetoric in these minutes and directives seeks to give the impression that Gestapo torture was a controlled process, and it invokes practices that the Gestapo knew were common in the United States and the United Kingdom. At Nuremberg, an Allied investigator confronted Dr. Werner Best, the Nazi governor of Denmark, with the Gestapo directives. Best, after all, was a recognized expert on policing. Didn't he know better? Best objected to the Allied officer's hypocrisy, pointing out that "similar methods were used in other countries."[73] Best was correct in one sense, of course; the U.S. Supreme Court case, *Ashcraft v. Tenessee* (1944) underlined the fact that some American police were all too familiar with these methods. But Best was also misleading. Actual Gestapo torture normally went far beyond these approved methods. There were indeed times and places where the Gestapo restricted itself to these techniques alone, but such cases of sweating were rare, as I indicate in the next chapter.

Best was misleading in another sense; "similar methods" were not common in most countries. Other states were not interested in sweating. Either they did not torture, or, if they did, they favored scarring techniques. Why use such time-consuming techniques when swifter, more painful techniques existed? In Hungary, police whipped and suspended victims during interrogation.[74] In Romania, an autocratic monarchy whipped and beat its opponents, whether they were Fascist or Communist.[75] And similar bloody practices appear in Italy, Yugoslavia, Poland, and Lithuania.[76]

Then there was revolutionary Russia in the 1920s. "This is how we examine here," said a cheka (secret police) interrogator. He had the person "placed, barefoot, on a red-hot frying pan." Then "he was beaten with a whip with metallic ends until his back, from the neck to the pelvis, was one mass of torn, dangling flesh."[77] Other practices included placing needles under fingernails, removing nails with pincers, pouring sealing wax on bodies, putting candles to the genitals, inserting enemas with powdered glass, branding victims with five-pointed stars, raping, burying alive temporarily, and striking the face with a nail-studded iron glove.[78] An observer concluded, "Each Che-Ka seems to have had its specialty in torture."[79]

Of all these specialties, there is one cheka method we remember with particular clarity today, though we may not know its origins. The cheka of Kiev "put a rat into an iron tube sealed with wire netting at one end, the other being placed against the victim's body, and the tube heated until the maddened rat, in an effort to escape, gnawed its ways into the prisoner's guts."[80] George Orwell adapts this technique in *Nineteen Eighty-Four* by changing one detail, placing the end of the tube on the face rather than on the stomach. In so doing, Orwell transforms a method of execution into a torture, but one that was never practiced quite that way in Russia.

This anecdote may serve to remind us that, in the study of torture, one must separate carefully what one imagines happened from the actual descriptions and distributions of techniques. Not everything one has heard about happened, and much that one has heard about did not happen when and where one thought it did. Sweating is a case in point. These were distinctive practices, and, in the 1920s and 1930s, they occurred rarely outside of Anglo-Saxon policing practices.

Sweating and Stealth in Russia

These then are the background practices to which Wolff and Hinkle refer: sweating, clean tortures, and psychological pressures. Police used such techniques to extract confessions for public trials. In Nazi trials, it did not matter that the defendants who confessed looked bruised and beaten; it was unlikely anyone else would see them afterward. In the United States and the United Kingdom, bruised and beaten defendants drew attention, so police had institutional incentives to develop a different set of techniques, and some clearly did.

The Soviet government used trials differently. It used them to explain government policy to the public. Show trials explained economic failures and justified huge purges. For example, after the fifty-three Shakhty engineers were convicted of sabotage in 1928, the government purged seven thousand engineers throughout the country. Such extremely public performances meant that, in these cases, the Soviet government could not avoid monitoring both at home and abroad. Indeed, it appears to have sought out public attention in these cases in order to demonstrate that it was far more open a society than it in fact was. At the height of the various purges in the 1930s, interrogators were torturing thousands, if not millions. They subjected them to relay interrogation, sleep deprivation, and overt torture.[81] Beatings "not uncommonly crippled the victim for life."[82] Some died under interrogation. Others were executed. The survivors went to brutal labor camps to starve, freeze, and die.[83]

But for show trial defendants, there had to be "special treatment."[84] There could be no signs of torture. The defendants had to confess voluntarily. Courtroom observers sometimes suspected confessions had been coerced, but those outside took the confessions at face value.[85] Even some of those who were eventually subjected to torture had themselves previously dismissed rumors of torture as "highly unlikely," naively believing that torture was "incompatible with the principles of democracy so solemnly proclaimed a short while before, as well as with the 'Stalinist solicitude for the human being.' "[86]

Coercing a statement by means of torture was by no means the end of the process. Perhaps more importantly, the defendants then had to stick to their confessions before the cameras and the press. This was by no means easy. The first show trial of the Stalin era was the trial of the Shakhty engineers. In this trial, only ten defendants confessed fully and six partially. One went mad prior to the trial, one committed suicide, some retracted their confessions in court, and the rest maintained their innocence.[87] In the Menshevik trial (1931), all fourteen defendants confessed.[88] In the Metro-Vickers trial (1933), all the Soviet engineers confessed, but only two of the six British engineers confessed fully. One of them repudiated his confession in court.[89] In 1934, the government turned to famous revolutionary figures from the Party. It tried Zinoviev, Kamenev, and their associates *in camera*, as their confessions fell short of what was desired for a public trial.[90] Finally, between 1936 and 1938, the government tried fifty-four well-known political figures.[91] In these trials, only one defendant, Krestinsky, retracted his confession.[92]

As this brief history suggests, interrogators made mistakes at first. Gradually they figured out how to get prisoners to stick to their confessions in public. The first element was a process of "very protracted interrogations, deprival of sleep, constant exposure to a powerful glare, much standing and simulations of impending execution."[93] To be precise, prisoners report being subjected to the following techniques in preparation for show trials.

Relay interrogation and sleep deprivation. Interrogations often happened at night. Few report getting more than a few hours of sleep, if that.[94] The interrogators were always fresh, bullying, questioning, insulting, humiliating, and threatening the victim hour after hour, day after day.[95] To the prisoner's frustration, each interrogator would start the case from the beginning and go over it repeatedly.[96] Alex Weissberg's interrogator could shout exactly the same question with precisely the same intonation for hours; "it was driving me mad."[97]

Light. The prisoner would answer questions under blinding floodlights.[98] In the prisoner's cell, a bright light fell on his face. "There is no escape from it. If at any time of the night I turned on my side, always the guard entered the cell and turned my head so that my eyes should directly face the lamp. He used to say: 'I must see your eyes.' "[99]

Positional tortures. Prisoners commonly stood for hours while questioned, what was dubbed *vystoika*.[100] This is an excruciating torture.[101] The ankles and feet swell to twice their size within twenty-four hours. Moving becomes agony. Large blisters develop. The heart rate increases, and some faint. The kidneys eventually shut down. When the prisoners returned to the cell, they had to sit without moving (*vysadka*). "My legs swelled from the 'standing' and the 'sitting.' "[102] They had to sleep in the prescribed manner, with hands on the blanket and face toward the light.[103]

Clean beating. Beating, if it occurred, was clean. "Special care was generally taken to see that the interrogation left no permanent visible marks."[104] Beating included kicks to the shins, slaps to the face, blows to the kidneys, and chokeholds.[105] Devices used included a rubber hose or a sandbag.[106] In 1937, a prisoner offered this example: "Klara lay down, pulled up her skirt to show hideous welts on her thighs and buttocks, and said, 'This is Gestapo.' Then she held out blue and swollen hands and said, "This is NKVD.' "[107] The Gestapo whipped; the

Soviet NKVD beat and beat hard, but it did not whip. Was this simply ideological conformity, the effort to "maintain the fiction that beating was not a regulation method, but was used only at the whim of the individual magistrate"?[108] Perhaps. It could be simply that whipping left permanent, visible welts. Bruised and swollen hands would return to normal. As one prisoner observed, "The NKVD obviously wished to avoid telltale evidence, such as would have been left by rubber clubs and similar weapons."[109]

Cold rooms and sweatboxes. Prisoners were put in cells that were very hot, freezing cold, or dark and wet.[110] In most cases, they were alone, but some cells housed several hundred men "in heat that chokes and suffocates, in stink that asphyxiates."[111]

Positional devices. Some report being put in straitjackets.[112] Some had their head wrapped in wet cloth; as the cloth dried, it compressed the head painfully.[113]

Salt, water, and alcohol. There were freezing baths of cold water and meals of salt herring (which fiercely dehydrates one).[114] In the case of alcoholics, interrogators simply withheld liquor.[115]

There was nothing mysterious about Soviet techniques, as Wolff and Hinkle correctly observed. Police elsewhere knew these techniques. The Soviet approach was simply more ideological.[116] The interrogators looked to generate false confessions for political reasons. They used similar physical techniques for the most part, though they did not use electric torture, the water cure, or drugs.[117] And as elsewhere, very few could resist these pressures:

> Time was their ally. . . . If there were some point at which torture must cease, then a prisoner might be able to summon up all his moral strengths and will power and hold out until then. There was no such point. I can hold out another night, and another night, and another night, he might think. But what then? What's the good of it? They have all the time in the world. At some point or other I must physically collapse.[118]

Unlike many American cases, very few prisoners subsequently withdrew their confessions in open court. Here we come to the other element of the interrogation, the psychological techniques that interrogators used to hold prisoners to their confessions, what was sometimes called the "Yezhov Method."[119]

Interrogators assessed a prisoner's character, raised his fears, and manipulated his weaknesses.[120] They established a relationship with the prisoner. Some wept along with prisoners as they confessed.[121] Interrogators played games. They feigned friendship or threatened aggressively (the hard-soft ploy). They rewarded cooperation and punished recalcitrance.[122] They used the confessions of less important prisoners to force more important ones to confess, and then used these against the holdouts (the prisoner's dilemma).[123] In the end, prisoners came to have a stake in confessing, and that is why they stuck to it in public.

Preparing so few for show trials consumed enormous time and resources. It had, remarked one prisoner, "one grave disadvantage—it took up a lot of time."[124] It required "the special squads of interrogators many months of relentless pressure to break down the resistance of the prospective main defendants."[125] Consequently, "Only a small proportion of prisoners are singled out for special treatment and N.K.V.D. men competent to deal with them are no doubt relatively few."[126]

No doubt. The government demoted and purged poor interrogators.[127] Interrogation was not a desirable job; many interrogators were young amateurs.[128] Yezhov's manual offered them no practical guidance, and many learned on the job. Each interrogator competed with the others to establish a good reputation.[129] If it looked like the prisoner might break, the interrogator persisted as long as he could before handing him over to the next man.

Wasteful as show trials were, there was an understandable political reason for extracting such confessions. Such public confessions destroyed defendants politically in a way that executing them would not. What was remarkable about the Stalinist purges was that judges wanted confessions from *everyone*, confessions that were never heard publicly and had no economic or political value. Judges had a legalistic fetish for confessions, and the police strove to satisfy it. Indeed, they preferred confessions rather than faking more elaborate charges. Confessions were easy to get, and implicated dozens more.

This generated an incredibly wasteful system devoted to the ritualistic production of confessions. At its peak, over one hundred thousand interrogators tortured thousands, even millions, none of whom were providing the state with any productive labor while they were busy confessing. Nor did retaining or cultivating expertise in interrogation seem to matter to the state. Over twenty thousand NKVD interrogators perished in the purges; the entire staff of the main Moscow prison was replaced four times.[130] It is hard to think of this as economically rational behavior.[131]

Lenin once said that the Soviets would adopt advanced industrial organization from America, what was called Taylorism, without the capitalist abuses.[132] The Soviets were never able to adopt Taylorism in industry, much less in interrogation.[133] Still interrogators liked to evoke the state's industrial rhetoric, implying that torture was a far more controlled process than it was in fact. For instance, Krivitsky, an NKVD agent who defected in the late 1930s, claimed that the Stalinist system adopted Taylorist techniques. He asserted, "This Third

Degree, improved by Stalin on the model of the latest American methods of mass production, had actually become known among us as the 'conveyor system' of examining prisoners."[134]

But Krivitsky is only parroting Lenin here, filing his "good citizen" report. It is a mistake to confuse the name of a practice, "the Conveyor" (a metaphor that suggests a modern mechanical assembly line), with what interrogators were actually doing, actions that were anything but economically rational. How a modern state engaged in a highly ritualized, wasteful process on such a massive scale defies easy explanation, certainly the convenient rationalizing gloss that Krivitsky puts on it.[135]

The Spread of the Russian Style

In 1945, Soviet armies occupied Eastern Europe, founding new Communist states. Soviet methods went along with them. In 1949, the Chinese Communist Party defeated the Nationalists and assumed power in China. All these states staged political trials and public confessions. Interrogators used bright lights, sleep deprivation, and relay interrogation, supplemented with the usual practices: beating, slapping, positional tortures (prolonged standing and sitting), sweatboxes, dark holes with rats, and salt diets.[136]

Over time, some nations supplemented the Russian style, improvising as well as drawing from past national practices of torture and interrogation. The most notable variations occurred in Romania, China, and Korea. These examples show, on the one hand, how Soviet modern could give way to bloodier methods. As governments stopped performing show trials, their torturers became less concerned with leaving marks. On the other hand, in the 1950s, when the Chinese anticipated international scrutiny of prisoner-of-war camps, they turned away from scarring tortures. Indeed, in some cases, they harnessed Soviet positional tortures and sweating techniques to generate public confessions from American POWs and filmed them for purposes of international propaganda.

To be specific, in Romania, guards beat prisoners with iron rulers, flogged with wires and wet ropes, and broke or removed teeth.[137] They also used the *falaka*.[138] This involved beating the soles of the feet with a heavy cable. The technique had been a familiar police torture in southeastern Europe since the Ottoman period, but it was never practiced in Russia. Soviet guards also did not usually handcuff their prisoners.[139] Romanian guards, however, used manacles that cut into the wrists, tightened with movement, or they held one in contorted positions for hours.[140] Sometimes they would also tie on a gas mask for hours, a device that made breathing difficult.[141] Guards also used the *maneg*, an exercise designed to exhaust prisoners.[142] Guards would force the prisoner to run around a small cell at a minimum speed for hours. Sometimes they would throw gravel on the floor.

When asked how Chinese interrogation differed from Soviet methods, one KGB officer replied simply and disingenuously, "The Chinese use torture."[143] As self-serving as the statement is, it properly recognizes that the Chinese added distinctive twists to Soviet tortures. The Soviets used forced standing that caused the legs to swell. The Chinese bound gauze strips to the ankles, which forced the ankles to contract against the swelling, causing pain more quickly.[144] The Chinese also forced prisoners to run between interrogations, usually wearing leg chains that cut and bruised.[145] The Chinese also used manacles.[146] They would tie the prisoner's hands behind his back, with his forearms side by side. This caused cuts in the arms, which in turn got infected. The hands swelled; any contact was agony. During questioning, interrogators gently "milked" the prisoner's sensitive fingers or put chopsticks and pencils between them. Sleep was impossible. Lying on one's side aggravated sore shoulders. Lying on one's back traumatized the swollen hands.

The most distinctive Chinese innovation was the way in which interrogators harnessed group pressure.[147] In the Soviet system, guards enforced sleep deprivation and positional tortures. In the Chinese system, cellmates performed these tasks. If the prisoner returned to the cell without manacles on his hand, they accepted him warmly. If he returned wearing manacles, cellmates chastised the recalcitrant prisoner. They beat, tortured, and starved him.[148] To prevent him from sleeping, cellmates took turns through the night pinching, poking, and slapping the prisoner.[149]

Chinese interrogators won cell cooperation by linking each member's progress to that of his cellmates. If there was any recalcitrance, "good" prisoners demonstrated their commitment by attacking the backslider. Group mutuality, confession, and public self-criticism have a long history in Chinese penal practice, stretching back into the imperial period. The Communist interrogators adapted old practices for new political purposes.[150]

Torture in the Korean War (1950–53) is the most interesting example of how other nations adapted the Russian style. The war pitted not only Koreans against each other, but also United Nations troops (American, British, and Turkish, to name but a few) against the Chinese on the Communist side. The conflict gradually drew worldwide attention, and, not surprisingly, clean tortures soon appeared in its wake.

In the first year of the war, North Koreans guards drove POWs on long, cold marches and housed them in disease-ridden shelters and water-filled caves.[151] Half the American troops captured died as prisoners, largely in North Korean camps.[152] North Korean interrogators tortured, slipping bamboo slivers under nails and hanging prisoners from the rafters by their hands.[153] One British prisoner was subjected to bone-breaking beatings and near suffocation with the water cure.[154] Another was forced to kneel for hours with his hands tied behind his back to a heavy board; he was beaten severely every time he moved.[155]

In the autumn of 1951, peace talks began. The Chinese soon learned that the UN negotiators were keenly interested in the condition of the POWs. The Chinese knew such information would raise disconcerting questions about the camps. By winter, the Chinese army assumed control of all foreign prisoners from the North Koreans. Overt torture "diminished, finally ceasing" except for the most recalcitrant.[156] The typical penalty was solitary confinement, in either an uncomfortable cell or a box.[157] Some prisoners also reported a routine for forced standing and sitting from 4:30 a.m. until 11:00 p.m., followed by a night in which guards routinely roused them from sleep "to make sure they were still there."[158]

For the recalcitrant, there was beating, forced running, forced standing with a rock over one's head, standing at attention for hours in freezing weather, forced kneeling in snow as guards poured water over the body.[159] Forced standing lasted up to thirty hours.[160] Sometimes guards forced prisoners to stand in water-soaked holes; the water would freeze gradually around the feet.[161] Other times, guards marched prisoners onto the Yalu and poured water over their feet, leaving them standing for hours with their feet frozen.[162]

Trussing became a clean art.[163] Hanging victims by the arms caused permanent damage. It dislocated shoulders and destroyed hands. Now guards forced the prisoner's head through a hangman's noose that was in turn tied to his hands. The victim choked slowly as the rope "tightened by the victim's own movement."[164] Sometimes guards would bind a prisoner's hands and then hook him so that he had to stand on his toes.[165] Guards also made the prisoner stand on his toes by tying his thumbs above him. If he brought down his heels, he dislocated his thumbs.[166] These techniques left some marks, but rope burns disappeared in time, and people break their thumbs in accidents too, and sometimes on purpose to discredit the authorities. Plausible deniability was part and parcel of the new art of trussing.

The Chinese also encouraged prisoners to repent and criticize their country. They recruited informants among the prisoners.[167] They applied group rewards and punishments.[168] When violations occurred, the guards did not always punish offenders. They punished the person who was most liked. Doing so "punishes everybody" and suggests that "this could happen to you, and you, and you."[169]

By 1953, 70 percent of the 7,190 U.S. POWs had criticized the American war effort at some point. Only 5 percent had resisted fully, while 15 percent had collaborated completely.[170] These numbers must be taken as suggestive since the official American measure for collaboration was a very low one. All it required was the corroborated accusation of an isolated but serious act of collaboration. Thus, someone who was a hard-core resistant the rest of the time would be classified as a partial collaborator.[171] In the follow-up studies on prisoners from Korea and China, analysts concluded that group pressure transformed those who were disposed, either by personal history or character, to embrace ideological indoctrination.[172] The American POWs in Korea were less vulnerable than those Americans incarcerated in China. The latter were often civilians who had lived in China for years and spoke Chinese, and so were more easily manipulated by their captors. The American soldiers had far more limited linguistic skills and little understanding of their captors or the society they came from. For the majority, indoctrination did not last much longer than the period of incarceration.

The Chinese also adapted Soviet modern for select prisoners, specifically seventy-eight U.S. aviators. In February 1952, Americans were shocked by Chinese film footage of American POWs with no apparent signs of torture freely confessing to using biological warfare in Korea. To get these confessions, interrogators subjected the prisoners to relay interrogation and sleep deprivation, some stretches lasting eighty-five days.[173] Prisoners were isolated in cold huts or water-soaked holes. They were forced to stand for hours, put before bright spotlights, doused with water in subzero weather, held in small boxes, put before firing squads, beaten, and trussed.[174] Interrogators humiliated and threatened them and intermittently offered rewards for cooperation (the hard-soft ploy).[175]

Of the seventy-eight aviators, thirty-eight confessed in part or in full to war crimes, and forty did not. These were poor results by Soviet standards. If the interrogators were exasperated by the resistance, they should not have been surprised, say Wolff and Hinkle. Soviet and Chinese interrogators manipulated prisoners to confess to what was partly true, but these interrogators wanted what was entirely fictitious, and "There was no way of looking upon it in any other fashion. It is notoriously difficult to get men to make such confessions."[176]

Nevertheless, the Chinese deployed with great success the confessions they did extract by means of clean tortures.[177] Many Americans took "at face value the Chinese contention that they did not commit atrocities or torture their captives."[178] It followed that, if so many Americans had been "brainwashed," this reflected some weakness in American character.[179] Conservatives blamed this weakness on socialist subversion beginning in the 1930s, while liberals placed the blame for weakness elsewhere, on American materialism.[180]

Either way, the enduring assessment was the myth that Americans had become soft in the post–World War II period, although there is little in the American performance in the Korean War to confirm this diagnosis.[181] This was certainly not the Chinese point of view as it appeared in their interrogation manuals.[182] Nor was it the official evaluation of experts hired by the U.S. military.[183] They saw no need for beefing up the toughness and discipline of U.S. troops.

Nevertheless, they did advise that "a program of political education was required to prepare military personnel to resist indoctrination efforts in the event of capture."[184] While the original recommendation emphasized political information to resist indoctrination "at an intellectual and philosophical level" improving the woeful knowledge of Americans of their own founding beliefs,[185] these programs soon became something quite different. As names such as "Countermeasures to Hostile Interrogation" and "Survival, Evasion, Resistance, Escape" suggest, these programs increasingly focused on creating physical pain and harsh survival conditions and, as I argue later in the book, became important conduits for the transfer of clean torture techniques among American troops.[186] It is hard not to conclude that these programs also became repositories of the post–Korean War national anxiety that American troops were soft, easily subject to brainwashing and "give-up-itis."[187]

Remembering Pavlov

Brainwashing brings to mind scientific techniques that can change human personalities. First coined by an undercover CIA operative, the word was useful for propaganda purposes.[188] But the term *brainwashing* had no practical purchase, referred to no specific techniques, as CIA director Allen Dulles knew. That is why he turned to Wolff and Hinkle. Dulles knew that the Chinese learned techniques from Soviet advisers. From where did the Soviets learn them?

Even stripped from this Cold War context, the question is a good one. The public nature of show trials and propaganda campaigns explains *why* torture was clean for carefully selected prisoners. But it does not explain *how* the NKVD chose to torture or what sources it drew on.

William Sargant argued that Soviet academics must have designed the Conveyor based on the work of I. P. Pavlov, the Nobel Prize–winning pioneer of operant conditioning. "The Communists must have found his mechanistic approach to the physiological study of behavior in dogs and men most helpful while pursing their policy of indoctrination."[189]

Wolff and Hinkle, however, found no evidence supporting this claim. Indeed, NKVD interrogators held theoretical psychiatry in profound contempt. The NKVD's techniques were powerful, but they had no roots in the Soviet academy.[190] This is not to say that Soviet psychiatry did not eventually play a role in torture. It did, but this happened much later, in the 1960s and 1970s. In that period, Soviet academicians administered psychoprisons for dissidents whom they diagnosed as "sluggish" schizophrenics.[191] But they were not advisers to torturers in the early twentieth century.

The story that the Soviets' Conveyor techniques grew from a Pavlovian origin is tenacious because it is a plausible but fictive chain of conspiratorial associations (Pavlov was Russian, the Soviet regime liked him, so they used his ideas). It also betrays a peculiar modern conceit about where evil comes from in our age: "the scientific specialist both as the fountain of all knowledge and the perpetrator of all evil."[192] This will not be the last time in this book we encounter this misleading theodicy.

Other analysts pointed to Russian police traditions as the source of the Conveyor.[193] Under the czars, however, torture meant whipping, a scarring practice that is entirely absent in the Conveyor. "In no country in the world was whipping so widely practiced, so savagely and so vindictively inflicted, as in the Russia of the Czars."[194] Nor did czarist police torture to generate false confessions. The security police, the Okhranka, wanted accurate security information quickly. "The Okhranka wants the truth," was the cardinal rule.[195] It used surveillance, fingerprinting, photography, and informants.[196] The early cheka employed bloody tortures, as we have seen. None of these police traditions resembles the clean techniques of the Conveyor. Indeed, the NKVD seemed unfamiliar with the technique at first. It had to learn how to master the techniques in a period of trial and error (1928–36).

Wolff and Hinkle name an alternative foreign origin for the Conveyor. One report suggested that Felix Dzherzhinsky, the first head of the cheka, drew on his encounters with the Polish police.[197] The Polish police were not unfamiliar with painful techniques that left few marks, but the evidence is slim.[198]

Nevertheless, it is true that many socialists had been prisoners in Europe and America. They knew these techniques firsthand from their own experiences. Eugene Lyons, an American socialist reporter, had seen sweating in American courtrooms. He recognized these techniques in Russia, despite his sympathies.[199] It would not be surprising if NKVD interrogators simply adapted techniques they had suffered elsewhere. These techniques were suited for public trials, and professional police in Europe. And America used them. Torturers like Krivitsky could think of themselves as thoroughly modern investigators, because the techniques they used distinguished them clearly from the whip-wielding interrogators of the czarist period.

So it may be that Krivitsky was right without knowing it. There may have been American roots to the Conveyor, but the connection, if it existed, was to well-known American police methods, not to Taylorist methods of industrial organization. The evidence, though, is not conclusive. Interrogators have known since the Inquisition that combining persistent interrogation with sleep deprivation will generate confessions.[200] Neither the techniques themselves, nor the combination, were invented from thin air by the Americans.

All one can say in the end is that the techniques that constituted the Conveyor were well known before 1928, and they were practiced primarily in the main Western democracies (the United States, the United Kingdom, and to a lesser extent France and Weimar Germany). This is not something that is generally remembered. Consider this recent statement that simply repeats Krivitsky's misleading metaphors and adds its own mistaken genealogies: "The advent of modern torture technique can be traced back to the Russian NKVD, which used sensory deprivation and multiple levels of brutality to induce stress before 'conveyor'-style questioning by relays of interrogators for days on end, thereby industrializing state terror."[201]

On the contrary, scientists did not even conduct sensory deprivation studies until the early 1950s, twenty years *after* the NKVD assembled the Conveyor, and the use of this term here to characterize Soviet positional tortures and sweating techniques is based on a popular, but mistaken, understanding of what sensory deprivation is and what techniques are required to induce it (as I argue in chapter 18). Even if this argument is unpersuasive, then those who look for the origins of modern torture should look earlier. Relay interrogation and sleep deprivation preceded the NKVD by some four hundred years. If this amounts to industrializing state terror, then credit should go to the Church of Scotland in the 1640s, whose interrogators first utilized these techniques on multiple suspects in sweeping witch hunts.[202]

But perhaps what is new here is modern police interest in combining sleep deprivation, relay interrogation, and other coercive physical techniques to produce confessions covertly. In this case then, credit for the advent of modern torture should go to police in the main democratic states. They practiced stealth torture, using the same techniques to generate false confessions, at least a decade before the NKVD turned to them. The NKVD's innovation was learning how to harness these techniques for eye-catching ideological purposes.

Whatever their origin, it is misleading to characterize sweating techniques as the first modern tortures. No doubt such techniques are useful when officials know what they want the prisoner to say, have many men to work on one individual, and have plenty of time. For my purposes, the history of modern sweating is a good example with which to begin the study of clean tortures. The movement, from American sweating to Russian and then Chinese sweating, neatly illustrates how important monitoring was in inducing the turn to covert torture.

But today police often use torture for a very different purpose, to gather accurate security information quickly. Under the constraints of limited time, many suspects, and few resources, sweating techniques are too time-consuming and inefficient. For these purposes, interrogators prefer techniques that are painful, quick, and labor-saving. Some of these techniques are old, such as the use of water, whips, or knives, but others are very modern indeed, including the use of electricity, sound, and drugs. These techniques have different histories and dates of origin than those associated with sweating, and require a different, separate telling. One can start that investigation by considering Gestapo torture. The Gestapo was not interested in confessions and show trials; its priority lay in gathering information. The tortures that appeared in various countries under Nazi rule introduce one to a broad range of modern tortures, some scarring and others that leave few marks. As with Soviet positional tortures and sweating techniques, it is important to separate out what was unique to Nazi torture and what was not. That is what I turn to next.

(1) The lash. (2) The bath.

—Captain M. Labussière at Nuremberg, 1946[1]

4 Whips and Water

In this chapter, I conduct an inventory of torture techniques of Nazi security agencies. Using documents from the Nuremberg trials supplemented with accounts of Resistance fighters across Europe, I identify characteristic techniques and how they spread (or failed to spread) country by country from 1933 to 1945.

Many believe that the Nazis were the preeminent modern torturers—indeed, we take it for granted nobody did anything worse or more cruelly than did the Nazis. But Nazi techniques were far from uniform, and they were not developed in isolation from other traditions of torture. Most important, as we will see in this and the next chapter, the torture techniques in Nazi-occupied France were deeply influenced by the French themselves. Moreover, when compared with techniques elsewhere, the techniques in France stand out; they are innovative, and the most distinctive (electrotorture and certain types of water torture) rarely occur outside of France. The title of this chapter, "Whips and Water," as well as the leading quote by Labussière, thus highlight the unity and diversity of Nazi torture: whips were the Gestapo's preferred weapon, while the bath was the innovation of Masuy, a notorious collaborator who worked with the Gestapo in France.

I will take up in detail in later chapters the question of how French torture techniques developed in the years prior to the war, and how French methods themselves spread during the war and afterward. Some of these methods will have an auspicious future in modern torture after the war. But this is largely unknown historical territory, and so best left for later. The aim in this and the next chapter is simply to describe the techniques that German Nazis did (or did not) pioneer and spread so that one can dispense with the common view that, to the extent torture still exists today, it is in its techniques and organization a stepchild of the Nazis.

Labussière's List

The most familiar inventory of Nazi tortures was presented at the Nuremberg tribunal. Prosecutors asked Captain M. Labussière of the French Resistance to describe the major methods of torture used in France. He listed six techniques.

First on the list is the lash. "(1) The lash."[2] Labussière records this without comment; everyone knew how common this practice was.

After whips, there was water torture:

> (2) The bath: the victim was plunged head-first into a tub full of cold water until he was asphyxiated. Then they applied artificial respiration. If he would not talk they repeated the process several times consecutively. With his clothes soaking, he spent the night in a cold cell.[3]

Colonel Rémy, a distinguished Resistance fighter, makes "the bath" sound innocuous compared to whips:

> The first [interrogation] lasted for about an hour. I had to lie on my stomach and was given about 120 lashes. The second interrogation lasted a little longer. I was lashed again, lying on my stomach. As I would not talk, they stripped me and put me in the bathtub. The 5th of May I was subject to a new interrogation at Loos. That day they hung me up by my feet and rained blows all over my body.[4]

So common was the bathtub, or *baignoire*, that French prisoners developed a new euphemism for torture: "Il a été *baigné* dimanche" (He was "washed" Sunday).[5]

Next there was electricity. "(3) Electric current: The terminals were placed on the hands, then on the feet, in the ears, and then one in the anus and another on the end of the penis."[6] Torturers typically used hand-cranked devices called magnetos to generate a charge.

Then comes, "(4) Crushing the testicles in a press specially made for the purpose. Twisting the testicles was frequent."[7] Pressing machines in general were very common in France. Others report "special handcuffs,"[8] "a machine to crush the ends of fingers,"[9] a bracelet composed of "balls of hard wood with steel spikes" that tightened around the wrist,[10] an iron headband that tightened around the skull,[11] and "a squeezing apparatus" for the whole body.[12]

After pressing, there was trussing, usually by the hands:

(5) Hanging: the patient's hands were handcuffed together behind the back. A hook was slipped through his handcuffs and the victim was lifted by a pulley. At first they jerked him up and down. Later, they left him suspended for varying, fairly long periods. The arms were often dislocated. In the camp, I saw Lt. Lefevre, who, having been suspended like this for more than four hours, had lost the use of both arms.[13]

Lastly, there was "(6) Burning with a soldering-lamp or with matches."[14] Others described toes burned with cotton wool pads dipped in gasoline, calves burned by blow torches, red hot pokers to the back, and "the electric bench where the feet are slowly roasted."[15]

Victims also mention that techniques Labussière does not, such as being attacked by dogs, having one's eyes pierced or burned out, having one's teeth filed down, salt poured into wounds, being cut with razors, having one's nails pulled out, and sweatboxes.[16]

Labussière ends his list with an iconographic image of a tortured teacher:

> On 2nd July my comrade Laloue, a teacher from Cher, came to the camp. He had been subject to most of these tortures at Bourges. One arm had been put out of joint and he was unable to move the fingers of his right hand as a result of the hanging. He had been subjected to flogging and electricity. Sharp pointed matches had been driven under the nails of his hands and feet. His wrists and ankles had been wrapped with rolls of wadding and the matches had been set on fire. While they were burning, a German had plunged a pointed knife into the soles of his feet several times and another lashed him with a whip. Phosphorous burns had eaten away several fingers as far as the second joint. Abscesses which had developed had burst, and this had saved him from blood poisoning.[17]

Just as the figures of martyred saints in Catholic churches tell the story of how Roman torturers persecuted Christians, on his body Laloue told the story of torture in France.

Documenting Nazi Torture

When writing his praised history of the Gestapo, Jacques Delarue recognized that Labussière's list had a limited scope: Labussière did not know what the Gestapo commonly did outside France. Few others have been as careful as Delarue.[18] When journalists describe "Gestapo torture," they find the Nuremberg transcripts and cite Labussière's list. They rarely ask, how common were these techniques outside of France?

This is not an easy question to answer.[19] There are two ways to reconstruct how Nazi security agencies tortured, from official documents (the "top-down" approach) or from survivor narratives (the "bottom-up" approach).

At Nuremberg, the French prosecutor conceded he could not use the top-down approach. "I shall not be able to prove this [the charge of systematic torture] by submitting German documents."[20] Many Gestapo headquarters, including those in Copenhagen, Vienna, and Berlin, were destroyed during the war. In some French and Czech cities, Germans and collaborators destroyed records before Resistance fighters stormed the headquarters.[21]

Moreover, a document outlining torture policy from one department would not necessarily apply to others. The Gestapo was a rat's nest of bureaucratic competition: "Each Gestapo 'office' worked for its own account, being bound by the internal partitioning and the rules of secrecy to ignore what happened in the neighboring branches."[22] The organization also changed incessantly during the war, and different regional offices became somewhat autonomous.[23] Moreover, the Gestapo was only one of several competing security organizations, all of which tortured.[24]

At any rate, the Allies found only three documents that described Nazi torture policy.[25] Meeting minutes from the Justice Ministry (June 1, 1937) outlined the policy for sharpened interrogations using a specified club.[26] A Gestapo form from Slovenia directed officers to complete it before "especially rigorous interrogations."[27] The form was blank. Lastly, Gestapo chief Müller's directive (June 12, 1942) amplified sharpened interrogations to include beating, sweating, and exhaustion exercises.[28]

At Nuremberg, defendants insisted they followed the milder 1937 standard, arguing that Müller's directive of 1942 did not correspond to what the police actually did.[29] From a different perspective, the prosecutors agreed that police did not follow Müller's 1942 directive. They knew that torture went well beyond what Müller authorized.[30] To prove that these horrors were official policy, they needed a different approach.

Consequently, prosecutors pioneered an approach that is now common in human rights documentation: they pieced survivor narratives into a pattern.[31] This was the bottom-up approach. Unique instances were not as valuable as several similar accounts from different times and places. That implied an official torture policy. "This systematic will can only be proved by showing that everywhere and in every case the German policy used the same methods."[32]

The Nuremberg tribunal did not agree with the prosecutors. In their final judgment, the judges brought down only one verdict affirming torture, this against Ernst Kaltenbrunner, for torture in the concentration camps. Outside the camps, "The worst Gestapo tortures were only semi-official."[33]

So "Gestapo torture" was not uniform across Europe, governed by a standard manual, or directed by specific orders from the center, but what exactly were the patterns? The record remains incomplete, but we can piece much of it together. Since Nuremberg, survivors have written their stories, and historians have reconstructed the Nazi occupation in their countries.

To inventory Nazi technique, one has to start where the French and Russian prosecutors stopped, adding even more stories. The bottom-up approach requires assembling multiple narratives to show patterns of usage. I have supplemented the Nuremberg record with a richer record of narratives from Resistance fighters across Europe than was available in the immediate aftermath of the war.[34] One can be certain that Nazi security agencies were not holding back when they tortured Resistance members for information. What techniques they had, they used.[35] These narratives thus offer the richest torture stories; prisoners remember the worst that was done to them. "Weapon focus," the tendency of people to "lock" their attention onto the weapon, is a well-documented finding in forensic settings; the extreme emotion intensifies and narrows memory.[36]

Of course, Resistance stories are not neutral. They present torturers in the most savage terms. But they remain reliable in many ways. If one bitter narrative after another from a particular region fails to mention techniques that were common elsewhere, we can reasonably conclude that these techniques were probably not practiced in that region. Likewise, one has greater confidence in multiple accounts of the same torture in the same place; single reports of unique tortures are less reliable.

One should remember that victims and witnesses do not always distinguish torture by the SA, SS, SD, police, and Gestapo. All this is called "Gestapo torture." Survivors do distinguish between torture by Germans and nationals of other countries that served as auxiliaries or allies.

The survey that follows suggests some straightforward conclusions. German security services showed little interest in clean tortures. "Gestapo torture" varied from region to region. Outside France, torture by security forces consisted mainly of diverse forms of flogging, beating, trussing, and the use of mechanical devices that cut, pressed, and burned. Again, outside France, water torture (the "bathtub") was rare, and electric torture was even rarer.

Torture in Germany

Most available narratives discuss Gestapo interrogation in Berlin. Narratives commonly mention whipping, sweating (sleep deprivation and relay interrogation), pressing devices, bright lights, positional tortures, and exhaustion exercises.

The Early Years (1933–34)

Interrogators slapped prisoners repeatedly during questioning under blinding lights. They ordered guards to kick, beat, and thrash prisoners. Arms were twisted. But above all there was whipping.[37] Jan Valtin, a Communist organizer, says each interrogator had a guard who whipped suspects. In Hamburg, the guards dipped their whips in water or petroleum jelly; wet whips cut deeper. In Berlin, guards used lead-filled whips. Valtin was first whipped on the back, head, and throat; his shirt was soaked with blood. Later, guards strapped him to a table and whipped his buttocks and thighs.[38]

Berlin Gestapo also used pressure devices. Wolfgang Szepansky, another Communist prisoner, remembers guards screwing finger presses and calf clamps to his body. His nails were pulled out. He was forced to stand through the night.[39] This was a standard positional torture. "Put the tips of your toes and the tip of your nose against the wall with your hands shackled behind your back, and stand straight. After you stand so for an hour your eyes bulge out of their caves and you feel as if huge rocks are pressing in on you from both sides." While a prisoner's back was turned, guards would unexpectedly bang his head against the wall, kick the shins, or slam carbines on the toes. One Hamburg guard placed cartridge shells in each shoe to aggravate the feet. In Berlin, this was standard: "kneeling for hours at a stretch on a police carbine, and at another time on a shallow box filled with nails."[40]

Lastly, there were exhaustion exercises: "She threw herself to the stone floor and scrambled back on her feet. A trooper swung his arms and barked commands: "Up-down! Up-down! We'll make you eat dirt you bitch. Up-down!"[41] Then there was the "Bear Dance." "It consisted of running and frog-leaping while carrying a pail full of water in manacled hands. . . . Each time water slopped over the rim of the bucket, I received a kick or a blow with a rubber truncheon."[42] Then there was "walking the plank," which was preceded by a rapid run to a mud hole. "Across it [the hole] led a narrow plank, which sagged downward in the middle. . . . I staggered out on the plank. After ten lurching steps, the trooper jumped with both feet on the end of the plank. I lost my balance and toppled into the mud."[43]

The Middle Years (1935–38)

Again, there was beating and whipping, by weapons including truncheons, whips, rifle butts, and sticks with rusty nails.[44] Prisoners also report sweating, sleep deprivation, and bright lights. The journalist Berhold Jacob, for instance, was "thrown into a brightly lighted cell," and interrogators "permitted him no sleep for sixteen nights."[45] Guards also used exhaustion exercises, for example, knee bends, the Bear Dance, and crawling distances on one's elbows.[46] The main positional torture was forced standing. In one case, the prisoner was forced to stand while wearing full work equipment and staring into the sun.[47] In another, guards drew marks on the floor and "made the student stand, the toes and heels of his shoes outlined by chalk marks, for two or three days. . . . If he moved from his place he was beaten mercilessly."[48]

The Final Years (1939–45)

Torture consisted of beating with truncheons, whipping, sweating, bright lights, positional tortures, and exhaustion exercises (knee bends, forced crawling, or carrying heavy weights).[49] One report describes thumbscrews and leg clamps that squeezed and broke the bone.[50] Helmuth von Moltke, a German aristocrat and noted military lawyer, reports being subjected only to sleep deprivation at Berlin and at Drögen, where all political interrogations took place, but he was well aware he was an exception. Torture of "blue-blooded swine" was routine after the failed plot to kill Hitler.[51]

Fabian von Schlabrendorf offers a unique account, describing two cutting devices. While his hands were tied behind his back, guards fastened a device that gripped all the fingers separately. Its interior was studded with pins. A screw caused the device to contract, driving the pins into the fingers. Schlabrendorf also describes a bed frame with "cylinders resembling stovepipes studded with nails on the inner surface." These were clamped around his legs, and a screw contracted the tubes "so that the nails pierced my legs from ankle to thigh."[52] The bed frame also expanded, stretching him gradually or with a jerk.

Torture in Nazi-Occupied Europe

German troops first occupied Austria and Czechoslovakia (1938–39), then Poland (September 1939), Denmark and Norway (April 1940), and then the Netherlands, Belgium, Luxembourg, and France (May–June 1940). Axis troops occupied Greece and Yugoslavia (April 1941) and then invaded Russia (June 1941). Then in 1944, Germany occupied its axis ally, Hungary.

The accounts below follow this chronology.[53] I document torture country by country, following each country's Nuremberg submission supplemented with Resistance accounts. As the Nuremberg tribunal singled out concentration camp torture as uniform and organized across Europe, I will present this penal regime in a final section.

Austria

"In sessions often lasting all night, political suspects were trampled and stamped on and badly beaten with belts, rubber hoses, or sticks."[54] The Viennese Gestapo preferred to strike blows at the cheeks, nose, throat, and back of the knees. It also favored grinding cigarettes slowly into the back of a hand, a torture practiced elsewhere in southeastern Europe as the "Prilep method," after the Bulgarian town where the technique was notorious.[55] Interrogators also hung people by their handcuffs.

Interrogators sweated valued prisoners. Captured American intelligence agents were subjected to a sweating regime without beating: solitary confinement, forced standing, starvation, death threats, and psychological pressure (the prisoner's dilemma), all to coerce confessions of espionage. One agent subsequently remembered this as early brainwashing.[56] A top Resistance leader "was tortured for days in the so-called Chamber of Mirrors where the prisoners were constantly exposed to strong light beams reflected by mirrors."[57] These stories suggest that interrogators practiced cleaner tortures on some prisoners, a pattern that will recur in some accounts from Poland and the Netherlands below. I will return to these incidents at the end of this chapter.

Czechoslovakia

Again, interrogation involved beating and whipping. A prisoner was "trampled, beaten with rubber hoses, [and] mutilated."[58] Interrogators pulled nails with special pliers.[59] Jan Filipek reports exhaustion exercises, "a senseless number of push-ups and deep knee bends."[60] Radomir Luza, a Czech Resistance fighter and a principal scholar on the Central European Resistance, concludes, "There was no basic difference between the Gestapo practices in Austria or in the Protectorate of Bohemia and Moravia."[61]

There was at least one exception. In January 1945, one of Luza's comrades, Jedilka, reported being subjected to a new technique. "For hours on end, the Gestapo used the infamous ice torture, which meant, as he sketchily described it, that he was repeatedly submerged in a bathtub of ice water, nearly drowned each time, prior to being kicked or subjected to some other more violent treatment."[62]

Poland

Beating was the most common method throughout Poland, beginning with beating of the face and proceeding to full-body beatings with cudgels, iron bars, whips, brass knuckles, and chains tipped with spiked balls.[63] Aleja Szucha, the

Gestapo headquarters in Warsaw, was notorious for distinctive tortures.[64] In the "pillar" (*slupek*), torturers suspended prisoners by the wrists from a pole so that they had to stand on their toes. Exhaustion exercises included repeated squats and the *zabki*, or "frog," introduced by Germans in the fall of 1940. The *zabki* required prisoners to squat and jump like frogs up and down the hall. Interrogators hooded the prisoner with a gas mask and then induced near asphyxiation by closing the air vent. They poured water in the noses and mouths of a prisoner or held his head under water, all of which techniques were called "sinking." Interrogators also burned with heated irons or cigarettes, removed nails with special pliers, or drove steel splinters under the nails.

Amid all this brutality, the Gestapo selectively practiced restraint. Between July 1942 and February 1943, the Gestapo arrested a Resistance network composed of Poles and Swedes. The Gestapo beat the Poles, but sweated the foreigners. One Swedish prisoner recalled "moments when he was close to losing his mind."[65] This was another instance where interrogators used techniques that left few marks on foreigners, in this case citizens of Sweden, a neutral power during the war.

In 1942, the Gestapo began interrogations at Pawiak prison.[66] Prisoners indicate that tortures became much more severe in the second half of 1942, once young Ukrainians began to work at Pawiak. "These mere boys showed so much ingenuity on their own account that the more experienced torturers often contented themselves with the role of spectator."[67] Torture included beating, whipping, hot irons, needles, the *slupek*, the *zabki*, forced boxing, crawling or walking on very hot metal surfaces, forced running (sometimes with a bag over the head to make breathing difficult), and eating salty foods or drinking vodka until the prisoner was sick.[68] One prisoner, tortured at Aleja Szucha and Pawiak in 1943, describes "so called 'Swings.' " These were "special electrical appliances" that burned the skin and electrified the body.[69] Other prisoners from this period confirm electrotorture, but do not describe the devices.[70]

Denmark

The official Danish report sums up interrogation concisely: "the whip or blows from a truncheon or rubber cudgel," as well as blows from a gun or a rifle butt. Beatings involved kicks to the head, groin and sexual organs.[71] "Particularly difficult prisoners were strapped face down over a table, hands and feet stretched and tied beneath it, and whipped or beaten."[72] Torturers used razors to slash hands and arms and crushed lighted cigarettes on the flesh. Sometimes guards used the *falaka*, applying blows to the flat of the feet.[73] They tied hands with barbed wire and handcuffs that tightened until the wrists were crushed.[74] Many tortures "caused permanent injuries."[75]

Norway

In Norwegian cities and villages, torturers beat, flogged, kicked, punched, broke fingers, stomped on stomachs, pulled out hair, pressed the cavity behind the ears, and twisted legs, arms, and ears.[76] The means included whips with leather or knotted straps, rubber-coated iron truncheons (large and small), chains, heavy ropes, canes, hose-piping, iron rods, steel springs, *Totenschläger* (large clubs dubbed "death-strikers"), and large sticks wrapped with cloth. One prisoner reported being subjected to the *falaka*.[77]

At Viktoria Terrasse, Gestapo headquarters in Oslo, "The fortunate endured no more than intense questioning, reinforced with threats and blows. . . . More commonly, victims were beaten and tortured as the first step of a harrowing experience."[78] One early account reports that torture at Viktoria Terrasse was graduated. First, interrogators sweated the prisoner under bright lights. Then came the sweatbox, either a dark cellar or tall narrow hotboxes where one stood for days. Then came violent techniques in a soundproof room with a dentist's chair.[79] No other account resembles this in the details.

Prisoners commonly report bone clamps.[80] Hans Cappelen, the sole Norwegian to testify at Nuremberg, described it as "a sort of home-made-wooden thing, with a screw arrangement, on my left leg; and they started to screw so that all the flesh loosened from the bones."[81] Several reports mention sticking pins under the nails or pulling them out.[82] Prisoners also performed exhaustion exercises, including repeated marching, standing at attention for hours, knee bends with heavy logs under each arm, and combinations of sprints and push-ups.[83]

Less commonly, guards burned prisoners using blowtorches, soldering lamps, and red-hot wires.[84] One report describes bare flesh pressed against the heated rods of an electric space-heater.[85] A U.S. citizen describes how torturers poured molten iron onto his palm, and then onto fresh wounds cut near the arteries. Then he was tied between two loudspeakers for forty-eight hours.[86]

The Norwegian government compiled a torture sequence.[87] Initially, the German government authorized beating. Then, in 1942, it authorized "calf-pinchers which had been tried by the Reichssicherheitshaupamt [the main office in Berlin]." Then in February 1945, orders authorized bathtub torture, "a method tried by the Gestapo in France and proved to be 'effective.' "[88]

This timetable corresponds to the survivor narratives. In the first Norwegian government report (1942), prisoners do not mention calf clamps. Cappellen, who was tortured 1941, provides the earliest account. The earliest bathtub torture dates from March 1945 at Viktoria Terrasse.[89]

The Netherlands

The official Dutch report mainly describes whipping and beating with truncheons, as do the Resistance accounts.[90] Sometimes victims had "their hands tied behind their back and then attached to a pole in a manner that their feet did not touch the ground."[91] Guards put prisoners in dark or overcrowded cells. They subjected them to forced standing and exhaustion exercises. They sprayed one prisoner with cold water.[92] Another witnessed them brand his brother with a red-hot iron.[93]

There were exceptions to the brutality, and again in these cases, the Gestapo turned to techniques that left few marks. "As a woman of a privileged class," Mona Parsons was subjected to sleep deprivation, relay interrogation, psychological pressure, and starvation.[94] Similarly, the Gestapo sweated a prized prisoner, a radio operator, subjecting him to a forty-hour interrogation.[95]

Luxembourg

The official Luxembourg report focuses on genocide, hostage taking, and summary execution; it does not itemize allegations of torture.[96] Nonetheless, a Resistance member describes the use at Villa Pauly, Gestapo headquarters, of suspension, slaps to the face, and kicks to the kidneys.[97]

Belgium

Resistance accounts emphasize beating or flogging, whether at the local Gestapo headquarters or at prisons.[98] At Breendonck, the main interrogation center, torturers suspended victims from a hook-and-pulley system. Interrogators then beat, whipped, and burned victims with cigarettes.[99] Exhaustion exercises were running ("the promenade"), crawling on elbows, and couché-debout (lie flat, get up, lie flat). The main positional torture was forced standing, sometimes at attention, often conducted in cold weather or in a water-filled trench.[100] Interrogators also subjected prisoners to ice-cold or boiling-hot showers.[101]

Prisoners also mention pressure devices, most notoriously the finger press at Breendonck, two padded plates that one tightened with a large ornate screw.[102] Less commonly, they describe "American cuffs" that tightened around the wrists as one moved.[103] Less frequently, police pulled nails and teeth, stuck pins, cut tongues, loosed dogs, and stuffed victims in a cold box or barrel.[104] One report describes shots to disorient the prisoner.[105] Another describes how interrogators withheld insulin shots, leading inadvertently to the prisoner's death.[106]

Herman Bodson, a Resistance fighter, states flatly, "I have never heard of the Paris method being used in Belgium."[107] The Nuremberg record bears him out.[108] Resistance stories do not report bathtub torture, and only two prisoners report electrotorture. A Belgian collaborator, Max Gunter, applied live wires to the stomach wound of Eugene Haessert.[109] Marguerite Paquet, interned at Breendonck between January and August 1943, states, "I received electric discharges with the aid of an instrument that ended in needle points."[110]

Yugoslavia

The official Yugoslav submissions describe how soldiers beat, mutilated, and burned civilians prior to massacring them.[111] Resistance accounts share this focus, although some also document interrogations. These consisted of beatings.[112]

Greece

Interrogations involved beating.[113] At Camp Haidari, Gestapo headquarters in Athens, violations were punished "with beatings and whippings, or by [Germans] unleashing their dogs."[114] In one case, German soldiers tied a woman's hands behind her back, and then suspended her from a rope.[115] Outside Athens, soldiers beat and looted.[116] Prisoners were placed in dark "punishment cells."[117] The Jews of Salonika were forced to stand in the sun for hours, and then soldiers "kicked and beat them or doused them in cold water. Some were forced to do physical exercises until they were exhausted."[118]

Russia

The Soviet prosecutor at Nuremberg focused his case on how Nazis mutilated soldiers and citizens before killing them.[119] Witnesses emphasized being suspended, beaten with rubber truncheons, and flogged with leather thongs wetted in water.[120] In Piyatagorsk, "a wide board was placed on the back of the shackled prisoner, and blows were struck on the board with heavy dumbbells."[121] At Kiev-Petchersk, interrogators spun the suspended prisoner around as they beat him. "The man became unconscious both from the insane speed of the rotation and from the beating."[122]

Lastly, the Soviet prosecutor asserted that in Odessa, the Nazis practiced electric torture. "The dial of the voltage control would be mercilessly turned to increase the voltage; the body of the interrogated would tremble and his eyes to protrude from their sockets."[123]

Unfortunately, this claim is problematic, because Odessa was not in occupied German territory. This much at least is indisputable. The Romanian Fourth Army took Odessa without German assistance after a terrible siege on October 16, 1941. From 1941 to 1944, Romania ruled Odessa.[124] Romania had its own feared political police, the Siguranta, whom the Odessans claimed "were as bad as the Gestapo."[125] One might conclude reasonably that the electrical machine used in Odessa belonged to the Siguranta. The prosecutor may have guessed as much since he was citing a document entitled "On the Atrocities Committed by the German and Romanian Invaders."[126]

But if Germans also used the Odessa machine, then the claim would have to be this. In October 1943, five divisions were separated from the German Sixth Army in the Ukraine. They fell back into Crimea, undertaking a frantic evacuation out to sea.[127] Some occupied Odessa during March 1944 before the city fell to Soviet forces on April 10.[128] They left behind the machine.

Could Germans have abandoned the Odessa machine after using it elsewhere? Perhaps, except that the Soviet prosecutor does not mention electric torture elsewhere in Russia, nor do the witnesses. This hypothesis seems unlikely, but so too is the alternative hypothesis that the Romanians brought the machine. Brutal as the Siguranta was, prisoners do not report electric torture.[129] Until the Russian documentation is available, the Odessa machine will remain a mystery.[130]

Concentration Camps

Camps had political departments that "acted as the long arm of the local *Gestapo* and 'looked after' the arrested man." Political prisoners could expect interrogation upon arrival and even after several months. Political departments also investigated Resistance organizations within camps. "Thus, being taken to a concentration camp did not mean that contact with the *Gestapo* had at last been ended."[131]

In Austria, police transferred prisoners to Mauthausen, where they "were mutilated, beaten to death, or hung for hours with their hands tied behind their backs."[132] In Poland, the Auschwitz interrogators tied a prisoner's hands to the feet and hung the body from a metal bar between two tables. As it swung freely, interrogators would beat the prisoner with metal strips and pour boiling water or oil into the nose. Interrogators also suspended prisoners, smashed teeth, and tore out fingernails.[133]

All camps had punishments for infractions.[134] Most prisoners commonly described institutionalized whipping. Camps usually had whipping posts, a wooden block or plank to which a prisoner would be tied while being whipped.[135] An Auschwitz prisoner describes a flogging machine, "a swinging apparatus manipulated by an SS."[136] Exhaustion exercises included drilling, running, and "gymnastics; flat on the belly, get up, lie down, up down, for hours."[137] Positional torture meant forced standing (standing at attention for hours) and forced kneeling (kneeling down with the hands outstretched, a heavy stone on each).[138] Guards commonly beat, whipped, and set dogs upon prisoners for any failure to obey.[139]

Auschwitz had two notorious additions in Block 11 for prisoners who tried to escape: the stake and *Stehzelle*, or standing cells. In the "stake," the prisoner's arms "were bent behind him and he was suspended by the wrists just above the ground." The *Stehzelle* were four narrow cells, each one three feet by three feet at the base. "Through small doors at the bottom, four prisoners at a time were pushed into it for the night; they could only stand up inside and by day went to work."[140] Similar boxes and stakes existed in other camps.[141]

At Ravensbrück, two individuals departed from these standard practices. Dorothea Binz, a guard who favored different styles of whips, punished minor infractions with an electric whip.[142] Ludwig Ramdor interrogated prisoners using narcotics and ordered them subjected to ice-cold, high-pressure hoses several times a week.[143] He also used water torture: "He tied women into a 'leap' with their heads bound tightly to their feet. Then he pushed their heads into a wash basin until they were on the verge of drowning."[144]

Remembering the War

In the previous chapter, I described an NKVD political prisoner, Klara, who explained the difference between Gestapo and NKVD technique to her fellow prisoners in 1937. She accurately illustrated NKVD beating technique, displaying her swollen hands. Now we can see that she also correctly identified standard Gestapo technique when she pointed to the whip marks on her thighs and said, "This is Gestapo."[145] Across Europe, Gestapo men flogged. Less common, but certainly still widespread, were methods of suspension, exhaustion exercises, burning (with lamps, wires, hot iron, or boiling oil) and piercing (with pins, nails, razors, studs, files, or pliers). Torture in the camps across Europe involved all these practices.

Sweating occurred at headquarters in Berlin, Drögen, Oslo, Warsaw, and Vienna. The Gestapo pulled its punches literally in cases involving foreigners (Poland, Austria), some rich or aristocratic prisoners (Germany, the Netherlands), and valued intelligence operatives (Netherlands, Austria). In these cases, interrogators subjected prisoners to relay interrogation, sweating, bright lights, and sleep deprivation.

Gestapo officers may have acted this way because they respected the humanity of these particular prisoners. This would be an instance of the dehumanization hypothesis, namely, that the Gestapo would torture people not like them differently than those who were more "like them." For people like them, they would use techniques that left fewer marks. But the Gestapo may also have acted this way not because it *had* these norms, but because it was aware *others* did and they would be observing what the Gestapo did. The rich and the noble and governments of neutral and allied powers, expected that people like them would be treated differently even when interrogated in war. This would be the international monitoring hypothesis, and it suggests that the Gestapo's behavior was not sincere, but opportunistic.

The evidence is unfortunately slim, but it is worth noting the Gestapo was hardly restrained in other cases involving similar people. For example, the Gestapo brutally tortured aristocrats involved in the attempt on Hitler's life in 1944. Interrogators poured molten metal on the hands of an American citizen in Norway in 1941, at a time when the United States was a neutral power. On the other hand, it was more restrained in cases of people who were not like them. For example, German guards subjected the Jews of Salonika to forced standing, extremes of temperature, and punitive exercises. Aside from the kicking and beating for the weak performers, this is a relatively clean regimen, but it is doubtful the Germans adopted this boot camp regimen because they identified with their prisoners. It is worth observing also, as the photographs indicate, that the prisoners performed these in public in Salonika, and the prisoners were headed for a far worse penal regimen in the camps. Similarly, the Gestapo in Oslo apparently began with sweating and other techniques that left few marks, but these were only the opening to a more harrowing experience for the Norwegian prisoners who failed to cooperate.

These discrepancies suggest that the international monitoring hypothesis is more plausible than the dehumanization hypothesis. The Gestapo's behavior was opportunistic and calculated, just as the NKVD's show trials were. What mattered to the Gestapo was who was watching these particular cases with interest. In the cases I documented, the Gestapo decided to torture, but stealthily, apparently meeting the expected norms.

Of course, cases of stealthy torture were even rarer in Nazi-occupied Europe than they were in the Soviet Union. The Gestapo, unlike the Soviet NKVD, did not use sweating as part of "an inquisitorial style of machinery for identifying the 'enemy within'" to domestic and international audiences.[146] The NKVD fought secret saboteurs within the Party and wanted to expose them to the world. The Gestapo knew its enemies and sought to dispose of them. In the 1930s, the Gestapo used ordinary bureaucratic methods, birth certificates and inherited police files, to identify Communists, Jews, homosexuals, and other internal enemies.[147] After 1939, it was even less interested in sweating false confessions from its prisoners. From the Resistance, it wanted true information. For this purpose, local Gestapo developed distinctive styles of torture.

The Gestapo in Norway commonly used bone clamps. Originally used in Germany, these came to Norway in 1941. Accounts from other countries do not mention them.

More generally, pressing devices appear in a northerly band stretching from Paris to Berlin to Oslo: the finger press (Belgium, France), wrist clamps (Denmark, Belgium), wrist clamps with spikes (France, Germany), headbands (France), squeezing apparatus (France), the bed frame (Germany, France), testicle presses (France), and bone clamps (Germany, Norway).

The Gestapo in Denmark regularly used the *falaka*. Only one account, from Norway, also mentions this technique.

The "Paris method" remains the most distinctive. When one reflects on Labussière's list in light of this survey, one realizes what is absent and what is uniquely present. Labussière does not highlight exhaustion exercises or positional torture, as prisoners from other regions do. He ranks bathtub torture and electric torture as the most common techniques after whipping, techniques that are rare outside France.

The bathtub torture was known to Resistance fighters in Norway, Belgium, and Czechoslovakia. It was, in the words of one Resistance fighter, "infamous."[148] But it apparently does not leave France until 1945, when we find one instance in Czechoslovakia (January 1945) and another in Norway (March 1945).[149] Outside France, prisoners do report being compressed by jets of water, forced to stand in cold water, or showered with cold or boiling water. The accounts do not single out water torture in the way Labussière does. Only Ramdor's techniques at Ravensbrück generate the horror French accounts express, and how he came by his technique is unknown.[150]

The hand-cranked magneto used for electric torture is again common in France, but not elsewhere. Setting aside the Odessa machine, whose provenance is mysterious, the magneto appears in a single Belgian account from Breendonck.[151] Many other accounts of this prison survive, as do photographs of the devices in the torture room, none of which identify an electric machine. If it was there, the device fell into disuse.

Resistance accounts remember the worst brutalities. Government reports itemize the worst techniques. If the Gestapo used electric torture across Europe, these reports would note it. They do not, contrary to popular belief. Perhaps, one day, evidence for this belief will appear, but the available record in the main European languages does not show it.

If the Gestapo favored electric torture, it had other choices besides the magneto. Dorothea Binz's electric whip was promising for a police that whipped, but this innovation remained a curiosity. Then there were the electric "swings" in Poland, which also did not appear elsewhere. Electroconvulsive therapy (ECT) machines also existed. After using them on incarcerated schizophrenics, Nazi doctors used them on thousands of German soldiers as the "Pansen cure." I will discuss this usage at length in chapter 6, but here it is sufficient to note that if the Gestapo ever used an ECT device in interrogation, no government or Resistance record of it appears. Even in France, where electric torture was common, torturers preferred hand-cranked magnetos, not ECT devices.

Outside France, Nazi interrogators rarely used the bathtub or magneto torture. So why do they appear in France? Who commonly used these tortures and why? It is important to know, as these are the tortures we will follow in many of the subsequent chapters. To answer these questions, we need to turn to the French Gestapo.

The bathtub, whether you will it or not, was still more humane.

—Masuy at his trial, 1947[1]

5   Bathtubs

After defeating France in 1940, the German government divided the country into two zones. Germany occupied the northern zone. A dependent government, Vichy, ran the southern zone.

In the northern zone, mainly in Paris, several French gangs conducted intelligence operations on behalf of the Germans. French historians refer to these gangs by their leaders: Lafont and Bonny, Masuy, or Berger. They are known collectively as the "French Gestapo." Then there were groups that operated outside of Paris. Vichy had a brutal security force, the Milice, and police squads, the most notorious of which was run by Inspector Marty in Toulouse.

In later generations, Frenchmen dismiss these torturers as "a miserable handful of traitors not worth mentioning."[2] Traitors they undoubtedly were, but historians certainly think they are worth mentioning for their inventive tortures. Jacques Delarue, the main French historian of the Gestapo, compares the French Gestapo to the medieval craft-torturers, noting how proudly they produced "variations and discoveries."[3] Alec Mellor, the postwar scholar of torture, singled out the Belgian torturer, Masuy. With Masuy, "Modern torture has found its first theoretician and this inhuman century had the doctrinaire that it merited." Mellor suggested that the twentieth century be dubbed "the Century of Masuy."[4]

In this chapter, I describe innovation in torture technique among the French gangs, for "in the domain of torture, the French agents were more refined and more cruel. They showed themselves more Nazi than the Nazis themselves."[5] First, I describe the two most inventive agents, Masuy and Marty. Masuy in Paris claimed a new approach to water torture. Marty in Toulouse brought electric torture to France. They used techniques that will dominate torture around the world after the war.

Then I describe how other French and German agents used these methods. In modern memory, the German Gestapo looms large as the progenitor of electric torture, if not all modern torture.[6] Remembering Masuy and Marty is one small step in remembering to whom that honor, if that is what one may call it, belongs.

Masuy's Bathtub

In 1947, Colonel Rémy, a famous Resistance fighter, published his wartime memoires. *Une affaire de trahison* opens with a photograph of a pair of brooding dark eyes staring out at the reader. Torture victims never forgot the eyes of Masuy.[7]

Christian Masuy was a pseudonym for George Delfanne, a Belgian national.[8] Masuy began his political career on the Allied side, smuggling refugees out of Germany into Belgium. Captured by the Abwehr, German military intelligence, he entered its service as a spy. Around 1942, the Abwehr assigned Masuy to one of its "purchasing bureaus" in Paris, enterprises through which the Germans collected strategic war materials from the black market. To these bureaus Germans relegated "satellite" services, including tracking the Resistance.[9]

Masuy's bureau was among "the most important and most dangerous."[10] At his headquarters, Masuy set about devising as many possible tortures as he could. He mentions electronic equipment, finger presses, and special pliers to remove nails. He was proudest of his distinctive approach to water torture, the bathtub. "The *baignoire*, whether you will it or not, was still more humane [than these other tortures]." Masuy's henchmen would hold the head under water and then Masuy would question them. "It was not rare that I obtained confessions after one or two immersions."[11]

The Gestapo was impressed enough to authorize using the bathtub in Norway and Czechoslovakia in 1945. After the war, Masuy and his chief assistants were executed, but the bathtub lived on in France and its colonies. In French Algeria and in Spain, it remained "the bathtub" (*la baignoire, la bañera*). In French Vietnam, it was dubbed "the submarine." By the 1960s, Latin Americans called the torture by both names.

Still, one is left somewhat puzzled by all this. What is so novel about nearly drowning a person? One wonders why the bathtub was so notorious among the Resistance and why Masuy thought his approach was so distinctive. To grasp its status, one needs to situate Masuy's technique among Western methods of water torture.

When Westerners think of water torture, they remember "Chinese water torture." In that artful Eastern technique, small drops of water fall on the forehead, slowly driving the victim mad. Less frequently remembered is that a sixteenth-century Italian lawyer, Hippolytus de Marsiliis, had independently proposed the torture of the drop and that French kings adopted it as a punishment for witches, sorcerers, and blasphemers.[12]

It was a torture without a future in European interrogation. Classical torturers wanted confessions of guilt. They were not oriental despots for whom torture meant the pleasure of watching one's enemy go mad. There was no percentage in a slow torture when there was cutting, burning, stretching, whipping, and piercing. The torture of the drop died out by the eighteenth century.

Today, we remember "Chinese water torture" because it captures a great fear about modern torture. It is a torture that reaches beyond the body and touches the mind. We would do better to think of Masuy instead. Masuy self-consciously harnessed water to touch the mind. This insight set him apart from many who preceded him in the field.

In the seventeenth century, European interrogators used water to cause pain in two ways, what I will call choking and pumping.[13] Choking involved covering the face with cloth, ladling water on it until the victim could not breath, and then removing it for questioning. Pumping involved forcibly filling the stomach and intestines with water. In pumping, victims' organs stretch and convulse, causing the most intense pain that visceral tissue can experience.[14] In the nineteenth century, torturers added a third variation: they showered prisoners from a great height with a solid stream of water, literally beating prisoners with water.[15] Nazi torturers, as documented in the previous chapter, adapted fire hoses and pressurized showers to produce the same effect.

The history of these techniques will be described later in this book. What is sufficient for the moment is that amid all this liquid horror, one other use of cold water was largely forgotten. Cold water can also induce psychological and physical shock. It is a familiar technique: throwing a pail of cold water on a body can shock an unconscious person to consciousness. Torturers knew the technique, but they had not thought to exploit it until Masuy.

Today many assume that shock treatment necessarily involves electricity. In the nineteenth century, shock treatment meant hydrotherapy. Asylum doctors prescribed it for "patients who seemed to need strong stimulation."[16] Noted French psychologists observed that these methods, because of "their exceptional and sometimes dangerous character, present the inconvenience that one cannot reproduce them many times for the same patient."[17] Ironically, doctors described electricity as a shock treatment because it resembled the effects of cold baths and douches.[18]

Masuy drew from this medical tradition. His victims choked, their stomachs swelled, but Masuy's main goal was to induce emotional shock. "The bathtub? I am not its inventor, but I knew how to bring this system to perfection by putting a very high degree of psychology in it. I use it because I know that all creatures are first of all and originally scared, and that fear exercises a paralyzing action and that it provokes pain and anguish."[19] Masuy complained that the Gestapo had abused *his* technique. In the hands of "those lard-heads," the bathtub became "a cruelty."

His bathtub technique was "experimental psychology."[20] He supervised to make certain that the bathtub "wasn't applied contrary to the proper spirit."[21] "The head held in the water, the patient suffocated. Then I warmed him up, and I comforted him with grog."[22] Masuy's "patient would be conscientiously dried in a bathrobe, warmed up, rubbed with eau de cologne, and consoled with Cognac." Masuy would then praise the victim for his courage, but remind him that it was useless, urge him to come clean, and if not, repeat the torture.[23] Masuy insisted, unlike many torturers of this period, that a doctor be present.[24] Efficiency was important, but he also had "the concern for not making people suffer," torturing men and women in the same professional way.[25]

So perhaps the twentieth century does deserve to be called "the Century of Masuy." Masuy understood that modern torture was fundamentally about emotional shock, not dramatic painful techniques like the Inquisitional water tortures. All this he dismissed as "mise-en-scène," showmanship.[26] Masuy strove to touch the minds of his victims. No wonder his victims could not forget his eyes. What Masuy did not anticipate was that electroshock, not water shock, would dominate the world.

Marty's Magneto

Pierre Marty was a successful police inspector in colonial Tunisia. As police commissioner of Bizerte in 1940, Marty had infiltrated and crushed Communist cells. After his return to France, the Vichy government appointed him as police chief of Montpellier on the Mediterranean (October 1943) and then as the top policeman in Toulouse (April 1944).[27]

Toulouse lay on the Spanish border. People running for their lives passed through the city, hiding in the countryside and hoping to find their way out of France. Police in the Resistance safeguarded routes over the Pyrenees and ignored false documents for Jews and Resistance fighters.[28] In effect, Toulouse was a "fief of the Resistance."[29]

In 1943, to counter the Resistance, Marty created an extralegal brigade of thugs, "the too famous 'special Marty brigade,' which he endowed with the famous electric machine and the black chamber, so many torture methods of his own invention."[30] The brigade was a parallel system alongside the regional police that he also managed. It beat victims with belts with brass buckles. It suspended, burned, and suffocated victims. It tore off nails, cut heels with knives, crushed genitals, and pierced flesh with pins.

"Besides these crude methods to make people talk under pain, the inspectors of the Marty Brigade had also thought of [*imaginer*] the electric machine," reported one near-contemporary account.[31] Marty's victims called it a thermocauterizer (*thermo cautère*).[32] Marty called it the "confectionary box" and "Radio London."[33] It consisted of "a magneto activated by a motor." One end was "attached to the wet hands of the patient, while the other pole, by means of a mobile wire, was placed on the most sensitive parts of the body and provoked deep burns."[34]

This is the earliest report of electric torture in France, though by no means in the French colonies. Magneto torture, as I will describe in chapter 7, was common in French Indochina long before it came to France. How Marty or his brigade came by it is unclear. Next to nothing is known about Marty's interrogation methods in colonial Tunisia or his earlier career.

What is certain is that, in southern France, Marty operated with two faces. The public face was that of the police superintendent, who insisted that the police should respect the law. At his trial, Marty asked the judges to consider the statistics. "My dossier will prove that I am the intendant who has tortured the least."[35]

Marty had another face. When a Toulouse police commissioner went to Marty to complain about the electrotorture of a prisoner, Marty said, "I forbid *you*, regular police, to use certain methods, but one way or another he is going to squeal."[36] Marty used the police for banal operations, and the brigade for extralegal ones, wanting "to leave the honor of the regular police intact."[37] Marty and five of his brigade were executed in 1948.

The French Gestapo and Electric Torture

Marty's magneto is the clearest example of what becomes a common French technique. Between 1943 and 1944, the technique appears in other cities, though it is often hard to determine the date or the instrument. The instances are listed below in order of clarity.

The Milice

Vichy created the paramilitary Milice in January 1943.[38] The Milice had an investigative wing, Bureau 51, which used electric torture. In the city of Vichy,

Henri Millou's team interrogated at the Chateau de Brosse and Commissaire Poinsot's team at the Petit Casino. Interrogations consisted of the bathtub, "whips, belts, the dynamo [a magneto] and the fridge [freezing prisoners in large commercial refrigerators]; their skin is torn off, their toes are crushed."[39]

Bureau 51 had investigative teams outside of the city of Vichy as well. In Paris, two Bureau 51 interrogators, a former bartender assisted by a former pimp, beat victims with mallets and broomsticks, flogged with leather belts, beat soles of feet (the *falaka*), broke teeth, squeezed skulls with metal bands, and pierced with pins and nails.[40] They also used an "aviation magneto," an electric device used to start plane engines.[41]

In Lyon, the team of Paul Touvier used whipping, forced standing on sharp objects, and a car dynamo to interrogate prisoners.[42] In Ariege in 1944, Milice interrogators submitted stubborn detainees to "a dynamo stuck on a [wooden] board."[43] The technique was "perfected at Foix," a town along the Pyrenees.[44] A report in 1944 describes a young girl beaten, choked, forced to hold buckets of water for hours, and electrified in Rennes.[45]

The Lafont-Bonny Gang

Henri Chamberlin, alias Henri Lafont, was the most notorious of the French Gestapo.[46] In 1942, he took on Pierre Bonny, a former police inspector, as his chief lieutenant. Lafont's gang came directly out of Fresnes Prison: One-Armed Jean, the Mammoth, Handsome Abel, Big Armed Jo, the Bloodthirsty (*le Sanguinaire*), and Glowing Nose (*Nez-de Braise*). There were also foreigners: a Dane, a Basque, an Armenian, a Jewish Bessarabian, and several Algerians.[47]

Torture at Lafont's headquarters began with beating and whips studded with nails. Interrogators filed teeth, cut the gums with razors, and struck teeth with mallets. Torturers then attached the victim's feet to a ring on the wall and banged his head repeatedly against the bricks. For the "difficult prisoners," Lafont employed the "electric bench" (*banc électrique*), which roasted feet, and the magneto: "Simple System. Plugging in of two wires, one on the finger, the other on the genitals. The crank was put into motion up until the confession."[48]

Lafont's headquarters attracted torturers. Violette Morris, a lesbian in the entourage of "Jo the Terror" and a former champion female discus-thrower, worked for Lafont in return for his permission to torture women with whips and lighters. Lafont disliked "perverts," preferring professional torturers.[49] At some point, Lafont hired a con man, Adolphe Cornet, "Fredo the Terror of Prison [*Gnouff*]." Fredo brought "the 'magneto to wipe off smiles' the functioning of which was confined to two assistants: Normand, ex-sergeant major of the L.V.F [Legion des Voluntaires Français] and Pierre Sibert, a fat professional killer."[50]

Other Gangs

Masuy possessed electrotorture equipment[51] although his victims remember bathtubs and beatings, not electrotorture.[52] Other Paris gangs did not use electrotorture. In the gang of Frederic Martin (alias Rudi de Mérode), torture began with blows, kicks, and then the bathtub.[53] Friedrich Berger's gang reversed the order: the bathtub first, followed by threats, whips, and cudgels. For the bathtub torture, Berger hired Rachid Zulgadar, an Iranian taxi driver nicknamed "King Kong," who had no difficulty holding heads under water.[54]

In Angers, Jacques Vasseur subjected prisoners to an electric helmet (*casque électrique*) that burned down to their scalps.[55] In Marseilles, the local Gestapo chief, Ernst Dünker (alias Delage), employed an Italian criminal, Giordano Bruno Gallino, nicknamed Geuele-en-or ("The Golden Maw") who specialized in electric torture.[56]

Other agents were less interested in electric torture, though this did not mean they were less inventive. Clara Knecht, a police spy, developed "an atrocious perfection of the bathtub torture . . . the bathtub of soapy water, in use at Rennes and other western cities."[57] In Montpellier, torturers brushed victims with a dog tooth brush and then shoved them in a vat of brine.[58] At the Alcazar in Lyon, torturers used an iron mask with screws that twisted the skull in different ways.[59]

In Bordeaux, a prisoner Pierre Touyaga was put to "tortures so refined and cruelly original by [Marcel] Fouquey that Fouquey, proud of his technical creativity, invents the neologism *touyaguer*, which the Deuxième Service had to use instead of *torturer*."[60] Lamote (also known as Pierre Paoli) at Bourges developed techniques so grotesque the Germans intervened sometimes to defend the victims. After using magnetos, and even experimenting once with Chinese water torture, he developed his signature razor technique, removing strips of skin from the heels.[61]

The Gestapo

It is clear, then, that French auxiliaries used electric torture commonly throughout France. The German Gestapo outside France rarely used electric torture. As one might expect, the German Gestapo inside France was more familiar both with the bathtub and with electric torture. German agents used bathtub torture in Paris, Nice, Bordeaux, Lyon, and Lille.[62] When it came to electrotorture, the Germans left that to the French.

Regional surveys of the Gestapo in France report no Germans using electrotorture in the regions of Angers, Bordeaux, Lille, Limoges, Lyon, Orleans, Rennes, Savoy, and Vichy.[63] Klaus Barbie in Lyon used the usual methods:

truncheons, whips, stretching tables, suspension, studded handcuffs, and pincers to tear nails.[64] German agents used electrotorture in one known case. In
Toulouse sometime after October 1943, four agents hung a victim by the feet,
burned his fingers, and subjected him to a magneto.[65]

At Nuremberg, the French prosecutor submitted fifty-seven affidavits of
torture victims from northern France. Fifty victims allege being flogged and
beaten. Six allege water torture. Only Albert Billot describes how a French
auxiliary, Verbrugge, tossed a live wire into the bathtub in which he sat.[66] In
the direct testimony to the Nuremberg judges, former French prisoners described two other cases of electric torture. Labussière describes how Laloue
received electric torture at Bourges, and Claeys, who was imprisoned in Poitiers,
had friends who had seen electric torture.[67] In these cases, unfortunately, one
cannot determine the agent, date, place, or device.

The Decline of Sweating and Stealth

In France, torture commonly meant whips, beating, and suspension. Beyond
that, it varied. Groups adopted different techniques and devices: the bathtub,
the electric helmet, the electric bench, the magneto, soldering irons, pliers,
presses, and unique razor methods.

The Gestapo inside France encouraged, but did not regulate, torture.
There was no German manual showing the French how to perform electrotorture or water torture. The competing French gangs became infernos of invention. Torture techniques spread from the bottom up, not from the top down.

Then torture became policy. On June 10, 1942, Karl Oberg, the supreme
head of the SS and the police in France, authorized sweating and regulated
beating, repeating Gestapo chief Müller's directive two days earlier.[68] This recommended approach, however, did not correspond to what was happening on
the ground. In France, more so than elsewhere, sweating was the last thing the
Gestapo did, and it is not hard to see why.

In war, interrogators want accurate, up-to-date information. Sweating takes
time, and Resistance fighters knew it. They developed a strategy now known
among guerrillas everywhere. They made a "contract" with arrested members:
Keep your mouth shut for as long as you can. Buy time with false or outdated
information. Give us 48 hours to change the names, codes, and places. Then
talk as much as you want. This strategy assumed that torture would *always*
work. It was a rule of prudence, not an empirical observation, and it seriously
undermined the quality of information that torturers could gather if someone broke.[69]

The strategy may seem obvious now, but it was not at the time.[70] As it spread, the Gestapo changed how it interrogated. "Interrogations were usually most severe during the first forty-eight hours after capture as the Gestapo understood that information obtained later would probably be out of date."[71] Interrogators ignored slow techniques like forced standing and pummeled the victim for as much information as they could get. "These tortures were all the more horrible because the Germans in many cases had no clear idea of what information they wanted and just tortured haphazard."[72] Such actions in turn pushed the Resistance to more extreme acts, including, in at least one case, torture of its own.[73]

In this context, sweating and clean tortures rapidly disappeared from the Reich.[74] Alec Mellor concluded that torture in France was dictated by a cold logic of war, just as Carl von Clausewitz, the nineteenth-century philosopher of war, predicted.[75] In war, Clausewitz argued, "There arises a sort of reciprocal action, which logically must lead to an extreme."[76]

To all this, there appears only one interesting exception. In Vichy, appearances mattered. Six months after Oberg legalized torture, the Vichy secretary general of the police was discouraging police torture. Once again, he complained, he was getting reports that threw "discredit upon the entire police force, sully the dignity of its functions, and reduce its authority."[77] Caught in the middle between the Resistance and the Germans, Vichy generated two systems of law enforcement: police for ordinary functions and the Milice for fighting the Resistance.[78] Marty, in this respect, was typical.

Did the concern for appearances encourage clean torture? Apparently it did for the Milice's Bureau 51. Writing shortly after the war, Elias Reval remembers that Leo Polin was subjected to the "supreme torture: sleep deprivation." It was "a cunning torture because it leaves no marks and one can't accuse anyone of responsibility."[79] This Vichy bureau also favored "electric torture, probably because it does not leave obvious traces and, that is to say, proof."[80]

In favor of Reval's conclusion, there is also the geographic distribution of electric torture in France. Outside Paris and Rennes, electric torture occurred mostly in the south (Toulouse, Marseilles, Foix, Lyon, Vichy) and along the Loire River valley (Bourges, Angers).

Aside from Bureau 51, Vichy electric users were not subtle. Reports describe roasted feet, burned fingers, and baked scalps. All the supplementary tortures—whipping, crushing, and beating—show that the torturers left deep scars. Where subtlety was needed, they abandoned the broken body, as if it was an accidental death.[81] Why Bureau 51 was so concerned with clean torture remains a mystery.

The German Gestapo and Modern Torture

The Gestapo did not torture "scientifically,"[82] if what one means by this is empirically confirmed rules that inevitably broke individuals. This survey confirms the American report after the liberation of Paris, which observed that interrogators were unsystematic and inefficient.[83] "All credible descriptions of torture involve crude techniques, easily learned at levels below official training."[84]

Gestapo interrogators were modern in that they applied pain without attention to what custom or law required. They expressed, like modern torturers everywhere, the growing autonomy of their profession from the law. Gestapo technique was also anachronistic, most closely resembling the torture of seventeenth-century European states. Whipping cut into sensitive skin tissue. Torches and heated wires aggravated sensory receptors. Pressure and suspension attacked the musculoskeletal system. Suspension deprived the muscles of blood and dislocated the shoulders and hands from the joints. Classical torturers would recognize all these common techniques.[85]

Usually, when observers talk about "scientific torture," they are gesturing at tortures that touch the mind or warp one's sense of self. At the very least, they describe methods that seize victims from within through drugs, sound, sweating, water torture, or electricity, the latter often presented as analogous to scientific shock treatment. German interrogators did not commonly use sweating, water torture, or electric torture in interrogation, much less electroconvulsive therapy, drugs, or sound. Many aspects of the Gestapo were modern, but torture was not one of them.[86]

The myth of the scientific Gestapo torture played on a predisposition to see Germans as efficient in everything. This reputation alone did more damage to the Resistance than torture. Many a fearful person became an informant rather than undergo "scientific" interrogation.[87]

The French Gestapo has a better claim to a place in the history of modern torture. To be sure, they did not everywhere seek to use torture cleanly, scientifically, or systematically. They did favor methods that gripped the subject from within. Masuy, in particular, understood why emotional shock mattered.

Remembering Nuremberg

To prove that German policy authorized organized torture, French prosecutors at Nuremberg set out to show that German torture was uniform and thus centrally planned. This was an excellent strategy in principle, but not in practice. Indeed, one can learn from the prosecution's mistakes.

The prosecution did not make clear what kind of uniformity it sought to establish. Was the prosecutor looking for identical practices, different practices that shared identical properties, or family resemblances? Too often, the prosecution waffled.[88] It is not surprising that it failed to persuade the judges, and in the end the judges returned only one guilty verdict on the charge of torture, against Kaltenbrunner for the penal regime in the concentration camps.[89]

The prosecution never defined precisely specific tortures among which it hoped to find uniformity. Whips, water, electricity, and razors all cause suffering, but they are not identical techniques. Too often, the prosecution's case was simply that victims suffered profoundly from torture. No doubt, but this did not mean interrogators used the same techniques to cause suffering and gather information. Uniformity of suffering does not imply uniformity of practice. Rather, it confuses the effects of torture with the means, yielding vague generalities.

Then there were simply empirical mistakes. For example, in listing torture in the Netherlands, Prosecutor Charles Dubost asserts that sometimes prisoners "were exposed to electrical current." He cites Document F-224 (RF 324), a document that contains no reference to electric torture.[90] Who knows what the Odessa machine is?

Subsequent writers have compounded the misleading impression that the Gestapo practiced French techniques throughout Europe. For example, Edward Crankshaw asserts that the more elaborate methods of torture were "practised with monotonous regularity in towns as far apart as Lyons [Lyon, France] and Stavanger [Norway], Amsterdam and Odessa. Thus, we find the testicle-crushing technique in almost universal use . . . again, there was a fairly elaborate exploitation of the principles of electricity."[91]

On the contrary, testicle-crushing devices were not found in Norway, Odessa, or Amsterdam. Electric torture was uncommon outside France. The Gestapo did use elaborate machines, but these varied across Europe. "There was no known case of the use of the rack," Crankshaw claims.[92] Clearly he had not read Schlabrendorf's memoirs.

The Nuremberg prosecutors chose a high standard to meet, namely, that torture methods were identical across Europe. This claim holds only for the concentration camps, as the tribunal judges correctly concluded. Elsewhere, there were only loose regional styles, most notably in Norway and France.

The Search for Electric Torture

In the last three chapters, I have shown that the great authoritarian states of the early twentieth century used stealth torture for show trials, UN inspections, and foreign newspapers. In these few instances, it served to "keep up appearances."[93]

The Russians and Chinese used clean tortures as the Spanish Inquisition would. They wanted to produce *false* confessions, and they did not mind using slow tortures to achieve this purpose. They did not share the concern of many modern torturers: to produce *accurate* intelligence with speed. The Germans did, but for that purpose, they preferred whips, truncheons, razors, and thumbscrews, not electricity and water torture. In their own ways then, Communists and Nazis were old fashioned.

In his history of the European Resistance, M.R.D. Foot asks rhetorically, "Was it one of them [the Gestapo] who invented the electric shock to the genitals, that has become a commonplace of over-sophisticated conduct since?"[94] That is unlikely. Nevertheless, the question Foot asks really does require an answer: who did invent electric torture? Or the other common clean tortures that use water, sound, drugs, light, and ice? I have described their use by the French Gestapo in this chapter, and their nonuse by Germans, to help dispense with the common assumption that German Nazis must have originated and spread all modern tortures. But that is a separate matter from pinpointing the ultimate origins of these methods. To what extent did the French Gestapo use methods invented prior to the war, and where did they come from?

That is what I turn to in the next two parts of this book, and I begin with electricity. For many, electricity is the emblematic modern torture. It involves mastering technology and science. It can be used to assault the mind while leaving few marks on the skin. To tell the story of electrotorture, then, is to tell the story of stealth torture as well as modern torture.

Unlike many tortures, electric torture requires easily identifiable instruments. Using survivor narratives in the Nuremberg fashion, one can compare these devices and map their movements. By examining the techniques that accompany them, one can also judge whether torturers intend to use these devices stealthily. When electrotorture is used with water or white noise, then torturers probably mean to be covert. When it is used with whips and razors, the torturers are not concerned with leaving marks.

In part III, I will show that electricity is not an easy power to harness for torture, much less use cleanly. Many instruments failed, and these failures illuminate the political factors that helped other instruments succeed. The French auxiliaries of the Gestapo will have their place in this story, but we will find that the nexus in which clean electrotorture appeared was democratic, not authoritarian (not, in other words, "the Gestapo"). We have already seen this origin in the case of sweating (chapter 3, "Lights, Heat, and Sweat"). In part IV, we will find that this pattern holds also for sound, drugs, light, ice, water, and positional torture.

III A History of Electric Stealth

Good Luck.

> —William Kemmler to the world upon being the first
>
> person execured on the electric chair, 1890[1]

6   Shock

In 1888, Thomas Edison recommended the electric chair to a New York State commission investigating alternatives to hanging. In 1890, New York State designated William Kemmler as the first victim of the chair. So at the dawn of the electric age, electricity found a legitimate place in punishment, and this would be portentous. The story of electrotorture is the story of how men took a power that killed and used it to forge simple tools that caused pain, but not death. My task in the next six chapters is to reconstruct the main elements of this largely forgotten history.

I begin with the birth of the electric chair, considering the advances that enabled men to control electric death. Then I describe several early electric devices that, despite common accounts, never caught on as torture instruments.

After evaluating these accounts, I turn in chapter 7 to the device that matters. Between 1930 and 1980, hand-cranked magnetos dominated the world of electrotorture. Stealthy magneto torture appeared first in the French colonial system. French interrogators adopted this practice in Vietnam in 1931 and carried it forward to Algeria in the 1950s. When seen from this perspective, the French Gestapo's preferences in torture are hardly surprising.

In chapter 8, I describe how other nations adopted the French style. The Vietnamese pass it on to the Americans, who carry the magneto forward to the Americas in the 1960s. North and South American torturers add their own variations. I also explore electrotorture devices outside the French style, notably in Argentina and South Africa.

In chapter 9, I trace how all these devices spread continent by continent from 1970 to 2000. Many authoritarian states, both capitalist and communist, now adopt electrotorture. This period of extraordinary innovation soon gives way to homogenization as stun technology sweeps the world.

In chapter 10, I describe how stun technology emerged, drawing on U.S. patent documents and narratives of the developers. The developers began their work in a hostile climate. In the 1960s, American police had been forced to abandon electric cattle-prods after political leaders condemned the practice. Americans also feared electrotorture from its sinister appearance in books and movies about asylums. One could not imagine tougher conditions in which to introduce the new technology. How stun developers overcame them is a remarkable story, far more revealing than the stories normally peddled about evil scientists and greedy corporations. In chapter 11, I describe how stun technology entered into torture in the United States and describe its effects on democratic life.

In the course of these chapters, I develop specific theses regarding the demand for and supply of clean tortures. I argue that clean electrotorture appeared mainly in contexts where publicity mattered, most notably in the colonies and foreign wars of democracies. It spread to authoritarian states in the 1970s as human rights monitoring intensified worldwide. I seek to show as well that electrotorture has tended to spread informally and from the bottom up. Torturers assembled or used electric devices based on what was available, what they remembered or heard, what they were accustomed to, and how much they thought they were monitored. Despite the higher degree of technological sophistication that characterizes stun technology, the spread of stun guns and Tasers is not an exception to this general trend.

The chapters that follow show how torture persisted in the face of public monitoring. They show the three ways torture appears in different democracies, the national security, juridical, and civic discipline models outlined in chapter 3. They go further, showing how these models of torture interact. Magneto torture used in wars abroad found its way back into regular policing in the home country, and stun guns used to impose civic discipline at home found their way into national security conflicts abroad.

All this, however, must be told with care. Let me begin, then, with the electric chair and the devices that appeared in its wake.

The AC/DC Controversy and the Electric Chair

In the 1880s, Thomas Edison and George Westinghouse competed to determine the nature of the socket that now resides in the wall of your home, whether it would yield direct (DC) or alternating (AC) current. One durable result of their struggle was the electric chair.

In this period, Edison dominated the field of commercial incandescent lighting. His company illuminated whole city blocks using direct current. Westinghouse challenged this dominance with a lighting system based on alternating current. His system could move high-voltage electricity over great distances on a small-diameter wire. The diameter of the wire was critical; copper prices were high, and AC systems promised enormous savings. Edison lobbied the states to pass laws limiting AC voltage to 200 volts while permitting 800 volts for DC. Such caps would have crippled Westinghouse's business.

Edison argued that caps were necessary because alternating current was "exceedingly dangerous."[2] He tapped into a great fear. In this period, accidental death by electricity was news.[3] Foreigners were appalled at the American statistics. A British observer cautioned his audience, "One must remember that in America life is held very cheap and that safeguards and protective legislation tend to be regarded as undue restriction upon industry and commerce."[4]

Edison found an ally in Harold P. Brown, a small-time consulting engineer, who was convinced that alternating current was fatal.[5] Brown's genius lay in spectacular, simple demonstrations. Brown began electrocuting dogs, first at Edison's laboratories and then in public lectures at Columbia University. Publicly electrocuting animals such as boa constrictors and elephants was not unusual in the late nineteenth century.[6] Brown's demonstration shocked onlookers because he used far more timid and less ferocious animals. He "made a Spanish bullfight seem a moral and innocent spectacle."[7]

Brown wired a seventy-six-pound dog in a cage. He then released five DC charges from an Edison dynamo (at 300, 400, 500, 700, and 1,000 volts respectively). At 1,000 volts, the dog's body contorted and "the experiment became brutal."[8] One spectator begged Brown to kill the dog. That was what he was waiting for. Brown killed the dog with a single charge of 330 AC volts. At his second demonstration, Brown dispatched three dogs with 400 AC volts. To avoid intrusion by the Society for the Protection of Cruelty against Animals, he performed it under the auspices of the New York City Department of Health.

In the meantime, another opportunity arose to discredit AC systems. In 1888, the state of New York established a commission to explore alternatives to hanging. The commission received two hundred recommendations from legal, medical, and electrical professionals. Doctors opposed lethal injection. Seventy-five respondents favored electrocution. Edison wrote saying he was opposed to the death penalty unless it was quick and painless; he recommended AC equipment. The idea was not new; *Scientific American* had already suggested it in 1876.[9]

The legislature authorized a machine. Frederick Peterson, a doctor who worked with Brown at Columbia, led the team, assisted by Arthur Kennelly (Edison's assistant) and Harold Brown. In the winter of 1888, Peterson's team electrocuted horses and calves at Edison's laboratory. The *New York Times* announced that the experiments proved "the alternating current to be the most deadly force known to science."[10] Then the team built an electric chair in Auburn prison. New York State designated William Kemmler, a murderer, to die in it. Brown insisted on using Westinghouse dynamos.

In a short time, Brown had put Westinghouse on the defensive. As one Westinghouse engineer mourned, "If we make it [AC] an instrument of death, women and others will oppose its introduction into the household."[11] Westinghouse paid for Kemmler's appeal to the Supreme Court, but the appeal failed.[12]

Kemmler was executed in August 1890. Executioners attached electrodes to his head and lower back. Not leaving anything to chance, executioners applied 7,000 volts for seventeen seconds. Yet within half a minute, Kemmler moved. " 'Great God! He is alive!' some one said; 'Turn on the current,' said another. . . . the unconscious wretch in the chair became as rigid as one of bronze. . . . The dynamo did not seem to run smoothly. . . . The stench was unbearable."[13]

Each side saw what it wanted.[14] The opponents condemned the execution as a barbarism, while Edison coolly suggested that executioners should attach electrodes to the hands to increase the speed of death.[15] In the seventh electrocution at Sing Sing in 1893, Charles McElvaine put his hands into electrified pockets. He did not die after a fifty-second shock. Executioners finished him by attaching electrodes to his head and calf.[16] This became the subsequent procedure. Normally, executioners set the charge for 2,000 to 2,200 volts at seven to twelve amperes. They then reduced the current and applied it repeatedly until the prisoner was dead.[17]

Edison also promoted electrocution in movies, reenacting the electrocution of McKinley's assassin and filming the electrocution of Topsy the elephant. These short films pioneered realist conventions now used for scientific documentary. In *Electrocuting an Elephant*, for example, the camera focused coldly on Topsy going rigid and falling down dead. It did not show the high emotion of the fifteen hundred onlookers at Coney Island in 1903. Nor did it reveal that Topsy had also eaten a carrot laced with 450 grains of potassium cyanide just before the switch was thrown.[18]

The Mystery of Electric Death

The electric chair soon became a symbol for death. States rapidly adopted the electric chair: Ohio (1896), Massachusetts (1898), New Jersey (1907), Virginia

(1908), North Carolina (1909), Kentucky (1910), and Arkansas, Indiana, Pennsylvania, and Nebraska (1913).[19]

Electric death itself remained a mystery. Of the twenty witnesses at Kemmler's execution, twelve were doctors waiting for the autopsy.[20] Kemmler was not simply the first person to die on the chair; he was the first controlled electrocution experiment on a human. Subsequent botched electrocutions intensified the debate.[21]

Reports showed that some persons could survive high voltages (like those struck by lightning), while others died after being exposed to lower voltages. It was not clear why this happened. In 1899, two research teams, one American and one Swiss, correctly identified the biological processes at work in these different deaths.[22]

After electrocuting numerous dogs, the teams concluded that alternating current at lower voltages normally killed through ventricular fibrillation. Electricity caused the heart's openings to flutter irregularly, interrupting the blood flow through the heart. This induced cardiac arrest. Fatality varied with animal's weight and age. Death was more likely with repeated shocks.

Direct current could kill in this way too, but alternating current was more dangerous. Shocks as low as 10 volts could produce ventricular fibrillation if the electrodes were in a line passing through the heart. High-voltage alternating current did not cause ventricular fibrillation. Rather, it caused "respiratory arrest, loss of consciousness, general paralysis, loss of reflexes and deep prostration."[23] Such damage, when permanent, was fatal.

All this may sound mysterious to the layperson, but the analogy to death by water may be helpful (even though the biological processes are different). One can die slowly of low-voltage shock in the same manner as a person slowly sinks and drowns in a freezing river. Or one can be damaged by the impact of a tremendous release of energy, as under a waterfall. Waterfalls do not drown one. They can stun and cause serious damage that, if permanent, is fatal.

In time, scientists learned that it was not the extent of the voltage (high or low), but the amperage, that is, the amount of current that passed through the body, that caused ventricular fibrillation. As little as 20 milliamps can be fatal.[24] High amperage killed even at low voltages. Again by analogy to water, it was not the height from which the water fell to the point of impact, but how cold the water freezing the body was. Even still water could kill.

This knowledge was critical for the future of electrotorture. Dead victims yielded no information. If a device is to be used to interrogate or intimidate, prisoners had to survive. Thus, a proper device had to deliver painful high voltages with low amperage. Ideally, torturers could regulate the charge and apply shock at their discretion to different parts of the body. Portability would be an advantage.

By the second decade of the twentieth century, several devices met these specifications. In what follows, I describe two sets of devices, those used by the police and those used by doctors.

Early Police Devices

In the thirty years after Kemmler's death, police stuck mainly to safer tortures. Typically, they used bright electric lights to sweat, burn, blind, and irritate suspects. In Paris, police took murder suspects to the morgue, where they suddenly switched on the lights to reveal the victim's body, hoping the shock would force a confession.[25]

When police applied electricity directly to the body, they drew on what was familiar. Some police constructed modified chairs. Argentine police borrowed devices from the stockyards.

American and Argentine police were among the first police forces to use clean electrotorture. In both cases, torturers sought to avoid detection by courts, journalists, or doctors. In the United States, police used electrotorture mainly in the 1920s. In Argentina, police adopted electrotorture during the "infamous decade" (1930–1943), as the oligarchic republic collapsed under fraud and coercion. In the 1930s, electrotorture also appeared in authoritarian states (Brazil, Portugal) or under near authoritarian conditions (Communist government in Republican Spain). Here police practice was scarring, suggesting that the torturers were not concerned with stealthiness.

Police elsewhere did not adopt these new devices. Modified chairs, for example, failed because judges and journalists could easily identify them, revealing that stealthy torture also required stealthy devices. The Argentine experience showed that, compared to other tortures, electrotorture was time consuming and labor intensive. Even though the Argentine device was flexible, nonlethal, portable, and clean, it languished for decades as a peculiar Argentine custom.

American birds, monkeys, and welcome mats. The early devices had short lives. In 1910, the anarchist philosopher Emma Goldman, who corresponded with many imprisoned anarchists, described a torture device called the "humming bird." It was "an electrical contrivance run along the human body," which probably hummed with current.[26] Until 1925, Dallas police used the "electric monkey"—so called because it was used "especially against Negroes"—which consisted of a storage battery with two terminals. The prisoner held one pole, and the other was pressed against his spine, giving what police called "a needle in the back."[27] Between 1922 and 1926, the Seattle police chief used a cell with an electrically wired carpet. When the carpet was switched on, "sparks fly and the prisoner leaps, screaming in agony, into the air. . . . It is not fatal, its effects are not lasting, and *it leaves no marks.*"[28]

British batteries. Cellular Prison in the Andamans was a labor colony for Indian prisoners. Failure to work led to beating, flogging, or being suspended by hand-cuffs, chained in fetters, or harnessed to grinding wheels. In 1912, Ullaskar Dutt refused to work. Having exhausted the usual methods, the warden had the prison doctor apply electrotorture using an electric battery.[29] Dutt went insane, and other prisoners do not report electrotorture after this date.

The Arkansas chair. In 1929, in Helena, Arkansas, the local sheriff charged James McAllister, an African-American, with the murder of his stepson. To induce a confession, McAllister was strapped and shocked on "an improvised electric chair." McAllister subsequently appealed his conviction, and at trial, he testified that his confession had been coerced. The presiding judge ordered the chair to be rolled into the courtroom, and Sheriff J. C. Barlow testified this piece of furniture came "with the office." Its purpose was to make suspects confess. Sheriff Barlow had inherited it from "a long line of former county Sheriffs"; he had rebuilt it and used it on three suspects.[30] This chair "leaves no marks."[31] As the survival of suspects shows, the device did not kill.

Other police in the American South sometimes used electric chairs as sites for interrogation. In Alabama, police whipped a man named Phillips at Atmore Prison Farm, and then bound him in the electric chair used for executions at Kilby Prison. After eight days and nights in the chair, he implicated four men charged with murder.[32] But the use of electric chairs for interrogation did not catch on, even though it was possible to build portable electric chairs that could be moved or hidden. For example, in 1940, the Mississippi state legislature authorized the building of a portable electric chair, one that would be trans-ported from county to county for authorized electrocutions. A Memphis firm built the chair, and it was first used in Lucedale, Mississippi, on October 11, 1940, and finally retired in 1954.[33] But there is no record of this chair being used for purposes of interrogation. The difficulty was that electric chairs drew a lot of attention. The arrival in town of Mississippi executioner Jimmy Thompson with his portable electric chair was an event not unlike the arrival of the circus. No doubt, someone would notice policemen rolling the electric chair into the interrogation room. What is certain is that other police departments did not adopt these devices as readily as, say, the rubber hoses that became ubiquitous in police interrogation.

The Spanish chair. In the 1930s, Spain was torn by civil war. A Republican government fought a Nationalist army led by General Franco. In the Republi-can areas, the Soviet NKVD organized Communist allies, secretly killing other socialists and anarchists. The Republican government was unable to prevent these operations. By 1938, the Military Investigation Service (SIM) tortured opponents in secret prisons, generating false confessions to discredit them.[34]

SIM tortures followed the Russian style: relay interrogation, sleep deprivation, sweatboxes, and forced standing or sitting.[35] SIM agents also beat with iron bars, flogged with rubber whips, broke teeth and bones, and burned paper on the soles of the feet.[36] They especially favored bathtub torture, *el suplicio del baño*.[37]

José Peirats adds that SIM agents had three special tortures for recalcitrant prisoners. The freezer was a cell with curved walls filled with freezing water in which the prisoner stood for hours. The noise box was a chest in which "one heard a terrifying cacophony of buzzers and bells." "The electric chair was a variation of the kind used in American penitentiaries, but which did not kill."[38]

Peirat correctly observes that "in those days they were innovations in police repression."[39] The difficulty is that other sources do not mention these tortures; Peirat's account stands alone. What is certain is that the Soviet NKVD was not interested in this local innovation; electricity is absent from Stalinist positional tortures and sweating.

In 1939, Nationalist forces under Franco took Barcelona, and following this date, prisoners report sleep deprivation, bright lights, cold baths, and electric shocks.[40] They do not mention the Spanish chair. It is possible Nationalist torturers may have briefly adapted the SIM's electric devices, abandoning them for other techniques in the late Franco era.[41]

Batteries in Portugal. Between 1932 and 1939, Antonio Salazar's secret police, the PIDE, tortured prisoners using whips, red-hot wires, hot lightbulbs, and electric wires tied to the genitals. Prisoners were severely scarred. One prisoner showed deep electrical injuries on his body made "by means of a wire connected to an electrical battery."[42] Prisoner reports after 1939 indicate that PIDE abandoned electrotorture for forced standing.[43]

Wired in Brazil. In 1935, the Brazilian military crushed a rebellion in its ranks.[44] Officers beat, whipped, and choked opponents. They pulled nails and teeth, stuck victims with pins, needles, and hot wires, and burned them with torches and cigars.[45] They also shocked at least four individuals "with live electric wires," badly burning an ear in one case.[46]

Exposing prisoners to live AC wires is potentially fatal, as the amperage is high. The interrogators were either unskilled or indifferent, probably both. The technique was local. Brazil's secret police did work with the Gestapo, particularly after 1937,[47] but the Germans did not use electrotorture until 1943. When they did, they sensibly used magnetos that had far lower amperage.

The picana eléctrica in Argentina. To move cattle through stockyards, Argentine cattlemen used a barbed goad, the *picana*. The electrified version replaced the barb with shock. The *picana eléctrica* was portable, easy to use, and generated low amperage. It was an ideal device for torture.

Argentine police adopt the *picana eléctrica* around 1935 in Buenos Aires. This date can be fixed fairly closely. In 1935, *Los Torturados* described recent cases of police torture, none of which involved *picanas*.[48] The first known victim was Estaban Filetti, charged with murder in 1935 or 1936. The second known victim was Humberto Vidone in Córdoba in 1939. He was "subjected to an electric machine brought from Buenos Aires that made him 'sing.' "[49]

The police device was "similar to the ones used to goad cattle in barnyards when they do not respond to the whip."[50] Meat and electricity were by then familiar companions. In the early twentieth century, European meatpackers experimented with electric stunning in abattoirs, and European corporations used electric refrigeration to ship huge cargoes of Argentine meat to Europe.[51] Experts determined that electrification did not affect the quality of ham, beef, and mutton.[52] In 1939, four Americans patented electric cattle-prods in Iowa, North Carolina, Indiana, and Wisconsin.[53] By this time, the *picana eléctrica* had already been in use in Argentina for several years.

There were two types of *picana*, one portable and the other powered by the mains and probably made for use in fixed dwellings like stockyards. The portable *picana* involved two cables running from an automobile battery. Torturers tied one cable to the victim's limb, and held the other or tied it to a rod similar to "that of a common welding machine."[54] Wherever torturers touched with the rod, direct current flowed through the body between the two cable ends. The second *picana* resembled "an electric gas lighter," with an insulated sleeve and a metal tip. This ran on alternating current from a wall socket. A transformer or "voltage reducer" kept the current within acceptable limits.[55]

DC *picanas* delivered between 12,000 and 16,000 volts with a thousandth of an ampere. The AC *picana* delivered about 10,000 volts.[56] Advertisers claim modern stun guns deliver up to 200,000 volts, so early *picanas* were modest by comparison.

Police transported *picanas* in suitcases. Operating *picanas* on humans required two people. One worked a bobbin, raising and reducing the voltage. The other applied the *picana* to the victim whom torturers had soaked and strapped to a table. The wand format made it easy to touch various body parts: the temples, ears, mouth, nose, nipples, stomach, genitalia, and legs. By contrast, cup electrodes had to be pasted on and could tear off during torture.

Still there were problems. Both Filetti and Vidone died after electrotorture.[57] Torturers had to learn not to kill their victims. Doctors monitored the torture process.[58]

Electricity also caused severe dehydration or damage to the tongue, making it difficult for victims to give information. Victims could bite the tongue severely as electricity forced the jaw to clamp down. Torturers sometimes made victims bite rubber or lead, but mostly, they sealed the mouth with plaster, what they dubbed "putting the lid on."[59]

Repeated electroshocks made muscles contract permanently, holding jaws rigidly in place. "Because the jaws are the first to tense up, we softened them with a good punch. We did it with this subject, but it didn't work. I grabbed him by the hair and hit his head over the table where he was tied. Think of this; it could have caused a concussion."[60]

As the muscles tightened with repeated shocks, bones snapped under pressure. Torturers had to take breaks to stretch the victim's body. "The secondary employees sit on the victim's knees while others hold the trunk. Nevertheless, arm and shoulder injuries are frequent."[61] Shocking was easy, but electrotorture was slow and labor intensive.

Mindful of journalists and doctors, torturers worked hard to "to avoid fractures, injuries, and lesions, which could indicate the contractions of the discharges."[62] *Picanas* did not normally generate sparks that burned the skin.[63] Just in case, torturers covered victims "with a thick cloth, to prevent the electric goad from leaving burn marks."[64] Police blindfolded victims so they could not say afterward what *picanas* looked like.[65]

Argentine police used *picanas* for decades, but *picanas* did not leave Argentina until the 1960s, when neighboring police in Uruguay adopted them. Between 1935 and 1970, police used electrified prods in only two other countries: Venezuela in the 1950s and the United States in the 1960s. In both cases, accounts pointed to an agrarian source of the devices, but as with Argentina, the precise provenance is hard to determine. The Venezuelan reports describe the device as the "*picana* of the employees in the slaughterhouses or stockyards for moving heads of cattle," and the Mississippi reports describe them as "cattle shockers."[66] By the 1970s, the Venezuelans abandoned the prod for the magneto. Neither police appears to have adopted its devices from Argentina, or used them for long (I describe both cases in chapter 8, "Currents").

The Mystery of Shock

In this section, I describe the contexts in which Europeans became concerned with medical electrical devices: in railway accidents, to treat battlefield injuries, and in asylums. Authorities were tempted to use electricity because these contexts yielded people with seemingly untreatable medical conditions: many were shock or "shell shock" victims, suffering from what we now call post-traumatic stress syndrome (PTSD).

Shock was more than a medical problem. It had political and economic implications as well. Politicians wanted to reduce the cost of military pensions and hospitalization. Railway companies wanted to reduce the cost of legal liability. Generals wanted able-bodied men fighting at the front. Hospital administrators wanted to reduce heavy burdens on the staff.

Some doctors concluded the best treatment for shock, and several other psychological conditions, was more shock, namely electroshock. In the next section, I consider the medical electroshock devices these doctors used. Then I consider whether police used these devices in the early twentieth century. Lastly, I consider the same question for the late twentieth century.

Industrial shock. In the late nineteenth century, train travel had many hazards, but among the most catastrophic was the railway accident. Some passengers had major physical injuries. Others had no visible physical damage, but claimed to suffer serious disabilities. These were victims of shock.

Train wrecks put into question deeply held beliefs, including faith in man's control over nature and the triumph of mechanization, and the trust in the discipline and skills of modern professionals operating complicated technology. Shock experienced as the result of railway accidents now "describes the kind of sudden and powerful event of violence that disrupts the continuity of an artificially/mechanically created motion or situation, and also the subsequent state of derangement."[67]

Shocked survivors raised complex legal liability questions in England in 1864 and in Germany in 1871.[68] Railway companies compensated the physically wounded, but balked at paying claims for people who had no visible injuries. Doctors debated whether the disorders were real.

Battlefield shock. The oldest use of the word *shock* is a military one. Shock occurred when two heavily armored knights or lines of soldiers collided in battle. Advances in cavalry (the stirrup) and infantry (new, more detailed military discipline) created powerful collisions that were unknown in the ancient world. With the advent of firearms, man-to-man collisions were augmented by shocks induced by bullets, cannonballs, grapeshot, artillery shells, grenades, bombs, and other types of military technology. Modern firearms generated almost instantaneous mass death, and many survivors, not surprisingly, were sent into shock. Some soldiers failed to notice painful, even life-threatening, wounds in battle. "The wounded man does not experience the wounding as such, but rather feels the concussion or a shock similar to an electric one."[69]

In 1914, a British surgeon coined the phrase *shell shock* to describe these strange psychological conditions. By 1915, he identified numerous symptoms of shell shock including amnesia, blindness, apparent paralysis, hearing and speech disorders, exhaustion, irritation, and constant headaches.[70] Shell shock survivors could not hold jobs, assist in family life, or have sexual relations.[71]

Shell-shocked soldiers raised the same complex questions as accident survivors. Doctors could treat and reintegrate the visibly injured: large black spectacles disguised scorched faces, "the artificial limbs of war-cripples did not creak, [and] empty sleeves were pinned up with safety pins."[72] Doctors could find nothing wrong with shell-shocked soldiers. Politicians balked at paying their medical pensions. Generals wanted these able-bodied men back at the front.

Medical shock. In the nineteenth century, some doctors used water shock on asylum patients, but many more criticized such techniques. Judging from the aftermath of battles and accidents, it was hard to imagine that shock had a medical value. All this changed in the twentieth century.

In 1919, the Austrian psychiatrist Dr. Wagner-Jaurreg won the Nobel Prize for pioneering "fever therapy." Wagner-Jaurreg successfully treated one dreaded disease by inducing another painful one. In this case, he treated acute neurosyphillis by inducing intense fevers for three weeks.[73] In 1927, another Viennese doctor, Manfred Sakel, treated diabetic drug addicts by inducing hypoglycemic shock. He reduced their blood's sugar content with insulin injections. In 1933, Sakel applied insulin shock therapy to schizophrenics, claiming great success.[74] In 1934, the Hungarian doctor Ladislas von Meduna, argued that epileptic convulsions improved schizophrenic patients. He artificially induced powerful convulsions by injecting Metrazol.[75]

Unlike Wagner-Jaurreg, Sakel, and Meduna never could explain why their shock treatments worked. Nevertheless, unlike psychotherapy, their approach could be used on a large scale for diseases impervious to treatment. By the late 1930s, many American and European hospitals adopted insulin and Metrazol therapy.[76]

William Sargant, a British psychiatrist, advocated insulin therapy for shell-shocked soldiers during World War II. "The most important lesson taught us by Dunkirk and the Battle of Britain of 1940–41 was never to let a neurotic pattern of thought or behaviour remain fixed in the patient's brain for a minute longer than necessary."[77] Doctors applied Sargant's modified shock insulin treatment to fifteen thousand American soldiers around the world.[78]

Sargant also recommended "front-line sedation" with barbiturates for shell shock. Barbiturates caused soldiers to relive their repressed memories. "After this discharge of pent-up emotions, especially battle terrors and possibly rage against their officers, soldiers would suddenly improve."[79] Sargant also had sedated patients imagine fictional battle scenarios. This produced "a greater emotional discharge" and was "more effective than the memory of the real event."[80]

Eventually, Sargant came to believe that Communists and Fascists planted fictional ideas in minds in this way, through shocking emotional discharge. During his work at Brixton Prison, Sargant had already seen British police plant false confessions in suspects' minds. In 1947, he observed the same effect at revivalist meetings and a snake-handling ceremony in Durham, South Carolina. Sargant claimed that Pavlov had discovered that shock reconfigured canine behavior in 1924.[81]

During the Cold War, Sargant's work became a best-seller.[82] Alongside his own intellectual journey (through shock therapy, schizophrenia, British sweating, shell-shocked soldiers, insulin and barbiturate treatment, Pavlov, religious revivalism, brainwashing), Sargant now offered another chain of discovery well suited to the times (through Pavlov, Stalinists, Chinese brainwashing).

By the early 1950s, shock therapy was an established treatment; even the Communists did it. Insulin therapy produced respiratory distress, epileptic seizures, and, sometimes, fatalities. It put extensive demands on the limited hospital staff. Metrazol therapy caused fewer deaths, but it had unpleasant side effects including fractures and respiratory problems. Many patients refused further treatment.[83] The question was if there was an alternative.

Early Medical Devices

In the late nineteenth century, the public viewed electricity in small doses as a therapeutic agent. For example, in the late 1880s, congressmen would "get freshened up" with an electric device while Congress was in session. The device was installed in the Capitol building next to the engine room. Congressmen claimed that "taking electricity" improved their brainpower, speechmaking, and listening capabilities.[84] Constituents could only hope.

With the advent of the electric chair, public enthusiasm vanished. Scientists doubted that electricity had any real health benefits.[85] Moreover, "The spectre of the electric chair was in the minds of all, and an imposing mass of medical literature enumerated the casualties, often fatal, ensuing upon electric discharges across the human body."[86]

Still, some doctors believed that electrical treatment solved important medical, political, and military problems. They used devices that were (largely) nonlethal, flexible, and probably portable.

Kaufmann machines. Fritz Kaufman was a German doctor during World War I. He treated shell-shocked soldiers who claimed that they could not move legs or arms. The "Kaufmann Cure" consisted of electroshock and exhaustion exercises.[87] Kaufmann used a device to apply powerful alternating currents to the paralyzed limb, several minutes at a time. A nurse monitored the controls; the precise machine is not known. Kaufmann barked out orders, making patients perform actual military drills. He then alternated electricity and exercises in one very long session until the patient moved the limb.

Once Kaufmann announced his cure in May 1916, it began a "triumphant march through Germany and Austria."[88] Doctors treated thousands of shell-shocked soldiers, even possibly Adolf Hitler.[89] Many soldiers viewed the Kaufmann cure "as a form of punishment."[90] Public indignation was intense. Alternating current caused cardiac arrest on occasion. More typically, as in Argentina, muscular contractions fractured legs, arms, and spines.[91]

Replying to criticisms, Kaufmann argued that shell-shocked soldiers put a "considerable burden on the military treasury." These men represented "a loss in the living work force at the state's disposal." He calculated that even a one hundred shell-shocked soldiers per German army corps cost 1,250,000 marks, an enormous sum.[92]

Yealland machines. Allied doctors also struggled with shell shock. Elites, like the poet Siegfried Sassoon, could afford private clinics and excellent psychotherapists.[93] This was hardly a solution for thousands of privates. Doctors opposed simply granting "pensions or gratuities to purely hysterical cases."[94] This affirmed the patient's hysteria, and cost more in the long run.

Treatment remained elusive. The French tried and rejected electrotherapy, arguing that such fancy equipment also confirmed the patient's fantasy that he had a real malady.[95] Some British and American doctors persisted with electrical treatments.[96] In England, Lewis Yealland claimed extraordinary results for patients who had been invalid for months if not years.[97]

Yealland applied direct current from a battery, though how he regulated it is unclear. He used attachments like roller, pad, and brush electrodes for the limbs.[98] In a typical case, Yealland treated a patient with a paralyzed leg on a couch. He electrified the limbs gently, then strongly, and then gently. As he applied electricity, he urged the patient to move the leg. The patient walked in less than an hour.[99]

Yealland acknowledged the treatment was painful, beginning his book with an often cited, horrifying case.[100] Yealland attached electrodes to the throat of a mute patient. The patient ripped out the wires at one point. Yealland prevented him from leaving the room, denied him water, and treated him for four hours until he spoke. Yealland pointed out that normally the cure was quick. His book documents fourteen cases cured in less than ten minutes, twelve in less than an hour. Only six cases took more than an hour, the longest being six hours. He cured soldiers of mutism, deafness, blindness, stammers, jerky gaits, and paralysis.

Electroconvulsive therapy (ECT) machines. In 1936, an Italian psychologist, Ugo Cerletti, was studying electrical alternatives to pharmacological shock therapy. He was hesitant; he had inadvertently killed a few dogs with 125 AC volts. While in Rome in 1937, colleagues told him that meat packers electrocuted pigs at the local slaughterhouse. Cerletti spent a day at the slaughterhouse electrocuting pigs. He concluded that killing them was by no means easy. Some pigs survived several electrocutions.

Cerletti's colleague, Lucio Bini, made the first ECT machine. He connected a voltmeter to a timer that divided the electric charge into tenths of seconds. The device produced 100–150 volts, enough to power a bulb. It was so simple Bini was unable to patent it.

Cerletti attached the electrodes to an incoherent schizophrenic. He used 70 volts for two seconds, and then a second shock (over the protests of the doctors and the patient himself) of 110 volts for five seconds. This second shock induced epileptic convulsions, after which the patient recovered his linguistic skills and asked where he was. In time, doctors released the patient.[101] Neither Cerletti nor any of his followers since have been able to explain how ECT treatment works.[102]

The Pansen cure. American and British hospitals adopted ECT machines almost immediately after Cerletti published his paper in 1940.[103] ECT found its greatest advocates in German military hospitals. By 1943, insulin was scarce, and German doctors needed an alternative for shock treatment.[104] At the reserve hospital at Ensen, Friedrich Pansen proposed using ECT devices as a quick cure for shell-shocked soldiers. The "Pansen cure" consisted of 300 milliamperes applied by electrodes to the head from a direct current machine.[105] The machine manufacturer is unknown.

At first, German generals resisted Pansen's cure. German military tradition gave soldiers the right to refuse medical treatment, which they did. Everyone remembered the Kaufmann cure. However, after the battles of Stalingrad and Kursk, the Wehrmacht needed every man at the front. On December 12, 1942, German leaders abolished the German soldier's right to refuse medical treatment, at least for ground troops. By 1943, the state was distributing ECT devices to all public asylums.[106]

The Pansen cure "began a veritable triumphal procession through the military hospitals. Ensen became much-visited location where countless numbers of doctors came to acquaint themselves with the new development in the field of therapy."[107] To promote the cure, Pansen persuaded a famous neuropathologist to shock himself publicly (at a tenth of what Pansen applied to soldiers). He also filmed the cure for Hitler in 1944, hoping "to convert the Führer" with his favorite medium.[108]

Pansen advised the K4 program, which exterminated the handicapped in institutions, and he drew his cure from experimentation on schizophrenics.[109] At Auschwitz, a Polish prisoner physician, a noted neurologist before incarceration, conducted similar research. Robert Lifton, a principal historian on the Nazi doctors, observes that this program was not therapy, but "a prelude to the gas chamber." Dr. Wilhelm König, the chief SS medical officer, approved the program because he believed the Polish physician would produce an interesting paper for which he could take credit.[110] Given the interest in the Pansen cure, this is not surprising.

After the war, a Canadian psychologist allegedly recommended to the American CIA director, "Each surviving German over the age of twelve should receive a short course of electroshock treatment to burn out any remaining vestige of Nazism."[111] Ironically, thousands of Germans soldiers had been so treated.

Defibrillators. In 1899, Prevost and Batelli discovered they could reverse ventricular fibrillation in the heart by applying high-voltage shock with a laboratory machine.[112] Their insight went unacknowledged for nearly fifty years. Then, in 1947, doctors reversed cardiac arrest with an experimental electrical device. In 1959, Kouwenhoven and his colleagues recommended combining defibrillators, close-chest cardiac massage, and mouth-to-mouth resuscitation. After this date, doctors commonly used defibrillators for cardiac arrest.

Transmitting Shock

Looking over this history, one can trace three chains of transmission between 1888 and 1945. On the police chain, devices move from animals (experimental devices) to murderers (the electric chair) and then to prisoners (modified chairs, live wires). On the medical chain, devices move from animals (experimental devices) to shell-shocked soldiers (Kaufmann and Yealland machines).

A third chain begins with devices from the commercial meat industry that move either to police interrogation (cattle prods in Argentina) or to medical treatment (ECT machines for schizophrenics and shell-shocked soldiers). This was the chain that mattered, yielding devices that are still widely used and abused around the world today.

Police devices, for their part, find few customers. The Gestapo and the Soviet NKVD were not interested in the activities of their respective satellites in Brazil, Portugal, and Spain. American police avoided the modified electric chairs. Doctors studied the chair, but did not use it for therapy. The *picana* languished in Argentina. The Argentine experience demonstrated that electrotorture was not simple, unless fatalities did not matter.

Common medical devices did not appear on the police chain. British doctors used electric machines, but policemen did not use electrotorture in the first seven decades of the twentieth century, in the United Kingdom, and electrotorture appears rarely in the colonies. German doctors also used Kaufmann and ECT machines, but public records do not describe German police using electric devices for interrogation until 1943. At that time, they used magnetos, not ECT machines.

Cerletti "discovered" ECT in Fascist Italy, but Mussolini's OVRA (Organizzazione di Vigilanza Repressione dell'Antifascismo) did not use ECT machines. American doctors adopted ECT in 1940, long after American police had abandoned electrotorture. French doctors did not use electrotherapy, and yet ironically the French Gestapo commonly practiced electrotorture. No police force ever used a defibrillator for institutionalized torture.

In short, the police and medical chains did not appear to intersect. Nevertheless, the electroshock doctors did change police practice. As they were under considerable professional scrutiny, doctors pioneered techniques that reduced visible damage. They used mouth guards, gels to avoid burns, and massage techniques to soften bodies after electroshock. Military doctors carried these techniques over into electrotorture, as the Argentine experience reveals.

Later Medical Devices

By the 1950s, various companies made ECT machines in Italy, France, Germany, and the United States.[113] In France, Jean Delay, a noted psychologist, championed ECT.[114] In 1948, two English surgeons developed the Page-Russell ECT technique. Page and Russell applied a one-second shock to produce an epileptic convulsion, and then followed it with five additional shocks during the convulsion.[115] Russell went on to found Ectron, a company that still manufactures ECT machines.

By 1953, one American ECT machine was the twice the size of a dictating machine. It cost $250 (approximately $1,788 in 2005 dollars). Other models were battery driven.[116] Today, Mecta (Lake Oswego, OR) and Somatics (Lake Bluff, IL) dominate the market. A Mecta 2003 runs between $8,000 to $10,000, depending on optional features. The Somatics Thymatron 2003 runs at about

$13,000. This fivefold cost increase in American machines reflects insurance costs, increased legal liability, reporting requirements, and government construction standards.[117]

The new machines have mechanisms that fraction time and electrical power into extremely small units. This increase in range yields microcharges, which older machines could not create, for use on minors. Still, some practitioners complain that the maximum thresholds allowable on machines are too low for treating some patients.[118] A 1971 study found maximum thresholds between 109 and 135 volts.[119]

More American doctors now use ECT as the cost of drugs and hospital stays has surged.[120] They have introduced new measures to reduce pain and physical damage.[121] To reduce muscular contractions that cause bone fractures, doctors prescribe muscle relaxants before the procedure. To reduce consciousness of electrical contact, doctors administer general anesthesia. Some have "abandoned the word *electroshock*, in part because no shock is involved."[122] Doctors also use a paralyzing agent that prevents seizures while permitting electrical contact with the brain.

Unlike most electrotorture, ECT can also induce memory loss, impaired judgment, disorientation, and confusion about time, place, or persons. Patients become oddly euphoric or apathetic.[123] To reduce these effects, doctors have adopted "continuous oxygenation (1953), unilateral electrode placement (1971), brief pulse energy currents (1976), and seizure duration monitoring (1982)."[124]

Public monitoring of ECT caused many of these changes. The public continues to identify shock treatment with authoritarianism, the fiercest critics being Scientologists.[125] Advocacy groups including former patients carefully monitor ECT doctors.[126] Psychoanalysts have also opposed shock treatment for decades. Both Freud and Sakel worked in Vienna, and their respective schools have long-standing enmities. In the Third World, where public monitoring is rare, doctors still practice unmodified ECT, a practice with a deservingly fearsome reputation.[127]

As in the early twentieth century, police do not use ECT machines for interrogation. It is seriously questionable why officers seeking accurate information would use a machine that induces confused judgment, inaccurate perceptions, and amnesia about recent events. Even if one simply hopes to induce terror, it is self-defeating if the victim is euphoric or cannot remember the torture.

Moreover, it is hard to understand why a police administrator would buy a ten-thousand-dollar machine with such a paltry charge when he can buy cheap, powerful, and unregulated devices for torture. Stun gun manufacturers sell devices for as low as thirty dollars and advertise huge discharges (between 50,000 and 200,000 volts). The modest old Argentine *picana* delivers 12,000 volts. Amateurs can use these devices without killing the victim, do not need to worry about how to attach electrodes, and do not have to fiddle with controls that look like "the flight deck of Concorde."[128] Only someone unfamiliar with the problems of torturers would think ECT machines "could be an excellent 'third degree' method to make someone talk."[129]

Torturers might value ECT machines "in situations where . . . *legitimacy* as a medical treatment is crucial."[130] Medically disguised torture like this is reported today only in Cuban and Chinese state psychiatric hospitals, as I discuss in chapter 19. Even here, there are alternatives. The Soviets had the longest history of warehousing dissidents in mental asylums for treatment. Soviet doctors, however, favored pharmacological shock, and rarely prescribed ECT.

Similarly, between 1950 and 1970, the CIA funded scientists in foreign countries to see if ECT machines could be used in brainwashing, most famously Ewen Cameron, a Canadian psychologist.[131] The agency paid Cameron about nineteen thousand dollars per year for five years in the late 1950s. By agency standards, this was a modest investment.[132] At Allan Memorial Institute in Montreal, Cameron broke down existing personalities with ECT machines ("depatterning").[133] Then he tried to induce new personalities ("psychic driving").[134] Instead, he produced damaged patients, 60 percent of whom could not remember anything about themselves six months to ten years prior to treatment.[135]

In the 1970s, specialists retrieved many CIA mind control projects through the Freedom of Information Act. They concluded that Cameron's research was implausible even by the professional standards of his time.[136] Indeed, by 1960, even Cameron endorsed ECT only to treat certain kinds of depression.[137] As for torture, the specialists conclude, police use ECT machines "infrequently, if at all."[138]

Remembering the Animals

The story of shock, medical and judicial, began as an animal story. Men electrified dogs, cows, horses, pigs, and even an elephant. It is also a story about the public's growing appetite for meat. The *picana eléctrica* comes directly out of Argentina's burgeoning beef industry. The ECT machine would not have existed "except for this fortuitous and fortunate circumstance of pigs' pseudo-electrical butchery" in Rome.[139]

Others would start the story of shock with scientists. In Algeria in the 1950s, the radical psychologist Frantz Fanon was certain that "psychiatrists in Algiers" used "electroshock treatments" on "numerous prisoners." He described procedures and symptoms that characterized ECT.[140] As the next chapter shows, Algerian prisoners and French torturers agree that electrotorture involved magnetos, not ECT machines. Like the French prosecutor at Nuremberg, Fanon reasoned mistakenly from the effects (reported electrotorture) to the devices (they are using the same devices as psychologists).

Another scientific story claims the CIA spread Dr. Cameron's depatterning methods worldwide, to the shah's Iran, Djibouti, El Salvador, and, inadvertently, Communist Vietnam. Most specifically, in the 1960s, the Moroccan secret police built torture chambers "identical to the one in the basement of the Allan Memorial Institute," and torturers used "Page-Russell electro shock machines" to gather "information about opponents to the King."[141]

The public record, which I document in the following chapters, is different.[142] In 2002, Ahmed Boukhari published his memoirs as a member of a Moroccan police torture unit in the 1960s. Boukhari identified only one torturer who used electrotorture, Oufkir. Oufkir was not a subtle torturer; he also liked pulling out teeth and using stilettos. Neither Boukhari nor numerous human rights reports describe anything resembling a scientific basement stocked with ECT machines.[143] The Iranian SAVAK and the Communist Vietnamese used cattle prods. American interrogators in Vietnam favored magnetos, and their technique does not resemble Cameron's depatterning. Salvadoran torturers probably also used magnetos. Public reports document no electrotorture in Djibouti. Even if one grants that torturers in these five places used ECT machines, this would constitute the smallest fraction of electrotorture worldwide. Today, torturers mainly use magnetos, cattle prods, and stun guns, none of which is related to Dr. Cameron or ECT machines.

The Cameron story is another version of a typical modern theodicy: the scientist as the source of all knowledge and evil. Cameron plays a role analogous to Pavlov in the story of brainwashing. The story unfolds with a similar chain of loose associations: Cameron used ECT devices—the CIA paid him—the CIA promoted torture—police everywhere use electrotorture. Admittedly plausible, it falls apart in the details.

The available evidence tells a different story. The accounts of early police devices suggest that torturers tinkered and borrowed until they found a device that fit their needs. The story of the Argentine *picana eléctrica* does not point to scientific procedures, but to a craft tradition. It took the police some years of tinkering before they finally figured out what to do. In this respect, it resembles the trial-and-error period of the Soviet NKVD, when it turned to sweating and clean tortures for false confessions. Moreover, the accounts indicate that machines do not fly off the shelves the moment they are invented, suddenly adopted by police everywhere. Nor is it sufficient for devices to be nonlethal, portable, scientific, painful, flexible, and leave few marks. Other factors play a role, including cost, maintenance, design (familiar or alarming), extent of monitoring (high or low), and effect (whether it induces amnesia).

All of these factors play a role in magneto torture, the device that eventually dominates electrotorture throughout the world. Let us now consider the real world of electrotorture.

(1) Il faut que la torture soit propre. [Torture must be clean.]

—Lecture notes, French reserve officer, 1959[1]

7 Magnetos

The *gégène* is an army signals magneto, used for communication purposes and also for torture. In the late 1950s, this word became notorious in France and Algeria. The term *gégéneur*, one who operates this device, became synonymous with torturer. However, electric torture by magneto began long before Algeria. As one French historian remarks, "The '*gégéneurs*' of Algeria invented nothing. In the 1930s, beneath the tropics, in the shelter of the French flag, all the degrading methods existed just fine."[2]

In this chapter, I document the history of magneto torture in the early twentieth century. I focus primarily on the French policing system between 1920 and 1965, when stealthy magneto torture was routine. From the start, French torturers took care to keep torture clean, which is to say, leave few marks. I also consider and seek to explain the behavior of the Japanese Kempeitai, the Hungarian police, and the British colonial police in Kenya during this period. They also favored magneto torture, but their use was not stealthy.

French police institutionalized electric torture in Vietnam during the 1930s. After documenting this history, I follow the trail of magneto torture out of Vietnam, first to France in World War II, then back to Vietnam in 1949, and then to Algeria in the 1950s, and finally back to Paris in the 1960s.

This trajectory of magneto torture is thought-provoking. A colonial technique found its way into domestic policing, traveling to France from Vietnam, not once, but twice. Nor will this be the last time a foreign army carries magneto torture out of Vietnam, as I will show in the next chapter. Let us consider first the magneto in the early twentieth century.

What Is a Magneto?

A magneto is a simple generator that produces a high-voltage spark. In the early twentieth century, magnetos were indispensable for starting machines. Viewers of old movies may recall seeing operators spin a handle on a phone before they spoke, or crank a handle on the hood of a car or spin a propeller on a plane to start the engine. In the course of the twentieth century, torturers adapted magnetos from all these devices for interrogation.

When one moves a coil of wire in a magnetic field, one produces an electric current in the wire. When a gap separates the wire ends, the voltage builds up until it is high enough to jump across the gap as a spark. In magnetos, cranking the handle rotated a coil of wire inside a ring of permanent magnets, and that in turn generated a spark from the wire. Other devices achieved the same result without permanent magnets, instead inducing a magnetic field in an outer coil of wire by the rotation of the inner coil, what Werner Siemens dubbed in 1867 "a self-exciting dynamo."[3] Yet other devices—transformers— took low voltage from an external source and changed it into a high-voltage spark. By 1886, Silvanus Thompson declared the differences were irrelevant. "The arbitrary distinction between so-called magneto-electric machines and dynamo-electric machines fails when examined carefully."[4] I shall call all these devices magnetos.

Automobile engines used magneto ignitions, until manufacturers replaced them with a coil ignition in the 1950s. Once the vehicle started, a chain from the main shaft cranked the magneto and generated high-tension current. A four-cylinder magneto ignition typically gave two sparks per revolution of the engine; it took four to eight volts and increased it by thousands of volts.[5] Cars also possessed several electrical systems, each with different energy requirements, and drivers preferred to start their cars without blowing out their radios and lights. "Commutated magnetos" had commutators that allowed the magneto's energy to supply the different systems at each one's particular requirements

Portable field telephone magnetos were common from the 1880s onward.[6] Each cranking generated a powerful, but short shock at very low amperage to ring the phone at the other end. The operator increased the voltage by cranking faster. Field magnetos also came equipped with wires ending in alligator clips, spring-loaded clips with serrated jaws. Torturers used these for quick, temporary attachments to various body parts.

By the early 1880s, most major armies had portable telephone sets and wire drums that were carried on horseback. By World War I, field telephones were ubiquitous. The German army, for example, had 6,350 men in communications units in August 1914. By 1918, there were 190,000 men handling communications.[7] Yet "during World War I, interrogation by dynamo did not exist."[8] Indeed, for some fifty years (1880–1930), soldiers and policemen did not think to use magneto torture. Between 1930 and 1945, the French, Japanese, and Hungarian police did use magnetos, but the kind of magneto did not seem to matter. Torturers used magnetos for cars, planes, refrigerators, and, in two Japanese cases, field telephones. By the 1950s, though, French torturers had settled on the field telephone as the primary form of magneto torture, a choice that would have a lasting effect on torture for the next three decades.

Indochina, 1931

In February 1930, colonial troops loyal to the Nationalist Party mutinied at military posts in northern Tonkin. This was called the Yen Bay Mutiny. The French reaction was swift and merciless. Foreign legionnaires arrived by the summer. Political disorder spread, as did a crime wave exacerbated by the world economic depression, and police repression increased dramatically.[9]

In 1931, a French journalist, Andrée Viollis, described the common tortures practiced in Vietnam. She concluded with a list of electric tortures, gathered from political prisoners:

> First, attach an end of wire to the arm or leg and introduce the other end into the genitals; pass current through them. Second, join together a whip of steel wires interlaced with an electric current; each blow of this instrument causes the patient such intense pain that he is reduced to asking for mercy and to confessing. Third, attach one [outlet] to the hands of the prisoner by a metallic wire that one plugs then into the circuit. Each time that one turns the commutator, the jolt is so violent that it is impossible to endure it for more than two or three times. These tortures were particularly honored and practiced daily during the year 1931 at the Police Commissariat at Binh-Donj (ville de Cholon).[10]

This is the earliest account of systematic state torture using electricity. The date is striking. It is four or five years before the Argentine police adopt the *picana eléctrica*, the Spanish SIM invents the electric chair, and the Brazilians use live wires. It is over a decade before Marty turns to magneto torture in Toulouse on behalf of Vichy. A decade before Dorthea Binz swung her electric whip at Ravensbrück, French torturers had fashioned one in Vietnam.

French colonial torture was not new. In Vietnam in the 1920s, as in France, police sweated and beat common criminals during interrogation. Increasingly the *passage à tabac* also fell on political prisoners. In a trial in 1927, for example, a gendarme testified that he walked in on two colonial Sûreté agents torturing a prisoner. This episodic torture became normal by 1930.[11]

Prisoners described the various tortures in articles in *La Lutte*, a left-wing Vietnamese journal in the 1930s. The most feared torture was the *crapaudine*. The prisoner is laid flat on his stomach. Torturers pull the arms and feet together behind the back until they touch. The body bends out like a bow. Then torturers press a foot against the ribs, "producing an unconscious muscular reaction (unconscious because 99 times out of 100, the victim loses consciousness), the reaction yields blood from the nose, mouth, the ears, and the anus."[12]

The *crapaudine* was a French military field punishment that had been abolished a decade or so earlier.[13] It means "the toad," though *à la crapaudine* means to cut open and broil. The Vietnamese called the torture appropriately the *lan mé ga*, "turning your guts inside out."[14] They had no doubts why the Sûreté favored it: It was "particularly loved by torturers because it leaves no apparent traces."[15]

Reports from *La Lutte* suggest that police stations differed in the cleanliness of their tortures. "In Saigon, tortures are performed with lots of know-how, and they have at least one goal: getting confessions without leaving marks."[16] Saigon torturers used clean tortures like the *crapaudine*, "diverse electric tortures," sleep deprivation, meals of salted rice to induce dehydration, starvation, and the *falaka*, the beating of the soles of the feet. Doctors were either unwilling or unable to diagnose the marks of torture as such.[17]

Such care was sometimes disregarded. For example, the Sûreté Générale subjected Tran Phu, the Communist Party secretary, to the *crapaudine*, then tried to bribe him, and then dehydrated him. Finally they burned his hands, tore his hair, slit the soles of his feet, put cotton soaked in alcohol in the slots, and burned it. Tran Phu died two days later.[18]

In the provinces, police were less clean. They whipped, pricked with pins, and pierced eardrums with thin *baguettes*. Even here though, there was some concern with cleanliness in torture. According to *La Lutte*, by the mid-1930s, "the beating of the soles of the feet" had been "imported to provinces from Saigon."[19] Local police also sometimes beat cleanly, or poured pimento-spiced *saumure* [brine] into orifices.

Viollis's list of standard tortures does not capture all the techniques prisoners report in *La Lutte*, but it mentions many of them.[20] This list also mentions four of the six standard tortures Labussière will itemize at Nuremberg: whipping, burning, suspension, and electric torture. Viollis omits the bathtub and testicle-crushing machines.

To be precise, Viollis distinguishes between "archaic" tortures and "modern" tortures, "all of which have been invented and practiced, notably by the Sûreté de Cholon."[21] Classical tortures include starvation, dehydration, the *fa-*

laka, pins under fingernails, "the wood press," "a funnel of petrol," suspension by the hands, and tongs that squeezed the temples until eyes popped out.[22] Tortures for young women included rape, suspensions by the toes, *falaka*, flogging, and "a nest of ants introduced into their intimate parts."[23]

Under modern tortures, Viollis lists the *crapaudine* (two styles); electrotorture; introducing "a spiral metal wire into the urinary tract" and pulling out brusquely; and a razor technique. This last involved the following steps: "With a razor blade, cut the skin of the feet in long furrows, fill up the wounds with cotton and set fire to the cotton."[24] What historians of the French Gestapo regarded as the peculiar technique of Lamote/Paoli was, according to Viollis, a standard practice in colonial Vietnam.

Viollis describes French police using not one, but *three* types of electrotorture. Two of them have no future in Vietnam: live wires and electric whipping. In 1936, *La Lutte* mentions only how "prisoners screamed before the 'magneto.' "[25] It seems interrogators settled on the one device that left the least marks and produced the lowest fatalities. The Saigon magneto does not appear to be a *gégène*, the army signals magneto. Viollis's description suggests a commutated magneto from an automobile.

So, in 1931, the French police in Vietnam were practicing stealthy magneto torture. In 1949, after an absence of fifteen years, the journalist Jacques Chégaray returned to Indochina. He visited a young officer in Tonkin in his post in the outback, at Phul-Cong.

> "You are a journalist from France? Delighted. Come see my home. Here, this is the lookout post; over there, the PC [command post] of the company."
>
> We enter; everything is in impeccable order. I congratulate him.
>
> "Here," he continues, "is my office. Table, typewriter, washbasin; and in the corner, the machine to make one talk."
>
> As I seem not to understand, he adds, "Yeah, sure, the dynamo [magneto]! It is a good handy way to interrogate the prisoners. The contact, the positive pole, and the negative pole; turn the handle and the prisoner spits [it out]."
>
> He resumes in the same tone: "Over there, the telephone; here, the rack for the maps of the general staff; over there, etc."[26]

One year after the execution of sinister Inspector Marty in Toulouse, this officer seems unaware that he is using exactly the same device Marty did. Should one say that the young officer in 1949 learned his technique in Paris from the French Gestapo? More likely, what one is looking at is something quite indigenous, so much a part of the office furniture in Indochina it was entirely acceptable.

Out of Indochina

Magneto torture first appeared in France in 1943, most probably introduced by the Marty Brigade in Toulouse, as I argued in part II. Magneto torture then spread rapidly through the French Gestapo and Milice. Most European electro-torturers in 1943 were French policemen (Marty, Poinsot, and Vasseur), former French soldiers (Normand and Touvier), or French criminals (Cornet and Gallino). Among them, the technique was well known. The question, then, is how magneto torture came to France. Perhaps it was Marty's independent innovation. However, in light of the French colonial police's extensive use of magneto torture in Indochina, it seems more plausible to think that it traveled through backroom apprenticeships in the French military and colonial police to France. Marty's Brigade was one conduit, but probably not the only one.

It is a tempting hypothesis, but the difficulty lies in connecting the dots between Vietnam in 1936 and France in 1943. Marty worked in North Africa before 1943, but little is known about his earlier history in the French colonial police. Moreover, some avenues of transmission can be eliminated. Outside of Indochina, between 1900 and 1943, prisoners do not report electrotorture in the Third Republic—not in France, or among the Legion's penal battalions in North Africa or in the *bagnards*, the grim prisons of French Guyana and New Caledonia.[27] One can also eliminate centralized training and transmission by the Sûreté. No one reports torture classes in Indochina. Torturers drew on what was at hand or what they had heard about. In a political crisis, they did not have the time to be inventive.

In favor of the hypothesis, however, there is some evidence that *other* torture techniques circulated by means of backroom apprenticeships, and that these techniques traveled between French police and the military as well as circulating geographically within the French colonial system. For example, the Foreign Legion prohibited the *crapaudine* in 1909 and, when the first attempt to stamp it out failed, again in 1920.[28] Yet police in Vietnam were still practicing it a decade later. Either legionnaires continued the practice surreptitiously (after all, it was a clean torture) or some old soldiers showed younger police how to do it. And there was the distinctive police razor technique: cutting slits on the soles and burning cotton soaked in alcohol in the slits or between the toes. This standard Vietnamese practice appears a decade later in Paoli's torture chambers in Bourges, as well as other French prisons.[29]

Additionally, what is striking is that the French torturers in Europe uniformly preferred magnetos for torture, even though they were indifferent as to the kind of magneto (unlike later French torturers, who strongly favored the field telephone). The Vichy Milice used a refrigerator magneto—probably from a commercial freezer. The Lyon Milice used a magneto from a Berliet car. The Paris Milice performed clean electrotorture with an aviation magneto. It was a magneto attached to a large steering wheel that the operator "drove." The device released less than one milliampere, but between ten thousand and fifteen thousand volts, roughly competitive with the *picana eléctrica*.[30] The Foix Milice used an odd dynamo that had three connections: to a lamp, to the victim's body, and to a white metal casing that was used as an electric prod.[31] All this suggests something of a craft tradition, in which people passed on a basic knowledge of how to torture using magnetos, but the device was determined largely by availability and chance.

So it is plausible to argue that magneto torture passed through the French colonial system from Indochina to France. Still, there is an alterative hypothesis that is worth exploring. The French Sûreté in Indochina was not the only Asian electrotorturer in the thirties. The Japanese military police, the Kempeitai, also used electrotorture, including, occasionally, magnetos. It is possible to speculate that they passed on magneto torture to the European torturers. To explore this hypothesis, one needs to reconstruct the pattern of Japanese torture in the 1930s and during World War II.

Korea, 1931

Let me start first with police torture in Japan and then turn to Korea. Reports suggest that while the Kempeitai did not use electrotorture in Japan, it did not hesitate to do so in Korea.

Japan

In 1928, a European observer identified the following tortures.[32] Police boxed suspects in a small space and poured water on their face until they confessed. They twisted arms, beat heads, pricked with sharp splinters, and poked with red-hot irons. They placed a flat timber over the ankles of a kneeling suspect and then pressed down until the joints came apart (ankle spreading).[33] In 1933, the novelist Kobayashi Takiji died in police custody. His body bore signs of beating, kicking, and hot tongs to the forehead. His fingers were broken. His thighs had a dozen holes "as if made by a nail or drill."[34]

Police also suspended prisoners by the fingers with the toes barely touching the floor; when the prisoner rested his heels, he pulled his fingers out of their socket. More severely, police roped the prisoner's hands behind his back and pulled him up to the ceiling, a procedure that slowly disjoins the shoulders.

Nishijima Shigetada, a Marxist activist, was suspended in this manner, beaten, and poked with a hot iron.[35]

Between 1941 and 1942, police arrested leftists and foreigners, subjecting them to torture.[36] Interrogation included continuous slapping (sometimes until the face was cut), suspension, beating, hair pulling, finger breaking, and forcing suspects to kneel for hours (with stamping on ankles). Interrogators pressed pencils between fingers and burned suspects with cigarettes. During the war, prisoners held on the Japanese mainland reported "water treatment" (Tokyo), burning (Kawasaki), suspension (Tokyo, Yokkaichi), kneeling on sharp instruments (Fukuoka, Omuta), having nails pulled (Yamani), and the knee spread (Tokyo).[37] Similar to the ankle spread, the knee spread required prisoners to kneel with a pole over the calves and beneath the thighs; the pole would sometimes be three inches in diameter. Guards then brought pressure on the thighs, sometimes by jumping on them, causing the knee joints to separate.[38] Lastly, it is worth noting that it was not prisoners alone who were subjected to some techniques. In 1946, Prime Minister Tojo observed, for example, that hard slapping, though forbidden, was also customary practice in the Japanese navy and army for training recalcitrant cadets.[39]

Korea

In 1910, Japan annexed Korea. During the period of "Military Rule" (1910–19), torture consisted primarily of flogging.[40] In March 1919, many Koreans protested for independence. In the period of "Cultural Rule" that followed, the Japanese repealed the Flogging Ordinance, but expanded police forces. Along with this came lengthy detention and torture.[41]

The first named cases of electrotorture appear in the 1930s.[42] Pak Se-yong, a twenty-four-year-year-old activist from Kijang, claimed that police subjected him to electrotorture in 1930.[43] Chong In-hwa, another activist, also described electrotorture in this period.[44] He claimed it happened while assisting the independence leader Kim Ku. The Japanese had exiled Kim Ku to China in 1919. In 1931 he began organizing the Korean Patriotic Corps. It seems likely that this was roughly when police tortured Chong In-hwa.

In 1942, Japanese arrested Westerners in Korea and Manchuria. Interrogators slapped them continuously and flogged them with rubber hoses and belts. They pumped the prisoners: they tied their knees to their chests, and then forced water down the throat with teakettle funnels. In Harbin, British and American prisoners described "electric treatment" that they characterized as "near-electrocution."[45]

Out of Korea

Prosecutors for the International Military Tribunal for the Far East (IMTFE), the sister to the Nuremberg tribunal, mapped Kempeitai torture after Korea. Interrogators in disparate regions shared a core style: beating, whipping, burning, forced kneeling (often on sharp objects), the knee spread, suspension, pumping stomachs with water (usually with a teapot), and magneto torture. Torture was not clean; it left permanent scars and injuries.

In mapping this pattern, the IMTFE prosecutors faced the same obstacles as the Nuremberg tribunal in finding documentary evidence of torture. During the war, the Japanese government generally ignored customary rules governing treatment of prisoners. This included denying visits to POW camps by neutral states designated by an enemy (in this case the Swiss government), restricting such visits when they were allowed, refusing to forward to the neutral states lists of prisoners taken and civilians interned, and censoring news relating to prisoners and internees, including letters from prisoners.[46] When the Japanese surrendered, the chief of the prisoner of war camps ordered all incriminating documentary evidence to be destroyed, and all those who "mistreated prisoners of war" were "permitted to take care of it by immediately transferring or by fleeing without trace."[47] The order was sent to camps in Formosa, Korea, Manchuria, North China, Hong Kong, Borneo, Thailand, Malaya, and Java.[48]

Consequently, the IMTFE prosecutors had to reconstruct the pattern of torture, grouping prisoner affidavits by region. They documented the core techniques not only among the Kempeitai throughout Asia, but also among other army and navy units, camp guards, and local police organized by the Kempeitai. "Such uniformity," concluded the IMTFE, "cannot have arisen by chance."[49] The IMTFE returned guilty verdicts on counts of torture. The summary that follows describes what the IMTFE found by region, starting with the occupation of China in 1937, followed by the regions occupied during World War II. I have supplemented these findings with prisoners' accounts where they are available.

China. In 1937, Japanese forces occupied Shanghai. The main tortures were beating (punches, slaps, kicks), flogging (with a hose, riding crop, bamboo bat, or stock), pumping stomachs with water, forced standing and kneeling, and electrotorture.[50] Torturers soaked prisoners, tied them to a painter's ladder, tied wires to the genitals, and then applied electricity with "a hand manipulated shocking coil."[51]

"Officers did not give explicit directions for questioning, but merely ordered so and so out for interrogation." Sergeants and interpreters adopted tortures as they saw fit: "Each handled the prisoner according to his own ideas."[52]

Supplementary tortures included burning with cigarettes, toenail removal, "rack torture," and "others too numerous to mention."[53]

Prisoners also reported "water treatment," burning, and electrotorture in Beijing, knee spreads and suspension in Nanking, and burning in Hanko and Nomonhan.[54]

Singapore and Malaysia. The main tortures were beating, flogging with knotted ropes and bamboo canes, burning with cigarettes and irons, forced sitting for hours on the floor, forced kneeling on sharp objects, needles under the nails, pumping with water (dubbed the "Tokio-wine treatment"), choking (with a wet cloth or in a tub or oil drum), suspension, and electrotorture.[55] There were two kinds of electrotorture. First, "An induction coil was used, one electrode being attached to the hand or foot and the other wire applied to various parts of the body." The second kind, "apparently more severe, was called the electric table or electric cap. There is evidence that this was used by [sic: but] not on any of our witnesses."[56]

"Every guard was a law unto himself."[57] Supplementary tortures included "ju-jitsu, twisting of limbs, bending back of fingers, twisting of sharp-edged wood between fingers, punching, repeated blows on the same spot, and so on." Later, interrogators would tear the scab with a frayed bamboo end, leaving permanent scars.[58] Prisoners also reported burning and suspension elsewhere in Malaysia, including Ipoh, Victoria Point, and Kuala Lumpur.[59]

Burma-Siam (Thailand) Railroad. Prisoners on this jungle project reported beating, flogging, genital burning, and pumping with water. Guards suspended prisoners, or stuck hot steel pins beneath the nails. Positional tortures included forced standing, holding heavy objects, and forced kneeling on sharp sticks while holding heavy rocks.[60] At Tavoy and Chumporn, prisoners were subjected to the knee spread and at Chumporn to electrotorture.[61]

Andaman and Nicobar Islands. Cellular Prison at Port Blair was a well-known British penal colony in the Indian Ocean. When the Japanese occupied the Andamans, they used the prison facilities there and at Kakana on the Nicobar Islands. Prisoners report the "water treatment," burning, knee spreads, and kneeling on sharp instruments.[62]

Vietnam (French Indochina). Prisoners were beaten, kicked, and flogged (with rods, truncheons, whips, belts, and rulers with metal edges). They were suspended by the thumbs, burned with cigarettes and lighted tapers, and forced to kneel for hours on broken bricks or sharp-edged wooden bars.[63] Then there was magneto torture. "The gendarme who worked the magneto and twisted my testicles was called the 'American.' I can recognize him."[64] Prisoners reported electrotorture, in particular, at detention centers in Hanoi and Mytho.[65] Interrogators also pumped stomachs with a teapot. They occasionally used the classical European technique, covering the face with cloth and then slowly soaking the cloth with water.[66] In one case, during pumping, torturers applied an electrified plate to the feet.[67]

The Philippines. Prisoners reported slapping, suspension, forced kneeling on sharp objects, forced knee spreads, having nails pulled, being pricked with sharp objects, forced standing and sitting, burning, squeezing skulls with rubber bands, and beating (with a huge variety of objects). Water torture included pumping stomachs with a hose (sometimes with soapy water) and choking (with a wet cloth or dunking in a tub or toilet bowl). Finger bandaging involved binding cartridges or pencils to fingers and then squeezing the hand gently or forcefully. "Sun treatment" involved tying prisoners to the ground with their faces toward the sun, propping the upper eyelid open with thin sticks, and forcing prisoners to stare at the sun for hours.[68]

Prisoners also report five types of electrotorture. One involved tying an EE5 telephone to the feet. This device was an old "lineman telephone," consisting of two binding posts to which one connected wires and a crank to generate a ring. When it rang, it delivered a shock. The shock lasted four to five minutes.[69] Three other electrotortures used the main power grid to electrify metal chairs, brass tabletops, and metal rings on the fingers. A fifth was exclusively for women; the torturer thrust an electrode "shaped like a curling iron up her vagina."[70]

Taiwan (Formosa). Torture included beating, water treatment, forced sitting, and forced standing with heavy buckets of water.[71] In 1945, a Korean described her torture as a comfort woman in Taiwan. A Kempeitai officer "pulled the phone cords and coiled them around my wrist and ankles. Then he said 'konoyaro'["you swine"] and turned the phone handle. My eyes and my body were shivering."[72]

Borneo. Here a Kempeitai torturer confessed to using pumping and electrotorture.[73] Torturers also used the ancient technique of beating lightly but repeatedly in the same spot until the flesh was highly sensitive. IMTFE affidavits list beating, flogging, suspension, burning (often with cigarettes), ankle spreading, knee spreading, forced sitting, pumping with water, and sometimes the Dutch style in choking.[74] Torturers varied pumping by feeding starved prisoners large amounts of uncooked rice, and then pumping them full of water ("rice torture").[75] Rice expands slowly when soaked. Guards also used a sweatbox ("Esau").[76]

Java. IMTFE affidavits report permanent scars from beatings, flogging (with a bamboo stick, dog whip, or ruler), scorching with cigarettes, pumping with water, and electrotorture.[77] "To prevent monotony, he [the interrogator] gave me electrization . . . if I am not gravely mistaken, it was altogether 39 times."[78] Prisoners report electrotorture in particular at camps in Batavia, Buitenzorg, and Semarang.[79]

Sumatra. Prisoners were beaten with cudgels, flogged, slapped, suspended, forced to stand at attention for hours, subjected to the water treatment and knee spreads, and burned with hot pokers.[80]

Micronesia, Timor, the Moluccas, the Solomons, and the Celebes. Torture on these islands consisted of severe beatings, floggings, pumping with water, hard slapping, burning with cigarettes, and suspension. Positional tortures included holding the "press up" position indefinitely, kneeling on sharp objects for hours, and standing, often while holding heavy objects.[81] On the Celebes, exhaustion exercises were common, in particular, crawling on one's stomach ("the lizard").[82]

The Kempeitai resembled a guild, with a high degree of group solidarity and coherence.[83] Unlike the Gestapo, regional Kempeitai did not become semiautonomous. They rarely used foreign auxiliaries for coercive interrogation.

Interrogators apprenticed in the field, learning core techniques. Uno Shintaro, a Kempeitai interrogator in China, states, "There really wasn't any concrete training for intelligence-gathering." Nevertheless, he took his responsibility seriously, selecting "capable soldiers and noncoms who understood Chinese and trained them" as he saw fit.[84] Prisoner affidavits also confirm that officers expected interrogators to produce results, but left the details to them.

If detailed torture manuals from a Kempeitai torture university exist, they are not widely available.[85] *Notes for the Interrogation of Prisoners of War* (1943), marked "Top Secret," authorizes torture, but does not regulate the practice. It leaves it to interrogators to produce results, offering no standardized procedures. It states simply, "The following are methods normally to be adopted: (a) Torture. This includes kicking, beating and anything connected with physical suffering."[86]

The Lost History of the Magneto

Looking back, one may safely conclude that magneto torture became common in Asia around the Great Depression. The French Sûreté and the Japanese

Kempeitai institutionalized it between 1930 and 1931. By 1945, the Japanese knew how to use a portable phone, what the French called the *gégène*, for torture.

We may never know whether the French in Indochina learned from the Japanese in Korea or the reverse. Or perhaps these were independent innovations. What is certain is that the two police used magneto torture differently. The Kempeitai did not care whether it left marks, whereas prisoners report that this mattered greatly to the French Sûreté. It is not clear why police in a French colony cared, while the police in a Japanese colony did not. But one might speculate that the conditions here resemble those mentioned elsewhere in the book as triggering stealth. Once again, we have police and troops of a democratic country using torture under conditions where there was, if not a free press, at least a vociferous alternative one that documented the treatment of prisoners. And authors like Viollis publicized torture well beyond the confines of Indochina, bringing the news back to France of the violence of the Yen Bay Mutiny.

The next country to adopt magneto torture was Hungary, possibly as early as 1941.[87] In 1943, Egon Balas, a Romanian prisoner, described the device as "a generator that one of the agents held in his lap while he turned its handle. . . . The faster the handle was turned, the stronger the current that coursed through my body." Torturers tied one wire to his ankle and applied the other to his head, neck, genitals, or inside his mouth. They used electrotorture to frighten and intimidate prisoners, not because it was clean.[88] Generally, Hungarian torture left scars.[89]

Next, the French Gestapo adopted the magneto, starting with Inspector Marty in Toulouse in 1943. The most plausible hypothesis is that magneto torture passed through the French colonial system from Indochina to France. This makes the most sense of the chronology, incidence, and frequency of the technique.

But let me now consider the alternative hypothesis I raised earlier in this chapter. Perhaps the Kempeitai passed it on to the Gestapo who then gave it to the French Gestapo. This hypothesis traces torture using established military connections between Axis powers. Tempting as this hypothesis might be, it is unconvincing in several respects.

This hypothesis does not explain why most early magneto torturers were French policemen, criminals, and legionnaires and why the first record of German officers using a magneto to conduct torture is in Toulouse in 1943. German military connections to the Japanese date to the early 1930s, but the Gestapo does not adopt these techniques from the Kempeitai at the same date. There certainly was ample opportunity. In March 1945, the U.S. War Department identified twelve different types of dynamos for field radio-telephones in the German military.[90]

Moreover, the Gestapo was unfamiliar with other common Kempeitai techniques. For example, Kempeitai agents favored pumping stomachs with water in every region of Asia; it was more common that electrotorture. The Main Security Office in Berlin treated Masuy's bathtub in 1943 as a discovery.

Following the military brass is not a reliable substitute for mapping the chronology and incidence of torture techniques. If it were, the parsimonious hypothesis would point to a Hungarian origin. Hungary was a more proximate Axis ally and it adopted magneto torture shortly before the Gestapo. Even this third hypothesis cannot explain the French character of magneto torture.

In the end, the pattern of the distribution of torture techniques suggests that the most plausible hypothesis is that magneto torture passed through the French colonial system from Indochina to France during World War II, and then spread to the German Gestapo and possibly to the Hungarians.

French and British Electrotorture after World War II

With the defeat of the Axis powers, magneto torture almost disappears world-wide. The main exception is in British and French colonies. The French used magneto torture in Vietnam as early as 1949, and there is at least one allegation of electrotorture in France as early as 1947 or 1948.[91] The British used electrotorture in Kenya in the early 1950s, including at least one use of magneto torture.

But the subsequent trajectory of British and French electrotorture varies significantly. British police in other colonies did not take up electrotorture, or, if they did, they quickly abandoned it. Although torture occurred in various British colonies, the British style did not include electrotorture (as I document in part IV). After their defeat in Vietnam, the French military carried over the routine use of magneto torture to Algeria, and the characteristic French usages here set the style for torturers worldwide for the next thirty years. Let me consider first the British usage, and then the French.

Until recently, it was not generally known that "electric shock was widely used" during the British counterinsurgency campaign in Kenya.[92] Difficult prisoners were sent to the Mau Mau Investigation Center, an intelligence unit run by the British Special Branch, which had "a way of slowly electrocuting a Kuke—they'd rough up one for days." One settler describes participating in this torture on one occasion, but "things got a little out of hand. By the time I cut his balls off he had no ears and his eyeball, the right one, I think was hanging out of its socket. Too bad, he died before we got much out of him."[93]

As this description suggests, electrotorture in Kenya occurred in the context of scarring tortures. Standard procedures included flogging, beating with sticks, cutting with knives, castration, shoving broken bottles, sand, and hot eggs into rectums and vaginas, wrapping suspects in coils of barbed wire, suspending prisoners by the feet until blood ran from their noses and ears. There are also occasional reports of other techniques that leave few marks, including sleep deprivation, forced standing, choking in water, the use of irritants such as pepper or soap, and punitive exercises, but these also occur amid other scarring tortures. British agents did not care whether they left marks or not. Indeed, torture was a public spectacle in many cases.[94]

The British counterinsurgency campaign in Kenya contrasts sharply in this respect with the French campaign in Algeria, where directives emphasized torturers should leave no marks. Moreover, unlike the French, British torturers did not appear to have a preferred device for electrotorture such as the army signals magneto or *gégène*. In the known cases, British torturers appear to use what was at hand, including the battery of a Land Rover and the generator of a police station.[95] One prisoner remembers a "small conductor" used at the Ruthigiti Post, and she offers a description that closely resembles magneto torture.[96]

There are few reports of British electrotorture before or after Kenya. There is only one report of British electrotorture before this date, at Cellular Prison in the Andaman Islands in 1912.[97] German prisoners at the London Cage (1940–48), a clandestine military prison with a brutal interrogation regimen, reported that they were "threatened with electrical devices," but none reported that interrogators used such devices on prisoners.[98] In the 1950s, the journalist Charles Foley heard rumors of electrotorture in Cyprus but was never able to confirm it.[99] Another journalist, John Barry, reports that a British Special Branch interrogator in Cyprus told him he had a "bad experience" with electrotorture once and abandoned it, "Nuff said."[100] Prisoners do not report electrotorture in Aden, and the only cases from Northern Ireland involve five men tortured between 1971 and 1972.[101] All this suggests that British torturers, for whatever reason, did not favor electrotorture.

This could not be said of the French colonial police and military; they not only favored magneto torture, but elected to use it in a particular form: the army signals magneto or *gégène*. It is difficult to know when after the war the French adopted torture by field telephone. An officer who served in Indochina before going to Algeria explained that colonial practices circulated not only among the Vichy French, but also the Free French.

> What happened afterward in Algeria were methods of torture that were imported in our units in 1939–1945 by a fringe of officers from the colonial army. I knew one of them. He was, to my knowledge, the first

one to use the *gégène*. In any case, it's a problem inherent in the colonial system. The English were worse than us! There was such hatred of the human beings in front of us that all methods were good for reaching our goals![102]

Indeed, what is certain is that torture quickly reappeared in French territories after the war: Algeria (1945), Indochina (1946), Madagascar (1947), and France (1947–48). By 1957, the *gégène* was the queen of torments.

Algeria. For most of the twentieth century, the French colonial police routinely beat Algerian suspects.[103] One colonial described seeing his father, a policeman in North Africa, beating and "torturing men in the grilling-hot courtyard of some Algerian police station."[104] General de Gaulle tried to reduce the inequities in 1944, but failed.[105] After the nationalist insurrection in Sétif in May 1945, police violence and torture was routine.[106] In August 1947, Algerian deputies compared police tactics to the Gestapo.[107] In 1950, a French prefect submitted "eighty complaints of acts of torture."[108]

France. Police textbooks after the war recommended sweating and beating.[109] Alec Mellor, the postwar torture scholar, recorded six cases between 1947 and 1948 where the police "used methods worthy of the Gestapo to compel confessions."[110] The most notorious was that of M. Cavailhié, who collaborated with the Abwehr, German Military Intelligence. At his trial, Cavailhié declared Paris police had beaten him. The judge was unmoved, replying that he should not have been surprised. As a member of the Abwehr, "he was used to it."[111] Then Cavailhié shocked everyone, alleging that police in Nice had subjected him to the *baignoire*, torture of the bathtub, and electrotorture.[112]

Madagascar. In 1947, the French army crushed a rebellion in Madagascar. In 1948, the Sûreté interrogated the three Madgascaran deputies, releasing their confessions as instigators of the rebellion. At their trial, the deputies withdrew their confessions, charging the Sûreté had tortured them, as well as the alleged witnesses, to make false confessions. They claimed agents beat them and then subjected them to the ordeal of the bathtub.[113] In the absence of telling marks, "It became hard for the public to decide where the truth lay."[114]

Indochina. In 1946, nationalist protests led to the first Indochinese War (1946–54). By 1949, Jacques Chégaray reported magneto torture in Vietnam. France withdrew its troops from Vietnam in 1954, soon redeploying many of these regiments to Algeria.[115] There was "not enough time for the 'bad habits' to be forgotten," observed a French historian.[116] Then came the Algerian Revolution and the *gégène*.

The Colonial Police and Wuillaume's List

The Algerian Revolution, and the place of torture in it, has been exceedingly well documented.[117] Here, I simply map changes in torture techniques during the revolution, and the main change was this. In 1954, torturers favored water torture over electrotorture. By 1957, torturers used the *gégène* almost exclusively for certain interrogations. In this section, I describe torture in 1954, and then I turn to the factors that led to the rise of the *gégène*.

In 1954, the French government sent Roger Wuillaume, the inspector general for administration, to investigate numerous allegations of police torture in Algeria. He spoke with prisoners and policemen.[118] All, either publicly or privately, confirmed that torture was routine. Wuillaume listed the standard tortures:

1. Imprisonment, for periods in excess of twenty-four hours, in some cases up to 15 or 20 days.
2. Beatings with fists, sticks or whips.
3. The *baignoire* [bathtub]. The person is held under water until he is practically suffocated or has even lost his consciousness.
4. The *tuyau* [water-pipe] method. A tube similar to a piece of gas piping is connected to a tap, or failing that a jerrican or other container. The victim's wrists and ankles are tied with his arms and legs bent and he is so held that his elbows are slightly below his knees; a thick stick is then passed between the elbows and knees. Once he is thus trussed up, he is rolled backward on to an old tyre or inner tube where he is firmly wedged. His eyes are bandaged, his nose is stopped up, the tube thrust into his mouth, and water passed through it until he is practically suffocated or loses consciousness.
5. Electrical method. Two electrical leads are connected to the mains [wall socket] and their bare ends applied like red-hot needles to the most sensitive parts of the body such as armpits, neck, nostrils, anus, penis or feet. Alternatively the two wires are wound one round each ear or one round each ankle or one round a finger and the other round the penis. If mains electricity is not available, the field electrical supply is used or the batteries of the signals W/T [wireless telegraphy] sets.[119]

Wuillaume observed that, judging by its frequency, police favored the *tuyau* or pumping with water over all other tortures.[120] Pumping, as I explained in chapter 5, produces the most intense pain visceral tissue can experience; this was why Inquisitional torturers valued it. In addition, pumping would not kill the victim, whereas live wires from the main power grid risked cardiac arrest.[121] Torturers recommended, as the safest electrical procedure, many pricks "as if using a red-hot needle."[122] Police favored using the mains over magnetos. Unlike Vietnam, the *gégène* was a secondary electrotorture device in 1954.

Wuillaume's list highlights clean tortures. Torturers explained to him how they prevented inadvertent death and left few marks. If there were bruises, the detention period was long enough for most to disappear.[123] Magistrates saw only prisoners who were "in good shape."[124] Wuillaume observed that the gendarmes cared less about leaving marks. Publicity mattered in the cities, whereas scars on peasants did not matter.[125]

In the absence of scars, Wuillaume was persuaded that pumping was similar to being deprived of a cigarette. Wuillaume recommended that the government legalize this standard Inquisitional torture. "I am inclined to think that these procedures can be accepted and that, if used in the controlled manner described to me, they are no more brutal than deprivation of food, drink and tobacco, which are however accepted."[126]

Wuillaume offered three arguments.[127] The usual roughing up (*passage à tabac*) had no effect on Algerians, who lived extraordinarily hard lives. Besides, these techniques were far more civilized than sweating. In the spirit of Masuy, Wuillaume argued that properly used, these techniques "produce a shock which is more psychological than physical and therefore do not constitute excessive cruelty."[128] Lastly, police told him they would inevitably turn to them, whether they were legal or not. Prohibiting them would simply drive them underground. Better, then, to legalize and regulate these techniques than to deny them hypocritically.

The Triumph of the *Gégène*

In February 1957, General Massu and his paramilitary troops ("Paras") assumed the policing of Algiers. Massu argued any means were acceptable in gathering information against terrorists. "Speed is critical," he insisted, and he authorized torture.[129] Massu had his staff bring a *gégène* to his office, where he tried it on himself.[130] " 'Was there really torture?' I can only reply in the affirmative, although it was never either institutionalised or codified. . . . I am not frightened of the word."[131]

At Camp Jeanne d'Arc, instructions itemized what mattered:

(1) Torture must be clean. (2) It must not happen in the presence of young soldiers. (3) It must not happen in the presence of sadists. (4) It must be carried out in the presence of an officer or someone responsible. (5) It must be humane, that is to say, it must stop the moment the man has talked — and, above all, it must leave no trace.

With these conditions satisfied you have a right to water and electricity.[132]

The police favored pumping with water, though "from September, 1956, on certain questionings were carried on exclusively by electricity."[133] After 1957, military torturers favored the *gégène* (slang for *génératrice*).[134]

In June 1960, a magistrate produced a *gégène* in court in Paris. It was "a curiously shaped object, a narrow, cylindrical machine which, from a distance, looked rather like a small duplicator minus its revolving drum. It had a small winding-handle or crank, and wires attached to terminals on one side."[135] The term *gégène* encompassed both magnetos from field telephones (EE8) and the larger "Wolf," which inflicted a different quality of pain.[136] "Instead of the sharp and rapid spasms that seemed to tear my body in two, a greater pain now stretched all my muscles and racked them for a longer time."[137]

Water and magnetos were nonlethal and clean. The *gégène* had a distinct advantage over water and other magnetos: it was intimately bound up in military practice. One might wonder what police were doing with a refrigerator magneto or why Paras spent so much time in the bathroom with the prisoner. Who would question why soldiers were carrying portable communications devices? Could there even be a modern army without the *gégène*?

Linkage is a simple principle: organize a situation such that one cannot do X (which is desirable) without also causing Y (which is not desired). Human and machines are woven together such that, to remove one element, one must undo the entire network. This raises the stakes. As a substitute is too costly and time-consuming, the status quo remains undisturbed.

The politicians were helpless. Paras used the *gégène* no matter how much politicians condemned it. By 1957, the *gégène* displaced pumping with water as the most frequent torture. In his famous torture memoir, Henri Alleg described five electrotorture sessions, far more than any other torture. He was choked with water only once.[138] In the sensational *Gangrene*, four prisoners described electrotorture, two did exhaustion exercises, and only one was choked with water.[139]

The *gégène* was portable, painful, flexible, multifunctional, free (indeed, government supplied), widely available, familiar to operate and maintain, and easily excusable. It generated far less amperage than the mains, reducing the risk of death. It left few marks. Torture advocates argued to a credulous public that electrotorture was "nothing serious."[140] When Massu saw Alleg in front of the Palais de Justice in 1970, he compared Alleg's "reassuring dynamism" with the scarred bodies of FLN victims. "Do the torments that he suffered count for much alongside the cutting off of the nose or of the lips, when it was not the penis, which had become the ritual present of the *fellaghas* to their recalcitrant 'brothers'? Everyone knows that these bodily appendages don't grow again.' "[141]

Nevertheless, magnetos required hands-on training. "The whole art consisted in handling it well."[142] In the absence of marks, soldiers sometimes misjudged how vulnerable the victim was, inadvertently killing her.[143] "I heard S—— say to the person who was working the magneto: "do it by little shocks: first you slow down then you start again."[144] Torturers had to sponge "with water in order . . . 'to leave no traces and increase the pain.' "[145] Other tricks of the trade included wrapping the body in a wet sheet, wrapping extremities in gloves or socks, and placing cardboard underneath the alligator clips.[146] Electrotorture also hardened muscles and locked jaws, sometimes so severely victims bit through the electrified wire in their mouth.[147] Torturers had to learn to loosen these.

Algeria, 1960

"Torture by electricity," wrote a French soldier, "first looked upon as useful, then as indispensable, has finally come to be considered matter-of-course, just as normal and proper as any other."[148] Henri Pouillot, who conducted a dozen torture sessions daily at Villa Sussini, calculated he subjected six hundred to a thousand individuals to magneto and water torture during his ten months of service (June 1961–March 1962).[149]

By 1960, the Paras had dramatically diversified the practice of electrotorture. Hafid Keramane, for example, offers a comprehensive list of tortures from this period. He identifies three broad classes of electrotorture.[150]

1. Magneto torture. Torturers strapped the victim down, soaked him, attached wires to his extremities, and cranked the magneto. Variants involved making the bound victim stand in a bucket of water or tying the victim to a metal ladder. The latter was applied mainly to young girls at the Villa Susini.
2. The electrified prod, typical of General Massu's headquarters, PC El Biar. The bound victim sat in a pool of water. Wearing rubber gloves and wooden clogs, torturers applied a long, electrified metal stick. "This operation sometimes leaves traces for more than 20 days."
3. The electric bath, *bain électrique*. Torturers placed the victim in a deep tub of water and then electrified it.

A fourth technique, especially favored by Sûreté in Paris, was the electric spit, *passer à la broche*. Torturers tied a victim's hand to his feet, slipped a pole in the bend of the knees, and rested the pole between two tables. Then they electrified the pole with one cable and pricked the body with the other end.[151]

Leulliette mentions that his torture group also used "an electric wire attached to a floor plug. Its role is to 'pleasure' the most important suspects."[152]

Keramane also enumerated the many kinds of water torture in this period:

1. Pumping. (*a*) Pouring water into the victim's mouth with cups or funnels. (*b*) Pumping by means of a hose (*tuyau*) inserted into the mouth from the tap. Torturers then folded the victim's legs against the bloated stomach, forcing water out of every orifice.
2. Choking with the bathtub, *baignoire*. (*a*) Plunging the head into the bathtub. (*b*) Putting young girls in a sack and plunging the sack into water. (*c*) Mounting the victim on the spit, head downward; the torturer swings the head into water and then withdraws it.
3. Choking on the *sauccison*, "the sausage." Torturers used a pulley to hoist victims by the feet, much like meat at the butchers. Then they dropped the victim from a great height into the sea or pool.

The manual *Guide provisoire de l'officier de renseignement* (1961) also defines three types of water torture: choking, pumping, and beating suspects with high-pressure jets.[153]

Keramane identified other tortures using fire, steel, and rope, but these left marks, perhaps not incriminating ones, but marks nonetheless.[154] Then Paras had to imprison those tortured long enough "for the marks to clear up."[155] Or they had to kill them surreptitiously: "They used to ask for volunteers to finish off the guys who had been tortured (there are no marks left that way and so no danger of a witch hunt later."[156] The accepted figure for "disappearances" during the Battle of Algiers alone is three thousand individuals.[157] Paras also knew how to use clubs to beat a suspect senseless without leaving marks.[158] But all this involved work. Electricity was easier and had, "despite all its horror, the advantage that its traces disappear if one takes the necessary care."[159]

Prisoners resisted stealth torture by tracking their wounds. Of course, torture victims have always authenticated their claims by describing their wounds, usually long broad scars made by whips, large burns, or notches cut out of the flesh. Algerian prisoners had to document smaller, transitory marks: scabs, numbness, and burns of uncertain origin.[160] Often specialists disagreed what these marks indicated.[161] Prisoners had to struggle to ensure their suffering would not go unacknowledged. Recording wounds, showing them to others, keeping the blood on the surface, being unclean, these became acts of resistance.

> "Take your handkerchief and clean up the blood—I don't want to see it. . . .
>
> *Salaud*, go and wash again. You did it on purpose. Your chest is still covered with blood."

And, in fact, I *had* done it on purpose, not being in any hurry to go back and be tortured.[162]

Remembering the Gestapo

The French government practiced torture, but France was not Nazi Germany. Its democratic character extended even to French torturers. They were always mindful of adverse publicity, favoring clean tortures. In a period cartoon, a French Para choked a suspect in a soapy bathtub. Next to him was a box of "Peace" detergent, advertised as "Great for Washing!"[163] Algerian torture was clean. Like shampoo, it disappeared down the drain. When asked to define torture forty years later, the French right-wing politician Jean Marie Le Pen (who was an officer during Battle of Algiers) stated torture was "a series of violent acts that cause physical injury to individuals, actions that destroy the personality and leave traces. Police and military interrogations do not fit this definition of torture."[164] Torture was Soviet brainwashing or what the Nazis did, but not what French paratroopers did, for they aimed neither to change personalities nor leave traces. Whatever Massu's faults, and he had many, at least he was never afraid of the word *torture* or of recognizing what it was the Paras did.

The image of Nazi torture played a multifaceted role in debates about the war. For opponents of the war, torture was a "Nazi virus."[165] The government bridled at the "scandalous comparison" to the Gestapo.[166] But even Massu's Paras embraced the Gestapo's disciplinary reputation, sometimes to invoke fear ("This is the Gestapo here!") and sometimes with regret ("them at least, they knew how to do it").[167] Older interrogators noted the irony. "I was tortured by the Nazis; now I do it myself."[168] Some took the lesson of the experience of the camps in a different direction. Paul Teitgin, the police prefect of an Algerian prefecture and a former prisoner at Dachau, resigned in protest in 1957.[169] Gaston Gosselin, a bureaucrat at the Ministry of Justice and another Dachau internee, leaked the devastating Red Cross report on torture in Algeria in 1960.[170] But they were the rare exception.

"Gestapo!" was not simply an accusation. It was also a historical thesis: the *reductio ad Hitlerum*, it all began with Hitler. "Many of the methods used in Algeria during the 1950s and early 1960s were similar if not identical to those alleged against the Gestapo."[171]

On the contrary, the two principal Algerian techniques, pumping stomachs with water and magneto torture, were uncommon Gestapo practices. They were, however, characteristic of other national policing traditions: American, French, and Japanese.

The history of torture rarely offers the simplicity of a *reductio*. Which police first devised portable electric instruments with low amperage for interrogation? That honor goes either to the American police (1920s), the Japanese in Korea (1931), or the French in Indochina (1931). Which state institutionalized electro-torture first? Either the Japanese or the French in their Asian colonies. Which state first adopted clean electrotorture to avoid public scrutiny? The first stealthy electrotorturers were either the American police in the South (for the modified chair), the French Sûreté in Saigon (for the magneto), or the Argentine police in Buenos Aires in 1935 (for the *picana eléctrica*). These police valued the fa-çade of democratic rule of law.

Those who remembered torture before the war knew there was more to modern torture than Nazis. In 1948, the unsympathetic judge of Cavailhié's trial knew his history better than most. "Mr. Cavailhié has spoken of grave matters: he has spoken of torture by electric current. The first time I heard of others speak of this, it was in Spain."[172] The judge remembered the Spanish chair, but even he no longer remembered the magneto from Indochina.

Those who came later could not resist the accusation, "Nazi!" Jean-Paul Sartre introduced Alleg's Algerian torture memoirs by invoking the Gestapo in the first sentence. "In 1943, in the Rue Lauriston (the Gestapo headquarters in Paris) Frenchmen were screaming in agony and pain: all France could hear them."[173] The German Gestapo was headquartered at 72 Ave. Foch, but no doubt a convenient error. Rue Lauriston was the headquarters of Henri Lafont, the most notorious of the French auxiliaries.

Vidal-Naquet, the finest scholar of the Algerian war, understood that reduc-ing torture to Hitler was "hardly the way to approach the problem."[174] He had read Jacques Chégaray's and Andrée Viollis's accounts of Vietnam. He knew that when evil came to visit, it did not always do so dressed in jackboots. Too often, it had a degree from Paris and invited you out for beer.

It was not uncommon for them to rig up a field telephone, and put one [wire] around a finger and the other around the scrotum and start cranking.

> —D. J. Lewis, former sergeant with the U.S.
> Ninth Military Police Company of the Ninth
> Infantry Division, stationed at Dong Tam, 1968–69[1]

8   Currents

Within one decade of the end of the Algerian war, magneto torture spread to Asia, Africa, South America, North America, Europe, and the Middle East. Sometimes it displaced other methods of electrotorture, and at other times, it marked the introduction of electrotorture, but in either case, it usually marked a shift in the entire torture regimen. If there was a distinctive *modern* style in torture, it was French modern: the field telephone magneto adapted with alligator clips, usually conjoined with water torture, either pumping (the tube, *tuyau*) or choking (the bathtub, *baignoire*). French modern was a stealthy style, one that was pioneered to avoid unwanted publicity and to create plausible deniability. In this respect, magneto torture became a marker for stealth torture wherever it went.

In the previous chapter, I showed how French forces carried magneto torture out of Vietnam to North Africa and Europe. In this chapter, I map a second route of distribution. I show how American forces carried magneto torture out of Vietnam to allied countries around the world.

As I will explain below, the South Vietnamese government tortured prisoners, and given the uniformity of techniques involved, it is not hard to conclude that this was government policy. As international attention focused on the war, South Vietnamese interrogators moved from visible techniques to stealth torture. Here they borrowed from the French colonial heritage, adapting techniques used by the French Sûreté in the 1930s and again by the French army in the 1940s and 1950s. After their arrival in Vietnam, some American interrogators also tortured and sought to leave no marks, especially as U.S. military monitoring for torture increased in the late 1960s. Interrogators adapted old techniques from

Table 8.1
Main Electrotorture Users, 1945–1979

User Type	1945	1950s	1960s	1970s
Magneto torture	France in Vietnam (**field telephone**)	France (**field telephone**)	France (**field telephone**) United States (**field telephone**, prod) S. Vietnam (**field telephone**) Brazil (**field telephone**) Israel South Korea (**field telephone**) Greece (**field telephone**)	United States (**field telephone**) S. Vietnam (**field telephone, peppermill**, prod) Brazil (**field telephone, peppermill**, prod, other) Israel (**field telephone**) South Korea (**field telephone**) Philippines (**field telephone**) Rhodesia (**magneto**, prod) Turkey (**peppermill**, prod) India (**generator**) Afghanistan (**field telephone, other devices**)
Convert to magneto torture		South Africa (live wire) UK in Kenya (battery, generator, magneto) Venezuela (**prod**, live wire, magneto) Spain (unknown)	South Africa (**magneto**)	South Africa (**field telephone**, various devices,) UK in Northern Ireland (likely magneto, prod) Venezuela (**field telephone**) Spain (telephone, transformer)
Likely magneto			Morocco Portugal	Morocco Indonesia Portugal Belgium Mexico

Table 8.1 (*cont'd*)

User Type	1945	1950s	1960s	1970s	
Unique users		USSR (ECT)		**Chile** (*parilla*, wires, likely magneto pre-1973) Cambodia (live wire)	Malawi (electric hat) Romania (ECT) Cuba (ECT, wires) Paraguay (iron bed)
Prod	Argentina	Argentina	Argentina Uruguay	Argentina Uruguay	Bolivia Greece Iran (**prod**, chair) Iraq
Likely prod					Egypt
Wires (source unknown)				**Burundi** Ecuador Cameroon El Salvador Colombia Ethiopia Djibouti Haiti	Libya Syria Mali Uganda Nicaragua Taiwan Zambia

Note: **Bold** marks a known preference for device type.

American policing in the 1920s and from French colonial policing by way of the South Vietnamese. Although it is rarely mentioned in the main American histories of the Vietnam War, U.S. soldiers both assisted others and employed themselves hand-cranked telephones for interrogations in Vietnam in 1960s.

The American and French roads out of Vietnam were probably not the only routes of transmission for magneto torture, though unquestionably they were two important axes along which torturers came to adopt hand-cranked telephones around the world. Other routes are less certain, but I will gesture to some possibilities in this and the next chapter as clues suggest.

What is certain is that by the 1970s, electrotorture became increasingly common. In the same decade that the United States and Western Europe embraced a human rights agenda and Amnesty International began its annual global audit of torture, torturers embraced electrotorture in large numbers. As the following chapter shows, this was only the beginning of a worldwide transformation.

Table 8.1 shows the progress of electrotorture around the world at midcentury. In the 1950s, only seven countries used electrotorture, and only one country, France, favored the field telephone magneto. By the 1960s, the police or military forces of eleven countries practiced electrotorture, and most of these forces adopted magneto torture (often field telephone magnetos or their smaller cousin, the "pepper mill") along with supplementary water tortures.

Between the 1960s and the 1970s, the number of countries using electrotorture quadrupled. Magnetos spread with this explosion, but so too did cattle prods, as I will explain. Between 1950 and 1970, torture using cattle prods is reported in only four countries, Argentina, Uruguay, Venezuela, and the United States. In the 1970s, this number increased to twelve. Many other electrotorture devices also appeared in this decade. I explain why these devices failed to catch on in the expanding torture market while cattle prods and magnetos did.

If we look back, the crucible for modern electrotorture in the twentieth century was clearly Vietnam. In the thirties, the French Sûreté pioneered stealthy torture, combining old clean tortures with electrotorture, and it was by French colonial routes that magneto torture came to Europe, not once, but twice. Then magneto torture passed on from the French-supported South Vietnamese government to American interrogators, who in turn carried magneto torture out of Vietnam.

South Vietnamese Torture

By 1963, no one doubted that the South Vietnamese government tortured prisoners.[2] South Vietnamese torture was painful and not particularly clean.[3] Torturers beat and whipped prisoners to death, particularly at Poulo Condor, a notorious prison island off the coast. Far from public scrutiny, guards crushed fingers and toes, removed teeth with pincers, stuck pins under nails and into knees, and burned flesh with lamps and cigarettes. They forced chopsticks, Coke bottles, and eels up orifices, and they exposed prisoners to ants. They suspended prisoners by the toes, testicles, or the hands ("ride in a Dakota"); then they beat and spun the victim ("slaughtering the pig" (1961), "the plane ride" (late 1960s).

Electric torture left burn marks. In 1961, a former prisoner from Poulo Condor described guards using an "electric flash" attachment from a camera that caused "severe pain and burnings."[4] In 1965, a prisoner on the mainland described how interrogators hooked wires to his appendages "and began to crank the dynamo."[5] Generally, they used "an army dynamo activated manually, in a manner so that one can augment or diminish at one's leisure the intensity of the current."[6]

From the fifties onwards, Vietnamese prisoners called water torture "ride in a submarine" or "taking the submarine," phrases that covered pumping and choking.[7] Torturers typically preferred pumping to choking.[8] One prisoner, tortured in 1960, describes the Dutch style of choking: they "tied me, face upward, to a plank. A towel was used to tie my head to the plank, a rubber tube led from a 200-liter barrel fixed to a stand. The water fell drop by drop onto the towel, soon flooding my face. To breathe, I sucked in water through my nose and mouth . . . my stomach started to swell like a balloon. . . . it was as if someone was twisting my entrails."[9] The water used in these operations was often soapy, salty, or mixed with lime, pepper, and excrement. Often interrogators stomped on bloated stomachs with hobnailed boots, a method bound to leave wounds.[10]

The Army Intelligence Bureau specialized in a unique innovation, the *chen ve,* "beneath the water or mud." Interrogators put a prisoner "into a large container with water up to his neck." Then "the container was violently struck on the side with a mallet until the prisoner fainted and blood spurted from his mouth."[11] The beating produced "great pressure on the body of the prisoner: the heart is shocked severely, the liver and kidneys swell and the bladder bursts."[12]

By the late 1960s, Vietnamese torture was stealthier. Interrogators forced prisoners to stand for hours before bright lights.[13] Guards beat prisoners inside a sack, a method that leaves "fewer superficial marks, but it seriously affects the internal organs."[14] They turned to the *falaka,* as the French had done in the 1930s, beating the soles of the feet; the prisoner "feels pain in three places—the feet, the knees and the heart, as the blood is forced up his body."[15] In 1973, three women put to the *falaka* "were beaten to death without any marks being left."[16]

Lastly, torturers used electrical and water torture more carefully. The *chen ve,* now called "the punching ball," became more common, as it "leaves much less visible traces, but is in fact more deadly."[17] By 1969, torturers also used a smaller magneto: "The 12 volt battery that is employed looks like a pepper mill."[18] It soon replaced field telephones: "All torture rooms are equipped with the same kind of generator, a machine that looks like a square pepper grinder."[19]

Magneto torture, water tortures, and *falaka* are familiar tortures from the French colonial period, though the *chen ve* appears to be a local innovation (I will discuss this technique further in chapter 13). Sources are quite clear that these techniques were favored because they were stealthy. And this concern with stealth is even more marked among accounts of American torture, and the reasons for it are spelled out somewhat more clearly. But the problem of American torture in Vietnam needs to be approached carefully. Let me begin with government records and the court martial record, and then turn to the testimonials of soldiers.

Vietnam, 1968

In 1965, General William Westmoreland acknowledged that news correspondents sometimes photographed American advisers standing by while Vietnamese interrogators tortured prisoners. In a letter to Major General Louis Walt, commander of the Third Marine Division, Westmoreland stated that he understood this presence was necessary to moderate the behavior of Vietnamese interrogators. "In any case," he added, "we should attempt to avoid photographs being taken of these incidents of torture and most certainly in any case to keep Americans out of the picture."[20]

On January 21, 1968, the *Washington Post* ran a photograph of a member of the First Air Cavalry Division "pinning a Vietnamese to the ground while two other Vietnamese placed a towel over his face and poured water into his nose."[21] This technique, what I call the Dutch style in choking in chapter 13, has a well-known history both in American policing and in East Asia. The American soldier was court-martialed on February 28, 1968.

On March 14, 1970, Lt. Gen. W. R. Peers reported to the secretary of the army the events leading to the notorious massacre at My Lai. Among other events, his report described how on March 19, 1968, "during the morning, an American assisted by an ARVN [Army of the Republic of Vietnam] interpreter interrogated detainees in the company position. A field telephone with leads attached to various parts of the body to produce electric shocks was one technique employed to obtain information." The report also states that the ARVN interpreter severely kicked and beat detainees, while probably "the same American using the field telephone" inflicted knife wounds on the back of the hands, in which he rubbed salt. The report distinguishes this torture from beatings conducted by a soldier after taking prisoners in the heat of battle.[22]

The discovery of American torture in Vietnam was shocking, and it led to a broader investigation. On May 21, 1971, in a report to the White House, Maj. Gen. Kenneth J. Hodson, the army judge advocate general, confirmed that American interrogators "on occasion" used electrical devices to torture Vietnamese during intelligence operations.[23] In fact, on August 13, 1971, investigators for the Army's Criminal Investigation Division (CID) had conducted an internal investigation of the 172nd Military Intelligence Detachment, and they reported that American and Vietnamese interrogators tortured Vietnamese detainees using "the transmission of electrical shock by means of a field telephone, a water-rag treatment which impaired breathing, hitting with sticks and boards, and beating detainees with fists."[24] Another internal inquiry by the CID identified twenty-nine members of the 173rd Airborne as suspects in confirmed cases of torture.[25]

Government reports also reveal certain deficiencies in the reporting of war crimes during the Vietnam War. Until March 25, 1966, the American commanders in Vietnam were only obliged to report war crimes of hostile forces. They were not obliged to report any war crimes, including torture, performed by U.S. forces and allies. After 1966, field commanders were obliged to report all war crimes, whether by hostile or U.S. forces. But until 1970, these new rules did not anticipate the possibility that the commander himself may have been involved, as Lieutenant William Calley was at My Lai. Commanders were responsible for reporting their own deficiencies, and there was no independent office to investigate adherence to the laws of war.[26] Nor were there meaningful punishments for failing to report war crimes, a factor that may also have contributed to "an attitude of laxness and indifference to such crimes."[27]

Under these circumstances, commanders could hide incidents of torture and other war crimes from their superiors with misleading bureaucratic reports and euphemisms.[28] In some cases, they no doubt did, and the My Lai incident is a case in point. Within "the Americal Division, at every command level from company to division, actions were taken or omitted which together effectively concealed from higher headquarters the events which transpired" during the military operation.[29] After 1970, new provisions did require immediate reports of injury or death to noncombatants by way of telephone or teletype, especially acts that "may be reasonably expected to arouse public interest or cause continuous or widespread adverse publicity."[30] But even with the changes, it is questionable whether they could prevent the cover-ups of the sort that followed My Lai.[31]

After My Lai, the military increased efforts to preserve documents, issued rules prohibiting destruction of records, and conducted studies of possible war crimes violations. This new concern is also reflected in the court martial record.

The vast majority of war crimes allegations investigated by the military were made after September 1969, when news of the My Lai incident broke. Of the 241 allegations of war crimes between 1965 and 1975, 191 (79 percent) were made after September 1969. Most allegations were not made by officers of the units involved, but by individuals long since separated from the service. Forty-seven allegations provided grounds for disciplinary actions, though in most cases investigators could not determine whether commanding officers knew of these incidents.

Even this more vigorous legal process left a great deal undisclosed. For instance, of the twenty-nine members of the 173rd Airborne suspected in con-firmed cases of torture, fifteen "admitted the acts." Records indicate, though, that only three were punished, and they received fines or reduction in rank. None served any prison time.[32]

In short, the official record of war crimes, including torture, is spotty at best, especially the records before 1969. "The real impetus to preserve the Viet-nam records came as a result of the tragic My Lai affair."[33] But this impetus was uneven. In 1991, C. A. Shaughnessy, a veteran staff member of the Vietnam Collection at the National Archives, concluded that the Vietnam War was far less documented even after 1969 than World War II or portions of the Civil War. He observed that many cubic feet of documents had been lost, destroyed, or misplaced, while other documents, removed for military historians, had been so jumbled their origin was unknown. Some documents that might shed light on torture in this period were still classified, especially those pertaining to the notorious CIA-managed Phoenix Program (described in chapter 21).[34] Since 1991, the situation has become more constrained. For example, the Vietnam war crimes records were declassified in 1994 but have been subsequently re-moved from the public shelves at the National Archives.[35]

All this is an important caution to those who depend solely on government documents to make their case. While government reports and court martial records are a good place to start in mapping American torture during the Viet-nam War, particularly after My Lai, it is equally clear that before 1969, "many such incidents escaped detection."[36] To understand the murky pre—My Lai history of American torture in Vietnam, we have to turn to the testimonial literature of Vietnam veterans.

Bell Telephone Hour

Many American soldiers did routine duties in Vietnam and did not participate in torture. As one MP said, the American torturers in Vietnam perpetuated a perception that all American soldiers were involved in war crimes. In fact, "The vast majority of us simply did our jobs there as best we could to survive and get on with our lives."[37] But some American soldiers observed or participated in the torturing of prisoners, and some have written or spoken about these incidents.

Using testimonial literature is fraught with problems. These accounts may be fraudulent or misleading. In the case of Vietnam, some soldiers and reporters fabricated stories or staged photographs for public consumption.[38] Moreover, in the wake of Senator John Kerry's campaign for president, pro- and anti–Vietnam War veterans exchanged new accusations of fabrications, primarily centering on the famous "Winter Soldier Investigation," which Kerry helped organize.

Despite all these concerns, there is no choice in the matter but to consider the testimonial literature. The gaps in the government record before 1969 are serious. Guenter Lewy, a historian of war crimes in Vietnam usually cited by conservative veterans, is highly critical of all testimonial literature in principle, preferring almost exclusively government documents.[39] Still, in practice, Lewy accepts some testimonial literature without question, or without corroborating government documents, most notably, torture accounts of American POWs in North Vietnam.[40] Moreover, he distinguishes among antiwar veterans' testimonies, regarding some as more reliable than others based on the contradictions he could identify.

This is a starting point for considering the veterans' testimonials. Some testimonials *are* less contested than others. In appendix D, I group various accounts of tortures in terms of their reliability. Here, I provide a summary report of the methods used and conclusions reached in appendix D.

Setting aside the known fabricated accounts, one must recognize that many of the remaining accounts describe American violence in the worst possible light. I have already outlined how I use testimonial literature like this in the case of Resistance stories from World War II (see chapter 4), and the procedures I follow here are no different. If one bitter narrative after another fails to mention techniques or procedures that were common elsewhere in the world, we can reasonably conclude that these techniques were probably *not* practiced in that region. Surely the narrators had every interest in saying everything they could to damage the U.S. government, and the absences and silences are telling. Furthermore, one has greater confidence in multiple accounts of the same torture in the same place; single reports of unique tortures are less reliable. Indeed, some well-known fabricated accounts are distinguishable by the fact that they mention unique tortures that appear in no other reports. Lastly, uniformity of practice indicates uniformity of intent, that is, some degree of planning and policy; this is the standard application of the Nuremberg rule, of course. Lewy applies this rule to North Vietnamese torture, but it applies equally to other cases. With these cautionary rules in mind, the testimonial story of American torture in Vietnam appears to be as follows.

American electrotorture in Vietnam began with some military interrogators adopting magneto torture in the Mekong region between 1963 and 1964.[41] This technique, particularly the use of field telephones for interrogations, spread among American units, peaking around 1967 or 1968. It was favored because it drew few marks, and so interrogators could avoid detection from their superiors at the base or in the field. Interrogators also adopted other clean techniques, such as slapping and stress positions, and after My Lai and similar scandals that publicized magneto and water torture in Vietnam, some of these lesser-known techniques became more prominent. Torture techniques migrated stateside, appearing sometimes in military training exercises. They were also discussed informally after interrogation training or indirectly through courses training soldiers to resist torture. In short, whether one takes the government record or the veterans' testimonials, one arrives at the same description of the American style of torture in Vietnam: electrotorture (by means of a field telephone magneto), water torture (particularly the Dutch style), and beating.

Veteran testimonials about torture rarely look upon the U.S. military and government in a favorable light. So it is surprising that no veteran mentions any figure like General Massu in Algeria, a general who knowingly allowed troops to use torture techniques for intelligence purposes. Nor do they identify any official army manuals, as in Algeria, that authorized torture techniques. None of the soldiers saw written orders to torture. One military interrogator stated flatly that the standard manual for interrogation listed no torture techniques and did not encourage torture. Thus, even if some veterans wanted to conclude that torture was U.S. government policy, the testimonial evidence as a whole does not suggest that torture was an official policy directed from Washington, DC.

Rather, the testimonial evidence suggests some commanders in Vietnam tolerated a subculture of torture among military interrogators. In this subculture, interrogators shared techniques and were highly dependent on ARVN interpreters and interrogators for advice and information. With the possible exception of the CIA, torture techniques appear to have migrated not from the top down, but laterally from unit to unit as the subculture expanded.

Midlevel officers, like Lieutenant Calley, tolerated this subculture of torture and even at times shielded it from scrutiny from headquarters. Just as it would be foolish to believe all testimonies equally, it is foolish to take the absence of official government accounts of torture before 1969 as evidence that some midlevel commanders were unaware of or did not even tacitly endorse the use of torture by interrogators. Not everything that governments do is written in records, especially in matters pertaining to torture. And the degree of uniformity in the techniques of torture suggests some level of official engagement, even if it did not involve senior commanders.

Serious flaws in American military recording of war crimes encouraged this situation. In 1964–65, for example, Donald Duncan, a Green Beret who became a prominent antiwar veteran, was outraged that his commanders participated in or failed to report torture by U.S. soldiers.[42] But the military regulations at the time did not oblige commanders to do so, nor did they anticipate that commanders might be involved in war crimes themselves.[43]

American interrogators were aware of general prohibitions against torture, but the combination of weak and unqualified leadership, incompetent planning, poor discipline, and peer bonding in the context of counterinsurgency warfare led to the appearance of torture.[44] These are classic conditions, as I explain in part V. Social psychologists have long known that divided or unclear lines of command, mixed messages about what is allowed, and lack of punishment for violations of rules are preconditions for torture in prison environments. Moreover, in counterinsurgency warfare, torturers tend to become a closed professional class, bound together by peer pressure and male bonding. Narrow professionalism drives bureaucratic devolution, as midlevel officers shield interrogators from scrutiny by superior officers while encouraging interrogators to do what is necessary to get intelligence. Interrogators torture more victims, more frequently, using a broader range of tortures while at the same time demanding more autonomy from superiors to conduct their business.

All these factors were present in Vietnam, and they allowed torture to spread, but just how widespread it was among military interrogators will be impossible to determine.[45] The stories do suggest that South Vietnamese and American torture subcultures informed each other. Increasing American sensitivity to torture coincides with the narrowing of South Vietnamese torture techniques to those that leave few marks. Conversely, American interrogators, in all probability, borrowed techniques used by the South Vietnamese. Other techniques, such as continuous slapping, or the "Taps," were not reported by prisoners of the South Vietnamese, but they were well known in American torture in the 1920s. American torturers showed little interest in other South Vietnamese techniques. These included, for the most part, scarring tortures such as whipping, but they also included customary practices such as the *falaka* and unusual innovations such as the *chen ve*.

Some stories about torture in Vietnam are probably apocryphal. For example, the most legendary "psychological" technique was the helicopter treatment. Interrogators would load two prisoners onto a helicopter, one of whom was disposable. They would threaten to throw the disposable suspect out of the helicopter if he did not talk, running toward the door and stopping short. Finally, they would throw him out. Then they would interrogate the person of real interest, who was now certain of imminent death.

The difficulty is that there is no documented incident involving this technique. In 1969, the *Chicago Sun-Times* and the *Washington Post* ran a story and photograph on this technique, but the photograph turned out to be staged.[46] The one veteran who repeatedly tells the helicopter story, K. Barton Osborn, turns out to be less than credible.[47] Among all the veterans accounts of torture described here, only three mention the technique, and both appear to have heard about it secondhand. They do not describe an instance they personally observed.[48]

Helicopter treatment became such a Vietnam legend that even today some remember descriptions of this torture vividly and believe it must have occurred. Perhaps; it is impossible to say that it did not occur at least once. But ironically, telephone torture, far more routine and also documented, barely impinged on modern memory. Some veterans even regarded it as an "urban legend."[49] Nevertheless, the government record and veterans' testimonials both point to a consistent American style of torture in Vietnam: electrotorture (by means of a field telephone magneto), water torture (particularly the Dutch style), and beating. This, as a French reporter recognized in 1973, is a torture style that is "most Algerian."[50]

Out of Vietnam Again

Magnetos are easy to spot in any torture narrative. They are the only electrotorture devices with distinctive cranks. They also make an inevitable grinding noise when they are cranked; even blindfolded victims can hear it. Unlike cattle prods and stun guns, torturers clamp or tie wires onto appendages.

With these markers in mind, here are the confirmed cases of magneto torture worldwide. Magneto torture occurred primarily in democratic contexts: in democracies engaged in ongoing guerrilla war (Spain, Israel, Turkey, India, Sri Lanka), in societies that had just transitioned from authoritarian to democratic government (Spain, Russia, Brazil, the Philippines), in consolidated democracies with sharp civic divisions (United States, Venezuela), and in societies with democratic governments that restricted participation to the white population (apartheid South Africa, Rhodesia-Zimbabwe). Between 1960 and 1980, magneto torture also occurred in five authoritarian contexts: Brazil (1964–87), South Korea (1964–87), Greece (1967–74), the Philippines (1972–86), and Soviet Afghanistan (1979–87). In four cases, Brazil, South Korea, Greece, and the Philippines, reports of electrotorture continued after the transition to democracy. In the 1990s, two other authoritarian governments turned to magneto torture, Turkmenistan and Yugoslavia, and electrotorture continued in Yugoslavia after the transition to democracy.

This distribution is consistent with the monitoring hypothesis, namely, that public monitoring leads institutions that favor painful coercion to use and combine procedures that evade detection by leaving few marks. Because public monitoring is greater in democracies, and because public monitoring of human rights is a core value in modern democracies, it is not surprising that where we find democracies torturing, we also find magneto torture in conjunction usually with water torture (as I will show in the next chapter). The French style in stealth torture helps interrogators avoid public monitoring, making it less likely that they will be found out or held responsible.

However, the distribution of magneto torture also raises the puzzle of why some authoritarian states adopted it in the 1960s where domestic public monitoring was not high. One possibility is that the United States was a universal distributor, furnishing all these authoritarian states with magnetos. Another, far more persuasive in my judgment, is that authoritarian states adopted these techniques because during this period the international public monitoring of human rights also intensified and these states were increasingly concerned about the impact of reports of torture on legitimacy and aid. I will weigh the merits of these hypotheses in the next chapter, but for the moment, I shall simply describe the empirical pattern of magneto torture. Below, I order the countries chronologically, based on the earliest available report of magneto torture in each state.

The United States. In 1966, police discovered that an Arkansas prison superintendent and his staff had used telephone torture in two penal institutions. The prison doctor had devised the Tucker Telephone, "an electrical generator taken from a ring-type telephone, placed in sequence with two dry cell batteries and attached to an undressed inmate . . . a crank was turned sending an electrical charge into the body of the inmate." Police determined that the staff "rung up" prisoners as early as June 1963.[51]

Chicago police investigators uncovered systematic torture in Area 2, a region comprising the south side of the city, between 1973 and 1986. Investigators grouped torture cases by technique, including electroshock (the earliest case being May 1973).[52] Victims described the device as a hand-cranked black box. In 1986, prisoners alleged that Jon Burge, a highly decorated Vietnam veteran and a top police commander, practiced magneto torture on detained suspects, showed his detectives how to perform various tortures, and chided them when they left marks.[53]

These cases suggest that war veterans brought magneto torture back from Vietnam to their civilian occupations as policemen and guards. For example, before he entered civilian policing, Burge had served two terms of duty in Vietnam, serving as a military policeman assigned with the Ninth Infantry. He studied military interrogation at Fort Gordon, Georgia, and "was familiar with electrical devices operated by a crank, saying he had used field telephones during his service in Vietnam." He "denied having heard of any torture that might have gone there."[54] One may be justly skeptical.

South Africa. In South Africa, prisoners described magneto torture as early as 1963. The *Observer*, a South African newspaper, reported three detainees gave "details of torture by electric shock methods which were first used in Algeria."[55] One said, "Every time I resisted answering the questions, they turned on the dynamo."[56] Magneto torture continued until the end of apartheid in 1989, particularly in Kwazulu-Natal, where a covert police unit commonly tortured with "a dynamo taken from a telephone."[57] Officers indicated that magnetos "were available from anyone at Telkom. I can go fetch you one now. It was an old crank telephone."[58]

South Korea. South Korea had the largest contingent of troops in Vietnam after the Americans, and these veterans did torture political prisoners in the 1960s.[59] In 1964, To Ye Jong reported torturers attached wires to his toes and "bandaged the part of my body where electric current ran so as not to leave the marks of electric torture."[60] Electrotorture is reported for the next two decades.[61] An officer of the Korean Central Intelligence Agency described using a khaki-colored telephone for night operations, including torture.[62] In 1989, the device was described as a "voltage generator."[63]

Brazil. Prisoners report electroshock by 1966–67.[64] By the late 1960s, torture victims reported seeing U.S. AID decals on the field telephones. In one case, American advisers described to Brazilian officers "the permissible levels the human body could withstand." One AID official was concerned enough to track orders from the police assistance program. "Electric shocks, he knew, were usually administered with military field telephones, and over those he had no control. He could try to prevent generators sent out with the U.S. AID decal if they were going to be used for torture."[65]

In the late 1960s, Brazilian torturers reported that the CIA would be upgrading their field telephones. They said that the CIA Technical Services Division in Panama was "developing devices to make the pain so sharp that a prisoner would break quickly."[66] By 1969, Brazilian torturers were using a new device, the *pimentinha*: "a magneto that produced low voltage and high amperage electricity; that, because it was a red box, . . . was called the 'little pepper.' "[67] This device resembled the Vietnamese "pepper grinder" that also appeared around this date. It is hard to believe this was coincidental.

In the 1980s, after the transition to democracy, police still used "electric shock, administered either directly with wires from a plug, or from a telephone mechanism which can be wound up to increase the current (the *pimentinha*)." In one case, television crews burst into a room and "took pictures of the telephone mechanism of the *pimentinha*." One human rights lawyer was also able to confiscate a *pimentinha*.[68]

Greece. Prisoners reported electroshock from 1967 onward.[69] In May 1968, a prisoner held by Salonika Security described having cables tied to his hands and feet, and then "with a machine that one of them turned, they caused electric current to be conducted to my lower extremities."[70]

Israel. Reporters described the French style in modern torture as early as 1969. "'Alligator' clips (electrical connections) were attached to his ears and genitals and electric current passed through them." Prisoners also reported "a waterhose inserted into the mouth and water poured down the throat. . . . an interrogator would then stand on his stomach, forcing the water back out of his mouth."[71] In the 1980s, a prisoner described the machine "as having a crank."[72] Blindfolded torture victims "remembered the sound of a machine before and during the application of the electricity." In 1992, military sources told a *Hadashot* reporter that interrogators used "a field telephone."[73]

Turkey. Interrogators turned to electrotorture in 1971, and it became more frequent after 1980. Torturers used "a magnetic field telephone," attaching it to sexual organs and the tongue, to the fingers, and to the small toe.[74] In May 1980, the *Democrat* newspaper ran a picture of a smaller torture device, a handcrank magneto. It resembles the Brazilian and Vietnamese pepper mills.[75] In 1995, the state minister for human rights, Azimet Köylüoglu, confirmed that interrogators commonly used the "magnetic telephone."[76]

Rhodesia/Zimbabwe. A former torturer confirmed interrogators used magneto torture as early as 1972. He would "pull a dynamo from his pack, attach alligator clips to the man's ears, and turn the crank."[77]

Venezuela. Electrotorture with cattle prods was routine in the 1950s, but one prisoner reported magneto torture in 1956.[78] By 1973, victims described "electric shocks through the use of a field telephone."[79]

The Philippines. Victims reported electrotorture starting in 1974. Torturers attached a wire to the forefinger and another to the penis. "Then followed the turning of the handle of the cranker dynamo, producing a [higher] current from low voltage."[80]

Spain. Electrotorture is reported briefly in 1958.[81] Subsequent accounts do not mention electrotorture in the late Franco era (General Franco died in 1975).[82] In the democratic period that followed, prisoners report electric torture with "a transformer-like, or telephone-like instrument."[83] In 2001, prisoners described being given electroshock mainly by means of wires, though occasionally they mentioned stun guns or prods.[84]

Afghanistan. The Khad was the first Communist police to adopt the French style in electric torture. In the early 1980s, prisoners said the commonest torture device looked "like an old-fashioned telephone with wires that are attached to the victim's body and a handle which is turned or pulled to apply the current."[85] They called it "the telephone box" and the "earphones." Soviet and East German manufacturers made them and supplied them to the police and the Khad.[86] At one headquarters, torturers used a machine the size of a typewriter with "a distinctive handle" and wires. "By turning the handle it would produce an electric current: the faster the handle was turned the stronger the electric current became."[87]

India. Police used electrotorture in the Punjab during the 1980s "by means of wires attached to a hand-cranked generator." This procedure was introduced in the Punjab in 1976 by a police captain who was afterward promoted.[88] Sikh and Kashmiri militants report electric torture starting in the mid-1980s. In 1991, fifteen Sikh militants "were given electric shocks, either with a magneto or from a mains socket."[89]

Sri Lanka. Tamil prisoners reported electric shock in Sri Lanka in the mid-1980s. They described the device as "a small telephone like device with a handle."[90]

Russia. After the collapse of the Soviet Union, Russian police adopted an electric "cranking machine." In 1994, a prisoner described it as "a small machine, with a handle" and clamps for attaching the wires to the ears. "At first they turned slowly, then faster. When they turned [it] quickly, I just lost consciousness."[91]

Yugoslavia. In 1998, a Kosovan clerk reported electrotorture in a Serbian prison. "They put metal bands around his wrists, and these were connected with wires to a generator with a voltmeter . . . somebody turned this generator to produce electricity."[92]

Turkmenistan. In 2002, officers here tortured a man who refused to swear an oath of military allegiance. They hooded him, beat him, and administered electroshocks using "wires from a field telephone."[93]

No doubt this chronology could be sharpened, but the trend toward magneto torture is unmistakable. Area specialists may also be able to clarify twenty-one other cases in the 1970s where police used wires and electrodes from an unknown source (see table 8.1).[94] Six of these police forces are possible magneto torturers.

To be specific, Indonesian and Mexican reports describe electrotorture in the field against guerrillas, where mains electricity would be unavailable.[95] This suggests magneto generators. Likewise, electrotorture by Belgian troops occurred during a NATO field exercise in 1971, also suggesting a magneto.[96] Prisoners in Northern Ireland describe how British interrogators used a portable machine, but as the use was indoors, it is difficult to determine whether it drew power from the mains or not.[97] British use of magnetos was not unknown, as British colonial police in Kenya had on occasion used magnetos in the 1950s.

Moroccan police adopted electrotorture as early as 1960 and continued using it throughout the 1970s.[98] It is difficult to ignore the close proximity in time and place to the French *gégéneurs* in Algeria.

In Chile, Amnesty International documented cases of police electrotorture under the governments of Eduardo Frei (1964–70) and Salvador Allende (1970–73). The earliest incident dated from 1969. In 1972, in a letter from Santiago Public Jail, left-wing guerrillas described tortures that "do not leave physical marks," notably clean beating, choking with water, and an electrical practice "detectives commonly call 'current' [*la corriente*]." Torturers wired appendages and electrified prisoners. They changed appendages frequently so as not to leave burns. Being blindfolded, prisoners were unable to describe the device.[99] Under the government of Augusto Pinochet, Chilean torturers favored an electrified bed, the *parilla*, but it is possible that this earlier device—seemingly light and portable, unlike the *parilla*—was a magneto.

The reports from other countries are too vague. Wires and clamps prove the devices were not stun guns or cattle prods, but it is possible that torturers simply used wall plugs. This was Khmer Rouge practice in the notorious Tuol Sleng prison in Cambodia.[100]

Variation within the French Style

Now this rather homogenous picture of electric torture needs to be qualified. The torturer's craft, like carpentry, painting, and other crafts, changes with times and places. There were some important national variations within the French style. These variations included the following.

Power. The Philippine magneto generated 90 volts.[101] The Israeli magneto could be set at least as high as 60 volts.[102] South African torturers claimed they could increase the voltage to 200 or 225 volts.[103] They also conducted electrotorture by hooking up wires to a car battery and accelerating an auto engine.[104] This would yield over a thousand volts. The Brazilians' "doublers of tension" fed an electronic circuit with simple radio batteries to achieve 500 to 1,000 volts. The *pimentinha* yielded only 100 volts, but at an alarming 10 amperes, a potentially fatal amperage. It could also be cranked in two directions, "thereby creating a counter electromotive force that doubled the original voltage of the machine."[105]

Contacts. French torturers used alligator clips or wrapped wire around the fingers. Other torturers found that clips offered too little electrical contact with the skin. They experimented with alternative contacts. For example, South African police tied each wire to a key and then placed each key on the victim's palms. The first shock contracts the muscles, forcing the hand closed. "While you keep turning the handle, he can't let go of it."[106] Brazilian torturers used Brillo scouring pads, inserting "a Bom Brill into a woman's vagina, hooking a field radio wire to the metal pad, and turning on the electric current."[107] Turkish and South African police used salt water to increase conductivity.[108] Argentine prisoners report that their torturers "threw water over us or washed us, 'to cool your body down so that you'll be sensitive again.' "[109]

Clean techniques. Some torturers hooded their victims so they could not describe their torture to others. Others used techniques to reduce burn or spark marks. Brazilians wrapped appendages in gauze, adopted wooden clothespins ("crocodiles"), and slipped fine wires between the teeth.[110] South Africans wrapped wire ends with cloth.[111] Many wet their victims. Turkish police recently adopted gel used for EKGs.[112]

Restraints. Hanging the prisoner on a bar is a method of trussing that dates from the slave trade (which I cover in part IV). Torturers bind the wrists to the ankles, pass a bar beneath crook of the knees, and then suspend the bar, with the prisoner's head hanging downward. This technique has various names, including *passer à la broche* (hanging from the spit) in France, and *pau de arara* (the parrot's perch) in Brazil.

In 1959, the Parsian Sûreté substituted a metal bar for the wooden one normally employed. They then electrified the bar and attached the wire to various appendages, passing current through the body.[113] American trainers made a similar point to Brazilian torturers: "the parrot's perch . . . was even more effective when combined with electric shocks."[114] Brazilians had tortured with the *pau de arara* since the 1940s, but it was a French innovation to combine it with electroshock.

Water supplements. Israeli and Brazilian interrogators supplemented magneto torture with pumping stomachs with a hose, while Spanish police favored choking in a tub.[115] Brazilians sometimes pumped by electrification: "A hose with running water was inserted into his nostrils and into his mouth, and he involuntarily breathed in every time he received an electric shock."[116]

Cattle Prods

Until the 1970s, few police employed cattle prods for intimidation and interrogation. Argentine police were the first, adopting prods in 1935 and remaining customary users for most of the twentieth century. Torture using the *picana eléctrica* was not an American invention, nor did the Brazilians introduce the practice to Argentina.[117]

In the early 1950s, the Venezuelan Guardia Nacional commonly used the *picana eléctrica* for torture. "Simple cables or a goad or *picana* of the employees in the slaughterhouses or stockyards for moving heads of cattle were connected to the most sensitive parts of the victim's body, which provokes a painful shock."[118] By the 1970s, the Venezuelans abandoned the prod for the magneto.

The first American cases occurred during the civil rights protests in the 1960s. The earliest case occurred June 1961, when officers at the Mississippi State Penitentiary used "cattle shockers" on two Chicago Freedom Riders.[119]

Uruguayan police adopted the *picana eléctrica* from Argentine police in the mid-1960s.[120] In 1971, they distributed these tools to the military. A military torturer "noticed the circulation of the appliance called the *picana eléctrica* (electric shock baton) in the different barracks where I happened to be. It was the novelty of the moment."[121] The prod also appeared in two other countries adjacent to Argentina, in Bolivia by 1976 and in Paraguay by 1986.[122] There was, in addition, one prod case in Brazil (1977) and another in Chile (1986), although in general, torturers in these countries favored other electroshock devices.[123] Outside the southern cone of Latin America, Mexican police remain the most common prod users, dubbing the device *la chicharra*, the buzzer.[124]

The prod made the greatest progress outside of the Americas. Prod torture is first reported in these countries on the following dates: Greece (1971), United Kingdom (1972), Vietnam (1972), Turkey (1977), Iran (1977), Rhodesia (1977),

Afghanistan (1978), Iraq (1979), Madagascar (1981–82), China (1986), Yugoslavia (1988), South Korea (1989), and Pakistan (middle to late 1980s).[125] What accounts for this rapid spread starting in the 1970s? To be sure, prods were nonlethal, portable, clean, painful, and flexible to use. They were also cheap, easy to maintain, and similar to police batons. All this does not explain the timing. The *picana eléctrica* had all these qualities in 1935, but it found no market.

The history of field telephones reveals one additional desirable quality in the age of human rights monitoring, what I have called linkage. As torturers came under greater scrutiny, they chose electric devices they could integrate into their regular duties. Until the 1960s, one could question what policemen were doing carrying electrified prods. In 1963, the Alabama police became the first police force to adopt cattle prods to control demonstrators.[126] By the 1970s, companies marketed electrified batons to police worldwide.[127] Prods became standard gear for nonlethal crowd control. Police could not be denied their legitimate use any more than soldiers could be deprived of field telephones. Police who tortured saw the advantages.

All things being equal, why did some police choose prods over portable telephones when they decided to use electrotorture? Cattle prods were hardly more "scientific" than telephones. As usual, police adopted devices based on habit, gossip, availability, and familiarity.

Uruguayan police, for example, began torturing "with a rudimentary electric needle that had come from Argentina." They adopted what they had heard was used nearby. In the mid-1960s, an American police adviser, Dan Mitrione, reinforced this habit. He arranged "for the police to get newer electric needles of varying thickness. Some needles were so thin they could be slipped between the teeth." The new needles were made by the CIA's Technical Services Division in Buenos Aires and delivered through the U.S. embassy's diplomatic pouch.[128] In 1971, police replaced the Argentine prods with new ones from American manufacturers.[129] About the same time, Brazilian police upgraded from field telephone magnetos to *pimentinhas*. In both countries, torturers favored what they knew how to use. It had become customary.

The Electric Cornucopia

In the 1970s, torturers invented many other electrotorture devices. Like prods and magnetos, these devices were nonlethal, clean, and painful. They lacked other critical qualities, and none of them found a niche in the world's torture markets. Some devices were not portable. Others were unfamiliar. Nor is it clear how they could be easily maintained, repaired, or replaced. They had characteristics that made them horrifying, but also easy to describe to journalists and activists. Stealth torture increasingly required stealthy devices, devices that fit into legitimate routine activities. These devices were too obvious.

The electric television. In 1972, Brazilian prisoners reported "a sort of television set in front of the chair which shoots forth electric charges which are very powerful, but which, as a result of distance, are not powerful enough to kill."[130]

The grill (parilla). After the Pinochet coup in 1973, Chilean torturers abandoned *corriente* for the *parilla*. The *parilla* is a metal grill with brass keys and metal plates connected to terminals. It delivered what "seemed like 200 volts." Electricity was delivered by means of metal bands or clothespins.[131] In her 1976 drawing of the *parilla* on which she was tortured, Sheila Cassidy showed an electric cable going to a transformer on the floor and then toward the wall.[132]

Modified chairs. The Brazilians developed a modified electrical chair, the "dragon chair." In 1966, Alves does not mention these chairs.[133] Two famous chairs appear in the 1970s. The Dragon Chair of São Paolo (1972) was a heavy chair made of corrugated iron. A wooden bar held the legs in place. Wires in the back electrified the chair. The Dragon Chair of Rio (1977) looked like a barbershop chair with foam rubber straps to cover the body.[134] The last chair on record is the Iranian Apollo Chair (1977).[135] Its only unique feature was a motorcycle helmet. Like many torturers elsewhere, Iranian police were not interested in screams. The helmet contained the noise while amplifying it for victims.

Electrotorture does not require a chair format, but these were irresistible showpieces. Protesters and journalists publicized descriptions endlessly, evoking the horror of the electric chair.[136] The chairs did not represent any technological advance, and Brazilians and Iranians abandoned them for other tortures by the 1980s.[137]

The electric skull, bag, and cap. These are South African devices. In 1957, a judge acquitted a defendant who had been given "electric shocks through a skull-shaped contraption placed on his head."[138] In 1976, in Soweto, a prisoner reported an electric cap. "They put something on my head, like a cap. I didn't see what it was. Then they came with a wet cloth and put it inside my mouth. Then I felt electric shocks going through my body."[139] In 1976, two prisoners at Zomba Prison in Malawi were also given "electric hat" torture.[140] In Johannesburg, Oshadi Phakathi reported she was "put in an electric frozen bag and suspended in the air by means of a heavy iron until I was suffocating."[141]

The electric refrigerator. This was another South African innovation from 1976. The prisoner was pushed into "a room with a door that looked like a butcher's refrigerator." In the dark, "I felt something like fingers touch me. With every touching I felt terrible shock. I screamed. I wet my pants on the second shock. There were three shocks in all. My whole body was wet when they opened the door."[142]

The Caroline and the spoon. These were Argentine inventions in the 1970s. The "Caroline" was a thick broom handle with two long wires than ran out of either end "like the antennae of a large insect." It was invented by a camp electrician and nicknamed "the electric cat."[143] No description of the electric spoon is available, but a prisoner reports that an army doctor would insert the spoon into the vagina of pregnant prisoners, cradle their fetuses, and deliver electric charges.[144]

The electric piano and microphones. In 1974, Brazilian prisoners described a "keyboard operated" electroshock device, dubbed the *pianola* ("little piano") and an "electric microphone" that delivered electric shocks to the prisoner, shocks "varying in intensity and duration according to sounds around him, including his own screams."[145] In 1983, an Afghan prisoner described a machine that "looked like a computer screen" with two small lamps, one yellow and one red. A device that "looked like a microphone" was wired to it. "When they pressed this microphone on my body I got strong electric shocks."[146]

Remembering Vietnam

In the 1980s, Americans flocked to movies of Rambo, the tormented Vietnam veteran played by Sylvester Stallone. In *First Blood: Part II* (1985), in a graphic and often praised torture scene, Lieutenant Colonel Podovsky and Captain Vinh subjected Rambo to electrotorture in Vietnam.[147] In fact, a POW history conducted for the U.S. Department of Defense identified only two cases of electrotorture conducted by the North during the entire Vietnam War, both occurring in 1969.[148] Though the Vietnamese did torture after the war, there were no reports of electrotorture even then.[149] Between 1950 and 1980, North Vietnamese, Soviets, indeed, most Communist societies that tortured prisoners, preferred Soviet positional tortures and sweating, often in conjunction with rope tortures, full suspension, flogging, and other disfiguring techniques.[150]

The irony in Rambo's electrotorture is that it was American, French, and South Vietnamese torturers who practiced electrotorture in Vietnam and who gifted it to the world. Perhaps Hollywood should not be faulted. Most torturers were also unaware that the common techniques they used, field telephone torture with water supplements, came to them by way of Vietnam and Algeria. In the social imaginary of torturers, Vietnam was simply a land of terror. Torturers remembered only legendary horrors like the helicopter treatment, and often inaccurately.[151] The Brazilians even invented an electrotorture dubbed "the Vietnam," but one that never existed in Indochina.[152]

Much that should have been remembered was forgotten. In 1997, an Amnesty International researcher came across an odd description of electric torture from Sri Lanka. The torture device looked like a telephone with a crank handle. The investigator wrote, "probably not a modern stun weapon, but apparently just as potentially damaging."[153] Just forty years after the Battle of Algiers, an Amnesty International researcher could no longer remember the word *magneto*. For by then the world of electrotorture had changed again.

The main thing is not to leave any marks.

— Hooded Brazilian police officer displaying

a stun gun, 2001[1]

9   Singing the World Electric

In the late twentieth century, torturers turned to electrotorture with far greater frequency than in the past. While it is difficult to estimate the increasing *magnitude* of electrotorture, one can map its expanding *scope*. Police or military interrogators in country after country turn to it. The surge occurred first in Latin America, the Middle East, and Asia in the late 1960s and early 1970s. African states followed in the 1980s. Lastly, in the 1990s, European states, especially the newly democratic states of Eastern Europe and the former Soviet Union, turned to electrotorture.[2]

The main task of this chapter is to document the expanding scope of electrotorture worldwide and to link this change to the development of stealth torture. However, before proceeding, I want to relate the preceding three chapters on electrotorture to the main claims of this book. This itemization clarifies what has already been established and provides a context for understanding the main claims in this chapter. It also helps identify what claims remain to be established, anticipating the purpose of the following two chapters on stun technology. Having provided this background understanding, I return to the daunting task of documenting the surge in electrotorture region by region and then consider plausible explanations for it.

When Electrotorture Was New

In the introduction, I distinguished between factual assertions (what I have called historical *claims* of this study), questions generated by these claims (what

I have called *puzzles*), and *explanations* of these puzzles. Keeping to the same format, I here summarize the claims of the preceding three chapters, and then turn to the puzzles and explanations.

Between 1890 and 1970, torturers adapted electric instruments for the purpose of torture. Some interrogators specialized in using electrotorture in a manner that did not leave marks. The instruments they preferred were not technologically sophisticated. Typically, they borrowed devices that came to them through routine usage: storage batteries, prods from the meat industry, and magnetos used to generate power for telephones, cars, refrigerators, and planes. More complex devices were rare and generally were abandoned over time. Examples include fancy electrical chairs, peculiar television sets, and electrified whips, swings, mats, belts, bags, caps, fridges, microphones, beds, and grills. These, it turned out, did not have a future. Likewise, medical devices rarely entered police and military interrogation, contrary to popular stories.

Stealthy electrotorture appeared first in American, Argentine, or French contexts, mainly in the late 1920s and 1930s. The French role in electrotorture was by far the most important, as French torturers pioneered the dominant form stealthy electrotorture took, namely, use of the magneto. French use of magneto torture seems to stretch almost unbroken from 1931 to 1960. Magneto torture was most common in the colonies of Vietnam and Algeria, but it also appeared in France twice, once during World War II (1943–45) and again during the Algerian conflict (1958–60).

American police used various electrotorture devices as early as 1910, but this practice more or less ceased in domestic policing by the 1930s, and the devices police used disappear. Between 1930 and 1960, there are no confirmed cases of American police and military using electrotorture at home or abroad.

When Americans return to the use of electrotorture in the 1960s, they turn to new devices. Some Americans adopted magneto torture, copying the French technique of using field telephones, or cattle prods. American telephone torture appears almost simultaneously domestically (the Tucker Telephone in the Arkansas prison system) and internationally in the Mekong Delta region of Vietnam. The earliest usage in both cases was apparently around 1963 or 1964. A little earlier, police in the American South turned to cattle prods for crowd control and occasionally torture (the earliest instance of which is June 1961). The next chapter will document further the rise and decline of police usage of the cattle prod in the 1960s.

American usage appears to be fragmentary and opportunistic, with different police and military interrogators using what was locally available. Of these various instances, the usage in Vietnam was by far the more important case, as electrotorture spread between military units in Vietnam, quietly tolerated by local officers, peaking in usage during the Tet Offensive in 1968. As in the

French case, magneto torture also traveled back to the United States through returning veterans, specifically to Chicago (1970–91). But more importantly, Americans played an important role in transmitting magneto torture to other places, most notably Brazil.

Of the three cases of stealthy electrotorture, the Argentine usage was the most localized of all. The *picana eléctrica* appeared first in the mid-1930s. It remained in almost continuous usage from that period onward, but police in neighboring countries were not interested in this device until the 1960s.

In the early twentieth century, this pattern of stealthy usage stands out against a violent background. Typically, other states that tortured either did not use electrotorture, or, if they did, used it without caring whether they left scars.

To be specific, the Japanese did not use electrotorture at home, but they did use it as part of a scarring regimen throughout their empire until 1945, starting with Korea in 1931 (see chapter 7, "Magnetos"). Nazi Germany did not use electrotorture as part of police interrogation domestically either (the sole known exception being Dorothea Binz's electric whip at Ravensbrück), but did occasionally resort to it in the conquered territories, most notably in France and Belgium (see chapter 4, "Whips and Water"). Nazi torture was generally scarring, and even in the few instances where Nazi torturers were stealthy, they did not use electrotorture. Auxiliary forces, most notably French and Ukrainian interrogators, used electrotorture more commonly, but again their torture was scarring (see chapter 4 and chapter 5, "Bathtubs"). The sole exception was Vichy's Bureau 51, where prisoners reported that it apparently mattered to their torturers whether they left marks or not.

Other early electrotorturers were the Portuguese secret police under Salazar (1932–39), the Brazilian police and military (1935), and the Spanish SIM in Republican Spain (probably as early as 1938) (see chapter 7). General Franco's police followed in the footsteps of the SIM in 1939, though their interest in electrotorture was sporadic at best (see chapter 6, "Shock" and chapter 8, "Currents"). All these police used techniques that left marks and deep scars, suggesting their interest in electrotorture was not about being stealthy. Venezuelan police also used prods in the early 1950s, but again the list of Venezuelan tortures from this period includes many scarring techniques, as I document later in this chapter.

Soviet police did not use electrotorture for interrogation domestically (see chapter 3). Though Soviet agents working in Spain may have been familiar with electrotorture conducted by the SIM (see chapter 6), they did not pass this technique back to the Soviet Union or to satellite states in their empire after World War II (for example, China or North Korea) (see chapter 3).

There was no electrotorture in the Austro-Hungarian Empire, though the Hungarians eventually adopted magneto torture perhaps as early as 1941 (see chapters 3 and 7). It is not clear whether the Hungarian police adopted this technique from somewhere or invented it on their own, but at any rate Hungarian torture left scars, as victims attest. And this usage ceases when Hungary becomes a Soviet client state.

Lastly, there is a sporadic history of British electrotorture stretching back to the beginning of the twentieth century. The first known instance comes from Cellular Prison, the penal colony of the Andaman Islands in 1912, and the device used was a storage battery (see chapter 7). This is among the earliest uses of electrotorture ever recorded. After World War II, British interrogators used electrotorture more extensively in Kenya in the 1950s. This usage was in conjunction with many scarring techniques, most notably flogging, so there is little evidence to suggest that the British interrogators intended to be stealthy. British interrogators elsewhere generally did not adopt electrotorture in the following decades, though there were sporadic reports from Cyprus (1955–56) and Northern Ireland (1972).

These claims yield the following generalizations. There is a long, though largely forgotten, history of electrotorture in democracies at home and abroad, a history that stretches from at least 1910 to the late twentieth century. This claim simply restates what I have already stated using the conventional designation of France, the United States, and the United Kingdom as the main democracies of modern history. One can dispute, if one likes, whether Argentina even had truly democratic governments after 1930. But as the Argentine usage was not influential in the early history of electrotorture, not much hangs on this point.

The French and American usage was more influential by far. The French and American torturers used magneto torture in conjunction with other techniques that left few marks, pioneering the way in stealthy electrotorture. By the late twentieth century, French-style magneto torture with a field telephone started appearing in countries around the world (see chapter 8), and as I will document in this chapter, other techniques that leave few marks tended to cluster around it. In this respect, French and American torturers were leaders in adapting and innovating stealthy electrotorture. This usage stands out against the backdrop of other states (authoritarian, Fascist, Communist, call them what you will) in the early twentieth century who either did not use electrotorture or used it in conjunction with scarring techniques.

Democratic states, then, were the first to pioneer clean electrotorture. But there is an important objection to consider here. The earliest French usage occurred first under colonial conditions that were hardly democratic, and generally these techniques rarely appeared in France itself. Likewise, the main instances of American electrotorture occurred in the context of a foreign war. If clean torture occurred primarily in the context of war and colonization, is it accurate to say that democracy and clean electrotorture go hand in hand?

This is a reasonable objection, but it only serves to restate the main empirical puzzle that follows from the historical claims. Why then, one may ask, does stealthy electrotorture appear first *in the colonies and foreign wars* of democracies and not *in the colonies and foreign wars* of authoritarian states? As with France and the United States, electrotorture does not appear domestically in fascist Japan or Soviet Russia at all, and there is only one major recorded instance of it in Nazi Germany. Why were authoritarian states uninterested in stealthy electrotorture? The Soviets, who had the keenest interest in stealthy torture, never used it for show trial preparations. And when electrotorture does appear in empires of authoritarian states, it is in the context of scarring techniques. Torturers serving these empires in conquered lands seem to have had little interest in the specifically *stealthy* use of electrotorture.

At any rate, French torturers used stealthy electrotorture domestically (even in Paris) as early as 1947 and as late as 1960. Stealthy American electrotorture appeared domestically first and reappeared again domestically after the 1970s (as I will document in chapter 11, "Stun City"). All this deserves an explanation. So again, we return to the original puzzle: Why does clean electrotorture occur first in democratic states (and, if one likes, the colonies and foreign wars of democratic states), and not in authoritarian states or their empires?

Explaining Clean Electrotorture

My main explanation for this historical pattern of clean electrotorture is the monitoring hypothesis. This hypothesis states that public monitoring leads institutions that favor painful coercion to use and combine clean procedures. This is because these methods make it less likely that torturers will be found out or held responsible. To the extent that public monitoring is not only greater in democracies, but that public monitoring of human rights is a core value in modern democracies, it is the case that where we find democracies torturing, we are also likely to find stealth torture.

The historical patterns of electrotorture I have described thus far fit this explanation. Prior to 1960, stealthy electrotorture appears mainly in democratic states, their colonies, or their foreign wars. Authoritarian states show no interest in clean electrotorture. Indeed, among all the documented cases of electrotorture between 1890 and 1960, there is only *one* case of clean electrotorture by an authoritarian state. Between 1943 and 1945, Vichy's Bureau 51 favored torture that left no marks, including electrotorture. Why Bureau 51 favored such techniques remains a mystery, since other French collaborators of the Nazis were hardly restrained.

One tempting alternative hypothesis would be to argue that regime type explains these outcomes, that democratic states (for whatever reason) always prefer clean electrotorture, while authoritarian states do not (the regime type hypothesis). But not all democracies are clean in their electrotorture in the early twentieth century. In the 1950s, the British used electrotorture in the context of a violent, scarring regimen that left many Kenyans broken for life. Conversely, some authoritarian states become cleaner in their torture over time. The South Vietnamese interrogators, for example, became increasingly more careful in the kind of evidence they left behind in the course of the 1960s.

What matters in these cases is whether the treatment of prisoners draws public attention. In Vietnam, General Westmoreland registered his concern with public perception as early as 1965. After the My Lai incident in 1968, American military concern with bad publicity intensified, even if the measures taken to control the torture of prisoners seem to have been, at best, inadequate. It would not be unreasonable to conclude that South Vietnamese officials also understood how foreign aid and legitimacy depended on controlling adverse publicity about torture of prisoners, although this is only speculation.

Conversely, the British treatment of the Mau Mau detainees did not draw much public interest at home, or for that matter, international interest. While detainees wrote articulately about their conditions, they did not get sympathetic coverage in the press. Some British MPs such as Barbara Castlereigh drew attention to the alleged abuses, but the British government so successfully repressed details of the torture that much of it was unknown until the early twenty-first century.[3]

Racism clearly was a factor in all this, as it was in French-occupied Algeria. Reports of torture of Algerians fell on indifferent ears. Public attention focused marvelously, though, once French police and Paras started torturing Europeans. The torture of Europeans in Oran, followed by the disappearance of Maurice Audin and the torture of Henri Alleg, led to a growing antitorture movement in France and drew international attention to prison conditions in Algeria (see chapter 1, "Modern Torture and Its Observers").

This seems to suggest yet another explanation for clean tortures. Perhaps torturers change their tactics depending on whether a person is like them or not (the dehumanization hypothesis). When the prisoner is like them, they use techniques that leave few marks. But when the person is viewed as an inferior, they are indifferent or deliberately leave scars. Sympathy, and not concern with public monitoring, drives the choices torturers make.

While there is no question racism played a part in colonial torture, it is too gross to account for the pattern of clean torture in colonies. While French police and military may have been cruelly indifferent to Arabs, Africans, and Asians, they pulled their punches in certain cases. French Paras used tortures

that left few marks more commonly in urban areas than in the Algerian countryside. The same distinction holds for the French Sûreté in Vietnam in the 1930s.

Should one conclude, then, that interrogators were less racist in urban
areas than in the countryside? This seems implausible given that, in Algeria
for example, we are often talking about the same units torturing in both places.[4]
It seems more plausible to argue that monitoring differed in urban areas from
monitoring in the countryside. There could be many possibilities; monitoring
may have been more frequent, comprehensive, specialized, and well informed.
We know that Algerian prisoners began documenting their scars, mindful that
no matter how small, these could verify their torture in courts and before the
press (chapter 7). It seems unlikely that this would have mattered if prisoners
were not equally mindful of the quality of public monitoring. Unfortunately,
all one can do is list the possible variables, and note that this distribution is
consistent with the view that public monitoring is more intensive in urban areas
than in distant regions.

At any rate, if torturers pull their punches when dealing with Europeans,
it may be because they know that the European public will notice this treatment
but will be indifferent to the treatment of non-Europeans. In this sense, the
dehumanization hypothesis is a variant of the monitoring hypothesis. Monitoring *will* differ depending on what the priorities of monitors are. As I argue in
part IV, some ancient societies pioneered painful physical techniques that left
few marks on women and children because of the treatment the public expected and demanded. Slave dealers preferred clean techniques because they
knew buyers would conclude scarred slaves were disciplinary problems and not
purchase them.

Public monitoring, then, is compatible with racist and sexist values; all that
matters here is that torturers know they are being watched according to some
set of values, and check their behavior accordingly. What is different about our
age is that the public monitoring now enforces a universal human rights regime.
Thus it is increasingly more difficult (though certainly not impossible) for police to excuse themselves for torturing someone because the person had the
wrong race or gender. Accordingly, one would expect interrogators to adopt
stealthy torture regimens for many more prisoners than in earlier centuries, and
those techniques originally reserved for women, children, or slaves to circulate
more widely. This, as I argue in part IV, is in fact the case.

However one slices it, then, the monitoring hypothesis provides the best
account of the distribution of clean or scarring torture in the early twentieth
century. Admittedly, a great deal is still unknown. It is not clear why Vichy's
Bureau 51 preferred clean torture. And we know too little about the circumstances in Vietnam in the 1930s and why the French Sûreté preferred leaving
no marks at this time. All one can say here is that European colonies were more

integrated with the colonial power than is commonly appreciated (as I explain in appendix B). What happened "out there" sometimes mattered to people in Paris and London. And while French Indochina was hardly a democracy, there was an alternative press that did draw torture and other human rights abuses to public attention.

Crafting Electrotorture

The preceding chapters also offer a more detailed understanding of how torturers choose their devices for torture and the kind of training they receive. Three cases in particular stand out: Argentina (1930–55), French Algeria (1955–60), and U.S. troops in Vietnam (1963–70).

Evidence from Argentina suggests that torturers learned to administer the *picana eléctrica* largely through trial and error as they interrogated prisoners (see chapter 6). There is little evidence of medical finesse here, as torturers punched jaws to prevent "lockjaw" and plastered mouths shut to prevent prisoners from biting off their tongues. Likewise, in Algeria, Wuillaume's report describes no police training in torture. Police learned the old-fashioned way in the course of interrogation. A little later, prisoners describe how French Paras learned on the job to turn magneto handles (see chapter 7). And, similarly, American interrogators appear to have learned how to operate magnetos by observing and imitating South Vietnamese interrogators and interpreters. In these three cases at least, there are no accounts of formal scientific training in electrical principles.

All this conforms well to the notion that torture is a craft, and police and military interrogators learn it mainly by imitation (the craft apprenticeship hypothesis). Less is known about training for electrotorture in other places and times, but the evidence appears to be similar. A Japanese interrogator states he received no formal training in torture and that he trained his own interrogators in China on the job. The Kempeitai manual offered no guidance in this respect either, authorizing torture but leaving it to the interrogators to pick what methods they wanted. American electrotorture in the early twentieth century appears haphazard and opportunistic (see chapter 3, "Lights, Heat, and Sweat"), as does the practice of the French Gestapo (1943–45) (see chapter 5).

Torture, in this respect, is similar to tailoring. Torturers may treat all prisoners to the same standard violence; torture becomes a "one size fits all" operation, with predictable, ill-fitting results. Or one can customize torture to the needs of the situation and the character of the prisoner. Either way, all the evidence suggests that, however it is performed, torturers learn their craft on the job. (In part V, I argue that this necessarily must be the case given the nature of pain.)

And as with tailoring, torturers develop certain styles based on past familiarity with the instruments, fashions of the day, and the needs of the situation.

To be specific, torturers generally preferred devices routinely available in ordinary life: cattle prods and magnetos. By the late 1950s, French electrototurers preferred a specific device that was multifunctional and linked to their routine activities, the field telephone or *gégène*. Indeed, the word *gégéneur* became synonymous with torturer. *Gégéneurs* preferred to combine electrototure with pumping or choking their victim in water. There are many different techniques that leave few marks, but the French preference for field telephone torture with various water tortures was so predictable that it is recognizable as a distinctive style in modern torture, what I have called French modern.

Why French torturers had such a distinctive preference is unclear; all one can say is that it became customary. But if we are to judge by the Paras' own self-descriptions, the Paras believed firmly that the Nazis were modern and scientific torture professionals (incorrectly, as I explain in chapter 5) and they, like most Frenchmen, took electrototure and water tortures to be quintessentially Nazi techniques (again incorrectly).

Given how quickly magneto torture spread in the wake of the Algerian war, it seems reasonable to think that many torturers were inspired by the French use of torture during the Battle of Algiers. Whether the Paras were in fact successful in the use of torture, or whether the Nazis were more successful than they were, are issues I leave for part V. For the moment it is sufficient to observe that nothing promotes a specific kind of torture technique like stories of its alleged success, and French modern came into the world with a formidable reputation and soon found imitators around the world.

Vietnam War stories seem to have also played a role in inspiring Brazilian torturers to use electrototure, but in a manner that never appeared in Vietnam. Torturers also played on the horrors of medical ECT torture, though again there is little evidence of ECT devices in their work.

The historical evidence points, then, mainly to imitation, familiarity, trial and error, rumor, gossip, and war stories. Institutional settings also played an important role in constraining, but not determining, outcomes. Electrototure appears quite often in the context of war and counterinsurgency, as one would predict. In these situations, immediate information is at a premium, and interrogators are likely to prefer techniques that cause immediate pain (e.g., electrototure) rather than those that take time to work (e.g., forced standing). Again, in situations where torturers adopt stealthy styles, they use electrical instruments that are routinely available and attached to their legitimate duties (riot batons and field telephones). Such qualities allow torturers to deny plausibly that they misused the devices, and this choice would be unintelligible in the absence of monitoring.

There are three alternative explanations to the craft apprenticeship hypothesis. One is that ideology plays some role in how torturers select their devices (the ideology hypothesis). In favor of this view is the absence of electrotorture in the Soviet Union and among its client states for much of the century. This is not absolute, of course, for some Soviet client states did use electrotorture by the 1970s, most notably Syria and Afghanistan. I will return to this claim at the end of this chapter.

Another explanation is that culture plays a role in the choice of technique (the cultural hypothesis). I will evaluate this claim more closely in part IV, where I consider torture techniques of great antiquity. Electricity, by contrast, is barely over a century old. If electrical pain is a cultural practice anywhere in the world, it must be in the United States, where it was invented. At the dawn of the electrical age, Americans were unique (and still are unique) in executing prisoners by electrocution. John Cover, the inventor of stun technology, took the initials of his favored childhood story of *Tom A. Swift and his Electric Rifle* to name his invention, the Taser. And I will document other elements of this electrical imaginary in American culture in the following chapter. But the point here is that this background understanding has not changed much over the century, and so it cannot be used easily to explain why American torturers changed their preferred devices from mats, storage batteries, and chairs in the 1920s to magnetos and prods in the 1960s to Tasers and stun guns in 1980s.

Perhaps Americans chose based on their evaluation of the scientific quality of these techniques (the scientific efficiency hypothesis). But the evidence for this claim is lacking. The evidence in the preceding chapters suggests that it was not sufficient for devices to be nonlethal, portable, scientific, painful, flexible, and leave few marks. Other factors played a role, including linkage, multifunctionality, cost, maintenance, design (familiar or alarming), extent of monitoring (high or low), and effect (whether it induces amnesia). Such considerations ruled out fancy electrical chairs, unique inventions such as electrical whips, and medical devices such as ECT machines.

In general, like torturers everywhere, American police generally favored low-tech devices (see chapter 3). Electricity was in this respect an exception to the rule. Moreover, it is difficult to explain why torturers preferred various high-tech devices, in some cases magnetos and in other cases prods, without appealing to some account based on availability, imitation, and reputation.

In short, electrotorture was a craft, and torturers learned their particular way of performing it on the job, by imitating their peers and experimenting on their own. Techniques spread from unit to unit, moving from the bottom up, rather than from the top down through centralized training. In many cases, local police appear to have turned to torture, even stealthy torture, on their own and without knowledge of their higher-ups. This appears to be the case for some American police (the 1920s); the colonial Sûreté in Vietnam (1930s) and Madagascar (1947); the French police in Nice (1947) and Algeria (the 1950s); the French military in Vietnam (the 1940s); American interrogators in Vietnam (1963–70); and police in Alabama and Mississippi (the 1960s).

In Algeria, of course, General Massu introduced the use of field telephones for electrotorture. But it would be more accurate to state that his officers introduced the *gégène* to *him,* and he then authorized its use. In fact, torture by magneto had a long history in the empire, and it, too, appears to have spread from the bottom up rather than from the top down. Algerian police had decided to adopt a stealthy regimen in torture long before the Paras arrived or the government itself became aware of it, as Wuillaume's report illustrated (see chapter 7). Local commanders, most notably Massu, eventually embraced it, and politicians learned to turn a blind eye.

There are, to be sure, other cases, where one can confirm political elites authorized torture (though not specifically electrotorture). One might cite here the Japanese Kempeitai manual and Gestapo chief Müller's directives regulating sharpened interrogations. But it is equally certain that in cases where the directives are known, torturers went beyond the authorized techniques. By 1960, French Paras had adopted a wider variety of techniques than Massu ever dreamed. No matter what the top authorities limit torture to, torture has a slippery slope, and torturers have strong incentives to adopt more extreme and diverse techniques (as I document in part V).

There is also little evidence that corporations and economic elites had a direct role in developing electrotorture before 1970. Thomas Edison played an important role in promoting the electric chair as a way of discrediting Westinghouse's alternating current. But beyond this, the evidence is scant. One can argue that the meatpacking, telephone, and transportation industries played an indirect role in making devices that were subsequently used for electrotorture. But it does not appear that corporate elites even noticed that cattle prods had an alternative market until the 1960s, and they were quite surprised to find out that law enforcement had any use for them as riot control devices, much less torture devices.

All this bears on yet another possible explanation for the spread of clean tortures, one that contests the monitoring hypothesis. One might argue that democratic states are ruled by an elite, who for whatever reason hide their domination through apparently law-abiding behavior. They are the ones who ordered lower-level agents to adopt clean techniques (the ruling elite hypothesis). But aside from Edison, there is no evidence that economic elites played such a direct role in the early history of electrotorture. And besides Massu, there is little evidence that political elites played such a role either.

Still, the decision to torture (stealthily or otherwise) is usually so buried in secrecy and so often lost to history that is hazardous to say more. Sometimes the decision comes from the lower-downs and is simply endorsed by the higher-ups; sometimes it comes from the higher-ups. In the case of electrotorture, on the whole, there seems more evidence that the lower-downs were more important. It is also worth observing that even Massu was well aware that domestic groups and the international press were observing the behavior of French troops in Algeria. He was aware, in other words, he was being monitored. The ruling elite hypothesis, in this sense, is not an *alternative* to the monitoring hypothesis.

Surging Forward

As I stated at the outset of this chapter, more countries started adopting electrotorture in the late twentieth century than ever before. In what follows, I argue that the turn to electrotorture is also a turn to stealthy torture. I hold that state officials, whether they were higher up or lower down, understood that bad publicity about torture affected foreign aid and global standing, and so torturers in authoritarian and democratic states alike chose cleaner techniques, including electrotorture. Let me call this the universal monitoring (UM) hypothesis.

One might distinguish this situation from the situation earlier in the twentieth century, when international monitoring was sporadic and selective, and scarring torture was the norm. Under these conditions, states only turned to clean techniques when they deliberately sought out international attention (Soviet show trials) or when they knew the foreign press was watching a particular incident (Nazi torture of Swedish prisoners). Authoritarian states were less likely to be cleaner than democratic states because they were far less accountable at home and abroad, and the history of electrotorture bears this out.

But by the 1960s, even some authoritarian states began adopting clean electrotorture, a trend that has continued since then. It coincides with the formation of an international human rights monitoring regime (see chapter 1). This international auditing of torture grew first in Europe in the 1960s. By the 1980s, one can speak of the formation of a global human rights consensus, enforced by numerous international and national auditors of human rights practices.

But two alternative explanations are also possible for the surge in electrotorture. One is that the surge was really driven by economic factors, not by universal monitoring. Corporations and economic elites, mobilizing commercial networks, flooded the world with slick advertising for cheap stun guns, and police and military customers worldwide responded in large numbers. This is yet another version of the ruling elite hypothesis, one that singles out economic elites.

Another explanation would be that a major state drove distribution and training in electrotorture around the world (the universal distributor [UD] hypothesis). Consider, for example, the list of countries that embraced electrotorture in the 1960s (provided in the previous chapter): France, the United States, South Vietnam, South Korea, Brazil, Israel, Greece, South Africa, Argentina, Morocco, Uruguay, and Portugal. Setting aside the old users (France, the United States, and Argentina), all the remaining countries were American allies. The United States could have been the universal distributor of electrotorture for the late twentieth century, shipping devices worldwide to its allies.

These versions of the UD hypothesis and ruling elite hypothesis are not incompatible. Indeed, since the stun industry was originally an American one, some prefer to roll them together and argue that the United States used its economic and political power to promote torture worldwide starting in the 1970s. I treat the two explanations separately.

In the following two chapters, I discuss the formation of the stun gun industry. I argue that the development of stun technology was far more problematic than is commonly described, and it is greatly misleading to argue that evil corporations simply made products that almost floated off the shelves to police stations everywhere around the world.

Nothing of the sort happened in the 1970s. U.S. government officials at virtually every level were indifferent if not downright hostile toward the promoters of stun technology. The inventors of stun technology had to overcome formidable obstacles to market their products, obstacles placed by the U.S. government itself. Moreover, the chronology of this chapter does not support the view that the stun industry promoted the spread of electrotorture; stun technology finally came of age in the mid-1980s, ten to twenty years after the surge in electrotorture had begun worldwide.

There is no question, of course, that stun guns and Tasers are very popular today, but would they be that interesting to torturers if they did not leave few marks and were not integrated into routine police activities? Without the facilitating conditions of global monitoring, would there even have been a torture market for these devices? The priority must go then to the "pull" of global monitoring rather than the "push" of economic and technological imperatives.

In this chapter, I focus on the political hypothesis that singles out the United States as a major universal distributor. We know that in one case, Brazil, American advisers introduced magneto torture to interrogators, and others have suggested that the CIA distributed electrical devices (though mistakenly identifying them as ECT devices; see chapter 6). It is not far-fetched to argue that this happened worldwide, and with increasing frequency, in the 1970s.

At the end of this chapter, I consider the most disciplined version of the UD hypothesis, advanced by Noam Chomsky. I offer three simple tests of this hypothesis, and the results indicate that this UD hypothesis is, at best, a partial explanation of the distribution of electrotorture in the 1970s. The UM hypothesis offers a more complete understanding of the actual distribution.

But first, I must document the distribution of electrotorture region by region. There can be no evaluating of any contending explanations without knowing the actual pattern on the ground. In many cases, all that we have are lists of known tortures used by the police and military, with little information regarding specific devices. These lists, however, are sufficient to determine whether there is a clustering of techniques that leave few marks around electrotorture, and whether they cluster in predictable ways (as in the style of French modern).

Wherever one documents a clustering of techniques that leave few marks, I conclude that the intent of torturers was not to leave scars. This does not rule out the possibility that torturers favored all these devices because they had some other hidden quality besides cleanliness. Perhaps techniques that leave few marks are inherently more painful (though, in assessing this possibility, the thought of boiling one's hand in oil gives one pause). Or perhaps torturers simply liked shiny American-made commercial products, but there are no reports of such consumer enthusiasm.

In what follows, I claim that torturers turned to electrotorture, and away from scarring methods, during the same decades when global audits of torture increased. Prods, magnetos, and stun guns usually spread in conjunction with other techniques that left few marks.[5] Region by region, torturers appear to have become increasingly concerned with the evidence they left behind.

The Americas

The major Latin American states all practiced electrotorture by the 1970s (table 9.1). In the next decade, they were joined by smaller states in Andean and Central America. As the steadily shifting lists of torture techniques below show, everywhere torturers shifted from open to stealthy brutality.

Argentina. In the early 1930s, torturers beat prisoners tied to chairs (*la silla*) and drove pegs (*los tacos*) into the kidneys that penetrated little by little into the flesh of the prisoner. They crushed hands with wooden presses (*las prensas*). They used wooden pincers to crush nipples and pull tongues (*la tenaza saca-lengua*). They drove red-hot needles into genitals (*las agujas caldeadas al rojo*). They rubbed the chest with strong hemp rope (*el serrucho*) or sandpaper and then aggravated the raw skin with alcohol and turpentine (*el papel de lija y aguarrás*). Prisoners were dunked headfirst into a barrel (*el tacho*) or confined to a small wet triangular cell (*el triángulo*).[6]

Table 9.1
Main Electroshock Users in the Americas, 1970–2004

	1970–1979	1980–1989	1990–1999	2000–2004
Previous user	United States (**magneto**, prod)	United States (**prod**, magneto)	United States (prod, magneto, **stun gun**)	United States (stun gun, stun belt)
	Argentina (prod)	Argentina (prod)	Argentina	Argentina (prod)
	Brazil (magneto)	Brazil	Brazil	Brazil (stun gun, wires)
	Uruguay (prod)	Uruguay (prod)	Uruguay (prod)	Uruguay
	Venezuela (magneto)	Venezuela	Venezuela (stun gun)	
Late user	Bolivia (prod)	Bolivia (prod)	Bolivia	Bolivia
	Chile ("current," *parilla*)	Chile (*parilla*)	Chile	Chile
	Colombia	Colombia (wires)	Colombia	Colombia
	Ecuador	Ecuador	Ecuador	Ecuador
	El Salvador	El Salvador	El Salvador	
	Mexico (wires)	Mexico	Mexico (prod, live wires)	
	Paraguay (iron bed)	Paraguay (prod)	Paraguay	Paraguay (prod)
	Cuba (ECT)	Cuba (wires, ECT)		
Later user		Guatemala	Guatemala	
		Honduras (wires)	Honduras	Honduras
		Peru	Peru	Peru
Latest user				Canada
Periodic user	Nicaragua	Nicaragua	Belize	
		Netherlands Antilles	Haiti	
		Grenada		
		Guyana		

Note: **Bold** marks a known preference for device type.

In 1935, the police adopted the *picana eléctrica*. By 1955, torturers favored it over all other techniques. They complemented it with pricking with a thin needle (*el pinchazo*), squeezing and strangling limbs with a wet towel (*la toalla mojada*), hand presses, and pricks under the nails (*la cuña*).[7] By 1976, common tortures were the *picana*, choking with water (*el submarino*), beating, kicking, cigarette burning, ice-cold baths, positional tortures, and sleep deprivation.[8] In 1990, torture consisted of electroshock (*máquina*), near-asphyxiation with a bag (*bolsa*), drugs, and clean beating and kicking.[9] "For example, they kicked me thousands of times on the legs, but they knew how to do it without making marks."[10] In 2002, police torture consisted of beatings, *picana*, and near asphyxiation.

Brazil. In the 1935, Getoelio Vargas's police showed little restraint. As documented in chapter 6, officers mainly beat, whipped, and choked opponents. They pulled nails and teeth, stuck victims with pins, needles, and hot wires, and burned them with torches, cigars, and electricity.[11] They also used a chair with hidden springs that suddenly threw the prisoner against the wall (*cadeira americana*, the American chair).[12] Cleanliness in torture only seemed to matter when a Brazilian senator condemned the violence; he was arrested, beaten with rubber clubs, and hidden for a week until his bruises cleared.[13]

In 1943, British and American agents helped Vargas's police interrogate a German spy ring.[14] Interrogators adopted American "third degree" techniques (*regime duro*). These were sleep deprivation or forced standing for two to three days, sometimes before bright lights. Other tortures were cigarette burns, kicks to the genitals, and clean beating.

In 1966, torturers used repeated electric shock, choking in water (*banho chinês*), exhaustion exercises (*ginástica*), and suspension (*pau de arara*). They also cuffed the victims in the ears with their palms in a concave position (*telefone*). They handcuffed them in uncomfortable positions to furniture for hours or days (*algemas*) and forced them to stand in front of bright lights (*sabão em pó*). They slipped alcohol into the anus (*churrasquinho*), pulled at flesh with pincers, and froze victims in meat lockers (*geladeira*).[15]

In 1979, the Archdiocese of São Paulo listed the main tortures as electric shock (magnetos, dragon chairs), pumping stomachs with water, slapping both ears (*teléfono*), forced standing (sometimes with heavy objects), suspension (*pau de arara*), and beating prisoners with a paddle (the *palmatoria*), an old slaver instrument that did not bruise the merchandise (discussed in part IV). The ordeal of the *geladeira* was now a machine like a meat locker that generated intense loud noises or persistent white noise. Less frequently, victims were subjected to snakes, insects, and drugs.[16]

In 2002, prisoners in São Paulo reported electrotorture, suspension on the *pau*, beating on the soles of the feet (*falaka*), sweatboxes (*cofrinho*), *teléfono*, exhaustion exercises, and clean beatings.[17]

Chile. In 1972, leftist guerrillas in Santiago Public Jail mainly used electricity (*la corriente*), choking, and "blows well applied to the kidneys, the stomach, and the liver," a beating style that would "not leave visible marks."[18] During the military coup (1973–74), torturers were either ferociously brutal or stealthy.[19]

When they were stealthy, torturers combined electroshock on the *parilla*, choking with water, punitive exercises, positional tortures (forced standing before bright lights), and drinking noxious substances.

Between 1974 and 1977, military torturers were more mindful of publicity. Torture consisted mainly of beating, *parilla*, choking with water (*submarino*), suspension, slapping the ears (*teléfono*), drugs, and near asphyxiation using plastic bags over the head ("dry submarine"). The degree of stealthiness varied with the degree of public monitoring. Torturers forced an English citizen to sign a document attesting she was not tortured, but for others, "brutal methods have continued to be used."[20]

From 1977 to 1990, torture consisted of beatings, *parilla*, suspension (*pau de arara*), *teléfono*, choking with water (*la bañera*), and, occasionally, *falaka*.[21]

Venezuela. In the 1950s, suspects were whipped, beaten with the plane of machetes, and forced to stand on sharp objects for hours (*el ring*, the sharp rims of an automobile wheel). These techniques left bloody wounds, and police transferred prisoners only after wounds healed. Other techniques were cleaner. Torturers used electroshock (*picana*, magneto), *falaka*, forced standing in front of bright lights in the sweat room (*capilla ardiente*), handcuffs that tightened with movement (*esposas italianas*). They stuffed prisoners into boxes of ice (*panela de hielo*). They also practiced sheet compresses (*la sabana*), wrapping prisoners in wet sheets and letting them slowly tighten around bodies as they dried.[22] By 1970, Venezuelan police had settled on a style: electroshock, beatings, near asphyxiation in a plastic bag ("dry submarine"), and burns with cigarettes.[23] Current practices include forced standing, suspension, electroshock, and the dry submarine.[24]

Less is known about the succession of torture techniques in other Latin American countries, but the lists that appear after the 1970s indicate that using torture techniques that left few marks became common. Colombian torturers used electroshock and disorienting drugs. More recently, they also used choking with water and a positional torture, *el chancho*, in which one lies parallel to the floor with head and tips of the toes straight. Uruguayan torturers preferred beatings, electric prods, pumping (*submarino*), and two positional tortures (forced standing (*planton*) and sitting on iron bars (*caballete*). A study of victims tortured between 1977 and 1983 reports that 89 percent of them had been subjected to water torture and electrotorture.[25]

Such trends also apply to the latecomers. Peruvian interrogators favored electroshock and choking in water (*ta tina*), often mixed with salt or hot peppers.[26] Mexican and Ecuadorian police combined electroshock with beatings, especially the *teléfono*, and choking (in water or with bags).[27] Bolivian police adopted the prod, the *falaka*, and positional tortures such as *el chancho*.[28]

Honduran torturers used electroshock, choking with water, *teléfono*, foam-covered batons, *falaka*, and sweatboxes.[29] Argentine police taught interrogators how to use a hood impregnated with noxious chemicals (the *capucha*).[30] Guatemalan torturers also used electroshock and the *capucha*. Paraguayan torturers used prods, choking (*pirenta*), the *falaka*, sweatboxes (*cajones, guardia*), positional torture (sitting in the fetus position for hours, *feto*), and exhaustion exercises (drawing heavy weights on a harness, *caballo*). They also wrapped suspects in plastic sheets and slipped them in cylinders (*secadra*).[31] In El Salvador, torturers used electrotorture, choking in water and plastic bags, positional torture (*el chancho*), suspension, sweating before bright lights, beatings, and exhaustion exercises.[32]

Cubans followed Soviet positional tortures and sweating techniques, and then, in the late 1970s, adopted psychoprisons that used various medical treatments (including pharmacological torture and ECT).[33] In 1981, José Morales Rodriguez was put into a water tank and electrified before being passed on to a psychiatric ward for pharmacological torture and ECT. This is the only reported case of Cuban electortorture outside of a medical context.[34]

Middle East and North Africa

In the Middle East and North Africa (table 9.2), torturers preferred to supplement electrotorture with the *falaka,* rather than water, a style one might call Mediterranean modern. One finds this combination repeatedly in the 1970s (Syria, Turkey, Morocco, and Iran), in the 1980s (Egypt, Iraq, Libya) and in the 1990s (Lebanon, Tunisia, Yemen, Saudi Arabia, and Kuwait after the Gulf War). Torturers also favored whipping with hoses (Egypt, Syria, Iraq, Tunisia). Some torturers also used water torture, including choking (Egypt, Lebanon, Saudi Arabia, Syria), cold showers (Syria, Israel), and high-pressure hoses (Turkey). Positional and restraint tortures also appeared in Israel, Lebanon, Morocco, Tunisia, Yemen, Saudi Arabia, Kuwait, and Iran. In the 1980s, Afghan torturers used plastic bags for near asphyxiation. Post-Taliban Afghan torture includes suspension and electroshocks.[35] In the 1990s, Moroccan and Algerian torturers varied choking, sometimes soaking the choke rag with chemicals or salt water (the *chiffon*).

Torture in democratic states was far cleaner than torture in authoritarian states.[36] In the 1970s, Israeli interrogators combined electrotorture, choking in water, *falaka*, cold showers, beating, and incarceration in refrigerator cells. By the 1990s, they abandoned these techniques for positional tortures known as the *shabeh*. Turkish interrogators' preferred technique was electrotorture combined with the *falaka*. By contrast, in authoritarian states, torturers used flogging, full

Table 9.2
Main Electroshock Users in the Middle East and North Africa, 1970–2004

	1970–1979	1980–1989	1990–1999	2000–2004
Previous user	Israel (magneto) Morocco (wires)	Israel (magneto) Morocco	Israel Morocco	Morocco
Late user	Afghanistan (magneto, prod, other) Egypt Iran (prod) Iraq (prod) Libya Syria (wires) Turkey (magneto)	Afghanistan Egypt Iran Iraq (prod) Libya Syria Turkey	Afghanistan Egypt (prod) Iran Iraq Libya Syria Turkey	Afghanistan Egypt Iraq Libya Syria Turkey
Late user		Algeria Jordan Lebanon Saudi Arabia Tunisia Yemen, P.D.R.	Algeria Jordan Lebanon (prod) Saudi Arabia (prod or stun gun) Tunisia Yemen	Algeria Jordan Lebanon Saudi Arabia Tunisia Yemen (prod)
Latest user				Canada
Periodic user		Kuwait UAE	Kuwait Qatar Palestine Authority	UAE

suspension (Egypt, Syria, Iraq), presses that crushed bones (Syria, Iraq), pliers to pluck nails (Algeria, Syria), boiling flesh (Egypt), striking with sharp instruments (Iraq, Egypt, Syria), heated grills and spits to roast victims (Iran, Iraq) or skewers that impaled them from the anus (Syria).

Among these states, Iranian torture followed a unique pattern.[37] Under the shah, torturers were mindful of bad publicity in international media. After the Islamic Revolution in 1979, this did not matter. Torturers beat and flogged, abandoning electricity. In the 1990s, domestic politics drove a new turn toward cleanliness in torture. The government now sought to make political opponents offer dramatic, seemingly voluntary, television recantations to demoralize the opposition. Iranian torture now involved standard Soviet positional tortures and sweating techniques as well as other clean torture techniques, such as sleep deprivation supplemented with beatings, the *falaka*, and, on rare occasions, electrotorture.[38]

Asia

In Asia (table 9.3), as in other areas, police were more likely than soldiers, especially those fighting wars on mountain frontiers and islands, to combine techniques that left few marks.

Southeast Asia. In the mountains of East Timor, Indonesian troops brutally tortured and killed guerrillas in the 1970s. By 1983, stealth mattered to the government. An interrogation manual urged soldiers to be mindful of adverse publicity. "Avoid taking photographs showing torture (*penyiksaan*) (of someone being given electric shocks, stripped naked and so on). Remember that such documentation/photographs should not be printed freely outside/in Denpasar [Bali, where Regional Command Headquarters I is located] and obtained by

Table 9.3
Main Electroshock Users in Asia, 1970–2004

	1970–1979	1980–1989	1990–1999	2000–2004
Previous user	S. Korea (phone magneto)	S. Korea	S. Korea	
Late user	Cambodia (live wires)	Cambodia	Cambodia (prod)	
	India (magneto)	India (magneto)	India (magneto)	India
	Indonesia (wires)	Indonesia	Indonesia (prod)	
	Philippines (magneto)	Philippines	Philippines	Philippines
	Taiwan	Taiwan	Taiwan (prod)	Taiwan (prod)
Later user		Bangladesh	Bangladesh	Bangladesh
		China	China	China
		(**stun gun**, prod, electric acupuncture)	(**stun gun, prod,** live wires, electric acupuncture, ECT)	(prod)
		Pakistan	Pakistan (prod)	Pakistan
		Sri Lanka	Sri Lanka (magneto, prod)	
Latest user			Nepal	Nepal
Periodic user	S. Vietnam		Vietnam (prods)	
		Burma/Myanmar	Burma/Myanmar	
		Laos		Laos
		Thailand		Thailand

Note: **Bold** marks a known preference for device type.

irresponsible members of society."[39] In camps, guards forced prisoners to perform exhaustion exercises (crawl on all fours) and stand for hours in the sun.
They choked them in water barrels. They placed buckets on the heads of prisoners and banged them very hard, a torture dubbed the Helmet.[40] Recent reports
also show regional variations in the cleanliness of torture, often including "the
effort to minimize signs of torture from the body of the victim . . . to avoid
"trouble" which most likely will be faced by the torturer."[41]

In the mid-1990s, after almost two decades, Vietnamese and Cambodian
police returned to electrotorture. In 1997, Vietnamese police shocked a defendant repeatedly with "electric shock batons in the anteroom before the trial."
Minutes later, he appeared before the judge, confessed to the murder of a police
officer, and pleaded for clemency.[42] Similarly, in 1995, Cambodian police used
electric batons to coerce a confession.[43] In 2000, investigators report electrotorture in Burma/Myanmar along with forced kneeling, forced standing, and choking in water or a plastic bag.[44]

East Asia. In the 1970s, Chinese interrogators used Stalinist torture and sweating techniques.[45] In the 1990s, a Tibetan monk walked out of China with a
satchel full of stun guns made in Taiwan and England. Palden Gyatso had
been imprisoned in Tibet for thirty years. He described how the Russian style
gave way to stun guns in the early 1980s.[46] Prods are now routine in Chinese
torture.[47] Taiwanese police started using electrotorture in the 1970s.[48] Medical
electrotorture is first reported in the late 1980s (electrical acupuncture) and
ECT since 1999.[49]

The Filipino police used electroshock, beating, exhaustion exercises,
choking in water, and the *falaka*.[50] South Korean interrogators combined electroshock, stomach pumping, forced standing or sitting, freezing, and sleep
deprivation.[51]

South Asia. In the 1980s, Sri Lankan government forces beat with sand-filled
plastic pipes (PVC piping), inserted chili into the orifices, and jumped prisoners with magnetos. In the 1990s, torture consisted of shock batons, the *falaka*,
and the dry submarine (in conjunction with petrol in the nostrils). Other times
troops were far less constrained, for example, whipping with barbed wire.[52]

Pakistan and India used electrotorture, particularly in the disputed Kashmir
region. Pakistani torturers adopted prods in the 1980s.[53] Pakistan and Bangladesh followed the Middle Eastern style of electroshock, *falaka*, and beatings.
Indian police occasionally used choking, but in general they adopted Mediterranean modern when it came to stealthy torture.[54]

In the 1990s, police in India and Pakistan developed a distinctive clean
torture to supplement electricity. They rolled a huge pestle (*ghotna*) used for

grinding corn and spices slowly down the thighs or calves, with the heaviest policemen standing on it. Usually the roller "was smooth and left no residual scar," but there were exceptions. Police used logs or steel tubes for the same purpose. Pakistani police also flogged with a *patta*, a leather strap with a wooden handle that bruised, but did not flay.[55]

Police in Nepal and Burma/Myanmar also adopted the roller.[56] In 2000, Nepalese police also used a weighted bamboo stick, the *belana*, in the same manner as the *ghotna*. They also choked with water, beat with nettles, and applied the *teléfono* and the *falaka*.[57]

Sub-Saharan Africa

Little is known about the surge in electrotorture in sub-Saharan Africa in the 1980s (table 9.4). Rwandan torturers used a specially rigged belt, and Burundans used an electric cable tied to the end of a stick.[58] In the 1990s, interrogators employed live wires (Chad and Zambia), prods (Nigeria), and transformers (Equatorial Guinea).[59] In 2002, torturers in the Cameroons used alligator clips or prods.[60] African torturers generally showed little concern for cleanliness in torture; scarring techniques were exceedingly common. In some cases, there are anecdotal reports of how external monitors shaped torture. In one report from Mobutu's Zaire, a prisoner says that "he was at first beaten with sticks before an officer stopped the beatings, saying, 'It will leave scars and we will get complaints from Amnesty International.' "[61] There are also some countries where torturers typically combined techniques that left few marks, suggesting their intent was to be stealthy. For example, torture in Zimbabwe now consists of shock, choking with water, positional tortures, and the *falaka*.[62] Evidence for stealthy torture is strongest in South Africa, and that is what I focus on here.

South Africa has a long history of electrotorture, one almost as long as that of France and Argentina. In the 1920s, the government used firearms, bombs and airplanes to suppress revolts. In the 1930s, the government shifted to brutal floggings with *sjamboks* or rhino-hide whips, violence that drew criticism from the English establishment.[63] Farmers also used *sjamboks* on their laborers, leaving many scarred for life. Torture became systematic by the 1950s, police and farmers sometimes interrogating suspects together.[64]

All this drew judicial and press criticism, including the often-drawn parallels between Afrikaners and Nazis.[65] Courts did try policemen, demonstrating that "policemen were not yet above the law and escalation in brutality."[66] Between 1946 and 1948, prosecutors charged 223 police, obtaining 174 convictions. Between 1956 and 1958, prosecutors charged 1,263 policemen, receiving 840 convictions.[67]

Table 9.4
Main Electroshock Users in Africa, 1970–2004

	1970–1979	1980–1989	1990–1999	2000–2004
Previous user	South Africa/ Namibia (field telephone)	South Africa/ Namibia	South Africa (prods, stun guns)	South Africa Namibia
Late user	Cameroon Ethiopia Malawi Uganda Zambia Zimbabwe/ Rhodesia	Cameroon Ethiopia Malawi Uganda Zambia Zimbabwe	Cameroon Ethiopia Malawi (prod) Uganda Zambia Zimbabwe	Cameroon (prod) Malawi (prod) Uganda Zimbabwe
Later user		Angola Chad Congo Guinea Kenya Mauritania Niger Rwanda Senegal Somalia Togo Zaire	Angola (prod) Chad Congo Guinea Kenya Mauritania Niger Rwanda Senegal Somalia Togo Zaire/Congo (prod)	Niger Rwanda Somalia Congo
Latest user			Sudan (prod) Nigeria (prod)	Sudan
Periodic user	Burundi Djibouti Mali	Burkina Faso Gabon Madagascar (prod) Mali Equatorial Guinea (transformer) Guinea-Bisau Comoros	Burundi Djibouti Lesotho	Burundi Eritrea

Too often, though, prosecutors chose only the most egregious cases. Courts were more willing to convict black policemen and dismiss cases against white officers. Ministers were willing to reinstate convicted officers.[68] In short, white police understood the bottom line: Torture, but be careful.

By the late 1950s, farmers and officers used near-asphyxiation with gas masks, pumping stomachs with water, whipping with hoses, the *falaka*, and electrotorture.[69] As a constable put it, first "we hit them. The second is electric shocks. The third is the gasmask."[70] Hooded prisoners could not see enough to testify who did what.

The first known case of electric torture occurred in the Orange Free State in 1954. A constable shocked an alleged cattle thief and then nearly asphyxiated him with a gas mask.[71] The first urban case occurred in 1955 in East London for a robbery suspect.[72] Other cases followed: 1956 (one case), 1957 (more than seven cases), 1961 (three), 1962 (one), and 1963 (four).[73]

Torturers used live wire, tying victims to tables or hanging them from the spit.[74] This was a dangerous process, leading to inadvertent deaths under interrogation and suspicious suicides.[75] The 1963 cases mark the beginning of magneto torture on political prisoners.

As international attention focused on apartheid, police interest in clean tortures grew. Police commonly beat, but were careful not to be too obvious. They also whipped with hose pipes, which would not leave welts. The next most common techniques were electrotorture, positional torture (such as forced standing), and near asphyxiation with gas masks and rubber tubes ("tubing"), and by choking with water.[76]

The Truth and Reconciliation Commission data shows the trend toward stealthiness. Of the three hundred witnesses the commission heard on torture between 1960 and 1973, electricity and positional torture appeared in a little less than one-third of all cases, and near asphyxiation occurred in one-sixth. Of the almost five hundred testimonies of torture between 1973 and 1984, positional torture appeared in two-fifths of all cases, and electrotorture in three-tenths and near asphyxiation in one-fifth. Of the eleven hundred witnesses the commission heard on torture between 1985 and 1989, electricity and near asphyxiation occurred with a little less than half, and positional torture with a quarter. Nationally, over the entire period (1960–89), electrotorture occurred in nine hundred out of twenty-two hundred cases, making it the most common torture after beating. Suffocation appeared in seven hundred cases and positional torture in six hundred.[77]

In the 1990s, such methods continued into the period that followed apartheid. Police, as well as private security officers, have subjected detainees to beatings and positional tortures, choked them with plastic bags (sometimes full of water), and shocked them with prods and stun guns (sometimes in combination with bags).[78]

Europe and Central Asia

Electrotorture appears most commonly in southern Europe and, after the Cold War, in Eastern Europe (table 9.5).[79] Southern European police usually supplemented electrotorture with water and the *falaka*. East European police favored gas masks.

Southern Europe. In the 1970s, Portuguese secret police (PIDE) used electrotorture, but Franco's Guardia Civile favored choking with water, clean beating,

Table 9.5
Main Electroshock Users in Europe and Central Asia, 1970–2004

	1970–1979	1980–1989	1990–1999	2000–2004
Previous user	Greece (prod) Portugal	Greece	Greece (stun gun) Portugal (stun gun) Portugal in Macao (prod)	Greece (stun gun)
Late user	Spain (transformer or magneto)	Spain Yugoslavia (prod)	Spain Yugoslavia/Serbia (magneto, prod, gun)	Spain Yugoslavia/Serbia
Later user		Albania Austria Italy Poland	Albania Austria (stun gun) Italy Poland	Poland
Latest user			Azerbaijan Bulgaria (prod) Croatia (prod) Cyprus (prod) Georgia Kazakhstan Moldova Russia (magneto) Tajikistan Turkmenistan Ukraine Uzbekistan (electric cap)	Bulgaria Croatia (prod) Cyprus Georgia Kazakhstan (wires) Moldova Russia Tajikistan Turkmenistan (field telephone) Ukraine (prod) Uzbekistan
Periodic user	Belgium Romania (ECT) United Kingdom	Hungary	Belgium Estonia Latvia	Romania Lithuania Slovakia (prod)

positional torture, and exhaustions exercises. After the Spanish transition to democracy, reports commonly mention electrotorture.[80] In 1983, one incident showed that stealth had arrived. Courts found that one prisoner had been "punched, kicked, hit with a telephone directory, hooded, partially asphyxiated with a plastic bag, submerged in water, and given electroshock."[81] His experience was almost encyclopedic, having suffered techniques that stemmed from French (magneto torture and choking with water), American (beating with a telephone directory), and Latin American policing (the dry submarine). In 2001, a torturer said to the guard attaching electrical wires to a prisoner, "Relax, the marks won't show on this guy, give him a bit more heat."[82]

In the 1980s, Italian police used stealth torture on prisoners as they transported them between prisons, including long beatings, pumping them with salt water, icy jets of water, and electroshock.[83] In 1981, Amnesty International received reports that two Albanian prisoners were subjected to electrotorture and forced standing. This was, Amnesty observed, a remarkably rare event, the only other incidents being two cases dating from 1958 and 1961.[84]

In the 1990s, international monitors documented electrotorture in Spain, Portugal, Greece, Cyprus, Yugoslavia, and Turkey.[85] The common combination was Mediterranean or French modern. In Cyprus in 1993 and again in 2000, the Committee for the Prevention of Torture (CPT) documented organized police violence to secure confessions using electric prods and the *falaka*. Police also practiced the Helmet, placing a metal bucket on the head and banging it. In 1993, the CPT documented Greek police using electrotorture and the *falaka* in Athens and Thessaloniki. Spanish torture, as usual, involved electricity, choking (bags and water), clean beating (including the *teléfono* and beating with telephone books or batons wrapped in newspaper or foam), suspensions, positional torture, and the *falaka*. Also in 1993, Italian troops regularly tortured Somali prisoners with dehydration, beatings, burning cigarettes on the soles of their feet, and electroshock.[86] Prisoners in Serbian prisons report *falaka*, choking in water, forced standing, and electrotorture.

Western Europe. Electrotorture is very rare in this region. British forces tortured five men with electricity in Northern Ireland between 1971 and 1972.[87] In 1971, Belgian troops tortured captured opponents during a NATO exercise. They used electroshock, suspension, and exposure in freezing weather for two days.[88] In 1995, sixteen Belgian soldiers were sentenced for torturing Somali citizens two years earlier. Torture included beating, suspension over a crocodile-infested river, positional torture, dehydration, and electroshock.[89]

The CPT and Amnesty International identified repeated electrotorture in Austria between 1989 and 1994.[90] Viennese police used stun guns and batons to shock illegal immigrants and citizens at the Bureau of Security. They choked detainees with water and bags. They also beat them using telephone books and other procedures that would not leave long-term marks.

Eastern Europe. During the Cold War, police stuck to Soviet positional tortures and sweating techniques. In 1947, a Romanian prisoner reported guards electrified the wet floor of his cell, and there is an undated case of electrotorture in Bulgaria.[91] If there was more police electrotorture, it has not been reported. Medical electrotorture is reported in 1953 at Kazan, one case in the 1960s, and three cases in Romania in 1978.[92] The Soviets and East Germans supplied the Aghan Khad with field telephone magnetos.[93] These police forces at least possessed the technical knowledge, even if there are no reports of its usage in Eastern Europe.

After the Cold War, many Eastern European police turn to routine electroshock. Russian police favor prolonged beating, suspension, magneto torture, and the *slonik* or elephant. This last involves hooding the prisoner with a gas mask and then inducing near asphyxiation by closing the air vent. The Moscow police prefer to use magneto torture "because it leaves only few marks that pass quickly."[94]

In the last fifteen years, investigators have documented police using electroshock in Russia, Poland, Estonia, Lithuania, Latvia, Bulgaria, Moldova, Georgia, Uzbekistan, and the Ukraine.[95] The combination of gas mask, beating, and electroshock is so characteristically East European that it might be called Slavic modern. Several countries have adopted this style, including Lithuania, Latvia, Moldova, Georgia, Uzbekistan, and Ukraine. Several also supplemented electricity with the *falaka* (as in the Mediterranean style). These include Poland, Lithuania, Latvia, Bulgaria, Georgia, Uzbekistan, and Ukraine. Uzbek police sometimes beat stealthily with wet towels, sandbags, and soda bottles filled with water.

Explaining the Surge

Figure 9.1 and table 9.6 illustrate the expanding scope of electrotorture by region and decade. They show that there was a surge in the use of electrotorture starting in the 1960s and continuing until the end of the twentieth century.

Could the surge simply be an effect of better global auditing after 1973? One cannot rule this out, but if electrotorture was more common before 1973, it was largely unknown to those who were covering torture at the time.

The global survey identified not only clustering of techniques that leave no marks (indicators of stealth), but also two new predictable, regional clusterings of specific techniques (what I have called styles of torture): Mediterranean

Table 9.6
Number of States using Electrotorture by Region, 1910–2000

	Americas	Middle East	Asia	Africa	Europe & Central Asia	Total
1910S	1	0	0	0	1	2
1920S	1	0	0	0	0	1
1930S	2	0	1	0	4	7
1940S	1	0	1	0	3	5
1950S	2	0	0	1	4	7
1960S	4	2	2	1	3	12
1970S	15	9	7	10	7	48
1980S	20	17	13	26	8	84
1990S	17	18	13	24	23	95

modern (electrotorture plus *falaka*) and Slavic modern (electrotorture plus gas mask asphyxiation).

Stealthy torture was most common among democratic states. It commonly appeared in democracies engaged in ongoing guerrilla wars, in societies that had just transitioned from authoritarian to democratic government, and in consolidated democracies with sharp civic divisions based on class or ethnicity. This corresponds to the typical conditions in which democracies turn to torture: to gather information in national security contexts, to induce false confessions, and to intimidate others and ensure civic discipline (see chapter 2, "Torture and Democracy"). The list of democratic states that used stealth torture includes all the magneto torturers identified in the previous chapter; French modern still has its admirers in the late twentieth century.

The democratic preference for stealthy torture should not be surprising. What needs to be explained is the fact that many authoritarian states also embrace electrotorture, and they do so in conjunction with other torture techniques that leave few marks. Among these countries are, in particular, Latin American states in the 1970s. It is tempting to explain this pattern in terms of intensified global monitoring of torture (the UM hypothesis) since the timing is so apt. But perhaps there is another explanation: the United States distributed electrotorture to authoritarian states.

Teasing apart the UM and the UD hypothesis is not easy since it is possible that the American "push" for stealthy torture responded to the American perception of increased auditing of torture, the "pull" of global monitoring. Moreover, many stealthy electrotorturers were French allies, too, and it would not

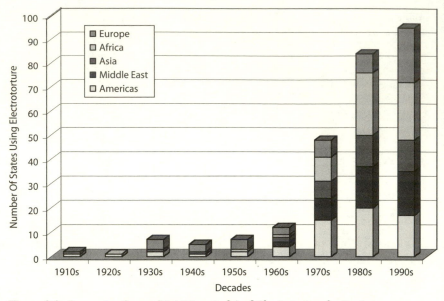

Figure 9.1. Increasing Scope (Not Magnitude) of Electrotorture by Region, 1910–2000

be hard to show that some received counterinsurgency assistance from the French as well. Why not argue that the French did it?

It is not sufficient, in other words, to state that the countries that were electrotorturers were also generally American allies. The evidence must be more direct. It must distinguish state involvement from the low-level borrowing and copying that characterizes much torture transmission. Torturers in the French Empire pioneered magneto torture by demonstrating how it could be done, but not, as far as we know, through direct training of torturers in other countries. There was no training camp for the Gestapo set up in Vietnam or North Africa. And though South Vietnamese torturers probably passed on magneto torture to American forces in Vietnam, this falls short of the claim that the South Vietnamese government had *a policy* of training American interrogators in torture.

Perhaps the best example of direct training comes from Brazil. In the 1960s, American operatives, including the CIA, played a critical role in introducing the Brazilians to field telephone torture, even supplying small hand-held magnetos (*pimentinhas*) that resembled the pepper mills of Vietnam. This suggests a straightforward test built on the Nuremberg principle, that uniformity of technique implies a policy of training in torture. It is reasonable to conclude one has identified a universal distributor whenever a state furnishes high levels of military aid and assistance *and* one establishes independently that all the states that received this assistance had identical torture techniques. In part II, I used this technique to demonstrate that the Soviet Union was a universal distributor, passing on the Russian style in sweating to Eastern Europe and East Asia, while the Nazis were not.

Noam Chomsky and Edward Herman make a similar case for the United States as a universal distributor in the 1970s. In *The Washington Connection and Third World Fascism*, on the inside cover, Chomsky and Herman post a remarkable graphic, entitled "The Sun and Its Planets: Countries Using Torture on an Administrative Basis in the 1970s, with Their Parent-Client Affiliations." At the center of this political solar system was the United States. This sun illuminated twenty-six "planets" that received American military aid and police training in the 1970s.[96] Applying the Nuremberg method, Chomsky and Herman argued that, since the planets received extensive American assistance and also tortured, one must reasonably conclude that the United States was the universal distributor of torture training.[97]

Chomsky and Herman offer a more plausible and precise UD hypothesis than most.[98] Unfortunately, it is still too vague. If uniformity of technique implies uniformity of will, then Chomsky and Herman must show that torturers were using the same techniques. Since a signature *American* technique in the 1970s was electric torture by magneto, and particularly by field telephone, one would expect this method to dominate electrotorture among the planets if American advisers were training torturers worldwide. This would be strong evidence that the United States was a universal distributor in the 1970s.

This suggests three tests: (1) Of the twenty-six planets, how many used field telephones for electric torture (the strong test)? (2) How many used the generic product, magnetos (the weaker test)? (3) How many planets used electric torture at all (including prods and live wire) (the weakest test)?

In fact, few planets practiced this signature American technique, or even magneto torture. Chomsky and Herman's hypothesis fails the strong and weaker test, as table 9.7 illustrates. It can only partly explain the distribution of electrotorture in the 1970s. In many instances, as I showed in the case of cattle prods in Uruguay in the previous chapter, Americans simply enhanced electrotorture practices that were already customary.

Chomsky and Herman's hypothesis passes the weakest test, showing that the vast majority of the planets (twenty-one out of twenty-six) adopted electrotorture in the 1970s. But this is a misleading impression. Twenty-six other countries that were not American "planets" (let me call them "stars") also used electrotorture (see table 9.8).[99] When one adds the stars to the planets, this yields a list of forty-seven countries that used electrotorture in the 1970s, and the majority of electrotorture users were *not* American client states, by Chomsky and Herman's

Table 9.7
Chomsky and Herman's U.S. "Planets" List and Electrotorture Users
(Grouped by Region)

Planet/Country	Field Telephone	Magneto	Electrotorture
Argentina	No	No (prod)	Yes
Bolivia	No	No (prod)	Yes
Brazil	Yes	Yes	Yes
Chile	No	No (parilla), Maybe before Pinochet (1973)	Yes
Colombia	Unclear	Unclear	Yes
Dominican Republic	No	No	No
Guatemala	No	No	No
Haiti	Unclear	Unclear	Yes
Mexico	Maybe	Maybe	Yes
Nicaragua	Unclear	Unclear	Yes
Peru	No	No	No
Paraguay	No	No (iron bed)	Yes
Uruguay	No	No (prod)	Yes
Venezuela	Yes	Yes	Yes
Tunisia	No	No	No
Morocco	Maybe	Maybe	Yes
Saudi Arabia	No	No	No
Iran	No	No (prod)	Yes
Turkey	Yes	Yes	Yes
South Vietnam	Yes	Yes	Yes
South Korea	Yes	Yes	Yes
Philippines	Yes	Yes	Yes
Indonesia	Maybe	Maybe	Yes
Spain	Yes	Yes	Yes
Portugal	Unclear	Unclear	Yes
Greece	Yes	Yes	Yes
Total Users	8	8	21

standards. The use of electrotorture in itself is not a sufficient marker for a hidden American hand in distributing torture devices.

What stands out when one looks at the complete list of electrotorturers is their absence in the Communist world. The vast majority of them fall firmly in the galaxy of the Free World. Table 9.8 lists the known "stars" that used electrotorture in the 1970s. If the weakest test should be the measure of confirmation, then the tip of the hat should go to the ideology hypothesis rather than to Chomsky and Herman. Perhaps, then, what needs to be explained is the Communist *aversion* to electrotorture, not the American promotion of it. In part IV, I document that the USSR was probably the most successful universal distributor in the twentieth century, distributing a Russian style in sweating and torture in many countries. The results here also seem to confirm this conclusion.

But one should hesitate before embracing any notion that Communists were inherently averse to electrotorture. Nine states in the Communist galaxy did use electrotorture in the 1970s, and there is no known reason why Communists should have an aversion to it. If there is an explanation for why torturers in the Communist world stuck to Stalinist techniques for so long, this probably has to do more with custom and habit than ideology.

Table 9.8
Electroshock Users Not on Chomsky and Herman's List, 1970–1980

Communist Galaxy	"Stars" in the Free World Galaxy
Afghanistan	Belgium
Cambodia	Burundi
Cuba	Cameroon
Egypt	Djibouti
Ethiopia	Ecuador
Iraq	El Salvador
Libya	Israel
Romania	Malawi
Syria	Mali
	Pakistan
	Rhodesia
	South Africa
	Taiwan
	Uganda
	UK in Northern Ireland
	United States
	Zambia
9	17

The more plausible explanation for the distribution of electrotorture remains the universal monitoring hypothesis. The reason that electrotorture appears more commonly in the "Galaxy of the Free World" is that there was a greater priority on stealthy torture. Here, a free press, activists, and international organizations checked state behavior by documenting torture. American advisers were also probably aware of this intensified monitoring. Even some Communist states in Europe were aware of the increased scrutiny (as I argue in part IV), and it is not surprising that some East European countries abandoned torture altogether.

On the other hand, some states in the Communist galaxy turned to brutal, scarring techniques. Iraq and North Korea did not depend on a good human rights record to maintain aid and legitimacy. This is again as the UM hypothesis would suggest. Where there is no accountability, torture will be scarring. The UM hypothesis also accommodates the great variety of electrical techniques in the 1970s. By the 1970s, it was well known that electrotorture left few marks, and the wild experimentation, as well as the spread of prods and magnetos, probably reflected this understanding.

As one looks back, it is ironic that Chomsky and Herman focused so strongly on the power of the universal distributor and discounted the effect of universal monitoring. They, of course, believed firmly that new mandarins controlled the media, shaping coverage to suit American interests.[100] It would be implausible on this view to think that human rights monitoring could have any lasting effects in the face of such a powerful constellation of interests. The irony is that they could not fully appreciate the critical effect of people like themselves and the movements they inspired.

Remembering the Cold War

During the Cold War, the great superpowers could not fight each other without risking nuclear annihilation. Instead, they fought each other through proxy allies throughout the world, and these allies often tortured their opponents. Only now can we see fully the devastation such proxy conflicts generated. But the bipolar character of the international system may also have enhanced the international human rights monitoring regime, especially during the period of détente. Both sides did present themselves as possessing a superior morality, and it was easier for critics to play states off against each other by appealing to their desire to win the "hearts and minds" of nonaligned states and to their interest in avoiding embarrassment at the United Nations. One could urge, for example, American politicians to do more to prevent torture because otherwise the Soviets would use it in their propaganda. The United States may have had a stronger incentive to urge its client states to be stealthier.

The end of the Cold War may have weakened the hand of human rights monitors. It is no doubt much harder to make the case to American politicians that torture is a bad idea because the government of Sudan, Cuba, or Iran might use it in their anti-American propaganda. This somehow does not have the same bite while one is engaged in the War on Terror.

This chapter produces some disconcerting evidence of this sort. The data in figure 9.1 show that, if one excludes Europe, there was a contraction in the scope of electrotorture in the 1990s. This result also appears in the long-term statistical project of documenting torture techniques worldwide by year, suggesting that the contraction began in the late 1980s and early 1990s.[101] At the moment, it is difficult to explain the sources of this contraction in scope. It does not appear to be due to a decline in torture worldwide. It may be related to the way torture techniques are documented by human rights agencies in the last decade (indeed, some of it no doubt is). But there is a possibility that the end of the Cold War intensified monitoring of torture in some regions, but also weakened the power of monitors in other regions. Perhaps this is why electrotorture increases in Eastern Europe, but seems to contract somewhat everywhere else.

Nevertheless, there are good reasons to believe that the scope of electric torture is not likely to change much more in the coming decade. Halfway through this decade, human rights monitors have reported electrotorture in sixty-six states, and more will likely follow by the end of the decade. All the evidence in this chapter suggests that once policemen and soldiers go electric in torture, they do not forget, despite changes in government or ideology.

Lastly, there has been a shift worldwide toward the acceptance of nonlethal electrical instruments. These devices are now no longer limited to torture, or more broadly, to policing. Consumers worldwide also purchase them as personal security devices. One cannot overestimate the availability of cheap stun technology worldwide. Today, many torturers use commercial batons and stun guns. Once torturers were devilishly imaginative tinkerers, but there has been a remarkable decline in imagination over the last three decades. Today, the cottage industry in electrotorture instruments has largely disappeared.

In the next two chapters, I use the example of the United States to investigate and discuss the new trend toward commercial electrical products in policing. I criticize the view that evil corporations simply made products that almost floated off the shelves to police stations everywhere around the world. The historical record does not bear out this suggestion. As I will document next, the stun industry came of age well after the surge in electrotorture had begun. In fact, the economic "push" was so tenuous that, more than once in its history, stun technology almost disappeared: The priority must go, then, to the "pull" of global monitoring rather than the "push" of economic and technological imperatives.

Nevertheless, the trends that have made our lives comfortable, even pleasurable, now also facilitate electrotorture elsewhere. Stun technology is here to stay, and some stun manufacturers have been unscrupulous in marketing their devices to countries that torture. Others, however, have been responsive to criticism that their products have promoted stealthy torture. They have introduced computerized means of monitoring these devices, a first in the history of electrotorture instruments. The question is whether agencies can intensify their monitoring of these instruments in this manner and whether such norms can be enforced on the stun industry as a whole. Before considering such detailed policy questions, one must document, as usual, the murky, often-forgotten history of modern electrotorture, separating myth and dreams from what is known and recorded.

My brothers believed in the dignity of man. How can those who

stood with them support a man whose agents used cattle prods and

dogs against human beings in Alabama?

> —Senator Edward Kennedy, on George Wallace's
>
> presidential campaign, 1968[1]

10 Prods, Tasers, and Stun Guns

Since the early 1950s, inventors have dreamed of a society in which nonlethal weapons were common. They dreamed of many devices similar to stun technology, devices that were nonlethal, portable, clean, painful, flexible, and easy to use. These dreams foundered in a context that resisted the diffusion of such weapons. After describing both the dreams and the context, I describe how technologies like stun guns and Tasers succeeded whereas so many other devices failed. In particular, I consider the work of John Cover, as remarkable a politician as he was an engineer, whose efforts made it possible to weave stun into the fabric of modern lives.

Among other things then, this chapter offers a chronology of the origins of the American stun industry, one that allows us to consider what role it played in the surge in electrotorture described in the previous chapter. It also corrects misleading accounts of the way stun technology was invented, offering a different narrative of technological innovation. In the next chapter, I explain how the stun industry wove the new technology into modern life and how it dealt with successive domestic torture scandals using stun guns. This leads to considering the effects of stun technology on democratic life and the policy questions that will increasingly confront all of us.

Electric Utopia

Inventors do not just imagine machines. They imagine consumers, competitors, salesmen, service providers—indeed, whole societies. They endow these actors with hopes, dreams, and purposes that their invention can satisfy. When they patent their idea, inventors express not only an engineering idea, but also a political scenario in which that design fits. Patents do not tell us much about the empirical sequence of innovation, but they do reveal visions. Until recently, reconstructing the succession of visions was an onerous task. Fortunately, IBM has now made available a database for American patents that allows one to reconstruct the successive visions of Stun City, and the picture it reveals is a remarkable tour of how electricity, policing, and security are bound together in the American cultural imaginary.

It was just before dawn in the town of Eutopia in the 1950s. Cattlemen were heading to the pens with their electric goads. These had new pistol grips and improved switches, flashlights to help them see in the dark, and, sometimes, a telescopic barrel for long reaches. They were compact, portable, and took little servicing.[2] As the sun rose, a postman warded off a big hairy dog with his "Electrified Stick."[3] In the police station, a suspect sat quietly tied to an electric restraint device that shocked him if he tried to move.[4] Nearby, at the army reserve, soldiers trained for stealthy commando-type assaults with electric spears and arrows.[5] In the woods nearby, a hunter disabled an injured and enraged bear with an electric rifle projectile.[6] At sea, Coast Guard divers warded off sharks with their "Electrical Shark Device" as they undertook dangerous underwater missions.[7]

Prosperous Eutopia grew into Stun City, and it had its problems, like all cities. In the 1960s, the violent and the insane would sometimes gather in the streets. Reluctantly, the police broke out their electric batons, their electric dart guns, and their electric liquid pistols to immobilize the unruly protesters humanely.[8] It was difficult, but no lives were lost.

In the 1970s, crime came to Stun City and this was unfortunate, but Stun City dealt with offenders humanely, as usual. On a fine spring day, a little old lady took her dog for a walk. When attacked in the hallway by a rapist, she immobilized him with her electrical finger glove and then held him on the floor with her electrical extension cane.[9] While waiting for building security, she activated her electrical "Anti-Pull Animal Leash Mechanism" to restrain her frantic dog that was pulling "excessively hard beyond a predetermined force."[10] On the street, a mugger attacked a businessman and fell down stunned, having touched his electrically charged suit.[11] The businessman held him in place with his electric umbrella until the police arrived.[12] A cab pulled up, and the cab driver ejected an unruly passenger, having first activated the passenger seat "rigged to give passengers a shock in the buttocks at the discretion of the driver."[13]

By the late 1970s, things had calmed down. Out on the farm, veterinarians were healing horses and dogs, preventing them from chewing their legs with electric bandages.[14] Farmers' children took out pests and birds with electrified jets of conductive liquid.[15] At the park, joggers and bicyclists enjoyed the sunny day, knowing they could easily ward off "menacing dogs and other animals" with their telescopic shock prods and electro-liquid pistols.[16]

If stun technology could have leapt from the imagination of inventors to the real world without difficulty, the patent history would be the history of the world we live in. *Well-meaning* corporations carried forward a *thoughtful* product through *honest* advertising and media to *just* states, *humane* police, and *decent and publicly minded* consumers. For stun corporations, this world would be utopia; for Amnesty International, it would be dystopia. In fact, this patent history presents the positive view of a story of scientific innovation used by critics of modern corporations, a general formula used since the 1960s: *greedy* corporations carry forward a *dangerously efficient* product by means of *deceptive* media and *unscrupulous* advertisers to *power-hungry* states, *indifferent* police, and, ultimately, *self-interested bourgeois* consumers.[17] Stripped of the nasty adjectives, the two stories of Stun City are identical.

But the point of beginning the story of stun technology with the patent history is that this is a *mythical* origin story: the patent history describes a world that never happened. Most of the devices never existed—there were no postmen with electric dog sticks in the 1950s or electric liquid riot control guns in the 1960s or electrical bandages for animals in the 1970s or telescopic shock prods in the 1980s. Patents articulate "a folklore on inventors, progress, discovery, property, and the like. We do not really know the relations between this metaphysics and folklore and the realities of technology."[18] Indeed, if the bright story of the Eutopia is a mythical history, then one should be equally cautious about swallowing darker stories that peddle the history of electric Dystopia, for the stories are identical once one sets aside the ethical evaluations.

To understand the real world of Stun City, we have to leave this fantasy origin behind. Let me begin first with the political and social context in which stun appeared. In the 1970s, the public was deeply hostile toward any electrical weapons in policing. This public attitude grew from the use of electrified batons for crowd control in civil rights protests in the 1960s. These electrified prods and batons did not use stun technology, but the public was not interested in the different ways in which such devices could be powered. It simply opposed their use, and this opposition was fairly effective. In 1978, British police observers noted that American police now depended heavily on new plastic batons.[19] What the British did not see or commend were electric batons; by 1972, those had "largely passed from the public scene."[20]

Electric-Free Protest

On June 21, 1961, the *Jackson Daily* reported that guards used "cattle shockers" on detained white teenage Freedom Riders at Parchman State Penitentiary in

Mississippi. Kenneth Shillman described how Felix Singer and Terry Sullivan were dragged along a concrete corridor, skin tearing off their bodies. "Electric shockers such as are used on livestock had first been used on them before they were dragged. . . . I saw the burns on Sullivan's arms and legs."[21]

In April 1962, Alabama police adopted electric prods publicly to "herd Negro demonstrators."[22] On May 4, 1963, the *New York Times* showed photos of Alabama highway patrolmen using prods on ten Freedom Walkers, giving the detained men repeated electric shocks. "As one of the Negroes flinched and twisted in the grip of the four troopers, an elderly toothless white man shouted from a roadside pasture: "Stick him again! Stick him again!"[23] Prods soon appeared in other civil rights conflicts.[24]

"Up to now," remarked the *New York Times*, "prods have rarely been used on human beings." Even Hot Shot Products, the main manufacturer of prods, was surprised. "We never manufactured them as a law enforcement device," asserted its president.[25] A year later, however, Hot Shots assigners patented an electrified police baton.[26]

These stock prods yielded between eight thousand and ten thousand volts, a figure that did not change significantly over the next two decades.[27] The *New York Times* reporter tried the device on himself, observing that it made him jump a foot, left his arm aching, and left two painful marks on the palm that lasted for more than a half hour.

"The usefulness in sit down, passive-resistance and campus riot situations is obvious, but has yet to be fully explored," remarked a police magazine.[28] By 1967, even advocates of nonlethal weapons were not optimistic: "The recent ill-feeling generated by the electrified baton and the use of dogs by some southern police forces for crowd control illustrates another unfortunate aspect of the use of new weapons."[29] By the 1970s, the prod had largely disappeared from descriptions of crowd control, and the record of torture using the prod also drops. While there are several accounts of torture using cattle prods in the 1960s, there is only one report of torture by prod (in New Orleans in 1973).[30] In 1992, *Soldier of Fortune* concluded that the prod's "initial successful use brought about its downfall. . . . The hostile press and other media then made the obvious negative comparison between people fighting for their political and civil rights and the treatment of cattle."[31]

In fact, demonstrators in other societies could expect to be rounded up with cattle prods. "It is being used in quantity by paramilitary police units abroad," wrote a specialist in policing with approval in 1971.[32] But for the last three decades of the twentieth century, American protesters enjoyed a civic experience the rest of the world has not enjoyed, the electric-free public protest. This remarkable experience ended, as nearly as one can tell, in November 2003, when Miami police used stun guns during public protests during the Free

Trade Area of the Americas summit. Like the civil rights protests, activists objected to the use of these new devices. "I think I'm in a third world country," remarked a protester expressing his peculiarly American entitlement.[33] And the use of electrical devices on middle-class protesters once again caught attention of the media, leading to public criticism of the Miami police's use of force.

But what the events in Miami also signaled was that American police had quietly adopted a new electrical technology in the 1990s, even if they had not up until that point deployed stun guns to regulate public protests. The question, then, is what made stun guns different from cattle prods, and why the inventors of stun succeeded when the marketers of cattle prods and electrical batons had failed so miserably in the 1960s.

Stun Technology

In 1972, John Cover filed to patent the Taser, and in 1977 filed to patent his unique circuitry, the power unit on which many stun devices are based.[34] In 1978, Gary Henderson and Guy Williams Jr. filed to patent two designs for stun guns.[35] These are the founding patents for stun technology.

Stun technology incapacitates the whole body for several minutes, an effect dubbed *electric curarization*, after the drug that induces paralysis.[36] Stun devices vary in their abilities to achieve this effect, but the general principle behind their use is immobilization ("stun").[37] By contrast, prods hurt only where they touch, confining the shock "to a small surface area which makes actual contact with the stick."[38] Cattle prods "do not incapacitate, but further agitate."[39] In short, prods get you moving; stun knocks you out or throws you to the ground in a spasm of flailing arms and legs.

Stun devices achieve this effect because of their unique circuitry. Stun devices loop energy from a low-voltage battery to produce "high intensity, short duration impulses; the non-incapacitating devices [prods] produce a continuous alternating current."[40] In a Taser, for example, a pulse lasts four to six microseconds (millionths of a second), for the remaining .999996 seconds, the current drops to zero. When the trigger is held down, current does not flow continuously as in a prod. Rather, as long as the trigger is held down, the Taser repeats at an average rate of fifteen pulses per second, although the rate varies from model to model. The Taser's low amperage renders it a nonlethal weapon.[41] All of this is achieved with a nine-volt battery.

How well stun technology works depends on the condition of the equipment, circumstances of use, point of physical impact, and the clothing and size of the person. Cover knew that it took at least 30,000 volts to cross the gap imposed by clothing.[42] The original Nova stun gun was advertised at 50,000 volts. There has since been, according to industry enthusiasts, an "ongoing competition among manufacturers in claiming the highest voltage. Some advertise 75,000, 150,000, even 250,000 volts! On testing, many of these devices are lucky to produce 30,000 v. . . . *All this hype over high voltage is aimed at a public which is easily misled over electrical terms.*"[43] One cannot get more energy out of nowhere, and there are apparently genuine technical limits on how many times current can be looped no matter how clever the circuitry.

Stun weapons, then, are different from prods. So how did these devices find widespread acceptance in the United States, given public hostility to prods? Social scientists describe innovation and diffusion as a sequence of events in which a technology moves from the world of science to the social and political realm. This sequence begins with identifying a basic need; then doing scientific research to make sure the device works; and then marketing the useful device to society. Then society responds by adopting or resisting it.[44] The history of prods roughly corresponds to this: manufacturers identified a basic need, handling livestock, and marketed it to farmers, who adopted it. Police in turn borrowed prods, and soon manufacturers marketed to them, but the public resisted, and the prod disappeared.

Adopting this perspective raises some mysteries in the case of stun technology. In the 1970s, there were two kinds of electroshock devices, prods and stun devices. It seems these devices should have had identical destinies: society would either embrace them or reject them. If Americans did not really oppose electroshock weaponry for policing, both weapons would be common today. And if they did, then both would languish. So why didn't Americans reject stun technology as they rejected prods, the first electric weapons used publicly in American policing? Perhaps Americans opposed electroshock weaponry for policing, but not as deeply as I have suggested. In that case, surely society would favor the weaker device (prods) over the stronger (stun). But in fact the reverse occurred. The *weaker* devices, prods, still languish in the United States despite the hopes of their proponents while consumers have embraced stun devices that totally demobilize a person and advertise voltages at least two orders greater than prods.[45]

Something is wrong in the way we are describing the sequence of innovation in the case of stun. To grasp what the error is, I now consider more closely the story of John Cover, the man who invented stun.

Covering America

John Cover was an independent inventor who imagined an electrical device that immobilized people when it struck them. He was inspired in part by a children's series about a young boy whose remarkable gadgets led him on many fine adventures. Indeed, Cover named his device after one of the books in this series, *Tom A. Swift and His Electric Rifle*.[46] But Cover was not a dreamer, or at least, not just one. He understood that the "social side" or diffusion (which according to social scientists comes last) was integral to the innovation of stun. From the start, Cover worked on the social side—not merely locating needs, but organizing existing consumers and creating anticipated ones. He incited and created needs to which his innovation responded. This was as much a part of his scientific work as that of identifying new materials, shaping new connections, and conducting different tests. Whenever Cover changed an element on the social side (whom he was cultivating, for example) he also had to change elements on the technical side (what kind of materials he used). Likewise, apparently simple "technical" decisions had effects on the social side.

In other words, for inventions to make it into the world, inventors like Cover have to make the whole package of people and things work together. The word *alliance* captures this chain of people and things that work together to make inventions possible. Cover was not so much inventing a "thing," or a series of things, as he was assembling alliances—or rather a series of alliances—that were simultaneously social and technological. Each model represented a scenario and a flag around which to mobilize resources and juxtapose them to make a "product."

For over two decades, Cover presented scenarios through which stun would come to America and then juxtaposed people and things to offer a socio-technical alliance to realize the dream. He was as much a general as an inventor. Cover organized quite a few alliances before he found one stable enough to use. He imagined the Taser as a heavy-duty crowd control device; a sleek flashlight gun for stewardesses; a potentially lethal weapon (no flashlight) that fired, among other things, electric nets; a nonlethal weapon for ordinary citizens (flashlight reincorporated for identifying muggers); a gun for personal security; and lastly, a nonlethal police special for taking out isolated, violent criminals.

After Cover assembled this last alliance, other manufacturers colonized this network to market their own variations of stun technology, and innovation followed the classic form (invention to diffusion), carried forward by the network as if the devices were powered by their own inherent utility. But Cover's story shows that there was nothing particularly magical about stun technology, and, in this respect, it serves as an important check on accounts that overstate the power of manufacturers and economic elites in marketing products.

Alliance 1

In 1966, Cover read that the Presidential Commission on Crime urged manufacturers to develop "non-lethal weapons to combat riots and civil unrest that was plaguing the country." A few days later, he read of a hiker who had lived after hours "frozen" to an electric power line.[47] Experimenting on himself, Cover discovered he could cause his muscles to contract involuntarily, rendering himself immobile.

By 1969, Cover had the general idea of a gun that fired darts on wires through which he could deliver current. The question was whether he *could* deliver the current *under riot conditions*. To zap a fully clothed individual, the current has to leap a gap sometimes more than an inch thick. Cover knew that at least thirty thousand volts were required to jump such gaps. *That* would require riot police to carry heavy equipment, which was out of the question. "If you try to supply even very small currents . . . at 30 kilovolts, you find it takes a lot of power—hundreds of watts—which then means your system is no longer portable."[48]

To reach his intended market, Cover had to create a portable power source that generated at least thirty-thousand volts. To do this, Cover manipulated a lower-power battery "through clever circuitry to deliver concentrated power dispensed in peak-energy, extremely-short pulses."[49] Cover's circuitry drew enough power out of a battery in short bursts (ten pulses per second) to cause muscle seizures. Pulsing reduced the need for equipment, and created a portable device (Model I).

This small chain of things worked together well, but it could not be easily allied with a human operator. No matter how Cover got the current, "extremely high voltages had to be safely confined within a tool small enough to be hand-held." This proved terribly difficult since "current under high voltage had the bad habit of leaking through the seams and shocking the user."[50] No one would use a device that shocked the operator in demonstrations. This alliance produced power at the cost of making the device difficult to carry and use.

Alliance 2

In 1970, Cover demonstrated the prototype Taser, (Model II) to military, police, secret service, and gun manufacturers. The police expressed the least interest. They "didn't want the Taser for themselves and they didn't want the general public to have them either." It was not hard "for an officer to see himself on the end of Taser tethers in confrontations, down in the street while hostile civilians disarmed him." What the police wanted was a *lethal* electrical weapon, "more firepower, not less."[51] It is not clear why they did not think that they would be even at more risk should such a lethal weapon fall into the hands of hostile civilians.

The military tests also did not go well. "In 1973, Cover was invited by the Army to Aberdeen proving grounds to try his system on primates. Cover was surprised to find that Rhesus monkeys proved able to partially function at electrical inputs that would have completely immobilized humans."[52] For a device that claimed to immobilize, this must have been a setback.

Alliance 3

By 1971, Cover was focusing on civilian usage, temporarily giving up on the police and military market. Airlines were looking for alternatives to combat the new trend in airplane hijacking. Air marshals could not fire guns in confined, pressurized cabins thirty thousand feet in the air. The Taser looked like an answer, but airlines wanted something even smaller than Model II, the heavy-duty device for riot control. They wanted a sleeker professional device, one that was light enough for cabin attendants to use. "It was back to the drawing board for Cover. His prototypes were in serious need of improvement."[53] Cover needed capital and a cost-efficient design. He proposed the "Taser flashlight" (Model III), mounting the dart gun on prefabricated flashlight components.

TWA placed a tentative order for five hundred guns at one thousand dollars a piece.[54] Cover found investors excited about the civilian market, but they were hesitant to invest in a gun. Cabin attendants could not fire guns without a license. Only gun dealers could sell guns. One could not import guns overseas without government approval.

Cover had always understood the device to be a weapon, if not a gun. Indeed, the Taser used rifle primer to fire the darts. Now, to make the sale, win venture capital, and purchase the components to assemble the devices, Cover asked the Treasury Department to rule that the Taser was *not* a gun. Guns fired bullets and were lethal. The Taser was a nonlethal weapon with tethered darts. In 1971, Treasury agreed Tasers were not guns.[55]

Alliance 4

The Treasury's ruling is hard to swallow in light of what Cover did next. In 1972, he filed a patent for a "weapon for immobilization and capture."[56] Model IV consists of a power supply, tethering wires, and harmless projectiles. "In different embodiments, the projectile can be a pellet, a net, or a combination of pellets and a net." Accompanying drawings show at least two types of pellets and two types of netting. The electrical impulses "would range in effect from immobilizing to potentially 'lethal' levels."[57] Nothing had been settled, it appears, about the lethality of the device. Cover suggested that the Taser could be potentially lethal (contrary to much subsequent Taser literature) and he expressed no interest in riot control.

Alliance 5

By 1973, Cover was also designing a personal security weapon "based on the Taser flashlight (TF-1) concept planned for the airlines with rechargeable batteries."[58] He built a flashlight into the device. The flashlight handle made it look professional and cut production costs. In 1974, Cover produced the "Public Defender." This model did not cast nets or fuzzy pellets, but darts. It sold for $199.50. Demo models appeared at the International Security Show in February 1975, and the device found a market not only among civilians but among police. By midyear, Taser Systems had sold two thousand devices to civilians, private security firms, and police.[59] The State Department flew four units to King Hussein in Jordan. China began negotiating for a deal. In October, Taser Systems struck a seven-figure deal with the Hertz family for exclusive rights to market the Taser in California and adjacent states.

This presumably is the point where corporations, states, and advertisers take over, spreading Model V across the globe. This development would coincide with the surge in electrotorture worldwide, confirming the hypothesis that economic elites had driven the surge. But that is not what happened next. Instead, all Cover's alliances fell apart, and the Taser came close to being nothing but junk.

In 1973, the Nixon administration had mandated new preboarding screening procedures for airlines—including the use of magnetometers. These procedures ended the rash of skyjackings nationally and then worldwide. Airlines "lost interest in the Taser."[60] In mid-1975, police, the gun industry and the National Rifle Association raised objections to the Taser in Washington. In the fall, the California attorney general classified the Taser as a "potentially lethal weapon" and banned it from his jurisdiction.[61] In December 1975, the U.S. Consumer Safety Products Commission (CSPC) halted all sales and began investigating the apparently hazardous product. The Hertz marketing deal collapsed, and Cover's investors had not recovered their start-up costs.

Alliance 6

The Taser went back to the laboratory. In April 1976, the CSPC decided that it would not ban the Taser. CSPC tests concluded that its maximum output was 10 percent of lethal value, though individual susceptibility varied and the hazard grew with repeated shocks.[62]

This good news was tempered by bad. The Treasury Department classified the Taser as a Title II weapon, in the same class as "machine guns, destructive devices, and certain other firearms." After all, Treasury and Cover had agreed in 1971 that the Taser was a firearm with tethered darts, but not a gun. "The

Taser didn't *look* like a gun since it had the shape of a straight-handled flashlight. In part, the Taser *was* a flashlight. A separate switch allowed a user to project a narrow beam as an aiming device. It *did* have a straight handle to reduce the cost of tooling."[63]

Cover now wanted the Taser to be a gun, not another kind of firearm or a flashlight. At first, Cover tried to sell Treasury on the idea of a bent handle attachment (TF-76) to make the Taser a gun, hoping to avoid the time-consuming and expensive step of bending the handle. Then he reluctantly asked the machinists to "tool an attachment that put a bend in the Taser's handle."[64] The Bureau of Alcohol, Tobacco and Firearms then reclassified the device (Model VI) as a Title I weapon (a conventional handgun).

So now the Taser was (again) a gun, but that killed all the prearranged marketing deals. Only gun shops could sell Tasers. The Department of State put the gun on the Munitions Control Act list, meaning it now had to approve all overseas sales, and foreign clients had to furnish their government's approval.[65] One could not sell, directly or indirectly, to unapproved countries, like Communist China.

More bad news followed.[66] Some police in medium-sized cities (Nashville, Akron) bought Tasers, but so did criminals, who used them in muggings and robberies in Miami, Dallas, New York, Long Island, and Iowa. Local grassroots movements rose against the weapon. Michigan and Hawaii banned Tasers. In Canada, it became a criminal offense to buy, sell, or possess one. The Los Angeles Police Department, the most technologically oriented American police force, considered and rejected the Taser twice. Cover's investors "had spent millions with little hope of recouping the investment. The foreign market was essentially dead. Police departments at that time had little interest in the Taser. Even the promising airline market died."[67] By 1979, Cover was trying to interest the California Department of Fish and Game in the TF-76Gx3 as a means of immobilizing deer. A device designed for short-range urban policing was adequate only for trapped deer, not animals wandering in the wild.[68]

Alliances 7 and 8

Stun technology would probably have vanished, except for a lucky opportunity. In 1982, the Los Angeles City Council banned police use of chokeholds during arrests. Records indicated that LAPD officers had killed fifteen people in the previous seven years while holding them in chokeholds.[69] The police department demonstrated "laxity in pursuing use-of-force alternatives."[70] Police switched to swinging metal batons but complaints of excessive force doubled. LAPD-related litigation costs soared from $891,000 to $ 11.3 million.[71]

Cover cultivated police interest in the Taser as a nonlethal alternative to batons. The LAPD once again ran field tests and encountered some problems. Policemen were not airline cabin attendants. They pressed triggers heavily with their thumbs, which could distort the internal mechanism and short out the unit. Others lifted their thumbs upon firing the Taser, cutting off current to the wires and rendering the device ineffective.[72]

Officers also complained that standard Tasers wouldn't stun individuals high on PCP ("Angel Dust").[73] They believed PCP addicts became animalized, that is, unnaturally strong, indifferent to danger, and impervious to pain. Government reports agreed.

The LAPD ordered seven hundred devices, but wanted a more powerful and durable technology. By 1983, Cover had redesigned the Taser again (Model VII). He "answered the problem presented by users of PCP" by increasing the Taser's power. The PS-83 "Police Special" was now a gun for subduing violent, unstable individuals. It was no longer a paramilitary crowd control weapon or a civilian safety device for cabin attendants or a flashlight (which "proved unreliable as an aiming device" and "a constant source of repair problems").[74]

Increasing the power increased the likelihood the device would fail to operate as designed. The internal chamber of Cover's circuitry was an engineer's nightmare. The spark gap worked at near capacity. It pitted and oxidized upon usage, and the capacitors could suddenly fail after regular use. Finding the right metal proved difficult and costly. Platinum staples were ideal, but too expensive. Steel corroded rapidly and required careful placement. Titanium steel worked, but was too brittle and snapped, not good for a portable police device. Adding nickel to the titanium steel helped, but decreased the gap and reduced the charge. Eventually, makers used argon gas in the chamber to reduce oxidization.

Current also could leak through the casing and shock the user. The TE-86 (Model VIII) was wrapped in a shrink-fit, polyolefin skin to prevent leakage.[75] Nevertheless, the TE-86 and earlier models had a delicate "internal high-voltage switching mechanism." A moderate impact could damage it, though this "may not be evident until it's used later." When an operator used the damaged Taser, high-voltage leakage shocked the user through the trigger or a seam in the device.[76]

Cover also built a stronger trigger and configured it to stay depressed as soon as the Taser was fired even if the officer lifted his thumb. If the current ran continuously, the live wires could shock the officer as he approached to handcuff the suspect.[77] Police had to learn to avoid the wires and reset the device upon use.

Finally, Taser batteries were not removable, and the device had to be serviced at the factory every two years.[78] Defective Tasers leaked shock. Spark gaps failed after heavy usage. Without the factory, the LAPD would have been the master of seven hundred pieces of junk within two years, and Taser Systems was in financial trouble.

Other stun manufacturers now colonized Cover's stable network of allies, starting in 1985 with the advent of the first commercial stun gun, the NOVA XR-5000. These competitors built far cheaper stun guns, guns that were soon implicated in police torture. But it should be clear that this date comes too late to account for the global surge in electrotorture. It started gathering steam in the late 1960s and expanded dramatically in the 1970s. What is more, the American stun torture scandals generated huge crises for the stun industry, scandals that increased company liability payments and drove customers, police and civilian, away. The stun industry may have come of age in the mid-1980s, but it had at least a decade to go before it overcame the obstacles in its path to become the global industry it is today.

In the next chapter, I consider how the stun industry colonized Cover's network and overcame the torture crisis, and why stun devices did not disappear from American policing as did the electrified baton. What is important here is that by the mid-1980s, Cover had established a stable, defendable scenario for stun technology. Stun devices were police specials for taking out isolated violent criminals. This is how we still think of stun technology today.

Remembering Eutopia

Too often the story of stun technology is told as if the *technological* product emerges full blown from the head of Zeus and then it was simply a *social* question of overcoming resistance. For Cover's hagiographers, resistance was substantial. For Cover's critics, it was minimal; capitalism generated a technological imperative against which resistance was necessary, but futile.

Cover did not distinguish artificially between "technical" and "social" questions. He knew his problem was to mobilize certain kinds of people and things in a socio-technical chain along a scenario he imagined. These elements were not givens, but had to be brought into existence or pushed out of the picture, depending on the scenario.

Cover's difficulties arose when his allies proved to be weak links. If any ally failed, then the Taser was a bunch of wires that belonged to the history of Eutopia. If the capacitors couldn't handle the electrical energy, if high voltage would not sit quietly in a small handheld device, if rhesus monkeys did not lie still before the army brass, if a trigger crushed under a policeman's thumb, if the casing or capacitors cracked when the device fell, if an investor or a customer vanished, if police could imagine themselves tethered by wild hippies to electric wires, if the factory that reserviced batteries went bankrupt, all that remained was mush.

Inventions, then, do not appear fully tested and ready to roll out from Evil Devices R Us. We can see more clearly, then, why we *do not* live either in Eutopia or Dystopia. For patents to make it into the world, inventors have to make the whole package of people and things work together. The more they do, the more inventors can argue that people are resisting something powerful (let us call it "a technological imperative"), and this is a "social problem." The more things and people resist what they are supposed to do, this is a "technical question" of getting the stun to "work." At this point, no one talks about "social resistance," much less "the inevitable march of technology."

You see those two little marks close together like vampire bites
on their bodies . . . those are stun gun marks.

— Defense attorney Nick Hentoff, on police violence

in Maricopa County Jails, Arizona, 1997[1]

11 Stun City

Over the last two decades, stun manufacturers have boldly redesigned their
products to open new markets and surmount new challenges, including bad
publicity and lawsuits. Stun guns are complex technological products, and their
design bears the history of the rich and litigious democratic society in which
they first appeared.

To reduce the risk of litigation, stun manufacturers created products that,
among other things, left few marks *when they were properly used*. This quality
set stun guns apart from mace, rubber bullets, and other nonlethal weapons,
where clean usage is difficult regardless of whether officers use them well or
poorly. As a result, this design characteristic also reduces the ability of authorities to oversee officers using these weapons. One can tell if stun guns are used
badly, but one cannot always tell after the fact that a stun gun, if it was used
correctly, has been used at all. This is true also of its use for torture.

Counting on police to act professionally on their own cannot make up for
this potential problem in oversight. On the contrary, a perverse professional
pride may drive police to use stun guns for torture because they have a reputation to preserve as officers who solve crimes. In Chicago, police officers praised
for their professionalism allegedly extorted confessions from suspects with
stealth torture for decades in the late twentieth century. Even though these
policemen used magnetos, not stun guns, the case shows that professional police can be driven to torture regularly, and that they can get away with it for
years in a modern democracy provided certain conditions are met.

In this chapter, I describe first the Chicago story and then various stun
torture scandals in the past two decades, showing that other officers counted

on the same conditions that prevailed in Chicago. Then, I describe how stun manufacturers confronted the bad publicity and redesigned their products. I argue that these changes have made it even more likely that torturers will use stun guns. Lastly, I consider how stun torture affects victims, communities, and democratic life.

Magneto Torture in Chicago

In 1990, the Chicago Police Department's Office of Professional Standards conducted a study of police torture in Area 2, a zone comprising most of south Chicago. Michael Goldston, the city investigator, identified fifty cases between 1973 and 1986 involving over thirty officers. Goldston grouped the incidents by torture technique (electrotorture, suspension, and "bagging," or near-asphyxiation with a plastic bag [the "dry submarine"]). He concluded that police violence was "systematic" and included "psychological techniques and planned torture."[2]

Other reports indicate detectives were extracting confessions of guilt by means of torture as early as 1968.[3] Flint Taylor, a lawyer for the People's Law Office, has updated Goldston's list, identifying over seventy incidents of alleged torture between 1973 and 1991, involving eighty-three prisoners and more than fifty-two officers.[4] Prisoners described magneto torture, bagging, suspension (including the strappado), whipping, beating, and clean beating (using phone books, rubber hoses, slapping, the *teléfono*, and the *falaka* in one case).

At least eleven men were sentenced to death and many others given long-term prison sentences based on confessions extracted by torture in Area 2. The Illinois judicial system was compromised. In 2003, Governor George Ryan commuted the death sentences of all 167 death row inmates, pardoning four Area 2 victims and commuting the sentences of the others.[5] Many other Area 2 victims remain in prison.

Most alleged incidents in Area 2 implicated Commander Jon Burge and those detectives whom he supervised. At the time of his dismissal, Burge was the commander of the Area 3 detective division, outranking 99 percent of all policemen in the city. Burge had been discharged honorably from military service in Vietnam, receiving the Bronze Star, the Vietnamese Cross of Gallantry, and the Purple Heart. He received his first police commendation in 1972 (for preventing a suicide), and a second commendation for an off-duty incident.[6] He and his detectives were also commended for "skillful interrogation" in Area 2.[7] When Burge and several of his men came to Area 3, prisoners reported torture there.

The officers allegedly involved, in other words, were career policemen, men who appeared to comply with professional rules, who were evaluated regularly by their supervisors, and who were even commended by the city for their conduct. By contrast, the prisoners who made allegations were hard to believe. Andrew Wilson, the most important victim, had spent most of his life in institutions, having been on the street for a total of four months in twenty-five years. He was impulsive, emotional, and adolescent; in short, "his ability to function in the community" was "severely limited."[8]

In 1982, police arrested Wilson for killing a police officer. According to Wilson, the commanding officer, Jon Burge, told his men not to assault him when he was arrested, adding "We'll get him at the station." There, other detectives beat Wilson and bagged him. Burge chided them for sloppy technique. Wilson reports Burge saying that "he wouldn't have messed my face up, he wouldn't have messed me up." Detectives then took Wilson to a room, clamped alligator clips to his right ear and nostril, and "turned a crank on the side of the box." Burge apparently told Wilson something like, "My reputation is at stake and you are going to make a statement."[9] Later, a detective connected the magneto to Wilson's fifth finger on each hand, "and then he kept cranking it and kept cranking it and I was hollering and screaming."[10] Then detectives used a black, round device, moving it "up and down like this, real gentle with it, but you can feel it, still feel it. Then he jabbed me with the thing and it slammed me . . . into the grill on the window."[11]

Wilson sued, but judges, juries, reporters, and the public did not believe him. Two separate civil trials failed to convict Burge, and it was only when investigators revealed the entire pattern of abuse in the 1990s that the Chicago police dismissed Burge and disciplined two other officers. No other officers allegedly involved have been disciplined. Several were promoted, and others retired with full benefits.[12] Unlike other cities, Chicago now cannot consider an officer's prior record of complaints when investigating new allegations of brutality, an arrangement the police union has insisted upon.[13]

Some might believe that practices like those in Chicago are common, that, as Alan Dershowitz claims, "torture is happening in every police station in America. It's called the third degree."[14] That overstates the case. The 1998 Human Rights Watch report examining police brutality in fourteen American cities did not announce findings as serious as those the Wickersham Commission reported in the 1930s, and few would agree that torture is as common in the United States now as it was then.[15] John Conroy, the reporter who closely followed the Chicago story, no doubt correctly observes that after Chicago, "no one can dispute that it [torture] happens here."[16] It happens under specific conditions. Unlike the southern police, the Chicago police could torture as long as they did because they used *stealthy* torture regimens on *inarticulate* subjects, with *criminal or institutional* histories, and in cases of *intense public disapproval of those crimes.*

Torture can be an open secret in a democratic society. Apparently, successive Chicago police superintendents suppressed internal investigations that revealed torture, successive state's attorneys knew of the torture but refused to investigate, and the state's Felony Review Unit knowingly elicited and used tortured confessions.[17] Approximately one-third of the current Cook County criminal court judges are former assistant state's attorneys or Area 2 detectives who were involved in the torture cases.[18] Courts and the public will also look the other way. Indeed, the alleged torture cases in Area 3, involving electrotorture, bagging, and clean beating, all occurred during or after Wilson's two unsuccessful civil suits.[19]

Some judges are now more sensitive to stealth torture: "We are seeing cases, like the present case, involving punching, kicking, and placing a plastic bag over a suspect's head to obtain confessions."[20] Combining stealth torture, racism, union politics, electoral ambitions, and public hysteria over crime is a winning package.

Stun and Torture

The first commercial stun gun, the NOVA XR-5000, appeared in 1985, just before the first trial of Detective Burge. The Chicago police did not use stun guns for torture, as far as can be determined.[21] But shortly afterward, several police and private security officers around the country did.[22] Like the Chicago police, they used them on *inarticulate* subjects, with *criminal or institutional* histories, and in cases of *intense public disapproval of those crimes.* In 1985, prosecutors indicted five NYPD officers on charges of using stun guns between 1985 and 1986 to torture African-American and Hispanic youths suspected of drug dealing. In 1985, a San Diego private security guard admitted using the "stun gun on transients."[23] In 1986, the LAPD discovered two officers had repeatedly shocked a Hispanic juvenile "in an attempt to force him to confess to stealing stereo parts."[24] In the 1990s, one Bronx clinic records that 11 percent of its patients reported "electrical torture," suggesting that stun torture was underreported in this period.[25] In 2004, Denver police allegedly used stun guns on handcuffed prisoners—including a pregnant woman—in squad cars or chained to the wall of booking rooms.[26]

Prison guards were also accused of tormenting inmates with stun batons, stun guns, stun belts, Tasers, and even electric shields.[27] In 1994, Maricopa County Jails began a pilot study using stun guns and pepper spray as a nonlethal *response* to violent acts by prisoners. Reports of excessive brutality soon followed, yielding two Department of Justice investigations, an Amnesty International report, and lawsuits. Both DOJ reports concluded that guards used devices as "compliance tools," that is, for conditions that were "not justified for passive or active resistance."[28] In short, they were used for torture.

These stories point to the rapid spread of stun weaponry in the 1980s, and this spread is surprising given how badly the inventor of stun technology himself was doing around 1985. Cover had tried for years to market the Taser, his version of stun technology, to police departments. By the mid-1980s, he had found at best a small niche market of a few hundred departments, but he was facing serious technical and financial obstacles in marketing the Taser. The Nova stun gun, by contrast, swept the field in 1985. Less than fifteen months after it was introduced, Nova had sold two hundred thousand units, mainly to police departments. Why were other stun manufacturers so much more successful than Cover?

Stun guns differ from Tasers in certain respects. Although they draw on Cover's circuitry, they fire no darts. They have a pair of electrodes no more than two inches apart, like cattle prods. If the electrodes are pressed against a nerve cluster, the device can immobilize the body involuntarily. However, stun guns must be held against the nerve cluster (usually the base of the neck or under the collarbone) for a minimum of three to four seconds. Only under this circumstance can one "stun," that is, make the subject "faint from pain [or] suffer a transient anemia (syncope)."[29] Otherwise, stun guns cause local pain where they touch, delivering the equivalent of powerful kicks and punches.[30] Stun guns, in this respect, are less likely than Tasers to immobilize subjects, unless the subject is close enough to strike the device against a nerve cluster. If the purpose of possessing such weapons is to immobilize with a full-body shock, the Taser is the better device.

So the early success of Nova was not due to any magical qualities stun guns possessed. In fact, the success was partly due to the way other stun manufacturers managed to ride Cover's success and colonize the networks he had established. Cover had managed to show how a technology using stun circuitry could be useful to police, and stun manufacturers adopted this rationale. Other stun manufacturers fudged the line between stun guns and Tasers, advertising that stun guns were "currently in use by over 400 progressive agencies and correctional facilities worldwide."[31] They also described the devices as "guns" like the Taser, even though technically they were not guns. Indeed, manufacturers had eliminated the gun design that characterized Cover's Tasers to reduce government regulation and costs (a Nova cost twenty-nine dollars, a Taser three hundred).[32] This made the "guns" easier to sell, not only to the police but to the general public. While the sale of Tasers was highly regulated (because it *was* classified as a gun), the new stun devices were called "guns" but sold in mail order catalogs and shops. Stun manufacturers also designed the new devices to use replaceable batteries, eliminating the need for costly factory servicing that drove costs up for the Taser. Soon manufacturers abroad produced even cheaper stun guns. These were not always reliable; the spark gap might fail after a few uses. Still, stun guns were easily replaceable, whereas Tasers were not.

But stun manufacturers assembled networks that went well beyond what Cover had ever imagined. Stun manufacturers built the new circuitry into portable CD players, radios, key chains, car doors, and umbrellas. They marketed stun guns to women, claiming, controversially, that it was a woman's best defense against rape.[33] The Myotron Venus, for example, was a small, pearl-colored stun device "designed to appeal primarily to women." The manufacturers insisted it was not a stun "gun," but the Venus was not easily distinguishable from the Nova guns in electrical output or physiological effects.[34] Women, guessed marketers, would not carry "guns" or cattle prods, which "are not easily carried in the pocket or purse."[35] The pearl-colored compact case in one's purse did the same work as a cattle prod, and indeed, for all intents and purposes, it *was* a cattle prod with a "feminine" design.

Stun companies also marketed stun guns as sex toys to those who favored electrotorture in voluntary sex play: "Just about every [sex] magazine includes ads for so-called 'stun guns.' "[36] Even among practitioners of sadomasochism, stun guns provoked controversy.

Electric S-M emerged in the mid-1970s around the figure of Tony DeBlase, a unique figure in American gay and S-M history.[37] DeBlase was one of the first members of the Chicago Hellfire Club (around 1976), named after the old sex-and-scandal club that counted among its distinguished members Benjamin Franklin. DeBlase also founded *Dungeon Master* magazine (1979–94) and later purchased and directed the classic leather magazine *Drummer* (1986–92). He hand-sewed the Leather Pride Flag (1989), the black-and-blue flag with the red heart that is ubiquitous in gay pride parades today. His *Fledermaus Anthology* (1982) is a classic in the S-M fiction genre and titled after his S-M pseudonym and academic specialization (DeBlase had a Ph.D. in Zoology and specialized in Iranian bats).

At the annual Infernos of the Hellfire Club, DeBlase organized S-M education lectures on Saturdays, pioneering a format that is now common. Inferno 8 (around 1978) included probably the first "electrotorture demo."[38] DeBlase catalogued Inferno practices in *Physical Interrogation Techniques*.[39] Although ostensibly a torture manual, DeBlase signaled the book's nature in his pseudonym, Richard Krousher ("Dick Crusher").[40]

DeBlase ran an S-M shop in Chicago between 1983 and 1986, claiming, "I was the first person to carry electrical toys."[41] He scoured midwestern rummage sales, looking for quack medical devices, especially "Violet Wands," dramatic devices that yielded purple light via small lightning bolts from Tesla coils, and had inventive attachments. DeBlase did not carry stun guns and searched, apparently fruitlessly, for magnetos.[42]

S-M practitioners adopted the DeBlase instruments, particularly the Violet Wands that are still highly prized. Many longtime users reject stun guns. "Should be returned to sci-fi props department, illegal and lethal," remarks one adviser.[43] "Could be used in an interesting psych scene, but I would personally not actually apply it to my partner," remarked another.[44] Some S-M users push the limits, and others suggest ways of toning down the devices. Stun guns, cattle prods, and magnetos are more the stuff of S-M fiction than common practice. Aside from DeBlase's work, S-M knowledge of these devices is rudimentary and often inaccurate.

Torturers, on the other hand, immediately appreciated stun guns. They saw them as modified cattle prods with Cover circuitry. The two narrowly spaced prods always distinguished them as "primarily pain-compliance tools with secondary effects on specific, target muscles or nerve centers."[45] These weapons caused pain (like prods), delivered a full-body shock with the right placement (like Tasers and magnetos), were nonlethal (and so idiot proof), were easily replaceable, did not look like guns, and left few marks.

Tasers and Torture

American police used Tasers just as they used stun guns, mainly on *inarticulate* subjects, with *criminal or institutional* histories, and in cases of *intense public disapproval*. In the first LAPD field tests, police used the Taser twenty-six times, "mainly against extremely violent mentals and drug-crazed suspects."[46] A 1987 study of LAPD practice documented 218 cases of Taser-related injuries. All patients were young men (average age being twenty-eight), and 86 percent had been using PCP that day.[47] A 1991 study of LAPD mortality data and Tasers recorded sixteen cases, all of them young men known to use illicit drugs, several with criminal histories; most were minorities (five Mexican-Americans, eight African-Americans).[48]

Increasingly, the LAPD police used Tasers not merely to immobilize, but to *diagnose* the use of PCP. If such a powerful device did not work, it stood to reason that the victim must be high on PCP. The practice of electric diagnosis, if one may call it that, led directly to the most famous police brutality case of the late twentieth century, the Rodney King affair.

On that fateful night, Sergeant Koon fired the Taser twice, and it failed to immobilize Rodney King. All the officers—Powell, Koon, and Briseno—became convinced that King was under the influence of PCP—and the main evidence they cite is that he managed to resist a swarm of officers and the Taser.[49] Once the officers made this diagnosis (in error, as it turned out), they proceeded to the next level of force: they beat King with metal batons.

The beating was particularly ferocious because the officers feared King had the superhuman strength of a PCP user.[50] Koon did not stop the beating at the thirty-fifth second of the video when King stopped rising, or at the sixty-fifth second, when Briseno stomped on King. The beating proceeded for another thirty seconds, a disconcertingly long time in an assault.

Koon explains the prolonged beating by saying he was busy delivering a third reminder jolt with the Taser.[51] When he heard his performance was taped, he was excited: " 'BITCHIN' I thought, 'This is great! They got it on tape! Now we'll have a live, in-the-field film to show police recruits. It can be a real life example of how to use escalating force properly.' "[52] The video offered a grimmer picture: "The sergeant was seen attempting to keep the wires from tearing or tangling, apparently preoccupied with his weapon [the Taser] [instead of with] controlling his officers."[53]

Using the Taser increased LAPD department's civil liability claims and payments, increased personnel complaints and demands for disability compensation, and destroyed the public image of the police, exactly the opposite of what a 1993 study concluded Taser usage would do.[54] LAPD officers stopped using Tasers.[55] In 2001, only 125 police agencies used them.[56]

For over a decade, Cover and his associates organized a string of struggling companies.[57] Police brutality scandals drove away investors and increased insurance premiums. In 1993, Rick and Tom Smith formed a small company, Air Taser, that adapted Cover's design to create a personal security device.[58] The air taser's darts were propelled by compressed air, not gunpowder. As a result, the Bureau of Alcohol, Tobacco and Firearms (BATF) ruled that the air taser was not a firearm, and so not subject to the same regulations as Tasers.

In 1998, Air Taser changed its name to Taser International and began sales to law enforcement agencies worldwide. It also started "Project Stealth," to develop an advanced taser "with much higher power to stop goal oriented, focused and extremely TASER technology resistant individuals."[59] In December 2000, Taser International began marketing the M26. This advanced taser included a password-protected data chip that recorded the time and date of the last 585 firings.[60] The X26, issued 2003, enhanced the dataport, incorporating data on the duration of each discharge and the temperature at the time of use for the last 2,000 firings. In addition, the new air cartridge released forty small confetti-like I.D. tags when it was fired, each one of which was marked with a unique serial number.[61]

The new air tasers reduced the cost of litigation and regulation while retaining the traditional features of Tasers. The data chips in particular "protects officers from unfounded allegations" and holds "officers accountable for use."[62] Sales soared. In the wake of 9/11, major airlines purchased air tasers for cockpit crews. By 2004, Taser International had sold air tasers to forty-three hundred law enforcement agencies worldwide. Taser International purchased the old Taser company, Tasertron. Taser International stock increased from $3.65 a share to $147 in three years.[63]

Taser International's data chip is an important step in the right direction for stun technology, as I will explain below. Whether these changes will spare it eventual litigation remains to be seen. The Taser's success thus far has depended on its use on inarticulate subjects, with criminal histories, in cases of public disapproval. However, firing a pair of darts in a crowded airplane cabin will be an entirely different matter, reproducing conditions similar to those that doomed police riot prods in the 1960s. Analysts at that time explained that electric technology would not find acceptance in democracies if devices endangered or antagonized bystanders, provoked angry responses if they were used poorly, and appeared cruel even if they were nondamaging.[64] The moment a cockpit crew uses the device on a middle-class passenger in a case of air rage or accidentally blinds a seated passenger, litigation, bad publicity and all the usual consequences will follow.

The more serious problem will continue to be the Taser's use in states that torture. Cover always maintained that the Taser was a poor torture device: "As a torture device, the Taser wasn't in the same league as the ubiquitous cattle prod or car battery, the instruments of choice in such places as Zimbabwe and Iraq. Even a field telephone could be (and often was in Viet Nam) easily modified to deliver excruciating pain via the hand-crank generator."[65] Unlike most stun spokesmen, Cover knew the competition and asked correctly why torturers would prefer Tasers to magnetos and cattle prods. The answer is that in most cases, they do not. What torturers prefer are stun guns, highly modified cattle prods that have Cover's unique circuitry.

Even so, the Taser can be a good torture device. While magnetos have been known to kill people, Taser defenders continually insist that not a single death can be directly attributed to a Taser.[66] For torture, that is invaluable, as is the ability to deliver a full-body shock. While magnetos have to be clipped and stun guns pressed against the flesh, Taser darts can be taped or hooked to the clothing with less danger of leaving marks. Certain dart attachments produce excruciating pain, especially when the current flows across a joint.[67] There are already reports of alleged police torture with Tasers in Colorado in 2004.[68] Recent Taser models, such as the M26 and the X26, possess "contact drive stun backup capability," that is, they can be used as stun guns, devices favored by torturers the world over.[69]

Burning Issues

As stun salesmen constantly remind us, stun devices are meant to be nonlethal weapons. Unlike a bullet, stun does not cut or lacerate the body: "There are no injuries, no cuts, no physical damage."[70] It leaves no scars or long-term burns.

Nevertheless, stun does leave short-term marks depending on how the weapon is applied. These "signature marks"[71] disappear rapidly. "Tasers and stun guns create wheals about the diameter of a pencil at the current's points of entry and exit. These are first and second degree burns which form thin scabs; they disappear in a week or two and are medically inconsequential (second-degree burns raise blisters; third degree burns leave scars)."[72]

Major stun gun companies put some effort into reducing these signature marks. The Nova Spirit stun gun "has answered the problem by recessing the [electric] probes into a 'tunnel.' " Stun Tech's Ultron II stun gun recesses two of its four probes along a reverse sloping wall. "Without this feature, the shunts can add a second pair of so-called signature marks." Some stun guns have rapid on-off switches that prevent the device from overheating.[73] Training is also available "to reduce liability and increase effectiveness."[74] Among other things, officers are advised to avoid targeting the face or use the device on people who will be perceived to be vulnerable (e.g., people in wheelchairs).[75]

Stun companies know they operate in a litigious society. They know from experience that stun torture jeopardizes their business and that police will abandon stun if they perceive it increases their liability. Most litigation has focused on visible damage, particularly deaths while police used Tasers or stun guns. Juries can easily understand deaths. Industry spokespersons bitterly contest the causes of these deaths, while critics charge that coroners do not adequately investigate stun deaths, sometimes under intense police pressure.[76]

In designing products, then, stun manufacturers think prospectively about reducing liability. For example, because some Tasers could also be used as stun guns, LAPD officers sued the city for compensation for any injuries they sustained while using Tasers as stun guns. They argued that "since the LAPD issues stun guns, and since using stun guns must involve physical contact, the LAPD has a policy of encouraging physical combat." To forestall this argument, Taser manufacturers designed an LAPD police special that replaces the stun prods with plastic plugs. Consequently, "This aspect won't be seen as a department *encouragement* for an officer to close with the suspect with all the attendant consequences of hand-to-hand combat."[77]

For legal reasons, stun manufacturers show the same design concerns with medically inconsequential signature marks. "These marks, or the lack of them, are legally consequential and can be crucial in the defense of a suit involving Taser or stun gun usage."[78] In wrongful-death suits, the absence of marks on the body undermines the claim that the victim died from electrocution.[79] Like-wise, John Murray and Barnet Resnick, two stun advocates, offer this caution regarding liability in cases of police brutality:

> People felt if they only pressed harder and longer, the suspect would stop struggling. . . . But long persistent reapplication of stun guns can leave a trail of blisters that will not only infuriate the recipient, they will arouse the ire of journalists and attorneys. These misuses of the NOVA weapon ended in the arraignment of several NYPD officers on charges of brutality. The press picked up the story and claimed that the stungun (in their minds, this included the Taser) was a torture device capable of causing serious burns.[80]

This is a misleading description of the actual NYPD events, but that is not important.[81] Murray and Resnick's complaint seems to be that the torturers pressed hard and long. This yielded evidence of torture, a trail of burns that attracted journalists and attorneys. They imply that if the torturers had used the stun guns properly, leaving fewer and less extreme marks, monitors would have no complaints about police behavior. Then who would? For no one would know that officers had been torturing suspects systematically for months. Complaints by youths with criminal records would hardly be credible.

How far can reducing signature marks help? Consider the case of Scott Norberg.[82] In 1996, Norberg died as officers confined him to a restraint chair in Maricopa County Jail in Arizona. Guards strapped a towel over his mouth and shocked him multiple times—eight to twenty times according to the inmates, two to six times according to the guards, and twenty-one times according to the medical examiner hired by Norberg's family. The coroner ruled Norberg's death was caused by accidental asphyxiation.

A profound ambiguity surrounded Norberg's death. Despite numerous witnesses, no one could say when and where the gun was pressed against Norberg's body. We cannot tell how many times the guns were used, and what role electricity played in his death. Nor can we tell whether 50,000 volts was "too much" or "too little" for the situation. Different figures—20,000 or 150,000—seem plausible; one simply cannot say.

Stun and Democracy

A fundamental rule in a democratic society is to apply no more force than is necessary to perform policing functions. For every weapon, public standards govern police usage, and anything more is unjustifiable violence. As democrats, we will disagree as to whether the standards have been met, but there is no disagreement about the standards themselves. Everyone, for example, agrees that the famous blow with a metal baton to Rodney King's head was illegitimate. Even Officer Powell agreed; he simply denied he struck it.[83] In Norberg's case, we could not identify what the standards of use were, much less whether guards had conformed to them.

Clear public standards of use are reasonable expectations for any punitive technology. Consider, for example, the tables by which the hangman determines the approximate drop of a body from the platform. Hanging has always been a difficult art. If the drop is too long, the rope tears the head out. If the rope is too short, the condemned strangles slowly.

In 1870, William Marwood solved the problem of excessive cruelty by offering clear standards. He drew up mathematical tables based on the weight, age, development, and muscular strength of the condemned.[84] The correct calculation snapped the neck without any additional pain, precisely the sentence that had been issued; anything more or less was actionable. Today, a metal device on the platform also allows hangmen to calculate in advance the length of the drop, from six to ten feet, to the closest half inch. Thanks to the new tables, nineteenth-century police chiefs went to bed at night comforted with the thought that those executed suffered neither more nor less than justice demanded.

Most police devices are unlikely to be as clearly regulated. In most cases, a third party can determine how a police officer used a weapon by examining the device, the victim's body, and the witnesses. One can tell if a gun has been fired, how many times, and where the bullets went. This information can then be checked against an officer's report and the victim's claims to see if more force than necessary was used.

One can think of similar measures in the case of mace, rubber bullets, and horses in riots: whether the crowd was retreating or advancing or whether the guns were aimed high or low. One can seek witnesses to verify whether police actions met or exceeded standards of use, a difficult process but one that has been performed successfully numerous times.

It is not possible to monitor stun usage in this way, and for particular reasons tied to the design of these devices. One cannot look at evidence from the victim's body because, unlike guns, these devices leave few forensic traces. Electrotorture "can be life-threatening even though no physical marks can be found at the objective examination—even shortly after torture."[85] Nor can one tell by examining a stun gun the number of discharges and their duration, or, in the case of Tasers, whether darts were released and the distance they traveled.

Stun guns, in particular, are silent. Some stun guns make loud sounds when tested, but not when they are pressed against a body. Even users cannot tell what the stun gun is doing. "Don't be alarmed," comforts a manufacturer, the stun gun "will still be doing its job."[86] Witnesses cannot really "see" what is happening, electricity being hard to observe with a human eye. They cannot tell whether the device is activated or discharged, or how much electroshock the victim is receiving and whether it is too much.

In short, when stun technology is used properly, judges, juries, and disciplinary review boards have a hard time evaluating whether police used these devices for purposes of torture. They can only weigh the officer's report against victims' claims, victims who often lack credibility. Many victims do not remember what happened to them clearly; some even report "total amnesia."[87]

When a technology evades third-party scrutiny, when it cannot be seen or heard or measured, it also evades precisely those legal standards that are used to protect us against ill-treatment and torture. It grants almost unlimited power to the user. When this power is not an accidental feature of the technology, but built into its design and a characteristic principle of its proper use, then its makers aim at weakening legal protections. No democracy, committed to limited government, can license such power without endangering itself.

For this reason, many stun weapons do not qualify as weapons police should use in a democracy—not because they are lethal or a torture technology, but because they are clean. When one combines cleanliness with nonlethal weaponry in this way, one profoundly undermines police supervision and evaluation. Commanding officers and desk sergeants may not know whether officers have been torturing suspects for months using stun technology, particularly if they are careful about the marks they leave. Twenty-first-century democrats, even chiefs of police, cannot rest at night as easily as nineteenth-century ones did.

This argument differs from others normally advanced against nonlethal weaponry. I am not here concerned with all nonlethal weapons, only stun devices. My argument accepts what stun manufacturers say at face value, namely that properly used, stun usage is nonlethal and nondamaging. Proper usage, by these very avowals, produces few marks and precisely the corrosive ambiguity that is so antidemocratic. My argument differs from those of stun gun critics who demand more oversight. Perhaps officers are easily tempted to use stun guns in situations that they could handle with lesser degrees of force.[88] If that is so, "more oversight" cannot check this temptation unless stun technology itself changes.

In this respect, the Taser International's data chip was an important step toward allowing third-party scrutiny. Considerable ambiguity, though, remains. For example, in 2004, Denver police officers confirmed that they had covered a prisoner's head with a pillowcase and that "they tased the highly intoxicated suspect at least eight times while he was handcuffed."[89] The prisoner claimed the officers tased him repeatedly in the back of a squad car until he "consented" to take a drug test (which proved negative). In this case, the data chip would agree with both the officers' and victim's reports, producing precisely the antidemocratic ambiguity. The data chip does not distinguish whether officers used the device as a taser (to fire darts) or as a stun gun, torturing the suspect on the back seat. It does not measure whether the darts were fired at a great distance or in close proximity. Nor does it catch cases where officers activated or threatened to use the device if compliance did not follow.

Additionally, mechanical recording is unhelpful unless recordkeeping procedures are adequate. Currently, no single agency tracks downloaded information from Tasers. Taser International asks police departments to submit their records voluntarily, but the records are incomplete as not all departments comply. And it is not clear how many police departments have in place policies for downloading materials locally to ensure no information is deleted. As an official with the International Association of Chiefs of Police stated, "That transfer really needs to have some standards and requirements, otherwise there's no security there."[90] In fall 2005, Taser International and Stinger Systems, an American stun gun manufacturer, introduced devices that allow audio-video recording.[91] They may address ambiguities that the data chip does not (though not all), and they suffer from the same recordkeeping deficiencies.

But No One Died

For twenty-five years, advocates of stun have argued that they meet a robust standard that qualifies their products for police usage in democracies. This standard is that no gun was fired and no one died. "These devices don't kill people," insists NOVA's president, John McDermit. Rick Smith, CEO of Taser International, argues that by restricting stun guns "that could save lives, we're actually degrading human rights."[92]

Tasers do save lives (the matter is much more debatable in the case of stun guns). Nevertheless, no one should be under any illusions about what the claim "no one died" means. What stun manufacturers are doing is reversing the traditional injunction of democratic policing—not "no more force than necessary," but "*any* force short of death is justified." In doing so they link lower mortality rates (surely desirable to a fair-minded public) to devices that leave few marks and are hard to monitor. This is another illustration of the principle of linkage discussed in chapter 7 ("Magnetos"): if you want X (which is desirable), you must also choose Y (which is not).

"No one died" is an appealing argument, and probably sincerely believed in most cases. It is also a troubling one. The argument amounts to saying that safer streets can be won when one doesn't secondguess professional police on the job, when one has no standards other than officer's report that weapons were used properly. "No one died" furnishes a clear standard to be sure, but in a way that cedes unlimited power to police in the name of professionalism.

The difficulty is that professionalism is no check on torture (as I will discuss further in part V). Belief that it is is simply empirically false. Many authoritarian states that torture have professional police, and many torturers are professionals.[93] As the Chicago case illustrates, certain qualities of professionalism can drive officers to torture. As Sargeant Koon illustrates, police in conflicts are poor judges of their own professional skills. Appeals to one's own professionalism have to be matched with oversight, and stun technology provides no easy way to exercise it.

Democratic policing preserves not only the lives of citizens, but also their liberties and their ability to pursue happiness. Stun manufacturers, by contrast, believe in the sanctity of life, but have, until recently, demonstrated *no* commitment to the rule of law beyond this minimal standard. Most enlightened dictators would have no difficulty endorsing their view. "I'm never going to kill you or anyone else, but have you met my professional police?" is not a democratic viewpoint. Until more stun companies follow Taser International's lead and start acting like democrats, police chiefs that adopt stun weapons are simply waiting for the next torture scandal.

Civic Shock

Stun technology combines nonlethal weaponry, increased professional autonomy, and an inevitable marked decrease in public accountability. If you want the first quality, which is surely desirable, you must will the others. On the other hand, stun figures in numerous activities that make life safer and even pleasurable for some. How then could one prohibit stun simply because a few misuse it? It is difficult not to yearn for the old days of racks and iron maidens. There was only one way to use an iron maiden.

Stun, then, frustrates regulation as well as third-party scrutiny, creating fertile conditions for police torture. The effects of stun run deeper. Stun discourages public outrage and political action. Victims find no affirmation in publicity. Where race, class, or status divides citizens, civic doubt is magnified. Is the person really a torture victim or simply exaggerating in preparation for a lawsuit? Some citizens probably care deeply, but are torn. While they would be quick to denounce torture in their city if certain it was occurring, no one wants to appear a fool.[94]

Friends and families of survivors may have, to varying degrees, similar doubts, wondering whether these physically capable survivors are simply lazy or morally weak. In marginal communities, where people measure others by their opposition to authority, stealth torture survivors seem hesitant and incapable. The older generation will remember scarring beatings, and wonder why survivors are unable to assume their family and community responsibilities. As a UN psychologist observes, "The associated feelings of shame, remorse, and guilt can cause severe mental trauma that would not have been experienced had the subjects been physically scarred."[95]

Contrast this condition with that of Bruce Shapiro, a survivor of violence, though not of torture:

> Anyone trying to deal with the reality of crime, as opposed to the fantasies peddled to win elections, needs to understand the complex suffering of survivors of traumatic crimes and the suffering and turmoil of their families. I have impressive physical scars . . . a broad purple line from my breastbone to the top of my pubic bone, an X-shaped cut into my side where the chest tube entered. . . . But the disruption of my psyche is more noticeable. For weeks, I awoke each night agitated, drenched in perspiration. For two months, I was unable to write. . . . Thought to all appearances normal, I feel at a long arm's remove from all the familiar sources of pleasure, comfort and anger that shaped my daily life. . . . What psychologists call post-traumatic stress disorder is, among other things, a profoundly political state in which the world has gone wrong, in which you feel isolated from the broader community by the inarticulable extremity of experience. . . . As a crime victim and a citizen, I want the reality of a safe community—not a politician's fantasy land of restitution and revenge.[96]

Shapiro also feels isolated from his community, but his scar authorizes his words and configures a different relationship to the world. It is a disconcerting, problematic relationship. Psychologists want to classify him. Politicians want to win elections advertising his wounds. Friends extend sympathy and recognition, though his suffering is beyond their grasp. What Shapiro does not appear to feel is doubt, remorse, shame, or guilt for who he is and how he behaves. This is an experience well beyond those who can show no such scars.

We have, then, violence that can leave marks and violence that does not, and the two variants yield two entirely different civic experiences. The phenomenon is not a new one. In chapter 6 ("Shock"), I discussed how war and railway accidents also yielded two classes of survivors, those with marks (the injured) and those without marks (shock or shell shock victims). The latter were lesser citizens, treated with less sympathy and public concern.

Stun technology, then, is not a shortcut to better community relations. Rather, it masks political and social inequity with frustration, paralysis, doubt, and fear. A 2002 Taser International study determined that 85 percent of those shocked with Tasers were unarmed and fewer than 5 percent were carrying guns.[97] Mayors—like those of Cincinnati and Denver—who advocate stun are not simply trading the bad publicity of a recent policing shooting for a torture lawsuit later.[98] They are creating conditions where stun torture will serve as a civic marker, as I describe in chapter 2 ("Torture and Democracy"). Lesser citizens will know who they are and where they belong.

Welcome to Stun City

Stun City is not a particularly just, kind, or comfortable place; it is not Eutopia. Homeless people live on the streets. Illegal immigrants desperately look for jobs. There are drug addicts, thieves, and terrorists. This said, a father is "thankful" thieves used stun guns on his son, a supermarket clerk, rather than the pistol they also had.[99] Stun salesmen market to the anxiety: "I'd rather have someone attack me with a stun gun than a .44 magnum."[100] Of course, not even the technology works the way it should in Stun City. Cheap stun guns break down. "Swap meet" stun guns sit in glove compartments and purses, their batteries dead. For many, these are more talismans than technology.

What is remarkable about the citizens of Stun City is not their anxiety or indifference, but their judgment. While an S-M lover will pass over the prospect of using stun guns on her sexual partner as dangerous torture, normal citizens of Stun City consider using these devices to solve arguments with their boyfriends. After all, "I could get mad at him one morning and shoot."[101] In Stun City, citizens call the *same* practice, stunning, different things depending on who suffers and the context in which it is applied.

Used during a public protest, stunning is still unquestionably torture.[102] Used publicly on a drug-crazed individual, it appears to induce a temporary "lucid interval"[103] or "a sedative effect,"[104] almost humane and medically effective assistance. Told by a credible citizen-prisoner to the press, stunning is outrageous.[105] Used quietly on immigrants in Vienna or a thief in Nicosia or New York—then it is the kind of story that anyone can pick up hanging around jailhouses. Used on an enraged businessman in an airline cabin, it will be called torture, but used on a foreigner in the same context, it will be a good antiterrorism precaution. Used by authoritarian states abroad, it is torture; but used at home, it is probably good policing. Citizens have a hard time "seeing" torture is happening in their neighborhoods, for twenty years in the case of Chicago.

Such differences occur because a clean torture technique leaves only the ability to use one's voice to alert others to torture. Those who are well positioned and articulate can persuade many they were tortured; those who are not, fail to persuade. Those who speak well win their place as citizens in democracies. The others do not count.

Observers offer two histories of Stun City and its peculiar practices. The first story situates Stun City in the history of reason and progress, in the technological drive to build better and safer devices for the public, dismissing the "techno-phobic rant" of critics.[106] The second story tells how Stun City drew on practices of authoritarian states and evil scientists who invented electrotorture.[107]

These stories play important roles in legitimating or delegitimating new electric technologies. To delegitimate these devices, one passes over the democratic usage of them, focusing on their export to horrible states where the technology appears alongside knives and guns. To legitimate these devices, one presents them as domestic conveniences like microwave ovens, ignoring their use in torture around the world.

Such narratives have long histories in Stun City. At the dawn of the electrical age, some regarded the electric chair as progress in the modern way of death, while others believed that it was "degrading of an agent which has done so much and is accomplishing more for the advancement of civilization than almost any other discovery in the history of the world."[108] Or to take a less remembered skirmish, in the 1970s, animal rights groups attacked Amnesty International's "horrendous and disgusting" electrical experiments on hogs. While Amnesty acknowledged that it had turned to science to "test human torture techniques," critics condemned its work as "valueless, serving no practical purposes whatsoever," invoking the image of mad science.[109]

Not surprisingly, some organizations, more mindful of credibility, have learned to craft more subtle stories.[110] Taser International understands the history of electrical torture and has accordingly inserted a data chip into instruments. Amnesty International acknowledges that these instruments have been useful for law enforcement in life-saving situations and simply wants them properly regulated. These positions are more nuanced, but they also presuppose the two origin myths of Stun City. For what makes these organizational positions more credible is precisely that they differ from the stereotypical positions. Each refinement, in this respect, succeeds because it re-entrenches the background picture.

The difficulty is that the background picture is a myth.[111] Electrotorture had no magical power to grow on its own in the absence of self-interest and accident. There was no "inevitable" march of technology. Nazis and Stalinists were not interested in electrotorture. Cruel psychologists (Cameron, Pansen, Cerletti) did not pioneer police electrotorture. Cover—the closest thing we have to a major scientist—was not the source of all unreason in the world.

In fact, electrotorture has more to do with democratic states—with their failed colonial adventures and with their desire to appear humane as they exercise violence at home. The vigilance with which lawyers defended their clients, communities denounced police brutality, and human rights activists monitored torture abroad—even this noble concern led torturers to adopt electrotorture around the world. In an age when we are apt to link all evil things to globalization and all nice things to democratization and human rights monitoring, it is important to see that electrotorture is more closely tied to the latter than to the former. Electrotorture tells us more about our civilization than we would like to know.

Other Stealth Traditions

On April 28, 2004, CBS aired pictures of torture from Iraq's Abu Ghraib prison in late 2003. This news report, as well as others that followed, identified many nonelectrical tortures. Each of these techniques has its discrete and often forgotten history, and the chapters that follow relate what is known about each technique. They also build on the conclusions I have drawn from the history of electrotorture, relating the history of these less familiar techniques to the central claims of this study.

Electrotorture is a good place to start the history of modern torture because it is its poster child. It is rooted in an invention essential to our daily lives, electricity. It is sustained by means of technology and scientific knowledge. To many, then, it is starkly emblematic of how torturers can adapt to modern conditions. But it would be a mistake to think that if we, for example, were able to control stun technology, we would be free of stealthy torture. As I have told the history of electrotorture, I have gestured toward many other techniques that leave no marks, techniques that tend to cluster around electrotorture as the century proceeds. Some of these techniques, such as the *falaka* and water torture, are low tech and among the earliest methods recorded, while others, such as the use of sound or drugs, are quite contemporary and high tech.

Naturally, then, the chapters that follow start at different places and times. They follow each technique from generation to generation until it appears alongside others in modern torture. Regrettably, the histories I can sketch are somewhat more partial and fragmented than what I offered in part 3 for electrotorture. From a methodological point of view, electrical instruments are easily identifiable, and this makes it easier to discuss how electrotorture developed, mutated, and spread. The same cannot be said, for example, about particular ways of beating with hands or sticks. But to the extent that one can discern coherent patterns, these histories support the general argument I advanced in part III. Indeed the conceptual story will be familiar:

Among my historical claims, I assert that many techniques appeared first in diverse contexts in democratic states: in prisons, police stations, ships at sea, military barracks, schools, and slave markets. If they did not appear first in these contexts (or if the context of their original invention is unknown), what is certain is that historians first record their use alongside other techniques for purposes of stealthy torture in democratic contexts. I also draw attention to what appears to be the expanding *scope* of these techniques in the 1960s and 1970s, appearing often far beyond the original contexts in which they circulated earlier. Often they appeared in authoritarian states that also used them in conjunction with other techniques that did not leave marks, the clustering pattern I take as indicating stealthy torture.

In documenting these patterns, I take it for granted that at this point, readers are familiar with the main cases of stealthy torture mentioned in parts II and III; I do not set out to reestablish that torture in the United States in the 1920s, French Algeria in the 1950s, or Vietnam in the late 1960s was stealthy. I do, however, draw attention to other cases that did not receive as close attention because electrotorture played a negligible role in them, for example, American torture in the Philippines in the Spanish-American War, British torture in India and Mandatory Palestine in the 1930s, authoritarian Greece in the 1960s, and Israel in the late twentieth century. In these cases, I describe, as far as is known, the range of techniques that cluster in the interrogation rooms.

I also assume that readers are familiar with the general distribution of scarring and clean tortures in the late twentieth century (documented in chapter 9, "Singing the World Electric"), for example, that much torture in Africa tended to be scarring, as did the torture of important Middle Eastern authoritarian states (Syria, Iraq), while authoritarian states in Latin America in the 1970s, democracies along the Mediterranean, and post-Communist democracies in Eastern Europe used clean tortures for the most part. But again, I draw attention to cases where authoritarian states with long-standing records of scarring tortures adopt techniques that leave few marks in the late twentieth century, for example, Saudi Arabia and the Gulf States in the 1990s.

Such changes of practice are, on my argument, hardly coincidental. The pattern, which occurs repeatedly in chapter after chapter in this part, fits with my general argument regarding monitoring. The monitoring hypothesis would predict that techniques that leave few marks would tend to appear mainly in democratic contexts before the late 1960s and early 1970s. This is because public monitoring leads institutions that favor painful coercion to use and combine clean torture techniques to evade detection, and, to the extent that public monitoring is not only greater in democracies, but that public monitoring of human rights is a core value in modern democracies, it is the case that where we find democracies torturing today, we will also be more likely to find stealthy torture.

Likewise, the universal monitoring hypothesis would predict that the market in clean techniques would flourish as the incentive for avoiding adverse publicity about torture and gaining legitimacy in the area of human rights grows in the late twentieth century. One would predict that techniques that once occupied relatively narrow niches (limited exclusively to slaves, children, or women, for example) would circulate more widely, that they would appear in authoritarian as well as democratic states, and that the chronology of this expanding scope would occur roughly around the 1960s and 1970s.

This is what occurs, and it indicates once again that a critically important event happened in this period: either the push of a universal distributor changed the world of torture or the pull of global human rights monitoring drove many torturers, in authoritarian and democratic states alike, to put a priority on using clean techniques. So in chapter 15 ("Forced Standing and Other Positions"), I consider possible universal distributors in this period and argue that the evidence for this hypothesis is lacking. This leaves the universal monitoring hypothesis as the main plausible argument for the turn to techniques that leave few marks.

One outstanding issue left over from part III is settling how torturers choose the kinds of techniques they do. Even if the priority is on stealth, torturers still have distinct preferences and apply different styles. Overall, the following chapters show that the world of torture is dominated by low-tech, not scientific, tortures. In fact, all the techniques that appeared at Abu Ghraib and other American facilities belong either to a family of tortures that descended from old West European military and police punishments, or to pre–World War II practices of French colonialism, or to native American policing practices from the nineteenth century. I have separated out each technical strand as clearly as possible and often close with how U.S. agents used these techniques in Iraq, Afghanistan, or elsewhere.

Torturers favor low-tech over high-tech tortures because, in general, low-tech procedures are harder to spot and easier to maintain, transmit, and transport. Monitoring drives invention and transmission of techniques, but it is not the only force shaping how torturers choose techniques. As I argued in part III, torture is a craft, not a science. Torture rarely involves formal learning and most often is mastered through trial and error on the job. In this context, torturers pick their techniques by imitating others, opportunistically adapting familiar procedures from other contexts, and following gossip and rumor about what techniques have fearsome reputations (the craft apprenticeship hypothesis). The alternative hypotheses would be that the choice of torture techniques is shaped by traditional culture, ideology, or scientific efficiency. The history of electrotorture offers some evidence in favor of the craft apprenticeship hypothesis, but I could not evaluate the alternative hypotheses directly in part III.

But in the following chapters I do, and conclude that the craft apprenticeship hypothesis does a fairly good job explaining the historical patterns of transmission. On the other hand, the alternative hypotheses are hard pressed to explain critical anomalies. The scientific hypothesis fails to explain why some high-tech techniques are abandoned while others succeed, given that they are all highly efficient in causing pain (chapters 18, "Noise," and 19, "Drugs and Doctors"). The cultural hypothesis does not explain why torturers abandoned traditional techniques like the *falaka* or why others adopted these culturally alien techniques (chapters 12, "Sticks and Bones, and 19). And the ideological hypothesis fails to make sense of the widely varying patterns of techniques in the Communist world, presumably a key case where common ideology would predict similar tortures (chapters 13, "Water, Sleep, and Spice," 15, and 19).

Lastly, the historical dominance of low-tech torture worldwide casts doubt on the apocalyptic claims that a science of torture has arrived and now dominates torture chambers around the world. Explanations of this sort are misleading or mistaken, usually because they are based on poor historiography (chapter 18). There is no science of torture currently. In part IV, I review all known torture manuals and training programs in the past century, and I argue that there is also little evidence of a behavioral science for training torturers in the real world. I then explain this historical pattern, showing why one cannot teach torture by the book and why a science of torture is unlikely in principle.

The chapters to follow do not simply buttress claims and explanations advanced in part III. First, I reconstitute for the first time histories of techniques that are never treated discretely, gathering together all that is known about each practice. Analysts cannot study torture when clean historical data is absent, and those that do often generate misleading and unreliable explanations. They rely too much on national memories and overgeneralize from single cases, muddying the waters.

The histories here try to get the patterns of appearance and distribution across time around the world as close to the surface as possible. The record is often fragmentary, and others perhaps may complete the distributions. Nevertheless, these histories are sufficient to check misleading memories and raise questions about common explanations of torture. They also complete another goal of this study, to provide a reliable sourcebook for others to use. Occasionally, I fill out the historical record with information that does not bear directly on the specific theses I argue. I note, for example, how certain torturers complement each other physically, and map their increasing frequency over time, for example, water torture and spice tortures, or sleep deprivation and forced standing. Nevertheless, I return at the end of each chapter to the main theses of this study, though some may wish to go directly to the summary evaluation in chapter 20, "The Supply and Demand for Clean Torture."

Second, I advance new, provocative points about stealth torture. Most importantly, I argue that torturers have changed the way monitors operate in the late twentieth century. As torture became stealthy, ordinary monitors could not easily confirm the suffering of victims. Increasingly, doctors and psychiatrists were drawn into monitoring as critical witnesses, affirming or denying torture. Stealth torture has disempowered ordinary observers, making monitoring a battle among experts, and the experts themselves now sometimes find themselves in jeopardy as states intimidate or kill them.

Monitors shaped the world of torture, and now torturers shape the world of monitors. Human rights monitoring is now an agonic struggle, and if nothing else, the chapters that follow reveal that stopping torture requires a great deal more than just monitoring. Among other things, it requires a public more literate in understanding what stealthy torture is and state officials who recognize the wasteful, corrupting, misleading, and falsely consoling results that torture generates. I take up these issues in part V.

The chapters that follow also raise a new methodological point, namely, distinguishing clearly between the legally authorized and illegal police use of techniques that cause intense physical pain. This problem did not arise in part III because no state has ever legally authorized its police to use electricity for purposes of punishment. Although *electrocution*, the electric way of death, is still legal in some places, *electrotorture* has never been legal anywhere. Occasionally, some have proposed giving each convicted criminal a just measure of electrical pain instead of a prison term, but no state has ever given this argument much consideration.[1] States have authorized police to use electrical batons for crowd control, but the presence of an electric baton in an interrogation room necessarily raises questions of illegal activity. It was only in the late twentieth century, with the advent of stun technology, when the line between legally authorized and illegal use of electrical weaponry blurred somewhat, particularly in prisons. Here guards have used stun technology to induce compliance and fear rather than deal with individuals who were actively or passively resisting. These cases have been intensely controversial in part, as I have argued, because it is rarely possible to monitor the use of stun technology.

For the most part, then, one can draw a clean line between legitimate and illegitimate police usage of electrical instruments: the use of electrical instruments for purposes of gathering information or securing confessions was always illegal and their use for purposes of intimidation illegal until fairly recently. That is not the case for many of the techniques discussed in the chapters that follow. States legally authorized police, prison guards, and military officials to use these painful techniques to intimidate, gather information, or extract false confessions from detained helpless individuals. They were, in short, legal tortures.

I do not undertake to explore the complete legal usage of these procedures in prisons or barracks in previous centuries. What is important for my purposes is that many clean techniques began in democratic states. Often there is no earlier record of them, or if there is, they first achieved notoriety as legal tortures in democratic states. It may seem puzzling that some democratic states legally punished criminals using tortures that left few marks. Legal punishments, after all, do not have to be stealthy; they are openly stated in the public record and often performed publicly.

But, in many cases, these punishments followed growing public outcry against the more common punishment, whipping and flogging, which left bloody scarring bodies open for all to see. Not surprisingly, prison wardens and military officials in democratic states were among the first to favor techniques that left few marks. The new punishments, usually instituted during the nineteenth century, were painful, but left few visible signs, and many could not judge how much pain was involved. It was only when public scandals, usually inadvertent deaths, made evident what was truly involved, that officials abandoned these techniques, at least legally. American prison officials who instituted the "baths" at Sing Sing and the British military commanders who instituted Field Punishment Number 1 (the "crucifixion") seemed especially sensitive to bad publicity.

But it is not simply that these cleaner techniques first appeared in democratic states as legal punishments. More importantly, these techniques survived and persisted among police and military of democratic states long after their usage was no longer legally permitted. When the legal usage stopped and the illegal usage began is often hard to date, but the persistence is unquestionable.

Lastly, long after police and military in democratic states had ceased using some techniques (legally or illegally), torturers in other countries continued using them. Establishing these continuities is an important part of the chapters that follow (especially in chapter 14, "Stress and Duress"). Modern democracies have long forgotten their own histories of torture. In fact, earlier democratic states showcased what could be done for later authoritarian states. Techniques, once legitimate in democratic states in previous centuries, cast a long shadow over the twentieth century. Later users often had no prior history of familiarity with these techniques; their penal codes never authorized such procedures. Yet in the late twentieth century, one finds them adapting techniques that first appeared in democratic states.

The fact that democratic states subsequently abolished the legal use of these techniques, then, does not alter the fact that they were leaders in adapting and innovating techniques that left few marks, techniques that found their way into stealthy torture. Those interested in the distinction between torture and punishment will find further discussion of this matter in appendix B, "Issues of Method."

Let me turn, then, to the specific histories. I begin with ancient practices and their modern adaptations to stealthy torture (chapters 12 and 13). These practices include whipping, paddling, the *falaka*, water tortures, sleep deprivation, and use of spices to aggravate wounds and tissues. In chapters 14 through 17, I cover the history of positional tortures, exhaustion exercises, and restraints. Since the revelations at Abu Ghraib, these techniques are usually all called "stress and duress" techniques, but the different practices have different trajectories. Then, in chapters 18 and 19, I describe the use of drugs and white noise (what is sometimes called "sensory deprivation"). I argue that these scientific tortures are far less common than the more plebeian techniques, and I ask why torturers tend to ignore the scientific and persist with the plebeian.

[The *falaka*], if skillfully done, breaks no bones, makes no skin lesions, and leaves no permanent and recognizable marks, but causes intense pain and swelling of the feet.

—European Commission of Human Rights, Opinion

in the Case against Greece, 1970[1]

12   Sticks and Bones

This chapter covers ways of striking other human beings with whips and sticks that leave few marks. These are old techniques, their origins lost to memory. What can be said is that in ancient societies, state officials and citizens used these methods, and often law and custom protected their rights to exercise such violence over others. But, for my purposes, what is remarkable is that these techniques persisted long after they were neither legal nor customary. Most typically, police and military used them to interrogate, intimidate, and secure false confessions from prisoners, often in conjunction with other techniques that left few marks.

Clean Whipping

As long as humans depended on the strength of animals for transportation and power, they used whips to motivate other humans and beasts of burden.[2] Whips enabled users to strike a controlled blow and make noises, soft or sharp and loud as was required, to direct activities.

Historically, overseers used longer whips for coordinating several workers, as they could reach out over distances and obstacles to the laggard in a group. Lash whips concentrated energy at the end of the thong when the whip was thrown, making a loud crack as the end accelerated past the speed of sound. They were commonly used to direct carriages and coaches, to supervise galleys and plantation gangs, and to move herds of cattle.

Shorter whips were for controlling a single worker, for example, domestic slaves, indentured kitchen help, or pack animals. They were also used in cases where longer whips might get entangled with the harness or rigging, as on sailing ships. Short whips were also used to punish criminals, exorcise demons, demonstrate penitence, motivate schoolchildren, discipline soldiers and sailors, and extract evidence from the behavior of animals as well as confessions from men and women in judicial proceedings.[3]

Short whips had a single flat thong or multiple light thongs attached to a handle with a hinge. These whips could bruise or cut the skin, but not beyond healing. They could be used to administer different blows, light or heavy, superficial or deep cutting, rhythmic or erratic. The famous whips, like the cat-o'-nine-tails, required considerable strength, extensive skill, and a flair for showmanship.[4]

In the West, Roman judges passed their tools to the Catholic Church, which adopted them for purposes of exorcism and penance.[5] The church passed on the short Roman whips (the *ferula* and the *scutica*) to generations of school-children.[6] Early modern floggers favored whips that tore the flesh and caused permanent injury, if not death. The British cat-o'-nine-tails was a two-piece whip with nine two-foot thongs attached to a wooden handle.[7] The "Thieve's Cat" had knots, and in crueler versions, braided lead bits, that cut into the flesh. The number of knots varied, one per thong on the army whip, three per thong for the navy. The South African cat had seven per thong.[8] The dreaded Russian "Great *Knout*" was a monstrously long whip with a hook at the tip that yanked out chunks of flesh with each blow.[9]

There was always a lesser tradition of clean whipping, whipping that bruised, but left few scars. Some slaves were too valuable to scar, and prospective buyers interpreted scarred slaves as disciplinary problems. In this tradition, floggers reduced the edges that might cut into the skin. The Romans whipped their valuable female slaves with silk sashes. Some American slave owners used a broad, soft "buckskin cracker" that "makes a very loud report and stings, but does not bruise the flesh."[10]

The British army used the broad sling of a fire-lock to whip ("Sling-Belting"), a punishment on par with paddling.[11] In the 1930s, British floggers adopted modern cat-o'-nine-tails. Its ends were "whipped" with silk thread rather than knotted, and British prisoners wore leather bands to protect the kidneys and neck.[12] Although the pain was severe, an evaluation of judicial whippings between 1931 and 1935 found that "blood did not flow during the whipping, probably due to the fact that the tails were not knotted."[13] In Canada, prison guards used the flat leather *ferula* until 1972.[14]

Democratic states abolished flogging gradually, but the process was not as quick as is sometimes imagined. The British abolished the cat as a military field punishment in 1881, but the 1914 army regulations permitted specific officers to apply up to thirty strokes for certain offenses.[15] British commanders flogged Indians soldiers during campaigns in Iraq in 1917 under this authority.[16] Unofficial flogging also occurred during the Burma campaign in 1943.[17] The British navy abolished all corporal punishment in 1949, but the caning of seaman cadets continued for some years in the 1950s.[18] England and Canada practiced judicial whipping for civilian males during the 1930s.[19] The practice continued in British colonies like Rhodesia, South Africa, and Singapore.

The French abolished military flogging in 1893, but numerous reports describe whipping in the Foreign Legion in the 1920s, particularly in the penal battalions.[20] Walter Kanitz, who served in the 1930s, claimed it had disappeared during his service.[21] The U.S. Army abolished military whipping in 1850, but the practice continued in prisons and work camps well into the early twentieth century.[22] Whipping remained legal in Delaware and Maryland until the 1960s. The last reported judicial flogging occurred in Delaware in August 1961, ten lashes for wife beating.[23]

In the twentieth century, clean whipping flourished even as overt whipping, legally authorized or illegal, disappeared. American police struck prisoners with rubber hoses, a technique now known worldwide. Manufacturers had made rubber hoses since the 1870s, but their use in torture was an American innovation, most documented cases coming from eastern and midwestern states in the 1920s (New York, Illinois, Ohio, and Missouri).[24] Here, police corded one end to create a nonslip handle and sometimes filled the hose with lead.[25] Lacking edges, rubber hoses would bruise, but not cut the skin. Today torturers use virtually anything that is flexible with a broad flat surface or rounded edges.

Paddles

Paddling makes deep bruises that will clear in a few weeks without any visible injury. "The punishment is dreadfully severe, but for all no blood is drawn."[26] To strike more painfully, beaters perforated the paddle with several holes. Solid paddles trapped the air between the flat head and the flesh, cushioning the blows.

Paddling was originally a nautical punishment, mainly for minor offenses such as quitting one's station during night watch. Among English sailors, "to cob" meant to strike or fight, and "cobbing" meant to strike the buttocks with a flat instrument.[27] The "cobbing board" was a flat piece of wood. Customarily, this was a stave of the cask with the bung-hole, a hole drilled into the cask for pouring out the liquid within. The stave would be cut in two and the beater would use the bung-hole end to strike the buttocks. Alternatively, sailors used a stocking full of sand, sometimes wet, to administer blows.[28]

The French also paddled, calling the instrument the *bâton de justice*.[29] In the 1920s, French investigators cobbed every witness in piracy cases in Korea using instruments "rather like a canoe paddle or a thick cricket bat, on a part where he could not be injured, but where the bruises would show up beautifully."[30] Ostensibly, witnesses insisted on this beating, arguing that bruises would allow them to give information on river piracy while telling their neighbors that the French had extracted the information under torture.

In an age where ships were the primary means of transportation, nautical punishments were soon imitated on land. British officers cobbed infantrymen for petty offenses, and Irish schoolchildren were paddled for failing to remove their hats, becoming the first of many schoolchildren to be cobbed.[31] During the Revolutionary War, American officers cobbed soldiers for crimes "characterized by meanness and low cunning."[32] Slave dealers also paddled slaves. American and Brazilian slave owners preferred the whip for plantation work and major offenses, but they used paddles for minor crimes and household discipline.[33] Some American prisons also used paddles in the late nineteenth century to intimidate as well as punish prisoners for poor contract work.[34] British sailors cobbed young trainees for being slow to leave the mess hall in the evening ("fork in the beam").[35] Most judicial cobbing, at land or at sea, ceased by the late nineteenth century, but paddling persisted into the twentieth century in fraternity hazing, military initiations, domestic castigation, and S-M games.

By the early nineteenth century, beaters carved paddles with shuttle necks, and many paddles had perforated heads. The Brazilian *palmatoria*, the American military paddle, and the slave-cobbing paddle all had several auger holes.[36] The paddles ranged in size from the size of tennis rackets to oars and included battledores, large flat paddlelike instruments used for putting bread in the oven. The largest were made of oak or hickory. They were two to three feet long, four to six inches wide at the head, with handles about a foot long. Modern *palmatorias* sometimes use rubber heads rather than the traditional wooden ones.[37]

Until the twentieth century, what mattered in paddling was the lack of permanent injury, not necessarily the fact that one could escape detection by outside observers. Many slave owners wet and sanded paddles before use, a practice that would definitely leave marks. Mrs. Mann of Missouri was famous for her occasionally lethal "six pound paddle."[38] Some prison paddles were filed to leave deep cuts.[39]

Stealthiness mattered most to slave dealers, who may have invented the perforated paddle for economic reasons.[40] A scarred slave was an troublesome one, and no one wanted to purchase trouble. The dealers used cobbing paddles and flopping paddles, the "flop" being a piece of leather a foot and one-half long and as broad as the palm of the hand, with a two-foot handle. These devices were used for "various offenses, especially the unpardonable one of 'not speaking up and looking bright and smart' when the buyers were choosing."[41]

Police turned to cobbing in the twentieth century, selecting classical or modern instruments. In the 1920s, Cleveland police used sausage-shaped sandbags made of silk along with rubber hoses, "these instruments being chosen because, when properly applied, they leave no marks."[42] The Chicago police were the first to discover that some telephone books were heavy enough to "stun a man without leaving a mark."[43] In 2003, this technique appeared again in a wish list of interrogation techniques offered by American interrogators with the Fourth Infantry Division in Tikrit, Iraq.[44] French police favored the *chaussette à clous*, socks filled with lead nails.[45] In the 1930s, Soviet police occasionally favored rubber hoses and sandbags.[46] In the 1960s, the Greeks beat prisoners with truncheon-shaped socks, rubber tubes, and rubber paddles.[47] In the last two decades, Spanish, French, Portuguese, and Austrian police have favored the telephone book, the Turkish police have used sandbags, and the newly democratic Bulgarian police beat suspects with rubber hoses.[48] Sri Lankan torturers cut PVC piping and pack it with sand, making a device that can "deliver a lot of force, but as it is applied over a relatively large surface area, there is little risk of permanent scarring."[49] Spanish torturers tape foam or telephone books around their batons.[50]

Brazilian military police revived paddling as a clean art in the late 1960s. Accounts of torture from 1966 to 1969 do not mention the *palmatoria*.[51] In 1969, an instructor demonstrated the *palmatoria* to eighty Brazilian interrogators in the context of several other clean techniques, and prisoners commonly reported the technique after that date.[52] Paddling also appears in the Indian subcontinent in the 1990s. The Sri Lankese torturers adopted large kitchen paddles or *akappai*, used for stirring big pots of rice, to beat prisoners, while Indian police turned to a device similar to the flopping paddle, a *patta*.[53]

Beating Feet

The soles of the feet are not thickly muscled, and so caning or whipping them is especially painful. Depending on the weight of the rod and the intensity and frequency of the blows, this practice can yield mildly swollen feet to broken bones that damage a person permanently. There are two traditional variants. In the Chinese style, the prisoner lies on his stomach with his legs bent, the soles of his feet facing upwards.[54] In Russia, where this style is used, it is still called a "Chinese" torture.[55] In the Middle Eastern style, the prisoner lies on his back, his feet bound by the ankles tightly to a pole. The pole may be suspended or held by two men, with the soles of the feet exposed outward.

Beating the soles of the feet is called the *falaka* or *falaqa* (Turkish, Arabic, Farsi), the *falanga* (Greek), and *karma* or *arma* (Moroccan Arabic). The Arabic term *falaqa* refers to the pole (*falaq* or *mikatra*) to which the extremities are bound in the Middle Eastern style.[56] In the Middle East, observers distinguish between the *falaka* and all other beating with sticks (*choob zadan* in Farsi, *çomak* in Turkish). Europeans, however, call both the specific and the general practice the bastinado, after the beating sticks (*baston, bastóne,* or batons).[57] For the sake of clarity, I use the term *falaka* for any technique that strikes only the feet.

Chinese started practicing the *falaka* regularly with the Sung (960–1279).[58] Iranians say the *falaka* arrived in their country with the Mongols, eight hundred years ago. There is no evidence of the *falaka* in the Arab world before the tenth century, after which it becomes exceedingly common.[59] All stations of Turkish and Persian society practiced it, Europeans noting it as early as 1537.[60] Ottoman women received the *falaka* by passing their extremities through a curtain, while Qajar princes received theirs lying upon a silk carpet.[61] The *falaka* became a proper supplement to a sound education, much as caning was to the English schoolmaster. In North Africa, the *falaka* was confined mainly to students in Koranic and Talmudic schools.[62]

The addition of the *falaq* in the Middle East made the *falaka* a potentially disfiguring technique. In cases where rulers demanded permanent damage, torturers looped the *falaq* on the shins, rather than at the ankles. Each blow against the soles of the feet drove the shins against the pole, shattering the bones. Usually rulers preferred mutilation and amputation, not the *falaka*. One considered oneself fortunate to be subjected only to the simple *falaka*, which was shameful, but not usually disfiguring. The shame passed quickly, for the punishment was so common.[63] Indeed, male peasants in Iran preferred the *falaka* to spanking (a punishment for women and children).[64]

Muslim armies passed the *falaka* on to the Indians and Europeans who lived along the Mediterranean. The claim that the ancient Greeks invented the *falaka* is false.[65] There is no evidence of the word or the practice before the Turkish conquest, after which *falanga* appeared commonly in Greek elementary schools.[66]

In British colonial India, Governor Warren Hastings applied the *falaka* to recalcitrant taxpayers. His torturers, charged Edmund Burke, threw "them with their heads downwards over a bar, beat them on the soles of the feet with rattans, until the nails fell from the toes."[67] The British army adopted the *falaka* by the mid—eighteenth century, dubbing it "booting." "It consisted in flogging a man on the soles of the feet," and was on par with cobbing. It was used principally in the cavalry.[68] English tourists did not hesitate going native with the *falaka*, beating locals who earned their displeasure—as Mark Twain observed in his trips in the Middle East.[69] The French also adopted the *falaka* in the Foreign Legion in North Africa and in the *bagnard* prisons of New Caledonia.[70]

In the 1930s, Europeans reported that the Yugoslavian and Hungarian police used the *falaka* regularly, the latter applying it to Slovaks during the occupation of Czechoslovakia in 1938.[71] The Vichy Milice used the "Arab torture" in France during the war, and the Nazis used the *falaka* mainly in occupied Denmark, and less commonly in Norway.[72] Romanian police used the *falaka* during both the Fascist and Communist periods.[73]

None of this usage shows much concern with clean use of the *falaka*. Beaters used broken bamboo, rhino-hide whips, heavy cables, or even barbed wire, devices that would leave their "mark for time."[74] Nevertheless, there was a tradition of clean *falaka*. In the Middle East, a "delicate consideration" toward women involved pouring water on the feet to soften them and leave few marks.[75] Chinese beaters repeatedly tapped lightly on the soles.[76] This procedure does not break the skin, but soon yields a penetrating pain, and beaters used to practice this delicate art by repeatedly striking blocks of tofu without breaking them. This practice was unknown outside of China.

The first modern police to use the *falaka* as part of a stealthy regimen was the French Sûreté in Vietnam in the 1930s. In 1936, the Vietnamese leftist journal *La Lutte* charged that "blows to the soles of the feet are imported from Saigon to the provinces" and the purpose of the beating was "to extract confessions without leaving a trace."[77] In the same year, British commanders in Palestine told police and troops to use "Turkish methods." "Suspects arrested for interrogation . . . were now tortured as a matter of course: the bastinado [*falaka*], suspending suspects upside down and urinating in their nostrils, extracting fingernails and pumping water into a suspect before stamping on him, became common place."[78] Aside from the extraction of nails, this regimen is a clean one. In the case of Mordhy Petcho, torturers poured water on the feet, suggesting that leaving marks was a concern.[79]

Clean *Falaka* appears in Venezuela, French-occupied Algeria, and South Africa in the 1950s, and among South Vietnamese interrogators and U.S. soldiers in Vietnam during the 1960s.[80] Chicago police allegedly used the *falaka* in at least one instance, against Paul Mike, in February 1982.[81] In 1969, a new supervisor discovered that clean *falaka* was a standard practice in the Massachusetts juvenile detention system: "A boy's feet were strapped to a bed frame and beaten on the bare soles with wooden paddles or the wooden backs of floor brushes." Secret files tersely recorded the beatings. "Donald 16, beaten on the soles of his bare feet with straps."[82]

In 1967, several countries charged that Greece was practicing systematic torture, a charge the government vehemently denied.[83] While the Council of Europe deliberated, Greek torturers sought "to avoid leaving marks, or at least not to permit the detainee to be released until the marks had disappeared." Greek torturers routinized the *falaka*, choosing rounded or flat objects such as garden hoses and belts to whip the feet. They wet the feet regularly to keep them soft and to reduce swelling. And when the victim lost feeling in his feet, torturers made him walk until sensation returned.[84]

Greece was the first modern state to show the full advantage gained by *falaka* in the age of human rights monitoring.[85] In a study of two hundred torture victims, Ole Rasmussen found that 83 percent of Greek prisoners received the *falaka*, but only 17 percent reported electrotorture. The Spanish Guardia Civile put 39 percent of its prisoners to the *falaka* and 18 percent to electricity. Among Chilean prisoners, only 8 percent reported the *falaka*, and 86 percent described electrotorture.[86]

After Greece withdrew from the Council of Europe in 1969, torture became considerably less stealthy. Torturers were "encouraged by superior officers to leave torture marks on their victims, then release them." The goal was now "to demoralize the student movement" by showing what could be done to them.[87]

The *falaka* is now ubiquitous because "the necessary tools are to be found lying around any police station," "pain in the sensitive areas is very intense," and "traces of the torture can be soon made to disappear." To reduce swelling, torturers make detainees walk or jump up and down barefoot in a pool of water. Others apply yoghurt or anti-inflammatory cream to the feet. "After a couple of days, that is when the detainees are usually released by the police or transferred to a prison, it is almost impossible—except for the expert eye—to perceive the swelling."[88]

In the Middle East and North Africa, *falaka* is still a customary practice, and it is integrated in both stealthy (e.g., Turkey and Israel) and unstealthy regimens (e.g., Syria and Iraq). Often it is combined with electrotorture. Iraqi torturers under Saddam Hussein, for example, subjected over half their prisoners to electricity (63 percent) and the *falaka* (75 percent).[89] The combination appears repeatedly in the 1970s (Syria, Israel, Turkey, Morocco, and Iran), in the 1980s (Egypt, Iraq, Libya) and in the 1990s (Lebanon, Tunisia, Yemen, Saudi Arabia, and Kuwait after the Gulf War).[90]

Likewise, in Europe, the *falaka*-electrotorture combination appears in Cyprus, Greece, Spain, Poland, Lithuania, Latvia, Bulgaria, Georgia, Yugoslavia, and the Ukraine. In 1993, Italian troops used this combination in Somalia. In all these cases, *falaka* appears in conjunction with other techniques that leave few marks. The *falaka* also appears as part of stealthy regimens that do not include electricity in Portugal, Macedonia, Romania, Slovakia, and Croatia.[91]

The *falaka* has also appeared in regions where it is not customary. In 1969, Brazilian instructors demonstrated to interrogators how to apply *palmatorias* to the flat of the feet.[92] In 1987, Human Rights Watch observers claimed *palmatorias* were used primarily to strike the soles of the feet, a considerable narrowing of its customary usage in Brazil.[93] Less frequently, the *falaka* appears in Argentina, Nicaragua, Chile, South Africa, and Rhodesia/Zimbabwe in the 1970s and in Paraguay, Honduras, and Bolivia in the 1990s. In the last two decades, it has appeared in torture in Ethiopia, Somalia, Kenya, Cameroon, and Mauritius.[94] Some of this usage is probably stealthy. In the Cameroons, for example, torturers apply it mainly to prisoners attracting domestic or international attention.[95] On the other hand, the *falaka* is far less common in Asian torture than it used to be, and the *falaka*/electrotorture combination appears only in the Philippines and South Korea in the 1970s and in Pakistan and Nepal in the 1990s.[96]

Remembering Slaves and Sailors

As long as human beings have beaten others with whips and sticks, they have on occasion chosen methods that left few marks. Slave dealers did so because they wanted to make a sale. Men did so to keep their women presentable and sexually desirable. Captains could not afford to mutilate able-bodied sailors for minor infractions when every hand was needed miles out at sea. Masters sometimes spared children scarring punishments on account of their weakness.

Some of these motivations furnish evidence for hypotheses I have already discussed. Slave dealers did not choose cobbing because they had sympathy for slaves (the dehumanization hypothesis), but because they knew buyers would be inspecting the goods. This was a highly limited case where monitoring drove torturers to stealth. Other cases may involve sympathy, for example, the clean beating of children. And several cases don't pertain to either monitoring or sympathy, for example, the utilitarian concern to avoid seriously damaging one's labor force at sea or the self-interested clean beating of women.

The main point here is that clean beating preceded human rights monitoring, but it never constituted more than a minor tradition in torture. In the twentieth century, police and military interrogators gave these practices a greater role in torture than they had enjoyed in the past. They replaced the old specialized instruments (cobbing paddles, whips) with instruments more easily disguised (rubber hoses and telephone books). They developed procedures to "lose" prisoners in the system until the bruises cleared.

These changes occurred first in democratic societies and then authoritarian ones. At the start of the twentieth century, American police adapted clean whipping and cobbing to police interrogation. British and French colonial police adapted the *falaka* as part of a stealthy interrogation regimen, seeking to avoid bad publicity at home. Then authoritarian states adapted the techniques of democratic police. Some, like Greece, did so to win legitimacy in Europe, while others recognized that bad publicity made it harder to secure economic and military aid from Western industrialized states.

The enlisted men began to use the old Filipino method of mild

torture, the water cure. Nobody was seriously damaged.

— President Theodore Roosevelt, on torture by American

troops in the Philippines, 1902[1]

13 Water, Sleep, and Spice

Modern water torture involves two main practices, pumping and choking. Pumping involves forcibly filling the stomach and intestines with water. A garden hose or teapot spout in the mouth is sufficient, but other methods of delivery are possible. Spanish inquisitors inserted a piece of absorbent linen into the gullet, forcing the mouth open as they poured water over it. In any case, once water is forced into the intestines in this manner, the organs stretch and convulse, causing "some of the most intense pain that visceral tissues can experience."[2] Victims feel their organs are being burned or cut on the inside. Pumping also induces "a state of shock" and generates "feelings of pain, feeling cold, shivering, and perspiration."[3]

Choking pushes pumping one step further by preventing breathing. Torturers submerge victims, either fully or partially in a pool of water, or suffocate victims under a wet cloth. Even a small amount of water in the glottis causes violent coughing, initiating a fight-or-flight response, raising the heart rate and respiratory rate and triggering desperate efforts to break free. The supply of oxygen available for basic metabolic functions is exhausted within seconds. While this is sometimes called "an illusion of drowning," the reality is that death will follow if the procedure is not stopped in time. Regardless, the prisoner involuntarily ingests large amounts of water, much as in pumping, with similarly painful results. Lastly, these effects are more pronounced when the prisoner is lying on his back and water is poured over the nose and mouth, as the nostrils serve "as a catch basin for small, but significant nonetheless, amounts of water."[4]

These techniques do not exhaust what can be done with water, and moderns have added some important new variations to water torture, using it to beat or freeze prisoners. At the same time, they have largely abandoned the ancient practice of boiling prisoners, a torture that causes visible blisters and burns.[5]

In this chapter, I also describe the history of spice torture and sleep deprivation, two techniques almost as old as water torture. Spice tortures often supplement other tortures. In pumping and choking for example, tortures sometimes add harsh irritants to the water. Likewise, sleep deprivation reduces the pain thresholds of prisoners, making it an obvious supplement to other tortures.

Pumping

In early modern Europe, authoritarian states counted pumping as one of the most fearful tortures.[6] Inquisitional interrogators called it the *Tormento de Toca* or *aselli*. In prerevolutionary France, pumping (*la question d'eau*) was one of two well-known interrogatory techniques.[7] With the passing of these states, pumping was largely forgotten until the early twentieth century.

In 1902, during the Spanish-American War, U.S. soldiers put funnels in the mouths of Filipinos, forcing buckets of water into their organs.[8] William Howard Taft, governor of the Philippines, carelessly conceded to the Senate that the "water cure" was the policy in some cases.[9] How American troops came upon this practice is not clear, but it is probable that the Americans adapted it from the Filipinos, who knew it from Spanish colonial history.

What is certain is that no one remembered that it was one of the most fearful tortures of the Inquisition. President Roosevelt called it a "mild torture."[10] War critics were outraged, but, painful as the torture was, Americans could not see damage, and pumping and choking took root among soldiers and policemen. During World War I, imprisoned conscientious objectors to the war enumerated the violence to which military personnel subjected them, "above all various forms of the water cure."[11] And in the 1920s, police subjected prisoners to pumping, "having an ordinary water hose thrust into the mouth or down the throat, the faucet opened and the stomach flushed."[12] The British Criminal Investigation Division (CID) pumped Arab and Jewish prisoners in Mandatory Palestine between 1936 and 1939.[13]

The Japanese police never pumped in Japan, but the Japanese Kempeitai commonly practiced it in Shanghai in 1937 and then throughout their dominions (Korea, Manchuria, Singapore, Malaysia, Java, Vietnam, Philippines, Micronesia, Borneo, and Burma) during the war.[14] Prisoners in Singapore dubbed the practice the "Tokio-wine treatment."[15] Interrogators used hoses and teakettles to funnel water down the throat. In Borneo, torturers fed starved prisoners large amounts of uncooked rice, and then pumped them full of water ("rice torture").[16] Rice expands slowly when soaked.

In the 1950s, the French police in Algeria called pumping stomachs the *tuyau* or "the tube" after the hose they ran from the tap.[17] Afterward, they would fold the legs against the bloated stomach, forcing water slowly out of every orifice. Roger Wuillaume reported that, judging by its frequency, police favored pumping over all other tortures in 1954–55.[18] The practice appears to fade between 1958 and 1959, but returns by late 1959.[19] One prisoner reported undergoing pumping combined with electrotorture. Each time he received a shock, he sucked in water involuntarily.[20]

In 1969, a Palestinian prisoner reported that Israeli interrogators inserted a water hose "into the mouth and water poured down the throat. . . . an interrogator would then stand on his stomach, forcing the water back out of his mouth."[21] In the 1970s, Brazilian interrogators pumped with a hose running through the nostrils into the mouth, sometimes combined with electrotorture.[22] In the 1980s, accounts of pumping come from South Korea, Italy, Chile, and Vietnam.[23] In the 1990s, prisoners reported pumping in Mexico and Chad.[24] In 2003, U.S. interrogators pumped a prisoner at a base in Afghanistan.[25] In 2004, Ugandan prisoners identified pumping (dubbed the "Liverpool") as a routine torture.[26]

Choking

The oldest European form of choking is "ducking," temporarily submerging the body in water. In 1189, during the Crusades, Richard I declared to his troops that he who "struck with the palm of his hand, without drawing blood, he shall be thrice ducked in the sea."[27] The Code of Oleron, the customary standards that governed European seafaring for the next several centuries, prescribed ducking for falling asleep at the watch and failing to observe proper dress.[28]

By the seventeenth century, British, Dutch, and French captains used "ducking by the yard arm" for minor infractions and rites of passage.[29] The Tasmanian Museum possesses a "ducking box" used in ships transporting convicts to Australia. The coffin-shaped box was pierced with holes and then dropped into the sea. Ducking for theft also persisted well into the nineteenth century.[30]

The Dutch pioneered a more economical method of choking. Torturers shoved a soaked cloth into a prisoner's mouth, ladling water on it until the victim nearly suffocated. They would then remove the cloth for questioning and reapply it as needed. Removing the cloth from a prisoner, observed a practitioner, "is like pulling his bowels through his mouth."[31] The Dutch used this technique on British merchants in the East Indies in 1622.[32] Italians also used it on heretics; the date of this usage is unclear.[33]

Uniquely among European peoples, the British adapted ducking for punishments on land, developing a ducking chair for this purpose.[34] The victim was strapped to a caged chair on the end of a long lever, and men then lowered the lever into a river or pond. The punishment was reserved for people who talked too much, such as some London astronomers who made false predictions in 1523. Increasingly, the punishment fell on nagging women.[35] The last woman ducked in England was Jenny Pipes in 1809 in Leominster, Herefordshire. Indian police, however, continued choking into the nineteenth century, dipping prisoners in "wells and rivers until the party is half-suffocated."[36]

The British, French, and Dutch navies also practiced a grimmer form of choking. Sailors hung the victim from the lowest beam (the yardarm) of the main mast on one side of the ship and then, using pulleys, dragged him with ropes beneath the ship's keel to the other side of the long beam. This was called "keelhauling."[37] Keelhauling was not some ancient nautical torture. It originated with the modern navy. The practice presupposed rigging that was invented for the giant British man-of-war, a battleship that was in use from the Tudor period to the mid–nineteenth century, when steamships replaced them.[38]

The British abolished keelhauling in 1720 and the French and the Dutch in 1750. The practice continued unofficially for some years afterward, but there are no British records of keelhauling after 1770, and the last Dutch record was in 1806.[39]

Americans often cited keelhauling in debates on corporal punishment as a specifically British barbarism, even though the practice had vanished by American independence.[40] Americans continued to practice traditional British punishments. Ducking nagging women, an old Puritan punishment, continued into the late nineteenth century. The last American ducked was Mrs. Mary Brady, a "common scold" in 1889, in Jersey City. The last Canadian ducked was Miss Annie Pope in Ottawa in 1890.[41]

In the 1850s, as the public mood turned against whips, the U.S. Navy abandoned whipping for other punishments, including showering. In this punishment, prisoners were doused "for long periods with bilge water."[42] In 1848, Sing Sing Prison in New York abandoned whips for showering recalcitrant prisoners. Guards attached a close-fitting hollow shield around the neck. Then they showered the prisoner with water, choking him as water accumulated around his chin and mouth.[43] It was "a process of gradual strangulation by drowning."[44]

In the 1920s, the Wickersham Commission described how some American police illegally tied down a victim and then slowly poured water into his nostrils "so as to strangle him, thus causing pain and horror for the purpose of forcing a confession."[45]

In the 1930s, Argentine police and Franco's interrogators in Spain dunked suspects headfirst into a barrels and wells.[46] Japanese police and Kempeitai choked prisoners in Japan, Singapore, Vietnam, Borneo, and the Philippines. Most typically, interrogators adopted the Dutch style in choking, using a wet cloth to choke victims and ladling water on the face, though occasionally they choked prisoners in tubs, oil drums, or toilet bowls.[47]

In 1943, Masuy, the Belgian torturer who ran black market operations for the Nazis in France, made choking his signature technique.[48] There were other methods. At Auschwitz, Gestapo agents hung prisoners upside down and forced boiling water or oil into the nostrils.[49] Pouring water into nostrils is also reported at Aleja Szucha in Poland.[50] And at Ravensbrück, Ludwig Ramdor had his own unique approach.[51]

It was Masuy's technique that spread through western Europe. Masuy maintained at his trial in 1947 that choking was "more humane" than plucking nails.[52] The Gestapo, not known for its humanity, authorized this method for Norway and Czechoslovakia in 1945 as the resistance struggles there intensified.[53] Gestapo interrogators also adopted the technique in Lille, Lyon, Nice, Bordeaux, and Paris. Other French collaborators also adopted Masuy's *baignoire*, including the Berger gang (Paris), Merode's gang (Paris), the Milice's Bureau 51 (Paris), and some agents in Rennes.

After the war, French police used the *baignoire* to produce false confessions in Madagascar (1947) and France (1947–48).[54] In Algeria, French interrogators pioneered the stealthy practice of combining electricity and water torture.[55] In the early 1950s, French police had various names for choking including the "swimming title" (*brevet de natation*), the "juice," (*le jus*), the "midnight bath" (*le bain de minuit*), and the "four o'clock bath" (*le bain de 4 heures*).[56] In the late 1950s, paratroopers used pumping and choking, including the *baignoire* and ducking (the sausage, *saussison*).[57] There is only one report of the Dutch cloth technique being used (in Paris in 1961).[58]

During the Korean War, one British prisoner reported being subjected to choking by Korean interrogators.[59] The British, for their part, used choking during the Cyprus emergency in the 1950s. They elected to use the Dutch style: "You might be half-suffocated with a wet cloth which forced you to drink with every breath you took."[60] British interrogators also briefly adopted this procedure in Northern Ireland in 1972.[61] In South Vietnam, prisoners reported water torture, dubbing it "taking the submarine," a phrase that covered pumping and choking.[62] Torturers typically favored pumping over choking.[63] American soldiers sometimes pumped and choked in Vietnam.[64]

In 1966, Brazilian torturers adopted choking (*banho chinês*, the Chinese bath).[65] Spanish police also choked prisoners in tubs, calling the torture the *bañera*, or bath.[66] In 1972, before the Pinochet coup, leftist guerillas in Santiago Public Jail charged that police used water choking.[67] Choking with water (the *bañera*) remained a standard torture for the next two decades.[68] Argentine torturers also used choking in the 1970s (*el submarino,* or the submarine).[69]

Uruguayan torturers were the most inclined toward water torture.[70] In Rasmussen's study of two hundred torture victims, he found that Uruguayan survivors reported water torture most frequently (89 percent). Survivors from other Latin countries reported this less commonly (25 percent of Spanish victims, 32 percent of Argentine victims, and 18 percent of Chileans). Torture victims from elsewhere (Iraq and Northern Ireland) did not report the practice.

Between 1970 and 1990, prisoners frequently reported choking in water, often in conjunction with electricity or other clean tortures. Choking appears in numerous countries, most notably Brazil, Chile, Argentina, Spain, Portugal, Mexico, El Salvador, Nicaragua, Peru, the Philippines, Indonesia, Chad, South Africa, Zimbabwe, Egypt, Lebanon, Israel, Syria, and Saudi Arabia.[71] Aside from Syria, what is notable about this list is the absence of countries from the Communist bloc, and this would seem to suggest an ideological disposition against water torture. But it seems more plausible to explain this pattern with respect to monitoring. Water torture was more common not because Communists had an ideological objection to water torture, but because non-Communist countries had far greater reasons to be concerned with human rights monitoring.

In the 1990s, monitors documented choking in water in Colombia, Ecuador, Honduras, Paraguay, Mexico, Venezuela, Spain, Austria, Moldova, Bulgaria, Albania, Syria, Sri Lanka, Burma/Myanmar, Bangladesh, and Nepal. In 2002, U.S. interrogators at Guantánamo requested approval to use the Dutch cloth technique, a technique with a long history in the American South. Secretary Rumsfeld rejected this request in December 2002.[72] Nevertheless, it seems plausible that other accounts describing interrogators sprinkling or pouring water on prisoners refer to unauthorized usage of this technique.[73] In 2005, a U.S. Navy SEAL indicated that the Dutch cloth technique was a familiar part of SEAL training.[74]

Possibly the most notorious account of choking in recent years has been the CIA technique known as "waterboarding." Journalists have offered different accounts of this authorized torture, but none of them coherent at this time. On June 28, 2004, the *New York Times* reported that the Justice Department specifically authorized CIA interrogators to use full-body ducking after 9/11. This technique was described as strapping prisoners to a board and then forcibly pushing them underwater, a technique they dubbed "waterboarding."[75] This description of waterboarding most closely resembles in its particulars the singular style of Ludwig Ramdor, the notorious Kripo investigator at Ravensbrück, though how the CIA came upon it is hard to know. On November 18, 2005, reporters for *ABC News* described waterboarding as a variant of the old Dutch cloth technique. "The prisoner is bound to an inclined board, feet raised and head slightly below the feet. Cellophane is wrapped over the prisoner's face and water is poured over him. Unavoidably, the gag reflex kicks in and a terrifying fear of drowning leads to almost instant pleas to bring the treatment to a halt."[76] The addition of the cellophane wrap to the face makes this account incoherent. It is not possible for a gag reflex to kick in if no water is reaching the mouth. If interrogators were using cellophane to cover the face, there would be no point in using water to choke the victim; the victim would be asphyxiating in any case.

The traditional technique requires the use of cloth to absorb the water, and it was clearly known to Guantánamo interrogators, so CIA interrogators may in fact be choking with water. But if they were choking with cellophane, this is a form of near asphyxiation using plastic, what is sometimes known as the dry submarine (discussed in chapter 16, "Fists and Exercises"). Only future prisoner or interrogator accounts will tell us more accurately whether what was used was the Dutch technique or the dry submarine.

Showers and Ice

Water has other uses in modern torture besides choking and pumping. Less commonly, torturers use water to freeze and beat prisoners.

Beating with water. In the nineteenth century, American jailers used to punish prisoners by choking them under long showers. At Sing Sing, jailers released a solid stream of cold water from a great height, literally beating prisoners with water.[77] The effect was similar to standing before a fire hose. The impact caused extensive bruises and eventually unconsciousness.[78] In 1858, guards at Auburn prison showered Simon Moore for thirty minutes, after which he collapsed and died. To avoid unwanted scandal, New York prisons reduced the shower heights and eventually abolished water punishments in 1882.[79]

Fire hoses deliver water with great force, enabling them to serve as effective substitutes for tall showers. In the late nineteenth century, American fire hoses could deliver water with pressures tested to 350 psi.[80] It was not long before they appeared in prison practice. In the early 1860s, the "shower bath" was a standard punishment at San Quentin. Prison guards stripped prisoners, tied them to the "ladder," and then "sprayed a stream of cold water from a one-and-one-half inch hose under great pressure against the victim's face, breast, and exposed genitalia." Prison records show a minimum of forty-two Hispanics received the "shower" punishment between 1872 and 1875, and Anglo prisoners also received the punishment. At San Quentin, flogging was abolished in 1880 and the "shower bath" in 1882.[81] But the practice was not forgotten. In 1918, for instance, military officers used fire hoses to beat imprisoned Molokans, a small religious sect of conscientious objectors, when they refused to stand for reveille. The hosing lasted for two hours.[82]

Although there may be earlier cases, the first known European cases of "hosings" come from British prisons in Ireland in 1923.[83] Guards used hosing again to quell a prison strike on Christmas Day 1939. Prisoners were "badly buffeted by the powerful jets and almost drowned."[84] Nazi prison camps, most notably Ravensbrück, also used fire hoses in this manner.[85]

The first official use of fire hoses for torture occurs in French colonial Algeria. The *Guide provisoire de l'officier de renseignement* (1961), a manual for intelligence officers, specifically recommended softening prisoners with "pressurized jets."[86] In recent decades, guards have used pressurized water to beat prisoners in South Vietnam, Israel, Turkey, and Italy. Turkish police use high-pressure hoses to "reawaken circulation" after suspension and electrotorture.[87] Most recently, American soldiers have used hoses on children in Iraqi prisons; one-fifteen-year-old allegedly "was soaked repeatedly with hoses until he collapsed."[88]

Freezing water. Between 1915 and 1921, "special" prisoners in the British penal colony of the Andamans were "forcibly taken to the water tanks and cold water was thrown on them for hours"; they were then returned to the cells naked.[89] Similarly, during World War I, some conscientious objectors held in military prisons reported they were held in ice water showers and baths until they fainted.[90] In the 1920s, a prisoner described how Chicago police subjected him to the "sand blast gun" and then the "ice water cure," which consisted of filling an ordinary bathtub with crushed ice and water, stripping the suspect, and immersing him.[91] Although it was not a common technique, Soviet interrogators in the 1930s did use freezing baths of cold water to extort confessions.[92] Franco's interrogators adopted this technique in 1939, and Nazi guards made prisoners stand in freezing pools of water or under freezing cold showers, especially in Belgian camps.[93] Between 1940 and 1948, British interrogators used "cold water showers" as part of a brutal interrogation regimen in a clandestine London prison for German POWs accused of war crimes (discussed in chapter 15, "Forced Standing and Other Positions").[94] French Paras also used cold showers occasionally in Algeria in the 1950s.[95] In the 1970s, Greek, Chilean, Israeli, and Syrian interrogators made prisoners stand under cold showers or in cold pools for long periods.[96] During a joint training exercise with American Special Forces, some West German border guards were subjected to various tortures, including "continual cold showers."[97] American forces doused prisoners in Iraq and immersed prisoners in Afghanistan.[98] Likewise, CIA interrogators left their subjects in cold cells, and "throughout the time in the cell the prisoner is doused with cold water."[99]

Ice tortures. During the Korean War (1950–53), Chinese commanders marched British and American POWs onto the frozen Yalu River in subzero weather and poured water over their feet. "The water immediately froze, the prisoners were left for hours with their feet frozen into the ice to 'reflect' on their crimes."[100] In 1953, a Bulgarian prisoner described how guards poured buckets of ice in the center of his cell and them made him stand in ice up to his knees for hours.[101] In the same year, in Venezuela, torturers invented the ice panel (*la panela de hielo*). Prisoners describe this as a coffinshaped box. Inside was "an immense panel of ice covered with sawdust and wrapped in hemp cloth. . . . They made me lie down face up on it."[102]

In January 1956, Greek reporters charged that British interrogators made prisoners stand on ice during the Cyprus Emergency.[103] In the late 1960s, the Greek military junta subjected its prisoners to the ordeal of ice. One prisoner asserted that torturers "doused her, almost naked, with icy water as she lay on ice."[104]

In the 1970s, two South African prisoners in Kwazulu-Natal reported being "wrapped in a cloth and put in dry ice" for hours.[105] In the 1980s, Filipino police adopted "forced lying on a block of ice."[106] The Soviet army and the Afghan Khad covered prisoners in snow.[107] In the 1990s, Turkish police also turned to chilling and smothering prisoners under large blocks of ice.[108] A Palestinian detained in 2000 reported that Israeli interrogators "brought pieces of ice and forced me to swallow a piece and rubbed another piece along my chest," after which they choked him for five minutes in the toilet bowl.[109]

Salt and Spice

Traditionally, torturers used irritants to make executions more painful.[110] Acid torture and toxic pumping continue this tradition. Acid torture is not a common modern torture, but when torturers use it, it is in authoritarian states where it does not matter whether victims are scarred or killed: Nazi-occupied France, Iran during the 1960s, Brazil and Argentina during the 1970s, and Madagascar, Syria, and El Salvador in the 1980s.[111] Similarly, pumping stomachs with toxic liquids (bleach or iodine) has been reported in Italy in the 1930s and Guatemala in the 1990s.[112]

Most modern use of irritants leaves few marks. The transition from scarring to clean irritants occurs earliest in British colonial India. In the eighteenth century, Governor Hastings's torturers sometimes fashioned their *falaka* rods from the *bechettea*, a highly caustic and poisonous plant. Beating with this rod created wounds that festered, leaving "a crust of leprous sores upon the body, and often ends in the destruction of life itself."[113] By the nineteenth century, police rubbed pepper in victims' eyes or packed chili powder in their nostrils, a practice that colonial police continued until the 1940s.[114]

Observers at the time correctly recognized that pepper torture marked a turn to stealthy torture, noting that the Indian police failed "ignominiously for some years, until the new police learnt to use the 'extra-legal' methods of the old police without being found out."[115] They incorrectly blamed such tortures on atavistic Indian tendencies. In fact, British citizens did not hesitate using the same techniques elsewhere. In the West Indies, British owners rubbed pepper into the eyes if slaves dozed at work.[116] In the nineteenth century, British captains had sailors rub salt into the wounds of a flogged man, a practice that continued into American slavery.[117]

Most torturers today prefer either common condiments (pepper, chili powder, curry powder, salt) or household cleaning supplies (alcohol, bleach, lye, ammonia, or soap). These can aggravate wounds without scarring prisoners. Some of them are antiseptics, allowing for plausible deniability when they are applied to open wounds. Torturers use irritants in several ways, most of them leaving few marks.

Insertion. In applying irritants, most modern torturers avoid the eyes, preferring to insert irritants into the nostrils, eyes, anus, or vagina. In the last four decades, prisoners have reported this kind of pepper torture in India, Pakistan, Sri Lanka, Greece, Somalia, and Tanzania.[118] In the 1960s and 1970s, Brazilian torturers slipped alcohol into the anus (the *churrasquino*, or barbecue); Israeli torturers applied sulfur to open wounds, while Syrians applied salt.[119] In the 1980s Burmese torturers applied salt and curry powder after whipping suspects.[120] In 1990s, Sri Lankan torturers rubbed salt into wounds.[121] In 2003, American soldiers applied pepper to the eyes of one prisoner at Abu Ghraib.[122]

Spiced wash. In the nineteenth century, American slave owners washed slaves down with red pepper and salt after floggings.[123] British captains also had errant sailors brushed down with cold brine.[124] In the 1930s, Argentine torturers rubbed down prisoners with sandpaper and a mixture of turpentine and alcohol (*el papel de lija y aguarrás*).[125] Guards poured vinegar onto the wounds of prisoners in the French exile prisons.[126] The sole report in recent decades is from Djibouti, where torturers allegedly dipped victims in vats of brine.[127] Some torturers, though, use salt washes for other purposes. In the 1970s, Turkish and South African police used salt water to increase conductivity in electrotorture.[128]

Spiced choking. Many modern torturers add irritants to the water with which they choke their victims. In the 1930s, British CID forced water with a "mild acid" down the nostrils of prisoners.[129] During World War II, Clara Knecht, a Nazi police spy in France, developed "an atrocious perfection of the bathtub torture . . . the bathtub of soapy water, in use at Rennes and other Western cities."[130] This technique reappeared in France's colonial struggles overseas. In the 1950s, Paras in Algeria sometimes used soapy or bleach water tubs, and South Vietnamese agents added soap, salt, or a mixture of lime, pepper, and excrement to their tubs.[131]

Today most prisoners report being choked in extremely dirty water. In the 1980s, Peruvian interrogators choked prisoners in water (*ta tina*) mixed with salt or hot peppers, and prisoners in Djibouti report being choked in vats of soapy water.[132] Similarly, Mexican police force carbonated water with chili pepper down the nasal passages (*tehuancanazo*).[133]

Spiced pumping. Mussolini's OVRA pumped prisoners with castor oil.[134] British police pumped Palestinian Arabs with beer.[135] Nazi torturers at Pawiak in Poland forced vodka down the throats of prisoners.[136] French Paras pumped alcohol.[137] In the Philippines, Japanese torturers occasionally pumped stomachs with soapy water.[138] In the 1980s, Italian police pumped prisoners with salt water when they transported them between prisons.[139] In the British and French cases, forced ingestion of alcohol probably also served as cultural humiliation.

Spiced ingestion. Torturers induce rapid dehydration by forcing prisoners to consume extremely salted meals. One might call this technique "dry pumping." Prisoners report salt diets in French Indochina (1930s, salted rice), in the Soviet Union (1930s, salted herring), Nazi-occupied Poland (1940s), French-occupied Algeria (1950s, salt), Greece (1960s), Syria (1970s), Turkey (1980s, salted cheese), and China (1990s).[140]

Spiced gas. In 1856, Louisiana's Pentonville Prison became the first to use pepper spray on prisoners in confined spaces. The governor "got some cayenne pepper and burnt it in a fumigating bellows, and then blew the smoke down the corridor where the fellow was."[141] During the Civil War, jailers confined some prisoners in cells next to furnaces that generated dark smoke.[142] This low-tech approach still persists in some countries. In Sri Lanka, for example torturers burn chilies over a fire and blow the irritant smoke into the eyes of the prisoner.[143]

At the turn of the century, Folsom Penitentiary in California created a "Chloride of Lime Cell," a cell whose floor was soaked with chloride of lime. Chloride of lime has a biting acrid smell, familiar to anyone who uses bleach, and within minutes the fumes affected the prisoner's breathing, burned the lining of his nose and throat, and stung his eyes.[144] Soviet army guards also used this procedure in military prisons.[145]

In the 1920s, Chicago police pioneered the technique of pumping tear gas into small cells.[146] Others placed a box over the prisoner's head and released a canister inside the box.[147] Advances in pumping technology now allow torturers to apply mace, pepper spray, or tear gas directly into keyholes or the mouth or face of prisoners. This technique appeared in Israeli prisons in the 1970s, American and Canadian prisons in the 1980s, and in Belgium and Taiwan in the 1990s.[148]

Torturers have also adapted the Dutch style in water choking for gassing. They pour water into a prisoner's mouth through a rag (*chiffon*) soaked in bleach, which caused the prisoner's throat to burn horrendously. The first recorded account of the *chiffon* comes toward the end of the Algerian war, in Paris in January 1961, but it was not forgotten. By the 1990s, Moroccan and Algerian torturers commonly used the *chiffon*.[149]

Guatemalan and Honduran torturers hood their prisoners in cloth bags doused with chemicals (the *capucha*), a technique allegedly taught to them by Argentine advisers.[150] Ukrainian torturers forced gas masks onto the heads of prisoners and then pumped ammonia up the breathing tube.[151]

Deprivation of Sleep

Describing his torture by sleep deprivation by the Soviet police, Menachem Begin observes that anyone subjected to this condition knows that "not even hunger or thirst are comparable to it."[152] Experts now agree that sleep deprivation "is a basic, and potentially dangerous, physiological need state, similar to hunger or thirst and as basic to survival."[153] Additionally, sleep deprivation reduces a body's tolerance for musculoskeletal pain, causing deep aches first in the lower part of the body, followed by similar pains in the upper body.[154] Animal tests suggest that REM sleep deprivation increases sensitivity to mechanical, thermal, and noxious electrical stimuli.[155]

Sleep-deprived people are highly suggestible (a condition not unlike drunkenness or hypnosis), making sleep deprivation ideal for inducing false confessions.[156] Sleep-deprived subjects also have vivid auditory and visual hallucinations, making this practice ideal for documenting such remarkable events such as secret pacts with the devil.[157] Hippolytus de Marsilliis (b. 1451), an Italian lawyer, is credited with introducing this technique into the Catholic Inquisition's toolkit.[158] But Inquisitional interrogators soon were aware of the unreliable character of sleep deprivation, and in particular the vivid hallucinations of subjects. The preferred technique of the Inquisition was the rack. It was Protestant countries that embraced sleep deprivation. The Calvinist Church of Scotland adopted sleep deprivation for witch interrogations in the 1640s, making it the first nation to apply sleep deprivation systematically. Scottish torture included standard instruments except for the rack, about which lawyers had doubts.[159] Sleep deprivation was legally less dubious. Guards took turns shaking and pricking victims, or victims were forced to walk perpetually for two days or more, combined with a limited diet. The English Parliament prohibited "swimming" witches in 1645, and so English witch hunters followed the Scottish model, combining sleep deprivation and forced sitting or walking to extort confessions.[160]

Sleep deprivation was not a common torture in the early modern period. Torturers preferred to whip, stretch, burn, pierce, cut, and brand their victims. In the modern era, common use of sleep deprivation occurred first in democracies or the colonies of democracies. In 1854, a British commission reported that it was a common practice among colonial police in India.[161] In the 1930s, French torturers in Saigon used sleep deprivation combined with electricity, *falaka*, meals of salt, and positional tortures on Vietnamese nationalists.[162] American police also revived sleep deprivation in the early twentieth century as newspapers condemned more coercive techniques.[163] Detectives took turns interrogating suspects for hours or days (in a stifling interrogation room, hence the sweating). They kept them awake by shining bright lights into their eyes, shaking them, or making constant noise.

Sweating appears in Europe in the 1930s. The British police were not unfamiliar with sweating, what they called "extended interrogation."[164] Likewise, Stalin's police sweated suspects, using sleep deprivation, like U.S. police, to generate false confessions for public trials. The Soviet style in sweating carried over into Communist states and then to revolutionary Iran in the 1990s.[165]

The Gestapo was the first to use sleep deprivation to gather military intelligence. The first reports appear in the late 1930s. In 1942, Gestapo chief Heinrich Müller authorized "sharpened interrogation" for terrorists, approving sleep deprivation, starvation, exhaustion exercises, regulated beating, and confinement in dark cells—but only to gather intelligence on those who had "plans hostile to the state," not to get confessions of guilt.[166]

Franco's police in Spain turned to sweating in 1939.[167] Between 1940 and 1948, British military interrogators in a clandestine London prison sought to extract confessions of war crimes from 3,573 German POWs. To this end, they subjected the prisoners to a regimen of sleep deprivation, forced standing, exhaustion exercises, cold water showers, and beatings.[168] In 1943, British and American agents introduced Brazilian police to sweating, helping them interrogate a German spy ring with sleep deprivation, forced standing, and clean beating.[169] This combination has since appeared in other countries, including Argentina, Portugal, and South Korea.[170] Sleep deprivation was a standard part of British interrogation in Northern Ireland in the 1970s and the current Israeli *shabeh* procedures.[171]

American courts finally barred sleep deprivation for domestic policing during World War II. In 1941 Tennessee police subjected one suspect, Ashcraft, to sleep deprivation and interrogation for thirty-six hours until he confessed he had killed his wife. In *Ashcraft v. Tennessee* (1944), the Supreme Court did not simply toss out the confession as unacceptable in any democratic society; it linked sweating directly to the practices of "certain foreign nations dedicated to an opposite policy," namely, "physical or mental torture."[172]

After 9/11, the U.S. military authorized sleep deprivation of prisoners for up to seventy-two hours, far longer than what Ashcraft was subjected to.[173] The CIA also authorized sleep deprivation in combination with standing handcuff restraints for more than forty hours.[174] Local commanders and interrogators, military and civilian, also took initiatives. At Camp Cropper, near Baghdad Airport, one prisoner being kept awake for ninety-six hours.[175] At Guantánamo, guards exercised sleep deprivation under the cover of moving detainees from one cell to another every hour or two, a technique called "the frequent-flier program."[176] In 2002, American interrogators on the ground in Afghanistan developed a technique they called "monstering." The commander "instituted a new rule that a prisoner could be kept awake and in the booth for as long as an interrogator could last." One "monstering" interrogator engaged in this for thirty hours.[177]

Remembering the Inquisition

Today, we prefer to remember pumping and sleep deprivation as Inquisitional tortures, not as modern tortures. Modern torturers practice these techniques on many more victims than Inquisitors ever bothered. Although they capture the modern imagination, these were relatively uncommon techniques compared to whips, ropes, and racks.

We also forget that modern torturers have not merely substituted funnels for pumping with rubber hoses. They have developed new water tortures (tortures with cold showers and ice) and added variations to classical techniques (the spiced *chiffon* or rice torture). They have introduced new methods of delivery, replacing showers with high-pressure jets and bellows with gas canisters.

Above all, modern torturers have favored clean variations, choosing cold over hot water and common condiments over caustic substances. This occurred in nineteenth-century British India, where the police were "tied down to a law invented by foreigners,"[178] and in the United States, where the public and the law demanded interrogation without violence. Water torture in stealthy regimens also appeared during the American war in the Philippines and the Arab Revolt in Mandatory Palestine, circumstances where democracies had to exercise violence mindful of public reaction at home. Authoritarian police, notably the Japanese Kempeitai, followed, but they valued these techniques because they were extremely painful. They did not exploit the clean characteristics of these tortures until the late twentieth century, when global human rights monitoring came of age.

Any straps or ropes used for this purpose must be of sufficient width
that they inflict no bodily harm and leave no permanent mark on
the offender.

—British War Office Memorandum on Field Punishment
Number 1 (the "crucifixion"), January 12, 1917[1]

14   Stress and Duress

Since April 2004, government reports and journalists have documented repeated instances of American torture in Iraq, Afghanistan, and elsewhere.[2]
The torture at Abu Ghraib stands out, but American soldiers at various Iraqi
camps have also resorted to torture. Most accounts describe sweating (using
light and noise to induce sleep deprivation), humiliation and degradation, use
of threatening dogs, and exposure to extremes of heat and cold, and some accounts describe water torture, *falaka*, electrotorture, and the use of spices. But
above all, reports and journalists describe repeatedly a class of techniques
known as "stress and duress." Stress and duress techniques can be grouped in
four categories:

1. Positional torture, such as forced standing, squatting or kneeling for
   hours, sometimes holding heavy objects. At Abu Ghraib, the famous pictures of the hooded men standing immobile on a box for hours with
   wires attached to their fingers models a version of this torture.[3] In military slang, practices like this were called "smoking the prisoner."[4]
2. Exercising ceaselessly until prisoners are exhausted. These include push-
   ups, knee bends, and forced crawling (what is traditionally called "the
   lizard").[5]
3. Restraint tortures, including handcuffing prisoners in standing positions
   or with the hands positioned above the head ("high cuffing") or suspending prisoners in uncomfortable ways. This category also includes
   positional devices, such as stuffing individuals into constrained spaces
   such as sleeping bags or "the coffin" at the U.S. detention center at
   Qaim near Syria.[6]

4. Beatings, including slapping, cuffs to the ears, and pressuring the abdomen, types of blows that leave few marks.[7]

These techniques are painful and may not mark the body permanently. One may well ask whether anyone would know very much about U.S. torture in Iraq and elsewhere in the absence of the unauthorized pictures taken at Abu Ghraib. Indeed, U.S. torture continued after the world was informed of Abu Ghraib, long after American officials assured the public that torture had stopped. As one sergeant with the Eighty-second Airborne testified, "We still did it, but we were careful."[8] An elite Special Operations unit, Task Force 6-26, was more direct. Soldiers posted placards on the detention area that said, "No Blood, No Foul." The slogan, as a Defense Department explained, reflected the task force's adage, "If you don't make them bleed, they can't prosecute for it."[9]

Whatever investigations ultimately reveal about who authorized these practices, the history of these techniques is easy to trace. In the following three chapters, I argue that most tortures that characterized Abu Ghraib belong to a family of tortures that descended from old west European military and police punishments, what I will call the lesser tradition in stress torture. This chapter covers the early history up to the 1950s, and the next three chapters consider how these techniques evolved in the late twentieth century.

I begin by contrasting the lesser tradition with the classic restraint tortures like the rack. I argue that Englishmen, Frenchmen, and Americans commonly chose these techniques in the nineteenth and early twentieth centuries as alternatives to flogging, a practice that increasingly fell into disrepute in these countries. Authoritarian states preferred far more sanguinary tortures, especially flogging. When they did adopt elements of the lesser tradition, they tended to modify the procedures in ways that would leave marks.

Great and Lesser Stress Traditions

The techniques used in Iraq are painful. Long-term restraint in virtually any position will produce screaming muscles. Forced standing causes the ankles and feet to swell to twice their size within twenty-four hours. Moving becomes agonizing and large blisters develop. The heart rate increases, and some people faint. The kidneys eventually shut down.[10]

These techniques constitute the lesser tradition in stress tortures, lesser not because they are less painful, but because they leave less in the way of visible marks. They differ, in this respect, from the great tradition in restraint tortures (the strappado, or full suspension), which leaves permanent, visible, injuries.

Full suspension by the wrists, for example, causes permanent nerve damage in fifteen minutes to an average-sized man. If prisoners are heavier, damage occurs more swiftly. In the "standing handcuffs," however, torturers allow the victims feet to touch the ground (sometimes barely). The earth thus shares the weight with the cuffs. This increases the time prisoners may be suspended, elongates the pain, and delays permanent injury, factors that matter in stealth torture.

Similarly, in the classic strappado, guards tie a victim's hands behind his back. They then hoist him from the ground by means of a hook and pulley, drop him to the floor and repeat the process. The strappado can easily dislocate the shoulders and maim victims permanently. However, the same approximate condition can be achieved, without overall damage and for a longer period of time, by raising the handcuffed hands behind the back until the prisoner is standing on his toes; his hands are then attached to a hook. I will call this position the reverse standing handcuffs.

Other lesser methods of trussing allow for long-term suspension with far less injury, including, hanging victims upside down and bucking, a method used in the slave trade. These methods, however, run the risk of causing suffocation as fluids clog the nasal passage and mouth.

Historically, authoritarian states have favored full suspension, the rack, the strappado, and hanging in crucifixion. The lesser techniques have characterized torture in democratic states.

British Stress Tortures

For centuries the British military, like most armies, disciplined their troops with whips. At sea, the British navy supplemented flogging with ducking and keelhauling. Eventually, these field punishments gave way to drilling and solitary confinement.

This well-known transition did not happen quickly and included several interim and unofficial punishments. Some have been covered in previous chapters, including cobbing, the soft strap, and *falaka*. There were others, and the list offered here is not meant to be exhaustive; I identify only those techniques that were to have a future in modern torture.

Early Military Tortures

In 1786, an anonymous officer said officers often applied to soldiers, without trial, three customary unofficial punishments for petty crimes: tying the neck and heels, riding the "Wooden Horse," and picketing.[11] They are also among the earliest forms of forced sitting, forced standing, and restraint tortures in Western armies.

In the Picket, guards drove a post into the ground. The prisoner mounted a stool near it barefooted, his right hand fastened to a hook on the post by a noose round his wrist or thumb. The wrist was drawn as high as it could be pulled. The stool was removed and a stump tapered to a sharp point was set in its place. The prisoner could relieve the strain on his hand by resting his bare heel on the sharp point of the stump. Conversely, the picket stump "though it did not break the skin put him to great torture; the only means of mitigation was by resting his weight upon his wrist, the pain of which soon became intolerable."[12] The cavalry and artillery typically used the Picket, and the typical time on the picket was fifteen minutes.

The Wooden Horse was a large trestle with a sharp ridge or angle eight or nine feet long. Sometimes it was customary to add wheels, a wooden horse's head, and a tail. The handcuffed prisoner straddled the ridge that dug into the cleft between his legs. Guards tied muskets to the legs to strain the thighs, or "as was jocularly said, [to keep] their horse from kicking them off."[13] It was reserved for the infantry, since these soldiers were unaccustomed to riding horses.

In "tying the neck and heels," the prisoner sat on the ground. Torturers placed a firelock (flintlock) over the neck and another on the back of the thighs. Torturers then pull the two firelocks together by means of a pair of cartouche-box straps. "In this situation, with his chin between his knees, has many a man been kept till blood gushed out of his nose, mouth and ears."[14]

At sea, captains used different positional and restraint tortures.[15] The most well known today is the "spread eagle," in which a sailor would be placed upon the rigging of the mizzenmast, his feet and arms stretched wide apart and secured by ropes. Another frequent variant involved shoving a capstan bar through a barrel and tying the prisoner's arms to it. The arms were extended backward "at the full length crosswise, and so tied to the bar."[16] Sometimes, sailors hung a basket of bullets or weights from the neck.

Military punishments also included drills (heavy marching or trotting round in a circle), forced standing (standing fully equipped in heavy marching order with face to the wall); carrying or dragging heavy objects (a log or capstan bar) for hours, moving cannon shot back and forth (the "shot drill"), being stuffed in a barrel, confinement to the dry room or black hole, and forced drinking of salt water.[17]

Then there were three positional devices, the Gag, the Wooden Collar, and the Whirligig. Some offenders were obliged to wear the Wooden Collar, two thick pieces of wood that fit around the neck and weighed sixty pounds. In gagging, torturers introduced a wood or iron ball into the mouth and fastened it with an improvised harness. The Whirligig was a circular wooden cage reserved for the camp prostitutes and dishonest supply merchants. The cage turned on a pivot, and "when set in motion wheeled round with such velocity that the delinquent became extremely sick, and commonly emptied his or her body through every aperture."[18]

Several of these tortures derive from Britain's interaction with China and India in this period. The Wooden Collar is an adaptation of the Chinese cangue.[19] "Tying the neck and heels" is one of the basic rope tortures of the traditional Indian *anundal*.[20] Similarly, the *falaka*, "dry room," and the "black hole" are East Indian punishments adapted by the British army.[21]

Many early British practices, official and unofficial, had serious liabilities. The Wooden Horse, the Picket and tying neck to heels could rupture shoulders, ruin wrists, or lame soldiers, making them useless for military service. Commanders preferred whipping, but as the public mood turned against whipping, the British military looked for alternatives. In this context, it settled on a restraint torture that was similar to the Capstan and had none of the liabilities of the Picket.

The Crucifixion

In 1881, the British military outlawed flogging as a field punishment, replacing it with a new schedule of punishments. The most severe involved the following procedure. Guards attached a soldier to a "fixed object" for two hours a day up to three months. The fixed object was usually a wheel of an artillery gun, though it could be "the wheels of a wagon, the pole of a tent, or a post driven into the ground."[22] Guards tied the soldier's hands and feet to the wheel and fed him bread and water. The War Office called this position "Field Punishment Number 1," but soldiers knew it as "the crucifixion."[23]

The internal debates in the War Office indicate that British generals and officials proposed several alternatives to flogging in the 1880s, all of which were clean, painful, and left no permanent injuries. These included shot drills, the crossbar (the Capstan), the spread eagle, stocks, being handcuffed behind the back, clean whipping, forced marching at night with the reliefs, imprisonment in irons or in a straight waistcoat, and the "Little Ease."[24] This last, the original suggestion for the crucifixion, consisted of "keeping a man in an uncomfortable position by means of irons around his neck, hands and feet."[25]

To facilitate the decision-making process, the British War Office also conducted a survey of field punishments of all major European powers as well as the United States, itemizing them by technique.[26] Among other punishments, investigators noted that some Austrian and German regiments used a practice similar to the Little Ease, a practice called "tying up" (*das Anbinden*). In Austro-Hungary, the soldier was forced to stand while bound to a wall, pillar, or tree by means of ropes or metal rings, with care taken to allow for circulation of blood and that enough space was left between the two inner ankles.[27] Likewise, in Germany, the prisoner was tied up "in an erect position, with his back to a wall, tree, or like object, in such a way that he cannot sit or lie down."[28]

These were comparatively new punishments, introduced with the abolition (for the most part) of military corporal punishment in Austro-Hungary (1868) and Germany (1872). British investigators were skeptical whether the Little Ease or tying up was effective in maintaining discipline and whether the Germans would in fact stick to it in practice. Indeed, they concluded:

> There is little doubt that in the next war in which Germany is engaged the military authorities will interpret the new paragraph 124 [allowing exceptions for corporal punishment] in a sense favourable to military discipline, and the German soldier will find himself still liable, as he was under the old system, to the tolerably severe corporal punishment of being wounded, and even killed, by his officer's sword, or shot by his comrades rifles, without previous trial.[29]

Officials in the War Office, however, were uncomfortable with the Little Ease, which was, in their words, "supposed to amount almost to torture."[30]

But after deliberation, in 1907, the British military approved Field Punishment Number 1. Crucifixion was a common punishment during World War I for offenses such as drunkenness and disobeying an order. In 1916, for example, a soldier who missed his train was subjected to crucifixion near the small village of Wickford in Essex. His hands were handcuffed and on each arm guards hung a pail of water. He was subjected to this eight hours a day on a diet of bread and water and guarded with soldiers with fixed bayonets.[31]

Scenes like this led to harsh public reactions. "I really think it wicked," wrote a Wickford resident, "that Englishmen who are giving up their all for King and Country to be treated so, worse than the most wicked criminal."[32] On the other hand, British generals objected to abolishing this field punishment. One argued that the punishment was necessary for disciplining offending soldiers.[33] Another warned that if officers had no choice but to send soldiers to prison, there would be manpower shortages.[34]

In January 1917, the War Office standardized Field Punishment Number 1. Hands were to be tied loosely, with six inches of play between them and the fixed object, if they were tied at all. Feet similarly should be tied, but loosely. If the prisoner was tied, ropes should not restrict his breathing. Irons were recommended, but if ropes and straps were used, they were to be broad enough to cause no physical harm and "leave no permanent mark on the offender."[35] Regulations for field punishments in 1949 indicate that British officers continued fixed object punishment well after World War II.[36]

Police and Prison Tortures

English police rarely sweated or beat in the course of interrogation in the early twentieth century.[37] Likewise, most British colonial policing was conducted without torture.[38] British policing also eliminated many sanguinary tortures customarily employed by the peoples they ruled. Precisely because authorities kept a sharp eye on policemen, when colonial police did turn to torture, they did so increasingly with stealth.

Positional and restraint torture was a perennial problem in British colonial India. In 1855, an investigative commission in Madras determined that police used mainly traditional procedures (the *anundal* and wooden screw presses called the *kittee*). The commission also identified several techniques that left few marks, including sleep deprivation, choking with water, exhaustion exercises, and irritating spices.[39] These were the techniques that had a future. In the early twentieth century, accounts describe prisoners being suspended upside down; having a baton smeared with chilies thrust into the anus; sitting for hours in dirty water up to the neck, and beatings.[40]

Between 1910 and 1930, Indian prisoners at the penal colony in the Andaman Islands reported fetters, crossbars, flogging, full-day cold baths, small cages, and the standing handcuffs.[41] The latter consisted of being "hung up to the wall" and standing eight hours a day with a one-hour break.[42] Positional devices included bar fetters and, more feared, crossbar fetters.[43] A bar fetter was a metal triangle that tied at three points, the ankles and the waist. It prevented one from bending one's legs; the punishment sometimes lasted months in the Andamans. This technique continues in Pakistan today.[44] Crossbar fetters involved an iron bar between the fetters that kept one's legs wide apart day and night. Lastly, there was being yoked to the oil mill. This forced one to walk in a circular motion for sixteen hours, with predictable dizziness and exhaustion.[45]

Prisons in Ireland used the crucifixion ("mock crucifixions"), standing handcuffs ("semi-hangings"), chain cuffs, and hosings in the 1920s.[46] In the early 1930s, a British prisoner held in India described standard tortures for refractory prisoners as the standing handcuffs, fetters, flogging, and solitary confinement. Beating and flogging often involved the "blanket parade": the prisoner was wrapped in a blanket and then beaten through the blanket with bamboo rods: "Although he receives all the pain of the beating, he has not wounds to show the superintendent to justify his complaint. And indeed it is not wise to complain; for complaints do not lead to rectification of evils, but to further punishment and torture."[47]

Similar conditions held in Mandatory Palestine. In the 1930s, police brutality (called "duffing up" after a notorious British officer) increasingly concerned the Anglican clergy, who emerged as "a self-appointed civil rights organization."[48] This brutality paled when compared to British military and police behavior after 1938.

British soldiers and police subjected prisoners to forced standing, forced sitting, *falaka*, pumping and choking with water, exposure to extremes of heat and cold, flogging with elastic bands, slapping, genital squeezing, as well as to being suspended and urinated upon.[49] The violence fell on all parties, the crowded Palestinian jails being the only Mandate facility truly shared by both Arabs and Jews. Aubrey Lees, the assistant district commissioner in Hebron and also the town coroner, offered the following list of tortures he gathered from prisoners and policemen: pumping, pumping with beer, genital squeezing after pumping, mild acid in nostrils, beating with rubber truncheons, breaking fingers and tearing, and rolling prisoners on a nailed plank.[50]

In London, the National Council for Civil Liberties and the Howard League for Penal Reform publicized accounts, and questions were asked in Parliament. The Colonial Office publicly dismissed the reports, but privately worried about what it called "Black and Tan tendencies" and even evidence of "third degree" interrogations.[51] The tortures bore no relation to the tortures of the Blacks and Tans or the British police in Ireland (1920–21).[52] Those tortures were bloody and highly visible, while many Palestinian tortures were clean and allowed for plausible denial. By World War II, police turned to "sublimated beating," but these procedures soon came to light in the Farran affair after the war.[53]

Nineteenth-century British prisons and reformatories preferred exhaustion exercises. Guards required prisoners to perform shifts on various devices, notably the treadmill (1817) and the crank (1840). The treadmill involved forced walking, what was similar to ascending an endless flight of steps. As one ascended the wheel, the previous step slid away. It exhausted the strongest of men in fifteen minutes. Turning the crank required turning a handle twenty revolutions a minute, for a total of ten thousand revolutions in 8.5 hours.[54] "No human being, whether adult or juvenile, could continue to perform such an amount of labor of this kind for several consecutive days."[55]

As in the Andamans, positional tortures did exist at the margins of the prison system. Failure to turn the crank could lead to being laced in a straitjacket and "strapped to the wall in a standing position for hours at a time."[56] Even after the crank and the treadmill were abolished, exhaustion exercises and forced standing were standard regimens for incorrigible youth into the early twentieth century.[57]

French Stress Tortures

French field punishments did not differ markedly from British ones in the eighteenth century. They included whips, choking with water (ducking and keelhauling) and cobbing (*bâton de justice*) and the Wooden Horse (*cheval de bois*), the latter being used for soldiers and prostitutes.[58]

And like the British, the French military gradually abandoned whipping in field punishments. The French navy flogged soldiers until 1848, when it was abandoned the practice except for prison hulks.[59] On land, flogging continued until 1893, when it was abolished. However, numerous reports, some no doubt exaggerated, describe whipping in the Foreign Legion in the 1920s, particularly in the penal battalions.[60] Walter Kanitz, who served in the 1930s, claimed it had disappeared during his service.[61]

What is certain is that over time beating and flogging became less frequent. In their place, French commanders adopted several positional and restraint tortures, tortures that were painful, but left few marks.

Military Tortures

The most notorious tortures were the *crapaudine* and the *silo*. Little is known about the origins of these techniques. By the 1920s, when most soldiers described them, they were considered barbaric survivals of another age.

In 1881, a British intelligence officer described the *silo* as an official punishment used exclusively in the Discipline Companies of Algeria for serious offenses. On the military base, the *silo* was "a subterranean chamber having an iron firmly fixed horizontally close to the floor." Prisoners were handcuffed in front or behind the back with each leg bound to the bar with an iron ring. "Men secured in this way can lie on their backs or sit up, but are unable to assume any other position." In the field, guards planted the bar in the ground, and "the culprits are attached to it as mentioned above, a tent being pitched over them for shelter."[62] Prisoners were held in this position for hours.

It appears that the *silo* underwent various transformations as a field punishment after this date. In the 1920s, soldiers describe the *silo* as a form of forced squatting used in the Foreign Legion. The *silo* was a funnel-shaped hole dug in the ground, broad at the top and narrowing to a point at the bottom. "A man could neither stand or lie down in it, but must half crouch in his own excrement through the heat of the day and the cold of the night."[63] In the early twentieth century, General François de Negrier found fifteen silos, each occupied with a soldier, at the Legion outpost at Saida during a surprise inspection.[64] Negrier ordered the holes filled in. Evidently the practice continued unofficially sometime after it was officially forbidden.

The *crapaudine* was an official field punishment.[65] *Crapaud* means "the toad," though *à la crapaudine* means to cut open and broil. In this restraint torture, the prisoner is laid flat on his stomach. Torturers pull the arms and feet together behind the back till they touch. The body bends out like a bow. The prisoners' "joints locked, their muscles went into spasms."[66] "Hours after I had been untied, the pains continued across my shoulders and back and all the next day, lying in my grave, I was unable to move and I thought that I must be paralyzed for ever."[67]

The *crapaudine* was officially abolished by 1910.[68] In 1920, Jacques Londres publicly protested the practice, suggesting that officers favored *crapaudine* despite the regulations. And even after this date, the *crapaudine* persisted in penal battalions.[69]

Forced standing followed the *crapaudine* and *silo* around 1910. The soldier was tied to a gun wheel, a wagon wheel, tree, or constructed rack. The guards would tie the hands behind the back, drawing the elbows upwards, or alternatively the arms would be stretched out and pulled back slightly, "an exceedingly awkward position, after a short time." The soldier would be left in the condition for eight hours or more under the sun, occasionally splashed with water.[70]

This position was "innocent-sounding, but singularly fiendish."[71] It caused excruciating pain to the shoulders and arms, since they soon had to bear the whole weight of the body. As the body sinks forward, breathing becomes difficult. Victims can only relieve the pain by standing straight as long as possible. In effect, victims cycle between excruciating pain in the lower part of the body and crushing weight in the shoulders or chest.[72]

This, as a British observer recognized, was the British crucifixion: "Crucifixion did not mean his being nailed to a cross, but tied up to a wheel of a gun and left in the blazing sun for hours."[73] As with the British crucifixion, there were unofficial variants. One was to weigh down the neck with a heavy bag of wet sand until the chin rested on the breastbone, making it difficult to breathe.[74] In a "Grade Three Punishment," soldiers dug a narrow slotlike hole, just large enough for a man to put one foot into it, about twelve inches deep. They then put the prisoner's left foot inside the hole and filled it up. The prisoner was left in the sun with his hands bound. "Now, that doesn't sound very terrible, does it? Yet, after half-an-hour of it, I have heard men screaming and raving."[75]

Exhaustion exercises and forced lying followed in the 1920s. The pack drill (*la pelote*) involved forced marching with heavy equipment or wet sandbags around the neck.[76] Other exhaustion exercises involved moving heavy bags of wet sand (the English "shot drill"), marching perpetually in a circle (the *plute*), running over sharp stones, and alternatively running and crawling in full gear over long distances.[77] One soldier saw the sack drill and other exercises performed in conjunction with sleep deprivation.[78]

Forced lying involved lying immobile in a shallow sand grave or on sharp stones for days. In the sand grave, the soldier was usually bound hand and foot and left exposed.[79] In other instances, prisoners were left unbound, but guarded. "One lies still without the slightest movement. The guard sees to that, throwing stones at the instance of even the merest motion."[80] Sometimes, soldiers would be covered with a low pup tent as a concession to the sun.[81] These procedures had various names: *la tombe, la tombeau, la tombeaux, la tombre,* and the inoffensive sounding "tent torture."[82]

To these approved field punishments, one must add several unofficial tortures that appear in the 1920s. Some were copied from North African practice, most notably the *falaka* and burying soldiers in the sand up to the neck.[83] Others report being held in sweat rooms and dark holes, being forced to drink salt water, having salt rubbed into their wounds, and being choked with gun fat to the throat.[84] Still others describe being hung by the thumbs with the toes barely touching the ground or, conversely, by the feet with the head barely touching the ground.[85]

Police and Prison Tortures

In the 1840s, reports of torture in the French prison system focused on two restraint tortures, the *piton* and the *piquet*. The *piquet* "consists in tying two detainees face to face with their arms in a cross."[86] The *piton* was a wooden table leaned up against the wall, where the prisoner was "crucified by means of straps which keep his arms and legs spread out." Further, "By tightening or loosening the straps, one can more or less control the blood circulation of the victim." The limbs of prisoners turned blue and swelled monstrously, but "one does not prolong it until the victim asphyxiates."[87] While the *piquet* was "particularly cruel," the *piton* was "most frequent." It was particularly notorious at the prison at Loos.[88]

Newspapers reported other tortures as well, though the nature of some has been lost to modern memory.[89] The prison at Mont-Saint-Michel used the classic *brodequins*. Other prisons appeared to have used various sweatboxes, judging by the names: the *etouffoirs* (chokers) of Melun, the *column* at Nimes, the *cage* at Saint-Lazare, and the *clock box* at Rouen. At Nimes, guards also applied cangues or iron collars to prisoners or forced prisoners to wear large postillion boots weighted down with fifty pounds and carry heavy sacks of rocks until they were completely exhausted.[90]

In 1848, the French government banned arbitrary punishments in prisons, especially the *piton*, cangues, and handcuffs behind the back, but these practices persisted during the Second Empire (1851–71). In 1859, Marquis La Rochefoucauld-Liancourt identified a range of "French imitations, always so unhappy," of British and American prison techniques. They included whipping, dark cells, the iron collar (weighing eighty pounds), and unique boxes. "One has invented boxes in which one makes women enter, and of which the higher plank is opened to allow only the head to pass through; other boxes hold the feet and hands in such a way that they can make no movements, and this immobility is one of the harshest tortures one can feel."[91] The Marquis also describes the "cage" in Lausanne, Switzerland, "a wooden box in which the prisoner was made to squat for a long time." This box had angular bars (creating discomfort) and sharp wooden blades that pricked the prisoner if he leaned on them ("It is to be noted, though, that the blades did not actually draw blood, since they were made of wood").[92] In 1869, a French lawyer recorded the case of a female prisoner at Rennes confined in a box so small she had to breathe through a pipe in the ceiling.[93]

After 1871, with the founding of the Third Republic, these techniques gave way to exhaustion exercises in the disciplinary room. Here, prisoners were made to walk around for eight hours a day in the cold. In 1880, the French government forbade guards from using whips and sticks on prisoners. Punishment was limited to solitary confinement, hard labor, and the guillotine.[94] Other unofficial practices soon appeared. Most famous was the notorious *passage à tabac*, systematic beating that often left few marks. Typical procedures included slaps, blows to the kidneys "with a wet towel so no mark is left," and kneeling handcuffed and barelegged for hours on the spokes of a bicycle wheel, a practice "excessively painful, but [which] leaves little trace."[95] In the *bagnards*, exile prisons in New Caledonia (New Guinea), French Guiana, and Poulo Condor off the coast of Vietnam, guards turned to less famous procedures that left few marks.

In the disciplinary rooms of New Caledonia, torture included the *falaka*, the *crapaudine*, and the *coubaril*.[96] In the *falaka*, the application of blows follows the Chinese style: the prisoner was tied to a bench, his feet exposed outwards, and blows struck to the sole of his feet.[97] Prisoners also reported being suspended upside down from trees with their heads touching the ground. To exacerbate the situation, guards rested the prisoner's head on an anthill.[98]

The Caledonian *crapaudine* involved suspending the bowed body from a tree branch, forcing the arms and legs to carry the full weight of the body.[99] A period magazine illustrated on its cover the *crapaudine* without suspension.[100] "Thus attached, the prisoner must painfully drag himself each time he wants to make any kind of movement. If he wants to eat a bit of bread thrown at him, he pushes it with one of his shoulders up to the closest wall and, pressing the crumb against the wall, he turns around halfway and bites the bread, just like a lizard going after its prey."[101]

The *coubaril* was a box that forced prisoners to bend backward for long periods. The box had two parts, a lower part in which the prisoner sat with his legs stretched out in stocks at the end and a top part that "folded down on him and didn't allow him to actually sit upright."[102] Guards held prisoners in *coubarils* for as many as sixteen days. Some *coubarils* had multiple seats (between two and ten seats).

The *bagnards* of French Guiana favored hot rooms and the "bench of justice." The latter consisted of a three-inch-wide steel shelf along the side of the cage in which prisoners lived. Guards forced the prisoner to squat on the bench, thrust his arms backward between the cage bars, and manacled his wrists together. He was tied like this for up to three hours at a time. This position caused "excruciating pain on the muscles of the arms, hips and legs," crippling prisoners for days, though not permanently so.[103]

In North Africa, the *crapaudine*, the *tombeau*, and the *tombe* persisted in labor camps in the 1930s as well as POW camps in the 1940s. Authorities prohibited the *tombeau* in February 1943, but it persisted in Saharan labor camps.[104]

In Vietnam in the 1930s, the French Sûreté commonly used the *crapaudine* on prisoners. They increased the pain, by putting a foot to the ribs and bowing out the body farther. Blood rushes out the nose, mouth, ears and anus. Prisoners dubbed it, appropriately, the *lan mé ga*, "turning your guts inside out."[105] They knew why the Sûreté favored it: it was "particularly loved by torturers because it leaves no apparent traces."[106] Other techniques involved sleep deprivation, salted meals, and the *falaka*, all used to get "confessions without leaving marks."[107]

American Stress Tortures

American positional tortures drew on slave tortures and British field punishments. Police introduced their own unique innovations. Let me consider these in turn.

Slave Restraint Tortures

A former slave, John Brown, lists the common tortures of slaves: whipping, branding, cobbing, flopping with the flopping paddle, spiced washes following whipping, the picket, and bucking.[108] All of these, save bucking, are familiar British practices, deriving mainly from nautical practice. To this list, one can also add the standing handcuffs ("hanging from the rafters") and forced standing (crucifixion).[109] "Some tie them up in a very uneasy posture, where they must stand *all night*, and they will then work them hard all day."[110]

In the slave picket, masters suspended slaves by the wrists from a tall pole, yanking victims up by means of a pulley. The left foot was drawn up and tied to the right thigh, toes pointing downward. A sharpened stump was placed beneath the victim, and if he "desires to rest, he can do so only by placing the foot that is at liberty at the sharp end of the stake." If the victim rested his foot on the sharp point, a bystander would force the foot downwards, often perforating "the heel or sole of the foot till the bone."[111]

The positional torture with a notorious future was bucking, what will be called the "parrot's perch." In bucking, the victim sits with the knees bent. The victim's hands are tied and brought down over the knees until the chin rests on the knees. A thick stick is then slipped over the elbows and below crook of the knees. The victim is rendered utterly immobile and soon experiences powerful strains and muscle spasms.

Bucking allows for easy transportation of a prisoner. Romans used to carry Christians into the amphitheaters in this way.[112] This ancient procedure persisted in the Mediterranean region until the twentieth century. In the 1930s, the Yugoslavian police favored bucking in administering the *falaka*. "He pulled my handcuffed hands down between my knees and inserted under my knees and over my hands an iron bar. Then he rolled me over like a ball, so that I lay immobilized on my back with my legs in the air. Having got me in this position, he began to beat me on the soles of my feet with a belt."[113]

By this time, bucking was also a common practice throughout the Americas. In the early nineteenth century, the French painter Jean Debret drew a remarkable portrait of a Brazilian master beating a bucked slave, a picture that was endlessly reproduced in American antislavery pamphlets.[114] Debret pictures what John Brown describes: the bucked slave "was turned first on one side then on the other, and flogged with willow switches and the cowhide, until the blood ran down in streams."[115] American drawings of bucking, however, show slaves being cobbed rather than whipped.[116]

Bucking was a standard military punishment in the United States in the 1850s.[117] In New York, Sing Sing Prison also practiced bucking around 1860. Guards practiced the true parrot's perch, suspending the pole with the prisoner's head swinging downward.[118]

Military Tortures

Some British military practices also appeared in American military contexts, including Cobbing and the Picket.[119] American forces also adopted the Wooden Horse. The English and the Dutch had practiced the Wooden Horse in the Americas. There was a public Wooden Horse set up in downtown New York, "a straight, narrow, horizontal pole, standing twelve feet high" with its upper edge sharpened "to intensify cruelty."[120] In September 1776, Paul Revere ordered two soldiers in the Continental army to be subjected to the Wooden Horse for playing cards on the Sabbath. They "rode the Wooden Horse for a quarter of an hour with a musket on each foot."[121] In drawing up the Articles of War, John Adams prescribed wooden collars, badges, and limited flogging.[122]

Nevertheless, born out of a war against the British, Americans were critical of some European military traditions such as keelhauling, flogging, and the Wooden Horse ("the Sawbuck"). By the 1840s, public and congressional sentiment turned against whipping in particular. The government abolished flogging in the navy by 1850 and in the army in 1861. Like the British and the French, the American military drew on old punishments and invented new ones.

Naval officers adopted gagging (from British practice); bucking (from slavers); straitjackets and showering (new correctional trends of the period) and sweatboxes (from Oriental practice).[123] Infantry officers practiced bucking and the standing thumb-cuffs, while two fixed object punishments, "the spread eagle" and "the rack," appeared in the artillery.[124] The American spread eagle involved tying the soldier to the spare wagon wheel and giving it a quarter turn so the victim hung by a foot and a wrist. In the "rack," the man was tied on his back over the wooden box at the rear of a wagon. His wrists were tied to the upper rims of the wheels and his feet to the lower, so his extremities were stretched over the edges of the box.

Then there were sweatboxes and choke boxes. During the Civil War, the military sweatbox was a cell near a very hot stove in which guards burned old boots and bones, producing intense smoke and heat.[125] And for alcohol-related offenses, the army used the old practice of the "drunkard's cloak" or "barrel shirt." Soldiers would cut a hole in a barrel for heads and hands, and force the prisoner to wear it for a prolonged period of time in public.[126]

In 1872, new regulations outlawed branding (e.g., D for Deserter), tattooing, sweatboxes, and excessive solitary confinement.[127] Exhaustion exercises soon became the substitute punishment. In 1881, the British War Office survey of field punishments described American punishments as varying with "the customs of the service." Thus the soldier, if convicted, was forced "to carry a loaded knapsack for a certain time" (pack drill), "stand on a barrel," or "suffer any other ignominy which would naturally result in a degree of bodily pain or fatigue, provided the same were not excessive and physically injurious."[128] Some soldiers were subjected to "the Log," forced standing while holding a log on one's shoulder.[129] At the Naval Academy, midshipmen were forced to do small arms drills late at night, marched in their underwear in freezing weather, and forced to stand at attention until a predetermined number had collapsed from exhaustion.[130]

Some nineteenth-century military punishments reappear in military prisons during World War I, along with several new ones. The harshest punishments appear to have fallen on those conscientious objectors who refused to serve even in noncombat roles. These men were typically sentenced to military prisons for desertion, insubordination, or making disloyal statements. For these men, the standard prescribed military punishment was the standing handcuffs.

Prisoners were handcuffed to their cell door eight to nine hours a day, in one case up to fifty days.[131] Those who spoke in solitary had their hands cuffed high above their heads with their back to the iron bars for the same number of hours, a technique American troops in Iraq today call "high cuffing."[132] Prisoners described high cuffing as excruciatingly painful, and even the general public, otherwise unsympathetic with these prisoners, found the practice appalling. The practice ceased almost immediately after World War I.[133]

Additionally, prisoners reported that enlisted men, with the tacit collusion of officers, tortured them in ways that are familiar from reports today. Soldiers beat and bayoneted them, dragged them like animals with a rope around the neck, chilled them in ice-cold baths or showers until they fainted, scrubbed them with lye or with hard brushes until the flesh was raw, beat them with high-pressure fire hoses, forced them to stand at attention for hours in great heat or cold, made them perform exhaustion exercises, beat them about the face until their eardrums burst, pressed their eyeballs, dunked them headfirst into latrines, held them for long periods in black holes and narrow cells in which they had to stand for hours, put them "to bed" under a mountain of blankets, hung them to the ceiling by the thumbs or in other ways, and, most frequently, subjected them to various "water cures," forms of pumping or choking first used by the military during the Spanish-American War.[134] Standard exhaustion exercises included forced running, "holding a spoon at arm's length for several minutes, waddling around the room in full squat position, standing on one foot for one hour with the other foot tied to the hip, transferring water by spoon from one bucket to another."[135]

Police and Prison Tortures

Shortly after the Civil War, a survey of prisons and reformatories in North America found prisons commonly used whips and dark cells. However, northeastern American prisons used other tortures, notably, bucking, showers, and the yoke, the "outrages of the inquisition and the inhumanities of the slave pen."[136]

Sing Sing officials, for example, experimented in this period with alternatives to whipping. Techniques came and went, including bucking, cobbing, gagging, the ball and chain, the iron hat, the iron jacket, and the yoke or crucifix. The latter two were positional torture devices drawing on Chinese cangues. Yokes were long iron bars, four inches wide, the heaviest being forty pounds, with staples for the neck and arms. The prisoner's arms were stretched along the bar's length. Even a short stint on a yoke could leave one immobilized for weeks. Like the barrel shirt, the iron jacket was "a bulky device fixed around the neck and worn by the inmate day and night."[137]

Other northeastern prisons used similar devices. Vermont prisons favored iron jackets.[138] Eastern State Penitentiary in Pennsylvania favored the iron gag. Here, the arms were drawn high behind the back and fastened to the iron gag. Relieving pressure to the arms forced the gag farther in the mouth, while pushing the gag out strained the arms.[139]

In the 1920s, some prisons abandoned the whip for the Wooden Horse, now called "riding the mule." A prisoner spent five to six hours "riding a narrow sharpened ridge pole," unable to move "or ease his position."[140] Southern prisons favored the whip, but some county wardens also handcuffed the hands and feet of prisoners "in an elevated position above their heads, while they are compelled to stand in an upright position."[141] In the 1920s, "female ward sweat boxes" were "boxes just large enough for a person of normal size to be confined" and "contained chains for the purpose of preventing prisoners incarcerated therein from assuming a squatting position." They were what later came to be called in Nazi Germany *Stehzelle*, or standing cells.[142] In Gainesville, Texas, the standing cell was in the dining room so that the prisoner could smell the food.[143]

California prisons routinized the cloth straitjacket in the late nineteenth century. In 1884, Folsom Penitentiary used "a coffin-shaped piece of canvas about four feet long, with brass eyelets down each side and internal pockets for the prisoner's hands."[144] The canvas was pulled tightly together, a process dubbed "cinching" by the prisoners.[145] In 1912, a prisoner described what it was like to be drawn up inside the "San Quentin Overcoat."[146]

> After they put me into the jacket they played tug of war with me. The rope broke and they got another. They lifted me off the floor and let me fall several times. This was to knock the wind out of me and to use my natural weight to tighten the jacket. The pain begins in five or ten minutes. It's a suffering of the kidneys. It seems as if someone is crushing them in his hands, or as if they were jumping and trying to get away from you. You[r] hands begin to feel twice their size. The hands and arms all go dead, then come to life with sharp, keen pains. You have sharp pains in your stomach, very sharp pains.[147]

In 1937, the chief warden at San Quentin practiced "the spot." He drew a circle of gray paint, two feet in diameter, in which offenders had to stand immobile for four hours, twice a day.[148]

These practices soon appeared in the course of interrogation, especially forced standing.[149] Clean beating included slapping, whipping with hoses, and beating with sandbags and telephone books. Police made prisoners perform exhaustion exercises. They used dark holes and coffin-shaped sweatboxes leaned against stoves. They also cinched straitjackets. "It leaves no marks and the police can always argue that the prisoner became so unruly that he had to be restrained. Also the average person does not regard the jacket as a means of inflicting pain."[150]

New American positional devices also appeared during this period (1860–1940). In July 1866, J. C. Gardner, the warden of the Oregon State Penitentiary, patented the infamous Gardner Shackle (later called the Oregon boot).[151] This device consisted of a heavy iron band (five to twenty-eight pounds) that locked around one ankle with an iron ring and braces that attached to the heel of the boot. This device kept the wearer off balance and deprived him of agility, preventing him from climbing over the prison walls easily. Wearing the shackle for extended periods of time caused extreme physical damage, and inmates were bedridden for weeks at a time in extreme pain. Oregon prisoners referred to the device as a "man killer" and described the process of wearing it as being "ironed out." By 1878, Oregon prison officials limited the use of the shackle for punishment and transportation. The device apparently underwent some modifications afterward. In 1931, the Wickersham Commission described the Oregon boot as an "iron frame, which does not touch the foot while it is at rest, but which if a man tries to run or walk away or suddenly jump will have a tendency to restrain him."[152] The last recorded case of a prisoner being ironed out was in 1939 in Mill City, Oregon, for purposes of transportation to Oregon State Penitentiary.

Then there were handcuffs. All modern handcuffs are based on the "Peerless" pattern (1912) that "flick" onto a prisoner's wrists. The Peerless pattern had ratchet teeth that allowed one to adjust it to the size of the wrist.[153] If the handcuff was not double locked, the ratchet teeth could move. By the early twentieth century, many prisoners describe being bound in handcuffs that tightened if they struggled or moved. They were often described as "American" handcuffs (and sometimes "German" or "Italian" handcuffs).

Authoritarian Adaptations

Positional tortures were not common beyond the United States, Britain, France, and their colonies in the nineteenth century. Most autocracies beat and flogged their prisoners and soldiers. Some Asian societies, including India, China, and Japan, practiced traditional, and often mutilating, restraint tortures. And even these became far less common by the early twentieth century, in some cases disappearing entirely.

This pattern does not change appreciably in the early twentieth century. In Europe, for example, authoritarian police continued to beat and whip their prisoners.[154] They preferred full suspension, pulling up prisoners with hooks and pulleys. Full suspension allowed one to whip, burn, and beat the prisoner on both sides as well as strain the wrists by spinning the body.

Authoritarian states first turn to the lesser tradition in stress tortures in the 1930s. For two reasons, it would be a mistake to regard these tortures as examples of how authoritarian states also used stealthy regimens. First, these were not the most common techniques. Whipping and beating with truncheons remained more common than positional tortures. Full suspension, with all its damaging consequences, was far more common than partial suspension. And these tortures paled in comparison to the violence that awaited prisoners later. Second, authoritarian usage tended to push positional tortures in a more sanguinary direction, supplementing these techniques in ways that left scars. Generally speaking, one must conclude that authoritarian states used these techniques not because they were clean, but because they were painful.

Japan. Like India and China, Tokugawa Japan had an ancient history of restraint tortures. The three most common were "Hugging the Stone," the "Lobster," and "Suspension." These restraint tortures, along with flogging, were practiced successively on prisoners, usually with intervals of a few days, until prisoners confessed.

In Suspension, torturers hung a prisoner from a beam with the wrists "tightly bound together behind his back with green hemp rope, which gradually cut into the flesh." The Lobster involved tying the arms and legs tightly for three or four hours "until the body became wan and pallid and gave signs of the approach of death." Hugging the Stone required a prisoner to kneel on a platform of three-cornered stones, his arms tightly braced by ropes, and then heavy slabs were gradually piled on his knees.[155]

In the 1920s, Japanese police practiced full suspension, but not the Lobster or Hugging the Stone. By the 1930s, Japanese military police flogged, beat, burned, pierced, shattered, and electrified victims.[156] Leaving the prisoner scarred did not matter.

Japanese torturers also used some techniques that left few marks. These included sweatboxes, finger bandaging, standing handcuffs, pumping, choking, and repeated slapping. The context suggests that torturers chose these techniques because they were customary or regarded them as painful. No available source suggests they favored them because they were stealthy procedures.

Japanese torturers also practiced positional tortures. In general, they favored forced kneeling over forced standing or sitting. As in Hugging the Stone, this positional torture was often done on a surface covered with sharp objects; sometimes the victim held heavy objects. This position also permitted the practice of the ankle spread, placing a board on the ankles and applying pressure until the ankles are disjoined. In some regions, exhaustion exercises were common, in particular, crawling on one's stomach ("the lizard").

Russia. Czarist police and the revolutionary cheka preferred whipping and beating, if not more mutilating tortures. Likewise, most Stalinist torture was not subtle; beatings often crippled victims for life. For a far smaller group selected to confess before public show trials, the NKVD developed a stealthy interrogation style, drawing on sweating procedures and other tortures well known to American and European police in the early twentieth century. One central element of this Soviet regimen in torture was standing and sitting for days.[157]

Spain. In 1938, the Republican secret police, the SIM, adopted the Soviet regimen to extract false confessions, including prolonged forced standing and sitting. It soon supplemented sweating with beatings with iron bars, flogging, burning, choking in water, and electrotorture. This pattern, in which Soviet positional tortures and sweating gave way to mutilating tortures, is one that will recur in other Communist societies after World War II.

Nazi Germany. The Nazis consistently favored flogging and beating throughout Europe.[158] Beyond this, Nazi torture varied, reflecting the fact that the Nazis often hired local auxiliaries who brought their own customary practices.

Sometimes, Nazis or their auxiliaries did draw on the lesser traditions in positional tortures. They forced prisoners to stand at attention or kneel for long hours, sometimes on sharp objects (Germany) and often holding heavy items (Germany, Norway, Belgium, the Netherlands, and the camps). Polish prisoners report the standing handcuffs, a position they called the *slupik*, or pillar. Concentration camp guards applied the reverse standing handcuffs, a practice called "the stake." The prisoner's arms "were bent behind him and he was suspended by the wrists just above the ground."[159]

Nazi torturers also used sweatboxes in Norway, Belgium, Greece, and the camps, including standing cells, or *Stehzelle*. The German cells were three by three feet at the base, with doors at the bottom. Prisoners were squeezed and had to stand until guards pulled them out by the feet.

Guards also forced prisoners to perform many different exhaustion exercises. These included the Bear Dance and the plank (Germany, 1933–35); *couché-debout* (Belgium, the camps); endless knee bends (Germany, Austria, Czechoslovakia, Norway, and Greece); the Lizard (Germany, 1935–39); endless push-ups (Czechoslovakia), squats and hopping squats (Poland), and march and run, what was sometimes called the "promenade" (Norway, Belgium, Yugoslavia, and the camps). Gestapo interrogators used exhaustion exercises for purposes of interrogation sometimes, but, in the context of camps, exhaustion exercises were also used to weed out the weak; they were part of the process of genocide.

Brazil. In stark contrast to the later twentieth century, there is little evidence of positional torture in Latin America in the early twentieth century. Most Latin American police beat, flogged, burned, pierced, and choked.[160] Vargas's police was no exception.[161]

In 1943, under the tutelage of American and British advisers, Brazilian police adopted "third degree" techniques to interrogate German spies. This procedure included forced standing and sleep deprivation for two or three days, sometimes before bright lights.[162] The turn to positional torture was portentous, for such procedures would become more common in the late twentieth century.

Remembering the Eighteenth Century

In 1976, *Time* magazine published drawings of major modern tortures.[163] One showed "the horseman," a man with his arms tied behind his back, straddling a long, narrow, horizontal bar suspended in the air. Another depicted a man forced to stand with his arms extended, holding weights. A third showed a bound man with a stick passed under his knees and over his forearms, hanging upside down. Yet another showed someone applying pressure to a prisoner's abdomen.

The first was an unofficial eighteenth-century British and French military punishment, the second was a nineteenth-century British field punishment, the third was an ancient slave punishment in the Americas, and the last was a police procedure well known to American and European police in the early twentieth century (as I will document in chapter 16, "Fists and Exercises"). They were, respectively, the Wooden Horse, the crucifixion, bucking, and the belly slap.

This chapter captured why different agents developed these procedures in democratic societies. Slave dealers wanted to make a sale. They did not want to damage the merchandise or leave scars that might indicate to potential buyers that the prisoner was a disciplinary problem. They chose clean techniques to avoid the scrutiny of potential buyers. Military and civilian prison officials were looking for alternatives to whipping as the public in France, Britain, and the United States became increasingly uneasy with flogging. The techniques they chose also left few marks, and not a few were borrowed from the abolished practice of slavery. What was important in these cases was that those at a distance could not judge how much pain was involved. It was only when public scandals, usually reports of inadvertent deaths, made evident what was truly involved that officials abandoned these techniques, at least officially.

By the end of the nineteenth century, Britain, France, and the United States had abolished most of these legal punishments. Sadly but inevitably, they survived and persisted among police and military of democratic states long after their usage was no longer legally permitted. It is, of course, often hard to date when the legal usage stopped and the illegal usage began, but the persistence is unquestionable. Police and military favored these clean tortures because they helped them evade detection by external monitors. This is a pattern I continue to document in the subsequent chapters.

All this casts a new light on the article in *Time* in 1976. *Time* named the tortures it depicted in Spanish and Portuguese, and it suggested that *authoritarian* states had invented *new* tortures. In fact, the article marks the moment when some authoritarian states adopted several *old* stress tortures of *democratic* societies. That has largely been forgotten. In 2004, a human rights monitor described the history of the techniques at Abu Ghraib like this: "Stress and duress interrogation techniques were invented in the dungeons of the world's most brutal regimes for only one purpose — to cause pain, distress, and humiliation without physical scars."[164]

On the contrary, most techniques that appeared at Abu Ghraib had appeared first in American prisons and plantations, British ships and bases, and French prisons and penal camps in the colonies. Authoritarian states in the early twentieth century had no prior familiarity with these techniques, and their penal codes rarely authorized such procedures. Their torturers occasionally adopted a few procedures, but they preferred flogging, beating, and mutilating tortures. Leaving no physical scars was not their pressing concern.

Using stress tortures as part of stealthy regimens became more common in authoritarian states only after World War II, and that is what *Time* and the world remember. But we forget how earlier democratic states had already showcased what could be done with stress and duress techniques, and how torturers in later authoritarian states had simply imitated them. Thus, clean stress techniques, once legitimate in democratic states in previous centuries, cast a long shadow over the twentieth century. Democratic states may have long abolished the legal use of these techniques, but this does not alter the fact that they were leaders in adapting and innovating clean "stress and duress" techniques that are now ubiquitous in stealthy torture. Documenting this transition in the late twentieth century is the task of the next three chapters.

I stand for 8–10 hours a day. Why is standing limited to 4 hours?

— Donald Rumsfeld, U.S. secretary of defense, comment

on memorandum authorizing stress positions

for Guantánamo internees, April 2003[1]

15   Forced Standing and Other Positions

In this chapter, I follow one major component of "stress and duress" techniques through the late twentieth century. Positional tortures require prisoners to assume normal human positions, but for abnormal periods of time. These positions include standing, sitting, kneeling, squatting, bowing, and lying. Some prisoners hold these positions voluntarily, fearing the consequences of disobedience. Others are bound in place. These tortures resemble restraint tortures, but restraint tortures differ in that the positions in which one is tied are not normal ones for human beings (suspension, for example).

Humans are not designed to stand utterly immobile, and even short periods of forced standing can be painful. Consider, for example, this report from a prisoner of the Gestapo in Hamburg in 1933–34. "Put the tips of your toes and the tip of your nose against the wall with your hands shackled behind your back, and stand straight. After you stand so for an hour your eyes bulge out of their caves and you feel as if huge rocks are pressing in on you from both sides."[2] Or this report from a volunteer in the French Foreign Legion in the 1920s describing what happens to men who have one foot fixed permanently to the ground and are forced to stand. "Now, that doesn't sound very terrible, does it? Yet, after half-an-hour of it, I have heard men screaming and raving."[3] Secretary Rumsfeld is fortunate he is not obliged to stand immobile. Swiftly, moving becomes painful, and soon the ankles and feet swell to twice their size, and large blisters appear within twenty-four hours. This, probably combined with dehydration, causes the kidneys to fail.[4]

In this chapter, I note the agents, locations, and date, to the extent possible, of various positional tortures. Unfortunately, positional tortures are hard to map.

They rarely involve specific technology (like electricity) or material (like water). Prisoners' accounts do not always highlight them. There may well be more cases than mentioned here. My goal is simply to map known trends and evaluate claims made about how positional tortures spread.

As I argued in part III, the dominant style in stealth torture today is French modern, that is, the combination of electrotorture and water torture, more recently supplemented with *falaka*, clean whipping, gas masks, and plastic bags. Few states today have favored "stress and duress" techniques over the dominant style. Those that have were either democratic states or states under international scrutiny, or both.

Old Users after the War

Positional torture continued among countries that practiced positional torture during and after World War II. Interrogators practiced positional tortures either at the margins of colonial systems (France, the United Kingdom) or as a domestic police practice (Japan, the Soviet Union, East Germany). Some countries resumed positional torture after a hiatus of two decades (Brazil, Spain) or more (the United States).

German and Japanese officers continued positional tortures in concentration camps until the war was lost and the camps disbanded. Prisoners in the United States, whether POWs or civilians, did not report positional tortures; if the practice existed, it was rare. In Morocco, the Free French practiced the *tombeau* "virtually under the shadow of the American flag," according to an American investigator in February 1943.[5]

The French camps imprisoned remnants of the old Foreign Legion and thousands of central European Jews and Spanish Republicans. The French used them as laborers to build a trans-Saharan railroad. A Jewish concentration camp survivor and Foreign Legion veteran described the model punishment as "the 'tomb,' which consisted in placing the victim in a kind of tomb dug by himself." Prisoners were "forced to stay in a horizontal position" for several days, guarded by an armed Moroccan or Senegalese sentry.[6] In 1942, an American Office of Strategic Services officer investigating one French camp reported that there were "two rows of such tombs, one meter apart."[7]

In 1943, French authorities prohibited the *tombeau* in labor camps (once again, for it had been abolished before the war as well).[8] The *tombeau* nevertheless persisted into the 1950s. Between 1952 and 1953, protests were lodged at the United Nations, and the practice was once again abolished.[9] At least one report from 1959 suggests that it persisted well into the Algerian war.[10]

French soldiers also adopted forced standing. In the first reported case in 1956, a prisoner describes how French soldiers made her stand for twelve hours with a hood over her head. Over the next four years, prisoners report being forced to kneel holding a chair, squat for hours inside a box, or stand for up to twenty-four hours, sometimes on one leg, or with one's hands in the air.[11]

Soviet interrogators used forced standing on Axis POWs throughout the war. "Physical torture to persuade German prisoners to join was not standard practice, but beatings, forced standing in the snow or cold, implied threat or execution were not that uncommon either."[12] After the war, interrogators used the Stalinist Conveyor system (positional tortures and sweating techniques) well into the 1950s.

The British had practiced forced standing as a military field punishment since 1907. Regulations for field punishments in 1949 indicate that British officers continued fixed object punishment after World War II. These regulations specify that a prisoner could be held in fetters or handcuffs and secured to an object "to prevent his escape." The duration could not exceed three months or, in the case of a commanding officer, twenty-eight days. Irons were recommended, but straps and ropes were permitted. Above all, "Every portion of a field punishment shall be inflicted in such a manner as is calculated not to cause injury or to leave any permanent mark on the offender."[13]

The technique, however, was not limited to British servicemen. Prisoners in Mandatory Palestine also reported being subjected to it in the 1930s. Between July 1940 and September 1948, British interrogators used forced standing as part of a brutal regimen to coerce German POWs to make statements about war crimes. Over thirty-five hundred German POWs went through a clandestine military prison in London, and one thousand made statements, which in some cases was the only evidence against them.

Recently revealed documents outline the techniques commonly used at the London office of the Combined Services Detailed Interrogation Centre, otherwise known as the "London Cage."[14] Prisoners were forced to stand at attention for up to twenty-six hours, forced to kneel as they were beaten about the head, deprived of sleep and food, exposed to extremes of heat and cold including cold-water showers, subjected to mock executions, and threatened with unnecessary operations and electrical devices.

In 1946, Capt. Fritz Knoechlein, as SS officer, submitted a written complaint stating that as he refused to confess, he was stripped of most clothes (in October), deprived of sleep for four days, starved, forced to perform rigorous exercises until he collapsed, forced to march in a tight circle for four hours, doused with cold water, beaten with a cudgel, forced to stand beside a large gas stove with all its rings lit, then confined in a shower that sprayed extremely cold water from the sides, as well as above, and then forced to run in circles while carrying heavy logs. Since some of these tortures followed his complaint, he heeded the guards' advice not to complain again. One may be skeptical of Knoechlein's complaints, as he was sentenced to death at the time, but his accounts do not differ substantively from those of other prisoners.

It is difficult to determine whether the British government endorsed these procedures. Lt. Col. Alexander Scotland supervised the Cage. Scotland had received an Order of the British Empire for his interrogation of German prisoners in World War I, and MI19, the department of the War Office responsible for gathering information from POWs, assigned Scotland to run the Cage. Scotland refused Red Cross inspections, arguing that his prisoners were either civilians or criminals within the armed forces, and so not protected by the Geneva Convention. An MI5 investigation concluded otherwise, noting that Scotland had repeatedly violated the Geneva Convention when he subjected prisoners to, among other things, forced standing. Scotland was never charged, and information pointing to war crimes in his memoirs was suppressed. Scotland may not have had the clear approval of MI19, but it is certain his superiors knew of the allegations of torture and then quietly overlooked events at the Cage.

In 1956, during the Cyprus emergency, British police units received copies of the 1949 regulations on fixed object punishment.[15] About the same time, there were accusations of similar procedures being applied to civilian prisoners. In January 1956, for example, an Athens newspaper charged that British police forced EOKA (Ethniki Organosis Kyprion Agoniston, or National Organization of Cypriot Fighters) prisoners in Cyprus "to stand on nails or on ice."[16] Forced standing then appeared in 1965 in Aden, where British troops made prisoners stand naked throughout interrogations. Prisoners also reported guards "forcing them to sit on poles 'directed towards' their anus."[17] But a military report of the Aden scandal did not even consider forced standing as abuse, focusing entirely on other allegations.[18]

What was a custom of the service (as the British expression goes) in the Middle East, though, was torture to the British in Korea. During the Korean War, British POWs had no difficulty describing their treatment as torture. After the war, the Joint Services Intelligence School at Maresfield began subjecting soldiers, particularly pilots, to known Soviet techniques, training them to resist the effects of these procedures.[19] This training is now known as "R21 techniques" or "resistance to interrogation."[20] Army Intelligence in turn trained Royal Ulster Constabulary (RUC) interrogators in Northern Ireland in the early 1970s, though it did not supervise actual interrogations.[21] The RUC used several positional tortures on numerous prisoners in Northern Ireland throughout the 1970s. These included forced sitting, forced squatting, and standing with hands raised.[22] In the late 1970s, RUC guards enforced the "imaginary chair" in which the prisoner has "to squat with his back to the wall for an hour" as if he was sitting in a chair.[23]

In 1946, a senior Japanese police official explained that humane treatment of suspects was among "luxuries which we [Japanese] cannot afford," and that sometimes police officials had to solve crimes "by methods that perhaps are not considered humane."[24] In 1947, an American intelligence researcher reported, "The Japanese police are still using third degree methods to extort confessions from people whom they believe guilty."[25]

What these methods were was unclear until an important study by the Japanese Federation of Bar Associations in the mid-1980s of one hundred cases, some going back to the early 1970s. This, and subsequent studies, revealed that Japanese police used a painful, but stealthy regimen of positional tortures, exhaustion exercises, and restraints for purposes of interrogation and intimidation. Prisoners reported forced immobility in several positions, including standing, sitting, squatting on the heels, but most commonly the customary kneeling position, or *seiza*.[26] Prison rules at Fuchu prison specified, "Do not on your own accord lie down in the cell. Moreover, do not lean against or sit on the bedding."[27]

Spanish Republicans used forced standing in the late 1930s, but accounts do not mention this practice under the Franco regime in the 1950s. In 1968, prisoners reported being forced to stand or kneel, and the practice becomes common the 1970s.[28] In the standing position, prisoners held their arms out horizontally, supporting heavy objects. In the kneeling position, prisoners rested on fine gravel stones or steel ball bearings or they were forced to hold heavy objects like telephone books.[29] Prisoners have continued to report forced immobility positions until the present, including standing (sometimes on tiptoes or with arms raised), prolonged standing with bent knees, and kneeling on a bar.[30]

In 1942, American and British advisers instructed Brazilian police in forced standing, but other incidents are not reported until 1966. After this date, prisoners report being made to stand for hours before bright lights (*sabão em pó*).[31] By 1970, guards made prisoners stand on tiptoe with four telephone books in each hand (nicknamed "Christ the Redeemer").[32] They also made prisoners stand on top of cans with bare feet, in which position they would beat them and burn them with cigarettes. They attached electric wires to prisoners. They applied electroshock if victims began to collapse in exhaustion. The jolts of electricity made the hooded victims' feet stick to the cans, contracted their muscles, and so forced them to stand up straight. "To all this the authorities gave the name of Viet Nam."[33]

When American interrogators turned to torture in the late twentieth century, their preferred style was French modern. American positional torture first reappeared domestically in the context of prisons, particularly prisons that primarily held non-American detainees for immigration violations. Edward Calejo, a prison guard in Miami's Krome Detention Center, described how he treated detainees in the early 1990s. "I mean, we make guys stand in line — they just stand there, just to stand there. 'Don't move,' you know. And we'd make them stand there all day long."[34] In addition to forced standing, Calejo described a regimen at Krome that included slapping, beating, pointless exercises, and humiliation.[35] In 1998, inmates at Florida's Jackson County Jail described a large concrete slab to which individuals were tied in a crucifix position. The slab had iron rings in the corners and leather straps for the arms and legs. As one prisoner stated, "Concrete. Cold, cold, cold. And they'll cut the AC up high, high, high, and you'll be butt-naked. . . . You're on your belly. . . . And when time to eat, they loose one hand. So you eat, and they strap you back. It's torture, man."[36] Other prisoners describe how guards shocked them with stun guns and electric shields while they were in this position.[37]

In the mid-1990s, American prisons adopted restraint chairs. These chairs tilt backward like lounge chairs, but have restraints for the wrists and ankles. "Shackle boards" or "restraint beds" also use four point restraints, but they are used mainly in Virginia prisons.[38] Prisoners report being strapped into restraint chairs as punishment or to incapacitate them while being tortured in some other manner. In August 1999, a judge ruled in a Tennessee case that confessions extracted while suspects are strapped in restraint chairs are invalid. In November 1999, a judge in Ventura County, California, issued a preliminary injunction banning their use in the county jail after a lawsuit alleged widespread abuse.[39]

In military interrogation, positional torture first occurs in Afghanistan. In December 2002, prisoners at Bagram airbase reported that interrogators kept them "standing or kneeling for hours."[40] Subsequent reports documented forced lying (Afghanistan), forced sitting, sometimes using padded restraint chairs (Guantánamo, Cuba), and forced standing or kneeling (Iraq).[41]

Positional torture in Abu Ghraib prison in Iraq involved the greatest variations.[42] It included forcing prisoners to hold boxes and balance themselves on MRE (Meals Ready to Eat) boxes with arms extended. One military policeman (MP) attached wires to the fingers of hooded prisoners, warning them that they would receive electroshock if they ceased to stand. Prisoners were also handcuffed to rails, bunks, or doors of their cell and forced to stand or lie for long periods.

Agents in these cases were MPs, allegedly directed by military intelligence or Special Forces units. In addition, two MPs "were put in charge because they were civilian prison guards and had knowledge of how things were supposed to run." Staff Sergeant Frederick, the group leader, had worked six years for the Virginia Department of Corrections.[43]

Positional Tortures in the Communist World

In the 1950s, Soviet advisers taught positional tortures to interrogators in other Communist states. If ideology shapes the distribution and transmission of torture techniques (the ideology hypothesis), one would expect to see great continuity in tortures in Communist states, with a pronounced preference for positional tortures. After all, interrogators shared not only ideological beliefs, but also common training from the leading Communist state. But this is not what occurred. Almost everywhere in the Communist world, positional tortures started disappearing by the 1960s. By the 1980s, if the practice of positional torture existed at all, it was a minor part of a far more horrific regimen. Here again, the evidence does not support the ideology hypothesis and suggests other factors were at work.

To be specific, there is no question that the Stalinist Conveyor system appeared in many Communist states following World War II. In the 1950s prisoners reported positional torture in Hungary (forced standing and sitting), East Germany (sitting), Bulgaria (standing), and Romania (standing on one foot, forced lying).[44] Such practices probably occurred elsewhere in Eastern Europe in this period.

Chinese interrogators forced prisoners to stand, wrapping gauze around the feet that caused increasing pain as the feet swelled from prolonged standing.[45] During the Cultural Revolution, prisoners were forced to bow forward with arms extended for prolonged periods, a painful groveling posture known as the "airplane."[46] Later prisoners report various coerced postures including standing, kneeling, lying on a shackle board (*di lao*, "tiger bed"), or sitting (sometimes on a low stool), standing on one foot, leaning against walls, or strapped to the floor with arms outstretched.[47]

In North Korea, American and British POWs reported forced standing holding a rock over one's head, standing at attention for hours in freezing weather, or standing in water-soaked holes.[48]

The North Vietnamese had adopted Soviet confessional techniques in the late 1940s, but prisoners do not report forced standing until 1965. In this year, American POWs report forced kneeling with hands in the air or, less frequently, sitting or standing.[49] Guards would sometimes place objects (pebbles or sticks) under the knees. One POW observed, "kneeling torture" was similar to "driving a long nail under the kneecap." The knees swelled to the size of a large grapefruit. "The sensitive human knee when in contact with rough, bare concrete for a longer period of time, generates great pain. . . . If you have any doubts about this, try kneeling on a broomstick with your hands in the air for 15 or 20 minutes."[50] After the war, guards in prison camps occasionally applied forced standing.[51]

In the late 1970s, Cambodian torturers took a different approach. Before the revolution, Cambodians greeted each other by pressing palms together (*sompeah*). When recognizing those of higher status (royalty, Buddhist monks, or an image of the Buddha), Cambodians raised the joined palms above the head and, sometimes, prostrated themselves (*thvay bongkum*, or paying homage). At Tuol Sleng interrogation center, this honorary gesture was rendered into a positional torture dubbed "paying homage to the wall," "to the chair," "to the table," or "to the image of dogs" or sometimes called *sompeah*. Holding this position for long periods was "enough in most cases to induce a full confession."[52]

In the Middle East, Syrian and Iraqi interrogators forced prisoners to stand on one leg for prolonged periods, sometimes with their hands in the air.[53] In Soviet-occupied Afghanistan, torturers forced prisoners to stand for long periods in snow or water.[54]

The preceding evidence may suggest that Communist states fully embraced the Stalinist style of positional tortures and sweating techniques, and so are evidence in favor of the ideology hypothesis. But this spread of positional tortures needs to be kept in perspective. In Romania, Bulgaria, Poland, Yugoslavia, and Albania, flogging and beating were far more common than positional tortures.[55] Afghani, Syrian, and Iraqi torturers beat, whipped, and shocked prisoners; burned and boiled their flesh; mutilated them with knives; crushed bones in presses; roasted victims on spits; or impaled prisoners in the anus with skewers.[56] Soviet allies in Africa (Ethiopia, Somalia, Angola, Mozambique) did not use positional tortures at all, choosing far more sanguinary techniques.[57]

The North Vietnamese preferred excruciating rope tortures that popped out the shoulder joints and "hell cuffs" that tightened until they cut to the bone, practices that continued after the war, while Cubans beat and disfigured prisoners and Cuban advisers in Vietnam used scarring flogging and water torture on American POWs.[58] In Cambodia, torture was a prelude to genocide. Tuol Sleng torturers applied beatings, full suspension, electrotorture, water torture, and mutilation with knives and sharp-edged presses.[59]

Between 1950 and 1980, Chinese torturers used rope tortures, fetters, tightening handcuffs, finger bandaging, and coffinlike wooden cupboards for sweatboxes.[60] By the 1980s, the Chinese turned to electrotorture, full suspension, standing handcuffs, reverse standing handcuffs, and restraint tortures.[61]

Forced standing and sleep deprivation did continue in the Soviet military as a routine punishment, but again this practice needs to be kept in perspective. It is hard to underestimate the level of brutality in Soviet army training. In 1990, Soviet papers reported that fifteen thousand soldiers died during the first five years of perestroika, four thousand in 1989 alone. These figures *did not* include those who died in combat in Afghanistan and elsewhere.[62]

All this is what one would expect under the monitoring hypothesis. Where there is no public monitoring and accountability, why bother being stealthy? However, during détente and perestroika, some countries became more mindful of publicity in specific cases. In the 1960s, Soviet authorities entirely abandoned Stalinist positional tortures and sweating for incarcerating dissidents in psychiatric institutions, a transition I discuss in a subsequent chapter. Romania, Cuba, and China adopted this practice as well. Torture was now disguised as medical treatment. Likewise, where avoiding monitoring mattered, Soviet army officers were fully capable of combining methods that left few traces.[63]

In some East European countries, torture became infrequent. For example, in its first annual audit of torture worldwide in 1973, Amnesty International reported that it had not received reports of torture in the past ten years from Hungary, Poland, or Czechoslovakia.[64] In its 1986 audit, Amnesty International reported forced standing only in Yugoslavia.[65]

In the 1990s, positional torture was still rare in Eastern Europe. In Albania, prisoners report fixed object restraints.[66] In Slovakia, prisoners report being forced to stand (sometimes with arms outstretched, knees bent, or on tiptoe) or to kneel on a chair.[67] Forced standing is occasionally reported in Yugoslavia and in provincial cities in Russia.[68]

Positional Tortures in the Non-Communist World

The survey of Communist states suggests that, although one may receive one's techniques from a common source (the universal distributor hypothesis), this training rapidly decays, especially in the absence of monitoring. And although a certain technique might be strongly associated with a common ideology (the ideology hypothesis), shared beliefs are insufficient to keep continuity in techniques. Monitoring seems to do a better job in explaining why torturers select scarring or clean tortures. And there is further evidence in favor of the monitoring hypothesis when one looks at the distribution of positional torture in the non-Communist world.

In this section, I cover the expanding scope (not magnitude) of positional tortures as the techniques appear in one state after another. The states covered in this section do not have common ideologies, so it is not likely that this preference for positional torture is driven by ideological considerations. I will consider at the end of this chapter whether a universal distributor hypothesis is confirmed by the evidence. Here, I simply make the historical claim that while positional torture was disappearing in Communist countries, positional torture was spreading rapidly to authoritarian and democratic states elsewhere, often in states where there was a known concern for leaving few marks. I list the known instances in chronological order, based on the date of the first report of positional torture.

Venezuela. Around 1953, Venezuela police adopted forced standing facing the wall, dubbing it the "Thirty-eighth Parallel."[69] Interrogators also forced prisoners to stand with arms extended or before bright lights for days, a torture called the "Hot Chapel" (*capilla ardiente*).[70] In 1998, a survey of 135 prisoners tortured in the previous three years reported positional tortures in ten cases, showing policemen had not forgotten this technique.[71]

In 1953, the most notorious positional torture was the Ring (*el ring*), which was used on "hundreds of prisoners,"[72] Prisoners mounted a truck or automobile wheel rim turned flat on its side. Barefooted, they balanced themselves on the rims, handcuffed behind the back. "At first, the position is just uncomfortable, but after some hours have passed the edge of the rim hurt the bottoms of the feet to the point of producing bloody wounds. Later the pain is unbearable. . . . The feet swell up to the ankles."[73]

Portugal. In 1953, Humberto Lopes, a Communist leader, reported that PIDE, the Portuguese secret police, forced him to stand for hours. Subsequently, two other prisoners, leaders in the Angolan and Portuguese Communist parties, made similar allegations. By the early 1960s, "statue torture" (*estatua*) and sleep deprivation were PIDE's main torture techniques.[74] For six days, says one prisoner, "I suffered the statue . . . on falling asleep, I would be woken at once or within a few minutes by having pins stuck in me or by shaking, or by sounds of knocking or tapping. In the end the slightest noise would waken me. I have since suffered from auditive hallucinations."[75]

As allegations of torture mounted, the Portuguese government invited Lord Russell to investigate. Lord Russell was a respected journalist who had covered Nazi torture. He assumed incorrectly that statue torture had to be performed in a *stehzelle*, a standing box like those the Nazis used. When he could not find one in PIDE prisons, he concluded the prisoners were lying.[76] Russell was a skilled observer, but unfamiliar with clean tortures like the Spot. His inexperience became embarrassingly obvious by the 1970s.

Portuguese prisoners knew why PIDE preferred forced standing. "I should explain that, as I was told by the PIDE agents, this [the statue] does not nowadays mean being required to stand all the time and being beaten when you sit or fall down, because that would leave marks."[77] In 1970s, in Mozambique, PIDE's main positional torture was prolonged kneeling on a broom handle with one's hands raised, dubbed the torture of the rod (*tortura da vara*).[78]

South Africa. South African police adopted positional tortures in the early 1960s. A 1989 study of 175 torture victims indicated that forced standing occurred in 50 percent of all cases. About 34 percent of the prisoners report being forced to crouch, stand on their toes with arms up stretched, do the imaginary chair, or hold heavy objects over their heads.[79] The Truth and Reconciliation Commission, which uses the broader category of posture tortures (positional and restraint tortures) records that posture tortures occurred in a little less that one-third of three hundred cases between 1960 and 1973, increased to almost two-fifths of almost five hundred cases between 1974 and 1984, and then declined to about one-fifth of about eleven hundred cases in the final years of apartheid.[80]

South African police developed several different posture tortures.[81] The earliest reported case (1961) involved kneeling and holding a chair over one's head while handcuffed.[82] In 1963, there was the imaginary chair: a prisoner had to crouch as if he was sitting in "a government chair, so I must not break it."[83] In 1964, a prisoner reported the Spot. Interrogators put a sheet of paper on the floor and made the prisoner stand on it for two days.[84] Interrogators also made prisoners stand on one leg.[85] Sometimes guards put pebbles or sand in the shoes.

The most common reports concerned "brick torture." "They turn two bricks towards each other like an inverted V—and you have to stand on that narrow edge while you are being interrogated, and you've got to balance yourself on your arches, which are killing you."[86] Sometimes a prisoner also held a brick over his head in this position. Another method, reported a police captain, "is where a person stands on a brick balancing on his heels or on his toes for hours."[87]

Greece. In 1967, a prisoner in Greece reported forced standing at the Heraclion Gendarmerie, a practice that became more common in the 1970s.[88] "They made me stand with one arm in the air, like the Statue of Liberty and I kept falling down."[89] Prisoners described standing at attention facing the wall or standing in the Spot.[90]

South Vietnam. In the late 1960s, prisoners reported interrogators making them stand for hours before bright lights.[91] Prisoners did not report Americans using positional torture.

South Korea. Starting in the late 1960s, prisoners reported forced standing and sitting.[92]

Uruguay. Forced standing (the *plantón*) begins as early as 1971. An army torturer, Lieutenant Cooper, indicated the *plantón* was a preferred method.[93] Just how common is revealed in Ole Rasmussen's survey of two hundred victims from eight countries, all tortured between 1970 and 1983. Most Uruguayans (89 percent) reported forced standing, as did the majority of victims from Spain and

Northern Ireland (60 percent and 61 percent respectively). In Greece, Chile, Argentina, and Iraq, only 10–20 percent of prisoners reported forced standing.[94]

Nicaragua. In 1973, a respected journalist reported he was forced to "squat for periods of many hours until he collapsed."[95]

Israel. In 1974, a Palestinian prisoner reported being forced to stand with his hands in the air.[96] The preferred GSS method in this period, however, remained French modern. After 1987, torture changed dramatically.[97] The GSS abandoned electricity for "tying up" techniques, *al-Shabeh*.

The *shabeh* consists of restraint tortures, positional tortures, exhaustion exercises, and clean beating, sometimes inflicted according to a specified schedule. It includes prolonged forced squatting (the *qambaz*, or Frog), forced sitting, and forced standing. It also includes *stehzelle*, narrow cells in which detainees must stand handcuffed or with their hands tied behind or above their head. *Khazayen*, or "coffin cells," can be as small as fifty by seventy centimeters.[98] In 1991, lawyers for a detainee received his medical record, including a form specifying the detainee's fitness for interrogation, which stated that the detainee "could be bound, hooded, and made to stand for long periods."[99]

In 1999, the High Court of Justice forbade certain elements of the *shabeh*. Subsequently, human rights groups have documented numerous cases where GSS officers applied not only the *qambaz* (now prohibited) and forced-sitting *shabeh*, but also prolonged forced standing with arms raised or standing with knees bent or on one leg, all performed without coffin cells.[100]

The Philippines. In 1975, prisoners reported being subjected to "lying on air" torture, also called the "San Juanico Bridge." This consisted of making prisoners lie with feet on one bed and head another bed.[101] In the 1980s, investigators describe "forced lying on blocks of ice."[102]

Information about other cases is somewhat more limited. Forced standing was routine in Argentina after 1976, but again the preferred techniques were French modern.[103] Though not reported in the initial reports after Pinochet's coup, forced standing became routine in Chile by the mid-1970s.[104] Iranian prisoners report forced squatting on an invisible chair ("the chair").[105]

In the 1980s, torturers in Paraguay required prisoners to sit in a fetus position (*feto*) for hours.[106] Bolivian torturers made prisoners lie parallel to the floor supported only by the head and tips of the toes (the Pig, *el chancho*).[107] In 1986, a monitoring group in El Salvador reported that 387 out of 433 prisoners interviewed (89 percent) reported forced standing and sleep deprivation. Some also reported the *chancho*.[108] Colombian torturers employed forced standing (*plantones*) in the 1980s. In 2003, Colombian prisoners reported being forced to bend forward with the head touching the ground and the hands tied behind the back (also called *el chancho*).[109] Detainees in Saudi Arabia also reported prolonged forced standing in the mid-1980s.[110]

In the 1990s, torturers in Burundi forced prisoners to "kneel for long periods on sharp bottle tops or pebbles."[111] In Sudan in the 1990s, prisoners reported being "beaten, whipped, and forced to stand for long periods."[112] In 1994, detainees in Indian Kashmir reported "forced standing or lying for hours in the snow, completely or partially naked."[113] In Pakistan, some prisoners detained in the 1990s reported enforced standing.[114] In Burma/Myanmar, a prisoner detained in the late 1990s reported being "forced to stand on tiptoe for hours on end, knees bent, and buzz like an aero plane." Later, he was forced to kneel on sharp stones.[115] In Tunisia, prison punishment included being "forced to remain all night facing the wall, standing in the hall near the guards, and sometimes completely naked."[116]

In 1999, Mexican prisoners reported prolonged standing and squatting.[117] In 1999, the Austrian Ministry of Justice prohibited restraint beds in prisons (also known as "cage beds," or *gitterbetten*). Prison officials claimed they had inherited them from a mental hospital in 1994 and denied that they used them. In 2001, a prisoner died after being tied to a bed using four-point restraints.[118] In 2002, prisoners in Cambodia were "forced to stand in the sun for long periods, or to stand on their own hands, or balance on one foot."[119] Lastly, there are the reports from American-occupied Iraq. For example, members of the Eighty-second Airborne forced detainees "to hold five-gallon water jugs with arms outstretched or do jumping jacks until they passed out."[120] In addition to American usage, Danish interrogators interrogated Iraqi prisoners allegedly using techniques including forced kneeling, exposure to extreme cold, "moderate physical pressure, loud music and standing for long periods of time."[121]

In reviewing these cases, it is hard not to notice that the spread of positional tortures begins in the 1960s and accelerates in the last three decades of the century. This chronology coincides with the emergence of a global human rights monitoring regime, and so favors the universal monitoring hypothesis. In the next section, I consider whether one can explain this pattern more persuasively with reference to a universal distributor, and find this argument unpersuasive.

It is more difficult to get a handle on the preference of some states for positional tortures over other techniques. Clearly, some states preferred positional torture over electrotorture (notably Portugal (1950s), Britain (1970s), and Israel (1990s)), while one knows from part I that many states trended in the opposite direction, favoring electrotorture and water torture over positional torture (France, Spain, South Africa, Latin America, and the United States).

It would be difficult to explain this preference by appealing to ideology, since it is difficult to find a shared ideology among these states. It would also be difficult to explain the preference for positional tortures with reference to efficiency. Positional tortures *are* labor-saving devices (the prisoner does the work), but they take time to have their effects. Torturers use them when they have plenty of time, mainly to intimidate prisoners or force a false confession. When they are short of time, torturers normally reach for devices like magnetos that cause immediate pain. This might explain why the Portuguese adopted positional tortures, since here the PIDE may just have wanted confessions.

But it fails to explain why the British or the Israeli interrogators turned to positional tortures. In both cases these states were confronting, by their own accounts, urgent civil emergencies where timeliness was critical. If one takes these states at their word, then one can only conclude that in these cases they reached for practices that they knew from their own histories or that had a fearsome reputation, and torturers persisted in their usage out of habit, as the craft apprenticeship hypothesis would suggest. Otherwise, one must conclude that, contrary to what these states alleged, the purpose of torture was to generate false confessions and torturers did not really operate under the urgency of a ticking time bomb.

The Universal Distributor Hypothesis Revisited

In the twentieth century, positional torture was most common in southern Europe, East Asia, and Latin America. It was less frequently reported in Africa, the Middle East, and South Asia. In the Communist world, which did not worry about public monitoring, torturers chose mutilating techniques over positional torture, and the Stalinist tradition of positional torture tended to fade over time. Elsewhere in the world, interrogators combined clean torture techniques in various ways, and here positional torture took root. It did so unevenly, appearing more commonly in some states than in others.

The country with the longest history in positional torture was Britain. In the Middle East, the British practiced forced standing between 1900 and 1975, first as a field punishment (Egypt) and then on political prisoners (Mandatory Palestine, Cyprus, and Aden). There are no reports of forced standing in British colonies in Southeast Asia or sub-Saharan Africa. Forced standing seems to have been a customary regional practice, one that did not receive much thought until it received attention from religious organizations (Mandatory Palestine), newspapers (Cyprus), and human rights organizations (Aden).

British troops also practiced forced standing in the British Isles, first as a field punishment, then during World War II at the London Cage, then in "resistance to interrogation" programs, and lastly, in Northern Ireland. Here again, aside from public objections during World War I, information about these practices was suppressed or went unnoticed until the 1970s. Then, "Changing attitudes coupled with more intense scrutiny of all security forces methods [by the media] rendered unacceptable methods which had hitherto attracted no attention."[122]

More generally, positional torture flourished at the margins of colonial systems (Britain, France) and in authoritarian states most proximate to European human rights monitors (Portugal, Spain, and Greece). It spread rapidly through Latin America after 1965, at about the same time that human rights monitoring become ubiquitous. Democratic states gave it a greater role in the same period (Spain, Israel, Japan, India, Colombia).

The history here supports the claim that what drives the spread of clean torture techniques is public monitoring (the monitoring hypothesis) and the chronology coincides with the emergence of an international human rights regime (the universal monitoring hypothesis). But the history also indicates some states played important roles in spreading positional tortures, and so there could be a single important universal distributor. Still, let me consider the possible universal distributors (the USSR, the UK, and the United States) and explain why I am not persuaded by this explanation.[123]

The Soviet Union

The most important universal distributor of positional tortures was the USSR. Certainly, Soviet interrogators played an important role in training interrogators elsewhere how to use Stalinist positional tortures and sweating techniques. Nevertheless, the most durable effect of Soviet intervention was probably indirect and inadvertent.

To be specific, direct Soviet training did not seem to last long, as allied interrogators gradually switched to other techniques. But the use of Stalinist techniques in the Korean War had an important effect in the non-Communist world, advertising the power of positional tortures ("brainwashing"). Forced standing appears in Venezuela and Portugal around 1953. Venezuelan torturers referenced the Korean War by calling forced standing the "Thirty-eighth Parallel." The French practiced forced standing before World War II, but prisoners do not report it after the war until 1956. These events seem hardly coincidental.

After the Korean War, British and American forces adopted training procedures for soldiers who might be subjected to Soviet techniques.[124] "Stress inoculation" programs, as they are now called, may have had the effect of making known techniques to soldiers who then brought that experience to bear in Northern Ireland, Afghanistan, and Iraq.

The Soviet example captures various ways torture can be transmitted. Sometimes torture is transmitted through training (China, Eastern Europe). Sometimes rumor is sufficient (Venezuela, France, Portugal). Some torturers apply the worst that was experienced by themselves or their mates to their prisoners (British and American positional torture; Israeli standing cells). In yet other cases, police reach for what is customary (Japan). All of this is much as the craft apprenticeship hypothesis would suggest.

The United Kingdom

British forces are also identified as universal distributors, carrying common interrogation techniques from Malaya (1948–60) to Kenya (1952–56) to Aden (1963–67) to Hong Kong (1967) to Northern Ireland (1971–74).[125] This claim, however, greatly overstates the degree to which British counterinsurgency training was centralized and standardized.[126] If British interrogation practices were standardized, one would expect standard techniques passed on in a developing trajectory from event to event. That is not what the record shows.

Prisoners at the London Cage (1940–48) were subjected primarily to forced standing and kneeling, beating, sleep deprivation, cold showers, exposure to extremes of heat and cold, and exhaustion exercises. On the other hand, no torture is reported during the British counterinsurgency in Malaya (1948–60). Torture in Kenya (1952–56) was sanguinary and flogging normally; sleep deprivation and positional tortures are not reported.[127] Cyprus (1956) involved beatings and public floggings, before interrogators turned to clean beating, forced standing, ice, and drugs. Interrogators in Hong Kong (1967) sweated suspects (sleep deprivation and relay interrogation). They did not use forced standing or beating. In Aden (1963–67), they did. RUC beating in Northern Ireland (1972–80) was part of a highly stealthy art, but British police practice at home did not show such sophistication.[128] There was also much "RUC 'freelancing'" with other "bizarre tortures," some of it amateurish.[129] And there were unique regional techniques, air conditioners in Aden and white noise generators in Northern Ireland.[130] British agents in Kenya slipped hot eggs into rectums and vaginas, a technique that then appears in Cyprus.[131] A British Special Branch interrogator in Cyprus claims to have come up with the "hot egg under the armpit" technique that still occasionally appears in the Mediterranean region, but this seems more likely to be an adaptation of the Kenyan approach.[132] It does not appear in subsequent British colonial conflicts. Lastly, electrotorture appeared widely in Kenya but not in Aden and in only a few incidents in Cyprus and Northern Ireland.

There is no obvious trajectory here. Calling all this "torture" gives the impression of continuity while disguising intrastate variations in what techniques interrogators chose in different conflicts. In fact, the pattern of torture confirms what is generally known about British counterinsurgency.

While the French developed a clear counterinsurgency doctrine, no comparable "British doctrine" emerged until long after Britain's counterinsurgency operations had ceased.[133] Most counterinsurgency campaigns were organized on an ad hoc basis. When asked to explain their methods, officers described them as "common sense" or "making it up as we went along," and could not cite precedents for their actions even when they existed. Interrogation practices, like other techniques, "were transmitted informally from one generation of soldiers and civil servants to the next."[134]

Why were counterinsurgency operations so improvised? First, the army promoted officers based on their ability to handle conventional troops. Prowess in irregular warfare was not valued. In addition, "The very decentralization that had made the British army and colonial administration such a flexible machine may have inhibited the collection and transmission of experience." Officers in Kenya "probably did not come into contact with district officers from Malaya or anywhere else in the empire." Lastly, district officers were territorial, and competing regiments "may have had a similar unwillingness to share experience."[135]

The United States

In 1942, American advisers trained Brazilian police in positional torture. And by the late twentieth century, many Latin American countries practiced positional torture (Venezuela, Brazil, Argentina, Chile, Colombia, Bolivia, Paraguay).

However, American training in positional torture is one, but probably the least significant, of several sources. By the 1960s, Americans interrogators preferred electrotorture and water torture. American interrogators in Vietnam did not use positional torture. Similarly, the Chicago police department, when it tortured in the early 1970s, preferred French modern.

In fact, Latin American torturers could have learned positional tortures from several sources. Venezuelans copied the practice from Korean War reports in the 1950s. South Africa and Argentina exchanged torture experts in the mid-1970s.[136] The Brazilians could have learned it from Portugal's PIDE. And world media reported extensively on British positional torture in Northern Ireland.

Remembering the Hooded Men

The famous hooded man at Abu Ghraib was forced to balance on a box with the threat of electric torture if he collapsed. Staff Sergeant Frederick testified that military interrogators told him to stage a mock electrocution. He then instructed two other guards to attach wires to the fingers and toes of the hooded man.[137] In fact, he was one of several prisoners subjected to this technique. Where did the MI men learn this technique?

In 2002, Secretary of Defense Rumsfeld received and approved a memorandum that recommended positional tortures for interrogations.[138] Perhaps Pentagon lawyers suggested forced standing because the European courts considered it simply ill-treatment in the case of the Irish hooded men. Or maybe military officers remembered it from stress inoculation training. Or maybe this was the CIA's memory of the Korean War.

One day we will know more about the memos. The American *practice* of positional torture in Iraq does suggest at least one history, one that does not exist if one just studies memos, and one that does not point to Communist North Korea or Northern Ireland.

The torture of the hooded man at Abu Ghraib has three components: hooding, standing balanced on a box, and having wires attached. Few countries hooded prisoners for torture in the early twentieth century. The Gestapo practiced hooding routinely at the Fortress Prison of Breendonck (Belgium), but it was generally uncommon. Hooding became more common after World War II, in the age of stealthy torture. Hooding does not simply confuse prisoners, making them more vulnerable and confused. It also deprives the prisoner of information about what was done, who did it, and where it happened, making their public testimony less useful.

In the 1950s, hooding appeared in South Africa and French-occupied Algeria (1950s). Torturers used it commonly in Brazil and Spain (1960s), Northern Ireland, Chile, Argentina, and Israel (1970s), and in many other countries since then (notably Bolivia, Zambia, Zimbabwe, Indonesia, El Salvador, and Honduras). Forced standing on an object is far less common than hooding. It was commonly practiced in only three countries in the twentieth century (chronologically): Venezuela (wheel rims), South Africa (bricks), and Brazil (cans). Attaching electric wires to force the victim to keep his balance was known only in Brazil ("the Vietnam"). Sometimes practices speak louder than words.

But again there must be some allowance made for the technique of striking without marking.

—Justice Kelly, Northern Ireland, March 1980,

judgment in the case of Edwin Brophy[1]

16   Fists and Exercises

In this chapter, I describe two additional "stress and duress" techniques in the late twentieth century. These techniques are striking bodies in ways that do not leave marks (clean beating) and forcing prisoners to exercise ceaselessly until they drop (exhaustion exercises).

Prisoners tend to report the worst that torturers do, and they may pass over common practices like those I discuss here. Likewise, human rights monitors have rarely reported elements of clean beating as distinctive techniques (the *teléfono* being the main exception). Considering everything else that happened to torture victims, clean beating hardly seemed worth reporting.

The existing accounts do suggest that clean beating has become more common in more countries or, at least, that prisoners regard these techniques as important enough to report today. Moreover, when one considers which police forces used the broadest range of clean beating procedures, one repeatedly finds democratic policemen, usually using these procedures alongside positional tortures such as forced standing.

Similarly, exhaustion exercises were largely unknown in torture in the early twentieth century. They appear first in colonies of democracies (Britain and France), democracies (the United States), and subsequently in two authoritarian states in the 1930s (Germany and Japan). In the 1950s, exhaustion exercises persisted only in the colonies of democratic states (France and Britain) and two authoritarian states (Romania and North Korea). They then appeared in authoritarian states under high levels of international scrutiny, first Spain and Greece in the 1960s, then spreading throughout Latin America and East Asia.

Clean Beating

Clean beating involves striking bodies with one's hands in ways that leave few long-term bruises. In 1931, the Wickersham Commission listed how the New York police practiced beating: "Punching in the face, especially a hard slap on the jaw; hitting with a billy; whipping with a rubber hose; kicking in the abdomen; tightening the necktie almost up to the choking point; squeezing the testicles. Methods are favored which do not leave visible marks, because these attract the attention of courts."[2] To this nearly comprehensive list of clean techniques, one might add cuffing the ears (*teléfono*) and bending the wrists (dorsiflexing).

Clean beating requires no special instruments (like positional torture) and produces immediate pain (like electrotorture). Inspectors may find objects (sandbags and shock batons), eliminate closets that could be used for standing cells, and identify serious bruises disguised by clothing. Clean beating has to be captured in the act, and the best check against it remains video cameras in interrogation rooms and on patrol cars.

Blows to Fleshy Areas

"Bruising only tends to occur where flesh meets bone; the stomach is a fleshy area unlikely to bruise, except along the costal margin where the stomach meets the rib cage."[3] When bruises do appear, police hold prisoners until the short-term marks disappear.

American police have long known that blows to the thighs, pressure to the abdomen, genital squeezing, and jaw squeezing leave few long-term marks.[4] In the 1920s, they preferred blows to the abdomen ("fist to the wind"), over the kidneys, and in the soft hollows above the hips. Some police padded their fists with boxing gloves, while others chose rubber hoses and sandbags because they left no "enduring traces."[5]

French police and Paras were also familiar with these clean techniques. Consider this account from Algeria in 1957: "A rain of punches, slaps landed all over my body. One of the inspectors having yelled out to watch out for traces, it was then a series of punches, from the knees to the genitals."[6] Soldiers also occasionally used the "blanket roll," wrapping a prisoner in a blanket and then beating him.[7]

British interrogators in Cyprus in 1956 were familiar with clean beating. A journalist visiting an Army prison explained how "H.M.T.'s," Her Majesty's torturers, operated. "You might be alternately maltreated and questioned by relays of men for one hour or four or twenty four. You might be beaten on the stomach with a flat board, you might have your testicles twisted, you might be half-suffocated with a wet cloth which forced you to drink with every breath you took. . . ."[8] Similarly, in Aden in 1965, Amnesty International investigators report, "hitting and twisting their [prisoner's] genital organs" was one of ten procedures used at interrogation centers.[9] In 1966, an American soldier stated he had learned various torture techniques through resistance to interrogation training at Fort Bragg, including the "delicate operation" of squeezing testicles in a jeweler's vice.[10]

In 1970, a prisoner described how Greek torturers "removed my shoes and some of my clothes, and they began to beat me again, while someone was giving instructions as to method: 'Beat him on the head and stomach. Be careful not to leave marks.' "[11]

Spanish police have beaten cleanly since the late 1960s.[12] In the 1970s, beating was combined with the Stool. The prisoner lies "down over a small stool, face upwards, either supported at the waist or at the spine. He is made to lie in this painful position for long periods." Police then strike the abdomen, head, and soles of the feet."[13] In 2002, an interrogator pointed out a policeman to a prisoner and said that he could "beat him all over his body without leaving marks."[14] In another case, an officer told a prisoner that his method "consists in pinching the testicles with two fingers; that leaves no traces, and the guy who endured it the longest without passing out held out for three minutes."[15]

In 1972, under the government of Salvador Allende, leftist guerillas in Santiago Public Jail described how police used "blows well-applied to the kidneys, the stomach and the liver," a beating style, they asserted, that would "not leave visible marks."[16] And in 1988, a prisoner reported that, after electrotorture, the guards delivered "blows to different parts of the body. So as not to leave marks, they hit with the hand, with the back or the palm of the hand, different parts of the body, like the abdominal region, the ribs, on the face, the jaw."[17]

Clean beating seems to be a feature of the Chicago police in the 1970s and 1980s. Prisoners reported beatings, along with other techniques that leave few marks (electrotorture, *falaka*, use of telephone books), but observers were unable to document the violence for years.[18] Japanese police also favored this kind of beating, including "poking [a prisoner] in the midriff with their fists," "kicking him around the hips and legs," "kneeing him in the thighs," and kicking in the buttocks.[19]

Clean beating was also routine in several British youth detention centers, where "boys were frequently punched in the stomach or slapped in the face as a form of punishment."[20] The Royal Ulster Constabulary (RUC) also used clean beating regularly on prisoners in Northern Ireland in the 1970s, including blows to the genitals, punches, and straight finger prods to the abdomen, a technique that "does not leave marks."[21] International attention overlooked these practices, focusing instead on the RUC's notorious Five Techniques (forced standing, hooding, sleep deprivation, deprivation of food and drink, and white noise).

Once European courts had condemned the Five Techniques, the RUC developed clean beating into a high art. Just how well the RUC beat can be gauged from one brutal case involving punches to the stomachs, kicks to the testicles, strikes to the head, bending over a table, and head banging. Six different doctors examined the prisoner in the next week, including one shortly after the beatings. Even the two who were certain his complaints were genuine found no bruising, swelling, or discoloration.[22]

The RUC adopted new positions like the Spanish Stool, now dubbed the "Crab." Prisoners would lie on their back across a chair while police punched their stomachs.[23] "They kept insisting that [a prisoner] was responsible for the murder at Dernagh crossroads and continued hitting him in the stomach, asking him if he knew it would leave no marks."[24]

The Israeli GSS also routinized clean beating in the early 1990s. In 1992, an Israeli paramedic assigned to an interrogation facility reported that he knew detainees were being beaten, but he could not prove it. "They would come out of the interrogation rooms and would tell me how the interrogators had hit them. When I took off their clothes and examined them, however, I couldn't find a thing."[25]

A Latvian soldier reported that, in the 1990s, Soviet sergeants also knew how to beat their recruits cleanly. Although they used fists, boots, and heavy military belt buckles, "these sergeants knew how to avoid provoking scars and other permanent marks."[26] In 1999, Romanian police beat prisoners using the blanket roll, and in 2000, Slovak police donned surgical gloves before beating a prisoner.[27]

In 1990, an Argentine prisoner reported, "They kicked me thousands of times on the legs, but they knew how to do it without making marks."[28] And Brazilians at the Lucélia Penitentiary in Sao Paulo reported that the usual treatment upon arrival was "blows and slaps, and later [being] forced to take a freezing bath to avoid the formation of hematomas [bruises]."[29] And in 2005, a Guantánamo detainee alleged that a doctor advised guards as they beat a prisoner about the face, saying, "Hit him *around* the eye, not *in* the eye."[30]

Slapping ("the Taps")

"Beating a person with the open hand will not leave marks at all on the face," observed an American interrogator who worked in Vietnam, "and you can beat a person almost senseless without leaving any obvious reddening of the skin."[31]

Slapping is hardly a new prison practice. Korean comfort women, Indian colonial recruits, and British POWs report Japanese practiced hard, sometimes fatal, slapping throughout Asia in the 1930s and 1940s.[32] In 1946, Prime Minister Tojo felt obliged to explain that slapping was a customary means of training for uneducated Japanese families as well as the Japanese army and navy. "I don't think it is a crime. It is something that comes from custom."[33] Since Japanese also practiced many scarring tortures, beaters probably did not intend to be stealthy.[34] Slapping was also common in North Vietnamese prison camps in 1968. "I welcomed this punishment," reported a U.S. POW, "because it left only welts and bruises."[35]

What is new is police interest in slapping as a stealthy technique. In the 1920s, Americans and French police were probably the first to recognize it could serve this purpose in conjunction with other tortures.[36] American police called rhythmic slapping "the Taps." While the point of contact remained sensitive for months, "by using a rubber hose or tire, no outward evidence of the punishment is discernible after a few hours."[37]

The Soviets adopted sweating, positional tortures, and slapping, in the 1930s.[38] French forces in Algeria combined slapping with other clean techniques, especially electrotorture, pumping, and choking.[39] American interrogators embraced slapping during the Vietnam War. As one Army interrogator observed, slapping was "a mark of sophistication that we acquired" after 1967 when interrogators used less electrotorture.[40]

In the 1970s and 1980s, "slapping the ears and face with open hand" was a standard procedure for the RUC in Northern Ireland.[41] In the last decade, the Committee for the Prevention of Torture (CPT) has recorded police slapping in several European countries, including Ireland, Spain, France, the Czech Republic, Romania, Slovakia, Ukraine, and Estonia.[42] In Israel, government authorities have designated "a slap to the face" as a legitimate interrogation technique, and prisoners report that it is commonly used.[43] Japanese police also practiced slapping in interrogation.[44] And Indonesia police employ hard slapping, often on both sides of the face, dubbed the "Japanese method."[45] In 1996, a Florida prison guard asserted that slapping about the face was a common practice at Miami's Krome Detention Center.[46] In 2003, interrogators with the Fourth Infantry Division stationed in Tikrit developed a wish list of interrogation methods including "open-hand strikes."[47] In 2005, CIA sources identified the "Attention Slap" and the "Belly Slap" as two authorized interrogation methods in which some CIA interrogators were trained. The Belly Slap was a "hard open-handed slap to the stomach," while the Attention Slap was also an open-handed slap, presumably to the face.[48]

Often, this slapping seems to be stealthy. As a Spanish prisoner put it, "Blows were mainly directed to my head. It looked like they didn't want to leave any marks on me, but they were very painful, as they hit me with all their strength."[49] Likewise, the purpose of CIA slapping was "to cause pain, but not internal injury." The fact that slapping is often accompanied by other clean techniques confirms this impression. CIA slapping, for example, is combined with forced standing, cold cells and showers, choking with water, and the shaking (to be covered below), all techniques that leave few marks.[50]

Cuffing the Ears (Teléfono)

This practice involves striking the ears simultaneously with the palms in concave positions. Like slapping, cuffing is not a new torture. Again, what is new is police interest in this technique.

Observers first noted cuffing during the British counterinsurgency campaign in Kenya. In 1955, in a prison, Captain Ernest Law stated, "I saw the chief warder clapping his hands with all his force simultaneously on both ears of these women. The force was enough to split the eardrums. I actually saw one woman pass her motion with fright."[51] Kenyan prisons used whips, so it is unlikely that the warden intended to be stealthy. It is more likely that he employed it mainly to cause pain.

North Vietnamese also cuffed ears, but their purpose was to cause pain and damage, not avoid marks. An American POW observed in 1965 that "they were trying to break his eardrums, and the slaps were so hard that he could not understand why they did not break. There was no blood; the eardrums remained intact. His ears rang and his head ached. The slapping went on and on."[52]

Cuffing was not a common British practice in Aden.[53] Nevertheless, one prisoner did report it in 1965, alleging interrogators "beat me with their open hands . . . banging on both ears at the same time." While detention medical records identified damage to the membranes of the ears, the interrogation center record stated that the prisoner had "no apparent injury," suggesting that marks did matter here.[54]

Torturers cuffed routinely in two states in the late 1960s, Spain and Brazil. Spanish interrogations sometimes began "with blows to the ears delivered with the palm of a hand, producing giddiness, panic, and permanent aural damage."[55] In 1966, a Brazilian journalist reported that cuffing the ears was a standard torture under the military junta. Prisoners called it the *telefone*.[56] In the last three decades, human rights monitors have documented the *teléfono* in Argentina, Chile, Uruguay, Honduras, El Salvador, Ecuador, Peru, and Mexico.[57]

The practice has occurred well outside Latin America, even if the term is not used. Prisoners in Chicago report that police used "ear cupping" in 1979 and 1986 as a supplement to other tortures.[58] Prisoners also reported the practice in Greece and Northern Ireland in the 1970s, Iran in the 1970s and 1980s ("the hammer"; *chakoshi*, or "the Welcoming Ceremony"; *khoshamadgoui*), the Philippines and Japan in the 1980s (where it is called *piang piang*), and Nepal and

Haiti (where it is called *kalot marrasa*) in the 1990s. In the 1990s, observers reported cuffing in Spain, Ireland, Tunisia, and Bulgaria.[59]

Dorsiflexing

"Dorsiflexing" is the technique by which the wrists are pulled back or forward. This may also be done with fingers, finger flexing. American police used dorsiflexing in the 1920s, and a criminologist at the time described it as "the Japanese art of twisting" which "when properly applied caused the most agonizing suffering and pain—and left no marks."[60] Between 1976 and 1979, the RUC routinely practiced dorsiflexing. An examining doctor found "no sign of any injuries or bruising, but there was a slight swelling around the joint where the wrists meets the hand, which could, he admitted, have been self-inflicted."[61] In the 1980s, prisoners reported finger flexing in Spain and Japan.[62] In 1993, a detainee described how Swiss policed "tried to force her to sign various documents by twisting her right wrist and forcing it down on the table."[63]

Violent Shaking (al-Hazz)

"The interrogator grabs the interrogee, who is sitting or standing [handcuffed], by his shoulders or by his shirt collar, and shakes him violently, so that his fists are beating the interrogee's chest and his head is thrown backwards and forwards."[64] Severe cases of violent shaking have all the usual, and potentially fatal, features of the more familiar "shaken infant syndrome." In prisoners, these are called "shaken adult syndrome."[65]

The Israeli GSS routinized violent shaking in the 1990s. Palestinians refer to this practice as *al-Hazz*, and various government documents affirm its use in interrogation today.[66] One prisoner underwent *al-Hazz* three times in one week and described its typical effects. The second time, he "passed out and fell to the floor." After receiving oxygen, he was interrogated again. This time, the interrogator shook him more gently, "but it affected me severely, and I lost all sensation in my head."[67] In 1995, Prime Minister Yitzhak Rabin stated that violent shaking was an "exceptional" measure used against eight thousand Palestinians.[68] In 2005, CIA sources listed "the Attention Grab" as one of six authorized interrogation techniques, a technique in which "the interrogator forcefully grabs the shirt front of the prisoner and shakes him."[69]

Eyeball Pressing

Eyeball pressing involves placing the thumbs over the lids and forcing them downwards. The earliest report is from a U.S. military detention center during

World War I, where soldiers used this "exquisite torture" on recalcitrant conscientious objectors.[70] Prisoners report eyeball pressing in North Vietnam (1968), Spain (1969), and Northern Ireland (1971).[71] The practice is reported again among British forces stationed in Iraq in 2003. Soldiers placed sandbags over faces of Iraqi prisoners, and one "poked his fingers in the victim's eyes." "I've seen the state of their faces when they took the sandbags off. Their noses were bent—they looked like haggises."[72]

Adapting "the Necktie"

In the early twentieth century, American police would choke detainees by "adjusting" their neckties until they almost strangled them. "The necktie" has largely disappeared; few detainees these days wear ties. Some police use their bare hands or stuff cloth in the mouths of prisoners, like the Japanese in the 1980s.[73] The French Paras eventually moved to soft scarves (chèches).[74] Those with a still cleaner touch choose three other methods of near asphyxiation that do not involve such effort.

Bagging. Police sometimes slip the prisoner's head into a cheap plastic bag, tie the bottom, and then remove it before the prisoner asphyxiates. American police called this technique "bagging," Latin Americans, *la bolsa* (the bag), and Western NGOs, the "dry submarine," *submarino seco*, a Spanish expression from the 1970s.

In Chicago, bagging was a common police practice for two decades. The official police investigation identifies this technique by name and incident. A more comprehensive analysis of all cases between 1972 and 1991 dates the first case of bagging from 1972 and its most routine use in the early 1980s.[75] These dates make the Chicago police among the earliest users of bagging.

In 1980, New Orleans police chained several detainees to chairs, beat them with fists and books, and, in two cases, " 'bagged' [them], a process whereby officers placed a bag over the victim's head and temporarily sealed the bottom."[76] In 1982, a British prisoner at a Birmingham police station claimed that "a plastic bag was repeatedly placed over his head until he agreed to sign a confession."[77] The CPT reports incidents of bagging in Spain, Austria (starting in the 1980s), and the Ukraine.[78] In 2000, the Spanish police's use of bagging exceeded that of electroshock.[79]

The earliest Latin American cases of bagging come from Argentina and Chile in the 1970s, after which the practice appears commonly in the region. In the 1990s, prisoners report bagging in Argentina, Venezuela, Mexico, and Paraguay.[80] Bagging also appears in Soviet-occupied Afghanistan ("the black bag," 1984), the Philippines (1987), Sri Lanka (1986), Botswana (1993), Burma (1999), Uzbekistan ("the bag of death," 2000), and China (2004).[81] As I explained in chapter 13, if CIA waterboarding involves the use of cellophane, as is sometimes alleged, then this too qualifies as a form of dry choking.[82]

Hooding. Where hooding is customary, police simply soak the cloth sack, making it difficult to breathe, a process called "sacking" in Israel.[83] An interrogator may also simply tie the sack at the neck.[84]

Gas masks. This involves hooding the prisoner with a gas mask and then closing the air vent. Ukranian guards at the Gestapo prison in Warsaw, Aleja Szucha, are the first recorded practitioners of gas mask asphyxiation.[85] In the 1950s, the practice appears in Communist Romania as a standard prison punishment.[86] It also appears in South Africa: As a constable put it, first "we hit them. The second is electric shocks. And the third is the gasmask."[87] South African and Romanian torturers did not seem to practice gas mask torture beyond the early 1960s.

Gas mask asphyxiation is unreported elsewhere for the next three decades, with the exception of a single report from China in 1986.[88] In the 1990s, the CPT documented multiple cases of gas mask torture in Lithuania, Latvia, Russia, Moldova, Georgia, and the Ukraine.[89] Russian police today call this practice "the elephant" (*slonik*), a term that describes how prisoners look. When confronted with evidence of gas mask torture, a Russian police detective replied, "Why would we need to use a gas mask when there are plastic bags?"[90]

Exhaustion Exercises

Discipline involves drilling, repeating exercises until one performs a task precisely and automatically.[91] And for centuries, drilling has been a punishment for inadequate soldiers, sailors, and cadets. What is new is that these drills should appear in torture chambers or prior to interrogation.

As in positional torture, detainees often perform exhaustion exercises because they fear worse consequences if they disobey. They are mistaken in this. Exhaustion exercises induce ferocious muscle cramps and physically weaken detainees, making them vulnerable to suggestion. A young woman forced to do hundreds of deep knee bends observed, "It leaves no marks, but it hurts horribly."[92]

Torturers rarely use only disciplinary exercises to torture; the point here is *not* to induce more discipline through training. The torturer's purpose is to harness discipline to cause pain, with few marks, and with the semivoluntary participation of the victim. Usually, guards beat and humiliate prisoners as they exercise. They slap, kick fleshy areas, strike abdomens, hit with books and rubber hoses, and use other typical clean procedures.

The main exhaustion exercises listed below will be familiar from military training. Again, this list probably has omissions. In the last three decades, for example, there are reports of exhaustion exercises in Singapore, South Korea, and Zimbabwe, but the kind of exercises are not specified.[93]

Continuous running. The first postwar account of punitive running dates from a British POW camp in Indonesia between August 1945 and February 1946. Japanese POWs doing hard labor report that they were forced to run two kilometers each time they were allowed to drink water. "To get there you had to run there, drink and run back. Many collapsed of sunstroke. Our skin blistered. We told them we weren't soldiers and asked to be excused from heavy labor." But "British army policy seemed to be to imbue in us the consciousness of our defeat, physically, mentally and even spiritually."[94] A German POW in the London Cage described among his tortures forced walking, in this case walking in a tight circle for hours.[95] POWs do not report punitive running in other British camps in Europe, and too little is known about the British POW camps in Kenya and Ethiopia.[96] Prisoners in Cyprus (1956) also do not report forced running.

In French Algeria, prisoners describe forced running in 1954 and 1957.[97] In 1965, observers in Aden reported that British soldiers forced prisoners "to run in circles until they were exhausted."[98] After 1971, prisoners in Northern Ireland also reported continuous running, often until the early morning hours. They describe running on the spot and around the room, as well as the "running urination exercise," in which one urinated while running around a pit. Others were made to do continuous step-ups using a chair.[99]

Among Communist countries, Romanians seem to be the only country to adopt continuous running (the *maneg*) in the 1950s.[100] Guards forced a prisoner to run around a small cell at a minimum speed for hours, a practice the French Foreign Legion called *la plute*. One American POW in North Korea described being tied to a jeep and forced to run after it.[101] POWs generally reported positional tortures, not exhaustion exercises.

In the late 1960s, Greek torturers chose forced running because it reduced numbness and swelling in the feet caused by intensive *falaka*. Between 1973 and 1974, Chilean soldiers made prisoners run up and down stairs or forced them to run across uneven floors blindfolded.[102] In the mid-1980s, Italian prisoners in the high-security lockup at Agrippa prison reported being forced to run continuously during the exercise period.[103]

Knee bends. The Gestapo preferred this procedure during interrogation in several European countries. After World War II, prisoners first report knee bends in the course of interrogation in Spain and Brazil in the mid-1960s. In Spain, knee bends were performed while holding one's arms extended to the side.[104] In Brazil, prisoners held telephone books on their palms as they performed the *ginastica*.[105] In 1999, Yemeni authorities were "forcing victims to repeatedly crouch and stand, causing severe leg pain."[106]

Prior to interrogation, American troops told detained Iraqis at a forward operating base (not Abu Ghraib) to do "repeated press ups and to repeatedly stand up from a crouching position and then return to the crouching position."[107] Members of the American Eighty-second Airborne preferred a variant exercise, forcing detainees to "do jumping jacks till they passed out."[108] A prisoner in Pakistan reported that police forced him to do deep knee bends five hundred times.[109] The Israeli GSS, Spanish police, and Iranian police practice a modified knee bend, telling detainees, for example, to "stand up and sit down 200 times."[110] In Iraq, American troops practiced the "ups and downs" on prisoners, forcing them "to stand up, then sit down, over and over again for periods of up to twenty minutes."[111]

The Bear Dance. This lumbering exercise is what was once called the shot drill (England), the *pelotte* (France), or the Bear Dance (Germany). It involves moving some distance while carrying heavy objects in both hands, such as stones, telephone books, or buckets of water. Usually guards trip or beat prisoners in transit, causing them to drop or spill the heavy objects. For instance, at the London Cage, British interrogators allegedly made at least two German POWs run in circles carrying heavy logs.[112] Algerian prisoners describe how French soldiers made them run pulling a trailer or carrying heavy blocks.[113] In the last two decades, such practices have appeared in Benin (*le rodeo*), Paraguay (*caballo*) Syria, and Israel.[114]

Handcuffed push-ups. "With handcuffs on and my eyes covered, they made me do as many push-ups as my body could bear."[115] This technique was first reported in Spain in the late 1960s and then in Chile (the "German torture") and El Salvador in the 1980s.[116] Ordinary sit-ups and push-ups are also not unknown. In Northern Ireland in the 1970s, RUC prisoners were forced to perform push-ups constantly late into the night.[117] Prisoners in South Africa reported push-ups and high jumps in the 1980s.[118] The Israeli GSS had prisoners perform deep sit-ups on chairs.[119] In the last few years, Spanish police have forced Basque detainees to perform push-ups and high jumps at police stations, and American troops also subjected detained Iraqis to push-ups before interrogation.[120]

Ducks, rabbits, and frogs. Some torturers force prisoners to walk long distances on their knees (France in Algeria, Brazil today).[121] More commonly, they do squat walking, sometimes called "frog marching," the "duck walk" (*el pato*), or "bicycle torture."[122] Torturers bind the prisoner's hands behind the back or under the knees. Then with clubs and blows, they force the prisoner to walk or hop about the room "like a rabbit."[123] Such practices were common in the 1970s in Spain (where it is still reported), Chile, and Northern Ireland.[124] South African prisoners describe frog jumping in police stations in the Western Cape (1974), the Transvaal (1985), and the Orange Free State (1986).[125] In the 1990s, Zambian and Indonesian police frog-marched prisoners.[126]

Lizards and dogs. Guards force prisoners to twist and crawl long distances, a practice the Japanese called "the lizard" during World War II. The lizard was a common exercise in what the French in Algeria cynically called "sports."[127] In the 1960s, the Spanish called it the "little walk."[128] In the last two decades, there are reports from Indonesia, Zambia, Benin, Japan, and American-occupied Iraq.[129] In 1991, for example, a Japanese prisoner was able to see his lawyer "only after a humiliating crawl for an hour and a half on the floor, all the way from his cell to the visiting room."[130] And at Abu Ghraib, General Taguba reported soldiers made prisoners "do strange exercises by sliding on their stomach, jump up and down."[131] Other prisoners report being made to crawl on all fours like a dog, sometimes on a leash.[132]

Remembering the Grunts and the Cops

Modern police and military power are based on drills and discipline. By patrolling, monitoring, and responding quickly, they control social spaces very effectively. This, as the French social theorist Michel Foucault once observed, allows early modern states to exercise power without employing overt sanguinary violence.[133]

In the twentieth century, this order is reversed. Instead of discipline replacing torture, discipline today often acts in a subsidiary role supporting torture. Exhaustion exercises are an excellent example of this reversal of elements. When torturers adopt them in various countries, they do not do so to replace whips, water tortures, electrotorture, the *falaka*, beatings, or positional tortures. It was democratic soldiers that pioneered this approach, drawing often on typical military punishments.

Similarly, the cleanest beaters have usually been democratic policemen. American and French police were probably the most skilled beaters in the early twentieth century. In the late twentieth century, the most consistent crafty beaters were the British RUC (1970–80), the Chicago police in Area 2 and 3 (1969–91), the Israeli GSS (1986 to present), Spanish police (1975 to present), and Japanese police (1970s to present).

Authoritarian states that adopted clean beating were those especially sensitive to international monitoring. The first reports come from authoritarian Spain and Greece in the 1960s and 1970s, two states under considerable scrutiny in Europe. After 1970, clean beating appears in authoritarian states (most frequently, Spanish-speaking countries) and then in newly democratized states in Eastern Europe. This is as the universal monitoring hypothesis would lead one to predict.

In most cases, the arm will regain its normal composure.

—Dirk von Schrader, *Elementary Field Interrogation,*

on the one-arm hang position[1]

17   Old and New Restraints

In this chapter, I describe the last component of "stress and duress" techniques in the late twentieth century, restraint tortures (bucking, the *crapaudine*, standing handcuffs, reverse standing handcuffs, the Wooden Horse, sweatboxes, and straitjackets). Torturers bend or partially suspend victims to induce strains and deep muscle cramps. Normally, they combine these methods with beatings and other procedures. These tortures constitute the lesser tradition in restraint not because they are less painful, but because they leave fewer telltale marks.

I describe when and where these techniques were first reported after World War II and what is known about their history. Some histories are deeply suggestive about origins and transmission, but the caveat from the previous chapters applies here: these are difficult practices to follow. Certainly, habit, custom, familiarity, and prior histories of suffering play important roles in how torturers work, but so do rumor, curiosity, and innovation. What one can say only is that such clean techniques, whether inherited, adapted, or invented, are now increasingly common.

Bucking (the Parrot's Perch)

Bucking involves tying the arms to the ankles and then sliding a stout pole behind the knees and over the elbows. In this position, the body is immobile. The body may be left on the ground or suspended with the head hanging downwards. In the nineteenth century, torturers supplemented bucking with whipping and cobbing, but modern torturers also use electricity, choking with water, and the *falaka* on bucked prisoners.

For centuries, slave dealers bucked prisoners for transport in the Mediterranean region and in the Americas. American military and police bucked prisoners routinely in the nineteenth century. In the 1920s, the Yugoslavian police bucked prisoners, suspended them between tables, and then beat them on the soles of the feet (*falaka*).[2]

After World War II, French torturers in Algeria employed bucking, what detainees called *passer à la broche*, being put on the spit. Victim affidavits report two cases in 1956, after which it is commonly reported.[3] Soldiers attached electrodes to the bucked prisoners, poured water in the nostrils, or beat the soles of the feet with a rubber hose (*falaka*). In the early 1960s, the Sûreté in Paris used a metal pole, which they electrified with one cable and pricked the body with the other end.[4]

In 1966, a Brazilian journalist listed bucking as a standard torture technique, calling it "the 'parrot's perch' [*pau de arara*], a method that in France is called *passer à la broche*, in which the prisoner has the bound wrists and ankles positioned in front similar to an upside down oarsman, and is suspended upon a stick, passed under the crook of the knees and suspended by two chairs or two tables."[5] In 1969, a Brazilian instructor demonstrated various torture techniques to a class of eighty interrogators. Using six prisoners, he demonstrated the parrot's perch, the *palmatoria* paddle, the *falaka*, forced standing on sharp cans (the Vietnam), magnetos, and water pumping. The instructor emphasized that these techniques were best used in combination: "the parrot's perch, for example, was even more effective when combined with electric shocks."[6]

Some suggest that Brazilians invented the parrot's perch "in Sao Paulo in the 1940s."[7] Certainly the phrase is Brazilian. It was unknown in Portuguese until the 1940s except as word for a plant.[8] In the 1940s, Brazilians used the phrase *pau de arara* to describe migrant laborers from Brazil's impoverished northeast who traveled to cities for work, or to refer to the covered trucks in which they traveled, definitions that appear in dictionaries by 1967.[9] It seems likely that the phrase became a jailhouse pun for torture, associating beating with a stick (*pao*) and bucking with torturing *nordestinos* (born in a *pau de arara*, as the songs go) sometime between the 1940s and 1966.

The Brazilians were not the first modern police force to use this method of trussing (that honor goes to the Americans or the Yugoslavs). Nor were they the first to combine the *pau* with electrotorture or the *falaka*. The French and the Yugoslavian police had already pioneered these practices. Lastly, Brazilian accounts of torture under Vargas in the 1940s do not mention the *pau*, although the possibility remains that it was used mainly on poor *nordestinos* and went largely unreported.[10]

What Brazilian torturers did do is revive bucking throughout Latin America in the 1960s. Since then, bucking has appeared in torture chambers in Chile (*pau de arara* with electricity), Argentina, Haiti (*djak*), and Mexico (the Roast Chicken, *pollo rostizado*).[11]

Police also buck in the Mediterranean region as well, where the practice was also once customary in Spain (the bar, *la barra*, usually with electricity and *falaka*), Lebanon, Morocco (the parrot, *le perroquet*), Tunisia (the "roasted" position, *roti*, conjoined with choking and *falaka*), and possibly Syria (the Chicken, *farruj*) and Egypt.[12]

In the 1960s bucking also appears in regions where it had not been reported before.[13] South African police used bucking ("the Chicken") with magneto torture.[14] In 1971, the Royal Ulster Constabulary bucked a prisoner: "They got a rope and laced it through his arms and legs and hung him to the rafters all trussed up like the way you would a chicken and kept hanging him there."[15] Iranian police used it on common thieves in the 1970s ("chicken barbecue," *djudje kabab*).[16]

South Korean police combined bucking with choking with water.[17] In the 1980s, Somali torturers called it the "Vig," distinguishing it from another torture dubbed the "Mig" (see below).[18] In recent years, prisoners have reported bucking in Yemen (Kentucky *Farruj* or Chicken) and Namibia ("Fried Chicken Style").[19] Kenyan and Pakistani police have combined bucking with the *falaka*.[20]

The *Crapaudine*

Here, guards tie the arms and legs, and then draw them together behind the back. Sometimes they insert a rod into the knot and twist it, bowing the body out farther. Prisoners rock on their stomachs like a boat. Torturers then lift and drop them, suspend them, apply electrotorture, beat them, or press against their backs with feet or chairs.

The *crapaudine* was a French Foreign Legion practice. Algerian prisoners report some surviving Legion techniques, including suspended *crapaudine* in an Algerian camp and two cases of being buried up to the neck (*silo*) between 1956 and 1957.[21]

Most recent accounts are from East Asia and Africa: Vietnam (1970s and 1980s), Chad (1980s), Tunisia, Cameroon, and Lebanon (1990s). The practice became notorious in Chad (the *Arbachatar*) and Lebanon (the Flying Carpet).[22] Suspended *crapaudine* was standard in Tunisia and Cameroon (the seesaw, *balançoire*).[23] Tunisian torturers sometimes placed a chair "between the back and the triangle of the feet and hands," bowing the body further.[24] The Vietnamese practiced the classic *crapaudine* (the Airplane Trip, *voyage en avion*, or the Airplane, *l'avion*) and the Double Airplane (*double avion*), a half tie, binding the left arm and right leg behind the back.[25]

It is suggestive that all these countries are former French colonies. However, the *crapaudine* has also appeared outside the Francophone world since the 1970s. It has appeared in China (*liankao*), Angola (*chinkwalia*), and Somalia (the MIG, after "the swept-back wings of the [Soviet] MIG aircraft").[26] Angolan torturers sometimes tied with wet rope that slowly contracted (*nguelelo*).[27] In the 1990s, prisoners from Equatorial Guinea also report the *crapaudine*.[28]

As these are postrevolutionary states, often with Marxist-Leninist roots, this may suggest ideology plays a role in how the *crapaudine* was transmitted (the ideology hypothesis). Suggestive as this link may be, there are many other non-Communist contexts in which the *crapaudine* has also appeared. Von Schrader's *Elementary Field Interrogation*, a privately published American torture manual that draws heavily on the Vietnam experience, dubs the *crapaudine* "Ulysses' Bow."[29] In 2004, a prisoner at Guantánamo described how guards "cuffed me in an act called the scorpion," probably an instance of the Bow.[30] In at least one instance, Brazilian torturers used the *crapaudine* with magneto torture (the "Chinese torture").[31] Iranian police suspended the prisoner and placed a weight on his back.[32] In the 1980s, the *crapaudine* was routine in Honduras ("the Iguana") and El Salvador (*avioncito*).[33] And the *crapaudine* was typical Israeli GSS practice in Gaza and most West Bank centers between 1988 and 1993, dubbed the "banana tie" since "the tied up body looks like a banana."[34] And the *crapaudine* appears now routinely in Uganda (*kandoya*), where torturers sometimes suspend the victims from the ceiling while they are tied in this position.[35]

Standing Handcuffs

The standing handcuffs, as prisoners in British colonial India called it, involved forcing a prisoner to stand with his hands or thumbs suspended above him. The reverse standing handcuffs involves tying the arms behind the back and then suspending the victim from a wall hook with his toes barely touching the ground. These practices do considerably less damage than full suspension.[36] Von Schrader calls these techniques the Bath of Flies (standing handcuff), the Stork (reverse standing handcuff), and the One-Arm Hang Position (the Picket).[37]

Since World War II, they have been reported in Chinese POW camps in North Korea (1952–53), French Algeria (1957–59), North Vietnam (1960s), Northern Ireland (1971), Brazil (1970s), the Philippines (1970s), El Salvador (1980s), Iran ("weights," *ghapani*, 1980s), and Israel (1980s–1990s). Recent accounts come from Mexico, China, Russia, and American-occupied Iraq ("high cuffing").[38] The most detailed account is that of CIA technique, in part because it was highly valued among interrogators. "Prisoners are forced to stand handcuffed and with their feet shackled to an eye bolt in the floor for more than 40 hours."[39]

In the mid-1990s the Israeli GSS routinely used the reverse *sitting* handcuffs, a procedure dubbed *qas'at al-tawlah* by Palestinians.[40] They forced the detainee to sit on the floor or kneel with his back toward a table, his arms tied behind his back. Interrogators then lifted his arms upward behind him and stretched them out on the table while forcing his body downward. Interrogators thus achieved the same effects as standing without the aid of the incriminating wall hook. To aggravate the pain, interrogators pushed the detainee's body downward with their feet or stretched out the detainee's legs.

Police also use simpler methods, for instance, cuffing the hands behind the back and then pulling the arms upward, as in one French case in the 1990s.[41] Or they handcuff tightly one arm over the shoulders to one arm under the shoulders, putting slow pressure on the upper chest (dubbed "Su Qin carries a sword on his back," *Su Qin bei jian*, in China).[42]

Sweatboxes

These boxes are very hot, cold, or wet. Some hold a prisoner immobile (like a coffin). Others allow some movement but are designed to be uncomfortable. They are built just short of human dimensions, making it impossible to fully extend oneself in any direction (what I will call "squeeze cells"). Others have uneven surfaces and sharp edges that make sitting painful. Some are cages, exposed to the elements, while others are dark holes.

East Asian torturers customarily used such boxes before World War II, and prisoners frequently report them in this region after the war. Chinese used them during the Korean War, and Chinese prisoners today relate accounts of squeeze cells (*xiaohao*, literally "small number"), dark cells (*heiwu*), and extremely hot or cold cells.[43] In Vietnam, they are dubbed variously dark cells, tiger cages, or Connex boxes. The latter are large metal freight containers abandoned in the thousands by American forces. They accommodate several prisoners and are outfitted with metal stocks. Being metal, the boxes heat up rapidly in the tropical sun.[44]

French Paras used a squeeze cage at the Perrin farm and prison in Algeria in the 1950s, and prisoners describe squeeze cells in the 1970s in South Vietnam, Iran ("coffin," *tabout* or "barrel," *boshke*), Israel, and Turkey ("tortoise cell").[45] The Portuguese PIDE used sweatboxes (the icebox, *frigideira*, and frying pan, *torradeira*) as the boxes heated in the day and cooled at night.[46] In the last three decades, prisoners also reported sweatboxes in Latin American countries such as Brazil (*cofrinho*), Honduras, and Paraguay (*cajones*, *guardia*).[47] During the Second Iraq War, American troops allegedly stuffed individuals into sleeping bags (the "sleeping bag technique") and housed prisoners "in cells so small that they could neither stand nor lie down," and others used a box known as "the coffin" at the U.S. detention center at Qaim near Syria.[48]

In 1966, Brazilians adapted refrigeration for sweatboxes. Prisoners were shoved naked into a meat locker chilled to freezing temperatures (the refrigerator, *geladeira*).[49] Mexican police employed refrigeration once in 1997.[50] And in 2005, the "Cold Cell" was identified as one of six authorized CIA interrogation techniques. This cell was kept chilled at fifty degrees Fahrenheit and the prisoner was regularly doused with cold water.[51]

Chilling can be achieved without using cold boxes. For example, during World War I, prisoners at Alcatraz were removed from the hole and left exposed on the windward side of the island for eight hours a day.[52] Since the 1960s, torturers have adapted air vents to put "the air in a state of war with me," in the words of one prisoner.[53] In the first recorded case in 1961, guards at Parchman, Mississippi's state penitentiary, blasted civil rights detainees with a fire hose, and then turned "the air-conditioning system on full blast" for three days.[54] In 1965, detainees in Aden reported that British guards kept them "undressed in very cold cells with air conditioners and fans running at full speed."[55]

In the early 1970s, South Vietnamese torturers held Vhuen Van Tai, the highest-ranking Vietcong officer captured, in a room outfitted with heavy duty air conditioners for four years; a CIA interrogator who interviewed him in 1972 in the room regularly described Tai as "thoroughly chilled."[56] In other countries, interrogators forced prisoners to stand or squat for long periods in front of blasting air conditioning units or fans, as in the Singapore (1970s), Philippines (1976), Taiwan (1980), South Africa (1980s), and Israel (1991 to present).[57] Nor has the technique been forgotten in the United States. Reports of AC torture include prisons for Immigration and Naturalization Service detainees in Florida and New Jersey in the 1990s, the American military prison at Guantánamo, and most recently by special units in Iraq, who soaked prisoners before chilling them.[58]

The history of the Israeli "Freezer" illustrates how traditional sweatboxes gave way to chilled boxes and then to chilling. In 1977, the Freezer was a small cold, dark cell (two feet square and five feet high) with sharp three-quarter-inch stones set into the concrete floor. "One could not normally stand on them," and sitting on them was uncomfortable.[59]

By 1991, cells no longer had sharp stones. On the West Bank, sweatboxes were tall and narrow *stehzelle* in which individuals had to stand for hours (sometimes hooded and tied to an overhead bar), while others were boxes in which individuals had to sit immobile. At Gaza Central Prison, though, standard treatment involved beatings with long periods in the "refrigerator," a standing box capable of very low temperatures.[60]

After 1998, prisoners describe chilling, but not boxes.[61] Sometimes this occurred in prison cells; "the GSS apparently has computerized control in over cell temperatures."[62] Some interrogators chilled the interrogation room once they left the room. "The door of the room was closed and cold air entered the room. This situation would continue until 5 p.m., after that they would transfer me to the cell."[63]

Adapting Old Restraints

Some restraint tortures draw on the same principles as much older devices such as straitjackets, whirligigs, and wooden horses.

Straitjackets. The Japanese restraint belt is a leather belt with two attached cuffs that produces "the same effect as a straight-jacket."[64] Prisoners are cuffed to the belt with leather straps, with one arm attached in front and one arm behind the back. They are bound in this position for weeks sometimes, forced to sit cross-legged and to eat in this fashion as well.

Spanish police occasionally use the "famous thermal blanket," in which a prisoner is wrapped and baked in an electric blanket. In 2001, a prisoner reported being taped into the blanket for long periods and intermittently subjected to bagging.[65] In Uzbekistan, guards wrapped a detainee "tightly in a rubber sheet or suit" and then doused him alternately with cold and extremely hot water, a technique U.S. soldiers once dubbed "the old cold water—hot water treatment."[66] In Paraguay, guards wrapped prisoners in plastic sheets and slipped them into cylinders (*secadra*).[67]

The Wooden Horse. This torture involves mounting a handcuffed prisoner on a pole or trestle. In 1956, a French soldier in Algeria listed standard tortures as being magnetos, caging and exposure to the sun, and "being stationed naked, straddling [*à cheval*] upon a pole, hands and feet tied up."[68] In 1959, a similar report lists the trestle (*le tréteau*) as a standard punishment at the Améziane detention camp.[69] In the 1970s, Uruguayan military and police also employed the Wooden Horse (the sawhorse, *la caballete*). But some police achieve the same effect by forcing the prisoners' legs to the sides, a process that appears commonly in India (*cheera*, "leg stretching") and is occasionally recorded in Northern Ireland and Israel.[70]

Alternative cuffs. "Handcuffs, wrist or ankle ties leave no mark if they are applied properly, and in some countries officers take care to prevent damage."[71] French torturers in Algeria sometimes used soft scarves and rags.[72] In India, police bind wrists and ankles with the detainee's turban cloth.[73] Spanish torturers now use disposable foam-covered plastic cuffs.[74] American prison guards have used the pliers meant to cut plasticuffs to depilate prisoners.[75]

Finger bandaging. Finger bandaging is an old East Asian technique. It takes advantage of swelling that occurs with tight cuffing. Torturers stroke the fingers, rub pencils along them, squeeze them (sometimes with bullets or pencils between them). This causes excruciating pain with few marks. Prisoners have described finger bandaging in China (1950s), South Korea (1970s), Burma/Myanmar (1990s), and Japan (1990s), and occasionally beyond Asia (e.g., Spain).[76]

Whirligigs. Violent spinning induces intense nausea and dizziness without leaving marks. In Communist Afghanistan in the 1980s, a prisoner reported an electric spinning chair. "The chair turned around in a circle. I was tortured like this for 15 days, between one and four in the morning."[77] Iranian guards had a spherical container in which the prisoner was tossed "like a ball in a lotto machine."[78] Such devices, though, are rare. More commonly torturers spin prisoners who are hoisted inside sacks, tied in a buck (the "helicopter technique" in South Africa), or suspended by the waist or the feet.[79]

The *Shabeh*

Palestinians use the term *shabeh* to characterize the interrogation style of the Israeli GSS in the last decade or so. The principle behind *shabeh* is a familiar one: build up small practices to create large, painful effects. As Nigel Rodley, the UN's special rapporteur on torture concluded in 1997:

> Each of these measures on its own may not provoke severe pain or suffering. Together—and they are frequently used in combination— they may be expected to induce precisely such pain or suffering, especially if applied on a protracted basis, of say, several hours. In fact, they are sometimes apparently applied for days or even weeks on end. Under those circumstances, they can only be described as torture."[80]

The small elements of *shabeh* include sweating, sleep deprivation (up to twenty-five days), clean beating, bagging, positional tortures, exhaustion exercises, exposure to extreme heat and cold, boxes, and old restraint techniques (standing cells, standing and reverse handcuffs, *Qas'at al-Tawlah*).

The most novel elements of *shabeh* are the use of noise and chair torture, that is, "being shackled to a chair in a variety of uncomfortable positions (that in time becomes painful)."[81] As I discuss noise in the following chapter, here I focus on chair tortures.

Most commonly, interrogators shackled detainees to small chairs for children. These chairs are smooth, and the front legs are shorter than the back.[82] Deep aches "develop in the lower part of the body which is always sliding downward." As in positional tortures, "The hands swell. The feet swell. The entire body aches. Pains in the lower back develop."[83] This *shabeh* prevents "the body and mind from all sleep and rest." While fewer interrogators have used this method in recent years, they do select smaller chairs for larger men, producing the same effects.[84]

Another technique is to have the handcuffed prisoner lie across a stool on the small of his back, his extremities hanging over the sides, and beat him.[85] Dubbed *al-Qas'ah*, this position produces the same effect as the banana tie without the binding.[86] In the last few years, interrogators have the prisoner hang off the seat of the interrogation chair. Some now use the "bending method." Here, the prisoner is forced to lean back at an angle on a chair with no backrest. "If I tried to return to normal, sitting position he pushed me back. This continued for a long time."[87]

Detainees who emerged from *shabeh* interrogations had "little physical proof of the experience. The few signs left on the prisoner's bodies evaporated after a shower, uninterrupted sleep, and standard prison rations."[88] This prevented detainees from questioning the government's account of interrogation processes and also neutralized them in their own communities. When prisoners had clear wounds of torture, "the community understood why they broke down and implicated friends in real or imagined crimes." But lacking such wounds, they could not explain their weakness. Nor could they explain why they refused to continue their nationalist activities, a damaging move in a society in which political struggle was a measure of social worth. "The associated feelings of shame, remorse and guilt can cause severe mental trauma that would not have been experienced had the subjects been physically scarred."[89]

In some countries, interrogators and prisoners alike call certain tortures "Palestinian Hanging."[90] This phrase describes practices that are not Israeli, usually damaging full suspension, much as *Chinese* or *German* is sometimes used to describe tortures that were never Chinese or German. Such adjectives play on fears, invoking popular misconceptions. Because *shabeh* produces frightening effects systematically without marks, Israeli torture too, like Chinese and German, is now legendary.

The novelty of the *shabeh* also contributes to this legend. *Elements* of the *shabeh* can be found in Israel's past practice or in other national styles, but nothing quite like the *shabeh*.

To be specific, between 1969 and 1988, Palestinians report an eclectic range of techniques, principally magneto torture, *falaka*, choking in water, cold soaking, and harsh beatings, and, less frequently, positional tortures, slapping, freezing boxes, and noise.[91] Torture varied regionally, less stealthy in Lebanon, and stealthier on the West Bank and Israel, where a Jewish suspect in a criminal case received electrotorture in 1983.[92] During the first Intifada, bone-breaking beatings and banana ties (*crapaudine*) were especially common.[93] In 1991, there was a spike in magneto torture in the Hebron area.[94]

By 1993, however, interrogation practice shifted sharply.[95] Prisoners no longer reported banana ties, choking in water, electrotorture, or the *falaka*. Moreover, they described a standardized process across all facilities. Sleep deprivation, which Menachem Begin had observed in his own prison days was incomparable even to hunger or thirst, was now routine.[96] Restraint and positional tortures were duly noted on daily schedule sheets.[97] The process had a "conveyorlike quality" though, in the case of juveniles, there were eclectic variations.[98]

The *shabeh* also departs from previous national styles. Some Israelis note correctly that the *shabeh* includes the British "Five Techniques" (forced standing, hooding, sleep deprivation, starvation and thirst, and white noise).[99] But the *shabeh* also includes many restraint tortures and harsh, systematic beatings, practices that are absent in the Five Techniques. The Five Techniques were used for four to five days; the GSS practices *shabeh* on detainees for weeks. The *shabeh* more closely resembles American practice in the 1920s, which included similar beating and restraint tortures, but American torture too did not last as long, nor did torturers keep schedules.

Shabeh also resembles Soviet modern (positional tortures and sweating) in duration and beating, but Stalin's interrogators did not use restraint tortures. Early Communist Chinese interrogators did use all these elements, but their use of shackling was scarring, and they did not use chair tortures. The principle behind *shabeh*, systematically using small effects to generate great pain, is well known in Chinese torture. It governed tortures such as the Death of a Thousand Cuts. But this famous death was highly visible. *Shabeh* combines a thousand *clean* practices to create social death.

Some *shabeh* practices resemble French techniques from the 1930s, what might be called French classic. The banana tie is the *crapaudine*, and the "bending method" is simply the *coubaril*, using the interrogation chair without the box or fetters.

Spanish, British, and Japanese police have sometimes combined positional tortures, exhaustion exercises, clean beating, and restraint tortures. The Spanish and British even used chair tortures like *al-Qas'ah* (the Stool, the Crab), and the Japanese police roped suspects in the "tipsy chair." "They made me sit in a funny position. The chair was tipsy, and I couldn't lean over or rest. They ordered me to confess."[100]

Nevertheless, British, Spanish, and Japanese interrogators did not use standing or reverse handcuffs, the bending method, the freezer, or standing cells. Only the Spanish used bagging routinely. Scheduling tortures is unknown in all these cases. "Small chair" torture, the most common Israeli *shabeh*, is unknown worldwide, save for one case from North Korea in 1953.[101]

In torture, much that is considered new is, in fact, quite old. But the *shabeh* is a remarkable exception, and is a unique new contribution to the world of modern torture.

Remembering the Allied POWs

Are stress and duress techniques torture? We had no difficulty calling them that when our enemies used these techniques. During World War II, we had no difficulty calling Japanese slapping a war crime. We recognized torture in German concentration camps (*stehzelle*, gas mask choking, and forced exercises), in French detention camps in the Sahara (the *tombeau*), and in Stalin's gulags (standing and sitting with sleep deprivation).

Our fathers knew torture when they saw it in North Korea (forced standing, finger bandaging, standing handcuffs, sweatboxes) and Vietnam (slapping, standing). Our American forefathers had no difficulty denouncing old British and French military punishments as torture (bucking, the Wooden Horse, the *crapaudine*, the crucifixion, and the spread eagle). And heirs to this tradition also knew these techniques for what they were. In 2003, in response to an email soliciting a wish list of coercive interrogation techniques, one interrogator with the 501st Intelligence Battalion replied, "We need to take a deep breath and remember who we are. . . . We are American soldiers, heirs of a long tradition of staying on the high ground. We need to stay there."[102]

Yet, in August 1, 2002, White House lawyers itemized techniques that would not, in their view, constitute torture under the Federal Torture Act, including forced standing, hooding, starvation, thirst, mind-altering drugs, sleep deprivation, shaking (*Al-Hazz*), the "frog crouch," and the Israeli *shabeh*.[103] And in 2004, Phillip Heymann, a former deputy attorney general in the Clinton administration, proposed that American interrogators use "highly coercive interrogation methods."[104] Although he does not give specific examples, Heymann and his coauthor characterized these methods as techniques that fall midway between torture (practices forbidden by statutory and treaty obligations) and noncoercive interrogation (as specified by the due process law of the U.S. Constitution). It is hard to see how Heymann's approach excludes the stress and duress techniques and other methods specified by White House lawyers.

Others at home and abroad characterized stress and duress techniques as "torture lite" or "moderate physical pressure," American and Israeli expressions that have found some currency in newspapers. But whether they are called by these names, or called "enhanced interrogation" or "highly coercive interrogation," all this is simply another way of saying they are clean, and therefore misleading, techniques to those who observe them at a distance. Their main value is that they are gray tortures that are hard to condemn. In the absence of visible marks, how can anyone tell how much pain prisoners are in? One should think twice before accepting government euphemisms for torture. One might well remember that other states notorious for torture also did not refer to their interrogation methods as torture. The Nazis used the expression "sharpened interrogation" and the French in Algeria insisted on the expression "pushed interrogation," and historians know what techniques these expressions covered.

But the story I have told in the previous four chapters is darker. "Stress and duress" techniques, which frequently occurred at Abu Ghraib, belong to a family of tortures that descended from old West European military and police punishments. Stress and duress techniques were not unknown in authoritarian states, but such states had little incentive to use them until the age of human rights monitoring. At this point, authoritarian tortures start drawing more heavily on the stress and duress techniques of democratic states.

To be precise, British and American officers pioneered the use of forced standing. American police pioneered beating with rubber hoses, ratchet cuffs, cinching, and many types of clean beating in the early twentieth century. The Protestant Church of Scotland first routinized sleep deprivation. British, American, and French militaries first favored exhaustion exercises as torture, not to mention using restraint tortures (bucking, the *crapaudine*, and the standing handcuffs). By the 1950s, the French had abandoned these classic techniques for French modern, the combination of electrotorture and water tortures. But British and American practice recurrently draws on this long tradition even today, and so it would be apt to call this style of torture Anglo-Saxon modern (combining sweating with stress and duress techniques). The Israeli *shabeh* is, from this perspective, a variant within this much longer tradition of torture, as is Soviet modern (the Stalinist "Conveyor" method).

In the decades that followed, these stress and duress techniques swept the globe. The tortures British and Americans and French first used on ships and bases, in police stations and penal colonies, in time came to be used on our soldiers in POW camps elsewhere. The procedures that first appeared in places like the American Midwest, Essex, or Algiers appeared again in East Asia, Nazi Germany, North Korea, and North Vietnam decades later. What our governments do now will have consequences for future generations of POWs. Without our marvelous capacity to forget the past, the present would indeed be unbearable.[105]

Please break my eardrum.

> — "B," middle-aged Japanese public servant, falsely
>
> arrested, but not charged, for murder[1]

 Noise

In this chapter, I discuss the place of unbearable noise in torture. First, I survey historical uses of noise, distinguishing unbearable noise from older usages. Next, I discuss CIA-funded sensory deprivation experiments that used noise in the 1950s, the devices produced for use in them, and reports of their subsequent application in torture. Lastly, I consider the important argument Tim Shallice makes about modern torture in "The Ulster Depth Interrogation Techniques and Their Relation to Sensory Deprivation Research," an argument subsequently popularized in John McGuffin's *The Guineapigs*.[2]

Low-Technology Noise

As long as human beings have tortured each other, they have used noise. Torturers have used noise to intimidate and surprise prisoners, to supplement sleep deprivation, to mask screams, and to cause pain without leaving traces. Rarely mentioned in premodern accounts of torture, these low-tech approaches to noisemaking are now increasingly common. The following are some typical uses.

Intimidating noise. "The police need to shout," observed an Argentine prisoner, "shouting helps them."[3] In the 1970s and 1980s, Japanese police circled suspects as a group, "banging hands or rulers on [the] table," while others cupped their hands around the suspect's ears and shouted "repeatedly in a loud voice from both sides, 'Killer! Killer! (Faintness and dizziness result, and ringing in the ears continued for sometimes afterward)."[4] Then there is the screaming. Many a prisoner has been shattered by screams nearby, especially when they imagined they were hearing screams of loved ones.

Surprising noise. Floggers cracked their lash whips to the left or right of a prisoner's head, making a loud crack as the end accelerated past the speed of sound. British captains fired a single gun over the head of a keelhauled sailor as he emerged from the sea "in order to astonish and confound him."[5] Since the 1970s, ear cuffing (the *teléfono*), once rare, has become common worldwide.[6] Torturers also use loud surprising noise to keep prisoners awake for many hours. Consider this incident from German-occupied Norway in 1942. "He had to sit down between two loud-speakers for forty-eight hours. As soon as he dropped they shook him." There were other men with him, "eight in all, as far as I remember. They all had to sit up straight."[7]

Masking sound. Torturers make sounds to mask screams. In 1944, Gestapo men beat up Walter Bauer, one of those implicated in the Hitler assassination plot, while "phonograph records with children's songs were played at full volume to drown out the screams of the tortured man."[8] Sometimes things went wrong. Consider this example from 1933 in Hamburg: " 'The phonograph is busted,' " a trooper reported. 'They'll hear him scream.' 'Then tie a towel around his head," Radam [the interrogator] directed, 'and jam a steel helmet over his face, and then all you fellows sing. Let him yell to his heart's content.' "[9]

Irritating noise. In the 1950s, the Portuguese PIDE combined sleep deprivation with noise, forced standing (the statue, *estatua*), exhaustion exercises (forced walking), starvation, and thirst.[10] Duration varied from two to seven days, often repeated after brief periods of rest. PIDE's use of noise was so consistent that prisoners came to call sleep deprivation "sound torture," *tortura de sono*. For six days, says one prisoner, "I suffered the statue . . . on falling asleep, I would be woken at once or within a few minutes by having pins stuck in me or by shaking, or by sounds of knocking or tapping. In the end the slightest noise would waken me. I have since suffered from auditive hallucinations."[11] So sensitive did prisoners become that officers only needed to shake their newspapers or drop a coin on the table to interrupt the prisoner's sleep.

Emotive noise. An Argentine prisoner reports that in the 1970s, Argentine guards would play over the PA system "slushy, romantic songs by Julio Iglesias to make the prisoners weep."[12] The music was played so loudly that it was also impossible to sleep.

Vibrating noise. In South Vietnam in the 1960s, the Army Intelligence Bureau specialized in the *chen ve* ("beneath the water or mud," "the punching ball").[13] Interrogators put a prisoner "into a large container with water up to his neck." Then "the container was violently struck on the side with a mallet until the prisoner fainted and blood spurted from his mouth."[14] The beating produces "great pressure on the body of the prisoner: the heart is shocked severely, the liver and kidneys swell and the bladder bursts."[15] Normally banging a barrel in this way would raise the water only a few inches, not enough to change the pressure in the barrel or cause this damage. It is possible that the *chen ve* tank generated a unique shattering vibration when the mallets struck a particular spot. The technical requirements for such a device make this unlikely.[16] But if such knowledge was known, it has now been lost.

Loud noise. "The Helmet" involves forcing a helmet or bucket onto the prisoner's head and beating it. The helmet generates loud, unbearable noise. The earliest possible case is from Venezuela in 1956, using a plastic bucket, the *tobo*. Torturers taunted the prisoner saying, "You can't say we were beating you. We stuck the *tobo* on you," and that "you may die of heart failure, an attack, a fainting fit, but nobody can accuse us of having killed you."[17]

Since then, the helmet has appeared worldwide. In 1968, an American Green Beret said that, among other torture techniques, he had been taught "to put a bucket on people's heads and bang on it."[18] In the 1970s, Indonesian guards in East Timor "placed buckets on the heads of prisoners and banged them very hard."[19] In 1992, police in Limassol, Cyprus, struck a metal bucket with sticks, and in an incident in France in 1996, French police "covered the head of a person with a bucket and beat the sides of the bucket repeatedly with a baton."

In the 1970s, Spanish torturers were probably the first to use the motorcycle helmet, a device not only suited for beating the head, but also so tightly constructed that it spared torturers from listening to screams. Spanish interrogators first used the helmet during the Motorcycle (*la moto*), a unique restraint torture. Victims were "made to wear a helmet which was hit repeatedly, producing a deafening noise."[20] The helmet then appears in electrotorture in the 1980s.[21] And most recently, interrogators have subjected prisoners to the helmet in the standing position. "They put a helmet on me and made me stand up. . . . the blows hurt me a lot and made me feel like fainting."[22]

The motorcycle helmet was also the only unique feature of the Apollo Chair, the clunky electrotorture device used by the shah's torturers in the 1970s. The only contemporaneous account describes how prisoners wore a motorcycle helmet while strapped to a bed, looking like an Apollo astronaut;[23] meanwhile, "various instruments are hammered against the helmet."[24] Prisoners were also stuffed into barrels (*boshke*) and guards then beat the barrel, what is described as "a further development of the apollo."[25] Postrevolutionary prisoners' reports do not describe the Apollo.[26]

High-Technology Noise

Low-tech noise, then, is common, and there is generally a marked preference among modern torturers for low-tech procedures. However, this is not what captures modern imagination. What captivates modern minds is high-tech noise. This includes placing subjects in boxes or rooms where they are bombarded with noise of all sorts from machines, or subjecting them to scientifically engineered noise that only machines can produce ("white noise"). It also includes noise that may not be heard by the human ear, but can cause serious bodily damage, what is called "high-intensity sound" or "infrasound." This is what is known about high-technology noise in the twentieth century.

Spain. In 1990, José Peirats described a box that existed in the SIM prisons in Republican Spain in the mid-1930s. The noise box was a chest in which "one heard a terrifying cacophony of buzzers and bells." Peirat correctly observes that "in those days they were innovations in police repression."[27] If confirmed independently of Peirats, this would make the SIM the inventors of the first high-tech torture box. The difficulty is that other SIM prisoners do not mention these tortures; Peirats's account stands alone. The noise box is also unknown in Stalinist torture, nor are there subsequent accounts from Franco's Spain.

Northern Ireland. In August 1971, British soldiers arrested 342 men. Twelve of them were taken to an unknown location and subjected to what is now notorious as the Five Techniques (forced standing, hooding, sleep deprivation, starvation and thirst, and white noise). Too often details of the case are forgotten.

The 342 prisoners were all subjected to beatings, exhaustion exercises, or positional tortures in various detention centers.[28] Then 12 men, three groups of 4, were hooded and transported. Sometimes they were told they would be tossed from the helicopter. Eventually, all were taken to a cold room and forced to take the search position, hands and legs wide apart, back rigid, and head held up. If they rested their head, guards banged them against the wall. If they closed their fists, guards beat the hand until it opened. If they fell, they were kicked until they stood up. Occasionally, guards struck them in the genitals, arms, or legs, for no perceptible reason. They held this position for hours and sometimes days without food or water. Lastly, the room was filled with white noise. Periodically, guards would take the men to interrogators who subjected them to beating and sweating. Toward the end of their detention, prisoners were not put in the search position. They were left lying on the floor, forced to sit in uncomfortable positions or hung by the handcuffs from a wall hook.[29]

Among the Five Techniques, the noise received the most attention.[30] Prisoners offered different descriptions of this sound: as compressed steam escaping ("noise like compressed-air engine in room. Very loud, deafening");[31] whirring ("a constant whirring noise like a helicopter blades going round");[32] droning ("low droning noise which sounded to me like an electric saw");[33] piercing ("a terrible high pitched noise");[34] and variable ("roaring at times and then it would calm down, and then roar up again").[35] Most men reported auditory hallucinations including church hymns, Sousa marches, an Italian tenor, protest poems, and a death service. Interrogators referred to the room as the "music box" and were aware the detainees were experiencing auditory hallucinations.[36]

Less attention has been paid to the not so dramatic effects of the tortures including blurred vision, intense loss of sensation, and intense swelling of the ankles to almost twice normal size.[37] To counteract the loss of sensation, guards forcibly exercised and beat the men until circulation was restored, and then put the prisoners back in position.[38] Less attention has also been paid to the "black room," used mainly for teenagers and schoolboys, who were "kept in isolation and complete darkness while tape recordings of people being beaten up are played through the walls."[39]

West Germany. In November 1971, federal border guards were "systematically tortured" as part of their training. During an exercise in Bavaria with American Special Forces, "They had been beaten and locked into tiny torture chambers, where they were subjected to continual cold water showers and unendurable noise. An officer was stripped and tied to a tree by his genitals."[40]

Brazil. *Geladeiras* were most common in the southern triangle of Guanabara (Rio City), São Paulo, and Minas Gerais.[41] In 1966, a journalist described the *geladeira* or icebox as a meat locker with subzero temperatures.[42] In 1972, a prisoner described the Rio *geladeira* as a small dark "soundproof cell" with "an electrical system that reproduced the most varied sounds, reminiscent of sirens, bombardments, etc. all this interspersed with periods of silence."[43] A Parisian lawyer, Georges Pinet, reported that the noises included "jet engines, screams of terror, deafening and nerve-shattering music and flashing lights combined with thirst, cold and hunger to create delirium. Then while the victim is under illusion of fantasies resulting from this delirium, a vision of water is offered him, and a feminine voice suggests that his thirst will be satisfied if he confesses or signs a declaration."[44]

In 1976, a prisoner, José Miguel Camolez, described the *geladeira* in Rio as a small windowless, soundproofed room, two meters by two meters, with an observation hole covered with dark glass. Inside, he heard "several different voices coming simultaneously from loudspeakers installed in the ceiling; they began to call him dirty names." He "began to protest immediately with loud shouts," and "the voices then stopped and were replaced by electronic noises so loud and so intense he could no longer hear his own voice." Then the sound stopped and the walls of room were battered "with great intensity for a long time with something like a hammer or a wooden shoe."[45] Others mention that the *geladeira* was "very cold," had a "very strong light," and produced varying sounds from "the noise of an airplane turbine to a strident factory siren."[46]

In 1977, prisoners described the *geladeira* as an observation room, a concrete room enclosed within another room. Everything was monitored with closed-circuit television. Prisoners were starved and had to defecate and urinate on the floor, but sleeping was allowed. Oxygen came through small holes in the wall and at night there were "bone chilling" and "diabolical" sounds that penetrated "the head like a corkscrew." The box would get extremely hot or cold randomly. Prisoners did not see their torturers. An official DOPS record from the period states that the *geladeira's* objective was the "destructuring" of the captive's personality.[47]

Israel. In 1977, two prisoners described how a sweatbox, the "Frigidaire," had been rigged to produce "a strange noise" that "disturbed their sleep." They likened it to "a kind of hissing noise from an engine, or maybe a buzzing noise."[48] No reports like this follow in the following decades. In the early 1990s, the only reported use of noise is to mask beatings. "They raised the volume of the cassette recorder to its highest level and the first beating round started."[49]

The GSS returns to noise in the mid-1990s, playing "blaring Western music" on loud speakers during the *shabeh* periods. According to one detainee, the music is "designed only to prevent sleep and to stupefy the senses of the detainees, especially 'Middle Eastern' detainees who are not used to this kind of music as it is so nerve-wracking."[50] Another claims that the purpose is to mask the screams of detainees.[51] In 2001, a Palestinian juvenile described how he was transported blindfolded and handcuffed in a jeep, "with my head next to the speaker of a tape recorder that they played at high volume for a few minutes."[52]

Mexico. In 1997, two prisoners described "unusual methods of torture" in addition to the regular fare (electrotorture, beatings, and starvation). One described being locked in a freezing icebox, while the other, "José X," was "tied up in a sound-proof room where he was made to stare into a spot light while heavy rock music was played loudly."[53]

Former Republic of Yugoslavia. In 1999, after the Kosovo war, British troops found white-noise rooms in Mali Alas, a village south of Pristina. These were "two small rooms about eight feet long and four feet wide. One of them was soundproofed with egg boxes that were painted green. There was nothing in the room except a large transistor and stereo." The battalion commander speculated, "It looked like a white noise room for psychological torture, subjecting people to non-stop, indescribable noise." The building was a youth detention center. It had 250 prisoners, but the Serbian staff had vanished and taken all the files on the youths held there.[54]

Dubai. In Dubai, a British firm was reported to have installed "prisoner disorientation equipment" in the Dubai Special Branch Headquarters. The room, called the House of Fun, is "a high-tech room fitted with a generator for white noise and strobe lights such as might be seen in a disco, but turned up to a volume capable of reducing the victim to submission within half an hour."[55]

U.S. military base at Guantánamo, Cuba. In 2004, a U.S. military official confirmed that a regular procedure at Camp Delta, the main prison facility, was to make "uncooperative prisoners strip to their underwear, having them sit in a chair with shackled hand and foot to a bolt in the floor, and forcing them to endure strobe lights and screamingly loud rock and rap music played through two close loudspeakers, while the air-conditioning was turned up to maximum levels."[56] One prisoner recalled, "I was left in a room and strobe lighting was put on and very loud music. It was a dance version of Eminem played repeatedly."[57]

American-occupied Iraq. In May 2003, U.S. military interrogators in Iraq subjected detainees to "a fearsome mix of Metallica and Barney the Dinosaur."[58] In 2004, two other military interrogators reported that music was used for sleep deprivation. Military intelligence troops "told guards to keep detainees awake and blast music at them."[59] Danish officers also allegedly used for interrogation "moderate physical pressure, loud music and standing for long periods of time."[60]

Some U.S. interrogators believed it was the noise that caused pain, not the sleep deprivation. "In training, they forced me to listen to the Barney I Love You song for 45 minutes. I never want to go through that again."[61] Others claimed the music was simply culturally offensive: "These people haven't heard heavy metal. They can't take it."[62]

These, then, are the possible candidates for high-technology noise in interrogation and torture, and it is in fact a fairly small set of cases. If there are more, they have not been widely reported.[63] Most of these accounts describe torturers operating in time-honored ways: using noises to scare (Northern Ireland, Brazil), to intimidate (Brazil), to mask beatings (Israel), and to supplement sleep deprivation (Israel, American-occupied Iraq). American soldiers playing Barney repeatedly and loudly do not represent a major technological advance over the Gestapo boys who played children's songs while they were beating up Bauer. They may be using louder machines, but the imagination is low-tech.

The Brazilian *geladeira* is another matter. It moves from being a freezer to a highly complicated machine in the late 1970s. Numerous prisoners confirm its use, making it the first high-technology noise box. Likewise, the British use of white noise in Northern Ireland is striking—not even the Brazilians used noise like this. The source of the noise remains unclear, though one prisoner reported the room was adjacent to a water-pumping station.[64] This noise reappears only in Israel and West Germany in the 1970s.

Peirats is the only prisoner so far who claims he was subjected to the SIM noise box, and José X the only one describing the Mexican sound room. Next to nothing is known about the "House of Fun" in Dubai police headquarters (1996) or the Yugoslavian white-noise room in the juvenile detention center (1999). Since they have been reported, prisoners have not come forward to describe this kind of torture.

Other claims about high-tech noise have been exaggerated. In 1974, British reporters described how the Portuguese PIDE studied the *torturo de sono* scientifically, making films of the victims for doctors to study.[65] A visitor to PIDE's facilities found "the organization's technical workshops and labs would probably have delighted a provincial detective service 20 years ago." The PIDE's data files were "manually operated," their interrogation rooms clumsily organized, the officers of "poor quality," and "their methods primitive." He concluded, "So much for the rumor that its officers were trained in CIA techniques."[66]

Some have claimed that the Iranian Apollo helmet amplified screams.[67] It is never clear from accounts if this is a mechanical feature or a psychological report. An alleged photograph of the Apollo, of unknown origin, fails to show any amplification mechanism. This photograph is unreliable because it shows a metal can, not a motorcycle helmet, and a chair rather than a bed.[68] In fact, the Apollo helmet probably was not different from the buckets and motorcycle helmets that preceded it.

In the 1970s, John McGuffin and Steve Wright warned that the British military was testing squawk boxes and photic drivers, devices of ultrasonic sound and light that caused dizziness, nausea, unconsciousness, and epilepsy.[69] The British army possessed thirteen squawk boxes (at a cost of two thousand pounds a piece) that were "highly directional and can therefore be aimed at particular people in the crowd."[70] Thirty years later, such devices are still on the drawing board, and the field of nonlethal sonics and photics is plagued with problems, including the problem of directionality.[71] At any rate, there are no reports of damaging "infrasound" used in torture.

The CIA and Sensory Deprivation Boxes

Putting aside the false leads, one can expand this small sample of high-technology sound by adding the CIA-sponsored sensory deprivation experiments that really did happen. And one might begin with John Marks's *The Search for the Manchurian Candidate* and Alan Scheflin and Edward Opton's *The Mind Manipulators*.[72]

These three authors are the most knowledgeable experts on the CIA experiments in brainwashing, excluding the CIA officers and consultants who wrote the reports and congressional staffers who investigated them. In the late 1970s, these authors gathered approximately sixteen thousand pages of declassified top secret U.S. Army and CIA material, "detailing the most massive experimentation program in history to tame the human mind."[73] Marks's collection is now publicly available at the National Security Archives at George Washington University, Washington, DC.

Among other experiments, these books describe the CIA's interest in specific high-tech boxes. These boxes represent two different strands of sensory deprivation research. Lilly's tank is an example of *sensory* deprivation (SD), the removal of all stimuli from the environment. Baldwin's box, by contrast, is an example of *perceptual* deprivation (PD), in which devices including white noise are used to *mask over* stimuli from the environment. The senses are not deprived, but they can no longer perceive. This is what we know about the boxes and their characteristic features.

Baldwin's Box

From the early 1950s, the CIA had been interested in SD research conducted by Donald Hebb, a psychologist as McGill University. Hebb put subjects in a sealed environment, a room or a large box, and deprived them of sensory input.[74] Goggles covered the eyes. Ears were muffed or exposed to constant low hum (white noise) that masked the environment. Padding prevented subjects from touching. The box blocked any external smells or sounds. The subjects could move and sleep, and they were periodically given meals and bathroom breaks. They were released when they wanted, and Hebb never left anyone in "the box" for more than six days.

At the National Institutes of Health (NIH), Maitland Baldwin also conducted SD research following Hebb's method. Unlike Hebb, Baldwin put an army volunteer in the box and refused to let him out. This persisted for forty hours. Finally, "after an hour of crying loudly and sobbing in a heartrending fashion," to use Baldwin's words, the soldier kicked his way out of the box. Baldwin became convinced that the box "could break any man, no matter how intelligent or strong-willed."

In 1955, Morse Allen of the CIA's Artichoke program contacted Baldwin. While Baldwin was certain the box would "almost certainly cause irreparable damage," he agreed to do further experiments if the agency "could provide the cover" and the subjects would do "terminal type" experiments.

In 1956, the CIA proposed building "a special chamber, in which all psychologically significant aspects of the environment can be controlled."[75] Numerous meetings discussed how and where to fund Baldwin, but the agency terminated the project when an agency medical officer criticized the project as "immoral and inhuman" and suggested that advocates for Baldwin might want to "volunteer their heads for use in Dr. Baldwin's 'noble' project."[76]

Baldwin eventually became an agency consultant on another project, but agency officers were wary of him because he was a "jack of all trades," an "eager beaver" with an obvious streak of "craziness." Baldwin performed lobotomies on apes and put them in the NIH box he had developed. Whether Baldwin used humans is unknown, but he did discuss "how lobotomized patients reacted to prolonged isolation" with an outside consultant.[77]

Lilly's Tank

John Lilly worked next door to Baldwin at the NIH, though there is no evidence Baldwin ever told Lilly what he was working on. For his SD experiments, Lilly invented a unique tank.[78] "Subjects floated in a tank of body-temperature water, wearing a face mask that provided air but cut off sight and sound." Lilly's tank reduced sensory inputs that Hebb's method could not. Hebb's method could not control the effects of gravity, or variable airflow as it passed over the body, or the tactile stimulation as the body heated up the bed. In the water tank, one floated, and the temperature remained consistent and identical to body temperature

Lilly used an abandoned World War II tank developed by the Office of Naval Research for studying the metabolism of underwater swimmers. He put himself in the tank first, maintaining that "he himself be the first subject of any experiment, and, in the case of the consciousness-exploring tank work, he and one colleague were the *only* ones."[79]

Like nearly every scientist working on the brain in the 1950s and 1960s, Lilly soon found "men from the secret agencies looking over his shoulders, impinging on the research."[80] In Lilly's case, CIA officials wanted to know,

"Could involuntary subjects be placed in the tank and broken down to the point where their belief systems or personalities could be altered?"[81] Lilly was more focused on the positive benefits of his research, and he soon realized that he could no longer work on the NIH without compromising his principles. He quit in 1958.

Other researchers adopted Lilly's tank, and one study in 1966 found that "only one subject lasted 10 hours, the median duration being under four hours." This is considerably shorter than forty hours in Baldwin's box. Tim Shallice, one of the strongest critics of SD research, concludes that Lilly's water tank was "the most severe situation used" in SD studies.[82]

Cameron's Psychic Driving Box

Ewen Cameron was a Canadian psychologist at McGill University. At the Allan Memorial Institute in Montreal, Cameron broke down personalities ("depatterning") and then tried to induce new personalities ("psychic driving"). He had used drugs and ECT machines for purposes of depatterning.[83] The damage was extensive. A follow-up study of Cameron's depatterned patients from the early 1960s showed that 60 percent could not remember anything about themselves as they had been six months to ten years prior to treatment.[84]

Cameron's depatterned patients did not interest the CIA. In 1958, the agency offered Cameron funding to take his research beyond this point. "Agency officials wanted to know if, once Cameron had produced the blank mind, he could then program in new patterns of behavior."[85] Unlike Baldwin, Cameron already had a cover and worked in a foreign country. He could find his own supply of subjects, and he was "willing to do terminal experiments in electroshock, sensory deprivation, drug testing, and all of the above combined."[86]

Cameron secured an agency grant of about nineteen thousand dollars a year for about five years, modest by CIA standards, but important to Cameron. He constructed a box along Hebb's design in the converted stables behind Allen Memorial where his assistant had a behavioral lab. He pumped in repeated verbal messages by means of continuous tape loops underneath pillows in "sleep rooms." Messages included negative and positive statements (e.g., "Madeleine you let your mother and father treat you as a child all through your single life," followed by "You mean to get well").[87] Cameron left one woman, Mary C, in the box for thirty-five days. Cameron wrote, "Although the patient was prepared by both prolonged sensory isolation (35 days) and by repeated depatterning, and although she received 101 days of positive driving, no favorable results were obtained."[88]

In fact, Cameron was able to destroy minds, but not rebuild them. No psychiatrist, as far is publicly known, accepts his theory of psychic driving. Even Donald Hebb observed: "That was an awful set off ideas Cameron was working with. It called for no intellectual respect. If you actually look at what he was doing and what he wrote, it would make you laugh. If I had a graduate student who talked like that, I'd throw him out." The difficulty was that while Cameron "was no good as a researcher," but "he was eminent because of politics."[89]

Beyond the Laboratory

The SD/PD boxes were fearsome devices. CIA interrogation manuals, the *Kubark* (1963) and the *Human Resources Exploitation Training Manual* (1983), specifically single out Lilly's water tank as being particularly effective in generating stress and anxiety.[90] One would expect, then, that these boxes would exist worldwide, if not in squeamish democratic states, then at least in authoritarian ones.

The evidence is otherwise. Among the handful of known cases, the Brazilian *geladeiras* most closely resemble the PD boxes. Like Cameron's box, their stated purpose was destructuring personalities. While this may have been true in theory, in practice, prisoners mainly described the unbearable noise ("one's ears would burst" or "such strident deafening sounds as to drive him mad").[91] The boxes retained their original character as sweatboxes to induce pain, generating extremes in cold or heat, even as more technology was added on. Camolez's 1976 account suggests that the operators of *geladeiras* were not always well skilled.

Other boxes that might fit this pattern appear in the 1970s in West Germany and Israel, but like the *geladeiras*, they do not make it into the 1980s. Too little is known about the boxes in Spain in the 1930s or Dubai, Mexico, and Yugoslavia in the 1990s.

No prisoner has ever reported being subjected to Lilly's SD water tank. In 1971, Shallice explained, "It is only good fortune that the Lilly-Shurley immersion technique would be inconvenient, expensive, difficult to rationalize away, and liable to suicide by drowning if used as an interrogation technique; it would be a really potent stressor."[92]

As I argued in part III with respect to electrotorture devices, highly technological inventions do not float effortlessly from the world of science to police forces. In the case of stun technology, success in laboratories rarely translated into success in the real world. It required someone of Cover's political and scientific skills to weave together networks that would sustain his inventions beyond the laboratory.

SD/PD boxes were painful, clean, and nonlethal. The *geladeira* was, in addition, capable of many functions. These boxes failed to catch on as torture devices. They were not portable, were unfamiliar to the users, were hard to maintain and repair, required a sophisticated support network, were too difficult to find or create, and were too visible in the world of monitoring (not directly linked to routine duties and had no obvious civilian usage). They lacked the quality of "everydayness" that enabled stun to succeed.

And there were easily more portable and simpler alternatives. Simple sleep deprivation and drugs can also produce hallucinations. There are also, as we have seen, simpler ways of subjecting prisoners to painful noise, including the helmet, the *boshke*, the *teléfono*, and loudspeakers. To this one might add that Cameron's specific approach produced retrograde amnesia, useful for "brain-washing" perhaps, but hardly useful if the interrogator was hoping to get information about the previous six months to ten years.

It is not surprising, in the end, that the only part of SD/PD experiments that appear in torture contexts is noise. Devices that produce noise require no special training, are cheap, ubiquitous, portable, easily explainable. Why use a PD chamber when you have a loudspeaker or a boom box?

There was only one SD/PD box that was able to transition to everyday use, though not for torture, and this was Lilly's water tank. While Lilly was performing his experiments in the 1950s, he reported that the water tank was profoundly relaxing and refreshing, two hours in the tank being equivalent to a full night's sleep. Lilly spent those two hours not simply in sleep, but also in various states of consciousness. He found he could voluntarily induce "waking dreams, hallucinations; total events could take place in the inner realities that were so brilliant and so 'real' they could possibly be mistaken for events in the outside world."[93]

Lilly never described his out-of-body experiences in scientific journals, but he did record them. Aldous Huxley, who corresponded with Lilly, compared Lilly's visionary work in the laboratory with Tibetan lamas, Hindu hermits, and Christian saints.[94] Lilly left the NIH only after consulting with two or three extraterrestrial beings; they suggested that he work with dolphins.[95] Lilly's pioneering work on dolphin intelligence was subsequently portrayed in *The Day of the Dolphin* (1973), with George C. Scott as Lilly. Paddy Chayefsky explored Lilly's mind-altering journeys in his novel *Altered States* (1978), which subsequently became a movie of the same name (1980).

In 1972, Glenn Perry, a shy computer programmer at Xerox, approached Lilly. He had read Lilly's *The Center of the Cyclone*, and asked if Lilly would give him specifications so he could build a tank of his own. Perry used the tank to overcome his shyness. He then started making Lilly floatation tanks, and Lilly named the company Samadhi.[96] In 1978, Lilly wrote *The Deep Self: Profound Relaxation and the Tank Isolation Technique*.[97]

The Lilly floatation tank became a New Age phenomenon. Today, numerous wellness retreats throughout the world have Lilly tanks. They are used for relieving pain and insomnia, and for meditation, self-analysis, and transcendental experiences. They are self-contained, require no plumbing, attach to standard electrical outlets, and are about the size of a double bed. Samadhi Tank Company sells various models including the Classic ($6,500) and the Eco Tank ($3,500), and a thriving secondhand market moves used tanks within two weeks.

Shallice knew that subjects reacted differently to SD/PD, that the painful anxiety and stress effects varied, and that the SD effects "depend critically upon how the subject conceives of the situation."[98] I doubt he imagined that the most fearsome SD box would be a popular home relaxation device for altered mind-states.

Principles and Guinea Pigs

In 1957, Harold Wolff and Lawrence Hinkle had established that isolation, sleep deprivation, nonspecific threats, depersonalization, and inadequate diets placed enormous stress on individuals. In 1971, Tim Shallice argued that interrogators achieved results with the Ulster prisoners in six days, whereas Soviet sweating and positional tortures, as Wolff and Hinkle had reported, took four to six weeks on average. This shorter time was due to "the greater intensity of the sleep deprivation and particularly of the isolation methods."[99]

Someone had improved upon Soviet techniques. The Five Techniques "were developed utilizing a knowledge of the sensory deprivation literature." They were "an example of the way all aspects of military operations are losing their craft-like character and being approached from a scientific perspective."[100] Shallice pointed to American military agencies, which had "pumped a considerable amount of money into the research for obvious reasons."[101]

John McGuffin popularized Shallice's thesis that knowledge of sensory deprivation experiments clarified incidents of torture in Ulster. Indeed, he went farther than Shallice, arguing that the Ulster incident *was* an experiment and the prisoners, guinea pigs.

Neither Shallice nor McGuffin had access to the unclassified CIA material that Marks, Scheflin, and Opton used six years later. They had not studied Soviet positional tortures and sweating techniques, and they used mainly Wolff and Hinkle's summary analysis. They did not know the place of sweating, sleep deprivation, or positional torture in British military history. They wrote before serious historical and archival work had been done on British counterinsurgency. After thirty years, one can look back at the actual development of torture technology and compare their claims to what we now know.

Shallice's argument has three empirical components: the Five Techniques were faster than the Soviet techniques; what drove this advancement was scientific research elsewhere; and American and British militaries funded this research. I consider these claims, and then turn to McGuffin's claim that the Ulster incident was an experiment and to even broader claims others derive from McGuffin, for instance, that American torture after 9/11, indeed most torture worldwide, expresses a science of torture. In retrospect, all these claims appear exaggerated, muddled, or mistaken.

1. *The Five Techniques were faster than Soviet techniques.* On the contrary, when traditional combination of positional torture and sweating is broken down into its component elements, the apparent time difference Shallice identifies vanishes. In the traditional regimen, interrogators wanted false confessions. Even if a prisoner confessed on the first day, interrogators would make the prisoner repeat the confession until they had the kind of confession desired for public trials.

Consider this typical interrogation process of a Portuguese prisoner in the early 1960s. He was subjected to the usual regimen of forced standing and sleep deprivation (sound torture, *tortura de sono*) in units lasting no more than three days (38.5, 54, 56, 56, and 71 hours respectively). In between there were various interrogations (30.5, 22, 27, 22, and 30 hours) and periods in isolation (37, 10, 10, and 20 days).[102]

While total incarceration was 94 days (13 weeks), the actual periods of forced standing and sleep deprivation were not significantly different from those of the Ulster detainees. Wolff and Hinkle had stated this themselves, noting that there are genuine physiological limits for how long human beings can stand immobile (not more than 2 or 3 days).[103] Archival studies showed that 90 percent of PIDE's victims developed the usual symptoms within 2 to 3 days, including nervous breakdowns, hallucinations, extreme anxiety, and disorientation in time and space.[104] If length of torture matters, in some cases the Ulster detainees stood longer, a testimony to their stamina, but not a point that assists Shallice's claim.

In short, the reason the Soviet regimen lasted four to six weeks was not because the techniques were slower, but because the purpose of torture was different. British interrogators wanted information and they wanted it quickly. Soviet interrogators were prepared to take their time.

Shallice is right to say that sleep deprivation and isolation are painful. This would not be news to old-school torturers, even if SD research clarifies why this is so. Moreover, forced standing is also painful and places temporal limits on torture, and Shallice does not even consider whether this could explain the time difference. Indeed, he seems unaware that Soviets used it.[105] And the claim that Soviet techniques were somehow milder and less severe from a psychological point of view will be news to those who underwent them.[106]

2. *What drives high-technology torture is scientific research.* On the contrary, monitoring, not science, drives high-technology torture. In part V, I consider whether a science of torture is even plausible. Looking backward, thirty years later, there is precious little evidence of a science of torture based on SD/ PD research. The failure of PD boxes to spread reminds one that science has no magical powers. Those committed to a scientific imperative would be hard pressed to explain the distribution and chronology of torture techniques that this book has documented so far.

Consider, for example, that of the Five Techniques, only one is new: unbearable noise. Most accounts of high-technology noise occur in states where monitoring mattered, either democratic states in military conflict or authoritarian states under increased scrutiny for their human rights records (Yugoslavia being the only exception). This supports my alternative hypothesis that what drives modern torture is monitoring, not science (the monitoring hypothesis).

More disturbingly, perhaps, all available accounts of high-technology noise (even the exaggerated ones) date from after August 1971, that is, after the firestorm of international publicity around the British Five Techniques. Peirats's 1990 account is the only one that describes high-technology noise before 1971, in Republican Spain in 1935 or 1936, and that remains difficult to confirm. Most other accounts of white noise fall between 1971 and 1977, a chronology that coincides with more intense international and domestic monitoring of human rights violations and fits within the parameters of the universal monitoring hypothesis. This pattern also suggests that torturers elsewhere learned this procedure not through centralized training in the science of noise torture, but by imitating what they heard in press and monitoring reports about the British Five Techniques (the craft apprenticeship hypothesis). Political activists, including McGuffin, may have been more influential than they ever knew.

This would not be the first time torturers learned of torture though media publicity. Between 1953 and 1956, there was another small spurt of imitation among torturers. The international publicity around forced standing in North Korea appears to have led to imitations in Venezuela, Portugal, and French-occupied Algeria. The rapid disappearance of white noise also suggests the fadlike character of torture as a stylized craft. Most telling perhaps, Israeli interrogators abandoned white noise entirely in the 1970s, and when they returned to noise in the 1990s, they chose rock music. Rock music may sound like white noise to some adults, but as far as is known, it does not have the same properties as white noise. If there was a science of white-noise torture, the Israeli GSS apparently was unconvinced.

3. *In the 1970s, American and British militaries were funding SD research.* On the contrary, military interest in SD had ended by the early 1960s. The CIA's initial interest in scientific research was consistently related to brainwashing, not interrogation. This was especially true in the case of SD/PD. The agency was not interested in Cameron's depatterning techniques (using drugs and ECT), only his promise to create new personalities through psychic driving.

Baldwin told the agency that such techniques could be used for torture in interrogation.[107] The agency was not interested: officials terminated his project, and some ridiculed his interest in torture.[108] Whatever Baldwin's subsequent consulting research aimed at, placing lobotomized simians in the box was not about extracting information that they knew. The CIA terminated funding for any Baldwin project by the end of the 1950s and for Cameron's projects by 1963. These were, as we now know, failures.

The CIA's KUBARK *Counterintelligence Interrogation* Manual (1963) does not mention either Cameron's or Baldwin's work. It uses three publicly available sources on SD, especially the work of John Lilly, all written between 1956 and 1961. The *Kubark's* writers discuss experiments by Hebb and Lilly to eliminate stimuli and mask "remaining stimuli, chiefly sounds, by a stronger but wholly monotonous overlay." They conclude, "The results of these experiments have little applicability to interrogation because the circumstances are dissimilar."[109] The experiments do yield some hypotheses, and these, they say, are worthy of more research.

If there were additional experiments, Marks, Scheflin, and Opton were unable to find them. One might expect that such additional research would be incorporated into the classified CIA interrogation manual from 1983, the *Human Resource Exploitation Training Manual*. The SD section simply summarizes the *Kubark* discussion. The hand-deleted sections mention Lilly's water tank and cite no additional literature.[110] In short, by 1971, when McGuffin and Shallice were raising the alarm, the CIA had already abandoned SD/PD research related to brainwashing, its main interest, and had rejected further proposals to apply this research to interrogation.

There is even less evidence of British military research in SD. Most of the techniques used in 1971, even combined in that form, were part of a long-standing Anglo-Saxon military and police tradition in torture (chapters 14–17). This tradition antedated not only SD research, but also the Soviet style in positional torture and sweating (chapter 3). The Anglo-Saxon tradition in stress and duress was passed down orally, in backrooms and barracks and after training classes, through generations of soldiers, not through centralized training, as the craft apprenticeship hypothesis suggests (chapter 15).

The only evidence of centralized training pertains to the R21 or stress inoculation training, which was then passed on to the RUC in Northern Ireland, but this does not show up in other parts of the empire (chapter 15). Shallice does not cite British military research on SD/PD equivalent to that of Baldwin, Lilly, or Cameron. In 1959, the British medical journal *Lancet* described how a governmental hospital reproduced Hebb's SD experiment using twenty volunteers.[111] Neither Shallice nor McGuffin cite this public study as a precursor to the events they are describing, and wisely so. Anyone who cites this single case, however nefarious, to illustrate a British science of torture must weigh this against a documented craft tradition of British torture spanning decades.[112]

4. *The Ulster incident was a sensory deprivation experiment.* In favor of this thesis is the extraordinary place of white noise. This cannot be explained away, as British counterinsurgency experts have proposed, by referring to venerable and ancient traditions.[113] The British had used forced standing, hooding, starvation and thirst, and sleep deprivation in other places, but there is no record of their use of sound before 1971. The references to the "music box" suggest that the guards were aware of the unique character of the noise.

If the Ulster incident was an experiment, it was not an SD/PD experiment. SD/PD boxes are kept at body temperature, but the prisoners were exposed to extremes of heat and cold.[114] Physical massage, sleep deprivation, and exhaustion exercises are not features of the classic SD/PD experiments, but the Ulster prisoners were subjected to all of these. Not even the CIA *Kubark* manual connects forced immobility and standing to sensory deprivation, discussing these practices instead under "Pain."[115] Forced immobility and beating has no place in experiments that aim at removing stimuli or at least masking over them.

McGuffin invents a phrase with no scientific standing, calling these procedures "SD 'auxiliary' techniques" and arguing that their purpose is to impede normal body functioning.[116] Procedures like beating and immobility are not even functional equivalents to the setup of SD/PD experiments. SD/PD experiments require preparations, but inducing greatly swollen joints, bruises, and kidney failure, or anything even remotely resembling these symptoms, is not among them. No doubt such effects impede normal bodily functioning, but in fact all torture techniques do. That is what makes them torture, and there is nothing special about the ones McGuffin identifies. One can, if one wishes, call all forms of torture, or even the very large class of stress and duress techniques, "sensory deprivation," but this act empties the term of any descriptive value.[117] Shallice, to his professional credit, never claimed that SD experiments resembled the Ulster incident, only that they clarified it.

Other features usually identified are too general. The boiler suit clothing, for example, does resemble what subjects wore in SD experiments. Baggy clothing was a standard practice for decades, since it made running difficult for escapees. In British practice, baggy clothing goes back at least as far as the gunnysack clothing of the Andaman penal colonies at the turn of the century.

The Ulster incident could have been an experiment, though not an SD one. It could have been an experiment in the painfulness of white noise. If that is so, it showed poor judgment.[118] Previous SD research had shown that white noise suppressed human sensitivity to pain. A torturer following the latest experimental results of the period would wisely have gone with SD rather than PD, since experimental results had shown "a 42¾ increase in pain sensitivity after four days of sensory deprivation in contrast to an increase of only 5¾ in a group of controls."[119]

The Ulster incident could have been an experiment in psychological regression. The *Kubark* manual, for example, does hypothesize that increased immobility might lead to more stress, that this might vary with individual characteristics, and that depriving subjects of human contact might make subjects more susceptible to the interrogator. Deprived of stimuli, a subject may regress and then "view the interrogator as a father figure."[120] This result would normally, the manual speculates, strengthen the subject's tendencies toward compliance. The RUC interrogators did not communicate their paternal benevolence well when they were beating and shouting at the prisoners. And none of the men reported regarding the interrogator as a benevolent father figure.

Lastly, the Ulster incident could have been an experiment in an unscientific sense. Some intelligence officer may have been trying out white noise to add to the usual toolkit, say for R21 training. This seems most plausible, conforming to what is generally known about British counterinsurgency work. Those who did this work were less like scientists, and more like magpies, reaching for whatever they thought might work in a pinch.

5. *American torture after 9/11, indeed torture globally, expresses a science of torture.* On the contrary, virtually all the techniques that appeared at Abu Ghraib and other American facilities belong either to a family of tortures that descended from old West European military and police punishments (Anglo-Saxon modern) or they descend from the pre–World War II practices of French colonialism (French modern). Most techniques are low tech, many rooted in native American policing going back to the nineteenth century. I have separated out each technical strand as clearly as possible in the last fourteen chapters, and, in many cases, the strands close with how U.S. agents used these techniques in Iraq, Afghanistan, or elsewhere. Again, I will not say that each history is complete, but these histories of recorded incidents are certainly more complete than anything that has been available hitherto.

In the absence of detailed histories of each technique, it has been tempting to connect the dots leading to American torture in the War on Terror very differently. This alternative history goes something like this: CIA reaction to Communist brainwashing—CIA-funded SD/PD experiments—the hooded men of Northern Ireland—School of the Americas—torture in Latin America and worldwide—torture in Afghanistan, Iraq, and Guantánamo.[121]

Histories of this sort usually embrace some version of Noam Chomsky's universal distributor hypothesis, but they are not Chomskyan histories. Chomsky argues the United States spread torture around the world, but he does not, so far as I know, claim as well that there is an American *science* of torture. The claim that such a science exists stands apart logically from any particular hypothesis about its method of transmission. And those who make this claim lean heavily on Shallice's and McGuffin's histories of torture, not on Chomsky. But that is not their only mistake. They also advance their case by collapsing the distinction between high-tech and low-tech torture, presenting low-tech tortures as if they express high-tech science. In this way, they see proof of an American universal distributor everywhere.

Studying torture techniques is not the same as, say, studying drugs. Opium is opium whether it is grown in Afghanistan or Southeast Asia. It may vary in quality, but basically it has the same chemical composition and the same physical effects. But in torture, these details matter. A telephone magneto is not a jerry-rigged device, nor is it an ECT machine, a stun gun, or a Taser.[122] Each has a different composition and usually different effects. This allows one to recognize the usage of each technique. More importantly, one can reconstruct the history of each instrument to determine whether transmission stories are true or false.

But histories of an American science of torture ironically pay no attention to the actual devices or their effects. By calling it all "electrotorture," they set the bar so low that, for example, evidence of magneto torture in Vietnam effortlessly becomes evidence of the fruits of CIA ECT experimentation.[123] They do not ask what relationship ECT could have to magneto torture. After all, ECT notoriously generates retrograde amnesia, and it is hardly a form of electrotorture appropriate if one was gathering information Vietcong prisoners remembered.

Similarly, white noise is not any loud or irritating noise; these do not have its unique properties. The presence of white noise was precisely what made McGuffin's charge of scientific torture plausible in Northern Ireland. For better or worse, there are no similar reports of white noise in American detention centers post-9/11.[124] This makes the case for a scientific basis, much less an SD basis, for these tortures even less plausible. If playing Barney, Metallica, or Eminem loudly was a form of SD experimentation, then Amnesty International should be looking for torture victims in the American suburbs. There will be lots of them.

One could multiply the examples based on the previous chapters. Choking in water (waterboarding) has no relationship with the effects of Lilly's water tank.[125] Forced standing is not sensory deprivation.[126] A cold box, even one with air conditioning, is not an SD chamber.[127] Nor is exposure to the elements in a cage or solitary in a small room.[128] Hooding is not sensory deprivation; sensory deprivation is not any kind of disorientation a prisoner feels; and the effects of sensory deprivation are not identical to any and all forms of fear, identity crisis, or post-traumatic stress disorder.[129] Whatever issues one may have with Chomsky's view of torture, his claims are, by contrast, specific and discrete enough to be testable.

Histories of an American science of torture rarely explain why they identify low-tech tortures with high-tech ones. They get no help here from McGuffin; whatever his faults, McGuffin knew high-tech practices like white noise were different from "auxiliary practices" like forced standing. He believed low-tech practices like forced standing were *supplements* to SD techniques, but the new histories treat these low-tech practices as *equivalents* to SD, a thesis McGuffin never advanced. Among recent writers, only Alfred McCoy recognizes the problem. He concedes that most torture techniques worldwide are "simple, even banal."[130] "Medieval and modern methods sometimes seem indistinguishable"; CIA prisons at Bagram do not look too different from Inquisitional prisons.[131] Everything gets mixed up, and so one cannot distinguish the scientific from the crude technique.

Perhaps one day someone will furnish a plausible standard for distinguishing the alleged scientific tortures from the incredible banality of torture in the field, but so far none of the answers are persuasive. Forced standing and other banal procedures are neither necessary supplements nor fundamental features of SD/PD-based scientific torture, as I already explained in the previous sections.[132] Some torturers do use instruments to force physical restraint (a rack), but this is not evidence of a modern scientific technique invented by the CIA.[133] No doubt, one can restrain people to stand with or without instruments, but *both* practices are centuries old (chapter 14). Inquisitional and CIA torturers may have different purposes, but having a different purpose is not evidence of a science of torture.[134] Having the intention to be scientific does not make it so anymore than wearing a white lab coat makes one a scientist.

Torture no doubt has a slippery slope, and torturers rapidly adopt more brutal and cruel procedures beyond the approved techniques.[135] Everything does get all mixed up. But conceding this does not help distinguish the scientific from the crude technique. Indeed, it counts against a science of torture existing at all. If nothing else, a science of torture means a precise way of regulating pain to achieve results. But, as I explain in chapter 21, the reason torturers drive toward excessive brutality is because they have no way to regulate pain and so depend on craft maxims.

If there is a slippery slope in torture, there cannot also be a science of torture. If a science of torture existed, the slippery slopes would be far less slick, if not disappear entirely; torturers would not have to guess. But in fact they do, and the slope kicks in. So either there was no major American breakthrough in the science of torture in the 1950s, or, a science of torture decays rapidly in the field. There are no other choices. What is certain is that high-tech devices rarely persist. Like unusual molecules that survive only in laboratory conditions, these devices dissipate when exposed to reality.

6. *Clean techniques express a psychological science of coercion.* On the contrary, clean techniques are not psychological techniques at all. The techniques I have covered in this book cause *physical* pain. Even sleep deprivation has specific effects on the body's physiological processes. It is not a technique of psychological regression.[136] It is true that all physical techniques of torture, clean or scarring, have psychological as well as physical effects. But psychological techniques of coercion have for the most part *only* psychological effects. Subjects may feel pressed, anxious, or fearful, but it is not as if their ankles swell up suddenly or blood starts pouring from their noses, or as if death ensues.

Clean tortures cause the same physical pain regardless of whether the pain is self-inflicted or inflicted by some other agent. One gets no nearer a psychological science of coercion by insisting on the "self-inflicted" nature of some techniques.[137] The voluntary nature of forced standing does not make this torture "psychological" any more than voluntarily sticking a knife into one's flesh is a psychological torture.

Clean tortures leave no marks, and the absence of marks does indeed have serious psychological and social consequences. But the fact that a physical technique leaves no marks does not make it a psychological technique.[138] A paddle or a fist applied to the body leaves marks if used one way, but not if used another way. Both strikes involve harsh physical blows, and it is absurd to refer to a clean blow as psychological and a scarring one as physical.

Similarly, waterboarding is not a psychological torture. Torturers, of course, have always favored this description; in his apology for French police torture in Algeria in 1955, Inspector Roger Wuillaume called water torture and electrotorture tortures that were "more psychological than physical."[139] Similarly, in February 2006, the *Wall Street Journal* editorial defended the administration's interrogation policies, arguing that waterboarding simply "induces a feeling of suffocation" and that all U.S. techniques, including waterboarding, are "psychological techniques designed to break a detainee."[140] Andrew Sullivan, the conservative blogger, led the charge for calling waterboarding what it was. When one's head is stuck under water, the painful sensation of near asphyxiation and fiery distension of the bowels is just that; it is not the psychological *appearance* of the *feeling* of a sensation of near asphyxiation. In a day or two, the editorial board got it.

Reporters and critics also mistakenly bought into this apologetic cant. One administration critic, for example, asserted that the point of waterboarding is "to induce the survival reflex of a near death experience and thus break the victim psychologically."[141] On the contrary, CIA waterboarding is no less a physical torture than the Inquisitional water torture. Both procedures cause extreme and intense pain, and that is why interrogators, classical and modern, favor it.

There are good reasons to keep the commonplace distinction between psychological fears and physical pain, not the least being that one would want to distinguish between torture and frivolous sentimental claims.[142] If one does not distinguish between psychological fears of pain and pain itself, it is just as logical to argue that any uncomfortable thought counts as torture as it is to argue that sticking someone's head under water is simply playing on their psychological fears of death. And when torture become such a slippery word, analytic discussion becomes meaningless.

None of this is to deny that there are not coercive psychological techniques. This book has mentioned more than a few, and perhaps someone will write a history of all of them one day. There are at least four distinct strands that deserve reflection, but one can look in vain for evidence of them in the histories of an American science of "psychological" torture. Almost inevitably, these accounts start and end with the CIA-sponsored studies of psychological experimentation, especially SD studies.[143]

The four strands of psychological techniques are the following.

First, there are old psychological techniques like the "Mutt and Jeff" approach, the long-standing stock of Anglo-Saxon policing from the 1920s. They still appear in the CIA *Kubark* manual and in more recent American military interrogation manuals.

Second, there is the method of psychological regression. The *Kubark* manual breaks new ground by framing the entire process of interrogation, coercive and noncoercive, around a specific theory: regression through frustration. How such a theory ended up becoming the conceptual core of *Kubark* is worthy of its own investigation. One fact, though, is certain. The *Kubark* writers discuss the specific theory of psychological regression without reference to theories of sensory deprivation; the sources they use are from a different tradition, psychoanalytic and Gestalt psychology.[144] Indeed, in 1941, long before SD/PD research, the noted Gestalt psychologist Kurt Lewin had clarified the situational factors that could force personalities to regress temporarily to earlier developmental states in children.[145] He had specified situational factors such as reduction of environmental background (dedifferentiation), creating internal conflicts (disorganization), altering perceptions of time, and shattering a belief in security and stability of the situation. Identical claims can also be found in *Kubark*.

Third, there are psychological techniques from colonial policing. British and French police had a long history of using cultural humiliation during incarceration, and successor states also adopted them sometimes. Cultural coercion includes forcing Muslims to eat pork and drink alcohol, remove veils from women, or remove the turbans of Sikhs.[146]

Last, there are techniques that characterized specialized military programs designed to shore up the fortitude of soldiers going into battle. These include British R-21 techniques as well as the American "countermeasures for hostile interrogation" and the SERE (Survival, Evasion, Resistance, Escape). Dr. Louis "Jolly" West, a UCLA neuropsychiatrist, designed one of the earliest, the program at the Air Force Survival School.[147] A full history of these programs has yet to be written. No one knows what range of psychological techniques these programs used, but some, such as spitting on Bibles, sound terribly similar to the abuse of Qurans that happened at Guantánamo.[148]

These distinct strands of psychological coercion, each with its own history, are no doubt part of a broad occupational shift among torturers. Classical torturers marked their victims' bodies as religion or custom required. They often branded or scarred in public, using bodies to advertise state power and deter others from similar behavior. By contrast, modern torturers favor pains, physical or psychological, that intimidate the prisoner alone. At times, they reach farther than mere behavioral compliance, seeking to apply physical pain in order to touch the mind or warp a sense of self, and thereby shape the self-understandings of prisoners and dispose them to willing, compliant action.

In this respect, modern torture, whether scientized or not, has a somewhat different emphasis than classical torture. But it does not pay to put too much weight on this or to call all modern torture psychological science. The trouble is that many specific practices, and even the overall emphasis, can also be found among some premodern torturers. For example, Catholic Inquisitors shared the orientation of modern torturers because, unlike the state torturers, they were concerned with saving souls.[149] So if one wanted to call *any* serious assault on identity a modern psychological science of coercion, then one would have to date its start with the Catholic Inquisition, not with the CIA.

More generally, it is a mistake to call any technique that strikes out at the mind a "scientific" one. If the word *science* means anything, it means minimally this: there are general rules, fixed in advance, that are sufficient for the correct choice in particular situations. These rules use a unit of measure, pain in this case, to explain and predict outcomes, a unit commensurable across all subjects regardless of its source. Nothing in the world of coercion, psychological or physical, comes close to this, and as I argue in chapter 21, it is unlikely anything ever will. Torture is, and will likely remain, a craft.

Remembering Evil

The CIA has done horrible things using scientists, especially in the 1950s and 1960s. It sponsored Bluebird, Artichoke, and MKULTRA, research projects that selected and destroyed the lives of innocents in the United States, Canada, and France. The CIA also prefers clean torture in the age of human rights monitoring; even if it did not transmit techniques, in many places it authorized them. The problem, then, is not that there are not hidden political conspiracies. Problems arise when one adopts methods and concepts that make it impossible to distinguish between real conspiracies and imagined ones, and this creates a frightening experience.

For example, today, "sensory deprivation" is confused with stress (standing, forced postures, freezing or hot boxes), disorientation (hooding, sleep deprivation), debility (being deprived of food and water), overstimulation (loud noises), and isolation (solitary in a small cell). The phrase is so general it simply evokes fear, much like "Chinese" or "Nazi" torture. Even torturers like to apply the scientific-sounding name to practices they have performed for centuries.

Sensory deprivation as a word for torture gains its power not from its descriptive accuracy, but from its implicit account of evil. It implies that most torture grew from irresponsible science in the service of arbitrary power. For some, this powerful, almost theological, account of evil is hard to shake, as I explain in chapter 24. And such evil does happen in the world of torture, as the next chapter on drugs shows, but not often.

For better or for worse, most torturers choose low-tech procedures that help them avoid detection and are easy to pass on through apprenticeship. Low-tech torture thrives on ignorance, custom, rumor, selective memory, poverty, and media publicity. It lives off the violence in stockyards, schools, barracks, and homes. These are less sensational sources of evil, but far greater dangers to life and limb today than sensory deprivation.

Under Stalin, to wind up in a special psychiatric hospital was
an unattainable dream.

> —Vladimir Gusarov, Soviet dissident committed to Kazan
>
> Psychiatric Prison Hospital, 1953–54[1]

19   Drugs and Doctors

In this chapter, I describe the place of drugs and doctors in torture. First, I
describe the use of drugs to extort confessions and gather information from
prisoners in the early twentieth century. I consider ordinary police usage
and then CIA use of these scientific tortures. Next, I survey what is known
about the use, spread, and incidence of pharmacological torture during the
Cold War, focusing in particular on pharmacological torture in the Soviet
Union. In the 1970s, pharmacological torture spread rapidly among countries
and then declined everywhere in the 1980s except in the Soviet Union and
other Communist countries. These authoritarian states replied to international
and domestic critics by justifying painful pharmacological treatments of dissidents as legitimate medical intervention in psychiatric cases. Monitoring then
played an important role in driving pharmacological torture in the context of
Communist psychoprisons.

    The Communist exception offers once again an opportunity to explore the
role of ideology in the choice of torture techniques (the ideology hypothesis).
Pharmacological torture happened within the context of psychiatric prisons,
and so I consider the development of psychiatric prisons in Communist countries more generally. As Gusarov says, Stalin had little interest in psychoprisons
when he could send people to labor camps and prisons for torture.[2] But after
Stalin's death, remanding dissidents to psychoprisons became more common, and this process intensified in particular during the period of détente
in the 1970s. Around this time, psychoprisons appeared in Romania, Cuba,
and China. If these changes coincided with a change in ideology, this does
not appear in the historical record. It seems more likely that other Commun-

ist countries imitated the Soviet example because the Soviets had shown successfully a way to fend off international human rights monitors. And in the last few years, there are reports of psychiatric detention of dissidents in post-Communist Turkmenistan and the Russian Federation. This pattern of imitation resembles the way other torture techniques have spread, even if, in this case, one is dealing with a high-tech torture. Torturer-doctors, like less scientific torturers, learned by observing and imitating others in their craft (the craft apprenticeship hypothesis).

The history of these events is also the history of how doctors and psychiatrists became human rights monitors and the emergence of a medical monitoring system that complemented the juridical one. Ordinary observers cannot always see traces of clean tortures, but doctors sometimes can. I conclude by examining three types of medical monitors (prison doctors, local civilian doctors, and international medical monitors), considering the achievements and limitations of each.

Police and Drugs

In 1922, Robert House, a Texan obstetrician, wrote the Texas Medical Society, claiming he had discovered that "it is impossible to lie" under the influence of scopolamine.[3] House maintained he had found a "humane third degree."[4] "If my assertion is correct," he said, "there is no justifiable reason for any person to be convicted upon circumstantial evidence, nor any excuse for the brutal third degree methods, nor any excuse for the state to permit a suspect to turn State's evidence."[5]

Scopolamine was a powerful sedative, belonging to the same family as nightshade and mandrake. Isolated by a German chemist in 1892, doctors soon used it to control trembling movements (such as those in Parkinson's disease) and to treat withdrawal symptoms from drug addiction. But its most important usage came in 1894, when German doctors began experiments in obstetrical deliveries. The German program involved putting women into a "twilight sleep" (*dämmerschlaf*) using scopolamine, and it quickly triggered controversy worldwide. Advocates claimed that women's accounts made "a man break down and weep because he would not have a baby," while opponents believed scopolamine posed lethal dangers to mother and child.[6] To determine the optimum dosage for delivery, experimenters developed a memory test to bring the patient as far away from consciousness but short of full unconsciousness. With watch in hand, experimenters methodically questioned the patient, asking her to recall and identify various items and events, until they were sure the powers of recollection were deadened.

House had been experimenting with scopolamine since 1897, first on addicts and then on pregnant women. In 1916, after having delivered a baby, House and the husband could not find the scales to weigh the child. The wife, "apparently sound asleep, spoke up and said, 'They are in the kitchen on a nail behind the picture.' "[7] House theorized scopolamine forced truthful statements, and tested his hypothesis by interrogating four hundred pregnant women.[8] Having received correct answers "in every case, without exception," he then experimented on a man suspected of two burglaries at the prison hospital in Dallas. The prisoner confessed to the first robbery, but not the second. House developed a standard medical interrogation technique, convinced he could "force the truth from any person, on any question."[9]

American police already knew that they could force confessions from addicts merely by withholding drugs.[10] But a drug that forced the truth was promising. Spectacular cases followed, including a suspected axe murderer (Alabama, 1924) and a recalcitrant murder suspect (Denver, 1935).[11] The *American Journal of Police Science* reprinted House's original letter in 1931. In 1932, Calvin Goddard, a writer of true crime stories, popularized scopolamine as "truth serum."[12] The public embraced the phrase. Noah, after all, had revealed his secret thoughts when he was drunk, and the Romans always said that in wine, there was truth (*in vino veritas*).[13] Why couldn't science have found a better truth serum than alcohol?

Popular accounts overlooked awkward cases. In 1928, for example, Hawaiian police encouraged a suspect to admit he wrote a ransom note; later evidence vindicated him and pointed to the real killer.[14] In 1932, doctors at the meetings of the Chicago Neurological Society noted the variable success rates and questioned the authenticity, as well as legality, of confessions obtained in this manner. One doctor described being present at one of House's experiments when the patient "lied consistently all through the sitting."[15] The most important experiment, conducted at the University of Wisconsin, concluded that personality, not scopolamine, was critical in interrogation. In general, "The subjects who were resistant to suggestions in the normal state were also resistant when under the influence of the drug. There was a fairly marked tendency for those who were susceptible in the normal state to be markedly more so when under the influence of scopolamine."[16]

Legal and medical attention turned to other drugs. For over a century, psychiatrists had used drugs (hashish, opium, cocaine, and mescaline) to break down unconscious resistances and bringing to light repressed psychological states.[17] In the 1930s, American and English psychiatrists were experimenting with sodium amytal and sodium pentothal, new barbiturates originally developed for anesthesia.[18] If these drugs could remove *unconscious* resistances, would they also remove *voluntary* inhibitions? Could one extract the truth from silent or deceptive criminals?

In postwar Belgium and France, people asked this question during the hunt for suspected war criminals. French and Belgian doctors knew narcoanalysis from treating shell shock; it was the standard Allied treatment in England, North Africa, and France during World War II (see chapter 6, "Shock").[19] Now in Belgium, a suspected traitor was "pitilessly pursued with a syringe and mercilessly drugged with various products."[20] In 1947, French doctors administered sodium pentothal to Henri Cens, a henchman for the notorious Inspector Marty.[21] Cens had been wounded in the brain with a bullet and subject to periodic epilepsy, but prosecutors suspected he was malingering. During narcoanalysis, he uttered one lucid word, "*oui* [yes]." Doctors concluded that Cens was paralyzed, but fit for trial and imprisonment.

The wartime experience refocused attention on narcoanalysis on both sides of the Atlantic.[22] In the United States, dramatic "truth serum" cases involving child murderers, lost amnesiac girls, and paralyzed combat pilots stoked the public imagination.[23] The noted British medical journal *The Lancet* weighed in, questioning a court case that admitted evidence gathered through narcoanalysis.[24] In 1958, the political prisoner Henri Alleg charged that doctors had administered sodium pentothal during his torture in Algiers, reopening yet another round of psychiatric debates.[25]

By the early 1960s, professional judgment was that narcoanalysis was unreliable.[26] The "truth drugs" only produced "a relaxed state of mind," similar to "acute alcoholism—boasting, loquaciousness and general rambling."[27] Even if such a drug existed, a detainee might "not only tell the truth, he might embroider it to such a degree that for criminal interrogation purposes the efficacy of the drug is completely destroyed."[28]

The CIA and Drugs

In October 1942, the Psychological Warfare Branch of MI5, British Intelligence, wrote the American National Research Council. They asked the committee to investigate "the feasibility of using drugs in the interrogation of prisoners of war."[29] John Marks, Alan Scheflin, and Edward Opton have used declassified documents to reconstruct the massive experimentation that followed.[30]

During and after World War II, the OSS, CIA, and U.S. Army investigated drugs extensively, sometimes experimenting on innocents without consent. Starting in the 1940s, the CIA tested over 150 chemical substances to see how they affected human beings. These experiments included ordinary substances (caffeine, coffee, nicotine, and alcohol), "poisons (belladonna, strychnine), narcotics (heroin), hallucinogens (LSD, marijuana, peyote), "truth serums" (scopolamine, sodium amytal, sodium pentothal), barbiturates, nitrous oxide ("laughing gas"), chloral hydrate, tranquilizers, hypnotics, depressants, cocaine, atropine, morphine, amphetamines, Harmaline (an alleged Soviet speech-inducing drug), and aktedron (the alleged speech-inducing drug given to Cardinal Jószef Mindszenty).[31]

This secret research began long before the postwar concern about Communist brainwashing and continued long after that hysteria passed. It involved 149 subprojects, at least 185 nongovernment researchers, eighty institutions, forty-four colleges and universities, fifteen research foundations affiliated with pharmaceutical or chemical corporations, twelve hospitals and clinics, and three penal institutions.[32]

Among other conclusions, this research closed the book on "truth drugs." Was there a drug that reveals secrets a subject wishes to keep secret? The CIA judgment was that "a careful evaluation of the psychological mechanisms involved leads to the conclusion that such a goal is beyond reasonable expectation from any drug."[33] There are no truth drugs. Reports did note that some drugs, particularly those that made one addicted or caused pain, could be used to torture a detainee during interrogation. A skilled interrogator could exploit any weakness or dependency in hopes of getting information.[34] In this respect, drugs did not differ from other torture tools.

The myth of truth serum persisted for other reasons. For example, in 1975, the U.S. Army updated its intelligence manuals using army documents compiled between 1965 and 1966.[35] One manual, *Handling of Sources*, recommended procedures discredited by the CIA, including hypnosis and "truth serum" (sodium pentothal), even citing the old folklore ("*in vino veritas*" [*sic*]).[36] The Spanish version circulated in Latin America for years under the title *Manejo de Fuentes* in various military training classes. This may explain why prisoners report being administered sodium pentothal in the 1970s in the Philippines, Brazil, Uruguay (combined with the paralyzing drug curare), and Chile (in conjunction with hypnosis).[37] But reports of sodium pentothal became infrequent in the 1980s, suggesting that torturers abandoned this practice regardless of the CIA's (outdated) advice.

Human rights activists also believed in the myth of truth serum. In 1974, for example, McGuffin expressed surprise at the amateurish ways torturers used drugs in Northern Ireland. After all, "Opportunities clearly existed for much more concentrated and scientific tests, using more sophisticated drugs, provided by the Drug Squad, than those obtainable by local Branch men themselves."[38] Similarly, another observer argued that the Uruguayan pentothal-curare technique was very effective: "Everyone gives in under this pressure."[39]

But if Uruguayans had discovered the holy grail of interrogations, they did not put away their electric prods, plastic bags, and bathtubs.[40] As for the British, the CIA had already answered the question put to it by MI5 in 1942. If the RUC acted like amateurs, it was because they were out of the loop.

The Decline of Pharmacological Torture

While drugs cannot force the truth, they can make one sick, chatty, relaxed, addicted, giddy, forgetful, restless, anxious, sleepy, sluggish, unconscious, incapacitated, uncomfortable, or dead. They can cause pain. Brazilian torturers, for example, injected alcohol into tongues (1940s) and ether into the scrotum (1960s), and induced violent contractions with drugs (1970s).[41]

Some torturers clearly worked with medical advice drawn from ECT procedures.[42] In the 1970s, Brazilians used muscle relaxants to reduce the muscular rigidity and bone fractures induced by electroshock.[43] Uruguayans paralyzed with curare derivatives.[44] Chilean doctors prescribed various drugs before and after torture, including Valium to prisoners with high blood pressure so they would work better with "the boys."[45] Some Argentine and Guatemalan prisoners report pharmacological torture.[46] In some countries, torturers gave detainees lethal doses of slow-acting drugs; the released prisoner, they hoped, would appear to die a natural death before he or she could make a fuss.[47]

What is striking, though, is that reports of pharmacological torture began to decline in the 1980s. In 1986, Robert Kirschner, a seasoned medical observer for human rights organizations, described most pharmacological torture as "sporadic and without any clear purpose."[48] Other sources corroborate Kirschner's observation, including patient studies, human rights reports, and torture manuals.

Patient studies. Anne Goldfield and her team examined six patient studies conducted between 1979 and 1985, comprising 319 patients from thirteen countries (Chileans being the largest group). Only 12 patients (3.8 percent) reported "nontherapeutic medical administration."[49] Danish doctors working with Amnesty International reported on 135 cases from several countries, all tortured in the 1970s and 1980s. Only 7 percent of all victims reported pharmacological torture. It ranked eleventh in a list of twelve techniques. Similarly, in his study of 200 patients, Rasmussen reported only 1 patient who described receiving an injection, and pharmacological torture is absent from the list of twenty-eight main types of torture.[50]

Human rights reports. In its global audit of torture for the 1980s, Amnesty International reported torturers used drugs only in El Salvador, Zaire, and Colombia.[51] Some later annual reports, like the 1993 report, do not mention pharmacological torture at all. Case studies also mark the decline. The Chilean National Commission on Truth and Reconciliation noted three phases of torture in Chile: the early period (1973–74), the middle period (1974–77), and the late period (1977–90). It noted that DINA (Direccíon de Inteligencia Nacíonal, or National Intelligence Directorate) used drugs mainly in the middle period, and the commission does not discuss drugs at all in its discussion of the late period.[52] Similarly, a recent study of fifty-one Pakistani torture victims identified only three who reported pharmacological torture.[53] Such examples can be multiplied.

Torture manuals. In 1975, the CIA announced that it had ceased experimenting with drugs in 1967 and all indirect participation had ended in 1973. To be sure, one can be justly skeptical of this; the CIA had made such claims before.[54] And even if true, the existing data surely had ongoing field utility.

But this field usage is not described in the declassified and unedited *Human Resources Exploitation Training Manual* (1983). The CIA distributed thousands of copies of this manual in Spanish in Central America. Under "Narcosis," it repeats the conclusions of CIA research: "There is no drug which can force every subject to divulge all the information he has."[55] It recommends tricking subjects by giving them placebo sugar pills, and telling them that it is a truth serum. It discusses no other drugs for interrogation. Likewise, Schrader does not discuss drugs in his notorious Vietnam era torture manual, *Elementary Field Interrogation.*[56]

Pharmacological torture has always had "a special fascination for those disposed to intrigue, both historically and in fiction. There was always a high probability that the deed would go undetected and the culprit go unpunished." This kind of clean torture simply became harder by the 1980s. As Kirschner observed, "With advances in pharmacology and toxicology, the drugs have become more sophisticated but the chances of detection have also increased."[57] This chronology favors the universal monitoring hypothesis.

Of course, it is possible that torturers worldwide embraced the CIA's final conclusion that drugs are not useful in extracting information. But this would be no reason to abandon pharmacological torture. Torturers would still be able to use drugs to cause pain, intimidate, and force false confessions. But pharmacological torture is not often reported even for these purposes, suggesting that Kirschner drew the right conclusion. With increased medical monitoring, specialized drugs have simply become easier to spot.

Soviet Pharmacological Torture

In this picture of overall decline in pharmacological torture, there is one very significant exception. In the USSR, doctors used "therapeutic drugs as a principal agent of punishment."[58] Soviet doctors commonly favored haloperidol (haldol). It creates intense restlessness, a condition where the patient cannot be still: "It is difficult to think, walk, or sit, and impossible to lie down."[59] Haloperidol also slows body movement and induces symptoms similar to Parkinson's disease, including frequent licking, neck spasms, and mastication.[60] While doctors can control these effects, Soviet doctors did not try. Another typical drug, Aminazin, made detainees intensely sleepy and groggy and "in sufficient quantities makes one a vegetable."[61] If dissidents did not look insane going in, they certainly looked that way afterward.

Soviet doctors also administered insulin shock treatments and induced intense fevers with sulfazin, a drug that also creates excruciating pain at the injection site.[62] Doctors used these drugs to coerce detainees to change their ideas or discourage a prisoner from telling "others about his fate."[63] To produce a greater loss of inhibitions, doctors administered drug cocktails of sodium amobarbital (amytal) with caffeine or mixes of lysergic acid (LSD-25), psilocybin, or peyote (mescaline).[64]

Soviet psychiatric treatment also included beatings, or as inmates joked darkly, "fisticine."[65] Doctors condoned beatings, but insisted that they must be done correctly. One doctor reprimanded an orderly: "Don't you know you're not supposed to beat people, especially if you don't know how to do it."[66] Mikhail Kukobaka describes the techniques of one orderly who was especially skilled, which included open-handed slaps, blows to the stomach, and near asphyxiation with a wet towel—all clean procedures.[67] Orderlies also used four-point restraints and wet wraps. This latter procedure involves wrapping strips of wet sheeting around patients and allowing them to dry out. As the sheets dry, they "squeeze the entire body in a vise."[68] Straitjackets were not used, but solitary confinement was common.[69]

None of these were new procedures. Jaeger, Meduna, and Sakel had invented fever and insulin shock therapy in Austro-Hungary in the 1930s.[70] Western asylums after World War II used drugs analogous to haloperidol and aminazin, and the Soviet tortures were "in many respects similar to those common for so long in mental institutions in this country [United States]."[71] Nor was the Soviet state's use of psychiatric prisons new; dissidents had been sent to psychiatric prisons since Stalin.

What was new was the Soviet state's use of psychiatric hospitals to inflict pharmacological torture. This was a shift from Stalinist torture. Stalinist torture did not involve drugs.[72] At most, interrogators manipulated preexisting addictions and revived unconscious prisoners with huge doses of stimulants.[73] Similarly, detainees interred in psychiatric hospitals in the Stalinist era do not report being subjected to any therapies. Most Stalinist era detainees regarded psychiatric interment as better than the "much harsher punishment" that waited for them in the death camps.[74] Naum Korzhavin even says that the doctors were "benevolent, not punitive," hoping "to pin a diagnostic label on him in order to prevent his dispatch to a labour camp."[75] Those in labor camps hoped in vain to be committed to the local psychiatric ward.[76]

In the 1950s, "medication was rarely used" in most hospitals, but when it was, it consisted of "sleep therapy," that is, large doses of sleeping pills.[77] The Leningrad psychiatric hospital was the exception, using sleep therapy, wet wraps, insulin shock, and sulfazine injections, but "in 1953, no one received any treatment at the Leningrad SPH."[78] Some ECT was reported at Kazan in the early 1950s; these incidents and the case of Victor Fainberg are the only reports of ECT.[79] After 1954, "Many patient-prisoners were hurriedly discharged, and the regimen became more relaxed."[80] Alexander Volpin was committed three times in the Khrushchev era, but he "was never seriously treated for mental illness." In 1960, he received "small amounts of reserpine, a drug then used as a tranquilizer." At another time, a sympathetic physician helped him "avoid treatment with haloperidol, a potent tranquilizer used for some major psychiatric disorders."[81]

Dr. Norman Hirt dates the new drug treatments with the case of Olga Iofe in 1969 at the Kazan Hospital. She was given "a chemical lobotomy." Hirt argues that "she was apparently a test case used coldly by the KGB to break down the law, to experiment with drugs, and to frighten other freedom fighters."[82] Similarly, two psychiatrists, Sidney Bloch and Peter Reddaway, compiled a list of 210 dissidents detained between 1962 and 1976, identifying the medical treatment where possible. They identify seventeen cases of pharmacological torture and another six possible cases. None of these cases occurred before 1968, and the largest number occurred in 1974.[83]

Sometime between 1960 and 1970, conditions in psychiatric institutions changed. By 1970, punitive medicine was a standard treatment. Soviet psychoprisons were no longer "oases of humanism" to which labor camp detainees could aspire.[84] By 1976, labor camps were far more desirable. "Along with me there were common criminals who simulated illness to get away from labor camps, but when they saw the side-effects—twisted muscles, a disfigured face, a thrust-out tongue—they admitted what they had done and were returned to camp."[85] A doctor explained the change to one prisoner: "You don't need any treatment, but if we don't give you any drugs, then when you're out here, you'll say you were healthy and that's why no treatment was prescribed."[86]

Given this historical sequence, it seems unlikely that ideology shaped the Soviet choice of torture technique. The practice of warehousing dissidents appears to begin at the margins of the Stalinist penal system, and this practice was almost abandoned in 1954 with de-Stalinization. Soviet pharmacological torture, that is, the use of punitive medicine, really began fifteen to twenty years *after* de-Stalinization. The question, then, is what does explain this chronology. The answer appears to be monitoring.

Communist Pyschoprisons

Unlike non-Communist countries, Soviet pharmacological torture had a clear purpose. It fit into a preexisting system of Soviet psychoprisons that sheltered it as a form of legitimate medical intervention. Western psychiatrists prefer to date the birth of Soviet psychoprisons from the establishment of the Kazan prison hospital (1930s) or the victory of Snezhnevksy's theory of sluggish schizophrenia (1950s), a theory that made it easier to commit dissidents.[87] These dates are based on a very specific criterion: the moment when doctors abused the *diagnosis* of madness. This criterion mattered to professionals. However, Soviet dissidents date the birth of the psychoprison by administrative rather than medical criteria, that is, when the state embraced psychoprisons. They identify political events: Party investigations of the hospitals (1955–56), state funding for more hospitals (1960s), and new regulations that expanded the acts for which one could be committed (1961).[88]

For Soviet authorities, psychiatric incarceration was a stealthy alternative to public trials: "Why bother with political trials when we have psychiatric clinics?"[89] In a courtroom, "The defendant might seize [the opportunity] to make an impassioned plea of his innocence."[90] Such defendants "were a great embarrassment to the organizers of these trials and provoked indignation both in the Soviet Union and abroad. Such trials, in fact, only led to the further spread of 'sedition.' "[91] So "the KGB found it convenient to divert about one in ten political cases via the psychiatric route."[92]

Publicizing individual cases did not necessarily help. In his autobiographical novel *Ward 7* (1965), Valeriy Tarsis explains how unhappy Soviet doctors became when "the foreign press got hold of" political cases like his. Release was impossible, since the KGB had secretly ordered the commitment. Now "it was up to her to produce a diagnosis, a treatment, and a history of the case . . . and what was she to do?"[93] Tarsis mentions two alternatives, force and "happiness pills," whose "long-term effects are anything but happy."[94] Similarly, in 1965, Yevgeni Belov, a student, disappeared on the way to pick up English friends at the airport. Authorities reported that he had been committed.[95] A well-publicized campaign failed to find him.

In fact, commitments and punitive medicine escalated in the 1960s.[96] Increasingly, dissidents concluded that they needed "the unambiguous condemnation of their detention by medical opinion in the free world."[97] In 1968, the human rights movement in the Soviet Union focused squarely on Soviet political psychiatry, writing international bodies and organizing public protests. They distributed their own case files and publicized new cases.[98] Lastly, Dr. Semyon Gluzman, a Soviet psychiatrist, joined the dissident Vladimir Bukovsky to write *A Manual on Psychiatry for Dissidents*. One of the most widely distributed pieces of underground samizdat, the manual offered dissidents advice on how to avoid psychiatric commitment.[99]

In 1972, the West German Psychiatric Association condemned political psychiatry. In 1975, Amnesty International classified misuse of psychiatric treatment as torture.[100] Détente, particularly the Helsinki process, intensified monitoring of human rights abuses, both East and West.[101] Alexander Podrabinek, for example, wrote his noted book *Punitive Medicine* as an addendum to the Helsinki Agreement (1975).[102] In 1977, the World Psychiatric Association (WPA) officially condemned Soviet psychiatry.

By 1972, the Soviet government had released the detainees that had drawn Western attention, and courts avoided committing famous dissidents.[103] At the same time, commented an account from the 1970s, "Sanctions against dissenters have mounted, paradoxically, since the advent of U.S.-Soviet détente in 1972."[104] For example, by 1976, Podrabinek had identified two hundred psychoprison cases over some thirty years.[105] Between 1975 and 1979, Amnesty International had documented one hundred more cases, and eighty-five more by 1983.[106] In eight years, the number committed was approaching the number known to be interred in the thirty years before 1976. Similarly, the number of psychoprisons had more than doubled between 1965 and 1975, from six to fifteen.[107]

This was not surprising, observed Podrabinek. "The 'politics of détente' proclaimed by the Soviet government did not result in any decrease of repression, but rather a more elaborate disguise of repression and intensification of camouflage and misinformation."[108] These actions led inexorably to disciplinary debates at world congresses where Western psychiatrists challenged diagnoses and Soviet psychiatrists appeared armed with case files.[109] Andrei Snezhnevsky despised his psychoanalytic critics: "Psychotherapy—now there's something that needs research!"[110]

Psychoanalysts paid special attention to pharmacological torture and ECT because these methods epitomized "a whole tradition; it symbolizes everything its opponents want psychiatry to give up."[111] Psychoanalysts had criticized phar-

macological treatment of schizophrenia since the 1930s. Their criticism was
now informed by memories of Nazi medical experimentation and postwar psychiatric abuse in American hospitals.[112]

In the end, critics of Soviet psychoprisons prevailed. In 1983, the Soviets
withdrew from the WPA, joined by the Cubans, who withdrew in solidarity.[113]
By 1989, Soviet political cases leading to psychiatric incarceration had ceased,
well-known dissidents had been released, the Soviet press had condemned political psychiatry, and Soviet psychiatrists were negotiating their reentry into
the WPA.[114]

The inheritance of the Soviet psychoprison still remains. Years after the
end of the Soviet Union, released dissidents were unable to drive cars, buy
houses, travel abroad, or get married; they remained stripped of these rights
because the original psychiatric diagnoses were never overturned.[115] Moreover,
the Soviets had shown how state officials could successfully disguise torture as
legitimate medical intervention. Other Communist societies soon adopted the
psychoprison model. Cuba and China still have psychoprisons today, even
though they do not necessarily use the same tortures. And more recently, officials in the Russian Federation and Turkmenistan have also warehoused dissidents in psychiatric hospitals. To be specific, the following are the known cases
of psychoprison incarceration in chronological order.

Hungary. In 1959, Lajos Ruff offered this unusual account. First, he was sweated
like many other prisoners. Then he was committed to a psychiatric ward. Orderlies there regularly administered to him a mix of scopolamine, mescaline, and
curare. They isolated him in a room with an unusual silver beam of light that
followed him about, and, at another point, they bound him in a straitjacket.
Ruff also stated that wetsheeting ("packing," as he called it) and ECT were
routine institutional procedures, but he was not subjected to these procedures,
nor was he beaten.[116]

Romania. In 1965, Amnesty International reported only that guards gave prisoners "drugs to make them talk in their sleep" and then placed a tape recorder in
the cell.[117] By the late 1970s, Romania had fully adopted the Soviet psychoprison. Most prisoners reported pharmacological torture, though in 1978,
Amnesty International documented three cases of ECT.[118]

Cuba. In 1969, a young cadet, Eduardo Yanes Santana, described being
subjected to pharmacological torture.[119] Brown and Lago record twenty-six
cases after this date, mostly from the late 1970s and early 1980s. Unlike East
European cases, these prisoners reported ECT almost as often as pharmacological torture.[120] Longtime prisoners noted the change. Arrested in 1959, Eugenio

de Sosa Chabau had consistently refused to participate in standard reeducation programs in several prisons. In 1977, guards confined him to solitary and gave him psychotropic drugs. He then observed orderlies apply ECT to the temples of six patients. When it came his turn, "Most of the shocks were applied to my testicles."[121]

China. Until the 1980s, prisoners rarely report drugs in torture. An exception to this was one case of "truthful words medicine" (*cheng yen yao*) in 1951.[122] Political psychiatry began in earnest in 1987. Various government ministries proposed a new uniform classification for mental offenders, including "romantic maniacs," "political maniacs," and "aggressive maniacs."[123] Treatment consisted of pharmacological torture, four-point restraints in beds, and electric needles applied to extremely painful acupuncture points, and since 1999, ECT.[124]

Russian Federation. In April 1998, police arrested Vasily Stetsik, editor-in-chief of the journal *The Truth about Human Rights*, in Novotroitsk, and charged him with murder. A former cellmate reported that Stetsik would instruct other prisoners about their rights and would advise them on how to submit complaints on prison conditions. A prison psychiatrist assigned him to the psychiatric ward, and since December 1998, he has been in various psychiatric prisons.[125]

Turkmenistan. In January 2004, Gurbandurdy Durdykuliyev wrote an open letter to the president and local governor, urging them to permit a demonstration in Balkanabad in mid-February. On February 13, plainclothes police arrested Durdykuliyev and confined him to a psychiatric hospital. He has been in various psychiatric hospitals since, diagnosed as suffering from "wild paranoia in an aggressive form."[126]

Lines of Defense

The events in this chapter point to the increasingly important role doctors and psychiatrists play in monitoring torture, identifying abuses, and exposing doctor-torturers to professional censure. Two contrasting events show this growing importance. In 1931, the Chicago Neurological Society contested the notion of a "truth serum," but it had no easy means of creating a national, much less an international, consensus against the use of drugs. And most states ignored such medical skepticism for at least another three decades. By contrast, in 1977, the World Psychiatric Association not only exposed Soviet pharmacological torture to the world, but also put Soviet practitioners, not to mention the Soviet government, under considerable pressure.

In a world of stealth torture, doctors become critical agents, supplementing what lawyers do. Not surprisingly, medical monitoring is also growing more complicated and more dangerous. Medical monitoring comes in three forms, and understanding the differences helps identify strengths and weaknesses of this medical regime.

Prison Doctors

Few doctors, including those who work on human rights, would give up private practice to become a prison doctor. Not even army doctors do this work willingly.[127] Prison doctors find themselves stuck between interrogators eager to enlist their assistance, authorities anxious to quell any criticism, and prisoners who are often unsympathetic and manipulative.

Nevertheless, these doctors are best situated to catch torture when it appears. For example, prison doctors in Northern Ireland revealed a pattern of stealthy torture in the late 1970s. These doctors were not disposed to believe prisoners, nor were they trained to identify clean techniques like dorsiflexing.[128] The doctors became suspicious and soon concluded "there was a conflict between their professional duties and their professional ethics."[129] They complained first in March 1977, and then considered resigning. Finally, in 1979, Dr. Robert Irwin released 150 cases from his files to the newspapers. The subsequent scandal brought down the Labour Government.[130]

More typical are those like the doctor described by a Basque prisoner: "I told him that they were hitting me and he said that if there were no marks then he couldn't do anything."[131] Another could not get the prisoner to trust him: "He tried to calm me down, but I don't believe him, I'm very scared. I'm about a half an hour in that room, sitting in the chair, shaking without being able to speak."[132] A third knew, but did not act: "Eh, they didn't hit you too hard; all you have are a few marks."[133]

Some doctors have been more directly implicated in torture and interrogation. Historians, monitors, and prisoners have described cases in Nazi-occupied Europe, French colonial Algeria, the United States, Northern Ireland, Chile, the Philippines, Turkey, Brazil, Israel, and South Africa.[134] Patient studies indicate 20–40 percent of all cases involve medical participation.[135]

In contexts like these, doctors have performed several important tasks.[136] They have examined detainees before and during torture. "Our problem is: should we heal this man who will again be tortured or should we let him die?"[137] They have offered advice as to the limits of torture for each detainee. They have advised torturers on how to leave fewer marks. They have issued false autopsies, false diagnoses (such as schizophrenia), and false certificates of good health when prisoners were released. Lastly, they have questioned detainees, administered drugs, caused pain, or offered sympathetic, but firm, advice that the detainee cooperate.

Local Monitors

Police sometimes release prisoners when they see no marks even though the trained medical eye can still document torture. For example, high levels of myoglobin in the urine strongly suggest severe muscle damage. This effect disappears within forty-eight hours, but when police maintain the prisoner was under close protective observation and the prisoner describes torture in nondirected questioning, few other events besides torture can explain this outcome.[138]

Local doctors thus become the next line of monitoring after prison doctors. However, civilian doctors rarely see prisoners immediately after interrogation. When they do, doctors are inexperienced and make mistakes in documenting torture.[139] Until recently, there were no uniform standards for torture reports.[140] Lastly, civilian doctors are vulnerable to torture and execution themselves.[141]

Occasionally, local doctors may have shaped police behavior. In 1991, for example, a Turkish medical research group reported that they could identify *falaka* using bone scintigraphy, a technique that reveals small fractures missed by conventional radiographs.[142] Even months in detention could not hide these effects. Subsequently, doctors in Izmir "reported fewer and fewer complaints of falanga [*falaka*] from new cases seeking medicolegal help, although electric torture may have become more prevalent and the total number of victims changed little."[143]

International Monitors

In 1973, Amnesty International began organizing doctors to monitor torture from abroad. In 1974, the first Amnesty medical group began work in Copenhagen. In 1975, the World Medical Association issued the Tokyo Declaration condemning doctors who participated in torture. Latin American doctors organized tribunals. The British Medical Association issued *The Torture Report* (1986), insisting doctors had a positive obligation to act against torture, not merely a duty to avoid doing it.[144] Doctors and torture was the topic of international conferences in Copenhagen (1986), Montevideo (1987), Paris (1989), and Tromsø (1991), as well as whole issues of the *American Journal of Forensic Medicine and Pathology* and the *Journal of Medical Ethics*.[145] By 1984, some four thousand physicians in thirty countries were engaged in examining victims, running missions to other countries, and doing research on treatment.[146] Gathering objective evidence became critical, and new Amnesty International reports were sometimes thick with medical observations.[147]

Soon the Danish researchers associated with Amnesty International became concerned with clean tortures.[148] Two Spanish prisoners alleged electricity, choking, bagging, and dorsiflexing, but "no physical marks can be found at the objective examination—even shortly after torture."[149] In a survey of twenty-two Greeks patients, researchers found objective findings in only half of them even though all reported being beaten or subjected to *falaka*.[150] An Argentine prisoner claimed that marks left by the electric *picana* disappeared during her eighteen days of detention. Argentine authorities rejected this claim, saying that "marks left by the *picana* (electric prod) last for more than 18 days."[151] Experiments showed that *picanas* left tiny reddish scars that vanished fairly quickly and could be confused with a dermal disease. American cattle prods "left no marks, and the modest power of .9 watts makes any tissue destruction unlikely."[152] All this was hardly reassuring.

Subsequent research focused on identifying the traces of *falaka* and electrotorture.[153] While it is not possible to identify a specific torture by a single lesion, specialists can identify many minute traces that confirm the prisoner's allegations of torture when taken together. For example, doctors can identify *falaka* injuries by observing microlesions with bone scintigraphy, identifying a thickening of the *planta facia* muscle with magnetic resonance imaging (MRI), documenting a flattening of the heels and changes in proprioception, and recording specific symptoms patients describe in nondirected interviews.[154]

Electrotorture has proven more difficult to identify. Doctors did not know at first if heat burns differed from electrical injuries; early research had suggested no distinctions.[155] In 1984, Danish researchers identified a distinctive pattern *beneath* the skin. Where the cathode of the baton touched the skin, bands of calcium accumulated on collagen fibers six days after exposure.[156] By 1987, researchers announced, "Thus, it is possible to verify even 'invisible' electrical torture."[157] Even so, identifying collagen calcification in electrical injury had to be done within fourteen days of the injury.[158] Injuries caused by wires disappeared more quickly.[159] Stun gun injuries did not leave the characteristic pattern.[160]

Researchers have now found other ways to identify electrical injuries.[161] Some tortures, however, remain hard to diagnose, notably specific restraint tortures.[162] Diagnosing clean tortures from abroad continues to be a difficult business. Victims are often poor and unable to travel, and those that do come don't seek treatment immediately. At the Rehabilitation Center for Torture Victims in Copenhagen, doctors see patients on average 10.5 years after their torture.[163]

Remembering the Prison Doctors

When we think about doctors in torture, we think about the Nazi doctors, Faustian figures who experimented for the sake of theoretical knowledge. We spend far less time reflecting on the dilemmas of prison doctors.[164] These earnest toilers of the vineyards do not run research programs and are not interested in theoretical science. They are far more likely than theoretical scientists to be involved in torture.

In the United States, for example, public concern until recently focused on how doctors prescribed drugs to prisoners before and during trials.[165] In January 2002, a British doctor expressed concern "on behalf of my medical colleagues in the US military forces. I have imagined what I might do if I were to find myself posted to Guantanamo Bay Cuba." He warned his colleagues not to assume that democracies would not torture and doctors would not be used in interrogations.[166]

In fact, almost immediately after 9/11, an FBI agent mused openly about using "truth serum": "Drugs might taint a prosecution, but it might be worth it."[167] In 2002, an American interrogator in Afghanistan insisted U.S. forces were providing scrupulous medical care, "adding in a deadpan voice, that 'pain control [in wounded patients] is a very subjective thing.'"[168] In 2003, medical personnel at Abu Ghraib treated tortured victims and recorded the evidence, but failed to report these incidents. "Rather than putting a stop to torture, they tacitly abetted it, by patching up victims and staying silent."[169]

In June 2003, an American counterintelligence agent for the California National Guard witnessed five incidents of torture at his base and requested a formal investigation. Commanding officers claimed he was "delusional," and gave him thirty seconds to withdraw his formal request. When he refused, he was ordered to see combat stress officers. Within thirty-six hours, he was ordered to lie in a gurney, strapped down, and medevacked by plane to a medical center outside Iraq. No "medevac" order was ever issued, in violation of army policy.[170]

In 2004, the International Committee of the Red Cross reported that, at Guantánamo "doctors and medical personnel conveyed information about prisoners' mental health and vulnerabilities to interrogators." Most notoriously, a group of psychologists, known as the Behavioral Science Consultation Team (BSCT, or "Biscuit"), advised the interrogators.[171]

Not all these acts involve participating directly in torturing, but why should that be far away? Some, including doctors, now argue that prison doctors should participate in torture when their duty to society outweighs their duties to their patients.[172]

V Politics and Memory

"Mind you, the devil is old; grow old to understand him."
This does not mean age in the sense of birth certificate . . .
one has to see the devil's ways to the end in order to realize
his power and his limitations.

— Max Weber, "Science as a Vocation"[1]

20 Supply and Demand for Clean Torture

So democracies torture. Policemen and soldiers of democratic states have used electrotorture, water torture, stress and duress techniques, drugs, and beatings. These public agents have used these and many other techniques to intimidate, to generate false confessions, and to gather strategic information. They have done so sometimes on their own, sometimes in collusion with local citizens, and sometimes with the quiet approval, if not explicit authorization, of their governments.

None of this is to say that democracies have a worse record than authoritarian states. Dictators deserve their reputation for greater violence and cruelty, as this book has amply documented. But this book has also established that democracies have a *different* history of torture, not an *absence* of history. Democracies torture, but they torture differently, favoring cleaner techniques to avoid scandal and to boost their legitimacy. The history of modern democratic torture is part of the history of stealth torture.

In the concluding chapters, I tackle some obvious questions that arise from the account I have given and that, if anything, have become more pressing in public debate ever since September 11, 2001. Does torture work? More generally, what are the effects of organized torture? I have at times implied certain answers to these questions in the previous chapters, but in what follows I bring together whatever is known from multiple disciplines that bears on these questions.

First, however, I am going to say more about what to make of the basic story I have recounted. We have the facts about modern torture at hand, but it may be helpful, even at the risk of some repetition, to say more about the dynamics that lie behind these facts. So I will reprise the major historical claims and explanations of this study, explaining why I find alternative explanations of the facts unpersuasive. I will also amplify some of my own explanations, pointing to further avenues of research.

Torture is an old and clever demon, and Weber's advice is especially apt to any social scientist entering into the dark looking for answers about it. It is all too easy to fall prey to false or misleading pictures of the practice of torture, and it is only by following its ways to the end that one recognizes the power of torture and its limitations.

Historical Claims

There are many clean torture techniques, that is, painful physical techniques that leave few marks. Most of these techniques are not technologically sophisticated and involve everyday instruments. Most appeared first among lists of British military punishments, in the context of American slavery, penal institutions or military punishments, and during policing and military operations in French and British colonies. In some cases, as with electrotorture, these techniques first appeared in the context of torture. In other cases, they were first used for other purposes, but police and military interrogators in democratic states soon adapted them for torture. This includes practices such as cobbing (*palmatoria*), bucking (the parrot's perch), spicing, forced standing, exhaustion exercises, ducking, the Wooden Horse, the *falaka*, the *crapaudine*, and sweatboxes. Eventually, these techniques appeared in torture chambers in many other states around the world.

To be sure, some clean techniques appeared first in the torture chambers of authoritarian states, but not many. Examples include pumping with water (the Catholic Inquisition), sleep deprivation (the Protestant Church of Scotland), and gas mask asphyxiation (Ukrainian torturers in Gestapo prisons in Poland). Here again, torturers in democratic states led the way in adapting these methods to modern torture, often in combination with other clean practices. The American police in the 1920s were the first to combine sleep deprivation and positional torture to coerce confessions in the modern age. American troops in the Philippines in 1901 were the first to adapt the practice of pumping, a Spanish Inquisitional practice that had probably survived in the Philippines, to gather information. Gas mask asphyxiation was very rare after World War II until it became a standard practice in torture in post-Soviet East European democracies.

There is, then, a long, unbroken, though largely forgotten history of torture in democracies at home and abroad, a history stretching back some two hundred years and involving the main democracies of modern times. The histories of the preceding chapters untangled and identified each strand, tracing each recorded usage from the first obscure references to the latest accounts from the American War on Terror. Others may find more recorded instances, but these histories are certainly more complete than anything that has been available hitherto.

More importantly, police and military in the main democratic states were leaders in adapting and innovating clean techniques. Again, the history of electrotorture illustrates this point quite clearly. The first police forces to use electrotorture were the American (ca. 1908), the British (1912), the French (1931), the Japanese (1931), and the Argentine police (1936). The first police to use clean electrotorture regularly were the domestic American police (1920s), the French Sûreté in Vietnam (1931), and the Argentine police (1936). The French in particular pioneered the dominant form of electric torture for forty years, torture by means of a field telephone magneto.

Some techniques may have been discovered simultaneously in authoritarian and democratic states. Asphyxiation by bagging can be credited either to the Chicago police (1972) or to the Chilean (1973) or Argentine (1975) police. But such cases are rare. The histories of many other techniques point to the role of democratic torturers as innovators. The seventeenth-century Dutch pioneered the practice of water choking with a linen napkin or *chiffon*, and the Americans and British pioneered the use of beating with high-pressure water in the nineteenth century. British prisons in India were the first to combine standing handcuffs and freezing baths. Other techniques include beating with a rubber hose (American police in the 1920s), dorsiflexing (the RUC in Northern Ireland in the 1970s), and the *shabeh* (Israel in the 1990s).

The claim that the main democracies were torture innovators is agnostic as to how other countries ended up with these techniques and by what route they arrived, if indeed they came from the outside. It does not imply a specific explanation for how torturers around the world came by the techniques they currently use (e.g., by means of CIA training, low-level transmission, or simple imitation). All it states is that the techniques now commonly used in interrogation rooms and prisons around the world had their roots in the main democratic states.

The alternative claim would be that authoritarian states invented and distributed these clean techniques. But the historical evidence for this is simply not there. Prior to and during World War II, clean torture techniques rarely appear in other countries notorious for torture, including Russia, Germany, the Austro-Hungarian Empire, and Japan and their colonies. When they do, they are just as quickly forgotten.

Again, the history of electrotorture illustrates this general observation. The Nazi Gestapo did not use electrotorture for interrogation until 1943. This was over a decade after the French police was using electrotorture, and instances of Gestapo torture using magnetos occur only and infrequently in Nazi-occupied France or Belgium (the first being in Toulouse in October 1943). What is more, Gestapo torture was scarring, not clean. Likewise, Japanese Kempeitai electrotorture, which began concurrently with the French practice in East Asia, was scarring, not clean.

Electrotorture is not the simple exception to the rule here. As part IV demonstrates, the same story could be told for every other clean technique. The main exception here was how the Soviets passed on Stalinist sweating and positional torture. After World War II, this style of torture appeared in several Communist countries in the 1950s, but the main point here is that this style soon gave way to brutal, scarring torture regimens. Generally speaking, authoritarian states until the late twentieth century showed little interest in techniques that were clean.

Lastly, I claim that clean torture techniques are far more common in the late twentieth century than they were at any time previously. There are of course, many scarring tortures around the world, but there are fewer reports of them, and some scarring techniques have entirely vanished. On the other hand, clean torture techniques have appeared in contexts quite different than the ones in which they were first customarily used, and other new coercive and clean methods have appeared alongside them.

This clustering of clean techniques appeared first in the context of democratic states. The important cases are American torture in various cities in the 1920s and possibly during the Spanish-American War, French torture in Indochina in the 1920 and 1930s, British torture in India and Mandatory Palestine before World War II, British torture in the London Cage between 1940 and 1948, and French torture in North African camps during and after World War II. Among authoritarian states before 1945, there are only two important examples of the clustering of clean techniques: the Stalinist methods used for show trials in the 1930s and the Nazi usage for a handful of Swedes in 1943. Generally speaking, though, torture in these states was scarring, and these examples were the exception.

In the two decades that followed World War II, clustering appears again mainly among the police and military of democratic states: in French torture in Madagascar in the 1940s and in Algeria in the 1950s, American torture in Vietnam in the 1960s, and British torture in Aden in the 1960s. That said, in some cases, democratic states favored scarring techniques, such as the British in Kenya in the 1950s. Clean Stalinist techniques appear in East European countries and East Asia, but these techniques are soon combined with scarring techniques. The main exception here is in the treatment of American POW pilots in North Korea, who are subjected to a clean regimen of torture.

During the 1960s, the clustering of clean techniques starts appearing more frequently in some authoritarian states: among South Vietnamese interrogators, in authoritarian Greece, in South Africa, and more generally among authoritarian states in Latin America. In the last three decades, this clustering has persisted in Latin America, in democratic states along the Mediterranean, and in post-Communist democracies in Eastern Europe. Some authoritarian states also have adopted these techniques with great skill, most notably, the Iranian police in the 1990s. And clean techniques now appear with greater frequency in authoritarian states where they were previously unknown, for example, in Saudi Arabia and the Gulf States.

Still, the police and military of democratic states remain the most disciplined consistent users of clean techniques. The best examples are British RUC torture in Northern Ireland in the 1970s, American police torture in Chicago in the 1970s and 1980s, Japanese police torture in the 1980s, torture by the Israeli GSS, the Spanish Guardia Civile, and Turkish police in the 1990s, and American CIA interrogators during the War on Terror.

I also claim that clean techniques do not cluster randomly, but appear frequently in predictable combinations. I call these predictable combinations *styles* of torture. The most important is the style I dub French modern, the combination of clean electrotorture with water torture. Again, these clean regimens appear with greater frequency in the late twentieth century.

My general claim, then, is this: Over the course of the century, torture has changed worldwide, the kind of sweeping change that is rare with any method of violence. Torturers, on their own or at the direction of others and for whatever reason, have turned more and more, as time has gone by, toward techniques that leave few marks.

This historical claim yields several puzzles. Why do clean tortures and democracy go hand in hand? Why did authoritarian states start using clean techniques in the late twentieth century? Why are there variations in the pattern of scarring or clean tortures between states and within states? How do torturers end up with the clean techniques they use? Why do clean techniques cluster in predictable styles? Why do some democracies torture while others do not? Each of these puzzles requires an explanation.

The Priority of Public Monitoring

Why do clean tortures and democracy go hand in hand? My explanation is this: public monitoring leads institutions that favor painful coercion to use and combine clean torture techniques. This is because these methods make it less likely that torturers will be found out or held responsible. To the extent that public monitoring is not only greater in democracies, but that public monitoring of human rights is a core value in modern democracies, it is the case that where we find democracies torturing today, we will also be more likely to find police and military using multiple clean techniques. I call this pattern of torture *stealth torture*.

The monitoring hypothesis explains why clean tortures tend to cluster in democratic contexts. More importantly, it also explains why some authoritarian states favored stealthy torture. For example, it explains why the Soviets favored clean torture for show trials, since in this case the Soviet government was deliberately seeking international attention. And it offers some tantalizing research avenues to explain variations in the pattern of clean and scarring within countries, for example, why torture in the countryside is scarring while torture in the cities is often consistently clean. On this view, one might hypothesize that in the cities, there are more journalists, doctors, and human rights organizations.

One piece of evidence in favor of the monitoring hypothesis is the historical pattern in which clean techniques tend to cluster together. This pattern of clustering occurs much as the monitoring hypothesis would predict. But clustering alone is insufficient without further historical documentation. One can be certain that when torturers combine scarring techniques with clean ones, they do not care whether they leave evidence behind. But this study has found more than one reason that people chose to combine clean techniques. Still, if one goes through the possibilities, the case for the monitoring hypothesis becomes increasingly compelling.

First, sometimes stories indicate that people pulled their punches because they did not want to reduce the labor force. Many nautical punishments were bruising, but not debilitating, because captains needed every hand while at sea. Captains of French Foreign Legion units deep in the desert may have favored such punishments for the same reason. Romans may have whipped their female slaves with silk sashes to keep them sexually desirable and usable. But there is little evidence that modern torturers used clean techniques because they were concerned about prison labor, or that such concerns have become more pronounced in the late twentieth century.

Second, it is possible that some people favored clean techniques out of racism. When it came to people *unlike them*, they were entirely unrestrained and used scarring tortures. But some could not bear to scar people *like them*, though they still had to do their job, and so they were clean. Now if this view is true, one would expect to find many testimonials to this effect in the late twentieth century, when cleaner techniques are much more common. But if there are any, I have not found them; no one seems to indicate that torturers chose cleaner techniques because they sympathetically identified with their prisoners. Nevertheless, the dehumanization hypothesis, as I call it, may explain some cases in the early twentieth century, and in the next section, I will discuss these cases a bit more closely.

Lastly, there are a handful of cases where it was entirely unclear why torturers used clean techniques consistently. We may never know why Vichy's Bureau 21 felt the strong need to be clean during World War II, as the testimonials suggest, when all around them torture was brutally scarring and no independent journalists or organizations kept an eye on their behavior. Perhaps further research will resolve these cases.

In the cases, I have documented above, historical sources tell us that the reason torturers favored clean techniques was that they were trying, with some success, to evade monitoring and preserve a thin veer of legitimacy. In short, both historical sources and the patterns of clustering favor the monitoring hypothesis. I will amplify this claim more in the next section. But first I want to offer two alternative explanations to the monitoring hypothesis, and explain why I find them unpersuasive.

One alternative explanation would be that the type of state affects the type of technique used. Democracies favor clean techniques but authoritarian states do not. I call this the regime type hypothesis, and the difficulty with this explanation is that it does not adequately explain the historical pattern of scarring and clean tortures. To be specific, some authoritarian states also use clean techniques, especially in the late twentieth century, and on this view, it is not at all clear why they should. Nor does this hypothesis adequately explain why the same democratic state favored exclusively clean techniques in some cases but scarring techniques in others. The British, for example, used scarring techniques in Kenya, but were considerably cleaner in Northern Ireland. The regime type hypothesis is simply too general to serve as an adequate explanation: yes, some examples fit, but others do not, and this hypothesis offers no explanation for the variations.

Another alternative explanation holds that democratic states are ruled by an elite who, for whatever reason, want to hide their exploitative state in the guise of a genuinely democratic government and so order lower-level agents to be stealthy and not make a mess. It is not torturers who mean to be stealthy, but their bosses, and the monitoring hypothesis simply gets the emphasis wrong. I call this alternative explanation the ruling elite hypothesis.

Now some accounts in this book favor this explanation, but the main point here is that this is not an *alternative* explanation for the pattern of clean and scarring torture. For if the difference between democratic and authoritarian states is that democratic elites want to wear a mask to disguise their tyranny, then one must ask why. And that brings one back to the fact that they believe they are being watched and judged by others in how well they respect human rights and they believe at least a thin veneer of legitimacy is necessary, one that includes stealth torture.

Public monitoring, then, is still the critical variable that makes elites behave as they do. The only disagreement between the monitoring hypothesis and the ruling elite hypothesis is who is making the decision to turn to stealth: lower-level or higher-level agents. The evidence offered in this study is that both political elites and lower-level police and military have, at different times, initiated stealth torture. General Massu and Secretary Rumsfeld ordered the use of clean techniques, but they are comparatively rare figures. More commonly, this study has documented how torture began with the lower-downs, and was simply ignored by the higher-ups. Examples of the latter include police torture in various American cities in the 1920s, police torture in Area 2 in Chicago in the 1970s and 1980s, and American torture in Vietnam in the 1960s.

The ruling elite hypothesis has another troubling feature that deserves closer consideration. If what makes democratic states different is that they are ruled by hidden elites who are mindful of publicity, how then does one explain why democratic elites sometimes favored scarring techniques, as the British did in Kenya? Or conversely, why do elites in some authoritarian states also feel the need to use cleaner techniques at times? The ruling elite hypothesis is vulnerable, then, to the same kinds of problems as the regime type hypothesis. It cannot explain variations in clean or scarring patterns between states and within states without appealing either to the monitoring hypothesis or to attitudinal claims about elites in democratic and authoritarian states.

Now perhaps if we had access to the deliberations of political elites, one might understand the logic of these choices, but we do not. The source material and the subject matter make it difficult to ascertain from where the initiative for torture came and which agents sustained it. All we can say is that this study finds some limited evidence for a political variant of the ruling elite hypothesis: some political elites in the main democracies, occasionally tacitly or overtly, endorse stealth torture.

On the other hand, this study fails to find much evidence for the economic variant of the ruling elite hypothesis. This variant states that an economic elite combines entrepreneurship with political and social networks to spread clean torture technology. But the evidence is otherwise.

For example, there is little evidence that corporations and economic elites had a direct role in developing electrotorture before 1970. Thomas Edison played an important role in promoting the electric chair as a way of discrediting Westinghouse's alternating current. But beyond this, the evidence is scant. One can argue that the meatpacking, telephone, and transportation industries played an indirect role in making devices that were subsequently used for elec-trotorture. But it does not appear that corporate elites even noticed until the 1960s that cattle prods had an alternative market, and they were quite surprised to find out that law enforcement had any use for them as riot control devices, much less torture devices. In short, for the first seventy years of electrotorture, economic elites did not play a direct role in promoting electrotorture.

More generally, this economic variant is based on a naive conception of the nature of torture technology, even of the high-tech variety. To be specific, very few clean techniques require major technical innovation—they can be taught in any backroom and require neither technological research nor corpo-rations. Electrotorture is very much the exception, as part IV makes amply clear. Nor does the history of most of these clean techniques show the involvement of entrepreneurs or technological innovation as the major push behind their diffusion. This is even the case for more highly sophisticated tortures such as drugs and sensory deprivation boxes. Nor does this account explain why some technologies that did involve corporate and scientific investment fail to take hold while others did not (unless one makes unverifiable claims about the atti-tudes of corporate elites). Why, for example, did corporate elites favor stun technology as opposed to sensory deprivation boxes?

Possibly the best (indeed only) evidence in this study that might sup-port the economic variant of the ruling elite hypothesis is that corporate elites played an important role in sustaining stun technology in the 1990s. There is definitely something to be said for this, provided one does not confuse this claim with a broader claim that corporate elites invented and promoted stun technology. The developmental history of stun technology does not support the broader claim. While the patent history for electric devices does suggest something like the inevitable march of technology, the story of Cover and the real patterns of innovation for high-tech electric stun devices bear no relation-ship to the patent history.

In fact, the American government officials were either uninterested in stun technology or actively placed obstacles in the path of its development, and Cover had a difficult time securing funding from any economic elite. By the late 1970s, stun technology would have entirely disappeared had it not been for a fortuitous combination of events that kept Cover's enterprise alive. By the mid-1980s, stun technology had a small market, but it would take another de-cade to become a global industry.

These objections to the economic variant raise puzzles of their own; namely, why is there such a priority on low tech in torture? And how are such low-tech tortures transmitted? I will have more to say on these issues later in the chapter. But let me first unpack further the monitoring hypothesis.

Variations among and within States

The monitoring hypothesis offers a more comprehensive understanding of the changing pattern of clean or scarring tortures than other accounts. My argument depends on positing a major shift in the overall pattern of torture in the late 1960s and the early 1970s. It is at this point that more states turn toward cleaner tortures. Let me call this transitional period for brevity's sake the Turn. The monitoring hypothesis explains the patterns of clean and scarring torture before the Turn, what accounts for the Turn, and also the pattern of clean and scarring torture that follows the Turn. I argue that before the Turn, one finds clean tortures primarily in democracies. The Turn marks the formation of the international human rights monitoring regime, and after the Turn, one finds clean techniques spread more broadly as states begin to take account of increased international scrutiny.

It is important in this context to explain apparent anomalies and exceptions. The most troubling cases for the monitoring hypothesis are cases where authoritarian states combine clean tortures or cases where democratic states use scarring tortures. The first cases are troubling because presumably authoritarian states do not have much in the way of domestic torture auditors, and so the use of clean techniques seems inexplicable. I argue that authoritarian states turned to clean torture primarily after the Turn, not due to domestic monitoring but due to increased international monitoring. And the main cases of clean authoritarian torture before the Turn can be explained with reference to the rare situation where these states believed their practices were being audited.

The second cases would be particularly troubling in democracies with highly active domestic auditors of torture. One would think that under these conditions democracies would resort to clean techniques, as the monitoring hypothesis suggests, rather than scarring techniques. In the known cases, often cases where a democratic power ruled a colony, racism drove public indifference to scarring tortures. Let me call this the dehumanization hypothesis. But this hypothesis is far too clunky to explain identical conditions where racist police used clean techniques on local populations. It cannot explain interstate and intrastate variation in clean or scarring tortures. I argue that the monitoring hypothesis does a more comprehensive job in explaining these patterns, and it can integrate the insights of the dehumanization hypothesis within its general framework.

Before the Turn

In this period, one finds torturers using clean regimens mainly in democracies or in the colonies of democracies. This is consistent with what the monitoring hypothesis would predict. In democracies, police and military are under greater scrutiny from journalists, courts, and communities, and so they are more careful in how they go about torturing. In authoritarian states, police and military are far less accountable to others for the violence they perform, and so there is no percentage in using clean techniques.

Why then do some authoritarian states adopt occasionally adopt clean torture regimens? The answer is that authoritarian states adopted clean regimens in the rare cases where prisoners drew international attention (particularly from democratic states) or where authoritarian rulers deliberately sought international attention regarding their treatment of prisoners. Let me call this the international monitoring hypothesis.

The international monitoring hypothesis explains the most important cases of clean torture among authoritarian states before the Turn. Stalin wanted the prisoners of the show trials to make their confessions spontaneously and without evidence of torture, and it was to this end that the Soviet Conveyor was designed. The Chinese wanted American POWs to confess to war crimes spontaneously, particularly the pilots, and to this end, Chinese torturers combined techniques that left little permanent damage. Faced with increased international scrutiny of its police practices by the Council of Europe, torturers in authoritarian Greece turned to clean techniques. Similarly, South Vietnamese turned to cleaner tortures after American journalists began documenting instances of South Vietnamese torture in the 1960s. It would appear that either the South Vietnamese government on its own, or with a forceful American prompt, concluded that open torture jeopardized its war effort.

There are cases where factors other than monitoring may explain the pattern of clean and scarring tortures. For example, in 1943, the Gestapo arrested a group of Poles and Swedes who were working together fighting the Germans. The Gestapo beat the Poles, but sweated the Swedes. Now it is possible that what drove the Gestapo in this instance was racism. The Gestapo officers acted this way because they identified with the Swedes as Aryans, and so chose cleaner techniques when they tortured them. On the other hand, they regarded the Poles as inferiors and chose brutal scarring techniques in their case.

This example illustrates the logic of the dehumanization hypothesis. It offers a plausible reason for why American slave owners used scarring techniques or why the British public did not lift a finger despite horrific reports of torture in Kenya in the 1950s. It also explains why the French public and press seemed generally uninterested in torture in Algeria, despite reports, until the police and Paras started torturing white Europeans; then they were keenly interested. In all these cases, cleaner tortures were for those "like us," and scarring tortures were for the "other." The dehumanization hypothesis may also explain certain gendered patterns of torture. For example, it points to the way in which norms of modesty shaped the way in which torturers administered *falaka* to female prisoners in the Middle East in the nineteenth century.

What is critical to establish in these cases is whether the torturers themselves possessed these norms or whether they were aware that others possessed these norms. For example, the Gestapo officers may have identified with the Swedish prisoners. That would be the strong version of the dehumanization hypothesis. But they may also have been aware that others identified with the Swedes and they would be observing and reacting to what the Gestapo did in this case. The rich and the noble, as well as governments of neutral and allied powers, expected that *their* people would be treated differently. The others do not matter so much. If this is the view, then the dehumanization hypothesis is not an alternative to the international monitoring hypothesis, since in both cases, it is international monitoring that is driving the use of cleaner procedures.

The strong version of the dehumanization hypothesis seems most firmly grounded when explaining the use of scarring tortures on "the other" rather than the use of clean tortures on the "same." Racism unquestionably shaped the indifference of Europeans and Americans, even when journalists, writers, and organizations reported on horrible abuses and tortures.

But the dehumanization hypothesis is hard pressed to explain when Europeans and Americans elected to combine clean techniques in the torture of Asians, Arabs, and Africans. The French police were combining clean techniques in the torture of Algerians four years before the first white Europeans were tortured. The French Paras used clean tortures in the urban areas more commonly than the Algerian countryside. The French Sûreté in Vietnam also used clean techniques on Asians in the 1930s, though it was more careful in urban areas than in the countryside.

Should one conclude that interrogators were less racist in urban areas than the countryside? This does not seem likely. In Algeria, for example, we are talking about the same units torturing in both places. It seems more plausible to argue that monitoring differed in the urban areas. It may have been more frequent, more comprehensive, more specialized, and better informed. We also know that prisoners began documenting their scars, no matter how small, and this practice of verifying one's torture would not have mattered if prisoners were not mindful of the quality of public monitoring. All this cannot be proven without the shadow of a doubt, but this explanation is more plausible than any other.

Moreover, this study has documented cases where indeed racists have pulled their punches not out of sympathy for victims, but because they knew others would be inspecting them. Slave dealers, for example, favored clean techniques because they knew they would have a harder time selling scarred slaves. White potential owners would regard scarred slaves as a disciplinary problem, and so would be less willing to buy them. Likewise, while the French public may have been indifferent to torture, the French government was fending off allegations of torture in the press and investigating police torture in Algeria as early as 1955.

This kind of monitoring is certainly limited in scope and rudimentary in practice, but it explains why torturers pulled their punches in the treatment of some "others." It also explains why torturers were careful about their treatment of some white Europeans. The Gestapo was not a selectively humane organization but rather one that was opportunistic, calculating, and mindful of cases that drew international interest. The French Paras were no different. And generally speaking, it is hard to find cases in the twentieth century where one can be certain that the reason torturers chose cleaner techniques was because they actually possessed certain racial norms or felt a certain kinship with their victims.

After the Turn

Torturers appear to be responsive to monitoring, and different monitoring regimes appear to bring to bear different kinds of values. What is different about our age is that there are many more monitors and that these monitors now enforce a universal human rights regime. Thus, it is increasingly difficult (though certainly not impossible) for police to excuse themselves for torturing someone because the person had the wrong race or gender. Let me call this the universal monitoring (UM) hypothesis.

The UM hypothesis claims that in the late 1960s and early 1970s, international human rights monitoring came of age. The last three decades might be called the golden age of human rights monitoring. Not only has the scope of human rights monitoring increased, but there are now many more accounting mechanisms to document human rights abuses whenever they occur. In response to increased monitoring, torturers worldwide have adapted by turning to cleaner techniques.

If the UM hypothesis is correct, one would expect that clean techniques that were originally reserved for women, children, or slaves would circulate more widely. One would also expect interrogators to adopt clean torture regimens for many more prisoners after the Turn than before. And in particular, one would expect even authoritarian states to adopt clean torture regimens in order to preserve legitimacy and foreign aid.

And this is in fact the pattern one finds on the ground. Perhaps the most striking surge is the surge in electrotorture starting in the late 1960s, beginning in Latin America (chapter 9). But one also finds the same chronology repeated with every other clean torture technique: these techniques appear more broadly after the Turn. Moreover, authoritarian states in the late twentieth century are far more likely than those in the early twentieth century to adopt

clean regimens of torture, which appear with greater frequency among democratic states as well.

In short, stealth torture appears to be a perverse effect of the growing robustness of international monitoring. By creating conditions in which observers
could monitor specific behaviors, the observers changed the behavior they
sought to document. When monitors exposed torture to pubic censure through
careful documentation, torturers responded by investing in less visible and
harder to document techniques.

In advancing this argument, I find three alternative explanations unpersuasive. The most sophisticated is the view that the United States distributed torture
techniques around the world in the 1960s and 1970s, and that this accounts for
the new pattern of clean torture techniques. This is a variant of a standard
hypothesis in the torture literature, what I have called the universal distributor
(UD) hypothesis. The UD hypothesis holds that one country, in this case the
United States, is the source of critical torture techniques around the world.

In chapter 9, I consider the most compelling version of the American UD
hypothesis, the argument advanced by Noam Chomsky and Edward Herman. If
the U.S. government were responsible for the distribution of torture techniques
worldwide, one would expect to find some strong resemblance in torture techniques between the countries that received the greatest American aid and military support. The difficulty is that one does not find it. If uniformity of practice
implies uniformity of intent, then in this case, it is rather hard to pin down
intent. What is more, the American UD hypothesis leaves unclear why the
United States would feel compelled to distribute cleaner torture techniques at
this time. Again, if this is because it wanted to reduce bad publicity that might
jeopardize its allies, then surely this is not an alternative to the universal monitoring hypothesis. Chomsky and Herman's account is open, in this respect, to
the same objections raised against other versions of the ruling elite hypothesis.

Setting aside the American UD hypothesis, I consider other possible candidates including the Soviet Union, the United Kingdom, and France. In each
case, I find the evidence wanting. The pattern of techniques is too varied to
suggest a single source. The main exception to this is in Soviet Union, which
seems to have been more successful than most in distributing its particular
regimen to its allies. The difficulty is that the Soviet UD hypothesis has the
wrong chronology and wrong pattern of clean versus scarring torture. Historically the pattern appears immediately after World War II, twenty years at least
before the Turn. And the regime decays rapidly in Communist countries and
it is pretty much gone by the 1970s, much as the monitoring hypothesis would
predict. Where there is no accountability, there is no percentage in being clean.

Common ideology also appears be a very poor guide in helping one understand the pattern of clean and scarring techniques. I repeatedly consider Com-

munist states as a test of the ideology hypothesis, and find that they varied enormously in their use of clean and scarring techniques or whether they tortured at all. I considered, in particular, one possible piece of evidence in favor the ideology hypothesis, for it appeared that very few Communist regimes used electrotorture, which was very common outside of the Communist world. But this had less to do with an alleged Communist distaste for electrotorture, and more to do with the fact that torturers elsewhere were more vulnerable to international scrutiny.

Lastly, it is possible that clean techniques existed widely before universal monitoring, but that analysts only noticed them when better documentation began. Universal monitoring meant more human rights audits of individual countries and more careful identification of specific torture techniques.

Here I can only stand by my research of torture before 1973. I am fairly confident, for example, I have found most of the cases electrotorture before this date. If there are others, I would certainly like to know about them. Increased auditing and documentation probably has identified more techniques than would have been possible before the Turn, and this is probably truest with the techniques that do not involve complicated devices, for example, positional tortures. I do not claim I have offered the last word on this. However, I do claim that I have offered sufficient coverage of each torture technique to show that there was a surge worldwide in the 1960s and 1970s.

I also cannot say definitively whether most intrastate variation in clean and scarring relates to different kinds of monitoring (e.g., frequent/infrequent; comprehensive/scattered; proximate/distant; internal to institution/external to institution; domestic/international; local knowledge based/foreign; or medical/nonmedical). It seems logical that different kinds of monitoring would affect the behaviors of torturers differently, and that these effects are distributed differently. The hostility of torturers toward doctors who track torture seems partial evidence toward the view that the kind of monitoring matters to torturers. And the repeated observation that clean techniques occur with greater frequency in cities than in the countryside (and almost never vice versa) is certainly suggestive; urban areas include, among other things, far greater prospect of scrutiny by unwanted eyes. But unfortunately we are some way from linking different kinds of monitoring to different patterns of torture.

National Styles of Stealth Torture

Torturers do not simply combine clean tortures. They combine them in predictable ways. One striking empirical pattern that emerges from the data is repeated clustering of clean techniques in predictable ways in various countries or regions, what I call *styles* of torture. The notion of styles is helpful because they highlight certain relationships, enabling some continuities and discontinuities to be seen more clearly. Certain combinations persist not only across time in a country but also appear in torture in other countries, some of them allies and some of them enemies of the original users.

The dominant styles today fall into two classes. One class is built around electrotorture, and I distinguish specific styles in the manner in which they supplement electrotorture. When electrotorture is commonly supplemented with water tortures, the style is French modern. This is the most common combination worldwide. When it is supplemented with gas masks, I call it Slavic modern, and when it is supplemented commonly with the *falaka*, Mediterranean modern.

The other class is based on stress and duress techniques usually supplemented with water tortures, beating with various instruments, noise, and drugs. Electrotorture is not part of this tradition normally. I call this style of torture Anglo-Saxon modern. The Stalinist Conveyor technique (Soviet modern), the tortures in the French Foreign Legion (French classic), and the Israeli *shabeh* belong to this tradition of torture.

As the names suggest, these predictable combinations of clean torture appeared first in French, British, or American contexts, that is, in democracies or in the colonies of democracies. The main authoritarian contribution to stealth torture was the Soviet psychoprison, the use of medical diagnoses to institute pharmacological torture. This inheritance persists today in several countries, though it is not nearly as widespread as French modern and Anglo-Saxon modern.

These three styles replaced older national styles that involved whips, burning, razors, and other scarring procedures. The German Gestapo and Japanese Kempeitai illustrate these older styles, styles that, as it turned out, did not have a future (see chapter 4, "Whips and Water," and chapter 7, "Magnetos").

If torturers chose clean techniques at random, then there would be no national styles. So why are there national styles? After all, there is no obvious reason why one technique appears regularly with another. The answer depends on what kind of practice one thinks torture is and how one believes torturers learn their art.

My explanation is that torture is a craft, not a science. In the next chapter, I explain in greater detail why torture is necessarily a craft based on what we know about pain, and that it is unlikely to be a science unless the nature of pain itself changes. Here, I simply advance the case that, currently, torture resembles other crafts in the way torturers learn their art. I call this the craft apprenticeship hypothesis.

I argue that torturers learn their craft on the job, by observing and imitating others like themselves. This shapes the decisions they later make when doing torture. Training in a craft is not simply a form of intentional communication, in which a master craftsman passes onto the apprentice technical knowledge of this or that practice. "The way we do things around here" is also a way of signifying belonging to a group, a reference to a shared identity. In torture, the importance of group bonding and peer solidarity is well known, and I will document this further in the next chapter.

Torturers rarely use one technique alone, and the way they combine techniques and the accepted limits of the common toolkit communicate who they are and index the community of practitioners to which they think they belong. Of course, one needs to be careful about the self-descriptions of torturers. "I learned this technique from the Gestapo" more often than not is a false story, even if the torturer felt a kinship with Nazi torturers. This is why there is no substitute for the empirical study of styles.

Generally speaking, the *bricolage* of torture includes inherited patterns from the past, improvised responses to political events, and adaptations from here and there that "fit" into how things are done. These are the elements that constitute a style of torture. When explaining why regional tailors differ in the way they make clothes, one might consider habit and training (this is how we do it here) and availability (we do what we can with what we've got). In the case of styles of torture, it is plausible to consider historical memory (the old sergeant tells me this is how the Nazis did it), habit and training (this is how we do it here), and availability (torturers do not have a great deal of time for experimentation, particularly in a crisis, and they reach for well-known techniques). As with tailoring, torturers develop certain styles based on past familiarity with their instruments, fashions of the day, and the needs of the situation. Torturers may treat all prisoners to the same standard violence; torture becomes a "one size fits all" operation, with predictable, ill-fitting results. But the more cunning torturers may customize torture to the needs of the situation and the character of the prisoner. These torturers will be the innovators who introduce new variations in style.

I will unpack the craft apprenticeship hypothesis further shortly. Here I want to consider three less plausible ways of explaining the fact that clean tortures come in certain predictable combinations.

One possibility is that state ideology explains why torturers choose the techniques that they do (the ideology hypothesis). Now I have already argued that ideology cannot adequately explain why torturers choose clean over stealthy torture techniques. It seems even more unlikely such a hypothesis could also explain why they favor some clean techniques over the others or why they would combine them together in particular ways.

Another possibility is that torturers choose their techniques based on a proven laboratory record of successful performance (the scientific efficiency hypothesis). This hypothesis presumes that torture is a science or is approaching one. But this hypothesis makes it very hard to understand the development of styles of torture and their continued variations. If torture is approaching a science, one would expect a gradual convergence of techniques as the scientific training in torture advances worldwide. After all, it seems inconceivable that states could resist mastering knowledge of scientific torture any more than states could resist research on nuclear weapons.

But if styles of torture are converging around one single scientific style, this study has been unable to document it. There is no doubt a convergence of some sort, a surge in clean techniques worldwide. But this is caused not by the *push* of scientific and technological advancements, but by the *pull* of universal monitoring. And this pull has yielded not one, but several different styles of clean torture. Moreover, there is little evidence that high-tech tortures are spreading. Electrotorture is very much the lone exception here. The priority of torturers remains on learning how to use low-tech methods, and I will explain why shortly.

A last possibility is that styles of torture are rooted in inherited patterns of penal practice (the cultural hypothesis). This hypothesis dovetails somewhat with the craft apprenticeship hypothesis. Torturers unquestionably combine techniques and develop styles based on inherited patterns from the past. How else can one explain why torturers in the Middle East turn to the venerable *falaka* instead of water torture? Or why South Asian torturers adopt the *ghotna*? Or why East Asian torturers occasionally use customary finger-bandaging and Chinese torturers in psychoprisons turn to electric acupuncture? All these ancient practices have entered into modern torture.

It also makes sense that former colonies persisted in the use of techniques that were customary before their independence. Torturers in former French colonies persisted in using the *crapaudine* and magneto torture, and former English colonies persisted in ducking (Canada and the United States) and the Wooden Horse (the United States) long after the British had abandoned these procedures. Likewise, this study has documented several cases where governing powers "go native" and start using local techniques. A particularly good example is the way in which colonial powers ended up with the torture techniques of other societies. The British adopted the *falaka*, spicing, and certain rope tortures from colonial India. The French adopted the *falaka* from the Vietnamese or from North African societies.

The difficulty with the cultural hypothesis is that it does not adequately explain why torturers abandon these techniques or why torturers with no cultural roots adopt these techniques. Why, for example, did torturers in other states adopt the *crapaudine*, states as different as Israel, China, Angola, and El Salvador? Why do American and French prisons adopt sweatboxes and cangues from East Asian practice? No cultural explanation suffices, and the problem becomes especially severe with respect to whole styles of torture. It is one thing for the style to appear in the country of an ally but quite another thing to explain why the same style appears in the torture chambers of one's enemy. It is not surprising, for example, to find that Anglo-Saxon modern appears in Israel, but it is much harder to explain why the same regimen appears in the Soviet Union, where there is little continuity in culture. And, of course, French modern appears in countries that have no relationship to France or its colonies.

The Strength of Low Technology

Let me now unpack the craft apprenticeship hypothesis further. In particular, I want to sketch how monitoring has affected the craft of torture and the way in which torturers learn and change their techniques. In particular, I argue that monitoring has reinforced the craft nature of torture. First, it has put a premium on torturers learning low-tech tortures. Second, it has heightened the importance of "on the job" training as opposed to centralized, formal training in the craft of torture.

Let me begin with a set of factual claims. This book has covered hundreds of cases of innovation and adaptation in torture. Repeatedly, certain qualities turned out to be necessary for successful innovation and adaptation. Successful devices were nonlethal, portable, left few marks on the body, and were labor saving, painful, and flexible to use. They were easily available, easy to maintain, and cheap to replace. It helped enormously when the procedures were familiar cultural practices or remembered by old hands.

Some devices could be used for other purposes besides torture (e.g., cattle prods). Others had the quality of linkage: they fit into routine duties of officers. Soldiers, for example, could not be deprived of field telephones without undermining military efficiency. Some tools had the important quality of everydayness. Torturers learned to use things that were literally part of the furniture of civilian life: lights, chairs, stools, telephone books, keys, fans, handkerchiefs, buckets, hoses, water, plastic bags, tires, clothes pins, tape, gauze, and spices.

Why did torturers choose procedures that made use of what was at hand? Because their simplicity and ordinariness was critical in an age of increased public scrutiny. Instruments had to be easy to hide, disguise, throw away, or move quickly. Governments could not easily control devices that had legitimate civilian functions, much less those that were integral to the activities of law enforcement. On the other hand, devices that did not survive were those that were too visible, had no obvious legitimate civilian functions, and was not integral to the activities of policemen and soldiers.

Whips, for example, underwent precisely this transition. Whips had been, for millennia, instruments of ordinary life. They were necessary for transportation and coordination of animals. But today we are most likely to see whips in circuses and ranches. They are no longer necessary for a policeman's function, say, to transport prisoners. In the age of tractors and automobiles, there is only one reason why police have whips, for purposes of punishment and torture.

These qualities of success explain why torturers generally prefer low technology to high technology in stealth torture, and why they prefer some high-technology devices to others. Sensory deprivation boxes were nonlethal, painful, and left few marks. But they proved to be too visible, not easily portable, unfamiliar to users, and hard to maintain and repair. They required a support network, and they were difficult to find and create. Police could not directly link them to their routine duties. They were not multifunctional or flexible, and they lacked the quality of everydayness (with the exception of Lilly's water tank, which would be at home in a New Age resort).

Electrotorture turned out to meet many more of these requirements, but not all electrical devices were the same. Electroconvulsive therapy (ECT) devices had the unhelpful quality of inducing retrograde amnesia, hardly a plus if one is interrogating someone for information. Police would have a hard time explaining why they had medical devices like a defibrillator in the interrogation room. Many other devices failed to catch on for similar reasons, including electrified chairs (United States, Spain, Brazil, Iran), mats (United States), beds (Chile), whips (Nazi Germany), swings (Nazi-occupied Poland), helmets (Nazi-occupied France, South Africa, Malawi), bags (South Africa), refrigerators (South Africa), televisions (Brazil), belts (Rwanda), sticks (Burundi), brooms (Argentina), and microphones (Soviet-occupied Afghanistan). Even the *picana eléctrica* did not appear in torture for decades outside of Argentina and Venezuela.

Most of these devices were inventions of tinkerers, not laboratories. This includes stun technology, which was the product of years of effort by a single man, John Cover. Cover never conceived of his scientific activity as a laboratory science separate from organizational and networking activities. Inciting and creating needs, organizing new allies and new consumers, were as integral to Cover's activities as choosing new materials, shaping new connections, and conducting specific kinds of tests.

Whenever Cover changed an element on the social side (whom he was cultivating, for example), he also had to change elements on the technical side (what kind of materials he used). Likewise, apparently simple "technical" decisions had effects on the social side. In other words, Cover was not so much inventing a "thing" or a series of things as he was assembling alliances— or rather a series of alliances—that were simultaneously social and technological. Taser models were flags around which he organized his alliances. He mobilized certain kinds of people and things in a socio-technical chain along a scenario he imagined. The elements of alliances were not "givens," but had to be brought into existence or pushed out of the picture, depending on the scenario. Eventually Cover created a successful scenario in which this high-technology product "worked." Others then colonized it, including torturers who appreciated immediately the cover the normal, legitimate use of stun weaponry provided them.

Successful alliances delivered "products." The stronger these networks were, the more convincingly Cover and his associates could argue that people were resisting something powerful ("a technological imperative"), and all this talk about torture was a "social and political problem." The more things and people resisted what they were supposed to do, this became a "technical question" of getting the devices to "work." At this point, no one talked about "social resistance," much less "the inevitable march of law enforcement technology."

By contrast, the laboratory scientists concerned with sensory deprivation (SD) boxes (Cameron, Baldwin, Lilly) imagined no scenarios other than the narrow concerns of their experiments. They did not reflect on the kinds of questions that troubled Cover, such as portability, flexibility, multifunctionality, everydayness, linkage, cost, maintenance, repair, and replacement. Nor did the CIA, with its extensive resources, bother to look into these questions.

Scientific as these products were, they did not float effortlessly under their own volition into the world. Torturers generally found no use for them within the context of their craft. If something survived, it was noise, and again it was torturer-tinkerers elsewhere in the world that adapted this one element that did survive the SD research. They adapted it using ordinary devices that were multifunctional, everyday, and easy to replace.

Some believe that modern torture tends toward high technology: "There seems to be constantly ongoing research in this field, aimed at developing more refined methods, which are effective in breaking down the victim's resistance, and which at the same time will leave only little or no visible trace."[2] But if there is, this book did not find it. The tortures at Abu Ghraib and elsewhere do not express a remorseless American science of torture. And more generally, the story of clean torture shows little evidence of a scientific "research and development" drive behind torture. In the world of increased public monitoring, torturers know that low tech is usually better than high tech.

The Power of Whispers

Clean torture is among the oldest kinds of stealthy violence. States turned to it earlier than they turned to stealth in other means of violence, and torture by stealth has spread more widely and involved a greater variety of techniques. Over the course of a century, torture has changed worldwide, the kind of sweeping change that is rare with any method of violence, but that is perhaps more remarkable in this case for its reliance on hidden networks. Techniques spread through backroom apprenticeships, networks of whispers, knowing glances, and the enabling power of averted eyes.[3]

In a world of public monitoring, networks of whispers do not leave behind evidence that connects government leaders directly to torture on the ground. Such networks diffuse responsibility among many different people. Formal training leaves behind written evidence, including training manuals, photographs, and letters authorizing training,

It also makes instructors far more visible to their enemies. Consider the cautionary story of Dan Mitrione.[4] In the 1960s, Mitrione was a notorious American police adviser who instructed Brazilian and Uruguayan police in formal torture classes. In 1970, Uruguayan guerrillas kidnapped and executed him. His body showed no signs of torture, binding, or mistreatment.

Informal apprenticeship has other advantages in recruitment and secrecy. Soldiers and doctors who might balk at being involved in torture can be drawn into it in small steps until they are as implicated as anybody else.[5] Such practices also tie torturers together in bonds of secrecy and fraternity.[6] Apprenticeship also creates regional argot for torture, "a language with new words and expressions so that they can talk about various things without being understood by outsiders."[7]

In short, word of mouth is far more effective in a world of public monitoring than torture by the book. The great disadvantage of backroom apprenticeship is that it passes on inaccurate information along with the accurate. This includes false rumors about origins, mythologies about how to leave no marks, and self-serving stories about the efficiency of this or that technique. Backroom apprenticeship is one of several reasons why organizations fail to learn from the experience of torture.

Torture folklore, for instance, is a source of the persistent demand that torture be used for national security purposes despite considerable evidence that it does not work, a matter I take up in the next few chapters. It is also the source of misleading accounts of origins. Take, for instance, the names for various tortures. The trickiest names are those that impute historical origins. The Chinese did not invent sleep deprivation or choking in water.[8] The Germans did not create a torture chair with moving parts.[9] Hooding was used long before torturers ever heard of sensory deprivation experiments, and sleep deprivation antedates World War II.[10] American soldiers in Vietnam did not practice forced standing with wires attached to one's fingers.[11] Other words are simply too general to be helpful guides. *Water cure*, the old American name for water torture, can refer to pumping, choking, choking with a napkin in the Dutch style, cold baths or showers in asylums, and beating with high-pressure showers. Names like *the crucifixion* or *Christ the Redeemer* can mean forced standing with arms extended (a positional torture) or suspension from the arms (a restraint torture).[12]

For those who believe that modern torture depends on more formal training, this study has found the following evidence regarding torture manuals and formal classes.

Manuals for Torture

Gestapo manuals sometimes described the psychology of interrogation, but did not describe torture techniques.[13] Soviet NKVD interrogation manuals did not describe torture techniques either.[14] The Vietnam era edition of the U.S. Army field manual on interrogation (FM 30-15) endorsed only psychological techniques (chapter 8).

Some documents reveal that torture was authorized, but they are generally poor guides to actual practices on the ground. The top secret *Notes for the Interrogation of Prisoners of War* (1943) authorizes the Japanese Kempeitai to use torture but offers no standardized procedures. It states briefly, "The following are methods normally to be adopted: (a) Torture. This includes kicking, beating and anything connected with physical suffering."[15] Japanese torture involved a great deal more than kicking and beating (chapter 7). The French manual, *Guide provisoire de l'officier de renseignement* (1961), apparently endorsed water tortures (choking, pumping, and high-pressure hoses), though the main torture in Algeria was electrotorture (chapter 7).

In 1937, the Gestapo and the lawyers for the Ministry of Justice agreed that interrogations could involve up to twenty-five blows with a standardized club.[16] In 1942, Gestapo chief Müller expanded the approved methods. They now included sleep deprivation, starvation, exhaustion exercises, and confinement in dark cells.[17] There are at best only a handful of Gestapo cases that would conform to such instructions (chapter 4). Similar problems arise when one compares the list of approved torture techniques from the Department of Justice and the Pentagon to the kinds of torture techniques reported in Iraq, Afghanistan, and Guantánamo (chapter 14).[18]

Two CIA interrogation manuals, the *Kubark* (1963) and the *Human Resources Exploitation Training Manual* (HRET) (1983), are now available on the Internet.[19] These manuals maintained that good interrogation requires the psychological regression of prisoners. They argued that pain is only valuable if it induces psychological regression, that individuals react to pain differently, and that pain may strengthen resistance rather than weaken it. Neither of these manuals offers specific instruction in torture techniques, but they do itemize them.

Kubark discusses "debility" (restraining prisoners for long periods, holding them in conditions that are extremely hot, cold, or moist, depriving them of sleep and food, and exhaustion exercises), "pain" (forced standing), "sensory deprivation" (Lilly's water tank), "narcosis" (the use of drugs and placebos), hypnosis, and the threat of ECT.

The unedited *HRET* is almost identical, except that it adds forced sitting on a stool under "Pain," and makes no references to drugs or ECT.[20] The CIA had concluded long before that ECT and drugs were not helpful in interrogation (chapters 18 and 19). The outdated reference to Lilly's water tank remained unchanged. The *HRET* was edited in 1985 to remove objectionable discussion of torture, but the Spanish version was not. In this same period, the U.S. Southern Command distributed various intelligence manuals under the army's "Project X" program, instructions that suggested beatings and included outdated discussion of truth serums.[21]

Project X was "a training package to provide counterinsurgency techniques learned in Vietnam to Latin American countries."[22] Much of it was drawn from FM 30-18, a classified army field manual on intelligence tactics. In 1982, the Reagan administration restored counterintelligence training, and administrators assigned the task to Victor Tise, a young officer from the U.S. Army Intelligence Center and School (USAICS) at Fort Huachuca. Tise was sent to the School of the Americas at Fort Gulick, Panama Canal Zone. He worked with Captain John Zandar, USAICS, and they were given a very short period of time to reconstitute a seven-week training program. Tise sent the material he received from USAICS to the Department of Defense for clearance, and the package was returned marked "approved but unchanged."[23] Hundreds of copies were subsequently distributed throughout Latin America.[24] Students came from Bolivia, Colombia, Costa Rica, Dominican Republic, Ecuador, Guatemala, Honduras, Mexico, Peru, and Venezuela.[25]

Unfortunately, the techniques listed in these manuals, whether approved or not, do not match typical procedures used by Latin American torturers (chapter 9). Take the Honduran case, where there is a direct link between the training manuals and soldiers on the ground, particularly the notorious Brigade 316. Honduran torturers typically used electroshock, choking with water, *teléfono*, foam-covered batons, *falaka*, sweatboxes, and hoods soaked with chemicals.[26] This list has at best only one common item with those listed in the *HRET*, sweatboxes. The techniques listed in the *HRET*, or as far as is known, Project X materials, do not seem to have interested Honduran torturers much.

Moreover, none of the CIA manuals offers anything resembling formal instruction in applying a torture technique. Take, for example, the claim that *Kubark* offers technical "directives" for applying electrotorture.[27] *Kubark* has three references to electricity in the entire text. One reference (under "Legal and Policy Considerations") prohibits using medical, chemical or electrical method or material to induce "acquiescence" without "prior Headquarters approval," and another suggests threatening detainees feigning mental problems with ECT therapy.[28] Lastly, an advisory early in the text reminds agents to make sure they know whether the voltage is 110 or 220 before mounting electrical equipment, wise advice for any traveler abroad who uses microphones and tape recorders, as the manual urges.[29]

One can put as sinister a twist on such statements as one likes.[30] But none of this amounts to formal training in using any electrical device, for example, an ECT machine. One also has to wonder why anyone would think it plausible that the CIA would use ECT devices for gathering intelligence, a device that typically causes retrograde amnesia in a prisoner. And no CIA manual refers to the most common electrotorture device of all, magnetos.

News stories that use *Kubark* and *HRET* to document American influence on torture demonstrate repeatedly the perils of using Google to teach the history of torture.[31] Indeed, what is true of electrotorture is also true of other techniques. For example, after 9/11, CIA and army interrogators requested permission to perform Dutch choking with a wet napkin ("waterboarding").[32] This torture does not appear in any pre-9/11 government document discussing interrogation, including *Kubark* and *HRET*. They represent native traditions, passed on orally, that came forward once government officials authorized torture.

Dirk von Schrader's pamphlet, *Elementary Field Interrogations*, represents some of this lore.[33] Given how difficult it is to find, it is hard to gauge what its effect has been on practice. The author was allegedly an operator in the notorious Phoenix Program in Vietnam.[34] He discusses a surprisingly narrow range of techniques (mostly restraint tortures), nothing remotely resembling the full range of tortures practiced on the ground during the Vietnam War (see appendix D).

Less representative, despite appearances, is Richard Krousher's *Physical Interrogation Techniques* (chapter 11).[35] Despite its encyclopedic appearance, this book is a catalog of American gay S&M practice in the 1970s and shows little understanding of the pressures to which interrogators are subject. Passive exercise machines and their supplements (electrified fishnet clothing) might be excellent stuff for a weekend at the club Inferno, but hardly the sort of thing that one might be using in Vietnam.

This, then, is as much as is known about manuals, and the conclusion must be that none of these manuals is a good guide to the actual practice of torture.

Programs seem to be better guides to torture, but there are few known reports of these. The known information can be divided into two kinds of programs, those in which governments instructed others in torture and those programs that used highly coercive techniques for other purposes and inadvertently became conduits for torture training.

Interrogation Programs involving Torture Training

There are only a handful of known instances in which interrogators were trained in classrooms to use specific techniques, techniques that did appear in later reports of torture. In the 1960s, Brazilians offered torture seminars that did demonstrate specific techniques.[36] Dan Mitrione offered similar seminars in Brazil and Uruguay. In the 1980s, "Mr. Bill," a CIA instructor, taught Honduran interrogators in Texas.[37] Lastly, in 2003, the CIA selected fourteen agents for the interrogation of a dozen top al-Qaeda suspects, and it trained them in six authorized torture techniques, including the Dutch method of choking with water.[38]

Studies of other known programs do not identify training in actual techniques, suggesting that these skills were picked up on the job. In 1959, a French program at Camp Jeanne d'Arc defined conditions under which soldiers could turn to water and electrical torture in Algeria, but apparently did not demonstrate the techniques.[39] Some Paras claim they received no directives on how to torture.[40] In the 1960s, the Greek junta instituted an official recruitment program for torturers.[41] This program has been exceptionally well documented. Soldiers were subjected to beatings, exhaustion exercises, and ritual humiliation. This prepared them to be less sympathetic when they assumed their roles as interrogators. However, recruits received no seminars on specific techniques.

Stanley Milgram, the noted psychologist, explained why such programs can transform ordinary men into torturers, demonstrating his point with ethically questionable experiments to generate obedience.[42] It is tempting, no doubt, to believe that the CIA paid Milgram to do this research and so encouraged Milgram to invent a behavioral science for training torturers.[43] Thomas Blass, Milgram's biographer, challenges every particular of these claims, stating that there is "not a shred of evidence that Milgram received CIA funding and I have no reason to believe that this claim has any foundation."[44]

Suppose, however, that the CIA did fund Milgram. What is certain is that there is little evidence of his work in the known programs for training torturers. Consider the Greek and Brazilian programs, the most explicitly documented programs for American client states. These have little in common, share no standardized content, bear little resemblance to Milgram's experiments, and in fact apply principles that Milgram showed were either superfluous or mistaken.

The Greeks beat their future torturers brutally to desensitize them; Milgram had shown that simple psychological mechanisms (e.g., distance from the victim) could induce the same effects without physical contact.[45] Why then go through the effort of physical abuse? Brazilian seminars demonstrated torture to new recruits using live victims; Milgram taught that proximity to the victim was more likely to induce disobedience. In fact, experiments that had subjects see or touch victims yielded the lowest rates of compliance.[46] If Milgram invented a behavioral science for training torturers, no one is reading him.

In addition, the amount of time trainees spend on actual interrogation is pitifully short. For example, notorious American "Project X" instructional packets break down how much time was spent on various types of training.[47] These packets show that very little time was spent on actual interrogation techniques. If Project X programs involved teaching torture techniques by the book, instructors were able to train students in a complete craft in less than two hours, a remarkable achievement for any professor.

Similarly, the Project X Intelligence Training Packet required about 177 hours of instruction. Interrogation of POWs and Document Exploitation was 32 hours, most of which was devoted to document and map management. Students received only 2 hours in "the Process of Interrogation." The Counterintelligence Packet required 145 hours, with 9 hours for "Interrogations," 1 hour of which was on interrogation techniques. The Intelligence for Stability Operations required 160 hours of training, 13 hours of which were for "Interrogation and Document Exploitation" overall.

In short, interrogation programs, even those that allow for torture, do not appear to be the main channels by which torturers learn their craft. There are very few formal programs for training torturers. The existing few have no standardized content and do not illustrate a behavioral science for training torturers. Even in American counterintelligence, where one would expect to find this training most clearly, the time spent on teaching interrogation of *any* sort is so short that it could not have been a program priority.

Resistance to Torture Programs

Another possibility is that torturers learned their craft indirectly. Some official programs, while not designed to train torturers in specific skills, may have shaped what techniques soldiers later chose for interrogation. In the wake of the Korean War, Americans and British instituted programs to prepare their soldiers for hostile interrogation, named "R21 Techniques," "countermeasures to hostile interrogation," "stress inoculation," or "Survival, Evasion, Resistance, Escape" (SERE). Soldiers volunteered for these programs, but the training was harsh, like the training Greek torturers received.[48] It seems plausible that volunteers learned to do unto others what was done unto them and then applied this lesson once torture was authorized.

It is hard to find direct official transmission from these programs to torturers. The only known case is a very recent one, the transmission of SERE techniques to interrogators at Guantánamo.[49] In the SERE program, American soldiers were hooded, deprived of sleep, starved, stripped of clothes, exposed to extreme temperatures and painful noise, choked with water (the Dutch method), and subjected to harsh interrogation including humiliation, sexual embarrassment, and desecration of religious symbols and books.[50] In this sense, these programs were "the closest thing on their [the Pentagon's] organizational charts to a school of torture," indeed far more so than the official interrogation programs at Fort Huachuca or a School of the Americas.

SERE techniques moved in two directions, laterally to Guantánamo and up the chain of command once torture was authorized. The lateral movement happened fairly early. On March 22, 2005, a former chief of the Interrogation Control Element at Guantánamo stated in a sworn statement that SERE instructors instructed Guantánamo interrogators. He stated that his predecessor "arranged for SERE instructors to teach their techniques to interrogators at GTMO. . . . The instructors did give some briefings to the Joint Interrogation Group interrogators." He also emphasized that neither he nor General Miller, who commanded the camp, thought SERE techniques "were appropriate."[51] Quite independently, FBI officials wrote several emails around the same period critical of Guantánamo interrogation, describing the tortures used as "SERE techniques."[52] And the SERE program's chief psychologist, Col. Morgan Banks, issued guidance in early 2003 for the military psychologists who helped devise the interrogation strategies at Guantánamo.

What exactly Banks or SERE instructors taught will remain unclear until transcripts and memos are released, but it seems generally that SERE techniques moved laterally from Fort Bragg, where SERE is located, to Guantánamo. At the same time, Guantánamo interrogators visiting the SERE school developed a wish list of techniques" for "high-profile, high-value" detainees."[53] This list included sleep deprivation, stress positions, and physical assault. This list was the basis for what Secretary of Defense Rumsfeld approved in December 2002 and advisers claimed was legal since the methods were already used in SERE training.

The only other known case of transmission suggests techniques in stress inoculation programs traveled indirectly, mainly by means of low-level lateral transmission. In the 1970s, Army intelligence officers appear to have passed on R21 techniques to police in Northern Ireland, who then used them to interrogate prisoners. But despite the attention this case has garnered, scholars have not identified high-level contacts between British military intelligence and the

RUC. And despite allegations to the contrary, it is hard to find any role played by British military psychologists, much less experts in sensory deprivation (see chapters 15 and 18). While it seems plausible that intelligence officers did transmit R21 techniques to RUC officers, it seems more than likely that this was done largely through backroom apprenticeship.

This study has identified many similar cases of low-level transmission between soldiers. Repeatedly, soldiers in various armies drew on their own brutal training or official military punishments in torturing others. Indeed, most accounts of torture transmission in Iraq and Afghanistan are stories of low-level transmission. Abu Ghraib MPs did not have formal classes in torture. For example, dog handlers at Abu Ghraib do not describe a training program for the use of dogs in torture and interrogation. Rather, they describe how a team of Guantánamo interrogators, so called "Tiger Teams," regularly told them to "scare up" prisoners according to an allegedly approved plan, and that a team staff sergeant was responsible for bringing the "lessons learned" at Guantánamo to MPs, including the use of dogs. This is typical backroom apprenticeship. Although the interrogation plan had been "approved by 'higher' [authorities]," the specific techniques followed "a fair amount of brainstorming" at the local level.[54]

Similar stories appear at other American camps in Iraq. Once soldiers knew harsher interrogation techniques were permitted, they drew on their own experiences in assembling their methods: "In training, they forced me to listen to the Barney I Love You song for 45 minutes. I never want to go through that again."[55] Here, soldiers learned from their trauma and passed it on. Others drew on what they knew or remembered from other contexts. Consider, for example, the interrogator who asphyxiated General Abed Hamed Mowhoush, an Iraqi prisoner, in a sleeping bag. "The sleeping bag technique" was originally the idea of a soldier "who remembered how his older brother used to force him into one and how scared and vulnerable it made him feel."[56] After he was charged, the interrogator claimed that "the sleeping bag technique" was a standard SERE technique called "close confinement," but one can be justly skeptical.[57]

American soldiers in Afghanistan also drew on what they knew or were familiar with. Soldiers with the Fourth Infantry Division in Afghanistan report that "there was no specific training on the treatment of detainees; the MPs relied on their common knowledge in this area."[58] The unit frequently used inexperienced personnel and hired interpreters off the street. "There were too many interrogations and not enough interrogators."[59] Even the trained interrogators felt they had too little training to deal with the situation. Indeed, officers "engaged in interrogations using techniques they literally remembered from the movies."[60]

Similar considerations may apply to CIA methods. Veteran CIA officials insist that "case officers aren't actually trained in interrogation techniques" and that they never knew "anyone who was a 'professional interrogator' in the agency."[61] As one decorated active case officer with twenty-five years experience says, "We're not trained interrogators—to be honest, in those situations I really had no idea what I'm doing and I'm not the only one who has had this experience."[62] Nevertheless, the CIA had a stress inoculation program at "The Farm," instituted in 1970 and run until the late 1990s, in which individuals were subjected to sleep deprivation, doused with cold water, forced to sit or stand for long periods, put in small coffinlike spaces, and given oversalted or contaminated food.[63] It seems plausible that in cases where agents wanted to torture, they drew on their own personal trauma at the Farm and taught these techniques to others.

In short, this study has found very limited evidence in favor of the thesis that torture training is transmitted through official manuals or centralized interrogation programs. Even cases of high-level transmission through stress inoculation programs are hard to find. This is surprising given the scope of this study, which covers nearly a century of modern torture around the globe. Perhaps others will uncover more programs and manuals eventually, but as far as the published evidence goes, the craft apprenticeship hypothesis remains the most plausible explanation for how most torture techniques get transmitted. Interrogators appear to pass on techniques largely through low-level transmission between ordinary soldiers and policemen or by means of simple imitation on the job.

Why Styles Change

Monitoring, then, has reinforced the craft nature of torture. Torturers favor low-technology items because they are harder to identify. They use high-tech devices for torture mainly when they allow plausible deniability, that is, they are multifunctional or can be associated with legitimate, routine activities. And methods of torture take increasingly hidden and circuitous routes. Formal, explicit training would be relatively easy to identify.

All this explains some general characteristics of modern torture, but it does not explain how torturers innovate within their craft. In particular, this book has documented several cases where torture subcultures changed dramatically. Why do torturers change techniques, even entire styles, say from Anglo-Saxon modern to French modern or psychoprisons? Now it is not possible to do an ethnography of torturers "on the job," so it is hard to be certain why torturers change and at whose orders. But the evidence does point to several reasonable possibilities driving the changes in torture techniques and styles, though none can be advanced with certainty.

Changing demands on police. Changes in the political environment in which police torture may change the techniques they use. For example, police in many places use sweating and forced standing to generate false confessions. But matters are different when one wants accurate information quickly. When suspects are many and resources few, sweating and positional torture become too time-consuming and inefficient. For these purposes, interrogators prefer techniques that are painful, quick, and labor-saving, for example, tortures involving electricity. Such factors may explain why South African torturers shifted away from forced standing to electrotorture in the 1970s (chapter 15). It may be in this case that there was a change in police goals, that is, police shifted from using torture to extract false confessions to using it to extract accurate information.

Imitating the news. Torturers appear to imitate what they read about in the news. For example, most available accounts of high-technology noise (even the exaggerated ones) date from after August 1971, that is, after the firestorm of international publicity around the British Five Techniques (chapter 18). This seems hardly coincidental. Similarly, known Chinese techniques from the Korean War appeared in the strangest places following the riveting stories of Chinese "brainwashing" of American and British POWs. Ice tortures appeared soon after in Bulgaria (1953), Venezuela (1953), and British-occupied Cyprus (1956). Forced standing appeared in Portugal (1953), Venezuela (1953), and French-occupied Algeria (1956). It is hard to see what other factor besides imitation could account for the appearance of these techniques in such disparate countries. Torturers, on this account, are opportunists, and are unlikely to pass up the chance to try out a new technique, especially if news reports describe it as fearsome. It is not surprising, then, to find a similar shift in Egyptian torture following the Abu Ghraib scandal as well.[64]

Learning from neighbors. Some torture subcultures borrow from their neighbors. Much as busy consumers might buy a certain kind of car or shop at a certain store because a neighbor recommends it, torturers are usually pressed for time and may rely unreasonably on recommendations of familiars or copy what they think has a successful track record nearby. Several cases have this kind of feel to them. In the 1960s, Uruguayans borrowed the *picana* from Argentine torturers. Romanian, Cuban, and Chinese officials copied the Soviet psychoprison, apparently without much prompting from the Soviets. American interrogators probably learned about the magneto not stateside, but from South

Vietnamese interrogators, who in turn copied the French colonists. The old "hot egg under the armpit" routine, first introduced by the British in Cyprus, persists in the Mediterranean region long after the United Kingdom had abandoned its colonies.

Soldiers going home. This study showed several instances in which returning troops brought torture techniques from colonial or international war to domestic policing. Soldiers brought these procedures to their civilian lives as detectives, correctional officers, and private security guards. French colonial techniques used in the 1930s appeared in the hands of the French Gestapo in the 1940s. French army tortures from Vietnam in the 1940s appeared in Algeria when the Paras assumed control in 1957, and eventually made it to the Parisian Sûreté by the early 1960s. The spillover effect also occurred in domestic violence, one policeman using on his wife and child the techniques he used at work.[65]

American troops probably brought back pumping and magneto torture from the Spanish-American and Vietnamese wars, respectively. Wartime experience also probably played a role in the electrotorture of an ordinary Israeli suspect in Tiberias in 1983. One can only wait to see what current wars will bring home.

What happens "over there," then, shows up in "a neighborhood near you." If this is a plausible description, the question is why soldiers would act in peacetime as they had in war. One possibility is that soldiers-turned-police need to produce results for bureaucratic advancement. This apparently was the case with the individual who introduced electrotorture into the Punjab in the 1970s (chapter 8). Another possibility is that such men have reputations to uphold. They were hired for being tough on criminals and knowing what needs to be done (chapter 2). Gender and self-perception may play important roles here.[66]

Learning from historical trauma. Imitating what enemies have done to one may also be a source of changing practices. For example, in the case of ice torture, it is tempting to draw a chain of transmission in which enemies copy enemies: Chinese used it on the British in North Korea (1952–53), British and Turkish interrogators on Greek Cypriots (1956), and Greek police on leftist students (1960s). This example suggests that torturers learn from trauma. They think of the worst that was done to them and they do it to their enemies. Here again, they may be responding to the pressures of time as well as reaching for what is familiar.

But learning from trauma appears to be a complex process, sometimes opening doors and at other times closing them. Some historical trauma appears to make torturers averse to certain techniques. Vietnamese and Algerian torturers did not turn to electrotorture for decades, and Israelis did not use standing cells until the 1990s even though they used sweatboxes. When they did adopt these old procedures, they used them in ways that varied just enough from their original to suggest they were not behaving as their ancient tormentors had.

Kinds of public attention. Some cases suggest that the proximity of monitors (national or international) and the kinds of monitors (medical or legal) may also change the techniques torturers prefer. For example, in Turkey, Izmir's police shifted from the *falaka* to electrotorture at about the same time that local medical monitors found bone scintigraphy identified the effects of *falaka*. The motive in this case was to escape detection by local medical monitors, and the behavior makes sense. Other cases are less plausible simply because the behavior makes no sense and the monitors too distant. For example, South African torturers probably did not add water to electrotorture and wrap electrodes in cloth because they were flipping through pages of *Forensic Science International* in their spare time and found out that the Danish researchers could now identify electrotorture forensically. The South African technique was old folk wisdom for cleanliness, but ineffective against Danish biopsy procedures for electric injury (chapter 19).[67]

Escaping detection is not the only way in which public monitoring can affect the kind of techniques used. Some kinds of torture depend on their legitimacy as medical treatments, and the doctors who administer them may insist on them simply because to do otherwise would damage their reputation. For example, in the 1950s, doctors involved in Soviet psychoprisons appear not to have treated dissidents with drugs, as they did other patients (chapter 19). This suggests they did not take seriously the diagnosis of sluggish schizophrenia at first. Soon Soviet doctors found themselves in a difficult spot, having complied with the Soviet state, but being pressured by international organizations, particularly those of doctors and psychiatrists, to justify their diagnoses. Having claimed dissidents were sluggish schizophrenics, Soviet doctors had to vindicate their judgment. Vindicating their judgment meant misrecognizing the mental disposition of dissidents and prescribing treatments to "cure them." This may explain the increase in pharmacological torture in the late 1960s and through the 1970s. Even today, it is difficult to know whether these men were sincere doctors or simply political agents of the Soviet state.

Government-to-government transfer. Occasionally, governments learn from each other at higher levels of contact. In 1963, South African torturers shifted from wires to magnetos in electrotorture, the same year that they initiated conversations with the French on counterinsurgency training.[68] After evaluating Uruguayan electrotorture instruments, Dan Mitrione urged the U.S. government to supply better prods and needles in the late 1960s, a change that a Uruguayan torturer observed who did not know of Mitrione (chapter 8). Nazi spies reported Brazilian police subjected them to positional tortures and sleep deprivation in the 1940s, a procedure not known in Brazil before this date but familiar to American and British advisers who were on site (chapter 15). And prisoners reported Stalinist sweating and positional torture independently of the presence of Soviet advisers in Republican Spain, Eastern Europe, and East Asia between 1935 and 1960 (chapter 3).

All these cases suggest that agents of one government passed on torture techniques to another. In all these cases, *independent* reports on the ground confirm the presence of a *signature* technique or procedure for *another* nation with whom the police had contact. The presence of foreign advisers matches patterns of reported torture. Thus, it seems likely that Brazilians police assisting at the National Stadium in Chile in 1973 passed on some distinctive techniques like the *pau*, but Argentine torturers probably did not learn any new tricks from Uruguayan visits in 1977 and 1978.[69] In the latter case there was no significant change in the actual practice of torture in Argentina, whereas distinctive techniques like the *pau* were unknown in Chilean torture.

Too often, however, observers, pointing only to patterns of military training and aid, assert that government-to-government transfer has occurred. Many use this approach to underline American responsibility for torture worldwide (chapters 9 and 18).

Much of this book shows the problems with stories that follow scientists and advisers. In the age of stealth, following the Cash, the Brass, and the Lab Coat is no substitute for reconstructing the patterns of torture on the ground. French counterinsurgency theory and training had a well-documented impact on strategic thought of South American militaries, but this does not mean that their procedures came directly from French Algeria.[70] Some French colonial techniques did make it to South America, but via U.S. training of Brazilian police (chapter 8).

The pattern on the ground shows little evidence for a universal distributor of torture techniques (chapters 9, 15). Some major powers, the United States and the USSR, had a regional impact in their own zones of influence for a short time. Other powers were considerably less successful. The German Gestapo employed auxiliary police in the regions it occupied, and these men brought their own national traditions. The German style, if that is what we may call leg clamps and racks, appeared mainly in the Lowlands, Norway, and northern France and disappeared after World War II (chapter 4). The Japanese Kempeitai left few traces on torturers who followed them, despite a fairly consistent toolkit wherever they were in Asia (chapter 8, 9).

Disciplinary Interventions

In the introduction I mentioned some important theses on modern torture and human rights monitoring beyond those discussed thus far. I also made alternatives claims. Here I list the specific theses again and discuss the alternative claims in light of the evidence presented in this study.

International human rights regimes do shape state behavior. Many ordinary observers hold that human rights monitoring has no effect on the practice of violence in states and the patterns that appear. This study suggests that human rights monitoring does. In particular it holds that the formation of a human rights regime had a dramatic impact on the spread of clean torture techniques worldwide.

An international regime is a set of implicit or explicit norms, principles, and decision-making processes that states set up to monitor certain issues in international politics. In chapter 2, I described how a set of norms, principles, and auditing organizations appeared in the last three decades of the twentieth century that focused on maintaining human rights, as well as monitoring and preventing abuses. The fundamental question in the study of international regimes is from where they get their ability to influence state behavior.

This study suggests that the human rights regime gained a great deal of its power through the influence exerted by a group of democratic states, particularly those in Europe, who linked a good human rights record with aid and recognition. Other states came to realize that compliance with a human rights regime was critical if they wished to preserve foreign aid, legitimacy, or membership in this community of states. Some eventually abandoned torture altogether. Others turned to stealth torture. But had these states not participated as they did, it seems unlikely torture in the late twentieth century would have looked any different than torture in the early twentieth century. At best, states would have turned to stealth torture only in extraordinarily high-profile cases or in cases where they were seeking international attention (the international monitoring hypothesis).

It is also clear that the international human rights monitoring system did not depend on the goodwill of either the United States or the Soviet Union. Rather, these superpowers felt compelled to comply because they claimed a superior morality, a commitment to human rights in terms of their own political and ideological traditions. Critics played them against each other. They appealed to their desire to win the "hearts and minds" of nonaligned states and to their interest in avoiding embarrassment at the United Nations.

Ironically, superpower competition during the Cold War allowed the human rights regime to flourish. And sadly, the end of the Cold War may have weakened the hands of international auditors, regardless of the events that followed 9/11. One can urge American politicians to avoid torture because the government of Sudan, Cuba, or Iran might use such stories to stoke anti-American sentiments. But this does not have the same bite as suggesting that the Soviets would use it in their anti-American propaganda.

The question is whether a superpower can, by its own actions, undermine an international regime such as global human rights monitoring. Does this international monitoring regime depend on the goodwill of a single dominant power such as the United States? Will the international human rights monitoring regime be weakened further? The answer is uncertain, but this study suggests that much depends on whether the state in question is a democracy or not. A victorious Soviet Union would probably have been less amenable to pressure from human rights monitors, and the international human rights monitoring regime would probably have faltered and shrunk back to the borders of Western Europe. But a victorious United States appears far more open to domestic and international pressure.

Domestic and international auditors can bring to bear on policymakers not only norms, but also accurate, documented information on violations. Specific, credible information and appeals to rights can shake public confidence, influence policymakers, and raise questions about government policy and legitimacy. The United States can evade human rights auditing, even damage it considerably, but as long as it is a democracy, it is unlikely to be impervious to such pressures. There is, in other words, grounds for hope that the human rights monitoring regime may survive this crisis.

No single nation is the primary, original distributor of modern torture technology. Repeatedly, in this study, I have gestured toward accounts that claim that some states have acted as universal distributors, passing torture techniques to others by means of military aid and training. These universal distributors included Nazi Germany, the Soviet Union, the United States, and the United Kingdom.

But these claims are greatly overstated. Torture techniques circulate by many means, but centralized international distribution by a single state is probably among the least important. There are a few exceptions. Stalinist sweating was remarkably uniform worldwide in the 1950s, suggesting Soviet advisers were the most influential teachers. American agents had far less influence, except in some parts of Latin America in the 1960s. Beyond this, there is little evidence that torture techniques used worldwide today stem from any universal distributor.

Torture is a craft, not a science. The empirical study of torture instruments and methods does not support the thesis that torture is becoming a science. Globally, and across the century, torture is dominated by low-tech, not high-tech, devices. These cluster in different national styles and are not converging on a single "scientific" style. There is no behavioral science for training torturers; torture is still a craft apprenticeship. There is no evidence of a breakthrough in scientific research on torture by the Soviets in the 1920s, the CIA in the 1950s, or by the RUC in the 1970s, but if there was, the scientific products of this effort (SD/PD boxes; white noise) did not survive long in the field (chapter 18). The known scientific projects were failures; the CIA had terminated them by the time activists raised the alarm. Arguments that low-tech tortures are really high tech or psychologically scientific are weak or implausible.

In chapter 21, I offer further behavioral evidence showing that even torturers know torture is not a science, and I argue that such a science is unlikely. But this argument is unlikely to persuade many who believe in a science of torture. Their belief is rooted in general preconceptions about technology and progress, including a secular theodicy, a peculiarly modern way of accounting for evil in the modern world (chapter 24). Empirical study can offer no answer that satisfies faith.

How well torture technology spreads depends on the strength of the socio-technical network that carries it forward. Scholars of technology hold that the development of high-technology products follows a certain sequence of stages, beginning with conception and innovation and ending in the diffusion of a finished product. But as I explained earlier in this chapter, this account does not adequately characterize how stun technology developed. The story of Cover showed how innovation and diffusion were activities performed simultaneously. Cover had to simultaneously create socio-technical networks to sustain innovations.

To know one's pain is to be able to describe it to oneself and others. Many would hold that being subjected to torture is a world-destroying experience. It is important for scholars to understand the ways torture produces this important effect. One important explanation is the thesis advanced by the cultural theorist Elaine Scarry. Scarry begins with the very simple observation that pain is private. No one can know my pain. Pain is an inherently inexpressible sensation, and experiencing it drives one into a prelinguistic silence. Torture in this sense drives one into prelinguistic silence, and this inability to express oneself does have significant political consequences. Most notably, this allows states to shape the terms in which prisoners (and repressed populations more generally) understand and describe their reality. Torture in this sense is world-destroying.

Over the last two decades, empirical studies of torture have put this account of torture into question in two important ways. These studies show that pain is neither necessary for torture to be world destroying, nor is it sufficient for torture to be world destroying.

To be specific, raw pain is not *necessary* to destroy a prisoner's sense of reality. In chapter 3 ("Lights, Heat, and Sweat"), I documented how police and interrogators can use powerful psychological techniques to break down a prisoner's sense of reality. There are other techniques that do not cause physical pain but shake one's confidence and self-understandings down to their foundations. These include isolation, mock executions, screams from other cells, and threats against one's family. In his important study of painful religious rituals, Ariel Glucklich shows how ascetics and mystics also used similar techniques that fall short of raw pain to unmake their profane selves, including isolation, ongoing prayer and chanting, and hard physical work. "Pain," as Glucklich says, "is one example in a range of methods, but it must neither be elevated above the others nor reduced to them." Indeed, it is far from evident that "pain is more effective in this process than any other means."[71] Indeed, as I argue in the next chapter, pain may in fact reinforce one's sense of self during torture.

This brings up the second objection: pain is not *sufficient* to destroy a prisoner's sense of reality. Several studies of torture victims have made this point.[72] For example, in his study of Irish republican prisoners, Allen Feldman shows how Irish republican prisoners harness the pain of torture to transform themselves. The Irish paramilitary prisoner exploited interrogation violence to achieve "self-detachment of his body," grounded himself more firmly in his cause, and moved "from being the object of violence to the subject position of the codifying agent," thereby "emptying it [state violence] of its ideological content."[73] Similarly, in her study of Palestinian prisoners, Lisa Hajjar argues that they "retained their agency because they comprehended their suffering as part of the national struggle in which they were actively engaged." To them, the torture chamber, far from being a space of complete subjection and world destruction, was a "shared political arena" in which "both interrogators and interrogees were participants rather than actors and objects."[74] Lastly, some victims describe how brutal torture induced in them intense spiritual and mystical states that helped them resist their tormentors.[75]

Glucklich explains why pain can enhance agency, how it can be self-transforming and world-creating. Pain, Glucklich argues, can be rendered meaningful, and "it is not only subject to verbal communication but also figures in our ability to empathize and share. In other words, the symbolic and experiential efficacy of pain derives from the way it bridges 'raw' sensation with our highest qualities as human beings in a community of other humans."[76]

There is, no doubt, something important about Scarry's claim that one should pay attention to the ability of torture victims to express themselves, but not the specific mechanics of pain to which she gestures, mechanics that are neither necessary nor sufficient to explain the outcome of torture. Linguistically, the inability to express oneself has many facets. The inexpressibility that matters in torture is the gap between speakers and their communities, not the gap between the brain and the tongue. Expressing pain is about the conventions that acknowledge the recognition of others, not about our certainty or doubt about whether others *have* pain. The failure to grasp pain is not a failing of the intellect, but the failing of spirit, the inclination to give up when the conventions one counts on break down.

Covert torture undermines the legal, medical, and narrative conventions that people counted on to express themselves. But often this would not have mattered if they had wounds to show as in classical torture, and it would be a mistake to think of all these problems as problems of language and expression. Pain does not seek a home simply in language, but a home in the body. Clean tortures deny precisely this physical home, tangling victims and their communities in doubts, uncertainties, and illusions. And it is possibly not accidental that Scarry's important study appeared in the mid-1980s, when these kinds of clean techniques began spreading worldwide, and her focus on expression was a first take on an important phenomenon.

This study has explored the disturbing political implications of this phenomenon, the truth that we are less likely to complain about violence committed by stealth. Indeed, we are less likely even to have the opportunity to complain. This is not because we are indifferent (though it is certainly possible), but because we are often uncertain whether violence occurred at all. We are, in effect, politically illiterate in stealth torture, and this has political consequences.

By turning to stealthy torture, state officials repeatedly impeded the ability of victims to make allegations of torture stick. Doctors were unable to affirm allegations even immediately after torture (chapters 17–19). Not even families and friends believed victims of the *shabeh* had suffered much (chapter 18). Unable to focus on electrical injuries from Tasers, lawyers had to concentrate on whether the devices were lethal: there was, at least, no arguing with a dead body (chapter 11). And what was the Soviet public to believe about political dissidents who had been diagnosed as mad (chapter 19)?

In the months after 9/11, human rights monitors repeatedly described allegations of American torture, victims shared stories with their communities in Iraq and Afghanistan, and even government officials conceded that they used "torture lite." The photographs from Abu Ghraib reminded the American public that "torture lite" was simply another way of saying "painful tortures that left no marks" (chapters 14–18). But even after Abu Ghraib, lawyers for Guantánamo detainees doubted allegations of torture until uncovered FBI emails confirmed them.[77] And today, Americans still have difficulty with the T-word, preferring instead *abuse, moderate physical pressure, enhanced interrogation, highly coercive interrogation,* and *pushed interrogation.*

All this enabled (and still enables) torture to continue before our eyes. But one can take heart that everyday actors did *not* remain silent in the face of the many problems they faced. Whatever the sources of the inexpressibility of pain, they have not been permanently disempowering. Throughout the twentieth century, torture victims persuaded others of the truth in the face of sneaky torturers, manipulative statesmen, societal discrimination, and paralyzed observers. The world came to trust them because they spoke the truth they knew and the pain they felt in the face of danger.[78]

This book is no substitute for the political communities fearless speech has created. Political communities are less durable than objects of worldly making such as this book, but infinitely more powerful.[79] Fearless speech has enhanced our ability to recognize, monitor, and criticize stealth torture. Acting, not making, creates our world, and this book traces the results of the actions of thousands, even millions, of others.

The Demand for Torture

At the outset of this book, I asked, "Why is it that torture persists despite an unprecedented age of democratization and human rights monitoring?" There are three main reasons for this: the demands for false confessions, for local security, and for accurate information. Torture has an elective affinity for these conditions. These conditions are sufficient to produce torture with a high degree of probability.

To be specific, sometimes torture persists because judicial systems value confessions too much and police set out to get them by any means (chapter 2). Police may not necessarily use torture, but it is exceedingly likely they will. In other cases, torture exists as an informal arrangement between neighborhood police and residents. Police torture immigrants, the homeless, and the poor, reminding them where they can and cannot go. Torture is not the only way to generate highly segmented city streets, divide up public spaces, and create semiprivate ones (gated communities and malls). But where such demands exist, torture is not too far away. In a globalized world, characterized by vast legal and illegal flows of people and goods, communities use torture to reduce civic insecurity (chapters 2, 10–11).

Stun City is only the most visible city in this empire of stealth torture. This routine civic violence does not catch the newspaper headlines like Abu Ghraib. Nevertheless, it is just as common as national security torture, and it is an open secret to people who live in many societies.[80] Asad's thesis that torture in modern democracies has nothing to do with the disciplining of citizens reveals a surprising unfamiliarity with the place of torture in the globalized world in which we live.[81]

Lastly, some demand that organizations use torture to extract accurate information, particularly in national emergencies. In chapter 21, I consider this policy question, gathering the scientific and social scientific evidence that bears on it. This evidence suggests that torture is the clumsiest method available, and interrogators would have better luck in some cases flipping coins or shooting randomly into crowds. In chapter 22, I then consider the cases cited by apologists, from the Battle of Algiers and the Gestapo to the current War on Terror. I show that the dynamics of torture are the same in these cases, and they offer little support for the claim that torture is a reasonable choice in national emergencies. In fact, stories of torture working are grounded in movies rather than history.

If torture for information does not work, why then do governments fail to learn? In part, because governments rarely gather or analyze information from coerced interrogation, and torturers regularly hide evidence of failure (chapter 23). Learning about torture mostly goes on through backroom apprenticeships, and this too passes on misleading folklore, as well as accurate information. It also passes on historical myths about torture's efficacy, myths lodged deep in the political and cultural anxieties of modern societies (chapter 24). Torture may not appear in every national emergency, but as long as modern democracies embrace these myths, torture is never far away.

After some months of practice, I manage to sense the precise
instant when the prisoner is going to crack, the fraction of the
second when he loses his grip.

—*Confessions of a Professional Torturer*[1]

21 Does Torture Work?

Torture can be used in three ways: to induce a false confession, to cause fear, and to elicit true information. Can organizations use torture to intimidate prisoners? Yes. Can organizations use torture to produce false confessions? Absolutely. With enough time, a human being can be trained to say anything. These cases of torture "working" are not the important ones.

The real question is whether organizations can apply torture to produce true information. Lt. Col. Roger Trinquier, one of the architects of interrogation during the Battle of Algiers, believed it did:

> If the prisoner gives the information requested, the examination is quickly terminated; if not, specialists must force his secret from him. Then, as a soldier, he must face the suffering, and perhaps the death, he has heretofore managed to avoid. . . . Science can easily place at the army's disposition the means for obtaining what is sought.[2]

Dan Mitrione, the American torture instructor in Uruguay, also had this view of torture: "You must cause only the damage that is strictly necessary, not a bit more. We must control our tempers in any case. You have to act with the efficiency and cleanliness of a surgeon and with the perfection of an artist."[3]

Can torture can be precise, scientific, professionally administered, and yield accurate information in a timely manner? Let me spell out the components of this position as empirical questions:

1. Can torture be scientific?
2. Can one produce pain in a controlled manner?

3. Does technology help torturers in this respect?
4. Can pain be administered respectfully and professionally?
5. Can interrogators separate deceptive from accurate information when it is given to them?
6. How accurately do co-operative prisoners remember information after torture?
7. Does this investigative method yield better results than others normally at an army's disposal?
8. If not, does this investigative method yield better results under conditions of constrained time?

The first four questions apply to all torture, whether it is for purposes of confession, intimidation, or information. The last four apply only to torture for information. If all, or even some, of these questions can be answered affirmatively, then torture does indeed work in a very interesting way.

In this chapter, I assemble what scientists and social scientists know empirically about the answers to each question, and this evidence gives no comfort to advocates of torture, no matter how they qualify the questions. Apologists often assume that torture works, and all that is left is the moral justification. If torture does not work, then their apology is irrelevant. Deciding whether one *ought* or *ought not* to drive a car is a pointless debate if the car has no gas.

Can Torture Be Scientific?

Some believe that science may hit upon the precise amount of pain to produce compliance. But there is little empirical evidence of a science of torture, only misleading folklore about pain.[4]

Extreme pain, as noted clinical psychologist Ron Melzack has shown, is far more complex than commonly supposed. Even massive injuries do not always produce pain. In one study, 37 percent of people who arrived at an emergency ward with injuries such as amputations, major lacerations, and fractures did not feel any pain for many minutes, or even hours. Similarly, soldiers with massive wounds sometimes do not feel their pain for a long time.[5]

Torturers know this, and they know this problem worsens as torture proceeds. Pain is not a constant, which they can simply increase. As the body is damaged, its ability to sense pain declines. More injury does not produce more pain, but its opposite. "I omitted to tell you (the investigators) that after one has received a certain amount of beating on the feet, the pain is no longer felt. . . . It is as if the body had become saturated with pain. The police know this, and this is why they apply the next stage, the running round in a circle to restore circulation in the feet."[6]

Desensitization from *falaka* is well documented, but prisoners and interrogators report similar effects from forced standing ("I lost all power of feeling"), piercing and acid ("I felt nothing"), electrotorture ("I had become almost as insensitive as a machine"), restraint tortures ("Your whole upper torso becomes numb. It's a relief. You feel no more pain"), burning flesh with acetylene torch ("It did not hurt too much because I was so feeble that I did not care"), and beating ("A beating is not effective torture because after the first few blows, you don't feel anything").[7]

Ordinarily, people are familiar with this phenomenon from exposure to intense cold. Coldness makes us less sensitive to nerve impulses and produces behavior indifferent to actual injury.[8] This is why the cold compress, a household remedy, works. Torture victims also know this effect: a session in the freezing *baignoire* makes one insensitive to blows immediately afterward.[9] Certain neurons have a suppressive effect in the case of intense coldness, an effect not unlike that of morphine. When scientists use a thermal grill to prevent the excitement of cold-specific cells, the pain from cold is intense.[10] Experimenters do not know why this happens, but certain neurological mechanisms evidently limit our perception of injury in the case of coldness. Similar mechanisms come into play with other kinds of pain.

Moreover, pain is not a single sensation, but, as Melzack observes, can variously feel like burning, throbbing, cutting, and dozens of other possible sensations.[11] Victims report playing these different sensations against each other, using one pain to distract themselves from another, much as a person might bite his hand as someone extracts a thorn. "In order to escape these sudden easing and sharp increases towards the maximum agony, I started to bang my head against the ground with all my force and each blow brought me relief."[12]

This counter-pain can be as simple as the irritating bites of many mosquitoes. In North Vietnam, for example, an American POW "was grateful for the mosquitoes" while he was in torture cuffs. As he rushed about the room brushing his body against the walls, "he almost forgot the agony of the torture cuffs in his constant effort to keep them [the mosquitoes] off him."[13]

While movies suggest a scale of pain—showing fancy machines with dials—the reality of pain is that it is not a set of units that you can "add" up. As Melzack and his colleague Patrick Wall conclude, "The word 'pain' represents a category of experiences, signifying a multitude of different unique experiences having different causes and characterized by different qualities varying along a number of sensory and affective dimensions."[14]

Lastly, torturers know that human beings differ unpredictably in their ability to endure extreme pain. They know that hard-core revolutionaries display "an unheard of physical resistance . . . how can one explain their incomprehensible stubbornness?"[15] This is highly problematic since such people are usually precisely the people from whom interrogators want information. Similarly, colonial torturers held that an Algerian peasant would be unmoved by tortures that would shatter Europeans, and this was why more painful torture was required: "In countries where the ordinary man shows such extraordinary resistance to all types of hardship, the above procedures [sleep deprivation, starvation, and threats] would have no more effect than simply hitting the man."[16]

Variations in enduring pain can be spelled out more precisely. Repeated experiments have considered variations in four thresholds of pain: when one first senses anything (the sensation threshold), when one senses the sensation as pain (the pain perception threshold), when the pain really hurts (the pain tolerance threshold), and when one holds on to see how much pain one can stand (encouraged pain tolerance).

We are pretty much alike in our ability to sense pain, the first two thresholds. We vary in our ability to endure pain, and vary even more when we are encouraged to stand it. Experiments with placebos show that people use psychological states like distraction or anxiety to reduce pain.[17] Past experiences and cultural beliefs enable some individuals to endure pain others could not. Religious pain (e.g., hook swinging) and athletic pain (the limping, but enduring football player) remind us that torture is not a unique phenomenon in this respect.[18]

In short, as the CIA *Kubark* manual observes, "Everyone is aware that people react very differently to pain." Indeed, "Individuals react differently even to such seemingly non-discriminatory stimuli as drugs." Life experience is the critical factor. "The man whose childhood familiarized him with pain may dread it less, than one whose distress is heightened by fear of the unknown. The individual remains the determinant."[19]

The notion of a science of torture rests on simple folklore about pain. This folklore teaches that all people avoid pain and seek pleasure, more injury produces more pain, and so it is simply a matter of calibrating the quantity of pain for each individual. These views do not make any sense in torture. The people interrogators most want to question are also the most likely to embrace and resist pain. More injury often produces less pain, especially over the course of an interrogation. Pain is not an undifferentiated sensation that is amenable to a scale. If there turns out to be a science of torture one day, it will look nothing like common folklore imagines it.

There is reason to think that a science of torture is a utopian idea. A science of torture requires at least this: general rules, fixed in advance, that identify the correct choice in particular situations. It also requires a unit that is commensurable regardless of its source. When I boil water, I have a common measure for heat whether it comes from a fire, a stove, or an electric burner. All I need to know are the laws that govern that particular liquid, and I can choose correctly in advance how much heat to apply.

Pain, unlike heat, is not a single commensurable unit; sensations vary depending on their source. Unlike boiling water, every person appears to have a different pain endurance threshold, and it changes over time. General rules fixed in advance are an illusion. Torturers can claim that they know in advance the precise moment when individuals will crack, but it is at best an idle boast.

Can Torture Be Restrained?

While torturers cannot be scientific, perhaps they can apply pain with care and restraint. For example, some American advisers in Vietnam believed that, while "severe forms of torture were counterproductive," South Vietnamese interrogators were able to apply "limited doses of physical abuse."[20] In fact, the dynamics of torture push in the opposite direction.

Because most torturers are aware that it is not possible to know how much pain individuals will take; that individuals become less sensitive over time, and eventually the window in which they can apply pain that day closes; and that different tortures yield different effects on different people and affect the same person differently at various times—in short, because torturers know the folk wisdom on pain is nonsense, they typically observe two simple rules.

First, everybody has a limit, so aim high as early as you can. Maximal pain eliminates marginal differences between people, and one need not be too precise. One need only push to the extreme. Individuals will then signal when they want to talk. Hence the usual advice to the prisoner, "When you want to talk, all you have to do is move your fingers."[21] The notion is to overtake an individual's limit rapidly before he becomes desensitized and slips beyond the interrogator's reach.

Second, because each technique affects different people in unpredictable ways, adopt a scattershot approach. Some pains are more noxious than others for the prisoner. It is just that torturers do not know which ones. To keep prisoners from anticipating their actions, torturers break usual rhythms and vary techniques.[22] "You have to have a flair for it," they say.[23] This is why torturers use a broad toolkit and even engage in silly experimentation ("mad dentist torture").[24]

As torturers push toward the extreme in pain, they encounter three limits that neither they, nor the prisoner, can anticipate: death, unconsciousness, and physical damage.

Dead bodies give no information. As Dan Mitrione puts it, "A premature death means a failure by the technician." It is a "luxury" if one knows one can let a prisoner die.[25] This has serious consequences for one's career as an interrogator. As an Israeli GSS interrogator explained, "However funny and disproportionate from the point of view of causing a person's death it may sound to you—it's a serious punishment in a service in which the worker's involvement is so great. He might even be kicked out of the service."[26]

Unconsciousness results in costly delays. "It's really a privilege to pass out," explained a French Resistance fighter. "It gives you a reprieve between blows. You don't feel anything or hear anything anymore. Of course he's still the stronger one, but at the same time there's nothing he can do against this temporary absence. He has to say to himself, 'Let's hope he snaps out of it.' "[27] Torturers understand the phenomenon well. "You know, you did well to pass out. Don't think that you will always be able to lose consciousness . . . get up!"[28]

Physical damage also results in delays. Like nurses who run out of places to stick the IV needle into the body, torturers run out of places where they can apply pain effectively. Consider these Gestapo men interrogating with a leg clamp in Norway.

> "Another turn of the screw." "How long will the leg hold?" "There it goes." "Rot! A leg can take a lot." But there is a limit. . . . "Shall we take the other leg straight away?" The one in brown asked the commandant as he removed the towel. "No."[29]

They saved the woman's other leg for interrogation another day. Or consider the complaint of this French torturer: "So you call in the Senegalese. Either they hit too hard and destroy the creature or else they don't hit hard enough and it's no good. "[30]

Maximal pain, scattershot approaches, inadvertent death, the delays inflicted by unconsciousness and physical damage are not accidental features of torture. They follow inevitably from rational responses to the realities of pain. Once the torture session starts, it necessarily devolves into an unrestrained hit-or-miss affair.

Given that individual torture sessions will necessarily be unrestrained, the only way to check the negative effects is to delay initiating the session. "You have to know when to lay it on and when to lay it off."[31] But this turns out to be paradoxical advice, roughly of the same order as "Look before you leap but he who hesitates is lost!" A careful dissection of this advice shows why.

Armchair philosophers may think naively that one wants to cause immediate, excruciating pain, but experienced professionals know that one exhausts other means before turning to torture. Khmer Rouge interrogators were certainly not ones to shrink from extreme torture, but their interrogation manual emphasizes the importance of trying to win the prisoner's cooperation first through misleading deceit.[32] A captured Chinese interrogation manual for the Korean War makes a similar point. "Good results can never be obtained by demanding a large amount of information from the POW immediately after he is captured on the battlefield." Again, Chinese interrogators tortured, but their interrogation policy recommended building confidence with the prisoner slowly, as "haste will only bring failure."[33] French torturers for the ancien régime also favored graded coercion, beginning with the display of instruments and moving by steps toward fearsome pain.[34]

The CIA *Kubark* explains why interrogation should start slowly and without torture: "Interrogatees who have withstood pain are more difficult to handle by other methods."[35] The U.S. Army study of American POWs, probably the largest study of a single group of tortured prisoners, draws the same conclusion. "Available evidence suggests, in fact, that torture may intensify, rather than weaken, the resistance of the prisoner, and that more skillful and experienced Communist interrogators avoid its use."[36] As Henri Alleg explained, "Each blow stupefied me a little more, but at the same time confirmed me in my decision not to give way to these brutes who flattered themselves they were like the Gestapo."[37] Immediate torture lowers expectations and enhances pain tolerance, as this successful Norwegian Resistance prisoner explained about Gestapo torture. "They use a leather strap, knotted." "Is it terribly painful?" "I'm almost used to it by now. The voice was toneless, as grey as his hair."[38] Having blown one's cards on a gamble, there will be little left to do. "One should always give them some hope," explained Dan Mitrione, "a distant source of light."[39]

Mitrione emphasizes how important it is to play on the *fear* of torture before one starts it. The experienced torturer knows that it is imprudent to be restrained once torture starts, but playing on fear before torture starts may save effort. This is especially reasonable given what torturers know about the physiological dynamics and psychological effects of pain. The experienced torturer holds back as long as possible, offering the slim possibility the victim may escape pain through cooperation. This is what torture apologists appear to mean when they insist that torture is simply "a psychological technique." What they are saying is that "we're not going to torture, but we sure as hell are going to make them *think* we are."[40]

But, it is as naive to believe that one avoids torturing merely by exploiting the fear of torture as it is to start torturing immediately. Professional torturers like Dan Mitrione know that fear of torture is not credible unless you are willing to go the distance. To constantly threaten torture without doing it is also counterproductive. As *Kubark* explains, "If an interrogatee is caused to suffer pain rather late in the interrogation process and after other tactics have failed, he is almost certain to conclude that the interrogator is becoming desperate. He may then decide that if he can just hold out against this final assault, he will win the struggle and his freedom."[41]

So then perhaps one should torture sooner than later, but that returns us to the place where we began. Look before you leap, but he who hesitates is lost. It sounds sage to say you have to know when to put it on and put it off, but it simply amounts to saying torturers have no objective way of knowing when to start or restrain their behavior. Torturers may *think* they are guided by some unknown, unique psychological insight that restrains them. But there is precious little behavioral evidence that torturers have anywhere near the psychological insight or self-control with which they credit themselves, as I show shortly. And if that is so, the bottom line is that there is no meaningful restraint in torture. There is no *fear* of torture without torture, and no *"little* torture" without *"more* torture" with all the inevitable consequences that this chapter documents.

Does Technology Help?

Technology can help with the conduct of torture: Modern instruments reduce the hard labor of torture, helping ensure that it is not lethal; and they guarantee that few marks will be left as evidence. Doctors can revive unconscious patients more quickly and sometimes prevent inadvertent damage or death. But there is no technology that can calculate the precise amount or kind of torture that will work with each human being. Using magnetos, stun guns, or white noise is painful, but that does not make torture a science, any more than wearing a white lab coat makes torturers scientists.

High-tech torturers push to the extreme just as torturers who use sticks and fists. Consider electrotorture. Sometimes, interrogators sound terribly restrained and precise: "Set it on 60 volts."[42] Even in this case, torturers followed the two basic rules of torture: push to the max and vary your techniques. When they were not successful with various voltages, they beat the prisoner, used the *falaka*, and then threatened to torture his brother. Setting the voltage at 60 turns out in retrospect to be a guess. Torturers were hoping to be in the ballpark, high enough to overtake the prisoner's pain threshold. In fact, electrotorturers have no idea where to set the dial. If they did, they would not ask victims to signal them when they are ready to talk.

Electrotorturers also must contend with inadvertent deaths, decreasing sensitivity to electrical injury, and costly delays due to unconsciousness. In a science or even restrained art of torture, interrogators would know where to put the dial for each individual. But this study has found no evidence that they do, and it is unlikely that they will unless the nature of human pain changes. What holds for electrotorture, the paradigmatic form of technological torture, is probably true for any other high technology. Indeed, if such a technology existed, it would surely be just as widespread as electricity.

Can Torture Be Professionally Conducted?

Torture might be a messy process, but it may still yield valuable intelligence. All that is required is that torture be conducted professionally and yield true results better than other ways of gathering intelligence. When one sets aside the myths of scientific or technological torture and the folklore about pain, this is the argument that really matters and to which the rest of this chapter is dedicated.

Professional policing involves applying no violence in excess of what the job requires. A professional arrest involves no more pain than necessary to restrain the victim safely, even if it looks like a messy process. A professional search might appear chaotic, but involves no more discomfort than is necessary to fulfill the task licensed by a warrant. Why then couldn't police implement "a torture warrant" in the same professional way?[43] The public could rest easy that in these cases no *excessive* coercion had been applied other than that required by the public interest.

To think professionalism is a guard against causing excessive pain is an illusion. Instead, torture breaks down professionalism. Professionals become less disciplined, more brutal, and less skilled while their organizations become more fragmented and corrupt. Usually, organizations and interrogators are worse off than before they started torturing despite their best intentions, an interesting demonstration of counter-finality.[44] In torture, the rhetoric of professionalism is common, but the behavioral and organizational indicators show a rapid decay in professionalism.

Failure to Observe Regulations

When governments authorize torture, they also offer a list of approved interrogation techniques. Professional police, they reason, will stick to these procedures. In fact, the empirical record shows something quite different. In cases where historians know the list of authorized techniques, the actual practice of torture on the ground regularly exceeds the authorized list.

The torturers at Abu Ghraib knew the list of approved tortures put out by the Pentagon, but they went far beyond these techniques, trying anything that worked. French instruction barely touched the wide range of techniques Paras used in Algeria. Gestapo chief Müller's list bore no relation to actual Gestapo torture. The notorious "Dutch" (Kang Kech Ieu), the manager of the Khmer Rouge's chief interrogation center, was also exasperated by the undisciplined behavior of his interrogators. The Tuol Sleng *Interrogators' Manual* complains that interrogators "emphasized torture over propaganda. . . .

Don't be so bloodthirsty that you cause their death quickly. You won't get the needed information."[45]

Similarly, CIA manuals taught widely in South America in the 1980s bore little relationship to the inventiveness of those who were trained using them. Consider, for example, the story of Florencio Caballero, an interrogator in a Honduran army death squad in the 1980s.[46] In Texas, Caballero's CIA instructor, "Mr. Bill," taught him American positional tortures and sweating techniques. Caballero insisted that they were all trained not to go beyond these techniques. Although Caballero and his unit practiced the American regimen, they rapidly moved on to electrotorture and burning flesh, among other things. His unit became undisciplined and brutal. "Somehow it had all gone wrong, even though it started well, even though 'the Americans' had good ideas." Caballero also insisted that he was a professional and that he did not enjoy torture.

The explanation for these historical cases is straightforward. As a victim feels less pain, torturers have to push harder, using more severe methods to overtake the victim's maximal pain threshold. Because victims experience different types of pain, torturers have to use a scattershot approach. No matter how professional torturers want to be, they must inevitably disobey any authorized limits for torture.

The historical evidence parallels the theoretical models of torture, models that mathematically sketch the incentives torturers have to behave professionally or not.[47] In the "game of torture," victims are either weak or strong and torturers are professionals, zealots, and sadists. Zealots torture for the cause, sadists do it for themselves, and professionals do not want to torture, but will if it is necessary. The state endorses torture for either intimidation or information. Once it does so, the incentives are such that torture "is carried out with positive probability"—regardless of the type of torturer. Even professionals succumb to the pressure to torture regardless. When the purpose is intimidation, "All types of torturers will behave sadistically."[48]

Some believe that all torture is the work of zealots and sadists, but studies of torturers point to the opposite conclusion.[49] Organizations prefer to recruit ordinary people as torturers. Zealots and sadists are disciplinary problems, hard to control and manage. The problem is that professionals soon start behaving like zealots and sadists.

Competitive Brutality

Professional police compete for reputation, career advancement, and bonuses. Ordinarily, this competitiveness may yield professional results, but, in torture, it leads to a destructive dynamic. Two police rivals might share credit for gathering different pieces of evidence that fit together, but interrogating prisoners is a zero-sum game: someone gets the credit for breaking the prisoner, while the other person does not. Pushing to the max is the only rational option. "Our problem is as follows: are you able to make this fellow talk? It's a question of personal success. You see, you're competing with the others. In the end, your fists are ruined."[50]

Rivalry between interrogators who torture feeds the drive toward unprofessional brutality. As one French torturer put it, each interrogator "thinks he is going to get the information at any minute and takes good care not to let the bird go to the next chap after he's softened him up nicely, when of course the other chap would get the honor and glory of it."[51] This phenomenon seems ubiquitous. Soviet prisoners observed a similar "keen competition between individual commissars."[52] Likewise, Indonesian torturers "competed with each other in their zeal to inflict torture."[53]

Underneath this behavior, one senses the effects of competitive masculinity. Police live in insular societies, with their own codes of secrecy and manhood, and in the case of interrogators, especially so.[54] Interrogators demonstrate their prowess through their own endurance in questioning prisoners, what American interrogators in Afghanistan dubbed "monstering."[55] Competitive masculinity drives violence as "each man is constantly proving his courage and toughness relative to others in his unit."[56]

Deskilling

Coercive interrogation undermines other professional policing skills: Why do fingerprinting when you've got a bat? It is simply easier to turn to torture than to do the hard, time-consuming work of surveillance, interviewing, verification, and intelligence analysis.

This phenomenon is not a new discovery. Investigators, judges, and secret services have known police torture leads to police deskilling from decades of investigations. James Stephens was perhaps the first to note it in the India Evidence Act of 1872. "It is far pleasanter to sit comfortably in the shade rubbing pepper into a poor devil's eyes than go about in the sun hunting up evidence."[57] Justice Frankfurter was more precise: a police that relies "too heavily on interrogation will not pursue or learn other crime detection methods, and the consequent danger that the police will feel themselves under pressure to secure confessions."[58] The CIA's unedited *Human Resources Exploitation Training* (*HRET*) manual explains, "The routine use of torture lowers the moral caliber of the organization that uses it and corrupts those that rely on it as the quick and easy way out."[59]

Deskilling has been best documented in the Japanese context (chapter 2). As Miyazawa observes, Japanese police "do little other than interrogate the suspect." The environment "precluded the development of other investigative skills."[60] Watson too remarked that reliance on coerced interrogation led to the neglect of "more objective methods of investigation such as gathering physical evidence and conducting forensic inquiries."[61] As professional skills decay, police rely more on interrogation to get information and, with it, increasing brutality. Torture is a shortcut that soon becomes a well-traveled road. This creates "a vicious cycle" in which the investigators are progressively deskilled.[62]

Narrow Professionalism

Not surprisingly, team leadership focuses on good results from torture, allowing leeway for brutality, competition, and deskilling in other areas. Organized torture in this respect produces a kind of tunnel vision, what might be called "narrow professionalism."[63] Each individual focuses on his task as an end in itself, "failing to see the wider consequences of his action while on the job."[64]

Narrow professionalism has striking effects on organizations that torture. It feeds the drive toward brutality as older hands encourage younger ones to do their job right. Authority, especially if it is proximate, can move ordinary people to engage in violence of which they would never have imagined themselves capable.[65] At the same time, torturers appeal to professionalism to reduce supervision of higher-ups in the chain of command.[66] We're professionals, they assert, leave us alone.

Intelligence teams of this sort rapidly become laws unto themselves, taking pride in their abilities to circumvent bureaucracies. Security organizations that have tortured, including Israeli, British, and American, have also felt justified in deceiving government officials and perjuring themselves in court.[67] As one U.S. Special Forces major and veteran of U.S.-sponsored Central American guerrilla insurgencies observed, such units "were on their own wave length. . . . You have two parallel chains of command, and one could wind up doing what they feel like doing."[68]

Not surprisingly, this triggers bureaucratic fragmentation and devolution. The Brazilian case is the best-documented example. Under the military junta in the 1960s, the government divided and reassigned tasks, eliminating conflict and giving each group its own specialization. In some cases, "Police and security responsibilities were so narrowly defined, that it was impossible for an agency to perform its task without violating another group's turf." Different parts of the internal security system "were able to—and in fact had to—turn against each other."[69]

Different intelligence units raided each other's prisons, looking for suspects to interrogate. Competition between intelligence agencies is a normal phenomenon, and usually a good one, producing multiple sources of information.

"There is nothing unusual in rivalry between two detectives or two police departments developing into cut-throat competition."[70] Narrow specialization when combined with torture triggered a "devolutionary spiral" that soon assumed a life of its own "as each locus of newly privatized social control and authority move[d] farther from the formal social-control system."[71] Units supported their activities with extortion, blackmail, and black market operations.[72] These trends triggered clandestine wars between units, and ultimately destabilized the Brazilian army.

Brazil is an extreme case, but it illustrates the corrosive effect torture has on professional and bureaucratic authority. The Brazilian military eventually intervened after two cases in which officers tortured their own soldiers or acted out of pleasure.[73] "Unless everyone in the army participates in torture, you very quickly develop two kinds of soldiers," the disciplinarians and the torturers, observed a Brazilian magazine editor. Disciplinarians, who promoted the military's everyday functioning, concluded, "The torturers were going to have to be isolated, marginalized and eliminated, *so as to save the Army.*"[74]

Works Better Than What?

The deprofessionalizing effects alone are serious enough to give any policy-maker pause before institutionalizing professional torture warrants. Still, these deprofessionalizing costs may be worth paying if torture is more effective than alternative methods of investigation.

The best source for information bar none is public cooperation. The loss of public cooperation can be compensated for somewhat with a well-articulated system of informants. Informants, of course, shape information to fit their own interests. But other methods are less helpful. Having more men or more technology may help at the margins, but they are no substitute for public cooperation.

Is torture more effective than these other ways of gathering information? Torture is definitely inferior. The top-secret *Notes for the Interrogation of Prisoners of War* (1943), the Japanese interrogation manual for the fascist Kempeitai, is quite clear on this. Torture "is only to be used when everything else has failed as it is the most clumsy [method]."[75]

To be specific, since the 1970s, a large body of American research has shown that unless the public specifically identifies suspects to the police, the chances that a crime will be solved falls to about 10 percent.[76] In England, three-fifths of all offenses are cleared by information given by witnesses and victims. Only a small percentage of crimes are discovered or solved through surveillance, fingerprinting, DNA sampling, forensic tests, house-to-house inquiries, and offender profiling. In England, this number constitutes as little as 5 percent of all detections.[77]

Police depend heavily on public cooperation for both crime detection and resolution.[78] "On their own, police are relatively helpless regardless of the resources they devote to criminal investigation."[79] Since the 1970s, researchers have been "unable, often at considerable cost, to show that the number of police, the amount of money spent on police, or the methods police use had any effect on crime."[80]

Nothing illustrates the power of public cooperation more clearly than the way the British police caught five men alleged to have planted bombs on London buses and trains on July 21, 2005.[81] Police captured the July 21 bombers using accurate public information, and they did this within ten days. Police identified Mukhtar Said-Ibrahim after his parents, Mohammed and Esha, contacted them; they turned in their son after seeing his picture on surveillance tapes. On July 22, Ibrahim's neighbor, Tanya Wright, gave a statement to the police that helped locate Ibrahim, and another suspect, Yasin Hassan Omar. Omar was then traced to Birmingham, where he was arrested six days later. Three commuters identified and chased a third suspect, Ramsi Muhammad, until they lost him in London traffic, and police later arrested Muhammad in the same flat as Omar. Police identified Hussein Osman, the fourth bomber, from video surveillance. They located him by tapping his brother-in-law's mobile, and Italian authorities arrested him.

Police captured their suspects without torture or an American-style Patriot Act. Parliament passed no new laws following the bombings. All arrests occurred under the Terrorism Act of 2000. All arrests happened within one week, between July 21 and July 31. In total, police arrested forty-four people, including the alleged bombers and thirteen men and women on suspicion of harboring them.[82] Prosecutors charged the bombers and three who aided them.[83] Of the remaining twenty-six individuals, twenty were released within twenty-four hours, and six were held longer, including one on an immigration charge. The only misstep came when police identified a suspect acting on their own suspicions and, tragically, ended up killing an illegal Brazilian immigrant, Jean Charles de Menezes, with no connection to the bombings.[84]

Police also suspected a feared fifth bomber who failed to carry out his mission with a live bomb, packed with explosives, nails and bolts. This is as clear a ticking time bomb case as one can imagine. Police found the bomb on July 25 searching the bushes near where other arrests had been made. Five days later, police arrested the fifth bomb suspect, Manfo Kwaku Asiedu.[85] It is unlikely the police would have been anywhere near the ticking bomb without the assistance of Ibrahim's parents and neighbor, commuters who identified Muhammad, and those who identified Osman's brother-in-law.

Police in long-term dictatorships also know the importance of public co-operation for solving crimes. Sometimes though, they cannot get public coop-eration for certain crimes (such as those against state property or socially toler-ated crime such as prostitution or alcoholism).[86] Consequently, long-term dictatorships tend to rely more heavily on an alternative human intelligence system—informants.[87] "The development of network informers is a major fea-ture of Communist control methods."[88] For example, during World War II, the Soviets completely shut down German counterintelligence with a dense network of informants, including 2 million informers in the military and 1.4 million civilian "resident agents."[89] During the Cold War, the KGB had ap-proximately 420,000 employees, but its grip "relied heavily on an extensive network of collaborators, who spied on colleagues and neighbors," a number as yet uncounted, but sure to be enormous.[90] In East Germany, the Stasi em-ployed more than 175,000 informers and one in every ninety-seven citizens served as an informer.[91]

Although long-standing dictatorships use torture for intimidation and false confessions, they also know that good intelligence requires humans willing to go to the government and work with it. Torturing destroys bonds of loyalty that keep information flowing, causing remaining sources to dry up. Mutual suspicion is not as reliable as public trust, but it is the next best thing as people cooperate to demonstrate their loyalty or evade suspicion.

Even guerrillas engaged in civil war know the importance of public cooper-ation for intelligence. Civil wars are won with civilian support, but they are fought *through* civilian populations. Indiscriminate violence is counterproduc-tive, for it encourages civilians to join the more discriminating actor. Selective violence is more valuable, making threats credible and generating fear among defectors. But this requires private information, information guerrillas do not have. "While it is possible to rely on cues, depend on spies and paid informers, or use torture, there is no substitute for the kind of information provided on a regular and voluntary basis by scores of local sympathizers."[92] The Iraqi insur-gency, for example, can strike selectively because many eyes tell it where sol-diers go. As a U.S. government report from 2004 states, insurgents gathered information mainly through "painstaking surveillance and reconnaissance" by "pro-insurgent individuals" working for the police and local administration, and so their "operational intelligence has proven to be quite good."[93]

Is Anything Better Than Nothing?

Torture for information may be the clumsiest method, it may produce serious institutional damage, but it may also be better than sitting on one's hands. As one RUC officer complained in Northern Ireland, "If you have a close-knit society which doesn't give information then you've got to find ways of getting it. Now the softies of the world complain—but there is an awful lot of double talk about it."[94] Critics of torture sometimes object that a prisoner who has information will always lie under torture. But surely he would lie in any case.[95] All things being equal, why not torture? Under these circumstances, the prisoner "is more likely to say something—anything—rather than remain silent or defiant."[96]

The problem of torture does not lie with prisoner who has information. It lies with the prisoner with *no information*. Such a person is also likely to lie, to say *anything*, often convincingly. The torture of the informed may generate no more lies than normal interrogation, but the torture of the ignorant and innocent overwhelms investigators with misleading information.

In these cases, nothing is indeed far preferable to "anything." "Anything" needs to be verified, and as the *Kubark* manual explains, "A time-consuming delay results." In the meantime, the prisoner can think of new, more complex falsehoods should this bid for relief fail.[97]

Especially problematic is the well-established tendency of people to inform on others to settle private feuds and old scores. This information is verifiable, but malicious. In civil war contexts, it is almost routine.[98] Local informants reason correctly that outsiders are unlikely to have independent means of verifying this information. Likewise, in interrogation, if one has to give a name, it might as well be the name of a real rival. Prisoners reason they are unlikely to be second-guessed. Interrogators will show successful arrest and kill rates and win praise from superiors, who will not ask too many questions afterward since they are invested in the information being accurate.[99]

Intelligence gathering is especially vulnerable to this deception. In police work, the crime is already known; all one wants is the confession. In intelligence, one must gather information about things that one does not know. It is surprising how much consensus there is on this problem, even among manuals that recognize that torture might sometimes be necessary. Here is a short list:

> Care must be exercised when making use of rebukes, invectives or torture as it will result in his telling falsehoods and making a fool of you. (*Notes for the Interrogation of Prisoners of War*, Japanese Kempeitai manual, found in Burma, 1943)[100]

> The use of force often has the consequence that the person being interrogated under duress confesses falsely because he is afraid and, as a consequence agrees to everything the interrogator wishes. (Indonesian interrogation manual, found in East Timor, 1983)[101]

> At best, use of force is a poor technique since it may induce the subject to tell what he thinks the interrogator wants to hear. The subject may not possess the information sought, but he will fabricate information to please the interrogator and bring an end to the force being applied. (*U.S. Army Field Manual 30–15 Intelligence Interrogations*)[102]

> Intense pain is quite likely to produce false confessions, concocted as a means of escaping from distress. (CIA *Kubark Counterintelligence Manual*, 1963)[103]

> Intense pain is quite likely to produce false confessions, fabricated to avoid additional punishment. (*Human Resources Exploitation Training Manual*, unedited, 1983)[104]

To this list, one might add some older injunctions. A Chinese legal text (ca. 217 b.c.) advises, "If in trying lawsuits it is possible by means of documents to track down his (or their) words, obtaining the facts of the person without using the bastinado is best; applying the bastinado is inferior, (for) when there is fear, (everything) is spoiled."[105]

It is, at any rate, surprising how hard it is to get *anything* under torture. In prerevolutionary France, for example, prosecutors sought to extract confessions for various charges in 785 cases between 1500 and mid-1700s. Standard tortures were pumping stomachs with water (*question d'eau*) and the bone-crushing use of splints (*brodequin*), though some provinces used thumbscrews, poured boiling oil on the feet, or drew them toward a fire. The percentage of cases culminating in confessions varied by province: Paris (3–9 percent), Brittany (8–9 percent), Roussillon (10–13 percent), and Toulouse, the highest (14.2 percent).[106] Most of the time, torturers were unable to get a confession. Similarly, interrogators at the London Cage got German prisoners to confess to past war crimes, without and with torture, for only 1,000 of the 3,573 prisoners. The remaining 70 percent refused despite threats, beatings, humiliation, exhaustion exercises, cold showers, extreme heat, mock executions, and forced standing, kneeling, and marching.[107] Those who imagine torture *usually* yields *something* are bound to be surprised by such low returns.

European prosecutors knew this problem for millennia. The Roman lawyer Ulpian, who did not shrink from endorsing torture in some cases, cautioned interrogators that torture "is a chancy and risky business and one which may be deceptive." He notes some will always lie under torture; others will "tell any kind of lie than suffer torture," and one "should not place confidence in torture applied to [a person's] enemies, because they readily tell lies." He advises that one can have confidence in coerced information only after the case has been investigated by other means.[108]

But other means of intelligence are *not* normally available under the circumstances in which torture for strategic information becomes a plausible choice. The clumsiest method becomes the best one because other more reliable methods have proven fruitless in anticipating the enemy's behavior. How then to weed out the inevitable lies under *these* conditions?

One alternative would be to try to keep prisoners separate and compare stories. But this will not do. As all stories are coerced, this strategy compounds misinformation rather than corrects it. Each lie reinforces the others. The Tuol Sleng interrogators produced precisely this hall of mirrors and described a vast internal conspiracy that still puzzles analysts today.[109]

The best alternative is to train interrogators to spot the truth with reasonable accuracy. Good interrogators can tell when prisoners really have no information, and they will not put them in a position where they would have to lie and taint the information. Trained interrogators can persist with other prisoners because they can tell that they are lying. Such skills would enable organizations to assemble the right bits of information, and they are a standard part of most modern interrogation training.

How Well Do Interrogators Spot the Truth?

The standard text for modern interrogation is Fred Inbau and John Reid's *Criminal Interrogation and Confessions.* Over the last sixty years, this book has become "the definitive police training manual in the United States, if not the Western World." Since it appeared in 1942, it has been rewritten as two series, with three editions in the first series and four in the second, totaling seven different manuals (1942, 1948, 1953, 1962, 1986, and 2001).[110]

Inbau and Reid do not endorse torture. Indeed, their aim has always been to reduce police incompetence, corruption, and brutality and enhance the police's efficiency and public image. To this end, they set out to put interrogation on a scientific basis.[111] Their manuals train interrogators to detect deception and understand the criminal psyche. Police trained in these techniques become human lie detectors. Reid and Associates claims today that those trained in this method have an 85 percent success rate in identifying deception.[112]

Since 1974, Reid and Associates has trained 150,000 law enforcement personnel in North America, Europe, Asia, and the Middle East. Other programs typically follow their method. Reid and Associates advertises courses that are "on the cutting edge of the most sophisticated and updated material on interrogation offered anywhere."[113]

Detecting deception is a very difficult task. Experiments show that most people are terrible at it. In 1980, a survey of all the available scientific literature found an accuracy rate (percentage of correct answers) of 57 percent. This is a low score since a 50 percent accuracy score would be the same as flipping a coin. In 2000, a second study of thirty-nine additional studies after 1980 found an almost identical accurate rate, 56.6 percent.[114]

More nuanced studies showed that people are more likely to believe statements are truthful and so people have high accuracy rates for true statements (67 percent) and worse rates for lies (44 percent). This number, 44 percent, is less than what would be generated by chance, and in these cases, flipping a coin would be *more* accurate than letting people guess.[115]

Psychologists have also tested professional lie-catchers. After all, ordinary people are not used to dealing with liars and are easily fooled. Psychologists have been particularly interested in police trained in the Inbau and Reid method, since 85 percent is an extraordinary accuracy rate.

Consistently, over twenty years, "Psychological research has failed to support the claim that individuals can attain such high average levels of performance in making judgment of truth and deception." On the contrary, "Training programs produce only small and inconsistent improvements in performance compared with a control condition and . . . police investigators and others with relevant on-the-job experience perform only slightly better than chance, if at all."[116]

Police accuracy rates generally fall between 45 percent and 60 percent. Some groups are better than others, notably interrogators for the U.S. Secret Service (64 percent), the CIA (73 percent), and sheriffs (67 percent).[117] In laboratory experiments, rates did not exceed chance levels when police interviewed suspects. Indeed, those who conducted interviews were less accurate than those who judged videotapes.[118] Police accuracy rates also did not improve in real criminal investigation settings. Police accuracy did not exceed chance levels (57 percent accuracy on average compared to 54 percent for untrained observers).[119]

The Dutch researcher Aldert Vrij reasoned that perhaps, in these studies, police were interrogating in unfamiliar contexts, dealing with unfamiliar suspects (e.g., foreign nationals), or working in low-stakes situations. He then chose familiar settings, in high-stakes situations with the typical suspects. Police detecting abilities improved (an accuracy rate of about 65 percent for detecting truths and lies), but remained "far from perfect, and errors in truth-lie detection were frequently made."[120] Police who reported extensive interrogation experience were modestly better than those who lacked it. Since the case material was sensitive, police did not allow Vrij to use a control group, and Vrij notes that laypersons may have the same success rate, making police success unremarkable.

Perhaps the most disturbing result of Vrij's research is that those police who followed the Inbau and Reid method were actually worse at detecting deception. "The more police followed their advice, the worse they were in their ability to distinguish between truth and lies."[121] Moreover, Vrij could find no relationship between their accuracy and the confidence police expressed in their judgment. Police displayed an overconfidence effect typical in deception studies and they were just as likely to have false beliefs about deception as laypersons.[122] Other studies have also suggested the "disturbing possibility that police training in the detection of truth and deception leads investigators to make prejudgments of guilt, with high confidence, that are frequently in error."[123]

Police turn out to be slightly better in contexts that are familiar with people they know, but that might be true for laypersons too. Those trained in the Inbau and Reid method are likely to be more prone to error, but just as confident about their opinion. Police may regard interrogation as an essential part of criminal investigation, but research does not even show this. A study funded by the British government examined 1,476 cases from London and Birmingham and concluded that police interrogation did not contribute greatly to the discovery or conviction of criminals. "Claims made for the efficacy of 'traditional' methods of detection are, save in a small minority of cases, nothing short of myths; most serious offences are discovered and cleared up without much investigative activity on the part of the police."[124]

Torturers have far less training or experience in interrogation than police, and so the prospect that they will be better at spotting deception is not good. Most torturers are ordinary soldiers and policemen, usually selected because they have endured hardship and pain, fought with courage, kept secrets, possessed correct political beliefs, and been trustworthy and loyal.[125] Known torture manuals offer them little training on spotting deception. Most are compiled stories about "the characteristic mistakes of poor interrogators."[126]

Not surprisingly, torturers interrogate with background assumptions and harvest self-fulfilling results. For example, the Chilean DINA in the early 1970s subjected Sheila Cassidy, an English citizen, to various tortures, especially electrotorture on the *parilla*. After several days, she broke down and revealed the names of the nuns and priests who had sheltered her. The devout interrogators could not believe her and continued torturing her for days afterward. "They found the truth more difficult to believe than the lies I had told them at first, and I received many gratuitous shocks because they could not believe the nuns and priests were involved."[127] The notion that one will stop torturing when one hears the right information presupposes that one has gathered circumstantial information that allows one to know the truth when one hears it. That is precisely what does not happen with torture.

It is possible to train people to be better lie detectors by reading microexpressions. These expressions are shorter than one-twenty-fifth of a second, and reading them requires slow-motion films.[128] Currently, multiple U.S. military agencies are funding programs to develop computerized cameras to track microexpressions. According to the psychologists receiving these grants, microexpressions "do not vary among cultures and races."[129] That would be news indeed, but all this funding is still speculative and has yet to yield the results claimed. What effect torture would have on reading microexpressions is anybody's guess.

What is plausible currently is that police who arrive with assumptions about the crime and follow folk wisdom on deception (the darting gaze, shiftiness, etc.) or the Inbau and Reid method are likely to be worse than others who come with an open mind and draw on their own extensive experience. Torturers are better off listing their questions and flipping a coin for each one.

How Well Do Cooperative Prisoners Remember?

Torturers gain information from individuals by exhausting them (sweating, positional tortures, sleep deprivation, exhaustion exercises) or applying traumatic pain (e.g., electrotorture). Uncooperative individuals may not give up, but they do make mistakes in judgment, accidentally revealing information. During World War II, for example, an Allied radioman gave what he remembered as the discarded security code under torture; it turned out to be the correct one.[130]

Such lapses in judgment and memory also occur among cooperative prisoners. Lawrence Hinkle, a neurologist who, along with Wolff, advised the CIA on brainwashing, puts it bluntly: "Any circumstance that impairs the function of the brain potentially affects the ability to give information, as well as the ability to withhold it."[131] In coerced interrogation, as the unedited CIA *HRET* manual explains, "The subject's ability to recall and communicate information accurately is as impaired as his will to resist."[132]

After torture, cooperative prisoners make two kinds of errors in relating information. They express high confidence in mistaken information, and they suffer peculiar lapses in memory remembering recent events. While prisoners *want* to cooperate, these problems are not in their control.

Lapses in Memory

Torture inhibits a prisoner's ability to communicate in two ways. Sometimes the prisoner cannot talk at all. "I was so paralyzed, my tongue could not work, so I could not speak, only groaned a bit, crying, naturally, always."[133] Interrogators are more troubled by its effects on thought. "I couldn't speak clearly or focus on ideas or think, and it was impossible to have a clear idea of what was happening around me."[134] Tortured co-operative prisoners forget even simple information about the recent past.

For example, Sheila Cassidy could not remember information she knew only weeks before her arrest even when she *wanted* to cooperate. After days on the electric *parilla*, "I found it quite impossible to lie for the shocks came with such frequency and intensity that I could no longer think. So they broke me." She decided to tell them the street address of where she had medically treated the man they wanted, but she could not remember. "Although I knew the street name, I had no idea of the number. Still furious, they realized that in truth I could not tell them where to go and once more they untied me."[135]

Cassidy's condition is probably an example of Ribot's gradient, a phenomenon documented in numerous quantitative studies since the 1970s. When there is trauma to the brain, the farther back the memory, the more likely it is to survive the trauma. The closer the memory is in time to the trauma, the less likely it is to survive. In 1881, Théodule Ribot formulated this as a law of regression: in memory, "The new perishes before the old."[136] Recent memories die before remote ones. For example, Princess Diana's bodyguard suffered head injuries during the crash that killed her. He remembered who he was, but not incidents immediately prior to the accident for months. Most of those appear to have been lost permanently.

The length of Ribot's gradient varies with the species, days or weeks in rats, months in monkeys, years or even decades in humans.[137] The degree of fragmentation also varies with each person and type of brain damage.[138] But generally, quantitative studies show that unique events are harder to remember than those that were repeated. Autobiographical memory and public events memory are affected only if the memory is recent. Subjects cannot overcome this inability by trying to remember.[139]

In terms of torture, the problem of retrograde amnesia has been particularly well documented in the case of electroconvulsive therapy.[140] In Dr. Cameron's experiments for the CIA, patients lost their memory for events that had occurred any time from the previous six months to ten years earlier.[141] All torture involves some trauma to the brain, but not necessarily to the hippocampus. Electrotorture, especially full-body shock as in Cassidy's case, is more likely to damage memory, as is beating to the head (slaps, violent shaking, etc.). Ribot's gradient does not occur for every kind of torture, but many techniques that cause pain also damage memory. By the time prisoners wish to cooperate, it may be too late.

The unedited *HRET* argues that while coercive interrogation impairs a prisoner, "He does not need mastery of all his mental and physical powers to know whether he is a spy or not."[142] No doubt, since memories of identity are old and more likely to survive trauma. During the First Gulf War, for example, Iraqi torturers repeatedly dropped bound U.S. POWs face first onto the floor, asking, "Pilot or Navigator?" Prisoners who broke remembered this bit of information correctly. But no interrogator should be surprised if prisoners cannot correctly remember a recent street address, name, or code even when they want to cooperate.

The Illusion of Knowing

While cooperative prisoners may experience memory losses, at least these are recognizable to both prisoners and interrogators. More problematic is false information that is unrecognizable to the cooperative prisoner, much less to the interrogator.

Sweating is the simplest form of coerced interrogation, combining repeated questioning and sleep deprivation. Strikingly, simple sweating increases the confidence of cooperative subjects who report false information as true, and they are unable to compensate for these errors. Researchers have long known that sleep deprivation generates major cognitive deficiencies similar to alcoholic inebriation, including heightened suggestibility and errors in judgment.[143] They also know that repeating statements leads subjects to increase the perception of their being true.[144] When the two are combined as in simple sweating, a peculiar phenomenon develops, "the illusion of knowing."[145]

Under repeated questioning, sleep-deprived subjects display "higher confidence, but not greater accuracy."[146] And subjects are more confident when experimenters repeat affirmative questions (Do you know John?) than nonaffirmative questions (You haven't met, have you?). Moreover, "Even guessing can fill gaps in memory, with vividness increasing each time the event is recalled, thus increasing confidence for false-alarm errors and causing lower 'don't know' rates; repeated imagining can lead to confident illusory recollections."[147]

Is it within the control of individuals to compensate for these cognitive deficiencies? Psychologists have been concerned with this question for reasons having nothing to do with torture or interrogation. The cognitive deficiencies of sleep deprivation have dangerous consequences in ordinary life. Drivers, machine operators, and nurses may act impulsively when making complex decisions, behave with less caution, lose track of time, tend to fixate, be unable to ignore irrelevant information, and register new information more slowly.[148] Can sleep-deprived individuals go more slowly, collect their thoughts, and indicate when they have less confidence than they remember?

It turns out that they cannot. Sleep loss causes cognitive deficiencies that are unknown to individuals. These effects do not change even when individuals know they are sleep deprived and proceed more cautiously. Indeed, when the question is repeated, they are likely to be more confident in their mistaken answer, not less. The results are "similar to the confident errors in memory caused by hypnosis," where hypnotized participants are "unaware that their responses are inaccurate."[149] It is no wonder, historically, that witch hunters favored sleep deprivation in their effort to document trysts with the Devil.[150]

Sleep-deprived individuals make errors because they lose the ability to tell where an idea came from, and so they judge the accuracy of the memory by their familiarity with it. "Judgment by familiarity can result in false eyewitness testimony, which is more likely when participants are stressed or distracted."[151] Third parties (jurors, interrogators) observing eyewitnesses are more likely to rely on confident cooperative witnesses than on uncertain ones, thereby compounding the original error.[152] Likewise, ordinary people believe confessions even when they know the confessions are coerced and have been told that they are inadmissible in court, even when they claim coerced confessions do not affect their decisions.[153]

The unedited *HRET* maintains, "Coercive techniques will rarely confuse a resistant subject so completely that he does not know whether his own confession is true or false."[154] In fact, subjects make precisely this mistake, confabulating details in their memory to fit questions even when coercion is absent.[155] Under coerced interrogation, this outcome is more likely, and interrogators following the *HRET*'s advice will place mistaken confidence in the cooperative prisoner's firm avowals.

Asking questions repeatedly is an ineradicable feature of most interrogations, and asking affirmative questions (do you know X? where is Y?) probably inevitable. Sweating is so common in torture it is practically routine, and prisoners who experience memory lapses from trauma are likely to remember fictions quite vividly. When combined with the typical unskilled torturer, all this is a recipe for retrieving extremely poor information. Because both interrogators and cooperative prisoners have high confidence in this information, others are unlikely to second-guess its accuracy. This is yet another manner in which torture produces mistaken information.

How Good Is the Intelligence Overall?

The analysis thus far suggests three different sources of error that systematically and unavoidably corrupt information gathered through torture. These are deceptive, but actionable information given by uncooperative or innocent prisoners; the well-documented weakness of most interrogators for spotting deception; and mistaken, but high-confidence, information offered by cooperative prisoners after torture.

Is there evidence that this does occur? In fact, there is statistical evidence that interrogators produce consistently poor information in battlefield conditions or emergencies involving torture.

South Vietnam

Starting in the mid-1960s, the CIA ran a clandestine operation in South Vietnam designed to eliminate the Vietcong (VC) infrastructure.[156] The Phoenix Program aimed to capture and kill VC operatives. Its managers coordinated intelligence across numerous organizations, both American and Vietnamese. Action squads then executed the information, performing "snatch and grab" operations or selective assassinations.

Phoenix managers left behind a unique database, one that recorded their own beliefs about the reliability of the intelligence they were using.[157] The database classified targets as confirmed or unconfirmed VC. The standards were simple: three independent pieces of intelligence were sufficient for a confirmed VC identification. The database showed 73,697 Vietnamese were targeted, 15,438 of them killed, and 22,000 arrested, a total of approximately 96,000 individuals. Phoenix was a highly sophisticated system for selecting and killing people. Even though the standards for target identification were low, Phoenix did not involve the random violence that characterized counterinsurgency operations in other conflicts. In this respect, the Phoenix database gives the best picture of how a sophisticated force selected a pool of suspicious individuals to interrogate and terminate during an insurgency.

Stathis Kalyvas and Matthew Kocher have recently analyzed the database results.[158] First, they observed that a simple cross-tabulation of confirmation and final status reveals a story of capricious violence. They found that only about 10 percent of all individuals targeted under the Phoenix Program were confirmed VC by the database's own standards. Among those eventually killed, 4.5 percent were confirmed VC. By contrast, Phoenix operatives had terminated 20 percent of the unconfirmed, and additionally large percentages had been captured or defected to the government (34 and 18 percent respectively). By the time the database closed in 1973, only 25 percent of the unconfirmed VC remained at large, and 94 percent of the confirmed VC also remained at large.

In simple terms, this means that 94 out of every 100 highly suspicious individuals managed to elude American and South Vietnamese teams by the database's own standards. Less suspicious individuals were twenty-four times more likely to be captured than highly suspicious ones. Less suspicious individuals were also five times more likely to be killed that highly suspicious ones. In terms of odds, "an individual had close to 32 times greater odds of being killed, and 26 times greater odds of being captured or killed, in the unconfirmed category."[159]

Kalyvas and Kocher explain this outcome by arguing that the Phoenix database was reasonably accurate in identifying real Vietcong agents and innocents and that real VC agents simply had greater resources to avoid being captured. Those in the unconfirmed category had fewer resources to draw on and so were completely exposed. Phoenix teams put the same amount of effort to catch members of both categories, but it was simply easier for them to find or kill the unconfirmed. The alternative explanation, far less reasonable, is to assume that Phoenix teams put more effort into hunting down unconfirmed persons than confirmed ones. In favor of Kalyvas and Kocher's view is that while defections to the South Vietnamese side were common among the unconfirmed, almost no one from the confirmed category defected, precisely what one would expect if this category was composed largely of real Vietcong.

Using this general interpretation of the data, Kalyvas and Kocher use a simple mathematical model to estimate the ratio of civilians to Vietcong victimized by the Phoenix operations. This model makes three assumptions. It assumes that the Phoenix database includes two stable and mutually exclusive groups, Vietcong and innocents and, consequently, that both the confirmed and unconfirmed VC categories can likewise be partitioned into Vietcong and innocents. Second, Kalyvas and Kocher assumed a constant proportion of victims for Vietcong and a constant proportion for innocents in each case independent of their confirmation status. They stipulate, in other words, that Phoenix's process of confirmation did not itself affect the rate of victimization. People got victimized because of their characteristics. Lastly, Kalyvas and Kocher assume that the real Vietcong were far less likely to be caught for the reasons described above and that the odds described above also accurately characterize the "odds ratio of innocents/Vietcong in the unconfirmed group to innocents/Vietcong in the confirmed group."[160]

Kalyvas and Kocher then graph all the possible solutions that are consistent with these assumptions. While there are thousands of possible combinations, they found these results fell in a fairly narrow range of possibilities. They estimate that the Phoenix Program "victimized *at least* 38 innocents for every 1 actual Vietcong agent (the intermediate solution is about 78 innocents for every 1 Vietcong)."[161] This is truly awesome perverse selection.

And how successful was Phoenix in eliminating Vietcong despite this incredible cost to the lives and well-being of innocents? The database results are consistent with various scenarios, including, at one extreme, no actual Vietcong killed despite having thirteen thousand real agents in the pool of suspects and, at the other extreme, nineteen hundred actual Vietcong agents terminated with eight thousand innocents dead. "In other words, the most optimistic (i.e., most accurately selective scenario) is that about 4.7 innocent persons were killed for every Vietcong agent. In the intermediate case, we have about 10.3 innocents killed for every rebel participant."[162]

These results suggest that the Phoenix database contained some incredibly poor information. Where did it come from? Poor information entered the database in two ways, in the *selection* of people and in the *methods* of interrogation.

The database suggests that the pool of individuals selected was composed of people with no information to give. Informants may have voluntarily fingered some, while others undoubtedly talked under torture.[163] In either case, identification and selection followed from "a morass of individual vendettas and settling of accounts."[164] Even if torture was completely effective, the database indicates that it would still be unreliable as a source of information because the way individuals are chosen in insurgencies guarantees many prisoners with no information. But it seems plausible that torture compounded the selection errors: the ignorant fingered the innocent and deceived the torturers, and the innocent were then interrogated or terminated.

If Phoenix was an effective program, as Moyar claims, it was not because Phoenix managers executed accurate information.[165] Phoenix's effectiveness came from selective violence. When violence is indiscriminate, it is hard to know what to do. When violence is selective, people *assume* the right people are being targeted and this discourages *anyone*, enemy or not, from doing *anything* that might make them fall under suspicion. Death squads are chillingly effective even if they are not accurate.

Northern Ireland

A similar pattern of error appears in British data for operations in Northern Ireland between 1970 and 1971.[166] In the first six months of the Troubles, official records identified the number arrested, those interrogated for 24–48 hours and released, those sent to internment camps for holding, and those detained for further interrogation. Prisoners in the last category were presumably those that the RUC believed were IRA members.

In the course of six months, the RUC arrested increasingly more suspects, but fewer individuals *it believed* were IRA members or sympathizers. In August, the RUC arrested 342 people, interrogated and released 116 (34 percent) and detained 226 (66 percent). By the end of October, the RUC had arrested 882, interrogated and released 466 (54 percent), sent 278 to internment camps (31 percent), and detained 128 for further interrogation (14.5 percent). By the end of January, the RUC had arrested 2,357 individuals, interrogated and released 1,600 (67.8 percent), interned 598 (25.3 percent), and detained 159 (6.7 percent).

In short, the RUC was arresting more and more individuals it concluded were innocents, an enormous waste of resources. Information accuracy decayed rapidly over the six-month period. The better rate for August, the first month, probably reflects the fact that police arrested based on previously known intelligence gathered without torture. If coerced interrogation produced these better results, then police would be releasing fewer prisoners each subsequent month rather than more.

Even in the August sweep, there were false positives, though not as many as the months that followed. Researchers have compared the names of the arrested individuals to independent sources, identifying who was an IRA member. Of the 342 individuals taken up in the August sweep, the British interrogated and detained 124 at the Crumlin Jail on suspicion of being IRA members. Of this number, there were 4 senior IRA members and 80 who were, in some way, linked to the IRA. Already by August then, 40 men, a little less than one-third, were there entirely by accident, but were tortured nevertheless. It would be surprising if the accidental arrest rate improved subsequently.

Again, the rapid slide in accuracy probably followed from the manner in which police selected and interrogated prisoners, each process compounding the other. RUC interrogation, whether short or long, often included beating, sweating, exhaustion exercises, and forced standing.[167] People, tortured or not, fingered other innocents simply because, in the words of an MI5 interrogator, they had "nothing to tell."[168] Eventually, the British government concluded that "detainees aren't valuable" as information sources in Northern Ireland and chose other methods for gathering intelligence.[169]

British Cyprus

In the 1960s, a group of government experts studied the intelligence records during the 1956 EOKA crisis. They acknowledged that the British "had the civilian population against them" and that any collaborator "was in great danger." Normal incentives did not apply. But coerced interrogation simply yielded poor data. Torture yielded talkers but "produced no result." As Peter Hamilton, the security adviser to the British colonial government in Cyprus put it, "The police intelligence system, including interrogation in Cyprus, was bad."[170]

Hamilton also concluded that the British could have dismantled EOKA and captured Grivas, the EOKA leader, using standard intelligence operations in six months. "Grivas could have been found; it was an answerable problem, tackled properly—a good military intelligence operation which the soldiers knew how to do would have produced the answer."[171] In fact, the critical break came in May and June 1956 when British troops captured Grivas's papers in a mountain raid. Special Branch used these documents to break up thirty units, killing or arresting twenty-two most wanted terrorists, and unmasking two EOKA police informants.[172]

These operations give us a remarkable glimpse into the way in which governments decide whom to arrest, torture, or kill. There is no clean torture of the enemy to produce consistently accurate information. What there is instead is messy, unselective, unprofessional torture that produces consistently unreliable information. This information sweeps up thousands of innocents along with a few of the enemy. The Phoenix Program targeted ninety-six thousand individuals, killing fifteen thousand. This figure includes at most nineteen hundred enemy soldiers and probably far less.

Messy torture for information poses an ethical dilemma, of course. One can ask whether bombing Vietnamese positions, killing twenty-five thousand civilians and seriously wounding another fifty thousand annually[173] is better or worse than killing fifteen thousand, including at most nineteen hundred enemy soldiers, over four years. Sometimes politicians must make harsh ethical decisions, but these bear no resemblance to the picture of interrogation and the ethical choices torture apologists describe. The Trinquier model for gathering intelligence—the model of scientific, professional, selectively administered, and accurate torture—is an illusion. The decision to torture for information in war is more like carpet-bombing a country flat.

Even When Time Is Short?

What if time is short, as with a "ticking bomb"? Does torture offer a shortcut? Constrained time changes none of the dynamics described thus far. Indeed, it intensifies them by limiting what torturers can do.

Physiological Limits

Physical interrogation methods, like psychological methods, take time, time that interrogators do not have in emergencies. Real torture—not the stuff of television—takes days, if not weeks. Even torturers know this, preferring to increase pain slowly with different techniques. "Many talk better after a week of solitary confinement than under torture by electricity."[174] Death squads are fast, but a torturer is "not like the killer who puts a notch in his gun each time he kills someone," as one Brazilian torturer put it.[175] In fact, "The torturer's work is relatively slow and methodical, whereas the murderer's is often quick and spontaneous. A torturer's work is never done."[176]

Short time changes a torturer's preferences. Torturers cannot use techniques that take time, like forced standing and sleep deprivation. They must push to maximal pain fast with techniques like whipping, harsh beating, violent shaking, and electroshock. These techniques are the only way to overtake the individual's pain threshold, but they also risk brain trauma. Ribot's gradient becomes especially troublesome in ticking time bomb cases, since here the memory torturers want to extract is a recent one.

Intensified torture also quickly produces insensitivity, unconsciousness, and inadvertent death. A victim of Japanese fascist police reported that it took only a half hour of forced kneeling for his legs to go "mercifully numb."[177] The Gestapo tortured repeatedly within first twenty-four to forty-eight hours, but after four sessions, a Norwegian Resistance fighter concluded that "pain had reached its limit—when it could hurt no more, what did it matter how it was inflicted?" As Yugoslav partisan Milovan Djilas, who was tortured by the pro-Nazi Ustaca, observes, "All individual acts of torture have their limits, just as our bodies have limits of endurance. When the infliction of pain reaches the latter limits, the body and spirit protect themselves by lapsing into unconsciousness. . . . This is the beginning of the victory over torturers and tortures alike."[178]

Interrogators know these medical problems cause costly delays, if not outright failure. They are cautious, and this makes them especially vulnerable to deception, for example, feigned unconsciousness, heart palpitations, madness, and epileptic seizures. Kubark devotes an entire section to "malingering." "The history of interrogation," it concludes, "is studded with stories of persons who have attempted, often successfully, to evade the mounting pressures of interrogation by feigning physical or mental illness."[179] Even pros like Klaus Barbie, the noted Nazi torturer, have been fooled in this manner.[180]

In time, malingering can be uncovered, but, as Kubark observes, many intelligence situations "make it difficult or next-to-impossible to summon medical or other professional assistance." The only real options are to wait (lose precious time) or apply more pain to test the truth (which may compound a genuine condition).[181] Threatening more torture is an empty threat under these conditions.[182]

Resource Limits

In the case of ticking time bombs, information is time sensitive. For decades, guerrilla organizations have made "torture contracts" with their members: If you get arrested, keep the interrogators busy for twenty-four hours and let us change the passwords and locations. Make them waste their time and resources. After a day, say whatever you want, since what you know will be useless. The value of interrogation declines much more rapidly in these circumstances, whether one tortures or not.

At the same time, constrained time makes interrogators even more vulnerable to verifiable, but malicious, information. There is too little time to verify anything by other methods. Those with limited interrogation experience, for example, soldiers, are least likely to distinguish lies from truths. In war, they are often interrogating in unfamiliar contexts with foreign suspects. In terrorism, police cannot easily identify terrorists; there are no "visibly detectable personality traits that would allow authorities to identify a terrorist." Recruiters favor terrorists "practically indistinguishable from normal people," weeding out the conspicuous and the mentally ill.[183]

One may decide to torture because *anything* is still better than nothing. Everything we know about information gathered under these conditions, from South Vietnam and Northern Ireland, indicates that anything is far worse than nothing. Verifying anything spreads resources more thinly, and following anything endangers one's company. Following anything also precipitates actions that increase hostility from noncombatants (unprovoked raids and arrests of the innocent), destroy public trust, and so further constrain intelligence operations. Consider the July 21 bombers from London and the hunt for the last ticking time bomb packed with explosives and nails. It is unlikely that the British police would have been anywhere near this bomb if they had a reputation for torture. Would, for example, the parents of Mukhtar Said Ibrahim have identified him if they knew police would torture him? That seems highly unlikely.

Psychological Limits

Hardcore believers, including presumably the common terrorist, do not break quickly. Likewise, "Persons of considerable moral or intellectual stature," remarks *Kubark*, "often find in pain inflicted by others a confirmation of the belief that they are in the hands of inferiors, and their resolve not to submit is strengthened."[184] Torture offers such individuals opportunities to show character.

"I know I would break under torture," you may say. If you do, then the reason you betrayed your friends has nothing to do with the actual pain, does it? You have decided when you would betray the cause long before you saw the torture chamber. "Almost always, one does not become a traitor *under* torture, but *before* torture," says Djilas. Indeed, "Most people prepare themselves to give in under torture before arrest, while they are still free."[185] Analysts who carefully studied detainees who broke under Soviet and Chinese torture came to similar conclusions.[186] During, before, and after incarceration, each prisoner displayed strengths and weaknesses largely dependent on his own character.

In these cases, torture was not the *cause* of cooperation. Preexisting character shaped the motivation to talk or not, and those that talked were simply looking for a plausible scenario to betray others. Torture provided one such scenario, but other fearsome scenarios would work just as well.

For example, during World War II, British counterespionage managed to identify almost every German spy without using torture—not just the 100 who hid among the seven thousand to nine thousand refugees coming to England each year, not just the 120 who arrived from friendly countries, but also the seventy sleeper cells that were in place before 1940. Only 3 agents eluded detection; 5 others refused to confess. The British then offered each agent a choice: Talk or be tried and shot. Many Germans chose to talk and became double agents. They radioed incorrect coordinates for German V missiles, directing them to land harmlessly in fields. But for this misdirection, the distinguished war historian John Keegan concludes, in October 1944 alone the Germans would have killed about 1,300 people and injured 10,000 others.[187]

There is no reason to think that torture, or even the fear of torture, would have yielded any better results. In fact, torturing probably yields worse results than threatening death. Masochists and hardcore believers will stay silent whether they are threatened with death or torture, but ordinary prisoners become more unmanageable after they are tortured. They often describe their relief to discover that they were made of sterner stuff. "I felt almost triumphant. I knew they would not break me; I did not care what else they did."[188] Even those who secretly anticipated they might break are sometimes surprised to find that the pain made them more intractable.[189] Once the fear was gone, they became less cooperative.

Kubark maintains that the more one knows about a prisoner's fears, the more one knows whether coerced or uncoerced interrogation is likely to succeed.[190] This is plausible, but then coerced and uncoerced interrogation depend on precisely the same practice, a psychological profile of what prisoners fear, and this is no argument for favoring *in principle* torture over a psychological technique under conditions of constrained time.

Besides, careful psychiatric profiles take time to complete, time that, in this case, is not available. So typically torturers substitute simple occupational categories for them.[191] Torture peasants first, then ask questions, for example, but question students first, then torture. These rules of thumb, playing on superficial similarities, are misleading guides for torture. It is well documented that people in the same category (e.g., students) react to torture differently. Conversely, as *Kubark* explains, "The same coercive method may succeed against persons who are very unlike each other."[192] Constrained time raises the stakes in how torturers categorize and approach prisoners, but the rudimentary psychology torturers use does not provide guidance.

Indeed, the torturer's paradox grips decision-making more tightly, making it difficult to know what to do next: Don't wait too long, but don't torture right away. Don't make the prisoner faint or die, but push to the max. Don't desensitize the prisoner, but hit hard. Look before you leap, but he who hesitates is lost. Under these conditions, *Kubark* concludes, torture is a "hit or miss" practice and "a waste of time and energy."[193]

In guerrilla war or terrorism, interrogators may turn to torture because physical techniques seem faster and more likely to extract accurate information and the prisoner is the *right* suspect (the enemy). In fact, physical methods offer little real advantage under time constraints; interrogators are even more vulnerable to deception than normal; and they confront an enemy that is hard to identify and spreads information unevenly between its members. Under these conditions, interrogators generate volumes of information that is "actionable," but just plain wrong.

Remembering the Questions

Torture cannot be scientific. It is unlikely interrogators can torture in a restrained manner. Technology does not help them in this respect. Torture has strong corrosive effects on professional skills and institutions. Clean, selective, professional torture is an illusion. This is true regardless of whether one uses torture to intimidate, interrogate, or extract false confessions.

For harvesting information, torture is the clumsiest method available to organizations, even clumsier in some cases than flipping coins or shooting randomly into crowds. The sources of error are systematic and ineradicable. Innocent and ignorant prisoners generate malicious information, using torturers to settle private scores. Only highly experienced interrogators can spot such deception. Cooperative prisoners are unlikely to remember well and may give false answers with confidence. Neither they nor interrogators easily detect these errors.

In short, organized torture yields poor information, sweeps up many innocents, degrades organizational capabilities, and destroys interrogators. Limited time during battle or emergency intensifies all these problems.

These results do not prove that torture never works to produce accurate information. That would misread the scientific and social scientific evidence, and, at any rate, impossibility arguments are hard to prove. What it does establish are the specific conditions where torture may work better than other ways of gathering intelligence.

Torture would work well when organizations remain coherent and well integrated, have highly professional interrogators available, receive strong public cooperation and intelligence from multiple independent sources, have no time pressures for information, possess enough resources to verify coerced information, and release innocents before they are tortured.

In short, torture for information works best when one would need it least, peacetime, nonemergency conditions. If the suspect really *is* the right person to interrogate, interrogation is more likely to yield accurate information if the person is an opportunist, not a hardcore believer, as in the notorious Daschner case in Germany in 2002.[194] Even then, torture has problems that cannot be eliminated, including desensitization, death, unconsciousness, the loss of memory caused by damage, and the production of information that is more reliable the more it pertains to the remote past, not the immediate present.

Whether one can justify torture ethically when there is no emergency or when other methods of gathering intelligence are available, is another matter. My guess is that it would be hard to persuade most people, especially a jury. Daschner could not.[195]

They said that it was accepted almost everywhere in the world that beating a suspect was often a quick way of getting him to talk.

—Reporter talking to Royal Ulster Constabulary detectives,

Northern Ireland, 1977[1]

22   What the Apologists Say

Torture apologists point to one powerful example to counter all the arguments against torture: the Battle of Algiers. In 1956, the Algerian FLN (National Liberation Front) began a bombing campaign in Algiers, the capital of French colonial Algeria, killing many innocent civilians. In 1957, General Jacques Massu responded with a counterinsurgency campaign in Algiers using torture. "By such ruthless methods, Massu smashed the FLN organization in Algiers and re-established unchallenged French authority. He did the job in seven months—from March to mid-October."[2]

It is hard to argue with success. Here were professional torturers who produced consistently reliable information in a short time. It was a breathtaking military victory against terrorism by a democracy that used torture. Yet the French won by applying overwhelming force in an extremely constrained space, not by superior intelligence gathered through torture. As noted war historian John Keegan said in his recent study of military intelligence, "It is force, not fraud or forethought, that counts" in modern wars.[3]

The real significance of the Battle of Algiers is rhetorical. It dates the startling moment when modern democracies began official torture apology. After 1957, politicians and generals regularly cited the battle to silence their critics.[4] Archives on the Algerian war are now partially open, and many French interrogators wrote their biographies in the 1990s.[5] The story they tell will not comfort generals who tell self-serving stories of torture's success.[6] In fact, the battle shows the devastating consequences of torture for any democracy foolish enough to institutionalize it.

After discussing the Battle of Algiers, I discuss several other common counterexamples, including Gestapo policing and current American counterintelligence operations. In each case, I argue that everything described in chapter 21 on the failure of torture to produce reliable information holds for these conflicts as well.

Remembering the Battle of Algiers

Torture by the French failed miserably in Vietnam, and the French army could never entirely secure the Algerian countryside.[7] Here were the same regiments, using the same techniques to gather information (magnetos and water torture), pitted against an enemy that used similar counterinsurgency tactics. So either torture really did not work or some additional factor made the difference in Algiers in 1957.

Among many torture apologists, only General Massu, with characteristic frankness, identified the additional factors.[8] In Vietnam, Massu said, the French posts were riddled with informants. Whatever the French learned by torture or other means, their enemy knew immediately. Long distances separated the posts. In Algiers, the Casbah was a small space that could be cordoned off. A determined settler population backed the army; half the population of Algiers in 1957 was European.[9] Unlike Vietnam, the army was not riddled with informants, and the FLN never knew what the army was doing.

The French army began by creating an awesomely efficient informant system of its own, called the Dispositif de Protection Urbaine (DPU).[10] Massu took a census in the Casbah and issued identity cards to everyone. He ordered soldiers to paint numbers on each block, and each block had a warden—usually a trustworthy Algerian—who reported all suspicious activities. "No Muslim was able to enter the European quarters without being reported."[11] From March through September, twenty thousand people daily left by the controlled exits.[12] Every morning, hooded informants, the *cagoulards*, identified any suspects as they tried to leave.[13] The FLN also inadvertently helped the French by calling a general strike, which revealed other sympathizers.[14] The French gained accurate intelligence through public cooperation and informants, not torture.

In fact, no rank-and-file soldier has related an incident in which he personally, through timely interrogation, produced decisive information that stopped a ticking bomb from exploding. "Just as the interrogation starts," observed one torturer, "they speak abundantly, cite the names of the dead or militants on the lam, indicate the placement of an old arms cache in which we will find only a couple documents without interest."[15] Detainees also named their private enemies—true information, but without utility to the French.[16]

The FLN military men had also been told, when forced to talk, to give up the names of their counterparts in the rival organization, the more accommodationist MNA (National Algerian Movement).[17] Not very knowledgeable in the subtleties of Algerian nationalism, the French helped the FLN liquidate the more cooperative organization, unknowingly driving a politics of extremism.[18]

The famous movie portrays the Algerian population as united behind the FLN and assumes that torture is why the French won the battle, but the real Battle of Algiers was a story of terror, collaboration, and betrayal by the local population. It was "a population that was cowed beyond belief and blamed the FLN leadership for having brought them to this pass."[19]

General Massu's strategy was not to go after the FLN bombers, but to identify and disable anyone who was even remotely associated with the FLN.[20] It was not a selective sweep. Massu arrested 30 to 40 percent of all males.[21] The smallest interrogation unit in Algiers had thousands of files and the largest possessed over one hundred thousand files.[22]

Police prefects found themselves unable to deny arrest warrants to Massu's men, armed with guns and files. Paul Teitgin, the police prefect of Algiers, issued eight hundred temporary detention orders (*arrêtés d'assignation*) for the eight months before the battle, seven hundred for the first three months of the battle, and then four thousand a month for the remaining months.[23] By the end of the battle, he had detained twenty-four thousand, most of whom (80 percent of the men and 66 percent of the women) were tortured.[24] The Casbah's total population was eighty thousand.[25]

These figures exclude others whom military units tortured extrajudicially.[26] The civilian judicial system collapsed under the weight of this torture. During the battle, the Court of Appeals in Algiers handled the fewest torture complaints of any appeals court in Algeria.[27] In one case, when the defendant displayed torture scars, the judge voided the confession.[28] But generally, judges were unable to "betray" the soldiers.[29] Similarly, doctors, whose task it was to monitor torture, were corrupted by participation.[30]

"What to do with these poor devils after their 'use'?" asked a French soldier.[31] Some torturers preferred to kill them.[32] By the end of the battle, about 13,000 Algerians (and some Frenchmen) were issued *dossier d'assignation* and sent to detention camps. Another 3,024 simply "disappeared," either being killed in prison or under torture.[33] These numbers again are based on those detained in civilian, not military, prisons.[34]

Information in the Battle of Algiers

In 1956, the chief FLN operative, Saadi Yacef, had assembled approximately 1,400 operatives in Algiers.[35] Even if every one of Yacef's operatives was among the 3,024 "disappeared,"[36] Massu killed more innocents than terrorists, arrested at least 22,600 other people who were not connected to the FLN, and tortured most of them. Despite arresting nearly one-third of a city quarter, the Paras were torturing about fifteen individuals for every one hit.

The number of false positives, then, was enormous, and these numbers are similar to those identified for the Phoenix Program in Vietnam and the British arrests in the first months of the Troubles (discussed in the previous chapter). In fact, the number of false positives is probably higher here because this analysis minimizes the *total* number of arrests, and it assumes that *all* the FLN members were captured and tortured. The figure of 24,000 arrests does not include those arrested or tortured in military prisons, on the one hand, and on the other, it is a matter of record that some FLN members died in shootouts and bomb explosions, and others became informants. The analysis probably underestimates how many innocents the Paras unwittingly tortured.

Nevertheless, Massu did break the FLN operation in Algiers. His victory followed from three factors, though weighing their importance is difficult. Arresting one-third of an entire city quarter in just nine months—a remarkable feat under any circumstances—creates a general feeling of terror that is hard to discount.[37] Persistent selective violence (e.g., the disappeared) was also a powerful deterrent, as the Phoenix Program demonstrates. Algerians presumed that the French were disposing of the *right* people, and few would risk even appearing remotely associated with the FLN. Lastly, the informant system led soldiers to many critical arrests. Paul Aussaresses, who coordinated intelligence during the first six months of the battle, repeatedly describes the role played by informants in the Algerian war.[38]

The role of informants is one of the least appreciated elements of the Battle of Algiers, and deserves some elaboration, before I turn to the role of torture in the conflict. In the first round of arrests, Aussaresses got secret, and probably illegal, access to police files naming some two thousand suspected Algerian nationalists.[39] Some information came from regular policing (forensic analysis, translated documents, routine identity checks, tracing handgun ownership, simple deceptions, police surveillance, and tapping prison cells).[40] Patrols also yielded some information.[41] For example, Yacef Saadi, the head of the FLN, dropped his handbag after an accidental encounter with a patrol; it contained fake ID cards, FLN documents, and his address book.[42]

But as police studies would predict, public cooperation and informants produced the critical information. Loyal bloc wardens provided accurate information on some FLN members.[43] But even more valuable were former FLN operators. Massu raised a "French-protected militia from turncoat F.L.N. members to terrorize the Moslem population of the Kasbah and hunt out all remaining suspects."[44] Some worked as informants in the prisons.[45] Others entered the Casbah clad inconspicuously in worker's dungarees (*blues de chauffe*) "to mingle with their former terrorist associates and lead Godard's intelligence operatives to the bosses' lairs. The technique was to achieve such success that the expression *la bleuite*, or "the blues," later assumed a particularly sinister connotation in the war as a whole."[46]

The deadliest *blues* were a former soldier and killer ("Surcouf"), a betrayed wife of a FLN militant ("Ourhia the Brown"), the former head of the western zone of Algiers until his capture in August (Hani Mohammed), and, most importantly, a former FLN chief of east Algiers (Gandreche Hacene, "Zerrouk" (FLN alias), "Safy the Pure").[47] These double agents tracked down "Mourad" and "Kamel," the new FLN bomb squad chief and his military deputy in August. *Blues* brought information in August that pointed the Paras to No. 3 Rue Canton, where the last FLN leader, Yacef, lay hidden. It was a *blue* who pointed the Paras to the last FLN refuge in October, where Ali la Pointe, Hassiba Ben Bouali, and twelve-year-old "Petit" Omar, snipping paper cutouts as usual, lay hid for hours.[48] And Ourhia snared the last FLN leader at large, Ben Hamida.[49]

Vittori's notorious personal torturer despised those who became informers upon the slightest physical threat. "I detest the squealers who offer their services to the strongest side and afterwards become efficient auxiliaries of the repression."[50] Trinquier, on the other hand, made it a point to recruit them. "Our best agents will be furnished to us by the enemy himself. During the course of interrogations, we should always bear in mind that the majority of individuals arrested, if we have enough flexibility, can change camp."[51] Once swept up by the French, some no doubt found serving as an informant was a compelling option, considering the alternatives of death or torture. Torturers helped recruit Algerians as informers who otherwise had no information to give. They created insular individuals who depended on the French for their survival and whom the French could easily track down if they needed to. How common this was is hard to say. Important informants such as Ourhia the Brown and Zerrouk joined voluntarily. Others needed only to appear intimidated. They worked out their terms in advance. "Call two gendarmes so that they can rough me up a bit, and I'll open."[52]

However informants were recruited, the informant network proved to be remarkably free from double agents and misleading information. Only one FLN double agent penetrated the informant network, and he was exposed in weeks.[53] Some informants named their private enemies.[54] In one case, vengeful Paras, acting on false information from informants, massacred civilians.[55]

But overall, the informant system was responsible for many critical arrests during the battle. "The cornering of Yacef, then of Ali la Pointe, in the final stages of the Battle of Algiers had been ultimately achieved by his [Captain Léger's] *blue* double agents." In his final act, Yacef named Safy the Pure as the military commander of the whole Algiers area. From this position, Léger and his superior, Yves Godard, penetrated the entire FLN structure. As they became familiar with how FLN factions distrusted each other, they fed "a most savage and self-perpetuating series of purges." They planted documents on dead accused traitors implicating other loyal leaders as traitorous *blues*. The FLN severed its own limbs for the next two years.[56]

French Interrogation Units

If the informant system was responsible for so many successes, what then was the source of all the false positives? Of course, Algerians may have given informers misleading information about their enemies, but since the informants proved repeatedly reliable, this seems hard to believe. The other source of tactical information was coerced interrogation, and it is hard not to conclude that torture was responsible for the many false positives. In what follows, I describe first the organizational consequences of coercive interrogation during the Battle of Algiers, showing that these were no different than other cases. Then I turn to the quality of the information interrogators produced through torture.

Interrogation was the responsibility of the Détachement Opérationnel de Protection (DOP), "specialists in the interrogation of suspects who wanted to say nothing," in Massu's words.[57] At its zenith, the DOP was about two thousand men. But there were so many suspects that each regimental interrogation team also tortured.[58] Pierre Leulliette, a young Para, was surprised at "the scale and frequency of the interrogations."[59]

One prisoner during the battle describes fifty to sixty interrogations over four nights.[60] Similarly, Henri Poulliot, who worked as a DOP lieutenant at the Villa Susini, says that soldiers conducted a dozen torture sessions a day, and he served months later (June 1961 through March 1962). He estimates between three thousand and five thousand sessions during his ten months at this notorious torture center.[61] Between January 1957 and February 1961, the Amezaine detention center, also notorious for torture, processed 108,175 prisoners, including 11,518 "nationalists" and 787 "suspects."[62] Many soldiers did routine duties in the Algerian war and did not participate in torture.[63] But assuming Poulliot's rates are standard across all detention centers, hundreds did.

Trinquier, the counterinsurgency expert who headed the DPU, believed that torturers could observe professional norms—applying only the pain necessary for information and then stopping.[64] But the stories of rank-and-file torturers confirm previous studies of the dynamics of torture. "I realized that torture could become a drug," remarked a French interrogator. "I understood then that it was useless to claim to establish limits and forbidden practices, that is, yes to electrotorture, but without abusing it, any further no. In this domain too, it was all or nothing."[65]

Similarly, the British counterinsurgency expert Brian Crozier praised the professional, "selective use of electricity."[66] But, one soldier observed, "torture by electricity, first looked upon as useful, then as indispensable, has finally come to be considered matter-of-course, just as normal and proper as any other."[67] Long after the battle was over, Poulliot estimates torturers still used water torture or electrotorture on one-fifth of all prisoners.[68]

Torturers knew that they had little time to get accurate information: "You've gotta go fast because otherwise it all disappears rapidly."[69] But they tortured for days and weeks (in the case of Henri Alleg for over a month) long after any valuable information could be retrieved.[70] As one would predict, engaging in torture discouraged using ordinary—and more effective—policing skills. For example, soldiers arrested a locksmith and tortured him for three days. In his pocket, the locksmith had bomb blueprints with the address of an FLN bomb factory in Algiers. The locksmith bought time, the bombers relocated, and the French raid three days later fell on open air.[71] Had the soldiers been able to read Arabic, they would have found the bomb factory days earlier. But they were too busy torturing.

Competitive brutality became the rule among interrogators and Paras who tortured.[72] Interrogators competed in producing new techniques and some "become dangerously creative perfectionists."[73] Unit commanders criticized "low output" torturers, who learned in time to speed up.[74] When interrogators believed the prisoner might break, they spared no violence.[75] One interrogator, who failed using torture, killed the prisoner when she subsequently cooperated with a rival interrogator who did not torture.[76] Soldiers tried to bribe prisoners with their own pay to advance their careers.[77] Those critical of torture were constantly harassed, and one described being sent on a mission that, unbeknownst to him, was suicidal.[78]

Interrogators insisted that they were not sadists, and, though a few tortured to settle personal scores, they were professionals.[79] It was time-consuming, hard work.[80] Nevertheless, it also produced a unique rush. "A strange taste was born in my mouth, while my saliva became pasty"; it was a "sort of pleasure" but something short of *jouissance*.[81] Groups of empowered young men, several interrogators observed, were easily the most dangerous predators on the earth.[82] Some tried to seduce female prisoners.[83] Others engaged in rape; Pouillot estimates sixty to one hundred rapes during his time at Villa Susini, three-quarters of them gang rapes.[84]

Officers insisted that torture occurred only when they were present, and sometimes they were.[85] But it was easy to ignore the rules.[86] "We thought certain interrogations shouldn't have happened and that more precise barriers should have been put up. Everyday morality was completely absent from our reasoning."[87] Interrogators continued torturing after their officers forbid it.[88] They usually tortured and killed at smaller, more distant posts because the "commanders aren't there to 'put the brakes.' "[89]

The French military fragmented under the competition associated with torture for information. Officers lost control over their charges, or the charges refused to follow higher command.[90] Parallel systems of administration emerged. Inevitably, intelligence agencies squabbled.[91] It became "out of the question" to coordinate intelligence: "Why aid a competitor in difficulty?"[92]

For example, theoretically, the DOP exercised a specialized task within the army. Practically, "no one [was] fooled" and its work necessarily broached other domains.[93] It drafted soldiers from the army, the air force, and the gendarmerie.[94] These services loathed DOP practice. They knew the DOP recruited without telling local commanders, and soldiers with DOP service were "difficult to command and readapt."[95] The DOP generated a "zone of lawlessness," which then spread "to other troops that work for it." By January 1958, it had its own private prisons and "veritable practical autonomy."[96] Then military planners gave the DOP its own commando units, and so it was able to "emancipate itself" from the command and "wage its own war."[97]

Coerced Information in the Algerian War

When his unit left the Battle of Algiers, Leulliette observed that Algerians would describe 1957 as "when the Casbah, the symbol of all they had most deeply in common, was day and night in a state of siege, when terror was absolute master, when every one of its inhabitants could every moment say to himself: 'Within an hour, men will perhaps be knocking at my door to take me away forever.' "[98] Pouillot gives a less dramatic, but colder summary: "Given the manner in which the arrests were performed, a majority of those who passed by the Villa had no information to give. That wasn't important. One of the objectives of the use of torture was to remind Algerians that, by definition, they were considered accomplices of the FLN. In principle it was necessary to humiliate them so that they know that the army had all the rights, without any limitation and that they, the victims, had only to submit."[99]

Was torture necessary for victory? No doubt, the journalist Edward Behr, no apologist for torture, is right to assert that it had an indispensable role in the battle.[100] But this value was as a method of intimidation. Torture cowed many into quiescence and, sometimes, transformed others into miserable, dependent individuals who gathered information for the French. "Torture was effectively adapted to the new form of warfare the army faced in Algeria. This was not because the war demanded more intelligence gathering than other conflicts, but because it required control over the civil population." Torture served "to make them understand—and remember—who wielded power." It was "above all a *political* form of violence."[101]

But torture was the clumsiest method for gathering intelligence. Even the notorious Colonel Marcel Bigeard, the first commander to use torture officially, asserted, "Infiltration and information obtained spontaneously from the population are the most useful methods. I repeat, the use of pushed interrogations [the euphemism for torture] is only valuable if one is dealing with someone who is certainly guilty and if the information can immediately be exploited."[102]

In practice, though, soldiers suspected virtually all Algerians: "They all have members of their numerous families who have gone to the other side."[103] Some were arrested "upon denunciation, for something often insignificant."[104] Others were arrested because they were too well dressed, bought a new car with unaccounted money, were traveling single file, or ran upon being approached.[105] "In an army prone to doubts" and unable to distinguish among Algerians, "torture infiltrated and developed.[106]

If interrogators possessed a file on a prisoner, he was a suspect.[107] Named prisoners were either agents, deceivers, or potential informants; the classification system did not include innocence.[108] Everyone *had* to speak. "As much as he doesn't confess, he is not a suspect, not guilty. Thus, don't give him the possibility of keeping quiet." It was "better to be mistaken and rough up an innocent" than to let oneself be deceived.[109]

Some did not say anything, but most talked under torture; interrogators, and even some victims, agree on this.[110] "Veritable word-mills. I have met many of them," sighs Vittori's professional torturer.[111] False leads came from several sources. Many had nothing to say and were willing to say "everything and anything" that bore "no correspondence to reality."[112] Interrogators soon released "a good chunk" of the prisoners.[113] Some denounced their enemies, instances of "debt settling."[114] Others successfully deceived interrogators, so "often they [the leads] are outdated or false."[115] Others were handed false confessions; they signed them, were tried and executed.[116] "One must not forget," points out Pouillot, "that sometimes the tortured people were not completely conscious."[117]

Then there were errors by interrogators. Some interrogators caused delays, including fatal ones, thanks to "a natural brutality."[118] Others assumed too much and, as studies suggest, could not distinguish truths and lies. For example, an interrogator supplied the names and asked the suspect to affirm them. "This café-owner"? "The grain and seed dealer"? "He answers all our questions. The city seems literally stuffed with FLN militants," Vittori's professional torturer says skeptically. "He's our best informant," whispers the captain.[119]

Verified names were actionable, and officers launched military operations.[120] Were they successful? "Sometimes, but very rarely," Pouillot says, "these interrogations probably allowed one to 'harvest' a piece of information that made one able to avoid an attack, because the detainee talked very early on, but generally the information gathered arrived too late to be used."[121] But what mattered, particularly in the spring of 1957, was the number arrested and weapons seized, which demonstrated units had acted.[122] "My duty was to arrest the maximum number of people to avoid attacks."[123] Aussaresses described the consequences: "That system of tallying successes contributed to creating even more childish rivalry, which was completely unacceptable."[124]

Sometimes information analysts could not believe truths they heard. They could not believe, for example, that Yacef had spent months only two hundred yards from army headquarters even though informants pointed out the FLN safe house in August.[125] The French raided the site in October. Information analysts were also slow to translate documents like the locksmith's blueprints. These documents indicated the location of the secret bomb factory at Impasse de la Granade, and had they been translated promptly and professionally, the Paras would have found this location immediately. Instead, they found it a week later after torturing two other prisoners. And even then they could not believe that a respected *bouchaga* like Mostefa Bouhired housed a secret bomb factory at his home at No. 5 Impasse de la Granade. Not knowing who or what they were looking for, they retreated when the women of the house objected strenuously to being woken up. The first raid failed, and when the Paras returned the next day, the residents were gone. They bagged eighty-seven bombs but lost the suspects.[126] Processing the coerced information, as one torturer observed, involved endless daily meetings and wasteful cross-checking.[127] Regular police work would have saved lives far earlier than torture.

The interrogator accounts confirm Alistair Horne's judgment: "From a purely intelligence point of view, more often than not the collating services are overwhelmed by a mountain of false information extorted from victims desperate to save themselves from further agony."[128]

Some prisoners spontaneously offered information in noncoercive interrogation.[129] As Vittori's professional torturer concluded, it all depended on psychology, that is, the environment and the previous dispositions of individuals.[130] One man was arrested and tortured twice and yielded nothing; then he willingly directed Paras to a group of outsiders.[131]

Interrogators rarely cite specific personal successes at retrieving valuable information through torture. No one cites his role in preventing a ticking time bomb from going off. Such rumored successes always happen elsewhere and are things interrogators have only heard about.[132] Some have false memories, for example, how Djamila Bouhired "spilled her guts" under electrotorture, when in fact she was never tortured.[133] In war, rumor exercises enormous power, and the loyalty that soldiers feel for each other reinforces the rumors. Even those who had never tortured believed it worked; they defended torture as if they, and not the interrogators they knew, stood accused of war crimes, though they knew nothing of the reality of torture.

Not even the interrogators knew how accurate the information was. "There were those who gave [talked under torture] who were smart; I never went to see if they gave the important stuff, or the principal stuff, or other stuff."[134] Vittori's professional torturer had his doubts and described unit morale as low.[135] To inspire soldiers, his commander invited two green DOP officers. The professional torturer describes their words with great bitterness: "They study the results obtained since the establishment of the DOP and every week, they give detailed summaries from which it emerges that the resistance of the FLN diminishes daily and that we save numerous human lives. We believe him, we who ask only to be convinced."[136]

A survey of the famous cases suggests as well that interrogators who did not torture were more successful in harvesting accurate, timely information. Although it is often forgotten, key FLN members were never tortured, including Yacef Saadi, Djamila Bouhired, Hadj Smain, Zahra, and Djamila Bouazza.[137] Djamila Bouhired and her interrogator developed an improbable romance during which she identified a bomb cache and gave up Djamila Bouazza, though not Yacef's hidden location.[138] Smain's interrogator tricked him into revealing Yacef's location.[139] Somewhat more suspect is Aussaresses's claim that Yacef Saadi immediately revealed Ali la Pointe's hideout in interrogation.[140] If this was so, why did it take five weeks (from August 24 to October 8) to raid it? This convenient memory must be squared with the documented role of Godard's informants, Aussaresses's intense dislike for Godard, and denials of Yacef Saadi, now an Algerian senator.[141] At any rate, if Yacef did betray Ali la Pointe, this was not because he was tortured.

Contrast these cases with the four important prisoners who were tortured, Ben M'hidi (the head of the FLN in Algiers), George Hadjadj (editor of the underground newspaper), Ali Boumandjel (the FLN foreign minister), and Henri Alleg (editor of the *Alger Républicain*). These prisoners gave up nothing other than their identity as opposition members, and two were killed to avoid bad publicity. The possible exception here is the case of Henri Alleg. The French interrogators wanted to know where Alleg had hidden, whom he had met there, and how to get into the safe house.[142] Alleg never revealed this information despite weeks of torture. When the torturers gave up after a month, they handed him to the notorious captain Roger Faulques, who interrogated Alleg without torture.[143] Faulques claims that at some point Alleg slipped once, accidentally confirming that "the man with the limp" worked on the Communist newspaper.[144] Alleg denies this, but perhaps he did not notice.[145] If Alleg did slip during his meeting with Faulques, this was not because of coercive interrogation. And, one might add, even if this information had been secured under torture earlier, it got the interrogators no closer to their main objective, namely, identifying the locations of the safe houses. One can always move the goalposts and claim success, but Faulques's claim that torture worked in Alleg's case has to be viewed with skepticism.

A few less important FLN members were more pliable under torture, but it is a dismal record even if one counts all the ambiguous accounts. As one would expect, the teenager Mohammed Bellamine gave up his three teenage accomplices in the stadium bombings. In three similar cases, individuals made unconfirmed allegations against several individuals at once, but given the large number of false positives, one should approach such accusations skeptically.[146] More plausibly, Ted Morgan claims that Paras found Ben M'Hidi by the unraveling of a string of tortured confessions: Abderrahmane, the metalworker, fingered Rabah, the mason, who fingered Boutaleb who gave Hamoud, who indicated Ben M'Hidi's safe house on Rue Claude Debussy, where Paras arrived with Ben M'Hidi's photo.[147] But in fact informers had already provided the critical information and the Paras who arrived at Rue Claude Debussy were on the trail of another man, Ben Khedda, and found Ben M'Hidi by accident.[148] All sources agree that the general location itself was useless had not loyal block wardens led the Paras to the safe house where they found Ben M'Hidi in pajamas.[149]

Didn't savage, unprofessional, hit-or-miss torture yield some valuable information not known by other means? Actually, there was one case in the final days of the battle in which torture did reveal critical secret information.

In September 1957, French soldiers captured "Djamal," an FLN messenger. Under torture, Djamal revealed the hideout of Yacef, the last FLN leader in Algiers. But that was not new. Informants had identified this FLN safe house months ago; the French had been too busy to raid it. The important information Djamal revealed was that the French government was secretly negotiating a peace settlement with the FLN. This shocking news deeply poisoned the military's relationship with the civilian government, a legacy that played no small part in the collapse of the Fourth Republic (May 1958) and in the attempted coup by some generals against President Charles de Gaulle (April 1961).

When asked whether torture was indispensable in wartime, General Massu replied in 2000: "No, when I think back about Algeria, it grieves me. We could have done things differently."[150] And Yves Godard, Massu's chief lieutenant, insisted there was "no need to torture" for information. Informants could have identified operatives, and then Godard would have given them a simple, draconian choice: Talk or die. The results would have been identical to torture and without damage to the army.[151] In fact, the British had used this strategy successfully during World War II.

Aussaresses praises torture's efficacy, but he does not cite specific successes either in Algiers or in Philippeville where he served earlier.[152] He describes two failures to extract information from specific suspects; he killed them both.[153] He describes how he personally executed Ben M'Hidi in his cell, but he does not mention that informants, not coerced information, clinched his arrest.[154] Similarly, Colonel Bigeard claims that he was personally present for each interrogation, that very few and only FLN operatives were tortured, and that he always had "good results."[155] Louisette Ighilahriz's recent account of her torture by Bigeard suggests he was not as discriminating as he affects.[156] Perhaps one day, researchers will document the exploits of Bigeard's unit using the newly opened Algerian archives; then one will know how much glory it deserved.

Saving Innocents, Losing Wars

The French won the Battle of Algiers using numerous informants along with massive force applied to a small, highly controlled zone. Few conflicts meet these conditions: the Warsaw Ghetto, Soweto, and Gaza City are the closest analogous situations. Routine torture contributed little accurate information, corrupted the French units that used it, and swept up many innocents.[157] As the CIA correctly concluded, "During the Battle of Algiers, the French Army used torture to neutralize a terrorist group within a matter of months. Unfortunately, along with the hundreds of terrorists that were arrested and tortured, so were hundreds of innocent civilians."

Some officers insisted that torturing was a more just policy than taking hostages randomly.[158] But during the battle, *at least* fifteen innocents were tortured for every one FLN operative. This is not random in a strict mathematical sense, but it does seem like sheer chance in every other respect.

French apologists believed one ought to torture only terrorists to save innocent lives.[159] But *ought* implies *can*, and organized torture in Algiers was not selective. Organized torture necessarily sweeps up thousands of innocents, and one gains no moral superiority claiming to save some innocents while torturing hundreds of others and quietly disposing of many more. What exactly, under these circumstances, is a government protecting innocents from?

Some soldiers, particularly those with settler families in Algeria, felt strongly that some innocents mattered more than others. "Would you not torture to save someone like you or related to you?" they often ask.[160] Perhaps there is a plausible case to make here. But too often this case is based on arbitrary genetic or national characteristics, and as far as I know, no torture apologist has made this case publicly since Gestapo chief Müller in 1942.

Some soldiers wanted to torture many more, while others wanted to torture with care.[161] One soldier called the first group the "cynics" and the second group the "humanists."[162] The cynics claimed the humanists were weak, and the humanists worried that releasing tortured prisoners increased public hostility and made operatives less likely to surrender.[163] "They're going to tell others, and from word of mouth the whole world will know," and their relatives and friends will "join the resistance," said one DOP officer.[164] The humanists preferred to kill the shattered prisoners. They dropped their bodies out at sea. Where there were no bodies, there could be no blame or ill will. But the bound bodies, "Bigeard's shrimps" as Teitgin called them, came in with the tide.[165] And as the numbers increased, the humanists stopped short of outright genocide: "One can't kill everyone."[166] The soldiers' humanism ran deep enough that they were conflicted.

In the end, the soldiers and officers blamed their leaders for exposing them to torture, noting its pernicious effects on their lives, their families, and their friends—a sense of betrayal that has not diminished with the years.[167] The politicians had to know what they were asking for when they unleashed "with impunity ten thousand combatants among a million city-dwellers with the mission to find some needles in an enormous haystack."[168]

Trinquier argued that the French defeat in Algeria could have been prevented if the army had not abandoned the DPU informant network after the Battle of Algiers.[169] Perhaps, since torture forced "loyal" Algerians to cooperate. But after the battle, they either ended their loyalty to France or were assassinated.[170] There was no DPU informant system to rebuild, and the French had unwittingly eliminated the accomodationist MNA. The FLN was the only alternative to the French. Torture forced a politics of extremes, destroying the middle that might have cooperated with the French. As Teitgin remarked, "Massu won the Battle of Algiers, but that meant losing the war."[171]

Outside of Algiers, cells were quickly reconstituted, within three months in some cases.[172] Either torture did not work there, or it created more hostility and more recruits. The "humanist" torturers had reasonable concerns. Patrick Kessel and Giovanni Pirelli's enormous volume assembles hundreds of affidavits and letters about torture, some written in barely literate French. They begin in 1954 and cover the entire Algerian conflict. Among so many documents, only a few prisoners described giving information, most of it false.[173] But the sense of being violated, betrayed, and wronged is palpable in page after page.

Gestapo Stories

During the Algerian war, a French torturer sighed wistfully about the Gestapo: "Them at least, they knew how to work; they weren't amateurs."[174] But the Gestapo was no more an exception to the dynamics of torture and policing than were the French Paras. "The Gestapo, like police anywhere, could not do its work without public support."[175] The Gestapo's enormous success against the

Resistance everywhere depended heavily on public cooperation and police informants (G-men or V-men). "Increased reliance on interrogation through torture during the war years reflects the declining professionalism of an overextended staff much watered down with neophytes."[176]

Himmler and Heydrich "rejected the mode of police spies, and chose instead an idealized secret service that every citizen willingly supported."[177] Public denunciations were "both a major source of Gestapo efficiency and an unmanaged more spontaneous driving force in initiating its actions."[178] In Düsseldorf, for example, public cooperation initiated at least 33 percent of all cases, while surveillance and informers another 15 percent. Official agencies accounted for another 34 percent and interrogation, coerced or uncoerced, 13 percent.[179] Similarly in Würzburg, public cooperation accounted for 64 percent of cases concerning "race defilement" and "friendship to Jews," 17 percent came from other agencies, especially the Nazi Party, 15 percent from interrogations, 4 percent from political evaluations, and 1 percent from surveillance.[180]

The Gestapo was brutal, but like many police, it played on minority outgroups and racism. Nor was public information always accurate; as in other contexts, people took the opportunity to dispose of their private enemies. In Würzburg, the Gestapo judged 41 percent of denunciations in racially related cases as unfounded. In light of such public cooperation, "The popular idea that the Gestapo always beat a confession out of its suspects becomes questionable."[181]

The spy net was also important, especially toward the war's end. Block wardens and reports of nonconformists generated about 7 to 10 percent of all cases.[182] In Düsseldorf, the Gestapo inherited well-placed police agents in the Communist Party. Most big trials "can be traced to betrayal by a very few individuals who were therefore highly valued by the Gestapo and preserved from exposure for as long as possible."[183]

In the two major studies, Gestapo interrogation accounted for 13–17 percent of all cases investigated. Gestapo training emphasized psychological techniques; for the period between 1934 and 1938, George Browder concludes, "Gestapo torture is quantitatively exaggerated."[184] Similarly, in his study of the Communist Party in the 1930s, Allan Merson observes, "What is remarkable is not that such betrayals by individuals under torture or blackmail, or perhaps by threats of their families, occurred in the illegal Communist organization, but that so few cases of it can be found."[185]

Case studies of the Gestapo in Saabrücken and Krefeld show that the Gestapo made headway into Communist and Jehovah's Witness communities through torture.[186] Nevertheless, "They did not always produce reliable results, especially when evidence was needed for court. Brutality could not compensate for inadequate technique."[187] In Krefeld, for example, the Gestapo arrested homosexuals based on previously compiled police lists and four denunciations, followed by accusations under interrogation. Although many were implicated, only four out of twelve accused were convicted in court, and only one sentenced to a concentration camp.[188]

Heydrich and Himmler worked hard to reduce Gestapo paperwork and information overloads. The Berlin main file required 250 clerks to maintain it. Detectives were "so overworked by reports and filing that they could do little real detective work," especially in smaller posts of one or two men.[189] Heydrich "did not greatly exaggerate when he claimed that his personnel did extensive overtime, rarely got allotted vacations and still could not keep up with the workload."[190]

The old Kripo detectives, the Gestapo's rival, were least comfortable with increasing deprofessionalization in policing. They jealously guarded their narrow bureaucratic territory, but this intensified interagency conflict.[191] Similarly, the SD (the SS security service, the Sicherheitsdienst) sometimes did not report offenders to the Gestapo.[192] Interagency *cooperation* required considerable effort, because "infighting of the Third Reich compounded normal bureaucratic rivalry." Since many Gestapo cases grew from interagency cooperation in the early years (15–34 percent), such rivalries must have taken their toll on the Gestapo's effectiveness.[193]

Stories from the Resistance

Beyond Germany, Resistance histories and survivor accounts reveal the powerful effects of informers and public collaboration.[194] Informers were far more devastating to the Resistance than torturers. Informers devastated the Resistance in Austria,[195] Czechoslovakia,[196] Poland,[197] Denmark,[198] Norway,[199] France,[200] Russia,[201] and the concentration camps.[202] For instance, during the bleakest period of the Nazi occupation of France (1943–44), the Gestapo had twenty-two hundred German agents, but some thirty thousand French agents.[203] Everywhere, the Resistance understood it had to kill informers and collaborators when possible.[204]

The German espionage network was quite broad.[205] The Gestapo entered Austria with a list of potential opposition leaders gathered since 1934, the initial arrests totaling nearly twenty thousand individuals, including three thousand long-term prisoners.[206] Similarly, American POWs were surprised to discover how much the Germans knew about them personally, including hometowns, bases where they trained, names of their parents and grandparents, and even their local football team and the latest scores.[207] Once in an occupied country, the Gestapo immediately used existing police files for the first round of arrests.[208] Some critical information came from documents members carried when captured.[209]

After 1938, bureaucratic devolution, deskilling, narrow professionalism, and information overloads overwhelmed the Gestapo. One Czech Resistance member discovered to his surprise that "all of their investigative procedures were relatively poor; ultimately they relied on violence. They were not very adroit in their questioning, suffered a lack of imagination and could exert no real psychological pressure on prisoners."[210] "These tortures were all the more horrible," remarked a French prisoner, "because the Germans in many cases had no clear idea of what information they wanted and just tortured haphazard."[211]

As one would expect, the devolutionary cycle led the Gestapo to rely ever more heavily on torture. The cases discussed subsequently are the known ones. Perhaps there are more; Resistance stories are selective. However, overall, these stories confirm what one might expect from the study of torture elsewhere. What is surprising is how *difficult* it is to find specific cases where torture produced information that was not known by other means. In a war that involved countless thousands, or even millions, of brutal interrogations, this is a poor track record. And in many cases, the voluntary betrayal is hard to parse out from the coerced.

Those who *were* tortured or knew the Gestapo's work were less pliable than those who, due to their own unique psychological disposition, merely *feared* the Gestapo by reputation and looked to the occasion of their arrest as a plausible scenario in which to betray others. Those who resisted often surprised themselves; it was unpredictable who would or would not break under torture.[212] Some broke because a particular torture, unbeknownst to the Gestapo, invoked a childhood fear; yet others changed under torture. Raymond Basset, a French Resistance member, said dental torture was so excruciating that "had they started to question me at that instant there was nothing I would not have told them." But the torturers got excited, kept his jaw rigid, and removed all the remaining teeth. When they were done, Basset was so angry he refused to talk at all.[213] Hardcore members did not normally break. In the cases discussed in what follows, Gestapo agents tortured leaders of the German, French, Belgian, Polish, and Danish Resistance. Among these, only one—Willy Lambrecht, leader of the Belgian Resistance—broke under torture.

Germany. In 1944, the Gestapo interrogated dozens of high state officials and military commanders in the plot to assassinate Hitler. These interrogations "were not especially productive. Even under the most brutal treatment, few prisoners revealed information not already known to the Gestapo."[214] For example, Schlabrendorf gave the name of General Henning von Tresckow after several months, but Tresckow was dead.

Carl Goerdler, a Resistance leader, revealed everything, probably voluntarily. He hoped to save innocents from mistaken arrest. The Gestapo arrested 7,000 people (including family members and other innocents), executed 4,980, and sent the rest to camps.[215] Despite Goerdler's information, Peter Hoffman, the main scholar on the German Resistance, concludes, "Six months from the start of their investigations, the Gestapo still had nothing like precise knowledge of the resistance movement."[216]

Austria. The main case of coerced interrogation came late in the war. In April 1945, during the siege of Vienna, a patrol commander disclosed the plan for a Resistance uprising behind German lines, but this did not prevent the city's collapse two days later to Soviet forces.[217] The Gestapo relied on informers to penetrate most cells, save one found by torturing a Croatian lieutenant in February 1945.[218]

Czechoslovakia. In 1942, the Resistance assassinated SS Obergruppenführer Heydrich.[219] A massive search operation was undertaken to find the assassins, covering an area of fifteen thousand square kilometers. The Germans searched thirty-six thousand homes. The search yielded 541 individuals who lacked proper papers or identification, 430 of whom were released later. The Germans also instituted strict control of road and railway transport as well as compulsory registration. Everyone over fifteen had to register with the police, and all seven thousand doctors in the region had to swear they had not treated an injured man fitting the description of the assassins. There were also 157 summary executions. Despite all this, the only significant arrest was Jan Zika. Zika was a member of the Central Committee of the Czech Communist Party, but unrelated to the assassins.

At this point, Heinz von Pannwitz, the officer heading the Prague Gestapo antisabotage section, made the suggestion that broke the case. Pannwitz had been a career policeman, and he knew what was required was human intelligence. He argued, "Our special squads . . . confirmed again and again the opinion of the criminologists that fear and anxiety kept back even those who might normally have been prepared to give some information no matter from what motive."[220] The Germans offered amnesty for intelligence as well as a substantial reward.

Within three days, the Germans had two thousand tips. Most leads turned out to be false. One false tip led the Gestapo to liquidate the village of Lidice, even though the Gestapo confirmed no Resistance members were there. But among the leads was an anonymous letter mailed by Karel Curda, a Resistance member who had parachuted in with the assassins, and naming the suspects.

Curda claimed he volunteered the information because he feared his family might be swept up in the terror.

Three days after mailing the letter, Curda voluntarily surrendered to the Gestapo at Prague and collected the large bounty. He identified safe houses, which the Germans promptly raided. During the raids, the key Resistance members committed suicide by swallowing cyanide tablets, but one surviving child knew too much. Young Ata Moravec was tortured, stupefied with alcohol, and shown his mother's head floating in a fish tank. He revealed to the Gestapo that his mother had told him to go to the catacombs of the Church of Karel Boromejsky if he was ever in trouble. This happened to be where the assassins had been hiding. The Gestapo besieged the church, killing the one hundred people in it, including Heydrich's assassins.

Between May 28 and September 1, 1942, the Germans arrested 3,188 individuals in the course of the terror. This rate of return for terror (one confirmed Resistance member captured for at least thirty innocents, provided one arrests and tortures in the thousands) is similar to other cases such as the Battle of Algiers. The Germans also executed 1,357 death sentences from among those arrested, a number that excludes the 252 relatives and helpers of the parachutists condemned to death a month later, the victims of the liquidated villages of Lidice and Lezáky and the 3,000 Jews deported to the east.

Poland. Among members of a Swedish cell operating in Poland, only one, Carl Herslow, confessed. Documents show that Herslow did not reveal all he knew and in some cases deliberately misled the Germans; the rest admitted nothing other than the irrefutable facts already known to interrogators.[221] In another case, Gestapo officers assembled written documents and coerced information from a courier to locate a Resistance leader. The latter did not break and revealed false information.[222] A partisan reported that those among them who tortured pro-Nazi Ukrainians rarely achieved any success, and often continued after the strategic purpose "had long been forgotten."[223]

Denmark. In December 1943, the Germans captured three recently arrived parachutists in Århus before they could take cyanide pills. Interrogators confronted each parachutist with a close associate of a Danish Resistance leader, and one "broke down completely and told everything he knew, almost without exception."[224] The Jutland Resistance (forty-four individuals), and groups associated with it, did not survive, nor do records of the subsequent infiltration operations nationwide. "It was tragic that it should have been the highly trained parachutists who gave away to the Germans more than any ordinary citizen unwittingly might have done."[225]

Another parachutist, under threats to his family, revealed an address that led to the arrest of a Danish Resistance leader, who did not speak.[226] This did not matter, for "in spite of their [the Gestapo's] failure to persuade most of the prisoners to reveal the names and addresses of their contacts, they were producing effective results."[227] This followed from "the activities of Danish informers combined with the tracking system of cross-referenced files."[228]

Norway. A Resistance member revealed the names of three friends under torture, one of whom was the informer who betrayed him. The main haul in this case was the hiding place for the radios.[229] In Oslo, one Resistance member broke in Masuy's *baignoire* "because he had a near hysterical fear of drowning from childhood."[230] He implicated doctors who helped the Resistance. They did not break.

France and Belgium. Colonel Rémy, whose Resistance cell Masuy decimated, reviewed his thirty members, identifying the three members who squealed. "Tilden" gave up everything and became a collaborator. "Alain" made a deal and got a refrigerator. Mésange gave up a precise license plate number ("What a memory!" remarks Rémy caustically).[231] Masuy claimed his torture methods always produced results.[232] Rémy believed accurate confessions were rare, and those who turned, out of greed or fear, were more dangerous than those put to torture.[233]

The writer Jean Amery broke on the hook at Breendonck, Belgium, but his cell was well organized and he knew only aliases. On the other hand, "I talked. I accused myself of invented absurd political crimes, and even now I don't know at all how they could have occurred to me, dangling bundle that I was."[234]

Henri Lafont, a French criminal, produced the greatest French success using torture. In 1941, he infiltrated the Marseilles Resistance on his own, where he found and tortured Lambrecht, leader of the Belgian resistance. Lambrecht broke. "It was an incredible feat; an uneducated French criminal had succeeded where the supposedly efficient German counterespionage agencies had so miserably failed."[235] The Germans arrested some six hundred people, and they rewarded Lafont with his own black market operation.

Some believe Gestapo torture in France was centralized, professionally administered, and invariant in practice.[236] But the successful torturers were not the Gestapo or even professional Vichy police. They were vagabonds and criminals, men who were neither disciplined nor willing to work under bureaucratic authority but highly imaginative when it came to pain.[237]

CIA Stories

The priority in America's War on Terror should be on developing human intelligence. European intelligence agencies know this, and the Battle of Algiers and the history of the Gestapo demonstrate its importance.[238] But American agencies chose a different path after 9/11. U.S. interrogators gave top Al Qaeda figures the "full coercive treatment," winning praise from Secretary of Defense Donald Rumsfeld and the Schlesinger Commission for their results.[239] Too little is known about specific cases, but the available evidence shows that American agencies could not overcome the critical problems of organized torture.

There are, as the previous chapter shows, two general problems that arise from organized torture. One is that it leads to organizational decay; torturers tend to disobey orders and regulations. This effect follows from the dynamics of pain, the competition among interrogators and agencies, and the narrow professionalism that torture as a vocation induces. The other general problem is that torture induces numerous false positives and buries interrogators in useless information.

In this section, I identify evidence revealing torture's devolutionary effects on U.S. operations, arguing that the slippery slope dynamics here do not differ from any other case. In the following three sections, I consider the quality of the information produced.

According to CIA sources, the agency selected fourteen CIA operatives and trained them in six authorized torture techniques. These included forceful shaking ("Attention Grab"), two types of slapping ("Attention Slap" and "Belly Slap"), forced standing, the cold cell, and most notoriously, waterboarding, that is, the Dutch method in choking. Interrogators had to send a cable and receive a reply each time before they could turn to a progressively harsher technique. The deputy director for operations had to authorize each step personally. Even some agency critics say that the operations were "relatively well-monitored and limited in use."[240] The agency limited torture only to a dozen high-value Al Qaeda targets. All of them confessed, none died, and all remain in CIA hands.

All this evokes the image of carefully regulated torture limited to fourteen individuals. But it would appear CIA officials have authorized the interrogation of others besides these fourteen, and "in reality, sources said, there are few known instances when an approval has not been granted."[241] Contrary to CIA claims, at least five CIA detainees have died in Iraq and Afghanistan.[242] In the "Salt Pit" case in Afghanistan, a CIA officer doused a detainee with water and left him standing all night. Death followed from hypothermia.

Focusing narrowly on the original fourteen CIA interrogators disguises two critical devolutionary effects of organized torture, the tendency of torturers to go beyond the approved methods and the tendency of those who are not authorized to torture to take matters in their own hands. In the Salt Pit case, the officer was apparently "young" and "untrained." It is unclear whether this means he was authorized to torture and went beyond approved methods or whether he was not authorized and took matters into his own hands.[243]

What seems certain is that the officer was not alone. Other U.S. servicemen state that they first learned their torture techniques by observing CIA field officers interrogating prisoners in Afghanistan, and they in turn used these methods on Afghan and Iraqi prisoners.[244] This is much as one would expect based on what is known from torture in other instances: interrogators move beyond the authorized techniques, and those not authorized to interrogate copy the torturers.

Consider, for example, the interrogation and death of the Iraqi major general Abed Hamed Mowhoush in 2003.[245] Chief Warrant Officer Lewis Welshoffer first questioned Mowhoush without torture about insurgent attacks. When Mowhoush did not cooperate, Welshoffer "took Mowhoush, his hands bound, before an audience of fellow detainees and slapped him," an attempt, in his words, "to show Mowhoush who was in charge."[246] Mowhoush, now publicly humiliated, said he would not be able to stop the attacks. Loss of face leads to inability to command, but Welshoffer appears to have taken this Middle Eastern truism as admitting that Mowhoush coordinated the attacks. He handed Mowhoush to a CIA agent called "Brian" and four "Scorpions," undercover CIA-trained Iraqi units who became increasingly involved in detainee torture. They beat Mowhoush senseless with fists, clubs, sledgehammer handles, pipes, and a rubber hose.[247] These techniques obviously are not among the six authorized CIA techniques, nor is it clear whether OGA ("other government employee," i.e., CIA agent) Brian was in fact one of the fourteen authorized CIA torturers, and if he was not, why he was authorized to torture and what disciplinary action was subsequently taken.

None of this bears any resemblance to the image of skilled and precise physical interrogation presented by CIA sources. At any rate, two days after these events, Welshoffer bound Mowhoush's hands and struck him repeatedly on the back of the arms in a painful spot near the humerus. He doused him with water. He then threatened to execute Mowhoush's son. He "fired a bullet into the ground near Mohammed's head within earshot, but just beyond the eyesight of Mowhoush."[248] This did not go as well as the identical scene in the TV series 24; Mowhoush did not confess. Finally, Welshoffer and another interrogator forced Mowhoush into a sleeping bag and bound the bag tightly with cords. Inadvertently, they asphyxiated him. One unnamed interrogator claimed he learned this technique from his brother, who tortured him as a child. Facing charges, however, Welshoffer said that he followed government-authorized "stress positions." Unfortunately, standard stress positions such as forced standing have nothing in common with sleeping bag asphyxiation. Then Welshofer claimed that "the sleeping bag technique" was a standard SERE technique called "close confinement."[249] He was closer to the truth when he observed that there were no specific rules for Iraqi interrogations and they "were looking for ideas outside the box."[250]

Another devolutionary effect of torture is competitive rivalry between agencies gathering information. Torture is a zero-sum game, and organizations have incentives to interrogate the prisoner before others do. In at least two instances, intelligence agencies seized prisoners from interrogators of other agencies. In Afghanistan, CIA operatives seized Ibn al Shaykh al Libbi while an FBI counterterrorism expert was interrogating him and flew him to an undisclosed country. In Iraq, intelligence agents, probably CIA, apparently removed prisoners without authorization from Abu Ghraib.[251]

Veteran CIA officers know these effects from past operations. One thirty-year CIA veteran described the aftermath of undercover CIA operations in Christian Maronite prisons in Lebanon. "Here's the important thing: When orders were given for that operation to stand down, some of the people involved wouldn't. Disciplinary action was taken."[252] Deprofessionalization is a typical result of organized torture, as interrogators zealously guard their freedom to do the job right.

Merle L. Pribbenow, a twenty-seven-year veteran of the CIA's clandestine Directorate of Operations, emphasized this effect: "If you talk to people who have been tortured, that gives you a pretty good idea not only as to what it does to them, but what it does to the people who do it. One of my main objections to torture is what it does to the guys who actually inflict the torture. It does bad things." Pribbenow observed that torture survivors often told him things that "they had not told their torturers, and I would ask, 'Why didn't you tell that to the guys who were torturing you?' They said that they [the torturers] got so involved that they didn't even bother to ask questions."[253] Frank Snepp, the CIA's top interrogator in Saigon, condemns torture for identical reasons. When South Vietnamese interrogators tortured one of his subjects, he was furious. "He can't talk. He's a wreck. I can't interrogate him."[254]

Engaging in torture produces a narrow professionalism, a kind of tunnel vision in which "torture becomes an end unto itself," to use Pribbenow's words.[255] Here, he echoed the French interrogator from Algeria described earlier in this chapter who asserted that torture was an all-or-nothing activity, and once one got into it, it was useless to try to establish limits and forbid certain practices.[256]

Some CIA veterans know the devolutionary and deprofessionalizing effects of torture that social scientists have documented independently. They also know what works in intelligence. "What real CIA field officers know firsthand is that it is better to build a relationship of trust . . . than to extract quick confessions through tactics such as those used by the Nazis and the Soviets."[257] Consider, for example, whether the parents of Muktar Said-Ibrahim, one of the July 21 bombers in London, would even have considered identifying their son to the British police if they knew he would be tortured.[258]

Torture undermines precisely this trust and makes it difficult to recruit informants for intelligence purposes. As Pribbenow puts it, "Foreign nationals agree to spy for us for many different reasons; some do it out of an overwhelming admiration for America and what it stands for, and to those people, I think, America being associated with torture does affect their willingness to work for us."[259]

While the CIA claims to have produced carefully regulated, professional, organized torture, the available public evidence suggests that the CIA has been unable to escape any of torturer's known devolutionary effects. The turn to torture split the ranks of the CIA and other military organizations.[260] As in Brazil in the 1970s, this conflict pits the torturers and their masters against the disciplinarians, the veteran military and intelligence officers who know the decaying discipline and deprofessionalization torture induces.[261] This split goes down to the rank-and-file members. When the agency selected officers for torture training, three wisely refused.[262] The limitations the CIA has placed on "enhanced interrogations" are almost identical to those imposed by Gestapo chief Müller in 1943 on the Gestapo's "sharpened interrogations," and there is no reason to believe that the CIA is likely to be any more successful than the Nazis in regulating torture.

The Interrogation of Al Qaeda

But perhaps the devolutionary and deprofessionalizing effects of organized torture must be borne given the necessities of war. Administration officials have claimed that "enhanced interrogations" have produced critical intelligence in the War on Terror. In 2004, Porter Goss, the director of the CIA, asked two national security experts to evaluate the CIA interrogation program's effectiveness. One, a former adviser to Republican Newt Gingrich (R-GA), concluded it was effective, and the other, a former deputy defense secretary under President Bill Clinton, "offered a more ambiguous conclusion."[263] The reports are not declassified, and both evaluators have declined to comment.

Consequently, until recently, there was "no way to corroborate these stories" of successful interrogation with enhanced techniques.[264] But three such stories can now be examined critically, the interrogations of Ibn al-Shaykh al-Libi, Abu Zubaydah, and Abdul Hakim Murad. I discuss them below, and these cases must be considered in light of what appears to be a pattern of what the CIA inspector general calls "erroneous renditions," that is, individuals seized on mistaken information and taken to locations where torture is routine. Since 2001, the CIA and allied intelligence agencies have picked up three thousand individuals worldwide, but it is impossible to know how many mistakes there have been.[265] Judging from the record in past conflicts, the numbers are likely to be high.

The Interrogation of Ibn al-Shaykh al-Libi and Abu Zubaydah

In late 2001, American soldiers captured al-Libi in Afghanistan and handed him over for interrogation. Jack Cloonan, an FBI counterterrorism expert, interrogated al-Libi without torture. According to Cloonan, al-Libi initially cooperated. He detailed information on the Al Qaeda training camps and staff in Afghanistan.[266]

Then CIA operatives seized al-Libi, removing him from Afghanistan to Egypt. Who then interrogated al-Libi is unclear. Some sources suggest CIA operatives interrogated him, while others say the CIA handed al-Libi over to Egyptian interrogators, a practice called extraordinary rendition.[267] In any case, al-Libi claims that he was subsequently tortured.[268]

Under interrogation, al-Libi reported "that Iraq had provided chemical and biological weapons training to the terrorist organization [Al Qaeda]."[269] The al-Libi interrogation became the "main source for intelligence, since discredited, that Iraq had provided training in chemical and biological weapons to members of the organization."[270]

On October 7, 2002, in a speech in Cincinnati, President George W. Bush said, "We've learned that Iraq has trained Al Qaeda members in bomb making and poisons and deadly gasses."[271] Earlier that week, the National Intelligence Estimate (NIE) on Iraq concluded that Saddam Hussein was not likely to provide such weapons to terrorists. The president rejected this conclusion, laying out the rationale for invading Iraq. "Iraq could decide on any given day to provide a biological or chemical weapon to a terrorist group or individual terrorists.[272]

Although the CIA cautioned that information came from "sources of varying reliability," administration officials, including CIA director George Tenet and Secretary of State Colin Powell, asserted the al-Libi claims "as matters of fact" in public statements to the Senate and to the United Nations respectively.[273] The president's phrase "any given day" became a standard administration refrain in making the case for war with Iraq.[274]

As it turns out, the United States found no weapons of mass destruction in Iraq, and both the 9/11 Commission and the Senate Select Committee on Intelligence concluded that, while Al Qaeda and Saddam Hussein's government contacted each other, they did not collaborate, certainly not in the way al-Libi claimed. Indeed, when confronted with this evidence, al-Libi recanted in January 2004. "He told us one thing at one time and another at another time."[275] But this was hardly al-Libi's fault. Dan Coleman, a former FBI counterterrorism agent, put it bluntly: "It was ridiculous for interrogators to think Libi would have known anything about Iraq. I could have told them that. He ran a training camp. He wouldn't have had anything to do with Iraq. Administration officials were always pushing us to come up with links, but there weren't any. The reason they got bad information is that they beat it out of him."[276] In the end, Al-Libi's false information helped persuade Americans to commit to a bitter conflict whose end is difficult to foretell.

As early as February 2002, an internal intelligence report warned the Bush administration that al-Libi statement was unreliable. Al-Libi's allegations lacked specific details on the Iraqi—Al Qaeda link, and the report concluded that al-Libi was "intentionally misleading the debriefers."[277] This is contested by two CIA sources with firsthand knowledge of al-Libi's statements. They say that al-Libi "sought to please his investigators, not lead them down a false path."[278] In plain language, this means, "If we had the right person with the right information, then he would tell the truth under torture." But that is precisely the problem in counterterrorism interrogation: too often interrogators do not know *who* they have in custody or *what* the person knows. And too often, overconfident interrogators take coerced confessions as the main evidence that they did indeed have the right person.

For example, Jordanian and American officials described Zein al-Abideen Muhammad Hassan, alias Abu Zubaydah, as a top Al Qaeda operative.[279] He turned out to be responsible for minor logistics, for example, travel for Al Qaeda wives.[280] He was also mentally deranged. He was "insane, a certifiable, split personality," keeping a diary in three voices, a young boy, a teenager, and a man.[281]

U.S. officials claimed they would not torture Abu Zubaydah.[282] But his capture provoked the first torture debate within the administration. President Bush asked one briefer, "Do some of these harsh methods really work?"[283] Meanwhile, Jay Bybee, head of the President's Office of Legal Counsel, provided a legal basis for the use of torture in a now notorious memorandum.[284] The CIA choked Abu Zubaydah with water, deprived him of sleep, inflicted deafening noise and harsh lights, and denied him medication.[285] And so, after two months, Abu Zubaydah spoke.[286] He talked about Al Qaeda connections to Saddam Hussein's Iraq and the Saudi royal family, as well as its ability to explode dirty atom bombs.[287] How could he be lying, since "Mr. Zubaydah and Mr. Libi, a Libyan, had worked closely together at Al Qaeda's Khalden terrorist camp in Afghanistan and are believed to share a knowledge of the terrorist network's plans for new attacks"?[288]

Abu Zubaydah implicated people worldwide, leading to their arrest.[289] He described major plots that targeted malls, banks, supermarkets, water systems, nuclear power plants, the Golden Gate Bridge, the Brooklyn Bridge, the Statue of Liberty, and major landmarks in Chicago.[290] Intelligence officials were delighted. Porter Goss, chair of the House Intelligence Committee, insisted, "The Abu Zubaydah story is a good story, with more to come."[291] Occasionally, some expressed doubts.[292] They were ignored; Abu Zubaydah was interrogated over one hundred times in his first year of incarceration.[293] Month after month, "The United States would torture a mentally disturbed man and then leap, screaming, at every word he uttered."[294]

President Bush asserts that Abu Zubaydah gave important information leading to the capture of Khalid Sheikh Mohammad ("KSM"), the alleged mastermind of the 9/11 attacks, and Ramsi bin al-Shibh, an alleged Al Qaeda operative.[295] But these claims do not square easily with other information. The key information leading to the capture of bin al-Shibh came to the CIA from the emir of Qatar, who took information "from the files of an al-Jazeera reporter (the Emir owns the network) who secretly visited both terrorists [al-Shibh and KSM] in the Karachi apartment where Binalshibh was subsequently captured in September 2002."[296] The instrumental person in KSM's capture was a tipster to whom the CIA paid a $25 million reward.[297] So what exactly did Abu Zubaydah contribute? Intelligence sources state that Zubaydah identified KSM by his alias, "Mukhtar," which was unknown to the CIA. But in fact, the CIA knew KSM's alias in August 2001, well before the 9/11 attacks and well before Abu Zubaydah was captured.[298] The information Abu Zubaydah gave was redundant, and the agency had failed to connect the dots, the typical deskilling that follows from torture.

All the problems discussed here are compounded if the CIA rendered prisoners to other agencies, as may have happened to Al-Libi. Extraordinary renditions violate two cardinal rules for gathering human intelligence: Do not surrender your assets and resources to others, and do not depend on intelligence from allied agencies without independent corroboration.[299] Failing to recognize these important warnings makes intelligence agencies even more susceptible to false information. One can only shake one's head in wonder as one hears that American agents apparently cited Syrian and Uzbek intelligence reports as if these agencies were entirely reliable sources.[300] Cultural familiarity and linguistic skill are not substitutes for professionalism.

The notion that one stops when one hears the right information presupposes that one knows the truth when one hears it. In gathering intelligence from al-Libi and Abu Zubaydah, U.S. interrogators were in the dark, and they heard what they wanted to hear. Whether the same will be said eventually about other Al Qaeda interrogations remains to be seen. Even American interrogators who would not shrink from torture are skeptical. If these operatives were revealing the entire organization roster, "We'd be seeing sweeping arrests in several different countries at the same time. Instead what we see is an arrest here, then a few months later an arrest there."[301]

The Interrogation of Abdul Hakim Murad

If the al-Libi case shows how trained CIA interrogators can generate and distribute false information, the Murad case illustrates how a police force is progressively deskilled through torture. Analyzing the Murad case is highly problematic because, as it turns out, apologists omit many historical details; the case has been studied as an example of mythmaking in the American media.[302] Here, I describe the Murad case as the apologists tell it using the sources they observe; even this rather minimalist approach reveals how problematic it is to cite this case as an example of torture working.

In 1995, Filipino police arrested Murad during a security search in advance of the pope's visit. They tortured him, and Murad revealed dramatic plots, including Al Qaeda plots to blow up planes. After 2001, Alan Dershowitz seized upon this example as his showpiece for how torture works. On CNN, Dershowitz crowed how the Filipinos "probably under our direction, tortured somebody and stopped 13 or 11 airplanes from being exploded over the Pacific Ocean and may have saved the life of the Pope."[303]

But the police had also seized a huge chemical and bomb making factory, an Arabic manual for building powerful liquid bombs, dozens of fake passports, and a computer encrypted and in Arabic. When these files were decrypted, they contained all the relevant information about the plots Murad later confessed to. They included objectives, flight schedules, and procedures, down to where to lay bombs and how to set the timer.[304]

Even so, the Filipino police tortured Murad for sixty-seven days. They beat him until they broke his ribs, burned him with cigarettes, lay him out on ice blocks, and pumped his stomach with water. Once they nearly killed him. Still Murad did not speak. He spoke only when a new team of interrogators introduced themselves as Mossad agents and said they were taking him to Israel.[305] This deception got Murad talking, and though it is hard to know why, some explanations seem far more plausible than others. Anyone who did not break after so many painful tortures was not likely moved by the fear that the Israeli interrogators might torture him by tying him to a chair for hours. Among reasons for Murad's cooperation, this seems the most unlikely. It seems more likely that Murad despised the thought of permanent incarceration among Jews or feared them or reasoned that his chances of release or prison privileges was better in Filipino prisons.

Whichever reason, it was Murad's imagination and personality, not actual torture, that got him talking, and, when he spoke, he told them what he probably concluded they already knew. After two months, the only new information Murad volunteered was that he also hoped to fly a small Cessna plane into the CIA building at Langley. Whether this expresses Murad's aspiration or invention, this plan is not in the computer. The computer also contained telephone numbers that eventually revealed Al Qaeda's finance officer and a money trail to Osama bin Laden.

One wonders, wrote the historian Jay Winik in 2001, "what would have happened if Murad had been in American hands."[306] One answer would seem to be that Americans would have decrypted the computer sooner. The computer was "the critical clue," and the *Washington Post* reporter who covered the story drew the proper conclusion: the War on Terror depended on developing "human resources."[307]

Virtually every case in which the FBI prevented a terrorist attack depended on "long term investigations that employed informants, undercover agents, and electronic surveillance."[308] Similarly, all known major international interdictions stemmed from "traditional, which is to say, good old fashioned cooperation with US allies"; the Defense Department's intelligence network contributed to none of them.[309] Dershowitz claims Jordanian intelligence used torture successfully in a major terrorist interdiction, but the main verifiable Jordanian successes, including locating Zarqawi, Al Qaeda's leader in Iraq, and preventing a bombing at Los Angeles airport, all combined "infiltration, electronic surveillance and counterintelligence."[310]

Working one's way into a terror cell is not unlike working one's way into organized crime. One has to turn potential terrorists into double agents and to win the confidence and cooperation of the communities that shelter them. Technology is no substitute for this. Nor is torture. There is no "denying the empirical reality that torture *sometimes* works," replies Dershowitz, "even if it does not always work. No technique of crime prevention always works."[311] No doubt, but most people know the great difference between techniques that usually work and techniques that work rarely if at all. This statement—especially in light of what really does work in policing after thirty years of research—is high-quality salesmanship. But it pales by comparison to the skill with which the Bush administration has successfully pitched the persistent failures of coercive interrogation programs as unqualified successes.

Abu Ghraib and Guantánamo

Since 2002, American soldiers have interrogated hundreds of Taliban fighters and Iraqi insurgents. Generals and interrogators have made dramatic claims about the results. "I'm talking about high-value intelligence here, distributed round the world," claimed General Geoffrey Miller, praising his Guantánamo interrogations. "Last month we gained six times as much intelligence as we did in January 2003."[312] Joe Ryan, who interrogated at Abu Ghraib in winter and spring 2004, was similarly ecstatic. "We are more productive right now than we have been since I have been here. Some intelligence things are really coming together and could shift a few things to our advantage."[313] Interrogators at other camps praised their special techniques, such as sleep deprivation or loud music: "They can't take it."[314] "Trust me it works."[315]

But by 2003, the noted war historian John Keegan already suspected that prisoners "have successfully overcome American efforts to break down their resistance to questioning." Ironically, he believed the Americans had failed because they were "culturally indisposed to employ torture and anyhow inhibited from so doing by domestic and international law."[316] Keegan was mistaken about the causes but, as far as we know, correct about the negligible results.

Abu Ghraib interrogations shed no light on the high-priority military questions, such as identifying the insurgency's leadership and locating Saddam Hussein.[317] A computer team and a program, "the Mongo Link," located Saddam Hussein by processing 62,500 relationships in the Saddam Hussein's circle.[318] And American forces located and killed Zarqawi using information gathered through Jordanian infiltration of Zarqawi's network, betrayal of local insurgent leaders, local tips, and electronic surveillance.[319]

Abu Ghraib MPs competed in torture, "staging contests to see how quickly a prisoner could be brought to tears."[320] And Abu Ghraib interrogators competed for information, bragging overconfidently about their successes. "Tonight I was sure I had the winning interrogation for information gathered. I came out with information to write three different reports. It paled in comparison to what the two other people wrote. I guess tonight was the night the detainees decided to all give up."[321] Interrogations, unsurprisingly, were "counterproductive."[322] In fact, army officials indicate that most useful battlefield intelligence came before prisoners got to Abu Ghraib. Once prisoners got there, "We got very little feedback." And if sonic torture was even partially as effective as some American soldiers claimed, many countries would be using it, but they do not. Praise of Metallica and Barney songs, as intelligence officer observed, is "the American equivalent of sending bagpipes into battle."[323]

Similarly, the Guantánamo interrogation system was "hopelessly flawed from the get-go," according to Lt. Col. Anthony Christino. Christino was the senior watch officer for the Joint Intelligence Task Force Combating Terrorism (JITF-CT). His task was to handle every piece of information that was "critical, time sensitive, intelligence." Christino concludes that the Guantánamo interrogations were overvalued and their results "wildly exaggerated."[324]

The hopeless flaws had two sources, poor selection of people to be interrogated and poor methods of interrogation. Government evaluations of each prisoner, completed as part of the Combatant Status Review Tribunals in 2004, reveal the selection problem. These show that government believes only 10 percent of the more than five hundred prisoners at Guantánamo were fighters. The evaluations identified 30 percent as members of terrorist organization and 60 percent as "associated with" terrorists. It identified 22 percent as Taliban, 33 percent as Al Qaeda, 28 percent as both, and 7 percent as either one or the other but unspecified, leaving 10 percent without any known association with a terrorist group by the government's own standards.[325]

Evaluations also show the case against many detainees is slim. Only about half of the prisoners (55 percent) committed hostile acts, and hostility is understood broadly. It includes wearing olive drab clothing, possessing a rifle, using a guesthouse, or possessing a model Casio watch that has appeared in terrorist bombings.[326] Consider, for example, the case of three Guantánamo detainees released in March 2004 to Great Britain. At Guantánamo, they had confessed to appearing "in a blurry video, obtained by American investigators, that documented some acolytes meeting with bin Ladin in Afghanistan." British intelligence officials, however, determined otherwise, establishing that the three men were living in England at the time the video was made. Subsequently, the three men told British authorities that "they had been coerced into making false confessions."[327]

Accusations by third parties, including other detainees, are common.[328] Al-Qahtani, the so-called twentieth hijacker, accused thirty fellow detainees, while another detainee accused more than sixty, approximately 10 percent of the entire prison population.[329] Although the U.S. military described Al-Qahtani's confession as vital intelligence in 2004, al-Qahtani retracted his confession in 2005, and records indicate interrogators coerced statements under torture.[330] All this suggests high rates of error as individuals accuse others. Even if torture were entirely reliable, the way the government selected individuals for detention guaranteed unreliable information since many had no information to give. In reality, torture probably compounded the errors implicit in the selection process.

"We're finding that the longer some stay, the more they talk," said General Miller, who headed Guantánamo.[331] No doubt. Guantánamo is a textbook case of what not to do. Social scientists know that interrogators with considerable interviewing experience are best at discerning lies from truths and that "the longer people are detained, the harsher the conditions, the worse the lack of a support system, the greater the risk that what they say will be unreliable."[332] But the interrogators at Guantánamo were young recruits, chosen not for their experience, but because "they're really committed to winning the mission."[333] And FBI interrogators, who used noncoercive means, complained bitterly that these military interrogators reduced prisoner cooperation by using coercive means. "Every time the FBI established a rapport with a detainee, the military would step in and the detainee would stop being cooperative."[334]

Afghanistan

Chris Mackey, an American interrogator, presents the most upbeat account of coerced interrogation in this conflict. But even he describes typical problems that drive slippery slopes in torture: competitive rivalry between agencies for bodies to interrogate; the difficulty of recruiting informants; and the tendency to regard interrogation as revenge.[335] Indeed, the interrogators from the 519th Military Intelligence Battalion who replaced Mackey's unit adopted similar interrogation procedures, and soon they were engaged in torture leading to the deaths of at least two prisoners.[336] If Mackey is right, Afghanistan is unlikely to be any exception to the social scientific evidence.

Mackey talks frankly about some problems in coerced interrogation, notably malingering and mental damage.[337] He admits that his unit kept lights on twenty-four hours and doused prisoners with water; he offers benign accounts of these actions, though he admits his is "not the most impartial position." Above all he insists, the interrogators practiced "trickery and deceit, but we never touched anyone."[338]

In fact, Mackey describes how his interrogators relied heavily on techniques psychological research has consistently shown to be unreliable. Mackey endorses the usual folklore on what deceptive behavior looks like.[339] He just *knew* some prisoners were terrorists before they even spoke.[340] He also believed sleep deprivation yields accurate information, praising his unit's use of it to judiciously break prisoners. There was "commonsense behind it: tired prisoners were simply more prone to slip."[341] Mackey seems unaware that even professional medieval inquisitors knew that repeated questioning during sleep deprivation guaranteed false information, and preferred the rack to a technique that produces illusions and hallucinations that prisoners convey with confidence.[342] Only witch hunters favored sleep deprivation because it produced, to their mind, accurate accounts of pacts with the Devil.

Mackey repeatedly claims that interrogators got "good stuff" from interrogation.[343] But his evidence is unpersuasive. As in many previous conflicts, some prisoners accurately identified private rivals and unrelated associates, for example, loan sharks and forgers in Pakistan.[344] And too often Mackey equates the fact that individuals talked with evidence that the talking was accurate and timely.[345] Given all this, it is questionable whether Mackey's unit was anywhere near as professional as he presents.

Indeed, Mackey describes only one verifiable case where military interrogators gathered timely, important information. In 2001 or early 2002, prisoners in Kandahar told Mackey's interrogators about a poison attack on the U.S. embassy in Rome. "It didn't seem feasible, but we passed the tip along. Weeks later, in late February, eight Moroccans were arrested in Rome. In their apartment, investigators found 8.8 pounds of cyanide-based compound, potassium ferrocyanide, a tourist map with the U.S. embassy circled and municipal maps indicating the location of underground utility lines near the embassy. . . . the talents of Hasegawa and Davis [two military intelligence interrogators at Bagram] were never questioned again."[346]

There were, in fact, two groups who set out to attack American installations in Rome.[347] One group consisted of three Iraqis, an Algerian and Tunisian who planned to use cyanide in operations: "Cyanide. That's poison!" one Iraqi said on a wiretapped phone line.[348] This group had long-standing ties to Al Qaeda. Subsequently, Italian police arrested a second group, all Moroccans, with potassium ferrocyanide, as Mackey says, in February 2002. Italian police found no connections between the Moroccans and Al Qaeda.

Mackey does not mention the first Iraqi plot. He mentions only the imminent Moroccan plot, praising the interrogators' professionalism. But this will not do. If, as Mackey claims, Hasegawa and Davis had learned of the imminent Moroccan plot from their prisoners, how was it possible for prisoners in Kandahar to know about a plot by a group with no known connection to Al Qaeda? If the Kandahar prisoners had any knowledge of a poison attack in Italy, all the evidence suggests that they were referring to the first plot organized by the Iraqis—a plot that was by then public knowledge in the West and probably also among Al Qaeda operatives everywhere. In fact, the Italian police had arrested the Iraqi—North African agents in March 2001, long before Mackey's unit even set foot in Afghanistan.

Mackey mentions none of this as he praises his interrogators for uncovering an imminent cyanide attack. Amateurs in the details of international terrorism, Hasegawa and Davis did not know the plot was probably old news, but Mackey presents it as news about the future. Nor does Mackey mention that potassium ferrocyanide, a gardening compound, has such small cyanide content that "if this substance had been put in the water network it appears that it would not have been capable of causing any damage whatsoever."[349] Nor does he mention that Italian police stopped both plots with traditional long-term police investigations begun in 1999 and that American intelligence, extracted by torture or otherwise, played no role in the arrests. Mackey is right that "the truth can be what you think it is,"[350] but he seems far less aware of this truth in practice.

Testimonial Literature from Other Conflicts

Beyond World War II, the Battle of Algiers, and the U.S. War on Terror, some have made extraordinary claims about torture's effectiveness in gathering information in various conflicts. When scrutinized, though, these claims remain ambiguous and misleading, if not mistaken.

Northern Ireland

The Parker Commission argued that interrogating the fourteen men arrested in August 1971 helped police solve eighty-five terrorist incidents, identified seven hundred additional IRA members, and enabled police to discover more arms and explosives than at any previous time.[351] Of course, none of the fourteen men claims to have said anything even remotely resembling this information, but suppose they lied.

Still, the number arrested, detained, and interrogated as suspected IRA is nowhere near seven hundred in the subsequent six months.[352] As for the arms cache discoveries, other explanations seem more plausible than accurate tips from coerced intelligence. For example, more arms flowed into the province once the conflict intensified. Between September and December 1971, shootings of police and soldiers increased tenfold; by 1972, this figure rose by 605 percent.[353] Normal policing would have located arms caches more frequently because stockpiles multiplied rapidly. The Parker Commission never gave good reasons for its beliefs or released data for third parties to confirm its conclusions.

Indeed, the British government eventually concluded that combating terrorism required infiltrating organizations with agents and adopting sophisticated eavesdropping methods. Tom Parker, a former officer for the MI5, the British Intelligence agency, observed that detainee interrogation backfired because many had nothing to tell. Interrogating and torturing detainees "did nothing but exacerbate the situation. Most of those interned went back to terrorism. You'll end up radicalizing the entire population."[354]

Vietnam

South Vietnamese officers and some American advisers claim torture worked effectively during the Vietnam War.[355] In his study of the Phoenix Program, Mark Moyar praises "the ability of the interrogators to distinguish fact from fiction," noting that this "allowed them to discern lies."[356] If that is so, such worldly discernment is nowhere evident in the Phoenix Program database, discussed in the previous chapter. In fact, the results here vindicate those American advisers who claimed that "torture did not provide any worthwhile intelligence and often yielded false information."[357]

The U.S. Army's field manual for intelligence (FM34-52) notes that simple direct questioning of prisoners was 85 percent to 95 percent effective in World War II and 90 percent to 95 percent effective in the Vietnam War.[358] Orrin Forrest, a CIA operative in South Vietnam, illustrated the power of this approach. Forrest successfully turned some important North Vietnamese cadres into true double agents, generating some small intelligence coups during the war. Forrest condemned the "incompetence and corruption" of interrogation centers, the "phony" statistics of confirmed VC terminated, and interrogators who had "no way of producing, except by beating the hell out of suspects, and then there was no way to verify the stories."[359] Over several years, he organized a professional team that did not torture and that built a database of some twenty thousand cards. Forrest attributes their success to public cooperation and constant cross-checking of facts.[360] "Every intelligence case officer, like every cop, knows that hard work can uncover leads and create results. But he also knows that more good information comes from walk-ins than from any other source. A witness you didn't know about decides to come forward, someone who participated in a crimes makes up his mind to confess, a foreign national with secrets to sell makes a contact, or an agent decides for one reason or another that he wants to defect."[361]

Forrest confirms that most people's motivations to give information, and when they will give it, are set well before they are interrogated. Forrest received his best information from an individual who defected after he killed a powerful North Vietnamese officer for the rape of his comrade.[362] Others were lovers or spouses of recent defectors who agreed to serve as double agents for the Americans.[363] Those who were captured gave information largely because they were exhausted and realistic about their situation, though there were lines they "wouldn't cross."[364]

Hard-core members did not break, as might be expected. Consider, for example, the case of Vhuyen Van Tai, the highest-ranking Vietcong intelligence officer captured.[365] The South Vietnamese used electrotorture, water torture, beatings, stress positions, and sleep deprivation. They kept him in a freezing refrigerated room with white walls and no windows for two years. Tai had been forced to surrender his false identity and cover story when confronted with other defectors; but under torture he never admitted his full identity, insisting that he was "a simple farmer who came south to support the liberation forces."[366] Torture "did not provide any other usable information." Frank Snepp, the CIA officer assigned to Tai, followed procedures and built a rapport with Tai. As agency veterans observe, "It was skillful questions and psychological ploys of the Americans, not any physical infliction of pain, that produced the only useful (albeit limited) information Tai ever provided."[367] One can only conclude, given his responsiveness to traditional interrogation techniques, that torture hardened his resistance, as in so many other cases.

Moyar argues that "so many Americans and Vietnamese interviewees testified to the effectiveness of torture that there can be no doubt that it extracted useful information in most cases."[368] But Moyar is overreaching, claiming more than his interviews can show. Those who torture or witness it have compelling reasons for believing in its effectiveness, not the least of which is to vindicate their involvement. There is no safety in just numbers of interviewees unless all the testimonials have corroborated specifics. Many Americans also want to believe in angels, indeed many more than those who believe in the effectiveness of torture, and one out of five believe they have seen an angel or know someone who has.[369] No one would suggest that government policy or military strategy should be based on the availability of angels. But somehow normal reasoning that applies to angels does not apply when devils are involved.

Israel

Israel is no more an exception to the general dynamics of policing and torture than any other country. Israel depends heavily on informers (ʿasafir), especially since the first Intifada.[370] "The amazing thing is that by now the existence of the birdies [informants] is well known and yet the system still works. People come out of interrogation, go into the regular prison and then tell their darkest secrets. I don't know why it still works, but it does."[371] Skilled interrogators of the General Security Service (GSS) are well aware of the dangers of torture for information, and caution against it.[372]

Typically officers charge Palestinian prisoners with stone throwing, assault, belonging to an illegal organization, or participating in a demonstration. But Israeli researchers surveying hundreds of cases concluded, "Many interrogations are not even aimed at extracting a confession to secure a conviction. Their purpose is general information gathering, random deterrence, intimidation or harm for its own sake." Indeed, the Landau Commission, the government commission that investigated torture allegations in the late 1980s, reported that interrogators released 50 percent of those detained.[373] A soldier of the Nahal Brigade (discussed in chapter 2, "Torture and Democracy") expressed the point of torture succinctly: "I didn't expect one of the Arabs to tell me something if we did not hit him. We just hit him. . . . I didn't expect that he would not throw stones the week after. We knew that they would hate us more than ever after this kind of thing."[374] This attitude is almost identical to that of the French DOP officer at the Villa Susini in Algeria discussed earlier in this chapter. Generally, those who do the torturing know their task is mainly to deter, intimidate, and punish, and they acknowledge this purpose more easily than their superiors.

GSS interrogators also confirm that noncombat military units also torture. "If a detainee dies from beating, then there is a reasonable chance that it was not during the GSS interrogations. A detainee goes through a lot of stations before reaching the 'interrogation cellars' of the GSS. He passes through the hands of non-combat units who have no more than the usual animal standard of kitchen and storeroom staff. They'll kill me for what I'm saying, but I mean it."[375]

Prisoners describe interrogation rooms as highly coercive environments "from which there is no escape until the interrogation ends."[376] Prime Minister Yitzhak Rabin confirmed, for example, that during the first Intifada, about eight thousand people were subjected to al-Hazz, or violent shaking.[377] In one survey of 477 prisoners, the vast majority describe being beaten (95.8 percent), forced to stand (92.9 percent), deprived of sleep (71 percent), or subjected to intense noise (71 percent), extremes of cold (92.9 percent), and heat (76.7 percent); pressure to the neck (68.1 percent); genital squeezing (66 percent); irritant gas (13.4 percent); instruments in penis or rectum (11.1 percent); and electroshock (5.9 percent). Most prisoners in this survey served less than five years, indicating they were convicted for "simple" crimes.[378] Another survey of 708 individuals (369 on the West Bank and 339 on the Gaza Strip) could not correlate the kind of torture with the seriousness of charges. Overall, 85 percent of prisoners arrested and 94 percent of those interrogated were subjected to various tortures.[379]

Those handed over for trial are usually convicted. Israel's military courts have a conviction rate of 96.8 percent in all cases, and the main evidence is usually a full confession by the accused. These numbers would be the envy of American and European prosecutors. This figure even tops Japanese confession rates (86 percent) and is similar to those found in Japan during and before World War II.[380]

False confessions are inevitable in contexts like these.[381] Some Palestinian prisoners confess to crimes they have not committed and, in this way, record their personal trauma or affirm their resistance. "Some are imaginary heroes, but they get sentenced for their imaginations."[382] But given the scale of the violence, torture no doubt generates many false confessions as well. The remaining difficulty is parsing out how often prisoners confess falsely, whether they confessed semivoluntarily or were coerced, and if so, whether by psychological or physical means.

Summing up the annual prisoner tallies, Lisa Hajjar estimates that Israeli military courts have prosecuted close to half a million Palestinians since 1967.[383] During the first Intifada, Israel had the highest rate of incarceration in the world.[384] Perhaps there are thousands of suicide bombers among these prisoners, but it seems more likely that torture in most cases was about routine intimidation and false confession, purposes for which it is well suited. The scale is greater, but the purpose of torture does not differ significantly from policing operations in other countries.

Some GSS interrogators and officials argue that torture regularly produced accurate information to stop "ticking bombs."[385] But in cases in which the GSS justified the arrest of named individuals as imminent "ticking bombs," interrogators routinely went home for the weekends and evenings, behavior that cannot be easily squared with claims that time was critical.[386] Other cases were ones "when we thought mistakenly that someone was a bomb."[387]

In 2001, a member of the Knesset asked the Israeli justice minister, in light of the High Court's ruling on torture, how many GSS petitions he had received indicating a "necessity defense" for violating interrogation rules in the previous two years. The minister replied that the attorney general had received none.[388] In January 2002, Alan Dershowitz claimed that the GSS had prevented "several attacks" through coerced interrogation, but, like so many others, he fails to identify any specific instances.[389] All this leaves two possibilities, neither reassuring for democrats. Either the GSS believed no one will ever prosecute its interrogators for violations and so could act with impunity despite the law, or the GSS regarded the cases of the previous two years, including the first nine months of the second Intifada, as routine violence, violence neither urgent nor easy to justify.

It took the GSS decades before it identified the first case remotely resembling a ticking time bomb, the case of Nasim Za'atari in 2003.[390] Za'atari was a Jerusalem resident who scouted potential targets for Hamas; he then disguised bombers and guided them to their targets. The case was a revelation, even though the government statement did not specify whether Za'atari's confession was coerced.[391] By 2005, the Justice Ministry routinely cited this case to silence its critics. Before that, "No known case like this has been recorded in Israel's history" and no new cases have been cited since.[392]

Standard government rhetoric now expands the notion of ticking time bomb to include not just specific individuals performing acts of terrorism, but anyone perceived to be associated with terrorism. "A ceasefire is a ticking bomb," observed an Israeli Foreign Ministry spokesman, as is the president of Iran.[393] In 1999, General 'Ali 'Issa, head of Lebanon's security services, used such Israeli statements to justify torturing an Israeli fighter pilot on the grounds that he had tactical military knowledge. When the pilot objected that he would be tortured anyways, the general replied, "You are absolutely right.. . . But now we do it with their [Israeli] approval. You are a ticking bomb, and your country permits us to torture you."[394] When the phrase "ticking time bomb" applies to anyone in war or peace, emergency or not, the phrase has become meaningless.

Remembering Abu Ghraib

After assuming command of Abu Ghraib, General Miller claimed that high-value intelligence increased by 50 percent once torture was abandoned.[395] Perhaps. General Miller always seems to make the politically correct statement at the proper time.[396] But the damage had been done. One Iraqi policeman who had been tortured mistakenly did not blame the Americans for arresting and torturing him, but "he trembles now when he sees a Humvee and he no longer trusts or works with the Americans."[397]

Whoever authorized torture in Iraq and elsewhere undermined the prospect of good human intelligence. Even if the torture produced more names ("actionable intelligence"), it also polarized the population, eliminating the middle that might cooperate. As we divided the world into "friends" and "enemies," we also alienated those who wished to be neither but hated our enemies just as much as we did.

The French have a plan. It succeeds tactically, but fails strategically.
To understand why, come to a rare showing of this film.

> —Flyer advertising the movie *The Battle of Algiers*, from
> the Directorate for Special Operations and Low
> Intensity Conflict, the Pentagon, September 2003[1]

23   Why Governments Don't Learn

In 1972, an RUC policeman threatened a prisoner with a technique that had "never failed yet." His magic technique was to set fire to a twig, blow it out, and stick it up the prisoner's nostrils five or six times. However, the prisoner said nothing under this torture and was released shortly thereafter.[2] But the policeman was unlikely to be daunted by this failure. As the previous chapters have suggested, torturers persist in using techniques even in the face of repeated failure. Because the policeman firmly *believed* the technique never failed, he was just as likely to try using the same trick the next day on another prisoner.

When officers resort to playing Metallica and lighting twigs, when the Pentagon watches Marxist-nationalist movies to understand how torture and terrorism work—one has to ask: why is it that governments never seem to learn or, at least, remember past failures? Why do many governments keep torturing for information? Or as Chris Mackey, the U.S. interrogator in Afghanistan, asks, "If coercion doesn't work, why would the agency [CIA] go to the trouble?"[3]

In these final chapters, I consider why we do not learn from past experience when it comes to torture. In this chapter, I consider failures in institutional learning: how knowledge does not accumulate and how it is neglected when it does. Next, I consider if institutions would learn better if governments legally regulated torture and subjected it to routine evaluation. But fortunately or unfortunately, the same factors that inhibit institutional learning about torture also make its public supervision impossibly difficult.

The best way to learn is to care for our memories of the past properly. As Alan Dershowitz rightly says in his introduction to the army report on the My Lai massacre in Vietnam, "We neither taught nor learned a lesson from the disaster of My Lai, and those who do not understand the lessons of the past are destined to repeat them."[4] In the following chapter, I consider how memories of the twentieth century powerfully shape our understanding of torture. These memories are often misleading, leading to false claims about modern torture's efficacy, as well as about its historical origins.

How Knowledge Does Not Accumulate

Several factors inhibit the accumulation of knowledge about torture: the informal way torture techniques are taught, the narrow professionalism of torturers, the competitiveness among interrogators, and operational flexibility in counterinsurgency warfare.

Militaries do learn from their mistakes in battle. They assess tactical and strategic mistakes, and then teach these lessons to officers and soldiers in the field. One would think similar learning would take place about torture, but it does not. Soldiers learn about torture not in schools, but through backroom apprenticeships. Backroom apprenticeship proves to be a very powerful method of education, gradually transforming torture techniques in the course of a century. This method of transmission is difficult to detect, a quality torturers value in an age of increased international scrutiny of human rights abuses. By the same token, torturers do not have the opportunity to evaluate their procedures objectively because so much training goes on in the dark. Torture is a craft that combines hundreds of discrete instruments and procedures, each with its own champions. Torturers learn each technique by imitation, custom, rumor, and accident. It is not surprising, then, that policemen attach magical properties to techniques even in the face of a record of failure ("a stick up the nose always works") and soldiers describe their fantasies as fact ("the Gestapo really knew how to torture").

Competitiveness also inhibits the accumulation of knowledge. Torturers do not give away their trade secrets to their rival interrogators. They resist when superiors begin to evaluate their alleged successes. Being narrow professionals, they demand autonomy to get the job done right.

Military promotions focus on battlefield successes with ordinary troops. Junior officers have little incentive to learn about interrogation, much less excel at it. This is a job usually assigned to specialized agencies. So when officers need information urgently, they adopt haphazard and juvenile approaches to interrogation.[5]

Counterinsurgency warfare also fragments knowledge. As units are more autonomous in this style of warfare, information is not pooled. Here, a French captain in Algeria pacifies a zone without torture, using informers and public cooperation combined with selective violence.[6] There, a French captain claims he had to torture. Under these conditions, soldiers easily misperceive what the group norm is and act accordingly.

Often the immediate and the local trump previous training and comprehensive analysis. Too often soldiers and policemen seem to engage in a version of the "drunkard's search." The drunkard staggers around under the spotlight looking hopelessly for his lost car keys. He should methodically search the dark path from the bar, but that is beyond his condition. He is drawn to the spotlight, the least likely place, because it is the only place he can search in his condition.

So, too, soldiers and policemen evaluate options during crises in the dark; they are drawn to the bright lights, to the dramatic but often fictional stories of torture's success. They ignore army manuals that caution against torture or well-grounded studies of what works in policing. When torture does not prove to be the key to success, they grumble that they would have succeeded had their organization been more supportive and given them more authority and had officers acted promptly on the good intelligence they delivered. Like the drunkard, they seem unaware that their failure followed from their muddled thinking.

How Knowledge Is Not Analyzed

If torture training was highly centralized, as critics like Noam Chomsky believe, institutions might know more about torture. For example, the CIA operatives who entered the information in the Phoenix Program database also recorded what they considered to be a baseline for accurate information. This allows one to determine how badly the program functioned by its own standards. Similarly, eventually scholars of the Franco-Algerian War will analyze Teitgin's twenty-four thousand arrest warrants, warrants that almost inevitably led to torture. They will compare what police thought they were doing against the previous history of those individuals.

In these cases, governments impeded research by classifying documents. Sadly, examples like the Phoenix Program, Teitgin's records, or the British arrest records for 1971–72 are few and normally see the light of public reason only after decades of secrecy. Full access to the French Algerian archives will probably take several more decades. And governments rarely assess torture programs publicly. The British government's report on interrogation in Northern Ireland in 1972 is a rare exception. Misleading as it is, the Parker Commission did try to measure the program's effectiveness in something other than generalities. Even here, though, researchers had to assess official claims without access to the data.

There may be secret, thorough reports of torture's effectiveness, but historians have yet to uncover them for any government. Those who believe in torture's effectiveness seem to need no proof and prefer to leave no reports. The secret documents historians do find, for example, the CIA's *Kubark* and *Human Resources Exploitation Training* manuals, suggest that government researchers do not do archival research to assess torture's effectiveness; instead they footnote public research. The blind, thus, lead the blind: scholars cannot access classified documents, and governments read scholars instead of analyzing their own data.

Governments also pillory human rights organizations for any mistake in their research, impugning the organization's credibility as a whole. Most organizations are understaffed, and lawyers are poor social scientists. Some hold that torture works, stipulating as truth what they cannot research, but claim it is irrelevant. For example, Manfred Nowak, the current UN special rapporteur on torture, holds that torture works, but values are more important. Common sense tells us, he says, that governments can verify intelligence information gathered under torture.[7] Values no doubt have their place, but making a virtue of one's ignorance has a great price. Government officials prefer a division of labor in which critics grow indignant and talk while they portray themselves as responsible people who know and do.

Occasionally some government officials leak information and some researchers find ways to get around government secrecy by meticulously reconstructing events or through statistically sophisticated indirect measurements. This evidence has long suggested that torture does not work as apologists claim, but the material has been scattered across several specialized disciplines. Policy debates have often passed over these studies, focusing instead on personal testimonials and historical cases. "The Battle of Algiers" and "the Gestapo" do not stand for careful studies of torture, weighing its merits against other police methods based on archival materials. They stand for memories and stories. Few people, for example, remember the important role Godard's *blues* played in the Battle of Algiers. They do not have big parts in the movie.

Violence is a complex phenomenon, not particularly amenable to truisms. Violence does not always breed more violence; sometimes it leads to less. To grasp what does or does not work, one has to descend into the details. Suppose in such and such a case torture failed. Did it fail because of its features or because *any* method of gathering information would have failed? In the Battle of Algiers, informants succeeded far more than torturers did in gaining the critical information, so the problem lies with torture. But one is fortunate so much information exists about the battle.

Such comparative information is not always available, and cases often lack clear baselines, making it difficult to judge what the cause of failure was. More commonly, one person lists successful counterinsurgency campaigns that used torture, while another lists a string of failed campaigns, a list that is usually considerably longer.[8] Rarely do debaters contend using identical examples.

How Torture Warrants Might Help

If governments gave more access to police and military archives, scholars would know more about how torture for information worked in Vietnam, Israel, Northern Ireland, and other conflicts. Studying modern torture would be like studying classical torture. By studying ancient documents similar to torture warrants, historians have documented the rates of coerced confession in early modern France, and they know that torture led to few confessions, true or false. Why not regulate modern torture for information and find out how well it works?

This is the best argument for getting legal warrants for torture. Alan Dershowitz first proposed the notion of torture warrants, but he has since been distracted by his argument against modern political hypocrisy.[9] Like other apologists, Dershowitz seems driven by a deep impatience with those who look the other way as someone else does the necessary dirty deed that works.[10] He seems to hold the view that torture is a necessarily evil, a tragic choice, the least bad choice among horrible choices, or a not unacceptable option considering the circumstances.[11] And he has spent much time vigorously defending this delicate wordsmithing from the widespread criticism he has garnered.[12]

If one wants to chastise the hypocrisy of others as one argues for torture warrants, then one has to prove that torture works.[13] But, logically, defending torture warrants does not depend on praising one's own moral clear-sightedness or defending the notion that torture works. Some governments *will* torture because they *believe* torture works better than anything else for getting information in some circumstances. If torture really doesn't work, then studying the torture warrant archives would show that. Warrants would require police to state their intent in torture. By stripping the secrecy from government torture, one can assess properly rates of failure. If it does not work, governments will stop torturing.

Torture warrants will also help answer another outstanding research question: how does torture affect interrogators? Torturers are hard to locate, dangerous to find, and even more difficult to interview. Researchers have interviewed small groups, but not large populations. They have also studied police working undercover as criminals; this work, though nowhere near as extreme, appears to have similar psychological and social consequences as torturing.[14] But creating torture warrants would necessarily require creating a large class of professionals who tortured, and this would be a unique opportunity to learn what torture does to interrogators directly.

So far, researchers know that torture traumatizes perpetrators "by inducing toxic levels of guilt and shame."[15] Why some have these feelings and others not is unclear, but some cases indicate that one's vulnerability is not within one's conscious control.

Frantz Fanon, for example, treated French torturers among his patients during the Algerian war. One policeman suffered from nightmares, extreme irritability, and intolerance to noise. Working up to ten hours each day torturing suspects, he grew impatient with his children, striking even his baby of twenty months with "unaccustomed savagery." He consulted a doctor only after he set upon torturing his wife one night. He knew quite well he suffered from spillover effects from his job, but he did not want to cease torturing, so he asked Fanon to show him how to continue torturing without the unfortunate side-effects.[16] In another case, a policeman was generally in good spirits during sessions until one day, Fanon found him trembling, sweating, and overcome with anxiety on the sidewalk. He had encountered one of his old victims in the hospital hallway. The policeman developed depression while orderlies found the victim in the hospital bathroom trying to commit suicide.[17]

Researchers speculate that when torturers act consistently with their moral or religious beliefs, they may escape torture unscathed. The Israeli interrogators who described their GSS days "as the best years of their life" and the Brazilian torturers who dehumanized their victims may never suffer from post-traumatic stress disorder (PTSD).[18] But the French cases suggest that whether they do or not is not something in their conscious control. A torturer's work apparently never ends; memories of applying extreme pain to others tick like a time bomb.

Setting aside PTSD, torturers are more vulnerable to job burnout than other violence workers. In a comparison of Brazilian torturers and killers, researchers found that the least burned out were those who facilitated violence, but did not actually perform it.[19] Rank-and-file cops were more burned out than those who simply ordered the violence, and torturers were more exhausted than killers. Putting a bullet in the head appears to be an easier occupation than questioning subjects daily.[20] Generally, torturers suffered from insomnia, hypersensitivity, nervousness, emotional problems, alcoholism, and potential suicidal behavior.[21] Some had resigned and others had burned out. Keeping their work lives secret deprived them of the support of friends and family, while their supervisors, who did none of the violence, drew richly on their support network. While the supervisors took pride in their work, the real torturers said the military brass had betrayed them and hung them out to twist in the wind. "We are society's toilet paper."[22]

Psychological studies of Greek torturers found a similar spread of disorders. Some torturers did not report stress or burnout.[23] Others had serious adjustment problems, including depression, anxiety, and stress, when they left the military context that supported their activities.[24] They were burdened by their secret history, fearing the hostility and isolation they experienced when they revealed their double life. One had constant nightmares, would wake up screaming from his sleep, and often wept in public, crying on one occasion, "What am I, a beast?"[25] One displayed maladaptive social behavior even after years of civilian life; indeed, he was accused of organizing the theft of funds at the company where he was employed.[26]

Anecdotal evidence from other conflicts suggests that other interrogators feel deeply betrayed. The French Paras never forgave Massu and the generals who sacrificed them.[27] Even today, psychologists working with DOP soldiers describe them as "spiritually wounded men, often ravaged by the weight of their guilt and shame."[28] As one Para who tortured put it recently, he will carry "the stain with him for the rest of his life"; others become "sociopaths with little regard for human life."[29] The Chilean air force and navy did not accept those "stained" (*manchado*) with torture back into the ranks because they judged these men lacked discipline and ethical values.[30] Uruguayan torturers were depressed and isolated once they left the occupational networks that supported their work.[31]

To be sure, many soldiers who do not torture also feel betrayed after wars, and the indifference to those who practice violence is probably quite old. As the weary voice of Ecclesiastes warned centuries ago: "I saw all the oppressions that are practiced under the sun. And behold, the tears of the oppressed, and they had no one to comfort them! On the side of their oppressors there was power, and there was no one to comfort them" (Eccles. 4:1). Presumably if one aims to regulate torture, one would also have to learn how to provide comfort and support to those doing society's dirty work. After wars, governments assist veterans associations and citizens organize ways to help veterans ease back into civilian life.

But as far as I know, no one, not even the philosophers, lawyers, and journalists who have justified torture in the name of national security, have ever organized, much less advocated, a Society for the Reintegration of Torturers. In these actions, even apologists reveal how much they share society's judgment that he who tortures is far beyond the pale, in the same company as cannibals. Although torturers may have performed something necessary and even justified at the time, they have also performed something monstrous, become walking abominations, and no integration can remove this stain. No one on the face of the planet wants to share their company, not even those who urged them forward.[32] Torture apologists accept the moral and psychological destruction of torturers as a necessity in crises, but they hardly think about them afterward. No doubt, many a soldier who has been urged to torture would find George Orwell's remarks about war all too apt: "One of the most horrible features of war is that all the war-propaganda, all the screaming and lies and hatred, comes invariably from people who are not fighting. . . . It is the same in all wars; the soldiers do the fighting, the journalists do the shouting, and no true patriot ever gets near a front-line trench."[33]

Lastly, social scientists have an even poorer understanding of how torture affects secondary bystanders. Establishing a class of professional torturers would allow social scientists to examine how torture affects their families and assistants. Fanon's study of a torturer's daughter indicated that she developed severe anxieties by her twenties. She spoke of her father's death with a lightheartedness that masked insensitivity to others.[34] Similarly, American advisers working in Turkey report that secretaries became traumatized typing up interrogation transcripts.[35] In these cases, torture is the gift that keeps on giving, shifting its effects from person to family and friends, from generation to generation. In this respect, torture appears to resemble some forms of domestic violence such as spousal battery and incest. But whether the cases above are common is anyone's guess.

Regulating Torture

The evidence so far is that torture does not work and often destroys interrogators and their families, but perhaps we are mistaken in our assessment. It would be hard to oppose torture warrants that would clearly confirm or reject these long-standing suspicions. Still, it might help to review what scholars know about the history of regulating torture before embracing the modest proposal of legalized torture warrants.

While it is not a large sample, the record indicates that governments regulate torture poorly. Once governments have the right to torture, officials have little professional incentive to check results. Professional torturers colonize bureaucratic, judicial, and legislative bodies designated to supervise them, making oversight difficult. And the populations liable to be tortured, however narrowly defined at first, grow over time.[36]

Greece and Rome

The Greeks and the Romans regulated torture by attaching it to the person, not the act. Rather than justify torture on the grounds that a crime was in progress, they justified torture on the notion that there were two kinds of people, one of which could never be tortured regardless of the crime. Slaves could be tortured, but citizens could not. The Romans extended the class that could be tortured to lower-end citizens, the *humiliores*, and in time, the emperors did not care about anyone's civic immunity.

The ancient regulation of torture involved a fairly strict belief in civic immunity, and through it, Greeks and Romans successfully regulated torture without putting their democratic life at risk for decades, even centuries. Moderns generally do not share the chauvinistic assumptions that Greek and Roman citizens had about their own superiority. Torture apologists would justify torture of citizens if necessity required it. It is unlikely they would embrace the Greek model of torture; they are more concerned about acts like terrorism, not civic immunity.

Early Modern Europe

Many authoritarian systems regarded torture as a suitable technique to gather information about criminal acts. Torture was legal and documented, but government officials did not generally *ask* whether torture produced accurate outcomes; they *knew* it. An interesting exception was witch hunting during the Spanish Inquisition. Inquisitors disciplined colleagues who tortured looking for witches, arguing there was little evidence of the existence of witches, and most confessions to pacts with the Devil were delusions. For example, Alonso de Salazar Frias, the Navarrese Inquisitor and a careful, scrupulous lawyer, reviewed thousands of witchcraft cases after an upsurge of witch executions on the French frontier between 1609 and 1610. He concluded, "I have not found the slightest evidence from which to infer that a single act of witchcraft has really occurred."[37]

Strongly centralized legal systems, like the Spanish and the English, were far better at checking coerced confessions for witchcraft than those that left local officials less supervised, as in France, Scotland, and the Spanish Netherlands.[38] Central authorities suspected the personal motives of regional elites who hunted witches. They were far less restrained when it came to secret fifth columns, Jesuits (in England), and secret Judaism and Islam (in Spain), and they knew how to use paranoia to mobilize a population to support the state. Spanish Inquisitors may sound almost like social scientists when they came to witches, but they did not think twice in the hunt for heretics.

Historians have recorded 81 cases of official torture in England between 1540 and 1604, and 785 official cases in France between 1500 and mid-1700s.[39] So Dershowitz claims that "there was far more torture in Medieval France than England because in France the practice was left to the discretion of local officials, whereas in England it required an extraordinary warrant, which was rarely granted."[40] Dershowitz hypothesizes that torture in "a formal, visible, accountable and centralized system is somewhat easier to control than an ad hoc, off-the-books, and under-the-radar-screen nonsystem."[41]

On the contrary, a strongly centralized system of legally regulated torture, which did not leave things to local officials, never held back the Spanish state. And torture would have been rare in the English system in *any* case, and would always have required considerable justification, whether there were warrants or not. After the 1140s, the English state gave greater responsibility to juries in determining outcomes, had no place for a state prosecutor, gave the judge a different role, and had broader rules of evidence. Circumstantial evidence could pile up until a jury found it convincing, whereas a continental judge could not find the defendant guilty until the prosecutorial system, including torture, played out to the end. Whereas on the Continent legally regulated torture made the resort to it common, "torture did not have a place in the law of England after 1166," writes Edward Peters, the noted expert on medieval torture. "The reforms of Henry II gave a procedure to the law of England that eliminated the use of torture in the very centuries in which continental legal reforms were drawing closer and closer to it."[42]

The emergence of our common-law system, not torture warrants, proved to be the bulwark against torture, leading to its steady elimination over time. As John Langbein, the modern expert on English torture, remarks, "The jury standard of proof gave England no cause to torture," and England "also developed no institutions to conduct torture."[43] The process complemented the procedures: "The English had no one to operate the torture chamber that they did not need." Contrary to Dershowitz, who selectively cites Langbein's research, Langbein writes, "What the English did not do was to regularize the use of torture in their criminal proceedings."[44]

Democratic oversight proved far more helpless in holding torturers accountable than a common-law system with its jury system of proof. The republican Italian city-states, like the Spanish and French monarchies, had a continental legal system that authorized torture. These democrats limited torture to a narrower range of crimes than the larger monarchies.[45] They discovered that, even in peacetime nonemergency conditions, executive officers used torture against innocent, decent citizens. Against certain grave accusations, there was no immunity. In the end, the *podestas* who tortured took over the republics.

Modern European States

Authoritarian states that legally regulated torture for information, not confession, also proved to be poor at it. In 1937, for example, the Gestapo agreed with the Justice Ministry to regulate procedures for "sharpened interrogation." Regulations required authorizations and even a form, of which a copy has survived. As torture was not a secret, one might expect to find documentary records, given how meticulously German bureaucrats worked. Records of the

Gestapo at Würtzburg, for example, show that officers documented public accusations and investigated them meticulously, finding many false ones. They also conducted interrogations, including, one assumes, sharpened ones. But if officers filled out forms for torture, there is no record of it there or, for that matter, anywhere else in Europe. And there is little evidence that officers limited torture interrogations to the classes of suspects Gestapo chief Müller stated could be tortured.

Democracies do not seem to have done a better job regulating torture either for information or for confession. In the Battle of Algiers, Teitgin's records show the alarming rate at which arrests speeded up as the battle proceeded until they peaked at four thousand a month for several months. Judges, doctors, and police prefects would not or could not hold back the demand from the Paras for arrests that led to torture. This is evidence enough that civil servants cannot exercise selective control once they have licensed armed men to exercise unlimited power over individuals. Successful torture turned out to be a wholesale operation, not a retail business.

The appeal of legalizing torture, like legalizing abortion, is that it makes rogue operations rare. Governments will "reduce and limit the amount of torture,"[46] and scholars could learn whether it really works. Cases like these suggest that legalizing torture makes rogue operations inevitable, and one is likely to learn even less. A professional torturer from Honduras, for example, could not understand why his CIA handlers insisted on his obtaining legal warrants before he interrogated and tortured prisoners. "Guerillas don't wait there with a pen to sign a judicial order. Our commander ordered us to kill them. We hid people from the Americans, interrogated them, then gave them to a death squad to kill."[47]

"Want to torture? Get a warrant," may sound like wise advice.[48] To interrogators, it sounds like a quaint practice to be avoided whenever possible. The Gestapo, which came closest to routinizing torture for information with paperwork, did not bother, and everywhere torturers push the institutionally prescribed limits on physical techniques. No matter how lax the rules governing torture are, a professional always insists that if he had greater power to arrest and cause pain, he would have gotten results sooner. Reading decrypted computer files, as in the Murad case, would not be on his agenda.

Variations in Regulative Failure

The limited evidence available suggests an additional point: torture for information appears more difficult to regulate than torture for confession. While both appear to lead down the slippery slope, the slope is steeper and slicker when torturers are seeking prospective information rather than confessions for crimes that already occurred.

Slippery slope arguments are contentious, and one must carefully distinguish between empirical and logical versions.[49] Logical versions are notorious fallacies. Typically, they hold that individuals slide down the slope because they cannot distinguish logically between a bad deed, the next worse deed, and the next worse until finally they slide into the abyss. In fact, most people understand that small shifts can accumulate to have terrible outcomes. And most police and soldiers can distinguish between approved and unapproved techniques, or coercive and uncoerced interrogation.

Nevertheless, police and soldiers do cross these lines, and the question is why. So far as analysts can tell, it is not because organizations recruit sadists to be torturers. What appears to happen is that ordinary individuals move from minor violations to the abyss through errors in judgment. Three factors cause these errors: ambiguous background context, desire to agree with the group, and confused self-understandings.

In the case of torture regulation, there appear to be at least three different slippery slopes. First, torturers go beyond the specified suspects to torture individuals not normally tortured. Second, torturers go beyond the approved techniques to a broader range of brutalities. Third, torturers break away from the bureaucratic oversight, creating their own semiautonomous organizations.

Going beyond the Specified Suspects

Regulated torture seems to increase in scope, incorporating ever more individuals (*humiliores*, not just slaves; good citizens, not just those of bad reputation; witnesses and relatives, not just suspects). The context in which torture occurs seems to play an important role in determining how sharp the slope is.

War conditions, for example, blur boundaries for soldiers; human beings do not come with labels "friend" and "enemy." Safety dictates assuming they are "enemy," and not surprisingly, the scope of torture for information in war rapidly expands, incorporating large numbers of innocents.

By contrast, most regulated confessional torture occurred against a stable background of peacetime chauvinism and racism, and authorities had an easier time keeping the scope of torture limited. Greeks and Romans knew who were citizens and who were slaves. In the Italian city-states, everyone knew who the families of bad reputation were; they were sometimes listed by name in the law books. Conditions of public hysteria made it more difficult to control torture. For example, in the great European witch hunts, local authorities arrested more individuals on charges of witchcraft that even Spanish Inquisitors would allow. During public paranoia, as in war, safety also requires assuming individuals are enemies first.

Going beyond Approved Torture Methods

Torture slopes toward greater brutality, but this slope varies. In confessional torture, torturers can take their time, slowly terrifying their victims. They have made the accusation; all that is required is the admission.

In torture for information, one is trying to prevent an imminent attack or save a threatened life. Time matters, and interrogators reach for what is rumored to have worked before regardless of whether it is approved. They will push the envelope wherever they can, trying to match the individual's pain threshold before it slips out of reach. The slope toward greater brutality is far sharper, particularly in the first forty-eight hours, when the information might be most valid. Anyone who thinks interrogators will obediently limit themselves to sterilized needles under the prisoner's nails displays a staggering naïveté about the dynamics of torture. Dershowitz, in particular, favors this showy suggestion,[50] but I know of no example of torture in the twentieth century, in peacetime or wartime, in which needles alone played a role in eliciting information, accurate or otherwise. It always takes a lot more.

Seeking Power as a Professional Class

The Catholic Church's Inquisitors, uniquely among torturers in Europe, became a power unto themselves. Once the pope gave them the power to absolve each other of their sins, the Inquisitors no longer needed secular torturers and often acted without approval of local bishops.[51] But beyond this, torturers in European confessional systems did not seek more power for themselves as a professional class. Some secular authorities, of course, used torturers to reinforce their own authority. In Italian city-states, *podestas* shored up their executive power this way, leading to the end of republicanism. And regional authorities in France, Scotland, and Spain expressed their autonomy from the state by exercising torture.

But where states have regulated torture for information, units that tortured commonly became political forces in their own right. Such factors as deskilling, competitive brutality, and narrow professionalism led to parallel systems of administration, creating states within states. This phenomenon occurred whether the practice was approved explicitly (the Gestapo, the French in Algeria) or tacitly (the Brazilian military, American counterinsurgency in Central America).

Torture in the context of counterinsurgency may be an especially toxic combination. Counterinsurgency units take pride in their ability to beat out competitive units, garner more praise from central authorities, and win more field autonomy for operations, especially in forward bases. Once they torture, they rapidly slide toward disaster.

Torture for information, then, has a steeper slope than confessional torture because it often occurs in fuzzy contexts, where groups are relatively autonomous, and when time is short. Regulating torture under these conditions is unlikely. English torture warrants, by contrast, were for judicial confessions, and it is not surprising that slope was less severe.

This bears directly on using torture warrants, since these warrants are to be used exclusively for gathering information.[52] Indeed, even some who endorse selective torture in emergencies understand that *regulating* torture for information is a fool's dream. Mark Bowden, for example, holds that "when the ban is lifted, there is no restraining lazy, incompetent or sadistic interrogators."[53] The results Abu Ghraib were inevitable in this respect. "When a prison, an army, or a government tacitly approves coercive measures as a matter of course, widespread and indefensible human-rights abuses become inevitable." This, he argues "is what happened in Israel, where a newly introduced regime of officially sanctioned 'aggressive interrogation' quickly deteriorated into a system of routine physical abuse."[54]

By contrast, Dershowitz maintains that his proposal of torture warrants would "maximize civil liberties"[55] and that, if it was in place, it would have prevented torture at Abu Ghraib,[56] Occasionally he also claims to find yet another example of torture working in the War on Terror.[57] But no one should be too concerned about these claims. On empirical matters pertaining to torture, Dershowitz's record has been worse than poor, and his work is typical in that respect. Indeed, whenever apologists claim empirical insight, everyone should simply ask them repeatedly for the evidence, check the sources, and then double-check the claim with other sources. Nothing apologists have advanced so far has withstood the light of day.

Stealth and the Regulation of Torture

Regulating torture will be more difficult in the twenty-first century. It is unlikely torturers will forget all the clean practices that helped them evade public scrutiny in this century. Indeed, governments may still prefer these to reduce public concern about torture.[58] Catching rule violations will be harder whether torture is legal and expected or whether it is forbidden.

Bowden, for example, believes that torture should remain illegal, but soldiers should do it when it is morally necessary and then submit to public trial. If the soldier was mistaken, he should be punished. If he was right, courts should let him go. In effect, Bowden proposes a balance of torture and risk. You might be right, but if you are wrong, your career is over. This would discourage lazy, incompetent interrogators, but protect the principled interrogator.[59] Morally justified torture thus resembles morally justified civil disobedience. Civil rights protesters break the law publicly and then submit their behavior to courts, and conscientious juries would release them too.

Stealth torture, though, undermines the balance of risk that Bowden proposes. Modern torturers specialize in techniques that leave no marks, and these torturers are at little risk of being "outed" if they are careful. And once torturers get away with clean practices, they tend to repeat them. This is the lesson of the Chicago torture scandals.

Moreover, I know of no modern professional torturer who voluntarily submitted to public scrutiny and took the heat. The historical record is that torturers come unwillingly and even then, rarely admit too much. When, for example, on the rare occasion French judges demanded Paras appear in court in Algeria, they said nothing to implicate themselves in torture, doctors often failed to find marks, and the courts regularly exonerated them.[60] And in practice there was no difference between the flak jacket philosophizing of the French Paras, so reminiscent of Bowden's argument, and government-approved torture, tacit or otherwise, in which close to twenty thousand were tortured in just one city in just one year. Perhaps there are soldiers like those Bowden describes in his stories, honorable men who just "torture a little" in an emergency and then take the consequences. But the sad reality is that like boasts of bravery, Bowden's opinion is too easy to hold when one faces little danger one's honor will be tested.

How Knowledge Does Not Matter

Governments may persist in torturing for information even when they know torture for information does not work. Not all problems of government are problems of knowledge. The notion that governments will stop when they know something does not work assumes a rationality that is all too often lacking. Sometimes officials find it expedient to torture regardless of what they know.

In the late 1950s, Paul Teitgin, the prefect of Algiers, caught Fernand Yveton, a Communist placing a bomb in the gasworks. Teitgin knew Yveton had a second bomb, and if Yveton had planted and exploded it, it would set off gasometers, killing thousands. Teitgin could not persuade Yveton to tell him where the other bomb was. Nevertheless, said Teitgin, "I refused to have him tortured. I trembled the whole afternoon. Finally the bomb did not go off. Thank God I was right."[61]

One can imagine what would have happened to Teitgin's career if the bomb had gone off. "You knew? You had the opportunity, and still you did nothing?" It would have done Teitgin no good to explain that torture produces false leads and wasted resources, that it damages police professionalism and integrity, or that Yveton might say nothing despite torture. Nor would it have helped Teitgin to say that he had started searches, authorized electronic surveillance, squeezed his informers, and interviewed all Yveton's associates.

In such a circumstance, Teitgin could have been much more reassuring if he had tortured Yveton *even though he knew torture did not work.* Teitgin could have said, "Well, I was doing something, I *even* had him tortured. Perhaps I should have tortured harder." Defending one's job against angry critics gives one powerful incentives to persist in torturing even if one knows it is ineffective. Torturing proves one is tough and resolute, willing to risk one's own soul for the public, even when everything seems hopeless.

Few can deny the power of doing "anything" under hopeless circumstances. But torture is not just anything. In practice, hiring torturers may be as helpful as hiring psychics in an emergency, another expertise police and CIA also use and with occasional success, according to testimonials.[62] But the terrorist's suffering is uniquely satisfying regardless of whether he reveals any information. Beneath the urbane, civilized appeal to torture for information, lurks a deeper impulse, born from fear and satisfied by pain.

When a public official is prepared to spill the blood of a detained, helpless individual, breaking bonds of law and morality, this appears to satisfy a debt incurred by the violence of a terrorist. For example, in September 1956, the newly appointed prefect of Oran, Pierre Lambert, directed a paramilitary unit to arrest forty individuals, the majority of European origin, including one pregnant woman. All were sympathizers or members of various leftist parties. Most were tortured, and torture in Oran was not a subtle operation. Prisoners were beaten, electrified in the body, throat, and sexual organs, showered with cold water, slapped heavily, and choked in a tub.[63] Only one prisoner confessed, but she insists that what information she gave was false and misleading.[64]

Critics assailed Lambert, particularly for torturing Europeans. In response, Lambert described a young Algerian grenade thrower who had caused numerous deaths. "This young Muslim was a little shaken by police, he talked, the grenades were seized, terrorists were arrested and the series of attacks stopped."[65]

Everyone knows Lambert's story now as the "ticking time bomb" story.[66] But the details of this miraculous case have been harder to find and ascertain. This young man's identity is never mentioned. Maybe he existed, maybe he did not. Maybe he spoke and spoke truly, maybe he did not. But it does not matter. What mattered was that the blood debt was satisfied. In Oran, the public did not look too closely at who actually paid this price, even if victims included many innocents.

When zealous public officials torture for information, it may look like they are responding rationally to ineffectiveness. But it is difficult to understand why *this* response (as opposed to so many others) is so satisfying without acknowledging that officials are also purging the wounded community's furious emotions with human sacrifices. As one active CIA officer observed in 2005, "The larger problem [with torture] here, I think, is that this kind of stuff just makes people feel better, even if it doesn't work."[67]

We will never know how common this motive is, for no public official in these times can admit to it, but, to use Machiavelli's words, resorting to human sacrifice is a prudent political practice that leaves observers "stunned and satisfied."[68] Strategic talk about torture in the face of terrorism turns out to have a deep undercurrent of blood lust. As Friedrich Nietzsche cautions, "It is a self-deception on the part of philosophers and moralists to imagine that by making war on decadence they therewith elude decadence themselves. This is beyond their powers: What they select as an expedient, as a deliverance, is itself only another expression of decadence—they alter its expression, they do not abolish the thing itself."[69]

Remembering the Soldiers

False prophets always appear during emergencies. They are not insincere. In fact, as the theologian Martin Buber reminds us, false prophets are nothing *but* sincere.[70] They are patriots who cannot abide the hypocrisy and stupidity of others. Like Hananiah, they break the yoke of Jeremiah that lies upon our shoulders and seek to reinforce our resistance in an hour of danger (Jeremiah 28).

We live in an age of false prophets. If the world of torture is as this book has described it, then the fate of all the Hananiahs who advocate torture is already sealed. They will be remembered only for what they said when it mattered most. In the midst of the Algerian war, a colleague of Pierre Lambert worried, "If one day he was accused, I hope he will be judged on the whole of his works in Algeria, and not on an isolated fact adroitly put in the forefront of attention [*monté en épingle*]."[71]

But the world remembers only Lambert's torture, Lartéguy's ticking time bomb story, Wuillaume's narrow professionalism, and Massu's war crimes. No one remembers Lambert was a compassionate socialist of uncommon energy, Lartéguy was a great war journalist, Wuillaume an accomplished civil servant, and Massu a patriotic general. What the world remembers is that they reinforced an illusion, and when it collapsed, so too did their people's resistance.

No less a tragic fate now overtakes America's flak jacket philosophers. This cost, and it is a great one, pales by comparison to what they have asked of the soldiers. The lives and families of Lynndie England, Samantha Harman, Chip Frederick, and other soldiers are probably ruined forever. "That's what we do. We sacrifice soldiers to save innocent lives," argued Alan Dershowitz on CNN. The families of these soldiers probably would choose differently than Dershowitz. Families are proud their relatives serve as soldiers, but few would sacrifice them as torturers.

As for the rest of us, now that the yoke is broken, we must ask what the hour demands of each of us. We might begin by learning from the mistakes of other democracies that have tortured. These democracies lost their wars because the brutality they licensed reduced their intelligence, compromised their allies, corrupted their military and government, and destroyed their soldiers on a bonfire of vanities, and they could not come to terms with that destruction.

When the politicians first heard of the torture, they denied it happened, minimized the violence, and called it ill treatment. When the evidence mounted, they tried a few bad apples, disparaged the prisoners, and observed that terrorists had done worse things. They claimed torture was effective and necessary and countercharged that critics were aiding the enemy. Some offered apologies, but accepted no responsibility. Others preferred not to dwell on past events.

The torture continued because these democrats could not institutionally recommit themselves to limited power at home or abroad. The torture interrogations yielded the predictable results, and the democracies remained mired in war despite overwhelming military superiority against a smaller enemy. Soon the politicians had to choose between losing their democracy and losing their war. That is how democracies lose wars.[72]

Leaders of dictatorships sign on to the Geneva Convention only out of prudential fear of what other states might do to their state. Leaders of democracies sign on to them not simply to restrain other states from torture, but to restrain themselves as well. They know that all human beings are capable of authorizing and performing torture. Respecting the rights of others is not coded into our DNA, but must constantly be reinforced by institutional checks and balances. As America's founders would have told us, we are our own worst enemy, and corruption arose in our democracy not because we failed to defeat others, but because we failed to restrain ourselves.

To articulate the past historically does not mean to recognize "the way it really was." (Ranke) It means to seize hold of a memory as it flashes up at a moment of danger.

—Walter Benjamin[1]

24 The Great Age of Torture in Modern Memory

The summer before I began writing this book, I spent time with a hunter in the bush north of the Alaska Range. He asked what kind of book I would be writing. I told him a history of torture techniques that left no marks. "I know what you mean, like tying a man down, pouring honey on his eyes and having ants eat them out." No, I replied cautiously, that would leave marks. He gave it another try. "How about tying someone with drops of water falling slowly on his forehead? Now that's torture."

The hunter offered me a remarkable lesson in modern memory. He did not know any technique I have described in this book. What the hunter remembered were tortures that lay beyond the horizons of this book. The memory of water torture came from travel books of the Far East, with chapters entitled "Chinese Horrors" and photographs of the refined Oriental cruelty.[2] Death by ants belonged to stories by soldiers of the French Foreign Legion.[3] Legionnaires killed their comrades rather than let them face such horrible deaths at the hands of the Berbers and the Tuaregs of the North African Rif.[4]

Passing from one person to another, these stories had finally made it to the hunter in the Alaskan bush in the twenty-first century.[5] By this time, Chinese water torture and death by ants were legends. Occasionally, some curious torturer tried them out once.[6] Typically they discovered that these techniques belonged to a different political context. Torture now is not about the ruler's pleasure, his satisfaction in the suffering of his enemies, the slow madness or painful death before his eyes over weeks. What modern torturers required was something different. If our hunter ever chose to work as a torturer, his employers would find that he was a poor one. He had the wrong memories.

But it is unlikely he would ever choose that profession. In the age the hunter remembered, torture was something other societies did. When Europeans and Americans encountered it—as in the story of Foreign Legionaries—it was something that was done "to us". Here was a blissful nineteenth-century memory residing untouched by the horrors of the twentieth century. The hunter also did not remember how modern the wars of the North African Rif were. He did not know that, between 1922 and 1927, Weimar Germans supplied the Franco-Spanish alliance with chemical weapons, and that alliance planes dropped these bombs on Berber and Tuareg civilians, exterminating them like so many ants.[7] Indeed, most people do not remember that horror.

Those of us who do remember the twentieth century, whether we are onlookers, torturers, or victims, have different memories. These memories float on vast seas of government secrecy, divided by lost continents of records destroyed in war and the many languages of the disappeared and the dead.

This book reconstituted these memories, linking them together. Each chapter closed with a lost memory, a reminder of how many memories of torture that we currently possess are misleading. These memories had us search for torture techniques in places they never were or pointed away from places where they were common. In this chapter, I present the overall cartography, a map of how moderns remember torture in the twentieth-first century. I show how our memory of modern torture slopes in one way, and how this slope impedes our ability to look to the past or understand the dangers of the present.

The Great Rift

World War II constitutes a great rift in modern memories of torture. Having read hundreds of biographies from the war, I understand why. One gets the impression that there was no time where things mattered more, where reality was more vivid and life more precious. For those who survived the war, what followed must have been relief, but also something infinitely less vital.

If the aftermath paled in contrast to the terrible events so many had lived through, life before the war was even more indistinct. This was the real rift, the washing out of the past. What people remembered was what was done "to us" *during* the war and what we did "to them" *after* the war. It took effort to remember what we were doing to others *before* the war or even during the war.

To be specific, in the aftermath of the Allied victory, the universal desire was to identify with the winners. What this amounted to, in part, was to fault the Germans for all the violence, including torture. Torture was "the method of the enemy," as a war poster pointedly asserted.[8] But if torture was the method of the enemy, then two corollaries followed.

One was that the Allies did not torture and had not recently. This played out differently for each ally. For the French, it meant forgetting colonial torture in Vietnam in the 1930s. For the British, "no Allied torture" meant holding up domestic policing as exemplary, while forgetting brutal prisons in India and Mandatory Palestine. It also meant suppressing any accounts of British wartime torture.

For example, when Lieutenant Colonel Scotland submitted his memoirs of the London Cage for government censorship in June 1950, War Office officials urged him to hide the manuscript, then threatened to prosecute him under the Official Secrets Act and sent Special Branch detectives to raid his retirement home. While MI5 concluded that Scotland had repeatedly breached the Geneva Convention, the Foreign Office wanted the book suppressed because it would assist "persons agitating on behalf of war criminals." Scotland deleted the incriminating passages and published the book seven years later, and the incident remained hidden until 2005.[9]

As for the Americans, no one wanted to hear about possible American military torture during World War II.[10] Americans consigned their torture to their prehistory, to the police of the 1920s or earlier. The difficulty here was that police had not forgotten those "third degree" practices. Repeated Supreme Court rulings in 1936, 1940, and 1944 reminded those who watched that police torture had not disappeared during the war, particularly in the American South.

Continental European states chose a different strategy. Here the problem was remembering too much suffering, not too little, and not just during the war. In the bloody aftermath of the Spanish Civil War, observers focused on Fascism and Franco's torture. Less often remembered, and sometimes vociferously denied by Communists, was how the SIM and its Stalinist agents practiced clean torture in the Republican zones. Likewise, Eastern Europe had been a scene of terror for years before the war, but after the war, all talk of torture was about the Gestapo. At Nuremberg, the Soviet Union scarcely distinguished between the Gestapo and the Romanian Siguranza.[11] This was the classic *reductio ad Hitlerum*, reduce it to Hitler and be done with it.

Some could not identify themselves with the winners, so here amnesia took a different form. The Japanese, for example, did not dwell on the Kempeitai or its torture in the years preceding the war. They focused instead on foreign policy, American occupation, or "later moments of excitation among the Chinese and South Koreans," offering the occasional "superficial criticism of the past."[12]

The second corollary to Allied victory was that as the Gestapo tortured "us," we resisted, all of us. This story of widespread resistance reinforced the myth of torture's effectiveness. If entire populations were resisting Nazi soldiers, if entire resistance networks were compromised, this *had* to be because Gestapo torture was so efficient. People had no other choice. Forgotten was how much the Gestapo drew on informants and turncoats from the local population. The Gestapo's success throughout Europe depended on people who "either collaborated with the occupying forces (a minority) or accepted with resignation and equanimity the presence and activities of the German forces (a majority). The Nazis could certainly never have sustained their hegemony over most of the continent for as long as they did had it been otherwise."[13]

The myth of modern torture's effectiveness, then, dovetails with the darkest chapter of European history, the extent of European collaboration with Nazi governments. Like every other successful police force, the Gestapo received far more assistance than anyone was prepared to admit after the war. It was far more politic to present Gestapo torture as a modern, frighteningly efficient machine that beat the truth out of anyone.

The Architecture of Amnesia

And so we emerged out of the war with the firm belief that the Gestapo invented modern torture and had used it successfully to produce reliable information. This built a slope into the way we told the history of modern torture afterward.

In fact, few modern techniques descend from the Gestapo, and Gestapo techniques had more in common with medieval than modern torture. The Gestapo was modern in many ways, but torture was not one of them. Still, our memories keep pointing the other way. If you are relating torture to modernity, wrote the anthropologist Talal Asad in 1997, if you hope to be convincing, then you should be looking at Gestapo torture and modern Germany.[14] New memories must "fit" the old.

This slope of modern memory sharply constrained subsequent research. Consider the "discovery" of colonial torture after the war. The Allies were as shocked as Claude Rains in *Casblanca* that torture was "still happening" in the colonies. Torture in Madagascar in 1947? An aberration. But it was increasingly hard to look the other way in Kenya, Cyprus, Aden, Algeria, and Vietnam. Since the Gestapo had invented modern torture, what was required was to trace the clues back to the Nazis.

Water torture? Look no farther than Masuy during the war and his notorious *baignoire*. Forced standing? Lord Russell links these reports immediately to the *Stehzelle* in Auschwitz, rather than reflecting even for a moment on the prewar history of British "crucifixion" or forced standing in Mandatory Palestine.[15] Torture by the CIA? Those practices, said Jesse Leaf, a CIA agent, "were based on German torture techniques from World War II."[16] Did the Japanese use electrototorture before the war? By the 1960s, even those who documented the horror of concentration camps could not remember this.[17] Electric torture came from the Nazis.[18] Then of course, it all fit.

This strategy was not always successful, and posed its own mysteries. Not all modern tortures, particularly the clean ones, can be linked to what the Nazis did. So researchers eliminated the possibilities. As the Allies did not torture before the war, the Germans were hardly clean, and the rest of the world was premodern, there remained only one possible source of tortures that left few marks: Stalinist Russia.

Here modern memory constrained in a different way, by reducing plausible sources of these clean tortures to just one. It discouraged exploring colonial torture (Vietnam or Mandatory Palestine) or Third World torture (the Argentine *picana eléctrica*, the Japanese magneto) or early capitalist adaptation of ancient techniques (the *falaka*, pepper, and the *palmatoria*) or prewar American techniques (positional torture) as examples of modern torture.

Stalin, it turned out, invented the future. Orwell, famously, drew on the Stalinist show trials for his classic account of modern torture, *Nineteen Eighty-Four*, but he was not the only one. The politics of the Cold War mapped neatly onto the great rift in modern memory of torture. British and American governments became obsessed with the secrets of Communist brainwashing even when their own internal reports indicated that Russian techniques were nothing mysterious and represented a common tradition in modern policing.

This narrowness of vision was by no means limited to conservatives. It also characterized leftist accounts of torture in capitalist states. In his remarkable critical survey of torture in the 1960s, Peter Deeley begins the chapter "Torture Today" with Stalinist torture and then proceeds to North Korea in the 1950s. He entirely omits the Nazi period, focusing instead on the post-Korean explosion: France in Algeria, British colonialism, and then American clients (South Africa, Spain, Israel, Greece, Brazil).[19] Subsequent narratives repeat this order of exposition, adding references to Northern Ireland and sensory deprivation experiments, and then American torture.[20]

Most were unable to see beyond the Stalinist horizons to British and French military practices or American police practices in the early twentieth century. Critical questions were never raised because it seemed fitting and right that, if it did not go back to the Nazis, it went back to Stalin. There were some exceptions. Writing immediately after the war, Alec Mellor still remembered other sources of torture before the war besides Nazism and Stalinism. He cites Argentina's *picana eléctrica*, prewar French and American police practice, competition for military intelligence among the Great Powers, and the Spanish Civil War. Few subsequent writers, aside from Peters, who knew Mellor's work, drew so broad a panorama of torture before 1939.

The rules of interpretive analysis were simple for any account of a torture method. If you cannot find it in Nazi Germany, then you will find it in Stalinist Russia. "Nazism and Stalinism mark a gash in history," write the French historians of torture, Daniel Bacry and Michel Ternisen.[21] On the contrary, they are a gash in our memory. The slope of postwar memory constrained where scholars looked, and each new story added to a complex city whose broad avenues followed and reinforced the contours of the landscape underneath. It was not long before some wondered whether this city had a designer.

The Designs of Genius

When Aristotle looked up at the heavens, he saw a design that pointed to a Prime Mover. How could something so logical not also have behind it a Creator? When moderns look at the world of torture, they also see an intelligent design, and that design speaks to them of an evil scientist.

William Sargant was the first to make the argument from design and identify the evil scientist by a name. His name was Pavlov, and he was the genius behind Soviet brainwashing. For if all modern torture goes back to Stalinism, who but Pavlov could have furnished the Soviets with the knowledge? Others looking at capitalist torture also saw a design, a clear architecture that spoke also of evil scientists. CIA employed scientists, particularly Dr. Ewen Cameron, had pioneered sensory deprivation and spread electroconvulsive therapy (ECT) devices to torturers around the world.

An evil genius designed modern torture on both sides of the Iron Curtain. Modern torture was not a craft. It was a remorseless science. And the scientist was the fount of all modern evil. The CIA scientists, in particular, were fascinating not because their wild experiments held so much promise, but because "of themselves." Amid all the exotic subjects of their experiments, they were "the most exorbitant subjects of all" with dreams "of access to total knowledge."[22]

Such Faustian images were not easy to abandon. Naïve scientific research, writes Tim Shallice, "could well hit on more effective procedures even though it had another aim," and unwittingly aid "the dominant class, or to use a term possibly more familiar in the USA, the military industrial complex."[23]

Science has undoubtedly unleashed some fearsome forces. One can be convinced of this truth, but still resist the belief that an evil scientific genius stands behind torture in the twentieth century. Noam Chomsky, for example, does not subscribe to this view, even though he is committed to a strong version of the universal distributor hypothesis. And Chomsky is quite right to resist such a temptation, for to reduce the nightmare of modern torture to an evil scientific genius is a leap of faith.

Michael Kerrigan's *The Instruments of Torture* (2001) wonderfully illustrates this faith in the argument from design. Even when he can identify no particular scientist, Kerrigan still *believes*. CIA psychologists *are* spreading ECT devices to torturers around the world. Even if there is no specific connection between lab and torture chamber, "the analogy between shock-therapy and torture is all to clear" and more pedestrian accounts of the origins of electric shock are mere "rationalization" that "cannot blind us."[24]

Anyone with a mustard seed of faith cannot abandon this modern theodicy in light of evidence; that is the nature of faith. One can always argue that even if no science of torture exists now, it will and "You'll see." Perhaps, the future is wide open. If one day this science comes to pass, we can be sure that some slippery slopes we see in torture would likely vanish. These slippery slopes, such as the expanding range of techniques, kick in because torturers have no way to regulate pain.[25] If nothing else, a science of torture means a precise way of regulating pain to achieve results. So the slopes would be far less slick, if not disappear entirely. That would be one sign that the apocalyptic future had arrived.

But we are nowhere near that point yet. Even McCoy, to his credit, describes powerfully corrosive slippery slopes in torture despite his view that it is now scientific.[26] The trouble is that making both claims at once is empirically incompatible and logically implausible. Either torture has been scientized, in which case we should not be seeing the slippery slopes. Or the slippery slopes we see exist, and we are nowhere near a science of pain. There are no other choices.

Moderns may not believe that the Creator rules the heavens, but many believe sincerely that the Devil presides over modern torture. Such theology asks us to struggle against torture in the wrong places. It paints the origin of modern torture in acts of hidden conspiracy beyond our reach, a misrepresentation that is as antidemocratic and disempowering as it is misleading. It draws our attention away from the contribution the very ordinary products and habits of our lives make to the continuing practice of torture in modern democracies, and it obscures our power to bring more justice to the lives of others, if we were willing to. Indeed, it has always been within our power to do so. Unfortunately, more often than not, we would rather believe in the Devil and his legions than confront the heavy burden of human responsibility.

Demons in the City

If a Devil presides over torture, he could not do it without his legion of demons. That is the story that all too often postatrocity trials tell us.

In the Frankfurt Auschwitz trial (1963–65), for example, prosecutors focused on the unique sadistic behavior of the guard Wilhelm Boger, but less so on similar acts by others. Boger received five consecutive life sentences for five instances of torture, but 4 years for helping select one thousand people for genocide from the trains. Dr. Franz Lucas, his codefendant, never tortured anyone, and many attested to his decency, but, as a doctor, he was far more involved in the railroad selections. Yet for these acts he received a lesser sentence than Boger, 3.5 years in prison.

People had no difficulty condemning Boger's sadism, for they could scarcely imagine acting in the same way, but they did not dwell on the fact that his behavior made him unlike many Nazi torturers and killers.[27] Responsibility, of course, is an individual matter, but inadvertently or not, focusing on exceptional behavior consoles us that none of us could behave like that. People can stand on the side of justice without thinking too hard about what ordinary people had done or how they benefited from torture.

Organizations also prefer to highlight exceptional individual behavior. For example, in 1994, as charges against Commander Burge and his associates accumulated, the City of Chicago abruptly changed positions. Rather than supporting Burge as it had in the past, the city turned to painting Burge's action "in the worst possible light, and thus outside the scope of his employment as a policeman, and thus outside the responsibility of the city and the realm of its treasury."[28] In this way, the city conveniently passed over organizational contexts that facilitated torture.

Jurors in the Chicago case behaved in an even more peculiar manner.[29] In delivering their verdict, jurors seemed genuinely torn between acknowledging the reality of torture and acting on that knowledge. Were the rights of Andrew Wilson, the victim of torture, violated? Yes. Was it routine police policy to torture detainees for killing policemen? Yes, but somehow the victim, Wilson, was not among the victims of that policy even though he was arrested on this charge. Were police involved in such routine policy? Yes, but not *these* policemen sitting in the courtroom.

The Chicago jurors did not relativize the meaning of torture, as Talal Asad suggests moderns do. They did not confuse torture with fox hunting and tough sports. They knew the distinction all too well. They were not desensitized, no longer shocked by what was "once shocking."[30] Nor did they play games with the rhetoric of justice. As long as Hammurabi, justice has always been about quantified pain: one took an eye for an eye, not two or more because that would be revenge.[31] But no one used this rhetoric, arguing that Burge had used no more pain than necessary. Jurors knew that what happened to Wilson was an inexcusable crime.

No, jurors had no doubt that Wilson's rights were violated, but they concluded this violation bore no relation to any *human* agent that he came into contact with during his incarceration. This is more disturbing than indifference, cultural relativism or self-deluding rhetoric.

In Chicago, torture happened "out there" without any relationship to anyone in particular. People knew it happened, and even understood how it shaped the topography of their city, but they could not find the person responsible. In early Christianity, demons stood for intangible hostile feelings that drove people unexpectedly in murky social conditions or shaped aberrant, recalcitrant individuals. The "horror of the demonic was its very facelessness,"[32] as Peter Brown, a distinguished scholar of classical antiquity, explains. Demons "did their business in the darkness."[33] Torture in Chicago and Auschwitz, as near as the trials could tell, was the work of demons.

Algerian Souvenirs

Novels and movies of the Franco-Algerian War have also contributed enormously to the modern imaginary of torture. *The Battle of Algiers*, *Lost Command*, and *The Centurions* powerfully shape how we remember, discuss, and think about modern torture even today. Too often, we recollect not actual events but these cultural artifacts.

In 1960, a war journalist and former paratrooper, Jean Lartéguy, wrote *Les Centurions*.[34] The novel's protagonist was Boisfeuras, a paratrooper tortured by Nazis and again by North Vietnamese Communists, who went on to fight against Algerian terrorists. In Lartéguy's imagination, the North Vietnamese were true masters of torture. Indeed, Paras attributed to them two exquisite tortures that were, in fact, unknown in their prisons: death by ants and oriental water tortures.[35]

Two scenes from Boisfeuras's adventures loom large in modern memory of torture, both of which illustrate what he learned at the feet of his North Vietnamese instructors. In one scene, Boisfeuras brutally and repeatedly slaps the beautiful Aicha, a thinly fictionalized Djamila Bouhired, to find bomb detonators. "I love you and hate you," Aicha says afterward. "You've raped me and I've given myself to you; you are my master and I shall kill you; you hurt me terribly and I want to start all over again."[36] Boisfeuras, the torturer, is the real man.[37] Muslim men learned to respect his forceful determination, and Muslim women learned to love him no matter how much he tortured them. Democracy and liberalism had not weakened Boisfeuras.

In the second pivotal scene, a dentist, Arouche, plants fifteen bombs in stores set to explode the next morning. But Boisfeuras, the Para, has been born again in Gestapo and Vietnamese prisons. After describing his own torture, Boisfeuras tortures Arouche, and "by the time the dentist was carried of on a stretcher, in the early hours of the morning, he has confessed everything; none of the fifteen bombs went off."[38] In the fictional history of torture, only one account describes torture working faster than this. In Alan Dershowitz's novel *Just Revenge*, the prisoner confesses to being a Nazi after being slapped powerfully across the face just once.[39]

Perhaps Lartéguy invented the ticking time bomb scenario after what he wished Teitgin had done to Yveton. Or perhaps he adapted Lambert's story of the grenade thrower of Oran. Lambert, as we now know, told the story to disguise the real police sweep, the gruesome torture of forty people; he suggested professionalism where there was none. And the people of Oran wanted the satisfaction that terrorists got what they deserved; they did not look too closely at Lambert's story, for that would disclose unpalatable horror.

Misrecognition (*méconnaissance*) is the sociological process by which people habitually pass off one kind of situation as another.[40] For life to go on, we proceed in *this* way. People misrecognize because they are invested in the particular way they think about themselves and others. Any other way of proceeding would be unthinkable or, at least, deeply disconcerting. Misrecognition lies at the borders of consent and coercion, just beyond consciousness, and yet is not an ideology. People partner in confirming each other's misrepresentation of the world, even if one person ends up somewhat worse off than before.

The Battle of Algiers, for example, tells the story of how a colonial paramilitary force wins a tactical victory against a nationalist revolutionary organization in a city quarter. The movie glosses over the betrayals, the key informers, the rival factions and rebel groups, and the popular anger against the rebels. This suits both sides of the conflict well. The revolutionary organization holds the view that it *was* the people, as the movie repeatedly reminds the viewer, and that it had no rivals. If it lost the battle despite such popular support, it *must have been* because torture worked. And the French veterans still cling to the notion that torture worked, producing timely information that saved innocents. Otherwise they had committed war crimes. Despite being enemies, both sides are deeply invested in the story that tells how professional, controlled torture delivered final victory to the French.

If *The Battle of Algiers* filled out the myth of professional torture in war, *Les Centurions* supplied the scenario that substituted the symbolic violence of the ticking bomb scenario for the messy, wholesale process of torture during the Algerian war. Many things in the novel happened as the Paras imagined they *should* have. In the real Battle of Algiers, Paras tortured Djamila Bouhired/Aicha; in the novel, she was just slapped around until she fell in love (Lartéguy in fact defended the soldiers accused of torturing Bouhired).[41] In the real battle,

General Aussaresses hanged the imprisoned Si Millial/Ben M'Hidi with his own hands in fear; in the novel, the revolutionary leader slit his wrists in despair. And, of course Boisfeuras applied torture selectively, collecting literally ticking bombs within hours of a true confession—though even those who have seen the famous *movie* of the battle and accept it implausibly as a real description of events know that no event like this occurred.

But too often fantasy sells better than reality. *Les Centurions* won the Prix Eve Delacroix in 1960 and sold half a million copies, a privilege no book on the real Algerian war can claim. It won praise for its military realism, and French Paras embraced the novel. The Battle of Algiers had been won, they claimed, by all the interrogators who, like Boisfeuras, had learned torture from "the Vietminh in the prison camps of Indochina" and "knew how to break a man's will."[42]

Reality embraced art, and then art became a historical movie. Columbia Tristar adapted it for a major Hollywood movie, *Lost Command*, in which Anthony Quinn (the Para) squares off against George Segal (the Terrorist). American servicemen praise the novel today; military reading lists place it alongside real classics such as Sun Tzu's *The Art of War*. Lartéguy's story has also appeared on many TV shows—most recently on Fox's *24*, now set in an American city. Then movies became guides to reality, as American soldiers drew on such shows to think of techniques with which to interrogate Afghan prisoners.[43]

When I argued in chapter 23 that Trinquier's model of efficient, selective, professional torture was fictional, I meant that literally. That is where you will find it: in novels, television series, and movies. But if it is fiction, how does it exercise the power of a black hole in modern memory? How does it bend all argument to its narrative, preventing light breaking beyond the edges to the realities of torture?

Certainly Lartéguy's story is convenient for various professionals. Philosophers and law professors love Lartéguy's fictional story for didactic purposes as a thought experiment for their students. Of course, they usually do not seem to have put much thought into what it would mean to talk about the ethics of torture as an abstract thought experiment. The rare exceptions here are Leonard Wantchekon and Andrew Healey, who model the complexity of choices and organizational context of torture far more clearly than anyone else.[44] They know that good thought experiments should involve knowledge, implicit or explicit, of the laws or processes that govern the entities they imagine, understanding of the scope of such processes, and all the relevant features of that world.[45] By contrast, the Lartéguy story assumes background conditions about the way torture works that are empirically implausible.[46] The philosopher Michael Levin no doubt spoke for many philosophers when a *Penthouse* reporter asked him how many books on torture he had read in using the Lartéguy story to justify the practice in *Newsweek*. "None," he replied.[47]

Bureaucrats and politicians like Lartéguy's story because it confounds their critics. They would scarcely get as far arguing that torture is unnecessary for us, but necessary for the tough, recalcitrant Arabs. And no one argues, as an American theologian did during the Spanish-American War, that a torture victim is a free agent because he "has it in his own power to stop the process" by spilling his guts.[48] Perhaps we are less openly racist or fooled by simple casuistry than our ancestors. But if that is so, why do we buy Lartéguy's story at all?

The deeper truth is that Lartéguy story feeds on a long-felt, common anxiety that democracy has made us weak and there are no real men anymore. "Radical terrorists will take advantage of our fussy legality, so we may have to suspend it to beat them. Radical terrorists mock our namby-pamby prisons, so we must make them tougher. Radical terrorists are nasty, so to defeat them we have to be nastier."[49] And shortly after 9/11, President Bush again raised this myth in an interview. "I do believe," he said, "there is an image of America out there that we are so materialistic, that we're almost hedonistic, that we don't have values, and that when struck, we wouldn't fight back. It was clear that bin Laden felt emboldened and didn't feel threatened by the United States."[50]

The point of Lartéguy's story is that failing to torture is the sissy's response; only a real man knows what to do. The question is whether Lartéguy is right that torture is the appropriate cure for this self-perceived weakness. This deserves some thought.[51]

Unlike traditional war, winning the War on Terror is not about winning more land or wealth. The War on Terror is about affirming our way of life, our fundamental identity of liberal democratic society. As President Bush observed in his speech to Congress on September 20, 2001, they "hate our freedoms— our freedom of speech, our freedom to vote and assemble and disagree with each other."[52] But this is not quite right. It is not the case that they simply "hate us for who we are, not what we do."[53] It is seriously doubtful that Osama bin Laden contemplated for a second that American society was just, good, or free any more than a school bully taking lunch money wonders for a second whether being smart has some virtue.[54] Rather, those who oppose our society believe that such societies are scam games, and they disguise violent coercion with talk of freedom. They are not surprised we torture because they predicted we would. What we *do* matters to them. The more we torture, the more credible they are.

And they have a point: if we cannot respect the rule of law, if we cannot fight with one hand tied behind our backs *and win*, who exactly are we? W. R. Kidd, whose influential book *Police Interrogation* shaped policing in the 1940s, spoke for many in the World War II generation who knew that torture was the method of the enemy. Shunning torture, Kidd wrote, "does not make us sissies. It takes more guts to control yourself and fight it out brain to brain that it does to slug it out.... If you resort to torture, you admit your victim is the better man." Kidd understood that one should win respect through interrogation, but he was certain that torture produced no respect. "When you 'break' a man by torture, he will hate you."[55]

The same point was made by Marine Major Sherwood Moran, the author of one of the "timeless documents" in military interrogation in 1943.[56] Moran specialized in interrogating Japanese prisoners, widely regarded as fanatical individuals from a hostile, alien culture, and Moran was exceedingly good at it. Far less successful interrogators forced them to stand during the entire interrogation and humiliated them. Moran observed that those who tried hardest to break the morale of prisoners not only made prisoners resist them more fiercely, but also they stupidly revealed to the prisoners their own weaknesses, specifically, the "fear that the prisoner will take advantage of you and your friendship." Moran's philosophy, by contrast, was "know their language, know their culture and treat the captured enemy as a human being."[57]

But at the end of the Korean War, Americans began to wonder whether the enemy had a point, whether Americans were not indeed weak, and so easily manipulated. Unlike World War II, Americans won no decisive victory in the Korean War, and many believed incorrectly that U.S. POWs had shown uncommon weakness in war.[58] Conservatives blamed socialist subversion. Liberals believed the postwar prosperity of American democracy had made Americans soft, and it was this myth that won out.

Although doubts about American valor have always existed in American history, the new myth implied that somehow American civilization itself had made American soldiers weak. Politicians and military officials were sensitive to it. Harsh programs like SERE set out to shore up these alleged shortcomings in toughness and character, and unwittingly then served as conduits for torture training. It was all too easy to see where this determination to overcome our self-perceived doubts would lead. In 1966, a military historian warned portentously that efforts "to eliminate the weaknesses allegedly revealed in POW camps in Korea might well strain to the breaking point" the principles on which American civilization is based.[59]

Those who do not think we can win by means of these principles harbor deep doubts, not about the strength of bin Laden, but about the founding beliefs of our civilization. They firmly believe in torture's efficacy, and they worry that we have become sissies and our enemies know it. "Don't be pussies," urged an American interrogator in Afghanistan.[60] They embrace Lartéguy's story because it shores up their shaken resolve as it did for the French Paras. But those who cure their fears by means of torture might do well to ponder the consequences of such myths. A captured Israeli fighter pilot said it best as his torturers called him a ticking time bomb and strapped him down to extract information. He thought, "Screw all these bigmouths with their ticking bombs."[61]

Caring for the Memories

It is easier, now, to chuckle at the memories of the Alaskan hunter because they are oddly refreshing. The hunter's memories are fixed firmly on the body and the pain it suffers. He does not share our modern obsession with self-identity that makes "brainwashing" such a terrifying phenomenon. We fear that one day techniques will alter our identities without our even being aware of it and that drugs will force out the truth despite our will.

The hunter's antiquated memories of torture serve as a helpful antidote for these more modern fears. Similarly, old books like Tiltman's *The Terror in Europe* (1932) free modern imagination from the enormous weight that Nazi Germany and Stalinism placed on our minds.[62] The past does not always rest "like a nightmare" upon the minds of the living, as Marx once claimed.[63] Sometimes it is simply forgotten.

But inconvenient, involuntary memories keep pouring into our leaky modern constructions, memories of ordinary people locked in forgotten prisons in obscure conflicts, often with few to remember their names and their pains when they were gone. There were memories of domestic slaves beaten with paddles in Brazil, Mennonites brutalized in U.S. military prisons during World War I, Chinese Americans tortured in hotels in the 1920s, Vietnamese Communists tortured by the Sûreté in the 1930s, anarchists suffering in SIM prisons during the Spanish Civil War, the prisoners of Admiral Horthy in Hungary, the first victims of the Argentine *picana*, soldiers in the French Foreign Legion, ordinary criminals in French *bagnards*, victims of the Japanese Kempeitai, Indian political prisoners in the British Andamans, and Arab villagers standing in the sun and clerks of the Irgun with stomachs of bloated water in Mandatory Palestine. There were all those who were tortured by the Gestapo across the vast expanse of Europe, but not in Paris or France, as well as those who remember being tortured by Hungarians and Romanians. And then there were all those tortured by the Allies, including the German POWs in the London Cage or Spanish Republicans and East European Jews in French labor camps in North Africa. These memories and many more were obscured by the architecture of modern memory.

If we cannot protect the memories of the dead, if we must repeat endlessly the myths of modern torture, then we will be unable to protect ourselves, much less future generations. The task of protecting so many forgotten people and facing so much horror is daunting, but the fact that these few voices survived destruction fans the spark of hope that not all is lost. I have gathered as many memories of modern torture as I can in one book, and this, as Aristotle explains in *Nichomachean Ethics*, is as far as a philosopher dares to go:

> Here, as in all other cases, we must set down the appearances (*phaino-mena*) and, first working through the puzzles, in this way go on to show, if possible, the truth of all the beliefs we hold about these experiences; and if this is not possible, the truth of the greatest number and the most authoritative. For if the difficulties are resolved and the beliefs are left in place, we will have done enough showing. (1145Â)[64]

No doubt, soon, some will relate other memories—for example, tales from secret CIA planes and safe houses around the world. But saying more now would be cold, strained speculation, and arid conspiracy theories cannot substitute for human memories of torture. Now I can return to those activities that, as David Hume suggested, cure the philosopher of the speculative vice and teach him the virtue of humility. "I dine, I play a game of back-gammon, I converse and am merry with my friends."[65] Only ordinary life teaches one about friendship and offers solace for the sadness of betrayal. A Russian soldier on a supply train in World War II observed rightly, "It's not for our brains to ponder these things. Without vodka, you can't figure it out."[66] Where then are my scotch, my accordion, my friends, and my surfboard?

A A List of Clean Tortures

This appendix lists the main coercive physical techniques covered in this study. It focuses exclusively on techniques that leave few marks. Upon first glance, some of these may not appear to leave few marks or, in some cases, not even constitute torture (such as forced standing or sleep deprivation). Those in doubt should consult the specific chapters on these techniques.

Those categories marked with an asterisk indicate classes of techniques that may or may not leave marks depending on how they are used. The list below excludes the list of scarring techniques discussed in this study; these would be too long to mention. It may suffice here to note that the main scarring techniques considered in this study involve burning (flames, irons, branding), cutting (knives, razors, pins), whipping (long or short whip, canes), boiling (in water or oil), and full restraints (strappado, full suspension, the rack, hell cuffs, and shackles).

Historically, some clean techniques listed below appear in predictable combinations. I call these combinations *torture regimens* or *styles of torture*. Styles are helpful as a heuristic device, highlighting continuities and discontinuities in the empirical record.

Modern styles of torture tend to fall into two classes. One class is built around electrotorture, and I distinguish specific styles in the manner in which they supplement it. When electrotorture is commonly supplemented with water tortures, the style is French modern; when it is supplemented with gas masks, Slavic modern; and when it is supplemented commonly with the *falaka*, Mediterranean modern. Anglo-Saxon modern is based around stress and duress techniques usually supplemented with water tortures, beating with various instruments, noise, and drugs. Electrotorture is not part of this tradition normally. The Stalinist Conveyor technique (Soviet modern), the tortures in the French Foreign Legion (French classic), and the Israeli *shabeh* belong to this tradition of torture.

*Electrotorture (Instruments)

Electric chair (Dragon chair, Apollo chair)
The Mains (live wire to a socket)
Magnetos (telephone or field telephone; car, airplane, refrigerator;
    also transformer or commutator)
Prods (Cattle prod, electrified police baton, *picana eléctrica*)
Stun gun, Taser, stun belt, electric shield, and other devices using
    Cover circuitry)
Other devices (electric hat, electric bag, *parilla*, electric whip, electric refrigerator, electric stick [homemade], electric belt [homemade],
    shock wand, electric plate, vaginal electrode, electric television

Beating (Instruments)

Sandbags, sand filled PVC piping
Telephone Books
*Falaka (beating on the soles of the feet)
*Clean whipping (rubber hose, broad belt, etc.)
*Paddles (*palmatoria*, cobbing)
Rollers (*Ghotna, Belana*)

Beating (Hands)

Covert beating (blows to fleshy areas—stomach, thighs)
Slapping (the Taps, the Attention Slap, the Belly Slap)
Teléfono (ear cuffing)
Dorsiflexing
Violent shaking (*al Hazz*, the Attention Grab)
Eyeball and Ear Press

Water Torture

Choking
Pumping
Showers and baths (hot and cold)
Fire hoses and pressure showers
Ice tortures and ice slabs

Dry Choking

Bagging
Hooding

Gas mask
"The Necktie"

Air

Refrigerated cells
Powerful fans
Computerized cooling systems

Exhaustion Exercises

Continuous running
Deep knee bends
The "Bear Dance"
Handcuffed push-ups
Constrained walking, frog marching and duck walks (the Duck,
      the Rabbit, and the Frog)
Constrained crawling (the Lizard and the Dog)

Positional Tortures

Forced standing (the crucifixion, the Spot, *vystoika*)
Forced sitting (simple *shabeh*, *vysadka*)
Forced lying (*le tombeau*)
Forced kneeling (*seiza*)
Forced squatting (*le silo*, the imaginary chair)
Forced bowing (the Airplane, *sompeah*)

Positional Devices

Standing cells (*stehzelle, khazayen*)
Straitjackets
Wet sheeting
The Oregon boot
Peerless "American Handcuffs"
Sweatboxes, choke boxes, and black holes

Restraints

Bucking (the parrot's perch)
The *Crapaudine* (Toad) (*l'avion*, the Banana Tie, *arbachatar*,
      Ulysses' Bow, *balançoire, liankao, chinkwalia, nguelelo*)
Standing handcuffs
Reverse standing handcuffs
The Wooden Horse, the sawhorse, the Sawbuck (*caballete*)
Soft cuffing (flexicuffs, foamcuffs)
Finger bandaging

Whirligigs
Shabeh and *qambaz* roping (chair tortures, bending method,
  Qas'at al-Tawlah)

Salts and Spices

Insertion
Spiced wash
Spiced choking
Spiced pumping
Spiced ingestion
Spiced gas

Drugs and Irritants

Sleep Deprivation

Noise

Low technology (noise, often loud, that is meant to intimidate, surprise,
  mask, irritate, vibrate)
High technology (white noise, infrasound)

Sensory Deprivation

Float tank (SD proper)
Perceptual deprivation (usually a box of some sort)

B Issues of Method

This appendix addresses four methodological questions about this study. What is the behavioral measure for grasping the *intent* of torturers to be stealthy? What is the measure for determining whether states are authoritarian or democratic? Which is the dependent variable in this study, torture or technologies of physical coercion? And what is the difference between torture and punishment? Appendix C discusses the organization of this study and offers a formal statement of each explanatory hypothesis and its rejected alternatives. In both appendices, I draw on and amplify claims made in the book in more analytic terms. Here, I address some frank questions about this work, consider tempting answers and interpretations, and reason my way back to the positions I hold in the book.

How Does One Know Whether Torturers Intend to Be Stealthy in the Course of Torture?

This study depends on establishing a behavioral measure for knowing the intent of torturers. Understanding the intent of torturers is difficult even when one can interview torturers directly. Even then, one can draw illegitimate inferences about the attitudes of torturers from their statements.[1] On the other hand, without any behavioral measure, a study of torturers would be based on subjective inferences—unverifiable "attitudinal claims" about what torturers decided, thought, or believed. The study would generate fictional patterns based on the writer's speculations, and an explanation of them would be pointless.

So the problem is real, whether one interviews torturers directly or studies their behavior. Establishing a consistent behavioral measure is a critical part of this project. I begin by distinguishing between *clean* and *scarring* torture. When torturers use electrotorture in conjunction with whips and razors, one can be certain that it is not being used stealthily. What would be the point of covert coercion with electricity when all the other techniques leave scars? On the other hand, when electrotorture is used in conjunction with other tortures that also do not leave marks, then one can be fairly certain that torturers favored cleanliness in torture.

Some materials can be clean or scarring depending on how they are used, and so one pays careful attention to *how* torturers behave. Boiling water leaves deep scars, while tepid water does not. Used one way, whips leave permanent lines, but another way they leave only bruises. Used one way, the *falaka* can shatter bones, but used another way its use is hard to identify afterward. A fist will leave major bruises on a face, but one can slap someone senseless without leaving marks. In the case of electrotorture, one looks for supplementary behavioral clues, for example, victims' reports that torturers used EKG gel, wooden clothespins, or wrapped fingers in gauze. This extra effort would be irrelevant if cleanliness did not matter.

Determining cleanliness is a necessary, but not sufficient, part of concluding that torturers aimed to be stealthy. There is more than one reason why torturers may want to be clean. It is helpful, of course, if torturers, victims, or witnesses report that torturers intended to be stealthy, but too often there is no evidence one way or the other. Historically, some torturers favored clean tortures for reasons not related to stealth. Motives included the need to maintain an undamaged labor force at sea, the desire for profit in the sale of slaves, or sympathy for someone who is "like us."

These motivations are absent and unreported in the modern age, but one must consider all the logical possibilities. If the other reasons are unconvincing, the case for stealthy intent in torture is all the more compelling. Moreover, some behaviors may suggest that torturers sought to be covert. For example, I argue that French torturers who did aim to be covert favored electrotorture devices that were multifunctional or linked to their routine activities. It is reasonable to conclude the same in other cases. There would be no reason to use consistently devices that were linked or multifunctional if plausible deniability was not a part of the user's agenda.

In short, the judgment of stealthiness is based on what is logical and what fits the available evidence. And in general, it is easier to show when torturers had no intent to be stealthy than to prove positively that they aimed at covert coercion. The evidence for stealthiness is circumstantial and contextual, and one can make mistakes. Thoroughness is the only insurance here.

Of course, the tortures studied here may all have some special quality X that has absolutely nothing to do cleanliness in torture. I can think of only one plausible alternative for quality X, and this is that these tortures are inherently more painful than, say, scarring the flesh with razors. But comparing pain objectively is difficult. Ordinary judgments are too subjective, and clinical psychologists have no easy answers. If torturers have done more experiments than psychologists, there is no record of it. If there is another special quality X equally as important as pain, a century of observers have failed to mention it.

Is the Main Claim of This Book about Torture or Technologies of Physical Coercion? Is It about Democracy or Public Monitoring?

Formally speaking, the pattern of procedures for painful coercion (clean/scarring) is the *dependent* variable (that is, what is to be explained). Public monitoring is the *independent* variable of this study (the factor in terms of which something is explained). Democracy is a dummy for public monitoring. It may appear that democracy can explain outcomes, but this is because of the many institutions in democracies that monitor government violence. Generally, regime type predicts outcomes imperfectly, as I explain in the introduction, and I reject a hypothesis framed in terms of regime types.

So the main explanatory claim is this: *Public monitoring leads institutions that favor painful coercion to use and combine clean torture techniques to evade detection, and, to the extent that public monitoring is not only greater in democracies, but that public monitoring of human rights is a core value in modern democracies, it is the case that where we find democracies torturing today, we will also be more likely to find stealthy torture.*

As this hypothesis suggests, "torture" is nothing *but* the technologies, the various means of applying pain, and any position that distinguishes between "torture" and "technologies of physical coercion" is based on an indefensible distinction. This is an important point, and I want to elaborate it here.

No particular practice is "torture" in itself. When a doctor pierces one's ears or cuts into one's flesh with a scalpel, when two drunk men in a bar test each other's endurance by holding onto a magneto wire as someone else turns the crank, when someone participates in a sleep deprivation experiment in a hospital—all these cases are not torture. Torture is a normative judgment. It identifies the moment when public authorities, or private individuals and professionals who quietly assist them, use these techniques on restrained individuals for state purposes (intimidation, false confessions, and information). It necessarily involves the use or abuse of public trust.

As an inherently normative concept, torture cannot serve as an empirical referent in the real world. At best, like murder, it can be used to group together nominally a class of objects of concern for analysis. Anyone seeking to explain murder generally would quickly spell out the empirical instances they are explaining. Serial murder, assassination, and the exclusive murder of women (femicide) describe patterns where one agent kills other agents using certain means for certain purposes, and social scientists offer explanations for each kind of murder. There is no general theory of "murder" (not even the *Encyclopedia of Violence, Peace and Conflict* has entries for "Murder" or "Killing"),[2] though there are many explanations for specific patterns. The study of "torture" is no different. Here again, the term *torture* delimits a field initially, and then one considers the different empirical patterns, variations in the aims and means of torturers, and offers an explanation for each. These results may lead one to redefine the boundaries of the field of research.

"Torture" in this sense is a helpful way of referring to an entire class of techniques once they enter the realm of public trust. But there are many legitimate uses of these techniques as well, and any account of their empirical distribution must disregard the normative/legal framework and look to how legitimate techniques pass into the realm of the state. If one looked simply at the patterns of state usage, then one would deliberately have chopped out half the empirical pattern.

The only reason one could do this is if one assumed torture was related to something else besides the techniques violators used—say for example, if one defined torture as simply the victims' experiences of unjustified pain. On this account, torture is a real empirical referent in the world. It is identical with victim's reports of suffering.[3] Torture then *would* be different from the techniques used to create it, and one would be uninterested in the distribution of techniques beyond state usage. But identifying torture with any report of suffering or indignity presents formidable methodological problems, as I explain in chapters 1 and 5, and an analysis built upon this foundation more closely resembles an ethical story no matter how much social scientific jargon is piled on it.

A related objection may also be implicit in the focus on the suffering of victims. This might be put something like this: What you are providing is a "how to" manual for torturers, focusing on the history and logic of techniques and machines. You are not really talking about torture, that is, the suffering of victims of the state. How can you justify this?

On the contrary, the whole point of explaining clean techniques and their history is to demonstrate that these are *painful* coercive techniques, and to alert others to the danger they represent. Until recently, most people believed victims of these techniques suffered little or no discomfort.

I argue that these techniques are deeply interwoven in our daily lives, that they have multiple sources stemming from ordinary industries and practices, and that there are deep interrelationships between the treatment of prisoners and our treatment of animals and the insane. Moreover, if, as I argue, knowledge of these techniques spreads laterally—hidden in pockets of society such as boarding schools, military camps, and fraternities—then we have to worry about *society* as much as *the state*. State authorities may authorize torture, but the knowledge of it rises from below once the authorization is given. It is one thing to stop the authorization of torture. This book draws attention to the harder issue of disturbing these deep pockets of social violence.

We can evade all these interrelationships by focusing strictly on the suffering of victims, but that is an ethically risky strategy. If the point of an ethical account is to make us think twice about what we are doing and how it is related to the injustices that others are doing or have done, then I think the histories I offer meet those standards.

Lastly, anyone who thinks this book even remotely resembles a "how to" torture manual is unfamiliar with torture manuals. They may wish to look at some real torture manuals, for example Dirk von Shrader's *Elementary Field Interrogation*, before making this charge. Such books are available on the Internet, and nothing I describe here is unknown or unfamiliar to those who practice torture. There is precious little evidence torturers spend their days trying to catch the latest medical literature on pain, much less pointers from social scientists. All this can only be worrisome to those who were unaware of these techniques and their diffusion or to those who spend their time worrying about what the state secretly knows. The reality is that states already know.

How Does One Tell the Difference between Torture and Punishment?

Not all punishments involve the deliberate, systematic infliction of physical torment on detained individuals by state officials. Other punishments include monetary fines, exile, shunning, isolation, hard labor, community service, penitential recitation ("I shall not . . ."), and other forms of ritual humiliation. What makes all these practices *punishment* is that states have authorized them, codifying their use in law or allowing their customary usage.

Not all punishments are torture, then, but some physical torments are legally authorized, and in this case one may speak of *legal torture* or torture as punishment. In these cases, states authorize agents to use their official powers to physically torment detained individuals systematically for public purposes (confession, intimidation, and information).

Sometimes states authorize officials to use punishments (physical and otherwise) during the course of investigation of crimes; these are judicial punishments. In other cases, they authorize agents to use them after public judgment; these are penal practices or punishment. Accordingly, one can divide legal torture into *judicial torture* and *penal torture*.

Of course, not all physical torments are authorized, and some techniques never have been. When state officials use them on detained individuals for confession, intimidation, and information, they are also torture, even though they are illegal. There is, of course, a gray area where officials turn a blind eye to the violent practices of others; call it unofficial torture or tolerated torture, if you like. Whether it is legal or illegal does not change the fact that the practice is torture from an ethical perspective.

It would be a mistake, then, to say all punishments are torture (for sometimes there is no direct physical torment) and conversely that all tortures are punishments (for many are not authorized by custom or law). Most importantly, the fact that a practice is *legally* authorized does not magically transform the practice into "not torture" any more than magic words uttered over an ass change it into a Ferrari.

In each case one must inquire whether physical torment is involved, whether the individual is helpless and detained, whether the agents who practice it are state or quasi-state officials, and whether it is put toward public purposes. If the answer in each case is yes, then it is torture, regardless of what it is called. If, in addition, the practice is legally authorized or authorized by custom, then it is a legal torture, and depending on whether it is practiced during investigation or after judgment, it is either judicial torture or penal torture. As to what to call painful practices that are neither punishment nor torture, I refer the reader to the discussion of "private torture" in chapter 1.

What Is the Measure for Determining Whether States Are Authoritarian or Democratic?

Democracy is a form of government based on amateurism (citizens rule in turn by means of lots or elections in a free choice among competitors) and participation (a significant segment of the society has access to these means). This is why France, the United States, and Britain as well as Greek, Roman, and Italian republics are classified as democracies. Even though suffrage was for most of their histories enormously limited compared to today, in their age, they represented the broadest extension of the principles of amateurism and participation.

In authoritarian states, by contrast, leaders are self-appointed or, if they were elected, are impossible to displace afterwards. Typically, this is justified by some claim besides amateurism, such as bureaucratic or military expertise, moral and religious authority, descent, or personal qualities of the ruler. Citizens do not choose their rulers by means of lots or elections in an open competition. Some authoritarian regimes do mobilize large populations to participate in national elections or referenda, but the outcomes are irrelevant to who decides what where, when, and how in politics.

These definitions are adequate as far as they go, but the problem is at the edges. Most states have various mixes of democratic and authoritarian elements. Some authoritarian states, for example, allow limited elections for some institutions, and some democratic states have elections that are less than fair. Social scientists debate what qualities can be classified as democratic and which authoritarian, how to characterize various mixes, and what conditions limit the scope of such characterizations.

Fortunately, my argument does not depend on use of regime type as the key independent variable. I do make the general claim that nonauthoritarian states typically have more domestic monitoring of government violence than authoritarian states, but this is noncontroversial. Standard definitions of authoritarianism often include the observation that such states are marked by the absence of competitive groups, organizations, and political parties that question the decisions of rulers or compete for power. Even those who think that the United States and other apparent democracies are really hidden authoritarian states run by political and economic elites acknowledge they differ from overt authoritarian states in this respect.

Moreover, the scope of this project precludes anything more than this simple distinction. This project surveys a broad range of institutional arrangements; not just the ones with which modern political scientists are familiar, but also governments such as interwar Hungary, and ancient Greece and Renaissance Italian city-states. These governments tried to implement principles of amateurism and popular participation. But comparisons beyond this are hazardous. More people probably voted in interwar Hungary, even as a percentage of the population, than ever did in Greek republics—should we then call Greek democracies undemocratic and a regime that eventually collapsed into a fascist dictatorship a democracy? To a certain extent, we have to accept the conventional designations that people offered at the time. Athens was democratic compared to Sparta or Persia. Interwar Hungary was less democratic than interwar France, but it was not Nazi Germany.

Some political scientists favor narrower distinctions; for example, they prefer to draw a line between consolidated and emerging democracies. Political scientists forged this tool in the late twentieth century in order to compare states in Latin America and Eastern Europe in the late 1980s and early 1990s to states such as France or Britain. But it is hardly suited for talking about Athenian democracy as it gradually lost its democratic way of life (neither consolidated or emerging) or interwar Hungary, which, even after decades, could not implement fully the principles of amateurism and participation in government (consolidated or emerging?). My simple claim that democracies generally have more monitors than authoritarian states is more than sufficient for the enormous scope of this project, whereas narrower tools, developed by political scientists in other decades for particular purposes, are not.

Despite these qualifications, some readers may question ways I use *democracy* in two specific instances. One pertains to the way I use the adjective *democratic* in some cases, and the other pertains to my characterization of the colonial projects of democratic states such as France and England.

Occasionally, I use phrases such as *democratic torturer* or *democratic police*. Some may be appalled at such phrases, and insist that one should speak of *torturers in democratic societies* and similarly *police in democratic societies*. This small debate over words stems from two very important ways of thinking about police and torture in democratic societies. Let me sketch out these two positions.

One may hold, in principle, that the police and military are an inherently authoritarian institution, and those that work in these institutions could not possibly be in any sense called democrats. This would be news to a lot of soldiers and policemen. It is quite possible for a torturer to believe and participate in democracy—to vote in the morning and torture in the afternoon, and we have regular examples about us all the time these days. Using phrases like *torturers in democratic societies* makes it sound like these people are aliens who happen to live alongside us rather than quite densely integrated with everyday life.

This is why I insist on phrases like *democratic torturer* and *democratic police*, disturbing as this usage may be. It would be nicer if such integration did not exist, but if we do not start coming to grips with phenomena this book describes, we better get ready for far worse things to come. Nor do I think this usage is unfamiliar or inaccurate. Families and corporations are not democracies either, but we have no difficulty speaking of democratic mothers and democratic businessmen. These are people who are committed to the principles of amateurism and participation in government even if the institutions in which they participate daily are not democracies.

Of course, someone may believe that *all* institutions in a democratic society should embody democratic principles, and by those standards, the phrase *democratic torturer* would be a contradiction in terms. But let us also concede that this is not an empirical position, but a normative one presented as an empirical objection. On this view, there are no democracies today and there never have been. I have no difficulty with advancing normative ideals of democracy, but I do worry when they blind one to the ways in which torture is integrated into existing democratic societies. Then they become excuses for not dealing with the real world.

Let me turn to the colonies of democratic states. It may be objected that the colonial projects of France and England were often authoritarian even if government in the home country was democratic. Local inhabitants did not participate in the governments that administered them. This is true of course, and sometimes relevant, and I try to highlight the differences that the fact made to torture.

But it is misleading to say that the line could be drawn as cleanly as this objection suggests because colonial societies had a complex relationship to the metropole. Settlers in Algeria voted in French elections as they did for their own municipal governments. If a court convicted you of a crime in democratic London or Paris, it was just as likely you could end up in Australia or New Guinea as in prison at home. If you served as a policeman in Tunis, you could be a policeman in Marseilles a few years later.

From the standpoint of the leaders of these empires, the populations that voted for them and the administrators that governed them, the British Empire or the French Empire were not just countries of others, but parts of the whole self. What happened "out there" mattered to those people in Paris and London and produced conflicts and even collapses of governments (consider, for example, the debate that raged in Victorian London about how Jamaican administrators reacted to a slave rebellion). This perspective is hard to appreciate now, especially if we believe that the colonies were really nations suffering under an authoritarian yoke. No doubt, the colonial projects were unjustifiable in a normative sense. I do not think I would incorporate that into an empirical typology.

To think of the British Empire as composed of a unit of democracy with various authoritarian colonial attachments is an anachronistic perspective, imposing a normative-liberationist view on a political system that simply did not think of itself in these terms. And when one imposes such a view onto the past, one misses precisely the connections that *Torture and Democracy* is about, that is, how certain techniques circulated between colonies, or between colonies and metropole. However unfamiliar this past may be to us, that, as the book argues, is the way things were.

C   Organization and Explanations

This appendix offers a formal statement of each explanatory hypothesis and rejected alternatives. Some might prefer to see all the historical facts grouped around these propositions. Let me acknowledge that behavioral social scientists write about such materials differently. In that tradition, I should summarize the history, pass over the "data," and get on with the theoretical explanation. Then the links between the history and the theoretical explanations would be much clearer.

I have sharpened the link between the historical material and theoretical hypotheses in the introduction to the book, the smaller introductions to parts II and IV, and chapters 9 and 20. This appendix may also be helpful as a guide to my main arguments. But generally, I have resisted this suggestion in favor of a plain-language text suited for ordinary educated readers. While I can certainly see the case for a social scientific reorganization of this study (hypothesis, alternative hypothesis, test, evidence, interpretation of results), social scientists are not my only audience. I appreciate the impatience of some more disciplinarily inclined readers, and it is fine to call the backbone of this manuscript "data" and demand more "theory." But there is a difference between "clean" and "dirty" data, and social scientists can summarize the data at their own peril. Torture is not like other topics in the social sciences, and too much of its history is wrapped in national mythology, accusation, and rumor. One could organize this study around a set of national case studies rather than study the empirical distribution of techniques worldwide. But then one would reproduce torture folklore in the guise of scholarship, and that is hardly a suitable basis for theorizing.

Here then is the argument in a nutshell. The backbone of this study is a set of factual empirical assertions, what I call *claims* (c). These claims generate *puzzles* (P) that in turn require *explanations*. I offer my own explanations (E) as well as alternative explanations (AE). Lastly, some of the explanations bear on debates in specific disciplines. They offer alternatives to the way people normally think about the issue at stake. I call these arguments *interventions* (I).

Empirical Claims

C1. There exist many painful physical techniques of interrogation or control that leave few marks. I call these *clean* techniques in contrast to *scarring* techniques.

C2. The vast majority of these techniques are not technologically sophisticated. They involve instruments that people commonly have at hand for other purposes.

C3. Most of these techniques appeared first among lists of British military punishments; in the context of American slavery, penal institutions, or military punishments; and during policing and military operations in French and British colonies. Virtually all the techniques that appear in conflicts in Afghanistan, Iraq, Algeria, and Northern Ireland, as well as in prisons in France, England, and the United States, are descended from these procedures or subsequent variants.

C4. There is a long, unbroken, though largely forgotten history of torture in democracies, at home and abroad, stretching back some two hundred years. This claim restates C3 using the conventional designation of France, England, and the United States as the main democracies of modern history, especially prior to World War II.

C5. The alternate claim would be that authoritarian states invented and distributed these clean techniques. However, prior to and during World War II, clean torture techniques rarely appear in other countries notorious for torture, including Russia, Germany, the Austro-Hungarian Empire, and Japan, or their colonies. When they do, they are just as quickly forgotten. Whatever one calls these states—whether one calls them monarchies, dictatorships, fascist, or communist states, totalitarian or authoritarian states—they are not conventionally or consistently designated as democracies before or after World War II.

C6. By the late twentieth century, the techniques that first appeared in the main democracies can be found in countries around the world. In addition, new coercive and clean techniques appeared alongside them in various countries.

C7. There are still many scarring torture techniques, but there are fewer reports of them by the late twentieth century, and some have vanished entirely.

c8. Torturers tend increasingly to use clean torture techniques in conjunction with each other. I call this tendency *clustering*. This clustering occurred first in the torture of modern democratic states in the early twentieth century and only rarely in authoritarian torture chambers. By the late twentieth century, similar clustering begins to appear among authoritarian states, although democratic torturers remain, by far, the most consistent users of clean techniques.

c9. Lastly, clean techniques do not cluster randomly but appear in predictable combinations. I call these predictable combinations regimens or *styles* of torture. For example, torturers tend to combine electrotorture with various water tortures, a style I call French modern after its first consistent users.

c10. Over the course of a century, then, torture changed worldwide, the kind of sweeping change that is rare with any method of violence. Torturers, on their own or at the direction of others and for whatever reason, have turned more and more toward techniques that leave few marks. This follows from c6 through c9 whether or not one concludes, as I argue, that stealthiness is what makes these techniques desirable. It is possible that these techniques have some other quality X in common besides leaving few marks, and this is why they are used more frequently. I consider this possibility in appendix B, but that is not critical to the factual claim here. All this claim states is that leaving few marks is *one* quality all these techniques obviously have in common and around which they may be grouped for purposes of analysis, even if this is not the only common element.

c11. In short, police and military in the main democratic states were leaders in adapting and innovating clean techniques. This follows from c4 and c6. French colonial police, for example, developed what became the dominant form of electric torture for forty years, torture by means of a field telephone magneto. They pioneered this clean technique in 1931 in Vietnam, before the Nazis came to power in Germany. This claim is agnostic on how other countries ended up with these techniques and by what route they arrived. It does not imply a specific explanation for how torturers came by the techniques they currently use, for example (by means of CIA training, low-level transmission between torturers, or simple imitation). All it states is that the techniques that are now commonly used worldwide had their roots in the main democratic states.

Puzzles

P1. Why do clean tortures and democracy go hand in hand?

P2. Why did other states that are not democracies start using these techniques? This yields two puzzles:

P2.1. Why did authoritarian states not use clean techniques in the early twentieth century?

P2.2. Why did authoritarian states start using these clean techniques in the late twentieth century?

P3. Why are there variations in the pattern of scarring or clean tortures within states?

P4. How do torturers end up with the clean techniques they use? Why are there styles of torture?

P5. Why do some democracies torture while others do not?

P6. Does torture work? This yields two puzzles:

P6.1. Can states successfully regulate torture?

P6.2. Can states use torture to generate successful outcomes?

Explanations and Alternative Explanations

Why do clean tortures and democracy go hand in hand? (P1)

E1. *Monitoring hypothesis.* Public monitoring leads institutions that favor painful coercion to use and combine clean torture techniques. These methods make it less likely that torturers will be found out or held responsible. To the extent that public monitoring is not only greater in democracies, but that public monitoring of human rights is a core value in modern democracies, it is the case that where we find democracies torturing today we will also be more likely to find police and military using multiple clean techniques. I call this pattern of torture *stealth* torture.

The main evidence in favor of this hypothesis is the historical pattern in which clean techniques appear and cluster together over time (C3, C4, C6, C7, and C8). Clustering, as I explain in appendix B, is one indicator of intent to be stealthy. Additional evidence includes testimonial literature and the lack of plausible alternative motives for torturers to combine clean techniques (as discussed in chapter 20).

AE1.1. *Regime type hypothesis.* The type of state bears a causal relationship to the type of technique. Democracies favor clean techniques but authoritarian states do not.

OBJECTION: AE1 cannot explain variation in the empirical distribution of clean and scarring tortures among states. For example, authoritarian states also use clean electrotorture techniques, but mainly in the late twentieth century, but on this explanation it is not clear why. Nor can this hypothesis explain why democratic states sometimes favor scarring techniques, as the British did in Kenya, and why at other times they favor exclusively clean ones, as the British did in Northern Ireland.

AE1.2. *Ruling elite hypothesis.* Democratic states are ruled by an elite who for whatever reason want to hide their exploitative state in the guise of a democratic government and so order lower-level agents to be stealthy and not make a mess.

OBJECTION: Not an alternative hypothesis. Public monitoring is still the critical variable that makes elites behave as they do. The only disagreement is who is making the decision to turn to stealth: lower-level or higher-level agents. The source material and subject matter make it difficult to ascertain. There is partial evidence for both political elites and lower-level policemen and military, though primarily favoring low-level agents.

One variant of this hypothesis places great emphasis on corporate, rather than political, elites. This hypothesis emphasizes how an economic hierarchy combines entrepreneurship with political and social networks to spread torture technology. This is by far the weakest and most unpersuasive variant of the ruling elite hypothesis. What drives this argument is in part a naive conception about the nature of torture technology. Very few clean techniques require major technical innovation—they can be taught in any backroom and require neither technological investment nor corporations (C2). Nor does the history of most techniques show the involvement of entrepreneurs or technological innovation as the major push behind their diffusion (C3, C4, C6, C7). This hypothesis also fails to explain why some technologies that involved corporate and scientific investment failed to take hold, while others did. While the patent history for electric devices does suggest something like the inevitable march of technology, the real patterns of innovation for high-tech electric stun devices bear almost no relationship to the patent history (see 13 below).

Why do other states that are not democracies start using these techniques? (P2)

Why do authoritarian states in the early twentieth century not use stealthy techniques? (P2.1)

E2.1. *International monitoring hypothesis.* In these states, police and military were far less accountable to others for the violence they performed, and so there was no percentage in using clean techniques. In the rare instances where cases drew international attention (particularly from democratic states) or where states deliberately sought international attention regarding their treatment of prisoners, they did use clean techniques. International monitoring, either unsolicited or deliberately sought, explains the rare cases of clean authoritarian torture.

AE2.1. *Dehumanization hypothesis.* This hypothesis predicts that torturers change tactics depending on whether the person is like them or not. When the prisoner is like "us," torturers try to leave few marks. When someone is "Other," they are indifferent or deliberately leave scars. Sympathy, not public monitoring, drives the choices torturers make.

OBJECTION: This hypothesis admits of a strong and a weak version. On the strong version, the torturers actually possess these norms, while on the weak version they are aware that others possess these norms and expect to see them enforced. The rich and the noble, as well as white Europeans and Americans, expected that *their* people would be treated differently. The others did not matter so much. The objection against the weak version is that this is itself the international monitoring hypothesis in a different guise.

The objection against the strong version is that there are too many cases where racist torturers treat identical "others" and "like us" differently. Nazis sweated women of privilege (Mona Parsons) and some German bureaucrats (von Moltke) even in the absence of public monitoring, but were merciless in other cases involving German aristocrats (the von Stauffenberg case). The strong version certainly explains why the Gestapo was brutal to some Europeans, or why colonial powers generally used scarring tortures on Africans, Arabs, or Asians. But racism and similar structural perceptions of the "other" are constants, and cannot explain variations in torture. This argument fails to distinguish between the routine racist treatment of certain groups and other cases where the torture went beyond the usual scale of brutality (for example, the treatment of the Kikuyu in Kenya, the French in the Algerian countryside) or cases where torturers sought to conceal evidence of torture (slave dealers in the Americas, the French in the cities of Algeria, the British in high-publicity cases in India). Should one conclude that French torturers, often the same units, were simply more racist when they went to the countryside? It seems more plausible that they were less worried about being observed or reported by unwanted eyes.

Why do authoritarian states start using these techniques in the late twentieth century? (P2.2)

E2.2. *Universal monitoring hypothesis.* International human rights monitoring comes of age in the 1970s; in response to increased monitoring, torturers turned increasingly to cleaner techniques. Even some authoritarian states learned to adapt their violent practices to preserve legitimacy and foreign aid. Torturers appear to be responsive to monitoring, and different monitoring regimes bring to bear kinds of values. Our age differs because there are many more monitors who now enforce a universal human rights regime. Thus, it is increasingly difficult for police to justify torturing prisoners because they have the wrong race or gender. By creating conditions in which observers could monitor specific behaviors, the observers changed the behavior they sought to document. When monitors exposed torture to pubic censure through careful documentation, torturers responded by investing in less visible and harder to document techniques.

AE2.2.1. *Universal distributor hypothesis.* A single power distributed these techniques globally in the late twentieth century to its authoritarian allies. The most important variant of this hypothesis is Chomsky and Herman's claim that the United States distributed torture techniques around the world in the 1960s and 1970s. Other possible candidates are the United Kingdom, the USSR, and France.

OBJECTION: Chomsky and Herman's thesis is a variant of the ruling elite hypothesis (AE1.2), and it is open to the same objections. Moreover, in this case, it is testable against the actual distribution of techniques, and the evidence suggests that it is false. The pattern of techniques is too varied to suggest a single source except in very specific regions of the world. This holds true for claims on behalf of the United Kingdom and France as well. There is a plausible case to be made for Soviet distribution, but this does not fit the chronology or the pattern identified in c5, c6, c7, and c8.

AE2.2.2. *Ideology hypothesis.* Ideology explains the turn to clean torture. For example, Marxist-Leninist thought disapproves of torture, and so Communist torturers prefer clean techniques so that they appear to comply with ideological requirements.

OBJECTION: This hypothesis cannot explain variation in techniques among states with the same ideology or variation across regions in the same state. Communist states vary enormously in their use of clean or scarring techniques or whether they torture at all.

AE2.2.3. *Better documentation hypothesis.* Clean torture preexisted universal monitoring in authoritarian states, but better systems of documentation since 1973 registered it for the first time.

OBJECTION: Increased auditing and documentation probably has identified more techniques than could have been identifed before the 1973, and this is probably truest with the techniques that do not involve complicated devices, for example, positional tortures. I have offered sufficient coverage of each major torture technique to show that, based on everything we know worldwide, there was a surge in the 1960s and 1970s.

When clean techniques appeared before the 1970s, they
typically occurred in democratic states (see C3–C7).

Why are there variations in the pattern of clean or scarring
tortures within states? (P3)

E3. *Monitoring hypothesis.* Torturers respond differently to different kinds of monitoring (frequent/infrequent; comprehensive/scattered; proximate/distant; internal to institution/external to institution; domestic/international; based on local knowledge/foreign; type of specialization (e.g., medical/nonmedical). It seems plausible to think that different variables affect monitoring. The hostility of torturers toward doctors who track torture seems partial evidence for the view that the kind of monitoring matters to torturers. The repeated observation that clean techniques occur with greater frequency in cities than in the countryside (and almost never the reverse) is certainly suggestive; urban areas include, among other things, far greater prospect of scrutiny by unwanted eyes. Unfortunately while the variables can be specified, we are a long ways from having an adequate tool to link some kinds of monitoring causally to different distributions of clean and scarring tortures.

AE3. *Regime type hypothesis.* States are mixes of authoritarian and democratic elements typically. Different types of states generate different domestic patterns of clean or scarring torture.

OBJECTION: Regime type does not explain variations in clean or scarring torture *among* states. If it cannot perform this fairly simple test, then how can it explain variations within states? And if it can, what precisely explains the variation here? The most plausible mechanism is that different regime types allow for greater or lesser freedom of the press, more or less independent judiciaries and citizen oversight, or greater or lesser autonomy for political parties, church groups, and nongovernmental associations concerned with human rights. But this is to say that different regime types generate different patterns of public monitoring and hence different patterns of clean or scarring torture. In that case, this is not an *alternative* hypothesis.

How do torturers end up with the stealthy techniques they use?
Why are there styles of torture? (P4)

E4. *Craft apprenticeship hypothesis.* Torturers learn their craft on the job, by observing and imitating others like them. This shapes the decisions they later make when they torture. Training in a craft is not simply a form of intentional communication, in which a master craftsman passes onto the apprentice simply technical knowledge of this or that practice. "The way we do things around here" is also a way of signifying belonging to a group, a reference to a shared identity. In torture, the importance of group bonding and peer solidarity is well known. The way torturers combine techniques and the accepted limits of the common toolkit communicate who they are and index the community of practitioners to which they think they belong.

Generally speaking, the *bricolage* of torture includes inherited patterns from the past, improvised responses to political events, and adaptations from here and there that "fit" into how things are done. These are the elements that constitute a style of torture. More specifically, torturers appear to choose their techniques based on how they were trained, what is immediately available, and what is attached to their legitimate routines (linkage and multifunctionality). Additional factors pertain to the institutional settings in which the craft is learned, which shape preferences for techniques that cause immediate pain as opposed to slower techniques. Lastly, memories of conflict (gossip, rumor, stories) and in particular collective national trauma shape the kinds of techniques torturers employ.

As with the craft of tailoring, torturers develop certain styles based on familiarity with their instruments, fashions of the day, and the needs of the situation. Torturers may treat all prisoners to the same standard violence; torture becomes a "one size fits all" operation, with predictable, ill-fitting results. But the more cunning torturers may customize torture to the needs of the situation and the character of the prisoner. These torturers will be the innovators who introduce new variations in style.

AE4.1. *Ideology hypothesis*. Torturers choose techniques that are the most coincident with the state's ideology. This is an identical claim to AE2.2.2.

OBJECTION: This hypothesis cannot explain intrastate and interstate variation in technical choice among states with the same ideology. For example, it is hard to explain why some Communist (and non-Communist) states adopted psychoprisons while others did not, or why the psychoprison was an ideological alternative better than Stalinist sweating and positional torture. It is difficult to fit the chronology of the rise of pharmacological torture in psychoprisons to ideological shifts in the Soviet polity.

AE4.2. *Cultural hypothesis*. Torturers choose techniques that fit their culture.

OBJECTION: This hypothesis dovetails with the craft apprenticeship hypothesis, as both hold that torturers combine techniques and develop styles based on inherited patterns from the past. There is considerable evidence in favor of this view, including the persistence of ancient practices in modern torture, the persistence of old colonial tortures in postcolonial contexts, or (conversely), the way colonial powers adopted the torture techniques of the societies they governed.

The objection to this hypothesis is that it cannot explain why torturers abandon long-standing cultural techniques or why torturers unfamiliar with these techniques and separated by time and place suddenly adopt them. This problem becomes especially severe when one considers whole styles of torture. It is one thing for the style to appear in the country of an ally, but quite another thing to explain why the same style appears in the torture chambers of one's enemy. It is not surprising, for example, to find that Anglo-Saxon modern appears in Israel, but it is much harder to explain why the same regimen appears in the Soviet Union, with little continuity in culture.

Above all, this hypothesis does not explain why torturers appear to have a preference for the *clean* version of a cultural practice instead of its *scarring* version. The history of the *falaka* illustrates all these points.

AE4.3. *Scientific efficiency hypothesis*. Torturers choose their techniques based on a proven laboratory record of successful performance. This hypothesis presumes that torture is a science or is approaching such status.

OBJECTION: This hypothesis cannot explain why torture is so often low tech. It also does not explain why torturers choose some scientific techniques but not others (e.g., magneto electrical generators over sensory deprivation boxes). Nor can it explain why torturers prefer the clean over the scarring version of a high-tech torture.

Lastly, this hypothesis makes it very hard to understand the development of styles of torture and their continued variations (C9). If torture is approaching the status of science, one would expect a gradual convergence of techniques as the scientific training in torture diffuses worldwide. After all, it seems inconceivable that states could resist mastering knowledge of scientific torture any more than states could resist research on nuclear weapons. But if styles of torture are converging around one single scientific style, this study has been unable to document it. This study does record a surge in clean techniques worldwide, but this development has fostered multiple styles of torture. And it is caused not by the *push* of scientific and technological advancements, but by the *pull* of universal monitoring. Moreover, there is little evidence that high-tech tortures are spreading. Electrotorture is very much the lone exception here. The priority of torturers remains learning how to use low-tech methods.

Why do some democracies torture while others do not? (P5)

E5. There are three sets of preconditions for torture in democratic states. At least one of these conditions is necessary (though not sufficient) for torture to occur. The three conditions are the following: the national security bureaucracy partially overwhelms the democratic institutions to which it is formally accountable (the national security model); the judicial system puts a high priority on confessions (the judicial model); the local police, either on their own or with the tacit consent of politicians or property owners, set about creating order (the civic discipline model). The models only indicate that torture has an elective affinity to such conditions. Pressing beyond this conclusion for a fine-grained causal account of the necessary *and* sufficient is currently not possible given the fragmentary knowledge of the empirical cases.

Does torture work? (P6)

Can states successfully regulate torture? (P6.1)

E6.1. *Slippery slope hypothesis*. Torture generates not one, but three slippery slopes. Torturers expand the range of victims that they are authorized to interrogate. They use greater variety of techniques than they are authorized to use. And they increasingly pursue their own interests, constituting themselves as a separate professional class and heightening bureaucratic devolution. These slopes are slicker and sharper in cases where the purpose of torture is prospective information rather than coerced confession about past events. Torture cannot be administered professionally, scientifically, or precisely; and it causes serious damage to the institutions that employ it. Empirically speaking, the strongest bulwark against these slippery slopes appears to be the common-law system and, more generally, legal systems that do not privilege prosecutorial power.

AE6.1. *State centralization hypothesis (Dershowitz thesis)*. States can control torture more easily in a formal, visible, accountable, and centralized system than in an ad hoc, under-the-radar nonsystem.

OBJECTION: There is no evidence for this thesis. State centralization does prevent local elites from using torture for their own purposes, but it does not stay the hand of centralized elites, who do not hesitate to use torture for their own purposes. Democratic accountability did not restrain torture in Italian city-states, but rather strengthened the hand of executive power, leading to an eventual end of the republican systems. Formal legal rules for torture, even in highly centralized states, are undermined by the various slippery slopes.

Can states use torture to generate successful outcomes? (P6.2)

E6.2. *Behavioral intimidation hypothesis.* I stipulate that torture can coerce others into behavioral compliance, whether in the form of false public confessions or behavioral obedience in public settings. But it does not work when what is sought is something other than superficial behavioral compliance. In particular, torture for *accurate* information is the clumsiest intelligence-gathering method, possibly even clumsier in some cases than flipping coins or shooting randomly into crowds.

This does not mean that on further empirical investigation these claims could not be qualified. Even some torture apologists stipulate that torture as intimidation does not work.[1] In particular, it seems an open question whether torture could intimidate a population if it were applied unselectively to everyone. If torture was inevitable no matter what one did, it is hard to see what incentives anyone would have for behavioral compliance. Stealthy torture appears to intimidate successfully because it is an example of *selective* deterrence, sending intimidating messages to those who behave or are assumed to behave in specific ways. The affected groups have incentives to act in ways such that they are not selected, while other parts of the population are entirely ignorant that what causes the higher degree of behavioral compliance is torture.

Likewise, while it seems plausible that torture can generate false confessions, in practice this appears to be considerably more difficult than commonly imagined. Data from the torture of criminals in ancien régime France, American pilots in North Korea, and German POWs tortured at the London Cage, all suggest that using torture to secure false confessions is exceedingly difficult no matter how draconian the methods. One relevant factor appears to be whether the false confession is entirely false or partly false (the latter being easier to secure).

AE6.2. *Military necessity hypothesis.* Torture is an effective tool for gathering intelligence in emergency conditions.

OBJECTION: On the contrary, there are three sources of error that are systematic and ineradicable. These are interrogator error, deception by uncooperative prisoners, and erroneous judgment by cooperative prisoners. These errors are undetectable to most interrogators, and they are intensified under conditions of limited time, as in battle or emergencies.

Torture for information works best when one would need it least, namely, during peacetime, nonemergency conditions. Torture would work well when organizations remain coherent and well integrated, have highly professional interrogators available, receive strong public cooperation and intelligence from multiple independent sources, have no time pressures for information, possess enough resources to verify coerced information, and release innocents before they are tortured. If the suspect really *is* the right person to interrogate, interrogation is more likely to yield accurate information if the person is an opportunist, not a hardcore believer. Even then, torture has problems that cannot be eliminated, including desensitization, death, unconsciousness, and memory loss caused by damage, in which case the most reliable information pertains to the more remote past, not the immediate present. Whether one can justify torture ethically when there is no emergency or when other methods of gathering intelligence are available, is another matter. My belief is that it is difficult to justify.

Interventions

11. *Political science, international politics.* The conventional wisdom is that contemporary human rights monitoring has no effect on the practice of violence in states and the patterns that appear.

   On the contrary, human rights monitoring does change patterns of torture. It does not always do so in the manner monitors intend. Monitoring may lead states to greater compliance to the rule of law and political sociability, but it may also generate patterns of covert torture. States may still repress, but they are mindful of the political implications of bad publicity for international legitimacy and international aid. International norms may also have another perverse effect. States that practice covert torture have little incentive to evaluate their repressive policies publicly, and so may foolishly pursue torture when its effects are at best neutral and sometimes counterproductive for state power.

   Additionally, this study suggests that the human rights regime gained a great deal of its power through the influence exerted by a group of democratic states, particularly those in Europe, who linked a good human rights record with aid and recognition. On the other hand, the international human rights monitoring system did not depend on the goodwill of either superpower, whether the United States or the Soviet Union.

Rather, these superpowers felt compelled to comply because they too claimed a certain commitment to human rights in terms of their own political and ideological traditions. Lastly, the competition between superpowers during the Cold War allowed the human rights regime to flourish. Both superpowers presented themselves as possessing a superior morality, and it was easier for critics to play states off against each other.

12. *Political science, international politics, history, European studies.* Conventional wisdom is that in the twentieth century, some states have acted as universal distributors, passing torture techniques to others by means of military aid and training. These universal distributors include Nazi Germany, the Soviet Union, the United States, and the United Kingdom.

   On the contrary, torture techniques circulate by many means, but centralized international distribution by a single state is probably among the least important. The Soviet Union is possibly the best candidate in this respect in terms of the breadth of its influence and uniformity of Stalinist technique across time and space. There is some partial evidence for the United States in Latin America. But beyond this, there is little evidence that torture techniques used worldwide today stem from a single universal distributor.

13. *Sociology, studies of diffusion.* Conventional wisdom is that high-technology products follow a certain sequence of stages, beginning with conception and innovation and ending in the diffusion of a finished product.

   On the contrary, this pattern cannot be found in the development of stun technology, the most high-technology device used in torture. The story of Cover showed that innovation and diffusion were performed simultaneously. Cover had to simultaneously create socio-technical networks to sustain their innovations.

14. *Sociology, human rights studies.* Conventional wisdom is that torture is a science, or has the potential of being a science.

   On the contrary, torture is a craft. The notion of a science of torture rests on simple folklore about pain. And given the nature of pain, there is every reason to believe that the notion of a science of torture is a utopian (or dystopian) dream. Technology may help in the conduct of torture by reducing labor, preventing unconsciousness, or preventing premature death. But no technology can calculate the precise amount or kind of torture that will work with each human being. Using magnetos, stun guns, or white noise is painful, but that does not make torture a science, any more than wearing a white lab coat makes torturers scientists.

15. *Philosophy/cultural studies.* Conventional wisdom is that torture is a world-destroying experience because pain is deeply isolating. After all, pain is private, and no one can know my pain. Pain is inherently inexpressible, and experiencing it drives one into a prelinguistic silence. This inability to express oneself has significant political consequences. Most notably, it allows states to shape the terms in which prisoners (and repressed populations more generally) understand and describe their reality.

On the contrary, empirical studies of torture have put this account of torture into question in two important ways. These studies show that pain is neither *necessary* for torture to be world destroying nor *sufficient* for torture to be world destroying. No doubt, one should pay attention to the ability of torture victims to express themselves, but the specific mechanics of pain are neither necessary nor sufficient to explain the final outcome of torture. Linguistically, the inability to express oneself has many facets. The inexpressibility that matters in torture is the gap between speakers and their communities, not the gap between the brain and the tongue. When conventions of speaking about pain break down, the state does indeed reap advantages by being able to preserve its legitimacy in the face of accusations of torture.

Expressing pain is about the conventions that acknowledge the recognition of others, not about our certainty or doubt about whether others *have* pain. If pain really did drive one into prelinguistic silence, one would not be able to grasp one's own pain; indeed one would not be able to distinguish between a sensation of pain and some other sensation X (the Wittgenstein thesis). To know one's pain is to be able to describe it to oneself and others. The failure to grasp pain is not a failing of the intellect, but the failing of spirit, the inclination to give up when the conventions one counts on break down. And what restores this capacity is a common political space in which people can express their pain to each other.

D   A Note on Sources for American Torture during the Vietnam War

This appendix evaluates sources on American torture in Vietnam. It is not concerned with allegations of massacre or other atrocities, and it would be inappropriate to extend the conclusions here to other forms of violence without careful reflection.

I have grouped the testimonial accounts in four categories. First, there are accounts that no one has questioned with regard to whether these soldiers served where they say or whether the facts are as they reported them. Then there is an identical set of accounts that differ only in that they were given in contexts that were less than impartial. Next there were soldiers who testified alongside others who fabricated or allegedly fabricated their stories. No one has directly questioned the veracity of the accounts themselves, but they are tarred by association with liars. Lastly, I consider the accounts made during the Winter Soldier investigation.

Once one separates out torture from other atrocity allegations and dispenses with the fabricated accounts, a fairly coherent picture of American torture emerges. The different sources conform quite well to the official reports and court martial records. They describe repeatedly the same range of techniques. Moreover, the evidence they present suggests that torture was not official U.S. policy in Vietnam, as it was in Algeria. The evidence veterans provided suggests an underground subculture of military interrogators who shared techniques tolerated and shielded by midlevel commanders. These soldiers were careful to hide what they did from superiors and were quite aware of military rules prohibiting torture. Torture techniques appear to have migrated not from the top down, but from unit to unit as interrogators imitated their interpreters, ARVN interrogators, and each other. These, then, are the accounts.

Uncontested Accounts

Lt. William Calley, who led the unit that committed the My Lai atrocities, describes American military police using electrotorture, choking in water, and stress positions. The military police "had an Army field telephone with a crank on it. They would wire up a Vietnamese wrists and (as they called it) would ring him up."[1] Some prisoners were held in small tiger cages covered with sandbags in which the individual had to squat for hours.[2] Interrogators also put a prisoner in a fifty-five-gallon drum filled with water and ran electricity through it, "and it would shoot him out," what was dubbed "a POW cannon."[3]

Leaving My Lai aside, the most extensive documentation of torture at a single area was in or around the headquarters of the Ninth Infantry Division at Dong Tam, fifty miles southwest of Saigon in the Mekong Delta between 1968 and 1969.[4] The events at Dong Tam drew attention in light of torture allegations against Jon Burge, a Chicago police commander and former Vietnam Vet who served with the Ninth Military Police of the Ninth Infantry Division at Dong Tam.

Allegedly, Burge used a handheld magneto to torture victims. Members of his unit in Vietnam remember this torture well. MPs describe field telephone torture, dubbed "the Bell telephone hour," in the manner of American corporate sponsorship of television programming. Although Philip Ash, the provost marshal, and Ray Merill, the deputy provost marshal of the Ninth MPs, received no reports of torture in this period, "Officers and enlisted men who served under Ash as company commander, executive officer, lieutenant and sergeant all told *the* [*Chicago*] *Reader* they'd heard of or witnessed field telephone interrogations."[5] MPs stated that it was common for MPs to be present during interrogations, and they described field telephone torture at Dong Tam and firebase Tigers Lair and Tan An. MPs do not describe performing the torture themselves, but they describe military interrogators using the technique, with or without ARVN members present. The common procedure was to attach one wire to the finger and the other to the breasts or testicles, but not to the ears.[6] Some mention other tortures; "we would pretty much do anything as long as we didn't leave scars on people."[7] None of these men describes performing torture themselves, and some, who are now law enforcement officials, strongly condemned it and, if they were in a position to stop interrogators at the time, did stop them.

When asked why they did not report torture, MPs described their powerless condition. "We would keep our mouth shut," since "it would have been my word against an officer's word, which the officer is always going to win. So what do you do?" They also emphasized that members of Military Intelligence "were held in the highest regard, they could walk on clouds." Those who did investigate corruption at the base were given another duty, usually more demeaning, and sometimes packed off elsewhere.[8]

Another cluster of testimonies relate to torture in the 172nd Military Intelligence Detachment. Robert Stemme Jr. reported that "it was pretty standard practice that people got slapped around or hit with things. . . . Field telephones—all those things—were tools of the trade."[9] Army investigators reported that another interrogator, Frederick Brown, described "water-rag and field telephone interrogation of detainees."[10] Staff Sgt. David Carmon also described water torture and magneto torture. For choking, he reported to investigators in December 1970, "I held the suspect down, placed a cloth over his face, and then poured water over the cloth, thus forcing water into his mouth."[11] In 2006, Carmon also described electrotorture techniques to the *Los Angeles Times*, indicating that interrogators generated electricity by turning "the phone crank."[12]

Lastly, Mark Moyar interviewed American advisers and their Vietnamese counterparts as part of his effort to reconstruct the operation of Project Phoenix, a counterinsurgency project designed to eliminate Vietcong infrastructure in the south. Moyar is generally sympathetic to Project Phoenix, and his aim is largely to defend the program against its critics. Nevertheless, Moyar sets out to explain why some Americans tortured more than others and why Americans generally tortured less than the South Vietnamese army. Because his analysis focuses primarily on why certain affective, cultural, and historical elements led some to torture more than others, his account is not particularly valuable in tracing torture techniques. But Moyar confirms that some Americans did torture. He observes that "advisers and veterans of U.S. military units said that American infantrymen were somewhat more likely to torture prisoners than were the American advisers, but they still were much less likely to do so than GVN personnel." Indeed, "All of the American advisers and their counterparts whom I interviewed said that few American advisers encouraged torture or tortured prisoners." Normally, Moyar reports, Americans left the interrogation and torture to the South Vietnamese personnel.[13]

Uncontested Accounts in Partisan Contexts

In 1967, the Russell Tribunal heard the testimony of three American soldiers that described torture. While the judges of the Russell Tribunal were hardly impartial, no questions have been raised about the two specific accounts. The accounts are as follows.

Donald Duncan, a sergeant in the American Special Forces, repeated roughly the account from his book, *The New Legions*.[14] Of his testimony, Guenter Lewy observes that Duncan refused to be led by the judges of the tribunal, insisting that he would only speak of things of which he had firsthand knowledge.[15] Nor does Duncan add anything more to this testimony in later interviews or in his testimony four years later at the Winter Soldier investigation.[16]

Duncan mainly described how he learned torture techniques through a classified course, Countermeasures to Hostile Interrogation, taught at Fort Bragg. The techniques he described were field telephone torture, spinning a man at the waist using a wide belt rope, extremes of temperatures ("the hot and cold treatment"), putting a bucket on the head and beating it, and crushing the testicles. The device for electrotorture was a "double E-A telephone, just a standard Army field set—battery operated—attaching the lead wires to the genitals."[17] Duncan emphasized that it "was always suggested that you do not mark a person. In other words, don't leave physical evidence on his body. Use those types of interrogation where if somebody were to see the prisoner immediately afterwards you couldn't tell that he had been abused."[18]

Intriguingly, Duncan does not describe one specific instance of American interrogators using the techniques he described from Fort Bragg. Duncan does describe two instances of American interrogation in Vietnam during his tour in 1965, both quick field interrogations. One involved beating the prisoner, and the other involved scratching the prisoner's chest with a long knife. In fact, Duncan states, Americans usually handed prisoners to their South Vietnamese counterparts, knowing they would be tortured for intelligence.[19]

Peter Martinsen, a military interrogator, describes the use of field telephones in interrogation involving U.S. officers and Vietnamese interpreters.[20] Martinsen's allegations often pertained to the members of the 172nd MI Detachment, and subsequent Army CID investigations indicated that members of this detachment did torture.[21]

Martinsen states, "Electrical torture was very common for a while in Vietnam, but was not very common towards the end of our assignment."[22] He indicates this technique fell out of favor and was replaced with continuous slapping. Martinsen describes two incidents that precipitated this change in his unit. In one, an overzealous interrogator was "wiring him [a prisoner], and he just fell over and died." This was problematic because "there is a log which must be kept in regard to the prisoners," and the death of a prisoner drew attention.[23] In a second case, a commander criticized a frustrated lieutenant who gave up electrotorture for inserting bamboos under the fingernails: "The prisoner had been scarred. The electrical torture generally does not leave scars, and beating generally does not leave scars, but the use of bamboo was forbidden, because it left marks and there was blood. After that, the use of extreme forms of electrical torture became less frequent. But it was understood that, if we did not leave scars, we could do exactly as we pleased."[24] Martinsen reports that he saw no cases of water torture.[25]

Martinsen appears in two other more controversial contexts. Although he picks up some new euphemisms for torture ("Bell Telephone Hour," "the Americal Rule"), his testimony does not change markedly from what he offered at the Russell Tribunal.[26] Martinsen adds only two new facts.

First he states that interrogators went to great lengths to hide torture from senior commanders. They were most concerned at military interrogation centers "because of the tight controls on keeping track of prisoners there."[27] And even in the field, interrogators tortured in tents to allow for plausible deniability by others. "This is just from a practical point of view, so unless you actually stick your head in you don't see what's going on."[28] Martinsen states that the U.S. Army field manual on interrogation (FM 30-15) endorsed only psychological techniques, and though he is skeptical of how seriously some commanders took it, the evasive behavior he describes would only occur if interrogators and their commanders knew that torture was prohibited.[29]

Martinsen also offers specific dates for shifts in torture techniques. During Operation Cedar Falls (January 1967), POW interrogators commonly used magneto torture. As newspaper accounts of torture mounted, torturers adopted continuous slapping. "Beatings were a mark of sophistication that we acquired later."[30] In Operation Manhattan (April–June 1967), "Electric torture wasn't used too much, as the major had put out the word to cool it a little bit."[31]

Other documents should also be mentioned in this context. Three collections of oral testimonials of veterans identify beating, magneto torture, and choking in water.[32] In a boastful account posted online, Dick Culver, an intelligence officer with the infantry in 1967, describes witnessing field telephone torture using an EE-8 Field Telephone applied to the prisoner's index fingers.[33] He describes how the interrogator eventually forced the prisoner to crank the magneto himself on fear of death, thereby electrotorturing himself. *Elementary Field Interrogation* is a torture manual written allegedly by a member of the U.S. Army Special Forces in the Phoenix Counterterrorism Program in the early 1970s.[34] It describes a surprisingly narrow range of techniques, including noise, slapping, and restraint tortures. It does not mention electrotorture.

Uncontested Accounts in Compromised Contexts

Lt. Col. Anthony Herbert describes only two instances of torture in interrogation around 1968.[35] He describes how he witnessed interrogators used the Dutch style of water torture on a prisoner, and provides a photograph of the incident taken by his helicopter pilot. In a second incident, he describes walking into an interrogation room to find an American interrogator and a Vietnamese interpreter using a handheld magneto (field telephone) on a prisoner. The only question regarding Herbert's testimonial is "not whether atrocities occurred but whether Herbert had reported them and had had his career ruined by a military establishment intent on concealing war crimes."[36] In fact, internal CID investigations found that military interrogators for the 173rd Airborne and 172nd Military Intelligence detachment tortured even if investigators could not substantiate Herbert's specific allegations.[37] Interrogators repeatedly "beat prisoners, tortured them with electric shocks and forced water down their throats." Soldiers also stated that "their captain approved of such methods and was sometimes present during torture sessions."[38]

Mark Lane's *Conversations with Americans* is the most notorious collection of soldier testimonials of the Vietnam War. Neil Sheehan has identified fabrications by Chuck Onan, Michael Schneider, Terry Whitmore, and Garry Giaminoto, though he recognizes that some of the other accounts ring true.[39] The fabricated accounts mention torture techniques known elsewhere, but never reported in Vietnam.[40]

The remaining testimonials of interrogation amount to this. Three soldiers describe magneto torture: "Take a field telephone, the TP 3-12, and put the connecting wire to it, then take the other end of the wire and attach it to a person's testicles and crank it—this causes a high-voltage shock, there is no amperage behind it, just voltage, but it is extremely painful."[41] One soldier describes water torture in the Dutch style, another the *falaka*, and the last electrotorture by car battery.[42] One soldier described killing POWs after torture if it was too difficult to bring them back.[43]

K. Barton Osborn testified about torture before the House Committee on Government Operations.[44] In the 1990s, the military released the results of its investigations of Osborn's allegations, and these indicate that Osborn misrepresented himself and what he had, or could have had, knowledge of.[45] The other witness at the hearing interviewed American interrogators and described the codependant relationship between American soldiers and South Vietnamese interrogators, noting that Americans were seen watching or assisting in torture. He describes how American interrogators used "what they call the good-guy bad-guy approach," treating the prisoners kindly, but threatening to hand them over to Vietnamese torturers if they did not cooperate.[46]

Osborn also testified before the Citizen Commission of Inquiry (sometimes called the Dellums Committee). Other testimonials delivered in this context have not been contested, and these describe beating, water torture, or magneto torture with field telephones. Ron Bartek, a military interrogator, described two incidents of torture. In one incident in 1968 or 1969, American interrogators used field telephone electrotorture, connecting wires to the groin and small of the back.[47] Bartek also described how other soldiers tortured him during Ranger training at Fort Benning. He described "having a cloth with a little wire embedded in it forced over my nose so I could not breath through my nose, and 5 gallons of water used to pour down my throat when I tried to breathe through my mouth."[48]

In these testimonials, veterans state that soldiers learned torture techniques after interrogation class stateside or through local apprenticeships in Vietnam. "After the regular classes or after any particular classes, say, on interrogation, the men in the class would gather outside with the instructor and say, 'Tell us, what is it really like. Then they would tell you the incidents of men being thrown out of helicopters, electrical torture, beating, etcetera.'"[49] Unit commanders did prohibit magneto torture, but there were limits. One lieutenant forbade magneto torture in his unit and was relieved after several months.[50]

The Winter Soldier Investigation

In Detroit in 1971, several soldiers described incidents of torture, though they refused to name the soldiers who had tortured.[51] These soldiers had served in different places in Vietnam at different times. They gave their own names and presented their discharge papers, identifying when and where they had served, and they detailed when and where torture occurred. The soldiers at Winter Soldier did not describe bizarre tortures never reported elsewhere, as in other accounts, and at least as far as torture is concerned, there is nothing here to make one question Senator Mark Hatfield's decision to read this account into the *Congressional Record* in 1971.

Recently, one soldier, Steve J. Pitkin, retracted his account in 2004 under mysterious conditions. I consider this incident below, along with allegations by Lewy, but so little is known about Lewy's and Pitkin's claims that it would be unreasonable to rely on either to assess the veracity of the veterans' accounts. The Pitkin retraction aside, the remaining stories offer this description of American torture.

Steve Noetzel offers the earliest account of American telephone torture, situating it in the Mekong Delta region between 1963 and 1964.[52] Soldiers who served in the mid-1960s repeatedly mention telephone torture and less commonly beating. There are two accounts describing the use of dogs in torture and singular accounts of suspension, water torture, and ear boring.[53] One soldier describes an incident of field interrogation using knives in which the prisoner was killed because the medics would have become suspicious.[54]

Don Dzagulones, a former military interrogator, gave the most detailed account of interrogation and torture. Dzagulones described field telephone torture as well as dehydration, which left "nothing that was traceable."[55] As in other testimonials, Dzagulones does not mention official training for torture. Rather, he describes how commanders in Vietnam exercised benign neglect ("If people did find out about it, they just let it go, because it was an accepted practice"). He also describes how he learned techniques off the books at Fort Meade in Maryland after the official instructors turned the class over to Vietnam veterans ("invariably the instruction would turn to various methods that they'd seen or heard or used in torturing people in Vietnam").[56] In the 1990s, Dzagulones repeated much of this original testimony, describing in particular the use of field telephones.[57]

Let me turn now to the criticisms of Winter Soldier. Guenter Lewy has sharply questioned the accounts soldiers provided. In particular, he sharply criticized the unwillingness of soldiers to name those who committed war crimes, arguing that in American jurisprudence, "guilt is always personal."[58] Lewy also summarized the results of the investigation of the Winter Soldier allegations by the Naval Investigative Service. "The most damaging finding consisted of the sworn statements of several veterans, corroborated by witnesses, that they had in fact not attended the hearing in Detroit. One of them had never been in Detroit all his life. He did not know, he stated, who might have used his name." The report also identifies another soldier, an African-American, who asserted that a member of the Nation of Islam helped him prepare his testimony.[59]

But the appearance of exactitude here is deceptive. Unlike other critics, such as Sheehan and Moyar, who have exposed fabricators by name using unclassified military files, Lewy does not give the names of the fake speakers at Winter Soldier, and guilt, as he so correctly states, is an individual matter. Collective sin belongs to theology, not history, and it is a mistake to tar everyone at Winter Soldier with the faults of specific individuals. In 2004, Lewy was no longer certain whether he saw the file that described these allegations. In an interview with the *Baltimore Sun*, Lewy states that he "does not recall if he saw a copy of the naval investigative report or was briefed on its contents."[60] The cursory bibliographic information, which offers neither the date of the investigation nor a reference number, suggests he never saw it.

Efforts to find this file have thus far failed. The *Sun*'s reporters were not able to secure it, and Paul O'Donnell, the spokesman for the Naval Criminal Investigative Service, reported that they "were searching for a copy of the report."[61] In addition, a military librarian with access to classified databases was unable to find the file listed in any database. Perhaps one day a FOIA request will recover this file and two other files Lewy cites.

The lack of names, the probable oral character of the summary, and the absence of the hard copy raise troubling questions about Lewy's allegations. Furthermore, during the 2004 presidential campaign, conservative groups put a great deal of energy into finding anyone who would discredit the Winter Soldier investigations. If, as Lewy insists, there were veterans who were outraged that someone used their name falsely to make claims of atrocities in Vietnam, this was the time for them to have come forward. But by the end of fall 2004, only one soldier came forward, Steven J. Pitkin.[62] If Pitkin's account is true, it does not fit the allegations in the NIS file. Pitkin does not state someone impersonated him at Winter Soldier; rather he retracts the account he offered there. So where were the several soldiers whose were so outrageously impersonated at Winter Soldier? And where was the African American who had received help from the Nation of Islam in preparing his testimony?

There are also troubling questions about the Pitkin affidavit. Pitkin apparently filed his affidavit twice. His first affidavit was filed on August 31, 2004, and it was immediately contested. Another veteran, Scott Camil, filed his own affidavit on September 11, 2004, pointing to falsehoods in the Pitkin affidavit.[63] Pitkin subsequently filed a new affidavit on September 15, 2004. This new affidavit was surprising in its own right since his close friend from the 1970s, Nancy Miller Saunders, believed he was dead.[64] At any rate, Pitkin's new affidavit states that he falsely described "incidents of rape, brutality, atrocities and racism" at the urging of presidential candidate John Kerry.[65] This is problematic for another reason: Pitkin's statement at Winter Soldier does not describe incidents of rape, brutality, or other atrocities. Pitkin speaks thrice in the transcripts of Winter Soldier. The first and longest testimony is a generic statement about the dehumanization caused by war. Here, Pitkin uses the word *atrocity* to describe U.S. press coverage and his army training stateside, but not to describe specific incidents of violence in Vietnam. The closest Pitkin comes to a specific allegation in this first testimony is the following statement:

> When I got to Nam, it was like black had turned into white because I was totally unprepared. I was put into a recon unit operating in the Mekong Delta. I hadn't been taught anything about the weather, the terrain. I had been taught a little bit about booby traps, but that's really up to the guy who lays them; they can just be anything. It was a hit and miss thing. You go over there with that limited amount of training and knowledge of the culture you're up against and you're scared. You're so scared that you'll shoot anything, that you'll look at your enemy and these people that you're sort of a visitor to. You'll look at them as animals and at the same time you're just turning yourself into an animal too.[66]

There are also no descriptions of rape or brutality towards Vietnamese in Pitkin's second and third speeches. Pitkin's second speech concerns lying in a hospital in Okinawa and receiving a beautiful letter from a girl about Woodstock. His third speech concerns how American soldiers damaged themselves to avoid fighting. He describes how soldiers burned, cut, and broke their legs. Given that this is Pitkin's testimony in its entirety, it is unclear what descriptions of rape and brutality the Pitkin affidavit is retracting.

One last fact raises questions about the political motivation behind the affidavit. Pitkin is the easiest veteran to associate with John Kerry at Winter Soldier because he is the only one to appear with him on film. It is thought-provoking that given all the soldiers Lewy claims were impersonated at Winter Soldier, only and especially Pitkin came forward to denounce it.

At the moment, then, Pitkin's affidavit seems unreliable and Lewy's claims about Winter Soldier are as nearly hearsay as the ones he is criticizing. Recently, a group of anti-Kerry veterans have received and made available some 21,477 pages of FBI documents on the Vietnam Veterans Against the War.[67] Perhaps in time, the lost file or FBI files similar to it will appear, allowing one to identify the liars. But the continued absence of the Naval Investigative File suggests that Lewy's contact deliberately misled him and Lewy mistakenly found the contact convincing.

Two other features of Lewy's discussion of torture are also troubling, suggesting that his assessment of American torture in Vietnam is less than even-handed. Despite his criticism of testimonials about American torture in South Vietnam, Lewy is quick to accept testimonial literature when it pertains to Communist torture. Unable to show North Vietnamese government documents authorizing torture, he argues nevertheless that the uniformity in the testimonial literature suggests that torture was government policy. Lewy faults gullible antiwar criticism, arguing that they should have known the North Vietnamese would torture given past testimonials about Communist practice during the Korean and Franco-Vietnamese wars.[68]

This is the standard application of the Nuremberg rule of course: uniformity of practice indicates uniformity of intent. Indeed, there are important continuities in Communist torture practices, although the testimonial literature also indicates significant variations during the Vietnamese and Korean conflicts, as I document in chapters 3 and 17. Lewy is right to criticize the antiwar critics on this point. By the same token, however, the French tortured in Vietnam as did the South Vietnamese, and the uniform pattern for the latter also strongly suggested that the South Vietnamese had an official torture policy too. Lewy mentions South Vietnamese torture in one sentence, stating only that the ARVN was known for their bad treatment and torture of captured VC. Lewy does not even mention French torture during the Vietnamese conflict.[69]

It seems odd that Lewy applies one set of rules for acceptable evidence and interpretation for Communist torture and quite another for American torture. Lewy is correct that retrospective testimony about the past is highly problematic, but so too is proximate testimony. Proximity to the incident may occlude judgment and perspective, and the real situation may become more apparent with time. General Massu believed that torture was effective and necessary at the time he acted in Algeria, but came, correctly, to the opposite conclusion thirty years later. Does this mean his later testimony is false or unreliable? Again, it is rather surprising that Lewy does not even mention this possibility, seeking to rule out all retrospective testimonial literature in principle when it comes to American veterans' testimonies of torture.[70]

All this is somewhat less than even-handed. Lewy is rightly anxious to correct outrageous allegations of atrocities in veterans' testimonies. The difficulty is that Lewy appears to bend too far in the opposite direction, throwing out the baby with the bathwater. Perhaps in the aftermath of the Vietnam War, tempers ran high and long-lasting dislikes did not easily dissipate. Ultimately though, the testimonial evidence does not disagree too much with the position Lewy wants to defend, namely, that torture was not official government policy issued from Washington, DC. The testimonial evidence describes instead a local, semiofficial policy that existed for all the reasons Lewy outlines.

Notes

Introduction

Unpublished sources from the Public Records Office at Kew, London are designated in the notes by the code PRO followed by the standard code designating the office of origin. The codes used in this study are CO (Colonial Office), FO (Foreign Office), and WO (War Office).

1. See Niccolo Machiavelli, "The Prince," in *Selected Political Writings*, trans. David Wootton (Indianapolis: Hackett, 1994), 55.
2. *Report of the Independent Commission of the Los Angeles Police Department* (Los Angeles: The Commission, 1991), ii. Ten years earlier, a similar chase from the same intersection ended in the driver's death, and no charges were brought in that case. Lou Cannon, *Official Negligence* (Boulder, CO: Westview, 1999), 97–100.
3. Cannon, *Official Negligence*, 27, 31–32; John Murray and Barnet Resnick, A *Guide to Taser Technology* (Whitewater, CO: Whitewater Press, 1997), 75–77, 83.
4. Cannon, *Official Negligence*, 26, 44.
5. Tom Owens with Rod Browning, *Lying Eyes* (New York: Thunder's Mouth Press, 1994), 121.
6. Stacey Koon with Robert Deitz, *Presumed Guilty* (Washington, DC: Regnery, 1992), 38.
7. Ibid., 41.
8. Ibid., 41–42.
9. Ibid., 42. See also Cannon, *Official Negligence*, 35–36.
10. Ibid., 187.

11. Steve Wright, "The New Trade in Technologies of Restraint and Electroshock," in A *Glimpse of Hell*, ed. Duncan Forrest (London: Amnesty International, 1996), 140.

12. Those who find the adjective *democratic* peculiar here may wish to consult appendix B, where I discuss my use of the words *democracy* and *democratic*.

13. Dana Priest and Barton Gellman, "U.S. Decries Abuse but Defends Interrogations: 'Stress and Duress' Tactics Used on Terrorism Suspects Held in Secret Overseas Facilities," *Washington Post*, December 26, 2002, A1, A14–A15; Amnesty International (AI), *United States of America: The Threat of a Bad Example*, AMR 51/114/2003, August 19, 2003; AI, *United States of America: "We don't torture people in America,"* AMR 51/128/2003, October 20, 2003; Alan Dershowitz, *Shouting Fire* (Boston: Little, Brown, 2002), 470–77; Alan Dershowitz, "Is There a Torturous Road to Justice?" *Los Angeles Times*, November 8, 2001, B19; Mark Bowden, "The Dark Art of Interrogation," *Atlantic Monthly*, October 2003, 51–76.

14. For further discussion of this point, see chapter 18, "Noise."

15. Darius Rejali, *Torture and Modernity: State, Society and Self in Iran* (Boulder, CO: Westview, 1994).

16. Brian Rappert, *Non-Lethal Weapons as Legitimizing Forces?* (London: Frank Cass, 2003); James Ron, *Frontiers and Ghettos* (Berkeley and Los Angeles: University of California Press, 2003).

17. AI, *Arming the Torturers: Electro-shock Torture and the Spread of Stun Technology*, ACT 40/01/97, March 4, 1997, 12.

18. James Ron, "Varying Methods of State Violence," *International Organization* 51.2 (1997): 296–97.

19. Truth and Reconciliation Commission, *Report* (London: Macmillan, 1999), 2:190.

20. Lawrence E. Hinkle and Harold G. Wolff, "Communist Interrogation and Indoctrination of 'Enemies of the State,' " *A.M.A. Archives of Neurology and Psychiatry* 76 (August 1956): 130, 135. See also Albert Biderman, *March to Calumny* (New York: Arno Press, 1979), 136–37.

21. Duncan Forrest, "The Methods of Torture and Its Effects," in Forrest, A *Glimpse of Hell*, 112.

22. Wright, "New Trade in Technologies," 139.

23. Cited in Doug Cassel, "Enforcing the International Prohibition against Torture," paper presented at the Conference on Investigating and Combating Torture, University of Chicago, March 4–6, 1999, 1.

24. Nigel Rodley, "Investigating and Combating Torture," paper presented at the Conference on Investigating and Combating Torture, University of Chicago, March 4–6, 1999, at which I was present. See also Eric Prokosch, "Amnesty International's Anti-torture Campaigns," in Forrest, A *Glimpse of Hell*, 33.

25. Priest and Gellman, "U.S. Decries Abuse"; AI, *United States of America: The Threat of a Bad Example*, AMR 51/114/2003

26. Mark Danner, *Torture and Truth: America, Abu Ghraib, and the War on Terror* (New York: New York Review of Books, 2004); Steven Strasser, ed., *The Abu Ghraib Investigations* (New York: Public Affairs, 2004); David Rose, *Guantánamo*

(New York: New Press, 2004); Michael Ratner and Ellen Ray, *Guantánamo* (White River Junction, VT: Chelsea Green, 2004); AI, *United States of America: Human Dignity Denied*, AMR 51/145/2004, October 27, 2004.

27. As this book goes to print, it appears that Porter Goss, the director of the CIA, asked two national security experts to evaluate the CIA interrogation program's effectiveness in 2004. These reports have not been released. Dana Priest, "Covert CIA Program Withstands New Furor," *Washington Post*, December 30, 2005, A01.

28. For similar arguments, see Daniel Thomas, *The Helsinki Effect: International Norms, Human Rights, and the Demise of Communism* (Princeton, NJ: Princeton University Press, 2001); and Thomas Risse, Stephen C. Ropp, and Kathryn Sikkink, *The Power of Human Rights* (New York: Cambridge University Press, 1999).

29. With one critical exception. See Ron, "Varying Methods."

30. Tim Shallice, "The Ulster Depth Interrogation Techniques and Their Relation to Sensory Deprivation Research," *Cognition* 1.4 (1972): 385–405; and John McGuffin, *The Guineapigs* (Harmondsworth, England: Penguin, 1974). For recent claims, see Wright, "New Trade in Technologies," 137, 140; Armen Victorian, "United States, Canada, Britain: Partners in Mind Control Operations," *MindNet Journal*, July 1996, http://www.heart7.net/mcf/mindnet/mn181.htm; Armen Victorian, *The Mind Controllers* (Miami, FL: Lewis International, 2000); Alfred McCoy, *A Question of Torture* (New York: Metropolitan, 2006), 5, 8, 50.

31. Geoffrey Abbott, *Rack, Rope and Red-hot Pincers* (London: Headline Books, 1993); Karen Farrington, *Dark Justice* (New York: Smithmark, 1996); Brian Innes, *The History of Torture* (New York: St. Martin's, 1998); Jean Kellaway, *The History of Torture and Execution* (New York: Lyons Press, 2000); and Michael Kerrigan, *The Instruments of Torture* (New York: Lyons Press, 2001).

32. Everett Rogers, *Diffusion of Innovations*, 4th ed. (New York: Free Press, 1992), 130–204.

33. Confirming similar claims by Bruno Latour, *Science in Action* (Cambridge: Harvard University Press, 1987); Bruno Latour, *Aramis or The Love of Technology*, trans. Catherine Porter (Cambridge: Harvard University Press, 1996); Bruno Latour, "*The Prince* for Machines as well as for Machinations," in *Technology and the Social Process*, ed. Brian Elliott (Edinburgh: Edinburgh University Press, 1988), 20–43; John Law, "On the Methods of Long Distance Control," in *Power, Action, Belief*, ed. John Law (London: Routledge and Kegan Paul, 1986), 234–63; John Law, "The Anatomy of a Socio-Technical Struggle," in *Science Observed: Perspectives on the Social Study of Science*, ed. Karin Knorr-Cetina and Michael Mulkay (London: Sage, 1983), 44–69.

34. "Statement of Mordehy Petcho," in *Case of Cohen and A. Laronovich and Case of M. Petcho*, PRO CO 733/413/6.

35. Ludwig Wittgenstein, *Philosophical Investigations*, trans. G.E.M. Anscombe (Oxford: Basil Blackwell, 1976), 89–124.

36. For example, Milovan Djilas, *Of Prisons and Ideas* (New York: Harcourt Brace Jovanovich, 1986), 4. For other accounts, see Darius Rejali, "Whom Do You Trust?

What Do You Count On?" in *On Nineteen Eighty-Four: Orwell and Our Future*, ed. Abbott Gleason, Jack Goldsmith, and Martha Nussbaum (Princeton, NJ: Princeton University Press, 2005), 155–79.

37. Elaine Scarry, *The Body in Pain: The Making and Unmaking of the World* (Oxford: Oxford University Press, 1985), 3, 4, 6, 45.

38. "To have pain," writes Scarry, "is to have *certainty*; to hear about pain is to have doubt" (ibid., 13). For Wittgenstein's response to such a claim, see Wittgenstein, *Philosophical Investigations*, remarks nos. 246, 251, 253, 289, 310, 403–9, and p. 189.

39. Veena Das, "Language and Body," in *Social Suffering*, ed. Veena Das, Arthur Kleinman, and Margaret Lock (Berkeley and Los Angeles: University of California Press, 1997), 88.

40. See Garath Williams, "Objects and Spaces: Reading Elaine Scarry's *The Body in Pain* in an Arendtian Light," unpublished paper, 2003.

Chapter 1
Modern Torture and Its Observers

1. Jason Barber, *Less than Human: Torture in Cambodia* (Pnom Penh: Cambodian League for the Promotion and Defense of Human Rights, 2000), 36.

2. Darius Rejali, *Torture and Modernity: Self, Society and State in Modern Iran* (Boulder, CO: Westview, 1994).

3. Ulpian, "Duties of Proconsul," in Edward Peters, *Torture*, 2nd ed. (Philadelphia: University of Pennsylvania Press, 1996), 215.

4. Ulpian, cited in ibid., 1.

5. Peters, *Torture*, 13–16; S. C. Todd, *The Shape of Athenian Law* (Oxford: Clarendon, 1993), 96, 172, 187; Steven Johnstone, *Disputes and Democracy* (Austin: University of Texas Press, 1999), 70–92; Page DuBois, *Torture and Truth* (New York: Routledge, 1991), 63; Virginia Hunter, *Policing Athens* (Princeton, NJ: Princeton University Press, 1994), 91–95, 181–84.

6. Sebastian Guazzini, "Tractatus ad Defensam Inquisitorum," in Peters, *Torture*, 251.

7. Cesare Beccaria, "Of Torture," in Peters, *Torture*, 265.

8. John Langbein, *Torture and the Law of Proof* (Chicago: University of Chicago Press, 1977), 3.

9. Chief Müller, "Decree of the Chief of the Security Police and the SD, 12 June 1942 regarding third degree methods of interrogation [1531-PS]," in International Military Tribunal (IMT), *Trial of the Major War Criminals* (Nuremberg, Germany: n.p., 1948), 27:326–27. English translation in *Germans against Hitler, July 20, 1944* (Bonn: Bundeszentrale für politische Bildung, [1969]), 190–91.

10. Alan Dershowitz, "Is There a Torturous Road to Justice?" *Los Angeles Times*, November 8, 2001, B19.

11. Cited in Peters, *Torture*, 2.

12. Martha Huggins, ed., *Vigilantism and the State in Modern Latin America* (New York: Praeger, 1991); Bruce Campbell, *Death Squads in Global Perspective* (New York: St. Martin's, 2000); T. David Mason and Dale Krane, "The Political Economy of Death Squads: Toward a Theory of the Impact of State-Sanctioned Terror," *International Studies Quarterly* 33.2 (1989): 175–98; Jeffery A. Sluka, ed., *Death Squad* (Philadelphia: University of Pennsylvania Press, 2000).

13. Deborah Blatt, "Recognizing Rape as a Method of Torture," *Review of Law and Social Change* 19.4 (1992): 821–65; Darius Rejali, "After Feminist Analyses of Bosnian Violence," in *The Women and War Reader*, ed. Lois Ann Lorentzen and Jennifer Turpin (New York: New York University Press, 1998), 26–33.

14. Anonymous (interviewed February 20, 1999), cited in Caroline Elkins, *Imperial Reckoning* (New York: Henry Holt, 2005), 183. See also Ted Morgan, *My Battle of Algiers* (New York: HarperCollins, 2005), 92.

15. Karl Marx, *Capital* (New York: International Publishers, 1070), 1:422–23.

16. James Walvin, *Slavery and the Slave Trade* (Jackson: University Press of Mississippi, 1983), 68–69; *Unchained Memories: Readings from the Slave Narratives* (Boston: Bullfinch Press, 2002), 87–89.

17. The UN definition of torture, for example, excludes the pain police cause incidentally while carrying out their lawful duties even though this too may result in indignity (Peters, *Torture*, 2).

18. Oregon Revised Statute 163.095(1)(e) (2001); Oregon Revised Statute 177.322 (2001).

19. IMT, *Trial*; John Marks, *The Search for the Manchurian Candidate* (New York: McGraw-Hill, 1980).

20. Daniel Thomas, *The Helsinki Effect* (Princeton, NJ: Princeton University Press, 2001), 87. See also Mary Ann Glendon, *A World Made New* (New York: Random House, 2001), 193–219; Paul Gordon Lauren, *The Evolution of International Human Rights*, 2nd ed. (Philadelphia: University of Pennsylvania Press, 2003), 237.

21. Pierre Vidal-Naquet, *Torture*, trans. Barry Richard (Harmondsworth, England: Penguin, 1963).

22. John McGuffin, *The Guineapigs* (Harmondsworth, England: Penguin, 1974), 78–116.

23. Andrée Viollis, *Indochine S.O.S.* (Paris: Gallimard, 1935).

24. H. Hessell Tiltman, *The Terror in Europe* (New York: Frederick A. Stokes, 1932).

25. Eugene Lyons, *Assignment in Utopia* (New York: Harcourt, Brace, 1937).

26. George Ryley Scott, *The History of Corporal Punishment*, 2nd ed. (London: Torchstream, 1954).

27. National Commission on Law Observance and Enforcement, *Report on Lawlessness in Law Enforcement* (Washington, DC: U.S. Government Printing Office, 1931).

28. Alec Mellor, *La Torture* (Paris: Horizons littéraires, 1949).

29. Vidal-Naquet, *Torture*, 142–43.

30. Peter Deeley, *Beyond Breaking Point* (London: Arthur Barker, 1971).

31. A. J. Langguth, *Hidden Terrors* (New York: Pantheon, 1978); Noam Chomsky and Edward Herman, *The Washington Connection and Third World Fascism*, 2 vols. (Montreal: Black Rose Press, 1979).

32. John Conroy, *Unspeakable Acts, Ordinary People* (New York: Knopf, 2000).

33. Vidal-Naquet, *Torture*, 142–43.

34. John Talbott, *The War Without a Name* (New York: Knopf, 1980), 98, 108.

35. Peter Benenson, introduction to *Gangrene* (London: Calberbooks, 1959), 38.

36. Amnesty International (AI), *1961–1976: A Chronology* (London, 1976), 3, 16.

37. AI, "About Us," http://www.amnesty.org.

38. Thomas, *The Helsinki Effect*, 50–51.

39. Ibid., 27–88; William Korey, *The Promises We Keep* (New York: St. Martin's, 1993).

40. James Ron, "Varying Methods of State Violence," *International Organization* 51.2 (1997): 280.

41. Jackie Smith, "Transnational Organizations," in *Encyclopedia of Violence, Peace, and Conflict* (San Diego: Academic Press, 1999), 3:591–602.

42. AI, *Report on Torture* (London: Duckworth, 1973).

43. Caroline Moorehead, "Crisis of Confidence," *Financial Times*, June 18, 2005, 18.

44. William Korey, *NGOs and the Universal Declaration of Human Rights* (New York: St. Martin's, 2001), 159–80.

45. Thomas, *The Helsinki Effect*, 91–157.

46. Jeri Laber, *The Courage of Strangers: Coming of Age with the Human Rights Movement* (New York: Public Affairs, 2002), 177–82, 376.

47. Vidal-Naquet, *Torture*, 143.

48. AI, *Torture Worldwide* (London, 2000), 100.

Chapter 2
Torture and Democracy

1. Walter Benjamin, "Theses on the Philosophy of History," in *Illuminations*, ed. Hannah Arendt, trans. Harry Zohn (New York: Schocken, 1968), 257.

2. For more on the distinction between democracy and authoritarian states, see appendix B. The puzzle is specified as puzzle 5 in appendix C.

3. George Kateb, "Undermining the Constitution," *Social Research* 70.2 (2003): 594.

4. Jacques Massu, *La vraie bataille d'Alger* (Paris: Plon, 1972), 175–83.

5. "Des cours sur une 'torture humaine' sont donnés aux stagiaires du camp Jeanne-d'Arc," *Le Monde*, December 20–21, 1959, 6. Translation available in *The Gangrene*, trans. Robert Silvers (New York: Lyle Stewart, 1960), 12–13.

6. Pierre Vidal-Naquet, *Torture*, trans. Barry Richard (Harmondsworth, England: Penguin, 1963), 98–106; Alistair Horne, *A Savage War of Peace* (New York: Viking, 1977), 273–99, 436–61.

7. Vidal-Naquet, *Torture*, 77–78.

8. Patrick Kessel and Giovanni Pirelli, *Le people algérien et la guerre* (Paris: François Maspero, 1962), 581.

9. Covered thoroughly in Sylvie Thénault, *Une drôle de justice* (Paris: Editions La Découverte, 2001).

10. Cited in *The Gangrene*, 77; see also 93.

11. Vidal-Naquet, *Torture*, 122–23. For other cases, see Kessel and Pirelli, *Le people algérien*, 435, 499.

12. Vidal-Naquet, *Torture*, 73, 112, 141; Pierre Vidal-Naquet, *La torture dans la république* (Paris: Editions de Minuit, 1972), 5; Henri Alleg, *The Question* (New York: George Braziller, 1958), 9–11; *The Gangrene*, 9–10.

13. Vidal-Naquet, *Torture*, 122.

14. Ibid., 86.

15. Cited in ibid., 100.

16. Vidal-Naquet, *Torture*, 17, 141–42.

17. Cited in ibid., 144.

18. Notably Jean Lartéguy, *The Centurions*, trans. Xan Felding (New York: E. P. Dutton, 1962). See Vidal-Naquet, *Torture*, 146.

19. Vidal-Naquet, *Torture*, 73.

20. Max Weber, *From Max Weber*, trans. H. H. Gerth and C. Wright Mills (New York: Oxford University Press, 1958), 226.

21. Vidal-Naquet, *Torture*, 149.

22. Ibid., 141.

23. John Conroy, *Unspeakable Acts, Ordinary People* (New York: Knopf, 2000), 212.

24. See Malcolm D. Evans and Rod Morgan, *Preventing Torture* (Oxford: Clarendon Press, 1998), 26–61; Stuart Creighton Miller, *Benevolent Assimilation* (New Haven, CT: Yale University Press, 1982), 167, 183, 184, 213, 225, 235; Richard Welch Jr., *Response to Imperialism* (Chapel Hill: University of North Carolina Press, 1979), 134–37; Peter Deeley, *Beyond Breaking Point* (London: Arthur Barker, 1971), 40–64; Hylah Jacques, "Spain: Systematic Torture in a Democratic State," *Monthly Review*, November 1985, 57–62; Amnesty International (AI), *India*, ASA 20/11/91 (London: Amnesty International 1992); AI, *Turkey*, EUR 44/39/92 (London, 1992); "Judge Rejects Bid to Extradite Chechen Rebel Leader," *Guardian* (London), November 13, 2003, http://www.guardian.co.uk/.

25. Guenter Lewy, *America in Vietnam* (Oxford: Oxford University Press, 1978), 324–31; Conroy, *Unspeakable Acts, Ordinary People*, 113–21; John Conroy, "Tools of Torture," *Chicago Reader*, February 4, 2005, 1, 24–27.

26. See Evans and Morgan, *Preventing Torture*, 26–60; and Talal Asad, "On Torture, or Cruel, Inhuman, and Degrading Treatment," in *Social Suffering*, ed. Veena Das, Arthur Kleinman, and Margaret Lock (Berkeley and Los Angeles: University of California Press, 1997), 296.

27. Philip Jones, *The Italian City-State* (Oxford: Clarendon Press, 1997), 377–80; Edward Peters, *Torture*, 2nd ed. (Philadelphia: University of Pennsylvania Press, 1996), 56–57.

28. Sebastian Guazzini, "Tractatus ad Defensam Inquisitorum," in Peters, *Torture*, 259.

29. Kenneth Pennington, *The Prince and the Law, 1200–1600* (Berkeley and Los Angeles: University of California Press, 1993), 42–44, 157–60; Trevor Dean, "Criminal Justice in Mid-Fifteenth-Century Bologna," in *Crime, Society and the Law in Renaissance Italy*, ed. Trevor Dean and K.J.P. Lowe (Cambridge: Cambridge University Press, 1994), 18–22; John K. Bracket, *Criminal Justice and Crime in Late Renaissance Florence, 1537–1609* (Cambridge: Cambridge University Press, 1992), 61–65; Guido Ruggiero, *Violence in Early Renaissance Venice* (New Brunswick, NJ: Rutgers University Press, 1980), 24; Henry Charles Lea, *A History of the Inquisition of the Middle Ages* (New York: Russell and Russell, 1958), 1:421–24.

30. For the United States, see National Commission on Law Observance and Enforcement, *Report on Lawlessness in Law Enforcement* (Washington, DC: U.S. Government Printing Office, 1931); and Human Rights Watch (HRW), *Shielded from Justice* (New York: Human Rights Watch, 1998). For Russia, see HRW, *Confession at Any Cost* (New York: Human Rights Watch, 1999), 20–42, 54–78, 103–11. For Japan, see Futaba Igarashi, "Forced to Confess," in *Democracy in Contemporary Japan*, ed. G. McCormack and Y. Sugimoto (Armonk, NY: M. E. Sharpe, 1986), 201–11.

31. Philip Zimbardo, "Coercion and Compliance: The Psychology of Police Confessions," in *The Triple Revolution Emerging*, ed. Robert Perrucci and Marc Pilisuk (Boston: Little, Brown, 1971), 492–508.

32. John Langbein, *Torture and the Law of Proof* (Chicago: University of Chicago Press, 1977).

33. Saul Kassin and Holly Sukel, "Coerced Confession and the Jury," *Law and Human Behavior* 21 (1997): 27–46.

34. David Bayley, *Forces of Order* (Berkeley and Los Angeles: University of California Press, 1976), 146–47.

35. Ibid., 150.

36. Gavan McCormack, "Crime, Confession and Control in Contemporary Japan," in McCormack and Sugimoto, *Democracy in Contemporary Japan*, 187.

37. Bayley, *Forces of Order*, 147.

38. McCormack, "Crime, Confession and Control," 187.

39. A. Watson, "The Dark Cloud over Japanese Criminal Justice: Abuse of Suspects and Forced Confessions," part 1, *Justice of the Peace and Local Government Law*, August 5, 1995, 516.

40. Karen Parker and Etienne Jaudel, *Police Cell Detention in Japan* (San Francisco: Association of Humanitarian Lawyers, 1989), 40.

41. Ibid., 9.

42. Bayley, *Forces of Order*, 151.

43. Setsuo Miyazawa, *Policing in Japan*, trans. Frank Bennett Jr. and John Haley (Albany: State University of New York Press, 1992), 20.

44. Parker and Jaudel, *Police Cell Detention*, 22–24.

45. Bayley, *Forces of Order*, 153; see 151–54.

46. Parker and Jaudel, *Police Cell Detention*, 12.

47. Peter Katzenstein and Ytaka Tsujinaka, *Defending the Japanese State* (Ithaca, NY: Cornell University Press, 1991), 144; Christopher Aldous, *The Police in Occupation Japan* (London: Routledge, 1997), 228, 284.

48. Parker and Jaudel, *Police Cell Detention*, 9–10. See also Chalmers Johnson, *Conspiracy at Matsukawa* (Berkeley and Los Angeles: University of California Press, 1972), 166–96; Miyazawa, *Policing in Japan*, 151–55.

49. Bayley, *Forces of Order*, 153.

50. Aldous, *Police in Occupation Japan*, 229.

51. See Igarashi, "Forced to Confess"; Miyazawa, *Policing in Japan*; Parker and Jaudel, *Police Cell Detention*; Aldous, *Police in Occupation Japan*, 226–30; Watson, "Dark Cloud," part 1, 516–19; A. Watson, "The Dark Cloud over Japanese Criminal Justice: Abuse of Suspects and Forced Confessions," part 2, *Justice of the Peace and Local Government Law*, August 12, 1995, 534–37; *A Typical Example of Human Rights Violations under the Daiyo-Kangoku System in Japan* (Tokyo: Japan Civil Liberties Union, 1991); AI, *Japan* (London, 1991); *What's Daiyo-Kangoku?* (Tokyo: Japan Federation of Bar Associations, 1993); HRW, *Prison Conditions in Japan* (New York: Human Rights Watch, 1995); F. Bennett, "Pretrial Detention in Japan," *Law in Japan* 23 (1990): 67–71.

52. Miyazawa, *Policing in Japan*, 234–35.

53. Ibid. See also Watson, "Dark Cloud," part 1, 516; and Johnson, *Conspiracy at Matsukawa*, 156.

54. Cited in Zimbardo, "Coercion and Compliance," 504.

55. Miyazawa, *Policing in Japan*, 225.

56. Ibid., 235.

57. Elise Tipton, *The Japanese Police State* (Honolulu: University of Hawaii Press, 1990), 137; see also 186. See also Bayley, *Forces of Order*, 152–53.

58. Miyazawa, *Policing in Japan*, 25; see also xi, 9, and 17.

59. Johnson, *Conspiracy at Matsukawa*, 151; Piet van Reenen, "Routine Police Torture: Towards a Personalistic Analysis and Strategy," *Human Rights Review* 4.1 (2002): 55–56.

60. Peters, *Torture*, 13–16; Steven Johnstone, *Disputes and Democracy* (Austin: University of Texas Press, 1999), 70–92; Page DuBois, *Torture and Truth* (New York: Routledge, 1991), 63; Virginia Hunter, *Policing Athens* (Princeton, NJ: Princeton University Press, 1994), 91–95, 181–84.

61. See Hunter, *Policing Athens*, 70–95.

62. Hannah Arendt, *The Human Condition* (Chicago: University of Chicago Press, 1958), 218 n. 53.

63. DuBois, *Torture and Truth*, 63. See also Hunter, *Policing Athens*, 181–84.

64. Freddie Parker, ed., *Stealing a Little Freedom* (New York: Garland, 1994), 113.

65. Spartacus Educational, *Slave Branding*, http://www.spartacus.schoolnet.co.uk/USASbranding.htm, updated May 2, 2002, accessed December 1, 2003.

66. Ibid. See also James Walvin, *Slavery and the Slave Trade* (Jackson: University Press of Mississippi, 1983), 99, 109–10; Daniel Mannix, *The History of Torture*

([New York]: Dorset, 1964), 179; John Hope Franklin and Loren Schwenger, *Runaway Slaves* (Oxford: Oxford University Press, 1999), 43, 194, 216–17.

67. Paul Finkelman, *Slavery in the Courtroom* (Washington, DC: Library of Congress, 1985), 171–73; William Andrews, *Bygone Punishments* (London: Philip Allan, 1931), 127–31; Linda Kealey, "Patterns of Punishment: Massachusetts in the Eighteenth Century," *American Journal of Legal History* 30.2 (1986): 163, 172. Such practices were also common in small European republics and relatively autonomous cities, for example in the northern and southern Netherlands (Pieter Spierenburg, "The Body and the State," in *The Oxford History of the Prison*, ed. Norval Morris and David Rothman [New York: Oxford University Press, 1995], 53). And there were analogous practices in authoritarian states. See Brian Innes, *The History of Torture* (New York: St. Martin's, 1998), 58–60; Alice Morse Earle, *Curious Punishments of Bygone Days* (Montclair, NJ: Patterson Smith, 1969), 86–95, 140.

68. Paul Chevigny, "Changing Control of Police Violence in Rio De Janiero and Sao Paulo, Brazil," in *Policing Change, Changing Police*, ed. Otwin Marenin (New York: Garland Publishing, 1996), 30.

69. William Greer, "Turmoil in Troubled Precinct Centers on 'The Strip,' " *New York Times*, April 26, 1985, B1.

70. Ibid.

71. "Brutality Charges Strain Bond of Trust; A Queens Neighborhood Divided," Associated Press, April 28, 1985, http://www.lexis-nexis.com/.

72. van Reenen, "Routine Police Torture," 54.

73. Miyazawa, *Policing in Japan*, 228.

74. Chevigny, "Changing Control," 26, 29.

75. Pierre Bourdieu and Loïs Wacquant, *An Invitation to Reflexive Sociology* (Chicago: University of Chicago, 1992), 167–68.

76. See, for example, Peter Taylor, *Beating the Terrorists?* (Harmondsworth, England: Penguin, 1980), 87–92, 123–42, 225–27, 266–68, 306–14.

77. HRW, *Confession at Any Cost*, 71–77, 110–11.

78. Charles Foley, *Island in Revolt* (London: Longmans, Green, 1962), 88.

79. van Reenen, "Routine Police Torture," 55.

80. HRW, *Confession at Any Cost*, 120.

81. Miyazawa, *Policing in Japan*, 227, 230.

82. Peter Andreas, "The Rise of the American Crimefare State," *World Policy Journal* 14.3 (1997): 39.

83. See Mike Davis, *City of Quartz* (New York: Vintage, 1992), 221–65; Les Johnston, *The Rebirth of Private Policing* (London: Routledge, 1992); Clifford Shearing, "Reinventing Policing: Policing as Governance," in Marenin, *Policing Change, Changing Police*; Clifford Shearing, "The Relation between Public and Private Policing," in *Modern Policing*, ed. Michael Tonry and Norval Morris (Chicago: University of Chicago Press, 1992); Rod Morgan and Tim Newburn, *The Future of Policing* (Oxford: Clarendon Press, 1997); Mark Shaw, *Crime and Policing in Post-Apartheid South Africa* (Bloomington: Indiana University Press, 2002); P. W.

Singer, "Corporate Warriors," Center for Strategic and International Studies, MIT, 2001–2.

84. Ibid.; see also Peter Andreas, *Border Games* (Ithaca, NY: Cornell University Press, 2000); Ronald Crelinsten, "The Discourse and Practice of Counter-Terrorism in Liberal Democracies," *Australian Journal of Politics and History* 44.1 (1998): 389–413.

85. Davis, *City of Quartz*, 250.

86. Johnston, *Rebirth of Private Policing*, 73–85.

87. Shaw, *Crime and Policing*, 102.

88. Louise I. Shelley, "Transnational Organized Crime," in *The Illicit Global Economy and State Power*, ed. Peter Andreas and Richard Friman (Lanham, MD: Rowman and Littlefield, 1999).

89. Ibid., 45. This, as Franchetti describes, was the genesis of the Mafia in southern Italy (Leopoldo Franchetti, *Condizioni politiche e administrative della Sicilia* [Firenze: G. Barbera, 1877]). Franchetti points out that the Mafia arose at a time when the state was unable to protect new middle-class property owners and many men trained in the use of violence were suddenly unemployed during the breakup of baronial estates and the transition to a market economy.

90. Mark Ragan, "Stun Gun Sales Shock Lawmen," *San Diego Union-Tribune*, May 9, 1985, A1.

91. Shaw, *Crime and Policing*, 96–101, 108.

92. Shearing, "Public and Private Policing," 425.

93. Asad, "On Torture," 296.

94. See the following reports made available by the European Committee for the Prevention of Torture (http://www.cpt.coe.int/en/): *Albania* (2000); *Austria* (1990, 1999); *Belgium* (1993, 1997, 2001); *Bulgaria* (1995, 1999); *Croatia* (1998); *Estonia* (1997); *France* (1991, 1996, 2000); *Georgia* (2001); *Greece* (1993, 1996, 1997, 2001); *Hungary* (1994, 1999); *Ireland* (1993, 1998); *Italy* (1992, 1995, 2000); *Latvia* (1999); *Lithuania* (2000); *Macedonia* (1998, 2001, 2002); *Moldova* (1998, 2000, 2001); *Poland* (1996, 2000); *Portugal* (1992, 1995, 1996, 1999); *Romania* (1995, 1999); *Russia* (2001); *Slovakia* (1995, 2000); *Switzerland* (1993); *Ukraine* (1998, 2000); *United Kingdom* (1994, 1997, 2001). See also Chevigny, "Changing Control"; Conroy, *Unspeakable Acts, Ordinary People*; HRW, *Confession at Any Cost*; AI, *Arming the Torturers*, ACT 40/01/97 (London, 1997), 7–11; AI, *Report on Torture* (London: Duckworth, 1973), 200; and AI, *India*.

95. See Katzenstein and Tsujinaka, *Defending the Japanese State*; Justin McCurry, "The Enemy Within," *Guardian* (London), December 30, 2003, http://www.guardian.co.uk/; Walter Ames, *Police and Community in Japan* (Berkeley and Los Angeles: University of California Press, 1981), 99; Japanese Civil Liberties Union, *Criminal Procedure and the Human Rights of Foreigners in Japan* (Tokyo: Japanese Civil Liberties Union, July 1991); Wayne Cornelius, "Japan: The Illusion of Immigration Control," in *Controlling Immigration*, ed. Wayne Cornelius, Philip Martin, and James Hollifield (Stanford, CA: Stanford University Press, 1994), 375–410.

96. Conroy, *Unspeakable Acts, Ordinary People*, 212–13.
97. Yehuda Meir, cited in ibid., 152–53.
98. Conroy, *Unspeakable Acts, Ordinary People*, 13–15, 139–42, 149–55, 205.
99. Ibid., 11–20.
100. Omri Kochva, cited in ibid., 209, 210; see also 212, 220.
101. Soldier cited in Conroy, *Unspeakable Acts, Ordinary People*, 142.
102. Omri Kochva, cited in ibid., 208; see also 14–15, 139, 201.
103. Zvi Barkai, cited in ibid., 155.
104. Ben Moshe, cited in ibid., 204.
105. Conroy, *Unspeakable Acts, Ordinary People*, 14.
106. Ben Moshe cited in ibid., 205.
107. Yehuda Meir, cited in ibid., 202–3.

Chapter 3
Lights, Heat, and Sweat

1. National Commission on Law Observance and Enforcement, *Report on Law-lessness in Law Enforcement* (Washington, DC: U.S. Government Printing Office, 1931), 256. Hereafter cited as Wickersham Commission.
2. Lawrence E. Hinkle and Harold G. Wolff, "Communist Interrogation and Indoc-trination of 'Enemies of the State,' " *A.M.A. Archives of Neurology and Psychiatry* 76 (August 1956): 115–74. The classified version, *Communist Control Techniques* (April 2, 1956) is available at the National Security Archives, George Washington University Library, Washington, DC. This report differs mainly in that it includes references to other CIA brainwashing studies, but the text is more or less the same. What McCoy means by calling the public version "sanitized" is anyone's guess. See Alfred McCoy, *A Question of Torture* (New York: Metropolitan, 2006), 46.
3. Hinkle and Wolff, "Communist Interrogation," 118.
4. Wickersham Commission, 30, 39, 61, 217.
5. Ibid., 72–75, 83.
6. Ibid., 153.
7. Ibid., 61 (Kansas City), 91–93 (New York), 102–4 (Buffalo), 120–22 (Detroit), 126 (Chicago), 144–47 (Los Angeles), 148–49 (San Francisco), 239 (Montgomery), 249 (St. Louis), 255 (Pittsburgh).
8. Ibid., 52–152, 238–59.
9. George Dougherty, former deputy commissioner of the New York Police Depart-ment, cited in ibid., 43.
10. Wickersham Commission, 92. See also Charles Franklin, *The Third Degree* (Lon-don: Robert Hale, 1970), 145.
11. See appendix B for further discussion of this methodological point.
12. "Report of the Committee on Lawless Enforcement of Law," *American Journal of Police Science* 1.6 (1930): 580. See also Emanuel Lavine, *The Third Degree* (Gar-den City, NY: Garden City Publishing, 1930), 50; F. Dalton O'Sullivan, *Crime*

Detection (Chicago: O'Sullivan Publishing House, 1928), 298; J. A. Larson, "Present Police and Legal Methods for the Determination of the Innocence or Guilt of the Suspect," *Journal of the American Institute of Criminal Law and Criminology* 16.2 (1925): 221.

13. Wickersham Commission, 118; see also 60–61, 153. See also Lavine, *The Third Degree*, 61–62; Thomas Repetto, *The Blue Parade* (New York: Free Press, 1978), 176–78; Oswald Villard, "Official Lawlessness," *Harpers*, October 1927, 610; Ernest Jerome Hopkins, *Our Lawless Police* (New York: Viking, 1931), 208, 211, 213–16; Larson, "Police and Legal Methods," 220, 239–42, 247–48.

14. Wickersham Commission, 126.

15. Ibid., 92, 118; Lavine, *The Third Degree*, 51–52; O'Sullivan, *Crime Detection*, 297; Richard A. Leo, "The Third Degree and the Origins of Psychological Interrogation in the United States," in *Interrogations, Confessions, and Entrapment*, ed. G. Daniel Lassiter (New York: Kluwer Academic, 2004), 45–47.

16. Wickersham Commission, 92, 118–20, 126; Lavine, *The Third Degree*, 50.

17. Wickersham Commission, 47, 153. See also O'Sullivan, *Crime Detection*, 298; Larson, "Police and Legal Methods," 220.

18. Wickersham Commission. 139.

19. Ibid., 239.

20. Villard, "Official Lawlessness," 611–12.

21. Wickersham Commission, 118–19, 151, 153; O'Sullivan, *Crime Detection*, 295; David Rothman, *Conscience and Convenience*, rev. ed. (New York: Aldine de Gruyter, 2002), 153, 155.

22. Wickersham Commission, 104; Larson, "Police and Legal Methods," 238–39.

23. Ibid., 92, 126; Lavine, *The Third Degree*, 50.

24. O'Sullivan, *Crime Detection*, 298; Larson, "Police and Legal Methods," 220.

25. Wickersham Commission, 67.

26. Larson, "Police and Legal Methods," 222.

27. Wickersham Commission, 38–39, 71–73, 141–43; Rothman, *Conscience and Convenience*, 152, 156; Larson, "Police and Legal Methods," 245; O'Sullivan, *Crime Detection*, 295; Daniel Mannix, *The History of Torture* ([New York]: Dorset, 1964), 186; Don W. Sears, "Legal Consequences of the Third Degree," *Ohio State Law Journal* 9 (1948): 515; *Report upon the Illegal Practices of the United States Department of Justice* (New York: Workers Defense Union, 1920), 11–16.

28. Wickersham Commission, 151. See also Peter Deeley, *Beyond Breaking Point* (London: Arthur Barker, 1971), 228; John MacDonald, *The Murderer and His Victim*, 2nd ed. (Springfield, IL: Charles C. Thomas, 1986), 136–37; Larson, "Police and Legal Methods," 221.

29. Wickersham Commission, 126; O'Sullivan, *Crime Detection*, 297; Leo, "Third Degree," 46.

30. Wickersham Commission, 69, 139.

31. Ibid., 151; O'Sullivan, *Crime Detection*, 296.

32. Rothman, *Conscience and Convenience*, 156; Mannix, *The History of Torture*, 184–85; Jack London, *Star Rover* (New York: Grosset and Dunlap, 1915), 51–60.

33. Wickersham Commission, 20. The full transcript of Sylvester's remarks and several other police chiefs at the meeting can be found in Larson, "Police and Legal Methods," 221–25.

34. Major Sylvester makes no reference to Freemasonry ceremonies in coining this phrase, contrary to Innes (Brian Innes, *The History of Torture* [New York: St. Martin's, 1998], 177). It is an American phrase and had no British equivalent. See United Kingdom, *Report of the Royal Commission on Police Powers and Procedure*, reprint ed. (New York: Arno, 1971), 100. The phrase does not originate with the Gestapo, or in Germany, or in Ireland in 1919, contrary to various claims (Larson, "Police and Legal Methods," 225; Kate Saunders, *Eighteen Layers of Hell* [London: Cassell, 1996], 44–45; Dirk von Schrader, *Elementary Field Interrogation* (n.p.: Delta, 1978), 27).

35. Wickersham Commission, 48, 104. For the similar impact of publicity on prison violence, see Rothman, *Conscience and Convenience*, 157.

36. Wickersham Commission, 127; see also 121–22.

37. Ibid., 118.

38. Ibid., 92.

39. Ibid., 104–10.

40. *Brown v. Mississippi*, 297 U.S. 279 (1936), 286.

41. *Chambers v. Florida*, 309 U.S. 227 (1939), 238–39.

42. *Ashcraft v. Tennessee*, 322 U.S. 143 (1944), 154. For earlier debates, see Wickersham Commission, 28.

43. Wickersham Commission, 53, 259–61; *Royal Commission*, 100; Patrick Devlin, *The Criminal Prosecution in England* (New Haven, CT: Yale University Press, 1958), 53; Ronald Kidd, *British Liberty in Danger* (London: Lawrence and Wishart, 1940), 151; George Ryley Scott, *The History of Torture* (London: Torchstream, 1940), 277; Stuart Bowes, *The Police and Civil Liberties* (London: Lawrence and Wishart, 1966); and Clive Emsley, "Police Forces and Public Order in England and France During the Interwar Years," in *Policing Western Europe*, ed. Clive Emsley and Barbara Weinberger (New York: Greenwood, 1991), 159–86.

44. Kidd, *British Liberty in Danger*, 152.

45. E. G. Hemmerde, cited in ibid., 151.

46. *Royal Commission*, 101.

47. Devlin, *Criminal Prosecution in England*, 53.

48. Scott, *The History of Torture*, 277.

49. William Sargant, *The Unquiet Mind* (Boston: Little, Brown, 1967), 118. See also William Sargant, *The Battle for the Mind* (Garden City, NY: Doubleday, 1957), 200–208. For Sargant's connection to British intelligence, see Michael Ignatieff, "What Did the CIA Do To His Father?" *New York Times Magazine*, April 1, 2001, 60.

50. Deeley, *Beyond Breaking Point*, 137–59.

51. Wickersham Commission, 111.

52. Jerome Skolnick and James Fyfe, *Above the Law* (New York: Free Press, 1993), 56–58. See also Wickersham Commission, 69, 121, 110–11 (hard-soft ploy), 167.

53. Anthony Storr, "Torture without Violence," *New Statesman*, March 12, 1960, 348.

54. Philip Zimbardo, "Coercion and Compliance: The Psychology of Police Confessions," in *The Triple Revolution Emerging*, ed. Robert Perrucci and Marc Pilisuk (Boston: Little, Brown, 1971), 492–509.

55. Scott, *The History of Torture*, 277.

56. Deeley, *Beyond Breaking Point*, 144–45, 157.

57. Ludovic Kennedy, *Ten Rillington Place* (New York: Simon and Schuster, 1961).

58. Ibid., 113. See also Storr, "Torture without Violence," 358.

59. Zimbardo, "Coercion and Compliance," 493.

60. Louis Ducloux, *From Blackmail to Treason*, trans. Ronald Matthews (London: Andre Deutsch, 1958), 87–88.

61. Alec Mellor, *La torture* (Paris: Horizons littéraires, 1949), 230.

62. Gérard de Lacaze-Duthiers, *La torture a travers les âges* (Herblay, Seine-et-Oise, France: Editions de l'idée libre, 1961), 79; Franklin, *The Third Degree*, 145.

63. Hsi-Huey Liang, *The Berlin Police Force in the Weimar Republic* (Berkeley and Los Angeles: University of California Press, 1970), 140.

64. Chief Müller, "Decree of the Chief of the Security Police and the SD, 12 June 1942 regarding third degree methods of interrogation [1531-PS]," in International Military Tribunal, *Trial of the Major War Criminals* (Nuremberg, Germany: n.p. 1948), 27:326–27. English translation in *Germans against Hitler, July 20, 1944* (Bonn: Bundeszentrale für politische Bildung, [1969]), 190–91.

65. George Browder, *Hitler's Enforcers* (New York: Oxford University Press, 1996), 17.

66. Liang, *Berlin Police Force*, 148–49; see also 117–18, 126, 137, 140, 149.

67. Ibid., 17.

68. Erich Lieberman von Sonnenberg, cited in Browder, *Hitler's Enforcers*, 29–30.

69. Ingo Muller, *Hitler's Justice* (Cambridge: Harvard University Press, 1991), 178.

70. Browder, *Hitler's Enforcers*, 38–39.

71. Muller, *Hitler's Justice*, 178–79.

72. Müller, "Decree," 27:326–27.

73. Cited in "Col. Neave Report: Final Report on the Evidence of Witnesses for the Defense," in International Military Tribunal, *Trial*, 42:56.

74. See István Pintér, *Hungarian Anti-Fascism and Resistance* (Budapest: Akadémiai Kiadó, 1986), 54; H. Hessell Tiltman, *The Terror in Europe* (New York: Frederick Stokes, 1932), 371–92; and Oscar Jászi, *Revolution and Counter-Revolution in Hungary* (New York: Howard Fertig, 1969).

75. See C. G. Costa-Foru, *Aus Den Folterkammern Rumäniens* (Vienna: Kulturpolitischer Verlag, 1925); Paul Held, *Quer Durch Rumänien* (Vienna: Münster-Verlag, 1925); Ion Ardeleanu, *Doftana* ([Bucharest]: Publishing House of Tourism, 1974); and Walter Bacon, "Romanian Secret Police," in *Terror and Communist Politics*, ed. Jonathan Adelman (Boulder, CO: Westview, 1984).

76. Tiltman, *The Terror in Europe*, 269–99, 337–407; Milovan Djilas, *Of Prisons and Ideas*, trans. Michael Boro Petrovich (San Diego: Harcourt Brace Jovanovich, 1986), 110.

77. Vcheka Weekly (Nolinsk, 1918), quoted in Lennard Gerson, *The Secret Police in Lenin's Russia* (Philadelphia: Temple University Press, 1976), 143–44.

78. Sergey Petrovich Melgounov, *The Red Terror in Russia* (Westport, CT: Hyperion Press, 1926), 112, 163–65, 180, 182, 185, 191; and Ronald Hingley, *The Russian Secret Police* (New York: Simon and Schuster, 1971), 128; George Leggett, *The Cheka* (Oxford: Clarendon, 1981), 198.

79. Melgounov, *Red Terror in Russia*, 178.

80. Leggett, *The Cheka*, 198. The original description is in Melgounov, *Red Terror in Russia*, 177. The practice is also alleged to be Chinese. See O'Sullivan, *Crime Detection*, 294.

81. Vladmir Tchernavin, *I Speak for the Silent*, trans. Nicholas Oushakoff (Boston: Hale, Cushman and Flint, 1935), 169–72; Antoni Ekart, *Vanished Without Trace* (London: Max Parrish, 1954), 35, 39–40; Victor Kravchenko, *I Chose Freedom* (New York: Charles Scribner's Sons, 1946), 271–73; Jerzy Gliksman, *Tell the West* (New York: Gresham Press, 1948), 282; Essad-Bey, *OGPU*, trans. Huntley Paterson (New York: Viking, 1933), 252; Robert Conquest, *The Great Terror* (New York: Oxford University Press, 1990), 121–23, 279; F. Beck and W. Godin, *Russian Purge and the Extraction of Confession*, trans. Eric Mosbacher and David Porter (New York: Viking, 1951), 48, 54; Hingley, *The Russian Secret Police*, 152; Nathan Leites and Elsa Bernaut, *Ritual of Liquidation* (Glencoe, IL: Free Press, 1954), 22; Boris Levytsky, *The Uses of Terror*, trans. H. A. Piehler (New York: Coard, McCann and Geoghegan, 1972), 120–21; K. F. Shteppa, "In Stalin's Prisons—Reminiscences," *Russian Review* 21.1 (1968): 45–46.

82. Hingley, *The Russian Secret Police*, 176. See also Shteppa, "In Stalin's Prisons," 45–46.

83. Elinor Lipper, *Eleven Years in Soviet Prison Camps* (Chicago: Henry Regnery, 1951), 162–91; Conquest, *The Great Terror*, 308–40; Hingley, *The Russian Secret Police*, 177; Daniel Bacry and Michel Ternisien, *La Torture* (Paris: Fayard, 1980), 117–18; Andrew Meier, *Black Earth* (New York: Norton, 2003), 159–308.

84. Zbigniew Stypulkowski, *Invitation to Moscow* (New York: Walker, 1962), 236; see also 266. See also Shteppa, "In Stalin's Prisons," 45; and Alex Weissberg, *Conspiracy of Silence* (London: Hamish Hamilton, 1952), 236, 399.

85. Eugene Lyons, *Assignment in Utopia* (New York: Harcourt, Brace, 1937), 121, 132, 379; Conquest, *The Great Terror*, 105–8; Hingley, *The Russian Secret Police*, 163, 181; Leondard Schapiro, *The Communist Party of the Soviet Union*, 2nd ed. (New York: Random House, 1971), 397–98, 431–32.

86. Shteppa, "In Stalin's Prisons," 44.

87. Lyons, *Assignment in Utopia*, 117, 124–26, 129, 133. See also Robert Tucker, *Stalin in Power* (New York: Norton, 1992), 77–78; and Hingley, *The Russian Secret Police*, 150–51. Hingley counts fifty-two defendants, not fifty-three. In fact, fifty-three engineers were charged, but Nekrasoff went mad, so only fifty-two appeared in court.

88. Tucker, *Stalin in Power*, 167; Raphael Abramovitch, *The Soviet Revolution, 1917–1939* (New York: International Universities Press, 1962), 382–87.

89. See Lyons, *Assignment in Utopia*, 564, Hingley, *The Russian Secret Police*, 151–52; Tucker, *Stalin in Power*, 166–67; and Tiltman, *The Terror in Europe*, 121–27.

90. Hingley, *The Russian Secret Police*, 159.

91. Conquest, *The Great Terror*, 71–108, 341–98; Hingley, *The Russian Secret Police*, 161.

92. For the debate over this retraction, see Conquest, *The Great Terror*, 343–54.

93. Leites and Bernaut, *Ritual of Liquidation*, 22.

94. Essad-Bey, *OGPU*, 250; Lipper, *Eleven Years*, 40–42; Gliksman, *Tell the West*, 282; Kravchenko, *I Chose Freedom*, 263; Hinkle and Wolff, "Communist Interrogation," 129; Shteppa, "In Stalin's Prisons," 45, 52, 55; El Campesino (Valentin Gonzalez), *Listen Comrades*, trans. Ilsa Barea (Melbourne: William Heinemann, 1952), 133–34, 140; R. V. Ivanov-Razumnik, *The Memoirs of Ivanov-Razumnik* (London: Oxford University Press, 1965), 87–88; Menachem Begin, *White Nights*, trans. Katie Kaplan (New York: Harper and Row, 1977) 107; Bacry and Ternisien, *La Torture*, 109–11, 117.

95. Stypulkowski, *Invitation to Moscow*, 260; Tchernavin, *I Speak*, 52, 107–8, 172; Beck and Godin, *Russian Purge*, 185; Lyons, *Assignment in Utopia*, 459; El Campesino, *Listen Comrades*, 140; Ivanov-Razumnik, *Memoirs of Ivanov-Razumnik*, 88–95.

96. Beck and Godin, *Russian Purge*, 185; Hinkle and Wolff, "Communist Interrogation," 134; Shteppa, "In Stalin's Prisons," 53.

97. Weissberg, *Conspiracy of Silence*, 230.

98. Gliksman, *Tell the West*, 282; Hinkle and Wolff, "Communist Interrogation," 132; Conquest, *The Great Terror*, 125.

99. Stypulkowski, *Invitation to Moscow*, 250.

100. Kravchenko, *I Chose Freedom*, 261; Lipper, *Eleven Years*, 41; Essad-Bey, *OGPU*, 251; El Campesino, *Listen Comrades*, 130–33; Tchernavin, *I Speak*, 161–62; Weissberg, *Conspiracy of Silence*, 236, 399; Shteppa, "In Stalin's Prisons," 45; Conquest, *The Great Terror*, 121; Hinkle and Wolff, "Communist Interrogation," 126; Bacry and Ternisien, *La Torture*, 116–17.

101. Hinkle and Wolff, "Communist Interrogation," 134.

102. Cited in Beck and Godin, *Russian Purge*, 185. See also Shteppa, "In Stalin's Prisons," 45, 52.

103. Stypulkowski, *Invitation to Moscow*, 250.

104. Beck and Godin, *Russian Purge*, 54–55.

105. Lyons, *Assignment in Utopia*, 459; Kravchenko, *I Chose Freedom*, 265.

106. Conquest, *The Great Terror*, 121; Vladmir Brunovsky, *The Methods of OGPU* (London: Harper and Brothers, [1931]), 131.

107. Tucker, *Stalin in Power*, 467–88.

108. Beck and Godin, *Russian Purge*, 54. See also Shteppa, "In Stalin's Prisons," 45.

109. Shteppa, "In Stalin's Prisons," 45.

110. Essad-Bey, *OGPU*, 249–50; El Campesino, *Listen Comrades*, 128–29, 189–91; Stypulkowski, *Invitation to Moscow*, 250; Brunovsky, *The Methods of OGPU*, 130–31; Lyons, *Assignment in Utopia*, 459; Conquest, *The Great Terror*, 277–78; Hinkle and Wolff, "Communist Interrogation," 129; Weissberg, *Conspiracy of Silence*, 399.

111. Lyons, *Assignment in Utopia*, 459.

112. El Campesino, *Listen Comrades*, 142; Brunovsky, *The Methods of OGPU*, 131.

113. Conquest, *The Great Terror*, 125.

114. Essad-Bey, *OGPU*, 250, El Campesino, *Listen Comrades*, 143.

115. Tucker, *Stalin in Power*, 169.

116. Hinkle and Wolff, "Communist Interrogation," 120.

117. Conquest, *The Great Terror*, 126; Leites and Bernaut, *Ritual of Liquidation*, 21–22.

118. Weissberg, *Conspiracy of Silence*, 236. See also Conquest, *The Great Terror*, 124.

119. Conquest, *The Great Terror*, 278. The method was named after Nikolai Yezhov, head of the NKVD.

120. Hinkle and Wolff, "Communist Interrogation," 136–42.

121. Schapiro, *Communist Party*, 431.

122. Gliksman, *Tell the West*, 281–82; Essad-Bey, *OGPU*, 248; Kravchenko, *I Chose Freedom*, 265, 270–71; Vladmir Tchernavin, *I Speak for the Silent*, trans. Nicholas Oushakoff (Boston: Hale, Cushman and Flint, 1935), 52–54, 159; Begin, *White Nights*, 108; Shteppa, "In Stalin's Prisons," 48; George Kitchin, *Prisoner of OGPU* (New York: Arno Press, 1970), 16–17; Brunovsky, *The Methods of OGPU*, 127–28; Tucker, *Stalin in Power*, 169–70, 315; Zbigniew Stypulkowski, *Invitation to Moscow* (New York: Walker, 1962), 277; Conquest, *The Great Terror*, 127, 278–79; Abramovitch, 382–87; and Schapiro, *Communist Party*, 397–99.

123. Trchernavin, 160–62, 172; Brunovsky, *The Methods of OGPU*, 127–28; Shteppa, "In Stalin's Prisons," 54; Tucker, *Stalin in Power*, 169–70, 315.

124. Weissberg, *Conspiracy of Silence*, 236; Conquest, *The Great Terror*, 279.

125. Tucker, *Stalin in Power*, 315. See also Hingley, *The Russian Secret Police*, 163.

126. Stypulkowski, *Invitation to Moscow*, 236.

127. Conquest, *The Great Terror*, 126, 131, 279; Beck and Godin, *Russian Purge*, 185; Hingley, *The Russian Secret Police*, 163; Gliksman, *Tell the West*, 285.

128. Hinkle and Wolff, "Communist Interrogation," 130–31, Lipper, *Eleven Years*, 37–38; Ivanov-Razumnik, *Memoirs of Ivanov-Razumnik*, 149.

129. Hinkle and Wolff, "Communist Interrogation," 123–24; Conquest, *The Great Terror*, 281; Stypulkowski, *Invitation to Moscow*, 237.

130. Conquest, *The Great Terror*, 279.

131. Ibid., 130–31.

132. Harry Braverman, *Labor and Monopoly Capital* (New York: Monthly Review Press, 1974), 12.

133. Don Van Atta, "Why Is There No Taylorism in the Soviet Union?" *Comparative Politics* 18.3 (1986): 327.

134. W. G. Krivitsky, *I Was Stalin's Agent* (London: Hamish Hamilton, 1939), 213.

135. For the general problems with economic accounts of terror and torture, see Darius Rejali, *Torture and Modernity: Self, Society and State in Modern Iran* (Boulder, CO: Westview, 1994), 167–70; Michael Taussig, "Culture of Terror—Space of Death, Roger Casement's Putumayo Report and the Explanation of Torture," *Comparative Studies in Society and History* 26 (1984): 479–84.

136. Jiří Pelikán, ed., *The Czechoslovak Political Trials, 1950–1954* (Stanford, CA: Stanford University Press, 1971), 80–81, 101, 129, 255; Stefan Korbonski, *Fighting Warsaw* trans. F. B. Czarnomski ([New York]: Funk and Wagnalls, 1956), 473–89; Ferenc A. Váli, *A Scholar's Odyssey*, ed. Karl Ryavec (Ames: Iowa State University Press, 1957), 154–63; Lajos Ruff, *The Brain-Washing Machine* (London: Robert Hale, 1959), 56–61, 77–78; Sargant, *Battle for the Mind*, 209–10; Lena Constante, *The Silent Escape*, trans. Franklin Philip (Berkeley and Los Angeles: University of California Press, 1995), 43, 55, 61; Annie Samuelli, *Woman Behind Bars in Romania*, 2nd ed. (London: Frank Cass, 1997), xvii; Michael Solomon, *Magadan* (Princeton, NJ: Vertex, 1971), 11, 19, 28; Corneliu Coposu with Doina Alexandru, *Confessions*, trans. Elena Popescu (Boulder, CO: East European Monographs, 1998), 72–73, 87–88, Teodor Gherasim, *Astride Two Worlds* (Tigard, OR: L. D. Press, 2000), 85–89, 119–20; Constantin Giurescu, *Five Years and Two Months in the Sighet Penitentiary*, trans. Mihai Farcas and Stephanie Barton-Farcas (Boulder, CO: East European Monographs, 1994); Claudio Nisida, *Le Torture* (Milan: Le Edizioni Del Borghese, [1960]), 25–198; Amnesty International (AI), *Prison Conditions in Rumania, 1955–64* (London, 1965), 8–11; Evgeni Genchev, ed., *Tales from the Dark* (Sofia, Bulgaria: Assistance Centre for Torture Survivors, 2003), 15, 71, 74, 77, 80, 82, 85, 86, 95, 103–4, 113–14, 123, 142; Robert Lifton, *Thought Reform and the Psychology of Totalism* (New York: Norton, 1961), 52, 20–25, 38–47, 486; Hinkle and Wolff, "Communist Interrogation," 148–49.

137. AI, *Prison Conditions in Rumania*, 11–12; Samuelli, *Woman Behind Bars*, xvii; Richard Wurmbrand, *From Suffering to Triumph* (Grand Rapids, MI: Kregel, 1991), 30; Silviu Craciunas, *The Lost Footsteps* (New York: Farrar, Straus and Cudahy, 1961), 130.

138. Wurmbrand, *From Suffering to Triumph*, 30; Coposu, *Confessions*, 72; Craciunas, *The Lost Footsteps*, 129; AI, *Romania*, EUR/39/02/87 (London, 1987), 21–23.

139. Hinkle and Wolff, "Communist Interrogation," 125–27, 155.

140. AI, *Prison Conditions in Rumania*, 11, 13–14; Samuelli, *Woman Behind Bars*, xvii–xviii; Solomon, *Magadan*, 28, 39; Richard Wurmbrand, *If Prison Walls Could Speak* (London: Hodder and Stoughton, 1972), 14.

141. Samuelli, *Woman Behind Bars*, xvii.

142. AI, *Prison Conditions in Rumania*, 11; Craciunas, *The Lost Footsteps*, 141–43.

143. Craciunas, *The Lost Footsteps*, 155.

144. Hinkle and Wolff, "Communist Interrogation," 155.

145. Lifton, *Thought Reform*, 23.

146. Hinkle and Wolff, "Communist Interrogation," 155.

147. Ibid., 148–91, 156–61; Michael Dutton, *Policing and Punishment in China* (Cambridge: Cambridge University Press, 1992), 282–83, 308–18; John Marks, *The Search for the Manchurian Candidate* (New York: McGraw-Hill, 1980), 130; Eugene Kinkead, *In Every War but One* (New York: Norton, 1959), 108–9.

148. Lifton, *Thought Reform*, 22–30, 49–50, 120–22, 159–61.

149. Ibid., 41.

150. Ibid., 392–98; Hinkle and Wolff, "Communist Interrogation," 167; W. Allyn Rickett, "Voluntary Surrender and Confession in Chinese Law: The Problem of Continuity," *Journal of Asian Studies* 30.4 (1971): 797–814; Dutton, *Policing and Punishment*, 178–84, 304–18. These practices also appear in the West. See Edgar H. Schein, *Coercive Persuasion*, with Inge Schneier and Curtis Barker (New York: Norton, 1961), 269–82; Frantz Fanon, *The Wretched of the Earth*, trans. Constance Farrington (New York: Grove Press, 1963), 287–89.

151. Anthony Farrar-Hockley, *The British Part in the Korean War* (London: HMSO, 1995), 2:265, 268; Hinkle and Wolff, "Communist Interrogation," 168, 169.

152. Farrar-Hockley, *British Part*, 2:268.

153. Ibid., 2:267–68; Raymond Lech, *Broken Soldiers* (Urbana: University of Illinois Press, 2000), 73, 77; Albert Biderman, *March to Calumny* (New York: Arno, 1979), 133–34.

154. Anthony Farrar-Hockley, *The Edge of the Sword* (London: Bucan and Enright, 1985), 184–88.

155. Ibid., 190.

156. Farrar-Hockley, *British Part*, 2:268; see also 2:272.

157. Ibid., 2:278; Farrar-Hockley, *Edge of the Sword*, 234; Lewis Carlson, *Remembered Prisoners of a Forgotten War* (New York: St. Martin's, 2002), 137, 138; Biderman, *March to Calumny*, 132, 134.

158. Biderman, *March to Calumny*, 132.

159. Carlson, *Remembered Prisoners*, 135, 174; Farrar-Hockley, *British Part*, 2:278; Farrar-Hockley, *Edge of the Sword*, 215–17; Lech, *Broken Soldiers*, 72, 91, 100, 174, 177; Biderman, *March to Calumny*, 132–34.

160. Biderman, *March to Calumny*, 133.

161. Carlson, *Remembered Prisoners*, 135.

162. Biderman, *March to Calumny*, 132.

163. Although there were exceptions. See Carlson, *Remembered Prisoners*, 201; Biderman, *March to Calumny*, 134.

164. Farrar-Hockley, *British Part*, 2:278; Biderman, *March to Calumny*, 133.

165. Biderman, *March to Calumny*, 133. I call this position the reverse standing handcuff in part 4.

166. Carlson, *Remembered Prisoners*, 174; Farrar-Hockley, *Edge of the Sword*, 217.

167. Biderman, *March to Calumny*, 48–53.

168. Farrar-Hockley, *British Part*, 2:270–78; Carlson, *Remembered Prisoners*, 198–99, 200–201.

169. Robert Fletcher, cited in Carlson, *Remembered Prisoners*, 175.

170. Marks, *Manchurian Candidate*, 125–26.

171. Biderman, *March to Calumny*, 27–38; H. H. Wubben, "American Prisoners of War in Korea: A Second Look at the 'Something New in History' Theme," *American Quarterly* 22.1 (1970): 10.

172. Lifton, *Thought Reform*, 236–39; Biderman, *March to Calumny*, 39–83, 138–39, 145–46; Hinkle and Wolff, "Communist Interrogation," 162–65; J.A.C. Brown, *Techniques of Persuasion* (Harmondsworth, England: Penguin, 1969), 282–84.

173. Kinkead, *Every War but One*, 160–61; Farrar-Hockley, *British Part*, 2:280.

174. Farrar-Hockley, *Edge of the Sword*, 217, 236–40, 254–63; Hinkle and Wolff, "Communist Interrogation," 168; Kinkead, *Every War but One*, 160–61, 161–62.

175. Kinkead, *Every War but One*, 160–61, 160–62; Carlson, *Remembered Prisoners*, 36–37; Hinkle and Wolff, "Communist Interrogation," 168.

176. Hinkle and Wolff, "Communist Interrogation," 169. This is also Biderman's conclusion in his study of 220 air force personnel repatriated in 1953 (*March to Calumny*, 136–37; Albert Biderman, "Effects of Communist Indoctrination Attempts," *Social Problems* 6.4 [1959]: 304–13). Biderman argues that psychological techniques were far more effective than coerced interrogation in securing confessions (Albert Biderman, "Social-Psychological Needs and 'Involuntary' Behavior as Illustrated by Compliance in Interrogation," *Sociometry* 23.2 [1960]: 120–47). See also Silverman's statistics on the difficulty of retrieving confessions, false or true, in the section "Is Anything Better Than Nothing?" in chapter 21, "Does Torture Work?"

177. Biderman, *March to Calumny*, 115–34, 189–214.

178. Wubben, "American Prisoners in Korea," 12; see also 19.

179. Biderman, *March to Calumny*, 139–46.

180. Wubben, "American Prisoners in Korea," 3–7, 18; Peter Karsten, "The American Democratic Citizen Soldier: Triumph or Disaster?" *Military Affairs* 30:1 (1966): 34–35, 38–39, 40 n. 31.

181. Biderman, *March to Calumny*, 221–23, 267–71; Wubben, "American Prisoners in Korea," 7–12, 13–17; Karsten, "American Democratic Citizen Soldier," 38, 40 n. 31.

182. Biderman, *March to Calumny*, 249–55.

183. Ibid., 262–67.

184. Biderman, "Effects of Communist Indoctrination," 312.

185. Ibid.

186. See, in particular, chapter 20, "The Supply and Demand for Clean Torture." Also chapter 15, "Forced Standing and Other Positions" and chapter 22, "What the Apologists Say."

187. Wubben, "American Prisoners in Korea," 5.

188. Marks, *Manchurian Candidate*, 125.

189. Sargant, *Battle for the Mind*, 30. The claim has been reiterated most recently in the *New York Times*. See M. Gregg Bloche and Jonathan H. Marks, "Doing Unto Others as They Did Unto Us," *New York Times*, November 14, 2005, A21.

190. Hinkle and Wolff, "Communist Interrogation," 116, 131, 171; Conquest, *The Great Terror*, 127.

191. Harvey Fireside, *Soviet Psychoprisons* (New York: Norton, 1979).

192. Lifton, *Thought Reform*, 388–89.

193. Hinkle and Wolff, "Communist Interrogation," 118–19; Marks, *Manchurian Candidate*, 130; Peter Suedfeld, "Changes in Intellectual Performance and in Susceptibility to Influence," in *Sensory Deprivation*, ed. John Zubek (New York: Meredith, 1969), 157.

194. George Ryley Scott, *The History of Corporal Punishment*, 2nd ed. (London: Torchstream, 1954), 52. See also Rene Fülöp-Miller, introduction to A. T. Vassilyev, *The Ochrana* (Philadelphia: J. B. Lippincott, 1930), 26, 29.

195. Charles Ruud and Sergei Stepanov, *Fontanka 16* (Montreal: McGill-Queens University Press, 1999), 61.

196. Until 1990, Western analysts could not access archives of the czarist police. None of the three new critical studies discusses Okhranka torture, and Daly suggests that it was a misperception to think that the Okhranka depended heavily on torture for information. See Ruud and Stepanov, *Fontanka 16*, 59–78; Jonathan Daly, *Autocracy under Siege* (DeKalb: Northern Illinois University Press, 1998), 50–51, 59–61, 72–97; Frederic Zuckerman, *The Tsarist Secret Police in Russian Society, 1880–1917* (New York: New York University Press, 1996), 12, 39–57.

197. Hinkle and Wolff, "Communist Interrogation," 120.

198. John Spivak, *Europe under the Terror* (New York: Simon and Schuster, 1936), 182–83. Compare with Essad-Bey, *OGPU*, 248.

199. Lyons, *Assignment in Utopia*, 21, 121.

200. Innes, *The History of Torture*, 144; Conquest, *The Great Terror*, 124.

201. Steve Wright, "The New Trade in Technologies of Restraint and Electroshock," in *A Glimpse of Hell*, ed. Duncan Forrest (London: Amnesty International, 1996), 137–38.

202. Diarmaid Macculloch, *The Reformation* (New York: Viking, 2003), 555.

Chapter 4
Whips and Water

1. International Military Tribunal (IMT), *Trial of the Major War Criminals* (Nuremberg: n.p., 1949), 6:173.

2. Ibid.

3. Ibid.

4. Ibid., 6:169.

5. Colonel Rémy [Gilbert Renault-Roulier], *Une affaire de trahison* (Monte Carlo: Raoul Solar, 1947), 235.

6. IMT, *Trial*, 6:173.

7. Ibid.

8. Ibid., 6:170, 37:293.

9. François d'Orcival, "Gestapo contre Résistance," in *Histoire secrète de la Gestapo*, ed. Jean Dumont, vol. 2 (Geneva: Editions de Crémille, 1971), 163.

10. IMT, *Trial*, 6:173.

11. Ibid., 6:170, 37:292. Although an independent innovation, this technique resembles the "death wreath" of the cheka at Amravir, the only other modern European record of a skull band. Sergey Petrovich Melgounov, *The Red Terror in Russia* (Westport, CT: Hyperion Press, 1926), 180.

12. IMT, *Trial*, 6:176.

13. IMT, *Trial*, 6:173.

14. IMT, *Trial*, 6:173. See also d'Orcival, "Gestapo contre Résistance," 163.

15. Roland Black, *Histoire et crime de la Gestapo parisienne* (Brussels: Bel Go-Suisses, 1945), 110. See also IMT, *Trial*, 6:160; James Gleeson, *They Feared No Evil* (London: Robert Hale, 1976), 145.

16. Jacques Delarue, *History of the Gestapo*, trans. Mervyn Savill (New York: Dell, 1964), 268; IMT, *Trial*, 6:167–69, 174.

17. IMT, *Trial*, 6:173.

18. Delarue, *History of the Gestapo*, 267–69.

19. My thanks to Dr. Jürgen Matthaus at the U.S. Holocaust Museum for his careful introduction to this problem.

20. IMT, *Trial*, 6:160. Prosecutors did sometimes use the "top-down approach" (IMT, *Trial*, 6:181 and 7:507).

21. See Fabrice Laroche, "Les Français de la Gestapo," in Dumont, *Histoire secrète*, 4:145; Milton Dank, *The French Against the French* (Philadelphia: J. B. Lippincott, 1974), 222; Philippe Aziz, *Au service de l'ennemi* (Paris: Fayard, 1972), 51; Marcel Hasquenoph, *La Gestapo en France* (Paris: De Vecchi Poche, 1987), 332; Milena Seborova, *A Czech Trilogy* (Rome: Christian Academy, 1990), 28. This was not an unusual procedure. In 1938, the Czech military also destroyed its files in advance of the Germans. An Abwehr major remarked, "That is what we expected. We would have done the same." Frantisek Moravec, *Master of Spies* (London: Bodley Head, 1975), 159–60.

22. Delarue, *History of the Gestapo*, 268–69. See also George Browder, *Hitler's Enforcers* (New York: Oxford University Press, 1996), 39, 68, 73, 90–91, 234.

23. See, for example, Paul Hehn, *The German Struggle against Yugoslav Guerillas in World War II* (Boulder, CO: East European Quarterly, 1979), 143; Mark Mazower, *Inside Hitler's Greece* (New Haven, CT: Yale University Press, 1993), 225.

24. The Gestapo was part of the Reich Security Office (RSHA) that also included its rival, the Kripo, or criminal police, and the SS Security Service (SD). The RSHA fit into the security-concentration camp system that included the SS, regional and local police, and the German military intelligence (Abwehr). For a "simplified" map of the German security service, see Michael Freeman, *Atlas of Nazi Germany*, consulting editor Tim Mason (New York: Macmillan, 1987), 153.

25. Since Nuremberg, historians have found no Gestapo torture manuals. Surviving manuals discuss only the psychology of interrogation (Browder, *Hitler's Enforcers*, 70). Two other texts, despite their titles, do not discuss interrogation or torture technique. See *The Gestapo and SS Manual*, trans. Carl Hammer (Boulder, CO: Paladin Press, 1996); and S. Vladimirov [pseud.], "Zapiski Sledovatelya Gestapo" [Notes of a Gestapo Interrogator], *Moskva* 6 (1971): 210–19; 7 (1971): 174–82; 8 (1971): 182–86. The only English translation is at the library of the Central Intelligence Agency at Langley.

26. Ingo Muller, *Hitler's Justice* (Cambridge: Harvard University Press, 1991), 178–79.

27. Edward Crankshaw, *Gestapo* (New York: Da Capo Press, 1994), 127. The form is discussed, but not included in the Nuremberg publications (see IMT, *Trial*, 7:506).

28. Chief Müller, "Decree of the Chief of the Security Police and the SD, 12 June 1942 regarding third degree methods of interrogation [1531-PS]," in IMT, *Trial*, 27:326–27. English translation in *Germans against Hitler, July 20, 1944* (Bonn: Bundeszentrale für politische Bildung, [1969]), 190–91.

29. IMT, *Trial*, 38:638; 42:56; Crankshaw, *Gestapo*, 130.

30. IMT, *Trial*, 7:507.

31. Ibid., 6:160, 165, 5:401.

32. Prosecutor Dubost, cited in ibid., 6:160.

33. Malise Ruthven, *Torture* (London: Weidenfeld and Nicolson, 1978), 290.

34. I used the U.S. Holocaust Museum Library and the Library of Congress. The LC catalog lists approximately two thousand underground Resistance stories from World War II. I have read whatever was available in English and French, as well as selective translations from German, Norwegian, Romanian, Polish, Italian, and Russian sources. This is approximately one-third of the collection. It would take mastery of many more European languages to complete this picture. My inventory is thus more complete than that of the Nuremberg prosecutors, but others are welcome to finish it.

35. Crankshaw, *Gestapo*, 130; Eric Johnson, *The Nazi Terror* (New York: Basic Books, 1999), 286.

36. Daniel Reisberg and Friderike Heuer, "The Influence of Emotion on Memory in Forensic Settings," in *Handbook of Eyewitness Psychology*, vol. 1: *Memory for Events*, ed. M. P. Toglia, J. D. Read, D. F. Ross, and R.C.L. Lindsay (Mahwah, NJ: Lawrence Erlbaum Associates, 2007); Daniel Reisberg and Friderike Heuer, "Memory for Emotional Events," in *Memory and Emotion*, ed. Daniel Reisberg and Paula Hertel (Oxford: Oxford University Press, 2004), 7–10. For memory of the trauma of torture generally, see Richard McNally, *Remembering Trauma* (Cambridge: Belknap Press of Harvard University Press, 2003), 211–13.

37. *In der Gestapo-Zentrale, Prinz-Albrecht-Strasse 8* (Berlin: Ev Akademie, 1989), 10–15, 39–45; Jan Valtin, *Out of the Night* (New York: Alliance, 1941), 515–17, 522–26, 547, 553, 565, 575–77, 581, 583–84; Anton Gill, *An Honorable Defeat* (New York: Henry Holt, 1994), 12–13; Allan Merson, *Communist Resistance in Nazi Germany* (London: Lawrence and Wishart, 1985), 139; Charles Hewitt Jr., "In the Hands of the Gestapo," in *Eye Witness*, ed. Robert Spiers Benjamin (New York: Alliance, 1940), 22.

38. Valtin, *Out of the Night*, 533–44.

39. *Gestapo-Zentrale*, 42–45.

40. Valtin, *Out of the Night*, 571–72, 559. Gisevius maintains that the Gestapo "beat," "doped," and "hypnotized" an anarchist named Lubbe. He bases this conclusion on how Lubbe appeared in court ("an empty husk"). See Hans Bernd Gisevius, *To the Bitter End*, trans. Richard Winston and Clara Winston (Boston: Houghton Mifflin, 1947), 80–81. However, sweating and positional torture can also produce

this result. Many also thought Stalin's victims were drugged, but there is no evidence for this claim either.

41. Valtin, *Out of the Night*, 514.

42. Ibid., 573.

43. Ibid., 560.

44. Johnson, *The Nazi Terror*, 206–7, 290; Martha Dodd, *Through Embassy Eyes* (New York: Harcourt Brace, 1939), 299–300; Friedrich Schlotterbeck, *The Darker the Night, the Brighter the Stars* (London: Victor Gollancz, 1947), 32–34; Eric Boehm, *We Survived*, reprint ed. (Santa Barbara, CA: ABC-Clio Information Services, 1985), 37–38; Michael Thomsett, *The German Opposition to Hitler* (Jefferson, NC: McFarland, 1997), 66; "Simpson Returns from Nazi Prison," *New York Times*, January 4, 1937, 3; Nikolaus Wachsmann, *Hitler's Prisons* (New Haven, CT: Yale University Press, 2004), 106.

45. Friends of Democracy, *The Gestapo, Hitler's Secret Police* (Kansas City, MO: Friends of Democracy, 1941), 10. See also Dodd, *Through Embassy Eyes*, 300; *Gestapo-Zentrale*, 74–75; Schlotterbeck, *Darker the Night*, 35.

46. Johnson, *The Nazi Terror*, 206; Boehm, *We Survived*, 37; Wachsmann, *Hitler's Prisons*, 108, 186.

47. Wachsmann, *Hitler's Prisons*, 109.

48. Dodd, *Through Embassy Eyes*, 300.

49. *Gestapo-Zentrale*, 87, 185–87; Wachsmann, *Hitler's Prisons*, 248–55; Johnson, *The Nazi Terror*, 241–43, 247, 348–50; Boehm, *We Survived*, 46, 136–37, 155–56, 167, 215–17, 140, 144; Eugen Budde and Peter Lutsches, "Der 20. Juli," in *Germans against Hitler, July 20, 1944* (Bonn: Bundeszentrale für politische Bildung, [1969]), 191; Fabian von Schlabrendorf, *The Secret War Against Hitler* (New York: Pitman, 1965), 310–12; Peter Hoffman, *History of the German Resistance, 1933–1945*, trans. Richard Barry (Cambridge: MIT Press, 1977), 522–23. Budde and Lutsches also believe drugs were mixed with food (191).

50. Boehm, *We Survived*, 197.

51. Helmuth James von Moltke, *Letters to Freya, 1939–1945*, ed. and trans. Beate Ruhm von Oppen (New York: Knopf, 1990), 21, 385.

52. Schlabrendorf, *Secret War Against Hitler*, 312.

53. As I was unable to find any documentation of Gestapo interrogation in Hungary (1944–45), I have omitted it.

54. Radomir Luza, *The Austrian Resistance, 1938–1945* (Minneapolis: University of Minnesota Press, 1984), 15–16. See also Carylyn Nuttall, "An Exercise in Futility," master's thesis, Emory University, 1972, 163.

55. Fritz Molden, *Exploding Star*, trans. Peter and Betty Ross (New York: William Morrow, 1979) 96–97, 100–104, 150, 224–25. For the Prilep method, see Barbara Jancar-Webster, *Women and Revolution in Yugoslavia, 1941–1945* (Denver: Arden, 1990), 134.

56. Floridmond Duke, *Name, Rank and Serial Number* (New York: Meredith Press, 1969), 67–104.

57. Walter Maass, *Country Without a Name* (New York: Frederick Ungar, 1979), 38.

58. Radomir Luza with Christina Vella, *The Hitler Kiss* (Baton Rouge: Louisiana State University Press, 2002), 66; see also 32–43, 94. See also Jan Filipek, *The Shadow of the Gallows* (Palm Springs, CA: Palm Springs Publishing, 1985), 44–57, 68–76; "Official Czechoslovak Report on German Crimes against Czechoslovakia," in IMT, *Trial*, 26:489–90; "Report of the Czechoslovakia Ministry of the Interior, Prague 09 July 1945 on Crimes Committed by the Allgemeine SS and the Waffen SS in Czechoslovakia, [959-D]," in IMT, *Trial*, 36:87–91; "Supplement to the Official Czech Report [60-USSR]," in IMT, *Trial*, 39:336–54; Radomir Luza, "The Czech Resistance Movement," and Anna Josko, "The Slovak Resistance Movement," in *A History of the Czechoslovak Republic, 1918–1948*, ed. Victor S. Mamtey and Radomir Luza (Princeton, NJ: Princeton University Press, 1973), 343–61, 362–83; Lewis M. White, ed., *On All Fronts* (Boulder, CO: East European Monographs, 1995), 45, 241; Jiri Dolezal and Jan Kren, *Czechoslovakia's Fight* (Prague: Czechoslovak Academy of Sciences, 1964); J. B. Muran, *We Fight On* (London: Lincolns-Prager, 1945).

59. Seborova, *A Czech Trilogy*, 28.

60. Filipek, *Shadow of the Gallows*, 76.

61. Luza, *The Austrian Resistance*, 18 n. 21. Luza cites to this end Oldrich Novák et al., eds., *KSC proti nacismu. KSC v dokumenetech nacistickyich bezpecnotnich a zpravodajskych organu* (Prague, 1971).

62. Luza, *The Hitler Kiss*, 194.

63. J. Gorecki, *Stones for the Rampart* (London: Polish Boy Scouts' and Girl Guides' Association, 1945), 57; Andrzej Czerkawski, *Aleja Szucha* (Warsaw: Sport i Turystyka, 1967), [6–8]; Regina Domanska, *Pawiak* (Warsaw: Ksiazka i Wiedza, 1988), 100, 102, 11; Zygmunt Sliwicki, *Meldunek z Pawiaka* (Warsaw: Panstwowe Wydawnictwo Naukowe, 1974), 89–90, 194; Sonia Games, *Escape into Darkness* (New York: Shapolsky, 1991), 213–15; Waldemar Lotnik, *Nine Lives* (London: Serif, 1999), 35, 102; *The Unseen and Silent*, trans. George Iranek-Osmecki (London: Sheed and Ward, 1954), 115; Joseph Tenenbaum, *Underground* (New York: Philosophical Library, 1952), 226, 426–27.

64. Czerkawski, *Aleja Szucha*, [6–8].

65. Józef Lewandowski, *The Swedish Contribution to the Polish Resistance Movement during World War Two (1939–1942)* (Stockholm: Almqvist and Wiksell International, 1979), 72, 76, 84.

66. Domanska, *Pawiak*, 111.

67. "Mira," "You Still Alive?" in *The Unseen and Silent*, 341.

68. Domanska, *Pawiak*, 98, 100–103, 111–12, 115, 116; Sliwicki, *Meldunek z Pawiaka*, 81, 89–90, 194. See also Leon Wanat, *Apel Wiezniow Pawiaka* (Warsaw: Ksiazka I Wiedza, 1976); Anna Sliwicka, *Cztery lata ostrego dyzuru* (Warsaw: Czytelnik, 1968); Adam Grzymala-Siedlecki, *Sto jedenascie dni letargu* (Kraków: Wydawnictwo Literackie, 1966).

69. "Mira," 101, 341.

70. Sliwicki, *Meldunek z Pawiaka*, 194; Domanska, *Pawiak*, 102–3.

71. "Official Memorandum by the Danish Government, 25 October 1945 concerning the crimes committed by the Germans [901-RF]," in IMT, *Trial*, 38:638. See also Robin Reilly, *The Sixth Floor* (London: Cassell, 2002), 93–95, 99–102, 104; David Lampe, *The Savage Canary* (London: Cassell, 1957), 63–64; 141; Harold Flender, *Rescue in Denmark* (New York: Simon and Schuster, 1963), 228; Christine Sutherland, *Monica* (New York: Farrar, Straus and Giroux, 1990), 156–57, 174; Birger Mikkelsen, *"A Matter of Decency"* (Elsinore, Denmark: Friends of the Sound, 1994), 40–43.

72. Reilly, *The Sixth Floor*, 93–94.

73. "Danish Government," 38:681.

74. Reilly, *The Sixth Floor*, 93, 95.

75. "Danish Government," 38:681.

76. IMT, *Trial*, 6:279–88; Tore Gjelsvik, *Norwegian Resistance, 1940–1945* (Montreal: McGill-Queens University Press, 1979), 144–45; Norwegian Government, *The Gestapo at Work in Norway* (Montreal: Royal Norwegian Government's Information Office, 1942), 13–16, 22–28; Hans Christian Adamson and Per Klem, *Blood on the Midnight Sun* (New York: Norton, 1964), 218–23, 218–23; Dorothy Baden-Powell, *Operation Jupiter* (London: Robert Hale, 1982), 150; Dorothy Baden-Powell, *Pimpernel Gold* (New York: St. Martin's, 1978), 103–4; Astrid Karlsen Scott and Tore Hang, *Defiant Courage* (Olympia, WA: Nordic Spirit Productions, 2000), 91, 95–98; Oluf Reed Olsen, *Two Eggs on My Plate* (Glasgow: Blackie, 1972), 27–28; Leif Hovelsen, *Out of the Evil Night*, trans. John Morrison (London: Blandford Press, 1959), 16; Sigrid Heide, *In the Hands of My Enemy*, trans. Norma Johansen, arr. Ethel Keshner (Middletown, CT: Southfarm Press, 1995), 52–55, 61; Per Hansson, *The Greatest Gamble*, trans. Maurice Michael (London: George Allen and Unwin, 1967), 118; Maynard M. Cohen, *A Stand against Tyranny* (Detroit: Wayne State University Press, 1997), 175, 185–86.

77. Norwegian Government, *Gestapo at Work*, 23.

78. Cohen, *A Stand against Tyranny*, 175.

79. Norwegian Government, *Gestapo at Work*, 31–32. The only element shared with other accounts is the dark cellar (Norwegian Government, *Gestapo at Work*, 19). Drummond also describes lights, but it is unclear on what this account is based (John D. Drummond, *But For These Men* [Morley, England: Elmfield Press, 1974], 69).

80. Heide, *Hands of My Enemy*, 64–65; Odd Bergfald, *Gestapo i Norge* (Oslo: Hjemmenes Forlag, 1978), 216, 218, 219, 221, 222, 225, 226.

81. Hans Cappelen, cited in IMT, *Trial*, 6:280.

82. IMT, *Trial*, 6:281; Norwegian Government, *Gestapo at Work*, 20; Scott and Hang, *Defiant Courage*, 96; Drummond, *But For These Men*, 69.

83. Norwegian Government, *Gestapo at Work*, 13–14.

84. IMT, *Trial*, 6:281; Norwegian Government, *Gestapo at Work*, 28.

85. Hansson, *The Greatest Gamble*, 67.

86. Norwegian Government, *Gestapo at Work*, 16–17.

87. Bergfald, *Gestapo i Norge*, 216–17.

88. Finn Palmstrom and Rolf Normann Torgersen, "Preliminary Report on Germany's Crimes against Norway [79-UK]," in IMT, *Trial*, 39:212–13.

89. Cohen, *A Stand against Tyranny*, 177–78.

90. "Statement of the Netherlands Government on the Prosecution and Punishment of the German War Criminals, [1726-PS]," in IMT, *Trial*, 27:517, 519–20, 524–30; Lore Cowan, *Children of the Resistance* (New York: Meredith Press, 1969), 125–26, 165; Corrie ten Boom with John Sherrill and Elizabeth Sherrill, *The Hiding Place* (London: Hodder and Stoughton and Christian Literature Crusade, 1971), 121–22; Graeme Warrack, *Travel by Dark* (London: Harvill Press, 1963), 170; Helen Moszkiewiez, *Inside the Getsapo* (Toronto: Macmillan of Canada, 1985), 82.

91. Walter Maass, *The Netherlands at War* (London: Abelard-Schumann, 1970), 85.

92. "Statement of Netherlands Government," 27:519, 525–30; Boom, *The Hiding Place*, 130; Maass, *The Netherlands at War*, 85.

93. "Statement of Netherlands Government," 27:520.

94. Andria Hill, *Mona Parsons* (Halifax, Nova Scotia: Nimbus, 2000), 88–89.

95. Pieter Dourlein, *Inside North Pole* (London: William Kimber, 1989), 108–15.

96. "Official Luxembourg Report concerning Crimes Committed by the Germans [77-UK]," in IMT, *Trial*, 39:137–55, esp. 152–54.

97. Colonel Rémy [Gilbert Renault-Roulier], *Une Épopée de la Résistance* (Paris: Grange Batelière, 1976), 1:73.

98. H. Paucot, "Rapport sur les atrocites allemandes commises pendant l'occupation [560-F and 517-F]," in IMT, *Trial*, 37:261–307; Colonel Rémy, *Une Épopée*, 1:139, 258, 264; Mark Bles, *Child at War* (San Francisco: Mercury House, 1989), 128, 154, 162–63; J. Schreuers, *My Country in Trouble* (New York: Carlton Press, 1962), 31–35, 43–47; Airey Neave, *Little Cyclone* (London: Hodder and Stoughton, 1954), 95, 129, 116; Allan Mayer, *Gaston's War* (Novato, CA: Presidio, 1988), 138–45; André Lamarche, *A vingt ans la guerre* (Liège: Impr. Solédi, 1986), 23–24; *Avenue Louise 347* (Brussels: Buch Edition, 1996), 39, 45, 46. For prison conditions in general, see Rémy, *Une Épopée*, 1:261–69; Lamarche, *A vingt ans la guerre*, 27–32; Roger-A Destroyer, *Parachutiste du roi* (Brussells: Charles Dessart, 1946), 134–37.

99. Bles, *Child at War*, 181–82, 124; IMT, *Trial*, 6:198–201; Jules Wolf, *Le process de Breendonck* (Brussells: Maison F. Larcier, 1973), 32–77; P. Lansvreugt and R. Lemaitre, *Le calvaire de Breendonck* (Brussells: Serge Baguette, 1945), 42, 45, 46; Adrien Henderickx, *1940–1945 Breendonck-Neuengamme* (Brussels: St. Pieters Leeuw, 1986), 24, 35; Victor Trido, *Breendonck* (Paris: Editions J. Dupuis, 1944), 67, 105; Jean Amery, *At the Mind's Limits*, trans. Sidney Rosenfeld and Stella P. Rosenfeld (Bloomington: Indiana University Press, 1980), 21–40. Breendonck's torture room has been well photographed. See Wolf, *Le process de Breendonck*; Trido, *Breendonck*, facing 25; Henderickx, *1940–1945 Breendonck-Neuengamme*, 34; Hervé Gérard, *La résistance belge face au nazisme* (Brussels: J-M. Collet, 1995), 85–86.

100. Rémy, *Une Épopée*, 2:246; Lansvreugt and Lemaitre, *Le calvaire de Breendonck*, 46; Wolf, *Le process de Breendonck*, 51, 58, 65, 67, 71.

101. Wolf, *Le process de Breendonck*, 32, 50, 66, 70; Lansvreugt and Lemaître, *Le calvaire de Breendonck*, 46.

102. Lansvreugt and Lemaitre, *Le calvaire de Breendonck*, 42; Henderickx, *1940–1945 Breendonck-Neuengamme*, 34. The best photograph is in Lord Russell, *Scourge of the Swastika* (New York: Philosophical Library, 1954), facing 181.

103. Mayer, *Gaston's War*, 138; Wolf, *Le process de Breendonck*, 37.

104. Schreuers, *My Country in Trouble*, 32; Lansvreugt and Lemaitre, *Le calvaire de Breendonck*, 41; Mayer, *Gaston's War*, 138–39; Wolf, *Le process de Breendonck*, 53, 70.

105. Schreuers, *My Country in Trouble*, 44.

106. Herman Bodson, *Agent for the Resistance*, ed. Richard Schmidt (College Station: Texas A&M University Press, 1994), 121–22.

107. Ibid., 73.

108. Paucot mentions five cases of the bathtub and one of bathtub and electricity, but all these cases happened in northern France, not in Belgium. See Paucot, "Rapport sur les atrocites," 37:282–83, 305 (Lille), 37:271–72 (Arras), 37:285 (Armentiere), 37:276–77, 286, 296 (Loos).

109. Bles, *Child at War*, 124, 126–27.

110. Cited in Wolf, *Le process de Breendonck*, 74.

111. "Report by the Yugoslav State Commission for Investigating the Crimes of the Occupying Power and Accomplices [36-USSR]" and "Extract from Report Number 5 by the Yugoslav State Commission for Investigating the Crimes of the Occupying Power and Accomplices [945-D]," in IMT, *Trial*, 39:273, 289 and 36:66–68, 70–71. See also Roy Neill, *Once Only* (London: Jonathan Cape, 1947), 240–41.

112. Vladimir Dedijer, *The War Diaries of Vladimir Dedijer* (Ann Arbor: University of Michigan Press, 1990), 1:430, 439, 474; Milos Achin, *The First Guerillas of Europe* (New York: Vantage, 1963), 101.

113. Christie Lawrence, *Irregular Adventure* (London: Faber and Faber, 1947), 266–67; Nicholas Hammond, *Venture into Greece* (London: William Kimber, 1983), 156.

114. Mazower, *Inside Hitler's Greece*, 227. See also Mary Henderson, *Xenia* (London: Weidenfeld and Nicholson, 1988), 68–74; Chris Jecchinis, *Beyond Olympus* (London: George G. Harrap, 1960), 200.

115. Henderson, *Xenia*, 70.

116. Mazower, *Inside Hitler's Greece*, 210–15; Amyntor, *Victors in Chains* (London: Hutchinson, n.d.), 26; William Jordan, *Conquest without Victory* (London: Hodder and Stoughton, 1969), 81–82; John Louis Hondros, *Occupation and Resistance* (New York: Pella, 1983), 153–59.

117. W. Byford-Jones, *The Greek Trilogy* (London: Hutchinson, 1946), 27–29.

118. Mazower, *Inside Hitler's Greece*, 239.

119. IMT, *Trial*, vol. 7, passim.

120. Ibid., 7:506–8.

121. A. N. Tolstoy, cited in ibid., 7:508.

122. IMT, *Trial*, 7:509–10.

123. Paul Krapyvny, in ibid., 7:509.

124. See Alexander Werth, *Russia at War, 1941–1945* (New York: E. P. Dutton, 1964), 813–25; and Keith Hitchins, *Rumania, 1866–1947* (Oxford: Clarendon Press, 1994), 473–74.

125. Werth, *Russia at War*, 822. See Walter Bacon, "Romanian Secret Police," in *Terror and Communist Politics*, ed. Jonathan Adelman (Boulder, CO: Westview, 1984), 135–41; and Nicholas Nagy-Talavera, *The Greenshirts and Others* (Stanford, CA: Hoover Institution Press, 1970), 297, 313. Romanian histories describe the Siguranta's legal organization. See Vasile Bobocescu, *Istoria Plitiei Române* (Bucharest: Editura Ministerului de Interne, 2000), 267–93; Tudor Danut, *Politia în Statul de Drept* (Bucharest: Editura Ministerului de Interne, 2000), 91–94; Lazar Cârjan, *Istoria Politiei Române* (Bucharest: Editura Vestala, 2000), 237–68.

126. The full reference is the Extraordinary State Commission, "On the Atrocities Committed by German and Romanian Invaders in the City of Odessa and in the Territory of the Odessa Regions [47-USSR]." Krapyvny was a "producer of news reels." See IMT, *Trial*, 7:509.

127. Hitchins, *Rumania, 1866–1947*, 489–90.

128. Werth, *Russia at War*, 813.

129. See Paul Held, *Quer Durch Rumänien* (Vienna: Münster-Verlag, 1925); Ion Ardeleanu, *Doftana* ([Bucharest]: Publishing House of Tourism, 1974); Jean-Paul de Longchamp, *La Garde de Fer* (Paris: SEFA, [1975]), 113, 118–19; Alexander Ronnett, *Romanian Nationalism*, 2nd ed. (Chicago: Romanian American National Congress, 1995), 37; Corneliu Codreanu, *La Garde de Fer* (Grenoble: I. Maril, Belmain, 1972), 139. Costa-Foru implies the Siguranta used electrotorture in the introduction, but no prisoner testimonials mentions it. C. G. Costa-Foru, *Aus Den Folterkammern Rumäniens* (Vienna: Kulturpolitischer Verlag, 1925), ii. Corneliu Coposu offers the only account of electric torture written between 1925 and 1960. Imprisoned in 1947, Coposu states that one of the "sanctioned methods" was "electrocutions, the method of placing you naked in a cell with a flooded floor connected to an electric wire that jerks you intermittent [*sic*]." This account of live wires bears no relation to the Odessa machine. Corneliu Coposu with Doina Alexandru, *Confessions*, trans. Elena Popescu (Boulder, CO: East European Monographs, 1998), 72.

130. The published proceedings of the Nuremberg tribunal do not include many supporting Soviet documents. But based on the prosecutor's description, the Odessa machine was *not* a magneto. Hand-cranked magnetos do not have voltmeters.

131. Józef Garlinski, *Fighting Auschwitz* (London: Julian Friedmann, 1975), 25. See also IMT, *Trial*, 21:516.

132. Luza, *Austrian Resistance*, 16. See also IMT, *Trial*, 6:233–38.

133. Garlinski, *Fighting Auschwitz*, 149, 157.

134. The Nuremberg tribunal heard reports on about twenty camps, including Auschwitz, Straflager, Mauthausen, Magdeburg, Belsen, Dora, Buchenwald, Sachsenhausen, Straffkommando, Vught, Aachen, Amrasch, Asperg, Cologne, Sonnenburg, Rheinbach, Münster, Lübeck Dietz-an-der-Lahn, and Radom. Witnesses included François Boix, Maurice Lampe, Hans Cappelen, Victor Dupont, Paul

Roser, Marie-Claude Vaillant-Couturier, and Alfred Balchowsky. See IMT, *Trial*, 6:183–318, 27:517–30, 36:74–76.

135. "Statement of Netherlands Government," 27:524; Seborova, *A Czech Trilogy*, 43–44, 46; Daniel Bacry and Michel Ternisien, *La Torture* (Paris: Fayard, 1980), 94.

136. Marie-Claude Vaillant-Couturier, cited in IMT, *Trial*, 6:213.

137. Ibid. See also IMT, *Trial*, 39:285; Thomsett, *German Opposition to Hitler*, 80.

138. Seborova, *A Czech Trilogy*, 43–44, 46; Russell, *Scourge of the Swastika*, 174.

139. IMT, *Trial*, 6:213, 39:285; Seborova, *A Czech Trilogy*, 118, 119, 123, 125–27; Sutherland, *Monica*, 212–13; Lotnik, *Nine Lives*, 108–9; Tenebaum, 267, 271; Hermann Langbein, *Against All Hope*, trans. Harry Zohn (New York: Paragon House, 1994), 213, 329, 331; Albert Nirenstein, *A Tower from the Enemy* (New York: Orion Press, 1959), 304, 318.

140. Garlinski, *Fighting Auschwitz*, 229. See also Russell, *Scourge of the Swastika*, 173–74.

141. Seborova, *A Czech Trilogy*, 45–46, Thomsett, *German Opposition to Hitler*, 80; Maass, *The Netherlands at War*, 85; Tenenbaum, *Underground*, 272.

142. Seborova, *A Czech Trilogy*, 119.

143. Lord Russell, *Scourge of the Swastika*, 202–3; Seborova, *A Czech Trilogy*, 118.

144. Seborova, *A Czech Trilogy*, 118. See also Lord Russell, *Scourge of the Swastika*, 203.

145. Robert C. Tucker, *Stalin in Power* (New York: Norton, 1992), 467–68.

146. Ruthven, *Torture*, 288.

147. Ibid.; Johnson, *The Nazi Terror*, 290; Browder, *Hitler's Enforcers*, 71–72; Nuttall, "An Exercise in Futility," 59–61.

148. Luza, *The Hitler Kiss*, 194.

149. No dates are given for the Polish "sinking" technique.

150. Ramdor may have devised it himself, or he may have come across it in reports at the RSHA. Since the RSHA authorized bathtub torture for Norway in 1945, it was familiar with the Paris method. Masuy developed the bathtub technique in Paris sometime in 1942. The RSHA assigned Ramdor as its agent to Ravensbrück in 1942 to monitor the camp and police the sector (Seborova, *A Czech Trilogy*, 117). All one can say is that Ramdor's technique did not precede Masuy's invention.

151. I pass over Haessert's torture in Belgium. Applying a live wire to a wound is not the same as using a specially designed device for electric torture.

Chapter 5
Bathtubs

1. Masuy, cited in Fabrice Laroche, "Les Français de la Gestapo," in *Histoire secrète de la Gestapo*, ed. Jean Dumont, vol. 4 (Geneva: Editions de Crémille, 1971), 28.

2. Cited in Milton Dank, *The French Against the French* (Philadelphia: J. B. Lippincott, 1974), 222.

3. Jacques Delarue, *History of the Gestapo*, trans. Mervyn Savill (New York: Dell, 1964), 269.

4. Alec Mellor, *La Torture* (Paris: Horizons littéraires, 1949), 221–22. See also Colonel Rémy's testimony in Marcel Hasquenoph, *La Gestapo en France* (Paris: De Vecchi Poche, 1987), 515.

5. André Caban, cited in Philippe Aziz, *Au service de l'ennemi* (Paris: Fayard, 1972), 14–15.

6. In this chapter, Gestapo still refers to the Reich's plainclothes political detectives. However, for the sake of clarity, I will sometimes use the redundant phrase "German Gestapo" to distinguish it from the French agents.

7. Colonel Rémy [Gilbert Renault-Roulier], *Une affaire de trahison* (Monte Carlo: Raoul Solar, 1947), facing 16.

8. For Masuy's life, see Laroche, "Les Français de la Gestapo," 26–28; Hasquenoph, *La Gestapo en France*, 154–56, 514–18; Jacques Delarue, *Trafics et crimes sous l'occupation* (Paris: Fayard, 1968), 46–53, 116–19.

9. Delarue, *Trafics et crimes*, 46.

10. Ibid.

11. Masuy, cited in Laroche, "Les Français de la Gestapo," 28.

12. Geoffrey Abbott, *Rack, Rope and Red-hot Pincers* (London: Headline Books, 1993), 110–11, 113; Brian Innes, *The History of Torture* (New York: St. Martin's, 1998), 63.

13. Abbott, *Rack, Rope*, 114–16; Innes, *The History of Torture*, 61–63; Michael Kerrigan, *The Instruments of Torture* (New York: Lyons Press, 2001), 83–86; Jean Kellaway, *The History of Torture and Execution* (New York: Lyons Press, 2000), 59; George Ryley Scott, *The History of Torture* (London: Torchstream, 1940), 171. I omit boiling, which was even by the Inquisition an antiquated technique (see Abbott, *Rack, Rope*, 109–10; Kellaway, *Torture and Execution*, 58).

14. Edward Peters, *Torture*, 2nd ed. (Philadelphia: University of Pennsylvania Press, 1996), 167.

15. *Sing Sing Prison* (New York: NY State Department of Correction, 1953), 5.

16. Edward Stainbrook, "The Use of Electricity in Psychiatric Treatment during the 19th Century," *Bulletin of the History of Medicine* 22.3 (1948): 163.

17. Jean Delay, B. Lainé, J. Puech, and J. Clavreul, "Recherches biologiques sur le choc émotionnel," *L'Encâephale* 42 (1953): 293.

18. Stainbrook, "Use of Electricity," 163.

19. Masuy, cited in Hasquenoph, *La Gestapo en France*, 35.

20. Masuy, cited in Mellor, *La Torture*, 220.

21. Mellor, *La Torture*, 218.

22. Masuy, cited in Laroche, "Les Français de la Gestapo," 28.

23. Mellor, *La Torture*, 218.

24. Ibid.

25. Hasquenoph, *La Gestapo en France*, 517.

26. Laroche, "Les Français de la Gestapo," 27.

27. Jean Estèbe, *Toulouse, 1940–1944* (Paris: Perrin, 1996), 155–56, 305; "Marty et sa brigade sanglante répondront de leurs crimes," *Dépêche du Midi*, June 14, 1948,

1; H. R. Kedward, *In Search of the Maquis* (Oxford: Clarendon Press, 1993), 84–87, 121–23, 191–94.

28. Henry Buisson, *La Police, son histoire* (Vichy, France: Wallon, 1949), 349.

29. Hasquenoph, *La Gestapo en France*, 433.

30. "200 victimes accuseront l'intendant Pierre Marty," *La Marseillaise du Centre* (Limoges), July 10, 1946, 1.

31. "Le procès Marty va évoquer les exactions," *Dépêche du Midi*, May 15–16, 1948, 2.

32. "Mauvaise journée pour Marty," *Dépêche du Midi*, June 25, 1948, 2.

33. Mellor, *La Torture*, 217.

34. "Le procès Marty," 2. See also "Marty et sa brigade," 2; and "Pathetique audience au procès Marty," *Dépêche du Midi*, June 29, 1948, 1.

35. "Marty a terminé son extraordinaire plaidoyer," *Dépêche du Midi*, June 23, 1948, 2.

36. "Le Commissaire Muller accuse Marty d'avoir torture Chappert," *Dépêche du Midi*, June 28, 1948, 1.

37. Estèbe, *Toulouse, 1940–1944*, 155.

38. Yann Stephan, *A Broken Sword* (Chicago: Office of International Criminal Justice, 1991), 37–40.

39. J. Delperrie de Bayac, *Histoire de la milice, 1918–1945* (Paris: Fayard, 1969), 243. See also Pierre Giolitto, *Histoire de la milice* (Paris: Perrin, 1997), 287–88, 292; Marc-André Fabre, *Dans les prisons de la milice* (Vichy: Wallon, 1944): 1–23 (reissued as *Dans les prisons de Vichy* [Paris: Albin Michel, 1995], 24–45).

40. Élias Reval, *Sixieme Colonne* ([Thonon, S.E.S,] 1945), 196–201.

41. Ibid., 199. See also Mellor, *La Torture*, 217; and Giolitto, *Histoire de la milice*, 286, 289, 292–93.

42. Giolitto, *Histoire de la milice*, 368–69; Marie France Etchegoin, "Les preuves qui accablent Touvier," *Nouvel Observateur*, April 23–29, 1992, 46.

43. André Laurens, *Un police politique sous l'occupation* (Foix, France: C.D.D.P, 1982), 162.

44. Giolitto, *Histoire de la milice*, 285.

45. Ibid., 286.

46. The best biography in English for Lafont is in Dank, *French Against the French*, 206–23. In French, see Jacques Delarue, "La Bande Bonny-Lafont," in *Resistants et collaborateurs*, ed. François Bédarida (Paris: Seuil, 1985), 62–69; Delarue, *Trafics et crimes*, 119–23; Hasquenoph, *La Gestapo en France*, 133–50; Roland Black, *Histoire et crime de la Gestapo parisienne* (Brussels: Bel Go-Suisses, 1945), 80–84, 108–11; Philippe Aziz, *Tu trahiras sans vergogne* (Paris: Fayard, 1970).

47. Hasquenoph, *La Gestapo en France*, 136–38; Fabrice Laroche, "Les Français de la Gestapo," in Dumont, *Histoire secrète*, 4:53–55; Aziz, *Tu Trahiras sans vergogne*, 65–79; André Brissaud, "Les traffics de la Gestapo," in Dumont, *Histoire secrète*, 2:222–25.

48. Jean, valet to Lafont, cited in Black, *Histoire et crime*, 110.

49. Laroche, "Les Français de la Gestapo," 65.

50. Aziz, *Tu trahiras sans vergogne*, 67. See also Hasquenoph, *La Gestapo en France*, 138; Laroche, "Les Français de la Gestapo," 59, 65.

51. Hasquenoph, *La Gestapo en France*, 516.

52. See, for example, Rémy, *Une affaire de trahison*, 137, 163–64, 185, 202, 234, 268 (bathtub); 62, 161, 185, 199, 200, 202, 366–67 (beating).

53. For Merode's biography, see Delarue, *Trafics et crimes*, 40–45; Hasquenoph, *La Gestapo en France*, 152–54.

54. For Berger's biography, see Delarue, *Trafics et crimes*, 123–29; Hasquenoph, *La Gestapo en France*, 150–52.

55. Hasquenoph, *La Gestapo en France*, 314.

56. Ibid., 232, 406; Pierre Guiral, *Libération de Marseille* (Paris: Librarie Hachette, 1974), 66.

57. Mellor, *La Torture*, 218.

58. Giolitto, *Histoire de la milice*, 285.

59. Ibid., 289.

60. de Bayac, *Histoire de la milice*, 273.

61. Aziz, *Au service de l'ennemi*, 53, 58; Hasquenoph, *La Gestapo en France*, 415. Lamote used the magneto in November 26, 1943, two months after Marty. For torture in Bourges, see Hasquenoph, *La Gestapo en France*, 411–18; Aziz, *Au service de l'ennemi*, 7–72; Jean Cathelin and Gabrielle Gray, *Crime et trafics de la Gestapo francaise* (Paris: Historama, 1972), 23–36; Yves Durand and Robert Vivier, *Libération de pays de Loire* (Paris: Librarie Hachette, 1974), 67–78.

62. Hasquenoph, *La Gestapo en France*, 337, 374, 409; Bruce Marshall, *The White Rabbit* (London: Cassell, 1988), 118–20; Pierre Bécamps, *Libération de Bordeaux* (Paris: Librarie Hachette, 1974), 115–16.

63. Hasquenoph describes regional Gestapos, Aziz covers the Gestapo in Bourges, Marseilles, and Saint-Etienne, and Cathelin and Gray describe specific regional incidents. See Aziz, *Au service de l'ennemi*; Hasquenoph, *La Gestapo en France*, 312–524; Cathelin and Gray, *Crime et trafics*, 1:115–251; 2:13–142; Charles Rickard, *La Savoie dans la Resistance*, 4th ed. (Edilarge S.A.: Editions Ouest-France, 1993), 179–92, 223, 287–88; Henri Michel directed a series on the Liberation by region in France (Henri Michel, ed., *La Libération de la France* [Paris: Librarie Hachette, 1973–74], 16 unnumbered volumes). Many studies describe Gestapo repression of the Resistance or specific victims between 1943 and 1944, the most specific being those on Bordeaux, Marseilles, and Limousin.

64. Hasquenoph, *La Gestapo en France*, 371.

65. Ibid., 438.

66. H. Paucot, "Rapport sur les atrocités allemandes commises pendant l'occupation," in International Military Tribunal (IMT), *Trial of the Major War Criminals* (Nuremberg: n.p., 1949), 37:271–72 (Renard), 37:276–77 (Guilbert), 37:285 (Rémy), 37:282–83 (Billot), 37:286 (Moutier), 37:296 (Duhamel), and 37:305 (Coussmacker).

67. IMT, *Trial*, 6:168, 173.

68. Hasquenoph, *La Gestapo en France*, 131; Malise Ruthven, *Torture* (London: Weidenfeld and Nicolson, 1978), 290.

69. Robin Reilly, *The Sixth Floor* (London: Cassell, 2002), 94; see also 102. See also François d'Orcival, "Gestapo contre Résistance," in Dumont, *Histoire secrète*, 2:161; M.R.D. Foot, *The Resistance* (New York: McGraw-Hill, 1977) 89; Stefan Korbonski, *Fighting Warsaw*, trans. F. B. Czarnomski (London: Allen and Unwin, 1956), 318; Józef Lewandowski, *The Swedish Contribution to the Polish Resistance Movement during World War Two (1939–1942)* (Stockholm: Almqvist and Wiksell International, 1979), 76.

70. The German Communists in the 1930s may have been the first to hit upon it. See Michael Balfour, *Withstanding Hitler in Germany, 1933–45* (London: Routledge, 1988), 80. Other Resistance movements learned it later, abandoning foolish alternatives. See Zbigniew Stypulkowski, *Invitation to Moscow* (New York: Walker, 1962), 44; and Christine Sutherland, *Monica* (New York: Farrar, Straus and Giroux, 1990), 173–74.

71. Reilly, *The Sixth Floor*, 94.

72. Claeys, cited in IMT, *Trial*, 6:167. See also Edward Crankshaw, *Gestapo* (New York: Da Capo Press, 1994), 130.

73. Stephan, *A Broken Sword*, 39. The one torture case involved a Maquis band that tortured and continuously raped a female German spy who had already been sentenced to death for some time. Eventually, a Maquis leader ordered that either the prisoner should be executed as sentenced or she would personally "come over and set her free" (Russell Braddon, *Nancy Wake* [London: Cassell, 1956], 209–10). In Poland too, this reciprocal logic drove Resistance partisans to torture. See Waldemar Lotnik with Julian Preece, *Nine Lives* (London: Serif, 1999), 69–72.

74. Sweating was most common in the early 1930s. See Jan Valtin, *Out of the Night* (New York: Alliance, 1941), 575–77; Eric Boehm, *We Survived*, reprint ed. (Santa Barbara, CA: ABC-Clio Information Services, 1985), 38; *Germans against Hitler, July 20, 1944* (Bonn: Bundeszentrale für politische Bildung, [1969]), 193; Allan Merson, *Communist Resistance in Nazi Germany* (London: Lawrence and Wishart, 1985), 53–53; George Browder, *Hitler's Enforcers* (New York: Oxford University Press, 1996), 70–71. Later accounts show far less interest in appearances. See Peter Hoffman, *The History of the German Resistance, 1933–1945* (Cambridge: MIT Press, 1977), 527; *Germans against Hitler*, 200, 209–11.

75. Mellor, *La Torture*, 221. See also Hasquenoph, *La Gestapo en France*, 516.

76. Carl von Clausewitz, *On War*, ed. Anatol Rapoport (Harmondsworth, England: Penguin, 1968), 103.

77. Cited in Mellor, *La Torture*, 237

78. Stephan, *A Broken Sword*, 39; Delarue, *History of the Gestapo*, 245, 253–54.

79. Reval, *Sixieme Colonne*, 175.

80. Ibid., 199.

81. Crankshaw, *Gestapo*, 131; Browder, *Hitler's Enforcers*, 38; Kedward, *Search*, 222; Bécamps, *Libération de Bordeaux*, 121; Hans Bernd Gisevius, *To the Bitter End*, trans. Richard and Clara Winston (Boston: Houghton Mifflin, 1947), 63–64.

82. John Drummond, *But For These Men* (Morley: Elmfield Press, 1974), 69.

83. Ruthven, *Torture*, 290.

84. Browder, *Hitler's Enforcers*, 70.

85. Peters, *Torture*, 163–64, 166–67.

86. The Gestapo had elaborate cross-referenced card files, technology to monitor telephone and wireless communications, and the ability to steam open mail undetected (Browder, *Hitler's Enforcers*, 71–73).

87. D'Orcival, "Gestapo contre Résistance," 2:161.

88. IMT, *Trial*, 6:160, 168, 169, 174, 178, 180 (same), 6:169, 180 (similar), 6:165 (uniform), 6:180, 181 (analogous), 6:166, 179, 180, 181 (identical), 5:401 (general rule).

89. Ruthven, *Torture*, 290.

90. IMT, *Trial*, 6:180. Dubost identifies all the methods in this document correctly save electricity. "Statement of the Netherlands Government on the Prosecution and Punishment of the German War Criminals" in English, 1726-PS, 27:502–46, and in French, 224-F, 36:617–717. De Menthon also generalizes from one incident in Paucot's report to the rest of Europe. See IMT, *Trial*, 5:401.

91. Crankshaw, *Gestapo*, 124. See also Werstein, who finds electric torture in Denmark (Irving Werstein, *That Denmark Might Live* [Philadelphia: Macrae Smith, 1967], 108).

92. Crankshaw, *Gestapo*, 129.

93. Lewandowski, *Swedish Contribution*, 84.

94. Foot, *The Resistance*, 89.

Chapter 6
Shock

1. Cited in "Far Worse than Hanging," *New York Times*, August 7, 1890, 1.

2. Theodore Bernstein, "Theories of the Causes of Death from Electricity in the Late Nineteenth Century," *Medical Instrumentation* 9.6 (1975): 269.

3. Ibid., 268.

4. A. J. Jex-Blake, cited in ibid., 267.

5. See Thomas Hughes, "Harold Brown and the Executioner's Current," *Business History Review* 31 (1958): 143–65. This section was written too late to take advantage of Mark Essig's excellent new study. See Mark Essig, *Edison and the Electric Chair* (New York: Walker, 2003).

6. See Hughes, "Harold Brown," 150; Carolyn Marvin, *When Old Technologies Were New* (New York: Oxford, 1988), 115, 117.

7. Hughes, "Harold Brown," 149.

8. "A Dog Killed with the Electric Current," *New York Times*, July 31, 1888, 1.

9. Marvin, *Old Technologies*, 150.

10. "Surer than the Rope," *New York Times*, December 6, 1888, 1.

11. Otto Moses, cited in Marvin, *Old Technologies*, 150.

12. William Schabas, *The Death Penalty as Cruel Treatment and Torture* (Boston: Northeastern University Press, 1996), 180–81. Contrary to common belief, the Supreme Court did not determine that electrocution was not a cruel and unusual form of punishment. Rather, it rejected Kemmler's appeal on the grounds that the penal practices of the states did not have to conform to the Eighth Amendment. Later, the Court reversed itself, but it never revisited Kemmler's claim that electrocution was a cruel death. Many state supreme courts have rejected similar judicial challenges, but the Supreme Court has remained silent.

13. "Far Worse Than Hanging," 1.

14. Marvin, *Old Technologies*, 149–51; Hughes, "Harold Brown," 164.

15. Hughes, "Harold Brown," 164.

16. Bernstein, "Theories," 269.

17. See Schabas, *Death Penalty*, 179; Robert Elliot, *Agent of Death* (New York: E. P. Dutton, 1940), 58–78; and Amos Squire, *Sing Sing Doctor* (New York: Doubleday, Doran, 1935), 215.

18. Michael Punt, "The Elephant, the Spaceship and the White Cockatoo," in *The Photographic Image in Digital Culture*, ed. Martin Lister (London: Routledge, 1995), 62–64.

19. Schabas, *Death Penalty*, 179.

20. Bernstein, "Theories," 269.

21. *Louisiana ex rel Francis v. Resweber*, 329 U.S. 459 (1947) lists the early cases. More recent cases include Francis (Lousiania, 1947); Dunkins (Alabama, 1989); Stephens (Georgia, 1984), Evans (Louisiana, 1983), Tafero (Florida, 1990).

22. Bernstein, "Theories," 270–72.

23. Ibid., 272.

24. http://www.cdc.gov/niosh/elecovrv.html. Voltage designates the difference of potential energy between the positive and negative poles. Amperage designates the amount of current that travels through the wire. Current is the number of electrons passing through something every second. The nature of the wire's material affects how easily current can flow through it. This resistance is measured in ohms. One ampere is the current produced by one volt on a wire with one ohm resistance.

25. Marvin, *Old Technologies*, 37.

26. Emma Goldman, "Prisons," in *Anarchism and Other Essays* (New York: Dover, 1969), 119.

27. National Commission on Law Observance and Enforcement, *Report on Lawlessness in Law Enforcement* (Washington, DC: U.S. Government Printing Office, 1931), 139 (hereafter cited as Wickersham Commission); Ernest Jerome Hopkins, *Our Lawless Police* (New York: Viking, 1931), 220.

28. *Seattle Union and Record*, 1920s, cited in Oswald Villard, "Official Lawlessness," *Harpers*, October 1927, 611–12.

29. Cited in S. N. Aggarwal, *The Heroes of Cellular Jail* (Patiala, India: Punjabi University Publication Bureau, 1995), 94.

30. "Judge Orders Destruction of Electric Chair Used by Arkansas Sheriff for Confessions," *New York Times*, November 23, 1929, 12.

31. Wickersham Commission, 239.

32. "Says Electric Chair Forced Confession," *New York Times*, December 10, 1929, 24.

33. Bernstein, "Theories," 270, 271; Donald Cabana, "The History of Capital Punishment in Mississippi," *Mississippi History Now* (Mississippi Historical Society, 2000–2004), http://mshistory.k12.ms.us/features/feature57/punishment.htm.

34. Burnett Bolloten, *The Spanish Civil War* (Chapel Hill: University of North Carolina Press, 1991), 216–21, 499–507, 601–10; Robert Conquest, *The Great Terror* (New York: Oxford University Press, 1990), 410; W. G. Krivitsky, *I Was Stalin's Agent* (London: Hamish Hamilton, 1939), 93–134; Franz Borkenau, *The Spanish Cockpit* (London: Faber and Faber, 1937), 239–40; Fenner Borckway, *Worker's Front* (London: Secker and Warburg, 1938), 123–25; David Cattell, *Communism and the Spanish Civil War* (Berkeley and Los Angeles: University of California Press, 1955), 132–34; Pierre Broué and Emile Témime, *The Revolution and the Civil War in Spain*, trans. Tony White (London: Faber and Faber, 1972), 311–15; Hugh Thomas, *The Spanish Civil War* (New York: Harper and Row, 1961), 176–77; John McGovern, *Terror in Spain* (London: Independent Labour Party, [1938?]), 8–13; Julián Gorkin, *El proceso de Moscú en Barcelona* (Barcelona: Aymá, 1974), 52–57.

35. Conquest, *The Great Terror*, 410; Patrick v. zur Mühlen, *Spanien war ihre Hoffnung* (Bonn: Verlag Neue Gesellschaft, 1983), 163; Julian Gorkin, *Canibales politicos* (Mexico City: Ediciones Quetzal, 1941), 235; José Peirats, *Anarchists in the Spanish Revolution* (London: Freedom Press, 1990), 233.

36. Conquest, *The Great Terror*, 410; Mühlen, *Spanien war ihre Hoffnung*, 163; Katia Landau, *Le stalinisme en Espagne* (Paris: Impr. Cerbonnet, 1938), 24–26.

37. Gorkin, *Canibales politicos*, 233–34; Landau, *Le stalinisme en Espagne*, 22–23.

38. Peirats, *Anarchists*, 233.

39. Ibid.

40. Tomasa Cuevas, *Prison of Women*, trans. and ed. Mary Giles (Albany: State University of New York Press, 1998), 79, 118, 183, 202–3.

41. Peter Deeley, *Beyond Breaking Point* (London: Arthur Baker, 1971), 104–17; *Franco's Prisoners Speak* (London: Spanish Ex-Servicemen's Association, 1960).

42. Armando Correia de Magalhaes, cited in Amnesty International (AI), *Prison Conditions in Portugal* (London, 1965), 22.

43. AI, *Prison Conditions in Portugal*, 21.

44. Shawn Smallman, "Military Terror and Silence in Brazil, 1910–1945," *Canadian Journal of Latin American and Caribbean Studies* 24.7 (1999): 13–20.

45. Elizabeth Cancelli, *O mundo da violência* (Brasília, DF: Editora Universidade de Brasília, 1993), 193–94; William Waack, *Camaradas* (São Paulo: Companhia das Letras, 1993), 300; Hastings, "Political Prisoners in Brazil," *Times* (London), July 10, 1936, 12.

46. "State Department Hit by Marcantonio," *New York Times*, April 13, 1936, A19. See also "Charge Murder in Brazil," *New York Times*, March 26, 1936, A24; Minna Ewert, "Political Prisoners in Brazil," *Times* (London), July 18, 1936, 8; Stanley

Hilton, *Brazil and the Soviet Challenge* (Austin: University of Texas Press, 1981), 81–82, 84.

47. For this connection, see Hilton, *Brazil and the Soviet Challenge*, 118–19.

48. General Toranzo, *Los Torturados* ([Buenos Aires?]: Editorial Estampa, 1935).

49. Court proceedings in the abduction of Martha Ofelia Stutz, Cordoba, Argentina, cited in M. H. Landaburu and J. C. Suárez Muscardit, "Las Torturas," *Esto Es*, November 22, 1955, 23.

50. Roberto Estrella [Valentín Vergara], *Tortura* (Tucumán, Argentina: Ediciones "Dos-Ve," 1956), 10.

51. See Dana Sycks, *Cattle Raising in Argentina* (Washington, DC: U.S. Government Printing Office, 1929), 10–13; Simon Hanson, *Argentine Meat and the British Market* (Stanford, CA: Stanford University Press, 1938).

52. R. Warrington, "Electrical Stunning," *Veterinary Bulletin*, October 1974, 617–18.

53. Russell Wright, 1939, "Prod," U.S. Patent 2,304,065 (filed June 22, 1939; issued December 8, 1942); Sidney Andrus, 1939, "Flashlight Attachment," U.S. Patent 2,253,315 (filed July 5, 1939; issued August 19, 1941); Leon Mongan, 1939, "Electric Prodder," U.S. Patent 2,208,852 (filed February 16, 1939; issued July 23, 1940); Ernest Jefferson, 1939, "Electric Animal Prod," U.S. Patent 2,204,041 (filed October 23, 1939; issued June 11, 1940). These supplanted the earlier prod designs; see, for example John Burton, "Electric Prod Pole," U.S. Patent 427,549 (filed March 18, 1890; issued May 13, 1890).

54. Raul Lamas, *Los Torturadores* (Buenos Aires: Editorial Lamas, 1956), 152.

55. Landaburu and Suárez Muscardit, "Las Torturas," 23; Estrella, *Tortura*, 10.

56. Estrella, *Tortura*, 10.

57. Landaburu and Suárez Muscardit, "Las Torturas," 23; Lamas, *Los Torturadores*, 152.

58. Estrella, *Tortura*, 10.

59. Ricardo Rodríguez-Molas, *Historia de la Tortura* (Buenos Aires: Editorial Universitaria de Buenos Aires, 1984), 117.

60. Dr. Alberto Caride, cited in ibid., 120.

61. Estrella, *Tortura*, 11. See also Rodríguez-Molas, *Historia de la Tortura*, 117.

62. Estrella, *Tortura*, 10–11.

63. Ibid., 11.

64. Rodríguez-Molas, *Historia de la Tortura*, 117.

65. Lamas, *Los Torturadores*, 152; Rodríguez-Molas, *Historia de la Tortura*, 117, 119.

66. Pablo Sulbarán, *La Tortura en Venezuela* (Caracas: Pub. Seleven, 1980), 162; Kenneth Shillman, cited in "New York Rider Relates Harrowing Tale of Life in Maximum Security," *Jackson Daily*, June 21, 1961, http://www.freedomridersfoundation.org/photos.articles.and.artifacts.html.

67. Wolfgang Schivelbusch, *The Railway Journey* (Berkeley and Los Angeles: University of California Press, 1986), 157–58.

68. See ibid., 134–50; and Allan Young, "Suffering and the Origins of Traumatic Memory," in *Social Suffering*, ed. Arthur Kleinman, Veena Das, and Margaret Lock (Berkeley and Los Angeles: University of California Press, 1997), 245–60.

This literature puts into question the notion that male hysteria was largely un-known in the nineteenth century. For this position, see Elaine Showalter, *The Female Malady* (Harmondsworth, England: Penguin, 1987), 167–68, 172.

69. Pirogoff, cited in Schivelbusch, *The Railway Journey*, 156.
70. Charles Myers, "Contribution to the Study of Shell Shock," *The Lancet*, February 13, 1915, 316–20, September 9, 1916, 461–67, March 18, 1916, 608–13; Charles Myers, *Shell Shock in France* (Cambridge: Cambridge University Press, 1940), 11–12, 25–29.
71. Myers, *Shell Shock in France*, 86–87; Modris Eksteins, *The Rites of Spring* (Boston: Houghton Mifflin, 1989), 213, 228, 254.
72. Ilya Ehrenburg, cited in Eksteins, *The Rites of Spring*, 254.
73. Gerald Grob, *Mental Illness and American Society, 1875–1940* (Princeton, NJ: Princeton University Press, 1983), 293. Wagner-Jaurreg treated nine cases; three recovered entirely, three improved, and three were unchanged (Max Fink, *Electroshock* [Oxford: Oxford University Press, 1999], 86.
74. Sakel gives two different dates for his insight, 1929 and 1927. See Manfred Sakel, *The Pharmacological Shock Treatment of Schizophrenia* (New York: Nervous and Mental Disease Publishing, 1938), 2; Manfred Sakel, *Schizophrenia* (New York: Philosophical Library, 1958), v, 190.
75. Grob, *Mental Illness*, 298.
76. Ibid., 299; William Sargant, *The Unquiet Mind* (Boston: Little, Brown, 1967), 55.
77. Sargant, *The Unquiet Mind*, 90.
78. Ibid.
79. Ibid., 88.
80. Ibid., 113.
81. Ibid., 118–19.
82. William Sargant, *The Battle for the Mind* (Garden City, NY: Doubleday, 1957).
83. Fink, *Electroshock*, 89; Grob, *Mental Illness*, 303–4; Robert Peck, *The Miracle of Shock Treatment* (Jericho, NY: Exposition Press, 1974), 17.
84. *Electrical Review*, cited in Marvin, *Old Technologies*, 131. See also J. F. Falton, "Origins of Electroshock Therapy," *Journal of the History of Medicine and Allied Sciences* 11 (1956): 229–30; and Ernest Harms, "The Origin and Early History of Electrotherapy and Electroshock," *American Journal of Psychiatry* 107 (1955): 933–34.
85. See Edward Stainbrook, "The Use of Electricity in Psychiatric Treatment during the 19th Century," *Bulletin of the History of Medicine* 22.3 (1948): 175.
86. Ugo Cerletti, "Old and New Information About ElectroShock," *American Journal of Psychiatry* 107 (1955): 89.
87. Hans Binneveld, *From Shell Shock to Combat Stress*, trans. John O'Kane (Amsterdam: University of Amsterdam, 1997), 107–8.
88. Ibid., 109.
89. Ibid., 128.
90. Ibid., 127–28.
91. Ibid., 110; Showalter, *The Female Malady*, 206.

92. Binneveld, *Shell Shock*, 108.

93. Ibid., 88–89, 116–21; Showalter, *The Female Malady*, 179–91.

94. Fred Mott, *War Neuroses and Shell Shock* (London: Oxford University Press, 1919), 277.

95. Binneveld, *Shell Shock*, 114; Myers, *Shell Shock in France*, 103.

96. See Mott, *War Neuroses*, 276–80; Myers, *Shell Shock in France*, 58; and E. E. Southard, *Shell-Shock and Other Neuropsychiatric Problems* (Boston: W. M. Leonard, 1919), 782–95.

97. Lewis Yealland, *Hysterical Disorders of Warfare* (London: Macmillan, 1918).

98. Southard, *Shell-Shock*, 782–84; Yealland, *Hysterical Disorders of Warfare*, 14, 16, 56, 129.

99. Yealland, *Hysterical Disorders of Warfare*, 126–30.

100. Ibid., 7–15. Binneveld presentation of Case A1 is more reliable that Showalter's. Showalter omits how grateful the patient was for speaking again. She adds instead that the patient was required to say thank you, a passage that does not occur on pp. 14–15. Similarly in Case G4, Yealland cures a man who could not speak or move steadily in ten minutes. While Showalter is rightly concerned for the patient's subsequent psychological condition, she does not mention that the patient spoke again, which was the point of Yealland's treatment. Rather, she passes over the physical cure, and writes as if Yealland was curing the patient of his dreams and had failed. See Binneveld, *Shell Shock*, 111–14; Showalter, *The Female Malady*, 176–78.

101. See Cerletti, "Old and New Information," 90–92; and L. Bini, "Experimental Researches on Epileptic Attacks Induced by the Electric Current," *American Journal of Psychiatry* 94 (1938): 172–74.

102. Fink, *Electroshock*, 80; Peck, *Miracle of Shock Treatment*, 28, 48; American Psychiatric Association, *The Practice of Electroconvulsive Therapy* (Washington, DC; American Psychiatric Association, 2001), 330.

103. Grob, *Mental Illness*, 304; Showalter, *The Female Malady*, 206; Sargant, *The Unquiet Mind*, 55, 79–81.

104. Gotz Aly, "Pure and Tainted Progress," in *Cleansing the Fatherland*, ed. Gotz Aly, Peter Chroust, and Christian Pross, trans. Belinda Cooper (Baltimore: Johns Hopkins University Press, 1994), 204–5.

105. Binneveld, *Shell Shock*, 128.

106. Aly, "Pure and Tainted Progress," 204.

107. Binneveld, *Shell Shock*, 128.

108. Ibid.

109. Ibid., 127. For the program, see Aly, Chroust, and Pross, *Cleansing the Fatherland*, 1–98, 156–237.

110. Robert Jay Lifton, *The Nazi Doctors* (New York: Basic Books, 1986), 298–300.

111. Gordon Thomas, *Journey Into Madness* (New York: Bantam, 1989), 152.

112. Bernstein, "Theories," 273.

113. Cerletti, "Old and New Information," 92.

114. Jean Delay, A. Djourno, and G. Verdeaux, "Les nouvelles technique de l'électro-choc," *L'Encâephale* 40 (1951): 426–83.

115. L.G.M. Page and R. J. Russell, "Intensified Electrical Convulsion Therapy," *The Lancet*, April 17, 1948, 597–98.

116. John Marks, *The Search for the Manchurian Candidate* (New York: McGraw-Hill, 1980), 25.

117. Fink, *Electroshock*, 108; *Rohovit v. Mecta*, 506 N.W. 2d 449 (1993 Iowa Sup.); Richard Abrams, *Electroconvulsive Therapy*, 3rd ed. (New York: Oxford University Press, 1997), 277–79. Abrams is the director and part owner of Somatics.

118. See Abrams, *Electroconvulsive Therapy*, 279; Harold Sackeim, "Are ECT Devices Underpowered?" *Convulsive Therapy* 7 (1991): 233–36.

119. Robert Davis, Thomas Deter, David Egger, Gary Tucker, and Robert Wyman, "Electroconvulsive Therapy Instruments," *Archives of General Psychiatry* 25.2 (1971): 97–99. See also Morris Fraser, *ECT* (Chichester, NY: John Wiley, 1982), 107–15. Public information on the electrical characteristics of modern machines is rare.

120. Fink, *Electroshock*, 109.

121. Peck, *Miracle of Shock Treatment*, 18; Peter Breggin, *Electroshock* (New York: Springer, 1979), 149; C. P. Freeman, *The ECT Handbook* (London: Royal College of Psychiatrists, 1995), 37–96.

122. Fink, *Electroshock*, xi.

123. Breggin, *Electroshock*, 139–48; American Psychiatric Association, *Practice of Electroconvulsive Therapy*, 59–75; Richard Weiner, "Retrograde Amnesia with Electroconvulsive Therapy," *Archives of General Psychiatry* 57.6 (2000): 591.

124. Fink, *Electroshock*, 95.

125. Ibid., 98–99.

126. Breggin *Electroshock*, 154.

127. Fink, *Electroshock*, 105; Darius Rejali, *Torture and Modernity* (Boulder, CO: Westview, 1994), 71.

128. Fraser, *ECT*, 111.

129. Psychologist advising the CIA, cited in Marks, *Search*, 25.

130. Alan Scheflin and Edward Opton, *The Mind Manipulators* (New York: Paddington Press, 1978), 392.

131. Similar experiments are alleged but unconfirmed in South Vietnam and France. See Thomas, *Journey Into Madness*, 258–59; Alfred McCoy, *A Question of Torture* (New York: Metropolitan, 2006), 65; and *Stanley Milton Glickman vs. USA et al*, 83 civ. 3458 (TPG), U.S. District Court, Southern District of New York. In the mid-1960s, Lloyd Cotter, a military psychologist, described traveling alone to Vietnam to teach South Vietnamese doctors how to apply ECT to schizophrenics at Bien Hoa Mental Hospital. See Lloyd Cotter, "Operant Conditioning in a Vietnamese Mental Hospital," *American Journal of Psychiatry* 124 (July 1967): 23–66. Cotter based his work on B. F. Skinner's research, showed no awareness of Cameron's work (which was well published in psychiatric journals at this time), and did mention Vietcong prisoners at the hospital. Thomas, however, asserts that

two CIA psychologists accompanied Cotter. They used Dr. Cameron's techniques on Vietcong prisoners in a separate ward, killing all of them. Marks and Scheflin and Opton do not mention any documents pointing to this event in their extensive studies of the declassified CIA scientific data.

132. Marks, *Search*, 133, 141.

133. D. Ewen Cameron, "Production of Differential Amnesia as a Factor in the Treatment of Schizophrenia," *Comprehensive Psychiatry* 1 (1960): 26, 27; D. Ewen Cameron, "The Depatterning Treatment of Schizophrenia," *Comprehensive Psychiatry* 3.2 (1962): 65–76.

134. Marks, *Search*, 137.

135. A. E. Schwartzman and P. E. Termansen, "Intensive Electroconvulsive Therapy: A Follow-Up Study," *Canadian Psychiatric Association Journal* 12 (1967): 218.

136. Marks, *Search*, 140–41; Scheflin and Opton, *The Mind Manipulators*, 383–84.

137. D. Ewen Cameron, "The Modern Psychiatric Conception of Depression," *Acta Neuropsiquiát* 2 (1960): 124.

138. Scheflin and Opton, *The Mind Manipulators*, 391.

139. Cerletti, "Old and New Information," 90.

140. Frantz Fanon, *A Dying Colonialism*, trans. Haakon Chevalier (New York: Grove Press, 1965), 138. Fanon does not repeat the claim in his later work with torture victims. See Frantz Fanon, *The Wretched of the Earth*, trans. Constance Farrington (New York: Grove Press, 1968), 283.

141. Thomas, *Journey Into Madness*, 258–59, 311, 328, 333–36. Thomas, a British journalist and a longtime friend of William Sargant, relates this information from a CIA operative, Buckley. Buckley mysteriously does not appear among the despositions, affidavits, or other sources Thomas lists (369–75). For Thomas's connection to Sargant, see Michael Ignatieff, "What Did the CIA Do To His Father?" *New York Times Magazine*, April 1, 2001, 60.

142. Thomas (*Journey Into Madness*, 336) claims that *Torture in the Eighties* corroborates most of Buckley's claims, but these it does not. See AI, *Torture in the Eighties* (London, 1984), 109–10 (Djibouti), 155–58 (El Salvador), 238–40 (Morocco). Vietnam is not listed.

143. Ahmed Boukhari, *Le Secret* (Neuilly-sur-Seine: Editions Michel Lafon, 2002), 90; "The Now Unsecret Policeman," *The Economist*, February 16, 2002, 44. For the human rights reports on Morocco, see chapter 9 ("Singing the World Electric").

Chapter 7
Magnetos

1. "Des cours sur une 'torture humaine' sont donnés aux stagiaires du camp Jeanne d'Arc," *Le Monde*, December 20–21, 1959, 6.

2. Alain Ruscio, "Du Tonkin à Alger, des 'violences de detail,' " *Le Monde Diplomatique*, June 2001, 10–11, www.monde-diplomatique.fr.

3. Silvanus Thompson, *Dynamo-electric Machinery* (London: E. and F. N. Spon, 1886), 1.

4. Ibid., 4.

5. Arthur Judge, *Motor Manuals*, vol. 4: *Car Maintenance and Repair* (London: Chapman and Hall, 1952), 156–57.

6. Helge Kragh, "Telephone Technology," in *National Military Establishments and the Advancement of Science and Technology*, ed. P. Forman and J. M. Sánchez-Ron (Dordrecht, Netherlands: Kluwer Academic, 1996), 42.

7. Ibid., 44.

8. Jacque Chégaray, "Les tortures en Indochine," in *Les crimes de l'armée française*, ed. Pierre Vidal-Naquet (Paris: François Maspera, 1954), 20.

9. Peter Zinoman, *The Colonial Bastille* (Berkeley and Los Angeles: University of California Press, 2001), 203–5.

10. Andrée Viollis, *Indochine S.O.S.* (Paris: Gallimard, 1935), 21.

11. Daniel Hémery, *Révolutionnaires vietnamiens et pouvoir colonial en Indochine* (Paris: François Maspero, 1975), 162.

12. Viollis, *Indochine S.O.S.*, 21. See also Hémery, *Révolutionnaires vietnamiens*, 164, 457–58.

13. See Erwin Rosen [Carlé], *In the Foreign Legion* (London: Duckworth, 1910), 228–30; and Charles Mercer, *Legion of Strangers* (New York: Holt, Rinehart and Winston, 1964), 191.

14. Viollis, *Indochine S.O.S.*, 21.

15. Hémery, *Révolutionnaires vietnamiens*, 164.

16. Ibid., 457.

17. Ibid., 164–65.

18. Ibid., 163.

19. Ibid., 457.

20. Some of these are unintelligible eighty years afterward, notably the "coup de ballon" and the torture "a la coco."

21. Viollis, *Indochine S.O.S.*, 20.

22. Ibid., 20.

23. Ibid., 22.

24. Ibid., 20.

25. Hémery, *Révolutionnaires vietnamiens*, 164.

26. Chégaray, "Les tortures en Indochine," 17–18.

27. See chapters 3 ("Lights, Heat, and Sweat") and 14 ("Stress and Duress"); for the *bagnards*, see Michel Devèze, *Cayenne* (Paris: René Julliard, 1965); Peter Redfield, *Space in the Tropics* (Berkeley and Los Angeles: University of California Press, 2000), 51–111; Jean-Claude Michelot, *La Guillotine sèche* (Paris: Fayard, 1981), 177–95; Michel Bourdet-Pléville, *Justice in Chains*, trans. Anthony Rippon (London: Robert Hale, 1960), 84–95; Gerard Lacourrège and Pierre Alibert, *Au temps des bagnes* (Paris: Editions Atlas, 1986), 133–50; Marion Godfory and Stanislas Fautré, *Bagnards* ([Paris]: Editions du Chêne, 2002), 130–37, 152–57.

28. Rosen, *In the Foreign Legion*, 228–30; Mercer, *Legion of Strangers*, 191.

29. Philippe Aziz, *Au service de l'ennemi* (Paris: Fayard, 1972), 53, 58; Marcel Hasquenoph, *La Gestapo en France* (Paris: De Vecchi Poche, 1987), 416; International Military Tribunal, *Trial of the Major War Criminals* (Nuremberg, Germany: n.p. 1949), 6:160, 167, 168.

30. Elias Reval, *Sixieme Colonne* (Thonon, S.E.S,] 1945), 199; Pierre Giolitto, *Histoire de la milice* (Paris: Perrin, 1997): 292–93.

31. André Laurens, *Un police politique sous l'occupation* (Foix: C.D.D.P, 1982), 162.

32. J. Ingram Bryan, *Japanese All* (New York: E. P. Dutton, 1928), 142–43.

33. This appears to be an old technique, also practiced in Korea before the Japanese occupied it. Homer Hulbert, *The Passing of Korea* (New York: Doubleday, Page, 1906), 66. See also Lord Russell, *The Knights of Bushido* (London: Cassell, 1958), 276.

34. Elise Tipton, *The Japanese Police State* (Honolulu: University of Hawaii Press, 1990), 26.

35. Theodore Friend, introduction to *The Kenpeitai in Java and Sumatra*, trans. Barbard Gifford Shimer and Guy Hobbs (Ithaca, NY: Cornell Modern Indonesia Project, 1986), 2.

36. Otto Tolischus, *Tokyo Record* (New York: Reynal and Hitchcock, 1943), 335–52, 392–93; Haruko Taya Cook and Theodore Cook, *Japan at War* (New York: New Press, 1992), 224, 230–31.

37. Leon Friedman, ed., *The Law of War* (New York: Random House, 1972), 2: 1084–86.

38. Ibid., 2:1085.

39. Russell, *The Knights of Bushido*, 160.

40. See Chulwoo Lee, "Modernity, Legality and Power in Korea under Japanese Rule," in *Colonial Modernity in Korea*, ed. Gi-Wook Shin and Michael Robinson (Cambridge: Harvard University Asia Center, 1999), 33; Raymond Lamont-Brown, *Kempeitai* (Gloucestershire, England: Sutton, 1998), 85.

41. Lee, "Modernity, Legality and Power," 37.

42. A Korean web page on the March 1919 protests lists electric torture as one of five techniques and also states three people (Yi Tal-jun, Pak Kyong-ok, and Kim To-il) died of torture, but it is not clear whether they died of electrotorture (Dangjin Times, http://www.djtimes.co.kr/44.htm, accessed March 27, 2004). Other sources tell the electrotorture story of Kim Tu-hwan. Kim Tu-hwan is a legendary figure, like Robin Hood and Al Capone, and his life is often fictionalized and romanticized. Officials at the Sodaemun Museum in Seoul confirmed that electrotorture was common in the colonial period, but could not offer dates or cases. These cases seem the most reliable. More research in this area would be welcome.

43. Personal web page, http://kes46.new21.net/intropds/t5/t5.htm, accessed April 9, 2004. Also consult Kijang-gun Office, www.gijang.busan.kr.

44. Yon-hong Chong, "Kohyang ttang" [My Old Home], http://www.suzinwon.com/gohyangddang.htm, accessed March 27, 2004.

45. Tolischus, *Tokyo Record*, 393–94.

46. Friedman, *The Law of War*, 2:1118–23.

47. Chief of the Prisoner of War Camps, Prisoner of War Administration Section, Military Affairs Bureau, Order, August 20, 1945, cited in Friedman, *The Law of War*, 2:1087.

48. Friedman, *The Law of War*, 2:1087.

49. R. John Pritchard and Sonia Magbanua Zaide, eds., *The Tokyo War Crimes Trial* (New York: Garland, 1981), 16:40101. See also Friedman, *The Law of War*, 2:1084.

50. Pritchard and Zaide, *Tokyo War Crimes Trial*, 6:14165–85; Harriet Sergeant, *Shanghai* (London: Jonathan Cape, 1991), 316–17, 334–36; Friedman, *The Law of War*, 2:1084–85.

51. William Bungey, cited in Pritchard and Zaide, *Tokyo War Crimes Trial*, 6:14168.

52. Commander C. D. Smith, cited in ibid., 6:14183.

53. Bungey, cited in ibid., 6:14169.

54. Friedman, *The Law of War*, 2:1084–85.

55. Pritchard and Zaide, *Tokyo War Crimes Trial*, 6:12915, 12921, 12937, 12940–42; Russell, *The Knights of Bushido*, 278; Friedman, *The Law of War*, 2:1085; Taman Budiman, *Memoirs of an Unorthodox Civil Servant* (Kuala Lumpur: Heinemann Educational Books, 1979), 123–24; Chin Kee Onn, *Malaya Upside Down* (Singapore: Federal Publications, 1976), 117.

56. Reverend J. L. Wilson, cited in Pritchard and Zaide, *Tokyo War Crimes Trial*, 6:12942.

57. Lieutenant P. V. Dean, cited in ibid., 6:12923.

58. Pritchard and Zaide, *Tokyo War Crimes Trial*, 6:12942–43.

59. Friedman, *The Law of War*, 2:1084–85.

60. Pritchard and Zaide, *Tokyo War Crimes Trial*, 6:12961, 13188–93; Cook and Cook, *Japan at War*, 101, 422–24; Friedman, *The Law of War*, 2:1084–85; Russell, *The Knights of Bushido*, photos following 48, 89–93; A. G. Allbury, *Bamboo and Bushido* (London: Robert Hale, 1955), 33–34, 68–69, 132.

61. Friedman, *The Law of War*, 2:1085.

62. Ibid., 2:1085–86.

63. Pritchard and Zaide, *Tokyo War Crimes Trial*, 7:15319–20, 15323, 15327, 15332, 15334, 15337–39, 15341, 15348–49, 15366, 15371–74, 15383, 15432, 15439; Friedman, *The Law of War*, 2:1085–86.

64. Limousin Francois, cited in Pritchard and Zaide, *Tokyo War Crimes Trial*, 7:15344–45; see also 15327, 15332, 15432.

65. Friedman, *The Law of War*, 2:1085.

66. Pritchard and Zaide, *Tokyo War Crimes Trial*, 7:15339, 15366, 15372–74, 15432; Jacques Le Bourgeois, *Saïgon sans la France* (Paris: Librairie Plon, 1949), 33, 36–37. For origins of the Dutch technique, see chapter 5.

67. Pritchard and Zaide, *Tokyo War Crimes Trial*, 7:15366.

68. Friedman, *The Law of War*, 2:1085–86; Russell, *The Knights of Bushido*, 185–91; Felisa Syjuco, *The Kempei Tai in the Philippines* (Quezon City, Philippines: New Day Publishers, 1988), 64–69; Stewart Wolf and Herbert Ripley, "Reactions Among Allied Prisoners of War Subjected to Three Years of Imprisonment and Torture by the Japanese," *American Journal of Psychiatry* 104 (1947): 182–83.

69. Syjuco, *Kempei Tai*, 68.

70. Ibid., 67–68.

71. Russell, *The Knights of Bushido*, 164–70; Friedman, *The Law of War*, 2:1085–86.

72. Yi Yongsuk, "I Would Rather Die," in *True Stories of the Korean Comfort Women*, ed. Keith Howard, trans. Young Joo Lee (London: Cassell, 1995), 91.

73. Pritchard and Zaide, *Tokyo War Crimes Trial*, 6:13515–17.

74. Ibid., 6:13405–13407; 13333–43; Russell, *The Knights of Bushido*, 191–204; Friedman, *The Law of War*, 2:1085–86.

75. Yuki Tanaka, *Hidden Horrors* (Boulder, CO: Westview, 1996), 26–27; Russell, *The Knights of Bushido*, 198.

76. Russell, *The Knights of Bushido*, 193–95.

77. Pritchard and Zaide, *Tokyo War Crimes Trial*, 6:13677–84; Russell, *The Knights of Bushido*, 162–64, 209–12; Friedman, *The Law of War*, 2:1085–86.

78. Major A. Zimmerman, cited in Pritchard and Zaide, *Tokyo War Crimes Trial*, 6:13684.

79. Friedman, *The Law of War*, 2:1085.

80. Lamont-Brown, *Kempeitai*, 128–29; Russell, *The Knights of Bushido*, 175–76, 181–84, 205–8; Friedman, *The Law of War*, 2:1085–86.

81. Pritchard and Zaide, *Tokyo War Crimes Trial*, 6:13843; Russell, *The Knights of Bushido*, 151–62, 172–80; Cook and Cook, *Japan at War*, 114–15; Friedman, *The Law of War*, 2:1085–86.

82. Russell, *The Knights of Bushido*, 178–79.

83. Friend, introduction, 2; Cook and Cook, *Japan at War*, 152–53.

84. Cook and Cook, *Japan at War*, 152–53.

85. The IMTFE found none (see Pritchard and Zaide, *Tokyo War Crimes Trial*, 16:14101). However, Lamont-Brown states that "torture methods were on the syllabuses of the Kempeitai training schools." Unfortunately, he simply reproduces Russell, who offered an identical torture list and spoke of "a Kempeitai training school where many methods of these methods of interrogation were learnt." But Russell also documented no primary documents other than the 1943 manual. See Lamont-Brown, *Kempeitai*, 20; Russell, *The Knights of Bushido*, 274.

86. Pritchard and Zaide, *Tokyo War Crimes Trial*, 6:14779.

87. István Pintér, *Hungarian Anti-Fascism and Resistance, 1941–1945* (Budapest: Akadémiai Kiadó, 1986), 54.

88. Egon Balas, *Will to Freedom* (Syracuse, NY: Syracuse University Press, 2000), 95–97.

89. See Pintér, *Hungarian Anti-Fascism*, 54; Balas, *Will to Freedom*, 95–97; Emanuel Böhm, *Human Rights Violations* (New York: Slovak Institute, Cleveland, 1986), 80–104; and Barbara Jancar-Webster, *Women and Revolution in Yugoslavia, 1941–1945* (Denver: Arden, 1990), 109–11.

90. U.S. War Department, *Handbook on German Military Forces* (Baton Rouge: Louisiana State University Press, 1990), 441, 452.

91. Chégaray, "Les tortures en Indochine," 17–18; Alec Mellor, *La Torture* (Paris: Horizons littéraires, 1949), 233.

92. Caroline Elkins, *Imperial Reckoning* (New York: Henry Holt, 2005), 66.

93. Anonymous interview, Naivasha, Kenya, January 14, 1999, cited in ibid., 87.

94. Elkins, *Imperial Reckoning*, 63–73, 80, 136, 147, 155–57, 187, 207–8, 245, 247–49, 251, 254–57, 322, 325; David Anderson, *Histories of the Hanged* (New York: Norton, 2005), 291–93, 310, 315–16.

95. Elkins, *Imperial Reckoning*, 80, 258.

96. Salome Maina, August 13, 2003, cited in ibid., 258.

97. S. N. Aggarwal, *The Heroes of Cellular Jail* (Patiala, India: Punjabi University Publication Bureau, 1995), 94.

98. Ian Cobain, "The Secrets of the London Cage," *Guardian* (London), November 12, 2005, 8. See chapter 15, "Forced Standing and Other Positions."

99. Charles Foley, *Island in Revolt* (London: Longmans, Green, 1962), 131.

100. Cited by John Barry, reporter at *Newsweek* (email correspondence, July 1, 2004).

101. John McGuffin, *The Guineapigs* (Harmondsworth, England: Penguin, 1974), 130–31.

102. Roger R., cited in *Ceux d'Algérie*, ed. Andrew Orr (Paris: Editions Payot, 1990), 36. There are rumors of Allied troops using magnetos during World War II. Peter Martinsen, an American interrogator in Vietnam, reported that World War II and Korean veterans explained field telephone torture to him (John Duffett, ed., *Against the Crime of Silence: Proceedings of the Russell International War Crimes Tribunal* (New York: O'Hare Books, 1968), 453. Fabien Brun describes a photograph in a Frankfurt police museum of Allied electrotorture of a German prisoner at the end of the war. (Fabien Brun, email message to author, February 7, 2002.) I have been unable to find this photograph, but that would be concrete documentation of magneto usage in this murky period. Hanson claims American troops who tortured in World War II operated under a "don't ask, don't tell understanding" and were rarely punished by commanding officers, so records are unlikely (Victor Davis Hanson, "Winning a War without Torture," *Washington Times*, December 3, 2005, http://www.washingtontimes.com).

103. Pierre Vidal-Naquet, *Torture*, trans. Barry Richard (Harmondsworth, England: Penguin, 1963), 29, 176.

104. Robert Bonnaud, cited in Vidal-Naquet, *Torture*, 30.

105. Vidal-Naquet, *Torture*, 29; Henry Buisson, *La Police, son histoire* (Vichy, France: Wallon, 1949), 350–71.

106. Jean Luc Einaudi, *La ferme Améziane* (Paris: L'Harmattan, 1991), 9–10; Annie Rey-Goldzeiguer, *Aux origines de la guerre d'Algérie, 1940–1945* (Paris: Éditions la Découverte, 2002), 298–306.

107. Mellor, *La Torture*, 233 n. 2.

108. Fonlupt-Esperaber, cited in Vidal-Naquet, *Torture*, 30.

109. Vidal-Naquet, *Torture*, 22; Mellor, *La Torture*, 239–40.

110. Georges Putrament, Polish ambassador, cited in Mellor, *La Torture*, 233. The six cases occurred on August 8 and 10, 1947, September 6, 1947, March 2, 1948, in Valence; March 11, 1948, in Metz (Mellor, *La Torture*, 231–33; see also 238–41).

111. Mellor, *La Torture*, 233.

112. Ibid., 234.

113. Raymond Rabemananjara, *Madagascar* (Paris: L'Harmattan, 2000), 42–60.

114. Virginia Thompson and Richard Adloff, *The Malagasy Republic* (Stanford, CA: Stanford University Press, 1965), 56.

115. Anthony Clayton, *France, Soldiers and Africa* (London: Brassey's Defense Publishers, 1988), 153–96; John Talbott, *The War Without a Name* (New York: Knopf, 1980), 6–7.

116. Ruscio, "Du Tonkin à Alger," 11. See also Denis Lefebvre, *Guy Mollet face à la torture en Algérie* ([Paris]: Bruno Leprince, 2001), 23.

117. The classic English sources are Vidal-Naquet, *Torture*; and Alistair Horne, *A Savage War of Peace* (New York: Viking, 1977). Vidal-Naquet's account, banned in France, appeared ten years later in French as *La torture dans la république* (Paris: Les Éditions de Minuit, 1972). The most famous torture narratives are also available in English: *The Gangrene*, trans. Robert Silvers (New York: Lyle Stewart, 1960); and Henri Alleg, *The Question* (New York: George Braziller, 1958), originally *La Question* (Paris: Éditions de Minuit, 1961).

In French, the most complete documentation on torture survivors is Patrick Kessel and Giovanni Pirelli, *Le people algérien et la guerre* (Paris: François Maspero, 1962), a compilation of hundreds of affidavits, some by Algerians who barely spoke French. Pierre Vidal-Naquet, *La Raison d'état* (Paris: Éditions de Minuit, 1962) is the best compilation of government documents. Other classic texts are Pierre Vidal-Naquet, *L'Affaire Audin* (Editions de Minuit, 1958); and Comité Maurice Audin, *Sans Commentaire* (Paris: Editions de Minuit, 1961). The notorious Wuillaume report is available in Vidal-Naquet, *La Raison d'état*, 55–68, and translated in full in Vidal-Naquet, *Torture*, 169–79. Notes to Alleg and Wuillaume are given first to the English and then to the French editions (FE).

118. Wuillaume, "Rapport," 169–70; 58–59 (FE).

119. Ibid., 172; 60–61 (FE). See also "Rapport de M. Mairey, Directeur de la Sûreté sur le fonctionnement des forces de police en Algerie," in Vidal-Naquet, *La Raison d'état*, 81.

120. Wuillaume, "Rapport," 173; 62 (FE).

121. Ibid., 177; 65 (FE).

122. Ibid., 176; 65 (FE).

123. Ibid., 173–74, 176; 62–63, 65 (FE).

124. Ibid., 174; 62 (FE).

125. Ibid., 172–74; 61–63 (FE).

126. Ibid., 177; 66 (FE).

127. Ibid., 170, 176; 58–59, 65 (FE). See also Vidal-Naquet, *La Raison d'état*, 82.

128. Ibid., 176; 65 (FE).

129. Cited in "Le rapport de M. Maurice Garçon à la premier commission de sauvegarde," in Vidal-Naquet, *La Raison d'état*. See also Horne, *Savage War of Peace*, 198; and Jacques Massu, *La vraie bataille d'Alger* (Paris: Plon, 1972), 163.

130. Massu, *La vraie bataille d'Alger*, 165.

131. Ibid., 167.

132. "Des cours sur une 'torture humaine,'" 6. English translation available in *Gangrene*, 12–13.
133. Frantz Fanon, *The Wretched of the Earth*, trans. Constance Farrington (New York: Grove Press, 1968), 283. See also Kessel and Pirelli, *Le people algérien*, 201.
134. Horne, *Savage War of Peace*, 199; Talbott, *War Without a Name*, 92; Jean-Pierre Cômes, *"Ma" guerre d'Algerie et la torture* (Paris: L'Harmattan, 2002), 56; Jean-Pierre Vittori, *Confessions d'un professionnel de la torture* (Paris: Ramsay "Image," 1980), 53.
135. Simone de Beauvoir and Gisele Halimi, *Djamila Boupacha*, trans. Peter Green (New York: Macmillan, 1962), 148.
136. See Vittori, *Confessions*, 53; Massu, *La vraie bataille d'Alger*, 165; and Hafid Keramane, *La Pacification* (Lausanne: La Cité Éditeur, 1960), 15.
137. Alleg, *The Question*, 59; 37 (FE).
138. Ibid., 53–56, 58–59, 69–72, 79, 81–82 (*gégène*), 60–61 (pumping); 31–32, 36–37, 49–52, 61, 63–64 (*gégène*) and 39–40 (pumping) (FE).
139. *Gangrene*, 40, 45, 50, 59, 79–80 (*gégène*), 43 (choking), 37, 53 (exhaustion exercises).
140. Robert Lacoste, cited in Horne, *Savage War of Peace*, 200.
141. Massu, *La vraie bataille d'Alger*, 168.
142. Vittori, *Confessions*, 53.
143. Vidal-Naquet, *Torture*, 130–32; Cômes, *"Ma" guerre d'Algerie*, 56.
144. Alleg, *The Question*, 72; 52 (FE). See also Vittori, *Confessions*, 53.
145. *Gangrene*, 80. See also Kessel and Pirelli, *Le people algérien*, 51, 103, 406.
146. Kessel and Pirelli, *Le people algérien*, 57, 191, 544.
147. Alleg, *The Question*, 69, 71; 49–50, 52 (FE); Pierre Leulliette, *St. Michael and the Dragon*, trans. John Edmonds (Boston: Houghton Mifflin, 1964), 288.
148. Leulliette, *St. Michael*, 287.
149. Henri Pouillot, *La Villa Susini* (Paris: Éditions Tirésias, 2001), 86.
150. Keramane, *La Pacification*, 14–20.
151. *Gangrene*, 40, 59, 79; Einaudi, *La ferme Améziane*, 22, 80–81; Vidal-Naquet, *La Raison d'état*, 81, 127; de Beauvoir and Halimi, *Djamila Boupacha*, 149, 191.
152. Leulliette, *St. Michael*, 287.
153. Vidal-Naquet, *La Raison d'état*, 286.
154. See also Kessel and Pirelli, *Le people algérien*, 38, 218, 386, 419 (knives), 198 (nail pulling), 201 (pins under nails), 239 (walking on glass), 18, 210–12, 388 (boiling water), 38, 191, 201, 406, 498, 500, 545 (burning), 54, 152, 193, 268, 352, 406, 430, 591 (bottle up the anus), 104, 209, 235, 269, 356, 419, 470 (dogs).
155. Cômes, *"Ma" guerre d'Algerie*, 83; see also 89.
156. Soldier, cited in Vidal-Naquet, *Torture*, 137.
157. Horne, *Savage War of Peace*, 220. For similar events in Paris, see Jean-Luc Einaudi, *Octobre 1961* (Paris: Fayard, 2001).
158. Leulliette, *St. Michael*, 287; Benoist Rey, *Les Égorgeurs* (Paris: Editions de Minuit, 1961), 61–62.
159. Keramane, *La Pacification*, 14.

160. See, for example, *Gangrene*, 61; Kessel and Pirelli, *Le people algérien*, 60, 100, 156, 187, 190, 191, 197, 350, 433, 581, 582, 585.
161. See, for example, de Beauvoir and Halimi, *Djamila Boupacha*, 104–5, 122.
162. *Gangrene*, 39.
163. Kristin Ross, *Fast Cars, Clean Bodies* (Cambridge: MIT Press, 1995), 109.
164. Jean Marie Le Pen, cited in Adam Primor, "Le Pen Ultimate," *Ha'aretz* (English edition), April 22, 2002, http://www.haaretzdaily.com.
165. Edmund Michelet, cited in Vidal-Naquet, *Torture*, 92. See also Kessel and Pirelli, *Le people algérien*, 41, 238, 455; John Ambler, *The French Army in Politics* (Columbus: Ohio State University Press, 1966), 175; Vidal-Naquet, *La Raison d'état*, 148; Lefebvre, *Guy Mollet*, 97; Comité Maurice Audin, *Sans Commentaire*, 105; Michel Biran, "Deuxième classe en Algerie," *Perspectives Socialistes*, November 1961, 29.
166. M. Mollet, cited in Vidal-Naquet, *Torture*, 72. See also Horne, *Savage War of Peace*, 205; Talbott, *War Without a Name*, 94; and Massu, *La vraie bataille d'Alger*, 168–69.
167. Paras cited in Alleg, *The Question*, 58; 36 (FE); and Cômes, *"Ma" guerre d'Algérie*, 70. See also Alleg, *The Question*, 110, 98 (FE); Horne, *Savage War of Peace*, 203; Kessel and Pirelli, *Le people algérien*, 55, 652.
168. *Gangrene*, 59. See also Déodat Puy-Montbrun, *L'honneur de la guerre* (Paris: Albin Michel, 2002), 286, 310; Pierre Le Goyet, *La Guerre d'algerie* (Paris: Perrin: 1989), 124.
169. Horne, *Savage War of Peace*, 204.
170. Caroline Moorehead, "Crisis of Confidence," *Financial Times*, June 18, 2005, 18.
171. Malise Ruthven, *Torture* (London: Weidenfeld and Nicolson, 1978), 291.
172. Cited in Mellor, *La Torture*, 234–35.
173. Jean Paul Sartre, introduction to Alleg, *The Question*, 13. The English edition treats the Sartre introduction as part of the original edition, but the first French edition carries a different introduction by an unknown author.
174. Vidal-Naquet, *Torture*, 92.

Chapter 8
Currents

1. D. J. Lewis, cited in John Conroy, "Tools of Torture," *Chicago Reader*, February 4, 2005, 25.
2. Jean Lacouture, *Vietnam*, trans. Konrad Kellen and Joel Carmichael (New York: Vintage, 1966), 97–98.
3. Ibid., 98; Nguyen Xuan Tram, *From Mainland Hell to Island Hell* (Hanoi: Foreign Languages Pubishing House, 1961), 27–28, 88–90; Jean-Pierre Debris and André Menras, *Rescapés des bagnes de Saigon* (Paris: Les Editeurs Français Reunis, 1973), 47–50, 129–31, 145–53; *In Thieu's Prisons* (Hanoi: Foreign Languages Publishing House, 1973), 74–76; Holmes Brown and Don Luce, *Hostages of War*

(Washington, DC: Indochina Mobile Education Project, 1973), 9–10, 17, 29, 71–72; *The Forgotten Prisoners of Ngyuen Van Thieu* (Paris: n.p., May 1973), 32–34; Nguyen Dinh Thi, ed., *Les Prisonniers politiques* (Paris: Sudestasie, 1974), 101–13, 285–87; Pham Tam, *Imprisonment and Torture in South Vietnam* (Nyack, NY: Fellowship of Reconciliation, 1969[?]), 8–9; Sydney Schanberg, "Saigon Torture in Jails Reported," *New York Times*, August 12, 1972, A1, A3; Nguyen Van Minh, "Jail Notes of a Young Vietnamese," *The Nation*, March 24, 1969, 350–62; Amnesty International (AI), *Report on Torture* (London: Duckworth, 1973), 154–56; John Duffett, ed., *Against the Crime of Silence: Proceedings of the Russell International War Crimes Tribunal* (New York: O'Hare, 1968), 403–25, 404–5, 561–63.

4. Tram, *Mainland Hell*, 88.

5. Truong Nhu Tang, *A Vietcong Memoir*, with David Chanoff and Doan Van Toai (New York: Vintage, 1986), 114.

6. Debris and Menras, *Rescapés des bagnes*, 147.

7. Tram, *Mainland Hell*, 26; Tam, *Imprisonment and Torture*, 8; *Forgotten Prisoners*, 33.

8. Pumping (Tam, *Imprisonment and Torture*, 8; Brown and Luce, *Hostages of War*, 9, 72; Lacouture, *Vietnam*, 98; *In Thieu's Prisons*, 76; Thi, *Les Prisonniers politiques*, 102–3; *Forgotten Prisoners*, 33) and choking (Debris and Menras, *Rescapés des bagnes*, 47, 50; Tram, *Mainland Hell*, 26; Duffett, *Crime of Silence*, 560).

9. "Imprisonment and Torture of Political Prisoners: Testimony by Mrs. Pham Thi Yen," in Duffett, *Crime of Silence*, 562. See also Citizens Commission of Inquiry (CCI), ed., *The Dellums Committee Hearings on War Crimes in Vietnam* (New York: Vintage, 1972), 32.

10. Tram, *Mainland Hell*, 26–27; *In Thieu's Prisons*, 72.

11. Tram, *Mainland Hell*, 88.

12. Tam, *Imprisonment and Torture*, 8.

13. Ibid., 8; Brown and Luce, *Hostages of War*, 17; Schanberg, "Saigon Torture," A1; Thi, *Les Prisonniers politiques*, 103; *Forgotten Prisoners*, 33.

14. Thi, *Les Prisonniers politiques*, 101.

15. Tam, *Imprisonment and Torture*, 8.

16. Brown and Luce, *Hostages of War*, 71. The most detailed report of South Vietnamese *falaka* dates from 1960 (see Duffett, *Crime of Silence*, 562). It describes *falaka* administered in the traditional East Asian style (see chapter 12).

17. *Forgotten Prisoners*, 33. See also Debris and Menras, *Rescapés des bagnes*, 148–49; and Tam, *Imprisonment and Torture*, 8.

18. Thi, *Les Prisonniers politiques*, 103.

19. Tam, *Imprisonment and Torture*, 8–9.

20. Westmoreland to Walt, August 14, 1965, Center for Military History, cited in Guenter Lewy, *America in Vietnam* (Oxford: Oxford University Press, 1978), 328.

21. "Incident on a Patrol: A Vietcong's Ordeal by Water," *Washington Post*, January 21, 1968, A1, A23. See also Lewy, *America in Vietnam*, 329.

22. W. R. Peers, *Report of the Department of the Army Review of the Preliminary Investigations into the My Lai Incident,* vol. 1: *The Report of the Investigation* (Washington, DC: Department of the Army, March 14, 1970), 7–15.
23. Kenneth J. Hodson, army judge advocate general, cited in Lewy, *America in Vietnam,* 329.
24. Ralph Scott, Criminal Investigator, "CID Report of Investigation of 172nd MI Detachment," August 23, 1971, Investigations Division, U.S. Army CID Agency, Washington, DC.
25. Deborah Nelson and Nick Turse, "A Tortured Past," *Los Angeles Times,* August 20, 2006, A1.
26. Lewy, *America in Vietnam,* 345–46.
27. Ibid., 346.
28. Ibid.
29. Peers, *Report,* 11-1. See also W. R. Peers, *The My Lai Inquiry* (New York: Notable Trials Library, 1993), 199–209.
30. MACV Directive 335-18, September 18, 1965; MACV Directive 335-1, January 5, 1966, cited in Lewy, *America in Vietnam,* 344.
31. Lewy, *America in Vietnam,* 348.
32. Nelson and Turse, "A Tortured Past," A1.
33. C. A. Shaughnessy, "The Vietnam Conflict: 'America's Best Documented War'?" *History Teacher* 24.2 (1991): 139.
34. See ibid., 141, 145. I have been unable to find several files Lewy cites that describe torture incidents; indeed I have been unable to confirm whether they exist in a government database, classified or not. These include JAGW 1971/1096 (May 21, 1971), Incl. 5, case 51; U.S. Department of Army, Office of the Judge Advocate General, International Affairs Division, files of atrocity allegations; and Office of the Director, Judge Advocate Division, Headquarters USMC, Winter Soldier Investigation files. It is surprising that such files have not been declassified over thirty years after the war ended, but they may also have been lost or destroyed.
35. Nelson and Turse, "A Tortured Past," A1.
36. Lewy, *America in Vietnam,* 345.
37. Conroy, "Tools of Torture," 26. See also Lewy, *America in Vietnam,* 324.
38. Lewy, *America in Vietnam,* 311–24.
39. Ibid., 319. Lewy is a standard source for conservative commentators, most notably Burkett and Whitley's *Stolen Valor,* the text commonly cited to debunk veteran's testimony of atrocities. See B. G. Burkett and Glenna Whitley, *Stolen Valor: How the Vietnam Generation was Robbed of Its Heroes and Its History* (Dallas: Verity Press, 1998).
40. Lewy, *America in Vietnam,* 332–41.
41. *Veterans Testimony on Vietnam,* 92nd Congress, 1st sess., *Congressional Record,* vol. 117, part 8 (April 5–19, 1971), 9989.
42. Donald Duncan, *The New Legions* (New York: Random House, 1967), 168, 181.
43. Lewy, *America in Vietnam,* 343–44.
44. Ibid., 328–31.

45. Ibid., 311.

46. Ibid., 321–22.

47. CCI, *Dellums Committee Hearings*, 111; House Committee on Government Operations, Subcommittee on Government Operations, *U.S. Assistance Programs in Vietnam: Hearings*, 92nd Cong., 1st sess. (1971), 319.

48. *Veterans Testimony on Vietnam*, 9954; Mark Baker, *Nam* (New York: Quill, 1982), 205–6; CCI, *Dellums Committee Hearings*, 41, 46. The closest account to this is tossing prisoners out of a helicopter in anger. See "Testimony and Questioning of David Kenneth Tuck," in Duffett, *Crime of Silence*, 405.

49. Conroy, "Tools of Torture," 25.

50. Madeleine Rebérioux, "De la torture française à la torture américaine," *Raison prâesente*, January 25, 1973, 92.

51. Arkansas State Police, cited in Tom Murton, "Prison Doctors," in *Humanistic Perspectives in Medical Ethics*, ed. Maurice Visscher (Buffalo: Prometheus, 1972), 248–49.

52. Michael Goldston, *History of Allegations of Misconduct by Area Two Personnel* (Chicago: Office of Professional Standards, Chicago Police Department, September 28, 1990). Available at http://humanrights.uchicago.edu/chicagotorture/ops.shtml.

53. John Conroy, *Unspeakable Acts, Ordinary People* (New York: Knopf, 2000), 68–70, 76–77, 162, 226–27.

54. Ibid., 61–62, 76–77.

55. Cited in Patrick Duncan, *South Africa's Rule of Violence* (London: Methuen, 1964), 25.

56. Laloo Chiba, cited in South Africa, Truth and Reconciliation Commission (TRC), *Report* (London: Macmillan, 1999), 2:198. See also Peter Deeley, *Beyond Breaking Point* (London: Arthur Baker, 1971), 87–88. The only possible case that is earlier is from 1956 (see Duncan, *South Africa's Rule*, 40).

57. TRC, *Report*, 3:197.

58. Frank Bennetts cited in ibid., 2:191; see also 3:610.

59. Suh Sung, *Unbroken Spirits*, trans. Jean Inglis (Lanham, MD: Rowman and Littlefield, 2001), 21; Robert Blackburn, *Mercenaries and Lyndon Johnson's "More Flags"* (Jefferson, NC: McFarland, 1994), 31–67, 158; Frank Baldwin, Diane Jones, and Michael Jones, *America's Rented Troops* (Philadelphia: American Friends Service Committee, [1975?]).

60. Testimony to South Korean Association for the Defence of Civil Rights, cited in *The White Paper on the Problem of Human Rights in South Korea* (Pyongyang: Foreign Languages Publishing House, 1977), 14. See also Catholic Committee on Human Rights, *Sabop sarin: 1975 nyon ui haksal* [Murder by the Judiciary: the Massacre in 1975] (Seoul: Hangmin-sa, 2001). The Sinch'on Museum in North Korea claims electrotorture as early as the Korean War. However, unlike the Vietnam War, there are no English testimonies from either U.S. soldiers or Korean prisoners, and so this claim is unreliable.

61. Chae-ryong Chong, *Chon Segye Komun* [Tortures of the World] (n.p.: Sisa Non-p'yong, n.d.), 68–80; *Sesang e salgo sipta* [I Want to Live in This World] (Seoul: Korean Christian Church Association Human Rights Committee, n.d.), 413; AI, *Report of an Amnesty International Mission to the Republic of Korea* (London, 1976), 28; *Pan komun pan p'ongnyok ingan sonon* [Antitorture. Antiviolence Manifesto on Humanity] (Seoul: Korean Christian Church Association Human Rights Committee, 1989), 23, 34.

62. Se-yong Yi, "Uimunsa-wi ga palk'in Inhyoktang Chaegonwi sagon chonmo" [The Fabricated Case of "Committee for Rebuilding the People's Revolution Party," Disclosed by the Truth Commission for Suspicious Deaths] September 13, 2002, http://search.seoul.co.kr/.

63. *Pan komun*, 34.

64. Marcio Alves, *Torturas e Torturados* (Rio de Janeiro: Empresa Jornalística, 1966), 26; A. J. Langguth, *Hidden Terrors* (New York: Pantheon, 1978), 125, 138–40, 164, 193, 207, 212–17; Deeley, *Beyond Breaking Point*, 95–104; AI, *Report on Allegations of Torture in Brazil* (London, 1972), 63.

65. Langguth, *Hidden Terrors*, 125, 139. For U.S. military and police aid to Brazil in this period, see Martha Huggins, *Political Policing* (Durham, NC: Duke University Press, 1998).

66. Langguth, *Hidden Terrors*, 139–40.

67. Gildásao Westin Cosenza, cited in Archdiocese of São Paulo, *Torture in Brazil*, trans. Jaime Wright (New York: Vintage, 1986), 18. See also Langguth, *Hidden Terrors*, 217.

68. Paul Chevigny, Bell Gale Chevigny, and Russel Karp, *Police Abuse in Brazil* (New York: Americas Watch Report, 1987), 33–34, 37; AI, *The Pain Merchants*, ACT 40/008/2003, 34, http://www.amnesty.org.

69. European Commission of Human Rights, *The Greek Case* (Strasbourg: Council of Europe, 1970), 122, 269–70, 303, 416.

70. Ibid., 220. Uniquely, Korovessis describes ECT, but what device he experienced seems unclear. See Pericles Korovessis, *The Method*, trans. Les Nightingale and Catherine Patrakis (London: Allison and Busaby, 1970), 49–50; European Commission of Human Rights, *The Greek Case*, 122, 138.

71. Deeley, *Beyond Breaking Point*, 83. For reports from the early 1970s, see AI, *Report of an Amnesty International Mission to Israel and the Syrian Arab Republic to Investigate Allegations of Ill-Treatment and Torture* (London, 1974), 19–27; "Israel Tortures Arab Prisoners," *Sunday Times* (London), June 19, 1977, A1, A17–20.

72. Jeffrey Dillman and Musa Bakri, *Israel's Use of Electric Shock Torture in the Interrogation of Palestinian Detainees*, 2nd ed. (Jerusalem: Palestine Human Rights Information Center, 1992), 16.

73. Doron Me'iri, "Torture Unit," *Hadashot*, February 24, 1992, in Dillman and Bakri, *Israel's Use*, 68.

74. Human Rights Watch, *Turkey* 9:4 (March 1997), 13.

75. See AI, *Against Torture*, ACT 04/13/84 (London, 1984), 3; and AI, *Arming the Torturers*, ACT 40/01/97 (London, 1997), 2.

76. Human Rights Watch, *Turkey*, 11.

77. Conroy, *Unspeakable Acts, Ordinary People*, 92.

78. Pablo Sulbarán, *La Tortura en Venezuela* (Caracas: Publicaciones Seleven, 1979), 192.

79. AI, *Report on Torture*, 200.

80. Prisoner's account, cited before House Committee on International Relations, Subcommittee on International Organizations, *Human Rights in the Philippines*, 94th Cong., 2nd sess. 1976, 5. See also AI, *Report of an Amnesty International Mission to the Republic of the Philippines* (London, 1976), 35.

81. Miguel Sanchez-Mazas, *Spain in Chains* (New York: Veterans of the Abraham Lincoln Brigade, 1960), 23.

82. Deeley, *Beyond Breaking Point*, 104–17; *Franco's Prisoners Speak* (London: Spanish Ex-Servicemen's Association, 1960); AI, *Report of an Amnesty International Mission to Spain* (London, 1975), 7–9, 17–22.

83. AI, *Report of an Amnesty International Mission to Spain*, EUR 41/03/80 (London, 1980), 15 (see also 38, 41, 43, 45, 47); Kepa Landa, Carlos Beristain, Rosa Olivares, and Jesús Zalakain, *La Tortura en Euskadi* (Madrid: Editorial Revolución, 2000), 176.

84. TAT—Torturaren Arkako Taldea [Group Against Torture], *Torture in Basque Country: Report 2001* ([Bilbao]: Graficas Lizarra, S.L, 2002), 18, 34, 45, 57, 59, 60, 62, 83, 151, 210 (wires); 146,147, 208 (prod).

85. AI, *Afghanistan*, ASA 11/04/86 (New York, 1986), 12; see also 13–14.

86. Barnett Rubin and Jeri Laber, *Tears, Blood and Cries* (New York: Helsinki Watch Committee, 1984), 146.

87. Shahdarak student, cited in AI, *Afghanistan*, 13. A picture of this device appears in M. A. Dadfar, *The Impaired Mind* (Peshawar, Pakistan: Psychiatry Center for Afghan Refugees, 1988), facing 19.

88. Human Rights Watch and Physicians for Human Rights, *Dead Silence* (New York: Human Rights Watch, 1994), 58, 64, 82, 87, 88.

89. Duncan Forrest, "Patterns of Abuse in Sikh Asylum-Seekers," *The Lancet*, 345.8944 (January 28, 1995): 225.

90. AI, *Arming the Torturers*, 2 n. 2.

91. Human Rights Watch, *Confession at Any Cost* (New York: Human Rights Watch, 1999), 33.

92. Jørgen Thomsen and Maiken Mannstaedt, *The Green Birds* (Århus, Denmark: Danish Medical Group, 2000), 110; see also 6, 159.

93. AI, *Report 2002*, http://www.amnesty.org.

94. I present these here in chronological order based on the date of the report of electrotorture: Portugal in Mozambique (1966) and then in Portugal (1975), Belgium (1971), United Kingdom (1972), Burundi (1973), Zambia (1973), Syria (1973, 1975, 1979), Taiwan (1974), Mexico (1974, 1976), Indonesia (1975), Nicaragua (1975), Morocco (1977), Ethiopia (1977), Ecuador (1978), Uganda (1978), Colombia (1978, 1979), Cameroon (1979), Djibouti (1979), El Salvador (1979), Haiti (1979), Libya (1979), Mali (1979). Aside from the sources mentioned here and in

the following notes in this section, the remaining reports come from Amnesty International annual reports of the year specified. AI, *Report on Torture*, 148 (Pakistan); AI, *Mission to Israel and Syria*, 11–18; AI, *Syria* (London, 1979), 12; *Tortura na colónia de Moçambique* (Porto: Ediçoes Afrontamento, 1977), 48, 69, 76; Alexandre Manuel, Rogério Carapinha and Dias Neves, *PIDE* (Fundão, Portugal: Jornal do Fundão, 1974), 187.

95. AI, *East Timor* (London, 1985), 53–54. AI, *Report on Torture*, 194.

96. AI, *Report on Torture*, 160.

97. Dennis Faul and Raymond Murray, *British Army and Special Branch RUC Brutalities* (Dungannon, Northern Ireland: the Compilers, 1972), 10, 36, 39, 40, 46.

98. Ahmed Boukhari, *Le Secret* (Neuilly-sur-Seine: Editions Michel Lafon, 2002), 90; "The Now Unsecret Policeman," *The Economist*, February 16, 2002, 44; AI, *Morocco* (London, 1977), 12–13, which includes accounts of electrotorture. For additional accounts of electrotorture, see AI, *Morocco* (London, 1979), 13; AI, *Morocco* (London, 1986), 2, 4, 8; AI, *Morocco* (London, 1991), 7.

99. Ejército de Liberación Nacional, "Denuncian torturas," *Punta Final*, August 1972, 28; AI, *Report on Torture*, 189–90.

100. I confirmed this myself at Tuol Sleng Genocial Museum in 2002.

101. House Committee, *Human Rights in the Philippines*, 5.

102. Dillman and Bakri, *Israel's Use*, 50.

103. TRC, *Report*, 2:191.

104. Ibid., 3, 191, 338.

105. José Milto Ferreira de Almeida, cited in Archdiocese of São Paulo, *Torture in Brazil*, 17, 18.

106. Frank Bennetts, cited in TRC, *Report*, 2:191.

107. Huggins, *Political Policing*, 172.

108. Duncan, 28; Human Rights Watch, *Turkey*, 13.

109. AI, *Testimony on Secret Detention Camps in Argentina* (London, 1980), 18.

110. Archdiocese of São Paulo, *Torture in Brazil*, 24; Langguth, *Hidden Terrors*, 164, 193.

111. TRC, *Report*, 2:213.

112. Human Rights Watch, *Turkey*, 13.

113. *Gangrene*, trans. Robert Silvers (New York: Lyle Stewart, 1960), 59.

114. Langguth, *Hidden Terrors*, 219.

115. See Deeley, *Beyond Breaking Point*, 83, 113; Archdiocese of São Paulo, *Torture in Brazil*, 18.

116. José Milton Ferreira de Almeida, cited in Archdiocese of São Paulo, *Torture in Brazil*, 18. See also Deeley, *Beyond Breaking Point*, 99; Archdiocese of São Paulo, *Torture in Brazil* , 32–35, 38–41.

117. Contrary to Ole Vedel Rasmussen, "Medical Aspects of Torture," *Danish Medical Bulletin* 37, Sup. 1 (1990): 9; and Jean Franco, "Gender, Death and Resistance," in *Fear at the Edge*, ed. Juan Corradi, Patricia Weiss Fagen, and Manuel Antonio Garretón (Berkeley and Los Angeles: University of California Press, 1992), 106.

118. Sulbarán, *La Tortura en Venezuela*, 162.

119. Kenneth Shillman, cited in "New York Rider Relates Harrowing Tale of Life in Maximum Security," *Jackson Daily*, June 21, 1961, http://www.freedomriders foundation.org/photos.articles.and.artifacts.html.

120. Langguth, *Hidden Terrors*, 251.

121. Lieutenant Julio Cesar Cooper, cited in AI, *Political Imprisonment in Uruguay* (London, 1979), 3. See also Kathleen Teltsch, "Uruguay Accused of Using Torture," *New York Times*, January 17, 1974, A12.

122. *Informe: Violacion de los derechos humanos en Bolivia* (Bolivia: Central Obrera Boliviana, 1976), 117; *Tortura en Paraguay* (Asunción, Paraguay: Comite de Iglesias Para Ayudas de Emergencia and International Human Rights Law Group, 1993), 26, 28, 55; AI, *Torture in the Eighties* (London, 1984), 169.

123. Archdiocese of São Paulo, *Torture in Brazil*, 19; Physicians for Human Rights, *Sowing Fear* (Sommerville, MA: Physicians for Human Rights, 1988), 56.

124. AI, *Mexico*, AMR 41/04/91 (London, 1991), 25.

125. George Sayos, cited in Amalia Fleming, *A Piece of Truth* (London: Jonathan Cape, 1972), 249; Faul and Murray, *British Army*, 10, 14, 47; Schanberg, "Saigon Torture," A1, A3; Reza Baraheni, *The Crowned Cannibals* (New York: Vintage, 1977), 14–15; Ali-Reza Nobari, *Iran Erupts* (Stanford, CA: Iran-America Documentation Group, 1978), 154, 160; AI, *Turkey* (London, 1977), 7; AI, *Rhodesia/Zimbabwe* (London, 1976), 10; AI, *Torture in the Eighties*, 141; AI, *Iraq* (London, 1981), 5, 19–20, 22, 24–27; Rubin and Laber, *Tears, Blood and Cries*, 145; *Sae-sang-ae Sal-go Sip-da*, 427; Mary Salinsky and Liv Tigerstedt, *Evidence of Torture* (Oxford: Alden Group, 2001), 29, 37. For China, Yugoslavia, and Iraq, see Amnesty International annual reports for the respective years.

126. Austin Wehrwein, "Prod Used in South 'Makes You Jump,' " *New York Times*, June 22, 1963, 10.

127. See, for example, Michael Dewar, *Internal Security Weapons and Equipment of the World* (New York: Charles Scribner's Sons, 1979), 43.

128. Langguth, *Hidden Terrors*, 251–53, 286. Mitrione also instructed Brazilian and Uruguayan police in torture techniques. He was later kidnapped and executed by Uruguayan guerrillas, though, interestingly, his body showed no signs of torture, binding, or mistreatment. See Archdiocese of São Paulo, *Torture in Brazil*, 14; and David Ronfeldt, *The Mitrione Kidnapping in Uruguay*, N-1571-DOS/DARPA/RC (Rand Corporation, August 1987), 49.

129. Lieutenant Julio Cesar Cooper, cited in AI, *Political Imprisonment in Uruguay* (London, 1979), 3.

130. Deeley, *Beyond Breaking Point*, 98.

131. Physicians for Human Rights, *Sowing Fear*, 56, 57, 76–77, 80 (*parilla*).

132. Sheila Cassidy, *Audacity to Believe* (Cleveland: Collins World, 1977), 174.

133. Alves, *Torturas e Torturados*, 26.

134. Deeley, *Beyond Breaking Point*, 98; Archdiocese of São Paulo, *Torture in Brazil*, 18–19; AI, *Torture in Brazil*, 30, 33, 40, 67.

135. Baraheni, *The Crowned Cannibals*, 148–49. This is not to be confused with the "Hot Table" that roasts bodies on a heated bed (Nobari, *Iran Erupts*, 148, 154).

136. See, for example, Ian Mather, " 'Religious' Torturers Use Shah's Police Techniques," *The Observer*, November 14, 1982, 13; Steve Wright, "The New Trade in Technologies of Restraint and Electroshock," in *A Glimpse of Hell*, ed. Duncan Forrest (London: AI, 1996), 139. An alleged photo of unknown origin bears no resemblance to Baraheni's description: a motorcycle helmet and a bed with vises on the sides (Brian Innes, *The History of Torture* [New York: St. Martin's, 1998], 145).

137. For Brazil, see Chevigny, Chevigny, and Karp, *Police Abuse in Brazil*. For Iran, see AI, *Iran*, MDE 13/03/87 (London, 1987), 9–10; AI, *Iran*, MDE 13/09/87 (London, 1987), 57–63, 70–94; AI, *Iran*, MDE 13/21/90 (New York, 1990), 44–48.

138. Harold Bloom, "The South African Police," *Africa South* 2.1 (1957): 10.

139. Student, cited in *Political Imprisonment*, 66.

140. AI, *Malawi* (London, 1976), 7.

141. Cited in AI, *Political Imprisonment in South Africa* (London, 1978), 63.

142. Mr. M, cited in *Political Imprisonment*, 65.

143. Iain Guest, *Behind the Disappearances* (Philadelphia: University of Pennsylvania Press, 1990), 40.

144. Tina Rosenberg, *Children of Cain* (New York: William Morrow, 1991), 89.

145. Marvine Howe, "Brazil Said to Continue Torture," *New York Times*, November 4, 1974, 2. While the device was allegedly "similar to a technique used in South Vietnam," there is no record of a keyboard-operated system of electroshock torture in South Vietnam. Other descriptions of the pianola suggest it was a simple "magneto machine," and in this sense the Vietnam reference makes sense. (See Howe, 2; and Jack Anderson, "Brazil Leaders Rule by Torture," *Washingon Post*, June 30, 1973, E35.)

146. AI, *Afghanistan*, 14.

147. Sylvester Stallone and James Cameron, *First Blood: Part II, Final Shooting Script*, http://www.hundland.com/scripts/Rambo-FirstBloodPart2.txt.

148. Stuart Rochester and Frederick Kiley, *Honor Bound* (Annapolis, MD: Naval Institute Press, 1999), 486, 487.

149. Aurora Foundation, *Report on the Violations of Human Rights in the Socialist Republic of Vietnam, April 1975–December 1988* (Atherton, CA: Aurora Foundation, 1989).

150. For North Vietnamese torture, see Rochester and Kiley, *Honor Bound*, rope torture (145–50, 157–59, 161, 163, 217–19, 224, 302, 305–6, 311, 312, 338, 353–55, 359, 363, 387, 457, 484, 487), fetters and hell cuffs (145–49, 160, 162, 211, 213–14, 218–19, 224, 299, 300, 305, 307, 311–12, 330–31, 334–35, 353, 387, 487, 484, 509), full suspension (145, 354), rack (219), standing cuffs (158, 159); Lewy, *America in Vietnam*, 337–38. The main exceptions were Syria (1970s onward) and Cambodia (1975–79), where electrotorture was common. See also chapter 9, "Singing the World Electric," and chapter 15, "Forced Standing and Other Positions."

151. Some confused interrogation with execution (Mark Lane, *Conversations with Americans* [New York: Simon and Schuster, 1970], 29; *Veterans Testimony on Vietnam*, 9949–50, 9953; CCI, *Dellums Committee Hearings*, 134; Leroy TeCube, *Year*

in Nam [Lincoln: University of Nebraska Press, 1999], 138; John McGuffin, *The Guineapigs* [Harmondsworth, England: Penguin, 1974], 65, 70), while others suggested that one would toss out the highest-ranking soldier first, which would leave one with the soldier with the least information (Lane, *Conversations with Americans*, 84).

152. Archdiocese of São Paulo, *Torture in Brazil*, 22.

153. AI, *Arming the Torturers*, 2 n. 2.

Chapter 9
Singing the World Electric

1. Amnesty International (AI), *The Pain Merchants*, ACT 40/008/2003 (London: International Secretariat, 2003), 38, http://www.amnesty.org.

2. The regional tables in this chapter are based on the annual reports, country reports, and *Concerns in Europe* series of Amnesty International (http://www.amnesty.org), the country reports of the European Committee for the Prevention of Torture (CPT) (http://www.cpt.coe.int/en/); three specialized Amnesty International reports (*Pain Merchants*; *Arming the Torturers*, ACT 40/01/97 [London, 1997]; *Torture in the Eighties* [London, 1984]; and historical sources as cited.

3. Caroline Elkins, *Imperial Reckoning* (New York: Henry Holt, 2005), 275–353; David Anderson, *Histories of the Hanged* (New York: Norton, 2005), 291–92, 321–22.

4. See, for example, Pierre Leulliette, *St. Michael and the Dragon*, trans. John Edmonds (Boston: Houghton Mifflin, 1964), 279–333.

5. Often reports do not describe devices clearly, and there are gaps in coverage. Also, whether a country is or is not listed does not mean that its police did not use stealthy torture, only that there was no reported electrotorture. In 2003, Amnesty International listed about ninety countries in which electrotorture has been practiced since 1990 (*Pain Merchants*, 90). Most of these are listed below, but I cannot confirm these incidents from Amnesty archives for Taiwan, Myanmar, Jordan, Canada, Haiti, Jamaica, and Netherlands Antilles.

6. Ricardo Molas, *Historia de la Tortura* (Buenos Aires: Editorial Universitaria de Buenas Aires, 1984), 98.

7. Raul Lamas, *Los Torturadores* (Buenos Aires: Editorial Lamas, 1956), 151–52.

8. AI, *Report of an Amnesty International Mission to Argentina* (London, 1977), 37.

9. AI, *The Attack on the Third Infantry Regiment Barracks at La Tabla* (New York, 1990), 8–13.

10. Sebastian Roaquín Ramos, cited in AI, *La Tabla*, 13.

11. Elizabeth Cancelli, *Omundo da violência* (Brasília, DF: Editora Universidade de Brasília, 1993), 193–94; William Waack, *Camaradas* (São Paulo: Companhia das Letras, 1993), 300; Hastings, "Political Prisoners in Brazil," *Times* (London), July 10, 1936, 12.

12. Cancelli, *Omundo da violência*, 194.

13. Stanley Hilton, *Brazil and the Soviet Challenge* (Austin: University of Texas Press, 1981), 83.

14. Stanley Hilton, *Hitler's Secret War in South America, 1939–1945* (Baton Rouge: Louisiana State University Press, 1981), 243, 247, 249, 251, 255–57.

15. Marcio Alves, *Torturas e Torturados* (Rio de Janeiro: Empresa Jornalística, 1966), 26–27.

16. Archdiocese of São Paulo, *Torture in Brazil*, trans. Jaime Wright (New York: Vintage, 1986), 16–24.

17. *Mise à jour des allegations de torture dans l'état de São Paulo* (São Paulo: Action des Chrétiens pour l'abolition de la torture, 2002).

18. Ejército de Liberación Nacional, "Denuncian torturas," *Punta Final*, August 1972, 28.

19. *Report of the Chilean National Commission on Truth and Reconciliation*, trans. Phillip E. Berryman (Notre Dame, IN: University of Notre Dame Press, 1993), 1:134.

20. AI, *Chile* (London, 1974), 63. See also Sheila Cassidy, *Audacity to Believe* (Cleveland: Collins World, 1977), 218, 236.

21. *Chilean National Commission*, 2:499–501, 644; AI, *Chile* (London, 1983), 9, 17–18; AI, *Chile*, AMR 22/03/87 (London, 1987), 7–8, 10, 19–28.

22. Pablo Sulbarán, *La tortura en Venezuela* (Caracas: Publicaciones Seleven, 1979), 160–204.

23. AI, *Report on Torture* (London: Duckworth, 1973), 200.

24. Ana Barrios B. and Eva Duart O., *La Tortura: 40 años de pena* (Caracas, Venezuela: Red de Apoyo por la Justicia y la Paz, 1998), 34–35.

25. Ole Vedel Rasmussen, "Medical Aspects of Torture," *Danish Medical Bulletin* 37, Sup. 1 (January 1990): 8–9.

26. See also *Tortura en El Peru* (Lima, Peru: Coodiandora Nacional de Derechos Humanos, 1995), 20–40, 81–108.

27. For recent Mexican accounts, see ACAT/Mexico, *La Tortura en Mexico 1996* (Mexico City: Accióndelos Cristanos para la Abolición de la Tortura, 1997), 4–37; *Images of Repression*, (Mexico City: Human Rights Centre "Miguel Agustin Pro Juarez," 1999), 175–87.

28. See also *Informe: Violacion de los derechos humanos en Bolivia* (Bolivia: Central Obrera Boliviana, 1976), 115–17.

29. See also *Reseña de la Tortura en Honduras en Los Noventa* (Tegucigalpa, Honduras: Comité de Familiares de Detenidos-Desaparecidos en Honduras, 1994), 7.

30. Ginger Thompson and Gary Cohn, "Torturers' Confessions," *Baltimore Sun*, June 13, 1995, 1A; Ginger Thompson and Gary Cohn, "Unearthed: Fatal Secrets," *Baltimore Sun*, June 11, 1995, 1A; and Ginger Thompson and Gary Cohn, "A Survivor Tells Her Story," *Baltimore Sun*, June 15, 1995, 1A.

31. See also *Tortura en Paraguay* (Asunción, Paraguay: Comite de Iglesias Para Ayudas de Emergencia and International Human Rights Law Group, 1993), 26, 28, 52–87. This source dates the first electrotorture case to 1975 (see *Tortura en Paraguay*, 55).

32. For a complete list, see *La Tortura en El Salvador* (San Salvador, El Salvador: Commision de Derechos Humanos de El Salvador, 1986), 37–49, 73.

33. See chapter 19, "Drugs and Doctors."

34. Charles J. Brown and Armando Lago, *The Politics of Psychiatry in Revolutionary Cuba* (New Brunswick, NJ: Transaction, 1991), 84.

35. AI, *Afghanistan*, ASA 11/003/2003, http://www.amnesty.org.

36. AI, *Turkey* (1977), 7; "Israel Tortures Arab Prisoners," *Sunday Times* (London), June 19, 1977, A1, A17–A20; Ali-Reza Nobari, *Iran Erupts* (Stanford, CA: Iran-America Documentation Group, 1978), 148, 154; AI, *Syria* (London, 1983), 3; AI, *Iraq* (London, 1981), 4–5; El Nadim Center, "Torture Inside and Outside Police Stations in Egypt, 1993–1996," *Torture* 7.2 (1997): 54–55; *Official Response to the Government of Egypt's Report on the UN, the Committee against Torture* (Giza, Egypt: The Human Rights Center for the Assistance of Prisoners, 2002), 53.

37. Darius Rejali, *Torture and Modernity* (Boulder, CO: Westview, 1994); Ervand Abrahamian, *Tortured Confessions* (Berkeley and Los Angeles: University of California Press, 1999).

38. Electrotorture is not mentioned in the most recent reports. Human Rights Watch, *"Like the Dead in Their Coffins"* (2004), http://hrw.org/reports/2004; Pia Moisander and Erik Edston, "Torture and Its Sequel—A Comparison between Victims from Six Countries," *Forensic Science International* 137 (2003): 136.

39. AI, *East Timor* (London, 1985), 54.

40. Ibid., 57. For earlier brutality, see AI, *Indonesia* (London, 1977), 107; John Taylor, *Indonesia's Forgotten War* (London: Zed, 1991), 107–9.

41. Lembaga Studi dan Advokasi (ELSAM), *Revealing Tortures by Public Officials* (Jakarta Selatan, Indonesia: ELSAM, 1996), 128; see also 124–27. See also AI, *Power and Impunity* (London, 1994), 68–78.

42. AI, *Arming the Torturers*, 12.

43. AI, *Report*, 1997, http://www.amnesty.org.

44. Hans Draminsky Petersen, Lise Worm, Mette Zander, Ole Harting, and Bjarne Ussing, *Human Rights Violations in Burma/Myanmar* (Århus, Denmark: Physicians for Human Rights, 2000), 20–21.

45. AI, *Political Imprisonment in the People's Republic of China* (London, 1978), 119–30.

46. For the picture of Palden Gyatso and his satchel of guns, see AI, *Arming the Torturers*; and AI, *Torture Worldwide* (London, 2000), 104. Gyatso's account can be found in Palden Gyatso with Tsering Shkya, *The Autobiography of a Tibetan Monk* (New York: Grove Press, 1997), 195–96, 215, 227. I confirmed the make of the guns and the date of their appearance in an interview with Palden Gyatso at Reed College in 1997.

47. AI, *Torture in China*, ASA 17/55/92 (New York: Amnesty International USA, 1992), 6, 12, 17, 23, 25, 27, 28, 29, 31; AI, *People's Republic of China*, ASA 17/004/2001 (London, 2001), 7, 14, 23; photographs in Falun Dafa Information Center, *Torture Methods Used on Falun Dafa Practitioners in Detention Centers and Forced Labor Camps in China*, http://back.faluninfo.net/torturemethods2/.

48. AI, *Taiwan (Republic of China)*, 2nd ed. (London, 1980), 9.

49. See chapter 19.

50. House Committee on International Relations, Subcommittee on International Organizations, *Human Rights in the Philippines*, 94th Cong., 2nd sess. 1976, 5; Richard Claude, Eric Stover, and June Lopez, *Health Professionals and Human Rights in the Philippines* (Washington, DC: American Association for the Advancement of Science, 1987), 31.

51. AI, *Report of an Amnesty International Mission to the Republic of Korea* (London, 1976), 28, 36–39.

52. In addition to Amnesty International reports, see also Michael Peel and Mary Salinsky, *Caught in the Middle* (Oxford: Alden Group, 2000), 23–27.

53. Mary Salinsky and Liv Tigerstedt, *Evidence of Torture* (Oxford: Alden Group, 2001), 29, 37.

54. Human Rights Watch and Physicians for Human Rights, *Dead Silence* (New York: Human Rights Watch, 1994), 77, 78 (choking), 61, 63, 72, 74, 86, 87 (*falaka*). Hereafter cited as *Dead Silence*.

55. Duncan Forrest, "Patterns of Abuse in Sikh Asylum-Seekers," *The Lancet*, 345.8944 (January 28, 1995): 225–26; Duncan Forrest, "Examination Following Specific Forms of Torture," in *The Medical Documentation of Torture*, ed. Michael Peel and Vincent Iacopino (London: Greenwich Medical Media, 2002), 166; Morten Ekstrøm, Hans Draminsky Petersen, and Majken Marmstaedt, *Torture Continues in Indian Held Kashmir* (Århus, Denmark: Physicians for Human Rights, 1994), 19; *Dead Silence*, 58, 63–65, 67, 70, 74, 83, 87.

56. Moisander and Edston, "Torture and Its Sequel," 136; Petersen et al., *Burma/Myanmar*, 21.

57. AI, *Nepal*, ASA 31/016/2002, http://www.amnesty.org.

58. AI, *Torture in the Eighties*, 126, 139–40.

59. *Zambia Human Rights Report*, 1998 (Lusaka, Zambia: Inter African Network for Human Rights and Development, Afronet, 1999), 19; Koude Koussetogue, *La Torture* (N'Djaména, Chad: Association Jeunessee Anti-Clivage, 1995), 10; Chukwuma Innocent, *Above the Law* (Lagos, Nigeria: Civil Liberties Organisation, 1994), 65; AI, *Guinea Ecuatorial: Torturas*, AFR 24/05/90/s (Madrid: Mundograf, 1992), 28.

60. Olivia Ball, *"Every Morning Just Like Coffee": Torture in Cameroon* (London: Medical Foundation for the Care of Victims of Torture, 2002), 44.

61. AI, *Arming the Torturers*, 12.

62. *Survivors of Torture in Mount Darwin District, Mashonaland, Central Province* ([Harare, Zimbabwe]: Amani Trust, 1997), 13.

63. South Africa. Police Commission of Inquiry, *Interim and Final Reports* (1937), 70–74; John Brewer, *Black and Blue* (Oxford: Clarendon Press, 1994), 133–38, 141, 146.

64. Brewer, *Black and Blue*, 216–17; Patrick Duncan, *South Africa's Rule of Violence* (London: Methuen, 1964), 92–97.

65. Brewer, *Black and Blue*, 220; Duncan, *South Africa's Rule*, 48; Brian Bunting, *The Rise of the South African Reich* (Harmondsworth, England: Penguin, 1964).

66. Brewer, *Black and Blue*, 218.

67. Duncan, *South Africa's Rule*, 29.

68. Brewer, *Black and Blue*, 218–19; Duncan, *South Africa's Rule*, 48; Harold Bloom, "The South African Police," *Africa South* 2.1 (1957): 7–17.

69. Duncan, *South Africa's Rule*, 26–30, 36–42, 50.

70. Cited in ibid., 31.

71. Brewer, *Black and Blue*, 215.

72. Ibid.; Duncan, *South Africa's Rule*, 42.

73. Brewer, *Black and Blue*, 215; Duncan, *South Africa's Rule*, 25–28, 37–42; Bloom, "The South African Police," 10–11; South Africa, Truth and Reconciliation Commission (TRC), *Report* (London: Macmillan, 1999), 2:191. For accounts from the mid-1960s, see Peter Deeley, *Beyond Breaking Point* (London: Arthur Baker, 1971), 84–87.

74. Duncan, *South Africa's Rule*, 40–42, 26–28.

75. Ibid., 41–42; Brewer, *Black and Blue*, 216.

76. TRC, *Report*, 2:192, 216, 218; *Political Imprisonment*, 65.

77. TRC, *Report*, 2:190.

78. AI, *Report*, 1997; AI, *Report*, 1998; AI, *Report*, 1999, http://www.amnesty.org.

79. I follow Amnesty International practice in grouping the new central Asian states with Europe. These states are members of the Commonwealth of Independent States (CIS) and the Organization for Security and Co-operation in Europe (OSCE).

80. See notes for the entry for Spain in chapter 8, "Currents."

81. See also AI, *Spain*, EUR 41/02/85 (London, 1985), 15.

82. TAT—Torturaren Arkako Taldea [Group Against Torture], *Torture in Basque Country: Report 2001* ([Bilbao]: Graficas Lizarra, S.L, 2002), 39.

83. AI, *Torture in the Eighties*, 208–9.

84. AI, *Albania* (London, 1984), 21.

85. AI, *Concerns in Europe*, EUR 01/006, 1997; *Concerns in Europe*, EUR 01/002/1998; and *Concerns in Europe*, EUR 01/001/1999, http://www.amnesty.org. Also European Committee for the Prevention of Torture (CPT) reports on *Cyprus* (1991, 1996, 2000), *Greece* (1993); *Turkey* (1999, 2001), http://www.cpt.coe.int/en/; Jørgen Thomsen and Maiken Mannstaedt, *The Green Birds* (Århus, Denmark: Danish Medical Group, 2000), 110 (see also 6–7, 159). See also TAT—Torturaren Arkako Taldea [Group Against Torture], *Torture in Basque Country: Report 2001* ([Bilbao]: Graficas Lizarra, S.L, 2002).

86. AI, *Concerns in Europe*, EUR 01/006, 1997; and *Concerns in Europe*, EUR 01/001/1998, http://www.amnesty.org.

87. John McGuffin, *The Guineapigs* (Harmondsworth, England: Penguin, 1974), 130–31.

88. "Six Accused of Torture in Military Exercise," *Times* (London), October 25, 1972, 8f; " 'Torture' Soldier to Sue," *Times* (London), November 1, 1972, 4; "Belgian Troops Found Guilty of Torture," *Times* (London), November 21, 1972, 7.

89. AI, *Concerns in Europe*, EUR 01/006, 1997.

90. CPT, *Austria* (1990, 1994), http://www.cpt.coe.int/en/; AI, *Austria*, EUR 13/01/89 (London, 1990), 31.

91. Corneliu Coposu with Doina Alexandru, *Confessions*, trans. Elena Popescu (Boulder, CO: East European Monographs, 1998), 72; Evgeni Genchev, ed., *Tales from the Dark* (Sofia, Bulgaria: Assistance Centre for Torture Survivors, 2003), 145.

92. See chapter 19.

93. Barnett Rubin and Jeri Laber, *Tears, Blood and Cries* (New York: Helsinki Watch Committee, 1984), 146.

94. Human Rights Watch, *Confession at Any Cost* (New York: Human Rights Watch, 1999), 32.

95. CPT, *Bulgaria* (1995, 1999), *Estonia* (1997), *Georgia* (2001), *Latvia* (1999), *Lithuania* (2000), *Moldova* (1998, 2000, 2001), *Poland* (1996, 2000), *Russia* (2001), *Ukraine* (1998, 2000), http://www.cpt.coe.int/en/; Human Rights Watch, "*And It Was Hell All Over Again . . .*" (New York: Human Rights Watch, 2000), 9–14; Yevgeny Zakharov, *On Torture and Cruel Treatment in the Ukraine*, trans. Vladmir Rublinetskiy (Kharkiv, Ukraine: Kharkiv Group for Human Rights Protection, 2002), 43.

96. Noam Chomsky and Edward Herman, *The Washington Connection and Third World Fascism* (Montreal: Black Rose, 1979).

97. Chomsky and Herman identify thirty-five countries that tortured in the 1970s. Those not on the list are Burundi, Guinea, Iraq, Malawi, Rhodesia, South Africa, the Soviet Union, Syria, and Uganda.

98. For other, less precise "major distributor" hypotheses for this period, see TRC, *Report*, 2:28; Paul Gordon, "The Killing Machine: Britain and the International Repression Trade," *Race and Class* 29.2 (1987): 31–52; and J Pieterse, "Israel's Role in the Third World," *Race and Class* 26.3 (1985): 9–29.

99. Chomsky and Herman mention several of these and classify them outside the U.S. orbit, most notably South Africa, Rhodesia, and Malawi. See Chomsky and Herman, *Washington Connection*, 361 and inside jacket cover. I exclude Namibia because this would be counting South African forces twice.

100. Ibid., 6–7, 11–24.

101. The Reed Torture Technique database maps the distribution of torture techniques by country, agent, and year worldwide. Like the qualitative data here, it measures the scope, not magnitude, of torture techniques. We are focusing first on mapping electrotortures and water tortures. The database, if it can surmount some substantial recording problems, will allow a more fine-grained testing of the hypotheses stated here as well as generate others (for example, the likelihood that electrotorture may reappear in the near future based on past record of usage).

Chapter 10
Prods, Tasers, and Stun Guns

1. John Herbers, "Kennedy Asks Vote Rejecting Wallace," *New York Times*, October 25, 1968, 25.
2. George Bartel, "Stock Prod," U.S. Patent 2,484,147 (filed May 26,1948; issued October, 11, 1949); John Juergens, "Livestock Prod," U.S. Patent 2,561,122 (filed October 29, 1948; issued July 17, 1951); William Abildgaard, "Livestock Prod," U.S. Patent 2,273,003 (filed July 12, 1953; issued January 31, 1956); George Bartel, "Electrical Stock Prod," U.S. Patent 2,981,465 (filed July 1, 1960; issued April 25, 1961); Perry Laten, "Electric Slapper," U.S. Patent 3,227, 362 (filed January 15, 1964; issued January 4, 1966). See also chapter 6, "Shock," note 53.
3. Russell Fagan and Roy Harrison, "Electrified Stick for Postman," U.S. Patent 3,119,554 (filed January 7, 1963; issued January 28, 1964).
4. Samuel Voll, "Combined Policeman's Club and Restraining Device," U.S. Patent 2,966,621 (filed April 3, 1958; issued December 27, 1960).
5. Thomas Ryan, "Electric Weapons," U.S. Patent 2,805,067 (filed November 19, 1952; issued September 3, 1957).
6. Ibid.
7. Frank Mountjoy, "Electrical Shock Device for Repelling Sharks," U.S. Patent 3,484,665 (filed April 26, 1967; issued December 16, 1969); Clarence Johnson, "Electric Anti-Shark Dart," U.S. Patent 3,771,249 (filed November 13, 1973; issued September 4, 1969).
8. La Verne Larsen and Thomas Olson, "Night Stick with Electric Shock Means," U.S. Patent 3,362,711 (filed September 24, 1964; issued January 9, 1968); "Electrical Anti-personnel Weapon," U.S. Patent 3,374,708 (filed January26, 1965; issued March 26, 1968); Kunio Shimizu, "Arrest Device," U.S. Patent 3,523, 538 (filed, December 6, 1966; issued August 11, 1970); Kunio Shimizu, "Baton-type Arrest Device," U.S. Patent 3,625, 222 (filed March 9, 1970; issued December 7, 1971).
9. Gerald Laird, "Self-Defense Apparatus," U.S. Patent 4,337,496 (filed April 10, 1980; issued June 29, 1982); Michael Petrez, "Electric Shock Protection Device," U.S. Patent. 3,722,788 (filed January 29, 1971; issued March 27, 1973); Alfred Levin, "Pocket-sized Non-Lethal Electrical Weapon," U.S. Patent 4,006,390 (filed November 20, 1975; issued February 1, 1977); Donald Lipscomb, "Stun Gun Cane," U.S. Patent D325297 (filed February 16, 1990; issued April 14, 1992).
10. John Coulbourn, "Anti-Pull Animal Leash Mechanism," U.S. Patent 3,874,339 (filed June 26, 1974; issued April 1, 1975).
11. Edward Kerls, "Security Garment," U.S. Patent 4,485,426 (filed December 29, 1983; issued November 27, 1984).
12. Morris Maynor Jr. "Electric Umbrella,' U.S. Patent 4,093,969 (filed October 28, 1976 and June 6, 1978).
13. John Murray and Barnet Resnick, *A Guide to Taser Technology* (Whitewater, CO: Whitewater Press, 1997), 110.

14. William Boyle, "Electric Shock Training Device for Animals," U.S. Patent 4,153,009 (filed August 8, 1977; issued May 8, 1979).

15. Juan Paniagua, "Projector of Fluid with Electric Charge, of Portable Type," U.S. Patent 3,971,292 (filed November 12, 1974; issued July 27, 1976).

16. Gary Ward, "Electric Shock Safety Device," U.S. Patent 4,719,534 (filed May 14, 1986; issued January 12, 1988). See also J. Samuel Batchelder, "Method and Apparatus for Delivering Electric Currents to Remote Targets," U.S. Patent 4,852, 454 (filed November 10, 1987; issued August 1, 1989); and Joseph Abboud, "Irritant Ejecting Stun Gun," U.S. Patent 4,982,645 (filed January 23, 1990; issued January 8, 1991); Peter Coakely and Norbert Wild Jr. "Portable Electromagnetic Stun Device and Method," U.S. Patent 5,625,525 (filed July 11, 1994; issued April 29, 1997).

17. See, for example, Amnesty International, *Arming the Torturers*, ACT 40/01/97 (London, 1997), 2–3.

18. Nathan Reingold, "U.S. Patent Office Records as Sources for the History of Invention and Technological Property," *Technology and Culture* 1 (1960): 166.

19. " 'Impact Weapons'–The Shape of Things to Come?" *Police* 11.4 (1978): 16–18.

20. Joseph Coates, "Non-Lethal Police Weapons," *Technology Review* 74.7 (1972): 55.

21. "New York Rider Relates Harrowing Tale of Life in Maximum Security," *Jackson Daily*, June 21, 1961, http://freedomridersfoundation.org/photos.articles.and.artifacts.html. Parchman was a prison farm, so police may have used prods available for stock on prisoners. I can find no earlier record of prod usage at Parchman or elsewhere in the South. See James Peck, *Freedom Ride* (New York: Simon and Schuster, 1962), 148; David Oshinsky, *"Worse Than Slavery"* (New York: Free Press, 1996), 233–37; Taylor Branch, *Parting the Waters* (New York: Simon and Schuster, 1988), 484; Seth Cagin and Philip Dray, *We Are Not Afraid* (New York: Macmillan, 1988), 128–29; James Farmer, *Lay Bare the Heart* (New York: New American Library, 1985), 7–31.

22. Austin Wehrwein, "Prod Used in South 'Makes You Jump,' " *New York Times*, June 22, 1963, 10.

23. Claude Sitton, "10 on Freedom Walk Seized at Alabama Line," *New York Times*, May 4, 1963, 1.

24. The *New York Times* record indicates most police prod usage occurred in Alabama in 1963 (three demonstrations) and 1965 (six demonstrations). It also reports, in this period, one incident in Mississippi and another in Georgia. See Claude Sitton, "Court in Americus, Ga., Told of Police Beatings," *New York Times*, November 1, 1963, 19; and John Herbers, "Non-Violence–Powerful Rights Weapon," *New York Times*, February 28, 1965, E4.

25. Wehrwein, "Prod Used in South," 10.

26. See Larsen and Olson.

27. Wehrwein, "Prod Used in South," 10; Michael Dewar, *Internal Security Weapons and Equipment of the World* (New York: Charles Scribner's Sons, 1979), 43.

28. Rex Applegate, "Nonlethal Police Weapons" *Ordnance*, July–August 1971, 64.

29. Joseph Coates, *Nonlethal Weapons for Use by US Law Enforcement Officers* (Arlington, VA: Institute for Defense Analyses, November 1967), 47.

30. "Black Suspect in Murder of a Police Officer Alleges that the Grand Jury Was 'Knowingly Deceived,'" *New York Times*, December 14, 1975, 51.
31. Rex Applegate, "Riot Control," 17 *Soldier of Fortune* (December 1992): 44–45.
32. Applegate, "Nonlethal Police Weapons," 64.
33. Cited in Tere Figueras, Sara Olkon, David Ovalle, and Martin Merzer, "Clashes Resume after Thousands March Peacefully," *Contra Costa Times*, November 20, 2003, http://www.contracostatimes.com.
34. John Cover, "Weapon for Immobilization and Capture," U.S. Patent 3,803,463 (filed July 10, 1972; issued April 9, 1974); John Cover, "Power Supply for Weapon for Immobilization and Capture," U.S. Patent 4,253,132 (filed December 29, 1977; issued February 24, 1981).
35. Gary Henderson and Guy Williams Jr., "Electrical Shocking Device with Audible and Visible Spark Display," U.S. Patent 4162515 (filed March 31, 1978; issued July 24, 1979); Gary Henderson and Guy Williams Jr., "Combined Electric Shocking Device for Personal Protection," U.S. Patent D257171 (filed March 31, 1978; issued September 30, 1980).
36. Phyllis Croft, "Problems of Electrical Stunning," *Veterinary Record* (1952): 255.
37. *Stun Guns* (Aurora, CO: T'Prina Technology, 1994); Murray and Resnick, *Guide to Taser Technology*, 43–71.
38. Dewar, *Internal Security Weapons*, 43.
39. Grafton Hull Jr. and Joseph Frisbie, "The Stun Gun Debate," *Police Chief*, February 1987, 46.
40. M. N. Robinson, C. G. Brooks, and G. D. Renshaw, "Electric Shock Devices and their Effects on the Human Body," *Medicine, Science and the Law* (1990): 299.
41. Murray and Resnick, *Guide to Taser Technology*, 75, 77.
42. Ibid., 22.
43. Ibid., 50.
44. Everett Rogers, *Diffusion of Innovations*, 4th ed. (New York: Free Press, 1992), 130–204.
45. Applegate, "Riot Control," 45.
46. Victor Appleton, *Tom Swift and His Electric Rifle or Daring Adventures in Elephant Land* (New York: Grosset, 1911).
47. Murray and Resnick, *Guide to Taser Technology*, 22.
48. John Cover, cited in ibid., 22.
49. Murray and Resnick, *Guide to Taser Technology*, 78.
50. Ibid., 23.
51. Ibid., 25.
52. Ibid., 111.
53. Ibid., 26.
54. Ibid., 25.
55. Ibid., 26.
56. Cover, "Weapon for Immobilization and Capture," 1.
57. Ibid.
58. Murray and Resnick, *Guide to Taser Technology*, 116.

59. Stockholm International Peace Research Institute (SIPRI), *Anti-Personnel Weapons* (London: Taylor and Francis, 1978), 203; Fred Ferretti, "Zap!" *New York Times Magazine*, January 4, 1976), 15–16; Murray and Resnick, *Guide to Taser Technology*, 27.

60. Ferretti, "Zap!" 14. See also William Minor, "Skyjacking Crime Control Models," *Journal of Criminal Law and Criminology* 66 (1975): 94–105; Robert Chauncey, "Deterrence," *Criminology* 12 (1975): 447–73.

61. Murray and Resnick, *Guide to Taser Technology*, 28.

62. Ibid.

63. Ibid., 30.

64. Ibid., 31.

65. Ibid.

66. SIPRI, 203; Ferretti, "Zap!" 13, 16; Murray and Resnick, *Guide to Taser Technology*, 33–35; Hull and Frisbie, "The Stun Gun Debate," 46, 48.

67. Murray and Resnick, *Guide to Taser Technology*, 32.

68. D. A. Jessup, J. W. Foster, and W. E. Clark, "An Electronic Means of Immobilizing Deer," Wildlife Investigation Laboratory, California Department of Fish and Game, April 1980.

69. Lou Cannon, *Official Negligence* (Boulder, CO: Westview, 1999), 95–107; Joseph White Jr., "Policy Formulation and the Theory of Unintended Consequences," Ph.D. diss., University of Southern California, 2000.

70. Ibid., 106.

71. Ibid., 105.

72. Murray and Resnick, *Guide to Taser Technology*, 36, 130, 160.

73. Ibid., 15–16, 117.

74. Ibid., 117.

75. Ibid.

76. Ibid., 160.

77. Ibid., 36, 130.

78. Ibid., 12.

Chapter 11
Stun City

1. Anne-Marie Cusac, "Shock Value," *The Progressive*, September 1997, http://www.infotrac.com.

2. Michael Goldston to Chief Administrator, Office of Professional Standards, in *History of Allegations of Misconduct by Area Two Personnel* (Chicago: Office of Professional Standards, Chicago Police Department, September 28, 1990). Available at http://humanrights.uchicago.edu/chicagotorture/ops.shtml.

3. John Conroy, *Unspeakable Acts, Ordinary People* (New York: Knopf, 2000), 162.

4. G. Flint Taylor, "Known Area 2 and 3 Torture Victims, 1972–1991 (9/15/04)," unpublished data.

5. Abdon Pallasch, Annie Sweeney, and Carlos Adovi, "Gov. Ryan Empties Death Row of all 167," *Chicago Sun-Times*, January 12, 2003, http://www.suntimes.com; "Illinois Gov. Ryan to Empty Death Row," *ABC News*, January 11, 2003, http://abcnews.go.com.

6. Conroy, *Unspeakable Acts, Ordinary People*, 61–62.

7. G. Flint Taylor, "U.S. Torture," *Police Misconduct and Civil Rights Law Reporter* 7.15 (2004): 174.

8. Jim Miller, social worker, cited in Conroy, *Unspeakable Acts, Ordinary People*, 65.

9. Conroy, *Unspeakable Acts, Ordinary People*, 69.

10. Ibid.

11. Ibid., 70. A "shock wand," a pre-stun-era electric device, has a roller for its head and delivers a powerful shock.

12. Amnesty International (AI), "Summary of Amnesty International's Concerns on Police Abuse in Chicago," AMR 51/168/1999, 1, http://www.amnesty.org.

13. Ibid.

14. Alan Dershowitz, cited in Jeremy Campbell, "Torture's the New Way Forward," *Evening Standard* (UK), December 4, 2001, 20.

15. Human Rights Watch, *Shielded From Justice* (New York: Human Rights Watch, 1998).

16. Conroy, *Unspeakable Acts, Ordinary People*, 34. For the full Chicago story, see Conroy, 21–26; 60–87, 158–68, 225–41. For other torture cases in the period before stun guns, see *Blyden v. Mancusi*, 186 F.3Á 252, 257 (2nd Cir. 1999); *Inmates, Attica Correctional Facility v. Rockefeller*, 453 F.2Á 12, 16, 18–19, 2nd Cir. 1971); *Singletary v. Parsons*, No. 81-496 (E.D. La. 1986); *U.S. v. McKenzie*, 768 F.2Á 602, 604 (5th Cir. 1985).

17. John Conroy, "Deaf to the Screams," *Chicago Reader*, August 1, 2003, 1, 18–20, 22, 24–25. For cases between 1950 and 1970, see Taylor, "U.S. Torture," 9–10, 13–14, 21–24; *People v. Walden*, 19 Ill. 2Á. 602 (1960); *Walden v. City of Chicago*, 04-C-0047 (N.D. Ill.); Henry Cohen, *Brutal Justice* (New York: John Jay Press, 1980), 9, 21, 51, 58; Daniel Mannix, *The History of Torture* ([New York]: Dorset, 1964), 184–88.

18. Taylor, "U.S. Torture," 19.

19. Taylor, "Known Area 2 and 3 Torture Victims."

20. Judge Dom Rizzi, cited in Conroy, *Unspeakable Acts, Ordinary People*, 238.

21. John Conroy, "Tools of Torture," and "The Mysterious Third Device," *Chicago Reader*, February 4, 2005, 1, 24–27.

22. For the New York event, see the following articles from the *New York Times* (http://www.lexis-nexis.com/): Robert McFadden, "Youth's Charges of Torture by an Officer Spur Inquiry," April 22, 1985, B3; Selwyn Raab, "Two More Officers Charged in Inquiry into Torture at a Queens Precinct," April 25, 1985, A1; Robert McFadden, "Brutality Inquiry Widened in Queens," April 28, 1985, A34; Selwyn Raab, "Five Police Officers Indicted by Jury in Torture Case," May 1, 1985, A1. See also Cusac, "Shock Value"; Mark Ragan, "Stun Gun Sales Shock Lawmen," *San*

Diego Union-Tribune, May 9, 1985, A1, http://www.lexis-nexis.com/; Marcia Chambers, "Stun-Gun Charges Prompt Police Inquiry in West," *New York Times*, December 22, 1986, B12, http://www.lexis-nexis.com/.

23. Ragan, "Stun Gun Sales," A1.

24. Cusac, "Shock Value," http://www.infotrac.com.

25. Anne-Marie Cusac, "Stunning Technology," *The Progressive*, July 18, 1996, 22.

26. Mark Silverstein, Legal Director, ACLU of Colorado to Penfield Tate and Federico Alvarez, Co-Chairs, Mayors Task Force on Police, March 15, 2004, http://www.aclu-co.org.

27. Cusac, "Shock Value"; Jaime Castillo, "Panel Examines Training of Correctional Officers," *San Antonio Express-News* (Texas), September 17, 1997, B2; Douglas Waller, Peter Hawthorne, Rachel Salaman, and Alexandra Stiglmayer, "Weapons of Torture," *Time*, April 6, 1998, 52–53; "Stun Gun—Police Feel a Backlash," *US News and World Report*, May 13, 1985, 10, http://www.lexis-nexis.com/; Ruth Marcus, "Controversy Accompanies Popularity of Cheap Electric Stun Guns," *Washington Post*, May 6, 1985, C1, http://www.lexis-nexis.com/; AI, *Arming the Torturers*, ACT 40/01/97 (London, 1997); AI, "USA: Use of Electro-shock Stun Belts," AMR 51/45/96 (London, 1997); Philip Anderson, "Torture in the County Jail," *Washington Post*, December 23, 1998, A23; Mark Silverstein, Legal Director, ACLU of Colorado to Gerry Whitman, Chief of Police, February 26, 2004, http://www.aclu-co.org; Stephen Hudak, "Shocking Restraint," *Plain Dealer* (Cleveland), December 25, 1996, 7B; Mark Dow, *American Gulag* (Berkeley and Los Angeles: University of California Press, 2004), 327–28; U.S. Department of State, *Second Periodic Report of the United States of America to the Committee Against Torture*, May 6, 2005, Article 2 (16-34), http://www.state.gov/g/drl/rls/45738.htm.

28. Brian Rappert, *Non-Lethal Weapons as Legitimizing Forces?* (London: Frank Cass, 2003), 219. For a comprehensive evaluation of the Maricopa County jails, see Rappert, 211–24. For the DOJ and Amnesty International reports, see Eugene Miller, *Response and Outline to Expert Penologist's Report* (Washington, DC: Department of Justice, 1996; George Sullivan, *Report of Corrections Consultant on the Use of Force in Maricopa County Jails, Phoenix, Arizona, May 14* (Washington, DC: Department of Justice, 1997); AI, *Ill-treatment of Inmates in Maricopa County Jails, Arizona*, AMR 51/51/97 (London, 1997).

29. John Murray and Barnet Resnick, *A Guide to Taser Technology* (Whitewater, CO: Whitewater Press, 1997), 46.

30. Ibid., 38–39, 47.

31. NOVA advertisement, cited in Murray and Resnick, *Guide to Taser Technology*, 38.

32. Murray and Resnick, *Guide to Taser Technology*, 39.

33. Ragan, "Stun Gun Sales," A1; "Self Defense is Topic," *San Diego Union-Tribune*, May 18, 1985, B3, http://www.lexis-nexis.com/; Richard Green, "Non-Lethal Gun Marketed for Citizen Self-Protection," *News-Times*, June 3, 1996, 2, http://www.newstimes.com.

34. *Stun Guns* (Aurora, CO: T'prina Technology, 1994), 10.

35. Alfred Levin, "Pocket-sized Non-lethal Electrical Weapon," U.S. Patent 4,006,390 (filed November 20, 1975; issued February 1, 1977).

36. "Information on Electrical Play," Sparks@thepentagon.com, 1988-1996, http://www.sexuality.org/1/bdsm/elecplay.html.

37. See "A Small Tribute to Tony DeBlase," Dave Barker, dave@leatheru.com, 2004, http://www.leatheru.com.

38. Jack Rinella, "Interview with Tony DeBlase," Charles Renslow, 1995, http://www.leatherarchives.org/Collections/Archival/Oral%20History/tony.htm.

39. Interview with Dr. Andrew Charles (longtime partner of Antony DeBlase) in discussion with the author, January 15, 2004.

40. Richard Krousher [Antony DeBlase], *Physical Interrogation Techniques* (Port Townsend, WA: Loompanics, 1985). This book should not be taken as a guide to torture in the late twentieth century. DeBlase fails to show the concern for cleanliness or the professional distance (he is clearly into humiliation) that characterizes torture in this period. Indeed, although the press that marketed the book specialized in extreme literature including neo-Nazi materials, the book did not sell. I treat DeBlase's introduction, however, as a philosophical defense of torture by an important liberal voice, much like Alan Dershowitz's defense. The rest of the book is a commentary for S-M practice.

41. Rinella, "Interview with Tony DeBlase."

42. Ibid.; Charles, interview; Krousher, *Physical Interrogation Techniques*, 63-70.

43. Miss X, "Electricity is . . . shocking . . . deadly . . . erotic," missx@kinkymissx.com, 2002-3, http://www.kinkymissx.com/Home/KinkyMissXPreviewTexts/Kinky MissXTextsElectrics.htm.

44. "Information on Electrical Play."

45. Murray and Resnick, *Guide to Taser Technology*, 44.

46. LAPD Technical Services Bureau Bulletin, November 17, 1980, cited in ibid., 36.

47. Gary Ordog, Jonathan Wasserberger, Theodore Schlafer, and Subramiam Balasubramanium, "Electronic Gun (Taser) Injuries," *Annals of Emergency Medicine* 16 (1987): 73-78. See also Eric M. Koscove, "The Taser Weapon," *Annals of Emergency Medicine* 14 (1985): 1205-8.

48. Ronald Kornblum and Sara Reddy, "Effects of the Taser in Fatalities Involving Police Confrontation," *Journal of Forensic Sciences* 36 (1991): 434-48.

49. Lou Cannon, *Official Negligence* (Boulder, CO: Westview, 1999), 29, 31-33, 47, 581.

50. Ibid., 31, 35, 448.

51. Stacey Koon with Robert Deitz, *Presumed Guilty* (Washington, DC: Regnery, 1992), 41. Murray and Resnick also recommend reminder joints in their Taser protocol. See Murray and Resnick, *Guide to Taser Technology*, 52.

52. Koon , *Presumed Guilty*, 22.

53. AI, *Arming the Torturers*, 9. See also Cannon, *Official Negligence*, 27, 580.

54. Greg Meyer, "Nonlethal Weapons Versus Conventional Police Tactics," Ph.D. diss., California State University, Los Angeles, 1991, iii.

55. Cannon, *Official Negligence*, 547.

56. Nick Budnick, "Taser Crazy," *Willamette Week*, February 4, 2004, 16; Teresa Riordan, "New Taser Finds Unexpected Home in Hands of Police," *New York Times*, November 17, 2003, C4, http://www.nytimes.com.

57. Murray and Resnick, *Guide to Taser Technology*, 38, 41.

58. "Corporate Background," http://www.airtaser.com.

59. Ibid.

60. *Advanced Taser Brochure* (Scottsdale, AZ: Taser International Brochure, 2004); "Dataport Download Software and Adapter," http://www.airtaser.com.

61. *X26 Brochure* (Scottsdale, AZ: Taser International, 2004), http://www.airtaser.com.

62. Sarah Kershaw, "As Shocks Replace Police Bullets, Deaths Drop but Questions Arise," *New York Times*, March 6, 2004, A1, http://www.nytimes.com.

63. Budnick, "Taser Crazy," 16; Riordan, "New Taser," C4.

64. Joseph Coates, *Nonlethal Weapons for Use by US Law Enforcement Officers* (Arlington, VA: Institute for Defense Analyses, November 1967), 40.

65. Murray and Resnick, *Guide to Taser Technology*, 32.

66. To be specific, not one case in over one hundred thousand uses (Steve Tuttle, "Taser International, Inc. Responds to Media Sensationalism Regarding Alleged TASER Technology in Custody Deaths," press release, Taser International, Scottsdale, AZ, April 28, 2004, http://www.airtaser.com). See also Murray and Resnick, *Guide to Taser Technology*, 63, 101–8; Rappert, *Non-Lethal Weapons*, 203–4, 207; Alex Berenson, "As Police Use of Tasers Soars, Questions over Safety Emerge," *New York Times*, July 18, 2004, 22. Nevertheless, there are serious questions about deaths that follow Taser usage (Berenson, 22).

67. Murray and Resnick, *Guide to Taser Technology*, 95–97.

68. Silverstein to Tate and Alvarez, March 15, 2004.

69. *Advanced Taser Brochure*; *X26 Brochure*; Murray and Resnick, *Guide to Taser Technology*, 132, 161.

70. "Hand-held Electronic 'Stun Gun' Non-Lethal," *Enforcement Journal* (1985): 31.

71. Murray and Resnick, *Guide to Taser Technology*, 62, 92.

72. Ibid., 39

73. Ibid., 114–15.

74. "Hand-held Electronic 'Stun Gun,' " 31. See also Murray and Resnick, *Guide to Taser Technology*, 59–69, 155–58.

75. Murray and Resnick, *Guide to Taser Technology*, 157–58.

76. See Rappert, *Non-Lethal Weapons*, 204–8; Terence Allen, "Effects of the Taser in Fatalities Involving Police Confrontation," *Journal of Forensic Sciences* 37 (1992): 956–58.

77. Murray and Resnick, *Guide to Taser Technology*, 136; for similar concerns expressed in Taser training, see 155–58.

78. Ibid., 62.

79. Ibid., 63.

80. Ibid., 39. See also Bart Rommell, *Dirty Tricks Cops Use (And Why They Use Them)* (Port Townsend, WA: Loompanics, 1993), 105.

81. The subjects were not struggling, but restrained and helpless. The public was not shocked simply by the burns, but by the multiple shocks used to force confessions.

82. Cusac, "Shock Value."

83. Cannon, *Official Negligence*, 579–81.

84. Harry Potter, *Hanging in Judgment* (New York: Continuum, 1993), 101–2. For the drop tables, see Richard Clark, "The History of Judicial Hanging in Britain," http://www.richard.clark32.btinternet.co.uk/hanging1.html.

85. Hans Draminsky Petersen and Peter Jacobsen, "Life-Threatening Torture without Visible Marks," *Scandinavian Journal of Social Medicine* 13 (1985): 88. See also Allen, "Effects of the Taser," 957; and Duncan Forrest, Bernard Knight, and Morris Tidball-Binz, "The Documentation of Torture," in *A Glimpse of Hell*, ed. Duncan Forrest (London: Amnesty International, 1996), 174–75.

86. "Nova Spirit," in Murray and Resnick, *Guide to Taser Technology*, 193.

87. Ordog et al., "Electronic Gun (Taser) Injuries," 76. See also Joseph Fried, "Stun-Gun Accuser Fails to Recall Details of Arrest," *New York Times*, April 22, 1986, B3.

88. Budnick, "Taser Crazy," 16, 20; Silverstein to Whitman, February 26, 2004; Jerome Skolnick and Jamese Fyfe, *Above the Law* (New York: Free Press, 1993), 40; Lawrence Hinman, "Stunning Morality," *Criminal Justice Ethics* 17.1 (1998): 3–14.

89. Silverstein to Tate and Alvarez, March 15, 2004.

90. Project Manager, Research Center for the International Association of Chiefs of Police, cited in Beth DeFalco, "Taser to Offer Stun Gun Cameras," Associated Press, November 6, 2005, http://www.lexis-nexis.com/.

91. Defalco, "Taser to Offer Cameras."

92. Cited in Douglas et al., "Weapons of Torture," 53. For similar arguments see Berenson, "Police Use of Tasers," 22; Murray and Resnick, *Guide to Taser Technology*, 13, 16–20, 34–35, 41–42, 63, 158.

93. Martha Huggins, Mika Haritos-Fatouros, and Philip Zimbardo, *Violence Workers* (Berkeley and Los Angeles: University of California Press, 2002), 101–35, 245–63.

94. John Darley and Bibb Latane, "Bystander Intervention in Emergencies," *Journal of Personality and Social Psychology* 8 (1968): 377–83; John Darley and Bibb Latane, "Group Inhibition of Bystander Intervention in Emergencies," *Journal of Personality and Social Psychology* 10 (1968): 215–21; John Darley and Bibb Latane, "When Will People Help in a Crisis?" *Psychology Today*, December 1968, 54–56, 70–71.

95. Senior Mental Health Officer, UN Relief and Works Agency (UNRWA) cited in James Ron, "Varying Methods of State Violence," *International Organization* 51.2 (1997): 295.

96. Cited in Vivian Stern, *A Sin Against the Future* (Boston: Northeastern University Press, 1998), 307. Shapiro was seriously wounded in a stabbing in Connecticut in 1994.

97. Berenson, "Police Use of Tasers," 22.

98. "Cincinnati Mayor Recommends Stun Guns," December 7, 2003, http://www.yahoo.com; Kershaw, "Shocks Replace Police Bullets," A1.

99. Scott Armstrong, "Stun Guns Getting More Popular—and Controversial," *Christian Science Monitor*, May 16, 1985, 23, http://www.lexis-nexis.com/.

100. Marcus, "Controversy Accompanies Popularity," C1. See also Ragan, "Stun Gun Sales," A1.

101. Green, "Non-Lethal Gun Marketed," 2.

102. Tere Figueras, Sara Olkon, David Ovalle, and Martin Merzer, "Clashes Resume after Thousands March Peacefully," *Contra Costa Times*, November 20, 2003, http://www.contracostatimes.com; Mark Shaw, *Crime and Policing in Post-Apartheid South Africa* (Bloomington: Indiana University Press, 2002), 108.

103. Ordog et al., "Electronic Gun (Taser) Injuries," 76.

104. Murray and Resnick, *Guide to Taser Technology*, 65.

105. Patrice Gaines-Carter and Martin Weil, "Stun-Gun Used on Minister," *Washington Post*, May 31, 1985, C3, http://www.lexis-nexis.com/.

106. Steve Tuttle, "Taser International, Inc. Demands Amnesty International Withdraw Its Misleading and Defamatory Statements," press release, Taser International, Scottsdale, AZ, June 2, 2004, http://www.airtaser.com. See also Murray and Resnick, *Guide to Taser Technology*.

107. See, for example, Steve Wright, "The New Trade in Technologies of Restraint and Electroshock," in Forrest, *A Glimpse of Hell*, 137–52; Steve Wright, *An Appraisal of Technologies of Political Control*, PE 166 499 (Luxembourg Directorate General for Research, European Parliament January 6, 1998); AI, *The Pain Merchants*, ACT 40/008/2003 (London: International Secretariat, 2003); and AI, *Stopping the Torture Trade*, ACT 40/002/2001 (London: International Secretariat, 2001) (http://www.amnesty.org).

108. Carolyn Marvin, *When Old Technologies Were New* (New York: Oxford University Press, 1988), 150.

109. "Amnesty International Denies Torturing Hogs," *New York Times*, May 31, 1977, A3. For an account of the experiments, see chapter 19, "Drugs and Doctors."

110. Brian Rappert, "Moralizing Violence," *Science as Culture* 13.1 (2004): 13–18.

111. Whether my story of electrotorture is the typical, "know it all" view of a positive social scientist, as Rappert says (Rappert, "Moralizing Violence"), others can judge. Social scientists have no magic wand that sets their accounts apart from those of ordinary people. But as far as I know, there are only three ways even ordinary people know a story they tell is true: it corresponds to what is known, it offers the most comprehensive perspective on other perspectives, and it allows people to get the job done: it fits, it's logical, and it works. Stories that don't meet these standards are false, illogical, or misleading. We may debate whether one of these is more suited to the study of human beings than others, but there are no other standards. Those are the standards I am applying here, and of course, I could be mistaken in how I have conducted my research. As near as I can tell, Rappert's criticism is not so much about how one *does* social science, but rather about how one *talks* about what one does when one does social science. Like most appeals to ethical humility in social science, Rappert offers no different way of *doing* the study of electrotorture; only an injunction to *talk* about it differently.

Such criticism is neither here nor there. This is playing status games, and far too many books of this sort are devoted to the rhetoric of social science than its conduct (the notable exceptions to this, being Michel Foucault and Pierre Bourdieu).

Part IV
Other Stealth Traditions

1. Graeme R. Newman, *Just and Painful* (New York: Macmillan, 1983).

Chapter 12
Sticks and Bones

1. European Commission of Human Rights (ECHR), *The Greek Case* (Strasbourg: Council of Europe, 1970), 415.
2. For the best account of whips and whipmaking, see David Morgan, *Whips and Whipmaking* (Cambridge, MA: Cornell Maritime Press, 1972); Ron Edwards, *How to Make Whips* (Centreville, MD: Cornell Maritime Press, 1997); and George Ryley Scott, *The History of Corporal Punishment* (London: Torchstream, 1954). These accounts correctly recognize whips as ordinary objects, situating them in both animal and human history. For accounts that focus exclusively on penal whipping, see Scott Claver, *Under the Lash* (London: Torchstream, 1954); Geoffrey Abbott, *Rack, Rope and Red-hot Pincers* (London: Headline Books, 1993), 123–47; Karen Farrington, *Dark Justice* (New York: Smithmark, 1996), 114–19; Brian Innes, *The History of Torture* (New York: St. Martin's, 1998), 96–103; Jean Kellaway, *The History of Torture and Execution* (New York: Lyons Press, 2000), 122–27; and Michael Kerrigan, *The Instruments of Torture* (New York: Lyons Press, 2001), 125–35.
3. For the criminal prosecution and judicial torture of animals, see George Ryley Scott, *The History of Torture* (London: Torchstream, 1940), 278.
4. Scott, *History of Corporal Punishment*, 83–84.
5. Peter Brown, *The Cult of the Saint* (Chicago: University of Chicago Press, 1981), 109.
6. Morgan, *Whips and Whipmaking*, 13; Kerrigan, *The Instruments of Torture*, 126. For a list of the Greek whips that preceded the Roman ones, see Virginia Hunter, *Policing Athens* (Princeton, NJ: Princeton University Press, 1994), 168, 238 n.24.
7. Farrington, *Dark Justice*, 114, 116; Morgan, *Whips and Whipmaking*, 15; Scott, *History of Corporal Punishment*, 60, 83; W.N.T. Beckett, *A Few Naval Customs, Expressions, Traditions and Superstitions*, 2nd ed. (Portsmouth, England: Gieves [1915]), 15, 82; Martin Dugard, *Farther Than Any Man* (New York: Pocket Books, 2001), 28.
8. Patrick Duncan, *South Africa's Rule of Violence* (London: Methuen, 1964), 33.
9. Scott, *History of Corporal Punishment*, 52–53; Abbott, *Rack, Rope*, 138.

10. Daniel Mannix, *The History of Torture* ([New York]: Dorset, 1964), 179. See also Scott, *History of Corporal Punishment*, 78.

11. Beckett, *Naval Customs*, 14.

12. Scott, *History of Corporal Punishment*, 60; Abbott, *Rack, Rope*, 127.

13. Abbott, *Rack, Rope*, 128.

14. Scott, *History of Corporal Punishment*, 64; Kerrigan, *The Instruments of Torture*, 126.

15. Scott, *History of Corporal Punishment*, 60, 93; Abbott, *Rack, Rope*, 131. Military flogging was not simply "abolished in 1881" (Kellaway, *History of Torture*, 125).

16. Abbott, *Rack, Rope*, 131.

17. Claver, *Under the Lash*, 264–69.

18. Abbott, *Rack, Rope*, 133; "Discipline: General (Code 78A): Punishment of Boys by Caning," PRO WO 32/15278.

19. Scott, *History of Corporal Punishment*, 60–64; Abbott, *Rack, Rope*, 127–28; Duncan, *Rule of Violence*, 33, 133.

20. Charles Mercer, *Legion of Strangers* (New York: Holt, Rinehart and Winston, 1964), 193; Geoffrey Bocca, *La Légion!* (New York: Thomas Crowell, 1964), 123; Alfred Perrott-White, *French Legionnaire* (Caldwell, ID: Caxton Printers, 1951), 94, James Armstrong with William Elliott, *Legion of Hell* (London: Sampson Low, Marston, [1936]), 202–3; Reginald Forbes, *Red Horizon* (London: Sampson Low, Marston, [1932]), 7, 25, 71.

21. Mercer, *Legion of Strangers*, 190. O'Balance denies flogging ever occurred in the Legion, while "Tiger" O'Reilly's account seems to see whips everywhere. Both accounts strain credibility (Edgar O'Balance, *The Story of the French Foreign Legion* [London: Faber and Faber, 1961], 240; William Elliott, *The Tiger of the Legion* [New York: Greenberg, 1930], 122–31, 210–16).

22. Scott, *History of Corporal Punishment*, 83; Abbott, *Rack, Rope*, 146–47; James Valle, *Rock and Shoals* (Annapolis, MD: Naval Institute Press, 1980), 41, 83; F. Dalton O'Sullivan, *Crime Detection* (Chicago: O'Sullivan Publishing House, 1928), 295.

23. Mannix, *The History of Torture*, 187; Robert Caldwell, *Red Hannah* (Philadelphia: University of Pennsylvania Press, 1947), 32–58, 69–82, 127–31.

24. Cornelius Willemse, *Behind the Green Lights* (New York: Knopf, 1931), 354; Thomas Repetto, *The Blue Parade* (New York: Free Press, 1978), 176–78; National Commission on Law Observance and Enforcement, *Report on Lawlessness in Law Enforcement* (Washington, DC: U.S. Government Printing Office, 1931), 60, 118, 126, 153. Hereafter cited as Wickersham Commission.

25. Abbott, *Rack, Rope*, 147, 185.

26. John Brown, *A Slave Life in Georgia*, ed. F. N. Boney (Savannah, GA: Beehive Press, 1991), 98.

27. Dugard, *Farther Than Any Man*, 28; *Falconer's Marine Dictionary* (1780), reprint ed. (New York: Augustus Kelley, 1970), 84; Francis Grose, *Classical Dictionary of the Vulgar Tongue* (New York: Barnes and Noble, 1963), 88–89.

28. Beckett, *Naval Customs*, 14; Frederick Marryat, *Frank Mildmay* (Ithaca, NY: McBooks, 1998), 38; Government of Canada, National Defence, *Cadet Instructor Cadre, Junior Officer Leadership Course*, (A-CR-050-003/PF-001: 2001), 4-4-8.

29. *Falconer's Marine Dictionary*, 84.

30. William Sands, *Undiplomatic Memories* (New York: Whittlesey House, 1930), 147.

31. Grose, *Dictionary*, 89; Claver, *Under the Lash*, 21, facing 146.

32. Elisha Black, cited in Jeptha Simms, *The Frontiersmen of New York* (Albany, NY: Geo. C. Riggs, 1883), 2:167.

33. Brown, *Slave Life in Georgia*, 58; Dwight Lowell Dumond, *Anti-Slavery* (Ann Arbor: University of Michigan Press, 1961), 111, 115, 254; Robert Conrad, *Children of God's Fire* (Princeton, NJ: Princeton University Press, 1983), 258–67, 294–95, 314; João Maurício Rugendas, *Viagem Pitoresca através do Brasil* (São Paulo: Livraria Martins, 1940); "Castigos Domesticos," plate 4/10.

34. *Sing Sing Prison* (New York: NY State Department of Correction, 1953), 6; Alexander Pisciotta, *Benevolent Repression* (New York: New York University Press, 1994), 37.

35. Beckett, *Naval Customs*, 75.

36. Black, cited in Simms, *Frontiersmen of New York*, 2:167, Brown, *Slave Life in Georgia*, 58; Rugendas, *Viagem Pitoresca*, plate 4/10; *Sing Sing Prison*, 6; J. Ralph Jones, "Portraits of Georgia Slaves," *Georgia Review* 21 (1967): 269; Paul Finkelman, *Slavery in the Courtroom* (Washington, DC: Library of Congress, 1985), 171; *Unchained Memories* (Boston: Bullfinch Press, 2002), 130; "Narrative and Testimony of Rev. Horace Moulton," in *American Slavery As It Is*, ed. Theodore Weld (New York: Arno, 1968), 20–21; Kenneth Serbin, *Secret Dialogues* (Pittsburgh: University of Pittsburgh Press, 2000), 186; A. J. Langguth, *Hidden Terrors* (New York: Pantheon, 1978), 219.

37. Archdiocese of São Paulo, *Torture in Brazil*, trans. Jaime Wright (New York: Vintage, 1986), 16.

38. Mrs. Mann, cited in "Letter of Rev. C. Stewart Renshaw," in Weld, *American Slavery As It Is*, 71.

39. Scott, *History of Corporal Punishment*, 57.

40. Ibid., 77–78; Scott, *History of Torture*, 132, 196.

41. Brown, *Slave Life in Georgia*, 98.

42. Wickersham Commission, 118.

43. Ibid., 126.

44. Josh White, "Soldier's 'Wish Lists' of Detainee Tactics Cited," *Washington Post*, April 19, 2005, A16.

45. Gérard de Lacaze-Duthiers, *La torture a travers les âges* (Herblay, Seine-et-Oise, France: Editions de l'idée libre, 1961), 79.

46. Robert Conquest, *The Great Terror* (New York: Oxford University Press, 1990), 121; Vladmir Brunovsky, *The Methods of OGPU* (London: Harper and Brothers, [1931]), 131.

47. ECHR, 102, 170, 241, 323.

48. See Amnesty International (AI), *Spain*, EUR 41/02/85 (London, 1985), 15; Human Rights Watch, *Turkey* 9:4 (March 1997), 11; European Committee for the Prevention of Torture, *Austria* (1990), *France* (1991), *Portugal* (1992), *Bulgaria* (1995), http://www.cpt.coe.int/en/.

49. Michael Peel and Mary Salinsky, *Caught in the Middle* (Oxford: Alden Group, 2000), 23.

50. TAT—Torturaren Arkako Taldea [Group Against Torture], *Torture in Basque Country: Report 2001* ([Bilbao]: Graficas Lizarra, S.L, 2002), 13, 15, 22, 24, 41, 43, 44, 49, 55, 56, 59, 62, 78, 83, 90, 92 (book); 51, 61, 75 (baton wrapped in foam or newspaper).

51. Marcio Alves, *Torturas e Torturados* (Rio de Janeiro: Empresa Jornalística, 1966), 26–27; Peter Deeley, *Beyond Breaking Point* (London: Arthur Baker, 1971), 95–104 (or during the Vargas period).

52. Langguth, *Hidden Terrors*, 219; Archdiocese of São Paulo, *Torture in Brazil*, 16; Paul Chevigny, Bell Gale Chevigny, and Russell Karp, *Police Abuse in Brazil* (New York: Americas Watch Report, 1987), 33, 58.

53. Duncan Forrest, "Patterns of Abuse in Sikh Asylum-Seekers," *The Lancet*, 345.8944 (January 28, 1995): 225–26; Patricia Lawrence, "Survivors' Tasks: Narratives from Sir Lankan Detention Camps," Conference of the Human Rights Program, University of Chicago, March 4–6, 1999, 6.

54. Brian McKnight, *Law and Order in Sung China* (Cambridge: Cambridge University Press, 1992), 338–39; Scott, *History of Corporal Punishment*, 55, 136. The practice did not exist during the Han or the Age of Disunion, but it may have existed among the Tang who preceded the Sung (Mark Lewis, email correspondence, July 29, 2004).

55. *Report on Torture in the Nyzshni Novgorod Province* (Nyzshni Novgorod, Russia: Nyzshni Novgorod Province Society for Human Rights, 1997), 6.

56. G. Lecomte, "Falaka," *The Encyclopedia of Islam* (Leiden: E. J. Brill, 1965), 2:763; Uriel Heyd, *Studies in Old Ottoman Criminal Law*, ed. V. L. Ménage (Oxford: Clarendon Press, 1973), 273; Mannix, *The History of Torture*, 162; Darius Rejali, *Torture and Modernity* (Boulder, CO: Westview, 1994), 184.

57. See, for example, Antony Réal, *The Story of the Stick in All Ages and Lands* (New York: J. W. Bouton, 1875), 182–202.

58. McKnight, *Law and Order*, 339; Scott, *History of Corporal Punishment*, 55, 136. The Sung penal codes specifically mention beating the soles of the feet, but the practice may have made explicit what was already common practice in the preceding centuries. The T'ang Penal Code (a.d. 653), like the Sung, favored routinized beating with light or heavy sticks over the more horrific punishments of earlier periods. The code, however, does not specify where the blows should fall. See *The T'ang Code*, 2 vols., trans. Wallace Johnson (Princeton, NJ: Princeton University Press, 1997). There are references to beating with sticks from earlier periods. See A.J.P. Hulsewe's *Remnants of Ch'in Law* (Leiden, the Netherlands: E. J. Brill, 1985), 184–85.

59. Lecomte, "Falaka," 763.

60. Heyd, *Old Ottoman Criminal Law*, 273 n. 5.

61. Mannix, *The History of Torture*, 161–62; Mary Sheil, *Glimpses of Life and Manners in Persia* (London: John Murray, 1856), 246.

62. Lecomte, "Falaka," 763.

63. McKnight, *Law and Order*, 338.

64. Francis Forbes-Leith, *Checkmate* (New York: Robert McBride, 1927), 82.

65. Korovessis states, "The first mention of the word is in classical Greek; Demosthenes lays down that no witness at a trial may be considered reliable if he has previously been given the *falanga*." Pericles Korovessis, *The Method*, trans. Les Nightingale and Catherine Patrakis (London: Allison and Busby, 1970), 13. On the contrary, Demosthenes says no such thing. Demosthenes says no citizen shall be subjected to *basanos*, the general term used for gathering legal testimony through torture (Demosthenes 29.40, 30.37, 37.40–42, 47.12, 17, 54.27). The word *falanga*, much less the practice, does not, as near as I can tell, appear in Demosthenes anywhere, and the practice is not mentioned among any list of punishments or tortures for slaves or citizens in classical Greece (Hunter, *Policing Athens*, 92, 154–84, 219 n. 43, 236–43). For a discussion of *basanos*, see Page DuBois, *Torture and Truth* (New York: Routledge, Chapman and Hall, 1991).

66. Lecomte, "Falaka," 763.

67. Edmund Burke, *Speeches on the Impeachment of Warren Hastings* (London: Henry G. Bohn, 1857), 1:187.

68. Claver, *Under the Lash*, 21; Beckett, *Naval Customs*, 11.

69. Mark Twain, *Innocents Abroad* (New York: Library of America, 1984), 425.

70. Angus McLean, *Vive la Legion* (London: Sampson Low, Marston, [1937]), 139; Zosa Szajkowski, *Jews and the Foreign Legion* (New York: Ktav, 1975), 112; Gerard Lacourrège and Pierre Alibert, *Au temps des bagnes* (Paris: Editions Atlas, 1986), 134–35.

71. H. Hessell Tiltman, *The Terror in Europe* (New York: Frederick Stokes, 1932), 382, 399. Emanuel Böhm, *Human Rights Violations* (New York: Orbis, 1986), 97.

72. Lieutenant Castor, cited in Pierre Giolitto, *Histoire de la milice* (Paris: Perrin, 1997), 293; "Official Memorandum by the Danish Government, 25 October 1945 concerning the crimes committed by the Germans [901-RF]," in International Military Tribunal, *Trial of the Major War Criminals* (Nuremberg, Germany: n.p., 1948), 38:681; Norwegian Government, *The Gestapo at Work in Norway* (Montreal: Royal Norwegian Government's Information Office, 1942), 23.

73. Richard Wurmbrand, *From Suffering to Triumph* (Grand Rapids, MI: Kregel, 1991), 30; Silviu Craciunas, *The Lost Footsteps* (New York: Farrar, Straus and Cudahy, 1961), 130; Corneliu Coposu with Doina Alexandru, *Confessions*, trans. Elena Popescu (Boulder, CO: East European Monographs, 1998), 72.

74. William Grimes, cited in Twain, *Innocents Abroad*, 425.

75. Richard Burton, cited in Mannix, *The History of Torture*, 161.

76. Henry Norman, *The Peoples and Politics of the Far East* (London: T. Fischer Unwin, 1900), 221; Kerrigan, *The Instruments of Torture*, 122–24; Innes, *The History of Torture*, 148.

77. *La Lutte*, April 29, 1936, cited in Daniel Hémery, *Révolutionnaires vietnamiens et pouvoir colonial en Indochine* (Paris: François Maspero, 1975), 457.

78. Charles Smith, "Communal Conflict and Insurrection in Palestine, 1936–1948," in *Policing and Decolonization*, ed. David M. Anderson and David Killingray (Manchester, England: Manchester University Press, 1992), 66, 71. See also Mac-Michaels to Parkinson, September 2, 1938, in *The Miska Case*, PRO CO 733/371/3; Cuban Legation, "Memorandum: Julio Jacobo Jabour," in *Conduct of British Troops and Police: General Representations*, PRO CO 733/428/1.

79. "Statement of Mordehy Petcho," in *Case of Cohen and A. Laronovich and Case of M. Petcho*, PRO CO 733/413/6.

80. Pablo Sulbarán, *La tortura en Venezuela* (Caracas: Publicaciones Seleven, 1979), 164; Duncan, *Rule of Violence*, 41; Patrick Kessel and Giovanni Pirelli, *Le people algérien et la guerre* (Paris: François Maspero, 1962), 287, 350; Holmes Brown and Don Luce, *Hostages of War* (Washington, DC: Indochina Mobile Education Project, 1973), 71; Pham Tam, *Imprisonment and Torture in South Vietnam* (Nyack, NY: Fellowship of Reconciliation, 1969[?]), 8; Mark Lane, *Conversations with Americans* (New York: Simon and Schuster, 1970), 27, 85.

81. G. Flint Taylor, "Known Area 2 and 3 Torture Victims, 1972–1991 (4/7/04)," unpublished data.

82. Jerome Miller, *Last One Over the Wall*, 2nd ed. (Columbus: Ohio State University Press, 1998), 96.

83. ECHR, 413–23; Daniel Thomas, *The Helsinki Effect* (Princeton, NJ: Princeton University Press, 2001), 50–51.

84. Amalia Fleming, *A Piece of Truth* (London: Jonathan Cape, 1972), 235, 239, 248, 250; Deeley, *Beyond Breaking Point*, 65, 68–69, 72; Korovessis, *The Method*, 82; ECHR, 37, 45, 89, 175.

85. ECHR, 101, 415, 416.

86. Ole Rasmussen, "Medical Aspects of Torture," *Danish Medical Bulletin* 37, Sup. 1 (January 1990): 9. Similarly, Deeley reports for Greece twenty-three confirmed instances and fifty-three allegations of *falaka* and four confirmed instances and three allegations of electrotorture (*Beyond Breaking Point*, 66). For Spanish use of the *falaka* in this period, see Deeley, 112, 114.

87. Thomas Plate and Andrea Darvi, *Secret Police* (Garden City, NY: Doubleday, 1981), 176.

88. Antonio Cassese, *Inhuman States* (Cambridge, MA: Polity Press, 1996), 64. See also, for example, *The Citizen is Egyptian* (Giza, Egypt: Human Rights Center for the Assistance of Prisoners Campaign against Torture, 2002), 46.

89. Rasmussen, "Medical Aspects of Torture," 9.

90. AI, *Report on Torture* (London: Duckworth, 1973), 170, 209, 217; "Israel and Torture," *Times* (London), June 19, 1977, 17, 20; AI, *Torture in the Eighties* (London, 1984), 218, 237, 238; AI, *Amnesty International Report, 1993* (London, 1993), 288; AI, *Arming the Torturers*, ACT 40/01/97 (London, 1997) 7–8; AI, *Yemen*, MDE 31/001/1997; AI, *Kuwait*, MDE 17/001/1996; AI, *Lebanon*, MDE 18/005/2003, http://

www.amnesty.org; *Torture in Nyzschni Novgorod*, 6; Human Rights Watch, *Confession at Any Cost* (New York: Human Rights Watch, 1999), 24.

91. European Committee for the Prevention of Torture (http://www.cpt.coe.int/en/), *Bulgaria* (1995, 1999); *Croatia* (1998); *Georgia* (2001); *Greece* (1993, 1996, 1997); *Latvia* (2000); *Lithuania* (2000); *Macedonia* (1998, 2001, 2002); *Poland* (1996; 2000); *Portugal* (1992); *Romania* (1995, 1999); *Slovakia* (1995); *Ukraine* (1998, 2000); *Cyprus* (1992); AI, *Concerns in Europe*, EUR 01/006, 1997; AI, *Concerns in Europe*, EUR 01/001/1998, http://www.amnesty.org; Jørgen Thomsen and Maiken Mannstaedt, *The Green Birds* (Århus, Denmark: Danish Medical Group, 2000), 7.

92. Langguth, *Hidden Terrors*, 217.

93. Chevigny, Chevigny, and Karp, *Police Abuse in Brazil*, 33.

94. Rasmussen, "Medical Aspects of Torture," 9; AI, *Report on Torture*, 107; AI, *Rhodesia/Zimbabwe* (London, 1976), 10; AI, *Torture in the Eighties*, 106–7, 169; AI, *Report, 1986* (London, 1986), 46; AI, *Report, 1993*, 69, 84, 207; Don Foster, *Detention and Torture in South Africa*, with Dennis Davis and Diane Sandler (New York: St. Martin's, 1987), 103; National Academy of Sciences and Institute of Medicine, *Scientists and Human Rights in Somalia* (Washington, DC: National Academy Press, 1998), 34; Human Rights Watch, *Playing with Fire* (New York: Human Rights Watch, 2002), 76; Olivia Ball, *"Every Morning Just Like Coffee": Torture in Cameroon* (London: Medical Foundation for the Care of Victims of Torture, 2002), 44–45.

95. AI, *Report, 1993*, 84.

96. House Committee on International Relations, Subcommittee on International Organizations, *Human Rights in the Philippines*, 94th Cong., 2nd sess. 1976, 5; AI, *Report of an Amnesty International Mission to the Republic of the Philippines* (London, 1976), 22; AI, *Report of an Amnesty International Mission to the Republic of Korea* (London, 1976), 28; AI, *Report, 1993*, 213; AI, *Nepal*, ASA 31/016/2002, http://www.amnesty.org; Mary Salinsky, *Evidence of Torture* (London: Medical Foundation for the Care of Victims of Torture, 2001), 37–38.

Chapter 13
Water, Sleep, and Spice

1. Theodore Roosevelt to Hermann Speck von Sternberg, July 19, 1902, in *The Letters of Theodore Roosevelt*, ed. Elting Morison (Cambridge: Harvard University Press, 1931), 3:298.

2. Edward Peters, *Torture*, 2nd ed. (Philadelphia: University of Pennsylvania Press, 1996), 167.

3. Medical officer, cited in Patrick Duncan, *South Africa's Rule of Violence* (London: Methuen, 1964), 51. The most famous personal account is that of William Lithgow, pumped in Malaga during the Spanish Inquisition. See George Ryley Scott, *The History of Torture* (London: Torchstream, 1940), 174–76.

4. U.S. Navy Seal, cited in John Crewdson, " 'Waterboarding' Spurs Debate on What Is Torture," *Chicago Tribune*, December 28, 2005, sec. 1, p. 5.

5. The main accounts are from Syria in the 1980s, Iran in the 1930s, Nazi-occupied Belgium, and French colonies in the early twentieth century. Gérard de Lacaze-Duthiers, *La torture a travers les âges* (Herblay, Seine-et-Oise, France: Editions de l'idée libre, 1961), 124; P. Lansvreugt and R. Lemaitre, *Le calvaire de Breendonck* (Brussels: Serge Baguette, 1945), 46; Jules Wolf, *Le process de Breendonck* (Brussells: Maison F. Larcier, 1973), 32; Darius Rejali, *Torture and Modernity* (Boulder, CO: Westview, 1994), 76; Donne Raffat, *The Prison Papers of Bozorg Alavi* (Syracuse, NY: Syracuse University Press, 1985), 95; Amnesty International (AI), *Torture in the Eighties* (London, 1984), 243. Boiling or "blistering" was also a British military punishment in the eighteenth century. Scott Claver, *Under the Lash* (London: Torchstream, 1954), 21. For accounts of earlier periods, see Geoffrey Abbott, *Rack, Rope and Red-hot Pincers* (London: Headline Books, 1993), 109–10; Jean Kellaway, *The History of Torture and Execution* (New York: Lyons Press, 2000), 58.

6. Abbott, *Rack, Rope*, 114–16; Kellaway, *History of Torture*, 59; Brian Innes, *The History of Torture* (New York: St. Martin's, 1998), 61–63; Michael Kerrigan, *The Instruments of Torture* (New York: Lyons Press, 2001); 83–86; Cecil Roth, *The Spanish Inquisition* (New York: Norton, 1964), 95.

7. Lisa Silverman, *Tortured Subjects* (Chicago: University of Chicago Press, 2001), 46.

8. Stuart Creighton Miller, *Benevolent Assimilation* (New Haven, CD: Yale University Press, 1982), 167, 183, 184, 213, 225, 235, 248, 250; Richard Welch Jr., *Response to Imperialism* (Chapel Hill: University of North Carolina Press, 1979), 134–37, 144, 147; Willard Gatewood Jr., *Black Americans and the White Man's Burden, 1898–1903* (Urbana: University of Illinois Press, 1975), 278–79; Moorefield Storey and Marcial Lichauco, *The Conquest of the Philippines by the United States, 1898–1925* (New York: G. P. Putnam's Sons, 1926), 147–48; Henry Graff, ed., *American Imperialism and the Philippine Insurrection* (Boston: Little, Brown, 1969), 64–135. For a depiction, see Kerrigan, *The Instruments of Torture*, 82. Squire says pumping was used on mutineers, but there is no report of this. See Gatewood, *Black Americans*, 287; Amos Squire, *Sing Sing Doctor* (New York: Doubleday, Doran, 1935), 258.

9. Graff, *American Imperialism*, 92–93.

10. Roosevelt, *Letters*, 2:298.

11. Norman Thomas, "Justice to War's Heretics," *The Nation*, November 9, 1918, 547. The incident is discussed in detail in chapter 15, "Stress and Duress."

12. F. Dalton O'Sullivan, *Crime Detection* (Chicago: O'Sullivan Publishing House, 1928), 298.

13. "Statement of Mordehy Petcho," in *Case of Cohen and A. Laronovich and Case of M. Petcho*, PRO CO 733/413/6; "British Methods in Palestine," *Yorkshire Post*, November 23, 1938, and "Nazi Press Libel on British Troops," *Daily Telegraph*, November 23, 1938, in *Conduct of British Police and Troops*, PRO CO 733/371/2; Aubrey Lees, letter, in *Accusation of Police Shooting of Unarmed Prisoner in Jaffa*,

PRO CO 733/371/4; Charles Smith, "Communal Conflict and Insurrection in Palestine, 1936–1948," in *Policing and Decolonization*, ed. David M. Anderson and David Killingray (Manchester, England: Manchester University Press, 1992), 71.

14. R. John Pritchard and Sonia Magbanua Zaide, eds., *The Tokyo War Crimes Trial* (New York: Garland, 1981), 6:14168, 14170, 14181–82, 14184 (Shanghai); 12940 (Singapore); 13342, 13407, 13523 (Borneo); 13684 (Java); 13843 (Timor); 13193 (Burma); 7:15339, 15372–73, 15432 (Vietnam); Harriet Sergeant, *Shanghai* (London: Jonathan Cape, 1991), 334–35; Otto Tolischus, *Tokyo Record* (New York: Reynal and Hitchcock, 1943), 393–94; Lord Russell, *The Knights of Bushido* (London: Cassell, 1958), 178, 276; Felisa Syjuco, *The Kempei Tai in the Philippines* (Quezon City: New Day, 1988), 67; Jacques Le Bourgeois, *Saïgon sans la France* (Paris: Librairie Plon, 1949), 37; Stewart Wolf and Herbert Ripley, "Reactions Among Allied Prisoners of War Subjected to Three Years of Imprisonment and Torture by the Japanese," *American Journal of Psychiatry* 104 (1947): 183.

15. Chin Kee Onn, *Malaya Upside Down* (Singapore: Federal Publications, 1976), 117.

16. Yuki Tanaka, *Hidden Horrors* (Boulder, CO: Westview, 1996), 26–27; Russell, *The Knights of Bushido*, 198; Pritchard and Zaide, *Tokyo War Crimes Trial*, 13407.

17. "Rapport de M. Mairey, Directeur de la Sûreté sur le fonctionnement des forces de police en Algerie," in Pierre Vidal-Naquet, *La Raison d'état* (Paris: Éditions de Minuit, 1962), 81; Hafid Keramane, *La Pacification* (Lausanne: La Cité Éditeur, 1960), 15.

18. Wuillaume's report is available in Vidal-Naquet, *La Raison d'état*, 55–68, and translated in full in Pierre Vidal-Naquet, *Torture*, trans. Barry Richard (Harmondsworth, England: Penguin, 1963), 169–79. Notes to Wuillaume are given first to the English and then to the French editions (FE). The references to the *tuyau* are in Wuillaume, "Report," 173; "Rapport," 62 (FE).

19. Patrick Kessel and Giovanni Pirelli, *Le people algérien et la guerre* (Paris: François Maspero, 1962), 15, 21, 57, 58, 97, 187, 201, 217, 262, 409, 410, 430, 434, 498, 549, 591.

20. Ibid., 201.

21. Peter Deeley, *Beyond Breaking Point* (London: Arthur Barker, 1971), 83.

22. José Milton Ferreira de Almeida, cited in Archdiocese of São Paulo, *Torture in Brazil*, trans. Jaime Wright (New York: Vintage, 1986), 18. See also Deeley, *Beyond Breaking Point*, 99.

23. AI, *Torture in the Eighties*, 208–9; AI, *Chile*, AMR 22/03/87 (London, 1987), 23, 26; Aurora Foundation, *Report on the Violations of Human Rights in the Socialist Republic of Vietnam* (Atherton, CA: Aurora Foundation, 1989), 58.

24. Koude Koussetogue, *La Torture* (N'Djaména, Chad: Association Jeunessee Anti-Clivage, 1995), 11; *Images of Repression* (Mexico City: Human Rights Centre "Miguel Agustin Pro Juarez," 1999), 178.

25. Duncan Campbell and Suzanne Goldenberg, "The Afghan Gulag," *Guardian* (London), June 23, 2004, 2.

26. Human Rights Watch, *State of Pain: Torture in Uganda* (March 2004), Vol. 16, No. 4(A), 23.

27. "Chinon. 1st Richard, 1189," cited in Claver, *Under the Lash*, 4; W.N.T. Beckett, *A Few Naval Customs, Expressions, Traditions and Superstitions,* 2nd ed. (Portsmouth, England: Gieves, [1915]), 8.

28. Travers Twiss, ed., *The Black Book of the Admiralty*, reprint ed. (Abingdon, England: Professional Books, 1985), 3:233, 437, 439.

29. Abbott, *Rack, Rope*, 113; N.A.M. Rodger, *The Safeguard of the Sea* (New York: Norton, 1998), 1:322, 406; James Valle, *Rock and Shoals* (Annapolis, MD: Naval Institute Press, 1980), 38; C. R. Boxer, "The Dutch East-Indiamen," in *Dutch Merchants and Mariners in Asia, 1602–1795* (London: Variorum Reprints, 1988), 98; John Byrn Jr., *Crime and Punishment in the Royal Navy* (Aldershot, England: Scolar Press, 1989), 80.

30. Tom Lewis, "Punishment in Navies," *Navy News*, October 15, 2001, http://www.defence.gov.au/news/navynews, available at http://www.navy.gov.au/reserves/historyDocuments/Naval_Discipline.doc.

31. Ernestus Eremundus Frisius, cited in Abbott, *Rack, Rope*, 115. See also Kerrigan, *The Instruments of Torture*, 85–87; Innes, *The History of Torture*, 62–63.

32. Scott, *The History of Torture*, 177–78; Innes, *The History of Torture*, 62.

33. Abbott, *Rack, Rope*, 115.

34. Europeans also submerged accused witches, a practice that continued in some places up to the 1800s (Abbott, *Rack, Rope*, 113–14). This method did not require a ducking chair, and it was not expected that the woman would survive. It was in other words a method of execution, not torture.

35. Abbott, *Rack, Rope*, 116–21; Innes, *The History of Torture*, 65; Alice Morse Earle, *Curious Punishments of Bygone Days* (Montrclair, NJ: Patterson Smith, 1969), 11–17; Mel Melconian, email message to Gulf 2000 mailing list, March 1, 2004, https://www1.columbia.edu/sec/cu/sipa/GULF2000/.

36. Madras Commission, cited in Innes, *The History of Torture*, 157.

37. Abbott, *Rack, Rope*, 112–13, Claver, *Under the Lash*, 111; Boxer, "The Dutch East-Indiamen," 98; Rodger, *Safeguard of the Sea*, 1:322; Beckett, *Naval Customs*, 41.

38. My thanks to Alex Golubitsky for this insight. For the specific ships, see Rodger, *Safeguard of the Sea*, 1:71; N.A.M. Rodger, *The Wooden World* (Annapolis, MD: Naval Institute Press, 1986), inside jacket.

39. Claver, *Under the Lash*, 111; Beckett, *Naval Customs*, 12. Byrn finds no evidence of it in his study of the Leeward Islands Station (*Crime and Punishment*, 64–88).

40. Valle, *Rock and Shoals*, 41.

41. Abbott, *Rack, Rope*, 120–21. See also Earle, *Curious Punishments*, 17–23.

42. Valle, *Rock and Shoals*, 83.

43. *Sing Sing Prison* (New York: NY State Department of Correction, 1953), 5; for an illustration, see Innes, *The History of Torture*, 64; or Norval Morris and David Rothman, *The Oxford History of the Prison* (Oxford: Oxford University Press, 1995), 172.

44. E. C. Wines and Theodore Dwight, *Report on the Prisons and Reformatories of the United States and Canada*, 1867, reprint ed. (New York: AMS Press, 1973), 166.

45. *Fisher v. State*, 145 Miss. 116, 110 So. 361 (1926). See also National Commission on Law Observance and Enforcement, *Report on Lawlessness in Law Enforcement* (Washington, DC: U.S. Government Printing Office, 1931), 67. Hereafter cited as Wickersham Commission.

46. Ricardo Molas, *Historia de la Tortura* (Buenos Aires: Editorial Universitaria de Buenas Aires, 1984), 98; Tomasa Cuevas, *Prison of Women*, trans. and ed. Mary Giles (Albany: State University of New York Press, 1998), 64.

47. Pritchard and Zaide, *Tokyo War Crimes Trial*, 6:12938, 12940 (Singapore), 15366 (Vietnam); Russell, *The Knights of Bushido*, 278; J. Ingram Bryan, *Japanese All* (New York: E. P. Dutton, 1928), 142–43; Syjuco, *Kempei Tai*, 67; Tanaka, *Hidden Horrors*, 26–27; Taman Budiman, *Memoirs of an Unorthodox Civil Servant* (Kuala Lumpur: Heinemann Educational Books, 1979), 124.

48. See chapter 5, "Bathtubs."

49. Józef Garlinski, *Fighting Auschwitz* (London: Julian Friedmann, 1975), 149, 157.

50. Andrzej Czerkawski, *Aleja Szucha* (Warsaw: Sport i Turystyka, 1967), [7].

51. Seborova states he tied "women into a 'leap' with their heads bound tightly to their feet" and then "pushed their heads into a wash basin" (Milena Seborova, *A Czech Trilogy* [Rome: Christian Academy, 1990], 118). This may be a peculiar tying technique (for it would be hard to put the head into a basin when it is tied to the feet. It is more likely that Ramdor tied women's *hands* to their feet; this would be typical bucking. See also Lord Russell, *Scourge of the Swastika* (New York: Philosophical Library, 1954), 203.

52. Masuy, cited in Fabrice Laroche, "Les Français de la Gestapo," in *Histoire secrète de la Gestapo*, ed. Jean Dumont (Geneva: Editions de Crémille, 1971), 4:28.

53. Finn Palmstrom and Rolf Normann Torgersen, "Preliminary Report on Germany's Crimes against Norway [79-UK]," in International Military Tribunal (IMT), *Trial of the Major War Criminals* (Nuremberg: n.p., 1949), 39:212–13; Maynard M. Cohen, *A Stand against Tyranny* (Detroit: Wayne State University Press, 1997), 177–78; Radomir Luza, *The Hitler Kiss*, with Christina Vella (Baton Rouge: Louisiana State University Press, 2002), 194.

54. Raymond Rabemananjara, *Madagascar* (Paris: L'Harmattan, 2000), 42–60; Alec Mellor, *La Torture* (Paris: Horizons littéraires, 1949), 234; Charles Franklin, *The Third Degree* (London: Robert Hale, 1970), 145.

55. Wuillaume, "Report," 172–73; "Rapport," 60–62 (FE); "Rapport de M. Mairey," 81–82.

56. Kessel and Pirelli, *Le people algérien*, 7.

57. Keramane, *La Pacification*, 16.

58. Kessel and Pirelli, *Le people algérien*, 580. The modern Algerian *chiffon* may be built on this late development, "an enduring legacy of French colonial times" (Kerrigan, *The Instruments of Torture*, 87). It is also a rarely recorded phenomenon during the Franco-Algerian War.

59. Anthony Farrar-Hockley, *The Edge of the Sword* (London: Bucan and Enright, 1985), 184–86.
60. Charles Foley, *Island in Revolt* (London: Longmans, Green, 1962), 131.
61. John McGuffin, *The Guineapigs* (Harmondsworth, England: Penguin, 1974), 135–38.
62. Nguyen Xuan Tram, *From Mainland Hell to Island Hell* (Hanoi: Foreign Languages Publishing House, 1961), 26; Pham Tam, *Imprisonment and Torture in South Vietnam* (Nyack, NY: Fellowship of Reconciliation, 1969[?]), 8; Jean-Pierre Debris and André Menras, *Rescapés des bagnes de Saigon* (Paris: Les Editeurs Français Reunis, 1973), 47–50.
63. Tam, *Imprisonment and Torture*, 8; Debris and Menras, *Rescapés des bagnes*, 148–49; Holmes Brown and Don Luce, *Hostages of War* (Washington, DC: Indochina Mobile Education Project, 1973), 9, 72; Jean Lacouture, *Vietnam*, trans. Konrad Kellen and Joel Carmichael (New York: Vintage, 1966), 98; *In Thieu's Prisons* (Hanoi: Foreign Languages Publishing House, 1973), 76; Nguyen Dinh Thi, ed., *Les Prisonniers politiques* (Paris: Sudestasie, 1974), 102–3; *The Forgotten Prisoners of Ngyuen Van Thieu* (Paris: n.p., May 1973), 33.
64. Mark Lane, *Conversations with Americans* (New York: Simon and Schuster, 1970), 85, 121; *Veterans Testimony on Vietnam*, 92nd Congress, 1st sess., *Congressional Record*, vol. 117, part 8 (April 5–19, 1971), 9993; Al Santoli, *Everything We Had* (New York: Random House, 1981), 70.
65. Marcio Alves, *Torturas e Torturados* (Rio de Janeiro: Empresa Jornalística, 1966), 26.
66. Deeley, *Beyond Breaking Point*, 113.
67. Ejército de Liberación Nacional, "Denuncian torturas," *Punta Final*, August 1972, 28.
68. *Report of the Chilean National Commission on Truth and Reconciliation*, trans. Phillip E. Berryman (Notre Dame: University of Notre Dame Press, 1993), 1:134, 2:500, 644; AI, *Chile* (London, 1983), 9,18.
69. AI, *Report of an Amnesty International Mission to Argentina* (London, 1977), 37; Ole Rasmussen, "Medical Aspects of Torture," *Danish Medical Bulletin* 37, Sup. 1 (January 1990): 9.
70. Rasmussen, "Medical Aspects of Torture," 9.
71. See chapter 9, "Singing the World Electric."
72. "U.S. Interrogation Techniques," *USA Today*, June 23, 2004, 4A.
73. Interrogator Questions for Staff Sergeant, HHOC, 101st MI, March 28, 2004, DOD-021589, available at http://www.aclu.org; Interrogator Questions to Sergeant, 101st, MI, March 29, 2004, DOD-021613, available at http://www.aclu.org.
74. Crewdson, "Waterboarding Spurs Debate," sec. 1, p. 5.
75. Toni Locy and John Diamond, "Memo Lists Acceptable 'Aggressive' Interrogation Methods," *USA Today*, June 28, 2004, 5A; Michael Slackman, "What's Wrong with Torturing a Qaeda Higher-Up?" *New York Times*, May 16, 2004, sec. 4, p. 4.
76. Brian Ross and Richard Esposito, "CIA's Harsh Interrogation Techniques Described," *ABC News*, November 18, 2005, http://abcnews.go.com.

77. *Sing Sing Prison*, 5; Scott, *The History of Torture*, 243.

78. Abbott, *Rack, Rope*, 111.

79. *Sing Sing Prison*, 5.

80. Paul Hashagen, "The Development of the Fire Hose," *Firehouse Magazine*, September 1998, http://www.firehouse.com/magazine/american/colonial2.html.

81. Clare McKanna Jr. "Crime and Punishment: The Hispanic Experience in San Quentin, 1851–1880," *Southern California Quarterly* 72.1 (1990): 9–10.

82. Norman Thomas, *The Conscientious Objector in America* (New York: B. W. Huebsch, 1925), 154.

83. John McGuffin, *Internment* (Tralee, Republic of Ireland: Anvil, 1973), 44.

84. Ibid., 71.

85. Russell, *Scourge of the Swastika*, 202–3; Seborova, *A Czech Trilogy*, 118–19; Mark Mazower, *Inside Hitler's Greece* (New Haven, CT: Yale University Press, 1993), 239; "Statement of the Netherlands Government on the Prosecution and Punishment of the German War Criminals, [1726-PS]" in IMT, *Trial*, 27:519.

86. Vidal-Naquet, *La Raison d'état*, 286.

87. Human Rights Watch, *Turkey* 9:4 (March 1997), 14. For the countries listed, see *Veterans Testimony on Vietnam*, 9993; "Israel and Torture," *Times* (London), June 19, 1977, 20; *Black Book on the Militarist "Democracy" in Turkey* (Brussels: Info-Türk, 1986), 252; AI, *Torture in the Eighties*, 209.

88. Neil Mackay, "Iraq's Child Prisoners," *Sunday Herald* (Glasgow), August 1, 2004, 16.

89. S. N. Aggarwal, *The Heroes of Cellular Jail* (Patiala, India: Punjabi University Publication Bureau, 1995), 155.

90. Thomas, *Conscientious Objector*, 154–55, 160; Gerlof Homan, *American Mennonites and the Great War, 1914–1918* (Waterloo, Ontario: Herald Press, 1994), 115, 118.

91. O'Sullivan, *Crime Detection*, 298.

92. El Campesino (Valentin Gonzalez), *Listen Comrades*, trans. Ilsa Barea (Melbourne: William Heinemann, 1952), 143.

93. Cuevas, *Prison of Women*, 79; Wolf, *Le process de Breendonck*, 32, 50, 66, 70; Lansvreugt and Lemaitre, *Le calvaire de Breendonck*, 46.

94. Ian Cobain, "The Secrets of the London Cage," *Guardian* (London), November 12, 2005, 8.

95. Kessel and Pirelli, *Le people algérien*, 432, 455, 549.

96. AI, *Torture in Greece*, PUB 61/00/77 (London, 1977), 47; AI, *Torture in the Eighties*, 243; AI, *Chile* (1987), 22, 25; "Israel and Torture," 17, 18, 20.

97. Dan van der Vat, "German Border Police Tortured in Training," *Times* (London), March 2, 1973, 5.

98. Antonio Taguba, *Executive Summary of Article* 15-6 Investigation of 800th Military Police Brigade, May 20, 2004, http://www.msnbc.msn.com; AI, *USA: Human Dignity Denied*, AMR 51/145/2004, October 27, 2004, 24, http://www.amnesty.org; Eric Schmitt, "Task Force 6-26: In Secret Unit's 'Black Room,' a Grim Portrait of U.S. Abuse," *New York Times*, March 19, 2006, sec. 1, p. 1; Eric Schmitt, "Pentagon Study Describes Abuse by Units in Iraq," *New York Times*, June 17, 2006, A1.

99. Ross and Esposito, "CIA's Harsh Interrogation Techniques."

100. Deeley, *Beyond Breaking Point*, 28; See also Farrar-Hockley, *Edge of the Sword*, 215–16; Lawrence E. Hinkle and Harold G. Wolff, "Communist Interrogation and Indoctrination of 'Enemies of the State,' " A.M.A. *Archives of Neurology and Psychiatry* 76 (August 1956): 169.

101. Evgeni Genchev, ed., *Tales from the Dark* (Sofia, Bulgaria: Assistance Centre for Torture Survivors, 2003), 108–10.

102. Pablo Sulbarán, *La tortura en Venezuela* (Caracas: Publicaciones Seleven, 1979), 161–62.

103. Deeley, *Beyond Breaking Point*, 51.

104. Ibid., 78.

105. South Africa, Truth and Reconciliation Commission, *Report* (London: Macmillan, 1999), 168, 178.

106. Richard Claude, Eric Stover, and June Lopez, *Health Professionals and Human Rights in the Philippines* (Washington, DC: American Association for the Advancement of Science, 1987), 31.

107. *Ill-Treated and Killed Soldiers in the Soviet Army* (Århus, Denmark: Physicians for Human Rights, 1991), 12; M. Osman Rostar, *The Pulicharkhi Prison*, trans. and ed. Ehsanullah Azari (Peshawar, Pakistan: Writers Union of Free Afghanistan, 1991), 35.

108. U.S. Department of State, Bureau of Democracy, Human Rights, and Labor, "Turkey Country Report on Human Rights Practices for 1997" (1998), http://www.hri.org/docs/USSD-Rights/; AI, "Turkey," EUR 44/36/00 (July 2000), http://www.amnesty.org.

109. Ya'el Stein, *Torture of Palestinian Minors in the Gush Etzion Police Station*, trans. Zvi Shulman (Jerusalem: B'Tselem, 2001), 9, 15.

110. For example, the use of alcohol and sulfur in the burning of witches. See Abbott, *Rack, Rope*, 182–83.

111. IMT, *Trial*, 6:168; Bahman Nirumand, *Iran*, trans. Leonard Mins (New York: Monthly Review Press, 1969), 164; Archdiocese of São Paulo, *Torture in Brazil*, 22; Deeley, *Beyond Breaking Point*, 97; AI, *Mission to Argentina*, 39; AI, *Torture in the Eighties*, 141, 156; AI, *Syria*, MDE /24/09/87 (London, 1987), 19.

112. H. Hessell Tiltman, *The Terror in Europe* (New York: Frederick A. Stokes, 1932), 292; AI, *Amnesty International Report*, 1993 (London, 1993), 142.

113. Edmund Burke, *Speeches on the Impeachment of Warren Hastings* (London: Henry G. Bohn, 1857), 1:188.

114. Abbott, *Rack, Rope*, 183; Innes, *The History of Torture*, 158, 160; Philip Zimbardo, "Coercion and Compliance: The Psychology of Police Confessions," in *The Triple Revolution Emerging*, ed. Robert Perrucci and Marc Pilisuk (Boston: Little, Brown, 1971), 504.

115. John Beames, *Memoirs of a Bengal Civilian* (London: Chatto and Windus, 1961), 145. See also Zimbardo, "Coercion and Compliance," 504; Edmund Cox, *Police and Crime in India* (New Delhi: Manu, 1976), 106, 183; Charles Henderson, "Con-

trol of Crime in India," *Journal of the American Institute of Criminal Law and Crimonology* 4.378 (May 1913–March 1914): 381.

116. Daniel Mannix, *The History of Torture* ([New York]: Dorset, 1964), 178.

117. "Chapter 6—Laws of the Sea and Punishments" in *Customs of the Navy*, http://www.readyayeready.com; *Unchained Memories* (Boston: Bullfinch Press, 2002), 92, 96; Dwight Lowell Dumond, *Anti-Slavery* (Ann Arbor: University of Michigan Press, 1961), 249.

118. AI, *Torture in the Eighties*, 142, 201; Deeley, *Beyond Breaking Point*, 77; Morten Ekstrøm, Hans Draminsky Petersen, and Majken Marmstaedt, *Torture Continues in Indian Held Kashmir* (Århus, Denmark: Physicians for Human Rights, 1994), 19; European Commission of Human Rights, *The Greek Case* (Strasbourg: Council of Europe, 1970), 121; AI, *India* (London, 1988), 9; National Academy of Sciences and Institute of Medicine, *Scientists and Human Rights in Somalia* (Washington, DC: National Academy Press, 1998), 36; Michael Peel and Mary Salinsky, *Caught in the Middle* (Oxford: Alden Group, 2000), 42; Chris Mackey and Greg Miller, *The Interrogators* (New York: Little, Brown, 2004), 196.

119. Deeley, *Beyond Breaking Point*, 83; Alves, *Torturas e Torturados*, 27; AI, *Syria*, 19.

120. Innes, *The History of Torture*, 54.

121. Peel and Salinsky, *Caught in the Middle*, 42.

122. Osha Gray Davidson, "The Secret File of Abu Ghraib," *Rolling Stone*, August 18, 2004, 48–51.

123. Dumond, *Anti-Slavery*, 249; J. Ralph Jones, "Portraits of Georgia Slaves," *Georgia Review* 21 (1967): 269, 270; John Brown, *A Slave Life in Georgia*, ed. F. N. Boney (Savannah, GA: Beehive Press, 1991), 35, 38, 58.

124. Chapter 6, "Laws of the Sea and Punishments."

125. Molas, *Historia de la Tortura*, 98–99.

126. Gerard Lacourrège and Pierre Alibert, *Au temps des bagnes* (Paris: Editions Atlas, 1986), 134.

127. Gordon Thomas, *Journey Into Madness* (New York: Bantam, 1989), 333.

128. Duncan, *South Africa's Rule*, 28; Human Rights Watch, *Turkey*, 11 n. 15; 13.

129. Aubrey Lees, letter, PRO CO 733/371/4.

130. Mellor, *La Torture*, 218 n. 1.

131. Tam, *Imprisonment and Torture*, 8; Kessel and Pirelli, *Le people algérien*, 268, 543, 544; Kristin Ross, *Fast Cars, Clean Bodies* (Cambridge: MIT Press, 1995), 109.

132. AI, *Torture in the Eighties*, 110.

133. AI, *Report*, 1993, 208; AI, *Torture in the Eighties*, 166; AI, *Mexico*, AMR 4100081, http://www.amnesty.org.

134. Peters, *Torture*, 167.

135. Aubrey Lees, letter, PRO CO 733/371/4.

136. Zygmunt Sliwicki, *Meldunek z Pawiaka* (Warsaw: Panstwowe Wydawnictwo Naukowe, 1974), 194.

137. Kessel and Pirelli, *Le people algérien*, 651–52.

138. Syjuco, *Kempei Tai*, 67.

139. AI, *Torture in the Eighties*, 208–9.

140. Daniel Hémery, *Révolutionnaires vietnamiens et pouvoir colonial en Indochine* (Paris: François Maspero, 1975) 164; Essad-Bey, *OGPU*, trans. Huntley Paterson (New York: Viking, 1933), 250; Regina Domanska, *Pawiak* (Warsaw: Ksiazka i Wiedza, 1988), 98; *Black Book*, 254; Kessel and Pirelli, *Le people algérien*, 406; AI, *Torture in Greece*, 47; AI, *Report of an Amnesty International Mission to Israel and the Syrian Arab Republic* (London, 1974), 13; Falun Dafa Information Center, *Torture Methods Used on Falun Dafa Practitioners in Detention Centers and Forced Labor Camps in China*, http://back.faluninfo.net/torturemethods2/.

141. Henry Mayhew, cited in Abbott, *Rack, Rope*, 19.

142. Wickersham Commission, 38–39.

143. Peel and Salinsky, *Caught in the Middle*, 24.

144. Abbott, *Rack, Rope*, 19; O'Sullivan, *Crime Detection*, 297.

145. *Ill-Treated and Killed Soldiers*, 24.

146. Wickersham Commission, 126.

147. Richard A. Leo, "The Third Degree and the Origins of Psychological Interrogation in the United States," in *Interrogations, Confessions, and Entrapment*, ed. G. Daniel Lassiter (New York: Kluwer Academic, 2004), 46.

148. "Israel and Torture," 17; AI, *Torture in the Eighties*, 177–79; Brian Rappert, *Non-Lethal Weapons as Legitimizing Forces?* (London: Frank Cass, 2003), 211–19; *Arming the Torturers*, ACT 40/01/97 (London, 1997), 35; Mark Dow, *American Gulag* (Berkeley and Los Angeles: University of California Press, 2004), 327; European Committee for the Prevention of Torture, *Belgium* (2001) http://www.cpt.coe.int/en/.

149. Kessel and Pirelli, *Le people algérien*, 580; AI, *Report*, 1993, 50, 213.

150. AI, *Torture in the Eighties*, 158; Ginger Thompson and Gary Cohn, "Unearthed: Fatal Secrets," *Baltimore Sun*, June 11, 1995, 10A.

151. European Committee for the Prevention of Torture, *Ukraine* (2000), http://www.cpt.coe.int/en/.

152. Menachem Begin, *White Nights*, trans. Katie Kaplan (New York: Harper and Row, 1977), 108.

153. J.A.E. Fleming, "Pharmacological Aspects of Drowsiness," in *Forensic Aspects of Sleep*, ed. Colin Shapiro and Alexander Smith (Chichester, NY: John Wiley and Sons, 1997), 152.

154. Martha Lentz, Carol Landis, James Rothermel, and Joen Shaver, "Effects of Selective Slow Wave Sleep Disruption on Muscolskeletal Pain and Fatigue in Middle Aged Women," *Journal of Rheumatology* 26. (1999): 1586–92; S. Hakki Onen, Abdelkrim Alloui, Annette Gross, Alain Eschallier and Claude Dubray, "The Effects of Total Sleep Deprivation, Selective Sleep Interruption and Sleep Recovery on Pain Tolerance Thresholds in Healthy Subjects," *Journal of Sleep Research* 10 (2002): 35–42.

155. S. Hakki Onen, Abedelkrim Alloui, Didier Jourdan, Alain Eschallier, and Claude Dubray, "Effects of Rapid Eye Movement (REM) Sleep Deprivation on Pain Sensitivity in the Rat," *Brain Research* 900 (2001): 261–67.

156. M. Blagrove and L. Akehurst, "Effects of Sleep Loss on Confidence-Accuracy Relationships for Reasoning and Eyewitness Memory," *Journal of Experimental Psychological: Applied* 6.1 (2000): 59–73; Shapiro and Smith, *Forensic Aspects of Sleep,* 29–64, 99–130.

157. Walter R. Gove, "Sleep Deprivation: A Cause of Psychotic Disorganization," *American Journal of Sociology* 75.5 (1970): 782–99; Roger Eastmen, "When Will I Sleep Again?" *Airline Pilot,* November 1987, 10–14; David Tyler, "Psychological Changes During Experimental Sleep Deprviation," *Diseases of the Nervous System* 16.10 (1955): 293–99.

158. Innes, *The History of Torture,* 44.

159. Christiana Larner, *The Enemies of God* (Baltimore: Johns Hopkins University Press, 1981), 107; Diarmaid Macculloch, *The Reformation* (New York: Viking, 2003), 555.

160. Innes, *The History of Torture,* 117–18.

161. Ibid., 157.

162. Hémery, *Révolutionnaires vietnamiens,* 164–65.

163. See chapter 3, "Lights, Heat, and Sweat."

164. Scott, *The History of Torture,* 277; Deeley, *Beyond Breaking Point,* 139; 157.

165. Ervand Abrahamian, *Tortured Confessions* (Berkeley and Los Angeles: University of California Press, 1999). See chapter 3, "Lights, Heat, and Sweat."

166. Chief Müller, "Decree of the Chief of the Security Police and the SD, 12 June 1942 regarding third degree methods of interrogation [1531-PS]," in IMT, *Trial,* 27:326–27.

167. Cuevas, *Prison of Women,* 79, 183, 202–3.

168. Cobain, "Secrets of London Cage," 8. See chapter 15, "Forced Standing and Other Positions."

169. Stanley Hilton, *Hitler's Secret War in South America, 1939–1945* (Baton Rouge: Louisiana State University Press, 1981), 249, 251, 255–57.

170. AI, *Mission to Argentina,* 37; AI, *Report of an Amnesty International Mission to the Republic of Korea* (London, 1976), 28, 36–39; Alexandre Manuel, Rogério Carapinha, and Dias Neves, *PIDE* (Fundão, Portugal: Jornal do Fundão, 1974), 70, 98, 108–10, 128, 152, 180, 196.

171. Yuval Ginbar, *Back to a Routine of Torture,* trans. Jessica Bonn (Jerusalem: Public Committee against Torture in Israel, 2003), 45, 48–50, 54, 58, 61; Yuval Ginbar, *Flawed Defense,* trans. Jessica Bonn (Jerusalem: Public Committee against Torture in Israel, 2001), 29–31, 35, 37, 38, 41.

172. *Ashcraft v. Tennessee,* 322 U.S. 143 (1944), 155.

173. Esther Schrader and Greg Miller, "U.S. Officials Defend Interrogation Tactics," *Los Angeles Times,* May 13, 2004, A11; "Officials: Interrogation Techniques May Be Banned," May 14, 2004, http://www.cnn.com.

174. Ross and Esposito, "CIA's Harsh Interrogation Techniques."

175. International Committee of the Red Cross, *Report of the ICRC on the Treatment by Coalition Forces of Prisoners of War and other Protected Persons by the Geneva Conventions in Iraq during Arrest, Internment and Interrogation* (February 2004),

15. See also " 'Big Steve' and Abu Ghraib," Salon.com, March 31, 2006, http:// www.salon.com.

176. Jane Mayer, "The Experiment," *New Yorker*, July 11 and 18, 2005, 70–71.

177. Greg Miller, "Bound by Convention," *Stanford Magazine*, November–December 2004, http://www.stanfordalumni.org/news/magazine/2004/novdec; see also Mackey and Miller, *The Interrogators*, 288–89.

178. Beames, *Bengal Civilian*, 145.

Chapter 14
Stress and Duress

1. In *Discipline: Field Punishment*, PRO WO 32/5460 (Part I).

2. The main reports are Antonio Taguba, *Executive Summary of Article 15-6 Investigation of the 800th Military Police Brigade*, May 2004, http://www.msnbc.msn.com/id/4894001/, 14–22; International Committee of the Red Cross (ICRC), *On the Treatment by Coalition Forces of Prisoners of War and Other Protected Persons by the Geneva Conventions in Iraq during Arrest, Internment and Interrogation* (February 2004), 10–15; Seymour Hersh, "Torture at Abu Ghraib," *New Yorker*, May 10, 2004, 42–48; Seymour Hersh, "Chain of Command," *New Yorker*, May 17, 2004, 38–43; Seymour Hersh, "The Gray Zone," *New Yorker*, May 24, 2004, 38–44; Mark Danner, "Torture and Truth," *New York Review of Books*, June 10, 2004, 46–47, 50; Mark Danner, "The Logic of Torture," *New York Review of Books*, June 24, 2004, 70–74; Mark Danner, "Abu Ghraib: The Hidden Story," *New York Review of Books*, October 7, 2004, 44–50; Matt Kelley, "Intelligence Agents Encouraged Abuse," Associated Press, May 30, 2004, http://web.lexis-nexis .com; Matt Kelley, "Four U.S. Soldiers Charged with Abuse," Associated Press, July 29, 2003, http://web.lexis-nexis.com; Terence Chea, "California Guardsman Alleges Abuse in Iraq," Associated Press, June 9, 2004, http://web.lexis-nexis.com; Josh White, "Three More Navy Seals Face Abuse Charges," *Washington Post*, September 25, 2004, A16; Chris Mackey and Greg Miller, *The Interrogators* (New York: Little, Brown, 2004), 195; Josh White, "Soldier's 'Wish Lists' of Detainee Tactics Cited," *Washington Post*, April 19, 2005, A16; Eric Schmitt, "3 in 82nd Airborne Say Beating Iraqi Prisoners Was Routine," *New York Times*, September 23, 2005, A1; Eric Schmitt, "Task Force 6-26: In Secret Unit's 'Black Room,' a Grim Portrait of U.S. Abuse," *New York Times*, March 19, 2006, sec. 1, p. 1; Eric Schmitt, "Pentagon Study Describes Abuse by Units in Iraq," *New York Times*, June 17, 2006, A1; Peter Sleeth, "Killing in Iraq Unleashes Soldiers' Fury," *Oregonian*, December 12, 2004, A01; Gen. Ricardo Sanchez to C2, Combined Joint Task Force Seven, Baghdad Iraq 09335; C3, Combined Joint Task Force Seven, Baghdad, Iraq 09355; and Commander 305th Military Intelligence Brigade, Baghdad, Iraq 09335, "CJTF-7 Interrogation and Counter-Resistance Policy," September 14, 2003, available at http://www.aclu.org; "US Faces Prison Ship Allegations," *BBC News*, June 29, 2005, http://news.bbc.co.uk; Neil Mackay, "Iraq's

Child Prisoners," *Sunday Herald* (Glasgow), August 1, 2004, 16; Matthew D. La Plante, "Utah GI Exposed Abuses at Prison," *Salt Lake Tribune*, August 2, 2005, A1; Scott Gold, "5 California Guardsmen Face Charges of Abusing Iraqis," *Los Angeles Times*, August 23, 2005, A1; and Human Rights Watch, *Leadership Failure: Firsthand Accounts of Torture of Iraqi Detainees by the US Army's 82nd Airborne Division* (September 2005), 17: 3(G). A full list of torture techniques (identified by government source) can be found in Emily Bazelon, Phillip Carter, and Dahlia Lithwick, "What is Torture?—An Interactive Primer on American Interrogation," Slate.com (accessed November 13, 2005), http://www.slate/com/id/2119122/sidebar/21119631.

Electrotorture was documented in Danner, "Abu Ghraib," 44; Gold, "5 California Guardsmen," A1; Miles Moffeit, "Wider Iraqi Abuse Shown," *Denver Post*, May 26, 2004, A1; T. Christian Miller, "Ex-Detainees Sue 2 U.S. Contractors," *Los Angeles Times*, June 10, 2004, A9; Luke Harding, "Torture Commonplace, Say Inmates Families," *Guardian* (London), May 3, 2004, 5; Ghaith Abdul-Ahad, "More Iraqis Allege Abuse by U.S. Military," Reuters, May 4, 2004, http://www.yahoo.com; Viveca Novak and Douglas Waller, "New Abuse Charges," *Time*, June 28, 2004, http://www.time.com/time/; Sam Hananel, "Amnesty International Seeks Military's Taser Files," Associated Press, November 29, 2004, http://www.yahoo.com; and Amnesty International, *USA: Human Dignity Denied*, AMR 51/145/2004, October 27, 2004, 24, http://www.amnesty.org. The use of irritants is documented in Osha Gray Davidson, "The Secret File of Abu Ghraib," *Rolling Stone*, August 18, 2004, 48–51.

3. ICRC, *Treatment by Coalition Forces*, 12, 15, 16; Taguba, *Executive Summary*, 15; Hersh, "Torture at Abu Ghraib," 44; Danner, "Torture and Truth," 47; Danner, "Logic of Torture," 71–72; Danner, "Abu Ghraib," 47.

4. Human Rights Watch, *Leadership Failure*, 5, 12.

5. Taguba, *Executive Summary*, 18; Danner, "Abu Ghraib," 47; Danner, "Logic of Torture," 71–72; Jackie Spinner, "Soldier: Unit's Role was to Break Down Prisoners," *Washington Post*, May 8, 2004, A1.

6. ICRC, *Treatment by Coalition Forces*, 12, 13; Taguba, *Executive Summary*, 14–16; Danner, "Torture and Truth," 47; Danner, "Logic of Torture," 71–72; Danner, "Abu Ghraib," 47; Moffeit, "Wider Iraqi Abuse Shown," A1; Ghaith Abdul-Ahad, Josh White, Christian Davenport, and Scott Higham, "Yet More Photos of US Brutality Published," *Washington Post*, May 21, 2004, A1.

7. ICRC, *Treatment by Coalition Forces*, 10, 12, 14, 15; Taguba, *Executive Summary*, 14; Danner, "Torture and Truth," 47; Danner, "Logic of Torture," 71–72; Douglas Jehl, Eric Schmitt, and Kate Zernike, "U.S. Rules on Prisoners Seen as a Back and Forth of Mixed Messages," *New York Times*, June 22, 2004, A6.

8. Schmitt, "3 in 82nd Airborne," A1; Schmitt, "Pentagon Study Describes Abuse," A1.

9. Schmitt, "Task Force 6-26," sec. 1, p. 1.

10. Lawrence E. Hinkle and Harold G. Wolff, "Communist Interrogation and Indoctrination of 'Enemies of the State,'" A.M.A. *Archives of Neurology and Psychiatry* 76 (August 1956): 134.

11. The Old Officer, "Cautions and Advices to Officers of the Army," in Scott Claver, *Under the Lash* (London: Torchstream, 1954), 13.

12. Claver, *Under the Lash*, 14. See also Karen Farrington, *Dark Justice* (New York: Smithmark, 1996), 115. Illustrated in Claver, *Under the Lash*, facing 16.

13. Claver, *Under the Lash*, 13; Farrington, *Dark Justice*, 115; and Alice Morse Earle, *Curious Punishments of Bygone Days* (Montclair, NJ: Patterson Smith, 1969), 119–27. Illustrated in Claver, *Under the Lash*, facing 12; and Earle, *Curious Punishments*, facing 119.

14. Old Officer, cited in Claver, *Under the Lash*, 13. See also Jean Kellaway, *The History of Torture and Execution* (New York: Lyons Press, 2000), 126; and George Ryley Scott, *The History of Torture* (London: Torchstream, 1940), 243–44.

15. Claver, *Under the Lash*, 113–17, 123; John Byrn, *Crime and Punishment in the Royal Navy* (Aldershot, England: Scolar Press, 1989), 79–80.

16. Claver, *Under the Lash*, 113.

17. Ibid., 35, 117; James Armstrong with William Elliott, *Legion of Hell* (London: Sampson Low, Marston, [1936]), 167.

18. Francis Grose, *Military Antiquities*, cited in Claver, *Under the Lash*, 11. Illustrated in Geoffrey Abbott, *Rack, Rope and Red-hot Pincers* (London: Headline Books, 1993), facing 86.

19. Claver, *Under the Lash*, 117.

20. Scott, *The History of Torture*, 111–16; Brian Innes, *The History of Torture* (New York: St. Martin's, 1998), 154; Daniel Mannix, *The History of Torture* ([New York]: Dorset, 1964), 159.

21. Claver, *Under the Lash*, 36; Mannix, *The History of Torture*, 160.

22. Commander and Chief of Egyptian Expeditionary Force to War Office, in *Discipline: Field Punishment*.

23. On Field Punishment Number 1, see PRO WO 32/5460; PRO WO 32/5461; PRO WO 32/9543.

24. War Office, *Minute Paper*, April 14, 1881, PRO WO 32/6045; War Office, "Suggestions for Punishments in Compliance with Confidential Minute dated 19.5.81," PRO WO 32/6045.

25. War Office, *Minute Paper*, 3.

26. See C. H. Ellice, *Memorandum on Various Methods [of Punishment?] adopted in Foreign Armies for Soldiers in the Field*, July 9, 1879, PRO WO 32/5460. There is also a subsequent handwritten report submitted by a captain in the Intelligence Branch that adds further details on French colonial punishments. See Captain J. S. Rothwill[?], *Means of Preserving Discipline in the Field in Foreign Armies*, January 12, 1881, PRO WO 32/6045.

27. Ellice, *Memorandum*, 5.

28. Ibid., 7.

29. Ibid., 9.

30. War Office, *Minute Paper*, 3.

31. Resident of Wickford to War Office, December 12, 1916, in *Discipline: Field Punishment*.

32. Resident of Wickford.

33. General Sir Haig to War Office, in *Discipline: Field Punishment*.

34. Commander and Chief of Egyptian Expeditionary Force.

35. War Office Memorandum, January 12, 1917, in *Discipline: Field Punishment*.

36. War Office and Admiralty, "Rules for Field Punishment," in *UK Police Unit; Cyprus*, PRO CO 1037/52.

37. See chapter 3, "Lights, Heat, and Sweat."

38. David Anderson and David Killingray, eds., *Policing the Empire* (Manchester, England: Manchester University Press, 1991).

39. Innes, *The History of Torture*, 154–55, 157–58.

40. Ibid., 155; Cecil Walsh, *Crime in India* (London: Ernest Benn, 1930), 282–84.

41. Barindra Kumar Ghose, *The Tale of My Exile* (Pendicherry, India: Arya Office, 1922), 76, 92–93, 98–99, 131; S. N. Aggarwal, *The Heroes of Cellular Jail* (Patiala, India: Punjabi University Publication Bureau, 1995), 104, 148, 153–55, 160, 205, 171; R. C. Majumdar, *Penal Settlement in Andamans* (New Delihi: Government of India, 1975), 143–257; Ujjwal Singh, *Political Prisoners in India* (Delhi: Oxford University Press, 1998), 57. There are, as Amitav Ghosh observes, resemblances between the procedures in the Andamans and those used a century alter at Abu Ghraib (see Amitav Ghosh, "The Theater of Cruelty," *The Nation*, July 18, 2005, 31–32). Ghosh draws attention mainly to issues of culture and meaning, focusing on nakedness, isolation, and tattooing; my focus is mainly on the physical techniques of torture, which as I argue, belong to the long traditon of Anglo-Saxon modern.

42. Shri Savarkar, *The Story of My Transportation for Life*, trans. V. N. Naik ([Bombay]: Sadbhakti, 1950), opposite 208. See also Aggarwal, *Heroes of Cellular Jail*, 104, 151, 155, 160, 205.

43. Aggarwal, *Heroes of Cellular Jail*, 104, 141, 154–55, 160. Illustrated in Savarkar, *Story of My Transportation*, opposite 80 and 306; and Aggarwal, following 110.

44. Mary Salinsky and Liv Tigerstedt, *Evidence of Torture* (London: Medical Foundation for the Care of Victims of Torture, 2001), 40.

45. Savarkar, *Story of My Transportation*, 143, 418; Aggarwal, *Heroes of Cellular Jail*, 92, 99, 148, 171.

46. John McGuffin, *Internment* (Tralee, County Kerry: Anvil, 1973), 44, 64.

47. Lester Hutchinson, *Conspiracy at Meerut* (New York: Arno, 1972), 70–71. The Mongols spread the practice of rolling victims in rugs and beating them to death. In the thirteenth century, the punishment was reserved for Mongol princes whose blood could not be shed. The Mongol ruler, Hülegü, applied this punishment to the last caliph of Baghdad in 1258, a story that became legendary in the Islamic world (see J. A. Boyle, *The Cambridge History of Iran* [Cambridge: Cambridge University Press, 1968], 5:349).

48. Naomi Shepherd, *Ploughing Sand* (New Brunswick, NJ: Rutgers University Press, 1999), 212. For more on policing in this period, see Shepherd, 272–73; Charles Smith, "Communal Conflict and Insurrection in Palestine, 1936–1948," in *Policing and Decolonization*, ed. David M. Anderson and David Killingray (Manchester, England: Manchester University Press, 1992), 63–66; Martin Kolinsky, *Law, Order and Riots in Mandatory Palestine, 1928–1935* (London: St. Martin's, 1993); James Lunt, *Imperial Sunset* (London: MacDonald, 1981). For Duff's own narratives, see Douglas Duff, *Sword for Hire* (London: John Murray, 1934); Douglas Duff, *Palestine Unveiled* (London: Blackie and Son, 1938); and Douglas Duff, *May the Winds Blow* (London: Hollis and Carter, 1948).

49. *Conduct of British Police and Troops*, PRO CO 733/371/2; *The Miska Case*, PRO CO 733/371/3; *Accusation of Police Shooting Unarmed Prisoner in Jaffa*, PRO CO 733/371/4; *Conduct of British Police and Troops: Searches for Arms*, PRO CO 733/413/3; *Conduct of British Police and Troops: Shooting of Hospital Patient*, PRO CO 733/413/5; *Case of Cohen and A. Laronovich and Case of M. Petcho*, PRO CO 733/413/6; *Conduct of British Police and Troops: General Representations*, PRO CO 733/428/1; *Palestine: Internal Matters*, PRO FO 371/21881. For other accounts, see Shepherd, *Ploughing Sand*, 213–15; Smith, "Communal Conflict," 66–71.

50. Aubrey Lees to Friend, November 1938, in *Accusation of Police Shooting Unarmed Prisoner in Jaffa*, PRO CO 733/371/4. For Lees' other reports, see Shepherd, *Ploughing Sand*, 213–14.

51. *Condition and Conduct: Lord Wedgood's Enquiry*, PRO CO 733/434/7.

52. See, for example, American Commission on Conditions in Ireland, *Evidence on Conditions in Ireland* (Washington, DC: Bliss Building, [1921]), 107–9, 778–83, 789–91. James Murdoch, who studied Japanese police torture in this period, observes that while torture was common in Japan, "There is nothing that the Japanese Gendarmerie (at all times a splendidly trained force) did in either Korea or Formosa that cannot be paralleled to the fullest extent by the acts of the "Blacks and Tans" and the "Auxilliaries" in Ireland in 1920–1." See James Murdoch, *A History of Japan*, revised and edited by Joseph Longford (London: Kegan Paul, Trench Trubner, 1926), 3:337–38 n. 1.

53. Alexander Rubowitz was allegedly tortured to death at the hands of Major Farran's counterinsurgency squad, but as his body was never found, the allegations could never be confirmed and the techniques are unknown. See Smith, "Communal Conflict," 76–77; PRO CO 537/3872 (Outrages: Case of Major Farran); PRO CO 537/2302 (Case of Major Farran); David Charters, "Special Operations in Counter-Insurgency: The Farran Case, Palestine 1947," *Journal of the Royal United Services Institute* 124 (1979): 56–61; Roy Farran, *Winged Dagger* (London: Collins, 1947); Sumner Welles, "End of British Rule in Palestine is Termed Urgent Task of U.N.," *New York Herald Tribune*, August 12, 1947, 25; "Zionists Ask Purge of Palestine Police," *New York Times*, June 16, 1947, 10; Julian Louis Meltzer, "U.N. Body Scores Palestine Terror; More Britons Shot," *New York Times*, June 30, 1947, 1, 2.

54. Abbott, *Rack, Rope*, 20–23; Innes, *The History of Torture*, 142–44.

55. Committee investigating Birmingham prison, cited in Innes, *The History of Torture*, 143.

56. Innes, *The History of Torture*, 143.

57. Stephen Humphries, *Hooligans or Rebels?* (Oxford: Basil Blackwell, 1981), 216, 223.

58. Claver, *Under the Lash*, 14.

59. Abbot, *Rack, Rope*, 135.

60. Charles Mercer, *Legion of Strangers* (New York: Holt, Rinehart and Winston, 1964), 190; Geoffrey Bocca, *La Légion!* (New York: Thomas Crowell, 1964), 123; Alfred Perrott-White, *French Legionnaire* (Caldwell, ID: Caxton Printers, 1951), 94; Armstrong, *Legion of Hell*, 167, 202–3; Reginald Forbes, *Red Horizon* (London: Sampson Low, Marston, [1932]), 7, 25, 71; Ex-Légionnairre 1384 [John Harvey] with W. J. Blackledge, *Hell Hounds of France* (London: Sampson, Low, Marston, [1932]), 29, 59, 198–202; Angus McLean, *Vive la Legion* (London: Sampson, Low, Marston, [1937]), 149–50, 220, 223–24.

61. Mercer, *Legion of Strangers*, 190. O'Balance denies flogging ever occurred in the Legion, while "Tiger" O'Reilly's account seems to see whips everywhere. As I commented in chapter 12, both accounts strain credibility (Edgar O'Balance, *The Story of the French Foreign Legion* (London: Faber and Faber, 1961), 240; William Elliott, *The Tiger of the Legion* [New York: Greenberg, 1930], 122–31, 210–16).

62. Rothwill, *Means of Preserving Discipline*, 9.

63. Mercer, *Legion of Strangers*, 191.

64. Erwin Rosen [Carlé], *In the Foreign Legion* (London: Duckworth, 1910), 228–29.

65. See ibid., 228–30; Mercer, *Legion of Strangers*, 191, 195; Hugh Mcleave, *The Damned Die Hard* (New York: Saturday Review Press, 1973), 160; Michael Donovan, *March or Die!* (London: Cassell, 1932), 81.

66. Mcleave, *The Damned Die Hard*, 160.

67. A. R. Cooper with Sydney Tremayne, *The Man Who Liked Hell* (London: Jarrolds, 1938), 121. See also Zosa Szajkowski, *Jews and the Foreign Legion* (New York: Ktav, 1975), 7–8.

68. Rosen, *In the Foreign Legion*, 230.

69. Mercer, *Legion of Strangers*, 191; Cooper, *Man Who Liked Hell*, 121.

70. Rosen, *In the Foreign Legion*, 230; McLean, *Vive la Legion*, 220; Armstrong, *Legion of Hell*, facing 206; Elliott, *Tiger of the Legion*, 218. Photographed in Armstrong, *Legion of Hell*, facing 220.

71. Armstrong, *Legion of Hell*, 202.

72. McLean, *Vive la Legion*, 220; Perrott-White, *French Legionnaire*, 123; O'Balance, *French Foreign Legion*, 240; Szajkowski, *Jews and Foreign Legion*, 112; Armstrong, *Legion of Hell*, 200–201.

73. McLean, *Vive la Legion*, 220.

74. Armstrong, *Legion of Hell*, 201.

75. Ibid., 202. See also Elliott, *Tiger of the Legion*, 217.

76. Forbes, *Red Horizon*, 162; Szajkowski, *Jews and Foreign Legion*, 10; McLean, *Vive la Legion*, 222; Rosen, *In the Foreign Legion*, 70–71, 242–43; Elliott, *Tiger of the*

Legion, 216; Ernst Löhndorff, *Hell in the Foreign Legion*, trans. Gerard Shelley (New York: Greenberg, 1932), 117; Jacques Weygand, *Légionnaire*, trans. Raymond Johnes (London: George Harrap, 1952), 64–65; Bennett Doty, *The Legion of the Damned* (New York: Century Co., 1928), 37.

77. Löhndorff, *Hell in Foreign Legion*, 116–17, 135, 174, 201, 207 251; O'Balance, *French Foreign Legion*, 240; Perrott-White, *French Legionnaire*, 123; Doty, *Legion of the Damned*, 37, 275.

78. Armstrong, *Legion of Hell*, 167–68.

79. Bocca, *La Légion!* 123; Ex-Légionnairre 1384, *Hell Hounds of France*, 31; Michael Alexander, *The Reluctant Legionnaire* (New York: E. P. Dutton, 1956), 147.

80. World Jewish Congress, "Eye Witness Report," cited in Szajkowski, *Jews and Foreign Legion*, 112.

81. Szajkowski, *Jews and Foreign Legion*, 8, 10; Perrott-White, *French Legionnaire*, 123; Mercer, *Legion of Strangers*, 191, 194; Cooper, *Man Who Liked Hell*, 120; McLeave, *The Damned Die Hard*, 160; G. Ward Price, *In Morocco with the Legion* (London: Jarrolds, 1934), 227.

82. *Tombre* (Alexander, *The Reluctant Legionnaire*, 147; Mercer, *Legion of Strangers*, 194); *Tombeau* (Bocca, *La Légion!* 123; Szajkowski, *Jews and Foreign Legion*, 112); *Tombeaux* (Szajkowksi, 102–3, 112); *Tombe* (Szajkowski, 8).

83. Löhndorff, *Hell in Foreign Legion*, 293–94; Szajkowski, *Jews and Foreign Legion*, 8, 112; Mclean, *Vive la Legion*, 139; James Wellard, *The French Foreign Legion* (Boston: Little, Brown, 1974), 17.

84. Löhndorff, *Hell in Foreign Legion*, 294; Szajkowski, *Jews and Foreign Legion*, 8, 10; Elliott, *Tiger of the Legion*, 214; Armstrong, *Legion of Hell*, 166, 200; Mclean, *Vive la Legion*, 223; Doty, *Legion of the Damned*, 275.

85. Feet (Perrott-White, *French Legionnaire*, 118; Mercer, *Legion of Strangers*, 191); thumbs (Armstrong, *Legion of Hell*, 167; Donovan, *March or Die!* 81); hands (Elliott, *Tiger of the Legion*, 129, 213).

86. Jacques-Guy Petit, *Ces Peines obscures* (Paris: Fayard, 1990), 500.

87. Schoelcher, speech, January 5, 1849, cited in ibid., 500.

88. Petit, *Ces Peines obscures*, 500.

89. Ibid.

90. Ibid., 501.

91. F.A.F. de la Rochefoucauld-Liancourt, *Histoire des torture au XIXme siècle* (Paris: Typographie de Morris, 1859), 214–15.

92. Ibid., 221.

93. Petit, *Ces Peines obscures*, 501.

94. Gerard Lacourrège and Pierre Alibert, *Au temps des bagnes* (Paris: Editions Atlas, 1986), 138. For accounts of the prisons, see Lacourrège and Alibert; Michel Devèze, *Cayenne* (Paris: René Julliard, 1965); Peter Redfield, *Space in the Tropics* (Berkeley and Los Angeles: University of California Press, 2000), 51–111; Jean-Claude Michelot, *La Guillotine sèche* (Paris: Fayard, 1981), 177–95; Michel Bourdet-Pléville, *Justice in Chains*, trans. Anthony Rippon (London: Robert Hale,

1960), 84–95; Marion Godfory and Stanislas Fautré, *Bagnards* ([Paris]: Editions du Chêne, 2002), 130–37, 152–57.

95. Charles Franklin, *The Third Degree* (London: Robert Hale, 1970), 145.

96. Lacourrège and Alibert, *Au temps des bagnes*, 135, 138–44.

97. Eric Fougère, *Le grand livre du bagne* (French Guiana: Editions Orphie, 2002), 88; Lacourrège and Alibert, *Au temps des bagnes*, 134–35. Though it is possible the *falaka* arrived with Arab transports (Godfory and Fautré, *Bagnards*, 136–37).

98. Lacourrège and Alibert, *Au temps des bagnes*, 141–44, 150.

99. Ibid., 141.

100. Fougère, *Le grand livre du bagne*, 74.

101. Procureur général Cordeil, cited in Lacourrège and Alibert, *Au temps des bagnes*, 141.

102. Lacourrège and Alibert, *Au temps des bagnes*, 144.

103. Abbott, *Rack, Rope*, 181–82.

104. Szajkowski, *Jews and Foreign Legion*, 166.

105. Andrée Viollis, *Indochine S.O.S.* (Paris: Gallimard, 1935), 21. See also Daniel Hémery, *Révolutionnaires vietnamiens et pouvoir colonial en Indochine* (Paris: François Maspero, 1975), 164, 457–58.

106. Hémery, *Révolutionnaires vietnamiens*, 164.

107. Ibid., 457.

108. John Brown, *A Slave Life in Georgia*, edited F. N. Boney (Savannah, GA: Beehive Press, 1991), 35–39, 54–59, 97–98, 157–59.

109. Dwight Lowell Dumond, *Anti-Slavery* (Ann Arbor: University of Michigan Press, 1961), 116, 251; J. Ralph Jones, "Portraits of Georgia Slaves," *Georgia Review* 21 (1967), 269.

110. "Narrative and Testimony of Rev. Horace Moulton," in *American Slavery As It Is* (New York: Arno Press, 1968), 20.

111. Brown, *Slave Life in Georgia*, 37.

112. Mannix, *The History of Torture*, 202.

113. Hilde Isolde Reiter, cited in H. Hessell Tiltman, *The Terror in Europe* (New York: Frederick Stokes, 1932), 400. See also Tiltman, 398.

114. Jean Baptiste Debret, *Viagem Pitoresca e Histórica ao Brasil* (São Paulo: Livraria Martins, 1941), vol. 1, plate 25; Kellaway, *History of Torture*, 123.

115. Brown, *Slave Life in Georgia*, 35. See also Jones, "Portraits of Georgia Slaves," 269.

116. Dumond, *Anti-Slavery*, 115, 254; Paul Finkelman, *Slavery in the Courtroom* (Washington, DC: Library of Congress, 1985), 171

117. James Valle, *Rocks and Shoals* (Annapolis, MD: Naval Institute Press, 1980), 79.

118. *Sing Sing Prison* (New York: NY State Department of Correction, 1953), 6; Norval Morris and David Rothman, *The Oxford History of the Prison* (Oxford: Oxford University Press, 1995), 173.

119. Earle, *Curious Punishments*, 132; Elisha Black, cited in Jeptha Simms, *The Frontiersmen of New York* (Albany, NY: Geo. C. Riggs, 1883), 2:167.

120. Earle, *Curious Punishments*, 128.

121. Ibid., 131.

122. Valle, *Rocks and Shoals*, 41.

123. Ibid., 83. The practice was not new in the United States; Puritans practiced gagging, and after its abolition in the army, it remained a common punishment for schoolchildren (see Farrington, *Dark Justice*, 121; Earle, *Curious Punishments*, 101–5).

124. Russell Weigley, *History of the United States Army* (New York: Macmillan, 1967), 231–32; Bruce Catton, *A Stillness at Appomattox* (Garden City, NY: Doubleday, 1954), 32–33, 135–36; Bell Irvin Wiley, *The Life of Billy Yank* (Baton Rouge: Louisiana State University Press, 1971), 195; Mackey and Miller, *The Interrogators*, 282–83.

125. National Commission on Law Observance and Enforcement, *Report on Lawlessness in Law Enforcement* (Washington, DC: U.S. Government Printing Office, 1931), 38. Hereafter cited as Wickersham Commission.

126. Earle, *Curious Punishments*, 134–35.

127. Valle, *Rocks and Shoals*, 84.

128. Ellice, *Memorandum*, 1. See also Rothwill, *Means of Preserving Discipline*, 23–24.

129. Fort Scott National Historic Site, "Guardhouse-Tools and Equipment," http://www.nps.gov/fosc/guard4.htm.

130. Valle, *Rocks and Shoals*, 91.

131. Norman Thomas, "Justice to War's Heretics," *The Nation*, November 9, 1918, 547; Judah Magnes, *Amnesty for Political Prisoners* (New York: National Civil Liberties Bureau, 1919), 9.

132. Norman Thomas, *The Conscientious Objector in America* (New York: B. W. Huebsch, 1925), 183, 185, 193, 195–96, 198.

133. Ibid., 183–87, 195–96.

134. Thomas, *Conscientious Objector*, 144–60, 183–98, 239–43; Thomas, "Justice to War's Heretics," 547–48; Magnes, *Amnesty for Political Prisoners*, 9; *The Facts about Conscientious Objectors in the United States (Under the Selective Service Act of May 18, 1917)* (New York: National Civil Liberties Bureau, 1918), 20; Gerlof Homan, *American Mennonites and the Great War, 1914–1918* (Waterloo, Ontario: Herald Press, 1994) 115, 118, 119. Kohn offers a complete list of prisoners and gathers as much as exists in the official government record. See Stephen M. Kohn, *American Political Prisoners* (Westport, CT: Praeger, 1994).

135. Homan, *American Mennonites*, 115.

136. E. C. Wines and Theodore Dwight, *Report on the Prisons and Reformatories of the United States and Canada, 1867*, reprint ed. (New York: AMS Press, 1973), 165.

137. *Sing Sing Prison*, 6.

138. Wines and Dwight, *Report on Prisons*, 165.

139. Morris and Rothman, *Oxford History of Prison*, 121, 123.

140. F. Dalton O'Sullivan, *Crime Detection* (Chicago: O'Sullivan Publishing House, 1928), 295.

141. *Macon Daily Telegraph*, cited in Frank Tannenbaum, *Darker Phases of the South* (New York: Negro Universities Press, 1969), 110.

142. Perryman Committee report, cited in ibid., 196.

143. Tannenbaum, *Darker Phases of the South*, 195. See also O'Sullivan, *Crime Detection*, 295.

144. Abbott, *Rack, Rope*, 18.

145. For an account of this process, see Jack London, *The Star Rover* (New York: Grosset and Dunlap, 1915), 52–55.

146. Abbott, *Rack, Rope*, 18.

147. Cited in ibid., 18–19.

148. Abbott, *Rack, Rope*, 19. Abbott's claim that the warden *invented* the Spot must be balanced against the claim that about the same time a Nazi prison guard applied the Spot to political prisoners in Germany. See Martha Dodd, *Through Embassy Eyes* (New York: Harcourt Brace, 1939), 299–300.

149. See chapter 3.

150. Mannix, *The History of Torture*, 184.

151. Oregon Department of Corrections Operations Division, "A Brief History of the Oregon Boot," http://www.oregon.gov/DOC/OPS/PRISON/osp_history3.shtml. O'Sullivan incorrectly describes the boot as a sixty-pound ball with a chain (*Crime Detection*, 296).

152. Wickersham Commission, 151.

153. Alex Nichols, *Handcuffs and Other Restraints* (London: Kingscourt, 2002), 9, 28.

154. See chapter 3.

155. Murdoch, *A History of Japan*, 3:337–38 n. 1. Illustrated in Innes, *The History of Torture*, 152.

156. See chapter 7, "Magnetos."

157. See chapter 3.

158. See chapter 4, "Whips and Water."

159. Józef Garlinski, *Fighting Auschwitz* (London: Julian Friedmann, 1975), 229.

160. See chapter 9, "Singing the World Electric."

161. See chapter 6, "Shock."

162. See chapter 9.

163. "Torture as Policy," *Time*, August 16, 1976, 31–34.

164. Tom Malinowski, "The Logic of Torture," *Washington Post*, June 27, 2004, B7.

Chapter 15
Forced Standing and Other Positions

1. Cited in Douglas Jehl, "Files Show Rumsfeld Rejected Some Efforts to Toughen Prison Rules," *New York Times*, June 23, 2004, A10.

2. Jan Valtin, *Out of the Night* (New York: Alliance, 1941), 571.

3. James Armstrong with William Elliott, *Legion of Hell* (London: Sampson Low, Marston, [1936]), 202.

4. Lawrence E. Hinkle and Harold G. Wolff, "Communist Interrogation and Indoctrination of 'Enemies of the State,' " *A.M.A. Archives of Neurology and Psychiatry* 76 (August 1956): 134.

5. Leslie Heath, "Concentration Camps," cited in Zosa Szajkowski, *Jews and the Foreign Legion* (New York: Ktav, 1975), 152.

6. Cited in ibid., 99–100; see also 102, 112–13.

7. Cited in ibid., 109.

8. Ibid., 166.

9. Michael Alexander, *The Reluctant Legionnaire* (New York: E. P. Dutton, 1956), 156.

10. Patrick Kessel and Giovanni Pirelli, *Le people algérien et la guerre* (Paris: François Maspero, 1962), 455.

11. Ibid., 103, 203, 286, 288, 376, 200, 435 495.

12. Arthur L. Smith Jr., *The War for the German Mind* (Providence, RI: Berghahn, 1995), 25.

13. War Office and Admiralty, "Rules for Field Punishment," PRO CO 1037/52.

14. Ian Cobain, "The Secrets of the London Cage," *Guardian* (London), November 12, 2005, 8.

15. War Office and Admiralty, "Rules for Field Punishment," in *UK Police Unit; Cyprus*, PRO CO 1037/52.

16. Cited in Peter Deeley, *Beyond Breaking Point* (London: Arthur Barker, 1971), 51.

17. Deeley, *Beyond Breaking Point*, 58.

18. The report was "Joint Directive on Military Interrogation in Internal Security Operations Overseas (1965, revised 1967). See Thomas Mockaitis, *British Counterinsurgency in the Post-Imperial Era* (Manchester, England: Manchester University Press, 1995), 103.

19. Desmond Hamill, *Pig in the Middle* (London: Methuen, 1985), 66.

20. David Leigh, "UK Forces Taught Torture Methods," *Guardian* (London), May 8, 2004, 1; James Morton, *Catching the Killers* (London: Ebury Press, 2001), 175–76.

21. Hamill, *Pig in the Middle*, 66–67; Mockaitis, *British Counterinsurgency*, 122; Peter Taylor, *Beating the Terrorists?* (Harmondsworth, England: Penguin, 1980), 20.

22. Dennis Faul and Raymond Murray, *British Army and Special Branch RUC Brutalities* (Dungannon, Northern Ireland: the Compilers, 1972), 5, 9, 12–50 passim; Stephen Johns, *Tory Torture in Ulster* (London: Socialist Labour League, 1971), 11, 15, 16, 19, 22, 23; John McGuffin, *The Guineapigs* (Harmondsworth, England: Penguin, 1974), 47.

23. Taylor, *Beating the Terrorists?* 220.

24. Cited in Walter Ames, *Police and Community in Japan* (Berkeley and Los Angeles: University of California Press, 1981), 31.

25. Intelligence Research Report, January 15, 1947, cited in ibid., 253.

26. See Futaba Igarashi, "Forced to Confess," in *Democracy in Contemporary Japan*, ed. G. McCormack and Y. Sugimoto (Armonk, NY: M. E. Sharpe 1986), 198–200, 202; Karen Parker and Etienne Jaudel, *Police Cell Detention in Japan* (San

Francisco: Association of Humanitarian Lawyers, 1989), 8, 12, 37, A-9; Human Rights Watch, *Prison Conditions in Japan* (New York: Human Rights Watch, 1995), 2, 7–8, 20–21, 24–25, 39; Amnesty International (AI), *Japan*, ASA 22/04/98 (New York: Amnesty International USA, 1998), 5.

27. *Handbook for Life in Prison*, Fuchu Prison, in Human Rights Watch, *Prison Conditions in Japan*, 78.

28. Miguel Sanchez-Mazas, *Spain in Chains* (New York: Veterans of the Abraham Lincoln Brigade, 1960), 23; AI, *Report of an Amnesty International Mission to Spain*, EUR 41/03/80 (London, 1980), 14.

29. Deeley, *Beyond Breaking Point*, 107, 114; AI, *Spain*, 51.

30. European Committee for the Prevention of Torture, *Spain* (1994), http://www.cpt.coe.int/en/; TAT — Torturaren Arkako Taldea [Group Against Torture], *Torture in Basque Country: Report 2001* ([Bilbao]: Graficas Lizarra, S.L., 2002), 26, 27, 47, 48 (stand bent); 14 (kneel on bar); 23, 29, 35, 37, 42, 42, 71, 83, 84, 90, 93 (stand).

31. Marcio Alves, *Torturas e Torturados* (Rio de Janeiro: Empresa Jornalística, 1966), 26–27.

32. Archdiocese of São Paulo, *Torture in Brazil*, trans. Jaime Wright (New York: Vintage, 1986), 24.

33. Ibid., 22.

34. Mark Dow, *American Gulag* (Berkeley and Los Angeles: University of California Press, 2004), 59.

35. Ibid., 59; see also 143–44.

36. Patrick Johnson, a Bahamian detainee, cited in Dow, *American Gulag*, 329.

37. Dow, *American Gulag*, 327–28.

38. AI, *The Pain Merchants*, ACT 40/008/2003 (London: International Secretariat, 2003), 16–19, http://www.amnesty.org; *Cruel and Inhuman Treatment: The Use of Four Point Restrain in the Onondaga County Public Safety Building, Syracuse, NY* (Boston: Physicians for Human Rights, 1993).

39. AI, *Stopping the Torture Trade* (New York: Amnesty International USA, 2001), 12.

40. Dana Priest and Barton Gellman, "U.S. Decries Abuse but Defends Interrogations: 'Stress and Duress' Tactics Used on Terrorism Suspects Held in Secret Overseas Facilities," *Washington Post*, December 26, 2002, A1, A14–A15.

41. Raymond Bonner, Don Van Natta, Jr., and Amy Waldman, "Questioning Terror Suspects in a Dark and Surreal World," *New York Times*, March 9, 2003, A1, A14; AI, *U.S.A.: The Threat of a Bad Example* (London, 2003), 2–3; Neil Lewis, "Broad Use of Harsh Tactics Is Described at Cuba," *New York Times*, October 17, 2004, A1; Josh White, "Guantanamo Force-Feeding Tactics Are Called Torture," *Washington Post*, March 1, 2006, A8.

42. Jackie Spiner, "Soldier: Unit Role Was to Break Down Prisoners," *Washington Post*, May 8, 2004, A1.

43. Seymour Hersh, "Torture and Abu Ghraib," *New Yorker*, May 10, 2004, 44.

44. Ferenc A. Váli, *A Scholar's Odyssey*, ed. Karl Ryavec (Ames: Iowa State University Press, 1957), 157; Lajos Ruff, *The Brain-Washing Machine* (London: Robert Hale, 1959), 59–60; Anna Funder, *Stasiland* (London: Granta, 2003), 24–28, 218, 226–27; William Sargant, *Battle for the Mind* (Westport, CT: Greenwood, 1957), 209–10; Lena Constante, *The Silent Escape*, trans. Franklin Philip (Berkeley and Los Angeles: University of California Press, 1995), 55; Annie Samuelli, *Woman Behind Bars in Romania*, 2nd ed. (London: Frank Cass, 1997), xvii; Teodor Gherasim, *Astride Two Worlds* (Tigard, OR: L. D. Press, 2000), 87; Evgeni Genchev, *Tales from the Dark* (Sofia, Bulgaria: Assistance Centre for Torture Survivors, 2003), 108–10; AI, *Prison Conditions in Rumania, 1955–64* (London, 1965), 21.

45. Hinkle and Wolff, "Communist Interrogation," 155.

46. David Chandler, *Voices from S-21* (Berkeley and Los Angeles: University of California Press, 1999), 132.

47. AI, *Torture in China*, ASA 17/55/92 (New York: Amnesty International USA, 1992), 8–9, 31, 22–23; AI, *People's Republic of China*, ASA 17/004/2001 (London, 2001), 7, 14; AI, *Stopping the Torture Trade*, 10–11; illustrated in Falun Dafa Information Center, *Torture Methods Used on Falun Dafa Practitioners in Detention Centers and Forced Labor Camps in China*, http://back.faluninfo.net/torturemethods2/.

48. See chapter 3, "Lights, Heat, and Sweat"; Lewis Carlson, *Remembered Prisoners of a Forgotten War* (New York: St. Martin's, 2002), 135, 174; Anthony Farrar-Hockley, *The British Part in the Korean War* (London: HMSO, 1995), 2:278; Anthony Farrar-Hockley, *The Edge of the Sword* (London: Bucan and Enright, 1985), 217, 234, 237, 260; Eugene Kinkead, *In Every War but One* (New York: Norton, 1959), 161–62; Raymond Lech, *Broken Soldiers* (Urbana: University of Illinois Press, 2000), 72, 91, 100, 174, 177.

49. Stuart Rochester and Frederick Kiley, *Honor Bound* (Annapolis, MD: Naval Institute Press, 1999), 146, illustrated facing 146, 299, 305, 338, 394 n. 335, 486; John Hubbell, *POW* (New York: Reader's Digest Press, 1976), 121, 211, 221, 231, 269, 279, 482, 505 (kneeling); 172, 494 (sitting); 115, 505 (standing).

50. George E. Day, *Return with Honor* (Mesa, AZ: Champlin Fighter Museum Press, 1989), 141.

51. Aurora Foundation, *Report on the Violations of Human Rights in the Socialist Republic of Vietnam* (Atherton, CA: Aurora Foundation, 1989), 58, 59.

52. Chandler, *Voices from S-21*, 130, 132.

53. AI, *Syria* (London, 1987), 20; AI, *Iraq* (London, 1981), 4–5.

54. AI, *Afghanistan*, ASA 11/04/86 (New York, 1986), 12; M. Osman Rostar, *The Pulicharkhi Prison*, trans. and ed. Ehsanullah Azari (Peshawar, Pakistan: Writers Union of Free Afghanistan, 1991), 18–22, 35–37.

55. AI, *Torture in the Eighties* (London, 1984), 207–8, 210–14, 222–24; AI, *Romania*, EUR/39/02/87 (London, 1987), 21–23.

56. AI, *Syria*, 18–21; AI, *Iraq*, 5, 17–29; AI, *Afghanistan*, 11–16; Rostar, *The Pulicharkhi Prison*, 34–47.

57. AI, *Torture in the Eighties*, 105, 111, 121–22, 127; AI, *Political Imprisonment in the People's Republic of Angola* (New York: Amnesty International USA, 1984), 21–22; AI, *Somalia*, AFR/52/26/88 (London, 1988), 3; Committee on Human Rights, National Academy of Sciences and Committee on Health and Human Rights, Institute of Medicine, *Scientists and Human Rights in Somalia* (Washington, DC: National Academy Press, 1988), 34.

58. Aurora Foundation, *Report*, 54–58, 142; AI, *Cuba*, AMR 25/26/92 (New York, 1992), 52–53; Rochester and Kiley, *Honor Bound*, 394, 397–407.

59. Chandler, *Voices from S-21*, 127–34. See also the paintings of Van Nath displayed at Tuol Sleng.

60. Hinkle and Wolff, "Communist Interrogation," 155; AI, *Political Imprisonment in the People's Republic of China* (London, 1978), 124–27. See chapter 3, "Lights, Heat, and Sweat."

61. AI, *Torture in China*, 6–7; AI, *Report, 1993* (London, 1993), 96; AI, *People's Republic of China* (2001), 4–25; Falun Dafa Information Center, *Torture Methods Used on Falun Dafa Practitioners in Detention Centers and Forced Labor Camps in China*, http://www.faluninfo.net/torturemethods/index.asp.

62. *Ill-Treated and Killed Soldiers in the Soviet Army* (Århus, Denmark: Physicians for Human Rights, 1991), 2, 19, 37. For another account of more brutal postwar Soviet interrogation, see Chris Mackey and Greg Miller, *The Interrogators* (New York: Little, Brown, 2004), 284.

63. *Ill-Treated and Killed Soldiers*, 12, 19, 24, 37.

64. AI, *Report on Torture* (London: Duckworth, 1973), 171.

65. AI, *Report, 1986* (London, 1986), 320.

66. European Committee for the Prevention of Torture, *Albania* (2000), http://www.cpt.coe.int/en/.

67. European Committee for the Prevention of Torture, *Slovakia* (1995), http://www.cpt.coe.int/en/.

68. AI, *Report, 1986*, 320; Jørgen Thomsen and Maiken Mannstaedt, *The Green Birds* (Århus, Denmark: Danish Medical Group, 2000), 15; *Report on Torture in the Nyzshni Novgorod Province* (Nyzshni Novgorod, Russia: Nyzshni Novgorod Province Society for Human Rights, 1997), 3.

69. Pablo Sulbarán, *La tortura en Venezuela* (Caracas: Publicaciones Seleven, 1979), 162, 172.

70. Ibid., 164, 166.

71. Ana Barrios B. and Eva Duart O., *La Tortura: 40 años de pena* (Caracas, Venezuela: Red de Apoyo por la Justicia y la Paz, 1998), 34–35.

72. Sulbarán, *La tortura en Venezuela*, 166.

73. Ibid., 166; see also 154, 166–67; illustrated on 169. Sulbarán borrows the English word *ring*, instead of calling it a *rim*, as an English speaker would.

74. AI, *Prison Conditions in Portugal* (London, 1965), 15–18; Alexandre Manuel, Rogério Carapinha, and Dias Neves, *PIDE* (Fundão, Portugal: Jornal do Fundão, 1974), 43, 97, 104, 113, 188.

75. Arnaldo Mesquita, cited in AI, *Prison Conditions in Portugal*, 18.

76. Lord Russell of Liverpool, *Prisons and Prisoners in Portugal* (London: Waterlow and Sons, 1963), 12–13.

77. Arnaldo Mesquita, cited in AI, *Prison Conditions in Portugal*, 15–16.

78. *Tortura na colónia de Moçambique* (Porto: Ediçoes Afrontamento, 1977), 86, 88, 90, 100, 101, 102.

79. Don Foster, *Detention and Torture in South Africa*, with Dennis Davis and Diane Sandler (New York: St. Martin's, 1987), 102–3.

80. South Africa, Truth and Reconciliation Commission (TRC), *Report* (London: Macmillan, 1999), 2:190.

81. Ibid., 2:192; 3:75, 168, 177, 351, 403–5, 410, 571, 591, 599, 621; 4:208, 210; Deeley, *Beyond Breaking Point*, 89–95; AI, *Political Imprisonment in South Africa* (London, 1978), 65; Foster, *Detention and Torture*, 84, 102–3, 131, 133.

82. Patrick Duncan, *South African's Rule of Violence* (London: Methuen, 1964), 42.

83. TRC, *Report*, 2:192.

84. Ibid., 2:199.

85. Ibid., 3:168.

86. Foster, *Detention and Torture*, 133.

87. Captain van Loggerenberg, cited in TRC, *Report*, 3:616.

88. European Commission of Human Rights, *The Greek Case* (Strasbourg: Council of Europe, 1970), 337

89. George Spiliotis, in Amalia Fleming, *A Piece of Truth* (London: Jonathan Cape, 1972), 248.

90. AI, *Torture in Greece*, PUB 61/00/77 (London, 1977), 44, 47–48.

91. Pham Tam, *Imprisonment and Torture in South Vietnam* (Nyack, NY: Fellowship of Reconciliation, 1969[?]), 8; Holmes Brown and Don Luce, *Hostages of War* (Washington, DC: Indochina Mobile Education Project, 1973), 17; Sydney Schanberg, "Saigon Torture in Jails Reported," *New York Times*, August 12, 1972, A1; Nguyen Dinh Thi, ed., *Les Prisonniers politiques* (Paris: Sudestasie, 1974), 103; *The Forgotten Prisoners of Ngyuen Van Thieu* (Paris: n.p., May 1973), 33.

92. Suh Sung, *Unbroken Spirits*, trans. Jean Inglis (Lanham, MD: Rowman and Littlefield, 2001), 2; AI, *Report of an Amnesty International Mission to the Republic of Korea* (London, 1976), 28.

93. AI, *Political Imprisonment in Uruguay* (London, 1979), 3; Ole Vedel Rasmussen, "Medical Aspects of Torture," *Danish Medical Bulletin* 37, Sup. 1 (January 1990): 8–9.

94. Rasmussen, "Medical Aspects of Torture," 8–9. See also AI, *Torture in the Eighties*, 175.

95. AI, *Report on Torture*, 203.

96. "Israel Tortures Arab Prisoners," *Sunday Times* (London), June 19, 1977, A18.

97. James Ron, "Varying Methods of State Violence," *International Organization* 51.2 (1997): 275–300.

98. Stanley Cohen and Daphna Golan, *The Interrogation of Palestinians during the Intifada* (Jerusalem: B'Tselem, Israeli Information Center for Human Rights in the Occupied Territories, 1991), 50, 54 (stand), 51 (sit), 47 (standing closet); Jeffrey

Dillman and Musa Bakri, *Israel's Use of Electric Shock Torture in the Interrogation of Palestinian Detainees*, 2nd ed. (Jerusalem: Palestine Human Rights Information Center, 1992), 3; B'Tselem, *Routine Torture: Interrogation Methods of the General Security Service* (Jerusalem: B'Tselem, Israeli Information Center for Human Rights in the Occupied Territories, 1998), 29–31, 45 (*qambaz*).

99. "Medical Fitness Form," cited in Melissa Phillips, *Torture for Security* (Ramallah, West Bank: al-Haq, 1995), 109.

100. Yuval Ginbar, *Back to a Routine of Torture*, trans. Jessica Bonn (Jerusalem: Public Committee against Torture in Israel, 2003), 46, 48–50, 53, 57, 59, 62, 63 (sit), 52, 54 (*qambaz*); Yuval Ginbar, *Flawed Defense*, trans. Jessica Bonn (Jerusalem: Public Committee against Torture in Israel, 2001), 38 (stand); 35, 37 (*qambaz*); 26, 29–35 (sit); B'Tselem, *Legislation Allowing the Use of Physical Force and Mental Coercion in Interrogations by the General Security Service* (Jerusalem: B'Tselem, 2000), 58, 63, 65 (sit), 61, 63, 65 (*qambaz*); Ya'el Stein, *Torture of Palestinian Minors in the Gush Etzion Police Station*, trans. Zvi Shulman (Jerusalem: B'Tselem, 2001), 9, 17.

101. AI, *Report of an Amnesty International Mission to the Republic of the Philippines* (London, 1976), 21.

102. Richard Claude, Eric Stover, and June Lopez, *Health Professionals and Human Rights in the Philippines* (Washington, DC: American Association for the Advancement of Science, 1987), 31.

103. AI, *Report of an Amnesty International Mission to Argentina* (London, 1977), 37.

104. AI, *Chile* (London, 1974), 63; *Chile*, AMR 22/03/87 (London, 1987), 26 (stand), 27 (kneel on stones); *Report of the Chilean National Commission on Truth and Reconciliation*, trans. Phillip E. Berryman (Notre Dame, IN: University of Notre Dame Press, 1993), 1:134.

105. Mohammad [pseud.], *The Argot of the Victim* (Copenhagen: Rehabilitation and Research Centre for Torture Victims, 1992), 17.

106. AI, *Torture in the Eighties*, 169.

107. Ibid., 146–47.

108. *La Tortura en El Salvador* (San Salvador: Commision de Derechos Humanos de El Salvador, 1986), 44, 48, 73.

109. AI, *Report, 1986*, 138; AI, *Columbia*, AMR 23/066/2003, November 24, 2003, http://www.amnesty.org.

110. AI, *Report, 1986*, 354.

111. AI, *Report, 1993*, 80.

112. Ibid., 270.

113. Morten Ekstrøm, Hans Draminsky Petersen, and Majken Marmstaedt, *Torture Continues in Indian Held Kashmir* (Århus, Denmark: Physicians for Human Rights, 1994), 19.

114. Mary Salinsky and Liv Tigerstedt, *Evidence of Torture* (London: Medical Foundation for the Care of Victims of Torture, 2001), 37.

115. Hans Draminsky Petersen, Lise Worm, Mette Zander, Ole Harting, and Bjarne Ussing, *Human Rights Violations in Burma/Myanmar* (Århus, Denmark: Physicians for Human Rights, 2000), 21.

116. *Letters from Tunisia's Gulags*, trans. Yusra Kherigi (London: Tunisian Information and Documentation Bureau, 1998), 16.

117. *Images of Repression* (Mexico City: Human Rights Centre "Miguel Agustin Pro Juarez," 1999), 175, 177, 184.

118. AI, *Pain Merchants*, 17.

119. Olivia Ball, *"Every Morning Just Like Coffee": Torture in Cameroon* (London: Medical Foundation for the Care of Victims of Torture, 2002), 44–45.

120. Eric Schmitt, "3 in 82nd Airborne Say Beating Iraqi Prisoners Was Routine," *New York Times*, September 23, 2005, A1.

121. "Investigations Continue into Iraqi Deaths," *RFE/RL Iraq Report*, Radio Free Europe/Radio Liberty, Prague, Czech Republic, 7:30, August 12, 2004, http://www.rferl.org/; see also "Danish Iraq Major Complained over Prisoners' Treatment," *BBC Monitoring Europe* (June 2, 2005), http://www.lexis-nexis.com/; "Danish Military Police Chief in Iraq 'Unaware of Abuse,' " *BBC Monitoring Europe* (August 25, 2005), http://www.lexis-nexis.com/; " Memory Lapses' in Danish Iraq Abuse Trial," *BBC Monitoring Europe* (September 8, 2005), http://www.lexis-nexis.com/; "Danish Iraq Interpreters Demand Compensation for 'Abuse' Interrogations," *BBC Monitoring International Reports* (July 7, 2006), http://www.lexis-nexis.com/.

122. Mockaitis, *British Counterinsurgency*, 122.

123. Although France also used positional tortures in the Foreign Legion, this practice died out among French torturers in the 1950s with the transition to French modern (electrotorture and water tortures). The mere fact that a state received French training in torture in the late twentieth century would not explain why a state adopted positional torture at this time.

124. Leigh, "UK Forces," 1; Donald Duncan, "The Whole Thing Was a Lie!" in *A Vietnam Primer*, 2nd ed. (San Francisco: Ramparts, 1968), 77.

125. McGuffin, *The Guineapigs*, 23–35. McGuffin's uses and overstates Deeley's more cautious analysis of British torture. See Deeley, *Beyond Breaking Point*, 43–64.

126. Mockaitis, *British Counterinsurgency*, 187–88; David M. Anderson and David Killingray, "Consent, Coercion and Colonial Control," in *Policing the Empire*, ed. David M. Anderson and David Killingray (Manchester, England: Manchester University Press, 1991), 2, 12–13; David Killingray, "Securing the British Empire," in *The Policing of Politics in the 20th Century*, ed. Mark Mazower (Providence, RI: Berghahn, 1997), 175–77, 180.

127. Captain Ernest Law, "Five Months Without Trial," in *Gangrene* (London: John Calder, 1959), 102–4, 116–24; John Stonehouse, "From the Documents on Hola," in *Gangrene*, 128–56; "Horrors of Hola Detention Camp," *Daily Nation* (Nairobi, Kenya), April 22, 2004, http://www.nationmedia.com.

128. RUC technique is covered in chapter 16, "Fists and Exercises." For police beating in England from the 1950s onwards, see Stuart Bowes, *The Police and Civil Liberties* (London: Lawrence and Wishart, 1966, 151–53, 158–63, 170.

129. McGuffin, *The Guineapigs*, 100; and John McGuffin, *Internment* (Tralee, County Kerry: Anvil, 1973), 123. In *Guineapigs*, McGuffin identifies "mad doctor" procedure (135), amphetamines (138), electrotorture (135), *falaka* (136), the Dutch style in choking (137, contra McGuffin, not a typical French technique).

130. Deeley, *Beyond Breaking Point*, 43–64; McGuffin, *Guineapigs*, 23–25.

131. Caroline Elkins, *Imperial Reckoning* (New York: Henry Holt, 2005), 66, 68.

132. Cited by John Barry, reporter at *Newsweek* (email correspondence, July 1, 2004). Some prisoners report being threatened with electric instruments in the London Cage, but did not report it being used (Cobain, "Secrets of London Cage," 8). Charles Foley reports rumors of electrotorture in Cyprus, but was never able to confirm it (*Island in Revolt* [London: Longmans, Green, 1962], 131). For current usage of the egg technique, see Antonio Cassesse, *Inhuman States* (Cambridge, MA: Polity Press, 1996), 64.

133. The seminal texts were Frank Kitson's *Low Intensity Operations* (London, Faber, 1971) and his memoirs, *Bunch of Five* (London: Faber, 1977). For French doctrine, see Roger Trinquier, *La guerre moderne* (Paris: La Table Ronde, 1961); *Modern Warfare*, trans. Daniel Lee (New York: Praeger, 1964).

134. Mockaitis, *British Counterinsurgency*, 187. See also Taylor, *Beating the Terrorists?* 20.

135. Ibid., 189.

136. TRC, *Report*, 2:196.

137. Suzanne Goldenberg, "Soldier says Abu Ghraib Interrogators Told Him to Stage Mock Electrocution," *Guardian* (London), October 21, 2004, 5.

138. Jehl, "Files," A10; "U.S. Interrogation Techniques" *USA Today*, June 23, 2004, 4A.

Chapter 16
Fists and Exercises

1. Cited in Peter Taylor, *Beating the Terrorists?* (Harmondsworth, England: Penguin, 1980), 310.

2. National Commission on Law Observance and Enforcement, *Report on Lawlessness in Law Enforcement* (Washington, DC: U.S. Government Printing Office, 1931), 92. Hereafter cited as Wickersham Commission.

3. Taylor, *Beating the Terrorists?* 117.

4. Wickersham Commission, 118; see also 61, 92. See also Richard A. Leo, "The Third Degree and the Origins of Psychological Interrogation in the United States," in *Interrogations, Confessions, and Entrapment*, ed. G. Daniel Lassiter (New York: Kluwer Academic, 2004), 46; and Emanuel Lavine, *The Third Degree* (Garden City, NY: Garden City Publishing, 1930), 50.

5. Wickersham Commission, 60; see also 59, 118.

6. Patrick Kessel and Giovanni Pirelli, *Le people algérien et la guerre* (Paris: François Maspero, 1962), 284; see also 3, 59, 498. See also Charles Franklin, *The Third Degree* (London: Robert Hale, 1970), 145.

7. Kessel and Pirelli, *Le people algérien*, 97, 103.

8. Charles Foley, *Island in Revolt* (London: Longmans, Green, 1962), 131.

9. Peter Deeley, *Beyond Breaking Point* (London: Arthur Baker, 1971), 58.

10. Donald Duncan, "The Whole Thing Was a Lie!" in *A Vietnam Primer*, 2nd ed. (San Francisco: Ramparts, 1968), 77.

11. Andreas Frangeas, cited in Amalia Fleming, *A Piece of Truth* (London: Jonathan Cape, 1972), 247. See also European Commission of Human Rights, *The Greek Case* (Strasbourg: Council of Europe, 1970), 146.

12. Deeley, *Beyond Breaking Point*, 105–14. This practice may have started as early as 1960. See Miguel Sanchez-Mazas, *Spain in Chains* (New York: Veterans of the Abraham Lincoln Brigade, 1960), 23.

13. Deeley, *Beyond Breaking Point*, 111.

14. TAT—Torturaren Arkako Taldea [Group Against Torture], *Torture en pays basque: Report 2000*, http://www.stoptortura.com/, 2002, 41.

15. Ibid., 44.

16. Ejército de Liberación Nacional, "Denuncian torturas," *Punta Final*, August 1972, 28.

17. Italo Moya Escanilla, cited in Physicians for Human Rights, *Sowing Fear* (Sommerville, MA: Physicians for Human Rights, 1988), 76.

18. G. Flint Taylor, "Known Area 2 and 3 Torture Victims, 1972–1991 (4/7/04)," unpublished data; Michael Goldston to Chief Administrator, Office of Professional Standards, in *History of Allegations of Misconduct by Area Two Personnel* (Chicago: Office of Professional Standards, Chicago Police Department, September 28, 1990), available at http://humanrights.uchicago.edu/chicagotorture/ops.shtml.

19. Cited in Futaba Igarashi, "Forced to Confess," in *Democracy in Contemporary Japan*, ed. G. McCormack and Y. Sugimoto (Armonk, NY: M. E. Sharpe, 1986), 201–2. See also Karen Parker and Etienne Jaudel, *Police Cell Detention in Japan* (San Francisco: Association of Humanitarian Lawyers, 1989), 37.

20. Amnesty International (AI), *Report, 1986* (London, 1986), 316.

21. Dennis Faul and Raymond Murray, *The RUC: The Black and Blue Book* ([Dungannon, Northern Ireland]: [Denis Faul], 1975), 27. See also Dennis Faul and Raymond Murray, *British Army and Special Branch RUC Brutalities* (Dungannon, Northern Ireland: the Compilers, 1972), 9, 12–50 passim; Stephen Johns, *Tory Torture in Ulster* (London: Socialist Labour League, 1971), 15.

22. Taylor, *Beating the Terrorists?* 73–74, 88–90, 92.

23. Ibid., 220, 221, 225, 248.

24. Ibid., 117.

25. Avshalom Benny, cited in James Ron, "Varying Methods of State Violence," *International Organization* 51.2 (1997): 286. See also Stanley Cohen and Daphna Golan, *The Interrogation of Palestinians during the Intifada* (Jerusalem: B'Tselem, Israeli Information Center for Human Rights in the Occupied Territories, 1991),

52; Yuval Ginbar, *Back to a Routine of Torture*, trans. Jessica Bonn (Jerusalem: Public Committee against Torture in Israel, 2003), 53, 59; Yuval Ginbar, *Flawed Defense*, trans. Jessica Bonn (Jerusalem: Public Committee against Torture in Israel, 2001), 25, 32, 36, 37; Samir Qouta, Raija-Leena Punamäki, and Eyad El Sarraj, "Prison Experiences and Coping Styles Among Palestinian Men," *Peace and Conflict* 3.1 (1997): 24–26.

26. *Ill-Treated and Killed Soldiers in the Soviet Army* (Århus, Denmark: Physicians for Human Rights, 1991), 12.

27. European Committee for the Prevention of Torture (CPT), *Romania* (1999), *Slovakia* (2000), http://www.cpt.coe.int/en/.

28. Sebastian Roaquín Ramos, cited in AI, *The Attack on the Third Infantry Regiment Barracks at La Tabla* (New York, 1990), 13.

29. *Mise à jour des allegations de torture dans l'état de São Paulo* (São Paulo: Action des Chrétiens pour l'abolition de la torture, 2002), 31.

30. Jane Mayer, "The Experiment," *New Yorker*, July 11 and 18, 2005, 62.

31. Mark Lane, *Conversations with Americans* (New York: Simon and Schuster, 1970), 157.

32. Lord Russell, *The Knights of Bushido* (London: Cassell, 1958), 160; see also 172–73, 192. See also Keith Howard, ed., *True Stories of the Korean Comfort Women*, trans. Young Joo Lee (London: Cassell, 1995), 76, Otto Tolischus, *Tokyo Record* (New York: Reynal and Hitchcock, 1943), 341, 345.

33. Russell, *The Knights of Bushido*, 160–61.

34. For the full list of tortures, see chapter 7, "Magnetos."

35. Charlie Plumb, *I'm No Hero*, with Glen DeWerff (Independence, MI: Independence Press, 1973), 152. See also Stuart Rochester and Frederick Kiley, *Honor Bound* (Annapolis, MD: Naval Institute Press, 1999), 364, 387; John Hubbell, *POW* (New York: Reader's Digest Press, 1976), 98, 140, 218, 309, 437, 439, 482, 493.

36. Wickersham Commission, 56, 92, 104, 121. See also chapter 3, "Lights, Heat, and Sweat."

37. Lavine, *The Third Degree*, 51–52; Ernest Jerome Hopkins, *Our Lawless Police* (New York: Viking, 1931), 208.

38. Victor Kravchenko, *I Chose Freedom* (New York: Charles Scribner's Sons, 1946), 265.

39. Kessell and Pirelli, *Le people algérien*, 43, 44, 59, 284.

40. Lane, *Conversations with Americans*, 157. See also Dirk von Schrader, *Elementary Field Interrogation* (n.p.: Delta, 1978), 24–25.

41. Faul and Murray, *The RUC*, 9; Amnesty, *Report, 1986*, 317; Johns, *Tory Torture in Ulster*, 15.

42. See the following reports made available by the CPT, http://www.cpt.coe.int/en/ : *Czech Republic* (1997), *France* (1991, 2000), *Estonia* (1997), *Ireland* (1993, 1998), *Romania* (1995, 1999), *Slovakia* (1995), *Spain* (June 1994). See also Niels Uildriks, "Police Torture in France," *Netherlands Quarterly of Human Rights* 17.4 (1999):

417; TAT—Torturaren Arkako Taldea [Group Against Torture], *Torture in Basque Country: Report 2001* ([Bilbao]: Graficas Lizarra, S.L., 2002), 13, 25, 59, 74, 78.

43. B"Tselem, *Routine Torture: Interrogation Methods of the General Security Service* (Jerusalem: B"Tselem, Israeli Information Center for Human Rights in the Occupied Territories, 1998), 28, 34; Ginbar, *Back to a Routine*, 45, 47, 52, 53, 57; Ginbar, *Flawed Defense*, 28, 32, 36, 40.

44. Igarashi, "Forced to Confess," 201; Parker and Jaudel, *Police Cell Detention*, 37.

45. Lembaga Studi dan Advokasi (ELSAM), *Revealing Tortures by Public Officials* (Jakarta Selatan, Indonesia: ELSAM, 1996), 34–35, 39.

46. Mark Dow, *American Gulag* (Berkeley and Los Angeles: University of California Press, 2004), 59.

47. Josh White, "Soldier's 'Wish Lists' of Detainee Tactics Cited," *Washington Post*, April 19, 2005, A16.

48. Brian Ross and Richard Esposito, "CIA's Harsh Interrogation Techniques Described," *ABC News*, November 18, 2005, http://abcnews.go.com.

49. TAT, *Torture in Basque Country*, 59.

50. Ross and Esposito, "CIA's Harsh Interrogation Techniques."

51. Captain Ernest Law, "Five Months Without Trial," in *Gangrene* (London: John Calder, 1959), 119.

52. Hubbell, *POW*, 121, 309.

53. Deeley, *Beyond Breaking Point*, 58.

54. Roderic Bowen, *Procedures for the Arrest, Interrogation and Detention of Suspected Terrorists in Aden* (London: Her Majesty's Stationery Office, 1966), 16.

55. Deeley, *Beyond Breaking Point*, 105.

56. Marcio Alves, *Torturas e Torturados* (Rio de Janeiro: Empresa Jornalística, 1966), 26–27.

57. Ole Vedel Rasmussen, "Medical Aspects of Torture," *Danish Medical Bulletin* 37, Sup. 1 (January 1990): 8–9; Pia Moisander and Erik Edston, "Torture and Its Sequel—A Comparison between Victims from Six Countries," *Forensic Science International* 137 (2003): 136. See also chapter 9, "Singing the World Electric."

58. Taylor, "Known Area 2 and 3 Torture Victims."

59. CPT (http://www.cpt.coe.int/en/): *Ireland* (1998), *Spain* (1997), *Bulgaria* (1999); TAT, *Torture in Basque Country*, 13, 51, 74; *Letters from Tunisia's Gulags*, trans. Yusra Kherigi (London: Tunisian Information and Documentation Bureau, 1998), 50; Igarashi, "Forced to Confess," 201, 202. For an account of the medical diagnosis of cuffing, see Duncan Forrest, "Examination Following Specific Forms of Torture," in *The Medical Documentation of Torture*, ed. Michael Peel and Vincent Iacopino (London: Greenwich Medical Media, 2002), 162.

60. F. Dalton O'Sullivan, *Crime Detection* (Chicago: O'Sullivan Publishing House, 1928), 297.

61. Taylor, *Beating the Terrorists?* 148.

62. AI, *Spain*, EUR 41/02/85 (London, 1985), 12, 13; Igarashi, "Forced to Confess," 201.

63. AI, *Switzerland*, EUR 43/02/94 (New York: Amnesty International USA, 1994), 18.

64. Ginbar, *Back to a Routine*, 45.

65. Forrest, "Examination," 166.

66. Cohen and Golan, *Interrogation of Palestinians*, 32; Ginbar, *Back to a Routine*, 45, 47, 49; Ginbar, *Flawed Defense*, 25, 37, 41; B'Tselem, *Routine Torture*, 31, 32, 37, 38.

67. Nawwaf al-Qaysi, cited in Cohen and Golan, *Interrogation of Palestinians*, 32.

68. Cited in B'Tselem, *Routine Torture*, 38.

69. Ross and Esposito, "CIA's Harsh Interrogation Techniques."

70. Norman Thomas, *The Conscientious Objector in America* (New York: B. W. Huebsch, 1925), 144.

71. Deeley, *Beyond Breaking Point*, 110; Faul and Murray, *The RUC*, 27; Hubbell, *POW*, 509.

72. Richard Norton-Taylor and Matthew Taylor, "British Soldier Gives New Details of Abuse of Jailed Iraqis," *Guardian* (London), May7, 2004, 4.

73. Parker and Jaudel, *Police Cell Detention*, 38; Igarashi, "Forced to Confess," 202.

74. Kessel and Pirelli, *Le people algérien*, 95, 281, 491, 578 (strangulation), 411–12 (*chèche*).

75. See Goldston; and Taylor, "Known Area 2 and 3 Torture Victims."

76. *U.S. v. McKenzie*, 768 F.2Á 602, 604 (5th Cir, 1985).

77. CPT, *United Kingdom* (1994), http://www.cpt.coe.int/en/.

78. CPT, *Ukraine* (2000), *Spain* (1991, April 1994, June 1994, 1997, 1998), Austria (1994), http://www.cpt.coe.int/en/; AI, *Austria*, EUR 13/01/89 (London, 1990), 25, 33, 34.

79. TAT, *Torture in Basque Country*, 13–210 passim. Early accounts from Deeley do not mention bagging.

80. Rasmussen, "Medical Aspects of Torture," 8–9; AI, *Report, 1986*, 235; "Torture as Policy," *Time*, August 16, 1976, 33 (illustrated); Ana Barrios B. and Eva Duart O., *La Tortura: 40 años de pena* (Caracas, Venezuela: Red de Apoyo por la Justicia y la Paz, 1998), 34–35; AI, *Report, 1993* (London, 1993), 307; AI, *Mexico*, AMR 41/04/91 (London, 1991), 1, 19, 25; AI, *Mexico*, 41/008/2001 (New York, 2001), 2, 5, 21; *Images of Repression* (Mexico City: Human Rights Centre "Miguel Agustin Pro Juarez," 1999), 175–79, 181–83, 185; *Tortura en Paraguay* (Asunción, Paraguay: Comite de Iglesias Para Ayudas de Emergencia and International Human Rights Law Group, 1993), 26.

81. Richard Claude, Eric Stover, and June Lopez, *Health Professionals and Human Rights in the Philippines* (Washington, DC: American Association for the Advancement of Science, 1987), 31; AI, *Report, 1993*, 73; Human Rights Watch, "*And It Was Hell All Over Again . . .*" (New York: Human Rights Watch, 2000), 12; Hans Draminsky Petersen, Lise Worm, Mette Zander, Ole Harting, and Bjarne Ussing, *Human Rights Violations in Burma/Myanmar* (Århus, Denmark: Physicians for Human Rights, 2000), 21; Michael Peel and Mary Salinsky, *Caught in the Middle* (Oxford: Alden Group, 2000), 24; AI, *Report, 1986*, 267; AI, *Afghanistan*, ASA 11/04/86 (New York, 1986), 14–15. Illustrated in Falun Dafa Information Center, *Torture*

Methods Used on Falun Dafa Practitioners in Detention Centers and Forced Labor Camps in China, http://back.faluninfo.net/torturemethods2/.

82. Ross and Esposito, "CIA's Harsh Interrogation Techniques."

83. Cohen and Golan, *Interrogation of Palestinians*, 55; B'Tselem, *Routine Torture*, 36; Stan Cohen, "Talking about Torture in Israel," *Tikkun* 6.6 (1991): 27.

84. Jeffrey Dillman and Musa Bakri, *Israel's Use of Electric Shock Torture in the Interrogation of Palestinian Detainees*, 2nd ed. (Jerusalem: Palestine Human Rights Information Center, 1992), 56–57; Don Foster with Dennis Davis and Diane Sandler, *Detention and Torture in South Africa* (New York: St. Martin's, 1987), 132.

85. Andrzej Czerkawski, *Aleja Szucha* (Warsaw: Sport i Turystyka, 1967), [6–8].

86. Annie Samuelli, *Woman Behind Bars in Romania*, 2nd ed. (London: Frank Cass, 1997), xvii.

87. Cited in Patrick Duncan, *South Africa's Rule of Violence* (London: Methuen, 1964), 31. See also Duncan, 26–30, 36–42, 50; South Africa, Truth and Reconciliation Commission (TRC), *Report* (London: Macmillan, 1999), 2:192, 216, 218; AI, *Political Imprisonment in South Africa* (London, 1978), 65.

88. AI, *Torture in the Eighties* (London, 1984), 185.

89. See chapter 9, "Singing the World Electric."

90. Sasha Sidorov, cited in Human Rights Watch, *Confession at Any Cost* (New York: Human Rights Watch, 1999), 28.

91. Michel Foucault, *Discipline and Punish*, trans. Alan Sheridan (New York: Vintage, 1979), 135–95.

92. AI, *Report of an Amnesty International Mission to Spain* (London, 1975), 9.

93. AI, *Singapore* (London, 1976), 7; AI, *Report, 1993*, 183; AI, *Torture in the Eighties*, 137, Parker and Jaudel, *Police Cell Detention*, 38.

94. Haruko Taya Cook and Theodore Cook, *Japan at War* (New York: New Press, 1992), 414.

95. Ian Cobain, "The Secrets of the London Cage," *Guardian* (London), November 12, 2005, 8.

96. For the British POW burden, see Arthur L. Smith, Jr., *The War for the German Mind* (Providence, RI: Berghahn, 1995), 11–12, 25. Villari maintains that Italian POWs reported that African camps were brutal, but Benuzzi gives a much milder account. Luigi Villari, *The Liberation of Italy* (Appleton, WI: C. C. Nelson, 1959), 181–83; Felice Benuzzi, *No Picnic on Mount Kenya* (New York: E. P. Dutton, 1953).

97. Kessel and Pirelli, *Le people algérien*, 20, 206.

98. Deeley, *Beyond Breaking Point*, 58.

99. Sean McKenna, cited John McGuffin, *The Guineapigs* (Harmondsworth, England: Penguin, 1974), 48.

100. AI, *Prison Conditions in Rumania, 1955–64* (London, 1965), 11; Silviu Craciunas, *The Lost Footsteps* (New York: Farrar, Straus and Cudahy, 1961), 141–43; Richard Wurmbrand, *From Suffering to Triumph* (Grand Rapids, MI: Kregel, 1991), 30.

101. Lewis Carlson, *Remembered Prisoners of a Forgotten War* (New York: St. Martin's, 2002), 174.

102. *Report of the Chilean National Commission on Truth and Reconciliation*, trans. Phillip E. Berryman (Notre Dame, IN: University of Notre Dame Press, 1993), 1:134.

103. AI, *Report*, 1993, 172.

104. AI, *Spain* (1975), 9; AI, *Report of an Amnesty International Mission to Spain*, EUR 41/03/80 (London, 1980), 15, 45, 46.

105. Alves, *Torturas e Torturados*, 26.

106. AI, *Yemen*, MDE 31/004/1999 (1999), www.amnesty.org.

107. Reuters bureau chief in Baghdad, cited in Mark Danner, "The Logic of Torture," *New York Review of Books*, June 24, 2004, 71.

108. Eric Schmitt, "3 in 82nd Airborne Say Beating Iraqi Prisoners Was Routine," *New York Times*, September 23, 2005, A1.

109. Mary Salinsky and Liv Tigerstedt, *Evidence of Torture* (London: Medical Foundation for the Care of Victims of Torture, 2001), 41.

110. Cohen and Golan, *Interrogation of Palestinians*, 54; TAT, *Torture en pays basque*, 64; Mohammad [pseud.], *The Argot of the Victim* (Copenhagen: Rehabilitation and Research Centre for Torture Victims, 1992), 9.

111. Hina Shamsi, *Command's Responsibility*, ed. Deborah Pearlstein (New York: Human Rights First, 2006), 22.

112. Cobain, "Secrets of London Cage," 8.

113. Kessel and Pirelli, *Le people algérien*, 202, 651.

114. AI, *Report*, 1986, 24, 188; AI, *Syria*, MDE/24/09/87 (New York, 1987), 20; Ya'el Stein, *Torture of Palestinian Minors in the Gush Etzion Police Station*, trans. Zvi Shulman (Jerusalem: B'Tselem, 2001), 9.

115. Physicians for Human Rights, *Sowing Fear*, 76.

116. Deeley, *Beyond Breaking Point*, 111; Physicians for Human Rights, *Sowing Fear*, 76; *La Tortura en El Salvador* (San Salvador, El Salvador: Commision de Derechos Humanos de El Salvador, 1986), 43.

117. Sean McKenna, cited McGuffin, *The Guineapigs*, 48. See also McGuffin, 54; and Taylor, *Beating the Terrorists?* 116, 165.

118. TRC, *Report*, 3:353.

119. Cohen and Golan, *Interrogation of Palestinians*, 54.

120. Danner, "Logic of Torture," 71; TAT, *Torture in Basque Country*, 54, 59, 83; TAT, *Torture en pays basque*, 44.

121. Kessell and Pirelli, *Le people algérien*, 215; *Mise à jour des allegations de torture*, 11.

122. Deeley, *Beyond Breaking Point*, 105; AI, *Spain* (1975), 9; AI, *Spain* (1980), 14.

123. Deeley, *Beyond Breaking Point*, 105.

124. Rasmussen, "Medical Aspects of Torture," 8–9; Deeley, *Beyond Breaking Point*, 105, 107; AI, *Spain* (1975), 9; AI, *Spain* (1980), 32, 49.

125. TRC, *Report*, 3:353, 404, 617; Foster, *Detention and Torture*, 103; TAT, *Torture in Basque Country*, 14.

126. *Zambia Human Rights Report, 1998* (Lusaka, Zambia: Inter African Network for Human Rights and Development, Afronet, 1999), 7; ELSAM, *Revealing Tortures*, 33.

127. Kessel and Pirelli, *Le people algérien*, 651.

128. Deeley, *Beyond Breaking Point*, 115.

129. John G. Taylor, *Indonesia's Forgotten War* (London: Zed, 1991), 108; AI, *Report, 1986*, 24, AI, *Torture in the Eighties*, 139; *Zambia Human Rights Report*, 7.

130. Human Rights Watch, *Prison Conditions in Japan* (New York: Human Rights Watch, 1995), 33.

131. Adel Nakhla, U.S. Civilian contractor, cited in Antonio Taguba, *Executive Summary of Article 15–6 Investigation of the 800th Military Police Brigade*, May 2004, http://www.msnbc.msn.com/id/4894001/, 18; Mark Danner, "Abu Ghraib: The Hidden Story," *New York Review of Books*, October 7, 2004, 47.

132. Danner, "Logic of Torture," 70; Danner, "Abu Ghraib," 47.

133. Foucault, *Discipline and Punish*, 195–230.

Chapter 17
Old and New Restraints

1. Dirk von Schrader, *Elementary Field Interrogation* (n.p.: Delta, 1978), 31.

2. H. Hessell Tiltman, *The Terror in Europe* (New York: Frederick Stokes, 1932), 382, 399.

3. Patrick Kessel and Giovanni Pirelli, *Le people algérien et la guerre* (Paris: François Maspero, 1962), 24, 98, 156, 217, 261, 268, 350, 352, 356, 406, 410, 411, 430, 434, 498, 584, 591.

4. *The Gangrene*, trans. Robert Silvers (New York: Lyle Stewart, 1960), 40, 59, 79; Pierre Vidal-Naquet, *La Raison d'état* (Paris: Éditions de Minuit, 1962), 81, 127; Simone de Beauvoir and Gisele Halimi, *Djamila Boupacha*, trans. Peter Green (New York: Macmillan, 1962), 149, 191.

5. Marcio Alves, *Torturas e Torturados* (Rio de Janeiro: Empresa Jornalística, 1966), 26. See also Archdiocese of São Paulo, *Torture in Brazil*, trans. Jaime Wright (New York: Vintage, 1986), 16–17.

6. A. J. Langguth, *Hidden Terrors* (New York: Pantheon, 1978), 219; see also 220.

7. Paul Chevigny, Bell Gale Chevigny, and Russel Karp, *Police Abuse in Brazil* (New York: Americas Watch Report, 1987), 5. See also "Torture as Policy," *Time*, August 16, 1976, 32.

8. *Grande Dicionário da Língua Portuguesa* (Lisbon: Editorial Confluência, 1945, updated 1954). For earlier usage, see Joao Fernandes Valdez, *Portuguese and English Dictionary* (Rio de Janeiro: Livraría Garnier, [1875]), and A *New Dictionary of the Portuguese and English Languages*, 3rd ed. (Rio de Janeiro: n. p., 1908). Although Jean Debret famously drew a picture of a slave in the *pau*, he does not call it by this name. Jean Baptiste Debret, *Viagem Pitoresca e Histórica ao Brasil* (São Paulo: Livraria Martins, 1941), vol. 1, plate 25.

9. For example, *Pequeno Dicionário Brasileiro da Língua Portuguêsa*, 11th ed. (Rio de Janeiro: Ed. Civiliação Brasileira, 1967). The *Moderno Dicionário da Língua Portuguesa* (São Paulo: Mehoramentos, 1998) now gives a rich list for the phrase: plant, perch for birds, poor *nordestinos*, their trucks, and the torture.

10. Elizabeth Cancelli, *Omundo da violência* (Brasília, DF: Editora Universidade de Brasília, 1993), 193–94; William Waack, *Camaradas* (São Paulo: Companhia das Letras, 1993), 300; Hastings, "Political Prisoners in Brazil," *Times* (London), July 10, 1936, 12; "State Department Hit by Marcantonio," *New York Times*, April 13, 1936, A19. See also "Charge Murder in Brazil," *New York Times*, March 26, 1936, A24; Minna Ewert, "Political Prisoners in Brazil," *Times* (London), July 18, 1936, 8; Stanley Hilton, *Brazil and the Soviet Challenge* (Austin: University of Texas Press, 1981), 81–82, 84; Stanley Hilton, *Hitler's Secret War in South America, 1939–1945* (Baton Rouge: Louisiana State University Press, 1981), 243, 247, 249, 251, 255–57.

11. Amnesty International (AI), *Chile* (London, 1983), 9; AI, *Chile*, AMR 22/03/87 (London, 1987), 9, 10 (illustration), 19, 21; *Report of the Chilean National Commission on Truth and Reconciliation*, trans. Phillip E. Berryman (Notre Dame, IN: University of Notre Dame Press, 1993), 1:134; AI, *Mexico*, AMR 41/04/91 (London, 1991), 26; AI, *Report, 1986* (London, 1986), 165; Ole Vedel Rasmussen, "Medical Aspects of Torture," *Danish Medical Bulletin* 37, Sup. 1 (January 1990): 8–9.

12. AI, *Report of an Amnesty International Mission to Spain*, EUR 41/03/80 (London, 1980), 15, 22, 27, 29, 38, 41, 43, 47, 51; AI, *Report, 1986*, 345; AI, *Morocco* (London, 1986), 2; Rasmussen, "Medical Aspects of Torture," 8–9; *Letters from Tunisia's Gulags*, trans. Yusra Kherigi (London: Tunisian Information and Documentation Bureau, 1998), 15, 50; AI, *Syria* (London, 1987), 19–20; Joanna Oyediran and Paul Hunt, *Evidence of Torture in Africa: A Summary of the Annual Report* (UN Special Rapporteur on Torture, 1991), 10.

13. Rasmussen, "Medical Aspects of Torture," 6, 9.

14. Peter Deeley, *Beyond Breaking Point* (London: Arthur Baker, 1971), 88; Don Foster with Dennis Davis and Diane Sandler, *Detention and Torture in South Africa* (New York: St. Martin's, 1987), 132; South Africa, Truth and Reconciliation Commission, *Report* (London: Macmillan, 1999), 3:178.

15. Desmond Smith, cited in Stephen Johns, *Tory Torture in Ulster* (London: Socialist Labour League, 1971), 11.

16. Mohammad [pseud.], *The Argot of the Victim* (Copenhagen: Rehabilitation and Research Centre for Torture Victims, 1992), 10.

17. AI, *Report of an Amnesty International Mission to the Republic of Korea* (London, 1976), 37.

18. National Academy of Sciences and Institute of Medicine, *Scientists and Human Rights in Somalia* (Washington, DC: National Academy Press, 1998), 34.

19. AI, *Yemen*, MDE 31/004/1999 (1999), www.amnesty.org; P. ya Nangoloh, ed., *Etopola: The Practice of Torture in Present Day Namibia*, rev. ed. (Windhoek, Namibia: National Society for Human Rights, 1994), 7, 13.

20. *Playing with Fire* (New York: Human Rights Watch, 2002), 76; Mary Salinsky and Liv Tigerstedt, *Evidence of Torture* (London: Medical Foundation for the Care of Victims of Torture, 2001), 39–40.

21. Kessel and Pirelli, *Le people algérien*, 201 (*crapaudine*), 210, 216 (buried to the neck).

22. Koude Koussetogue, *La Torture* (N'Djaména, Chad: Association Jeunessee Anti-Clivage, 1995), 1, 10; AI, *Chad*, AFR 20/004/2001 (London, 2001), 28–29; AI, *Arming the Torturers*, ACT 40/01/97 (London, 1997), 6.

23. Olivia Ball, *"Every Morning Just Like Coffee": Torture in Cameroon* (London: Medical Foundation for the Care of Victims of Torture, 2002), 34.

24. Cited in *Letters from Tunisia's Gulags*, 50.

25. Christian de Goustine, *La torture* (Paris; Le Centurion, 1976), 93; Aurora Foundation, *Report on the Violations of Human Rights in the Socialist Republic of Vietnam* (Atherton, CA: Aurora Foundation, 1989), 57.

26. AI, *Political Imprisonment in the People's Republic of China* (London, 1978), 127; AI, *Torture in China*, ASA 17/55/92 (New York: Amnesty International USA, 1992), 16; illustrated in Falun Dafa Information Center, *Torture Methods Used on Falun Dafa Practitioners in Detention Centers and Forced Labor Camps in China*, http://back.faluninfo.net/torturemethods2/; AI, *Somalia*, AFR/52/26/88 (London, 1988), 3; AI, *Political Imprisonment in the People's Republic of Angola* (London, 1984), 22.

27. AI, *Angola*, 22.

28. AI, *Guinea Ecuatorial: Torturas*, AFR 24/05/90/s (Madrid: Mundograf, 1992), 31.

29. von Schrader, *Elementary Field Interrogation*, 34–35. Von Schrader, probably a pseudonym, was allegedly a U.S. Army Special Forces soldier who worked in the Phoenix Counterterrorism Program and was removed from Cambodia when the section chief of Special OPS Group anticipated that guerrillas would put a bounty on him. For a description of the Phoenix program, see chapter 21, "Does Torture Work?"

30. Redacted to Redacted, "FBI SA's RE: Detainee Abuse Allegation," June 29, 2004, http://aclu.org/torturefoia/released/fbi.html (accessed December 22, 2004).

31. Archdiocese of São Paulo, *Torture in Brazil*, 24.

32. Mohammad, *Argot of the Victim*, 12–13.

33. *Reseña de la Tortura en Honduras en Los Noventa* (Tegucigalpa, Honduras: Comité de Familiares de Detenidos-Desaparecidos en Honduras, 1994), 7; *La Tortura en El Salvador* (San Salvador, El Salvador: Commision de Derechos Humanos de El Salvador, 1986), 42, 73.

34. Stanley Cohen and Daphna Golan, *The Interrogation of Palestinians during the Intifada* (Jerusalem: B'Tselem, Israeli Information Center for Human Rights in the Occupied Territories, 1991), 52, 53 (illustration).

35. Human Rights Watch, *State of Pain: Torture in Uganda* (March 2004), 16:4(A): 23.

36. See chapter 14, "Stress and Duress."

37. von Schrader, *Elementary Field Interrogation*, 30–33.

38. See chapter 3, "Lights Heat, and Sweat" and chapter 14, "Stress and Duress";
    Kessel and Pirelli, *Le people algérien*, 217, 406; Johns, *Tory Torture in Ulster*, 15;
    Archdiocese of São Paulo, *Torture in Brazil*, 23–24; Stuart Rochester and Frederick
    Kiley, *Honor Bound* (Annapolis, MD: Naval Institute Press, 1999), 158, 159; John
    Hubbell, *POW* (New York: Reader's Digest Press, 1976), 465; AI, *Report of an
    Amnesty International Mission to the Republic of the Philippines* (London, 1976),
    22–25; AI, *Mexico*, 26; AI, *The Pain Merchants*, ACT 40/008/2003 (London: Inter-
    national Secretariat, 2003), 19, http://www.amnesty.org; AI, *Iran*, MDE 13/08/87
    (London, 1987), 10; Mohammad, *Argot of the Victim*, 14–15; Cohen and Golan,
    Interrogation of Palestinians, 47, 48, 50, 54;. Mark Danner, "Abu Ghraib: The
    Hidden Story," *New York Review of Books*, October 7, 2004, 47; illustrated in Falun
    Dafa Information Center, *Torture Methods*.

39. Brian Ross and Richard Esposito, "CIA's Harsh Interrogation Techniques De-
    scribed," *ABC News*, November 18, 2005, http://abcnews.go.com.

40. B'Tselem, *Routine Torture: Interrogation Methods of the General Security Service*
    (Jerusalem: B'Tselem, Israeli Information Center for Human Rights in the Occu-
    pied Territories, 1998), 26–27.

41. Niels Uildriks, "Police Torture in France," *Netherlands Quarterly of Human
    Rights* 17.4 (1999): 417.

42. AI, *Torture in China*, 17, 26; Kate Saunders, *Eighteen Layers of Hell* (London:
    Cassell, 1996), 40.

43. AI, *Torture in China*, 1992, 8–9, 11. Illustrated in Falun Dafa Information Center,
    Torture Methods.

44. Aurora Foundation, *Report*, 55–57, 60, 139, 142. For accounts during the Vietnam
    War, see Rochester and Kiley, *Honor Bound*, 386, 488.

45. Kessel and Pirelli, *Le people algérien*, 200; *Black Book on the Militarist "Democ-
    racy" in Turkey* (Brussels: Info-Türk, 1986), 252; "Israel Tortures Arab Prisoners,"
    Sunday Times (London), June 19, 1977, A19; Darius Rejali, *Torture and Modernity*
    (Boulder, CO: Westview, 1994), 71; Mohammad, *Argot of the Victim*, 9, 16; Donald
    Duncan, "Un béret vert parle," *Les Temps Modernes* 261 (1968): 1492.

46. Alexandre Manuel, Rogério Carapinha, and Dias Neves, *PIDE* (Fundão, Portu-
    gal: Jornal do Fundão, 1974), 19, 134.

47. AI, *Torture in the Eighties*, 164, 169; *Mise à jour des allegations de torture dans
    l'état de São Paulo* (São Paulo: Action des Chrétiens pour l'abolition de la torture),
    2002), tabulated data, 3.

48. Miles Moffeit, "Wider Iraqi Abuse Shown," *Denver Post*, May 26, 2004, A1;
    Ghaith Abdul-Ahad, "More Iraqis Allege Abuse by U.S. Military," Reuters, May
    4, 2004, http://www.yahoo.com; Eric Schmitt, "Pentagon Study Describes Abuse
    by Units in Iraq," *New York Times*, June 17, 2006, A1; M. Gregg Bloche and Jona-
    than H. Marks, "Doing Unto Others as They Did Unto Us," *New York Times*,
    November 14, 2005, A21.

49. Alves, *Torturas e Torturados*, 26–27; Archdiocese of São Paulo, *Torture in Brazil*,
    19–20.

50. *Images of Repression* (Mexico City: Human Rights Centre "Miguel Agustin Pro Juarez," 1999), 21.

51. Ross and Esposito, "CIA's Harsh Interrogation Techniques."

52. Norman Thomas, *The Conscientious Objector in America* (New York: B. W. Huebsch, 1925), 241.

53. Cited in Allegra Pacheco, "Israeli Justice on Torture," in *MER Monthly Magazine*, January 1999, http://www.middleeast.org/archives/1999_01_13.htm.

54. James Peck, *Freedom Ride* (New York: Simon and Schuster, 1962), 149; David Oshinsky, *"Worse Than Slavery"* (New York: Free Press, 1996), 234.

55. Deeley, *Beyond Breaking Point*, 58.

56. Frank Snepp, *Decent Interval* (New York: Random House, 1977), 31. See also Frank Snepp, *Irreparable Harm* (New York: Random House, 1999), 185–86.

57. AI, *Singapore* (London, 1976), 7; Foster, *Detention and Torture*, 103; AI, *Torture in the Eighties* (London, 1984), 203; AI, *Philippines*, 21, 35.

58. Mark Dow, *American Gulag* (Berkeley and Los Angeles: University of California Press, 2004), 143, 329; Neil A. Lewis, "Broad Use of Harsh Tactics Is Described at Cuba," *New York Times*, October 17, 2004, A1; Eric Schmitt, "Task Force 6-26: In Secret Unit's 'Black Room,' a Grim Portrait of U.S. Abuse," *New York Times*, March 19, 2006, sec. 1, p. 1; Eric Schmitt, "Pentagon Study Describes Abuse by Units in Iraq," *New York Times*, June 17, 2006, A1.

59. Mohammad abu-Ghabiyr, cited in "Israel Tortures Arab Prisoners," 19.

60. Cohen and Golan, *Interrogation of Palestinians*, 47–49; Melissa Phillips, *Torture for Security* (Ramallah, West Bank: al-Haq, 1995), 23, 96, 118–22.

61. Yuval Ginbar, *Back to a Routine of Torture*, trans. Jessica Bonn (Jerusalem: Public Committee against Torture in Israel, 2003), 57; B'Tselem, *Routine Torture*, 37. For earlier reports, see Phillips, *Torture for Security*, 107.

62. Yuval Ginbar, *Flawed Defense*, trans. Jessica Bonn (Jerusalem: Public Committee against Torture in Israel, 2001), 41. See also B'Tselem, *Legislation Allowing the Use of Physical Force and Mental Coercion in Interrogations by the General Security Service* (Jerusalem: B'Tselem, 2000), 58; Ginbar, *Back to a Routine*, 50–51, 57.

63. Samer Duqan, cited in Ginbar, *Back to a Routine*, 50–51.

64. AI, *Japan*, ASA 22/04/98 (London, 1998), 9. See also Human Rights Watch, *Prison Conditions in Japan* (New York: Human Rights Watch, 1995), 26–28, 64. Illustrated in HRW, *Prison Conditions in Japan*, 27; AI, *Japan*, title page.

65. TAT—Torturaren Arkako Taldea [Group Against Torture], *Torture in Basque Country: Report 2001* ([Bilbao]: Graficas Lizarra, S.L, 2002), 50.

66. Human Rights Watch, *"And It Was Hell All Over Again . . ."* (New York: Human Rights Watch, 2000), 16; Donald Duncan, "The Whole Thing Was a Lie!" in *A Vietnam Primer*, 2nd ed. (San Francisco: Ramparts, 1968), 77.

67. AI, *Torture in the Eighties*, 169.

68. Jean Muller, *Le dossier* (Paris: Cahiers du Témoignage Chrétien, 1957), 17.

69. Kessel and Pirelli, *Le people algérien*, 406. Photograph available in First Lieutenant J. C. Cooper, "Statement on Torture in Uruguay," AMR/52/16/79 (London: Amnesty International, 1979), 1.

70. Human Rights Watch and Physicians for Human Rights, *Dead Silence* (New York: Human Rights Watch, 1994), 59, 63, 64, 67, 69, 70, 74, 77, 78, 80, 82, 87, 88; Duncan Forrest, "Examination Following Specific Forms of Torture," in *The Medical Documentation of Torture*, ed. Michael Peel and Vincent Iacopino (London: Greenwich Medical Media, 2002), 165–66; Ginbar, *Flawed Defense*, 36; Dennis Faul and Raymond Murray, *The RUC: The Black and Blue Book* ([Dungannon, Northern Ireland]: [Denis Faul], 1975), 17.

71. Forrest, "Examination," 163.

72. Kessel and Pirelli, *Le people algérien*, 411–12, 584.

73. Forrest, "Examination," 163.

74. TAT, 38, 49, 50, 76. For an account of the new cuffs, see AI, *Pain Merchants*, 19–23; and Alex Nichols, *A Guidebook to the Handcuffs and Other Restraints of the World* (Malvern, Worcestershire, England: Kingscourt, 2002), 234–40.

75. Dow, *American Gulag*, 143–44.

76. Lawrence E. Hinkle and Harold G. Wolff, "Communist Interrogation and Indoctrination of 'Enemies of the State,' " *A.M.A. Archives of Neurology and Psychiatry* 76 (August 1956): 155; Hans Draminsky Petersen, Lise Worm, Mette Zander, Ole Harting, and Bjarne Ussing, *Human Rights Violations in Burma/Myanmar* (Århus, Denmark: Physicians for Human Rights, 2000), 21; AI, *Korea*, 28; Futaba Igarashi, "Forced to Confess," in *Democracy in Contemporary Japan*, ed. G. McCormack and Y. Sugimoto (Armonk, NY: M. E. Sharpe, 1986), 202; Karen Parker and Etienne Jaudel, *Police Cell Detention in Japan* (San Francisco: Association of Humanitarian Lawyers, 1989), 37.

77. AI, *Afghanistan*, ASA 11/04/86 (New York, 1986), 13–14. See also M. A. Dadfar, *The Impaired Mind* (Peshawar, Pakistan: Psychiatry Center for Afghan Refugees, 1988), 46.

78. Mohammad, *Argot of the Victim*, 16.

79. South Africa, Truth and Reconciliation Commission, 3:178; Duncan, "Un béret vert parle," 1485.

80. Cited in B'Tselem, *Routine Torture*, 38. See also Lea Tsemel, "An Open letter to Abu Jerry," *Middle East Report* 213 (Winter 1999): 2–3.

81. Ginbar, *Back to a Routine*, 46. See also Cohen and Golan, *Interrogation of Palestinians*, 50–54, "Israeli Interrogation Methods: Interview with Bashar Tarabieh," *Middle East Report* 201 (October–December 1996): 29.

82. Illustrated in Ginbar, *Back to a Routine*, 55; B'Tselem, *Routine Torture*, 28, 38; *The Case Against Torture in Israel*, ed. and trans. Allegra Pacheco (Jerusalem: Public Committee Against Torture in Israel, 1999), 85.

83. Affidavit of Felah Abu Ramila, in Pacheco, *Case Against Torture*, 87–88.

84. Ginbar, *Back to a Routine*, 53, 59; Ginbar, *Flawed Defense*, 30, 41; B'Tselem, *Legislation*, 57.

85. Cohen and Golan, *Interrogation of Palestinians*, 52, 53 (illustrated); B'Tselem, *Routine Torture*, 35, Ginbar, *Flawed Defense*, 40.

86. Ginbar, *Back to a Routine*, 45.

87. Salim, cited in Cohen and Golan, *Interrogation of Palestinians*, 54; Ginbar, *Flawed Defense*, 38; Ginbar, *Back to a Routine*, 45, 47, 54, 64–69, illustrated on 64; B'Tselem, *Routine Torture*, 36, 38.

88. James Ron, "Varying Methods of State Violence," *International Organization* 51.2 (1997): 286.

89. Senior Mental Health Officer, UN Relief and Works Agency, in Jerusalem, cited in ibid., 295.

90. *Militarist "Democracy" in Turkey*, 250; Salinsky and Tigerstedt, *Evidence of Torture*, 39.

91. Ron, "Varying Methods," 286; Phillips, *Torture for Security*, 45–52; "Israel Tortures Arab Prisoners," A17–A20; Jeffrey Dillman and Musa Bakri, *Israel's Use of Electric Shock Torture in the Interrogation of Palestinian Detainees*, 2nd ed. (Jerusalem: Palestine Human Rights Information Center, 1992), 3–4.

92. Dillman and Bakri, *Israel's Use*, 10.

93. Ron, "Varying Methods," 284; John Conroy, *Unspeakable Acts, Ordinary People* (New York: Knopf, 2000), 139–56; Dillman and Bakri, *Israel's Use*, 2, 10.

94. Dillman and Bakri, *Israel's Use*, 1–3.

95. Ron, "Varying Methods," 285–86; Malcolm D. Evans and Rod Morgan, *Preventing Torture* (Oxford: Clarendon Press, 1998), 50.

96. Menachem Begin, *White Nights*, trans. Katie Kaplan (New York: Harper and Row, 1977), 108. See chapter 13, "Water, Sleep, and Spice."

97. Copies of which are reproduced in B'Tselem, *Routine Torture*, 24, 28; B'Tselem, *Legislation*, 65.

98. Ron, "Varying Methods," 289; Ya'el Stein, *Torture of Palestinian Minors in the Gush Etzion Police Station*, trans. Zvi Shulman (Jerusalem: B'Tselem, 2001), 8–9, 14–17.

99. B'Tselem, *Legislation*, 43.

100. Cited Parker and Jaudel, *Police Cell Detention*, 37.

101. Anthony Farrar-Hockley, *The Edge of the Sword* (London: Bucan and Enright, 1985), 184.

102. Josh White, "Soldier's 'Wish Lists' of Detainee Tactics Cited," *Washington Post*, April 19, 2005, A16. See also Scott Horton, "Washington, Honor and the Treatment of Prisoners," *New York Law Journal* 234 (August 16, 2005): 2; David Hackett Fischer, *Washington's Crossing* (Oxford: Oxford University Press, 2004), 370–71, 375–79, 378.

103. J. S. Bybee, Office of Legal Counsel, Department of Justice to Alberto Gonzales, Counsel to the President, "RE: Standards of Conduct for Interrogation under 18 U.S.C. § 23402340A," August 1, 2003, in Mark Danner, *Torture and Truth* (New York: New York Review of Books, 2004), 139–42.

104. Phillip Heyman and Juliette Kayyem, *Protecting Liberty in an Age of Terror* (Cambridge: MIT Press, 2005), 35–38. The conclusions of the Heyman report were apparently embraced by Congresswoman Jane Harman, the ranking minority member on the House Permanent Select Committee on Intelligence, in a speech at Georgetown (Jane Harman, "Intelligence Gathering in the Fog of Law," deliv-

ered at Georgetown University, February 7, 2005), but then subsequently abandoned. See also Joseph Lelyveld, "Interrogating Ourselves," *New York Times*, June 12, 2005, sec. 6, p. 43.

105. Friedrich Nietzsche, *On the Genealogy of Morals*, ed. Walter Kaufmann (New York: Vintage, 1969), 57–58.

Chapter 18
Noise

1. Futaba Igarashi, "Forced to Confess," in *Democracy in Contemporary Japan*, ed. G. McCormack and Y. Sugimoto (Armonk, NY: M. E. Sharpe, 1986), 201.

2. Tim Shallice, "The Ulster Depth Interrogation Techniques and their Relation to Sensory Deprivation Research," *Cognition* 1.4 (1972): 385–405; John McGuffin, *The Guineapigs* (Harmondsworth, England: Penguin, 1974).

3. Jacobo Timmerman, *Prisoner Without a Name, Cell without a Number* (New York: Vintage, 1982), 83.

4. Igarashi, "Forced to Confess," 201.

5. W.N.T. Beckett, *A Few Naval Customs, Expressions, Traditions and Superstitions*, 2nd ed. (Portsmouth, England: Gieves, [1915]), 40–41.

6. See chapter 16, "Fists and Exercises."

7. "Witness F," cited in Norwegian Government, *The Gestapo at Work in Norway* (Montreal: Royal Norwegian Government's Information Office, 1942), 17.

8. Peter Hoffman, *History of the German Resistance, 1933–1945*, trans. Richard Barry (Cambridge: MIT Press, 1977), 523.

9. Jan Valtin, *Out of the Night* (New York: Alliance Book Co., 1941), 576.

10. Alexandre Manuel, Rogério Carapinha, and Dias Neves, *PIDE* (Fundão, Portugal: Jornal do Fundão, 1974), 70, 98, 108–10, 128, 152, 180, 196; Amnesty International (AI), *Prison Conditions in Portugal* (London, 1965), 15–18.

11. Arnaldo Mesquita, cited in AI, *Prison Conditions in Portugal*, 18. For a more modern example, see Human Rights Watch, *Georgia* 6:11 (August 1994), 7.

12. Iain Guest, *Behind the Disappearances* (Philadelphia: University of Pennsylvania Press, 1990), 42.

13. *The Forgotten Prisoners of Ngyuen Van Thieu* (Paris: n.p., May 1973), 33. See also Jean-Pierre Debris and André Menras, *Rescapés des bagnes de Saigon* (Paris: Les Editeurs Français Reunis, 1973), 148–49; and Pham Tam, *Imprisonment and Torture in South Vietnam* (Nyack, NY: Fellowship of Reconciliation, 1969[?]), 8.

14. Nguyen Xuan Tram, *From Mainland Hell to Island Hell* (Hanoi: Foreign Languages Publishing House, 1961), 88.

15. Tam, *Imprisonment and Torture*, 8.

16. Resonant destruction is literally rocket science. The sound of the main engines of the Space Shuttle would kill anyone standing near the launch pad (Tony Phillips, "Guitars and Rockets Have Surprising Similarities," *USA Today*, November 9,

2005, http://www.usatoday.com). Something smaller would have to be exceedingly well tuned.

17. Pablo Sulbarán, *La Tortura en Venezuela* (Caracas: Publicaciones Seleven, 1980), 190.

18. Donald Duncan, "Un béret vert parle," *Les Temps Modernes* 261 (1968): 1485.

19. AI, *East Timor* (London, 1985), 54.

20. AI, *Report of an Amnesty International Mission to Spain*, EUR 41/03/80 (London, 1980), 15.

21. AI, *Spain*, EUR 41/02/85 (London, 1985), 18.

22. Jon Zubiaurre Agirre, cited in TAT—Torturaren Arkako Taldea [Group Against Torture], *Torture in Basque Country: Report 2001* ([Bilbao]: Graficas Lizarra, S.L, 2002), 25. See also TAT, 46, and TAT—Torturaren Arkako Taldea [Group Against Torture], *Torture en pays basque: Report 2000*, http://www.stoptortura.com/, 2002, 74.

23. Reza Baraheni, *The Crowned Cannibals* (New York: Vintage, 1977), 148–49.

24. Mohammad [pseud.], *The Argot of the Victim* (Copenhagen: Rehabilitation and Research Centre for Torture Victims, 1992), 8.

25. Ibid., 9.

26. Contrary to Ian Mather, " 'Religious' Torturers Use Shah's Police Techniques," *The Observer*, November 14, 1982, 13. AI, *Iran*, MDE 13/08/87 (London, 1987), 10; AI, *Iran*, MDE 13/09/87 (London, 1987); AI, *Iran*, MDE 13/21/90 (New York, 1990); Human Rights Watch, "*Like the Dead in Their Coffins*," (2004), http://hrw.org/reports/2004; Darius Rejali, *Torture and Modernity* (Boulder, CO: Westview, 1994), 113–33.

27. José Peirats, *Anarchists in the Spanish Revolution* (London: Freedom Press, 1990), 233.

28. Denis Faul and Raymond Murray, *The Hooded Men* (Dungannon, Co. Tyrone: Denis Faul, 1974), 1.

29. McGuffin, *The Guineapigs*, 63, 67, 71.

30. Ibid., 112, 119, 123.

31. Patrick Shivers, cited in Faul and Murray, *The Hooded Men*, 6. See also testimony by Rodgers and Shannon (McGuffin, *The Guineapigs*, 96, 98); and Hannaway (Faul and Murray, *The Hooded Men*, 46).

32. Joseph Clarke, cited in Faul and Murray, *The Hooded Men*, 52; see also Hannway's testimony (44).

33. Patrick McClean, cited in Faul and Murray, *The Hooded Men*, 17; see also Hannway's testimony (44).

34. Michael Montgomery, cited in Faul and Murray, *The Hooded Men*, 31. See also Donelly's testimony (McGuffin, *The Guineapigs*, 23).

35. William Shannon, cited in McGuffin, *The Guineapigs*, 95.

36. Faul and Murray, *The Hooded Men*, 40; McGuffin, *The Guineapigs*, 74.

37. McGuffin, *The Guineapigs*, 58, 63, 66.

38. Ibid., 58, 61, 63, 69, 94.

39. Ibid., 135.

40. Dan van der Vat, "German Border Police Tortured in Training," *Times* (London), March 2, 1973, 5; James Morton, *Catching the Killers* (London: Ebury Press, 2001), 175–76.

41. Martha Huggins, *Political Policing* (Durham, NC: Duke University Press, 1998), 171.

42. Marcio Alves, *Torturas e Torturados* (Rio de Janeiro: Empresa Jornalística, 1966), 26.

43. Cited in Archdiocese of São Paulo, *Torture in Brazil*, trans. Jaime Wright (New York: Vintage, 1986), 21.

44. Georges Pinet, cited in McGuffin, *The Guineapigs*, 74n.

45. José Miguel Camolez, cited in Archdiocese of São Paulo, *Torture in Brazil*, 20.

46. Archdiocese of São Paulo, *Torture in Brazil*, 20.

47. Huggins, *Political Policing*, 166–67, 171.

48. "Israel Tortures Arab Prisoners," *Sunday Times* (London), June 19, 1977, A19.

49. Ramzi Da'na, cited in Jeffrey Dillman and Musa Bakri, *Israel's Use of Electric Shock Torture in the Interrogation of Palestinian Detainees*, 2nd ed. (Jerusalem: Palestine Human Rights Information Center, 1992), 56.

50. Felah Abu Ramila, cited in *The Case Against Torture in Israel*, ed. and trans. Allegra Pacheco (Jerusalem: Public Committee Against Torture in Israel, 1999), 86–87. See also B'Tselem, *Routine Torture: Interrogation Methods of the General Security Service* (Jerusalem: B'Tselem, Israeli Information Center for Human Rights in the Occupied Territories, 1998), 37, 38; B'Tselem, *Legislation Allowing the Use of Physical Force and Mental Coercion in Interrogations by the General Security Service* (Jerusalem: B'Tselem, 2000), 58, 63.

51. "Israeli Interrogation Methods: Interview with Bashar Tarabieh," *Middle East Report* 201 (October–December 1996): 29.

52. Mufid Hamamreh, cited in Ya'el Stein, *Torture of Palestinian Minors in the Gush Etzion Police Station*, trans. Zvi Shulman (Jerusalem: B'Tselem, 2001), 15.

53. *Images of Repression* (Mexico City: Human Rights Centre "Miguel Agustin Pro Juarez," 1999), 21.

54. Michael Evans, "The 'White Noise' Torture Room," *Times*, June 19, 1999, http://web.lexis-nexis.com/.

55. Duncan Forrest, "The Methods of Torture and Its Effects," in *A Glimpse of Hell*, ed. Duncan Forrest (London: Amnesty International, 1996), 112.

56. Neil A. Lewis, "Broad Use of Harsh Tactics is Described at Cuba," *New York Times*, October 17, 2004, A1.

57. Asif Iqbal, cited in Vikram Dodd and Tania Branigan "Questioned at Gunpoint, Shackled, Forced to Pose Naked," *Guardian* (London), August 4, 2004, 1.

58. Cited in Julian Borger, "Metallica Is Latest Interrogation Tactic," *Guardian* (London), May 20, 2003, 11.

59. Lara Jakes Jordan and Matt Kelley, "U.S. Allies Also Accused in Prison Abuse," Associated Press Online, May 28, 2004, http://www.lexis-nexis.com/. See also International Committee of the Red Cross, *On the Treatment by Coalition Forces of Prisoners of War and Other Protected Persons by the Geneva Conventions in Iraq*

during Arrest, Internment and Interrogation (February 2004), 12–13; Eric Schmitt, "Pentagon Study Describes Abuse by Units in Iraq," *New York Times*, June 17, 2006, A1.

60. "Investigations Continue into Iraqi Deaths," *RFE/RL Iraq Report*, Radio Free Europe/Radio Liberty, Prague, Czech Republic, 7:30, August 12, 2004, http://www.rferl.org/.

61. Cited in Borger, "Metallica," 11.

62. Sgt. Mark Hadsell, Psychological Operations Company, cited in "Sesame Street Breaks Iraqi POWs," May 20, 2003, http://www.bbc.co.uk. See also Eric Schmitt, "Task Force 6-26: In Secret Unit's 'Black Room,' a Grim Portrait of U.S. Abuse," *New York Times*, March 19, 2006, sec. 1, p. 1.

63. One possibility is an obscure reference to the "piripipi," a noise torture used in the secret detention camps in Argentina in the 1970s. The only reference to it I have found does not describe it in sufficient detail to determine whether this is low-tech or high-tech noise. See AI, *Testimony on Secret Detention Camps in Argentina* (London, 1980), 18.

64. McGuffin, *The Guineapigs*, 98.

65. Antonio de Figueiredo and Jonathan Steele, "Torture Films Found at Police HQ," *Guardian* (London), May 3, 1974, 4.

66. "How Not to Run Your Secret Police," *The Economist*, May 18, 1974, 31–32.

67. "Torture as Policy," *Time*, August 16, 1976, 33; Steve Wright, "The New Trade in Technologies of Restraint and Electroshock," in Forrest, *A Glimpse of Hell*, 139.

68. Brian Innes, *The History of Torture* (New York: St. Martin's, 1998), 145; Mohammad, *Argot of the Victim*, 8.

69. McGuffin, *The Guineapigs*, 149; Steve Wright, "New Police Technologies," *Journal of Peace Research* 15.4 (1978): 310.

70. McGuffin, *The Guineapigs*, 149.

71. Brian Rappert, *Non-Lethal Weapons as Legitimizing Forces?* (London: Frank Cass, 2003), 47–55; William J. Broad, "Oh, What a Lovely War. If No one Dies,' *New York Times*, November 3, 2002, sec. 4, p. 3; Corey S. Powell, "War Without Death," *Discover*, April 1999, 32. The only recent evidence of sonic weaponry appeared inadvertently when pirates tried to take the *Seabourn Spirit*, a cruise ship, off the coast of Somalia. The ship's crew "triggered a sonic weapon, which sent out ear-splitting bangs to repel the pirates" (David Smith, "Pirates Shoot at Briton's Cruise Liner," *The Observer*, November 6, 2005, 1). How common these weapons are on cruise ships is unreported.

72. John Marks, *The Search for the Manchurian Candidate* (New York: McGraw-Hill, 1980); Alan Scheflin and Edward Opton, *The Mind Manipulators* (New York: Paddington Press, 1978).

73. Affidavit of Alan W. Scheflin in *Stanley Milton Glickman vs. USA et al*, 83 civ. 3458 (TPG), U.S. District Court, Southern District of New York.

74. Marks, *Search for Manchurian Candidate*, 137–38. See also Donald Hebb, *A Textbook of Psychology*, 2nd ed. (Philadelphia: W. B. Saunders, 1966), 151–55, 250, 251 (illustration); W. H. Bexton, W. Heron and T. H. Scott, "Effects of Decreased

Variation in the Sensory Environment," *Canadian Journal of Psychology* 8.2 (1954): 70–76.

75. Undated untitled CIA document, cited in Scheflin and Opton, *The Mind Manipulators*, 149. The date and description closely conform to Baldwin's box and Cameron's psychic driving chamber, both of which existed. Scheflin and Opton believe this memo refers to a third, unknown, laboratory possibly built by Dr. Louis West (149–50).

76. Cited in Marks, *Search for Manchurian Candidate*, 138.

77. Marks, *Search for Manchurian Candidate*, 202.

78. John Lilly, *The Scientist* (Berkeley, CA: Ronin, 1978), 98–102.

79. Marks, *Search for Manchurian Candidate*, 143.

80. Ibid., 142.

81. Ibid., 143.

82. Shallice, "Ulster Depth Interrogation Techniques," 399.

83. For Cameron's own accounts of depatterning and psychic driving, see respectively D. Ewen Cameron, "Production of Differential Amnesia as a Factor in the Treatment of Schizophrenia," *Comprehensive Psychiatry* 1 (1960): 26, 27; and D. Ewen Cameron, Leonard Levy, and Leonard Rubenstein, "Effects of Repetition of Verbal Signals upon the Behavior of Chronic Psychoneurotic Patients," *Journal of Mental Science* (1960): 742–54.

84. A. E. Schwartzman and P. E. Termansen, "Intensive Electroconvulsive Therapy: A Follow-Up Study," *Canadian Psychiatric Association Journal* 12 (1967): 218.

85. Marks, *Search for Manchurian Candidate*, 140.

86. Ibid., 141.

87. Cameron, Levy, and Rubenstein, "Effects of Repetition," 743.

88. Ewen Cameron, cited in Marks, *Search for Manchurian Candidate*.

89. Cited in ibid., 137.

90. *KUBARK Counterintelligence Interrogation* (Langley, VA: Central Intelligence Agency (CIA), July 1963), 87–90 (hereafter *Kubark*); *Human Resource Exploitation Training Manual* (Langley, VA: Central Intelligence Agency, July 1963), 1983), K.6–7. Available at the National Security Archives, http://www2.gwu.edu/~nsarchiv/NSAEBB/NSAEBB122/ (hereafter cited as *HRET*).

91. Archdiocese of São Paulo, *Torture in Brazil*, 20.

92. Shallice, "Ulster Depth Interrogation Techniques," 399.

93. Lilly, *The Scientist*, 103.

94. Aldous Huxley, *Moksha*, ed. Michael Horowitz and Cynthia Palmer (Los Angeles: J. P. Tarcher, 1982), 57, 155, 195.

95. Lilly, *The Scientist*, 103–8. Lilly's account of the dialogue of the Three Beings is on pp. 109–13.

96. "Samadhi Floatation Tank Home," http://www.samadhitank.com.

97. John Lilly, *The Deep Self* (New York: Simon and Schuster, 1977).

98. Shallice, "Ulster Depth Interrogation Techniques," 395.

99. Ibid., 390.

100. Ibid., 386.

101. Ibid., 400; see also 399.

102. Manuel, Carapinha, and Neves, *PIDE*, 98.

103. Lawrence E. Hinkle and Harold G. Wolff, "Communist Interrogation and Indoctrination of 'Enemies of the State,' " *A.M.A. Archives of Neurology and Psychiatry* 76 (August 1956): 134.

104. de Figueiredo and Steele, "Torture Films Found," 4.

105. Shallice, "Ulster Depth Interrogation Techniques," 389.

106. John Conroy, *Unspeakable Acts, Ordinary People* (New York: Knopf, 2000), 129.

107. Marks, *Search for Manchurian Candidate*, 138.

108. Ibid.

109. *Kubark*, 88.

110. *HRET*, K.6–7.

111. S. Smith and W. Lewty, "Perceptual Isolation in a Silent Room," *The Lancet*, September 12, 1959, 342–45.

112. Alfred McCoy, *A Question of Torture* (New York: Metropolitan, 2006), 53–54.

113. Desmond Hamill, *Pig in the Middle* (London: Methuen, 1985), 66; Thomas Mockaitis, *British Counterinsurgency in the Post-Imperial Era* (Manchester, England: Manchester University Press, 1995), 122.

114. Faul and Murray, *The Hooded Men*, 1–2.

115. *HRET*, K.9–11.

116. McGuffin, *The Guineapigs*, 33, 36.

117. "The whole SD process was a 'package deal' " (McGuffin, *The Guineapigs*, 123).

118. The same could be said of the American interrogator in Iraq who suggested "white noise" for his interrogation "wish list" (Josh White, "Soldier's 'Wish Lists' of Detainee Tactics Cited," *Washington Post*, April 19, 2005, A16). Again, the practice belies the supposed utility, as all documented cases in which interrogators used noise involved music, not white noise.

119. John Zubek, "Sensory and Perceptual Motor Process," in *Sensory Deprivation: Fifteen Years of Research*, ed. John Zubek (New York: Meredith, 1969), 232.

120. *Kubark*, 88, 90.

121. See, for example, Vikram Dodd, "Torture by the Book," *Guardian* (London), May 6, 2004, 23; Andrew McLeod, "Victim of Latin American Torture Claims Abu Ghraib Abuse Was Official US Policy," *Sunday Herald* (Scotland), December 12, 2004, http://www.commondreams.org; Alfred W. McCoy, "America's Road to Abu Ghraib," September 9, 2004, http://www.Tomdispatch.com; Alfred W. McCoy, "Torture at Abu Ghraib Followed CIA's Manual," *Boston Globe*, May 14, 2004, A11; McCoy, *A Question of Torture*, 5, 8, 12, 49–50, 58–60; Naomi Klein, "The US Has Used Torture for Decades," *Guardian* (London), December 10, 2005, http://www.guardian.co.uk/; Neil MacMaster, "Torture: From Algiers to Abu Ghraib, *Race and Class* 46.2 (2004): 15; Armen Victorian, *The Mind Controllers* (Miami, FL: Lewis International, 2000); Armen Victorian, "United States, Canada, Britain: Partners in Mind Control Operations," *MindNet Journal* 1.81 (July 1996), http://www.heart7.net/mcf/mindnet/mn181.htm. The earliest adaptation of the classic narrative to post-9/11 torture was Joe Vialls, "Rift between US Govern-

ment and Special Forces: Rumsfeld Orders 'British' Torture for Afghan Prisoners,"
January 19, 2002, http://www.geocities.com/torturevictims/cuba.html.

122. Nor should one confuse any of these torture devices with typewriters, tape recorders, and other devices that depend on the availability of a proper wall plug (see
McLeod, "Victims").

123. McCoy, A *Question of Torture*, 65–68. For earlier versions of the same confusion
between ECT and magneto torture, see Pericles Korovessis, *The Method*, trans.
Les Nightingale and Catherine Patrakis (London: Allison and Busby, 1970), 49–
50; and Miguel Sanchez-Mazas, *Spain in Chains* (New York: Veterans of the Abraham Lincoln Brigade, 1960), 23.

124. The closest plausible claim is that prisoners and guards had to listen to the jet
engines of a plane for thirty hours in transport from Afghanistan to Guantánamo
(Vialls, "Rift"). This is white noise and it fell on everyone equally. But nothing
like this appears in U.S. prisons.

125. Walter Pincus, "Waterboarding Historically Controversial," *Washington Post*, October 5, 2006, A17.

126. Victorian, "United States, Canada, Britain"; Klein, "US Has Used Torture"; Vialls, "Rift"; McCoy, A *Question of Torture*, 8.

127. McCoy, A *Question of Torture*, 70.

128. Vialls, "Rift"; M. Gregg Bloche and Jonathan H. Marks, "When Doctors Go to
War," *New England Journal of Medicine* 352.1 (January 6, 2005): 4.

129. MacMaster, "Torture," 15; Klein, "US Has Used Torture"; Bloche and Marks,
"Doctors Go to War," 4; McCoy, A *Question of Torture*, 8, 90.

130. McCoy, A *Question of Torture*, 8, 59.

131. Ibid., 58–59.

132. Ibid., 52, 58.

133. Ibid., 59.

134. Ibid.

135. Ibid., 13–14, 58, 60.

136. Dodd, "Torture by the Book," 23.

137. McCoy, A *Question of Torture*, 8, 32, 45.

138. Ibid., 7, 9.

139. R. Wuillaume, "The Wuillaume Report," in Pierre Vidal-Naquet, *Torture*, trans.
Barry Richard (Harmondsworth, England: Penguin, 1963), 176.

140. "A 'Tortured' Debate," *Wall Street Journal*, February 6, 2006, http://www.wsj.com.

141. McCoy, A *Question of Torture*, 59. There is no evidence, one way or another, to
indicate whether CIA torture was less ritualistic than Inquisitional, as McCoy
claims. There are no ethnographies of CIA interrogators in the field akin to historical accounts of Inquisitors at work. Torturers as a whole are a superstitious lot,
and it is just as plausible that CIA interrogators had their own rituals.

142. See chapter 1, "Modern Torture and Its Observers."

143. See, for example, McCoy, A *Question of Torture*, 32, 50–52, 70.

144. These are sources numbered 13, 15, and 27 in the *Kubark* bibliography.

145. Kurt Lewin, *The Complete Social Scientist*, ed. Martin Gold (Washington, DC: American Psychological Association, 1999), 221–24.

146. Darius Rejali, "The Real Shame of Abu Ghraib," Time.com, May 20, 2004, http://www.time.com.

147. Rebecca Lemov, *World as Laboratory* (New York: Hill and Wang, 2005), 199.

148. Jane Mayer, "The Experiment," *New Yorker*, July 11 and 18, 2005, 63–67.

149. See Henry Charles Lea, *A History of the Inquisition of the Middle Ages* (New York: Russell and Russell, 1958), 1:415. Contrary to McCoy, *A Question of Torture*, 59.

Chapter 19
Drugs and Doctors

1. Vladimir Gusarov, "It Was Better Under Stalin," in Harvey Fireside, *Soviet Psychoprisons* (New York: Norton, 1979), 155.

2. See also Zhores Medvedev, "Psycho-adaptation or Democratisation?" in *A Question of Madness*, ed. Zhores Medvedev and Roy Medvedev, trans. Ellen de Kadt (New York: Norton, 1971), 198–99.

3. Cited in Jean Rolin, *Police Drugs*, trans. Laurence Bendit (London: Hollis and Carter, 1955), 17. House's original letter was published in the *Texas Medical Journal*, September 1922.

4. Robert House, cited in Andre Moenssens, "Narcoanalysis in Law Enforcement," *Journal of Criminal Law, Criminology and Police Science* 52.4 (1961): 454.

5. House, cited in Gilbert Geis, "In Scopolomanie Veritas: The Early History of Drug-Induced Statements," *Journal of Criminal Law, Criminology, and Police Science* 50:4 (1959): 351. House hated informants (see Geis, 351 n. 40). For a full list of House's writings, see Geis, 350 n. 37.

6. Geis, "In Scopolomanie Veritas," 348.

7. Robert House, cited in Rolin, *Police Drugs*, 17.

8. Robert House, "Use of Scopolamine in Criminology," *American Journal of Police Science* 2.4 (1931): 329.

9. Robert House, cited in Rolin, *Police Drugs*, 17. See also House, "Use of Scopolamine," 329.

10. National Commission on Law Observance and Enforcement, *Report on Lawlessness in Law Enforcement* (Washington, DC: U.S. Government Printing Office, 1931), 256.

11. Peter Deeley, *Beyond Breaking Point* (London: Arthur Baker, 1971), 228; for other accounts, see John M. MacDonald, *The Murderer and His Victim*, 2nd ed. (Springfield, IL: Charles C. Thomas, 1986), 136–37.

12. Calvin Goddard, "How Science Solves Crime: Truth Serum or Scopolamine in Interrogation of Criminal Suspects," *Hygeia* 10 (1932): 337–40. The term had been used earlier (House, "Use of Scopolamine," 330).

13. Rolin, *Police Drugs*, 11.

14. Deeley, *Beyond Breaking Point*, 228.

15. Rolin, *Police Drugs*, 19.

16. Clark L. Hull, *Hypnosis and Suggestibility* (New York: Appleton Century Crofts, 1933), 100.

17. Rolin, *Police Drugs*, 12–15, 22–23.

18. Ibid., 24–27.

19. Ibid., 27–28; Edward Saher, *Narcoanalysis* (The Hague: Martinus Nijhoff, 1950), 10; Roy Grinker and John Spiegel, *Men Under Stress* (Philadelphia: Blakiston, 1945), 389–406.

20. Rolin, *Police Drugs*, 115.

21. For the account of Marty and his brigade, see chapter 5, "Bathtubs."

22. See Saher, *Narcoanalysis*, 1–2, 7–20; Rolin, *Police Drugs*, 49–68, 80–135; Macdonald, *Murderer and His Victim*, 135–38; J. P. Gagnieur, "The Judicial Use of Psychonarcosis in France," *Journal of Criminal Law and Crimonology* 40.3 (1949): 370–80; *La narcose et ses application judiciaires* (Paris: Société Internationale de Criminologie, February 15, 1951); C. W. Muehlberger, "Interrogation under Drug Influence," *Journal of Criminal Law, Criminology and Police Science* 42.4 (1951): 513–28; George Dession, Lawrence Freedman, Richard Donnelly, and Frederick Redlich, "Drug-Induced Revelation and Criminal Investigation," *Yale Law Journal* 62.3 (1953): 315–47; Jean-Claude Lauret and Raymond Lasierra, *La torture et les pouvoirs* (Paris: Balland, 1973), 429–36.

23. Rolin, *Police Drugs*, 20–21; David Dressler, "The Drug That Makes Criminals Talk," *Saturday Evening Post*, December 27, 1947, 16–17, 43–44.

24. "Nothing But the Truth," *The Lancet*, March 21, 1953, 585–86.

25. Henri Alleg, *The Question* (New York: George Braziller, 1958), originally *La Question* (Paris: Éditions de Minuit, 1961), 92 (77–79, French edition); Deeley, *Beyond Breaking Point*, 226. Contrary to Fanon and others, this is the only known report from Algeria. See Lauret and Lasierra, *La torture et les pouvoirs*, 436; Frantz Fanon, *The Wretched of the Earth*, trans. Constance Farrington (New York: Grove Press, 1968), 284.

26. Moenssens, "Narcoanalysis in Law Enforcement," 454. Critics included F. E. Inbau and John Reid, the writers of what is now the standard police interrogation manual worldwide, and John Larson, the inventor of the modern polygraph test. See John Larson, *Lying and Its Detection* (Chicago: University of Chicago Press, 1932), 204–20; and John M. MacDonald, "Truth Serum," *Journal of Criminal Law, Criminology, and Police Science* 46.2 (1955): 260–61.

27. Deeley, *Beyond Breaking Point*, 228.

28. Ibid., 225.

29. Cited in Alan Scheflin and Edward Opton, *The Mind Manipulators* (London: Paddington Press, 1978), 135.

30. Scheflin and Opton, *The Mind Manipulators*, 106–212; John Marks, *The Search for the Manchurian Candidate* (New York: Times Books, 1979), 6–7, 21–44, 48, 55, 58–73, 105, 109, 118–22, 145, 155, 169–80, 198.

31. Scheflin and Opton, *The Mind Manipulators*, 126.

32. Ibid., 126, 142–43.

33. Cited in ibid., 136.

34. Ibid., 129–30.

35. Carlos Osorio, "Chronology of Events Related to Seven Army Spanish Language Manuals and CIA Manuals to Train Latin American Military in Intelligence and Interrogation Techniques Through the School of the Americas, Military Training Teams, and CIA Trainers," unpublished manuscript, National Security Archive, George Washington University, Washington, DC, January 23, 1997.

36. "Fact Sheet Concerning Training Manuals Containing Materials Inconsistent with US Policy," available at the National Security Archives, George Washington University, Washington, DC. The relevant passages are on the following pages: *Handling of Sources*, 147–48, and *Manejo de Fuentes*, 122–23.

37. Deeley, *Beyond Breaking Point*, 102; Eric Stover, *The Open Secret* (Washington, DC: American Association for the Advancement of Science, 1987), 28–29; Douglas Colligan, "The New Science of Torture," *Science Digest*, July 1976, 46–47; Amnesty International (AI), *Report on Allegations of Torture in Brazil* (London, 1973), 29, 35–36; AI, *Chile* (London, 1974), 63; AI, *Report of an Amnesty International Mission to the Republic of the Philippines* (London, 1976), 22, 31, 32; Archdiocese of São Paulo, *Torture in Brazil*, trans. Jaime Wright (New York: Vintage, 1986), 22.

38. John McGuffin, *The Guineapigs* (Harmondsworth, England: Penguin, 1974), 138.

39. Colligan, "New Science of Torture," 46–47.

40. AI, *Political Imprisonment in Uruguay* (London, 1979).

41. William Waack, *Camaradas: Nos Arquivos de Moscou* (São Paulo: Companhia das Letras, 1993), 300; A. J. Langguth, *Hidden Terrors* (New York: Pantheon, 1978), 230; Archdiocese of São Paulo, *Torture in Brazil*, 34.

42. See "Shock," chapter 6.

43. Archdiocese of São Paulo, *Torture in Brazil*, 35.

44. Colligan, "New Science of Torture," 46–47.

45. AI, *Chile* (London, 1983), 23. See also Stover, *The Open Secret*, 27–29.

46. AI, *Report of a Mission to Argentina, 6–15 November 1976* (London, 1977), 39; Robert Kirschner, "The Use of Drugs in Torture and Human Rights Abuses," *American Journal of Forensic Medicine and Pathology* 5.4 (1984): 313–14.

47. Jørgen Tomsen, Karin Helweg-Larsen, and Ole Vedel Rasmussen, "Amnesty International and the Forensic Sciences," *American Journal of Forensic Medicine and Pathology* 5.4 (1984): 306; Albert Jonson and Leonard Sagan, "Torture and the Ethics of Medicine," in *The Breaking of Bodies and Minds*, ed. Eric Stover and Elena Nightingale (New York: W. H. Freeman, 1985), 32; Michael Alan Green, "Sudden and Suspicious Deaths Outside the Deceased's Own Country—Time for an International Protocol," *Forensic Science International* 20 (1982): 71–75.

48. Kirschner, "Use of Drugs," 313.

49. Anne Goldfeld, Richard Mollica, Barbara Pesavent, and Stephen Faraone, "The Physical and Psychological Sequelae of Torture," *Journal of the American Medical Association* 259.18 (May 13, 1988): 2725–29.

50. Tomsen, Helweg-Larsen, and Rasmussen, "Amnesty International," 306; Ole Vedel Rasmussen, "Medical Aspects of Torture," *Danish Medical Bulletin* 37, Sup. 1 (January 1990): 8, 10.

51. AI, *Report,* 1986 (London, 1986), 155, AI, *Torture in the Eighties* (London, 1984), 133, 151.

52. *Report of the Chilean National Commission on Truth and Reconciliation,* trans. Phillip E. Berryman (Notre Dame, IN: University of Notre Dame Press, 1993), 1:134; 2:499–501, 644.

53. Mary Salinsky and Liv Tigerstedt, *Evidence of Torture* (London: Medical Foundation for the Care of Victims of Torture, 2001).

54. Scheflin and Opton, *The Mind Manipulators,* 169.

55. *Human Resource Exploitation Training Manual* (Langley, VA: Central Intelligence Agency, July 1963, 1983), K.12–K13. Available at the National Security Archives, http://www2.gwu.edu/~nsarchiv/NSAEBB/NSAEBB122/.

56. Dirk von Schrader, *Elementary Field Interrogation* (n.p.: Delta, 1978).

57. Kirschner, "Use of Drugs," 313.

58. Ibid., 314.

59. Former SPH prisoner, cited in Alexander Podrabinek, *Punitive Medicine* (Ann Arbor, MI: Karoma, 1980), 90.

60. Podrabinek, *Punitive Medicine,* 90; see also 33, 149.

61. Fireside, *Soviet Psychoprisons,* 55. See also Podrabinek, *Punitive Medicine,* 33, 89–90, 149; Kirschner, "Use of Drugs," 314.

62. Podrabinek, *Punitive Medicine,* 33, 92–94, 146, 149; Fireside, *Soviet Psychoprisons,* 55, 82–84, 125–26; Kirschner, "Use of Drugs," 313–14.

63. Sidney Bloch and Peter Reddaway, *Russia's Political Hospitals* (London: Victor Gollancz, 1977), 364 (Ivankov, Jankauskas).

64. Kirschner, "Use of Drugs," 314; Podrabinek, *Punitive Medicine,* 85–87.

65. Mikhail Kukobaka, "Memoirs," in Fireside, *Soviet Psychoprisons,* 176.

66. Cited in Fireside, *Soviet Psychoprisons,* 88. See also Podrabinek, *Punitive Medicine,* 147.

67. Kukobaka, "Memoirs," 177.

68. Fireside, *Soviet Psychoprisons,* 82; see also Podrabinek, *Punitive Medicine,* 33, 66–67, 94–95, 154.

69. Podrabinek, *Punitive Medicine,* 33, 65, 94–95.

70. See chapter 6, "Shock."

71. Kirschner, "Use of Drugs," 315.

72. Lawrence E. Hinkle and Harold G. Wolff, "Communist Interrogation and Indoctrination of 'Enemies of the State,'" *A.M.A. Archives of Neurology and Psychiatry* 76 (August 1956): 118.

73. Deeley, *Beyond Breaking Point,* 226; Robert Tucker, *Stalin in Power* (New York: Norton, 1992), 169.

74. Fireside, *Soviet Psychoprisons,* 67.

75. Sidney Bloch and Peter Reddaway, *Soviet Psychiatric Abuse* (Boulder, CO: Westview, 1984), 18.

76. Gusarov, "Better Under Stalin," 155; See also Podrabinek, *Punitive Medicine*, 65.

77. Podrabinek, *Punitive Medicine*, 65.

78. Ibid., 137; see also 66–67. See also Sidney Bloch and Peter Reddaway, "Psychiatrists and Dissenters in the Soviet Union," in Stover and Nightingale, *Breaking of Bodies*, 135.

79. Podrabinek, *Punitive Medicine*, 65, 85–95, 150; Fireside, *Soviet Psychoprisons*, 79. Bloch and Redaway's survey of 210 dissidents in psychoprisons describes no cases of ECT (*Russia's Political Hospitals*, 347–98).

80. Podrabinek, *Punitive Medicine*, 70.

81. Bloch and Reddaway, "Psychiatrists and Dissenters," 139.

82. Hirt, cited in Fireside, *Soviet Psychoprisons*, 40.

83. To be specific: 1968 (2), 1970 (1), 1972 (2), 1973 (3), 1974 (5), 1975 (3) (Bloch and Reddaway, *Russia's Political Hospitals*, 347–98).

84. Gusarov, "Better Under Stalin," 155.

85. "Meeting of Leonid Plyushch with Psychiatrists at N.Y. Academy of Sciences, March 26, 1976," in Fireside, *Soviet Psychoprisons*, 125.

86. Dr. A. L. Zeleneyev, cited in Podrabinek, *Punitive Medicine*, 85.

87. Fireside, *Soviet Psychoprisons*, xvi–xvii, 12–14; Bloch and Reddaway, *Russia's Political Hospitals*, 40; Reddaway and Bloch, "Psychiatrists and Dissenters," 149–50; Walter Reich, "The World of Soviet Psychiatry," in Stover and Nightingale, *Breaking of Bodies*, 213–14, 218. For discussion of Snezhnevkyism and the diagnosis of sluggish schizophrenia, see Harold Merskey and Bronislava Shafran, "Political Hazards in the Diagnosis of 'Sluggish Schizophrenia,'" *British Journal of Psychiatry* 148 (1986): 247–56; Greg Wilkinson, "Political Dissent and 'Sluggish' Schizophrenia in the Soviet Union," *British Medical Journal* 293 (September 13, 1986): 641–42; Sidney Bloch, "Soviet Psychiatry and Snezhnevskyism," in *Soviet Psychiatric Abuse in the Gorbachev Era*, ed. Robert van Voren (Amsterdam: International Association on the Political Use of Psychiatry, 1989), 55–61.

88. Podrabinek, *Punitive Medicine*, 70–72, 140; Fireside, *Soviet Psychoprisons*, 37–38 (Medvedev); Gusarov, "Better Under Stalin," 155, 158.

89. Dr. Morozov, cited in Fireside, *Soviet Psychoprisons*, 8.

90. Fireside, *Soviet Psychoprisons*, xvii.

91. Medvedev, "Psycho-adaptation or Democratisation?" 199.

92. Fireside, *Soviet Psychoprisons*, xvii. Also Medvedev, "Psycho-adaptation or Democratisation?" 199–200; and Fireside, *Soviet Psychoprisons*, 64.

93. Valeriy Tarsis, *Ward 7*, trans. Katya Brown (New York: E.P. Dutton, 1965), 107–8.

94. Ibid., 122.

95. Bloch and Reddaway, *Soviet Psychiatric Abuse*, 20; Robert van Voren, "The History of Political Psychiatry in the USSR," in van Voren, *Soviet Psychiatric Abuse*, 19.

96. Podrabinek, *Punitive Medicine*, 72.

97. H.J.N. Andreyev, "Political Dissent and 'Sluggish' Schizophrenia in the Soviet Union," *British Medical Journal* 293 (September 27, 1986): 822.

98. Fireside, *Soviet Psychoprisons*, 64; Friedrich Weinberger, foreword to van Voren, *Soviet Psychiatric Abuse*, 7; Fireside, *Soviet Psychoprisons*; I. F. Stone, "Betrayal by Psychiatry," *New York Review of Books*, February 10, 1972, 7–14.

99. Fireside, *Soviet Psychoprisons*, 33, 35. Full manual available in Fireside, *Soviet Psychoprisons*, 92–118.

100. AI, *Prisoners of Conscience in the USSR* (London, 1975).

101. Fireside, *Soviet Psychoprisons*, 89; Daniel C. Thomas, *The Helsinki Effect* (Princeton, NJ: Princeton University Press, 2001).

102. Fireside, *Soviet Psychoprisons*, 150.

103. van Voren, "History of Political Psychiatry," 20.

104. Fireside, *Soviet Psychoprisons*, 63; see also 8.

105. Podrabinek, *Punitive Medicine*, 155–83.

106. AI, *Political Abuse of Psychiatry in the USSR*, EUR 46/01/83 (New York: Amnesty International USA, 1983), 3.

107. Podrabinek, *Punitive Medicine*, 140.

108. Ibid., 135.

109. Fireside, *Soviet Psychoprisons*, 64.

110. Reich, "World of Soviet Psychiatry," 207.

111. Scheflin and Opton, *The Mind Manipulators*, 392; Fireside, *Soviet Psychoprisons*, xv. See also chapter 6, "Shock."

112. See, for example, "Connecticut Rejects Charges of Abuses at Mental Hospital," *New York Times*, June 22, 1969, 42; "Hospital Crimes Found in Chicago," *New York Times*, June 1, 1969, 31; Jessica Mitford, "The Torture Cure," *Harper's*, August 1973, 16, 18, 24–26, 28, 30.

113. Fireside, *Soviet Psychoprisons*, 1; Bloch and Reddaway, *Soviet Psychiatric Abuse*, 197; Charles J. Brown and Armando Lago, *The Politics of Psychiatry in Revolutionary Cuba* (New Brunswick, NJ: Transaction, 1991), 3–4.

114. Peter Reddaway, "Soviet Psychiatry and the WPA after Vienna, 1983–1989," in van Voren, *Soviet Psychiatric Abuse*, 73–85; Robert van Voren, "Soviet Psychiatry Criticized in the Soviet Press," in van Voren, *Soviet Psychiatric Abuse*, 62–72; Alexander Podrabinek, "Soviet Psychiatric Abuse during the Gorbachev Era," in van Voren, *Soviet Psychiatric Abuse*, 103; Rupert Cornwell, "Russia's Unholy Fools," *Independent Magazine*, March 25, 1989, 24–27.

115. Victoria Pope, "Mad Russians," *U.S. News and World Report*, December 16, 1996, 38–43.

116. Lajos Ruff, *The Brain-Washing Machine* (London: Robert Hale, 1959), 56–61, 74, 77–78, 91, 95.

117. AI, *Prison Conditions in Rumania, 1955–64* (London, 1965), 11.

118. AI, *Romania* (New York: Amnesty International USA, 1978), 14–18 (hospitals), 19–22, 26 (pharmacological torture), 21 (ECT); Nanci Adler and Gerard Mueller, "Psychiatry Under Tyranny," *Current Psychology* 12.1 (1993): 3–18.

119. Brown and Lago, *Politics of Psychiatry*, 99–100.

120. Ibid., 18, 22–25, 45–120 passim. Fifteen prisoners reported pharmacological torture, while eleven reported electrotorture.

121. Cited in ibid., 60.

122. "Chinese 'Truth Drug,'" *Times* (London), July 12, 1952, A3.

123. *Dangerous Minds* (New York: Human Rights Watch and Geneva Initiative on Psychiatry, 2002), 117–25.

124. Ibid., 123–25.

125. AI, *Vasily Stetsik*, October 2, 2002, EUR 46/017/2002, http://www.amnesty.org.

126. AI, *Turkmenistan: Appeal Cases*, November 24, 2004, EUR 61./008/2004, http://www.amnesty.org.

127. Peter Taylor, *Beating the Terrorists?* (Harmondsworth, England: Penguin, 1980), 149–50.

128. Ibid., 148–49, 213, 246, 266.

129. Ibid., 206. Specifically, see 65–66, 102, 114, 118, 154, 167, 184–85, 196–97, 203, 209, 213, 221, 225–26, 248, 251–52, 261, 272, 275, 284, 315–18, 334–35.

130. Ibid., 179, 187–92, 240–43, 273–79, 321–22.

131. Unai Lopez de Okariz Lopez, cited in TAT—Torturaren Arkako Taldea [Group Against Torture], *Torture in Basque Country: Report 2001* ([Bilbao]: Graficas Lizarra, S.L, 2002), 50.

132. Iratxe Sorzabal, *Torture in Basque Country*, 148.

133. Aitor Lorente, cited in TAT—Torturaren Arkako Taldea [Group Against Torture], *Torture en pays basque: Report 2000*, http://www.stoptortura.com/, 2002, 50.

134. Eric Boehm, *We Survived*, reprint ed. (Santa Barbara, CA: ABC-Clio Information Services, 1985), 193; Herman Bodson, *Agent for the Resistance*, ed. Richard Schmidt (College Station: Texas A&M University Press, 1994), 121–22; Benoist Rey, *Les Égorgeurs* (Paris: Les Éditions de Minuit, 1961); Emanuel Lavine, *The Third Degree* (Garden City, NY: Garden City Publishing, 1930), 61–69; Tom Murton, "Prison Doctors," in *Humanistic Perspectives in Medical Ethics*, ed. Maurice B. Visscher (Buffalo, NY: Prometheus, 1972), 248–65; Dennis Faul and Raymond Murray, *British Army and Special Branch RUC Brutalities* (Dungannon, Northern Ireland: the Compilers, 1972), 61–64; Stover, *The Open Secret*, 23–34, 75; Richard Claude, Eric Stover, and June Lopez, *Health Professionals and Human Rights in the Philippines* (Washington, DC: American Association for the Advancement of Science, 1987), 27–30; Paul Mansour, "Turkish Doctors Collude in Torture," *British Medical Journal* 314 (March 8, 1997): 695; Vincent Iacopino, Michele Heisler, Shervin Pishevar, and Robert Kirschner, "Physician Complicity in Misrepresentation and Omission of Evidence in Torture in Postdetention Medical Examinations in Turkey," *Journal of the American Medical Association* 276.5 (1996): 396–402; Fred Charatan, "Brazil Challenges Doctors Accused of Torture," *British Medical Journal* 318 (March 20, 1999): 757; Human Rights Watch, *Torture and Ill-Treatment, Israel's Interrogation of Palestinians from the Occupied Territories* (New York: Human Rights Watch, 1994): 216–19; *Dilemmas of Professional Ethics as a Result of Involvement of Doctors and Psychologists in Interrogation and Torture* (Jerusalem: Public Committee Against Torture in Israel, 1993); Ruchama Marton, "The White Coat Passes Like a Shadow," in *Torture*, ed. Neve Gordon and Ruchama Marton with John Jay Neufeld (London: Zed, 1995), 33–40; Melissa Phillips, *Tor-*

ture for Security (Ramallah, West Bank: al-Haq, 1995), 109; Mikki van Zyl, Jeanelle de Gruchy, Sheila Lapinsky, Simon Lewin, and Graeme Reid, *The Aversion Project* (Cape Town: Van Zyl, DeGruchy, Lapinsky, Lewin, Reid, 1999).

135. Rasmussen, "Medical Aspects of Torture," 43; Knud Smidt-Nielsen, "The Participation of Health Personnel in Torture," *Torture* 8.3 (1998): 93; P. B. Vesti, "Extreme Man-Made Stress and Anti-Therapy," *Danish Medical Bulletin* 37.5 (1990): 466–68.

136. AI, *Doctors and Torture*, ACT 75/001/2002 (London, 2002); British Medical Association, *Medicine Betrayed* (London: Zed, 1992); Richard Goldstein and Patrick Breslin, "Technicians of Torture: How Physicians Become Agents of State Terror," *The Sciences*, March–April 1986, 14–19; Jonson and Sagan, "Torture and Ethics," 31–35.

137. Rey, *Les Égorgeurs*, 53.

138. Michael Simpson, "Methods of Investigating Allegations of Electric Shock Torture," *Torture* 4.1 (1994): 28. See also Grethe Skylv, "The Physical Sequelae of Torture," in *Torture and Its Consequences*, ed. Metin Başoğlu (Cambridge: Cambridge University Press, 1992), 45; G. H. Malik, I. A. Sirwal, A. R. Reshi, M. S. Najar, M. Tanvir, and M. Altaf, "Acute Renal Failure Following Physical Torture," *Nephron* 63 (1993): 434–37.

139. Simpson, "Methods of Investigating Allegations," 28; Sklyv, "Physical Sequelae of Torture," 47–48; Tomsen, Helweg-Larsen, and Rasmussen, "Amnesty International," 306–7, 311.

140. Robert Kirschner and Michael Peel, "Physical Examination for Late Signs of Torture," in *The Medical Documentation of Torture*, ed. Michael Peel and Vincent Iacopino (London: Greenwich Medical Media, 2002), 149–58; Duncan Forrest, "Examination Following Specific Forms of Torture," in Peel and Iacopino, 159–70.

141. AI, *Harming the Healers*, ACT 75/02/00c (London, 2000); Joshua Phillips, "A Torture Path to Justice," *Washington Post Magazine*, August 17, 2003, 6–11, 19–25; Henrick Døcker, "Turkey Continues Harassment, Arrests and Torture of Medical Doctors," *Torture* 10.2 (2002): 53.

142. Veli Lök, Mehmet Tunca, Kamil Kumanloglu, Emre Kapkin, and Gurkan Dirik, "Bone Scintigraphy as Clue to Previous Torture," *The Lancet* 337 (April 6, 1991): 847; Semih Aytaçlar and Veli Lök, "Radiodiagnositic Approaches in the Documentation of Torture," in Peel and Iacopino, *Medical Documentation of Torture*, 207–20; Gurcan Altun and Gulay Durmus-Altun, "Confirmation of Alleged Falanga Torture by Bone Scintigraphy," *International Journal of Legal Medicine*, 117.6 (2003): 365–66.

143. Mehmet Tunca and Veli Lök, "Bone Scintigraphy in Screening of Torture Survivors," *The Lancet* 352 (December 5, 1998): 1859. See also Human Rights Watch, *Turkey* 9:4 (March 1997), 12.

144. *The Torture Report* (London: British Medical Association, 1986). See also "Doctors and Torture," 319 (August 14, 1999): 397–98.

145. "Human Rights and the Forensic Scientist," *American Journal of Forensic Medicine and Pathology* 5.4 (1984); "Proceedings of the International Symposium on Torture and the Medical Profession," *Journal of Medical Ethics* 17 (December 1991): Supplement.

146. Tomsen, Helweg-Larsen, and Rasmussen, "Amnesty International," 305.

147. See, for example, AI, *Tortured to Death in Uruguay* (London, 1976); AI, *Report of an Amnesty International Mission to Spain*, EUR 41/03/80 (London, 1980). For the importance of medical protocols, see Green, "Sudden and Suspicious Deaths," 71–75; Kirschner, "Use of Drugs," 314–15; L. M. Cathcart, P. Berger, and B. Knazan, "Medical Examination of Torture Victims Applying for Refugee Status," *Canadian Medical Association Journal* 121 (July 21, 1979): 179–84; Ole Vedel Rasmussen, Karin Helweg-Larsen, Jørgen Kelstrup, Pia Carlé, and Lars Adam Rehof, "The Medical Component in Fact-Finding Missions," *Danish Medical Bulletin* 37.4 (1990): 371–73.

148. Tomsen, Helweg-Larsen, and Rasmussen, "Amnesty International," 306.

149. Hans Draminsky Peterson and Peter Jacobsen, "Life-Threatening Torture without Visible Marks," *Scandinavian Journal of Social Medicine* 13 (1985): 88.

150. Hans Draminsky Peterson, Ulrik Abildgaard, Gedske Daugaard, Per Jess, Henrik Marcussen and Marianne Wallach, "Psychological and Physical Long-Term Effects of Torture," *Scandinavian Journal of Social Medicine* 13 (1985): 91.

151. AI, *Report of an Amnesty International Mission to Argentina* (London, 1977), 53.

152. P. Dyhre-Poulsen, O. V. Rasmussen, and L. Rasmussen, "A Study of an Instrument Used for Electrical Torture," in *Evidence of Torture* (London: Amnesty International, 1977), 29; A. R. Kjaersgaard and I. K. Genefke, "Victims of Torture in Uruguay and Argentina," in AI, *Evidence of Torture*, 20–26.

153. O. V. Rasmussen, A. M. Dam, and I. L. Nielsen, "Torture: A Study of Chilean and Greek Victims," in *Evidence of Torture*, 12; Ole Vedel Rasmussen and Grethe Skylv, "Signs of Falanga Torture," *The Lancet* 340 (September 19, 1992): 725; P. Marstrand-Bølling, "La torture dentaire," *Médicine et Hygiène*, March 21, 1979, 1042, 1045–46.

154. Kirstine Amris and Karen Prip, *Falanga Torture* (Copenhagen: International Rehabilitation Council for Torture Victims, 2003).

155. K. G. Nielsen, O. Nielsen, and H. K. Thomsen, "Device and Methods for the Measurement of Energy Transfer in Experiments Involving Thermal and Electrical Injuries of Skin," *Forensic Science International* 17 (1981): 203–9; L. Danielson, H. K. Thomsen, O. Nielsen, O. Aalund, K. G. Nielsen, T. Karlsmark, and I. K. Genefke, "Electrical and Thermal Injuries in Pig Skin," *Forensic Science International* 12 (1978): 211–25.

156. See also L. Danielson, H. K. Thomsen, O. Nielsen, O. Aalund, K. G. Nielsen, T. Karlsmark, and I. K. Genefke, "Early Epidermal Changes in Heat and Electrically Injured Pig Skin," *Forensic Science International* 17 (1981): 133–52; L. Danielson, H. K. Thomsen, O. Nielsen, O. Aalund, K. G. Nielsen, T. Karlsmark, and I. K. Genefke, "Tracing the Use of Electrical Torture," *American Journal of Forensic Medicine and Pathology* 5.4 (1984): 333–37; L. Danielson, H. K. Thomsen,

O. Nielsen, O. Aalund, K. G. Nielsen, T. Karlsmark, and I. K. Genefke, "Immediate Dermal Changes in Pig Skin after Exposure to Moderate Amounts of Heat and Electrical Energy," *Journal of Investigative Dermatology* 87.4 (1986): 528–33; L. Danielson, H. K. Thomsen, O. Nielsen, O. Aalund, K. G. Nielsen, T. Karlsmark, E. Johnson, and I. K. Genefke, "Ultrastructural Changes in Dermal Pig Skin After Exposure to Heat and Electrical Energy and Acid Based Solutions," *Forensic Science International* 38 (1988): 235–43; L. Danielson, H. K. Thomsen, O. Nielsen, O. Aalund, K. G. Nielsen, T. Karlsmark, and I. K. Genefke, "The Occurrence of Calcium Salt Deposition on Dermal Collagen Fibres Following Electrical Energy to Porcine Skin," *Forensic Science International* 39 (1988) 245–55; L. Danielson, H. K. Thomsen, O. Nielsen, O. Aalund, K. G. Nielsen, H. Lyon, T. Ammitzbøl, R. Møller, T. Karlsmark, and I. K. Genefke, "Electrically-Induced Collagen Calcification in Pig-Skin: A Histopathologic and Histochemical Study," *Forensic Science International* 39 (1988): 163–74; L. Danielson, H. K. Thomsen, J. L. Thomsen, Larry E. Balding, and T. Karlsmark, "Diagnosis of Electrical Skin Injuries: A Review and Description of a Case," *American Journal of Forensic Medicine and Pathology* 12.3 (1991): 222–36.

157. Eugene F. Roth Jr., Inge Lunde, Gudrun Boysen, and Inge Kemp Genefke, "Torture and Its Treatment," *American Journal of Public Health* 77.11 (1987): 1404.

158. Karlsmark, T., H. K. Thomsen, L. Danielsen, O. Aalund, O. Nielsen, K. G. Nielsen, and I. K. Genefke, "The Morphogensis of Electrically and Head-Induced Dermal Changes in Pig Skin." *Forensic Science International* 39 (1988): 175; Tonny Karlsmark, "Electrically Induced Dermal Changes," *Danish Medical Bulletin* 37.6 (1990): 517.

159. Danielson et al, "Morphogensis," 175; Karlsmark, "Electrically Induced Dermal Changes," 507–19.

160. Lis Danielsen, discussion with the author at the Rehabilitation and Research Centre for Torture Victims in Copenhagen, Denmark, September 2004.

161. Lis Danielsen, "The Examination and Investigation of Electric Shock Injuries," in Peel and Iacopino, *Medical Documentation of Torture*, 191–206; Lis Danielsen, Monika Gniadecka, Henrik Klem Thosmen, Frants Pedersen, Søren Strange, Kristian Gynther Nielsen, and Hans Draminsky Petersen, "Skin Changes Following Defibrillation," *Forensic Science International* 134 (2003): 134–41; John Conroy, *Unspeakable Acts, Ordinary People* (New York: Knopf, 2000), 78–81.

162. Sklyv, "Physical Sequelae of Torture," 43–44; Forrest, "Examination," 164–65.

163. Henrik Ronsbo, Rehabilitation and Research Center for Torture Victims, personal communication, September 2004.

164. Robert Jay Lifton, "Doctors and Torture," *New England Journal of Medicine* 351.5 (July 29, 2004): 415–16.

165. Frederic Parker and Charles Paine, "Informed Consent and the Refusal of Medical Treatment in the Correctional Setting," *Journal of Law, Medicine, and Ethics* 27.3 (1999): 240–51.

166. Tom Marshall, "Doctors in Guantanamo Bay Are at Risk of Being Accessories to Torture," *British Medical Journal* 324 (January 26, 2002): 235.

167. Damian Whitworth, "U.S. May Resort to Torture; Silent Suspects Frustrate Police," *Times* (London), October 22, 2001, A1. See also Drake Bennett, "The War in the Mind," *Boston Globe*, November 27, 2005, K1.

168. Dana Priest and Barton Gellman, "U.S. Decries Abuse but Defends Interrogations: 'Stress and Duress' Tactics Used on Terrorism Suspects Held in Secret Overseas Facilities," *Washington Post*, December 26, 2002, A14.

169. M. Gregg Bloche, "Physician: Turn Thyself In," *New York Times*, June 10, 2004, 240–43; Kathleen Auerhahn and Elizabeth D. Leonard, "Docile Bodies? Chemical Restraints and the Female Inmate," *Journal of Criminal Law and Criminology* 90.2 (2000): 600. For further reading on U.S. medical personnel in torture after 9/11, see Stephen Miles, *Oath Betrayed* (New York: Random House, 2006).

170. Terence Chea, "California Guardsman Alleges Abuse in Iraq," Associated Press, June 9, 2004, http://web.lexis-nexis.com; David DeBatto, "Whitewashing Torture?" December 8, 2004, http://www.salon.com.

171. Neil A. Lewis, "Red Cross Finds Detainee Abuse in Guantánamo," *New York Times*, November 30, 2004, A1. See also Joe Stephens, "Army Doctors Implicated in Abuse," *Washington Post*, January 6, 2005, A08; M. Gregg Bloche and Jonathan H. Marks, "Doctors and Interrogators at Guantanamo Bay," *New England Journal of Medicine* 353.1 (July 7, 2005): 6–8; American Psychiatric Association, "APA Statement on Psychiatric Practices at Guantanamo Bay," *Medical News Today*, June 29, 2005, http://www.medicalnewstoday.com.

172. Michael L. Gross, "Doctors in the Decent Society," *Bioethics* 18.2 (2004): 181–203; Jagdish Sobti, B. C. Chaparwal, and Erik Holst, "Study of Knowledge, Attitude and Practice Concerning Aspects of Torture," *Journal of the Indian Medical Association* 98.6 (2000): 334–35, 338–39.

Chapter 20
Supply and Demand for Clean Torture

1. In *From Max Weber*, ed. H. H. Gerth and C. Wright Mills (New York: Oxford University Press, 1946), 152.

2. Jørgen Tomsen, Karin Helweg-Larsen, and Ole Vedel Rasmussen, "Amnesty International and the Forensic Sciences," *American Journal of Forensic Medicine and Pathology* 5.4 (1984): 306.

3. See also Piet van Reenen, "Routine Police Torture," *Human Rights Review* 4.1 (2002): 54; Martha K. Huggins, Mika Haritos-Fatouros, and Philip Zimbardo, *Violence Workers* (Berkeley and Los Angeles: University of California Press, 2002), 173–75.

4. A. J. Langguth, *Hidden Terrors* (New York: Pantheon, 1978), 251–53, 286; Archdiocese of São Paulo, *Torture in Brazil*, trans. Jaime Wright (New York: Vintage, 1986), 14; and David Ronfeldt, *The Mitrione Kidnapping in Uruguay*, N-1571-DOS/DARPA/RC (Rand Corporation, August 1987), 49.

5. Richard Goldstein and Patrick Breslin, "Technicians of Torture: How Physicians Become Agents of State Terror," *The Sciences*, March–April 1986, 14–19.

6. Huggins, Haritos-Fatouros, and Zimbardo, *Violence Workers*, 29–62, 161–92.

7. Mohammad [pseud.], *The Argot of the Victim* (Copenhagen: Rehabilitation and Research Centre for Torture Victims, 1992), 4. Aside from this study, such argot has never been subjected to systematic analysis.

8. James Armstrong, *Legion of Hell*, with William Elliott (London: Sampson Low, Marston, [1936]), 167; Marcio Alves, *Torturas e Torturados* (Rio de Janeiro: Empresa Jornalística, 1966), 26; Amnesty International (AI), *Report of an Amnesty International Mission to Argentina* (London, 1977), 39.

9. AI, *Syria* (London, 1987), 18–19.

10. James Morton, *Catching the Killers* (London: Ebury Press, 2001), 175.

11. Archdiocese of São Paulo, *Torture in Brazil*, 22.

12. See chapter 15, "Forced Standing and Other Positions"; Archdiocese of São Paulo, *Torture in Brazil*, 24; *Black Book on the Militarist "Democracy" in Turkey* (Brussels: Info-Türk, 1986), 252.

13. George Browder, *Hitler's Enforcers* (New York: Oxford University Press, 1996), 70; *The Gestapo and SS Manual*, trans. Carl Hammer (Boulder, CO: Paladin Press, 1996); and S. Vladimirov [pseud.], "Zapiski Sledovatelya Gestapo" [Notes of a Gestapo Interrogator], *Moskva* 6 (1971): 210–19; 7 (1971): 174–82; 8 (1971): 182–86. The only English translation is at the library of the Central Intelligence Agency at Langley.

14. Lawrence E. Hinkle and Harold G. Wolff, "Communist Interrogation and Indoctrination of 'Enemies of the State,'" *A.M.A. Archives of Neurology and Psychiatry* 76 (August 1956): 123–24; Robert Conquest, *The Great Terror* (New York: Oxford University Press, 1990), 281.

15. R. John Pritchard and Sonia Magbanua Zaide, eds., *The Tokyo War Crimes Trial* (New York: Garland, 1981), 6:14779.

16. Ingo Muller, *Hitler's Justice* (Cambridge: Harvard University Press, 1991), 178–79.

17. Chief Müller, "Decree of the Chief of the Security Police and the SD, 12 June 1942 regarding third degree methods of interrogation [1531-PS]," in International Military Tribunal, *Trial of the Major War Criminals* (Nuremberg, Germany: n.p. 1948), 27:326–27. English translation in *Germans against Hitler, July 20, 1944* (Bonn: Bundeszentrale für politische Bildung, [1969]), 190–91.

18. "U.S. Interrogation Techniques," *USA Today*, June 23, 2004, 4A.

19. *KUBARK Counterintelligence Interrogation* (Langley, VA: Central Intelligence Agency, July 1963) (hereafter *Kubark*); *Human Resource Exploitation Training Manual* (Langley, VA: Central Intelligence Agency, July 1963, 1983), available at the National Security Archives, http://www2.gwu.edu/~nsarchiv/NSAEBB/NSAEBB122/.

20. See also Alfred McCoy, *A Question of Torture* (New York: Metropolitan, 2006), 92–94.

21. Memorandum from Werner E. Michel, Deputy Secretary of Defense, Intelligence Oversight to Richard Cheney, Secretary of Defense, "Improper Materials

in Spanish-Language Intelligence Manuals," March 10, 1992, 2–3. Available at the National Security Archives, http://www2.gwu.edu/~nsarchiv/NSAEBB/NSAEBB122/.

22. Ray W. Pollari to Principal Deputy for Intelligence, "USSOUTHCOM CI Training," August 1, 1991, 1. Available at the National Security Archives, http://www2.gwu.edu/~nsarchiv/NSAEBB/NSAEBB122/.

23. Ibid.

24. Ibid.

25. Michel, 2. See also "Report on the School of the Americas," Office of Congressman Joseph P. Kennedy II, available at the National Security Archives, George Washington University, Washington, DC.

26. See also *Reseña de la Tortura en Honduras en Los Noventa* (Tegucigalpa, Honduras: Comité de Familiares de Detenidos-Desaparecidos en Honduras, 1994), 7; Ginger Thompson and Gary Cohn, "Torturers' Confessions," *Baltimore Sun*, June 13, 1995, 1A; Ginger Thompson and Gary Cohn, "Unearthed: Fatal Secrets," *Baltimore Sun*, June 11, 1995, 1A; and Ginger Thompson and Gary Cohn, "A Survivor Tells Her Story," *Baltimore Sun*, June 15, 1995, 1A.

27. Neil MacMaster, "Torture: From Algiers to Abu Ghraib," *Race and Class* 46.2 (2004): 15.

28. *Kubark*, III.2 and IX.K, par. 6.

29. *Kubark*, VII.C3, par. 4.

30. See Andrew McLeod, "Victim of Latin American Torture Claims Abu Ghraib Abuse Was Official US Policy," *Sunday Herald* (Scotland), December 12, 2004, http://www.commondreams.org; and McCoy, A *Question of Torture*, 12, 50–52, 62.

31. Vikram Dodd, "Torture by the Book," *Guardian* (London), May 6, 2004, 23; Peter Grier and Faye Bowers, "How Interrogation Tactics Have Changed," *Christian Science Monitor*, May 27, 2004, http://www.csmonitor.com; McLeod, "Victim of Latin American Torture."

32. Toni Locy and John Diamond, "Memo Lists Acceptable 'Aggressive' Interrogation Methods," *USA Today*, June 28, 2004, 5A; Michael Slackman, "What's Wrong with Torturing a Qaeda Higher-Up?" *New York Times*, May 16, 2004, sec. 4, p. 4; "U.S. Interrogation Techniques," *USA Today*, June 23, 2004, 4A.

33. Dirk von Schrader, *Elementary Field Interrogation* (n.p.: Delta, 1978).

34. For a description of Phoenix, see chapter 21, "Does Torture Work?"

35. Richard Krousher [Antony DeBlase], *Physical Interrogation Techniques* (Port Townsend, WA: Loompanics, 1985).

36. Langguth, *Hidden Terrors*, 219–20.

37. James LeMoyne, "Testifying to Torture," *New York Times*, June 5, 1988, sec. 6, p. 45.

38. Brian Ross and Richard Esposito, "CIA's Harsh Interrogation Techniques Described," *ABC News*, November 18, 2005, http://abcnews.go.com.

39. "Des cours sur une 'torture humaine' sont donnés aux stagiaires du camp Jeanne d'Arc," *Le Monde*, December 20–21, 1959, 6.

40. Ted Morgan, *My Battle of Algiers* (New York: HarperCollins, 2005), 143–44.

41. Mika Haritos-Fatouros, "The Official Torturer," *Journal of Applied Social Psychology* 18.13 (1988): 1107–20; Mika Haritos-Fatouros, *The Psychological Origins of Institutionalized Torture* (London: Routledge, 2003).

42. Stanley Milgram, "Behavioral Study of Obedience," *Journal of Abnormal and Social Psychology* 67.4 (1963): 371–77; Stanley Milgram, *Obedience to Authority* (New York: Harper and Row, 1974).

43. McCoy, A *Question of Torture*, 47–49.

44. Thomas Blass, "Unsubstantiated Allegations on CIA-Milgram Link," listserv of the Society for Personality and Social Psychology, September 15, 2006, http://www.spsp.org/; forwarded by Thomas Blass (email correspondence to author, September 21, 2006). Blass wrote the only biography of Milgram, and he is the most important authoritative source on Milgram's life. His listserv posting focuses on McCoy's *Question of Torture*. He argues that McCoy makes his case "without citing any evidence and using 'guilt by association' " and that his book contains "unqualified and unsupported claims that Milgram had 'intelligence connections.' " The book uses "some questionable presentational devices," for example, the "use of time-compression to make dubious connections, selective use of information from my book, and to my knowledge, plain misstatements of fact." Blass itemizes each criticism in detail in his listserve posting. He is especially astonished that McCoy uses Blass's book as source evidence for his account of Milgram: "To my astonishment, [*Question of*] *Torture* bases its speculative claims against Milgram on a simple, benign set of circumstances that is detailed on pages 65–70 of my biography of him." See Thomas Blass, *The Man Who Shocked the World* (New York: Basic Books, 2004).

45. Milgram, *Obedience to Authority*, 39–43.

46. Ibid., 34–35. This finding is confirmed by many others. See Sheldon Levy, "Conformity and Obedience," *Encyclopedia of Violence, Peace and Conflict* (New York: Academic Press, 1999), 1:432.

47. U.S. Army Intelligence Center and School, Fort Huachuca, AZ, "Foreign Intelligence Assistance Program Project X: Annual List of Instructional Material," August 1977, available at the National Security Archives, George Washington University, Washington, DC.

48. The most detailed information about the SERE program comes from studies conducted by Charles A. Morgan III and his team at Yale. They studied the responses of soldiers subjected to SERE techniques. See Charles A. Morgan III, Maj. Gary Hazlett, Sheila Wang, E. Greer Richardson, Paula Schnurr, and Steven Southwick, "Symptoms of Dissociation in Humans Experiencing Acute, Uncontrollable Stress: A Prospective Investigation," *American Journal of Psychiatry* 158.8 (2001): 1239–47; Charles A. Morgan III, Gary Hazlett, Anthony Doran, Stephan Garrett, Gary Hoyt, Paul Thomas, Madeolon Baranoski, and Steven Southwick, "Accuracy of Eyewitness Memory for Persons Encountered during Exposure to Highly Intense Stress," *International Journal of Law and Psychiatry* 27 (2004): 265–79.

49. Jane Mayer, "The Experiment," *New Yorker*, July 11 and 18, 2005, 67–71; M. Gregg Bloche and Jonathan H. Marks, "Doing Unto Others as They Did Unto Us,"

New York Times, November 14, 2005, A21; Mark Benjamin, "Torture Teachers," Salon.com, June 29, 2006, http://www.salon.com.

50. Mayer, "The Experiment," 63–67.

51. Benjamin, "Torture Teachers."

52. FBI agent, cited in Bloche and Marks, "Doing Unto Others," A21.

53. Gen. James T. Hill, Chief of the United States Southern Command, cited in ibid., A21.

54. Josh White, "Abu Ghraib Dog Tactics Came from Guantanamo," *Washington Post*, July 27, 2005, A14. See also Josh White, "Abu Ghraib Tactics Were First Used at Guantanamo," *Washington Post*, July 14, 2005, A1; James R. Schlesinger, "Final Report of the Independent Panel to Review DOD Detention Operations (The Schlesinger Report)," in Mark Danner, *Torture and Truth* (New York: New York Review of Books, 2004), 333–34.

55. Cited in Julian Borger, "Metallica Is Latest Interrogation Tactic," *Guardian* (London), May 20, 2003, 11.

56. Josh White, "Documents Tell of Brutal Improvisation by GIs," *Washington Post*, August 3, 2005, A01.

57. See Bloche and Marks, "Doing Unto Others," A21.

58. Platoon Leader, 4th Infantry Division, cited in "Memorandum for Chief, Inspections Division, Subject: 4th Infantry Division Detainee Operations Assessment Trip Report (CONUS Team), DOD 015969 (DAIG 385) (hereafter cited as CONUS Team) (available at http://www.aclu.org). See also CONUS Team, DOD 015964–65; 015967; 015977–78 (DAIG 380–81, 383, 393–94).

59. CONUS Team, DOD 105973 (DAIG 394).

60. Platoon Leader, 4th Infantry Division, cited CONUS Team, DOD 015973 (DAIG 389). See also Christine Kearney, "ACLU Releases Iraq Prisoner Abuse Report Documents," September 15, 2005, http://www.aclu.org.

61. CIA case officer, cited in Jason Vest, "CIA Veterans Condemn Torture," *National Journal* 37.47–48 (November 19, 2005): 3652.

62. Ibid., 3653.

63. Mark Bowden, "The Dark Art of Interrogation," *Atlantic Monthly*, October 2003, 72; Larry C. Johnson, ". . . And Why It Should Never Be One," *Los Angeles Times*, November 11, 2005, B11. McCoy speculates that the techniques at the CIA Farm came from the *Kubark* manual (*A Question of Torture*, 53). The techniques used at the Farm appear in many places in American history. The fact that they also appear in *Kubark* does not establish any causal link.

64. See, for example, Emad Mekay, "Abu Ghraib Tactics Inspire Torture in Neighbor Egypt," Inter Press Service, June 22, 2004, http://ww.commondreams.org.

65. Frantz Fanon, *The Wretched of the Earth*, trans. Constance Farrington (New York: Grove Press, 1968), 267–70.

66. Huggins, Haritos-Fatouros, and Zimbardo, *Violence Workers*, 81–160.

67. Michael A. Simpson, "Methods of Investigating Allegations of Electric Shock Torture," *Torture* 4.1 (1994): 27–29. See Lis Danielsen's response: Lis Danielsen, "Commentary," *Torture* 4.1 (1994): 29.

68. South Africa, Truth and Reconciliation Commission, *Report* (London: Macmillan, 1999), 195. The TRC maintains that French contact also caused the shift toward forced standing and sweating, a change that also occurs in this period.

69. AI, *Argentina*, 56–57; AI, *Testimony on Secret Detention Camps in Argentina* (London, 1980), 28; AI, *Chile* (London, 1974), 58–59.

70. Contrary to MacMaster, "Torture," 8. See Eric Stener Carlsen, "Through a Glass Darkly: Reflections of French Torture Ideology in the Argentine Dirty War," unpublished manuscript, presented at "Investigating and Combating Torture: Exploration of a New Human Rights Paradigm," Human Rights Program, University of Chicago, March 1999.

71. Ariel Glucklich, *Sacred Pain* (Oxford: Oxford University Press, 2001), 43.

72. See Allen Feldman, *Formations of Violence* (Chicago: University of Chicago Press, 1991), 138–46; Veena Das, "Language and Body," in *Social Suffering*, ed. Veena Das, Arthur Kleinman, and Margaret Lock (Berkeley and Los Angeles: University of California Press, 1997), 88; Lisa Hajjar, *Courting Conflict: The Israeli Military Court System in the West Bank and Gaza* (Berkeley and Los Angeles: University of California Press, 2005), 184–217; Darius Rejali, "Whom Do You Trust? What Do You Count On?" in *On Nineteen Eighty-Four: Orwell and Our Future*, ed. Abbott Gleason, Jack Goldsmith, and Martha Nussbaum (Princeton, NJ: Princeton University Press, 2005), 155–79. For similar accounts of pain and meaning in nontorture contexts, see Glucklich, *Sacred Pain*, 44–48; and Arthur Frank, *The Wounded Storyteller* (Chicago: University of Chicago Press, 1995).

73. Feldman, *Formations of Violence*, 144.

74. Hajjar, *Courting Conflict*, 189.

75. See Langguth, *Hidden Terrors*, 208; Milovan Djilas, *Of Prisons and Ideas*, trans. Michael Boro Petrovich (San Diego: Harcourt, Brace, Jovanovich, 1986), 9.

76. Glucklich, *Sacred Pain*, 44.

77. Carol Leonnig, "Further Detainee Abuse Alleged," *Washington Post*, December 26, 2004, A1.

78. Michel Foucault, *Fearless Speech*, ed. Joseph Pearson (Los Angeles, CA: Semiotext(e), 2001).

79. Garath Williams, "Objects and Spaces: Reading Elaine Scarry's *Body in Pain* in an Arendtian Light," manuscript.

80. The phenomenon is just as common in dictatorships as it is in democracies. See Darius Rejali, *Torture and Modernity* (Boulder, CO: Westview, 1994), 62–112.

81. Talal Asad, "On Torture, or Cruel, Inhuman, and Degrading Treatment," in Das, Kleinman, and Lock, *Social Suffering*, 296.

Chapter 21
Does Torture Work?

1. Jean-Pierre Vittori, *Confessions d'un professionnel de la torture* (Paris: Ramsay "Image," 1980), 57. Vittori published this anonymous manuscript unedited; I have

follwed convention here and cited Vittori as the author, bbut readers should be aware that Vittori is not the professional torturer who penned the text.

2. Roger Trinquier, *La Guerre Moderne* (Paris: La Table Ronde, 1961), 39, 42; Roger Trinquier, *Modern Warfare*, trans. Daniel Lee (New York: Praeger, 1964), 21–22, 23.

3. Manuel Hevia Cosculluela, *Pasaporte 11333* (Havana: Editorial de Ciencias Sociales, 1978), 287. Translation from A. J. Langguth, "Torture's Teachers," *New York Times*, June 11, 1979, A19.

4. See also chapter 18, "Noise."

5. Ronald Melzack and Patrick Wall, *The Challenge of Pain* (Harmondsworth, England: Penguin, 1982), 15–19.

6. Peter Deeley, *Beyond Breaking Point* (London: Arthur Baker, 1971), 69.

7. Quotes are in order from prisoner cited in F. Beck and W. Godin, *Russian Purge and the Extraction of Confession*, trans. Eric Mosbacher and David Porter (New York: Viking, 1951), 185; Amnesty International (AI), *Chile* (London, 1974), 58; Henri Alleg, *The Question* (New York: George Braziller, 1958), 79 (originally *La Question* [Paris: Éditions de Minuit, 1961], 61); Capt. Konrad Trautman, cited in Stuart Rochester and Frederick Kiley, *Honor Bound* (Annapolis, MD: Naval Institute Press, 1999), 148; International Military Tribunal, *Trial of the Major War Criminals* (Nuremberg, Germany: n.p., 1949), 6:279–88; American POW, cited in Mark Baker, *Nam* (New York: Quill, 1982), 183.

8. Giorgio Bini, Giorgio Cruccu, Karl-Erik Hagbarth, Wolfgang Schady, and Erik Torebjörk, "Analgesic Effect of Vibration and Cooling on Pain Induced by Intraneural Electrical Stimulation," *Pain* 18 (1984): 239–48; Patricia Osgood, Daniel Carr, Arthur Kazianis, James Kemp, Nancy Atchison, and S. K. Szyfelbem, "Antinociception in the Rat Induced by a Cold Environment," *Brain Research* 507 (1990): 11–16.

9. Colonel Rémy [Gilbert Renault-Roulier], *Une affaire de trahison* (Monte Carlo: Raoul Solar, 1947), 200.

10. A. D. Craig, E. M. Reiman, A. Evans, and M. C. Bushnell, "Functional Imaging of an Illusion of Pain," *Nature* 384.6606 (November 21, 1996): 258–60; Kenneth L. Casey, "Resolving a Paradox of Pain," *Nature* 384.6606 (November 21, 1996): 217–18.

11. Melzack and Wall, *The Challenge of Pain*, 56–69.

12. Alleg, *The Question*, 72.

13. John Hubbell, *POW* (New York: Reader's Digest Press, 1976), 164.

14. Melzack and Wall, *The Challenge of Pain*, 71.

15. Vittori, *Confessions*, 107.

16. R. Wuillaume, "The Wuillaume Report," in Pierre Vidal-Naquet *Torture*, trans. Barry Richard (Harmondsworth, England: Penguin, 1963), 176; Pierre-Alban Thomas, *Les désarrois d'un officier en Algérie* (Paris: Éditions du Seuil, 2002), 94. For similar arguments, see Gideon Levy, "We Are the Shin-Bet: Extracts from *Ha'aretz* Supplement, January 5, 1990," in Stanley Cohen and Daphna Golan, *The Interrogation of Palestinians during the Intifada* (Jerusalem: B'Tselem, Israeli Information Center for Human Rights in the Occupied Territories, 1991), 113.

17. Melzack and Wall, *The Challenge of Pain*, 30–43; Lawrence E. Hinkle and Harold G. Wolff, "Communist Interrogation and Indoctrination of 'Enemies of the State,' " A.M.A. *Archives of Neurology and Psychiatry* 76 (August 1956): 169.

18. Ariel Glücklich, *Sacred Pain* (New York: Oxford University Press); Geoffrey Oddie, *Popular Religion, Elites and Reform: Hook-Swinging and Its Prohibition in Colonial India* (New Delhi: Manohar, 1995).

19. *KUBARK Counterintelligence Interrogation* (Langley, VA: Central Intelligence Agency, July 1963), 93 (hereafter *Kubark*); see also 82–83. For characteristic sources of value prisoners draw on to resist torture, see Darius Rejali, "Ordinary Betrayals," *Human Rights Review*, July–September 2000, 8–25; and Samir Qouta, Raija-Leena Punamäki, and Eyad El Sarraj, "Prison Experiences and Coping Styles Among Palestinian Men," *Peace and Conflict*, 3.1 (1997): 19–36.

20. Mark Moyar, *Phoenix and the Birds of Prey* (Annapolis, MD: Naval Institute Press, 1997), 102.

21. Alleg, *The Question*, 60.

22. See, for example, Thomas C. Wright and Rody Oñate, *Flight from Chile*, trans. Irene B. Hodgson (Albuquerque: University of New Mexico Press, 1998), 81–82.

23. Case No. 4, cited in Frantz Fanon, *The Wretched of the Earth*, trans. Constance Farrington (New York: Grove Press, 1968), 269.

24. John McGuffin, *The Guineapigs* (Harmondsworth, England: Penguin, 1974), 135.

25. Mitrione, cited in Cosculluela, *Pasaporte 11333*, 287; Langguth, "Torture's Teachers," A19.

26. GSS interrogator, cited in Levy, "We Are the Shin-Bet," 112.

27. Louise Aubrac with Betsy Wing, *Outwitting the Gestapo*, trans. Konrad Bieber (Lincoln: University of Nebraska Press, 1993), 176.

28. Alleg, *The Question*, 62.

29. Sigrid Heide, *In the Hands of My Enemy*, trans. Norma Johansen, arr. Ethel Keshner (Middletown, CT: Southfarm Press, 1995), 65–66.

30. Case No. 4, cited in Fanon, *Wretched of the Earth*, 269.

31. Ibid.

32. David Hawk, "The Tuol Sleng Extermination Centre," *Index on Censorship* 15.1 (1986): 27; Edward Peters, *Torture*, 2nd ed. (Philadelphia: University of Pennsylvania Press, 1996), 270–71.

33. *The Task of POW Interrogations*, cited in Albert Biderman, *Marchy to Calumny* (New York: Arno, 1979), 255.

34. Michel Foucault, *Discipline and Punish*, trans. Alan Sheridan (New York: Vintage, 1979), 40–41; Lisa Silverman, *Tortured Subjects* (Chicago: University of Chicago Press, 2001), 46.

35. *Kubark*, 95; also Moyar, *Phoenix*, 106; Mark Bowden, "The Dark Art of Interrogation," *Atlantic Monthly*, October, 2003, 64; Inspection to CIRG, "Counterterrorism Division GTMO Inspection Special Inquiry," July 13, 2004, http://aclu.org/torturefoia/released/fbi.html (accessed December 22, 2004); Stephen Budiansky, "Truth Extraction," *Atlantic Monthly*, June 2005, 32.

36. Albert Biderman, "Communist Techniques of Coercive Interrogation," cited in Biderman, *March to Calumny*, 136.

37. Alleg, *The Question*, 58.

38. Heide, *Hands of My Enemy*, 61.

39. Dan Mitrione, cited in Cosculluela, *Pasaporte 11333*, 285.

40. I set aside the specious claim that torture itself is a psychological technique. See chapter 18, "Noise."

41. *Kubark*, 95.

42. Jeffrey Dillman and Musa Bakri, *Israel's Use of Electric Shock Torture in the Interrogation of Palestinian Detainees*, 2nd ed. (Jerusalem: Palestine Human Rights Information Center, 1992), 50.

43. Alan Dershowitz, *Shouting Fire* (Boston: Little, Brown, 2002), 476–77.

44. Jon Elster, *Nuts and Bolts for the Social Sciences* (Cambridge: Cambridge University Press, 1989), 95.

45. Cited in Peters, *Torture*, 270–71.

46. James LeMoyne, "Testifying to Torture," *New York Times*, June 5, 1988, sec. 6, p. 45.

47. Leonard Wantchekon and Andrew Healey, "The 'Game' of Torture," *Journal of Conflict Resolution* 43.5 (1999): 596–609.

48. Ibid., 596.

49. See Mika Haritos-Fatourous, "The Official Torturer," *Journal of Applied Social Psychology* 18.13 (1988): 1107–20; Mika Haritos-Fatouros, *The Psychological Origins of Institutionalized Torture* (London: Routledge, 2003), 90–116; Martha K. Huggins, Mika Haritos-Fatouros, and Philip Zimbardo, *Violence Workers* (Berkeley and Los Angeles: University of California Press, 2002), 136–91; Moyar, *Phoenix*, 38; George Browder, *Hitler's Enforcers* (New York: Oxford University Press, 1996), 70; Lawrence Weschler, *A Miracle, A Universe* (New York: Penguin, 1991), 67.

50. Case No. 4, cited in Fanon, *Wretched of the Earth*, 269.

51. Ibid., 268.

52. Zbigniew Stypulkowski, *Invitation to Moscow* (New York: Walker, 1962), 237.

53. Cited in John G. Taylor, *Indonesia's Forgotten War* (London: Zed, 1991), 109.

54. Jerome Skolnick and James Fyfe, *Above the Law* (New York: Free Press, 1993), 89–113; Niels Uildriks and Hans van Mastrigt, *Policing Police Violence* (Deventer, the Netherlands: Kluwer, 1991), 160–62.

55. Chris Mackey and Greg Miller, *The Interrogators* (New York: Little, Brown, 2004), 288–89; Greg Miller, "Bound by Convention," *Stanford Magazine*, November–December 2004, http://www.stanfordalumni.org/news/magazine/2004/novdec.

56. Martha K. Huggins, "Torture 101," conference paper, American Association for the Advancement of Science, Washington, DC, June 28, 2004, 17. See also R. Ramirez, *What It Means to Be a Man* (New Brunswick, NJ: Rutgers University Press, 1999), 77.

57. Cited in Philip G. Zimbardo, "Coercion and Compliance: The Psychology of Police Confessions," in *The Triple Revolution Emerging*, ed. Robert Perrucci and Marc Pilisuk (Boston: Little, Brown, 1971), 504.

58. Cited in ibid.

59. Introduction to *Human Resource Exploitation Training Manual* (Langley, VA: Central Intelligence Agency, July 1963, 1983), sec. I.C. Available at the National Security Archives, http://www2.gwu.edu/~nsarchiv/NSAEBB/NSAEBB122/ (hereafter cited as *HRET*).

60. Setsuo Miyazawa, *Policing in Japan*, trans. Frank Bennett Jr. and John Haley (Albany: State University of New York Press, 1992), 234–35.

61. A. Watson, "The Dark Cloud over Japanese Criminal Justice: Abuse of Suspects and Forced Confessions," part 1, *Justice of the Peace and Local Government Law* 159 (August 5, 1995): 516.

62. Miyazawa, *Policing in Japan*, 235. See also Chalmers Johnson, *Conspiracy at Matsukawa* (Berkeley and Los Angeles: University of California Press, 1972), 156.

63. Senior RUC Officer, cited in Peter Taylor, *Beating the Terrorists?* (Harmondsworth, England: Penguin, 1980), 193.

64. Martha K. Huggins, *Political Policing* (Durham, NC: Duke University Press, 1998), 177–78; Zygmunt Baumann, *Modernity and the Holocaust* (Ithaca, NY: Cornell University Press, 1989), 159–61.

65. See Stanley Milgram, "Behavioral Study of Obedience," *Journal of Abnormal and Social Psychology* 67.4 (1963): 374; Stanley Milgram, *Obedience to Authority* (New York: Harper and Row, 1974), 59–60, 138–43; Wim Meeus and Quintent Wraajimakers, "Obedience in Modern Society: The Utrecht Studies," *Journal of Social Issues* 51.3 (1995): 155–75; and Charles Hofling, Eveline Brotzman, Sarah Dalrymple, Nancy Graves, and Chester Pierce, "An Experimental Study in Nurse-Physician Relationships," *Journal of Nervous and Mental Disease* 143.2 (1966): 171–80.

66. Huggins, Haritos-Fatouros, and Zimbardo, *Violence Workers*, 206–8.

67. John Conroy, *Unspeakable Acts, Ordinary People* (New York: Knopf, 2000), 60–87; Taylor, *Beating the Terrorists?* 156, 225–27, 268, 337–39; Jean Maria Arrigo, "A Consequentialist Argument Against Torture Interrogation of Terrorists," conference paper, Joint Services Conference on Professional Ethics, Springfield, VA, January 30–31, 2003, available at http://www.au.af.mil/au/awc/awcgate/jscope/arrigo03.htm (accessed January 1, 2007).

68. F. Andy Messing, cited in Martin Edwin Anderson, "Is Torture an Option in War on Terror?" *Insight Online*, May 27, 2002; reposted May 14, 2004, http://www.insightmag.com.

69. Huggins, *Political Policing*, 177–78.

70. Louis Ducloux, *From Blackmail to Treason*, trans. Ronald Matthews (London: Andre Deutsch, 1958), 87.

71. Huggins, *Political Policing*, 180, 186.

72. Ibid., 180, 186; Weschler, *A Miracle, A Universe*, 66.

73. A battalion commander tortured two soldiers to death while investigating whether they had smoked marijuana, while a security agent took sexual advantage of a family member who had come to plead for a prisoner (Weschler, *A Miracle, A Universe*, 67). The military also felt pressured by two highly public cases, the unexpected deaths of Wladimir Herzog, a journalist, and Manoel Fiel Filho, a

metalworker. These cases led President Giesel to dismiss the commander of the São Paulo—based Second Army, General Ednardo D'Ávilla Mello (Archdiocese of São Paulo, *Torture in Brazil*, trans. Jaime Wright [New York: Vintage, 1986], 56). Kenneth Serbin argues that the death of Alexandre Vannuchi Leme, a student at the University of São Paulo, was more important than Herzog's death. Kenneth Serbin, *Secret Dialogues* (Pittsburgh: University of Pittsburgh Press, 2000), 199–212.

74. Elio Gaspari, deputy director of Veja, in Weschler, *A Miracle, A Universe*, 67.

75. R. John Pritchard and Sonia Magbanua Zaide, eds., *The Tokyo War Crimes Trial* (New York: Garland, 1981), 6:14779.

76. David Bayley, *Forces of Order* (Berkeley and Los Angeles: University of California Press, 1976), 10.

77. Rod Morgan and Tim Newburn, *The Future of Policing* (Oxford: Clarendon Press, 1997), 117–18.

78. Peter W. Greenwood and Joan Petersilia, "The Criminal Investigation Process: Volume I: Summary and Policy Recommendations," in *What Works in Policing*, ed. David Bayley (New York: Oxford University Press, 1998), 75–107; Wesley Skogan and George Antunes, "Information, Apprehension, and Deterrence," in Bayley, *What Works in Policing*, 108–37; Peter Katzenstein and Ytaka Tsujinaka, *Defending the Japanese State* (Ithaca, NY: Cornell University, East Asia Series, 1991), 150.

79. Bayley, *What Works in Policing*, 8. See also Skogan and Antunes, "Information, Apprehension, and Deterrence," 123–25; Colin Loftin and David McDowall, "The Police, Crime and Economic Theory: An Assessment," in Bayley, *What Works in Policing*, 10–25.

80. David Bayley, *Police for the Future* (Oxford: Oxford University Press, 1994), 9.

81. "Attack on London: Profiles of the Five Men in Custody; The July 21 Suspects," *Guardian* (London), July 30, 2005, 4.

82. "Arrests Since July 7," *Guardian* (London), August 1, 2005, 4.

83. Rosie Cowan, "Big Security Ring for Bomb Hearing," *Guardian* (London), August 9, 2005, 1.

84. Clare Dyer, "No Officers to Face Charges over De Menezes," *Guardian* (London), July 15, 2006, http://www.guardian.co.uk/.

85. "Attack on London," 4; Rosie Cowan, "Bomb Suspects Appear in Court," *Guardian* (London), August 12, 2005,14.

86. Walter D. Connor, *Deviance in Soviet Society: Crime, Delinquency and Alcoholism* (New York: Columbia University Press, 1972), 151–52, 255–57; C. V. Hearn, *Russian Assignment* (London: Robert Hale, 1962), 26, 84–86; Jianhong Liu, Lening Zhang, and Steven F. Messner, eds., *Crime and Social Control in a Changing China* (Westport, CT: Greenwood, 2001), 23–56, 100–101, 129–30.

87. Connor, *Deviance in Soviet Society*, 75–76, 123–24.

88. Biderman, *March to Calumny*, 48.

89. Robert Stephan, *Stalin's Secret War* (Lawrence: University Press of Kansas, 2004), 61.

90. Amy W. Knight, *Spies Without Cloaks* (Princeton, NJ: Princeton University Press, 1996), 5–6. For informants and the NKVD, see Boris Levytsky, *The Uses of Terror*, trans. H. A. Piehler (New York: Coward, McCann and Geoghegan, 1972), 137–39; and Len Maks, *Russia by the Back Door*, trans. Rosamond Batchelor (London: Sheed and Ward, 1954), 217.

91. I use the latest figure. Estimates range from 125,000 to 500,000 informers. See Peter Finn, "Piecing Together a Paper Trail," *Washington Post*, December 7, 2003, A30; Glenn Frankel, "East German Party Leader Admits Spy Role," *Washington Post*, March 14, 1990, A32; Glenn Frankel, "East Germany Haunted by Stasi Legacy," *Washington Post*, March 31, 1990, A1; and Marc Fischer, "East Germans Face Pain of Redefining Pasts," *Washington Post*, January 19, 1992, A20.

92. Stathis Kalyvas, "The Logic of Violence in Civil War," unpublished manuscript, March 2000, 12, available at http:// www.nd.edu/~cmendoz1/datos/papers/kalyvas.pdf (accessed January 7, 2007).

93. Seymour Hersh, "The Gray Zone," *New Yorker*, May 24, 2004, 39–40.

94. Cited in Desmond Hamill, *Pig in the Middle* (London: Methuen, 1985), 67.

95. Bayley, *Forces of Order*, 145.

96. Richard Krousher [Antony DeBlase], *Physical Interrogation Techniques* (Port Townsend, WA: Loompanics, 1985), 2.

97. *Kubark*, 94.

98. Kalyvas, "The Logic of Violence," 8–10; Peter Hart, *The IRA and Its Enemies* (Oxford: Clarendon Press, 1998), 303–15.

99. Cited in Conroy, *Unspeakable Acts, Ordinary People*, 113–14.

100. Pritchard and Zaide, *Tokyo War Crimes Trial*, 6:14779. The full manual is available in Raymond Toliver with Hanns Scharff, *The Interrogator* (Fallbrook, CA: Aero, 1978), 360–65.

101. AI, *East Timor* (London, 1985), 53–54.

102. Cited in Krousher, *Physical Interrogation Techniques*, 1–2.

103. *Kubark*, 94.

104. HRET, K-10.

105. Cited in A.J.P. Hulsewe's *Remnants of Ch'in Law* (Leiden, the Netherlands: E. J. Brill, 1985), 183.

106. Silverman, *Tortured Subjects*, 89–90, 192.

107. Ian Cobain, "The Secrets of the London Cage," *Guardian* (London), November 12, 2005, 8.

108. Ulpian, *Duties of the Proconsul*, Book 8, 23–24, in Peters, *Torture*, 217. See also Hulsewe, *Remnants of Ch'in Law*, 184.

109. David Chandler, *Voices from S-21* (Berkeley and Los Angeles: University of California Press, 1999), 47–51, 104–9, 113–14, 177 n. 24.

110. Richard A. Leo, "The Third Degree and the Origins of Psychological Interrogation in the United States," in *Interrogations, Confessions, and Entrapment*, ed. G. Daniel Lassiter (New York: Kluwer Academic, 2004), 63–64.

111. Leo, "Third Degree," 70–79.

112. Christian Meissner and Saul Kassin, "You're Guilty, So Just Confess," in Lassiter, *Interrogations, Confessions, and Entrapment*, 90.

113. 1994 promotional brochure, cited in Leo, "Third Degree," 76.

114. Samantha Mann, Aldert Vrij, and Ray Bull, "Detecting True Lies," *Journal of Applied Psychology* 89.1 (2004): 137.

115. Ibid.

116. Meissner and Kassin, "You're Guilty," 90.

117. Mann, Vrij, and Bull, "Detecting True Lies," 137. See also Aldert Vrij, *Detecting Lies and Deceits* (Chichester, NY: John Wiley, 2000), 96. For a particularly detailed study of interrogator's error and bias, see Biderman's account of U.S. Army interrogators debriefing U.S. POWs returning from the Korean War (*March to Calumny*, 203–14).

118. Meissner and Kassin, "You're Guilty," 90.

119. Vrij, *Detecting Lies and Deceits*, 77–79, 95–96; 145; Aldert Vrij and Samantha Mann, "Who Killed My Relative?" *Psychology, Crime and Law* 7 (2001): 119–32.

120. Mann, Vrij, and Bull, "Detecting True Lies," 146.

121. Ibid.; see also 50–51, 77–79.

122. Ibid., 145; Lucy Akehurst, Ray Bull, Aldert Vrij, and Günter Köhnken, "Lay Persons' and Police Officers' Beliefs Regarding Deceptive Behaviour," *Applied Cognitive Psychology* 10 (1996)" 461–71; Lucy Akehurst, Ray Bull, Aldert Vrij, and Günter Köhnken, "The Effects of Training Professional Groups and Lay Persons to Use Critera-Based Content Analysis to Detect Deception," *Applied Cognitive Psychology* 18 (2004): 877–91.

123. Meissner and Kassin, "You're Guilty," 90.

124. Michael McConville and John Baldwin, "The Role of Interrogation in Crime Discovery and Conviction," *British Journal of Criminology* 2 (1982): 167.

125. Huggins, Haritos-Fatouros and Zimbardo, *Violence Workers*, 136–91; Haritos-Fatouros, *Institutionalized Torture*, 31–89; Conroy, *Unspeakable Acts, Ordinary People*, 88–122; Lemoyne, "Testifying to Torture," 45; Levy, "We Are the Shin-Bet," 108–13; Moyar, *Phoenix*, 88; "Yossi's Testimony," in Cohen and Golan, *Interrogation of Palestinians*, 101–7; F. Allodi, "Somoza's National Guard," in *The Politics of Pain*, ed. F. D. Crelinsten and A. P. Schmid (Leiden, the Netherlands: Center for the Study of Social Conflict, 1993), 113–27; Wolfgang Heinz, "The Military, Torture and Human Rights," in Crelinsten and Schmid, 65–97.

126. *Kubark*, 1.

127. Sheila Cassidy, *Audacity to Believe* (Cleveland: Collins World, 1977), 189. See also Vrij, *Detecting Lies and Deceits*, 95; Roger Koppl, "Epistemic Systems," *Episteme* 2.2 (2005): 91–106.

128. Vrij, *Detecting Lies and Deceits*, 40–41, 68.

129. Pratap Chatterje, "Meet the New Interrogators," CommonDreams.org, November 4, 2005.

130. Pieter Dourlein, *Inside North Pole* (London: William Kimber, 1989), 111.

131. Lawrence Hinkle Jr. "The Physiological State of the Interrogation Subject As It Affects Brain Function," in *The Manipulation of Human Behavior*, ed. Albert Biderman and Herbert Zimmer (New York: John Wiley and Sons, 1961), 20.

132. *HRET*, K-3.

133. Hans Cappelen, cited in International Military Tribunal, *Trial*, 6:279–88.

134. Alfred Malbrich Baltra, cited in AI, *Chile*, AMR 22/03/87 (London, 1987), 9.

135. Cassidy, *Audacity to Believe*, 189.

136. Théodule Ribot, *Diseases of Memory*, trans. William Huntington Smith (New York: Appleton, 1882), 127.

137. Martijn Meeter and Jaap Mure, "Consolidation of Long-Term Memory," *Psychological Bulletin* 130.6 (2004): 845; Larry Squire, "Memory and the Hippocampus: A Synthesis from Findings with Rats, Monkeys and Humans," *Psychological Review* 99 (1992): 222; Jeansok J. Kim and Michael Fanselow, "Modality-Specific Retrograde Amnesia of Fear," *Science* 256 (May 1, 1992): 675–77.

138. Meeter and Mure, "Consolidation of Long-Term Memory," 843, 845; Nancy Rempel-Clower, Stuart Zola, Larry Squire, and David Amaral, "Three Cases of Enduring Memory Impairment after Bilateral Damage Limited to the Hippocampal Formation," *Journal of Neuroscience* 16.16 (August 15, 1996): 5233–55.

139. Squire, "Memory and the Hippocampus," 219–20, 222–23.

140. Ibid., 221; A. E. Schwartzman and P. E. Termansen, "Intensive Electroconvulsive Therapy: A Follow-Up Study," *Canadian Psychiatric Association Journal* 12 (1967): 218; Richard Weiner, "Retrograde Amnesia with Electroconvulsive Therapy," *Archives of General Psychiatry* 47 (2000): 391.

141. See chapter 6, "Shock."

142. *HRET*, K-3.

143. Mark Blagrove and Lucy Akehurst, "Effects of Sleep Loss on Confidence-Accuracy Relationships for Reasoning and Eyewitness Memory," *Journal of Experimental Psychology: Applied* 6.1 (2000): 68; Gisli Gudjonsson, *The Psychology of Interrogations and Confessions* (West Sussex, England: Wiley, 2003), 389–90.

144. Blagrove and Akehurst, "Effects of Sleep Loss," 60.

145. Ibid., 68. See also Mark Blagrove, Dominic Cole-Morgan, and Hazel Lambe, "Interrogative Suggestibility: The Effects of Sleep Deprivation and Relationship with Field Dependence," *Applied Cognitive Psychology* 8 (1994): 169–79.

146. Blagrove and Akehurst, "Effects of Sleep Loss," 61.

147. Ibid.

148. Ibid., 69.

149. Ibid.

150. Christiana Larner, *The Enemies of God* (Baltimore: Johns Hopkins University Press, 1981), 107–8.

151. Blagrove and Akehurst, "Effects of Sleep Loss," 69.

152. Ibid., 70.

153. Saul Kassin and Holly Sukel, "Coerced Confession and the Jury," *Law and Human Behavior* 21 (1997): 27–46.

154. *HRET*, K-3.

155. Gudjonsson, *The Psychology of Interrogations*, 158–243; Gisli Gudjonsson, "Suggestibility and Compliance among Alleged False Confessors and Resistors in Criminal Trials," *Medicine, Science and Law* 31 (1991): 147–51; S. M. Kassin and K. L Kiechel, "The Social Psychology of False Confessions," *Psychological Science* 7 (1996): 125–28.

156. See Moyar, *Phoenix*, 47–55; David Elliott, *The Vietnamese War*, vol. 2: *Revolution and Social Change in the Mekong Delta, 1930–1975* (Armonk, NY: M. E. Sharpe, 2003), 1136–39; William Blum, *Killing Hope* (Monroe, ME: Common Courage Press, 1995), 130–33.

157. Phung Hoang Management System, January 1969–June 1972, Public Use Version, Records of the Office of the Secretary of Defense (RG330) NARA Electronic Records Division.

158. Stathis Kalyvas and Mathew Kocher, "Abusi USA: Il modello Vietnam in Iraq," *Il Manifesto*, June 21, 2005, 5; Stathis Kalyvas and Mathew Kocher, "Violence and Insurgency: Implications for Collective Action," unpublished manuscript, April 10, 2006.

159. Kalyvas and Kocher, "Violence and Insurgency," 20.

160. Ibid., 22.

161. Ibid., 26.

162. Ibid., 27.

163. Moyar, *Phoenix*, 64–107. See also chapter 8, "Currents."

164. Elliott, *Revolution and Social Change*, 1138.

165. Moyar, *Phoenix*, 242–78. For a more typical critical view, see Elliott, *Revolution and Social Change*, 1136–39; and Sam Adams, *War of Numbers* (South Royalton, VT: Steerforth Press, 1994), 177–78.

166. John McGuffin, *Internment* (Tralee, County Kerry: Anvil, 1973), 86–87.

167. See chapter 15, "Forced Standing and Other Positions," and chapter 16, "Fists and Exercises."

168. Tom Parker, MI5 officer, cited in Jane Mayer, "Outsourcing Torture," *New Yorker*, February 14 and 21, 2005, 116.

169. Ibid.

170. Peter Hamilton, British Colonial security adviser, cited in Deeley, *Beyond Breaking Point*, 54.

171. Ibid. See also David M. Anderson, "Policing and Communal Conflict," in *Policing and Decolonisation*, ed. David M. Anderson and David Killingray (Manchester, England: Manchester University Press, 1992), 210; and David Killingray, "Securing the British Empire," in *The Policing of Politics in the 20th Century*, ed. Mark Mazower (Providence, RI: Berghahn, 1997), 176.

172. Anderson, "Policing and Communal Conflict," 209.

173. Neil Sheehan, *A Bright Shining Lie* (New York: Random House, 1988), 617.

174. Pierre Leulliette, *St. Michael and the Dragon*, trans. John Edmonds (Boston: Houghton Mifflin, 1964), 289.

175. Cited in Huggins, Haritos-Fatouros, and Zimbardo, *Violence Workers*, 144.

176. Huggins, Haritos-Fatouros, and Zimbardo, *Violence Workers*, 144.

177. Otto Tolischus, *Tokyo Record* (New York: Reynal and Hitchcock, 1943), 343.

178. Milovan Djilas, *Of Prisons and Ideas*, trans. Michael Boro Petrovich (San Diego: Harcourt, Brace, Jovanovich, 1986), 9.

179. *Kubark*, 101.

180. Charles Rickard, *La Savoie dans la Resistance*, 4th ed. (Edilarge S.A.: Editions Ouest-France, 1993), 186.

181. AI, *Chile*, AMR 22/03/87 (London, 1987), 8–9.

182. Cassidy, *Audacity to Believe*, 180.

183. Rex A. Hudson, *The Sociology and Psychology of Terrorism* (Washington, DC: Federal Research Division, Library of Congress, 1999), 68–69. Available at http://www.loc.gov/rr/frd/pdf-files./Soc_Psych_of_Terrorism.pdf.

184. *Kubark*, 94. See also *Kubark*, 95; Antonio Cassese, *Inhuman States* (Cambridge, MA: Polity Press, 1996), 70, 72; and the statements of Paul Copher, U.S. intelligence liaison officer to the Turkish National Police on the interrogation of Nalan Gurtas in 1979 in Arrigo, "Consequentialist Argument."

185. Djilas, *Of Prisons and Ideas*, 5.

186. Hinkle and Wolff, "Communist Interrogation," 169; Robert Lifton, *Thought Reform and the Psychology of Totalism* (New York: Norton, 1961), 115–16, 131–32, 149–51; J.A.C. Brown, *Techniques of Persuasion* (Harmondsworth, England: Penguin, 1969), 283; Nathan Leites and Elsa Bernaut, *Ritual of Liquidation* (Glencoe, IL: Free Press, 1954), 22. Similar conclusions resulted from "truth serum" studies. Clark L. Hull, *Hypnosis and Suggestibility* (New York: Appleton Century Crofts, 1933), 100.

187. John Keegan, *Intelligence in War* (New York: Knopf, 2003), 331–33. See also Ben Macintyre, "The Truth the Tin Eye Saw," *Times* (London), February 10, 2006, 20.

188. Tolischus, *Tokyo Record*, 343.

189. *Kubark*, 94–95; Moyar, *Phoenix*, 106.

190. *Kubark*, 83.

191. See, for example, Vittori, *Confessions*, 107–9; *Kubark*, 15–29; and Darius Rejali, *Torture and Modernity* (Boulder, CO: Westview, 1994), 68–69.

192. *Kubark*, 83.

193. Ibid.

194. Richard Bernstein, "Kidnapping Has Germans Debating Police Torture," *New York Times*, April 10, 2003, sec. 1, p. 3; Peter Finn, "Police Torture Threat Sparks Painful Debate in Germany," *Washington Post*, March 8, 2003, A19.

195. Mark Landler, "Police Official Guilty of Torture by Threat," *New York Times*, December 21, 2004, A8.

Chapter 22
What the Apologists Say

1. Peter Taylor, *Beating the Terrorists?* (Harmondsworth, England: Penguin, 1980), 156.

2. Brian Crozier, *A Theory of Conflict* (New York: Charles Scribner's Sons, 1974), 159, 160.

3. John Keegan, *Intelligence in War* (New York: Knopf, 2003), 334.

4. Sylvie Thénault, *Une drôle de justice* (Paris: Éditions la Découverte, 2001), 134; Raphaëlle Branche, *La torture et l'armée pendant la guerre d'Algérie* (Paris: Gallimard, 2001), 218–23.

5. More interrogators and torturers have written or spoken about the Algerian conflict than virtually any other. Recent autobiographies include Jean-Pierre Vittori, *Confessions d'un professionnel de la torture* (Paris: Ramsay "Image," 1980); Jean-Pierre Cômes, *"Ma" guerre d'Algérie et la torture* (Paris: L'Harmattan, 2002); Pierre-Alban Thomas, *Les désarrois d'un officier en Algérie* (Paris: Éditions du Seuil, 2002); Henri Pouillot, *La Villa Susini* (Paris: Éditions Tirésias, 2001); Hélie de Saint Marc, *Mémoires* (Paris: Perrin, 1995); Ted Morgan, *My Battle of Algiers* (New York: HarperCollins, 2005); and Paul Aussaresses, *The Battle of the Casbah* (New York: Enigma, 2002). These supplement older accounts from soldiers such as Pierre Leulliette, *St. Michael and the Dragon*, trans. John Edmonds (Boston: Houghton Mifflin, 1964); Benoist Rey, *Les Égorgeurs* (Paris: Les Éditions de Minuit, 1961); Jean Muller, *Le Dossier* (Paris: Cahier du Témoignage Chrétien, 1957); Gérard Périot, *Deuxième classe en Algérie* (Paris: Flammarion, 1962); Michel Biran, "Deuxième classe en Algérie," *Perspectives Socialistes*, November 1961, 1–45; Jean Faure, *Au pays de la soif et de la peur* (Paris: Flammarion, 2001). In addition, there are two sets of interviews (see Claude Dufresnoy, *Des Officier Parlent* [Paris: René Julliard, 1961]; Andrew Orr, *Ceux d'Algérie* [Paris: Éditions Payot, 1990]) and extracts of psychiatric records (see Frantz Fanon, *The Wretched of the Earth*, trans. Constance Farrington [New York: Grove Press, 1968], 264–70).

6. See Marcel-Maurice Bigeard, *"J'ai mal à la France"* (Ostwald, France: Les Éditions du Pylogone, 2001); Déodat Puty-Montbrun, *L'Honneur de la guerre* (Paris: Éditions Albin Michel, 2002); Pierre Le Goyet, *La guerre d'Algérie* (Paris: Perrin, 1989), and, of course, Jacques Massu, *La vrai bataille d'Alger* (Paris: Plon, 1972).

7. Alistair Horne, *A Savage War of Peace* (New York: Viking, 1977), 339–40.

8. Massu, *La vrai bataille d'Alger*, 164; Horne, *Savage War of Peace*, 199.

9. Branche, *La torture et l'armée*, 110. For settler views, see Aussaresses, *Battle of the Casbah*, 77, 88.

10. Roger Trinquier, *Modern Warfare*, trans. Daniel Lee (New York: Praeger, 1964), 30–33, 37–38, 44–49; Aussaresses, *Battle of the Casbah*, 93, 157; Massu, *La vrai bataille d'Alger*, 135; Horne, *Savage War of Peace*, 198–99.

11. Trinquier, cited in Horne, *Savage War of Peace*, 198. See also John Ambler, *The French Army in Politics* (Columbus: Ohio State University Press, 1966), 172.

12. Branche, *La torture et l'armée*, 117.

13. Horne, *Savage War of Peace*, 199.

14. Morgan, *My Battle of Algiers*, 137–38.

15. Vittori, *Confessions*, 108.

16. Leulliette, *St. Michael*, 295; Ambler, *French Army in Politics*, 175.

17. Herve Hamon, *OAs* (Paris: Éditions du Seuil, 2002), 55. For the FLN-MNA rivalry, see Mohammad Harbi, *Une vie debout*, vol. 1: 1945–1962 (Paris: Éditions la Découverte, 2002); Adam Schatz, "The Torture of Algiers," *New York Review of Books*, November 21, 2002, 55.

18. Aussaresses claims he made efforts to recruit MNA once the FLN strategy was clear, but he does not mention success (*Battle of the Casbah*, 80–81).

19. Edward Behr, *The Algerian Problem* (London: Hodder and Stoughton, 1961), 118. See also Horne, *Savage War of Peace*, 220.

20. Ambler, *French Army in Politics*, 222; Cômes, "*Ma" guerre*, 191.

21. Behr, *The Algerian Problem*, 117.

22. Vittori, *Confessions*, 51.

23. Branche, *La torture et l'armée*, 121–22. These warrants allowed one-week detention without remand before a judge on charges.

24. Ibid., 125, 144.

25. Behr, *The Algerian Problem*, 117.

26. Branche, *La torture et l'armée*, 123.

27. Thénault, *Une drôle de justice*, 95. See also Aussaresses, *Battle of the Casbah*, 126–27.

28. Morgan, *My Battle of Algiers*, 172–74.

29. Thénault, *Une drôle de justice*, 159; see also 136–37, 139; and Patrick Kessel and Giovanni Pirelli, *Le people algérien et la guerre* (Paris: François Maspero, 1962), 435, 499.

30. Aussaresses, *Battle of the Casbah*, 131; Rey, *Les Égorgeurs*, 42–43, 53; Biran, "Deuxième classe en Algérie," 31; Kessel and Pirelli, *Le people algérien*, 60, 354, 408, 453.

31. Thomas, *Les désarrois*, 93.

32. Sous-Lieutenant F., D.O.P officer., cited in Dufresnoy, *Des Officier Parlent*, 32; see also 45.

33. Branche, *La torture et l'armée*, 123, 144. Aussaresses says Teitgin's figures were based on lists he supplied. Yves Godard, *Les paras dans la ville*, vol. 1: *Les Trois Batailles d'Alger* (Paris: Libarie Arthème Fayard), is the only person who disputes these figures. See Aussaresses, *Battle of the Casbah*, 123, 163; Horne, *Savage War of Peace*, 202.

34. Branche, *La torture et l'armée*, 118; Aussaresses, *Battle of the Casbah*, 84.

35. Horne, *Savage War of Peace*, 184.

36. Aussaresses, *Battle of the Casbah*, 129; Orr, *Ceux d'Algérie*, 77.

37. Horne, *Savage War of Peace*, 218.

38. Aussaresses in *Battle of the Casbah* describes their importance for success in Philippevile in 1955 (12, 22, 24–25, 30–32, 42, 45) and in Algiers (78, 80–81, 90, 93, 96, 157, 162). Contrary to Le Goyet, who claims, "In Algiers, we only had one method: make the suspects talk at any price" (*La guerre d'Algérie*, 125).

39. Aussaresses, *Battle of the Casbah*, 85–86.

40. Horne, *Savage War of Peace*, 193; Aussaresses, *Battle of the Casbah*, 116, 108, 111, 149; Morgan, *My Battle of Algiers*, 153, 154, 157, 204, 229.

41. Morgan, *My Battle of Algiers*, 204, 229.

42. Ibid., 186; see also 204.

43. Horne, *Savage War of Peace*, 194.

44. Behr, *The Algerian Problem*, 118.

45. Orr, *Ceux d'Algérie*, 200.
46. Horne, *Savage War of Peace*, 212.
47. Ibid., 259, Morgan, *My Battle of Algiers*, 218–19, 224–34. For other informers, see Aussaresses, *Battle of the Casbah*, 96.
48. Horne, *Savage War of Peace*, 212, 216, 218; Aussaresses, *Battle of the Casbah*, 80–81, 90, 162; Morgan, *My Battle of Algiers*, 227–29, 232.
49. Morgan, *My Battle of Algiers*, 234.
50. Vittori, *Confessions*, 109.
51. Trinquier, *Modern Warfare*, 37; see also 33.
52. Horne, *Savage War of Peace*, 191. See also Leulliette, *St. Michael*, 294.
53. Horne, *Savage War of Peace*, 216.
54. Aussaresses, *Battle of the Casbah*, 95.
55. Horne, *Savage War of Peace*, 209; Morgan, *My Battle of Algiers*, 197.
56. Horne *Savage War of Peace*, 260–61.
57. Massu, *La vrai bataille d'Alger*, 165.
58. Horne, *Savage War of Peace*, 199; Massu, *La vrai bataille d'Alger*, 165; Raphaëlle Branche, "Torture and Other Violations of the Law by the French Army during the Algerian War," in *Genocide, War Crimes and the West*, ed. Adam Jones (London: Zed, 2004), 140.
59. Leulliette, *St. Michael*, 288.
60. Kessel and Pirelli, *Le people algérien*, 217.
61. Pouillot, *La Villa Susini*, 86.
62. Benjamin Stora, *La gangrène et l'oubli* (Paris: Éditions la Découverte, 1992), 57–58.
63. Aussaresses, *Battle of the Casbah*, 120, 128; Hamon, *OAs*, 55; Cômes, *"Ma" guerre*, 168; Orr, *Ceux d'Algérie*, 184.
64. Trinquier, *Modern Warfare*, 21–22.
65. Cômes, *"Ma" guerre*, 83.
66. Crozier, *A Theory of Conflict*, 159.
67. Leulliette, *St. Michael*, 287; Pouillot, *La Villa Susini*, 67.
68. Pouillot, *La Villa Susini*, 86.
69. Soldier, cited in Orr, *Ceux d'Algérie*, 197.
70. Leulliette, *St. Michael*, 289; Horne, *Savage War of Peace*, 193; Henri Alleg, *The Question* (New York: George Braziller, 1958), 113.
71. Horne, *Savage War of Peace*, 193.
72. Leulliette, *St. Michael*, 288–89; Vittori, *Confessions*, 54–55; Biran, "Deuxième classe en Algérie," 29–30; Horne, *Savage War of Peace*, 201, 206.
73. Vittori, *Confessions*, 54; see also 56.
74. Biran, "Deuxième classe en Algérie," 30.
75. Vittori, *Confessions*, 57; Fanon, *Wretched of the Earth*, 268–69.
76. Cômes, *"Ma" guerre*, 70–72; 156–58.
77. Fanon, *Wretched of the Earth*, 268–69.
78. Dufresnoy, *Des Officier Parlent*, 131; Cômes, *"Ma" guerre*, 112.

79. Orr, *Ceux d'Algérie*, 74–75, 196–98, 201, 203; Faure, *Au pays*, 17; Vittori, *Confessions*, 56; Cômes, "*Ma*" *guerre*, 72; Aussaresses, *Battle of the Casbah*, xiii.

80. Fanon, *Wretched of the Earth*, 268, Leulliette, *St. Michael*, 286, 289; Morgan, *My Battle of Algiers*, 169–70.

81. Cômes, "*Ma*" *guerre*, 83. See also Leulliette, *St. Michael*, 281–84, 286, 288; Pouillot, *La Villa Susini*, 67.

82. Dufresnoy, *Des Officier Parlent*, 57, 139; Orr, *Ceux d'Algérie*, 87.

83. Horne, *Savage War of Peace*, 212.

84. Pouillot, *La Villa Susini*, 86.

85. Bigeard, *J'ai mal*, 184, 187, 192; Saint Marc, *Mémoires*, 217; Puty-Montbrun, *L'Honneur de la guerre*, 309; Faure, *Au pays*, 17; Orr, *Ceux d'Algérie*, 197.

86. Leulliette, *St. Michael*, 283.

87. Saint Marc, *Mémoires*, 219; see also Orr, *Ceux d'Algérie*, 33, 75, 184.

88. Thomas, *Les désarrois*, 89–92.

89. Biran, "Deuxième classe en Algérie," 28.

90. Ambler, *French Army in Politics*, 223.

91. Cômes, "*Ma*" *guerre*, 46–47; Branche, *La torture et l'armée*, 199; Aussaresses, *Battle of the Casbah*, 101–3.

92. Cômes, "*Ma*" *guerre*, 46.

93. Branche, *La torture et l'armée*, 197.

94. Ibid., 200–201, 205, 211.

95. Ibid., 202.

96. Ibid., 198, 203.

97. Ibid., 211. See also Thénault, *Une drôle de justice*, 105.

98. Leulliette, *St. Michael*, 296–97.

99. Pouillot, *La Villa Susini*, 84–85.

100. Behr, *The Algerian Problem*, 117.

101. Branche, "Torture and Other Violations," 144.

102. Bigeard, *J'ai mal*, 186. For Bigeard's first use, see Saint Marc, *Mémoires*, 216–17.

103. Dufresnoy, *Des Officier Parlent*, 5. See also Pouillot, *La Villa Susini*, 85; and Morgan, *My Battle of Algiers*, 84.

104. Sous-Lieutenant F of the DOP, cited in Dufresnoy, *Des Officier Parlent*, 32. See also Pouillot, *La Villa Susini*, 67.

105. Leulliette, *St. Michael*, 287–88; Vittori, *Confessions*, 45–46; Dufresnoy, *Des Officier Parlent*, 5, 45.

106. Cômes, "*Ma*" *guerre*, 172.

107. Pouillot, *La Villa Susini*, 67.

108. Vittori, *Confessions*, 107–8; Leulliette, *St. Michael*, 288.

109. Chief Sergeant T., cited in Vittori, *Confessions*, 46.

110. Vittori, *Confessions*, 107–8; Cômes, "*Ma*" *guerre*, 56; Pouillot, *La Villa Susini*, 83; Orr, *Ceux d'Algérie*, 76; Dufresnoy, *Des Officier Parlent*, 32; Rey, *Les Égorgeurs*, 78; Aussaresses, *Battle of the Casbah*, 128; Kessel and Pirelli, *Le people algérien*, 53.

111. Vittori, *Confessions*, 109.

112. Cômes, *"Ma" guerre*, 56, 158. See also Vittori, *Confessions*, 48; Dufresnoy, *Des Officier Parlent*, 5, 32, 45; Thomas, *Les désarrois*, 93; Godard, *Les Trois Batailles*, 239.

113. Officer-Cadet G, in Dufresnoy, *Des Officier Parlent*, 45. See also Pouillot, *La Villa Susini*, 67.

114. Pouillot, *La Villa Susini*, 84.

115. Thomas, *Les désarrois*, 92; Vittori, *Confessions*, 108.

116. Thomas, *Les désarrois*, 93; Vittori, *Confessions*, 158; Pouillot, *La Villa Susini*, 84; Thénault, *Une drôle de justice*, 153; Aussaresses, *Battle of the Casbah*, 127; Morgan, *My Battle of Algiers*, 212.

117. Pouillot, *La Villa Susini*, 84.

118. Vittori, *Confessions*, 46. See also Cômes, *"Ma" guerre*, 56, 72; Aussaresses, *Battle of the Casbah*, 129.

119. Vittori, *Confessions*, , 48.

120. Thomas, *Les désarrois*, 93; Orr, *Ceux d'Algérie*, 200; Aussaresses, *Battle of the Casbah*, 92.

121. Pouillot, *La Villa Susini*, 85.

122. Cômes, *"Ma" guerre*, 89.

123. *Pied-noir* soldier, cited in Orr, *Ceux d'Algérie*, 197.

124. Aussaresses, *Battle of the Casbah*, 123.

125. Trinquier, *Modern Warfare*, 15; Morgan, *My Battle of Algiers*, 229.

126. Horne, *Savage War of Peace*, 193. Morgan collapses the two incidents and counts sixty-seven, not eighty-seven bombs (see *My Battle of Algiers*, 151–52, 159).

127. Vittori, *Confessions*, 50–57.

128. Horne, *Savage War of Peace*, 204–5.

129. Aussaresses, *Battle of the Casbah*, 143, 157; Cômes, *"Ma" guerre*, 63, 72, 106, 156–58; Jean-Yves Alquier, *Nous avons pacifié Tazalt* (Paris: Robert Laffont, 1967), 168–218.

130. Vittori, *Confessions*, 46, 54, 107–9.

131. Périot, *Deuxième classe en Algérie*, 225–26.

132. Puty-Montbrun, *L'Honneur de la guerre*, 285–300; Orr, *Ceux d'Algérie*, 43, 197, 200; Saint Marc, *Mémoires*, 216–17; Rey, *Les Égorgeurs*, 16. The most extreme example is Morgan, whose only personal account involves killing the man he was interrogating (*My Battle of Algiers*, 91–92). This failure does not prevent him, however, from repeatedly affirming torture's efficacy (xix, 151) and accepting at face value descriptions of cases in which he did not participate.

133. Orr, *Ceux d'Algérie*, 43, 198. For Bouhired's interrogation, see Horne, *Savage War of Peace*, 211–12.

134. *Pied-noir* soldier, in Orr, *Ceux d'Algérie*, 198.

135. Vittori, *Confessions*, 56. See also Dufresnoy, *Des Officier Parlent*, 51.

136. Vittori, *Confessions*, 56.

137. Morgan, *My Battle of Algiers*, 186–87, 229, 265.

138. Horne, *Savage War of Peace*, 211–12; Morgan, *My Battle of Algiers*, 229.

139. Aussaresses, *Battle of the Casbah*, viii, 162; Morgan, *My Battle of Algiers*, 229; Neil McDonald, "Pontecorvo's Battle," *Quadrant Magazine*, June 2004, http://www.quadrant.org.au.

140. Aussaresses, *Battle of the Casbah*, 67–72, 149–50, 159–62; Morgan, *My Battle of Algiers*, 265, 231–32.

141. Morgan, *My Battle of Algiers*, 207.

142. Alleg, *The Question*, 45, 47, 74, 94–98.

143. Ibid., 110–12; Morgan, *My Battle of Algiers*, 206.

144. Morgan, *My Battle of Algiers*, 206.

145. Alleg, *The Question*, 110–12.

146. See, for example, Morgan *My Battle of Algiers*, 163, 170, 223.

147. Ibid., 158–60.

148. Horne, *Savage War of Peace*, 194.

149. Ibid.; Morgan, *My Battle of Algiers*, 159–60.

150. Beauge Florence, "Le général Massu exprime ses regret pour la torture en Algérie," *Le Monde*, June 22, 2000.

151. Godard, *Les Trois Batailles*, 239.

152. Aussaresses, *Battle of the Casbah*, 20, 120–21.

153. Ibid., 29, 129–30.

154. Ibid., 141.

155. Bigeard, *J'ai mal*, 184, 187–89, 192.

156. Louisette Ighilahriz with Anne Nivat, *Algérienne* (Paris: Fayard, 2001); Schatz, "The Torture of Algiers," 52.

157. *Human Resource Exploitation Training Manual* (Langley, VA: Central Intelligence Agency, July 1963, 1983), introduction, B, pars. 3 and 4. Available at the National Security Archives, http://www2.gwu.edu/~nsarchiv/NSAEBB/NSAEBB122/.

158. Thomas, *Les désarrois*, 128.

159. See, for example, Aussaresses, *Battle of the Casbah*, 17; and Le Pen in Philippe Bourdrel, *Le livre noir de la guerre d'Algérie* (Paris: Plon, 2003), 189.

160. Saint Marc, *Mémoires*, 218; Puty-Montbrun, *L'Honneur de la guerre*, 284; Orr, *Ceux d'Algérie*, 33, 75, 89, 196.

161. Dufresnoy, *Des Officier Parlent*, 32, 45; Leulliette, *St. Michael*, 291.

162. Leulliette, *St. Michael*, 291.

163. Pouillot, *La Villa Susini*, 84–85; Dufresnoy, *Des Officier Parlent*, 6, 32; Thomas, *Les désarrois*, 93–94; Cômes, "Ma" guerre, 57, 174; Orr, *Ceux d'Algérie*, 43, 76–77; Horne, *Savage War of Peace*, 205; Godard, *Les Trois Batailles*, 239; Muller, *Le Dossier*, 13; Rey, *Les Égorgeurs*, 73.

164. Sous-Lieutenant F., DOP officer, cited in Dufresnoy, *Des Officier Parlent*, 32. See also Dufresnoy, *Des Officier Parlent*, 45.

165. Teitgin, cited in Thomas, *Les désarrois*, 134. See also Aussaresses, *Battle of the Casbah*, 121, 126–27, 143, 151–52; and Morgan, *My Battle of Algiers*, 139.

166. Sous-Lieutenant F., DOP officer, cited in Dufresnoy, *Des Officier Parlent*, 32.

167. Horne, *Savage War of Peace*, 206; Dufresnoy, *Des Officier Parlent*, 56–57, 139; Pouillot, *La Villa Susini*, 131–32.

168. Godard, *Les Trois Batailles*, 239. See also Bigeard, *J'ai mal*, 187, 190–91; Le Goyet, *La guerre d'Algérie*, 125; Hamon, *OAS*, 54.

169. Trinquier, *Modern Warfare*, 49.

170. Horne, *Savage War of Peace*, 206; Périot, *Deuxième classe en Algérie*, 225.

171. Horne, *Savage War of Peace*, 205–7.

172. Branche, *La torture et l'armée*, 216.

173. Kessel and Pirelli, *Le people algérien*, 8, 54, 280, 265, 284, 411, 406–7, 430, 452.

174. Cômes, "Ma" guerre, 70.

175. George Browder, *Hitler's Enforcers* (New York: Oxford University Press, 1996), 69.

176. Ibid., 71.

177. Ibid., 234.

178. Ibid., 68.

179. Robert Gellately, *The Gestapo and German Society* (Oxford: Clarendon Paperbacks, 1990), 134–35; Browder, *Hitler's Enforcers*, 68–69.

180. Gellately, *Gestapo and German Society*, 162.

181. Browder, *Hitler's Enforcers*, 71.

182. Ibid., 68, 73.

183. Allan Merson, *Communist Resistance in Nazi Germany* (London: Lawrence and Wishart, 1985), 51.

184. Browder, *Hitler's Enforcers*, 70–71; see also 38–39.

185. Merson, *Communist Resistance*, 51. See also Browder, *Hitler's Enforcers*, 70–71; *In der Gestapo-Zentrale, Prinz-Albrecht-Strasse 8* (Berlin: Ev Akademie, 1989), 10–15, 39–45; Jan Valtin, *Out of the Night* (New York: Alliance, 1941), 515–17, 522–26, 547, 553, 565, 575–77, 581, 583–84.

186. Browder, *Hitler's Enforcers*, 70; see Eric Johnson, *The Nazi Terror* (New York: Basic Books, 1999), 182–83, 190–91, 241–43.

187. Browder, *Hitler's Enforcers*, 70.

188. Johnson, *The Nazi Terror*, 290.

189. Browder, *Hitler's Enforcers*, 76.

190. Ibid., 76; see also 38, 72–74.

191. Ibid., 40–41, 245.

192. Ibid., 68.

193. Ibid.; see 38, 73, 90–91, 234.

194. Milton Dank, *The French Against the French* (Philadelphia: J. B. Lippincott, 1974), Martin Conway, *Collaboration in Belgium: Léon Degrelle and the Rexist Movement, 1940–1944* (New Haven, CT: Yale University Press, 1993); Gerhard Hirschfeld, *Nazi Rule and Dutch Collaboration*, trans. Louise Willmott (Oxford: St. Martin's, 1988); Henry Lloyd Mason, *The Purge of the Dutch Quislings* (The Hague: Nijhoff, 1952); Vojtech Mastny, *The Czechs under Nazi Rule* (New York: Columbia University Press, 1971), 214–21; Rab Bennett, *Under the Shadow of the Swastika* (New York: New York University Press, 1999); Tadeusz Piotrowski, *Poland's Holocaust* (Jefferson, NC: McFarland, 1998); David Littlejohn, *The Patri-*

otic Traitors (Garden City, NY: Doubleday, 1972); Hans Christian Adamson and Per Kelm, *Blood on the Midnight Sun* (New York: Norton, 1964), 185–275; István Deák, Jan T. Gross, and Tony Judt, eds., *The Politics of Retribution in Europe* (Princeton, NJ: Princeton University Press, 2000).

195. Carylyn Nuttall, "An Exercise in Futility: The Austrian Resistance to the Nazis, 1938–1940," master's thesis, Emory University, 1972, 58–59, 138, 177–78, 201, 230, 268, 275, 298, 301–2; Walter Maass, *Country Without a Name* (New York: Frederick Ungar, 1979), 37; Fritz Molden, *Fires in the Night*, trans. Harry Zohn (Boulder, CO: Westview, 1989), 3–4, 6, 33, 44–47, 60.

196. Radomir Luza with Christina Vella, *The Hitler Kiss* (Baton Rouge: Louisiana State University Press, 2002), 39; Mastny, *Czechs under Nazi Rule*, 213–19.

197. *The Unseen and Silent*, trans. George Iranek-Osmecki (London: Sheed and Ward, 1954), 115; Sonia Games, *Escape into Darkness* (New York: Shapolsky, 1991), 212–19; Joseph Tenenbaum, *Underground* (New York: Philosophical Library, 1952), 426–27, 457; T. Bor-Komorwoski, *The Secret Army* (Nashville, TN: Battery Press, 1984), 46–47.

198. Birger Mikkelsen, "*A Matter of Decency*" (Elsinore, Denmark: Friends of the Sound, 1994), 40, 42–43; David Lampe, *The Savage Canary* (London: Cassell, 1957), 146, 182; Robin Reilly, *The Sixth Floor* (London: Cassell, 2002), 98.

199. Astrid Karlsen Scott and Tore Hang, *Defiant Courage* (Olympia, WA: Nordic Spirit Productions, 2000), 90–91, 95–98; Tore Gjelsvik, *Norwegian Resistance, 1940–1945* (Montreal: McGill-Queens University Press, 1979), 144.

200. Marcel Hasquenoph, *La Gestapo en France* (Paris: De Vecchi Poche, 1987), 326, 332; Louise Aubrac with Betsy Wing, *Outwitting the Gestapo*, trans. Konrad Bieber (Lincoln: University of Nebraska Press, 1993), 61–62.

201. S. Vladimirov [pseud.], "Zapiski Sledovatelya Gestapo" [Notes of a Gestapo Interrogator], *Moskva* 6 (1971): 210–19; 7 (1971): 174–82; 8 (1971): 182–86.

202. Józef Garlinski, *Fighting Auschwitz* (London: Julian Friedmann, 1975), 27, 138–39, 202.

203. Colin Nettelbeck, "Getting the Story Right," in Gerhard Hirschfeld and Patrick Marsh, *Collaboration in France* (Oxford: St. Martin's, 1989), 260.

204. Reilly, *The Sixth Floor*, 100; Nathaniel Hong, *Sparks of Resistance* (Odense: Odense University Press, 1996), 54, 79 n. 128; Hermann Langbein, *Against All Hope*, trans. Harry Zohn (New York: Paragon House, 1994), 216–17, 338; Russell Braddon, *Nancy Wake* (London: Cassell, 1956), 209–10.

205. Raymond Toliver, *The Interrogator*, with Hanns Scharff (Fallbrook, CA: Aero, 1978), 51–113, 127–29, 133–34, 193–95, 202–5, 213, 356–57. For other accounts see R. H. Bailey, ed., *Prisoners of War* (Alexandria, VA: Time-Life Books, 1981); C. F. Dillon, *A Domain of Heroes* (Sarasota, FL: Palm Island Press, 1995); F. D. Murphy, *Luck of the Draw* (Trumbull, CT: FNP Military Division, 2001); and D. A. Foy, " 'For You the War is Over': Treatment and Life of the United States Army and Air Corps Personnel Interned in POW Camps in Germany, 1942–1945," Ph.D. diss., University of Arkansas, 1981.

206. Nuttall, "An Exercise in Futility," 59–60; Radomir Luza, *The Austrian Resistance, 1938–1945* (Minneapolis: University of Minnesota Press, 1984), 14.

207. George Klare, "Questions," in *Interrogations, Confessions, and Entrapment*, ed. G. Daniel Lassiter (New York: Kluwer Academic, 2004), 21–23.

208. Frantisek Moravec, *Master of Spies* (London: Bodley Head, 1975), 159–60; Nuttall, "An Exercise in Futility," 59–60.

209. Hervé Gérard, *Une mission tres secrete* (Brussels: Editions J. M. Collet, 1985), 195; J. Gorecki, *Stones for the Ramart* (London: Polish Boy Scouts' and Girl Guides' Association, 1945), 55–57.

210. Jan Filipek, *The Shadow of the Gallows* (Palm Springs, CA: Palm Springs Publishing, 1985), 72.

211. M. Claeys, cited in International Military Tribunal (IMT), *Trial of the Major War Criminals* (Nuremberg: n.p., 1949), 6:167. See also Edward Crankshaw, *Gestapo* (New York: Da Capo Press, 1994), 130–31; Józef Lewandowski, *The Swedish Contribution to the Polish Resistance Movement during World War Two (1939–1942)* (Stockholm: Almqvist & Wiksell International, 1979), 71; and chapter 5, "Bathtubs."

212. Filipek, *Shadow of the Gallows*, 72; Garlinski, *Fighting Auschwitz*, 148, 151, 157, 202; Scott and Hang, *Defiant Courage*, 90–91, 95–98; Merson, *Communist Resistance*, 67; Luza, *The Hitler Kiss*, 66, 78, 194; Gérard, *Une mission tres secrete*, 195; Molden, *Fires in the Night*, 100; IMT, *Trial*, 6:280; Gjelsvik, *Norwegian Resistance, 1940–1945*, 107, 145; Vladimir Dedijer, *The War Diaries of Vladimir Dedijer* (Ann Arbor: University of Michigan Press, 1990), 1:430–31, 439, 474; Chris Jecchinis, *Beyond Olympus* (London: George G. Harrap, 1960), 200; Mary Henderson, *Xenia* (London: Weidenfeld and Nicholson, 1988), 68–74; Milena Seborova, *A Czech Trilogy* (Rome: Christian Academy, 1990), 28; Lewis M. White, ed., *On All Fronts* (Boulder, CO: East European Monographs, 1995), 45, 55, 241; Sigrid Heide, *In the Hands of My Enemy*, trans. Norma Johansen, arr. Ethel Keshner (Middletown, CT: Southfarm Press, 1995), 67; Maynard M. Cohen, *A Stand against Tyranny* (Detroit: Wayne State University Press, 1997), 178; Max Manus, *Nine Lives Before Thirty* (Garden City, NY: Doubleday, 1947), 288; Adamson and Klem, *Blood on Midnight Sun*, 218–23; Dorothy Baden-Powell, *Pimpernel Gold* (New York: St. Martin's, 1978), 103–5; Oluf Reed Olsen, *Two Eggs on My Plate* (Glasgow: Blackie, 1972), 27–29; Per Hansson, *The Greatest Gamble*, trans. Maurice Michael (London: George Allen and Unwin, 1967), 118; Airey Neave, *Little Cyclone* (London: Hodder and Stoughton, 1954), 116, M.R.D. Foot, *The Resistance* (New York: McGraw-Hill, 1977), 89, J. Schreuers, *My Country in Trouble* (New York: Carlton Press, 1962), 45–46; André Lamarche, *A vingt ans la guerre* (Liège: Impr. Solédi, 1986), 24; Herman Bodson, *Agent for the Resistance*, ed. Richard Schmidt (College Station: Texas A&M University Press, 1994), 121–22; Andria Hill, *Mona Parsons* (Halifax, Nova Scotia: Nimbus, 2000), 88–89; Lore Cowan, *Children of the Resistance* (New York: Meredith Press, 1969), 125; Corrie ten Boom with John Sherrill and Elizabeth Sherrill, *The Hiding Place* (London: Hodder and Stoughton and

Christian Literature Crusade, 1971), 121–22; Graeme Warrack, *Travel by Dark* (London: Harvill Press, 1963), 170.

213. Foot, *The Resistance*, 89.

214. Michael Thomsett, *The German Opposition to Hitler* (Jefferson, NC: McFarland, 1997), 229.

215. Ibid., 234–35.

216. Peter Hoffman, *History of the German Resistance, 1933–1945*, trans. Richard Barry (Cambridge: MIT Press, 1977), 519.

217. Gordon Shepherd, *The Austrian Odyssey* (London: Macmillan, 1957), 167.

218. Molden, *Fires in the Night*, 224.

219. See Callum MacDonald, *The Killing of SS Obergruppenführer Reinhard Heydrich* (New York: Free Press, 1988), 177–80, 189–97, 206; and Mastny, *Czechs under Nazi Rule*, 213–19.

220. MacDonald, *The Killing of Heydrich*, 189.

221. Lewandowski, *Swedish Contribution*, 75–77.

222. Gorecki, *Stones for the Ramart*, 55–57.

223. Waldemar Lotnik, *Nine Lives* (London: Serif, 1999), 71–72.

224. Jørgen Haestrup, *Secret Alliance*, trans. Alison Borch-Johansen (New York: New York University Press, 1976), 2:307.

225. Svend Truelsen, cited in Christine Sutherland, *Monica* (New York: Farrar, Straus and Giroux, 1990), 156–57.

226. Reilly, *The Sixth Floor*, 95.

227. Ibid., 105–6; see also 98–104. See also Mikkelsen, *A Matter of Decency*, 42–43.

228. Reilly, *The Sixth Floor*, 98.

229. Leif Hovelsen, *Out of the Evil Night*, trans. John Morrison (London: Blandford Press, 1959), 16.

230. Cohen, *A Stand against Tyranny*, 77.

231. Colonel Rémy [Gilbert Renault-Roulier], *Une affaire de trahison* (Monte Carlo: Raoul Solar, 1947), 232.

232. Masuy, cited in Fabrice Laroche, "Les Français de la Gestapo," in *Histoire secrète de la Gestapo*, ed. Jean Dumont (Geneva: Editions de Crémille, 1971), 4:28.

233. See also François d'Orcival, "Gestapo contre Résistance," in Dumont, *Histoire secrète*, 2:161.

234. Jean Amery, *At the Mind's Limits*, trans. Sidney Rosenfeld and Stella P. Rosenfeld (Bloomington: Indiana University Press, 1980), 36.

235. Dank, *French Against the French*, 212.

236. See Hasquenoph, *La Gestapo en France*, 131, 225, 337.

237. See chapter 5, "Bathtubs."

238. Max Hastings, "In the Fight against al-Qaida We Need People, Not Tanks," *Guardian* (London), October 17, 2005, 28.

239. James R. Schlesinger, "Final Report of the Independent Panel to Review DOD Detention Operations (The Schlesinger Report)," in Mark Danner, *Torture and Truth* (New York: New York Review of Books, 2004), 364; Mark Bowden, "The Dark Art of Interrogation," *Atlantic Monthly*, October, 2003, 55. For similar stories,

see Bowden, 73; Raymond Bonner, Don Van Natta Jr., and Amy Waldman, "Questioning Terror Suspects in a Dark and Surreal World," *New York Times,* March 9, 2003, A14; Josh White, "Abu Ghraib Tactics Were First Used at Guantanamo," *Washington Post,* July 14, 2005, A1.

240. Brian Ross and Richard Esposito, "CIA's Harsh Interrogation Techniques Described," *ABC News,* November 18, 2005, http://abcnews.go.com.

241. Ibid.

242. Ibid.; Hina Shamsi, *Command's Responsibility,* ed. Deborah Pearlstein (New York: Human Rights First, 2006), 1, 5, 9, 11, 14.

243. Ross and Esposito, "CIA's Harsh Interrogation Techniques."

244. Eric Schmitt, "3 in 82nd Airborne Say Beating Iraqi Prisoners Was Routine," *New York Times,* September 23, 2005, A1; Human Rights Watch, *Leadership Failure: Firsthand Accounts of Torture of Iraqi Detainees by the US Army's 82nd Airborne Division* (September 2005) 17: 3(G), 5–6, 11.

245. See Shamsi, *Command's Responsibility,* 6–9. Arthur Kane, "Guardsman: CIA Beat Iraqis with Hammer Handles," *Denver Post,* July 27, 2005, A9; Dana Priest and Josh White, "Before the War, CIA Reportedly Trained a Team of Iraqis to Aid US," *Washington Post,* August 3, 2005, A12; Josh White, "Documents Tell of Brutal Improvisation by GIs," *Washington Post,* August 3, 2005, A01.

246. Shamsi, *Command's Responsibility,* 7.

247. Kane, "Guardsman," A9; Priest and White, "Before the War," A12; White, "Documents," A01.

248. Shamsi, *Command's Responsibility,* 8.

249. Ibid., 7–8; M. Gregg Bloche and Jonathan H. Marks, "Doing Unto Others as They Did Unto Us," *New York Times,* November 14, 2005, A21.

250. Welshofer, cited in Shamsi, *Command's Responsibility,* 6.

251. Joe Ryan, CACI interrogator at Abu Ghraib, blog entry dated March 8, 2004, http://talkleft.com/new_archives/006886.html, http://nyc.indymedia.org/newswire/display/95152/index.php. Interrogators in the field refer to the CIA not by name, but as the OGA, "other governmental agency," and that is how I am reading Ryan's references here.

252. CIA officer cited in Jason Vest, "CIA Veterans Condemn Torture," *National Journal* 37.47–48 (November 19, 2005): 3653.

253. Merle L. Pribbenow, CIA officer, cited in ibid., 3652.

254. Frank Snepp, CIA interrogator, cited in ibid., 3653.

255. Pribbenow, cited in ibid., 3652.

256. Cômes, "Ma" guerre, 83.

257. Larry C. Johnson, veteran CIA officer and deputy director of the State Department's Office of Counterterrorism, ". . . And Why It Should Never Be One," *Los Angeles Times,* November 11, 2005, B11.

258. I discuss this case in the section entitled "Works Better Than What?" in chapter 21, "Does Torture Work?"

259. Vest, "CIA Veterans Condemn Torture," 3652.

260. For CIA objectors, see ibid., 3651–53; Johnson, "Why It Should Never Be One," B11; Sarah Baxer and Michael Smith, "CIA Chief Sacked for Opposing Torture," *Times* (London), February 12, 2006, 24; David Cloud, "Colleagues Say CIA Analyst Played by the Rules," *New York Times*, April 22, 2006, sec. 1, p. 1; David Rose, "MI6 and CIA 'Sent Student to Morocco to be Tortured,' " *The Observer*, December 11, 2005, 20; Douglas Jehl, "Report Warned CIA on Interrogation Tactics," *New York Times*, November 9, 2005, A1; Monisha Bansal, "Former Senior CIA Officials Back Anti-Torture Amendment," CNSNews.com, December 9, 2005; Mark Follman, "America Can't Take It Anymore," Salon.com, December 5, 2005. For other military organizations, see Pamela Hess, "Former Generals Promote Anti-Torture Bill," UPI, December 13, 2005, http://www.upi.com; Matthew D. LaPlante, "Expert Interrogator by Army's Prisoner Treatment," *Salt Lake Tribune*, August 4, 2005, A1; Karen J. Greenburg, "The Achilles Heel of Torture," tomdispatch.com, August 25, 2005; Joe Conason, "Officers and Veterans Defy Bush's Neocons," *New York Observer*, August 4, 2005, 5; Josh White, "Military Lawyers Fought Policy on Interrogations," *Washington Post*, July 15, 2005, A01; Charlie Savage, "Split Seen on Interrogation Techniques," *Boston Globe*, March 31, 2005, A12; David Kronke, "Unit's Military Expert Has Fighting Words for Bush," *Los Angeles Daily News*, March 27, 2006, www.dailynews.com.

261. Vest, "CIA Veterans Condemn Torture," 3653; Anatol Lieven, "Need for a New Force in US Politics: Spies and Generals Protest," *Le Monde Diplomatique*, June 9, 2006, http://mondediplo.com.

262. Ross and Esposito, "CIA's Harsh Interrogation Techniques."

263. Dana Priest, "Covert CIA Program Withstands New Furor," *Washington Post*, December 30, 2005, A01.

264. Bowden, "Dark Art of Interrogation," 55.

265. Dana Priest, "Wrongful Imprisonment: Anatomy of a CIA Mistake," *Washington Post*, December 4, 2005, A01; Jane Mayer, "Outsourcing Torture," *New Yorker*, February 14 and 21, 2005, 118–20.

266. John Cloonan, interview with Chris Lydon, "Open Source," Boston Public Radio, November 4, 2005, http://www.radioopensource.org; Mayer, "Outsourcing Torture," 114–16.

267. Douglas Jehl, "Qaeda-Iraq Link US Cited is Tied to Coercion Claim," *New York Times*, December 9, 2005, A1; Rosa Brooks, "In the End, Torture Hurts Us," *Los Angeles Times*, November 25, 2005, B15.

268. Brooks, "In the End," B15; Jehl, "Qaeda-Iraq," 1.

269. Dana Priest, "Al Qaeda-Iraq Link Recanted," *Washington Post*, August 1, 2004, A20.

270. Douglas Jehl, "High Qaeda Aide Retracted Claim of Link with Iraq," *New York Times*, July 31, 2004, A1.

271. Cited in Priest, "Al Qaeda—Iraq Link Recanted," A20.

272. Ken Gude, "They Got What They Wanted," Center for American Progress, August 5, 2004, http://www.americanprogress.org.

273. Jehl, "Aide Retracted Claim,"A1; Brooks, "In the End," B15.

274. Gude, "They Got What They Wanted."

275. Senior intelligence officer, cited in Priest, "Al Qaeda—Iraq Link Recanted," A20.

276. Dan Coleman, ex-FBI agent, cited in Mayer, "Outsourcing Torture," 116.

277. Douglas Jehl, "Report Warned Bush Team about Intelligence Doubts," *New York Times*, November 6, 2005, sec. 1, p. 14.

278. Ross and Esposito, "CIA's Harsh Interrogation Techniques."

279. See, for example, "A Master Terrorist is Nabbed," *New York Times*, April 6, 2002, A14; Judith Miller, "Dissecting a Terror Plot from Boston to Amman," *New York Times*, January 15, 2001, A1; David Johnston, "FBI Chief Says Al Qaeda Aide's Arrest Will Help Prevent Attacks by Terrorists," *New York Times*, April 4, 2002, A14.

280. Barton Gellman, "The Shadow War, in a Surprising New Light," *Washington Post*, June 20, 2006, C1. This chapter was written before Ron Suskind released his book on this incident. See Ron Suskind, *The One Percent Doctrine* (New York: Simon and Schuster, 2004).

281. Top FBI Al-Qaeda analyst to senior bureau official, cited in Gellman, "Shadow War," C1.

282. Philip Shenon, "Officials Say Qaeda Suspect Has Given Useful Information," *New York Times*, April 26, 2002, A12.

283. President Bush, cited in Gellman, "Shadow War," C1.

284. David Johnston, "Uncertainty about Interrogation Rules Seen as Slowing the Hunt for Information on Terrorists," *New York Times*, June 28, 2004, A8.

285. Gellman, "Shadow War," C1; Eric Schmitt, "There Are Ways to Make Them Talk," *New York Times*, June 16, 2002, sec. 4, p. 1; Don Van Natta Jr., "Interrogation Methods in Iraq Aren't All Found in Manual," *New York Times*, May 7, 2004, A13; Douglas Jehl and David Johnston, "White House Fought New Curbs on Interrogations, Officials Say," *New York Times*, January 13, 2005, A1.

286. Bonner, Van Natta, and Waldman, "Questioning Terror Suspects," A14.

287. Gerald Posner, "Scrutinizing the Saudi Connection," *New York Times*, July 27, 2004, A15; Philip Shenon, "CIA Warned White House that Links Between Iraq and Qaeda were 'Murky,'" *New York Times*, Jun 20, 2004, A7; Philip Shenon, "Qaeda Leader Said to Report A-Bomb Plans," *New York Times*, April 23, 2002, A9; James Risen and Philip Shenon, "US Says It Halted Qaeda Plot to Use Radioactive Bomb," *New York Times*, June 11, 2002, A1.

288. James Risen and Philip Shenon, "Terrorists Yields Clues to Plots, Officials Assert," *New York Times*, June 11, 2002, A1.

289. Gellman, "Shadow War," C11; Risen and Shenon, "US Says"; Ian Fisher, "Qaeda Suspect's Bosnian Wife Says He's No Terrorist," *New York Times*, January 28, 2002) A3; James Risen, "Morocco Detainee Linked to Qaeda," *New York Times*, June 19, 2002, A8; Keith Richburg, "French Terror Suspect Allegedly Confessed to Bin Laden Link," *Washington Post*, October 3, 2001, A10.

290. Shenon, "Qaeda Suspect," A12; Judith Miller and Philip Shenon, "Qaeda Leader in US Custody Provokes Alert," *New York Times*, April 20, 2002, A1; Philip Shenon, "FBI Warns of a Threat by a Leader of Al Qaeda," *New York Times*, April

25, 2002, A16; Al Baker, "Qaeda Tip Caused Alert in New York," *New York Times*, May 23, 2002, A1; Judith Miller, "US Received Tip on Qaeda Threats Against Landmarks, *New York Times*, August 13, 2002, A16; Eric Lichtblau and David Johnston, "Confidential Advisory Warns Officials of Rise in Possible Terror Threats," *New York Times*, February 6, 2003, A23.

291. Porter Goss, cited in Shenon, "Officials Say," A12.

292. Johnson, "Why It Should Never Be One," A8; Maureen Dowd, "Summer of All Fears," *New York Times*, June 12, 2002, A29.

293. Schmitt, "There Are Ways," 1.

294. Ron Suskind, cited in Gellman, "Shadow War," C1.

295. George W. Bush, "Speech on Trials for Enemy Combatants," September 6, 2001, http://mypetjawa.mu.nu/archives/184556.php.

296. Ron Suskind, "The Unofficial Story of al-Qaeda 14," Time.com, September 12, 2006.

297. Dan Eggen and Dafna Linzer, "Secret World of Detainees Grows More Public," *Washington Post*, September 7, 2006, A18.

298. Ibid.

299. Reuel Marc Gerecht, "Against Rendition," *Weekly Standard*, May 16, 2005, 23–25. This, of course, is not an argument against torture. Even those who think torture produces accurate information would be hard pressed to defend extraordinary rendition as opposed to "in house" torture on these grounds. For an especially detailed account of how prisoners rendered to Moroccan security services confess to terrorist involvement, see Human Rights Watch, *Morocco* (October 2004) 16:6(E), 57–62.

300. Mayer, "Outsourcing Torture," 116; Gerecht, "Against Rendition," 24.

301. Bowden, "Dark Art of Interrogation," 56.

302. Stephanie Athey, "The Terrorists We Torture: The Tale of Abdul Hakim Murad," *South Central Review* 24.1 (forthcoming 2007).

303. *CNN Newnight with Aaron Brown*, May 18, 2004, http://www.cnn.com. See also Alan Dershowitz, *Why Terrorism Works* (New Haven, CT: Yale University Press, 2002), 137; Michael Slackman, "What's Wrong with Torturing a Qaeda Higher-Up?" *New York Times*, May 16, 2004, sec. 4, p. 4.

304. All this information is stated in the same *Washington Post* article Dershowitz regularly cites, but Dershowitz omits it. See Dershowitz, *Why Terrorism Works*, 249 n. 10; Matthew Brzezinski, "Bust and Boom," *Washington Post Magazine*, December 30, 2001, W09.

305. Peter Maass, "If A Terror Suspect Won't Talk, Should He Be Made To?" *New York Times*, March 9, 2003, sec. 4, p. 4. This information was also in the article Dershowitz cites, but also is omitted in his discussion. See Dershowitz, *Why Terrorism Works*, 249 n. 10; Doug Struck, Howard Schneider, Karl Vick, and Peter Baker, "Borderless Network of Terror; Bin Laden Followers Reach Across Globe," *Washington Post*, September 23, 2001, A1.

306. Jay Winik, "Security Comes Before Liberty," *Wall Street Journal*, October 23, 2001, A26.

307. Brzezinski, "Bust and Boom," W09.

308. Jim McGee, "Ex-FBI officials criticize tactics on terrorism," *Washington Post*, November 28, 2001, A1.

309. Chris Nelson, "Rumsfeld's 'Secret CIA,'" *The Nelson Report*, January 24, 2005, cnelson@samuelsinternational.com. See also Eric Lipton, "Lessons from Canada," *New York Times*, June 11, 2006, sec. 4, p. 3.

310. Struck et al., "Borderless Network of Terror," A1. See also Dexter Filkins, Mark Mazzetti, and Richard Oppel, "The Raid Surveillance and Betrayal Ended Hunt," *New York Times*, June 9, 2006, A6. Dershowitz gives no citation for the alleged Jordanian success from torture, and his reference to Chapman does not include this information (Dershowitz, *Why Terrorism Works*, 249 n. 11; Steve Chapman, "No Tortured Dilemma," *Washington Times*, November 5, 2001, A18). Nor does Chapman include any mention of how the Philippine police helped "crack the 1993 World Trade Center bombings by torturing a suspect," as Dershowitz claims in note 11. The citation is in error.

311. Dershowitz, *Why Terrorism Works*, 137.

312. General Miller, cited in David Rose, "Guantanamo Bay on Trial," *Vanity Fair*, January 2004, 133.

313. Joe Ryan, a CACI Abu Ghraib interrogator, posted his diary online for three months until the Abu Ghraib crisis became headline news and then removed it from the Web. Various sites have since reconstituted pages from cached files. The dates and current URLs are as follows: March 7–18 (http://talkleft.com/new_archives/oo6886.html, http://nyc.indymedia.org/newswire/display/95152/index.php), March 21–April 2 (http://www.indymedia.org.uk/en/2004/06/292976.html), and April 11–26 (http://www.disinfopedia.org/wiki.phtml?title=Joe_Ryan_Iraq_Diary_April_2004).

314. Sgt. Mark Hadsell, PsyOps, cited in "Sesame Street Breaks Iraqi POWs," *BBC News*, May 20, 2003, http://www.bbc.co.uk.

315. U.S. operative cited in Julian Borger, "Metallica Is Latest Interrogation Tactic," *Guardian* (London), May 20, 2003, 11. See also Greg Miller, "Bound by Convention," *Stanford Magazine*, November–December 2004, http://www.stanfordalumni.org/news/magazine/2004/novdec.

316. Keegan, *Intelligence in War*, 361.

317. Douglas Jehl and Eric Schmitt, "Prison Interrogations in Iraq Seen as Yielding Little Data on Rebels," *New York Times*, May 24, 2004, A1.

318. Ed Vulliamy, Paul Harris, Jason Burke, and David Rose, "Secrets of the 'Hollow Man' Emerge from Saddam's Cell," *The Observer* (London), December 21, 2003, 16.

319. Filkins, Mazzetti, and Oppel, "Raid Surveillance," A6; Dan Murphy and Mark Sappenfield, "A Long Trail to Finding Zarqawi," *Christian Science Monitor*, June 9, 2006, 11; Ned Parker and Michael Evans, "Death of a Terrorist," *Times* (London), June 9, 2006, 1; Ned Parker, "Betrayal Led US Bombers to Hideout of Iraq's Most Wanted Man," *Times* (London), June 9, 2006, 4; Solomon Moore and

Greg Miller, "U.S. Tracks Aide to Zarqawi's Doom," *Los Angeles Times*, June 9, 2006, A1.

320. Chris Mackey and Greg Miller, *The Interrogators* (New York: Little, Brown, 2004), 475.

321. Ryan, March 15, 2004. See also April 16, 2004.

322. Jehl and Schmitt, "Prison Interrogations," A1. See also Anthony Lagouranis, *New York Times*, March 1, 2006, A19.

323. Ralph Peters, former colonel, U.S. Army Intelligence, cited in Borger, "Metallica."

324. Martin Bright, "Guantanamo Has 'Failed to Prevent Terror Attacks,' " *Guardian* (London), October 3, 2004, 1. See also David Rose, *Guantánamo* (New York: New Press, 2004), 11; David Rose, "Guantanamo Bay on Trial," 90, 133.

325. Lolita Baldor, "More Than Half of Guantanamo Detainees Not Accused of Hostile Acts," Associated Press, February 9, 2006, http://web.lexis-nexis.com. The CSRT reports can be found at http://www.defenselink.mil/pubs/foi/detainees/index.html.

326. Baldor, "More Than Half"; Greg Miller, "Documents Reveal the Stories of Prisoners at Guantanamo Bay," *Los Angeles Times*, March 4, 2006, A1.

327. Mayer, "Outsourcing Torture," 116.

328. William Fischer, "Reports Find Tenuous Terror Ties at Guantanamo, Inter Press Service, February 22, 2006, http://web.lexis-nexis.com.

329. Ibid.; Adam Zagorin, " '20th Hijacker' Claims that Torture Made Him Lie," Time.com, March 3, 2006, 1.

330. Interview with Adam Zagorin, "Inside Guantanamo Bay," *The Newshour with Jim Lehrer*, June 13, 2005, http://www.pbs.org.

331. General Miller, cited in Robert Burns, "U.S. Fighting Intelligence War in Cuba," Associated Press Online, November 25, 2003, http://web.lexis-nexis.com.

332. Gisli Gudjusson, cited in Rose, "Guantanamo Bay on Trial," 134.

333. General Miller, cited in Rose, "Guantanamo Bay on Trial," 133.

334. Inspection to CIRG, "Counterterrorism Division GTMO Inspection Special Inquiry," July 13, 2004.

335. Mackey and Miller, *The Interrogators*, 184, 194–95, 224, 218 (rivalry); 299–306, 318–20, 324–25 (informers); and 175–76 (interrogation as revenge).

336. Mackey and Miller, *The Interrogators*, 471, 476; Tim Golden, "In US Report, Brutal Details of 2 Afghan Inmates' Deaths," *New York Times*, May 20, 2005, A1; Tim Golden, "Army Faltered in Investigating Detainee Abuse," *New York Times*, May 22, 2005, sec. 1, p. 1; Tim Golden, "Years after 2 Afghans Died, Abuse Case Falters," *New York Times*, February 13, 2006, A1; Miller, "Bound by Convention."

337. Mackey and Miller, *The Interrogators*, 218, 232–33, 282–83.

338. Ibid., 468.

339. Ibid., 108–12, 168.

340. Ibid., 472.

341. Ibid., 288.

342. Christiana Larner, *The Enemies of God* (Baltimore: Johns Hopkins University Press, 1981), 107–8; Diarmaid Macculloch, *The Reformation* (New York: Viking, 2003), 555–56.

343. Mackey and Miller, *The Interrogators*, 216; see also 204, 278, 477.

344. Ibid., 193.

345. Ibid., 282–85.

346. Ibid., 172–73.

347. Daniel Williams, "Italy Probing Source of False Documents," *Washington Post*, July 13, 2002, A14; Melinda Henneberger, "Investigators Show that US Embassy Is Vulnerable," *New York Times*, February 27, 2002, A9; Melinda Henneberger, "Four Arrested in Plot Against US Embassy in Rome," *New York Times*, February 21, 2002, A15; Sheila Pierce, "Italian Police Arrest Moroccans, Seize Chemical," *Washington Post*, February 21, 2002, A14; Sheila Pierce, "Four Tunisians Convicted on Terror Charges; Men Tied to Al Qaeda by Italian Authorities," *Washington Post*, February 23, 2002, A16.

348. Cited in Williams, "Italy Probing Source," A14.

349. Emilio de Mese, cited in Pierce, "Italian Police Arrest Moroccans," A14.

350. Mackey and Miller, *The Interrogators*, 426.

351. Crozier, *A Theory of Conflict*, 157.

352. See chapter 22, "Does Torture Work?"

353. John Conroy, *Unspeakable Acts, Ordinary People* (New York: Knopf, 2000), 46. RUC interrogators made similar claims in the summer of 1977, but these will have to wait the declassification of their records. See Taylor, *Beating the Terrorists?* 156, 193, 205–6.

354. Tom Parker, MI5 officer, cited in Mayer, "Outsourcing Torture," 116–18.

355. Mark Moyar, *Phoenix and the Birds of Prey* (Annapolis, MD: Naval Institute Press, 1997), 102–3; Bowden, "Dark Art of Interrogation," 59–60.

356. Moyar, *Phoenix*, 60.

357. Ibid., 101. See also Martin Edwin Anderson, "Is Torture an Option in War on Terror?" *Insight Online*, May 27, 2002; reposted May 14, 2004, http://www.insightmag.com.

358. van Natta, "Interrogation Methods in Iraq," A11.

359. Orrin Forrest and David Chanoff, *Slow Burn* (New York: Simon and Schuster, 1990), 55–56.

360. Ibid., 111–14, 135.

361. Ibid. 122.

362. Ibid., 122–29.

363. Ibid., 172–76.

364. Ibid., 121; see also 132.

365. See Vest, "CIA Veterans Condemn Torture," 3652; Frank Snepp, *Decent Interval* (New York: Random House, 1977), 31, 35–36; and Frank Snepp, *Irreparable Harm* (New York: Random House, 1999), 185–86.

366. Vhuyen Van Tai, cited in Snepp, *Interval*, 36.

367. Pribbenow, cited in Vest, "CIA Veterans Condemn Torture," 3652. See also Snepp, *Harm*, 186.

368. Moyar, *Phoenix*, 60.

369. George Gallup Jr. and Jim Castelli, *The People's Religion* (New York: Macmillan, 1989); "Survey: Vast Majority of Americans Believe in Angels" *Star Tribune* (Minneapolis), December 19, 2001, http://www.startribune.com. For polls on torture, see Richard Morin and Claudia Deane, "American Split on How to Interrogate," *Washington Post*, May 28, 2004, A20; Abraham McLaughlin, "How Far Americans Would Go To Fight Terror," *Christian Science Monitor*, November 14, 2001, 1; Alisa Solomon, "The Case Against Torture," *Village Voice*, December 4, 2001, 56.

370. Lisa Hajjar, *Courting Conflict: The Israeli Military Court System in the West Bank and Gaza* (Berkeley and Los Angeles: University of California Press, 2005), 198–99; Samir Qouta, Raija-Leena Punamäki, and Eyad El Sarraj, "Prison Experiences and Coping Styles Among Palestinian Men," *Peace and Conflict* 3.1 (1997): 24; Joseph Lelyveld, "Interrogating Ourselves," *New York Times*, June 12, 2005, sec. 6, p. 66. For how informants are recruited, see Chris McGreal, "Web of Betrayal, Blackmail and Sex that Killed Two Lovers Who Turned Informed," *Guardian* (London), June 3, 2006, 16.

371. Michael Koubi, GSS interrogator, cited in Bowden, "Dark Art of Interrogation," 68–69.

372. Bowden, "Dark Art of Interrogation," 62–69; B'Tselem, *Legislation Allowing the Use of Physical Force and Mental Coercion in Interrogations by the General Security Service* (Jerusalem: B'Tselem, 2000), 49; "Psychology and Sometimes a Slap," *New York Times*, December 12, 2004, sec. 4, p. 7.

373. Stanley Cohen and Daphna Golan, *The Interrogation of Palestinians during the Intifada* (Jerusalem: B'Tselem, Israeli Information Center for Human Rights in the Occupied Territories, 1991), 23. See also Hajjar, *Courting Conflict*, 202.

374. Omri Kochva, cited in Conroy, *Unspeakable Acts, Ordinary People*, 209, 210; see also 212, 220.

375. Cohen and Golan, *Interrogation of Palestinians*, 110.

376. James Ron, *Torture and Ill-treatment* (New York: Human Rights Watch, 1994), 15.

377. B'Tselem, *Routine Torture: Interrogation Methods of the General Security Service* (Jerusalem: B'Tselem, Israeli Information Center for Human Rights in the Occupied Territories, 1998), 38.

378. Eyad Saraj, "Torture and Mental Health," in *Torture*, ed. Neve Gordon and Ruchama Marton with John Jay Neufeld (London: Zed, 1995), 104–7; Hajjar, *Courting Conflict*, 190–95.

379. Melissa Phillips, *Torture for Security* (Ramallah, West Bank: al-Haq, 1995), 21–24, 81.

380. See chapter 2, "Torture and Democracy."

381. Gisli Gudjonsson, *The Psychology of Interrogations and Confessions* (West Sussex, England: 2003), 175, 582–89.

382. Hajjar, *Courting Conflict*, 204–5.

383. Ibid., 185–86.

384. Middle East Watch, *Prison Conditions in Israel and the Occupied Territories* (New York: Human Rights Watch, 1991), 16.

385. Yuval Ginbar, *Back to a Routine of Torture*, trans. Jessica Bonn (Jerusalem: Public Committee against Torture in Israel, 2003), 47; B'Tselem, *Legislation*, 48; Cohen and Golan, *Interrogation of Palestinians*, 22–23; Gideon Levy, "We Are the Shin-Bet: Extracts from *Ha'aretz* Supplement, January 5, 1990," in Cohen and Golan, *Interrogation of Palestinians*, 108–13.

386. B'Tselem, *Routine Torture*, 15, 22; Yuval Ginbar, *Flawed Defense*, trans. Jessica Bonn (Jerusalem: Public Committee against Torture in Israel, 2001), 35.

387. Ginbar, *Back to a Routine*, 48.

388. Ginbar, *Flawed Defense*, 39.

389. Alan Dershowitz, "Want to Torture? Get a Warrant," *San Francisco Chronicle*, January 22, 2002, A19

390. Lelyveld, "Interrogating Ourselves," 43.

391. The Israeli statement asserted only that the methods used were "not torture in international law" (ibid.).

392. Cohen and Golan, *Interrogation of Palestinians*, 23. See also B'Tselem, *Legislation*, 5.

393. David Faranga, Israeli Foreign Ministry spokesman, cited in "Hamas and Islamic Jihad Agree to Ceasefire," *Guardian* (London), June 27, 2003, http://www.guardian.co.uk/; and Amir Oren, "Targeting Ahmadinejad," Haaretz.com, April 23, 2006. See also Ibrahim Barzak, "Palestinian Officials: Hamas Truce Soon," Associated Press, July 24, 2003, http://www.yahoo.com; Chris McGreal, "Israel Dismisses Intifada Truce," *Guardian* (London), June 30, 2003, 2.

394. Ronny Talmor, "How a Bomb Ticks," in B'Tselem, *Legislation*, 71. First appeared in *Tarbut Ma'ariv*, October 1, 1999.

395. Dexter Filkins, "General Says Less Coercion of Captives Yields Better Data," *New York Times*, September 7, 2004, A12.

396. For General Miller's credibility problems when it comes to speaking about torture, see Stephen J. Hedges, "General Contradicted His Sworn Testimony on Pentagon," *Chicago Tribune*, July 15, 2005, http://www.chicagotribune.com; Lolita Baldor and John J. Lumpkin, "Reprimand of Guantanamo Chief Urged, Nixed," Associated Press, July 13, 2005, http://www.lexis-nexis.com/; White, "Abu Ghraib Tactics," A01; and Pete Yost, "Lawyers Nix Please for Abu Ghraib Testimony," Associated Press, March 3, 2006, http://www.lexis-nexis.com/.

397. Yehiya Kadoori Hamoodi, cited in Deborah Sontag, "How Colonel Risked his Career by Menacing Detainee and Lost," *New York Times*, May 27, 2004, A11.

Chapter 23
Why Governments Don't Learn

1. Michael T. Kaufman, "What Does the Pentagon See in 'Battle of Algiers'?" *New York Times*, September 7, 2003, WK3.

2. Dennis Faul and Raymond Murray, *The RUC: The Black and Blue Book* ([Dungannon, Northern Ireland]: [Denis Faul], 1975), 40.

3. Chris Mackey and Greg Miller, *The Interrogators* (New York: Little, Brown, 2004), 477.

4. Alan Dershowitz, introduction to W. R. Peers, *The My Lai Inquiry* (New York: Notable Trials Library, 1993), iii.

5. As the British experience suggests. See chapter 15, "Forced Standing and Other Positions."

6. Jean-Yves Alquier, *Nous avons pacifié Tazalt* (Paris: Robert Laffont, 1967), 168–218.

7. Manfred Nowak, "Folter als spezifische Ausprägung von Gewalt," presented at Foltern: Internationale Konferenz des Graduiertenkollegs, Humboldt University, Berlin, April 27–29, 2006.

8. Brian Crozier, *A Theory of Conflict* (New York: Charles Scribner's Sons, 1974).

9. Alan Dershowitz, *Why Terrorism Works* (New Haven, CT: Yale University Press, 2002), 141, 149, 152–54; Alan Dershowitz, "Is It Necessary to Apply 'Physical Pressure' to Terrorists—and Lie About It?" *Israel Law Review* 23 (1989): 192–200; Alan Dershowitz, "Stop Winking at Torture and Codify It," *Los Angeles Times*, June 13, 2004, M5; Alan Dershowitz, *Shouting Fire* (Boston: Little, Brown, 2002), 476–77; Alan Dershowitz, "My Evolving Theory of Rights," *Boston Globe*, November 29, 2001, A18.

10. Dershowitz, *Shouting Fire*, 471; Oliver Moore, "Arar Sues US Government," *Globe and Mail Update*, January 22, 2004, http://www.globeandmail.com. See also David B. Rivkin Jr. and Lee A. Casey, "It's Not Torture, and They Aren't Lawful Combatants," *Washington Post*, January 11, 2003, A19; Mark Bowden, "The Dark Art of Interrogation," *Atlantic Monthly*, October 2003, 70; Mark Bowden, "The Lessons of Abu Ghraib," *Atlantic Monthly*, July–August 2004, 33–36; Anne Applebaum, "The Torture Myth," *Washington Post*, January 12, 2005, A21; Mirko Bagaric and Julie Clarke, "Not Enough (Official) Torture in the World? The Circumstances in which Torture is Morally Justifiable," *University of San Francisco Law Journal* 39.3 (2005): 581–616.

11. Dershowitz, *Why Terrorism Works*, 132–33, 141; Dershowitz, "When Torture is the Least Evil of Terrible Options," *Times Higher Education Supplement*, June 11, 2004, 20; Alan Dershowitz, "Yes, It Should Be 'On the Books,'" *Boston Globe*, February 16, 2002, A15; Alan Dershowitz, "Is There a Torturous Road to Justice?" *Los Angeles Times*, November 8, 2001, B19; Dershowitz, "Stop Winking," M5; Irwin Block, "Allow Judges to Issue 'Torture Warrants' in Terror Cases," *Montreal Gazette*, December 9, 2003, A7.

12. Dershowitz, "Yes, It Should Be," A15; Dershowitz, "My Evolving Theory," A18; Alan Dershowitz, "Warrant Would Make Those Using Torture Accountable," *Financial Times*, June 8, 2002, 8; Alan Dershowitz, "We Need a Serious Debate About the Use of Torture," *Guardian* (London), November 30, 2001, 23. For some critical appraisals, see William Schulz, "The Torturer's Apprentice," *The Nation*, May 13, 2002, 25–27; Jeremy Waldron, "The Great Defender," *New Times Book*

Review, February 3, 2002, 13; Christopher Hitchens, "In Case Anyone's Forgotten: Torture Doesn't Work," *Guardian* (London), November 14, 2001, sec. 2, p. 5; Jeremy Campbell, "Torture's the New Way Forward," *Evening Standard* (London), December 4, 2001, 20; Robert Reno, "Two Moralists Display Their Immorality," *Newsday*, February 5, 2002, A30; "Letters to the Editor," *San Francisco Chronicle*, January 31, 2002, A18.

13. Dershowitz, *Why Terrorism Works*, 138.

14. Gary Marx, *Undercover* (Berkeley and Los Angeles: University of California Press, 1988). These similarities include major psychological and identity problems (163, 169, 170, 171), guilt and anxiety (160), high personal cost of isolation and secrecy (161), high job stress (161), exaggerated sense of one's own power (163), low morale (167), bureaucratic devolution (161), rejection by professionals afterward (168, 170), failed social reintegration (169, 170), criminal activity (163), and anger, bitterness, and feelings of betrayal (170).

15. Richard McNally, *Remembering Trauma* (Cambridge: Belknap Press of Harvard University Press, 2003), 86.

16. Frantz Fanon, *The Wretched of the Earth*, trans. Constance Farrington (New York: Grove Press, 1968), 267–70.

17. Ibid., 264–67.

18. Gideon Levy, "We Are the Shin-Bet: Extracts from *Ha'aretz* Supplement, January 5, 1990," cited in Stanley Cohen and Daphna Golan, *The Interrogation of Palestinians during the Intifada* (Jerusalem: B'Tselem, Israeli Information Center for Human Rights in the Occupied Territories, 1991), 113; Martha K. Huggins, Mika Haritos-Fatouros, and Philip Zimbardo, *Violence Workers* (Berkeley and Los Angeles: University of California Press, 2002), 227–28.

19. Huggins, Haritos-Fatouros, and Zimbardo, *Violence Workers*, 215–31.

20. Ibid., 144, 221–27.

21. Ibid., 215–21.

22. Brazilian torturer, cited in ibid., 221.

23. See, for example, the case of "A" in Mika Haritos-Fatouros, *The Psychological Origins of Institutionalized Torture* (London: Routledge, 2003), 88.

24. Ibid., 93, 95, 97, 101, 105, 113–16, 203.

25. "D," cited in ibid., 97.

26. Haritos-Fatouros, *Psychological Origins*, 101.

27. Alistair Horne, *A Savage War of Peace* (New York: Viking, 1977), 206.

28. Beauge Florence, "350,000 anciens d'Algérie souffriraient de trouble psychiques lies à la guerre," *Le Monde*, December 28, 2000.

29. Ted Morgan, *My Battle of Algiers* (New York: HarperCollins, 2005), xix; see also 169–70.

30. Wolfgang Heinz, "The Military, Torture and Human Rights," in *The Politics of Pain*, ed. F. D. Crelinsten and A. P. Schmid (Leiden, the Netherlands: Center for the Study of Social Conflict, 1993), 84.

31. Aldo Martin, "Individual Depression after an Active Role in Violation of Human Rights," unpublished paper, Seventh International Symposium on Caring for Sur-

vivors of Torture, Cape Town, South Africa, 1995; Huggins, Haritos-Fatouros, and Zimbardo, *Violence Workers*, 212–13.

32. Hannah Arendt, *Eichmann in Jerusalem*, rev. ed. (Harmondsworth, England: Penguin, 1979), 278–79.

33. George Orwell, *Homage to Catalonia* (Boston: Harcourt, Brace, 1952), 65, 66.

34. Fanon, *Wretched of the Earth*, 277.

35. Jean Maria Arrigo, "A Consequentialist Argument Against Torture Interrogation of Terrorists," conference paper, Joint Services Conference on Professional Ethics, Springfield, VA, January 30–31, 2003, note 62, available at http://www.usafa.af.mil/jscope/JSCOPE03/Arrigo03.html.

36. Peters makes this case especially clearly with the notion of the ever-growing class of people subject to *crimen exceptum*, exceptional crimes. See Edward Peters, *Torture*, 2nd ed. (Philadelphia: University of Pennsylvania Press, 1996). Similar trends follow American legislation restricting other civil liberties. See David Cole, *Enemy Aliens* (New York: New Press, 2003).

37. Diarmaid Macculloch, *The Reformation* (New York: Viking, 2003), 556.

38. Ibid., 552–56; Edward Peters, *Inquisition* (Berkeley and Los Angeles: University of California Press, 1988), 92.

39. John Langbein, *Torture and the Law of Proof* (Chicago: University of Chicago Press, 1977), 81; Lisa Silverman, *Tortured Subjects* (Chicago: University of Chicago Press, 2001), 89–90, 192.

40. Dershowitz, "Yes, It Should Be," A15. Dershowitz claims this thesis is in Langbein, but I cannot find it.

41. Dershowitz, *Why Terrorism Works*, 158.

42. Peters, *Inquisition*, 59.

43. Langbein, *Law of Proof*, 78–79.

44. Ibid., 73.

45. See chapter 2, "Torture and Democracy."

46. Alan Dershowitz, "Want to Torture? Get a Warrant," *San Francisco Chronicle*, January 22, 2002, A19.

47. James LeMoyne, "Testifying to Torture," *New York Times*, June 5, 1988, sec. 6, p. 45.

48. Dershowitz, "Want to Torture?" A19.

49. John Kleinig, *The Ethics of Policing* (Cambridge: Cambridge University Press, 1996), 174–81; Lawrence Hinman, "Stunning Morality," *Criminal Justice Ethics* 17.1 (1998): 3–14.

50. Dershowitz, *Why Terrorism Works*, 144.

51. Henry Charles Lea, *A History of the Inquisition of the Middle Ages* (New York: Russell and Russell, 1958), 1:421–25.

52. Dershowitz, "Torturous Road to Justice?" B19.

53. Bowden, "Dark Art," 76.

54. Bowden, "Abu Ghraib," 35–36.

55. Dershowitz, *Why Terrorism Works*, 141.

56. Dershowitz, "Torture Least Evil," 20.

57. Especially Dershowitz, *Why Terrorism Works*, 137, 249 nn. 10 and 11. Compare these claims with chapter 22, "What the Apologists Say," especially notes to the section "The Interrogation of Al Qaeda."

58. James Ron, "Varying Methods of State Violence" *International Organization* 51.2 (1997): 286–87, 294.

59. Possibly an example of the sort Bowden has in mind, the only one I can find is this: Deborah Sontag, "How Colonel Risked his Career by Menacing Detainee and Lost," *New York Times*, May 27, 2004, A11.

60. Pierre Vidal-Naquet, *Torture*, trans. Barry Richard (Harmondsworth, England: Penguin, 1963), 64, 78–79, 127–34; "Henri Alleg," in Simone de Beauvoir and Gisele Halimi, *Djamila Boupacha*, trans. Peter Green (New York: Macmillan, 1962), 203–7.

61. Horne, *Savage War of Peace*, 204.

62. "Experimental Analysis of Extrasensory Perception," August 1961, Subproject 136, MKULTRA, Central Intelligence Agency; John Marks, *The Search for the Manchurian Candidate* (New York: Times Books, 1979), 211–12; Armen Victorian, *The Mind Controllers* (Miami, FL: Lewis International, 2000), 103–46; Charles Sellier and Joe Meier, *The Paranormal Sourcebook* (Chicago: Contemporary Books, 1999), 127–34.

63. Patrick Kessel and Giovanni Pirelli, *Le people algérien et la guerre* (Paris: François Maspero, 1962), 49–63; Sylvie Thénault, *Une drôle de justice* (Paris: Éditions la Découverte, 2001), 60; Vidal-Naquet, *Torture*, 70.

64. Affidavit of Gabrielle Benichou Gimenez, October 4, 1956, in Kessel and Pirelli, *Le people algérien*, 53–55.

65. Joseph Begarra to Guy Mollet (1957), in Denis Lefebvre, *Guy Mollet face à la torture en Algérie, 1956–1957* (Paris: Bruno Leprine, 2001), 97. See also Vidal-Naquet, *Torture*, 145–46.

66. See "Algerian Souvenirs" in chapter 24, "The Great Age of Torture in Modern Memory."

67. CIA case officer, cited in Jason Vest, "CIA Veterans Condemn Torture," *National Journal* 37.47–48 (November 19, 2005): 3653.

68. Niccolò Machiavelli, *The Prince*, trans. Robert Adams (New York: Norton, 1977), 22. See also Vidal-Naquet, *Torture*, 81; Orlando Patterson, *Rituals of Blood* (New York: Basic Civitas, 1998), 218–23; Michael Taussig, *The Nervous System* (New York: Routledge, 1992), 116; Michael Taussig, *Magic of the State* (New York: Routledge, 1997).

69. Friedrich Nietzsche, *Twilight of the Idols and The Anti-Christ*, trans. R. J. Hollingdale (Harmondsworth, England: Penguin, 1968), 34.

70. Martin Buber, "False Prophets," in *Israel and the World* (New York: Schocken, 1963), 116.

71. Begarra to Mollet, 98.

72. See Gil Merom, *How Democracies Lose Small Wars* (Cambridge: Cambridge University Press, 2003).

Chapter 24
The Great Age of Torture in Modern Memory

1. Walter Benjamin, "Theses on the Philosophy of History," in *Illuminations*, ed. Hannah Arendt, trans. Harry Zohn (New York: Schocken, 1968), 257.
2. See, for example, Henry Norman, *The Peoples and Politics of the Far East* (London: T. Fischer Unwin, 1900), 219–30.
3. Jacques Weygand, *Légionnaire*, trans. Raymond Johnes (London: George Harrap, 1952), 135; Hugh Mcleave, *The Damned Die Hard* (New York: Saturday Review Press, 1973), 137; Charles Mercer, *Legion of Strangers* (New York: Holt, Rinehart and Winston, 1964), 237; Zosa Szajkowski, *Jews and the Foreign Legion* (New York: Ktav, 1975), 7–8.
4. Weygand, *Légionnaire*, 135; G. Ward Price, *Extra-Special Correspondent* (London: George G. Harrap, 1957), 190–91.
5. For the power such stories in the nineteenth century, see Michael Taussig, "Culture of Terror—Space of Death. Roger Casement's Putumayo Report and the Explanation of Torture," *Comparative Studies in Society and History* 26.3 (1984): 467–97.
6. Occasional reports are from the Foreign Legion (James Armstrong with William Elliott, *Legion of Hell* [London: Sampson, Low, Marston (1936), 207–8]), American prisons (F. Dalton O'Sullivan, *Crime Detection* [Chicago: O'Sullivan Publishing House, 1928], 297), South Vietnam (Pham Tam, *Imprisonment and Torture in South Vietnam* [Nyack, NY: Fellowship of Reconciliation, 1969(?)], 8), Greece (Amalia Fleming, *A Piece of Truth* [London: Jonathan Cape, 1972], 235–36; European Commission of Human Rights, *The Greek Case* [Strasbourg: Council of Europe, 1970], 298), East Germany (Anna Funder, *Stasiland* [London: Granta, 2003], 226–27), Turkey (Human Rights Watch, *Turkey* 9:4 [March 1997], 11); El Salvador (Amnesty International [AI], *Report, 1986* [London, 1986], 125), and Equatorial Guinea (AI, *Report, 1993* [London, 1993], 125; Chris Mackey and Greg Miller, *The Interrogators* [New York: Little, Brown, 2004], 180).
7. Rudibert Kunz and Rolf-Dieter Müller, *Giftgas gegen Abd el Krim* (Freiburg: Verlag Rombach, 1990).
8. Colonel Rémy, *Une Épopée de la Résistance* (Paris: Éditions Atlas, 1979), 2:195.
9. Ian Cobain, "The Secrets of the London Cage," *Guardian* (London), November 12, 2005, 8.
10. There are uninvestigated rumors of American troops using torture during World War II. Whether this is interrogator lore or reality is hard to know. See John Duffett, ed., *Against the Crime of Silence: Proceedings of the Russell International War Crimes Tribunal* (New York: O'Hare, 1968), 453; Victor Davis Hanson, "Winning a War without Torture," *Washington Times*, December 3, 2005, http://www.washingtontimes.com. Hanson claims American troops who tortured in World War II operated under a "don't ask, don't tell" understanding and they were rarely punished by commanding officers, so records are unlikely. Fabien Brun describes a photograph in a Frankfurt police museum of Allied electrotorture of

a German prisoner at the end of the war, but I have been unable to find it (Fabien Brun, email message to author, February 7, 2002).

11. See chapter 4, "Whips and Water."

12. R.J.B. Bosworth, *Explaining Auschwitz and Hiroshima* (London: Routledge, 1994), 189. See also Saburo Ienaga, *The Pacific War, 1931–1945* (New York: Pantheon, 1978).

13. Tony Judt, "The Past Is Another Country: Myth and Memory in Postwar Europe," in *The Politics of Retribution in Europe*, ed. István Deák, Jan T. Gross, and Tony Judt (Princeton, NJ: Princeton University Press, 2000), 295.

14. Talal Asad, "On Torture, or Cruel, Inhuman, and Degrading Treatment," in *Social Suffering*, ed. Veena Das, Arthur Kleinman, and Margaret Lock (Berkeley and Los Angeles: University of California Press, 1997), 289.

15. Lord Russell of Liverpool, *Prisons and Prisoners in Portugal* (London: Waterlow and Sons, 1963), 6–8, 12–13.

16. Seymour Hersh, "Ex-Analyst Says CIA Rejected Warning on Shah," *New York Times*, January 7, 1979, A3.

17. See Paul Gregson, *Orgies of Torture and Brutality* (London: Walton Press, 1965), 247–54.

18. Marcio Alves, *Torturas e Torturados* (Rio de Janeiro: Empresa Jornalística, 1966), 26, 145; *The Gangrene*, trans. Robert Silvers (New York: Lyle Stewart, 1960), 59.

19. Peter Deeley, *Beyond Breaking Point* (London: Arthur Barker, 1971), 13–117.

20. John McGuffin, *The Guineapigs* (Harmondsworth, England: Penguin, 1974), 12–35; Peter Taylor, *Beating the Terrorists?* (Harmondsworth, England: Penguin, 1980), 20; John Conroy, *Unspeakable Acts, Ordinary People* (New York: Alfred Knopf, 2000), 255; Steve Wright, "The New Trade in Technologies of Restraint and Electroshock," in *A Glimpse of Hell*, ed. Duncan Forrest (London: Amnesty International, 1996), 137–38; Alfred McCoy, *A Question of Torture* (New York: Metropolitan, 2006), 1–107.

21. Daniel Bacry and Michel Ternisen, *La torture* (Paris: Fayard, 1980), 125.

22. Rebecca Lemov, *World as Laboratory* (New York: Hill and Wang, 2005), 220–21.

23. Tim Shallice, "The Ulster Depth Interrogation Techniques and their Relation to Sensory Deprivation Research," *Cognition* 1.4 (1972): 403.

24. Michael Kerrigan, *The Instruments of Torture* (New York: Lyons Press, 2001), 153–54. For similar analogies between ECT and electrotorture, see Pericles Korovessis, *The Method*, trans. Les Nightingale and Catherine Patrakis (London: Allison and Busby, 1970), 49–50; Miguel Sanchez-Mazas, *Spain in Chains* (New York: Veterans of the Abraham Lincoln Brigade, 1960), 23.

25. See chapter 21, "Does Torture Work?"

26. McCoy, *A Question of Torture*, 13–14, 58, 60. See also chapter 18, "Noise."

27. Devin Pendas, " 'I didn't know what Auschwitz was': The Frankfurt Auschwitz Trial and the German Press, 1963–1965," *Yale Journal of Law and Humanities* 12.2 (2000): 439–40.

28. Conroy, *Unspeakable Acts, Ordinary People*, 235.

29. Ibid., 167.

30. Asad, "On Torture," 297.

31. Friedrich Nietzsche, *On the Genealogy of Morals and Ecce Homo*, trans. Walter Kaufmann (New York: Vintage, 1969), 64–73.

32. Peter Brown, *The Cult of Saints* (Chicago: University of Chicago Press, 1981), 112.

33. *Vita sancti Severi Viennensis presbyteri* (1886) cited in ibid., 112.

34. Jean Lartéguy, *The Centurions*, trans. Xan Felding (New York: E. P. Dutton, 1962).

35. Ted Morgan, *My Battle of Algiers* (New York: HarperCollins, 2005), 95. Again, in a curious inversion, the first reports of ants in torture refer to French police, and then subsequently to the South Vietnamese police. See Andrée Viollis, *Indochine S.O.S.* (Paris: Gallimard, 1935), 22 and also chapter 8, "Currents."

36. Lartéguy, *The Centurions*, 470.

37. For similar torrid scenes in other novels of this period, see Pierre Vidal-Naquet, *Torture*, trans. Barry Richard (Harmondsworth, England: Penguin, 1963), 146.

38. Lartéguy, *The Centurions*, 481.

39. Alan Dershowitz, *Just Revenge* (New York: Warner, 1999), 127–28.

40. Pierre Bourdieu, *Outline of a Theory of Practice*, trans. Richard Nice (Cambridge: Cambridge University Press, 1989), 21–22, 195–96.

41. Vidal-Naquet, *Torture*, 146.

42. Morgan, *My Battle of Algiers*, ix, 156; see also 95.

43. "Memorandum for Chief, Inspections Division, Subject: 4th Infantry Division Detainee Operations Assessment Trip Report (CONUS Team), DOD 015973 (DAIG-389).

44. Leonard Wantchekon and Andrew Healey, "The 'Game' of Torture," *Journal of Conflict Resolution*. 43.5 (1999): 596–609.

45. Rachel Cooper, "From Though Experiments to Real Experiments," *Studies in History and Philosophy of Biological and Biomedical Sciences* 30.2 (1999): 263–71; Rachel Cooper, "Thought Experiments," *Metaphilosophy* 36.3 (2005): 328–47.

46. While I have spelled these out as clearly as I can, other philosophers have long made this point. See Henry Shue, "Torture," *Philosophy and Public Affairs* 7.2 (1978): 141; Jeremy Waldron, "Security and Liberty: The Image of Balance," *Journal of Political Philosophy* 11.2 (2003): 206–8; Jeremy Waldron, "Torture and Positive Law: Jurisprudence for the White House," revised manuscript, delivered at Boalt Hall GALA Workshop, September 30, 2004, 34–37.

47. Joe Spieler, "Prof. Michael Levin," *Penthouse*, October 1982, 134. For Levin's original argument, see Michael Levin, "The Case for Torture," *Newsweek*, June 7, 1982, 13.

48. Rev. Homer Stunz, " 'The Water Cure' from a Missionary Point of View," cited in Stuart Creighton Miller, *Benevolent Assimilation* (New Haven, CT: Yale University Press, 1982), 248.

49. Anne Applebaum, "The Torture Myth," *Washington Post*, January 12, 2005, A21. For similar French observations, see Roger Trinquier, *La guerre moderne* (Paris: La Table Ronde, 1961), translated by Daniel Lee as *Modern Warfare* (New York: Praeger, 1964).

50. President George W. Bush, cited in Bob Woodward and Dan Balz, " 'We Will Rally the World,' " *Washington Post*, January 28, 2002, A01.

51. It is suggestive that those who seem especially attracted to Lartéguy's story are often men from professions the public perceives as being the occupations for nerds and sissies, namely, actors, lawyers, and academics. For an exploration of the sources of the modern anxiety about manliness in democracies and how torture appears to respond to it, see Darius Rejali, "Torture Makes the Man," *South Central Review* 24.1 (forthcoming 2007).

52. George W. Bush, "Address to a Joint Session of Congress and the American People, September 20, 2001, http://www.whitehouse.gov/news/releases/2001/09/20010920-8.html.

53. Victor David Hanson, "They Hate Us for Who We Are, Not What We Do," *Chicago Tribune*, January 18, 2005, http://www.victorhanson.com.

54. See Darius Rejali, "Friend and Enemy, East or West: Political Realism in the Work of Osama bin Ladin, Carl Schmitt, Niccolo Machiavelli, and Kai Ka'us ibn Iskandar," *Historical Reflections* 3 (2004): 425–43. In a rare moment of clarity, even Hanson, "Winning a War," makes this point, though he is blissfully unaware of its implications.

55. W. R. Kidd, *Police Interrogation* (New York City: R. V. Basuino, 1940), 49.

56. Stephen Budiansky, "Truth Extraction," *Atlantic Monthly*, June 2005, 32.

57. Ibid., 35.

58. Albert Biderman, *March to Calumny* (New York: Arno, 1979), 115–34, 189–214, 221–23, 265–71; Peter Karsten, "The American Democratic Citizen Soldier: Triumph or Disaster?" *Military Affairs* 30:1 (1966): 34–40; H. H. Wubben, "American Prisoners of War in Korea: A Second Look at the "Something New in History" Theme," *American Quarterly* 22.1 (1970): 3–19.

59. Karsten, American Democratic Citizen Soldier," 39.

60. Cavenaugh, cited in Mackey and Miller, *The Interrogators*, 191; see also 180–81.

61. Ronny Talmor, "How a Bomb Ticks," in B'Tselem, *Legislation Allowing the Use of Physical Force and Mental Coercion in Interrogations by the General Security Service* (Jerusalem: B'Tselem, 2000), 71. First appeared in *Tarbut Ma'ariv*, October 1, 1999.

62. H. Hessell Tiltman, *The Terror in Europe* (New York: Frederick A. Stokes, 1932).

63. Karl Marx, "The Eighteenth Brumaire of Louis Bonaparte," in *Selected Writings*, 2nd ed., ed. David McClellan (Oxford: Oxford University Press, 2000), 329.

64. The translation is Martha Nussbaum's in *The Fragility of Goodness* (Cambridge: Cambridge University Press, 1988), 240.

65. David Hume, *A Treatise on Human Nature*, ed. David Fate Norton and Mary J. Norton (Oxford: Oxford University Press, 2000), 175 (I.4.7, par. 9).

66. The last phrase is an old Russian saying ("Ni, eto ne nashego uma delo. Bez Vodki ne razerschcya"). Aleksander Topolski, *Without Vodka* (Ottawa, Canada: UP Press, 1999), 1.

Appendix B
Issues of Method

1. Martha K. Huggins, Mika Haritos-Fatouros, and Philip Zimbardo, *Violence Workers* (Berkeley and Los Angeles: University of California Press, 2002), 45–62, 81–118, 192–209.
2. *Encyclopedia of Violence, Peace, and Conflict*, 3 vols. (San Diego: Academic Press, 1999).
3. For a very self-conscious use of this sense of torture, see Anatoly Koryagin, "Toward Truly Outlawing Torture," *Science* 241.4871 (September 9, 1988): 1277.

Appendix C
Organization and Explanations

1. Mirko Bagaric and Julie Clarke, "Not Enough (Official) Torture in the World? The Circumstances in which Torture is Morally Justifiable," *University of San Francisco Law Journal* 39.3 (2005): 4, 28–29.

Appendix D
A Note on Sources for American Torture during the Vietnam War

1. William Calley with John Sack, *Lieutenant Calley: His Own Story* (New York: Viking, 1971), 77
2. Ibid., 95.
3. Ibid., 78; see also 96.
4. John Conroy, "Tools of Torture," *Chicago Reader*, February 4, 2005, 1, 24–27.
5. Ibid., 24.
6. Ibid., 25.
7. Dennis Carstens, cited in Conroy, "Tools of Torture,"25.
8. D. J. Lewis, cited in ibid., 25.
9. Deborah Nelson and Nick Turse, "A Tortured Past," *Los Angeles Times*, August 20, 2006, A1.
10. Ibid.
11. Staff Sgt. David Carmon, testimony to Army CID Investigators, December 1970, cited in Nelson and Turse, "A Tortured Past," A1.
12. Ibid., A1.
13. Mark Moyar, *Phoenix and the Birds of Prey* (Annapolis, MD: Naval Institute Press, 1997), 96.
14. "Testimony and Questioning of Donald Duncan," in *Against the Crime of Silence: Proceedings of the Russell International War Crimes Tribunal*, ed. John Duffett (New York: O'Hare, 1968), 403–25, 457–513; Donald Duncan, *The New Legions* (New York: Random House, 1967), 156–61, 166–69, 180–81.

15. Guenter Lewy, *America in Vietnam* (Oxford: Oxford University Press, 1978), 313.

16. Duncan, *Veterans Testimony on Vietnam*, 92nd Congress, 1st sess., *Congressional Record*, vol. 117, part 8 (April 5–19, 1971), 9997; Donald Duncan, "Un béret vert parle," *Les Temps Modernes* 261 (1968): 1483–97.

17. Duffett, *Crime of Silence*, 464.

18. Ibid.

19. Ibid., 470–73.

20. "Testimony and Questioning of Peter Martinsen," in Duffett, *Crime of Silence*, 425–57.

21. Nelson and Turse, "A Tortured Past," A1; Ralph Scott, Criminal Investigator, "CID Report of Investigation of 172nd MI Detachment," August 23, 1971, Investigations Division, U.S. Army CID Agency, Washington, DC.

22. "Testimony of Martinsen," 431.

23. Ibid., 429.

24. Ibid., 428.

25. Ibid., 447.

26. Martinsen offered testimony at the Citizens Commission of Inquiry (Dellums Committee) and in Lane's *Conversations with Americans* (New York: Simon and Schuster, 1970), on avoiding scarring (146–47, 153), slapping (153, 157), field telephone torture (146, 148, 150, 153–54, 157, 158); Citizens Commission of Inquiry (CCI), ed., *The Dellums Committee Hearings on War Crimes in Vietnam* (New York: Vintage, 1972), 144, 146 (field telephone torture).

27. Martinsen, cited in CCI, *Dellums Committee Hearings*, 146.

28. Martinsen, cited in Lane, *Conversations with Americans*, 153, 157.

29. CCI, *Dellums Committee Hearings*, 147–48. Martinsen's first account of the manual is sketched out in Duffett, *Crime of Silence*, 433.

30. Martinsen, cited in Lane, *Conversations with Americans*, 157–59.

31. Martinsen, cited in CCI, *Dellums Committee Hearings*, 147.

32. Mark Baker, *Nam* (New York: Quill, 1982), 198–200 (beating), 215 (magneto); Al Santoli, *Everything We Had* (New York: Random House, 1981), 25 (beating), 70 (choking); Richard Stacewicz, *Winter Soldiers* (New York: Twayne, 1997), 105 (choking), 118 (magneto).

33. Dick Culver, "Infantry Officer by Trade, Intelligence Officer by Accident," http://www.jouster.com/Culvers/intelligence.htm.

34. Dirk von Schrader, *Elementary Field Interrogation* (n.p.: Delta, 1978).

35. Anthony B. Herbert with James T. Wooten, *Soldier* (New York: Holt, Rinehart and Winston, 1973), 293–95 (water torture), 351–52 (magneto).

36. Lewy, *America in Vietnam*, 323–24; Nelson and Turse, "A Tortured Past," A1.

37. Nelson and Turse, "A Tortured Past," A1; Scott, "CID Report."

38. Nelson and Turse, "A Tortured Past," A1.

39. Neil Sheehan, review of *Conversations with Americans*, *New York Times Book Review*, December 27, 1970, 5, 19.

40. For example, reports of wet sheet squeezing (Lane, *Conversations with Americans*, 115), a technique not seen outside of asylums and most recently reported in Soviet psychoprisons. See chapter 19, "Drugs and Doctors."

41. Joseph Arthur Doucette Jr., cited in Lane, *Conversations with Americans*, 85; for the other instances of magneto torture, see 121, 197.

42. Lane, *Conversations with Americans*, electrotorture with car battery (217), water (121), *falaka* (85).

43. Ibid., 85.

44. CCI, *Dellums Committee Hearings*, 106–32; "Statement of K. Barton Osborn," House Committee on Government Operations, Subcommittee on Government Operations, *U.S. Assistance Programs in Vietnam: Hearings*, 92nd Cong., 1st sess., 1971, 315–21.

45. Moyar, *Phoenix*, 93–97. McCoy defends Osborn's testimony (Alfred McCoy, *A Question of Torture* [New York: Metropolitan, 2006], 67–68).

46. House Committee, *Assistance Programs*, 106–7.

47. "Statement of Ron Bartek," in CCI, *Dellums Committee Hearings*, 68.

48. Ibid., 67.

49. "Statement of Michael Uhl," in CCI, *Dellums Committee Hearings*, 100.

50. Ibid., 102.

51. Senator Mark Hatfield of Oregon read the complete transcript of the "Winter Soldier Investigation" (Detroit, January 31–February 2, 1971) into the *Congressional Record*. See *Veterans Testimony on Vietnam*, 92nd Congress, 1st sess., *Congressional Record*, vol. 117, part 8 (April 5–19, 1971), 9947–10055. The edited version is available under Vietnam Veterans Against the War, *The Winter Soldier Investigation* (Boston: Beacon Press, 1972). The references to torture are *Veterans Testimony*, 9949–50, 9956–58, 9988–89, 9993, 9995–96, 10000, 10002, 10010, 10025, 10032, 10036, 10050.

52. *Veterans Testimony*, 9989. See also CCI, *Dellums Committee Hearings*, 136.

53. *Veterans Testimony*, magneto torture (9957, 9989, 9993, 9995–96, 10000, 10025, 10032), beating (9952, 9958, 10010), dogs (10000, 10025), water (9993), suspension (10002), ear boring (9949).

54. Ibid., 9995.

55. Don Dzagulones, cited in *Veterans Testimony*, 9996; see also 9993.

56. Ibid., 9995.

57. John Conroy, *Unspeakable Acts, Ordinary People* (New York: Knopf, 2000), 113–21.

58. Lewy, *America in Vietnam*, 315.

59. Ibid., 317.

60. Tom Bowman, "Kerry went from soldier to anti-war protester," *Baltimore Sun*, February 14, 2004), 6A.

61. Ibid.

62. "Affidavit of Steven J. Pitkin," Number DD235268, County of Palm Beach, State of Florida, September 15, 2004, http://ice.he.net/~freepnet/kerry/.

63. "Affidavit of Scott Camil, County of Alachua, State of Florida, September 11, 2004, available at http://ice.he.net/~freepnet/kerry/.

64. Nancy Miller Saunders, "A Convenient Recantation," December 7, 2004, http://www.onlinejournal.com.

65. "Affidavit of Steven J. Pitkin."

66. Steven J. Pitkin in *Veterans Testimony*, 10008.

67. "Complete VVAW FBI Files," http://ice.he.net/~freepnet/kerry/.

68. Lewy, *America in Vietnam*, 332–41.

69. Ibid., 328.

70. Ibid., 391.

Selected Bibliography

Unless it is an important or unique source, this bibliography does not list annual global reports, country reports (such as the annual country reports of the European Committee for the Prevention of Torture http://www.cpt.coe.int/en/), or regional reports (such as Amnesty International's *Concerns in Europe* reports (http://www.amnesty.org).

"200 victimes accuseront l'intendant Pierre Marty." *La Marseillaise du Centre* (Limoges), July 10, 1946, 1.

Abbott, Geoffrey. *Rack, Rope and Red-hot Pincers*. London: Headline Books, 1993.

Abdul-Ahad, Ghaith. "More Iraqis Allege Abuse by U.S. Military." Reuters, May 4, 2004, http://www.yahoo.com.

Abrahamian, Ervand. *Tortured Confessions*. Berkeley and Los Angeles: University of California Press, 1999.

ACAT/Mexico. *La Tortura en Mexico 1996*. Mexico City: Accióndelos Cristanos para la Abolición de la Tortura, 1997.

Achin, Milos. *The First Guerillas of Europe*. New York: Vantage, 1963.

Adamson, Hans Christian, and Per Klem. *Blood on the Midnight Sun*. New York: Norton, 1964.

Adelman, Jonathan, ed. *Terror and Communist Politics*. Boulder, CO: Westview, 1984.

Aggarwal, S. N. *The Heroes of Cellular Jail*. Patiala, India: Punjabi University Publication Bureau, 1995.

Alexander, Michael. *The Reluctant Legionnaire*. New York: E. P. Dutton, 1956.

Allbury, A. G. *Bamboo and Bushido*. London: Robert Hale, 1955.

Alleg, Henri. *La Question*. Paris: Éditions de Minuit, 1961. Translated as *The Question* (New York: George Braziller, 1958).

Alquier, Jean-Yves. *Nous avons pacifié Tazalt*. Paris: Robert Laffont, 1967.

Altun, Gurcan, and Gulay Durmus-Altun. "Confirmation of Alleged Falanga Torture by Bone Scintigraphy." *International Journal of Legal Medicine* 117.6 (2003): 365–66.

Alves, Marcio. *Torturas e Torturados*. Rio de Janeiro: Empresa Jornalística, 1966.

Ambler, John. *The French Army in Politics*. Columbus: Ohio State University Press, 1966.

American Commission on Conditions in Ireland. *Evidence on Conditions in Ireland*. Washington, DC: Bliss Building, [1921].

Amery, Jean. *At the Mind's Limits*. Translated by Sidney Rosenfeld and Stella P. Rosenfeld. Bloomington: Indiana University Press, 1980.

Ames, Walter. *Police and Community in Japan*. Berkeley and Los Angeles: University of California Press, 1981.

Amnesty International. *1961–1976: A Chronology*. London: Amnesty International, 1976.

———. *Against Torture*. ACT 04/13/84. London: Amnesty International, 1984.

———. *Arming the Torturers: Electro-shock Torture and the Spread of Stun Technology*. ACT 40/01/97. London: Amnesty International, 1997.

———. *Doctors and Torture*. ACT 75/001/2002. London: Amnesty International, 2002.

———. *Evidence of Torture*. London: Amnesty International, 1977.

———. *Harming the Healers*. ACT 75/02/00c. London: Amnesty International, 2000.

———. *Power and Impunity*. London: Amnesty International, 1994.

———. *Report on Torture*. London: Duckworth, 1973.

———. *Stopping the Torture Trade*. ACT 40/002/2001. London: International Secretariat, 2001.

———. *The Pain Merchants*. ACT 40/008/2003. London: International Secretariat, 2003.

———. *Torture in the Eighties*. London: Amnesty International, 1984.

———. *Torture Worldwide*. London: Amnesty International, 2000.

Amris, Kirstine, and Karen Prip. *Falanga Torture*. Copenhagen: International Rehabilitation Council for Torture Victims, 2003.

Amyntor. *Victors in Chains*. London: Hutchinson, n.d.

Barrios B., Ana, and Eva Duart O. *La Tortura: 40 años de pena*. Caracas, Venezuela: Red de Apoyo por la Justicia y la Paz, 1998.

Anderson, David. *Histories of the Hanged*. New York: Norton, 2005.

Anderson, David, and David Killingray, eds. *Policing the Empire*. Manchester, England: Manchester University Press, 1991.

———, eds. *Policing and Decolonisation*. Manchester, England: Manchester University Press, 1992.

Andreas, Peter. "The Rise of the American Crimefare State." *World Policy Journal* 14.3 (1997): 37–45.

———. *Border Games*. Ithaca, NY: Cornell University Press, 2000.

Andreas, Peter, and Richard Friman, eds. *The Illicit Global Economy and State Power*. Lanham, MD: Rowman and Littlefield, 1999.

Andrews, William. *Bygone Punishments*. London: Philip Allan, 1931.

Andreyev, H.J.N. "Political Dissent and 'Sluggish' Schizophrenia in the Soviet Union." *British Medical Journal* 293 (September 27, 1986): 822.

Applebaum, Anne. "The Torture Myth." *Washington Post*, January 12, 2005, A21.

Applegate, Rex. "Nonlethal Police Weapons." *Ordnance*, July–August 1971, 62–66.

———. "Riot Control." *Soldier of Fortune* 17 (December 1992): 43–47, 71–73.

Archdiocese of São Paulo. *Torture in Brazil*. Translated by Jaime Wright. New York: Vintage, 1986.

Ardeleanu, Ion. *Doftana*. [Bucharest]: Publishing House of Tourism, 1974.

Arendt, Hannah. *The Human Condition*. Chicago: University of Chicago Press, 1958.

Armstrong, James, with William Elliott. *Legion of Hell*. London: Sampson Low, Marston, [1936].

Arrigo, Jean Maria. "A Consequentialist Argument Against Torture Interrogation of Terrorists." Conference paper, Joint Services Conference on Professional Ethics, Springfield, VA, January 30–31, 2003. http://www.au.af.mil/au/awc/awcgate/jscope/arrigo03.htm.

Aubrac, Louise, with Betsy Wing. *Outwitting the Gestapo*. Translated by Konrad Bieber. Lincoln: University of Nebraska Press, 1993.

Auerhahn, Kathleen, and Elizabeth D. Leonard. "Docile Bodies? Chemical Restraints and the Female Inmate." *Journal of Criminal Law and Criminology* 90.2 (2000): 599–634.

Aurora Foundation. *Report on the Violations of Human Rights in the Socialist Republic of Vietnam*. Atherton, CA: Aurora Foundation, 1989.

Aussaresses, Paul. *The Battle of the Casbah*. New York: Enigma, 2002.

Avenue Louise 347. Brussels: Buch Edition, 1996.

Aziz, Philippe. *Au service de l'ennemi*. Paris: Fayard, 1972.

———. *Tu trahiras sans vergogne*. Paris: Fayard, 1970.

B'Tselem. *Legislation Allowing the Use of Physical Force and Mental Coercion in Interrogations by the General Security Service*. Jerusalem: B'Tselem, Israeli Information Center for Human Rights in the Occupied Territories, 2000.

———. *Routine Torture: Interrogation Methods of the General Security Service*. Jerusalem: B'Tselem, Israeli Information Center for Human Rights in the Occupied Territories, 1998.

Bacry, Daniel, and Michel Ternisien. *La Torture*. Paris: Fayard, 1980.

Baden-Powell, Dorothy. *Operation Jupiter*. London: Robert Hale, 1982.

Bailey, R. H., ed. *Prisoners of War*. Alexandria, VA: Time-Life Books, 1981.

Baker, Mark. *Nam*. New York: Quill, 1982.

Baldwin, Frank, Diane Jones, and Michael Jones. *America's Rented Troops*. Philadelphia: American Friends Service Committee, [1975?].

Balfour, Michael. *Withstanding Hitler in Germany, 1933–45*. London: Routledge, 1988.

Ball, Olivia. *"Every Morning Just Like Coffee": Torture in Cameroon*. London: Medical Foundation for the Care of Victims of Torture, 2002.

Baraheni, Reza. *The Crowned Cannibals*. New York: Vintage, 1977.

Barber, Jason. *Less than Human: Torture in Cambodia*. Pnom Penh: Cambodian League for the Promotion and Defense of Human Rights (LICADHO), 2000.

Başoğlu, Metin, ed. *Torture and Its Consequences*. Cambridge: Cambridge University Press, 1992.

Baumann, Zygmunt. *Modernity and the Holocaust*. Ithaca, NY: Cornell University Press, 1989.

Bayac, J. Delperrie de. *Histoire de la milice, 1918–1945*. Paris: Fayard, 1969.

Bayley, David. *Forces of Order*. Berkeley and Los Angeles: University of California Press, 1976.

———. *What Works in Policing*. New York: Oxford University Press, 1998.

Bazelon, Emily, Phillip Carter, and Dahlia Lithwick. "What is Torture?—An Interactive Primer on American Interrogation." Slate.com, http://www.slate/com/id/2119122/sidebar/21119631 (accessed November 13, 2005).

Beames, John. *Memoirs of a Bengal Civilian*. London: Chatto and Windus, 1961.

Beauvoir, Simone de, and Gisele Halimi. *Djamila Boupacha*. Translated by Peter Green. New York: Macmillan, 1962.

Beck F., and W. Godin. *Russian Purge and the Extraction of Confession*. Translated by Eric Mosbacher and David Porter. New York: Viking, 1951.

Beckett, W.N.T. *A Few Naval Customs, Expressions, Traditions and Superstitions*. 2nd ed. Portsmouth, England: Gieves, [1915].

Begin, Menachem. *White Nights*. Translated by Katie Kaplan. New York: Harper and Row, 1977.

Behr, Edward. *The Algerian Problem*. London: Hodder and Stoughton, 1961.

"Belgian Troops Found Guilty of Torture." *Times* (London), November 21, 1972, 7.

Benjamin, Walter. *Illuminations*. Edited by Hannah Arendt. Translated by Harry Zohn. New York: Schocken, 1968.

Bennett, F. "Pretrial Detention in Japan." *Law in Japan* 23 (1990): 67–71.

Benuzzi, Felice. *No Picnic on Mount Kenya*. New York: E. P. Dutton, 1953.

Bergfald, Odd. *Gestapo i Norge*. Oslo: Hjemmenes Forlag, 1978.

Bexton, W. H., W. Heron, and T. H. Scott. "Effects of Decreased Variation in the Sensory Environment." *Canadian Journal of Psychology* 8.2 (1954): 70–76.

Biderman, Albert. "Effects of Communist Indoctrination Attempts." *Social Problems* 6.4 (1959): 304–13.

———. "Social-Psychological Needs and 'Involuntary' Behavior as Illustrated by Compliance in Interrogation." *Sociometry* 23.2 (1960): 120–47.

Bigeard, Marcel-Maurice. *"J'ai mal à la France."* Ostwald, France: Les Éditions du Pylogone, 2001.

Bini, L. "Experimental Researches on Epileptic Attacks Induced by the Electric Current." *American Journal of Psychiatry* 94 (1938): 172–74.

Binneveld, Hans. *From Shell Shock to Combat Stress*. Translated by John O'Kane. Amsterdam: University of Amsterdam, 1997.

Biran, Michel. "Deuxième classe en Algerie" *Perspectives Socialistes*, November 1961, 2–44.

Black Book on the Militarist "Democracy" in Turkey. Brussels: Info-Türk, 1986.

Black, Roland. *Histoire et crime de la Gestapo parisienne*. Brussels: Bel Go-Suisses, 1945.

"Black Suspect in Murder of a Police Officer Alleges that the Grand Jury Was 'Knowingly Deceived.' " *New York Times,* December 14, 1975, 51.

Blackburn, Robert. *Mercenaries and Lyndon Johnson's "More Flags."* Jefferson, NC: McFarland, 1994.

Blagrove M., and L. Akehurst. "Effects of Sleep Loss on Confidence-Accuracy Relationships for Reasoning and Eyewitness Memory." *Journal of Experimental Psychological: Applied* 6.1 (2000): 59–73.

Blatt, Deborah. "Recognizing Rape as a Method of Torture." *Review of Law and Social Change* 19.4 (1992): 821–65.

Bles, Mark. *Child at War.* San Francisco: Mercury House, 1989.

Bloch, Sidney, and Peter Reddaway. *Russia's Political Hospitals.* London: Victor Collancz, 1977.

———. *Soviet Psychiatric Abuse.* Boulder, CO: Westview, 1984.

Bloche, M. Gregg. "Physician: Turn Thyself In." *New York Times,* June 10, 2004, 240–43.

Bloche, M. Gregg, and Jonathan H. Marks. "Doctors and Interrogators at Guantanamo Bay." *New England Journal of Medicine* 353.1 (July 7, 2005): 6–8.

———. "Doing Unto Others as They Did Unto Us." *New York Times,* November 14, 2005, A21.

Bloom, Harold. "The South African Police." *Africa South* 2.1 (1957): 8–20.

Blum, William. *Killing Hope.* Monroe, ME: Common Courage Press, 1995.

Bobocescu, Vasile. *Istoria Plitiei Române.* Bucharest: Editura Ministerului de Interne, 2000.

Bocca, Geoffrey. *La Légion!* New York: Thomas Crowell, 1964.

Bodson, Herman. *Agent for the Resistance.* Edited by Richard Schmidt. College Station: Texas A&M University Press, 1994.

Boehm, Eric. *We Survived.* Reprint. Santa Barbara, CA: ABC-Clio Information Services, 1985.

Böhm, Emanuel. *Human Rights Violations.* New York: Slovak Institute, Cleveland, 1986.

Bolloten, Burnett. *The Spanish Civil War.* Chapel Hill: University of North Carolina Press, 1991.

Bonner, Raymond, Don Van Natta Jr., and Amy Waldman. "Questioning Terror Suspects in a Dark and Surreal World." *New York Times,* March 9, 2003, A1, A14.

Boom, Corrie ten, with John Sherrill and Elizabeth Sherrill. *The Hiding Place.* London: Hodder and Stoughton and Christian Literature Crusade, 1971.

Borckway, Fenner. *Worker's Front.* London: Secker and Warburg, 1938.

Borger, Julian. "Metallica Is Latest Interrogation Tactic." *Guardian* (London), May 20, 2003, 11.

Borkenau, Franz. *The Spanish Cockpit.* London: Faber and Faber, 1937.

Bor-Komorwoski, T. *The Secret Army.* Nashville, TN: Battery Press, 1984.

Boukhari, Ahmed. *Le Secret.* Neuilly-sur-Seine, France: Editions Michel Lafon, 2002.

Bourdet-Pléville, Michel. *Justice in Chains.* Translated by Anthony Rippon. London: Robert Hale, 1960.

Bourdet-Pléville, Michel. *Justice in Chains*. Translated by Anthony Rippon. London: Robert Hale, 1960.

Bourdieu, Pierre, and Loïc Wacquant. *An Invitation to Reflexive Sociology*. Chicago: University of Chicago, 1992.

———. *Outline of a Theory of Practice*. Translated by Richard Nice. Cambridge: Cambridge University Press, 1989.

Bourgeois, Jacques le. *Saïgon sans la France*. Paris: Librairie Plon, 1949.

Bowden, Mark. "The Dark Art of Interrogation." *Atlantic Monthly*, October 2003, 51–76.

———. "The Lessons of Abu Ghraib." *Atlantic Monthly*, July–August 2004, 33–36.

Bowen, Roderic. *Procedures for the Arrest, Interrogation and Detention of Suspected Terrorists in Aden*. London: Her Majesty's Stationery Office, 1966.

Bowes, Stuart. *The Police and Civil Liberties*. London: Lawrence and Wishart, 1966.

Boxer, C. R. *Dutch Merchants and Mariners in Asia, 1602–1795*. London: Variorum Reprints, 1988.

Bracket, John K. *Criminal Justice and Crime in Late Renaissance Florence, 1537–1609*. Cambridge: Cambridge University Press, 1992.

Braddon, Russell. *Nancy Wake*. London: Cassell, 1956.

Branche, Raphaëlle. "Torture and Other Violations of the Law by the French Army during the Algerian War." In *Genocide, War Crimes and the West*. Edited by Adam Jones. London: Zed, 2004.

———. *La torture et l'armée pendant la guerre d'Algérie*. Paris: Gallimard, 2001.

Brewer, John. *Black and Blue*. Oxford: Clarendon Press, 1994.

British Medical Association. *Medicine Betrayed*. London: Zed, 1992.

Broad, William J. "Oh, What a Lovely War. If No one Dies." *New York Times*, November 3, 2002, sec. 4, p. 3.

Broué, Pierre, and Emile Témime. *The Revolution and the Civil War in Spain*. Translated by Tony White. London: Faber and Faber, 1972.

Browder, George. *Hitler's Enforcers*. New York: Oxford University Press, 1996.

Brown, Charles J., and Armando Lago. *The Politics of Psychiatry in Revolutionary Cuba*. New Brunswick, NJ: Transaction, 1991.

Brown, Holmes, and Don Luce. *Hostages of War*. Washington, DC: Indochina Mobile Education Project, 1973.

Brown, J.A.C. *Techniques of Persuasion*. Harmondsworth, England: Penguin, 1969.

Brown, John. *A Slave Life in Georgia*. Edited by F. N. Boney. Savannah, GA: Beehive Press, 1991.

Brown, Peter. *The Cult of Saints*. Chicago: University of Chicago Press, 1981.

Brunovsky, Vladmir. *The Methods of OGPU*. London: Harper and Brothers, [1931].

Bryan, J. Ingram. *Japanese All*. New York: E. P. Dutton, 1928.

Budiansky, Stephen. "Truth Extraction." *Atlantic Monthly*, June 2005, 32–35.

Budiman, Taman. *Memoirs of an Unorthodox Civil Servant*. Kuala Lumpur: Heinemann Educational Books, 1979.

Buisson, Henry. *La Police, son histoire*. Vichy, France: Wallon, 1949.

Bunting, Brian. *The Rise of the South African Reich*. Harmondsworth, England: Penguin, 1964.

Burke, Edmund. *Speeches on the Impeachment of Warren Hastings*. 2 vols. London: Henry G. Bohn, 1857.

Burkett, B. G., and Glenna Whitley. *Stolen Valor: How the Vietnam Generation was Robbed of Its Heroes and Its History*. Dallas: Verity Press, 1998.

Byford-Jones, W. *The Greek Trilogy*. London: Hutchinson, 1946.

Byrn, John, Jr. *Crime and Punishment in the Royal Navy*. Aldershot, England: Scolar Press, 1989.

Caldwell, Robert. *Red Hannah*. Philadelphia: University of Pennsylvania Press, 1947.

Calley, William, with John Sack. *Lieutenant Calley: His Own Story*. New York: Viking, 1971.

Campbell, Bruce. *Death Squads in Global Perspective*. New York: St. Martin's, 2000.

Campbell, Duncan, and Suzanne Goldenberg. "The Afghan Gulag." *Guardian* (London), June 23, 2004, 2.

Cancelli, Elizabeth. *O Mundo Da violência*. Brasília, DF: Editora Universidade de Brasília, 1993.

Cannon, Lou. *Official Negligence*. Boulder, CO: Westview, 1999.

Cârjan, Lazar. *Istoria Politiei Române*. Bucharest: Editura Vestala, 2000.

Carlson, Lewis. *Remembered Prisoners of a Forgotten War*. New York: St. Martin's, 2002.

Cassese, Antonio. *Inhuman States*. Cambridge: Polity Press, 1996.

Cassidy, Sheila. *Audacity to Believe*. Cleveland: Collins World, 1977.

Cathelin, Jean, and Gabrielle Gray. *Crime et trafics de la Gestapo francaise*. 2 vols. Paris: Historama, 1972.

Catholic Committee on Human Rights. *Sabop sarin: 1975 nyon ui haksal* [Murder by the Judiciary: The Massacre in 1975]. Seoul: Hangmin-sa, 2001.

Cattell, David. *Communism and the Spanish Civil War*. Berkeley and Los Angeles: University of California, 1955.

Catton, Bruce. *A Stillness at Appomattox*. Garden City, NY: Doubleday, 1954.

Cerletti, Ugo. "Old and New Information About Electroshock." *American Journal of Psychiatry* 107 (1955): 89.

Chandler, David. *Voices from S-21*. Berkeley and Los Angeles: University of California Press, 1999.

"Charge Murder in Brazil." *New York Times*, March 26, 1936, A24.

Charters, David. "Special Operations in Counter-Insurgency: The Farran Case, Palestine 1947." *Journal of the Royal United Services Institute* 124 (1979): 56–61.

Chea, Terence. "California Guardsman Alleges Abuse in Iraq." Associated Press, June 9, 2004, http://web.lexis-nexis.com.

Chevigny, Paul, Bell Gale Chevigny, and Russel Karp. *Police Abuse in Brazil*. New York: Americas Watch Report, 1987.

"Chinese 'Truth Drug.'" *Times* (London), July 12, 1952, A3.

Chomsky, Noam, and Edward Herman *The Washington Connection and Third World Fascism*. 2 vols. Montreal: Black Rose Press, 1979.

Chong, Chae-ryong. *Chon Segye Komun* [Tortures of the World]. N.p.: Sisa Nonp'y-ong, n.d.

Chukwuma Innocent. *Above the Law*. Lagos, Nigeria: Civil Liberties Organisation, 1994.

The Citizen is Egyptian. Giza, Egypt: Human Rights Center for the Assistance of Prisoners Campaign against Torture, 2002.

Citizens Commission of Inquiry, ed. *The Dellums Committee Hearings on War Crimes in Vietnam*. New York: Vintage, 1972.

Claude, Richard, Eric Stover, and June Lopez. *Health Professionals and Human Rights in the Philippines*. Washington, DC: American Association for the Advancement of Science, 1987.

Claver, Scott. *Under the Lash*. London: Torchstream, 1954.

Clayton, Anthony. *France, Soldiers and Africa*. London: Brassey's Defense Publishers, 1988.

Coates, Joseph. "Non-Lethal Police Weapons." *Technology Review* 74.7 (1972): 49–56.

———. *Nonlethal Weapons for Use by US Law Enforcement Officers*. Arlington, VA: Institute for Defense Analyses, November 1967.

Cobain, Ian. "The Secrets of the London Cage." *Guardian* (London), November 12, 2005, 8.

Codreanu, Corneliu. *La Garde de Fer*. Grenoble: I. Maril, Belmain, 1972.

Cohen, Henry. *Brutal Justice*. New York: John Jay Press, 1980.

Cohen, Maynard M. *A Stand against Tyranny*. Detroit: Wayne State University Press, 1997.

Cohen, Stan. "Talking about Torture in Israel." *Tikkun* 6.6 (1991): 23–30, 89–90.

Cohen, Stanley, and Daphna Golan. *The Interrogation of Palestinians during the Intifada*. Jerusalem: B'Tselem, Israeli Information Center for Human Rights in the Occupied Territories, 1991.

Cole, David. *Enemy Aliens*. New York: New Press, 2003.

Colligan Douglas. "The New Science of Torture." *Science Digest*, July 1976, 46–47.

Colonel Rémy [Gilbert Renault-Roulier]. *Une affaire de trahison*. Monte Carlo: Raoul Solar, 1947.

———. *Une Épopée de la Résistance*. 2 vols. Paris: Grange Batelière, 1976.

Cômes, Jean-Pierre. *"Ma" guerre d'Algérie et la torture*. Paris: L'Harmattan, 2002.

Comité Maurice Audin. *Sans Commentaire*. Paris: Editions de Minuit, 1961.

Connor, Walter D. *Deviance in Soviet Society: Crime, Delinquency and Alcoholism*. New York: Columbia University Press, 1972.

Conquest, Robert. *The Great Terror*. New York: Oxford University Press, 1990.

Conrad, Robert. *Children of God's Fire*. Princeton, NJ: Princeton University Press, 1983.

Conroy, John. "Deaf to the Screams." *Chicago Reader*, August 1, 2003, 1, 18–20, 22, 24–25.

———. "Tools of Torture" and "The Mysterious Third Device." *Chicago Reader*, February 4, 2005, 1, 24–27.

———. *Unspeakable Acts, Ordinary People*. New York: Knopf, 2000.

Constante, Lena. *The Silent Escape*. Translated by Franklin Philip. Berkeley and Los Angeles: University of California Press, 1995.

Cook, Haruko Taya, and Theodore Cook. *Japan at War*. New York: New Press, 1992.

Cooper, A. R., with Sydney Tremayne. *The Man Who Liked Hell*. London: Jarrolds, 1938.

Coposu, Corneliu, with Doina Alexandru. *Confessions*. Translated by Elena Popescu. Boulder, CO: East European Monographs, 1998.

Cornwell, Rupert. "Russia's Unholy Fools." *Independent Magazine*, March 25, 1989, 24–27.

Cosculluela, Manuel Hevia. *Pasaporte 11333*. Havana, Cuba: Editorial de Ciencias Sociales, 1978.

Costa-Foru, C. G. *Aus Den Folterkammern Rumäniens*. Vienna: Kulturpolitischer Verlag, 1925.

Cotter, Lloyd. "Operant Conditioning in a Vietnamese Mental Hospital." *American Journal of Psychiatry* 124 (July 1967): 23–66.

Cowan, Lore. *Children of the Resistance*. New York: Meredith Press, 1969.

Cox, Edmund. *Police and Crime in India*. New Delhi: Manu Publications, 1976.

Craciunas, Silviu. *The Lost Footsteps*. New York: Farrar, Straus and Cudahy, 1961.

Crankshaw, Edward. *Gestapo*. New York: Da Capo Press, 1994.

Crelinsten, F. D., and A. P. Schmid. *The Politics of Pain*. Leiden, the Netherlands: Center for the Study of Social Conflict, 1993.

Crelinsten, Ronald. "The Discourse and Practice of Counter-Terrorism in Liberal Democracies." *Australian Journal of Politics and History* 44.1 (1998): 389–413.

Cruel and Inhuman Treatment: The Use of Four Point Restrain in the Onondaga County Public Safety Building, Syracuse, NY. Boston: Physicians for Human Rights, 1993.

Cuevas, Tomasa. *Prison of Women*. Translated and edited by Mary Giles. Albany: State University of New York Press, 1998.

Cusac, Anne-Marie. "Shock Value." *The Progressive*, September 1997, 28–31.

———. "Stunning Technology." *The Progressive*, July 1996, 18–23.

Czerkawski, Andrzej. *Aleja Szucha*. Warsaw: Sport i Turystyka, 1967.

Dadfar, M. A. *The Impaired Mind*. Peshawar, Pakistan: Psychiatry Center for Afghan Refugees, 1988.

Danielsen, Lis, Monika Gniadecka, Henrik Klem Thosmen, Frants Pedersen, Søren Strange, Kristian Cynther Nielsen, Hans Draminsky Petersen. "Skin Changes Following Defibrillation." *Forensic Science International* 134 (2003): 134–41.

Dank, Milton. *The French Against the French*. Philadelphia: J. B. Lippincott, 1974.

Danner, Mark. *Torture and Truth*. New York: New York Review of Books, 2004.

Danut, Tudor. *Politia în Statul de Drept*. Bucharest: Editura Ministerului de Interne, 2000.

Das, Veena, Arthur Kleinman, and Margaret Lock, eds. *Social Suffering*. Berkeley and Los Angeles: University of California Press, 1997.

Davidson, Osha Gray. "The Secret File of Abu Ghraib." *Rolling Stone*, August 18, 2004, 48–51.

Davis, Mike. *City of Quartz*. New York: Vintage, 1992.

Day, George E. *Return with Honor.* Mesa, AZ: Champlin Fighter Museum Press, 1989.

Dean, Trevor. "Criminal Justice in Mid-15th Century Bologna." In *Crime, Society and the Law in Renaissance Italy.* Edited by Trevor Dean and K.J.P. Lowe. Cambridge: Cambridge University Press, 1994.

Debris, Jean-Pierre, and André Menras. *Rescapés des bagnes de Saigon.* Paris: Les Editeurs Français Reunis, 1973.

Dedijer, Vladimir. *The War Diaries of Vladimir Dedijer.* Ann Arbor: University of Michigan Press, 1990.

Deeley, Peter. *Beyond Breaking Point.* London: Arthur Barker, 1971.

Delarue, Jacques. "La Bande Bonny-Lafont." In *Resistants et collaborateurs.* Edited by Francois Bédarida. Paris: Seuil, 1985.

———. *History of the Gestapo.* Translated by Mervyn Savill. New York: Dell, 1964.

———. *Trafics et crimes sous l'occupation.* Paris: Fayard, 1968.

Delay, Jean, A. Djourno, and G. Verdeaux. "Les nouvelles technique de l'électrochoc." *L'Encâephale* 40 (1951): 426–83.

Delay, Jean, B. Lainé, J. Puech, and J. Clavreul. "Recherches biologiques sur le choc émotionnel." *L'Encâephale* 42 (1953): 289–319.

Dershowitz, Alan. "Is There a Torturous Road to Justice?" *Los Angeles Times*, November 8, 2001, B19.

———. *Shouting Fire.* Boston: Little, Brown, 2002.

———. "Want to Torture? Get a Warrant." *San Francisco Chronicle*, January 22, 2002, A19.

———. *Why Terrorism Works.* New Haven, CT: Yale University Press, 2002.

"Des cours sur une 'torture humaine' sont donnés aux stagiaires du camp Jeanned'Arc." *Le Monde*, December 20–21, 1959, 6.

Destroyer, Roger-A. *Parachutiste du roi.* Brussells: Charles Dessart, 1946.

Devèze, Michel. *Cayenne.* Paris: René Julliard, 1965.

Devlin, Patrick. *The Criminal Prosecution in England*, New Haven, CT: Yale University Press, 1958.

Dewar, Michael. *Internal Security Weapons and Equipment of the World.* New York: Charles Scribner's Sons, 1979.

Dilemmas of Professional Ethics as a Result of Involvement of Doctors and Psychologists in Interrogation and Torture. Jerusalem: Public Committee Against Torture in Israel, 1993.

Dillman, Jeffrey, and Musa Bakri. *Israel's Use of Electric Shock Torture in the Interrogation of Palestinian Detainees.* 2nd ed. Jerusalem: Palestine Human Rights Information Center, 1992.

Dillon, C. F. *A Domain of Heroes.* Sarasota, FL: Palm Island Press, 1995.

Dinh Thi, Nguyen, ed. *Les Prisonniers politiques.* Paris: Sudestasie, 1974.

Djilas, Milovan. *Of Prisons and Ideas.* Translated by Michael Boro Petrovich. San Diego: Harcourt Brace Jovanovich, 1986.

Dodd, Martha. *Through Embassy Eyes.* New York: Harcourt Brace, 1939.

Dolezal, Jiri, and Jan Kren. *Czechoslovakia's Fight.* Prague: Czechoslovak Academy of Sciences, 1964.

Domanska, Regina. *Pawiak*. Warsaw: Ksiazka i Wiedza, 1988.

Donovan, Michael. *March or Die!* London: Cassell, 1932.

Doty, Bennett. *The Legion of the Damned*. New York: Century Co., 1928.

Dourlein, Pieter. *Inside North Pole*. London: William Kimber, 1989.

Dow, Mark. *American Gulag*. Berkeley and Los Angeles: University of California Press, 2004.

Dressler, David. "The Drug That Makes Criminals Talk." *Saturday Evening Post*, December 27, 1947, 16–17, 43–44.

Drummond, John. *But For These Men*. Morley, England: Elmfield Press, 1974.

DuBois, Page. *Torture and Truth*. New York: Routledge, 1991.

Duffett, John, ed. *Against the Crime of Silence: Proceedings of the Russell International War Crimes Tribunal*. New York: O'Hare Books, 1968.

Dufresnoy, Claude. *Des Officier Parlent*. Paris: René Julliard, 1961.

Dugard, Martin. *Farther Than Any Man*. New York: Pocket Books, 2001.

Duke, Floridmond. *Name, Rank and Serial Number*. New York: Meredith Press, 1969.

Dumond, Dwight Lowell. *Anti-Slavery*. Ann Arbor: University of Michigan Press, 1961.

Dumont, Jean, ed. *Histoire secrète de la Gestapo*. 5 vols. Geneva: Editions de Crémille, 1971.

Duncan, Donald. "Un béret vert parle." *Les Temps Modernes* 261 (1968): 1482–97.

———. *The New Legions*. New York: Random House, 1967.

Duncan, Patrick. *South Africa's Rule of Violence*. London: Methuen, 1964.

Dutton, Michael. *Policing and Punishment in China*. Cambridge: Cambridge University Press, 1992.

Earle, Alice Morse. *Curious Punishments of Bygone Days*. Montclair, NJ: Patterson Smith, 1969.

Einaudi, Jean Luc. *La ferme Améziane*. Paris: L'Harmattan, 1991.

———. *Octobre 1961*. Paris: Fayard, 2001.

Ejército de Liberación Nacional. "Denuncian torturas." *Punta Final*, August 1972, 28.

Ekart, Antoni. *Vanished Without Trace*. London: Max Parrish, 1954.

Ekstrøm, Morten, Hans Draminsky Petersen, and Majken Marmstaedt. *Torture Continues in Indian Held Kashmir*. Århus, Denmark: Physicians for Human Rights, 1994.

El Campesino [Valentin Gonzalez]. *Listen Comrades*. Translated by Ilsa Barea. Melbourne: William Heinemann, 1952.

El Nadim Center. "Torture Inside and Outside Police Stations in Egypt, 1993–1996." *Torture* 7.2 (1997): 54–55.

Elkins, Caroline. *Imperial Reckoning*. New York: Henry Holt, 2005.

Elliot, Robert. *Agent of Death*. New York: E. P. Dutton, 1940.

Elliott, David. *The Vietnamese War*. Vol. 2: *Revolution and Social Change in the Mekong Delta, 1930–1975*. Armonk, NY: M. E. Sharpe, 2003.

Elster, Jon. *Nuts and Bolts for the Social Sciences*. Cambridge: Cambridge University Press, 1989.

Emsley, Clive, and Barbara Weinberger, eds. *Policing Western Europe*. New York: Greenwood, 1991.

Essad-Bey. *OGPU*. Translated by Huntley Paterson. New York: Viking, 1933.

Essig, Mark. *Edison and the Electric Chair*. New York: Walker, 2003.

Estèbe, Jean. *Toulouse, 1940–1944*. Paris: Perrin, 1996.

Estrella, Roberto [Valentin Vergara]. *Tortura*. Tucumán, Argentina: Ediciones "Dos-Ve," 1956.

Etchegoin, Marie France. "Les preuves qui accablent Touvier." *Nouvel Observateur*, April 23–29, 1992, 46.

European Commission of Human Rights. *The Greek Case*. 2 vols. Strasbourg: Council of Europe, 1970.

Evans, Malcolm D., and Rod Morgan. *Preventing Torture*. Oxford: Clarendon, 1998.

Evans, Michael. "The 'White Noise' Torture Room." *Times* (London), June 19, 1999, http://web.lexis-nexis.com/.

Ewert, Minna. "Political Prisoners in Brazil." *Times* (London), July 18, 1936, 8.

Ex-Légionnairre 1384 [John Harvey] with W. J. Blackledge. *Hell Hounds of France*. London: Sampson, Low, Marston, [1932].

Fabre, Marc-André. *Dans les prisons de la malice*.Vichy: Wallon, 1944. Re-issued as *Dans les prisons de Vichy* (Paris: Albin Michel, 1995).

The Facts about Conscientious Objectors in the United States (Under the Selective Service Act of May 18, 1917). New York: National Civil Liberties Bureau, 1918.

Falton, J. F. "Origins of Electroshock Therapy." *Journal of the History of Medicine and Allied Sciences* 11 (1956): 229–30.

Fanon, Frantz. *A Dying Colonialism*. Translated by Haakon Chevalier. New York: Grove Press, 1965.

———. *The Wretched of the Earth*. Translated by Constance Farrington. New York: Grove Press, 1963.

Farran, Roy. *Winged Dagger*. London: Collins, 1947.

Farrar-Hockley, Anthony. *The British Part in the Korean War*. 2 vols. London: HMSO, 1995.

———. *The Edge of the Sword*. London: Bucan and Enright, 1985.

Farrington, Karen. *Dark Justice*. New York: Smithmark, 1996.

Faul, Dennis, and Raymond Murray. *British Army and Special Branch RUC Brutalities*. Dungannon, Northern Ireland: The Compilers, 1972.

———. *The RUC: The Black and Blue Book*. [Dungannon, Northern Ireland]: [Denis Faul], 1975.

Faure, Jean. *Au pays de la soif et de la peur*. Paris: Flammarion, 2001.

Feldman, Allen. *Formations of Violence*. Chicago: University of Chicago Press, 1991.

Ferretti, Fred. "Zap!" *New York Times Magazine*, January 4, 1976, 13–16.

Figueiredo, Antonio de, and Jonathan Steele. "Torture Films Found at Police HQ." *Guardian* (London), May 3, 1974, 4.

Filipek, Jan. *The Shadow of the Gallows*. Palm Springs, CA: Palm Springs Publishing, 1985.

Finkelman, Paul. *Slavery in the Courtroom*. Washington, DC: Library of Congress, 1985.

Fireside, Harvey. *Soviet Psychoprisons*. New York: Norton, 1979.

Fischer, David Hackett. *Washington's Crossing*. Oxford: Oxford University Press, 2004.

Fleming, Amalia. *A Piece of Truth*. London: Jonathan Cape, 1972.

Flender, Harold. *Rescue in Denmark*. New York: Simon and Schuster, 1963.

Florence, Beauge. "Le général Massu exprime ses regret pour la torture en Algérie." *Le Monde*, June 22, 2000.

Foley, Charles. *Island in Revolt*. London: Longmans, Green, 1962.

Foot, M.R.D. *The Resistance*. New York: McGraw-Hill, 1977.

Forbes, Reginald. *Red Horizon*. London: Sampson Low, Marston, [1932].

The Forgotten Prisoners of Ngyuen Van Thieu. Paris: n.p., May 1973.

Forrest, Duncan. "Patterns of Abuse in Sikh Asylum-Seekers." *The Lancet* 345.8944 (January 28, 1995): 225–26.

———, ed. *A Glimpse of Hell*. London: Amnesty International, 1996.

Forrest, Orrin, and David Chanoff. *Slow Burn*. New York: Simon and Schuster, 1990.

Foster, Don, with Dennis Davis and Diane Sandler. *Detention and Torture in South Africa*. New York: St. Martin's, 1987.

Foucault, Michel. *Discipline and Punish*. Translated by Alan Sheridan. New York: Vintage, 1979.

———. *Fearless Speech*. Edited by Joseph Pearson. Los Angeles: Semiotext(e), 2001.

Fougère, Eric. *Le grand livre du bagne*. French Guiana: Editions Orphie, 2002.

Foy, D. A. " 'For You the War is Over': Treatment and Life of the United States Army and Air Corps Personnel Interned in POW Camps in Germany, 1942–1945." Ph.D. diss., University of Arkansas, 1981.

Franco's Prisoners Speak. London: Spanish Ex-Servicemen's Association, 1960.

Frank, Arthur. *The Wounded Storyteller*. Chicago: University of Chicago Press, 1995.

Franklin, Charles. *The Third Degree*. London: Robert Hale, 1970.

Franklin, John Hope, and Loren Schwenger. *Runaway Slaves*. Oxford: Oxford University Press, 1999.

Friedman, Leon, ed. *The Law of War*. 2 vols. New York: Random House, 1972.

Friends of Democracy. *The Gestapo, Hitler's Secret Police*. Kansas City, MO: Friends of Democracy, 1941.

Funder, Anna. *Stasiland*. London: Granta, 2003.

Games, Sonia. *Escape into Darkness*. New York: Shapolsky, 1991.

Gangrene. London: Calberbooks, 1959.

The Gangrene. Translated by Robert Silvers. New York: Lyle Stewart, 1960.

Garlinski, Józef. *Fighting Auschwitz*. London: Julian Friedmann, 1975.

Gatewood, Willard, Jr. *Black Americans and the White Man's Burden, 1898–1903*. Urbana: University of Illinois Press, 1975.

Geis, Gilbert. "In Scopolomine Veritas: The Early History of Drug-Induced Statements." *Journal of Criminal Law, Criminology, and Police Science* 50.4 (1959): 347–57.

Genchev, Evgeni, ed. *Tales from the Dark*. Sofia, Bulgaria: Assistance Centre for Torture Survivors, 2003.

General Toranzo. *Los Torturados*. [Buenos Aires?]: Editorial Estampa, 1935.

Gérard, Hervé. *La résistance belge face au nazisme*. Brussels: J-M. Collet, 1995.

Gerecht, Reuel Marc. "Against Rendition." *Weekly Standard*, May 16, 2005, 21–26.

Germans against Hitler, July 20, 1944. Bonn: Bundeszentrale für politische Bildung, [1969].

Gerson, Lennard. *The Secret Police in Lenin's Russia.* Philadelphia: Temple University Press, 1976.

The Gestapo and SS Manual. Translated by Carl Hammer. Boulder, CO: Paladin Press, 1996.

Gherasim, Teodor. *Astride Two Worlds.* Tigard, OR: L. D. Press, 2000.

Ghose, Barindra Kumar. *The Tale of My Exile.* Pendicherry, India: Arya Office, 1922.

Ginbar, Yuval. *Back to a Routine of Torture.* Translated by Jessica Bonn. Jerusalem: Public Committee against Torture in Israel, 2003.

————. *Flawed Defense,* Translated by Jessica Bonn. Jerusalem: Public Committee against Torture in Israel, 2001.

Giolitto, Pierre. *Histoire de la milice.* Paris: Perrin, 1997.

Gisevius, Hans Bernd. *To the Bitter End.* Translated by Richard and Clara Winston. Boston: Houghton Mifflin, 1947.

Gjelsvik, Tore. *Norwegian Resistance, 1940–1945.* Montreal: McGill-Queens University Press, 1979.

Gleeson, James. *They Feared No Evil.* London: Robert Hale, 1976.

Gliksman, Jerzy. *Tell the West.* New York: Gresham Press, 1948.

Glucklich, Ariel. *Sacred Pain.* Oxford: Oxford University Press, 2001.

Godard, Yves. *Les paras dans la ville.* Vol. 1: *Les Trois Batailles d'Alger.* Paris: Libarie Arthème Fayard.

Goddard, Calvin. "How Science Solves Crime: Truth Serum or Scopolamine in Interrogation of Criminal Suspects." *Hygeia* 10 (1932): 337–40.

Godfory, Marion, and Stanislas Fautré. *Bagnards.* [Paris]: Editions du Chêne, 2002.

Golden, Tim. "Army Faltered in Investigating Detainee Abuse." *New York Times,* May 22, 2005, sec. 1, p. 1.

————. "In US Report, Brutal Details of 2 Afghan Inmates' Deaths." *New York Times,* May 20, 2005, A1.

Goldfeld, Anne, Richard Mollica, Barbara Pesavent, and Stephen Faraone. "The Physical and Psychological Sequelae of Torture." *Journal of the American Medical Association* 259.18 (May 13, 1988): 2725–29.

Goldman, Emma. *Anarchism and Other Essays.* New York: Dover, 1969.

Goldstein, Richard, and Patrick Breslin. "Technicians of Torture: How Physicians Become Agents of State Terror." *The Sciences,* March–April 1986, 14–19.

Goldston, Michael. *History of Allegations of Misconduct by Area Two Personnel.* Office of Professional Standards, Chicago Police Department, September 28, 1990.

Gordon, Neve, and Ruchama Marton with John Jay Neufeld. *Torture.* London: Zed, 1995.

Gorecki, J. *Stones for the Rampart.* London: Polish Boy Scouts' and Girl Guides' Association, 1945.

Gorkin, Julian. *Canibales politicos.* Mexico City: Ediciones Quetzal, 1941.

————. *El proceso de Moscú en Barcelona.* Barcelona: Aymá, 1974.

Goustine, Christian de. *La torture.* Paris: Le Centurion, 1976.

Gove, Walter R. "Sleep Deprivation: A Cause of Psychotic Disorganization." *American Journal of Sociology* 75.5 (1970): 782–99.

Goyet, Pierre le. *La Guerre d'algerie*. Paris: Perrin: 1989.

Graff, Henry, ed. *American Imperialism and the Philippine Insurrection*. Boston: Little, Brown, 1969.

Greer, William. "Turmoil in Troubled Precinct Centers on 'The Strip.'" *New York Times*, April 26, 1985, B1.

Grinker, Roy, and John Spiegel. *Men Under Stress*. Philadelphia: Blakiston, 1945.

Grzymala-Siedlecki, Adam. *Sto jedenascie dni letargu*. Kraków: Wydawnictwo Literackie, 1966.

Gudjonsson, Gisli. *The Psychology of Interrogations and Confessions*. West Sussex, England: Wiley, 2003.

———. "Suggestibility and Compliance among Alleged False Confessors and Resistors in Criminal Trials." *Medicine, Science and Law* 31 (1991): 147–51.

Guest, Iain. *Behind the Disappearances*. Philadelphia: University of Pennsylvania Press, 1990.

Gyatso, Palden, with Tsering Shkya. *The Autobiography of a Tibetan Monk*. New York: Grove Press, 1997.

Haestrup, Jørgen. *Secret Alliance*. Translated by Alison Borch-Johansen. New York: New York University Press, 1976.

Hajjar, Lisa. *Courting Conflict: The Israeli Military Court System in the West Bank and Gaza*. Berkeley and Los Angeles: University of California Press, 2005.

Hakki Onen, S., Abdelkrim Alloui, Annette Gross, Alain Eschallier, and Claude Dubray. "The Effects of Total Sleep Deprivation, Selective Sleep Interruption and Sleep Recovery on Pain Tolerance Thresholds in Healthy Subjects." *Journal of Sleep Research* 10 (2002): 35–42.

Hakki Onen, S., Abedelkrim Alloui, Didier Jourdan, Alain Eschallier, and Claude Dubray. "Effects of Rapid Eye Movement (REM) Sleep Deprivation on Pain Sensitivity in the Rat." *Brain Research* 900 (2001): 261–67.

Hamill, Desmond. *Pig in the Middle*. London: Methuen, 1985.

Hammond, Nicholas. *Venture into Greece*. London: William Kimber, 1983.

Hansson, Per. *The Greatest Gamble*. Translated by Maurice Michael. London: George Allen and Unwin, 1967.

Haritos-Fatouros, Mika. "The Official Torturer." *Journal of Applied Social Psychology* 18.13 (1988): 1107–20.

———. *The Psychological Origins of Institutionalized Torture*. London: Routledge, 2003.

Harms, Ernest. "The Origin and Early History of Electrotherapy and Electroshock." *American Journal of Psychiatry* 107 (1955): 933–34.

Hart, Peter. *The IRA and Its Enemies*. Oxford: Clarendon Press, 1998.

Hasquenoph, Marcel. *La Gestapo en France*. Paris: De Vecchi Poche, 1987.

Hastings. "Political Prisoners in Brazil." *Times* (London), July 10, 1936, 12.

Hearn, C. V. *Russian Assignment*. London: Robert Hale, 1962.

Hehn, Paul. *The German Struggle against Yugoslav Guerillas in World War II*. Boulder, CO: East European Quarterly, 1979.

Heide, Sigrid. *In the Hands of My Enemy*. Translated by Norma Johansen. Arranged by Ethel Keshner. Middletown, CT: Southfarm Press, 1995.

Held, Paul. *Quer Durch Rumänien*. Vienna: Münster-Verlag, 1925.

Hémery, Daniel. *Révolutionnaires vietnamiens et pouvoir colonial en Indochine*. Paris: François Maspero, 1975.

Henderickx, Adrien. *1940–1945 Breendonck-Neuengamme*. Brussels: St. Pieters Leeuw, 1986.

Henderson, Charles. "Control of Crime in India." *Journal of the American Institute of Criminal Law and Crimonology* 4.378 (May 1913–March 1914): 378–400.

Henderson, Mary. *Xenia*. London: Weidenfeld and Nicholson, 1988.

Hersh, Seymour. "Chain of Command." *New Yorker*, May 17, 2004, 38–43.

———. "The Gray Zone." *New Yorker*, May 24, 2004, 38–44.

———. "Torture at Abu Ghraib." *New Yorker*, May 10, 2004, 42–48.

Hewitt, Charles, Jr. "In the Hands of the Gestapo." In *Eye Witness*. Edited by Robert Spiers Benjamin. New York: Alliance, 1940.

Heyd, Uriel. *Studies in Old Ottoman Criminal Law*. Edited by V. L. Ménage. Oxford: Clarendon Press, 1973.

Hill, Andria. *Mona Parsons*. Halifax, Nova Scotia: Nimbus, 2000.

Hilton, Stanley. *Brazil and the Soviet Challenge*. Austin: University of Texas Press, 1981.

———. *Hitler's Secret War in South America 1939–1945*. Baton Rouge: Louisiana State University Press, 1981.

Hingley, Ronald. *The Russian Secret Police*. New York: Simon and Schuster, 1971.

Hinkle, Lawrence E., and Harold G. Wolff. "Communist Interrogation and Indoctrination of 'Enemies of the State." *A.M.A. Archives of Neurology and Psychiatry* 76 (August 1956): 115–74.

Hinman, Lawrence. "Stunning Morality." *Criminal Justice Ethics* 17.1 (1998): 3–14.

Hirschfeld, Gerhard, and Patrick Marsh. *Collaboration in France*. Oxford: St. Martin's, 1989.

Hoffman, Peter. *History of the German Resistance, 1933–1945*. Translated by Richard Barry. Cambridge: MIT Press, 1977.

Hofling, Charles, Eveline Brotzman, Sarah Dalrymple, Nancy Graves, and Chester Pierce. "An Experimental Study in Nurse-Physician Relationships." *Journal of Nervous and Mental Disease* 143.2 (1966): 171–80.

Homan, Gerlof. *American Mennonites and the Great War, 1914–1918*. Waterloo, Ontario: Herald Press, 1994.

Hondros, John Louis. *Occupation and Resistance*. New York: Pella, 1983.

Hong, Nathaniel. *Sparks of Resistance*. Odense: Odense University Press, 1996.

Hopkins, Ernest Jerome. *Our Lawless Police*. New York: Viking Press, 1931.

Horne, Alistair. *A Savage War of Peace*. New York: Viking, 1977.

House, Robert. "Use of Scopolamine in Criminology." *American Journal of Police Science* 2.4 (1931): 329.

Hovelsen, Leif. *Out of the Evil Night*. Translated by John Morrison. London: Blandford Press, 1959.

"How Not to Run Your Secret Police." *The Economist*, May 18, 1974, 31–32.

Howard, Keith, ed. *True Stories of the Korean Comfort Women*. Translated by Young Joo Lee. London: Cassell, 1995.

Hubbell, John. *POW*. New York: Reader's Digest Press, 1976.

Hudson, Rex A. *The Sociology and Psychology of Terrorism*. Washington, DC: Federal Research Division, Library of Congress, 1999. Available at http://www.loc.gov/rr/frd/pdf-files/Soc_Psych_of_Terrorism.pdf.

Huggins, Martha. *Political Policing*. Durham, NC: Duke University Press, 1998.

———, ed. *Vigilantism and the State in Modern Latin America*. New York: Praeger, 1991.

Huggins, Martha, Mika Haritos-Fatouros, and Philip Zimbardo. *Violence Workers*. Berkeley and Los Angeles: University of California Press, 2002.

Hughes, Thomas. "Harold Brown and the Executioner's Current." *Business History Review* 31 (1958): 143–65.

Hulbert, Homer. *The Passing of Korea*. New York: Doubleday, Page, 1906.

Hull, Grafton, Jr., and Joseph Frisbie. "The Stun Gun Debate." *Police Chief*, February 1987, 46–49.

Human Resource Exploitation Training Manual. Langley, VA: Central Intelligence Agency, July 1963, 1983. Available at the National Security Archives, http://www2.gwu.edu/~nsarchiv/NSAEBB/NSAEBB122/.

"Human Rights and the Forensic Scientist." *American Journal of Forensic Medicine and Pathology* 5.4 (1984): 295.

Human Rights Watch. *"And It Was Hell All Over Again . . ."* New York: Human Rights Watch, 2000.

———. *"Like the Dead in Their Coffins."* 2004. http://hrw.org/reports/2004.

———. *Confession at Any Cost*. New York: Human Rights Watch, 1999.

———. *Dangerous Minds*. New York: Human Rights Watch and Geneva Initiative on Psychiatry, 2002.

———. *Playing with Fire*. New York: Human Rights Watch, 2002.

———. *Prison Conditions in Japan*. New York: Human Rights Watch, 1995.

———. *Shielded from Justice*. New York: Human Rights Watch, 1998.

———. *Torture and Ill-Treatment: Israel's Interrogation of Palestinians from the Occupied Territories*. New York: Human Rights Watch, 1994.

———. *Turkey* 9:4 (March 1997).

Human Rights Watch and Physicians for Human Rights. *Dead Silence*. New York: Human Rights Watch, 1994.

Humphries, Stephen. *Hooligans or Rebels?* Oxford: Basil Blackwell, 1981.

Hunter, Virginia. *Policing Athens*. Princeton, NJ: Princeton University Press, 1994.

Hutchinson, Lester. *Conspiracy at Meerut*. New York: Arno, 1972.

Hylah Jacques. "Spain: Systematic Torture in a Democratic State." *Monthly Review*, November 1985, 57–62.

Iacopino, Vincent, Michele Heisler, Shervin Pishevar, and Robert Kirschner. "Physician Complicity in Misrepresentation and Omission of Evidence in Torture in Postdetention Medical Examinations in Turkey." *Journal of the American Medical Association* 276.5 (1996): 396–402.

Ignatieff, Michael. "What Did the CIA Do To His Father?" *New York Times Magazine*, April 1, 2001, 56–59.

Ill-Treated and Killed Soldiers in the Soviet Army. Århus, Denmark: Physicians for Human Rights, 1991.

Images of Repression. Mexico City: Human Rights Centre "Miguel Agustin Pro Juarez," 1999.

In der Gestapo-Zentrale, Prinz-Albrecht-Strasse 8. Berlin: Ev Akademie, 1989.

In Thieu's Prisons. Hanoi: Foreign Languages Publishing House, 1973.

"Incident on a Patrol: A Vietcong's Ordeal by Water." *Washington Post*, January 21, 1968, A1, A23.

Informe: Violacion de los derechos humanos en Bolivia. Bolivia: Central Obrera Boliviana, 1976.

Innes, Brian. *The History of Torture*. New York: St. Martin's, 1998.

International Committee of the Red Cross. *Report of the ICRC on the Treatment by Coalition Forces of Prisoners of War and other Protected Persons by the Geneva Conventions in Iraq during Arrest, Internment and Interrogation*. February 2004.

International Military Tribunal. *Trial of the Major War Criminals*. 42 vols. Nuremberg: n.p., 1949.

"Israel Tortures Arab Prisoners." *Sunday Times* (London), June 19, 1977, A17–A20.

"Israeli Interrogation Methods: Interview with Bashar Tarabieh." *Middle East Report* 201 (October–December 1996): 29.

Ivanov-Razumnik, R.V. *The Memoirs of Ivanov-Razumnik*. London: Oxford University Press, 1965.

Jancar-Webster, Barbara. *Women and Revolution in Yugoslavia, 1941–1945*. Denver: Arden Press, 1990.

Japanese Civil Liberties Union. *Criminal Procedure and the Human Rights of Foreigners in Japan*. Tokyo: Japanese Civil Liberties Union, July 1991.

Jászi, Oscar. *Revolution and Counter-Revolution in Hungary*. New York: Howard Fertig, 1969.

Jecchinis, Chris. *Beyond Olympus*. London: George G. Harrap, 1960.

Johns, Stephen. *Tory Torture in Ulster*. London: Socialist Labour League, 1971.

Johnson, Chalmers. *Conspiracy at Matsukawa*. Berkeley and Los Angeles: University of California Press, 1972.

Johnson, Eric. *The Nazi Terror*. New York: Basic Books, 1999.

Johnston, Les. *The Rebirth of Private Policing*. London: Routledge, 1992.

Johnstone, Steven. *Disputes and Democracy*. Austin: University of Texas Press, 1999.

Jones, J. Ralph. "Portraits of Georgia Slaves." *Georgia Review* 21 (1967): 268–73.

Jones, Philip. *The Italian City-State*. Oxford: Clarendon Press, 1997.

Jordan, Lara Jakes, and Matt Kelley. "U.S. Allies Also Accused in Prison Abuse." Associated Press Online, May 28, 2004, http://www.lexis-nexis.com/.

Jordan, William. *Conquest without Victory*. London: Hodder and Stoughton, 1969.

"Judge Orders Destruction of Electric Chair Used by Arkansas Sheriff for Confessions." *New York Times*, November 23, 1929, 12.

Kalyvas, Stathis. "The Logic of Violence in Civil War." Unpublished manuscript, March 2000. Available at www.nd.edu/~cmendoz1/datos/papers/kalyvas.pdf.

Kalyvas, Stathis, and Mathew Kocher. "Abusi USA: Il modello Vietnam in Iraq." *Il Manifesto*, June 21, 2005, 5.

————. "Violence and Insurgency: Implications for Collective Action." Unpublished manuscript, April 10, 2006.

Karlsmark, Tonny. "Electrically Induced Dermal Changes." *Danish Medical Bulletin* 37.6 (1990): 507–20.

Karlsmark, T., H. K. Thomsen, L. Danielsen, O. Aalund, O. Nielsen, K. G. Nielsen, and I. K. Genefke. "The Morphogensis of Electrically and Head-Induced Dermal Changes in Pig Skin." *Forensic Science International* 39 (1988): 175–88.

Karsten, Peter. "The American Democratic Citizen Soldier: Triumph or Disaster?" *Military Affairs* 30.1 (1966): 34–40.

Kassin, S. M., and K. L. Kieche. "The Social Psychology of False Confessions." *Psychological Science* 7 (1996): 125–28.

Kealey, Linda. "Patterns of Punishment: Massachusetts in the Eighteenth Century." *American Journal of Legal History* 30.2 (1986): 163–86.

Kedward, H. R. *In Search of the Maquis*. Oxford: Clarendon Press, 1993.

Kellaway, Jean. *The History of Torture and Execution*. New York: Lyons Press, 2000.

Kelley, Matt. "Intelligence Agents Encouraged Abuse." Associated Press, May 30, 2004, http://web.lexis-nexis.com.

Kennedy, Ludovic. *Ten Rillington Place*. New York: Simon and Schuster, 1961.

The Kenpeitai in Java and Sumatra. Translated by Barbard Gifford Shimer and Guy Hobbs. Ithaca, NY: Cornell Modern Indonesia Project, 1986.

Keramane, Hafid. *La Pacification*. Lausanne: La Cité Éditeur, 1960.

Kerrigan, Michael. *The Instruments of Torture*. New York: Lyons Press, 2001.

Kessel, Patrick, and Giovanni Pirelli. *Le people algérien et la guerre*. Paris: François Maspero, 1962.

Kidd, Ronald. *British Liberty in Danger*. London: Lawrence and Wishart, 1940.

Kidd, W. R. *Police Interrogation*. New York: R. V. Basuino, 1940.

Kinkead, Eugene. *In Every War but One*. New York: Norton, 1959.

Kirschner, Robert. "The Use of Drugs in Torture and Human Rights Abuses." *American Journal of Forensic Medicine and Pathology* 5.4 (1984): 313–14.

Kitchin, George. *Prisoner of OGPU*. New York: Arno Press, 1970.

Kleinig, John. *The Ethics of Policing*. Cambridge: Cambridge University Press, 1996.

Knight, Amy W. *Spies Without Cloaks*. Princeton, NJ: Princeton University Press, 1996.

Kohn, Stephen M. *American Political Prisoners*. Westport, CT: Praeger, 1994.

Kolinsky, Martin. *Law, Order and Riots in Mandatory Palestine, 1928–1935*. London: St. Martin's, 1993.

Korbonski, Stefan. *Fighting Warsaw*. Translated by F. B. Czarnomski. [New York]: Funk and Wagnalls, 1956.

Korovessis, Pericles. *The Method*. Translated by Les Nightingale and Catherine Patrakis. London: Allison and Busaby, 1970.

Koryagin, Anatoly. "Toward Truly Outlawing Torture." *Science* 241.4871 (September 9, 1988): 1277.

Koussetogue, Koude. *La Torture*. N'Djaména, Chad: Association Jeunessee Anti-Clivage, 1995.

Kravchenko, Victor. *I Chose Freedom*. New York: Charles Scribner's Sons, 1946.

Krivitsky, W. G. *I Was Stalin's Agent*. London: Hamish Hamilton, 1939.

KUBARK Counterintelligence Interrogation. Langley, VA: Central Intelligence Agency, July 1963. Available at the National Security Archives, http://www2.gwu.edu/~nsarchiv/NSAEBB/NSAEBB122/.

Laber, Jeri. *The Courage of Strangers: Coming of Age with the Human Rights Movement*. New York: Public Affairs, 2002.

Lacaze-Duthiers, Gérard de. *La torture a travers les âges*. Herblay, Seine-et-Oise, France: Editions de l'idée libre, 1961.

Lacourrège, Gerard, and Pierre Alibert. *Au temps des bagnes*. Paris: Editions Atlas, 1986.

Lacouture, Jean. *Vietnam*. Translated by Konrad Kellen and Joel Carmichael. New York: Vintage, 1966.

Lamarche, André. *A vignt ans la guerre*. Liège, Belgium: Impr. Solédi, 1986.

Lamas, Raul. *Los Torturadores*. Buenos Aires: Editorial Lamas, 1956.

Lamont-Brown, Raymond. *Kempeitai*. Gloucestershire, England: Sutton, 1998.

Lampe, David. *The Savage Canary*. London: Cassell, 1957.

Landa, Kepa, Carlos Beristain, Rosa Olivares, and Jesús Zalakain. *La Tortura en Euskadi*. Madrid: Editorial Revolución, 2000.

Landaburu, M. H., and J. C. Suárez Muscardit. "Las Torturas." *Esto Es*, November 22, 1955, 23.

Landau, Katia. *Le stalinisme en Espagne*. Paris: Impr. Cerbonnet, 1938.

Langbein, Hermann. *Against All Hope*. Translated by Harry Zohn. New York: Paragon House, 1994.

Langbein, John. *Torture and the Law of Proof*. Chicago: University of Chicago Press, 1977

Langguth, A. J. *Hidden Terrors*. New York: Pantheon, 1978.

———. "Torture's Teachers." *New York Times*, June 11, 1979, A19.

Lansvreugt, P., and R. Lemaitre. *Le calvaire de Breendonck*. Brussells: Serge Baguette, 1945.

Larner, Christiana. *The Enemies of God*. Baltimore: Johns Hopkins University Press, 1981.

Larson, John. *Lying and Its Detection*. Chicago: University of Chicago Press, 1932.

———. "Present Police and Legal Methods for the Determination of the Innocence or Guilt of the Suspect." *Journal of the American Institute of Criminal Law and Criminology* 16.2 (1925): 219–71.

Lartéguy, Jean. *The Centurions*. Translated by Xan Felding. New York: E. P. Dutton, 1962.

Lassiter, G. Daniel, ed. *Interrogations, Confessions, and Entrapment*. New York: Kluwer Academic, 2004.

Latour, Bruno. *Aramis or The Love of Technology*. Translated by Catherine Porter. Cambridge: Harvard University Press, 1996.

———. *Science in Action*. Cambridge: Harvard University Press, 1987.

Laurens, André. *Un police politique sous l'occupation*. Foix: C.D.D.P, 1982.

Lauret, Jean-Claude, and Raymond Lasierra. *La torture et les pouvoirs*. Paris: Balland, 1973.

Lavine, Emanuel. *The Third Degree*. Garden City, NY: Garden City Publishing, 1930.

Lawrence, Christie. *Irregular Adventure*. London: Faber and Faber, 1947.

Lea, Henry Charles. *A History of the Inquisition of the Middle Ages*. New York: Russell and Russell, 1958.

Lech, Raymond. *Broken Soldiers*. Urbana: University of Illinois Press, 2000.

Lecomte, G. "Falaka." In *The Encyclopedia of Islam*, 2:763–64. Leiden: E. J. Brill, 1965.

Lee, Chulwoo. "Modernity, Legality and Power in Korea under Japanese Rule." In *Colonial Modernity in Korea*. Edited by Gi-Wook Shin and Michael Robinson. Cambridge: Harvard University Asia Center, 1999.

Lefebvre, Denis. *Guy Mollet face à la torture en Algérie*. [Paris]: Bruno Leprince, 2001.

Leggett, George. *The Cheka*. Oxford: Clarendon, 1981.

Leigh, David. "UK Forces Taught Torture Methods." *Guardian* (London), May 8, 2004, 1.

Leites, Nathan, and Elsa Bernaut. *Ritual of Liquidation*. Glencoe, IL: Free Press, 1954.

Lelyveld, Joseph. "Interrogating Ourselves." *New York Times*, June 12, 2005, sec. 6, pp. 36–43, 60, 66–69.

Lembaga Studi dan Advokasi (ELSAM). *Revealing Tortures by Public Officials*. Jakarta Selatan, Indonesia: ELSAM, 1996.

Lemov, Rebecca. *World as Laboratory*. New York: Hill and Wang, 2005.

LeMoyne, James. "Testifying to Torture." *New York Times*, June 5, 1988, sec. 6, p. 45.

Lentz, Martha, Carol Landis, James Rothermel, and Joen Shaver. "Effects of Selective Slow Wave Sleep Disruption on Muscolskeletal Pain and Fatigue in Middle Aged Women." *Journal of Rheumatology* 26.7 (1999): 1586–92.

Letters from Tunisia's Gulags. Translated by Yusra Kherigi. London: Tunisian Information and Documentation Bureau, 1998.

Leulliette, Pierre. *St. Michael and the Dragon*. Translated by John Edmonds. Boston: Houghton Mifflin, 1964.

Levin, Michael. "The Case for Torture." *Newsweek*, June 7, 1982, 13.

Levytsky, Boris. *The Uses of Terror*. Translated by H. A. Piehler. New York: Coard, McCann and Geoghegan, 1972.

Lewandowski, Józef. *The Swedish Contribution to the Polish Resistance Movement during World War Two (1939–1942)*. Stockholm: Almqvist & Wiksell International, 1979.

Lewis, Neil A. "Broad Use of Harsh Tactics Is Described at Cuba." *New York Times*, October 17, 2004, A1.

Lewis, Neil A. "Red Cross Finds Detainee Abuse in Guantánamo." *New York Times*, November 30, 2004, A1.

Lewy, Guenter. *America in Vietnam*. Oxford: Oxford University Press, 1978.

Liang, Hsi-Huey. *The Berlin Police Force in the Weimar Republic*. Berkeley and Los Angeles: University of California Press, 1970.

Lifton, Robert Jay. "Doctors and Torture." *New England Journal of Medicine* 351.5 (July 29, 2004): 415–16.

———. *The Nazi Doctors*. New York: Basic Books: 1986.

———. *Thought Reform and the Psychology of Totalism*. New York: Norton, 1961.

Lilly, John. *The Scientist*. Berkeley, CA: Ronin, 1978.

Lipper, Elinor. *Eleven Years in Soviet Prison Camps*. Chicago: Henry Regnery, 1951.

Liu, Jianhong, Lening Zhang, and Steven F. Messner, eds. *Crime and Social Control in a Changing China*. Westport, CT: Greenwood, 2001.

Locy, Toni, and John Diamond. "Memo Lists Acceptable 'Aggressive' Interrogation Methods." *USA Today*, June 28, 2004, 5A.

Löhndorff, Ernst. *Hell in the Foreign Legion*. Translated by Gerard Shelley. New York: Greenberg, 1932.

Lök, Veli, Mehmet Tunca, Kamil Kumanloglu, Emre Kapkin, and Gurkan Dirik. "Bone Scintigraphy as Clue to Previous Torture." *The Lancet* 337 (April 6, 1991): 847.

London, Jack. *Star Rover*. New York: Grosset and Dunlap, 1915.

Longchamp, Jean-Paul de. *La Garde de Fer*. Paris: SEFA, [1975].

Lotnik, Waldemar. *Nine Lives*. London: Serif, 1999.

Lunt, James. *Imperial Sunset*. London: MacDonald, 1981.

Luza, Radomir. *The Austrian Resistance, 1938–1945*. Minneapolis: University of Minnesota Press, 1984.

Luza, Radomir, with Christina Vella. *The Hitler Kiss*. Baton Rouge: Louisiana State University Press, 2002.

Lyons, Eugene. *Assignment in Utopia*. New York: Harcourt, Brace, 1937.

Maass, Peter. "If A Terror Suspect Won't Talk, Should He Be Made To?" *New York Times*, March 9, 2003, 4:4.

Maass, Walter. *Country Without a Name*. New York: Frederick Ungar, 1979.

———. *The Netherlands at War*. London: Abelard-Schumann, 1970.

Macculloch, Diarmaid. *The Reformation*. New York: Viking, 2003.

MacDonald, John. *The Murderer and His Victim*. 2nd ed. Springfield, IL: Charles C. Thomas, 1986.

Mackey, Chris, and Greg Miller. *The Interrogators*. New York: Little, Brown, 2004.

Magnes, Judah. *Amnesty for Political Prisoners*. New York: National Civil Liberties Bureau, 1919.

Majumdar, R.C. *Penal Settlement in Andamans*. New Delhi: Government of India, 1975.

Malik, G. H., I. A. Sirwal, A. R. Reshi, M. S. Najar, M. Tanvir, and M. Altaf. "Acute Renal Failure Following Physical Torture." *Nephron* 63 (1993): 434–37.

Malinowski, Tom. "The Logic of Torture." *Washington Post*, June 27, 2004, B7.

Mamtey, Victor, and Radomir Luza. *A History of the Czechoslovak Republic, 1918–1948.* Princeton, NJ: Princeton University Press, 1973.

Mann, Samantha, Aldert Vrij, and Ray Bull. "Detecting True Lies." *Journal of Applied Psychology* 89.1 (2004): 137–49.

Mannix, Daniel. *The History of Torture.* [New York]: Dorset, 1964.

Mansour, Paul. "Turkish Doctors Collude in Torture." *British Medical Journal* 314 (March 8, 1997): 695.

Manuel, Alexandre, Rogério Carapinha, and Dias Neves. *PIDE.* Fundão, Portugal: Jornal do Fundão, 1974.

Manus, Max. *Nine Lives Before Thirty.* Garden City, NY: Doubleday, 1947.

Marenin, Otwin. *Policing Change, Changing Police.* New York: Garland, 1996.

Marks, John. *The Search for the Manchurian Candidate.* New York: McGraw-Hill, 1980.

Marshall, Bruce. *The White Rabbit.* London: Cassell, 1988.

Marshall, Tom. "Doctors in Guantanamo Bay Are at Risk of Being Accessories to Torture." *British Medical Journal* 324 (January 26, 2002): 235.

Marstrand-Bølling, P. "La torture dentaire." *Médicine et Hygiène* (March 21, 1979): 1042, 1045–46.

"Marty et sa brigade sanglante répondront de leurs crimes." *Dépêche du Midi,* June 14, 1948, 1.

Marvin, Carolyn. *When Old Technologies Were New.* New York: Oxford University Press, 1988.

Marx, Gary. *Undercover.* Berkeley and Los Angeles: University of California Press, 1988.

Marx, Karl. *Capital.* 3 vols. New York: International Publishers, 1070.

Mason, T. David, and Dale Krane. "The Political Economy of Death Squads: Toward a Theory of the Impact of State-Sanctioned Terror." *International Studies Quarterly* 33.2 (1989): 175–98.

Massu, Jacques. *La vraie bataille d'Alger.* Paris: Plon, 1972.

Mather, Ian. " 'Religious' Torturers Use Shah's Police Techniques." *The Observer,* November 14, 1982, 13.

Mayer, Allan. *Gaston's War.* Novato, CA: Presidio, 1988.

Mayer, Jane. "The Experiment." *New Yorker,* July 11 and 18, 2005, 60–71.

———. "Outsourcing Torture." *New Yorker,* February 14 and 21, 2005, 106–23.

Mazower, Mark. *Inside Hitler's Greece.* New Haven: CT: Yale University Press, 1993.

———, ed. *The Policing of Politics in the 20TH Century.* Providence, RI: Berghahn, 1997.

McConville, Michael, and John Baldwin. "The Role of Interrogation in Crime Discovery and Conviction." *British Journal of Criminology* 2 (1982): 165–75.

McCormack, G., and Y. Sugimoto, eds. *Democracy in Contemporary Japan.* Armonk, NY: M. E. Sharpe, 1986.

McCoy, Alfred. *A Question of Torture.* New York: Metropolitan, 2006.

McGovern, John. *Terror in Spain.* London: Independent Labour Party, [1938?].

McGuffin, John. *The Guineapigs.* Harmondsworth, England: Penguin, 1974.

McGuffin, John. *Internment*. Tralee, Ireland: Anvil, 1973.

McKanna, Clare, Jr. "Crime and Punishment: The Hispanic Experience in San Quentin, 1851–1880." *Southern California Quarterly* 72.1 (1990): 1–18.

McKnight, Brian. *Law and Order in Sung China*. Cambridge: Cambridge University Press, 1992.

McLean, Angus. *Vive la Legion*. London: Sampson Low, Marston, [1937].

Mcleave, Hugh. *The Damned Die Hard*. New York: Saturday Review Press, 1973.

McNally, Richard. *Remembering Trauma*. Cambridge: Belknap Press of Harvard University Press, 2003.

Medvedev, Zhores, and Roy Medvedev. *A Question of Madness*. Translated by Ellen de Kadt. New York: Norton, 1971.

Meeus, Wim, and Quintent Wraajimakers. "Obedience in Modern Society: The Utrecht Studies." *Journal of Social Issues* 51.3 (1995): 155–75.

Meier, Andrew. *Black Earth*. New York: Norton, 2003.

Melgounov, Sergey Petrovich. *The Red Terror in Russia*. Westport, CT: Hyperion Press, 1926.

Mellor, Alec. *La Torture*. Paris: Horizons littéraires, 1949.

Melzack, Ronald, and Patrick Wall. *The Challenge of Pain*. Harmondsworth, England: Penguin, 1982.

Mercer, Charles. *Legion of Strangers*. New York: Holt, Rinehart and Winston, 1964.

Merom, Gil. *How Democracies Lose Small Wars*. Cambridge: Cambridge University Press, 2003.

Merson, Allan. *Communist Resistance in Nazi Germany*. London: Lawrence and Wishart, 1985.

Michel, Henri, ed. *La Libération de la France*. 16 vols. Paris: Librarie Hachette, 1973–74.

Michelot, Jean-Claude. *La Guillotine sèche*. Paris: Fayard, 1981.

Mikkelsen, Birger. "*A Matter of Decency*." Elsinore, Denmark: Friends of the Sound, 1994.

Milgram, Stanley. "Behavioral Study of Obedience." *Journal of Abnormal and Social Psychology* 67.4 (1963): 371–78.

———. *Obedience to Authority*. New York: Harper and Row, 1974.

Miller, Jerome. *Last One Over the Wall*. 2nd ed. Columbus: Ohio State University Press, 1998.

Miller, Stuart Creighton. *Benevolent Assimilation*. New Haven, CT: Yale University Press, 1982.

Minh, Nguyen Van. "Jail Notes of a Young Vietnamese." *The Nation*, March 24, 1969, 350–62.

Mise à jour des allegations de torture dans l'état de São Paulo, São Paulo: Action des Chrétiens pour l'abolition de la torture, 2002.

Mitford, Jessica. "The Torture Cure." *Harper's*, August 1973, 16, 18, 24–26, 28, 30.

Miyazawa, Setsuo. *Policing in Japan*. Translated by Frank Bennett Jr. and John Haley. Albany: State University of New York Press, 1992.

Mockaitis, Thomas. *British Counterinsurgency in the Post-Imperial Era*. Manchester, England: Manchester University Press, 1995.

Moenssens, Andre. "Narcoanalysis in Law Enforcement." *Journal of Criminal Law, Criminology and Police* Science 52.4 (1961): 453–58.

Moffeit, Miles. "Wider Iraqi Abuse Shown." *Denver Post,* May 26, 2004, A1.

Mohammad [pseud.]. *The Argot of the Victim.* Copenhagen: Rehabilitation and Research Centre for Torture Victims, 1992.

Moisander, Pia, and Erik Edston. "Torture and Its Sequel—A Comparison between Victims from Six Countries." *Forensic Science International* 137 (2003): 136.

Molden, Fritz. *Exploding Star.* Translated by Peter Ross and Betty Ross. New York: William Morrow, 1979.

———. *Fires in the Night.* Translated by Harry Zohn. Boulder, CO: Westview, 1989.

Møller, R., T. Karlsmark, and I. K. Genefke. "Electrically-Induced Collagen Calcification in Pig-Skin: A Histopathologic and Histochemcial Study." *Forensic Science International* 39 (1988): 163–74.

Moltke, Helmuth James von. *Letters to Freya, 1939–1945.* Edited and translated by Beate Ruhm von Oppen. New York: Knopf, 1990.

Moravec, Frantisek. *Master of Spies.* London: Bodley Head, 1975.

Morgan, Ted. *My Battle of Algiers.* New York: HarperCollins, 2005.

Morgan, Charles A., III, Gary Hazlett, Anthony Doran, Stephan Garrett, Gary Hoyt, Paul Thomas, Madeolon Baranoski, and Steven Southwick. "Accuracy of Eyewitness Memory for Persons Encountered during Exposure to Highly Intense Stress." *International Journal of Law and Psychiatry* 27 (2004): 265–79.

Morgan, Charles A., III, Gary Hazlett, Sheila Wang, E. Greer Richardson, Paula Schnurr, and Steven Southwick. "Symptoms of Dissociation in Humans Experiencing Acute, Uncontrollable Stress: A Prospective Investigation." *American Journal of Psychiatry* 158.8 (2001): 1239–47.

Morgan, Rod, and Tim Newburn. *The Future of Policing.* Oxford: Clarendon Press, 1997.

Morris, Norval, and David Rothman. *The Oxford History of the Prison.* New York: Oxford University Press, 1995.

Morton, James. *Catching the Killers.* London: Ebury Press, 2001.

Moszkiewiez, Helen. *Inside the Gestapo.* Toronto: Macmillan of Canada, 1985.

Mott, Fred. *War Neuroses and Shell Shock.* London: Oxford University Press, 1919.

Mühlen, Patrick v. zur. *Spanien war ihre Hoffnung.* Bonn: Verlag Neue Gesellschaft, 1983.

Muller, Ingo. *Hitler's Justice.* Cambridge: Harvard University Press, 1991.

Muller, Jean. *Le dossier.* Paris: Cahiers du Témoignage Chrétien, 1957.

Muran, J. B. *We Fight On.* London: Lincolns-Prager, 1945.

Murdoch, James. *A History of Japan.* 3 vols. Revised and edited by Joseph Longford. London: Kegan Paul, Trench Trubner, 1926.

Murphy, F. D. *Luck of the Draw.* Trumbull, CT: FNP Military Division, 2001.

Murray, John, and Barnet Resnick. *A Guide to Taser Technology.* Whitewater, CO: Whitewater Press, 1997.

Myers, Charles. "Contribution to the Study of Shell Shock." *The Lancet,* February 13, 1915, 316–20; September 9, 1916, 461–67; March 18, 1916, 608–13.

Myers, Charles. *Shell Shock in France*. Cambridge: Cambridge University Press, 1940.

Nagy-Talavera, Nicholas. *The Greenshirts and Others*. Stanford, CA: Hoover Institution Press, 1970.

Nangoloh, P. ya, ed. *Etopola: The Practice of Torture in Present Day Namibia*. Rev. ed. Windhoek, Namibia: National Society for Human Rights, 1994.

La narcose et ses application judiciaires. Paris: Société Internationale de Criminologie, February 15, 1951.

National Academy of Sciences and Institute of Medicine. *Scientists and Human Rights in Somalia*. Washington, DC: National Academy Press, 1998.

National Commission on Law Observance and Enforcement. *Report on Lawlessness in Law Enforcement*. Washington, DC: U.S. Government Printing Office, 1931.

Neave, Airey. *Little Cyclone*. London: Hodder and Stoughton, 1954.

"New York Rider Relates Harrowing Tale of Life in Maximum Security." *Jackson Daily*, June 21, 1961.

Nichols, Alex. *A Guidebook to Handcuffs and Other Restraints of the World*. Malvern, Worcestershire, England: Kingscourt, 2002.

———. *Handcuffs and Other Restraints*. London: Kingscourt, 2002.

Nietzsche, Friedrich. *On the Genealogy of Morals*. Edited and translated by Walter Kaufmann. New York: Vintage, 1969.

Nisida, Claudio. *Le Torture*. Milan: Le Edizioni Del Borghese, [1960].

Nobari, Ali-Reza. *Iran Erupts*. Stanford, CA: Iran-America Documentation Group, 1978.

Norwegian Government. *The Gestapo at Work in Norway*. Montreal: Royal Norwegian Government's Information Office, 1942.

"Nothing But the Truth." *The Lancet*, March 21, 1953, 585–86.

"The Now Unsecret Policeman." *The Economist*, February 16, 2002, 44.

Nuttall, Carylyn. "An Exercise in Futility: The Austrian Resistance to the Nazis." Master's thesis, Emory University, 1972.

O'Balance, Edgar. *The Story of the French Foreign Legion*. London: Faber and Faber, 1961.

O'Sullivan, F. Dalton. *Crime Detection*. Chicago: O'Sullivan Publishing House, 1928.

Olsen, Oluf Reed. *Two Eggs on My Plate*. Glasgow: Blackie, 1972.

Onn, Chin Kee. *Malaya Upside Down*. Singapore: Federal Publications, 1976.

Orr, Andrew, ed. *Ceux d'Algérie*. Paris: Editions Payot, 1990.

Oshinsky, David. *"Worse Than Slavery."* New York: Free Press, 1996.

Osorio, Carlos. "Chronology of Events Related to Seven Army Spanish Language Manuals and CIA Manuals to Train Latin American Military in Intelligence and Interrogation Techniques Through the School of the Americas, Military Training Teams, and CIA Trainers." Unpublished manuscript. National Security Archive, George Washington University, Washington, DC, January 23, 1997.

Owens, Tom, with Rod Browning. *Lying Eyes*. New York: Thunder's Mouth Press, 1994.

Oyediran, Joanna, and Paul Hunt. *Evidence of Torture in Africa: A Summary of the Annual Report*. UN Special Rapporteur on Torture, 1991.

Pacheco, Allegra, ed. *The Case Against Torture in Israel*. Translated by Allegra Pacheco. Jerusalem: Public Committee Against Torture in Israel, 1999.

Page, L.G.M., and R. J. Russell. "Intensified Electrical Convulsion Therapy." *The Lancet* (April 17, 1948): 597–98.

Pan komun pan p'ongnyok ingan sonon [Antitorture, Antiviolence Manifesto on Humanity]. Seoul: Korean Christian Church Association Human Rights Committee, 1989.

Parker, Freddie, ed. *Stealing a Little Freedom*. New York: Garland, 1994.

Parker, Karen, and Etienne Jaudel. *Police Cell Detention in Japan*. San Francisco: Association of Humanitarian Lawyers, 1989.

Patterson, Orlando. *Rituals of Blood*. New York: Basic Civitas, 1998.

Peel, Michael, and Mary Salinsky. *Caught in the Middle*. Oxford: Alden Group, 2000.

Peel, Michael, and Vincent Iacopino, eds. *The Medical Documentation of Torture*. London: Greenwich Medical Media, 2002.

Peers, W. R. *Report of the Department of the Army Review of the Preliminary Investigations into the My Lai Incident*. Vol. 1: *The Report of the Investigation*. Washington, DC: Department of the Army, March 14, 1970.

Peirats, José. *Anarchists in the Spanish Revolution*. London: Freedom Press, 1990.

Pelikán, Jirí, ed. *The Czechoslovak Political Trials, 1950–1954*. Stanford, CA: Stanford University Press, 1971.

Pendas, Devin. " 'I didn't know what Auschwitz was': The Frankfurt Auschwitz Trial and the German Press, 1963–1965." *Yale Journal of Law and Humanities* 12.2 (2000): 397–446.

Pennington, Kenneth. *The Prince and the Law, 1200–1600*. Berkeley and Los Angeles: University of California Press, 1993.

Périot, Gérard. *Deuxième classe en Algérie*. Paris: Flammarion, 1962.

Perrott-White, Alfred. *French Legionnaire*. Caldwell, ID: Caxton Printers, 1951.

Peters, Edward. *Inquisition*. Berkeley and Los Angeles: University of California Press, 1988.

———. *Torture*. 2nd ed. Philadelphia: University of Pennsylvania Press, 1996.

Petersen, Hans Draminsky, and Peter Jacobsen. "Life-Threatening Torture without Visible Marks." *Scandinavian Journal of Social Medicine* 13 (1985): 87–88.

Peterson, Hans Draminsky, Ulrik Abildgaard, Gedske Daugaard, Per Jess, Henrik Marcussen, and Marianne Wallach. "Psychological and Physical Long-Term Effects of Torture." *Scandinavian Journal of Social Medicine* 13 (1985): 91.

Petersen, Hans Draminsky, Lise Worm, Mette Zander, Ole Harting, and Bjarne Ussing. *Human Rights Violations in Burma/Myanmar*. Århus, Denmark: Physicians for Human Rights, 2000.

Petit, Jacques-Guy. *Ces Peines obscures*. Paris: Fayard, 1990.

Phillips, Joshua. "A Tortured Path to Justice." *Washington Post Magazine*, August 17, 2003, 6–11, 19–25.

Phillips, Melissa. *Torture for Security*. Ramallah, West Bank: al-Haq, 1995.

Physicians for Human Rights. *Sowing Fear*. Sommerville, MA: Physicians for Human Rights, 1988.

Pintér, István. *Hungarian Anti-Fascism and Resistance.* Budapest: Akadémiai Kiadó, 1986.

Pisciotta, Alexander. *Benevolent Repression.* New York: New York University Press, 1994.

Plate, Thomas, and Andrea Darvi. *Secret Police.* Garden City, NY: Doubleday, 1981.

Plumb, Charlie, with Glen DeWerff. *I'm No Hero.* Independence, MI: Independence Press, 1973.

Podrabinek, Alexander. *Punitive Medicine.* Ann Arbor, MI: Karoma Publishers, 1980.

Pope, Victoria. "Mad Russians." *U.S. News and World Report,* December 16, 1996, 38–43.

Potter, Harry. *Hanging in Judgment.* New York: Continuum, 1993.

Pouillot, Henri. *La Villa Susini.* Paris: Éditions Tirésias, 2001.

Powell, Corey S. "War Without Death." *Discover,* April 1999, 32.

Price, G. Ward. *In Morocco with the Legion.* London: Jarrolds, 1934.

Priest, Dana, and Barton Gellman. "U.S. Decries Abuse but Defends Interrogations: 'Stress and Duress' Tactics Used on Terrorism Suspects Held in Secret Overseas Facilities." *Washington Post,* December 26, 2002, A1, A14–A15.

Pritchard, R. John, and Sonia Magbanua Zaide, eds. *The Tokyo War Crimes Trial,* 22 vols. New York: Garland, 1981.

"Proceedings of the International Symposium on Torture and the Medical Profession." *Journal of Medical Ethics* 17 (December 1991): Supplement.

Puy-Montbrun, Déodat. *L'Honneur de la guerre.* Paris: Éditions Albin Michel, 2002.

Qouta, Samie, Raija-Leena Punamäki, and Eyad El Sarraj. "Prison Experiences and Coping Styles Among Palestinian Men." *Peace and Conflict* 3.1 (1997): 19–36.

Raab, Selwyn. "Five Police Officers Indicted by Jury in Torture Case." *New York Times,* May 1, 1985, A1.

Rabemananjara, Raymond. *Madagascar.* Paris: L'Harmattan, 2000.

Raffat, Donne. *The Prison Papers of Bozorg Alavi.* Syracuse, NY: Syracuse University Press, 1985.

Rappert, Brian. *Non-Lethal Weapons as Legitimizing Forces?* London: Frank Cass, 2003.

Rasmussen, Ole Vedel. "Medical Aspects of Torture." *Danish Medical Bulletin* 37, Suppl. 1 (1990): 1–88.

Rasmussen, Ole Vedel, and Grethe Skylv. "Signs of Falanga Torture." *The Lancet* 340 (September 19, 1992): 725.

Ratner, Michael, and Ellen Ray. *Guantánamo.* White River Junction, VT: Chelsea Green, 2004.

Réal, Antony. *The Story of the Stick in All Ages and Lands.* New York: J. W. Bouton, 1875.

Rebérioux, Madeleine. "De la torture française à la torture américaine." *Raison prâesente,* January 25, 1973, 90–92.

Reenen, Piet van. "Routine Police Torture: Towards a Personalistic Analysis and Strategy." *Human Rights Review* 4.1 (2002): 52–73.

Reilly, Robin. *The Sixth Floor.* London: Cassell, 2002.

Rejali, Darius. "After Feminist Analyses of Bosnian Violence." In *The Women and War Reader*. Edited by Lois Ann Lorentzen and Jennifer Turpin. New York: New York University Press, 1998.

———. "Friend and Enemy, East or West: Political Realism in the Work of Osama bin Ladin, Carl Schmitt, Niccolo Machiavelli and Kai Ka'us ibn Iskandar." *Historical Reflections* 3 (2004): 425–43.

———. "Ordinary Betrayals." *Human Rights Review*, July–September 2000, 8–25.

———. "The Real Shame of Abu Ghraib." Time.com, May 20, 2004. http://www.time.com.

———. *Torture and Modernity: Self, Society and State in Modern Iran*. Boulder, CO: Westview, 1994.

———. "Whom Do You Trust? What Do You Count On?" In *On Nineteen Eighty-Four: Orwell and Our Future*. Edited by Abbott Gleason, Jack Goldsmith, and Martha Nussbaum. Princeton, NJ: Princeton University Press, 2005.

Repetto, Thomas. *The Blue Parade*. New York: Free Press, 1978.

Report of the Chilean National Commission on Truth and Reconciliation. Translated by Phillip E. Berryman. Notre Dame: University of Notre Dame Press, 1993.

"Report of the Committee on Lawless Enforcement of Law." *American Journal of Police Science* 1.6 (1930): 575–93.

Report of the Independent Commission of the Los Angeles Police Department. Los Angeles: The Commission, 1991.

Report on Torture in the Nyzshni Novgorod Province. Nyzshni Novgorod, Russia: Nyzshni Novgorod Province Society for Human Rights, 1997.

Reseña de la Tortura en Honduras en Los Noventa. Tegucigalpa, Honduras: Comité de Familiares de Detenidos-Desaparecidos en Honduras, 1994.

Reval, Élias. *Sixieme Colonne*. [Thonon, S.E.S,] 1945.

Rey, Benoist. *Les Égorgeurs*. Paris: Editions de Minuit, 1961.

Rey-Goldzeiguer, Annie. *Aux origines de la guerre d'Algérie, 1940–1945*. Paris: Éditions la Découverte, 2002.

Rickard, Charles. *La Savoie dans la Resistance*. 4th ed. Edilarge S.A.: Editions Ouest-France, 1993.

Risse, Thomas, Stephen C. Ropp, and Kathryn Sikkink. *The Power of Human Rights*. New York: Cambridge University Press, 1999.

Robinson, M. N., C. G. Brooks, and G. D. Renshaw. "Electric Shock Devices and their Effects on the Human Body." *Medicine, Science and the Law* (1990): 285–300.

Rochester, Stuart, and Frederick Kiley. *Honor Bound*. Annapolis, MD: Naval Institute Press, 1999.

Rochefoucauld-Liancourt, F.A.F. de la. *Histoire des torture au XIXme siècle*. Paris: Typographie de Morris, 1859.

Rodger, N.A.M. *The Safeguard of the Sea*. New York: Norton, 1998.

Rodríguez-Molas, Ricardo. *Historia de la Tortura*. Buenos Aires: Editorial Universitaria de Buenos Aires, 1984.

Rogers, Everett. *Diffusion of Innovations*. 4th ed. New York: Free Press, 1992.

Rolin, Jean. *Police Drugs*. Translated by Laurence Bendit. London: Hollis and Carter, 1955.

Rommell, Bart. *Dirty Tricks Cops Use (And Why They Use Them)*. Port Townsend, WA: Loompanics, 1993.

Ron, James. "Varying Methods of State Violence." *International Organization* 51.2 (1997): 275–300.

Ronfeldt, David. *The Mitrione Kidnapping in Uruguay*. N-1571-DOS/DARPA/RC. Rand Corporation, August 1987.

Rose, David. *Guantánamo*. New York: New Press, 2004.

Rosen, Erwin [Carlé]. *In the Foreign Legion*. London: Duckworth, 1910.

Rosenberg, Tina. *Children of Cain*. New York: William Morrow, 1991.

Ross, Brian, and Richard Esposito. "CIA's Harsh Interrogation Techniques Described." *ABC News*, November 18, 2005. http://abcnews.go.com.

Ross, Kristin. *Fast Cars, Clean Bodies*. Cambridge: MIT Press, 1995.

Rostar, M. Osman. *The Pulicharkhi Prison*. Translated and edited by Ehsanullah Azari. Peshawar, Pakistan: Writers Union of Free Afghanistan, 1991.

Roth, Eugene F., Jr., Inge Lunde, Gudrun Boysen, and Inge Kemp Genefke. "Torture and Its Treatment." *American Journal of Public Health* 77.11 (1987): 1404.

Rothman, David. *Conscience and Convenience*, Rev. ed. New York: Aldine de Gruyter, 2002.

Rubin, Barnett, and Jeri Laber. *Tears, Blood and Cries*. New York: Helsinki Watch Committee, 1984.

Ruff, Lajos. *The Brain-Washing Machine*. London: Robert Hale, 1959.

Ruggiero, Guido. *Violence in Early Renaissance Venice*. New Brunswick, NJ: Rutgers University Press, 1980.

Russell of Liverpool, Lord. *The Knights of Bushido*. London: Cassell, 1958.

———. *Prisons and Prisoners in Portugal*. London: Waterlow and Sons, 1963.

———. *Scourge of the Swastika*. New York: Philosophical Library, 1954.

Ruthven, Malise. *Torture*. London: Weidenfeld and Nicolson, 1978.

Ruud, Charles, and Sergei Stepanov. *Fontanka 16*. Montreal: McGill-Queens University Press, 1999.

Sae-sang-ae Sal-go Sip-da. Seoul: Korean Christian Church Association Human Rights Committee, n.d.

Saher, Edward. *Narcoanalysis*. The Hague: Martinus Nijhoff, 1950.

Saint Marc, Hélie de. *Mémoires*. Paris: Perrin, 1995.

Salinsky, Mary, and Liv Tigerstedt. *Evidence of Torture*. Oxford: Alden Group, 2001.

Samuelli, Annie. *Woman Behind Bars in Romania*. 2nd ed. London: Frank Cass, 1997.

Sanchez-Mazas, Miguel. *Spain in Chains*. New York: Veterans of the Abraham Lincoln Brigade, 1960.

Sands, William. *Undiplomatic Memories*. New York: Whittlesey House, 1930.

Santoli, Al. *Everything We Had*. New York: Random House, 1981.

Sargant, William. *The Battle for the Mind*. Garden City, NY: Doubleday, 1957.

———. *The Unquiet Mind*. Boston: Little, Brown, 1967.

Saunders, Kate. *Eighteen Layers of Hell*. London: Cassell, 1996.

Savarkar, Shri. *The Story of My Transportation for Life*. Translated by V. N. Naik. [Bombay]: Sadbhakti, 1950.

"Says Electric Chair Forced Confession." *New York Times*, December 10, 1929, 24.

Scarry, Elaine. *The Body in Pain*. Oxford: Oxford University Press, 1985.

Schabas, William. *The Death Penalty as Cruel Treatment and Torture*. Boston: Northeastern University Press, 1996.

Schanberg, Sydney. "Saigon Torture in Jails Reported." *New York Times*, August 12, 1972, A1, A3.

Schapiro, Leondard. *The Communist Party of the Soviet Union*. 2nd ed. New York: Random House, 1971.

Scheflin, Alan, and Edward Opton. *The Mind Manipulators*. New York: Paddington Press, 1978.

Schivelbusch, Wolfgang. *The Railway Journey*. Berkeley and Los Angeles: University of California Press, 1986.

Schlabrendorf, Fabian von. *The Secret War Against Hitler*. New York: Pitman, 1965.

Schlotterbeck, Friedrich. *The Darker the Night, the Brighter the Stars*. London: Victor Gollancz, 1947.

Schmitt, Eric. "3 in 82nd Airborne Say Beating Iraqi Prisoners Was Routine." *New York Times*, September 23, 2005, A1.

Schrader, Dirk von [pseud.]. *Elementary Field Interrogation*. N.p.: Delta, 1978.

Schreuers, J. *My Country in Trouble*. New York: Carlton Press, 1962.

Schwartzman, A. E., and P. E. Termansen. "Intensive Electroconvulsive Therapy: A Follow-Up Study." *Canadian Psychiatric Association Journal* 12 (1967): 218.

Scott, Astrid Karlsen, and Dr. Tore Hang. *Defiant Courage*. Olympia, WA: Nordic Spirit Productions, 2000.

Scott, George Ryley. *The History of Corporal Punishment*. 2nd ed. London: Torchstream, 1954.

———. *The History of Torture*. London: Torchstream, 1940.

Sears, Don W. "Legal Consequences of the Third Degree." *Ohio State Law Journal* 9 (1948): 514–24.

Seborova, Milena. *A Czech Trilogy*. Rome: Christian Academy, 1990.

Serbin, Kenneth. *Secret Dialogues*. Pittsburgh: University of Pittsburgh Press, 2000.

Sergeant, Harriet. *Shanghai*. London: Jonathan Cape, 1991.

"Sesame Street Breaks Iraqi POWs." *BBC News*, May 20, 2003. http://www.bbc.co.uk.

Shallice, Tim. "The Ulster Depth Interrogation Techniques and their Relation to Sensory Deprivation Research." *Cognition* 1.4 (1972): 385–405.

Shapiro, Colin, and Alexander Smith. *Forensic Aspects of Sleep*. Chichester, NY: John Wiley and Sons, 1997.

Shaughnessy, C. A. "The Vietnam Conflict: 'America's Best Documented War'?" *History Teacher* 24.2 (1991): 135–47.

Shaw, Mark. *Crime and Policing in Post-Apartheid South Africa*. Bloomington: Indiana University Press, 2002.

Shearing, Clifford. "The Relation Between Public and Private Policing." In *Modern Policing*. Edited by Michael Tonry and Norval Morris. Chicago: University of Chicago Press, 1992.

Sheehan, Neil. *A Bright Shining Lie*. New York: Random House, 1988.

———. Review of *Conversations with Americans*. *New York Times Book Review*, December 27, 1970, 5, 19.

Shepherd, Gordon. *The Austrian Odyssey*. London: Macmillan, 1957.

Shepherd, Naomi. *Ploughing Sand*. New Brunswick, NJ: Rutgers University Press, 1999.

Showalter, Elaine. *The Female Malady*. Harmondsworth, England: Penguin, 1987.

Shteppa, K. F. "In Stalin's Prisons—Reminiscences." *Russian Review* 21.1 (1968): 38–58.

Shue, Henry. "Torture." *Philosophy and Public Affairs* 7.2 (1978): 124–43.

Silverman, Lisa. *Tortured Subjects*. Chicago: University of Chicago Press, 2001.

Simms, Jeptha. *The Frontiersmen of New York*. Albany, NY: Geo. C. Riggs, 1883.

"Simpson Returns from Nazi Prison." *New York Times*, January 4, 1937, 3.

Sing Sing Prison. New York: NY State Department of Correction, 1953.

Singer, P. W. "Corporate Warriors." Boston: Center for Strategic and International Studies, MIT, 2001–2.

Singh, Ujjwal. *Political Prisoners in India*. Delhi: Oxford University Press, 1998.

Sitton, Claude. "Court in Americus, Ga., Told of Police Beatings." *New York Times*, November 1, 1963, 19.

———. "10 on Freedom Walk Seized at Alabama Line." *New York Times*, May 4, 1963, 1, 9.

"Six Accused of Torture in Military Exercise." *Times* (London), October 25, 1972, 8È.

Skolnick, Jerome, and James Fyfe. *Above the Law*. New York: Free Press, 1993.

Slackman, Michael. "What's Wrong with Torturing a Qaeda Higher-Up?" *New York Times*, May 16, 2004, sec. 4, p. 4.

Sliwicka, Anna. *Cztery lata ostrego dyzuru*. Warsaw: Czytelnik, 1968.

Sliwicki, Zygmunt. *Meldunek z Pawiaka*. Warsaw: Panstwowe Wydawnictwo Naukowe, 1974.

Sluka, Jeffery A., ed. *Death Squad*. Philadelphia: University of Pennsylvania Press, 2000.

Smallman, Shawn. "Military Terror and Silence in Brazil, 1910–1945." *Canadian Journal of Latin American and Caribbean Studies* 24.7 (1999): 13–20.

Smidt-Nielsen, Knud. "The Participation of Health Personnel in Torture." *Torture* 8.3 (1998): 93.

Smith, Arthur L., Jr. *The War for the German Mind*. Providence, RI: Berghahn, 1995.

Snepp, Frank. *Decent Interval*. New York: Random House, 1977.

Sobti, Jagdish, B. C. Chaparwal, and Erik Holst. "Study of Knowledge, Attitude and Practice Concerning Aspects of Torture." *Journal of the Indian Medical Association* 98.6 (2000): 334–35, 338–39.

Solomon, Michael. *Magadan*. Princeton, NJ: Vertex, 1971.

Giurescu, Constantin. *Five Years and Two Months in the Sighet Penitentiary*. Translated by Mihai Farcas and Stephanie Barton-Farcas. Boulder, CO: East European Monographs, 1994.

South Africa. Police Commission of Inquiry. *Interim and Final Reports*. 1937.

South Africa. Truth and Reconciliation Commission. *Report*. 5 vols. London: Macmillan, 1999.

Southard, E. E. *Shell-Shock and Other Neuropsychiatric Problems*. Boston: W. M. Leonard, 1919.

Spinner, Jackie. "Soldier: Unit's Role was to Break Down Prisoners." *Washington Post*, May 8, 2004, A1.

Squire, Amos. *Sing Sing Doctor*. New York: Doubleday, Doran, 1935.

Stacewicz, Richard. *Winter Soldiers*. New York: Twayne, 1997.

Stainbrook, Edward. "The Use of Electricity in Psychiatric Treatment during the 19th Century." *Bulletin of the History of Medicine* 22.3 (1948): 156–77.

Stein, Ya'el. *Torture of Palestinian Minors in the Gush Etzion Police Station*. Translated by Zvi Shulman. Jerusalem: B'Tselem, 2001.

Stephan, Robert. *Stalin's Secret War*. Lawrence: University Press of Kansas, 2004.

Stephan, Yann. *A Broken Sword*. Chicago: Office of International Criminal Justice, 1991.

Stern, Vivian. *A Sin Against the Future*. Boston: Northeastern University Press, 1998.

Stone, I. F. "Betrayal by Psychiatry." *New York Review of Books*, February 10, 1972, 7–14.

Stora, Benjamin. *La gangrène et l'oubli*. Paris: Éditions la Découverte, 1992.

Storey, Moorefield, and Marcial Lichauco. *The Conquest of the Philippines by the United States, 1898–1925*. New York: G. P. Putnam's Sons, 1926.

Storr, Anthony. "Torture without Violence." *New Statesman*, March 12, 1960, 358.

Stover, Eric. *The Open Secret*. Washington, DC: American Association for the Advancement of Science, 1987.

Stover, Eric, and Elena Nightingale. *The Breaking of Bodies and Minds*. New York: W. H. Freeman, 1985.

Strasser, Steven, ed. *The Abu Ghraib Investigations*. New York: Public Affairs, 2004.

Struck, Doug, Howard Schneider, Karl Vick, and Peter Baker. "Borderless Network of Terror; Bin Laden Followers Reach Across Globe." *Washington Post*, September 23, 2001, A1.

Stun Guns. Aurora, CO: T'Prina Technology, 1994.

Stypulkowski, Zbigniew. *Invitation to Moscow*. New York: Walker, 1962.

Sulbarán, Pablo. *La Tortura en Venezuela*. Caracas: Publicaciones Seleven, 1979.

Sung, Suh. *Unbroken Spirits*. Translated by Jean Inglis. Lanham, MD: Rowman and Littlefield, 2001.

Survivors of Torture in Mount Darwin District, Mashonaland, Central Province. [Harare, Zimbabwe]: Amani Trust, 1997.

Sutherland, Christine. *Monica*. New York: Farrar, Straus and Giroux, 1990.

Syjuco, Felisa. *The Kempei Tai in the Philippines*. Quezon City, Philippines: New Day, 1988.

Szajkowski, Zosa. *Jews and the Foreign Legion*. New York: Ktav, 1975.

Talbott, John. *The War Without a Name*. New York: Knopf, 1980.

Tam, Pham. *Imprisonment and Torture in South Vietnam*. Nyack, NY: Fellowship of Reconciliation, 1969[?].

Tanaka, Yuki. *Hidden Horrors*. Boulder, CO: Westview, 1996.

Tang, Truong Nhu, with David Chanoff and Doan Van Toai. *A Vietcong Memoir*. New York: Vintage, 1986.

Tannenbaum, Frank. *Darker Phases of the South*. New York: Negro Universities Press, 1969.

TAT—Torturaren Arkako Taldea [Group Against Torture]. *Torture en pays basque: Report 2000*. http://www.stoptortura.com/, 2002.

———. *Torture in Basque Country: Report 2001*. [Bilbao]: Graficas Lizarra, S.L, 2002.

Taussig, Michael. "Culture of Terror—Space of Death, Roger Casement's Putumayo Report and the Explanation of Torture." *Comparative Studies in Society and History* 26.3 (1984): 479–84.

Taylor, G. Flint. "Known Area 2 and 3 Torture Victims, 1972–1991 (9/15/04)." Unpublished data.

———. "U.S. Torture." *Police Misconduct and Civil Rights Law Reporter* 7.15 (2004): 169–80.

Taylor, John. *Indonesia's Forgotten War*. London: Zed, 1991.

Taylor, Peter. *Beating the Terrorists?* Harmondsworth, England: Penguin, 1980.

Tchernavin, Vladmir. *I Speak for the Silent*. Translated by Nicholas Oushakoff. Boston: Hale, Cushman and Flint, 1935.

Teltsch, Kathleen. "Uruguay Accused of Using Torture." *New York Times*, January 17, 1974, A12.

Tenenbaum, Joseph. *Underground*. New York: Philosophical Library, 1952.

Thénault, Sylvie. *Une drôle de justice*. Paris: Editions La Découverte, 2001.

Thomas, Daniel. *The Helsinki Effect: International Norms, Human Rights and the Demise of Communism*. Princeton, NJ: Princeton University Press, 2001.

Thomas, Hugh. *The Spanish Civil War*. New York: Harper and Row, 1961.

Thomas, Norman. *The Conscientious Objector in America*. New York: B. W. Huebsch, 1925.

———. "Justice to War's Heretics." *The Nation*, November 9, 1918, 547–49.

Thomas, Pierre-Alban. *Les désarrois d'un officier en Algérie*. Paris: Éditions du Seuil, 2002.

Thompson, Ginger, and Gary Cohn. "Torturers' Confessions." *Baltimore Sun*, June 13, 1995, 1A.

———. "A Survivor Tells Her Story." *Baltimore Sun*, June 15, 1995, 1A.

———. "Unearthed: Fatal Secrets." *Baltimore Sun*, June 11, 1995, 1A.

Thomsen, Jørgen, and Maiken Mannstaedt. *The Green Birds*. Århus, Denmark: Danish Medical Group, 2000.

Thomsett, Michael. *The German Opposition to Hitler*. Jefferson, NC: McFarland, 1997.

Tiltman, H. Hessell. *The Terror in Europe*. New York: Frederick A. Stokes, 1932.

Timmerman, Jacobo. *Prisoner Without a Name, Cell without a Number*. New York: Vintage, 1982.

Tipton, Elise. *The Japanese Police State*. Honolulu: University of Hawaii Press, 1990.

Todd, S. C. *The Shape of Athenian Law*. Oxford: Clarendon, 1993.

Tolischus, Otto. *Tokyo Record*. New York: Reynal and Hitchcock, 1943.

Toliver, Raymond, with Hanns Scharff. *The Interrogator*. Fallbrook, CA: Aero, 1978.

Tomsen, Jørgen, Karin Helweg-Larsen, and Ole Vedel Rasmussen. "Amnesty International and the Forensic Sciences." *American Journal of Forensic Medicine and Pathology* 5.4 (1984): 305–10.

Tortura en El Peru. Lima, Peru: Coodiandora Nacional de Derechos Humanos, 1995.

La Tortura en El Salvador. San Salvador: Commision de Derechos Humanos de El Salvador, 1986.

Tortura en Paraguay. Asunción, Paraguay: Comité de Iglesias Para Ayudas de Emergencia and International Human Rights Law Group, 1993.

Tortura na colónia de Moçambique. Porto, Portugal: Ediçoes Afrontamento, 1977.

"Torture as Policy." *Time*, August 16, 1976, 31–34.

The Torture Report. London: British Medical Association, 1986.

" 'Torture' Soldier to Sue." *Times* (London), November 1, 1972, 4.

Tram, Nguyen Xuan. *From Mainland Hell to Island Hell*. Hanoi: Foreign Languages Publishing House, 1961.

Trido, Victor. *Breendonck*. Paris: Editions J. Dupuis, 1944.

Trinquier, Roger. *La Guerre Moderne*. Paris: La Table Ronde, 1961. Translated by Daniel Lee as *Modern Warfare* (New York: Praeger, 1964).

Tucker, Robert. *Stalin in Power*. New York: Norton, 1992.

Tunca, Mehmet, and Veli Lök. "Bone Scintigraphy in Screening of Torture Survivors." *The Lancet* 352 (December 5, 1998): 1859.

Twiss, Travers, ed. *The Black Book of the Admiralty*. 4 vols. Reprint ed. Abingdon, England: Professional Books, 1985.

Tyler, David. "Psychological Changes During Experimental Sleep Deprivation." *Diseases of the Nervous System* 16.10 (1955): 293–99.

A Typical Example of Human Rights Violations under the Daiyo-Kangoku System in Japan. Tokyo: Japan Civil Liberties Union, 1991.

Uildriks, Niels. "Police Torture in France." *Netherlands Quarterly of Human Rights* 17.4 (1999): 411–23.

Uildriks, Niels, and Hans van Mastrigt. *Policing Police Violence*. Deventer, the Netherlands: Kluwer, 1991.

Unchained Memories. Boston: Bullfinch Press, 2002.

United Kingdom. *Report of the Royal Commission on Police Powers and Procedure*. Reprint ed. New York: Arno, 1971.

The Unseen and Silent. Translated by George Iranek-Osmecki. London: Sheed and Ward, 1954.

U.S. Congress. *Congressional Record*. 92nd Congress, 1st sess. Vol. 117, pt. 8 (April 5–19, 1971).

U.S. Congress. House. Committee on Government Operations. Subcommittee on Government Operations. *U.S. Assistance Programs in Vietnam: Hearings.* 92nd Cong., 1st sess. 1971.

———. House. Committee on International Relations. Subcommittee on International Organizations. *Human Rights in the Philippines,* 94th Cong., 2nd sess. 1976.

"U.S. Interrogation Techniques." *USA Today,* June 23, 2004, 4A.

Váli, Ferenc A. *A Scholar's Odyssey.* Edited by Karl Ryavec. Ames: Iowa State University Press, 1957.

Valle, James. *Rock and Shoals.* Annapolis, MD: Naval Institute Press, 1980.

Valtin, Jan. *Out of the Night.* New York: Alliance, 1941.

Vat, Dan van der. "German Border Police Tortured in Training." *Times* (London), March 2, 1973, 5.

Vest, Jason. "CIA Veterans Condemn Torture." *National Journal* 37.47–48 (November 19, 2005): 3651–53.

Vesti, P. B. "Extreme Man-Made Stress and Anti-Therapy." *Danish Medical Bulletin* 37.5 (1990): 466–68.

Vidal-Naquet, Pierre. *L'Affaire Audin.* Editions de Minuit, 1958.

———. *La Raison d'état.* Paris: Éditions de Minuit, 1962.

———. *Torture.* Translated by Barry Richard. Harmondsworth, England: Penguin, 1963.

———, ed. *Les crimes de l'armée française.* Paris: François Maspera, 1954.

Villard, Oswald. "Official Lawlessness." *Harpers,* October 1927, 605–14.

Villari, Luigi. *The Liberation of Italy.* Appleton, WI: C. C. Nelson, 1959.

Viollis, Andrée. *Indochine S.O.S.* Paris: Gallimard, 1935.

Visscher, Maurice. *Humanistic Perspectives in Medical Ethics.* Buffalo: Prometheus, 1972.

Vittori, Jean-Pierre. *Confessions d'un professionnel de la torture.* Paris: Ramsay "Image," 1980.

Vladimirov, S. [pseud.]. "Zapiski Sledovatelya Gestapo" [Notes of a Gestapo Interrogator]. *Moskva* 6 (1971): 210–19; 7 (1971): 174–82; 8 (1971): 182–86.

Voren, Robert van. *Soviet Psychiatric Abuse in the Gorbachev Era.* [Amsterdam: International Association on the Political Use of Psychiatry, 1989].

Vrij, Aldert. *Detecting Lies and Deceit.* Chichester, NY: John Wiley, 2000.

Waack, William. *Camaradas: Nos Arquivos de Moscou.* São Paulo: Companhia das Letras, 1993.

Wachsmann, Nikolaus. *Hitler's Prisons.* New Haven, CT: Yale University Press, 2004.

Waldron, Jeremy. "Security and Liberty: The Image of Balance." *Journal of Political Philosophy* 11.2 (2003): 191–210.

———. "Torture and Positive Law: Jurisprudence for the White House." Delivered at Boalt Hall GALA Workshop, September 30, 2004.

Waller, Douglas, Peter Hawthorne, Rachel Salaman, and Alexandra Stiglmayer. "Weapons of Torture." *Time,* April 6, 1998, 52–53.

Walsh, Cecil. *Crime in India.* London: Ernest Benn, 1930.

Walvin, James. *Slavery and the Slave Trade*. Jackson: University Press of Mississippi, 1983.

Wanat, Leon. *Apel Wiezniow Pawiaka*. Warsaw: Ksiazka I Wiedza, 1976.

Wantchekon, Leonard, and Andrew Healey. "The 'Game' of Torture." *Journal of Conflict Resolution* 43.5 (1999): 596–609.

Warrack, Graeme. *Travel by Dark*. London: Harvill Press, 1963.

Watson, A. "The Dark Cloud over Japanese Criminal Justice: Abuse of Suspects and Forced Confessions." *Justice of the Peace and Local Government Law*, August 5, 1995, 516–19, and August 12, 1995, 534–37.

Weber, Max. *From Max Weber*. Translated by H. H. Gerth and C. Wright Mills. New York: Oxford University Press, 1958.

Wehrwein, Austin. "Prod Used in South 'Makes You Jump.'" *New York Times*, June 22, 1963, 10.

Weigley, Russell. *History of the United States Army*. New York: Macmillan, 1967.

Weiner, Richard. "Retrograde Amnesia with Electroconvulsive Therapy." *Archives of General Psychiatry* 57 (2000): 391–92.

Weissberg, Alex. *Conspiracy of Silence*. London: Hamish Hamilton, 1952.

Welch, Richard, Jr. *Response to Imperialism*. Chapel Hill: University of North Carolina Press, 1979.

Weld, Theodore, ed. *American Slavery As It Is*. New York: Arno, 1968.

Wellard, James. *The French Foreign Legion*. Boston: Little, Brown, 1974.

Weschler, Lawrence. *A Miracle, A Universe*. New York: Penguin, 1991.

Weygand, Jacques. *Légionnaire*. Translated by Raymond Johnes. London: George Harrap, 1952.

What's Daiyo-Kangoku? Tokyo: Japan Federation of Bar Associations, 1993.

White, Josh. "Abu Ghraib Dog Tactics Came from Guantanamo." *Washington Post*, July 27, 2005, A14.

———. "Soldier's 'Wish Lists' of Detainee Tactics Cited." *Washington Post*, April 19, 2005, A16.

———. "Three More Navy Seals Face Abuse Charges." *Washington Post*, September 25, 2004, A16.

White, Lewis M., ed. *On All Fronts*. Boulder, CO: East European Monographs, 1995.

The White Paper on the Problem of Human Rights in South Korea. Pyongyang: Foreign Languages Publishing House, 1977.

Whitworth, Damian. "U.S. May Resort to Torture; Silent Suspects Frustrate Police." *Times* (London), October 22, 2001, A1.

Wiley, Bell Irvin. *The Life of Billy Yank*. Baton Rouge: Louisiana State University Press, 1971.

Willemse, Cornelius. *Behind the Green Lights*. New York: Knopf, 1931.

Williams, Garath. "Objects and Spaces: Reading Elaine Scarry's *The Body in Pain* in an Arendtian Light." Unpublished paper, 2003.

Wines, E. C., and Theodore Dwight. *Report on the Prisons and Reformatories of the United States and Canada, 1867*. Reprint ed. New York: AMS Press, 1973.

Wittgenstein, Ludwig. *Philosophical Investigations*. Translated by G.E.M. Anscombe. Oxford: Basil Blackwell, 1976.

Wolf, Jules. *Le process de Breendonck*. Brussells: Maison F. Larcier, 1973.

Wolf, Stewart, and Herbert Ripley. "Reactions Among Allied Prisoners of War Subjected to Three Years of Imprisonment and Torture by the Japanese." *American Journal of Psychiatry* 104 (1947): 180–93.

Wright, Steve. *An Appraisal of Technologies of Political Control*. PE 166 499. Luxembourg Directorate General for Research, European Parliament, January 6, 1998.

———. "New Police Technologies." *Journal of Peace Research* 15.4 (1978): 310.

Wright, Thomas C., and Rody Oñate. *Flight from Chile*. Translated by Irene B. Hodgson. Albuquerque: University of New Mexico Press, 1998.

Wubben, H. H. "American Prisoners of War in Korea: A Second Look at the 'Something New in History' Theme." *American Quarterly* 22.1 (1970): 3–19.

Wurmbrand, Richard. *From Suffering to Triumph*. Grand Rapids, MI: Kregel, 1991.

———. *If Prison Walls Could Speak*. London: Hodder and Stoughton, 1972.

Yealland, Lewis. *Hysterical Disorders of Warfare*. London: Macmillan, 1918.

Yi, Se-yong. "Uimunsa-wi ga palk'in Inhyoktang Chaegonwi sagon chonmo" [The Fabricated Case of "Committee for Rebuilding the People's Revolution Party," Disclosed by the Truth Commission for Suspicious Deaths]. September 13, 2002.

Zakharov, Yevgeny. *On Torture and Cruel Treatment in the Ukraine*. Translated by Vladmir Rublinetskiy. Kharkiv, Ukraine: Kharkiv Group for Human Rights Protection, 2002.

Zambia Human Rights Report, 1998. Lusaka, Zambia: Inter African Network for Human Rights and Development, Afronet, 1999.

Zinoman, Peter. *The Colonial Bastille*. Berkeley and Los Angeles: University of California Press, 2001.

Zubek, John, ed. *Sensory Deprivation: Fifteen Years of Research*. New York: Meredith Corporation, 1969.

Zyl, Mikki van, Jeanelle de Gruchy, Sheila Lapinsky, Simon Lewin, and Graeme Reid. *The Aversion Project*. Cape Town: Van Zyl, DeGruchy, Lapinsky, Lewin, Reid, 1999.

Index